W9-ARP-586

Fodor's 2011

CALIFORNIA

Fodor's Travel Publications, New York, Toronto, London, Sydney, Auckland
www.fodors.com

Be a Fodor's Correspondent

Your opinion matters. It matters to us. It matters to your fellow Fodor's travelers, too. And we'd like to hear it. In fact, we need to hear it.

When you share your experiences and opinions, you become an active member of the Fodor's community. That means we'll not only use your feedback to make our books better, but we'll publish your names and comments whenever possible. Throughout our guides, look for "Word of Mouth," excerpts of your unvarnished feedback.

Here's how you can help improve Fodor's for all of us.

Tell us when we're right. We rely on local writers to give you an insider's perspective. But our writers and staff editors—who are the best in the business depend on you. Your positive feedback is a vote to renew our recommendations for the next edition.

Tell us when we're wrong. We're proud that we update most of our guides every year. But we're not perfect. Things change. Hotels cut services. Museums change hours. Charming cafés lose charm. If our writer didn't quite capture the essence of a place, tell us how you'd do it differently. If any of our descriptions are inaccurate or inadequate, we'll incorporate your changes in the next edition and will correct factual errors at fodors.com immediately.

Tell us what to include. You probably have had fantastic travel experiences that aren't yet in Fodor's. Why not share them with a community of like-minded travelers? Maybe you chanced upon a beach or bistro or B&B that you don't want to keep to yourself. Tell us why we should include it. And share your discoveries and experiences with everyone directly at fodors.com. Your input may lead us to add a new listing or highlight a place we cover with a "Highly Recommended" star or with our highest rating, "Fodor's Choice."

Give us your opinion instantly at our feedback center at www.fodors.com/feedback. You may also e-mail editors@fodors.com with the subject line "California Editor." Or send your nominations, comments, and complaints by mail to California Editor, Fodor's, 1745 Broadway, New York, NY 10019.

You and travelers like you are the heart of the Fodor's community. Make our community richer by sharing your experiences. Be a Fodor's correspondent.

Happy Traveling!

Tim Jarrell, Publisher

FODOR'S CALIFORNIA 2011

Editors: Maria Teresa Hart, *lead editor*; Rachel Klein, Matthew Lombardi, Jess Moss

Writers: Cheryl Crabtree, Lisa M. Hamilton, Reed Parsell, Christine Vovakes, Sura Wood, Bobbi Zane, Maren Dougherty, Maria Hunt, Amanda Knoles, Christine Pae, AnnaMaria Stephens, Claire Deeks van der Lee, Denise M. Leto, Fiona G. Parrott, Sharron Wood, Cindy Arora, Tanvi Chheda, Alene Dawson, Elline Lipkin, Lea Lion, Susan MacCallum-Whitcomb, Laura Randall
Editorial Contributors: Denise M. Leto, Amanda Theunissen, Laura Randall, Claire van der Lee, Erica Duecy

Production Editor: Jennifer DePrima
Maps & Illustrations: David Lindroth and Mark Stroud, *cartographers;* Bob Blake, Rebecca Baer, *map editors;* William Wu, *information graphics*
Design: Fabrizio La Rocca, *creative director*; Guido Caroti, Siobhan O'Hare, *art directors*; Tina Malaney, Nora Rosansky, Chie Ushio, Jessica Walsh, Ann McBride, *designers*; Melanie Marin, *senior picture editor*
Cover Photo: (Drakes beach, Point Reyes National Seashore): David W. Hamilton/Tips Italia/Photolibrary
Production Manager: Angela L. McLean

COPYRIGHT

ISBN 978-1-4000-0485-0

ISSN 0192-9925

SPECIAL SALES

This book is available at special discounts for bulk purchases for sales promotions or premiums. Special editions, including personalized covers, excerpts of existing books, and corporate imprints, can be created in large quantities for special needs. For more information, write to Special Markets/Premium Sales, 1745 Broadway, MD 6-2, New York, New York 10019, or e-mail specialmarkets@randomhouse.com.

AN IMPORTANT TIP & AN INVITATION

Although all prices, opening times, and other details in this book are based on information supplied to us at press time, changes occur all the time in the travel world, and Fodor's cannot accept responsibility for facts that become outdated or for inadvertent errors or omissions. So **always confirm information when it matters,** especially if you're making a detour to visit a specific place. Your experiences—positive and negative— matter to us. If we have missed or misstated something, **please write to us.** We follow up on all suggestions. Contact the California editor at editors@fodors.com or c/o Fodor's at 1745 Broadway, New York, NY 10019.

PRINTED IN SINGAPORE

10 9 8 7 6 5 4 3 2 1

CONTENTS

MAPS

ABOUT THIS BOOK

Our Ratings

Sometimes you find terrific travel experiences, and sometimes they just find you. But usually the burden is on you to select the right combination of experiences. That's where our ratings come in.

As travelers we've all discovered a place so wonderful that its worthiness is obvious, a place is so unique that superlatives don't do it justice. These sights, properties, and experiences get our highest rating, **Fodor's Choice**, indicated by orange stars.

Black stars highlight sights and properties we deem **Highly Recommended,** places that our writers, editors, and readers praise for consistency and excellence.

By default, there's another category: any place we include in this book is by definition worth your time, unless we say otherwise. And we will.

Disagree with any of our choices? Care to nominate a place or suggest that we rate one more highly? Visit our feedback center at www.fodors.com/feedback.

Budget Well

Hotel and restaurant price categories from ¢ to $$$$ are defined in the opening pages of each chapter. For attractions, we always give standard adult admission fees; reductions are usually available for children, students, and senior citizens. Want to pay with plastic? **AE, D, DC, MC, V** following restaurant and hotel listings indicate whether American Express, Discover, Diners Club, MasterCard, and Visa are accepted.

Restaurants

Unless we state otherwise, restaurants are open for lunch and dinner daily. We mention dress only when there's a specific requirement and reservations only when they're essential or not accepted—it's always best to book ahead.

Hotels

Hotels have private bath, phone, TV, and air-conditioning and operate on the European Plan (aka EP, meaning without meals), unless we specify that they use the Continental Plan (CP, with a Continental breakfast), Breakfast Plan (BP, with a full breakfast), or Modified American Plan (MAP, with breakfast and dinner) or are all-inclusive (including all meals and most activities).

We always list facilities but not whether you'll be charged an extra fee to use them.

Listings
★ Fodor's Choice
★ Highly recommended
⊠ Physical address
✛ Directions or Map coordinates
🕮 Mailing address
☎ Telephone
🖷 Fax
⊕ On the Web
✑ E-mail
🗟 Admission fee
☉ Open/closed times
Ⓜ Metro stations
▭ Credit cards

Hotels & Restaurants
🏨 Hotel
➷ Number of rooms
ৎ Facilities
🍴 Meal plans
✕ Restaurant
🖎 Reservations
𝌠 Dress code
⌇ Smoking
🍸 BYOB

Outdoors
⛳ Golf
⛺ Camping

Other
☚ Family-friendly
⇨ See also
⊠ Branch address
☞ Take note

Experience
California

WHAT'S NEW IN CALIFORNIA

Kitchen Confidential

Great dining is a staple of the California lifestyle, and a new young generation of chefs is challenging old ideas about preparing and presenting great food. Two trends are emerging. Young chefs like William Bradley (Addison, Del Mar) pick fresh and locally sourced food, while others such as Bruno Chemel, who recently opened Baume in Palo Alto, showcase molecular gastronomy. Another trend for small plates and tapas means you can have a Spanish appetizer followed by a Chinese entrée. James Beard award–winning Bradley Ogden embraces the farm-to-table locavore movement at Root 246 in Solvang. And what some consider the original locavore chef—Thomas Keller of French Laundry—has expanded south to Beverly Hills, where he opened the elegant Bouchon in 2009, followed by a more-affordable Bar Bouchon downstairs, serving upscale pub grub.

Kidding Around

California's theme parks work overtime to keep current and attract patrons of all ages. Legoland California Resort leads the pack by adding attractions every year and opening its first water park in 2010. Coming soon to the Carlsbad resort is a Lego-theme hotel.

Disneyland, using its high-grossing movie profits, renovated and reopened three of its most popular attractions: Abraham Lincoln, the Disney Gallery, and Sleeping Beauty's Castle.

Grape Expectations

A whole new crop of vintners and winemakers are making headlines, especially since some of them work their magic in unlikely places such as the Sierra foothills and at higher elevations in the Coast mountains. Notable is vintner Ann Kraemer, whose Shake Ridge old-vine zinfandels and tempranillo, sold under the venerable Yorba Family name, are turning heads in the Bay Area. Others include Mendocino-based Stuart Bewley noted for the lusty Alder Springs Syrah that emerges from his 4,400-foot hillside.

Suite Dreams

New or renewed hotels continue to be the big story across the state, despite challenges caused by the deep recession. Hyatt, tapping into guests' desires for elegant digs where personal service abounds, opened boutique Andaz hotels in West Hollywood and San Diego. Meanwhile, the Ace Hotel and Swim Club lures young Palm Springs visitors with 1960s chic decor and the matching party atmosphere. In San Francisco, the historic St. Francis hotel just completed a $40-million renovation of rooms and public areas. You can ski in and ski out of the Ritz-Carlton Highlands at Lake Tahoe; the resort, opened in December 2009, is set midway up the mountain at Northstar.

All Aboard

Riding the rails can be a satisfying experience, particularly in California where the distances between destinations can run into the hundreds of miles. You can save money on gas and parking, avoid freeway traffic, and see some of the best the state has to offer.

The best trip is on the new, luxuriously appointed Coast Starlight, a long-distance train with sleeping cars that runs between Seattle and Los Angeles, passing some of California's most beautiful coastline as it hugs the beach. For the best surfside viewing, get a seat or a room on the left side of the train and ride south to north from San Diego to Oakland.

Amtrak has frequent Pacific Surfliner service between San Diego and Los Angeles and San Diego to Santa Barbara. These are coach cars, but many of the trains have been upgraded and are comfortable and convenient, especially if you want to get off and on the train at several destinations—Anaheim near Disneyland, downtown Los Angeles, coastal Ventura and Santa Barbara, San Luis Obispo, and Oakland (just a BART ride to San Francisco).

Head for the Hills

Things are looking up for visitors to California's alpine recreation areas, thanks to a host of enhancements. As part of a fittingly gigantic redevelopment project, Mammoth Mountain opened its Top of the Sierra Interpretive Center in spring 2007 (at an altitude of 11,053 feet, they do mean *top*); and the Westin Monache hotel, anchor of the Village at Mammoth, is just steps from the gondola.

It's Easy Being Green

The Golden State is glowing green all over. It's the only state in the nation to mandate green building codes for all new construction to reduce greenhouse emissions. California Road Trips maps 12 green itineraries including the Ultimate Eco Tour of the North Coast; Natural Wonderland revealing the rugged beauty of the High Sierra; and Farm Fresh, drives that takes you to orchards that produce some of the best and most succulent fruit in the world.

Santa Barbara's car-free program can save you up to 50% on lodging, meals, and, of course, transportation. Palm Desert is also pushing green, not only in sustainable construction but also in encouraging use of golf carts for local transportation.

Homegrown Hospitality

Agritourism in California isn't new (remember, Knott's Berry Farm once *was* a berry farm), but it is on the rise, with farm tours and agricultural festivals sprouting up everywhere.

Wine country is a particularly fertile area—spurred by the success of vineyards, the area's lavender growers and olive-oil producers have started welcoming visitors. Sonoma Farm Tours include walking the land and a farm-driven dinner with paired wines.

In the Central Valley, America's number-one producer of stone fruit, you can travel themed tourist routes (like Fresno County's Blossom Trail) and tour herb gardens, fruit orchards, organic dairies, and pumpkin patches.

In Southern California public gardens bloom abundantly year-round.

State of the Arts

California's beauty-obsessed citizens aren't the only ones opting for a fresh look these days: its esteemed art museums are also having a bit of work done.

Following a trend set by the de Young Museum in San Francisco and the Getty Villa in L.A., Long Beach's Museum of Latin American Art doubled its exhibition space. Meanwhile, San Jose's Institute of Contemporary Art and the Museum of Contemporary Art in San Diego (MCASD Downtown) have both expanded into new digs. And the Palm Springs Museum of Art has morphed into a world-class showcase for contemporary work. Keep your eye on the Museum of Contemporary Art in Los Angeles, they have high expectations of a new director who no doubt has some revisions in mind.

WHAT'S WHERE IN SOUTHERN CALIFORNIA

The following numbers refer to chapters.

2 San Diego. San Diego's historic Gaslamp Quarter and Mexican-theme Old Town have a human scale—but it's big-ticket animal attractions like SeaWorld and the San Diego Zoo that pull in planeloads of visitors.

3 Orange County. The real OC is a diverse destination with premium resorts, first-rate restaurants, strollable waterfront communities, and kid-friendly attractions.

4 Los Angeles. Go for the glitz of the entertainment industry, but stay for the rich cultural attributes and myriad communities of people from different cultures.

5 The Central Coast. Three of the state's top stops—swanky Santa Barbara, Hearst Castle, and Big Sur—sit along the scenic 200-mi route.

6 Channel Islands National Park. Only 60 mi northwest of Los Angeles, this park accessible only by boat seems worlds away from urban sprawl and tangled freeways.

13 The Inland Empire. The San Bernardino Mountains provide seasonal escapes at Lake Arrowhead and Big Bear Lake, and the Temecula Valley will challenge your ideas of "California Wine Country."

14 Palm Springs and the Desert Resorts. Golf on some of the West's finest courses, lounge at some of its most fabulous resorts, and experience the simple life at primitive desert parks.

15 Joshua Tree National Park. Proximity to major urban areas—as well as world-class rock climbing and nighttime celestial displays—help make this one of the most visited national parks in the United States.

16 The Mojave Desert. In this hardscrabble country, material pleasures are in short supply, but Mother Nature's stark beauty more than compensates.

17 Death Valley National Park. America's second-largest national park isn't just vast and lonely—it's beautiful and often the hottest place in the nation.

19 The Southern Sierra. In the Mammoth Lakes region, sawtooth mountains and deep powdery snowdrifts combine to create the state's premier conditions for skiing and snowboarding.

20 Yosemite National Park. The views immortalized by photographer Ansel Adams—of towering granite monoliths, verdant glacial valleys, and lofty waterfalls—are still camera-ready.

21 Sequoia and Kings Canyon National Parks. The sight of ancient redwoods towering above jagged mountains will take your breath away.

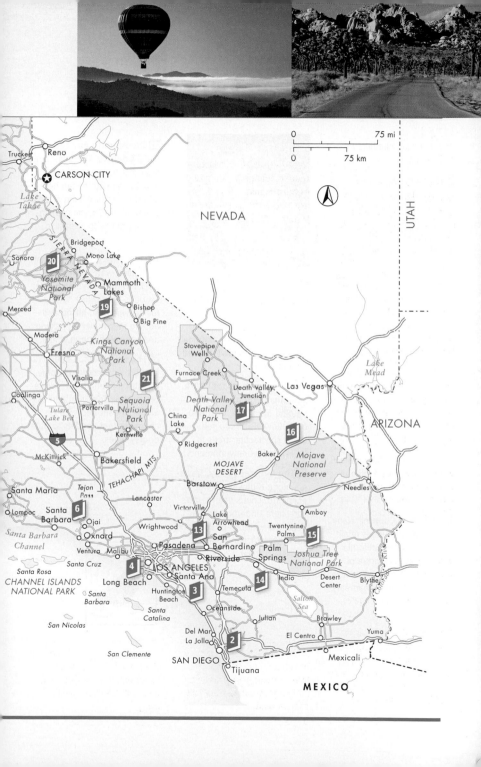

WHAT'S WHERE IN NORTHERN CALIFORNIA

The following numbers refer to chapters.

7 Monterey Bay Area. Postcard-perfect Monterey, Victorian-flavored Pacific Grove, and exclusive Carmel all share this stretch of California coast. To the north, Santa Cruz boasts a boardwalk, a UC campus, ethnic clothing shops, and plenty of surfers.

8 San Francisco. To see why so many have left their hearts here, you need to veer off the beaten path and into the city's neighborhoods—posh Pacific Heights, the Hispanic Mission, and gay-friendly Castro.

9 The Bay Area. The area that rings San Francisco is nothing like the city—but it is home to some of the nation's great universities, fabulous bay views, and Alice Waters's Chez Panisse.

10 The Wine Country. Napa and Sonoma counties retain their title as *the* California wine country, by virtue of award-winning vintages, luxe lodgings, and epicurean eats.

11 The North Coast. The star attractions here are the natural ones, from the secluded beaches and wave-battered bluffs of Point Reyes National Seashore to the towering redwood forests.

12 Redwood National Park. More than 200 mi of trails, ranging from easy to strenuous, allow visitors to see these spectacular trees in their primitive environments.

18 The Central Valley. Travelers along Highway 99 will enjoy attractions like Fresno's Forestiere Underground Gardens, the wineries of Lodi, and white-water rafting on the Stanislaus River.

22 Sacramento and the Gold Country. The 1849 gold rush that built San Francisco and Sacramento began here, and the former mining camps strung along 185 mi of Highway 49 replay their past to the hilt.

23 Lake Tahoe. With miles of crystalline water reflecting the peaks of the High Sierra, Lake Tahoe is the perfect setting for activities like hiking and golfing in summer and skiing and snowmobiling in winter.

24 The Far North. California's far northeast corner is home to snowcapped Mount Shasta, the pristine Trinity Wilderness, and abundant backwoods character that appeals to outdoorsy types.

1

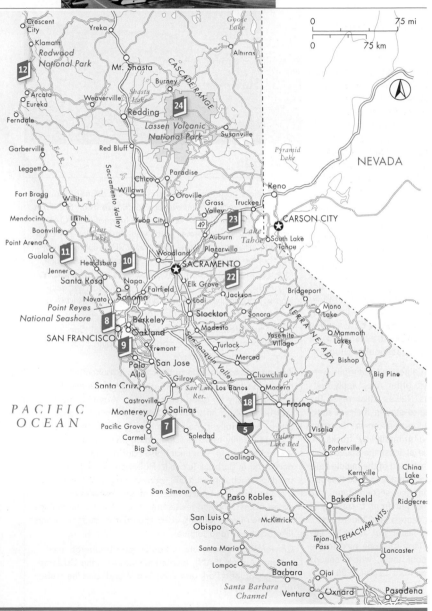

Crescent
City
Yreka
Goose Lake
75 mi

Klamath
0   75 km

Redwood National Park
12
Mt. Shasta
Alturas

Burney
CASCADE RANGE

Arcata
Weaverville
Shasta Lake
24

Eureka
Redding

Ferndale
Lassen Volcanic National Park
Susanville
NEVADA

Garberville
Red Bluff
Pyramid Lake

Leggett

Fort Bragg
Chico
Paradise
Reno

Willits
Willows
Oroville

Mendocino
Ukiah
Grass Valley
Truckee
CARSON CITY

Boonville
Yuba City
49
23
Lake Tahoe

Point Arena
Clear Lake
Auburn
South Lake Tahoe

Gualala
11
Healdsburg
Woodland
Placerville

Jenner
10
SACRAMENTO

Santa Rosa
Napa
Elk Grove
22

Novato
Fairfield
Lodi
Bridgeport

Point Reyes National Seashore
Sonoma
Jackson
Mono Lake

8
Berkeley
Stockton
Sonora
SIERRA NEVADA
Mammoth Lakes

SAN FRANCISCO
Oakland
Modesto
Yosemite Village

9
Fremont
Turlock
Bishop

Palo Alto
San Jose
Merced
Big Pine

Santa Cruz
Gilroy
San Joaquin Valley
Chowchilla

Castroville
San Luis Res.
Los Banos
Madera

PACIFIC OCEAN
Monterey
Salinas
18
Fresno

Pacific Grove
7
Soledad
5
Visalia

Carmel
Tulare Lake Bed
Porterville

Big Sur
Coalinga

Kernville
China Lake

San Simeon
Paso Robles
Bakersfield
Ridgecrest

San Luis Obispo
McKittrick
TEHACHAPI MTS.

Santa Maria
Tejon Pass
Lancaster

Lompoc
Santa Barbara
Ojai

Santa Barbara Channel
Ventura
Oxnard
Pasadena

CALIFORNIA PLANNER

Driving Around

Driving may be a way of life in California, but it isn't cheap (gas prices here are usually among the highest in the nation). It's also not for the fainthearted; you've surely heard horror stories about L.A.'s freeways, but even the state's scenic highways and byways have their own hassles. For instance, on the dramatic coastal road between San Simeon and Carmel, twists, turns, and divinely distracting vistas frequently slow traffic; in rainy season, mudslides can close the road altogether ⚠ Never cross the double line when driving these roads. If you see that cars are backing up behind you on a long two-lane, no-passing stretch, do everyone (and yourself) a favor and use the first available pullout.

On California's notorious freeways, other rules apply. Nervous Nellies must resist the urge to stay in the two slow-moving ones on the far right, used primarily by trucks. To drive at least the speed limit, get yourself in the middle lane. If you're ready to bend the rules a bit, the second (lanes are numbered from 1 starting at the center) lane moves about 5 mi faster. But avoid the far-left lane (the one next to the carpool lane), where speeds range from 75 MPH to 90 MPH.

Flying In

Air travelers beginning or ending their vacation in San Francisco have two main airports to choose from: San Francisco International (SFO) or Oakland International (OAK) across the Bay. The former lands you closer to the city core (ground transportation will take about 20 minutes versus 35); but the latter is less heavily trafficked and less prone to pesky fog delays. Both airports are served by BART, the Bay Area's affordable rapid-transit system. So your decision will probably rest on which one has the best fares and connections for your particular route.

If your final destination is Monterey or Carmel, San Jose International Airport (SJC), about 40 mi south of San Francisco, is another alternative.

Around Los Angeles, the options grow exponentially. LAX, the world's fifth-busiest airport, gets most of the attention—and not usually for good reasons. John Wayne Airport (SNA), about 25 mi south in Orange County, is a solid substitute—especially if you're planning to visit Disneyland or Orange County beaches. Depending on which part of L.A. you're heading to, you might also consider Bob Hope Airport (BUR) in Burbank (close to Hollywood and its studios) or Long Beach Airport (LGB), convenient if you're catching a cruise ship. The smaller size of these airports means easier access and shorter security lines. Another advantage is that their lower landing costs often attract budget carriers (like Southwest and JetBlue).

Convenience is the allure of San Diego's Lindbergh International Airport (SAN), located minutes from the Gaslamp Quarter, Balboa Park and Zoo, Sea World, and the cruise ship terminal.

WHEN TO GO

Because they offer activities indoors and out, the top California cities rate as all-season destinations. Ditto for Southern California's coastal playgrounds. Dying to see Death Valley? It's best appreciated in spring when desert blooms offset its austerity and temperatures are still manageable. Early spring—when the gray whale migration overlaps with the end of the elephant seal breeding season and the start of the bird migration—is the optimal time to visit Point Reyes National Seashore. Yosemite is ideal in the late spring because roads closed in winter are reopened, the summer crowds have yet to arrive, and the park's waterfalls—swollen with melting snow—run fast. Autumn is "crush time" in Napa and Sonoma valleys. Snowfall makes winter peak season for skiers in Mammoth Mountain and Lake Tahoe, where runs typically open around Thanksgiving. (They sometimes remain in operation into June.)

Climate

It's difficult to generalize much about the state's weather beyond saying that precipitation comes in winter and summers are dry in most places. As a rule, inland regions are hotter in summer and colder in winter, compared with coastal areas, which are relatively cool year-round. As you climb into the mountains, seasonal variations are more apparent: winter brings snow (at elevations above 3,000 feet), autumn is crisp, spring can go either way, and summer is sunny and warm, with only an occasional thundershower in the southern part of the state.

Microclimates

Mountains separate the California coastline from the state's interior, and the weather can sometimes vary dramatically within a 15-minute drive. On a foggy

summer day in San Francisco, you'll be grateful for a sweater—but head 50 mi north inland to Napa Valley, and you'll likely be content in short sleeves. Day and nighttime temperatures can also vary greatly. In August, Palm Springs' thermometers can soar to 110°F at noon, and drop to 75°F at night. Temperature swings elsewhere can be even more extreme. Take Sacramento. On August afternoons the mercury hits the 90s and occasionally exceeds 100°F. Yet as darkness falls, it sometimes plummets to 40°F.

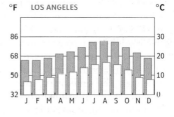

CALIFORNIA TODAY

The People

California is as much a state of mind as a state in the union—a kind of perpetual Promised Land that has represented many things to many people. In the 18th century, Spanish missionaries came seeking converts. In the 19th, miners rushed here to search for gold. And, in the years since, a long line of Dust Bowl farmers, land speculators, Haight-Ashbury hippies, migrant workers, dot-commers, real estate speculators, and would-be actors came chasing their own dreams.

The result is a population that leans toward idealism—without necessarily being as liberal as you might think. (Remember, this is Ronald Reagan's old stomping ground.) And despite the stereotype of the blue-eyed, blond surfer, California's population is not homogeneous either. Ten million people who live here (more than 28% of Californians) are foreign born—including former Governor Schwarzenegger. Almost half hail from neighboring Mexico; another third emigrated from Asia, following the waves of Chinese workers who arrived in the 1860s to build the railroads and subsequent waves of refugees from the Vietnam War.

The Politics

What's blue and red and green all over? California: a predominantly Democratic state with an aggressive "go green" agenda. When he left office in 2010, Governor Arnold Schwarzenegger left a legacy of pushing a number of environmental initiatives including controls on gas emissions. He also left the state in financial ruin, due in large measure to constitutional constraints and political infighting; as a result in 2010 taxpayers tried to take charge of the matter by launching a spate of ballot measures designed to change the

way the state does business. A constitutional convention was even in the works. All this activity will present challenges to the next governor when he or she takes office in 2011.

The Economy

Leading all other states in terms of the income generated by agriculture, tourism, and industrial activity, California has the country's most diverse state economy. Moreover, with a gross state product of more than $1.8 trillion, California would be one of the top 10 economies *in the world* if it were an independent nation. But due to its wealth and productivity California took a large hit in the recession that began in 2007. This affected all levels of government from local to statewide and resulted in reduction of services that Californians have long taken for granted. Most obvious to visitors are the state parks, most of which have reduced open hours and increased fees.

But the Golden State's economic history is filled with boom and bust cycles—beginning with the mid-19th-century gold rush that started it all. Optimists already have their eyes on the next potential boom: "green companies" focused on alternative energy, renewables, electric cars, and the like.

The Culture

Cultural organizations thrive in California. San Francisco—a city with only about 775,000 residents—has well-regarded ballet, opera, and theater companies, and is home to one of the continent's most noteworthy orchestras. Museums like San Francisco Museum of Modern Art (SFMOMA) and the de Young also represent the city's ongoing commitment to the arts. Art and culture thrive farther south in San Diego as well. Balboa Park alone

holds 15 museums, opulent gardens, and three performance venues, in addition to the San Diego Zoo. The Old Globe Theater and La Jolla Playhouse routinely originate plays that capture coveted Tony awards in New York.

But California's *real* forte is pop culture, and L.A. and its environs are the chief arbiters. Movie, TV, and video production have long been centered here since the dawn of the 20th century. Capitol Records set up shop in L.A. in the 1940s, and this area has been instrumental in the music industry ever since. And while these industries continue to influence national trends, today they are only part of the pop culture equation. Web sites are also a growing part of that creativity—YouTube and MySpace are California creations.

The Parks and Preserves

Cloud-spearing redwood groves, snow-tipped mountains, canyon-slashed deserts, primordial lava beds, and a seemingly endless coast: California's natural diversity is staggering—and efforts to protect it started early. The first national park here was established in 1890, and the National Park Service now oversees 30 sites in California (more than in any other state). When you factor in 278 state parks—which encompass underwater preserves, historic sites, wildlife reserves, dune systems, and other sensitive habitats—the number of acres involved is almost as impressive as the topography itself.

Due to encroaching development and pollution, keeping these natural treasures in pristine condition is an ongoing challenge. For instance, Sequoia and Kings Canyon (which is plagued by pesticides and other agricultural pollutants blown in from the San Joaquin Valley) has been named America's "smoggiest park" by the National Parks Conservation Association, and the Environmental Protection Agency has designated it as an "ozone non-attainment area with levels of ozone pollution that threaten human health." Another threat to the parks was California's 2009–10 budget crisis; most parks survived, but with restricted operating hours and increased entrance fees.

The Cuisine

California gave us McDonald's, Denny's, Carl's Jr., Taco Bell, and, of course, In-N-Out Burger. Fortunately for those of us with fast-clogging arteries, the state also kick started the organic food movement. Back in the 1970s, California-based chefs put American cuisine on the culinary map by focusing on freshly prepared seasonal ingredients.

Today, this focus has spawned the "locavore" or sustainable food movement—followers try to only consume food produced within a 100-mi radius of where they live, since processing and refining food and transporting goods over long distances is bad for both the body and the environment. This isn't much of a restriction in California, where a huge variety of crops grow year-round. Some 350 cities and towns have certified farmers' markets—and their stalls are bursting with a variety of goods. California has been America's top agricultural producer for the last 50 years, growing more fruits and vegetables than any other state. Dairies and ranches also thrive here, and fishing fleets harvest fish and shellfish from the rich waters offshore.

CALIFORNIA TOP ATTRACTIONS

San Diego

(A) San Diego is a thoroughly modern metropolis set on the sunny Pacific, filled with tourist attractions (think the Zoo, SeaWorld, and Legoland) and blissful beaches. But this is also a city steeped in history—in 1769 Spaniards established a settlement here near Old Town, site of the first Spanish outpost and now a state park dedicated to illustrating San Diego's raucous early days. The city's rousing downtown dining and entertainment district, the Gaslamp Quarter, is a contemporary recreation of bawdy Stingaree of the late 1800s.

Channel Islands National Park

(B) This five-island park northwest of Los Angeles is a remote but accessible eco escape. There are no phones, no cars, and no services—but there are more than 2,000 species of plants and animals (among them blue whales and brown pelicans), plus ample opportunities for active pursuits. On land, hiking tops the itinerary. Underwater preserves surround the park, so snorkeling, scuba diving, fishing, and kayaking around lava tubes and natural arches are other memorable options.

Los Angeles

(C) Tinsel Town, Lala Land, City of Angels: L.A. goes by many names and has many personas. Recognized as America's capital of pop culture, it also has highbrow appeal with arts institutions like the Getty Center, the Geffen Contemporary at MOCA, Walt Disney Concert Hall, the Norton Simon Museum, and Huntington Library. But you can go wild here, too—and not just on the Sunset Strip. Sprawling Griffith Park, Will Rogers State Historic Park, and Malibu Lagoon State Beach all offer a natural break from the concrete jungle.

Palm Springs and Beyond

(D) Celebrities used to flee to the desert for rest, relaxation, a few rays of sun, and to indulge in some high jinks beyond the watchful eyes of the media. You don't have to spend much time in Palm Springs to realize those days are *long* gone. In this improbably situated bastion of Bentleys and bling, worldly pleasures rule. Glorious golf courses, tony shops and restaurants, decadent spa resorts—they're all here. Solitude seekers can still slip away to nearby Joshua Tree National Park or Anza-Borrego Desert State Park.

Death Valley

(E) On the surface, a vacation in Death Valley sounds about as attractive as a trip to hell. Yet for well-prepared travelers, the experience is more awe-inspiring than ominous. Within the largest national park in the contiguous United States you'll find the brilliantly colored rock formations of Artists Palette, the peaks of the Panamint Mountains, and the desolate salt flats of Badwater, 282 feet below sea level. You can't get any lower than this in the Western Hemisphere—and, in summer, you can't get much hotter.

San Francisco

(F) Population-wise, San Francisco is smaller than Indianapolis. But when it comes to sites (and soul), this city is a giant. Start working through the standard travelers' "to do" list by strolling across the Golden Gate Bridge, taking a ferry to Alcatraz, and hopping on the Powell–Hyde cable car. Just leave enough time to explore the diverse neighborhoods where San Francisco's distinctive personality—an amalgam of gold-rush history, immigrant traditions, counterculture proclivities, and millennial materialism—is on display.

Yosemite National Park

(G) Nature looms large here, both literally and figuratively. In addition to hulking Half Dome, the park is home to El

Capitan (the world's largest exposed granite monolith, rising 3,593 feet above the glacier-carved valley floor) and Yosemite Falls (North America's tallest cascade). In Yosemite's signature stand of giant sequoias—the Mariposa Grove—even the trees are Bunyanesque. Needless to say, crowds can be super-size.

Lake Tahoe
(H) Deep, clear, and intensely blue, this forest-rimmed body of water straddling the California–Nevada border is one of the continent's prettiest alpine lakes. That environmental controls can keep it that way is something of a miracle, given Tahoe's popularity. Throngs of outdoor adventurers flock to the California side to ski, hike, bike, and boat. On the Nevada side, where casinos are king, gambling often wins out over fresh-air activities— but natural wonders are never far away.

Point Reyes National Seashore
(I) Aside from the namesake seashore, this Marin County preserve encompasses ecosystems that range from woodlands and marshlands to heathlike grasslands. The range of wildlife here is equally diverse— depending on when you visit, expect to see gray whales, rare Tule elk, and almost 500 species of birds. December through March you can also see male elephant seals compete for mates.

Wine Country
(J) Although the vineyard-blanketed hills of California's original Wine Country are undeniably scenic, the wine itself (preferably accompanied by the area's famed cuisine) remains the big draw here. Budding oenophiles can educate their palettes on scores of tours and tasting sessions—provided they can elbow their way through the high-season hordes.

CALIFORNIA'S TOP EXPERIENCES

Hit the Road
Kings Canyon Highway, Redwood Highway, Tioga Pass, 17-Mile Drive, the Lake Tahoe loop: California has some splendid and challenging roads. You'll drive through a tunnel formed by towering redwood trees on the Redwood Highway. If you venture over the Sierras by way of Tioga Pass (through Yosemite in summer only), you'll see emerald green meadows, gray granite monoliths, and pristine blue lakes—and very few people.

Ride a Wave
Surfing—which has influenced everything from fashion to moviemaking to music—is a quintessential California activity. You can find great surf breaks in many places along the coast between Santa Cruz and San Diego. But one of the best places to try it is Huntington Beach. Lessons are widely available. If you're not ready to hang 10, you can hang out at "Surf City's" International Surfing Museum or stroll the Surfing Walk of Fame.

Go for the Gold
Though California's gold rush ended more than a hundred years ago, you can still feel the '49er fever on the western face of the Sierra Nevada in Columbia, a well-preserved town populated by costumed interpreters, where you can pan for gold or tour a mine. Or visit Bodie, an eerie ghost town in the eastern Sierra that remains in a state of "arrested decay."

Think Globally, Eat Locally
Over the years California cuisine has evolved from a mere trend into a respected gastronomic tradition: one that pairs local, often organic or sustainable, ingredients with techniques inspired by European, Asian, and increasingly Indian and Middle Eastern cookery.

Embrace Your Inner Eccentric
California has always drawn creative and, well, eccentric people. And all that quirkiness has left its mark in the form of oddball architecture that makes for some fun sightseeing. Begin by touring Hearst Castle—the beautifully bizarre estate William Randolph Hearst built above San Simeon. Scotty's Castle, a Moorish confection in Death Valley, offers a variation on the theme; as does Marta Becket's one-woman Armargosa Opera House. And Lake Tahoe's Vikingsholm (a re-created Viking castle) is equally odd.

Get Reel
In L.A. it's almost obligatory to do some Hollywood-style stargazing. Cue the action with a behind-the-scenes tour of one of the dream factories. (Warner Bros. Studios' five-hour deluxe version, which includes lunch in the commissary, is just the ticket for cinephiles.) Other must-sees include the Kodak Theatre, home of the Academy Awards; Grauman's Chinese Theatre, where celebs press feet and hands into cement for posterity's sake; Hollywood Boulevard's star-paved Walk of Fame; and the still-iconic Hollywood sign. Celebrity sightings abound throughout SoCal; look for the paparazzi.

People-Watch
Opportunities for world-class people-watching abound in California. Just saunter the rainbow-flagged streets of San Francisco's Castro neighborhood or the century-old boardwalk in time-warped, resiliently boho Santa Cruz. Better yet, hang around L.A.'s Venice Boardwalk, where chain-saw jugglers, surfers, fortune-tellers, and well-oiled bodybuilders take beachfront exhibitionism to a new high (or low, depending on your point of view). The result is pure eye candy.

QUINTESSENTIAL CALIFORNIA

The Beach

California's beach culture is, in a word, legendary. Of course, it only makes sense that folks living in a state with a 1,264-mi coastline (a hefty portion of which sees the sun upward of 300 days a year) would perfect the art of beach-going. True aficionados begin with a reasonably fit physique, plus a stylish wardrobe consisting of flip-flops, bikinis, wet suits, and such. Mastery of at least one beach skill—surfing, boogie boarding, kayaking, Frisbee tossing, or looking fab while catching rays—is also essential. As a visitor, though, you need only a swimsuit and some rented equipment for most sports. You can then hit the beach almost anywhere, thanks to the California belief in coastal access as a birthright. The farther south you go, the wider, sandier, and sunnier the beaches become; moving north they are rockier and foggier, with colder and rougher surf.

The Automobile

Americans may have a love affair with the automobile, but Californians have an out-and-out obsession. Even when gas prices rev up and freeway traffic slows down, their passion burns as hot as ever. You can witness this ardor any summer weekend at huge classic- and custom-car shows held statewide. Even better, you can feel it yourself by taking the wheel. Drive to the sea following Laguna Canyon Road to Laguna Beach; trace an old stagecoach route through the mountains above Santa Barbara on Highway 154; track migrating whales up the coast to Big Sur; or take 17-Mile Drive along the precipitous edge of the Monterey Peninsula. Glorious for the most part, but authentically congested in some areas in the south, Highway 1 runs almost the entire length of the state, hugging the coast most of the way.

Californians live in such a large and splashy state that they sometimes seem to forget about the rest of the country. They've developed a distinctive culture all their own, which you can delve into by doing as the locals do.

1

The Wine

If California were a country, it would rank as the world's fourth-largest wine producer, after Italy, France, and Spain. In those countries, where vino is barely considered an alcoholic beverage, wine drinking has evolved into a relaxing ritual best shared with friends and family. A modern, Americanized version of that mentality integrates wine into daily life in California, and there are many places to sample it. The Napa and Sonoma valleys come to mind first. However, there are other destinations for oenophiles who want a vintage vacation. You can find great wineries around Santa Barbara County, Monterey Bay, Gold Country's Shenandoah Valley, and the Inland Empire's Temecula Valley, too. All are respected appellations, and their winery tours and tastings will show you what all the buzz is about.

The Outdoors

One of California's greatest assets—the mild year-round weather enjoyed by most of the state—inspires residents to spend as much time outside as they possibly can. They have a tremendous enthusiasm for every imaginable outdoor sport, and, up north especially, fresh-air adventures are extremely popular (which may explain why everyone there seems to own at least one pair of hiking boots). But the California-alfresco creed is more broadly interpreted, and the general rule when planning any activity is "if it can happen outside, it will!" *Plein air* vacation opportunities include dining on patios, decks, and wharves; shopping in street markets or elaborate open-air malls; hearing almost any kind of music at moonlight concerts; touring the sculpture gardens that grace major art museums; and celebrating everything from gay pride to garlic at outdoor fairs.

IF YOU LIKE

One-of-a-Kind Accommodations

Hoteliers statewide have done their utmost to create accommodations that match the glories of the region's landscape, in the process creating lodgings that boast character as well as comfort. Some are unconventional, while others are genuine old-school gems.

Hotel Del Coronado, Coronado. This turreted beauty is a veritable Victorian extravaganza that inspired L. Frank Baum's description of Oz. Iconic architecture aside, Hotel Del is also famous as the filming locale for *Some Like It Hot,* and it has hosted most of the U.S. presidents in the last century. Today it caters more to tour groups than Tinsel Town stars, but fans remain loyal.

Mission Inn, Riverside. This sprawling Spanish Revival estate has welcomed a who's who of politicos. Ronald and Nancy Reagan spent their wedding night here; Richard and Pat Nixon were married in its chapel; and eight U.S. heads of state have patronized its Presidential Lounge.

Movie Colony Hotel, Palm Springs. Hollywood's 1930s heyday comes alive at this glamorous boutique hotel designed by Albert Frey, who created mid-century minimalism in Palm Springs. The glam now attracts a lively clientele and has a cool vibe.

Fairmont San Francisco, San Francisco. This Nob Hill hotel got off to a shaky start (the 1906 earthquake delayed its opening by exactly a year), but it's hosted groundbreaking events like the drafting of the United Nations Charter and Tony Bennett's debut of "I Left My Heart in San Francisco."

Off-the-Beaten-Path Adventures

Mother Nature has truly outdone herself in California. But at the state's most popular sites, it can be hard to approach her handiwork with a sense of awe when you're encircled by souvenir hawkers and camera-wielding tourists. Step off the beaten path, though, and all you'll be able to hear will be the echo of your own voice saying "wow."

Hiking. Steam is the theme at Lassen Volcanic National Park: especially along the 3-mi Bumpass Hell Trail, which has hot springs, steam vents, and mud pots. If you're looking for a cooler hiking experience (temperature-wise), it's hard to top the rugged beauty of Point Reyes National Seashore.

Climbing. Joshua Tree National Park is California's epicenter for climbing; within the park there are hundreds of formations and thousands of routes to choose from. No experience? No problem. J-Tree outfitters offer crash courses for beginners.

Kayaking. Paddling around the lichen-covered sea caves of Channel Islands National Park or surreal tufa towers of Mono Lake, you'll feel like you're on another planet. But kayaking in San Francisco or La Jolla proves you needn't travel far to lose the mob.

Ballooning. Wanna get high? Hot-air ballooning—whether over Wine Country, Temecula, Palm Desert, Mammoth Lakes, or Shasta Valley—lets you sightsee from a totally new perspective.

Amusement Parks

You're on vacation, so why not enjoy some carefree pleasures? For concentrated doses of old-fashioned fun, indulge in creaky waterfront amusements—like Musée Mécanique on San Francisco's Fisherman's Wharf and the antique carousel at Santa Monica Pier. Or opt for a full day at an over-the-top theme park.

Disneyland, Anaheim. Walt Disney set the gold standard for theme parks, and his original "magic kingdom" (the only one built during his lifetime) remains at the top of its class due to innovative rides, animatronics, and a liberal sprinkling of pixie dust.

Legoland California, Carlsbad. Dedicated to the plastic bricks that have been a playtime staple for almost 60 years, this park has more than 50 Lego-inspired attractions (including the popular Volvo Jr. Driving School, Fun town Fire Academy, plus get-all-wet Splash Battle and Treasure Falls) and some 15,000 Lego models ranging from teeny working taxis to a 9-foot-tall dinosaur.

San Diego Wild Animal Park, Escondido. Get up close and personal with lions and tigers at this huge park where animals appear to be roaming free. You can feed a giraffe, talk to the gorillas, and track herds of elk as they cross the plain. Cheetahs bound, hippos huff, and zebras zip.

Santa Cruz Beach Boardwalk, Santa Cruz. Having celebrated its centennial in 2007, the state's oldest amusement park is a sentimental favorite. Expect vintage rides (most notably a 1911 carousel and wooden roller coaster) alongside contemporary attractions, as well as corn dogs, cotton candy, and loads of kitsch.

Spas

Ancient Romans coined the word "spa" as an acronym for *solus per aqua* (or "health by water"). There's plenty of the wet stuff in the Golden State, yet California spas—like California kitchens—are known for making the most of any indigenous ingredient. The resulting treatments are at once distinctive, decadent, and most importantly, relaxing.

The Golden Door, Escondido. Relax and renew at this destination spa tucked into a secluded canyon north of San Diego. Serenity and simplicity rule here, where every moment reflects its Zen-like ambience.

Glen Ivy Hot Springs Spa, Corona. Forget Club Med. In the Inland Empire, it's Club Mud that counts. The outdoor bath at this historic day spa couples red clay from Temescal Canyon with naturally heated, mineral-rich water from its own thermal springs.

Post Ranch Inn & Spa, Big Sur. Like its organic architecture, this luxe retreat's spa treatments are designed to capture the tone of Big Sur. Case in point, the Crystal and Gemstone Therapy. It combines Native American tradition (a ceremonial burning of sage) with an aromatherapy massage that employs jade collected from nearby beaches and essences of local wildflowers.

Spa Terra, Napa. While other Wine Country spas often overlook vineyards, the one at the new Meritage Resort occupies an estate cave 40 feet below them. Appropriately, the facility specializes in vinotherapy treatments incorporating—you guessed it—the fruit of the vine.

GREAT ITINERARIES

SOUTHERN CALIFORNIA DREAMING

Los Angeles, Palm Springs, and San Diego
Day 1: Arrival/Los Angeles

As soon as you land at LAX, make like a local and hit the freeway. Even if L.A.'s top-notch art, history, and science museums don't tempt you, the hodgepodge of art-deco, beaux-arts, and futuristic architecture begs at least a drive-by. Heading east from Santa Monica, Wilshire Boulevard cuts through a historical and cultural cross-section of the city. Two stellar sights on its Miracle Mile are the encyclopedic Los Angeles County Museum of Art and the fossil-filled La Brea Tar Pits. Come evening, the open-air Farmers Market and its many eateries hum. Hotels in Beverly Hills or West Hollywood beckon, just a few minutes away.

Day 2: Hollywood and the Movie Studios

Every L.A. tourist should devote at least one day to the movies and take at least one studio tour. For fun, choose the special-effects theme park at Universal Studios Hollywood; for the nitty-gritty, choose Warner Bros. Studios. Nostalgic musts in half-seedy, half-preening Hollywood include the Walk of Fame along Hollywood Boulevard, the celebrity footprints cast in concrete outside Grauman's Chinese Theatre, and the 1922 Egyptian Theatre (Hollywood Boulevard's original movie palace). When evening arrives, West Hollywood's restaurants are stoked up and the Sunset Strip club scene couldn't get any hotter—the parking nightmare proves it.

Day 3: Beverly Hills and Santa Monica

Even without that extensive art collection, the Getty Center's pavilion architecture, hilltop gardens, and frame-worthy L.A. views would make it a dazzling destination. Descend to the sea via Sunset Boulevard for lunch along Santa Monica's Third Street Promenade, followed by a ride on the historic carousel on the pier. The buff and the bizarre meet on the boardwalk at Venice Beach (strap on some Rollerblades if you want to join them!). Rodeo Drive in Beverly Hills specializes in exhibitionism with a heftier price tag, but voyeurs are still welcome.

Day 4: Los Angeles to Palm Springs

Freeway traffic permitting, you can drive from the middle of L.A. to the middle of the desert in a couple of hours. Somehow in harmony with the harsh environment, mid-century "modern" homes and businesses with clean, low-slung lines define the Palm Springs style. The city seems far away, though, when you hike in hushed Tahquitz or Indian canyons; cliffs and palm trees there shelter rock art, irrigation works, and other remnants of Agua Caliente culture. If your boots aren't made for walking, you can always practice your golf game or indulge in some sublime spa treatments at an area resort instead.

Day 5: The Desert

If riding a tram up an 8,516-foot mountain for a stroll or even a snowball fight above the desert sounds like fun to you, then show up at the Palm Springs Aerial Tramway before the first morning tram leaves (later, the line can get discouragingly long). Afterward stroll through the Palm Springs Art Museum where you can see a shimmering display of contemporary studio glass, an array of enormous

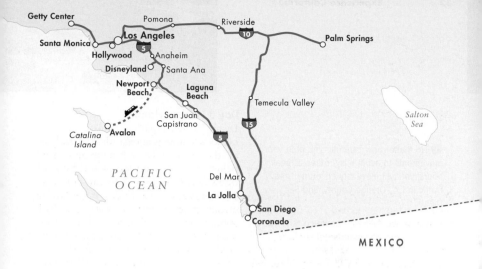

Native American baskets, and significant works of 20th-century sculpture by Henry Moore and others.

Day 6: Palm Springs to San Diego

South through desert and mountains via the Palms to Pines Highway on your way to San Diego, you might pause in the Temecula Valley for lunch at a local winery. Otherwise go straight for the city's nautical heart by exploring the restored ships of the Maritime Museum at the waterfront downtown. Victorian buildings—and plenty of other tourists—surround you on a stroll through the Gaslamp Quarter, but the 21st century is in full swing at the quirky and colorful Horton Plaza retail and entertainment complex. Plant yourself at a downtown hotel and graze your way through the neighborhood's many restaurants and nightspots.

Day 7: San Diego Zoo and Coronado

Malayan tapirs in a faux-Asian rain forest, polar bears in an imitation Arctic—the San Diego Zoo maintains a vast and varied collection of creatures in a world-renowned facility comprised of meticulously designed habitats. Come early, wear comfy shoes, and stay as long as you can stand the sea of children. Boutique-y Coronado—anchored by the grand Hotel Del Coronado—offers a more adult antidote.

Tea, cocktails, or perhaps dinner at the Del makes a civilized end to an untamed day.

Day 8: SeaWorld and Old Town

Resistance is futile: you're going to Sea-World. So what if it screams commercial? This humongous theme park, with its walk-through shark tanks and killer-whale shows, also screams fun. Surrender to the experience and try not to sit in anything sticky. Also touristy (but with genuine historical significance), Old Town drips with Mexican and early Californian heritage. Soak it up in the plaza at Old Town San Diego State Historic Park; then browse the stalls and shops outside the park at Bazaar del Mundo and San Diego Avenue.

Day 9: La Jolla to Laguna Beach

Positioned above an idyllic cove, La Jolla invites lingering. So slow down long enough to enjoy its shop-lined streets, sheltered beaches, and cultural institutions like the low-key Birch Aquarium at Scripps and the well-curated Museum of Contemporary Art. At Mission San Luis Rey, in Oceanside, and Mission San Juan Capistrano you can glimpse life as it was during the Spanish missionary days. Once a haven for artists, Laguna Beach still abounds with galleries. Its walkable downtown streets would abut busy Main

TIPS

❶ No matter how carefully you plan your movements to avoid busy routes at peak hours, you will inevitably encounter heavy traffic in L.A., Orange County, and San Diego.

❷ Allow yourself twice as much time as you think you'll need to negotiate LAX.

Beach Park if the Pacific Coast Highway didn't run through the middle of town.

Day 10: Catalina Island

Having spent so much time looking at the ocean, it's high time you got out *on* it—a quick excursion to Catalina, 75 minutes from the coast, will do the trick. Get an early start, catching the boat from Newport Beach, then use the day to explore this nostalgia-inducing spot. The harbor town of Avalon has a charming, retro feel, while the island's mountains, canyons, and coves are ideal spots for outdoor adventures. Take the 4:30 boat back to the mainland and overnight in Anaheim.

Day 11: Disneyland

Disney's original park is a blast even without kids in tow. So go ahead: skirt the lines at the box office—advance-purchased ticket in hand—and storm the gates of the Magic Kingdom. You can cram the highlights into a single day if you arrive at opening time with a strategy already mapped out. Alternatively, you can spend your final full day next door at Disneyland's sister park, California Adventure, which is a fitting homage to the Golden State. In either case, cap your holiday with a nighttime toast at Downtown Disney.

Day 12: Departure/Los Angeles

Pack up your Mouseketeer gear and give yourself ample time to reach the airport. Without traffic the 35-mi drive from Anaheim to LAX *should* take about 45 minutes. But don't count on it.

GREAT ITINERARIES

SIERRA RICHES: YOSEMITE, GOLD COUNTRY, AND TAHOE

Day 1: Arrival/San Francisco

Straight from the airport, drop your bags at the lighthearted Hotel Monaco near Union Square and request a goldfish for your room. Chinatown, chock-full of dim sum shops, storefront temples, and open-air markets, promises unfamiliar tastes for lunch. Catch a Powell Street cable car to the end of the line and get off to see the bay views and the antique arcade games at Musée Mécanique, the hidden gem of otherwise mindless Fisherman's Wharf. No need to go any farther than cosmopolitan North Beach for cocktail hour, dinner, and live music.

Day 2: San Francisco

A Union Square stroll packs a wallop of people-watching, window-shopping, and architecture-viewing. In Golden Gate Park, linger amid the flora of the conservatory and the arboretum, soak up some art at the de Young Museum, and find serene refreshment at the Japanese Tea Garden. The Pacific surf pounds the cliffs below the Legion of Honor art museum, which has an exquisite view of the Golden Gate Bridge—when the fog stays away. Sunset cocktails at the circa-1909 Cliff House include a prospect over Seal Rock (actually occupied by sea lions). Eat dinner elsewhere: Pacific Heights, the Mission, and SoMa teem with excellent restaurants.

Day 3: Into the High Sierra

First thing in the morning, pick up your rental car and head for the hills. A five-hour drive due east brings you to Yosemite National Park, where Bridalveil Fall and El Capitan, the 350-story granite monolith,

greet you on your wa lage. Ditch the car and pick up information and refreshment before hopping on the year-round shuttle to explore. Justly famous sights cram Yosemite Valley: massive Half Dome and Sentinel Dome, thundering Yosemite Falls, and wispy Ribbon Fall and Nevada Fall. Invigorating short hikes off the shuttle route lead to numerous vantage points. Celebrate your arrival in one of the world's most sublime spots with dinner in the dramatic Ahwahnee Hotel Dining Room.

Day 4: Yosemite National Park

Ardent hikers consider John Muir Trail a must-do, tackling the rigorous 12-hour round-trip to the top of Half Dome in search of life-changing vistas. The merely mortal hike downhill from Glacier Point on Four-Mile Trail or Panorama Trail, the latter an all-day trek past waterfalls. Less demanding still is a drive to Wawona for a stroll in the Mariposa Grove of Big Trees and lunch at the 19th-century Wawona Hotel. In foul weather, take shelter in the Ansel Adams Gallery and Yosemite Museum; in fair conditions, drive up to Glacier Point for a breathtaking sunset view.

Day 5: Gold Country South

Highway 49 traces the mother lode that yielded many fortunes in gold in the 1850s and 1860s. Step into a living gold-rush town at Columbia State Historic Park, where you can ride a stagecoach and pan for riches. Sutter Creek's well-preserved downtown bursts with shopping opportunities, but the vintage goods displayed at J. Monteverde General Store are not for sale. A different sort of vintage powers the present-day bonanza of Shenandoah Valley, heart of the Sierra Foothills wine country. Taste your way through

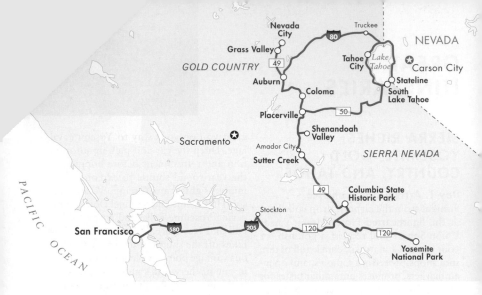

zinfandels and Syrahs at boutique wineries such as Domaine de la Terre Rouge, Renwood, and Sobon Estate. Amador City's 1879 Imperial Hotel places you firmly in the past for the night.

Day 6: Gold Country North

In Placerville, a mineshaft invites investigation at Hangtown's Gold Bug Mine, while Marshall Gold Discovery State Historic Park encompasses most of Coloma and preserves the spot where James Marshall's 1849 find set off the California Gold Rush. Old Town Auburn, with its museums and courthouse, makes a good lunch stop, but if you hold out until you reach Grass Valley you can try authentic miners' pasties. A tour of Empire Mine State Historic Park takes you into a mine, and a few miles away horse-drawn carriages ply the narrow, shop-lined streets of downtown Nevada City. Backtrack to Auburn or Placerville to overnight in historic or modern lodgings.

Day 7: To the Lake

Jewel-like Lake Tahoe is a straight shot east of Placerville on Highway 50; stop for picnic provisions in commercial South Lake Tahoe. A stroll past the three magnificent estates in Pope-Baldwin Recreation area hints at the sumptuous lakefront summers once enjoyed by the elite. High above a glittering cove, Emerald Bay State Park offers one of the best lake views as well as a steep hike down to (and back up from) Vikingsholm, a replica 9th-century Scandinavian castle. Another fine, old mansion—plus a nature preserve and many hiking trails—lies in Sugar Pine Point State Park. Tahoe City offers more history and ample dining and lodging choices.

Day 8: Lake Tahoe

With advance reservations, you can tour the ultraluxe 1936 Thunderbird Lodge and its grounds. The picture-perfect beaches and bays of Lake Tahoe-Nevada State Park line the Nevada shoreline, a great place to bask in the sun or go mountain biking. For a different perspective of the lake, get out on the azure water aboard the stern-wheeler MS *Dixie II* from Zephyr Cove. In South Lake Tahoe, another view unfurls as the Heavenly Gondola travels 2½ mi up a mountain.

Keep your adrenaline pumping into the evening with some action at the massive casinos clustered in Stateline, Nevada.

Day 9: Back to the City

After a morning of driving, return your rental car in San Francisco and soak up some more urban excitement. Good options include lunch at the Ferry Building, followed by a visit to the San Francisco Museum of Modern Art, or lunch in Japantown followed by shopping in Pacific Heights. People-watching excels in the late afternoon bustle of the Castro and the Haight. Say good-bye to Northern California at one of the plush lounges or trendy bars in the downtown hotels.

Day 10: Departure/San Francisco

Check the weather before you start out for the airport: Fog sometimes causes delays at SFO. On a clear day, your flight path might give you one last fabulous glimpse of the City by the Bay.

TIPS

❶ Try to time your trip for late spring or early fall to avoid the worst of the crowds and the road-closing snowfalls in Yosemite and around Lake Tahoe. Yosemite's falls peak in spring and early summer, while fall brings the grape harvest in the Sierra Nevada foothills.

❷ Parking in San Francisco is expensive and scarce. When you fly in, take a shuttle or taxi from the airport to the city, then use the excellent public transportation to get around. Car rental from downtown locations costs no more than at the airport.

❸ For a visit in any season, reserve your hotel or campground accommodations in Yosemite as far in advance as possible—up to a year ahead. Staying in the park itself will cost extra, but it will also save you precious time and miles of driving from the gateway communities.

❹ If you can stay longer, extend your Tahoe-area stay with a day in the Nevada mining boomtowns around Virginia City and a night amid the bright lights of Reno.

THE ULTIMATE ROAD TRIP

CALIFORNIA'S LEGENDARY HIGHWAY 1

by Cheryl Crabtree

One of the world's most scenic drives, California's State Route 1 (also known as Highway 1, the Pacific Coast Highway, the PCH) stretches along the edge of the state for nearly 660 miles, from Southern California's Dana Point to its northern terminus near Leggett, about 40 miles north of Fort Bragg. As you travel south to north, the water's edge transitions from long, sandy beaches and low-lying bluffs to towering dunes, craggy cliffs, and ancient redwood groves. The ocean changes as well; the relatively tame and surfable swells lapping the Southern California shore give way to the frigid, powerful waves crashing against weatherbeaten rocks in the north.

Map labels:
Ft. Bragg
Mendocino
SONOMA COUNTY
Point Reyes National Seashore
MARIN COUNTY
Marin Headlands
Sacramento
San Francisco
Santa Cruz
17-Mile Drive
Monterey
Carmel
Big Sur
Fresno
Hearst San Simeon State Historical Monument
San Luis Obispo
Santa Barbara
Santa Monica
Los Angeles
Long Beach

HIGHWAY 1 TOP 10

- Santa Monica
- Santa Barbara
- Hearst San Simeon State Historical Monument
- Big Sur
- Carmel
- 17-Mile Drive
- Monterey
- San Francisco
- Marin Headlands
- Point Reyes National Seashore

(opposite) Highway 1 near Mill Creek, Big Sur

Give yourself lots of extra time to pull off the road and enjoy the scenery

For more information, please see our Highway 1 CloseUps in chapter 4 (Los Angeles), chapter 7 (Monterey Bay Area), and chapter 8 (San Francisco).

STARTING YOUR JOURNEY

You may decide to drive the road's entire 660-mile route, or bite off a smaller piece. In either case, a Highway 1 road trip allows you to experience California at your own pace, stopping when and where you wish. Hike a beachside trail, dig your toes in the sand, and search for creatures in the tidepools. Buy some artichokes and strawberries from a roadside farmstand. Talk to people along the way (you'll run into everyone from soul-searching meditators, farmers, and beatniks to city-slackers and working-class folks), and take lots of pictures. Don't rush—you could easily spend a lifetime discovering secret spots along this route.

To help you plan your trip, we've broken the road into three regions (Santa Monica to Carmel, Carmel to San Francisco, and San Francisco to Fort Bragg); each region is then broken up into smaller segments—many of which are suitable for a day's drive. If you're pressed for time, you can always tackle a section of Highway 1, and then head inland to U.S. 101 or I-5 to reach your next destination more quickly.

WHAT'S IN A NAME?

Though it's often referred to as the Pacific Coast Highway (or PCH), sections of Highway 1 actually have different names. The southernmost section (Dana Point to Oxnard) is the Pacific Coast Highway. After that, the road becomes the Cabrillo Highway (Las Cruces to Lompoc), the Big Sur Coast Highway (San Luis Obispo County line to Monterey), the North Coast Scenic Byway (San Luis Obispo city limit to the Monterey County line), the Cabrillo Highway again (Santa Cruz County line to Half Moon Bay), and finally the Shoreline Highway (Marin City to Leggett). To make matters more confusing, smaller chunks of the road have additional honorary monikers.

Just follow the green triangular signs that say "California 1."

HIGHWAY 1 DRIVING

- Rent a convertible. (You will not regret it.)
- Begin the drive north from Santa Monica, where congestion and traffic delays pose less of a problem.
- Mind your manners on the freeway. Don't tailgate or glare at other drivers, and don't fly the finger.
- If you're prone to motion sickness, take the wheel yourself. Focusing on the landscape outside should help you feel less queasy.
- If you're afraid of heights, drive from south to north so you'll be on the mountain rather than the cliff side of the road.

San Diego

WORD OF MOUTH

"Unlike most east coast or Midwest big cities, you will be surprised that [in San Diego] the actual traffic downtown is much less difficult that trying to get to or from downtown from an outlying area. . . . The actual downtown area is quite small. Downtown (or Hillcrest, my favorite) is close to Balboa Park (and its Zoo), to the bay, to the ocean, etc."

—d_claude_bear

WELCOME TO SAN DIEGO

TOP REASONS TO GO

★ **Beautiful beaches:** San Diego's shore shimmers with crystalline Pacific waters rolling up to some of the prettiest stretches of sand on the West Coast.

★ **Good eats:** Taking full advantage of the region's bountiful vegetables, fruits, herbs, and seafood, San Diego's chefs surprise, dazzle, and delight diners with inventive California-colorful cuisine.

★ **History lessons:** The well-preserved and reconstructed historic sites in California's first European settlement help you imagine what the area was like when explorers first arrived.

★ **Stellar shopping:** Horton Plaza, the Gaslamp Quarter, Seaport Village, Coronado, Old Town, La Jolla . . . no matter where you go in San Diego, you'll find great places to do a little browsing.

★ **Urban oasis:** Balboa Park's 1,200 acres contain most of San Diego's museums and its world-famous zoo.

1 Balboa Park. San Diego's cultural heart is where you'll find most of the city's museums and its world-famous zoo.

2 Downtown. San Diego's downtown area is delightfully urban and accessible, filled with walkable A-list attractions like the Gaslamp Quarter, Horton Plaza, and the harbor.

3 Coronado. Home to the Hotel Del, this island-like peninsula is a favorite celebrity haunt.

4 Harbor and Shelter Islands & Point Loma. Yachts and resorts, fast food shacks and motels—plus gorgeous views of Coronado and the downtown skyline.

5 Mission Bay. Home to 27 mi of shoreline (and SeaWorld), this 4,600 acre aquatic park is San Diego's monument to sports and fitness.

6 Old Town. California's first permanent European settlement is now preserved as a state historic park.

7 La Jolla. This luxe, bluff-top enclave fittingly means "the jewel" in Spanish. Come here for fantastic upscale shopping and unspoiled stretches of the coast.

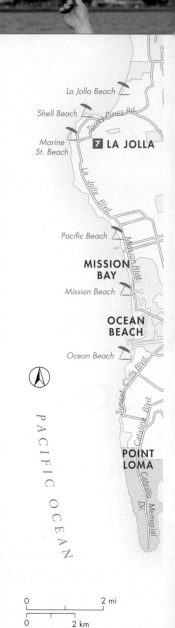

2

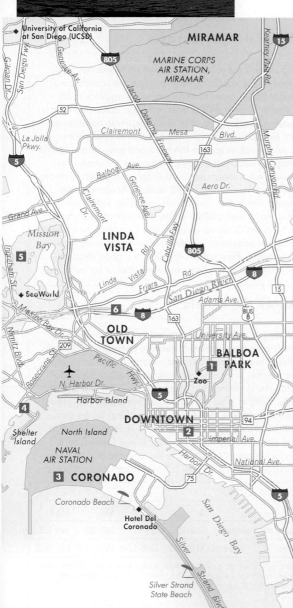

GETTING ORIENTED

Exploring San Diego may be an endless adventure, but there are limitations, especially if you don't have a car. San Diego is more a chain of separate communities than a cohesive city, and many of the major attractions are miles apart. Walking is good for getting an up-close look at how San Diegans live, but true Southern Californians use the freeways that crisscross the county. Interstate 5 runs a direct north–south route through the coastal communities from Orange County in the north to the Mexican border. Interstates 805 and 15 do much the same inland. Interstate 8 is the main east–west route. Routes 163, 52, and 94 serve as connectors.

SAN DIEGO PLANNER

Getting Around

If you're going to drive around San Diego, study a map before you hit the road. The freeways are convenient and fast most of the time, but if you miss your turnoff or get caught in commuter traffic, you'll experience a none-too-pleasurable hallmark of Southern California living—freeway madness.

The San Diego Trolley, which runs south to San Ysidro, has expanded north from Old Town to beyond Mission San Diego and San Diego State University; commuter Coaster trains run frequently between downtown San Diego and Oceanside, with convenient stops in the charming coastal towns of Solana Beach, Encinitas, and Carlsbad; and the bus system covers almost all of the county.

The Sprinter offers commuter train service between Oceanside and Escondido. Making connections to see the various sights can be daunting, however. Since the coast is itself a major attraction, consider staying there if you're carless. The great distances between sights render taxis too expensive for general transportation, although cabs are useful for getting around once you're in a given area. Old Town Trolley Tours has a hop-on, hop-off route of popular spots around the city.

About the Restaurants

San Diego's unbeatable sunny and warm weather combined with gorgeous ocean views and the abundance of locally grown produce make it a satisfying place to be a chef or a diner. While most of the top restaurants offer seasonal California cuisine, San Diego also boasts excellent examples of ethnic cuisines available at all prices. Local specialties include fish tacos and spiny lobster. While "Appropriate Dress Required" signs are sometimes displayed in the entrances to restaurants, this generally means nothing more than clean and reasonably neat clothing. Meal prices in San Diego have caught up with those of other major metropolitan areas, especially in districts like La Jolla, the Gaslamp Quarter, and Coronado, where high rents and popularity with the tourists lead to more expensive entrées. Reservations are always a good idea; we mention them only when they're essential or not accepted.

About the Hotels

When you make reservations, ask about specials. Many hotels promote discounted weekend packages to fill rooms after convention and business customers leave town. Since the weather is great year-round, don't expect substantial discounts in winter. That being said, you can find affordable rooms in even the most expensive areas. If an ocean view is important, request it when booking, but be aware that it will cost significantly more. You can save on hotels and attractions by visiting the San Diego Convention & Visitors Bureau Web site (⊕ www.sandiego.org) for a free Vacation Planning Kit with a Travel Value Coupon booklet.

WHAT IT COSTS

	¢	$	$$	$$$	$$$$
Restaurants	under $10	$10–$18	$19–$27	$28–$35	over $35
Hotels	under $100	$100–$199	$200–$299	$300–$400	over $400

Dining prices are for a main course at dinner, excluding 8.75% tax. Lodging prices are for a standard double room in high (summer) season, excluding 10.5% tax.

2

Updated by
Maren Dough-
erty, Maria
Hunt, Amanda
Knoles,
Christine Pae,
AnnaMaria
Stephens,
Claire Deeks
van der Lee,
Bobbi Zane

San Diego is a big California city—second only to Los Angeles in population—with a small-town feel. It also covers a lot of territory, roughly 400 square mi of land and sea. To the north and south of the city are 70 mi of beaches. Inland, a succession of chaparral-covered mesas are punctuated with deep-cut canyons that step up to savanna-like hills, separating the coast from the arid Anza-Borrego Desert.

The San Diego area, the birthplace of California, was claimed for Spain by explorer Juan Rodríguez Cabrillo in 1542 and eventually came under Mexican rule. You'll find reminders of San Diego's Spanish and Mexican heritage throughout the region——in architecture and place-names, in distinctive Mexican cuisine, and in the historic buildings of Old Town.

In 1867 developer Alonzo Horton, who called the town's bay front "the prettiest place for a city I ever saw," began building a hotel, a plaza, and prefab homes on 960 downtown acres. The city's fate was sealed in 1908, when President Theodore Roosevelt's Great White Fleet sailed into the bay. The U.S. Navy, impressed by the city's excellent harbor and temperate climate, decided to build a destroyer base on San Diego Bay in the 1920s. The newly developed aircraft industry soon followed (Charles Lindbergh's plane *Spirit of St. Louis* was built here). The military, which operates many bases and installations throughout the county (which, added together, form the largest military base in the world), continues to contribute to the local economy.

PLANNING

GETTING HERE AND AROUND
AIR TRAVEL
The major airport is San Diego International Airport, called Lindbergh Field locally. The airport's three-letter code is SAN. Major airlines depart and arrive at Terminal 1 and Terminal 2; commuter flights identified on your ticket with a 3000 sequence flight number depart

from a third commuter terminal. A red shuttle bus provides free transportation between terminals.

Airport San Diego International Airport (☎ *619/400–2400* ⊕ *www.san.org*).

Airport Transfers Cloud 9 Shuttle/SuperShuttle (☎ *800/974–8885* ⊕ *www.cloud9shuttle.com*). **Coronado Livery** (☎ *619/435–6310*). **Five Star** (☎ *619/294–3300 or 866/281–4288* ⊕ *www.fivestarshuttle.com*). **San Diego Transit** (☎ *619/233–3004, 619/234–5005 TTY and TDD* ⊕ *www.sdcommute. com*). **Access Shuttle** (☎ *619/282–1515* ⊕ *www.accessshuttle.net*).

BUS AND TROLLEY TRAVEL

The Greyhound terminal is downtown at Broadway and 1st Avenue, a block from the Civic Center trolley station.

San Diego County is served by a coordinated, efficient network of bus and rail routes that includes service to Oceanside in the north, the Mexican border at San Ysidro, and points east to the Anza-Borrego Desert. Under the umbrella of the Metropolitan Transit System, there are two major transit agencies: San Diego Transit and North County Transit District (NCTD). The bright-red trolleys of the San Diego Trolley light-rail system serve downtown San Diego, Mission Valley, Old Town, South Bay, the U.S. border, and East County. The trolley system connects with San Diego Transit bus routes.

Bus and Trolley Contacts Greyhound (☎ *619/515–1100* ⊕ *www.greyhound. com*). **North County Transit District** (☎ *800/266–6883* ⊕ *www.gonctd. com*). **San Diego Transit** (☎ *619/233–3004, 800/568-7097 TTY and TDD* ⊕ *transit.511sd.com*). **Transit Store** (☎ *619/234–1060*).

CAR TRAVEL

When traveling in the San Diego area, it pays to consider the big picture to avoid getting lost. Water lies to the west of the city. To the east and north, mountains separate the urban areas from the desert. Interstate 5, which stretches from Canada to the Mexican border, bisects San Diego. Interstate 8 provides access from Yuma, Arizona, and points east. Drivers coming from Nevada and the mountain regions beyond can reach San Diego on I–15. During rush hour there are jams on I–5 and on I–15 between I–805 and Escondido.

TAXI TRAVEL

Taxi stands are at shopping centers and hotels; otherwise you must call and reserve a cab. The companies listed below do not serve all areas of San Diego County. If you're going someplace other than downtown, ask if the company serves that area.

Taxi Companies Orange Cab (☎ *619/291–3333* ⊕ *www.orangecabsandiego. com*). **Silver Cabs** (☎ *619/280–5555* ⊕ *www.sandiegosilvercab.com*). **Yellow Cab** (☎ *619/234–6161* ⊕ *www.driveu.com*).

TRAIN TRAVEL

Amtrak serves downtown San Diego's Santa Fe Depot with daily trains to and from Los Angeles, Santa Barbara, and San Luis Obispo. Connecting service to Oakland, Seattle, Chicago, Texas, Florida, and points beyond is available in Los Angeles. Amtrak trains stop in San Diego North County at Solana Beach and Oceanside.

Coaster commuter trains, which run between Oceanside and San Diego Monday–Saturday, stop at the same stations as Amtrak plus others. The Sprinter runs between Oceanside and Escondido daily.

Information Amtrak (🕾 *800/872-7245* ⊕ *www.amtrak.com*). **Coastert** (🕾 *800/266-6883* ⊕ *www.sdcommute.com*). **Metrolink** (🕾 *800/371-5465* ⊕ *www.metrolinktrains.com*). **Oceanside Transit Center** (🕾 *760/722-4622* ⊕ *www.sdcommute.com*). **Santa Fe Depot** (🕾 *619/239-9021*). **Solana Beach Amtrak Station** (🕾 *858/259-2697*).

TOURS

Recommended Tours/Guides Daytripper (🕾 *619/299-5777 or 800/679-8747* ⊕ *www.daytripper.com*). **San Diego Scenic Tours** (🕾 *858/273-8687* ⊕ *www.sandiegoscenictours.com*). **Secret San Diego** (🕾 *619/917-6037* ⊕ *www.wheretours.com*).

Boat Tours Classic Sailing Adventures (🕾 *800/659-0141* ⊕ *www.classicsailingadventures.com*). **H&M Landing** (🕾 *619/222-1144* ⊕ *www.hmlanding.com*). **Hornblower Cruises & Events** (🕾 *619/234-8687 or 800/668-4322* ⊕ *www.hornblower.com*).

Bus and Trolley Tours Centre City Development Corporation Downtown Information Center (🕾 *619/235-2222* ⊕ *www.ccdc.com*). **Gray Line San Diego** (🕾 *800/331-5077* ⊕ *www.sandiegograyline.com*). **Old Town Trolley Tours** (🕾 *619/298-8687* ⊕ *www.trolleytours.com*).

Walking Tours Coronado Walking Tours (🕾 *619/435-5993* ⊕ *www.coronadowalkingtour.com*). **Gaslamp Quarter Historical Foundation** (🕾 *619/233-4692* ⊕ *www.gaslampquarter.org*). **Offshoot Tours** (🕾 *619/239-0512* ⊕ *www.balboapark.org*). **Urban Safaris** (🕾 *619/944-9255* ⊕ *www.walkingtoursofsandiego.com*).

VISITOR INFORMATION

City Contacts San Diego Convention & Visitors Bureau (🕾 *619/232-3101* ⊕ *www.sandiego.org*). **San Diego Convention & Visitors Bureau International Visitor Information Center** (🕾 *619/236-1212* ⊕ *www.sandiego.org*). **San Diego Visitor Information Center** (🕾 *800/827-9188* ⊕ *www.infosandiego.com*).

San Diego County Contacts California Welcome Center Oceanside (🕾 *760/721-1101 or 800/350-7873* ⊕ *www.oceansidechamber.com*). **Carlsbad Convention & Visitors Bureau** (🕾 *800/227-5722* ⊕ *www.visitcarlsbad.com*). **Coronado Visitor Center** (🕾 *619/437-8788* ⊕ *www.coronadovisitorcenter.com*). **Del Mar Regional Chamber of Commerce** (🕾 *858/793-5292* ⊕ *www.delmarchamber.org*). **Encinitas Chamber of Commerce** (🕾 *760/753-6041* ⊕ *www.encinitaschamber.com*). **Promote La Jolla, Inc.** (🕾 *858/454-5718* ⊕ *www.lajollabythesea.com*).

EXPLORING SAN DIEGO

DOWNTOWN

Nearly written off in the 1970s, today downtown San Diego is a testament to conservation and urban renewal. The turnaround began with the revitalization of the Gaslamp Quarter Historic District and massive redevelopment that gave rise to the Horton Plaza shopping center and the San Diego Convention Center, as well as to elegant hotels, upscale condominium complexes, and trendy restaurants and cafés. Like many modern U.S. cities, downtown San Diego's story is as much about its rebirth as its history.

Although many consider downtown to be the 16½-block Gaslamp Quarter, it actually comprises eight neighborhoods, also including East Village, Little Italy, and Embarcadero. Considered the liveliest of the bunch, Gaslamp's Fourth and Fifth avenues are peppered with trendy nightclubs, swanky lounge bars, chic restaurants, and boisterous sports pubs.

Nearby, the most ambitious of the downtown projects is East Village, encompassing 130 blocks between the railroad tracks up to J Street, and from 6th Avenue east to around 10th Street. Sparking the rebirth of this former warehouse district was construction of the San Diego Padres' baseball stadium, PETCO Park. As the city's largest downtown neighborhood, East Village is continually broadening its boundaries with its urban design of redbrick cafés, spacious galleries, rooftop bars, sleek hotels, and warehouse restaurants.

There are reasonably priced ($4–$7 per day) parking lots along Harbor Drive, Pacific Highway, and lower Broadway and Market Street. Most restaurants offer valet parking at night, but beware of fees of $15 and up.

SIGHTS TO SEE

❶ **Embarcadero.** The bustle of Embarcadero comes less these days from the activities of fishing folk than from the throngs of tourists, but this waterfront walkway—comprised of Seaport Village and the San Diego Convention Center—remains the nautical soul of the city. There are several seafood restaurants here, as well as sea vessels of every variety—cruise ships, ferries, tour boats, and Navy aircraft carriers.

On the north end of the Embarcadero at Ash Street you'll find the **Maritime Museum.** South of it, the **B Street Pier** is used by ships from major cruise lines—San Diego has become a major cruise-ship port, both a port of call and a departure point. The cavernous Cruise Ship Terminal has a cruise-information center. The occasional sight of several massive vessels lined up side-by-side is unforgettable, but note that security is tight on embarkation days, and only passengers with tickets are allowed in the cruise terminal on such occasions.

Tickets for harbor tours and whale-watching trips are sold at the foot of Broadway Pier. The terminal for the Coronado Ferry lies just beyond, between Broadway Pier and B Street Pier. One block south of Broadway Pier at Tidelands Park is Military Heritage Art, a collection of works that commemorate the service of the U.S military.

Be sure to enjoy a walk along San Diego's lovely waterfront sometime during your visit.

Lining the pedestrian promenade between the Cruise Ship Terminal and Hawthorn Street are 30 "urban trees" sculpted by local artists. Docked at the Navy pier is the decommissioned USS *Midway*, now the home of the San Diego Aircraft Carrier Museum.

The pleasant Tuna Harbor Park offers a great view of boating on the bay and across to any aircraft carriers docked at the North Island naval base.

The next bit of seafront greenery is a few blocks south at **Embarcadero Marina Park North**, an 8-acre extension into the harbor from the center of Seaport Village. It's usually full of kite fliers, in-line skaters, and picnickers. Seasonal celebrations, including San Diego's Parade of Lights, the Port of San Diego Big Balloon Parade, the Sea and Air Parade, and the Big Bay July 4 Celebration, are held here and at the similar **Embarcadero Marina Park South**.

Providing a unique shopping experience, **Seaport Village** covers 14 acres of waterfront retail stores, restaurants, and cafés.

The **San Diego Convention Center,** on Harbor Drive between 1st and 6th avenues, is a waterfront landmark designed by Canadian architect Arthur Erickson. The backdrop of blue sky and sea complements the building's nautical lines. The center often holds trade shows that are open to the public, and tours of the building are available.

⑤ Gaslamp Quarter Historic District. When the move for downtown redevelopment gained momentum in the 1970s, there was talk of bulldozing the Gaslamp's Victorian-style buildings and starting from scratch. (The district has the largest collection of Commercial Victorian–style

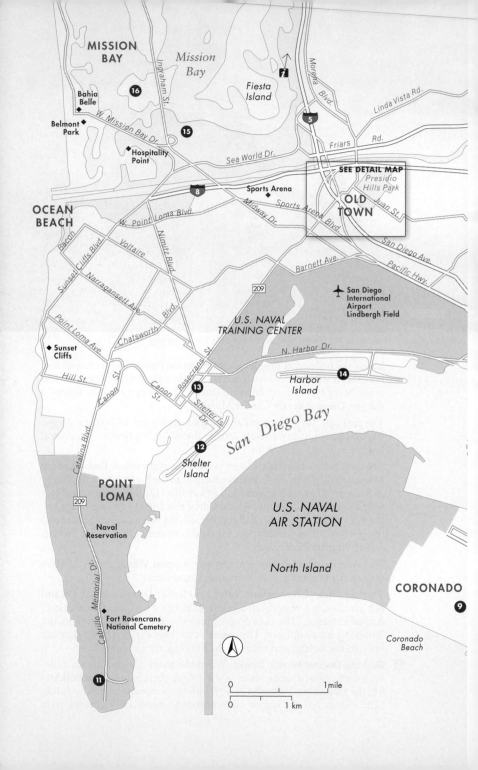

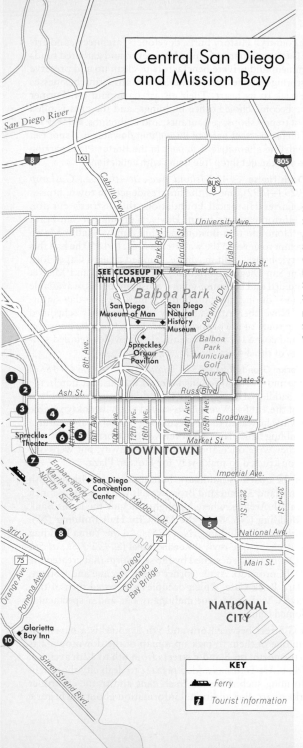

Central San Diego and Mission Bay

San Diego River

Balboa Park

SEE CLOSEUP IN THIS CHAPTER

San Diego Museum of Man

San Diego Natural History Museum

Spreckles Organ Pavilion

Balboa Park Municipal Golf Course

University Ave.

Morley Field Dr.

Upas St.

Date St.

Russ Blvd.

Ash St.

Broadway

Market St.

Spreckles Theater

DOWNTOWN

Imperial Ave.

San Diego Convention Center

Embarcadero Marina Park North South

National Ave.

San Diego-Coronado Bay Bridge

NATIONAL CITY

Main St.

Glorietta Bay Inn

Silver Strand Blvd.

KEY

Ferry

Tourist information

buildings in the country.) History buffs, developers, architects, and artists formed the Gaslamp Quarter Council, however, and gathered funds from the government and private benefactors to clean up and preserve the quarter, restoring the finest old buildings and attracting businesses and the public back to its heart. Their efforts have paid off. Former flophouses have become choice office buildings, and the area is filled with hundreds of trendy shops, restaurants, and nightclubs. ■TIP➔ Although there is metered street parking throughout downtown, a spot can be difficult to find. One alternative is to park in the Horton Plaza parking structure, where you can get three free hours with validation.

William Heath Davis House (✉ *410 Island Ave., at 4th Ave., Gaslamp Quarter* ☎ *619/233–4692*), one of the first residences in town, houses the Gaslamp Quarter Historical Foundation, the district's curator. Before Alonzo Horton came to town, Davis, a prominent San Franciscan—born in Honolulu to a Boston shipping family—had made an unsuccessful attempt to develop the waterfront area. In 1850 he had this prefab saltbox-style house, built in Maine, shipped around Cape Horn and assembled in San Diego (it originally stood at State and Market streets). Audio-guided and brochure-guided museum tours are available with admission ($5) during museum hours, which are Tuesday–Saturday 10–6 (10–4 November–April), Sunday 9–3. Regularly scheduled two-hour walking tours of the historic district leave from the house on Saturday at 11 and cost $10. The museum also provides detailed self-guided tour maps of the district for $2.

The Victorian **Horton Grand Hotel** (✉ *311 Island Ave.* ☎ *619/544–1886*) was created in the mid-1980s by joining together two historic hotels, the Brooklyn Kahle Saddlery Hotel and the Grand Horton Hotel, built in the boom days of the 1880s; Wyatt Earp stayed at the Brooklyn Kahle Saddlery Hotel while he was in town speculating on real estate ventures and opening gambling halls. The two hotels were not originally located at this address; they were once about four blocks away, but were dismantled and reconstructed to make way for Horton Plaza.

The majority of the quarter's landmark buildings are on 4th and 5th avenues, between Island Avenue and Broadway. If you don't have much time, stroll down 5th Avenue, where highlights include the **Louis Bank of Commerce Building** (No. 835), the **Old City Hall Building** (No. 664), the **Nesmith-Greeley Building** (No. 825), and the **Yuma Building** (No. 631). The Romanesque-revival **Keating Hotel** (✉ *432 F St., at 5th Ave., Gaslamp Quarter*) was designed by the same firm that created the famous Hotel Del Coronado. At the corner of 4th Avenue and F Street, peer into the Hard Rock Cafe, which occupies a restored turn-of-the-20th-century tavern with a 12-foot mahogany bar and a spectacular stained-glass domed ceiling.

The section of G Street between 6th and 9th avenues is a haven for galleries; stop in one of them to pick up a map of the downtown arts district. Just to the north, on E and F streets from 6th to 12th avenues, the evolving Urban Art Trail has added pizzazz to drab city thoroughfares by transforming such things as trash cans and traffic controller boxes into works of art. For additional information about the historic

area, call the **Gaslamp Quarter Association** (☎ *619/233–5227*) or log on
to their Web site (🌐 *www.gaslamp.org*). ✉ *614 5th Ave.*

6 **Horton Plaza.** This downtown shopping, dining, and entertainment multilevel maze-like mall fronts Broadway and G Street from 1st to 4th
avenues and covers more than six city blocks. Designed by Jon Jerde
and completed in 1985, Horton Plaza is far from what one would imagine a shopping center—or city center—to be. A collage of pastels with
elaborate, colorful tile work on benches and stairways, banners waving
in the air, and modern sculptures marking the entrances, Horton Plaza
rises in uneven, staggered levels to six floors; great views of downtown
from the harbor to Balboa Park and beyond can be had here.

Macy's and Nordstrom department stores anchor the plaza, and an
eclectic assortment of more than 130 clothing, sporting-goods, jewelry,
book, and gift shops flank them. Other attractions include the country's largest Sam Goody music store, a movie complex, restaurants,
and a long row of take-out ethnic food shops and dining patios on the
uppermost tier—and the respected San Diego Repertory Theatre below
ground level. The beautifully renovated historic 1920s Balboa Theater,
contiguous with the shopping center, seats 1,400 and offers live arts
and cultural performances throughout the week.

The mall has a multilevel parking garage; even so, lines to find a space
can be long. Entering the parking structure on G Street rather than 4th
Avenue generally means less traffic and more parking spaces. Parking validation is complimentary whether you spend a bundle or just
window-shop. Validation machines throughout the center allow for
three hours' free parking; after that it's $8 per hour. If you use this
notoriously confusing fruit-and-vegetable–themed garage, be sure to
remember at which produce level you've left your car. If you're staying
downtown, the Old Town Trolley Tour will drop you directly in front of
Horton Plaza. ✉ *324 Horton Plaza* ☎ *619/238–1596* 🌐 *www.westfield.
com/hortonplaza* ☉ *Mon.–Fri. 10–9, Sat. 10–8, Sun. 11–7.*

3 **International Visitor Information Center.** One of the two visitor information
centers operated by the San Diego Convention and Visitors Bureau (the
other is in La Jolla), this is the best resource for information on the
city. The staff members and volunteers who run the center speak many
languages and dispense information on hotels, restaurants, and tourist
attractions, including those in Tijuana, and provide discount coupons
for many. The office, located across from the Broadway Pier, also has
a change machine inside if you need to feed your meter. ✉ *1040 1/3
W. Broadway, at Harbor Dr.* ☎ *619/236–1212* 🌐 *www.sandiego.org*
☉ *June–Sept., daily 9–5; Oct.–May, daily 9–4.*

2 **Maritime Museum.** A must for anyone with an interest in nautical history,
this collection of restored and replica ships affords a fascinating glimpse
of San Diego during its heyday as a commercial seaport. The museum's
headquarters are the *Berkeley,* an 1898 ferryboat moored at the foot of
Ash Street. The steam-driven ship, which served the Southern Pacific
Railroad in San Francisco until 1958, played its most important role
during the great earthquake of 1906, when it saved thousands of people
from the fires that had engulfed San Francisco by carrying them across

Fodor's Choice
★

The *Star of India*, the oldest active sailing ship in the world, still occasionally plies San Diego Bay.

San Francisco Bay to Oakland. It now holds permanent exhibits on West Coast maritime history and complementary rotating exhibits.

The oldest active sailing ship in the world, the *Star of India*, is often considered a symbol of the city. An iron windjammer built in 1863, the ship made 21 trips around the world in the late 1800s, when she traveled the East Indian trade route, shuttled immigrants from England to New Zealand, and served the Alaskan salmon trade. Saved from the scrap yard and painstakingly restored, the Star of India is the oldest active iron sailing ship in the world.

You can take to the water in the museum's other sailing ship, the *Californian*. This replica of a 19th-century revenue cutter that patrolled the shores of California is designated the state's official tall ship. Weekend sails, typically from noon to 4, cost $42. Tickets may be purchased online or at the museum on the day of sail. They're most popular on sunny days, when it's recommended to show up at least one hour ahead of desired departure. ⊠ *1492 N. Harbor Dr.* ☎ *619/234–9153* ⊕ *www. sdmaritime.org* ⊠ *$14 includes entry to all ships except the Californian* ⊙ *9–8, until 9* PM *Memorial Day to Labor Day.*

❹ **Museum of Contemporary Art, San Diego.** A the downtown branch of the
FodorśChoice city's contemporary art museum, explore the works of international and
★ regional artists in a modern, urban space that is easily accessible by San Diego's trolley system. The Jacobs Building—once the baggage building at the historic Santa Fe Depot—gives artists flexible space to create large-scale installations. MCSAD showcases established and emerging artists in rotating exhibitions, as well as permanent site-specific commissions by Jenny Holzer and Richard Serra. Free cell phone audio tours

and podcasts are available for most exhibits; if you don't have an iPod with you, the museum will lend you one. ■**TIP→** Admission is good for seven days, and includes both the downtown and La Jolla locations. ⊠ *1001 Kettner Blvd.* ☎ *858/454–3541* ⊕ *www.mcasd.org* ☛ *$10; ages 25 and under are free; free 3rd Thurs. of the month 5–7* ☉ *Thurs.–Tues. 11–5, 3rd Thurs. until 7. Closed Wed.*

❼ **Seaport Village.** On a prime stretch of waterfront that spreads out across
☾ 14 acres connecting the harbor with hotel towers and the convention center, the three bustling shopping plazas of Seaport Village are designed to reflect the New England clapboard and Spanish mission architectural styles of early California. A ¼-mi boardwalk that runs along the bay and 4 mi of paths lead to specialty shops—everything from a kite store and swing emporium to a shop devoted to hot sauces—as well as snack bars and restaurants, many with harbor views; there are more than 60 in all. Seaport Village's shops are open daily 10 to 9; a few eateries open early for breakfast, and many have extended nighttime hours, especially in summer. Restaurant prices here are high and the food is only average, so your best bet is to go elsewhere for a meal. Live music can be heard daily from noon to 4 at the main food court. If you happen to visit San Diego in late November or early December, you might be lucky enough to catch Surfing Santa's Arrival and even have your picture taken with Santa on his wave. Every year in April catch the Seaport Buskers Fest, featuring a wide array of street performers.

The **Seaport Village Carousel** has 54 animals—lots of horses plus a giraffe, dragon, elephant, dog, and others—hand-carved and hand-painted by Charles Looff in 1895. Tickets are $2. Strolling clowns, balloon sculptors, mimes, musicians, and magicians are also on hand throughout the village to entertain kids. ⊠ *849 W. Harbor Dr.* ☎ *619/235–4014 office and events hotline* ⊕ *www.seaportvillage.com.*

Hillcrest. Northwest of Balboa Park, Hillcrest is San Diego's center for
OFF THE
BEATEN
PATH
the gay community and artists of all types. It truly is one of the city's most interesting neighborhoods. University, 4th, and 5th avenues are filled with cafés, a superb collection of restaurants (including many outstanding ethnic eateries), and boutiques (among which are several indie bookstores selling new and used books along 5th below University).

CORONADO

Although it's actually an isthmus, easily reached from the mainland if you head north from Imperial Beach, Coronado has always seemed like an island and is often referred to as such. Located just 15 mi east of downtown San Diego, Coronado was an uninhabited sandbar until the late 1800s; it was named after Mexico's Coronado Islands.

As if freeze-framed in the 1950s, Coronado's quaint appeal is captured in its old-fashioned storefronts, well-manicured gardens, and charming Ferry Landing Marketplace. Today's residents, many of whom live in grand Victorian homes handed down for generations, can usually be seen walking their dogs or chatting with neighbors in this safe, non-gated community. Naval Air Station North Island was established in 1911 on Coronado's north end, across from Point Loma, and was the

site of Charles Lindbergh's departure on the transcontinental flight that
preceded his famous solo flight across the Atlantic. Coronado's long
relationship with the U.S. Navy and its desirable real estate have made it
an enclave for military personnel; it's said to have more retired admirals
per capita than anywhere else in the United States.

Coronado is accessible via the arching blue 2.2-mi-long San Diego–
Coronado Bay Bridge, which handles some 68,000 cars each day. The
view of the harbor, downtown, and the island is breathtaking, day and
night. Until the bridge was completed in 1969, visitors and residents
relied on the Coronado Ferry, which today has become quite popular
with bicyclists, who shuttle their bikes across the harbor and ride Coronado's wide, flat boulevards for hours.

San Diego's Metropolitan Transit System runs a shuttle bus, No. 904,
around Coronado; you can pick it up where you disembark the ferry
and ride it out as far as Silver Strand State Beach. Bus No. 901 runs
daily between the Gaslamp Quarter and Coronado.

You can board the ferry, operated by **San Diego Harbor Excursion** (☎ 619/
234–4111, 800/442–7847 in CA ⊕ www.sdhe.com), at the Broadway
Pier on the Embarcadero in downtown San Diego; you'll arrive at the
Ferry Landing Marketplace in Coronado. Boats depart every hour on
the hour from the Embarcadero and every hour on the half hour from
Coronado, daily 9–9 from San Diego (9–10 Friday and Saturday),
9:30–9:30 from Coronado (9:30–10:30 Friday and Saturday); the fare
is $3.50 each way. Service to Coronado also departs from the conven-
tion center every other hour. Buy tickets at the Broadway Pier, 5th Ave.
Landing, or the Ferry Landing Marketplace. The company also offers
water-taxi service weekdays 9:30 AM–8 PM, Friday and Saturday until
10 PM. Later hours can be arranged. The fare is $7 per person. Call
☎ 619/235–8294 to book.

SIGHTS TO SEE

❾ **Coronado Museum of History and Art.** The neoclassical First Bank of
Commerce building, constructed in 1910, holds the headquarters and
archives of the Coronado Historical Association, a museum, the Coronado Visitor Center, the Coronado Museum Store, and Tent City Restaurant. The collection celebrates Coronado's history with photographs
and displays of its formative events and major sights. Two galleries have
permanent displays, while a third hosts traveling exhibits. For information on the town's historic houses, pick up a copy of the inexpensive
*Promenade Through the Past: A Brief History of Coronado and its
Architectural Wonders* at the museum gift shop. The book traces a
60-minute walking tour of the architecturally and historically significant
buildings that surround the area. The tour departs from the museum
lobby on Wednesday at 2 PM and costs $10. ⊠ *1100 Orange Ave.*
☎ *619/435–7242* ⊕ *www.coronadohistory.org* 🎫 *Donations accepted*
☉ *Weekdays 9–5, Sat.–Sun. 10–5.*

❽ **Ferry Landing Marketplace.** This collection of shops at the ferry landing
is on a smaller scale than Seaport Village, but you do get a great view
of the downtown San Diego skyline. Located along the San Diego Bay,
the little shops and restaurants resemble the gingerbread domes of the

Continued on page 63

BALBOA PARK
SAN DIEGO'S CULTURAL HEART

Acres of lush gardens, dozens of top attractions, and stunning architecture . . . no trip to San Diego is complete without a visit to Balboa Park.

SAN DIEGO'S TREASURE TROVE

Overlooking downtown and the Pacific Ocean, San Diego's sprawling, 1,200-acre Balboa Park is one of the world's great urban green spaces. It's home to most of the city's museums (so many that it's been dubbed "the Smithsonian of the West"), the Tony Award-winning Globe Theatre, and the world-famous San Diego Zoo.

The incredibly varied landscape here includes collections of palm trees, arid areas dotted with sagebrush and cactus, ornate rose gardens . . . and a canyon. Balboa Park was formally established as "City Park" in 1868, though much of the development that you see here today—including the lovely Spanish Renaissance style architecture—was a result of the 1915 Panama-California Exposition.

San Diegans spend years exploring this local treasure. And even though you'll just be scratching the surface, a visit here should definitely be on your itinerary.

(Above) Casa del Prado; (Previous page) The Alcazar Garden.

BEST BETS

Here at Balboa Park's attractions sorted by interest. *Numbers correspond with map and photo/descriptions on next page.*

ARTS AFICIONADOS
Globe Theatre, 7
Museum of Photographic Arts, 24
San Diego Art Institute, 20
San Diego Museum of Art, 14
SDAI: Mus. of the Living Artist, 27
Spanish Village Art Center, 18
Spreckels Organ Pavilion, 16
Timken Museum of Art, 21

ARCHITECTURE BUFFS
Bea Evenson Fountain, 3
Cabrillo Bridge, 5
California Building and Tower, 6
Casa de Balboa, 22
House of Charm, 26
House of Hospitality, 8

CULTURAL EXPLORERS
Centro Cultura de la Raza, 29
House of Pacific Relations, 9
Mingei International Mus., 28

HISTORY JUNKIES
Museum of San Diego History, 25
San Diego Museum of Man, 6
San Diego Nat. History Mus., 19
Veterans Mus., 30

NATURE LOVERS
Alcazar Garden, 1
Botanical Building, 4
Japanese Friendship Garden, 10
Inez Grant Parker Mem. Rose Garden, 11
Palm Canyon, 12

SCIENCE & TECHNOLOGY GEEKS
Reuben H. Fleet Science Ctr., 23
San Diego Air and Space Mus., 33
San Diego Automotive Mus., 32

KIDS OF ALL AGES
San Diego Zoo, 15
Carousel, 2
Miniature Railroad, 17
San Diego Model Railroad Mus., 13
San Diego Hall of Champions, 34
Marie Hitchcock Puppet Theater, 31

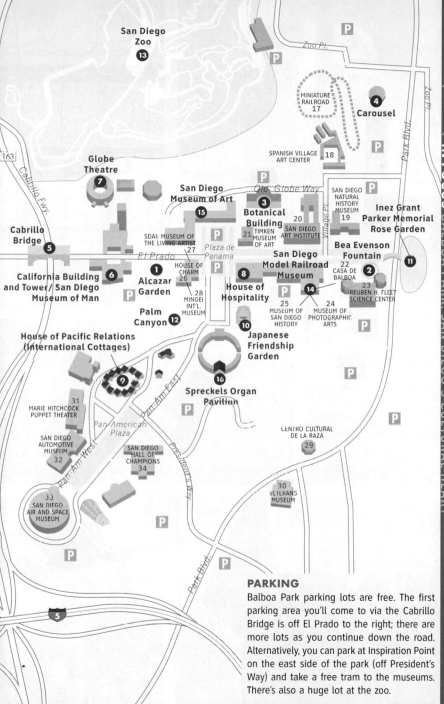

San Diego Zoo **13**

MINIATURE RAILROAD **17**

Carousel **4**

SPANISH VILLAGE ART CENTER **18**

Globe Theatre **7**

San Diego Museum of Art **15**

SAN DIEGO NATURAL HISTORY MUSEUM **19**

Inez Grant Parker Memorial Rose Garden

Botanical Building **3**

20 SAN DIEGO ART INSTITUTE

Cabrillo Bridge **5**

SDAI: MUSEUM OF THE LIVING ARTIST **27**

21 TIMKEN MUSEUM OF ART

Bea Evenson Fountain

Plaza de Panama

San Diego Model Railroad Museum **8**

22 CASA DE BALBOA **2** **11**

California Building and Tower/San Diego Museum of Man **6**

El Prado **1**

HOUSE OF CHARM **26**

Alcazar Garden

28 MINGEI INT'L. MUSEUM

House of Hospitality

23 REUBEN H. FLEET SCIENCE CENTER

Palm Canyon **12**

14

Japanese Friendship Garden **10**

25 MUSEUM OF SAN DIEGO HISTORY

24 MUSEUM OF PHOTOGRAPHIC ARTS

House of Pacific Relations (International Cottages)

9

Spreckels Organ Pavilion **16**

Pan-American Plaza

31 MARIE HITCHCOCK PUPPET THEATER

CENTRO CULTURAL DE LA RAZA

29

SAN DIEGO AUTOMOTIVE MUSEUM 32

SAN DIEGO HALL OF CHAMPIONS 34

30 VETERANS MUSEUM

33 SAN DIEGO AIR AND SPACE MUSEUM

PARKING

Balboa Park parking lots are free. The first parking area you'll come to via the Cabrillo Bridge is off El Prado to the right; there are more lots as you continue down the road. Alternatively, you can park at Inspiration Point on the east side of the park (off President's Way) and take a free tram to the museums. There's also a huge lot at the zoo.

16

14

21

TOTUS MUNDUS AGIT HISTRIONEM

Old Globe Theatre

7

12

8

19

TIPS AND TOP ATTRACTIONS

Balboa Park's immense size and myriad attractions all but require a premeditated plan of attack. Here are a few resources for planning a successful visit:

Your First Stop. Before your visit, be sure to call the Balboa Park Visitors Center (619/239–0512) or visit their Web site (www.balboapark. org) for more information.
Fueling Up. The park is filled with dining options; you'll find everything from hot dog stands to fine dining at The Prado (in the House of Hospitality, which is also home to the Balboa Park Food and Wine School (www. balboawinefood.com).
Free Tuesdays. Most of the park's museums offer free admission one Tuesday each month (on a rotating schedule); call ahead for more information.

TOP ATTRACTIONS
Balboa Park is filled with amazing sights, but these are a few of our favorites.

❶ **Alcazar Garden.** Modeled after the grounds of Spain's Alcazar Castle, this lush spot's tiled fountains, formal boxed gardens, and shady pergola encourage lingering.

❷ **Carousel.** All but two of the hand-carved animals on the park's 1910 carousel are originals.

❸ **Bea Evenson Fountain.** A favorite of barefoot children, this fountain in the Plaza de Balboa shoots cool jets of water 50 feet.

❹ **Botanical Building.** Sunlight streams through this graceful redwood-lath structure onto more than 2,000 orchids, ferns, and other tropical plants.

❺ **Cabrillo Bridge.** The park's official (and pedestrian-friendly) gateway soars 120 feet above the canyon floor.

❻ **California Building and Tower/San Diego Museum of Man.** The dramatic tower flanking the glittering dome of this 1915 structure is a San Diego icon. Inside is the park's highly respected anthropological institution.

❼ **Globe Theatre.** Founded in 1935 and modeled after Shakespeare's original, this Tony Award-winning theatre stages productions throughout the year.

❽ **House of Hospitality.** The park's visitor center is inside this intricately detailed landmark, originally built for the 1915 Panama-California Exposition and rebuilt in 1990.

❾ **House of Pacific Relations (International Cottages).** Originally built for the 1935 California Pacific Exposition, each of these 32 cottages represents a different country and hosts festive cultural events.

❿ **Japanese Friendship Garden.** The serenity of this peaceful Japanese-style garden—replete with walking paths, cherry trees, a Koi pond, and a traditional teahouse—is well worth the small admission price.

⓫ **Inez Grant Parker Memorial Rose Garden.** This gorgeous garden contains 125 varieties of roses…and more than 1,750 individual bushes.

⓬ **Palm Canyon.** Wander the winding paths of this shadowy canyon to see 450 tropical palms representing 58 different species.

⓭ **San Diego Model Railroad Museum.** The world's largest operating model railroad museum is exhilarating for kids and adults alike.

⓮ **San Diego Museum of Art.** The region's oldest and largest art museum holds an impressive collection—ranging from old masters to contemporary artists.

⓯ **San Diego Zoo.** More than 4,000 rare and endangered animals reside at this zoo, famous for its natural habitats and progressive conservation efforts.

⓰ **Spreckels Organ Pavilion.** A civic organist has performed free Sunday concerts on this outdoor 4,530-pipe organ since 1917.

2

IN FOCUS BALBOA PARK: SAN DIEGO'S CULTURAL HEART

Numbers correspond with photos and the map on the previous page.

LIONS AND TIGERS AND PANDA BEARS: THE WORLD FAMOUS SAN DIEGO ZOO

The San Diego Zoo, on a hilly 100-acre corner of Balboa Park, is one of the park's treasures. Operated by the nonprofit Zoological Society of San Diego, the conservation-focused zoo features more than 4,000 rare and endangered animals.

Occupying natural habitats rather than being cooped up in cages, they represent some 800 species from around the planet. While the zoo's adorable pandas get top billing, there are plenty of other cool creatures to see here, from teeny-tiny mantella frogs to larger-than-life African elephants.

STAR ANIMAL ATTRACTIONS

Polar Bear Plunge: Check out the agile swimmers from the underwater viewing room.

Absolutely Apes: Arboreal orangutans and siamangs—each with their own distinct and vocal personality—swing around in a rain forest ecosystem.

Owens Rain Forest Aviary: San Diego has some of the largest free-flight aviaries in the world, including this one featuring 200 birds from the Southeast Asian jungle.

Gorilla Tropics: Observe the complex social dynamics of gorillas in this unique natural habitat, which simulates an African rain forest. Nearby you'll find pygmy chimpanzees, or bonobos, thought to be the most intelligent primates after humans.

Koala Exhibit: The zoo has the largest number of koalas outside Australia.

Monkey Trails: This elaborate exhibition is like venturing deep into African and Asian forests. From a safe distance, you can spy on monkeys, elusive clouded leopards, rare albino hippos, and venomous snakes.

(Above) Hippo underwater at the San Diego Zoo

PANDA-MONIUM

The zoo currently has five pandas (on loan from China) at its Giant Panda Research Station—the most in the United States—and has had five successful panda births. The bears you'll likely see during your visit are Bai Yun ("White Cloud"); Gao-Gao ("Big-Big"), a rambunctious rescued bear; Su Lin ("A Little Bit of Something Very Cute"), born to Bai Yun and Gao-Gao in 2005; Zhen Zhen ("Precious"), born in 2007; and Yun Zi ("Son of Cloud") in 2009; to the same proud parents.

ZOO TIPS

If you want to see it all, give it a full day. To experience everything the zoo has to offer—or most of it, anyway—you'll need at least five hours.

Do your homework: Check the zoo's Web site for details on unique events like the summertime Nighttime Zoo, themed sleepover parties, and sunrise strolls, as well as info on admission deals.

Avoid ticket lines: Purchase and print tickets online using the zoo's Web site.

Picnic before (or after) your visit: The zoo doesn't allow any outside food. There's a wide variety of food available for purchase inside the zoo—but prices are steep.

Prioritize: When you arrive, grab a park map and plot your route (or, better yet, plan ahead with the interactive map on the zoo's Web site).

Wear comfortable shoes: Even if you utilize the zoo's aerial trams, buses, and moving walkways, you'll still be hoofing it quite a bit.

GETTING AROUND THE ZOO

The Skyfari, an aerial gondola lift, offers a bird's-eye view of the grounds and quick transportation. A double-decker, open-roof guided tour bus provides a narrated overview of much of the property; express buses stop at five points in the zoo every 20 minutes. Of course, you can also walk everywhere—just be aware that the terrain is occasionally hilly, and the zoo is *huge*.

PRACTICALITIES

✉ 2920 Zoo Dr.

☎ 619/234–3153, 888/697–2632 giant panda hotline

🌐 www.sandiegozoo.org

💲 $37 includes zoo, Children's Zoo, and animal shows, plus guided bus tour, unlimited express bus rides, and Skyfari Aerial Tram rides; zoo free for children under 12 in Oct.; $70 pass good for admission to zoo and San Diego Wild Animal Park within 5 days

💳 AE, D, MC, V

🕐 July–Sept., daily 9–9; Sept.–May, daily 9–4; Children's Zoo and Skyfari ride generally close 1 hr earlier.

SAN DIEGO WILD ANIMAL PARK

About 30 minutes north of the zoo, the 1,800-acre San Diego Wild Animal Park is an extensive wildlife sanctuary where animals roam free—and guests can get up close and personal in escorted caravans and on backcountry trails. *See listing in this chapter.*

DID YOU KNOW?

Rosebud! If some of the buildings in Balboa Park look strangely familiar, it may be because they were stand-ins for portions of Charles Foster Kane's estate, Xanadu, in Orson Welles' classic *Citizen Kane.* Shown here is the California Building and Tower/Museum of Man.

Hotel Del Coronado. If you want to rent a bike or in-line skates, stop in at **Bikes and Beyond** (✉ *1201 1st St. #122* ☎ *619/435–7180*). ✉ *1201 1st St., at B Ave.* ☎ *619/435–8895.*

❿ **Hotel Del Coronado.** One of San Diego's best-known sites, the hotel has
Fodor'sChoice been a National Historic Landmark since 1977. It has a colorful history,
★ integrally connected with that of Coronado itself, making it worth a visit even if you don't stay here. "The Del" was the brainchild of financiers Elisha Spurr Babcock Jr. and H. L. Story, who saw the potential of Coronado's virgin beaches and its view of San Diego's emerging harbor. They purchased 4,100 acres in 1885 for $110,000 and threw a lavish July 4 bash for prospective investors. By the end of the year they had roused public interest—and had an ample return on their investment. The hotel opened in 1888, just 11 months after construction began.

The Del's distinctive red-tile roofs and Victorian gingerbread architecture have served as a set for many movies, political meetings, and extravagant social happenings. It's speculated that the Duke of Windsor may have first met Wallis Simpson here. Eleven presidents have been guests of The Del, and the film *Some Like It Hot*—starring Marilyn Monroe, Jack Lemmon, and Tony Curtis—used the hotel as a backdrop. Tours of the Del are available Tuesday at 10:30 and Friday–Sunday at 2 for $15 per person. Reservations are required through the Coronado Visitor Center (☎ *619/437–8788*). ✉ *1500 Orange Ave.* ☎ *619/435–6611* ⊕ *www.hoteldel.com.*

HARBOR AND SHELTER ISLANDS AND POINT LOMA

The populated outcroppings that jut into the bay just west of downtown and the airport demonstrate the potential of human collaboration with nature. Point Loma, Mother Nature's contribution to San Diego's attractions, has always protected the center city from the Pacific's tides and waves. It's shared by military installations, funky motels and fast-food shacks, stately family homes, huge estates, and private marinas packed with sailboats and yachts. Newer to the scene, Harbor and Shelter islands are landfill. Created out of sand dredged from the San Diego Bay in the second half of the past century, they've become tourist hubs—their high-rise hotels, seafood restaurants, and boat-rental centers looking as solid as those anywhere else in the city.

SIGHTS TO SEE

⓫ **Cabrillo National Monument.** This 160-acre preserve marks the site of the
☾ first European visit to San Diego, made by 16th-century explorer Juan
Fodor'sChoice Rodríguez Cabrillo (circa 1498–1543)—historians have never conclu-
★ sively determined whether he was Spanish or Portuguese. Cabrillo, who had earlier gone on voyages with Hernán Cortés, landed at this spot, which he called San Miguel, in 1542. Today the site, with its rugged cliffs and shores and outstanding overlooks, is one of the most frequently visited of all the national monuments.

The **visitor center** presents films and lectures about Cabrillo's voyage, the sea-level tide pools, and migrating gray whales. **Interpretive stations** have been installed along the walkways that edge the cliffs. The moderately steep **Bayside Trail**, 2½-mi round-trip, winds through coastal

San Diego's myriad coastal trails and paths provide great views of natural and man-made wonders alike.

sage scrub, curving under the cliff-top lookouts and taking you ever closer to the bay-front scenery. You cannot reach the beach from this trail and must stick to the path to protect the cliffs from erosion and yourself from thorny plants and snakes—including rattlers. You'll see prickly pear cactus and yucca, black-eyed Susans, fragrant sage, and maybe a lizard or a hummingbird. The climb back is long but gradual, leading up to the **Old Point Loma Lighthouse.**

The western and southern cliffs of Cabrillo National Monument are prime whale-watching territory. A sheltered **viewing station** has wayside exhibits describing the great gray whales' yearly migration from Baja California to the Bering and Chukchi seas near Alaska. High-powered telescopes help you focus on the whales' water spouts. More accessible sea creatures can be seen in the **tide pools** at the foot of the monument's western cliffs. Drive north from the visitor center to Cabrillo Road on the left, which winds down to the Coast Guard station and the shore. ✉ *1800 Cabrillo Memorial Dr., Point Loma* ☎ *619/557–5450* ⊕ *www. nps.gov/cabr* 💰 *$5 per car, $3 per person entering on foot or by bicycle* ☉ *Park daily 9–5.*

🄬 **Harbor Island.** Following the success of nearby Shelter Island—created in 1950 out of material left behind from dredging a channel in San Diego Bay during the 1930s—the U.S. Navy decided to use the residue that resulted from digging berths deep enough to accommodate aircraft carriers to build another recreational island; the result is the 1½-mi-long peninsula known as Harbor Island. Restaurants and high-rise hotels now line its inner shore. The bay shore has pathways, gardens, and picnic spots for sightseeing or working off the calories from the various indoor or outdoor food fests held here. On the west point, Tom Ham's Lighthouse restaurant has a U.S. Coast Guard–approved beacon shining from its tower.

⓭ **Scott Street.** Running along Point Loma's waterfront from Shelter Island to Liberty Station on Harbor Drive, this thoroughfare is lined with deep-sea fishing charters and whale-watching boats. It's a good spot to watch fishermen (and -women) haul marlin, tuna, and puny mackerel off their boats.

⓬ **Shelter Island.** Shelter Island—actually a peninsula—supports towering mature palms, a cluster of resorts, restaurants, and side-by-side marinas. It's the center of San Diego's yacht-building industry, and boats in every stage of construction are visible in the yacht yards. A long sidewalk runs from the landscaped lawns of the **San Diego Yacht Club** (tucked down Anchorage Street off Shelter Island Drive) past boat brokerages to the hotels and marinas that line the inner shore, facing Point Loma. On the bay side, fishermen launch their boats or simply stand on shore and cast. Families relax at picnic tables along the grass, where there are fire rings and permanent barbecue grills. Within walking distance is the huge Friendship Bell, given to San Diegans by the people of Yokohama, Japan, in 1960.

MISSION BAY AND SEAWORLD

Mission Bay Park is San Diego's monument to sports and fitness. This 4,600-acre aquatic park has 27 mi of shoreline including 19 of sandy beach. Playgrounds and picnic areas abound on the beach and low grassy hills of the park. On weekday evenings joggers, bikers, and skaters take over. In the daytime, swimmers, water-skiers, anglers, and boaters—some in single-person kayaks, others in crowded powerboats—vie for space in the water. One Mission Bay caveat: swimmers should note signs warning about water pollution; on occasions when heavy rains or other events cause pollution, swimming is dangerous.

SIGHTS TO SEE

⓯ **SeaWorld San Diego.** One of the world's largest marine-life amusement parks, SeaWorld is spread over 189 tropically landscaped bay front acres—and it seems to be expanding into every available square inch of space with new exhibits, shows, and activities. **Journey To Atlantis** involves a cruise on an eight-passenger "Greek fishing boat" down a heart-stopping 60-foot plunge to explore a lost, sunken city. After this journey serenaded by dolphins calls, you view a 130,000-gallon pool, home to exotic Commerson's dolphins, a small black-and-white South American species known for speed and agility.

The majority of SeaWorld's exhibits are walk-through marine environments. Kids get a particular kick out of the **Shark Encounter,** where they come face-to-face with sandtiger, nurse, bonnethead, black-tipped, and white-tipped reef sharks by walking through a 57-foot clear acrylic tube that passes through the 280,000-gallon shark habitat. The hands-on **California Tide Pool** exhibit gives you a chance to get to know San Diego's indigenous marine life. At **Forbidden Reef** you can feed bat rays and go nose-to-nose with creepy moray eels. At **Rocky Point Preserve** you can view bottlenose dolphins, as well as Californian sea otters. At **Wild Arctic,** which starts out with a simulated helicopter ride to a research post at the North Pole, beluga whales, walruses, and polar bears can be viewed in areas decked out like the wrecked hulls of two 19th-century sailing ships. **Manatee Rescue** lets you watch the gentle-giant marine mammals cavorting in a 215,000-gallon tank. Various **freshwater and saltwater aquariums** hold underwater creatures from around the world. And for younger kids who need to release lots of energy, **Sesame Street Bay of Play at SeaWorld,** opened in 2008, is a hands-on fun zone that features three family-friendly Sesame Street–themed rides.

SeaWorld's highlights are its large-arena entertainments. You can get front-row seats if you arrive 30 minutes in advance, and the stadiums are large enough for everyone to get a seat in the off-season. Introduced in 2006 and starring Shamu the Killer Whale, **Believe** features synchro-nized whales and brings down the house. Blue Horizons, new in 2010, brings dolphins, pilot whales, tropical birds and aerialists together in a spectacular performance.

Another favorite is *Sesame Street presents Lights, Camera, Imagina-tion! in 4-D,* a new film that has Cookie Monster, Elmo, and other Sesame Street favorites swimming through an imaginary ocean and flying through a cinematic sky. **Clyde and Seamore's Risky Rescue,** the sea lion and otter production, also is widely popular.

Not all the shows are water-oriented. **Pets Rule!** showcases the antics of more common animals like dogs, cats, birds, and even a pig. One segment of the show actually has regular house cats climbing ladders and hanging upside down as they cross a high wire. The majority of the animals used in the show were adopted from shelters.

The 30-minute Dolphin Interaction Program ($190) lets you feed, touch, and give behavior signals to bottlenose dolphins. A less expen-sive treat ($39 adults, $19 children) is the **Dine With Shamu** package, which includes a buffet lunch and allows you the thrill of eating while the whales swim up to you or happily play nearby.

Shipwreck Rapids, SeaWorld of San Diego's first adventure ride, offers plenty of excitement—but you may end up getting soaked. For five minutes, nine "shipwrecked" passengers careen down a river in a raft-like inner tube, encountering a series of obstacles, including several waterfalls. There's no extra charge, making this one of SeaWorld's great bargains—expect long lines. Those who want to head to higher ground might consider the **Skytower,** a glass elevator that ascends 265 feet; the views of San Diego County are especially spectacular in early morning and late evening. The **Bayside Skyride,** a five-minute aerial tram ride that leaves from the same spot, travels across Mission Bay. Combined admission for the Skytower and the tram is $5.

SeaWorld is chockablock with souvenir shops and refreshment stands (the only picnic grounds are outside the park entrance), so it's hard to come away from here without spending a lot of money on top of the hefty entrance fee. The San Diego 3-for-1 Ticket ($121 for adults, $99 for children ages 3 to 9) offers five consecutive days of unlimited admission to SeaWorld, the San Diego Zoo, and the San Diego Wild Animal Park. This is a good idea, because if you try to get your money's worth by fitting everything in on a single day, you're likely to end up tired and cranky. Many hotels, especially those in the Mission Bay area, also offer SeaWorld specials that may include rate reductions or two days' entry for the price of one. ✉ *500 Sea World Dr., near west end of I–8, Mission Bay* ☎ *800/257–4268* ⊕ *www.seaworld.com* 🖅 *$69 adults, $59 kids; parking $12 cars; 1-hr behind-the-scenes walking tours $13 extra* 🖃 *AE, D, MC, V* ☉ *Daily 10–dusk; extended hrs in summer.*

16 Vacation Isle. Ingraham Street bisects this island. The water-ski clubs congregate at **Ski Beach** on the east side of the island, where there's a parking lot as well as picnic areas and restrooms. Ski Beach is the site of the annual Bayfair (formerly called the Thunderboat Regatta), held in September. At a pond on the south side of the island, children and young-at-heart adults take part year-round in motorized miniature boat races. ✉ *Mission Bay.*

OLD TOWN

San Diego's Spanish and Mexican roots are most evident in Old Town, the area north of downtown at Juan Street, near the intersection of interstates 5 and 8, that was the site of the first European settlement in Southern California. Although Old Town was largely a 19th-century phenomenon, the pueblo's true beginnings took place much earlier and on a hill overlooking it, where soldiers from New Spain established a military outpost in May 1769. Two months later Father Junípero Serra established the first of the California's missions, San Diego de Alcalá.

On San Diego Avenue, the district's main drag, art galleries and expensive gift shops are interspersed with tacky curio shops, restaurants, and open-air stands selling inexpensive Mexican pottery, jewelry, and blankets. The Old Town Esplanade on San Diego Avenue between Harney and Conde streets is the best of several mall-like affairs constructed in mock Mexican-plaza style. Shops and restaurants also line Juan and Congress streets. Bazaar del Mundo, a much-loved collection of shops holding handmade arts and crafts is at 4133 Juan Street.

Access to Old Town is easy thanks to the nearby Transit Center. Ten bus lines stop here, as do the San Diego Trolley and the Coaster commuter rail line. Two large parking lots linked to the park by an underground pedestrian walkway ease some of the parking congestion, and signage leading from I–8 to the Transit Center is easy to follow.

SIGHTS TO SEE

5 El Campo Santo. The old adobe-wall cemetery established in 1849 was until 1880 the burial place for many members of Old Town's founding families—as well as for some gamblers and bandits who passed through town. ✉ *North side of San Diego Ave. S, between Arista and Ampudia Sts., Old Town.*

1 Junípero Serra Museum. The hill on which San Diego's original Spanish presidio (fortress) and California's first mission were perched is now

TIP SHEET: SEAWORLD SAN DIEGO

Who Will Especially Love This Park?

The park, on 180 tropically landscaped acres, caters to adults and kids of all ages. The Sesame Street Bay of Play—for toddlers less than 42 inches tall—is a two-acre area with familiar television characters, live performances, Sesame Street rides, and interactive educational exhibits like the California Tide Pool.

What's This Really Gonna Cost?

In addition to tickets, you'll need to pay $12 for parking. Meals are about $6–$20 per person. There are also additional fees for Bayside Skyride ($3) and Skytower ($3); you can buy a combo ticket for both for $5. SeaWorld offers a broad range of public and private tours and animal interaction experiences, which start at $13 per person for a one-hour Behind-the-Scenes tour and run up to $190 per person for the Dolphin Interaction Program.

TOP 5 ATTRACTIONS:

Believe: This multimedia Shamu show blends killer whale behaviors with theatrical set pieces, music, and choreography. For an additional $19–$36, you can Dine with Shamu.

Penguin Encounter: Enjoy a close-up look at 250 penguins representing five species—including the only successful emperor penguin breeding colony outside Antarctica.

Shark Encounter: This 280,000-gallon tank is home to 12 shark species that swim above and around you as you walk through a clear acrylic tube.

Wild Arctic: Board a simulated jet helicopter, and disembark at a realistic Arctic research station with beluga whales, polar bears, walruses, and seals.

Blue Horizons: Super-intelligent bottlenose dolphins and pilot whales perform for huge crowds.

TIPS:

Cool Down: If it's hot when you visit, be sure to ride Journey to Atlantis, a cruise on an eight-passenger Greek ship that plunges 60 feet to the lost city—creating a nice, refreshing splashdown.

Up, Up and Away: Don't miss the Bayside Skyride over Mission Bay. It's an extra $3, but well worth the time and money—you'll get a great overview of the park and surrounding area.

Get Good Seats: Arrive at shows at least 30 minutes early to get front-row seats.

Save Some Cash: Look for SeaWorld specials at Mission Bay area hotels; some offer reduced rates and/or two-days-for-the-price-of-one admission deals. Be sure to ask when you book.

Elmo's Flying Fish, in SeaWorld's Sesame Street Bay of Play.

Acrobatic dolphins perform in SeaWorld's Dolphin Discovery show.

the domain of a Spanish mission–style museum established, along with Presidio Park, by department store magnate and philanthropist George Marston in 1929 to commemorate the history of the site from the time it was occupied by the Kumeyaay Indians through its Spanish, Mexican, and American periods. Artifacts include Kumeyaay baskets, Spanish riding gear, and a painting that Father Serra would have viewed in Mission San Diego de Alcalá. The education room has hands-on stations where kids can grind acorns in *metates* (stones used for grinding grain), dig for buried artifacts with archaeology tools, or dress up in period costumes—one represents San Diego founding father Alonzo Horton. Ascend the tower to compare the view you'd have gotten before 1929 with the one you have today. The museum, now operated by the San Diego Historical Society, is at the north end of Presidio Park, near Taylor Street. ⊠ *2727 Presidio Dr.* ☎ *619/297–3258* ⊕ *www.sandiegohistory. org* ⊠ *$5* ⊙ *Weekends 10–5.*

❸ **Old Town San Diego State Historic Park.** The six square blocks on the site
Ⓒ of San Diego's original pueblo are the heart of Old Town. Most of the
Fodor's Choice 20 historic buildings preserved or re-created by the park cluster around
★ **Old Town Plaza,** bounded by Wallace Street on the west, Calhoun Street on the north, Mason Street on the east, and San Diego Avenue on the south. The plaza is a pleasant place to rest, plan your tour of the park, and watch passersby. The noncommercial houses are open daily 10–5; none charges admission. Free tours depart daily from the Robinson-Rose House at 11 and 2.

The **Robinson-Rose House** (☎ *619/220–5422*), on Wallace Street facing Old Town Plaza, was the original commercial center of Old San Diego,

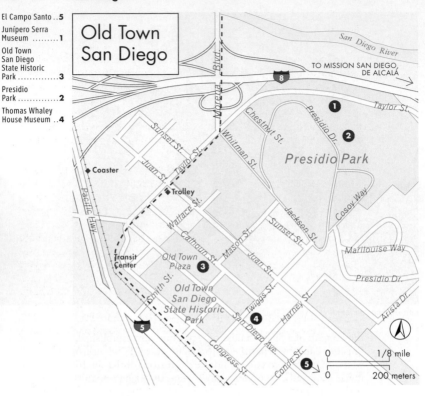

housing railroad offices, law offices, and the first newspaper press. Built in 1853 but in ruins at the end of the 19th century, it has been reconstructed and now serves as the park's visitor center and administrative headquarters. It contains a model of Old Town as it looked in 1872, as well as various historic exhibits. Just behind the Robinson-Rose House is a replica of the Victorian-era Silvas-McCoy house, originally built in 1869.

The **Casa de Estudillo** (⊠ *4001 Mason St., Old Town*), the largest and most elaborate of the original adobe homes, was built on Mason Street in 1827 by San Diego's first County Tax Assessor, Jose Antonio Estudillo, in collaboration with his father, the commander of the San Diego Presidio, José Maria Estudillo. The **San Diego Union Museum** (⊠ *Twigg St. and San Diego Ave., Old Town*) is in a New England–style, wood-frame house prefabricated in the eastern United States and shipped around Cape Horn in 1851. The building has been restored to replicate the newspaper's offices of 1868, when the first edition of the *San Diego Union* was printed.

Also worth exploring in the plaza area are the free Cosmopolitan Hotel, Seeley Stable, **Dental Museum, Mason Street School, Wells Fargo History Museum, First San Diego Courthouse, Casa de Machado y Silvas**

Commercial Restaurant Museum, and the **Casa de Machado Y Stewart.** Ask at the visitor center for locations.

② Presidio Park. The hillsides of the 40-acre green space overlooking Old Town from the north end of Taylor Street are popular with picnickers, and many couples have taken their wedding vows on the park's long stretches of lawn, some of the greenest in San Diego. You may encounter enthusiasts of the sport of grass-skiing gliding over the grass and down the hills on their wheeled-model skis. It's a nice walk from Old Town to the summit if you're in good shape and wearing the right shoes—it should take about half an hour. You can also drive to the top of the park via Presidio Drive, off Taylor Street.

If you do decide to walk, look in at the Presidio Hills Golf Course on Mason Street. It has an unusual clubhouse that incorporates the ruins of Casa de Carrillo, the town's oldest adobe, constructed in 1820. At the end of Mason Street, veer left on Jackson Street to reach the **Presidio Ruins,** where adobe walls and a bastion have been built above the foundations of the original fortress and chapel. Also on-site are the 28-foot-high Serra Cross, built in 1913 out of brick tiles found in the ruins, and a bronze statue of Father Serra. Before you do much poking around here, however, it's a good idea to get some historical perspective at the Junípero Serra Museum, just to the east. Take Presidio Drive southeast of the museum and you'll come to the site of Fort Stockton, built to protect Old Town and abandoned by the United States in 1848. Plaques and statues also commemorate the Mormon Battalion, which enlisted here to fight in the battle against Mexico. ⊠ *1 block north of Old Town.*

④ Thomas Whaley House Museum. Thomas Whaley was a New York entrepreneur who came to California during the gold rush. He wanted to provide his East Coast wife with all the comforts of home, so in 1857 he had Southern California's first two-story brick structure built, making it the oldest double-story brick building on the West Coast. The house, which served as the county courthouse and government seat during the 1870s, stands in strong contrast to the Spanish-style adobe residences that surround the nearby historic plaza and marks an early stage of San Diego's "Americanization." A garden out back includes many varieties of Old Garden roses from before 1867, when roses were first hybridized. Considered the most haunted building in San Diego, the house is open to visitors in the evenings . . . just in case you want to try to bump into a ghost. Starting at 7 PM, admission is by guided tour offered every half hour with the last tour departing at 9:30 PM. ⊠ *2476 San Diego Ave.* ☎ *619/297–7511* ⊕ *www.whaleyhouse.org* ☑ *$6 before 5, $10 after 5.* ☾ *Sept.–May, Mon.–Tues. 10–5, Thurs.–Sun. 10–10; June–Aug., daily 10–10.*

LA JOLLA

La Jollans have long considered their village to be the Monte Carlo of California. Its coastline curves into natural coves backed by verdant hillsides dotted with homes worth millions. Although La Jolla is a neighborhood of the city of San Diego, it has its own postal zone and a coveted sense of class; the ultrarich from around the globe own second homes here—the seaside zone between the neighborhood's bustling downtown and the cliffs above the Pacific has a distinctly European flavor—and old-monied residents maintain friendships with the visiting film stars and royalty who frequent the area's exclusive luxury hotels and private clubs. The town has a cosmopolitan air that makes it a popular vacation resort.

To reach La Jolla from I–5, if you're traveling north, take the La Jolla Parkway exit, which veers into Torrey Pines Road, and turn right onto Prospect Street. If you're heading south, get off at the La Jolla Village Drive exit, which also leads into Torrey Pines Road.

Prospect Street and Girard Avenue, the village's main drags, are lined with expensive shops and office buildings. Through the years the shopping and dining district has spread to Pearl and other side streets. Although there is metered parking on the streets, parking is otherwise hard to find.

SIGHTS TO SEE

3 **Birch Aquarium at Scripps.** The largest oceanographic exhibit in the United States, maintained by the Scripps Institution of Oceanography, sits at the end of a signposted drive leading off North Torrey Pines Road just north of La Jolla Village Drive. More than 60 tanks are filled with colorful saltwater fish, and a 70,000-gallon tank simulates a La Jolla kelp forest. Besides the fish themselves, attractions include a gallery based on the institution's ocean-related research, and interactive educational exhibits on climate change and global warming. ⊠ *2300 Expedition Way* ☎ *858/534-3474* ⊕ *www.aquarium.ucsd.edu* ⊠ *$12, parking free for 3 hrs* ⊗ *Daily 9–5, last ticket sold at 4:30.*

4 **La Jolla Caves.** It's a walk of 145 sometimes slippery steps down a tunnel to Sunny Jim, the largest of the caves in La Jolla Cove and the only one reachable by land. This is a one-of-a-kind local attraction, and worth the time if you have a day or two to really enjoy La Jolla. The man-made tunnel took two years to dig, beginning in 1902; later a shop was built at its entrance. Today La Jolla Cave Store, a throwback to that early shop, is still the entrance to the cave, which was named Sunny Jim after a 1920s cartoon character. The shop sells souvenirs and jewelry and watercolors by local artists. ⊠ *1325 Coast Blvd.* S ☎ *858/459-0746* ⊕ *www.cavestore.com* ⊠ *$4* ⊗ *Daily 10–5.*

5 **La Jolla Cove.** This shimmering blue inlet is what first attracted everyone to La Jolla, from Native Americans to the glitterati; it's the secret to the village's enduring cachet. You'll find the cove—as locals always refer to it, as though it were the only one in San Diego—beyond where Girard Avenue dead-ends into Coast Boulevard, marked by towering palms that line a promenade where people strolling in designer clothes are as common as Frisbee throwers.

Fodor's Choice
★

Smaller beaches appear and disappear with the tides, which carve small coves in cliffs covered with ice plants. Pathways lead down to the beaches. Keep an eye on the tide to avoid getting trapped once the waves come in. A long layer of sandstone stretching out above the

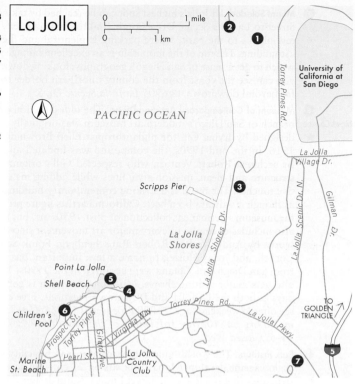

waves provides a perfect sunset-watching spot. Be careful, these rocks can get slippery.

An underwater preserve at the north end of La Jolla Cove makes the adjoining beach the most popular one in the area. On summer days, when water visibility reaches up to 20 feet, the small beach is covered with blankets, towels, and umbrellas, and the lawns at the top of the stairs leading down to the cove are staked out by groups of scuba divers, complete with wet suits and tanks. The **Children's Pool,** at the south end of the park, has a curving beach protected by a seawall from strong currents and waves. Since the pool and its beach have become home to an ever-growing colony of Harbor seals, it cannot be used by swimmers. It is however the best place on the coast to view these engaging creatures. ■**TIP→** Take a walk through Ellen Browning Scripps Park, past the groves of twisted junipers to the cliff's edge. Perhaps one of the open-air shelters overlooking the sea will be unoccupied, and you can spread your picnic out on a table and enjoy the scenery. ✢ *From Torrey Pines Road, turn right on Prospect, then right on Coast Blvd. The park is located at the bottom of the hill* ☎ *619/235-1169* ⊕ *www.sandiego. gov/lifeguards/beaches/cove.shtml* ☉ *4* AM*–8* PM.

⑦ Mount Soledad. La Jolla's highest spot can be reached by taking Nautilus Street to La Jolla Scenic Drive South, and then turning left. Proceed a few blocks to the park, where parking is plentiful and the views are astounding. The top of the mountain is an excellent vantage point from which to get a sense of San Diego's geography: looking down from here you can see the coast from the county's northern border to the south far beyond downtown. ⊠ *6905 La Jolla Scenic Dr. S.*

⑥ Museum of Contemporary Art, San Diego. The oldest section of La Jolla's branch of San Diego's modern art museum was originally a residence, designed by Irving Gill for philanthropist Ellen Browning Scripps in 1916. In the mid-1990s, the compound was updated and expanded by architect Robert Venturi, who respected Gill's original geometric structure and clean, mission-style lines while adding his own distinctive touches. The result is a striking contemporary building that looks as though it's always been here. California artists figure prominently in the museum's permanent collection of post-1950s art, but the museum also includes examples of every major art movement since that time— works by Andy Warhol, Robert Rauschenberg, Frank Stella, Joseph Cornell, and Jenny Holzer, to name a few. Important pieces by artists from San Diego and Tijuana were acquired in the 1990s. The museum also gets major visiting shows. Museum admission is good for seven days at both the La Jolla and Downtown locations. Free exhibit tours are offered weekends at 2. ⊠ *700 Prospect St.* ☎ *858/454–3541* ⊕ *www. mcasd.org* ⊠ *$10, free 3rd Thurs. of the month 5–7* ⊙ *Thurs.–Tues. 11–5, Closed Wed.*

Fodor's Choice
★

① Salk Institute. The world-famous biological-research facility founded by polio vaccine developer Jonas Salk sits on 27 cliff-top acres. The twin structures that modernist architect Louis I. Kahn designed in the 1960s in consultation with Dr. Salk used poured concrete and other low-maintenance materials to clever effect. The thrust of the laboratory–office complex is outward toward the Pacific Ocean, an orientation that is accentuated by a foot-wide "Stream of Life" that flows through the center of a travertine marble courtyard between the buildings. Architects-to-be and building buffs enjoy the free tours of the property; register online two days in advance. You can, however, stroll at will through the dramatic courtyard—simultaneously monumental and eerie. ⊠ *10010 N. Torrey Pines Rd.* ☎ *858/453–4100 Ext. 1287* ⊕ *www.salk.edu* ⊠ *Free* ⊙ *Grounds weekdays 8:30–5, free architectural tours Mon.–Fri. at noon. Reservations required.*

② Torrey Pines State Natural Reserve. *Pinus torreyana,* the rarest native pine tree in the United States, enjoys a 1,700-acre sanctuary at the northern edge of La Jolla. About 6,000 of these unusual trees, some as tall as 60 feet, grow on the cliffs here. The park is one of only two places in the world (the other is Santa Rosa Island, off Santa Barbara) where the Torrey pine grows naturally. The reserve has several hiking trails leading to the cliffs, 300 feet above the ocean; trail maps are available at the park station. Wildflowers grow profusely in spring, and the ocean panoramas are always spectacular. When in this upper part of the park, respect the various restrictions. Not permitted: picnicking, smoking, leaving the trails, dogs, alcohol, or collecting plant specimens.

Fodor's Choice
★

A surfer prepares to head out before sunset at La Jolla's Torrey Pines State Beach and Preserve.

You can unwrap your sandwiches, however, at Torrey Pines State Beach, just below the reserve. When the tide is very low, it's possible to walk south all the way past the lifeguard towers to Black's Beach over rocky promontories carved by the waves (avoid the bluffs, however; they're unstable). **Los Peñasquitos Lagoon** at the north end of the reserve is one of the many natural estuaries that flow inland between Del Mar and Oceanside. It's a good place to watch shorebirds. Volunteers lead guided nature walks at 10 and 2 on most weekends. ⊠ *N. Torrey Pines Rd.* ⊹ *Exit off I–5 onto Carmel Valley Rd. going west, then turn left (south) on Old Hwy. 101* ☎ *858/755–8219* ⊠ *Parking $10* ☉ *Daily 8–dusk.*

WHERE TO EAT

CORONADO AND SOUTH BAY

$$$$ ✕ **1500 Ocean.** The fine-dining restaurant at Hotel Del Coronado offers
AMERICAN   a memorable evening that showcases the best organic and naturally raised ingredients the region has to offer. Chef Brian Sinnott, who honed his technique in San Francisco, presents sublimely subtle dishes such as chilled king crab with compressed Asian pear salad; wild prawns with kale, smoked bacon, and shelled beans; and Kurobuta pork tenderloin with creamy polenta. The interior, at once inviting and elegant, evokes a posh cabana, while the terrace offers ocean views. An excellent international wine list and equally clever desserts and artisanal cheeses

BEST BETS FOR SAN DIEGO DINING

With hundreds of restaurants to choose from, how will you decide where to eat? We've selected our favorite restaurants by price, cuisine, and experience in the Best Bets list below. In the first column, Fodor's Choice properties represent the "best of the best" in every price category. Bon appétit!

Fodor's Choice ★

Bread & Cie ¢, p 79
George's California Modern $$$$, p. 84
Nine-Ten $$$, p. 84
Ortega's Mexican Bistro $, p. 82

Best By Price

¢

Bread & Cie, p. 79
El Zarape, p. 79

$

Michele Coulon Dessertier, p. 84
Ortega's Mexican Bistro, p. 82

$$

Sushi Ota, p. 83

$$$

Nine-Ten, p. 84

$$$$

1500 Ocean, p. 75
George's California Modern, p. 84

Best By Cuisine

AMERICAN

George's California Modern $$$$, p. 84
Nine-Ten $$$, p. 84

CAFÉS

Bread & Cie ¢, p. 79
Michele Coulon Dessertier $, p. 84

FRENCH

Bertrand at Mister A's $$$$, p. 77

LATIN/MEXICAN

El Zarape ¢, p. 79
Ortega's Mexican Bistro $, p. 82

SEAFOOD

Oceanaire Seafood Room $$$, p. 78

Best By Experience

BEST WATER VIEWS

George's California Modern $$$$, p. 84
Marine Room $$$$, p. 84

BEST BRUNCH

Bread & Cie ¢, p. 79
Nine-Ten $$$, p. 84

BEST OUTDOOR DINING

1500 Ocean $$$$, p. 75
Osteria Romantica $, p. 84

ROMANTIC

Bertrand at Mister A's $$$$, p. 77
Chez Loma $$$, p. 77
George's California Modern $$$, p. 84

complete the experience. ⊠ *Hotel Del Coronado, 1500 Orange Ave.* ☎ *619/522–8490* ▤ *AE, D, DC, MC, V* ⊘ *No lunch* ✛ *6D.*

$$$ ✗ **Chez Loma.** A favorite with guests at nearby Hotel Del Coronado, this
FRENCH restaurant is tucked away on a side street. Chez Loma is located in a former private home with lots of windows, soft lighting, and an upstairs Victorian parlor where coffee and dessert are served. The more elaborate dishes among the carefully prepared French bistro menu are boeuf bourguignon, rack of lamb with balsamic marinade, and roasted salmon in a horseradish crust. A specially priced early dinner menu and two choices of fixed-price menus for $40 or $45 offer more value. ⊠ *1132 Loma Ave.* ☎ *619/435–0661* ▤ *AE, D, MC, V* ⊘ *No lunch* ✛ *D6.*

DOWNTOWN

$$$$ ✗ **Bertrand at Mister A's.** Restaurateur Bertrand Hug's sumptuous 12th-
FRENCH floor dining room atop Banker's Hill offers serene decor, contemporary paintings, and a view that stretches to Mexico, making it perfect for a sunset cocktail. Chef Stephane Voitzwinkler creates luxurious seasonal dishes such as lobster strudel, black truffle macaroni and cheese, and Wagyu rib-eye steak with béarnaise sauce. The dessert list encompasses a galaxy of sweets. Service, led by the charming Hug, is expert and attentive. ⊠ *2550 5th Ave., Banker's Hill* ☎ *619/239–1377* ⌕ *Reservations essential* ▤ *AE, MC, V* ⊘ *No lunch weekends* ✛ *E5.*

¢ ✗ **Bread on Market.** The baguettes at this artisanal bakery near the
CAFÉ PETCO Park baseball stadium are every bit as good as the ones you'd buy in Paris. Focaccia and other superior loaves are the building blocks for solid but pricey sandwiches, which range from the turkey special with honey mustard and cranberry sauce to a vegan sandwich with locally grown avocado. The menu extends to a daily soup, a fruit-garnished cheese plate, and an appetizing Mediterranean salad. If you have a sweet tooth, try the peanut butter and chocolate chip cookies, coconut macaroons, and biscotti with hazelnut and chocolate. ⊠ *730 Market St., East Village* ☎ *619/795–2730* ▤ *AE, D, MC, V* ⊘ *No dinner* ✛ *E5.*

$$$ ✗ **Candelas.** The scents and flavors of imaginative Mexican cuisine
MEXICAN with a European flair permeate this handsome, romantic restaurant and nightspot in the shadow of San Diego's tallest residential towers. Candles glow everywhere around the small, comfortable dining room. There isn't a burrito or taco in sight. Fine openers such as cream of black bean soup, and salad of watercress with bacon and pistachios warm diners up for local lobster stuffed with mushrooms, jalapeño peppers, and aged tequila; or tequila-flamed jumbo prawns over creamy, seasoned goat cheese. The adjacent bar pours many elegant tequilas, offers entertainment, and has become a popular, often jam-packed nightspot. They also serve a Mexican-style breakfast on weekends. ⊠ *416 3rd Ave., Gaslamp Quarter* ☎ *619/702–4455* ▤ *AE, D, DC, MC, V* ⊘ *No lunch weekends* ✛ *H3.*

$ ✗ **Monsoon.** An exceptionally attractive restaurant, Monsoon delights
INDIAN with features such as a waterfall on the back wall that splashes like a cloudburst. Folding doors allow some tables to share the outdoor atmosphere of the terrace, but at a distance from the sidewalk. The menu

offers many dishes not easily found at local Indian eateries, including a sweetly spiced mango soup, banana curry, and lamb curry. The dozens of curries and similar dishes are spiced to taste, and baked-to-order breads should not be missed. ⊠ *729–733 4th Ave., Gaslamp Quarter* ☎ *619/234-5555* ⊟ *AE, D, MC, V* ✛ *H2.*

$$$ ✗ **Oceanaire Seafood Room.** Engineered to recall an ocean liner from the
SEAFOOD 1940s, Oceanaire is a bit put-on, but admirable for the long bar serving up classic cocktails, oysters, and sashimi, and a carefully prepared menu that offers up to 25 daily "fresh catches," and many specialties ranging from convincing Maryland crab cakes and oysters Rockefeller to richly stuffed California sole, a luxurious one-pound pork chop, and irresistible hash brown potatoes. Executive Chef Sean Langlois creates a daily menu that may include the deliciously hot, spice-fired "angry" lobster. Service is a casual thing in San Diego, which makes the professional staff here all the more notable. ⊠ *400 J St., Gaslamp Quarter* ☎ *619/858-2277* ⊟ *AE, D, MC, V* ☾ *No lunch* ✛ *H3.*

$$$$ ✗ **Rainwater's on Kettner.** San Diego's premier homegrown steak house
STEAK HOUSE also ranks as the longest-running of the pack, not least because it has
★ the luxurious look and mood of an old-fashioned Eastern men's club. The cuisine is excellent: open with the signature black-bean soup with Madeira. Continue with the tender, expertly roasted prime rib, superb veal's liver with onions and bacon, broiled free-range chicken, fresh seafood, or the amazingly succulent pork chops, all served in vast portions with plenty of hot-from-the-oven cornsticks on the side. The prime steaks sizzle, as does the bill. (Though the menu also offers a selection of light entrées that are a bit easier on the wallet.) ⊠ *1202 Kettner Blvd., Downtown* ☎ *619/233-5757* ⊟ *AE, MC, V* ☾ *No lunch weekends* ✛ *F1.*

$ ✗ **The Tin Fish.** On the rare rainy day, the staff takes it easy at this eatery
SEAFOOD less than 100 yards from the PETCO Parkbaseball stadium (half of the 100-odd seats are outdoors.) Musicians entertain some evenings, making this a lively spot for dinners of grilled and fried fish and shellfish, as well as seafood burritos and tacos. The quality here routinely surpasses that at grander establishments. Service hours vary with the day of the week, the weather, and whether it's baseball season or not, but generally Tin Fish is open from 11 to 8 Sunday through Thursday and until 11 PM on weekends. ⊠ *170 6th Ave., Gaslamp Quarter* ☎ *619/238-8100* ⌂ *Reservations not accepted* ⊟ *AE, D, MC, V* ✛ *H3.*

LITTLE ITALY

$$ ✗ **Buon Appetito.** This charmer serves Old World–style cooking in a
ITALIAN casual but somewhat sophisticated environment. Choose a table on the breezy sidewalk or in an indoor room jammed with art and fellow diners. Baked eggplant *all'amalfitana*, in a mozzarella-topped tomato sauce, is a dream of a dish, and in San Diego, tomato sauce doesn't get better than this. Consider also *branzino* (sea bass) in a mushroom sauce, hearty seafood cioppino, and expert osso buco paired with affordable and varied wines. The young Italian waiters' good humor makes the experience fun. ⊠ *1609 India St., Little Italy* ☎ *619/238-9880* ⊟ *AE, MC, V* ✛ *E5.*

$$$$ ✕ **Po Pazzo.** An eye-catching creation from leading Little Italy restaura-
ITALIAN teurs Joe and Lisa Busalacchi, Po Pazzo earns its name, which means
"a little crazy," by mixing a lively bar with a restaurant serving modern Italian fare. A steak house with an accent, this stylish eatery offers
attractive salads and thick cuts of prime beef, as well as a top-notch
presentation of veal chops Sinatra style with mushrooms, tomatoes,
and onions; and Sicilian rib-eye steak that defines richness. It's fun but
pricey, although the Sunday brunch buffet leads into a $24.95 prime-
rib dinner. ⊠ *1917 India St., Little Italy* ☎ *619/238–1917* ☰ *AE, D,
MC, V* ♣ *E5.*

UPTOWN

$ ✕ **Bombay Exotic Cuisine of India.** Notable for its elegant dining room with
INDIAN a waterfall, Bombay employs a chef whose generous hand with raw and
cooked vegetables gives each course a colorful freshness reminiscent of
California cuisine, though the flavors definitely hail from India. Try the
tandoori lettuce-wrap appetizer and any of the stuffed *kulchas* (a stuffed
flatbread). The unusually large selection of curries may be ordered with
meat, chicken, fish, or tofu. The curious should try the *dizzy noo shakk*,
a sweet and spicy banana curry. Try the family-style tasting menu, which
includes appetizer, tasting portions of four entrees, naan, and mango
mousse desert for $29 per person. ⊠ *Hillcrest Center, 3960 5th Ave.,
Suite 100, Hillcrest* ☎ *619/298–3155* ☰ *AE, D, DC, MC, V* ♣ *F4.*

¢   ✕ **Bread & Cie.** There's a brisk East Coast air to this artsy, urban bakery
CAFÉ and café that put itself on the map by being one of San Diego's first and
Fodor's Choice best artisan bread bakers. Owner Charles Kaufman is a former New
★ Yorker and filmmaker, who gave Bread & Cie a sense of theater by putting bread ovens imported from France on center stage. The mix includes
warm foccacia covered in cheese and vegetables, crusty loaves of black
olive bread, gourmet granola with Mediterranean yogurt, bear claws,
and first-rate cinnamon rolls. Lunch on house-made quiche, paninis
filled with pastrami, turkey, and pesto, or Brie and honey, washed down
with tea, coffee, and upscale soft drinks. ⊠ *350 University Ave., Hillcrest* ☎ *619/683–9322* ☰ *D, DC, MC, V.* ♣ *E4*

¢   ✕ **El Zarape.** There's a humble air to this cozy Mexican walk-up taque-
MEXICAN ria, but one bite of the signature scallop tacos and you'll realize something special is happening in the kitchen. Seared bay scallops mingle
with tangy white sauce and shredded cheese in a satiny corn tortilla. Or
perhaps you'll prefer sweet pieces of lobster meat in oversize quesadillas; burritos filled with chiles rellenos, or the original beef, ham, and
pineapple Aloha burrito. No matter, nearly everything is fantastic at
this busy under-the-radar eatery that's part of a developing independent
restaurant row in University Heights. Mexican beverages, including the
sweet-tart hibiscus-flower drink *jamaica* and the cinnamon rice drink
horchata, and house-made flan and rice pudding round out the menu.
⊠ *4642 Park Blvd., University Heights* ☎ *619/692–1652* ☰ *AE, MC,
V* ♣ *E4.*

$ ✕ **Hash House A Go Go.** Expect to wait an hour or more for weekend
AMERICAN breakfast at this splashy Hillcrest eatery, whose walls display photos of
farm machinery and other icons of Middle America, but whose menu

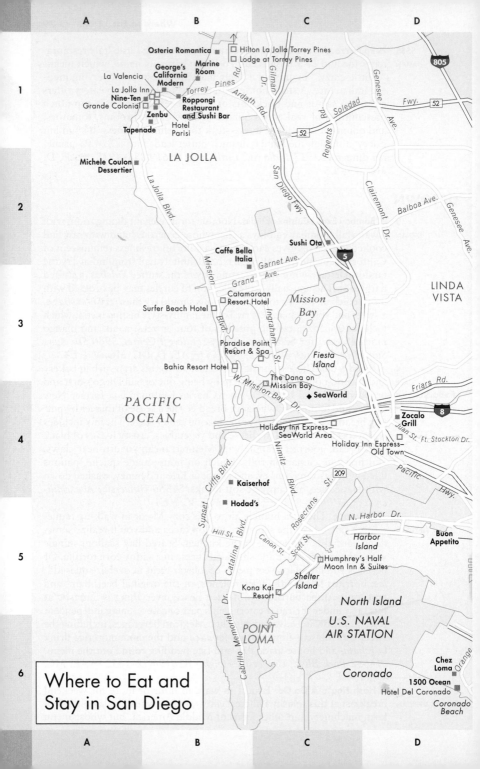

Where to Eat and Stay in San Diego

A

- Osteria Romantica — A1
- George's California Modern — A1/B1
- La Valencia — A1
- La Jolla Inn — A1
- Nine-Ten — A1/B1
- Grande Colonial — A1
- Zenbu — B1
- Marine Room — B1
- Roppongi Restaurant and Sushi Bar — B1
- Hotel Parisi — B1
- Tapenade — A1
- Hilton La Jolla Torrey Pines — C1
- Lodge at Torrey Pines — C1
- Michele Coulon Dessertier — A2
- LA JOLLA
- Caffe Bella Italia — B2/B3
- Sushi Ota — C2
- Catamaraan Resort Hotel — B3
- Surfer Beach Hotel — A3
- Mission Bay — C3
- LINDA VISTA — D2
- Paradise Point Resort & Spa — B3
- Fiesta Island — C3
- Bahia Resort Hotel — A3
- The Dana on Mission Bay — B4
- SeaWorld — C4
- Zocalo Grill — C4
- Holiday Inn Express–SeaWorld Area — B4
- Holiday Inn Espress–Old Town — C4
- PACIFIC OCEAN
- Kaiserhof — B5
- Hodad's — B5
- Buon Appetito — D5
- Harbor Island — C5
- Humphrey's Half Moon Inn & Suites — C5
- Kona Kai Resort — B5
- Shelter Island — B5
- North Island — C6
- U.S. NAVAL AIR STATION — C6
- POINT LOMA — A6
- Coronado — C6
- Chez Loma — D6
- 1500 Ocean — D6
- Hotel Del Coronado — D6
- Coronado Beach — D6

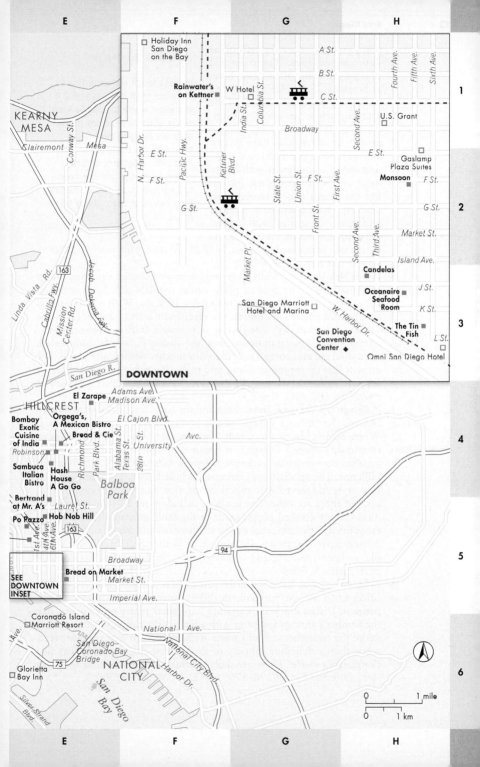

takes an up-to-the-minute look at national favorites. The oversized portions are the main draw here; at breakfast, huge platters carpeted with fluffy pancakes sail out of the kitchen, while at noon customers favor the overflowing chicken potpies crowned with flaky pastry. The parade of old-fashioned good eats continues at dinner with hearty meat and seafood dishes, including the grand sage-flavored fried chicken, bacon-studded waffles, and meat loaf stuffed with roasted red pepper, spinach, and mozzarela with a side of mashed potatoes. ⊠ *3628 5th Ave., Hillcrest* ☎ *619/298–4646* ▤ *AE, MC, V* ✢ *E4.*

> **BUDGET DINING**
>
> In these tough economic times, there are great deals available if you know where to look. To keep diners at the table, many restaurants are bringing back happy hour, with discounts (up to 50%) on drinks, appetizers, or small plates during the late afternoon and early evening. Some eateries have even instituted all-day happy hours.

$ ✕ **Hob Nob Hill.** That Hob Nob never seems to change suits San Diego
AMERICAN just fine; this is the type of place where regulars delight in ordering
★ the same meal they've been ordering for 20 years. With its dark-wood booths and patterned carpets, the restaurant seems suspended in the 1950s, but you don't need to be a nostalgia buff to appreciate the bargain-price American home cooking—dishes such as Waldorf salad, fried chicken, and corned beef like your mother never really made. The crowds line up morning, noon, and night. Reservations are suggested for Sunday breakfast. ⊠ *2271 1st Ave., Middletown* ☎ *619/239–8176* ▤ *AE, D, DC, MC, V* ✢ *E5.*

$ ✕ **Ortega's, A Mexican Bistro.** Californians have long flocked to Puerto
MEXICAN Nuevo, the "lobster village" south of San Diego in Baja California.
🕭 When a member of the family that operates several Puerto Nuevo
Fodor'sChoice restaurants opened Ortega's, it became an instant sensation, since it
★ brought no-nonsense, authentic Mexican fare straight to the heart of Hillcrest. The specialty of choice is a whole lobster prepared steamed Baja-style and served with superb beans, rice, and made-to-order tortillas, but there are other fine options, including melt-in-the-mouth carnitas (slowly cooked pork), made-at-the-table guacamole, and grilled tacos filled with *huitlacoche* corn mushrooms and Mexican herbs. The pomegranate margaritas are a must, as is the special red salsa if you like authentic spice. ⊠ *141 University Ave., Hillcrest* ☎ *619/692–4200* ▤ *AE, MC, V* ✢ *E4.*

$$ ✕ **Sambuca Italian Bistro.** This cozy, candlelit restaurant, with reasonable
ITALIAN prices and a well-prepared menu, differs more than a bit from the competition. Dishes marked "signature" are particularly noteworthy, like the Sambuca shrimp appetizer with a lime-garlic sauce. Creamy flavors make the four-cheese fusilli pasta with lobster an extravagant treat, while there's delicious subtlety to the roasted chicken with brandied Gorgonzola sauce. There are daily specials on weekdays. ⊠ *3888 4th Ave., Hillcrest* ☎ *619/298–8700* ▤ *AE, D, MC, V* ✢ *E4.*

BEACHES

$$ ✕ **Caffe Bella Italia.** Contemporary northern Italian cooking as prepared

ITALIAN in Italy is the rule at this simple restaurant near one of the princi-
pal intersections in Pacific Beach. The menu presents Neapolitan-style
macaroni with sausage and artichoke hearts in spicy tomato sauce,
pizzas baked in a wood-fired oven, linguine with clams, mussels, white
fish and salmon, plus formal entrées like chicken breast sautéed with
marsala and mushrooms, and slices of rare filet mignon tossed with
herbs and topped with arugula and Parmesan shavings. Impressive daily
specials include beet-stuffed ravioli in creamy saffron sauce. ✉ *1525
Garnet Ave., Pacific Beach* ☎ *858/273–1224* ▬ *AE, D, DC, MC, V*
☾ *No lunch* ✛ *B3.*

¢ ✕ **Hodad's.** No, it's not a flashback. The 1960s live on at this fabulously

AMERICAN funky burger joint founded in that era: an unrepentant hippy crowd
☺ sees to it. Walls are covered with license plates, and the amiable servers
with tattoos. Still, this is very much a family place, and Hodad's clien-
tele often includes toddlers and octogenarians. Huge burgers are the
thing, loaded with onions, pickles, tomatoes, lettuce, and condiments,
and so gloriously messy that you might wear a swimsuit so you can
stroll to the beach for a bath afterward. The mini-hamburger is good,
the double bacon cheeseburger absolutely awesome, as are the onion
rings and seasoned potato wedges. ✉ *5010 Newport Ave., Ocean Beach*
☎ *619/224–4623* ▬ *AE, MC, V* ✛ *B5.*

$$ ✕ **Kaiserhof.** Without question this is the best German restaurant in San

GERMAN Diego County, and the lively bar and beer garden work to inspire a
★ sense of *Gemütlichkeit* (happy well-being). Tourist board–style posters
of Germany's romantic destinations hang on the wall, Spaten and Paul-
aner flow from the tap. Gigantic portions are accompanied by such side
dishes as potato pancakes, bread dumplings, red cabbage, and spaetzle.
Entrées include sauerbraten, Wiener schnitzel, goulash, a great Reuben
sandwich, and smoked pork chops, plus excellent daily specials such
as crisp pork schnitzel with tart red cabbage. Weekday happy hour
includes German beers on tap and a generous buffet. Reservations are
a good idea. ✉ *2253 Sunset Cliffs Blvd., Ocean Beach* ☎ *619/224–0606*
▬ *AE, MC, V* ☾ *Closed Mon. No lunch Tues.–Thurs.* ✛ *B4.*

$$ ✕ **Sushi Ota.** Wedged into a mini-mall between a convenience store and

JAPANESE a looming medical building, Sushi Ota initially seems less than auspi-
cious. Still, San Diego–bound Japanese business people frequently call
for reservations before boarding their trans-Pacific flights. Look closely
at the expressions on customers' faces as they stream in and out of the
doors, and you can see the eager anticipation and satisfied glows that
are products of San Diego's best sushi. Besides the usual California
roll and tuna and shrimp sushi, sample the sea urchin or surf clam
sushi, and the soft-shell crab roll or the *omakase* tasting menu. Sushi
Ota offers the cooked as well as the raw. There's additional parking
behind the mall. It's hard not to notice that Japanese speakers get the
best spots, and servers can be abrupt. ✉ *4529 Mission Bay Dr., Pacific
Beach* ☎ *858/270–5670* ⚓ *Reservations essential* ▬ *AE, D, DC, MC,
V* ☾ *No lunch Sat.–Mon.* ✛ *C2.*

LA JOLLA

$$$$
AMERICAN
Fodor's Choice
★

✗ **George's California Modern.** Formerly George's at the Cove, an extensive makeover brought a new name and sleek updated look to this eternally popular restaurant overlooking La Jolla Cove. Hollywood types and other visiting celebrities can be spotted in the sleek main dining room with its wall of windows. Simpler, more casual preparations of fresh seafood, beef, and lamb reign on the new menu chef Trey Foshee enlivened with seasonal produce from local specialty growers. Give special consideration to succulent roasted chicken with escarole, local swordfish with prosciutto-wrapped gnocchi, and cider-glazed Niman Ranch pork chops. For more informal dining and a sweeping view of the coast try the rooftop Ocean Terrace. ⊠ *1250 Prospect St.* ☎ *858/454–4244* ⌂ *Reservations essential* ▤ *AE, D, DC, MC, V* ⊗ *No lunch in main restaurant, only Ocean Terrace* ✣ *B1.*

$$$$
FRENCH

✗ **Marine Room.** Gaze at the ocean from this venerable La Jolla Shores mainstay and, if it's during an especially high tide, feel the waves race across the sand and beat against the glass. Long-running chef Bernard Guillas takes a bold approach to combining ingredients. Creative seasonal menus score with "trilogy" plates that combine three meats, sometimes including game, in distinct preparations. Exotic ingredients show up in a variety of dishes, including Bengali cashew-spiced prawns, sesame-peppered ahi tuna, and a rack of lamb with violet mustard. ⊠ *2000 Spindrift Dr.* ☎ *858/459–7222* ▤ *AE, D, DC, MC, V* ✣ *B1.*

$
CAFÉ
☺

✗ **Michele Coulon Dessertier.** A "dessertier" confects desserts, a job that Michele Coulon does exceedingly well with organic produce and imported chocolate in the back of a small, charming shop in the heart of La Jolla. Moist chocolate-chip scones, the colorful raspberry pinwheel bombe (a molded dessert of cake, jam, almond macaroons, and ice-cream filling), the berry-frangipane tart, and a decadent chocolate mousse cake are a few treats. This is not just a place for dessert, however. Lunch is served weekdays (the store is open 9–4), and the simple menu includes quiche Lorraine (baked fresh daily) and salads. ⊠ *7556 Fay Ave.* ☎ *858/456–5098* ▤ *AE, D, MC, V* ⊗ *Closed Sun. No dinner* ✣ *A2.*

$$$
AMERICAN
Fodor's Choice
★

✗ **Nine-Ten.** Many years ago, the elegant Grande Colonial Hotel in the heart of La Jolla "village" housed a drugstore owned by actor Gregory Peck's father. In the sleekly contemporary dining room that now occupies the space, acclaimed Chef Jason Knibb serves satisfying seasonal fare at breakfast, lunch, and dinner. At night the perfectly executed menu may include tantalizing appetizers like lobster risotto or Maine scallops with cauliflower custard. The kitchen's creative flair comes through with dishes such as jerk pork belly with habeñero gelée, and *sous vide* salmon in an orange-olive oil emulsion. Delicious desserts include rosewater panna cotta with lychee raspberry sorbet. ⊠ *910 Prospect St.* ☎ *858/964–5400* ▤ *AE, D, DC, MC, V* ✣ *B1.*

$
ITALIAN

✗ **Osteria Romantica.** The name means "Romantic Inn," and with a sunny location a few blocks from the beach in La Jolla Shores, the look suggests a trattoria in Positano. The kitchen's wonderfully light hand shows up in the tomato sauce that finishes the scampi and other dishes, and in

The quality of the food complements the spectacular views at George's California Modern.

the pleasing Romantica salad garnished with figs and walnuts. Savory pasta choices include lobster-filled *mezzelune* (half moons) in saffron sauce, and wonderfully rich spaghetti *alla carbonara* The breaded veal cutlets crowned with chopped arugula and tomatoes is a worthy main course. The warm, informal service suits the neighborhood. ⊠ *2151 Avenida de la Playa* ☎ *858/551–1221* ▭ *AE, D, MC, V* ✛ *B1.*

$$ ✕ **Roppongi Restaurant and Sushi Bar.** A hit from the moment it opened, Roppongi serves global cuisine with strong Asian notes. The contemporary dining room, done in wood tones and accented with a tropical fish tank, Buddhas, and other Asian statuary, has a row of comfortable booths along one wall. It can get noisy when crowded; tables near the bar are generally quieter. Order the imaginative Euro-Asian tapas as appetizers, or combine them for a full meal. Equally delicious are the crispy tofu, pan-seared scallops on potato pancakes, and the Mongolian duck quesadilla. Well-executed entrées include grilled flat-iron steak with shishito peppers and macadamia-crusted mahi mahi with mango chutney. The creative sushi bar rocks. ⊠ *875 Prospect St.* ☎ *858/551– 5252* ▭ *AE, D, DC, MC, V* ✛ *B1.*

ASIAN

$$$ ✕ **Tapenade.** Named after the Provençal black olive-and-anchovy paste, Tapenade specializes in the fresh cuisine of the south of France. The sunny cuisine matches the unpretentious, light, and airy room, lined with 1960s French movie posters, in which it is served. Fresh ingredients, a delicate touch with sauces, and an emphasis on seafood characterize the menu, which changes frequently. If you're lucky, it may include wild boar stewed in red wine, lobster with white corn sauce flavored with Tahitian vanilla, pan-gilded sea scallops, and desserts like chocolate

FRENCH

fondant and profiteroles. The two-course "Riviera Menu," served at lunch for $21.95, is a fabulous steal. ⊠ *7612 Fay Ave.* ☎ *858/551–7500* ▤ *AE, D, DC, MC, V* ☺ *No lunch weekends* ✛ *B1.*

$$ ✕ **Zenbu.** There's a cool California vibe to this cozy, moodily lighted
ASIAN sushi and seafood restaurant that serves some of the freshest fish in town and attracts a who's who of La Jolla. Restaurateur Matt Rimel runs a commercial fishing company, and uses his connections to bring varied seafood from all over the world that excels whether raw or cooked. Seasonal specialties include buttery *otoro* tuna belly and local sea urchin fresh from its spiny shell. Sushi, which can be pricey, ranges from simple nigiri to beautiful sashimi plates and original rolls like Salmon Spider, which combines soft-shell crab with fresh salmon. Cooked dishes run from noodle bowls and grass-fed Montana prime sirloin seared at the table on a hot stone, to whole fried rockfish or local spiny lobster dynamite. ⊠ *7660 Fay Ave., Suite 1* ☎ *858/454–4540* ▤ *AE, D, DC, MC, V* ☺ *No lunch* ✛ *B1.*

OLD TOWN

$$ ✕ **Zocalo Grill.** Try for a table by a fireplace on the covered terrace, but
MEXICAN the contemporary cuisine tastes just as good anywhere in the spacious and handsome eatery. Instead of cooking the carnitas the traditional way—simmered in well-seasoned lard—Zocalo braises them in a mixture of honey and Guinness beer. Recommended starters include artichoke fritters and crisp shrimp skewers with pineapple-mango relish. The chicken enchiladas suisas with green salsa and tamarind-glazed salmon are typical of the Latin-influenced entrées. This is one of the best bets in Old Town. ⊠ *2444 San Diego Ave.* ☎ *619/298–9840* ▤ *AE, D, DC, MC, V* ✛ *D4.*

WHERE TO STAY

CORONADO

$$$$ ⊡ **Coronado Island Marriott Resort.** Near San Diego Bay, this snazzy hotel
☾ has rooms with great downtown skyline views. Despite a location in the shadow of the Coronado Bridge, this hotel offers a serene South Seas ambience. The lobby holds sofas that invite lounging, and the grounds support mature tropical plants. A redesigned pool area has fire pits, and the large rooms and suites are in low-slung buildings redone in a cheerful island-inspired fashion. The resort runs $6 water taxis that drop you off downtown on weekends and daily in summer. **Pros:** spectacular views; hotel spa; close to water taxis. **Cons:** not in downtown Coronado; tricky to find. ⊠ *2000 2nd St.* ☎ *619/435–3000 or 800/543–4300* ⊕ *www.marriotthotels.com/sanci* ⤳ *273 rooms, 27 suites* ☖ *In-room: a/c, refrigerator (some), Wi-Fi. In-hotel: restaurant, room service, bar, tennis courts, pools, gym, spa, water sports, bicycles, laundry service, parking (paid)* ▤ *AE, D, DC, MC, V* ✛ *E6.*

$$$ ⊡ **Glorietta Bay Inn.** The main building on this property is an Edwardian-style mansion built in 1908 for sugar baron John D. Spreckels, who

BEST BETS FOR SAN DIEGO LODGING

Here are our top lodging recommendations by price and experience. The very best properties—in other words, those that provide a particularly remarkable experience in their price range—are designated in the listings with a Fodor's Choice logo.

Fodor'sChoice ★

Calamaran Resort Hotel, p. 95

Grande Colonial, p. 92

Hotel Del Coronado, p. 88

Lodge at Torrey Pines, p. 95

Best By Price

$

Gaslamp Plaza Suites, p. 88

Holiday Inn Express—Old Town, p. 92

$$

The Dana on Mission Bay, p. 96

Humphrey's Half Moon Inn and Suites, p. 90

$$$

Catamaran Resort Hotel, p. 95

Grande Colonial, p. 92

Hotel Del Coronado, p. 88

$$$$

Hotel Parisi, p. 93

La Valencia, p. 93

Lodge at Torrey Pines, p. 95

Best By Experience

BEST HOTEL BAR

Grande Colonial, p. 92

La Valencia, p. 93

BEST BEACH

Hotel Del Coronado, p. 88

Paradise Point Resort & Spa, p. 96

BEST FOR KIDS

Coronado Island Marriott Resort, p. 86

Paradise Point Resort & Spa, p. 96

BEST FOR ROMANCE

Hotel Del Coronado, p. 88

Hotel Parisi, p. 93

Lodge at Torrey Pines, p. 95

BEST OLD HOTELS

Glorietta Bay Inn, p. 86

Hotel Del Coronado, p. 88

La Valencia, p. 93

Diego. Rooms in the mansion and
are quaintly furnished; some have
acent to the Coronado harbor and
but is much smaller and quieter than
Tours ($12) of the island's historical
ree mornings a week. Cookies and lem-
eat views; friendly staff; close to beach.
all; lots of traffic nearby. ✉ 1630 Glori-
r 800/283–9383 ⊕ www.gloriettabayinn.
m: a/c, kitchen (some), refrigerator, DVD,
dry service, parking (paid) ▭ AE, D, MC,

Victorian-styled "Hotel Del," situated along
as much of a draw today as it was when it
esort is always alive with activity, as guests—
European royalty, and celebrities—and tour-
ists marvel iful architecture, surrounding sparkling sand, and
gorgeous ocean views. About half of the resort's accommodations are
in the more charming, original Victorian building, where each room is
unique in size and footprint. Rooms in the California Cabana buildings
and Ocean Towers, built in the mid-1970s, have a Pottery Barn–style
look with marble bathrooms. These rooms are closer to the pool and the
beach, making them a good option for families with children. Luxury
enhancements include a spa with an infinity pool and Beach Village: 78
lavish beachfront villas and cottages that feature fully equipped kitchens, fireplaces, spa-style baths with soaking tubs, Bose sound systems,
and private ocean-view terraces. **Pros:** romantic; on the beach; hotel
spa. **Cons:** some rooms are small; expensive dining; public areas are
very busy. ✉ 1500 Orange Ave. ☎ 800/468–3533 or 619/435–6611
⊕ www.hoteldel.com ⇥ 757 rooms, 65 suites, 43 villas, 35 cottages
⚘ In-room: a/c, safe, Wi-Fi. In-hotel: 5 restaurants, room service, bars,
pools, gym, spa, beachfront, water sports, bicycles, children's programs
(ages 4–17), Internet terminal, laundry service, parking (paid) ▭ AE,
D, DC, MC, V ♻ D6.

DOWNTOWN

$ ⌸ **Gaslamp Plaza Suites.** On the National Register of Historic Places,
this 10-story structure a block from Horton Plaza was built in 1913
as one of San Diego's first "skyscrapers." The public areas have old
marble, brass, and mosaics. Although most rooms are rather small, they
are well decorated with dark-wood furnishings that give the hotel an
elegant flair. You can enjoy the view and a complimentary Continental
breakfast on the rooftop terrace. Book ahead if you're visiting in summer. **Pros:** historic building; good location; well priced. **Cons:** books up
early; smallish rooms. ✉ 520 E St., Gaslamp Quarter ☎ 619/232–9500
or 800/874–8770 ⊕ www.gaslampplaza.com ⇥ 12 rooms, 52 suites
⚘ In-room: a/c, refrigerator, DVD, Wi-Fi. In-hotel: bar, laundry service,
parking (paid) ▭ AE, D, DC, MC, V ⦿ CP ♻ H2.

$$ ⌘ **Holiday Inn San Diego on the Bay.** A 2007 renovation brought new beds and bath fixtures to this hotel on the Embarcadero, across the street from the Cruise Ship terminal and the Maritime Museum. The hotel, made up of three high-rise towers reached by dated elevators, has spacious rooms with balconies and hard-to-beat views. Although the hotel grounds are nice, if fairly sterile, the bay is just across the street and offers boat rides, restaurants, and picturesque walking areas. The hotel is close to the airport and Amtrak station. Restaurants on site include Ruth's Chris Steakhouse and Elephant & Castle. **Pros:** large rooms; great views; kids eat free. **Cons:** not centrally located. ⊠ *1355 N. Harbor Dr., Embarcadero* ☎ *619/232–3861 or 800/877–8920* ⊕ *www. holiday-inn.com* ↝ *600 rooms, 10 suites* ⚹ *In-room: a/c, refrigerator, Wi-Fi. In-hotel: 3 restaurants, room service, bar, pool, gym, laundry facilities, Wi-Fi hotspot, parking (paid)* ⊟ *AE, D, DC, MC, V* ⊹ *F1.*

$$$ ⌘ **Omni San Diego Hotel.** The product of burgeoning downtown growth, this modern masterpiece occupies the first 21 floors of a 32-story high-rise overlooking PETCO Park baseball stadium. Though built for the business traveler, the hotel attracts a fair share of sports fans (it's connected to the stadium by a sky bridge). The modern lobby is simply stunning; all rooms have windows that open to the breeze, and most have views of the ocean, bay, the downtown skyline, or the PETCO outfield. Spacious, pleasantly decorated rooms include DVD players and bathrobes. The pool terrace has a stone fireplace, outdoor dining, and plenty of padded chaise loungers. **Pros:** great views; good location; modern setting. **Cons:** busy; crowded during baseball season. ⊠ *675 L St., Gaslamp Quarter* ☎ *619/231 6664 or 800/843–6664* ⊕ *www. omnihotels.com* ↝ *478 rooms, 33 suites* ⚹ *In-room: a/c, safe, DVD, Internet, Wi-Fi. In-hotel: restaurant, room service, bar, pool, gym, laundry service, Wi-Fi hotspot, parking (paid), some pets allowed* ⊟ *AE, D, DC, MC, V* ⊹ *H3.*

$$$ ⌘ **San Diego Marriott Hotel and Marina.** This 25-story twin-tower hotel next to the convention center and marina has everything a businessperson—or leisure traveler—could want. As a major site for conventions, the complex can be hectic and impersonal, and the hallways can be noisy. Lending some tranquility are a pair of lagoon-style pools nestled between cascading waterfalls. The standard rooms are smallish, but pay a bit extra for a room with a balcony overlooking the marina and bay and you can have a serene, sparkling world spread out before you. **Pros:** great location; many amenities; Roy's Hawaiian Fusion Restaurant. **Cons:** small rooms; very busy. ⊠ *333 W. Harbor Dr., Embarcadero* ☎ *619/234–1500 or 800/228–9290* ⊕ *www.marriotthotels.com/sandt* ↝ *1,300 rooms, 54 suites* ⚹ *In-room: a/c, safe, refrigerator (some), Internet. In-hotel: Wi-Fi hotspot, parking (paid), some pets allowed* ⊟ *AE, D, DC, MC, V* ⊹ *H3.*

$$$ ⌘ **U.S. Grant.** Stepping into the regal U.S. Grant not only puts you in the lap of luxury, but also back into San Diego history; the 100-year-old building is on the National Register of Historic Sites. A 2006 total renovation reintroduced the hotel's original grandeur and opulence. The lobby is a confection of luxurious French fabrics, crystal chandeliers, and Italian Carrera–marble floors. Guests sip tea and martinis here Thursday through Sunday afternoons. Rooms feature custom Italian linens, operatic lighting, and original French and Native American artwork, and the sunny baths are elegantly designed with marble-tile shower enclosures and stone sinks. The Grant Grill restaurant boasts a fusion of grilled specialties and fresh regional cuisine. The venue's 1940s-style New York decor has a glamorous appeal, with African mahogany walls and plush seating. **Pros:** modern rooms; great location; near shopping and restaurants. **Cons:** the hotel's many special events can make for a hectic atmosphere. ⊠ *326 Broadway, Downtown* ☎ *619/232–3121 or 800/237–5029* ⊕ *www.luxurycollection.com/ usgrant* ⟲ *270 rooms, 47 suites* ↻ *In-room: a/c, safe, DVD (some), Internet, Wi-Fi. In-hotel: restaurant, room service, bar, gym, laundry service, Wi-Fi hotspot, parking (paid)* ▭ *AE, D, DC, MC, V* ✛ *H1.*

$$$ ⊡ **W Hotel.** Come here for the trendy decor, fruity drinks, and upscale rooms. The W chain's urban finesse adapts to San Diego with nautical blue-and-white rooms with beach-ball pillows and goose-down comforters atop the beds. The Beach bar has a heated sand floor and fire pit, but the pool is tiny by San Diego standards. The lobby doubles as the surf-and-sand chic Living Room lounge, a local hipster nightspot where non–hotel guests have to wait behind a velvet rope. Be sure to get a room on an upper floor—the scantily-clad crowd parties into the night. The hotel restaurant, Rice, serves stylish Asian and Latin cuisine, and the Away Spa caters to both body and spirit. **Pros:** large lobby that's fun for people-watching; modern rooms; spa. **Cons:** expensive parking; not centrally located. ⊠ *421 West B St., Downtown* ☎ *619/398–3100 or 877/822–0000* ⊕ *www.whotels.com/sandiego* ⟲ *258 rooms, 20 suites* ↻ *In-room: a/c, safe, DVD, Internet, Wi-Fi. In-hotel: restaurant, room service, bars, gym, spa, laundry service, parking (paid)* ▭ *AE, D, MC, V* ✛ *G1.*

HARBOR ISLAND, SHELTER ISLAND, AND POINT LOMA

$$ ⊡ **Holiday Inn Express–SeaWorld Area.** In Point Loma near the West Mission Bay exit off I–8, this is a surprisingly cute and quiet lodging option despite proximity to bustling traffic. The three-story building is only about a half mile from both SeaWorld and Mission Bay. Geared towards leisure travelers, rooms offer firm and soft pillows, and include standard sleeper sofas. Hot buffet breakfast is included. **Pros:** near SeaWorld; free breakfast; good service. **Cons:** not a scenic area; somewhat hard to find. ⊠ *3950 Jupiter St., Point Loma* ☎ *619/226–8000 or 800/320–0208* ⊕ *www.seaworldhi.com* ⟲ *69 rooms, 2 suites* ↻ *In-room: a/c, refrigerator, Wi-Fi. In-hotel: pool, laundry facilities, laundry service, Wi-Fi hotspot, parking (free)* ▭ *AE, D, DC, MC, V* ⦿❘ *CP* ✛ *C4.*

$$ ⊡ **Humphrey's Half Moon Inn & Suites.** This sprawling South Seas–style resort has grassy open areas with palms and tiki torches. A $20 million upgrade in 2008 put new bedding, carpeting, flat-screen TVs, microwaves, and granite vanities in guest rooms. In addition, some rooms have bay views and some have kitchens. The Grand Marina Suite can accommodate up to eight in 1,000 square feet with a full kitchen. Locals throng to Humphrey's for the brunch, jazz lounge, and the outdoor jazz and pop concerts from May through October. **Pros:** water views;

Hotel del Coronado

U.S. Grant

near marina; nightlife on property. **Cons:** vast property; not centrally located. ⊠ *2303 Shelter Island Dr., Shelter Island* ☎ *619/224– 3411 or 800/542–7400* ⊕ *www. halfmooninn.com* ⚓ *128 rooms, 54 suites* ⚐ *In-room: a/c, safe, kitchen (some), refrigerator, Wi-Fi. In-hotel:*

restaurant, room service, bar, pool, gym, bicycles, laundry facilities, Internet terminal, parking (paid) ⊟ *AE, D, DC, MC, V* ✛ *C5.*

$$ 🏨 **Kona Kai Resort.** This 11-acre property blends Spanish and Mediterranean styles. The spacious and light-filled lobby, with its neoclassical end tables, velvet sofas, and Oriental carpets over faded terra-cotta tiles, opens onto a lush esplanade that overlooks the hotel's adjacent marina. The rooms are well appointed, if a bit small, though most have balconies and look out onto either the marina or San Diego Bay. The attractive hotel is popular for business meetings. In summer, a two- to four-night minimum stay might be in effect. **Pros:** quiet area; near marina; water views. **Cons:** not centrally located; small rooms. ⊠ *1551 Shelter Island Dr., Shelter Island* ☎ *619/221–8000 or 800/566–2524* ⊕ *www.resortkonakai.com* ⚓ *124 rooms, 5 suites* ⚐ *In-room: a/c, refrigerator, Wi-Fi. In-hotel: restaurant, room service, bar, pool, gym, spa, beachfront, bicycles, Wi-Fi hotspot, parking (paid)* ⊟ *AE, D, DC, MC, V* ✛ *C5.*

OLD TOWN AND VICINITY

$ 🏨 **Holiday Inn Express–Old Town.** Already an excellent value for Old Town, this cheerful property throws in such perks as a free breakfast buffet. Rooms have a European feel; a $1 million renovation in 2007 added new carpet, linens, and bathroom granite and fixtures. When you've had enough of the heated pool off the shaded courtyard, you can tackle the historic park's attractions and restaurants nearby. **Pros:** good location; hot Continental breakfast. **Cons:** smallish rooms; few nightlife options. ⊠ *3900 Old Town Ave.* ☎ *619/299–7400 or 800/465–4329* ⊕ *www.hioldtownhotel.com* ⚓ *125 rooms, 2 suites* ⚐ *In-room: a/c, refrigerator, Internet. In-hotel: pool, laundry facilities, laundry service, Wi-Fi hotspot, parking (paid)* ⊟ *AE, D, DC, MC, V* 🍽 *CP* ✛ *D4.*

LA JOLLA

$$$ 🏨 **Grande Colonial.** This white wedding cake–style hotel has ocean views
Fodor's Choice and is in the heart of La Jolla village. Built in 1913 and expanded and
★ redesigned in 1925–26, the Colonial is graced with charming European details: chandeliers, a marble hearth, mahogany railings, oak furnishings, and French doors. The 18 club-level suites—called the Little Hotel by the Sea—offer additional amenities: complimentary valet parking, luxury bath products, snack baskets, and a full breakfast. **Pros:** near shopping; near beach; superb restaurant. **Cons:** somewhat busy street. ⊠ *910 Prospect St.* ☎ *858/454–2181 or 800/826–1278* ⊕ *www. thegrandecolonial.com* ⚓ *52 rooms, 41 suites* ⚐ *In-room: a/c, safe,*

kitchen (some), Wi-Fi. In-hotel: restaurant, room service, bar, pool, laundry service, parking (paid) ☰ *AE, D, DC, MC, V* ⊹ *B1.*

$$$
Fodor'sChoice
★

☷ **Hilton La Jolla Torrey Pines**. The hotel blends discreetly into the Torrey Pines cliff top, overlooking the Pacific Ocean and the 18th hole of the Torrey Pines Golf Course, site of the 2008 U.S. Open. Oversize accommodations are simple but elegant; most have balconies or terraces. The menu at the hotel's restaurant, the Torreyana Grille, changes with the seasons; Caesar salad and filet mignon are regulars, but you're likely to find lobster pot stickers and coffee-lacquered duck breast as well. **Pros:** ocean view; near golf; large rooms. **Cons:** not centrally located. ✉ *10950 N. Torrey Pines Rd.* ☎ *858/558–1500 or 800/774–1500* ⊕ *www.hilton. com* ➷ *382 rooms, 12 suites* ♿ *In-room: a/c, safe, Wi-Fi. In-hotel: restaurant, room service, bars, tennis courts, pool, gym, laundry service, Wi-Fi hotspot, parking (paid)* ☰ *AE, D, DC, MC, V* ⊹ *B1.*

$$$$

☷ **Hotel Parisi.** A Zen-like peace welcomes you in the lobby, which has a skylighted fountain and is filled with Asian art. The studio-style suites are decorated according to the principles of feng shui; you can order a massage, a yoga session, or the on-staff psychologist from room service. Favored by celebrities, the hushed, earth-tone suites have flat-screen TVs, granite bathrooms, Frette linens, and ergonomic tubs. The rooms are set back enough from the street noise, but in the ocean-view suites you have to look over buildings across the street to view the Pacific. A European buffet breakfast is served daily. **Pros:** upscale amenities; modern decor; in-room spa services. **Cons:** one-room "suites"; staff can be aloof. ✉ *1111 Prospect St.* ☎ *858/454–1511* ⊕ *www.hotelparisi.com* ➷ *24 suites* ♿ *In-room: a/c, safe, DVD, Wi-Fi. In-hotel: room service, parking (paid)* ☰ *AE, D, MC, V* ❍❘ *CP* ⊹ *B1.*

$$$

☷ **La Jolla Inn.** One block from the beach and near some of the best shops and restaurants, this European-style inn with a delightful staff sits in a prime spot in the village of La Jolla. Many rooms have sweeping ocean views from their balconies; one spectacular penthouse suite faces the ocean, the other village. Enjoy the delicious complimentary Continental breakfast in your room or on the upstairs sundeck. **Pros:** near beach; kids stay free; free parking. **Cons:** keyed entry on village rooms; busy area; dated rooms. ✉ *1110 Prospect St.* ☎ *858/454–0133 or 888/855–7829* ⊕ *www.lajollainn.com* ➷ *21 rooms, 2 suites* ♿ *In-room: a/c, kitchen (some), refrigerator, Internet, Wi-Fi (some). In-hotel: room service, bicycles, laundry facilities, laundry service, parking (free)* ☰ *AE, D, DC, MC, V* ❍❘ *CP* ⊹ *B1.*

$$$$

☷ **La Valencia.** This pink Spanish-Mediterranean confection drew Hollywood film stars in the 1930s and '40s with its setting and views of La Jolla Cove. Many rooms, although small, have a recently updated neutral color scheme with colorful accents, mod brocade-pattern chairs, and flat-screen TVs. The personal attention provided by the staff, as well as the plush robes and grand bathrooms, make the stay even more pleasurable. The hotel is right in the middle of the shops and restaurants of La Jolla village. Rates are lower if you're willing to look out on the village rather than the ocean. Be sure to have a cocktail while gazing at the ocean in Le Sala Bar and stroll the tiered gardens in back. **Pros:** upscale rooms; views; near beach. **Cons:** expensive; lots of

Lodge at Torrey Pines

La Valencia Hotel

La Valencia Hotel

Grande Colonial

Catamaran Resort Hotel and Spa

traffic outside. ⊠ *1132 Prospect St.* ☏ *858/454–0771 or 800/451–0772*
⊕ *www.lavalencia.com* ⤳ *93 rooms, 10 suites, 15 villas* ⟐ *In-room: a/c,*
safe, DVD, Wi-Fi. In-hotel: 3 restaurants, room service, bar, pool, gym,
laundry service, parking (paid) ⊟ *AE, D, MC, V* ✛ *B1.*

$$$$ ⛬ **Lodge at Torrey Pines.** This beautiful Craftsman-style lodge sits on
Fodor's Choice a bluff between La Jolla and Del Mar and commands a coastal view.
★ You know you're in for a different sort of experience when you see
the Scottish kilted doorman. The warm and understated rooms are
spacious and furnished with antiques and reproduction turn-of-the-
20th-century pieces. The service is excellent, and the restaurant, A. R.
Valentien (named after a San Diego plein-air artist of the early 1900s),
serves fine California cuisine. Beyond the grounds are the Torrey Pines
Golf Course and scenic trails that lead to the Torrey Pines State Beach
and Reserve. The village of La Jolla is a 10-minute drive away. **Pros:**
upscale rooms; good service; near golf. **Cons:** not centrally located;
expensive. ⊠ *11480 N. Torrey Pines Rd.* ☏ *858/453–4420 or 800/995–*
4507 ⊕ *www.lodgetorreypines.com* ⤳ *164 rooms, 6 suites* ⟐ *In-room:*
a/c, safe, kitchen (some), Internet, Wi-Fi. In-hotel: 2 restaurants, bars,
golf course, pool, gym, spa, Wi-Fi hotspot, laundry service, parking
(paid) ⊟ *AE, D, DC, MC, V* ✛ *B1.*

MISSION BAY AND THE BEACHES

$$ ⛬ **Bahia Resort Hotel.** This huge complex on a 14-acre peninsula in Mis-
☾ sion Bay Park has studios and some suites with kitchens; many have
wood beam ceilings and a tropical theme, and most have balconies
or other outside seating. The hotel's Victorian-style stern-wheeler, the
Bahia Belle, offers guests complimentary cruises on the bay at sunset.
Room rates are reasonable for a place so well located—within walk-
ing distance of the ocean—and with so many amenities. Guests at the
Bahia can use the spa and fitness center at the sister hotel, the Cata-
maran. **Pros:** some rooms right on the beach; good value; free parking.
Cons: not centrally located ⊠ *998 W. Mission Bay Dr., Mission Bay*
☏ *858/488–0551 or 800/576–4229* ⊕ *www.bahiahotel.com* ⤳ *243*
rooms, 77 suites ⟐ *In-room: a/c, safe, kitchen (some), refrigerator, Inter-*
net, Wi-Fi. In-hotel: restaurant, room service, bars, tennis courts, pool,
gym, beachfront, water sports, bicycles, children's programs (5–12),
Wi-Fi hotspot, parking (free) ⊟ *AE, D, DC, MC, V* ✛ *B3.*

$$$ ⛬ **Catamaran Resort Hotel.** Exotic macaw parrots perch in the lush lobby
☾ of this appealing hotel on Mission Bay. Tiki torches light the way through
Fodor's Choice grounds thick with tropical foliage to the six two-story buildings and
★ the 14-story high-rise. The South Seas theme continues in the room
design, while the Catamaran Spa, where the almost 10,000-square-
foot facilities are devoted to treatments such as Lomi Lomi massage
and seaweed body wraps, and has an Asian decor accented by beautiful
mosaics, Buddhas, and gilt ceilings. The fitness center offers sweeping
views of Mission Bay's beach; yoga and Pilates take place outside on the
secluded lawn. A classical or jazz pianist plays weekends at the Moray
Bar, and the Atoll Restaurant is a favorite for Sunday brunch. Among
the resort's many summertime activities are free cruises on Mission Bay
aboard the Bahia Belle stern-wheeler and Friday-night Hawaiian luaus

on the lawn. **Pros:** recently upgraded rooms; spa; free cruises. **Cons:** not centrally located. ✉ *3999 Mission Blvd., Mission Beach* ☎ *858/488–1081 or 800/422–8386* ⊕ *www.catamaranresort.com* ⤳ *311 rooms, 50 suites* ♿ *In-room: a/c, safe, kitchen (some), refrigerator (some), Internet, Wi-Fi. In-hotel: restaurant, room service, bar, pool, gym, spa, beachfront, bicycles, parking (paid)* ⊟ *AE, D, DC, MC, V* ⊹ *B3.*

$$ 🔲 **The Dana on Mission Bay.** There's a modern chic feel to the earth-toned lobby of this beach hotel, making it feel you've arrived somewhere much more expensive. The resort's rooms all have sofa sleepers—great for families—and bay views. The Bay View suites also have wet bars with granite counters and two flat-screen TVs. Some rooms are fairly standard hotel fare; be sure to ask for one of the newer Courtyard rooms, which are in two-story buildings without elevators. SeaWorld and the beach are within walking distance; there are also shuttles to SeaWorld, cruise terminals, and the airport. The Marina Village Conference Center across the street offers meeting and banquet rooms with bay views. **Pros:** free parking; water views; two pools. **Cons:** slightly confusing layout; not centrally located. ✉ *1710 W. Mission Bay Dr., Mission Bay* ☎ *619/222–6440 or 800/445–3339* ⊕ *www.thedana.net* ⤳ *259 rooms, 12 suites* ♿ *In-room: a/c, refrigerator, Wi-Fi. In-hotel: 2 restaurants, room service, bar, pools, bicycles, laundry service, Wi-Fi hotspot, parking (paid)* ⊟ *AE, D, DC, MC, V* ⊹ *C4.*

$$$ 🔲 **Paradise Point Resort & Spa.** The beautiful landscape at this 44-acre
☾ resort on Vacation Isle has been the setting for a number of movies. The botanical gardens have ponds, waterfalls, footbridges, waterfowl, and more than 600 varieties of tropical plants—a pleasant backdrop for the Balinese spa. Many recreation activities are offered, including five pools, and there's access to a marina. The rooms' bright fabrics and wood floors are cheery and many overlook the water. **Pros:** water views; pools; good service. **Cons:** not near commercial areas; summer minimum stays; motel-thin walls. ✉ *1404 W. Vacation Rd., Mission Bay* ☎ *858/274–4630 or 800/344–2626* ⊕ *www.paradisepoint.com* ⤳ *462 cottages* ♿ *In-room: a/c, safe, refrigerator, Internet. In-hotel: 3 restaurants, room service, bars, tennis courts, pools, gym, spa, beachfront, bicycles, WiFi hotspot, parking (paid)* ⊟ *AE, D, DC, MC, V* ⊹ *C3.*

$$ 🔲 **Surfer Beach Hotel.** Choose this place for its great location—right on bustling Pacific Beach. Guest rooms were updated in 2006 but are still rather simple, though they include pillow-top beds, upholstered headboards, and retro accents and flat-screen TVs. Most have balconies, but can look out on an ugly rooftop; get a higher room to take advantage of the ocean view. The slightly larger junior suites have leather sofas for lounging and wet bars with microwaves, refrigerators, and coffeemakers. While the two-bedroom Sunset Suite has bare bones decor, it includes a full kitchen and large sundeck that's perfect for warm-weather get-togethers. Take a break from the crowds on the beach and relax by the hotel's outdoor swimming pool. World Famous, the on-site restaurant, specializes in seafood and steaks and also serves up breakfast and lunch with an ocean view. **Pros:** beach location; view rooms; pool. **Cons:** busy area; dated rooms. ✉ *711 Pacific Beach Dr., Pacific Beach* ☎ *858/483–7070 or 866/251–2764* ⊕ *www.surferbeachhotel.*

com ↝*53 rooms, 16 suites* ⅋ *In-room: no a/c, refrigerator, Wi-Fi.*
In-hotel: restaurant, bar, pool, beachfront, laundry facilities, parking
(paid), some pets allowed ⊨ *AE, D, DC, MC, V* ⊹ *B3.*

NIGHTLIFE AND THE ARTS

2

Downtown is the obvious neighborhood for party animals of all ages.
Its streets are lined with sleek lounges, massive nightclubs, and quirky
dive bars. The Gaslamp Quarter is party central, with the most bars
and clubs located on its 16-block stretch. The late-night commotion is
spreading to East Village, the area surrounding PETCO Park. A few
neighborhoods on the outskirts of downtown—Golden Hill, Hillcrest,
and North and South Park, in particular—offer plenty of hip underground treasures for intrepid visitors.

The beach areas tend to cater to the casual and collegiate, though certain
haunts have their share of former flower children and grizzled bikers.
Hillcrest is the heart of San Diego's gay community, and home to loads
of gay-popular bars. Coffeehouses are another important element of San
Diego nightlife culture, especially for the under-21 set. Singer Jewel got
her start in local coffee shops, and plenty of other acts have launched to
fame from an active area music scene, including pop-punkers Blink-182
and Grammy-winning gospel group Nickel Creek.

Locals rely on alt-weeklies like the *Reader* and *San Diego CityBeat*,
as well as glossy monthlies like *San Diego* and *Riviera* magazines for
nightlife info. You can't buy booze after 2 AM, which means last call
is around 1:30. Smoking is only allowed outside, and even then it can
be tricky. And be sure to hail a taxi if you've tied one on—drunk driving laws in California are stringent. ■TIP→ All of San Diego's trendiest,
flashiest, busiest clubs and bars have dress codes and require identification.
Call ahead for details.

NIGHTLIFE

CASUAL BARS AND PUBS

Fodor'sChoice **The Waterfront** (✉ *2044 Kettner Blvd., Little Italy* ☎ 619/232–9656) is
★ San Diego's oldest neighborhood bar. It's not actually on the waterfront,
but has been the workingman's refuge in Little Italy since the days
when the area was the Italian fishing community. Because the bar is
considered a local landmark, developers actually constructed an apartment building around it rather than tear it down. It's also famous for
its bar burgers, and it's still the hangout of some working-class heroes,
even if most of the collars are now white. There's live jazz and blues
many evenings.

COFFEEHOUSES

★ **Brockton Villa Restaurant** (✉ *1235 Coast Blvd., La Jolla* ☎ 858/454–7393),
a palatial café overlooking La Jolla Cove, has indoor and outdoor seating, as well as scrumptious desserts and coffee drinks; the beans are
roasted in San Diego. It closes at 9 most nights.

CLOSE UP

Craft Beer Capital

San Diego claims to be the craft beer–making capital of the planet. What exactly *is* a craft beer? The term can include brews from small family-operated breweries—where you might get something different every time you go in for a sip of suds—to some fairly large, commercial operations that turn out standard (although still not mainstream) brews. Most craft brewmeisters started out as home beer makers, and the beer produced for sale reflects abundant creativity (and sometimes outright experimentation) in the use of grain, hops, and other things that go into a great glass of beer.

The brew culture continues to grow in San Diego, and enthusiasts are noticing. Escondido-based **Stone Brewing** (⊕ www.stonebrew.com) was declared the best brewery on the planet by readers of Beer Advocate magazine in 2009, and other San Diego breweries on the list are AleSmith (⊕ www.alesmith.com) and O-Brien's Pub (⊕ www.obrienspub.net) in Kearny Mesa. The largest and oldest of the San Diego craft brewers is **Karl Strauss Brewing** (⊕ www.karlstrauss.com), which operates a number of brew-pubs in the region.

So if you're looking for a cold one, you've come to the right place.

Fodor'sChoice ★ **Extraordinary Desserts** (⊠ *2929 5th Ave., Hillcrest* ☎ *619/294–2132* ⊠ *1430 Union St., Little Italy* ☎ *619/294–7001*) lives up to its name, which explains why there's a line at this café, even though it has ample seating. Paris-trained Karen Krasne turns out award-winning cakes, tortes, and pastries of exceptional beauty (many are decorated with fresh flowers). The Japanese-theme patio invites you to linger over yet another coffee drink. A branch in Little Italy has a patio with teak chairs, a bar serving wine and bubblies, and a wider selection of savory nibbles.

DANCE CLUBS

Cafe Sevilla (⊠ *555 4th Ave., Gaslamp Quarter* ☎ *619/233–5979*) brings a Latin flavor to the Gaslamp Quarter with its mix of contemporary and traditional Spanish and Latin American music. Get fueled up at the tapas bar before venturing downstairs for dancing. This is the best place in San Diego to take salsa lessons.

On Broadway (⊠ *615 Broadway, Gaslamp Quarter* ☎ *619/231–0011*), a huge club in a former bank building, used to be the hottest destination in town, but looks more and more like a dinosaur as the Gaslamp evolves around it. Still, on Friday and Saturday nights—the only nights it's open—sexily clad twentysomethings wait in a line that sometimes reaches around the block. Cover charges are steep and ordering drinks is a hassle, but the cool decor—marble floors, Greek columns, and original vault doors mixed with modern design elements—make it worth a visit, as do the computerized light shows, leviathan sound system, and skilled DJs.

Stingaree (⊠ *6th Ave. and Island St., Gaslamp Quarter* ☎ *619/544–0867*), a posh Gaslamp Quarter destination, occupies a historic warehouse in the former Red Light District. The owners spent a gazillion dollars creating this smashing three-story space with translucent "floating" staircases and floor-to-ceiling water walls. There's a high-end restaurant and a dance club inside (the music tends to be of the Top 40 variety). Dress nicely—the air of exclusivity at this hangout is palpable, and to further prove the point, drinks are steep.

GAY

★ **Bourbon Street** (✉ *4612 Park Blvd., University Heights* ☎ *619/291–0173*) is a popular place to meet old friends or make new ones. Several scenes exist in this one bar. The front area is a karaoke spot. The outdoor courtyard draws crowds that gather to watch and comment on whatever is showing on the large-screen TV. Weekends, a back area known as the Stable Bar has DJs who turn the small room into a makeshift dance floor.

Urban Mo's Bar and Grill (✉ *308 University Ave., Hillcrest* ☎ *619/491–0400*) rounds up country-music cowboys for line dancing and two-stepping on its wooden dance floor—but be forewarned, yee-hawers, Mo's can get pretty wild on Western nights. There are also techno and pop nights, but Mo's real allure is in the creative drinks ("Gonse Fishing"—served in a fishbowl, for example) and the breezy patio where love (or something like it) is usually in the air.

HIP LOUNGES AND TRENDY SINGLES BARS

Altitude Skybar (✉ *660 K St., Gaslamp Quarter* ☎ *619/696–0234*), at the San Diego Marriott Gaslamp Quarter, occupies the hotel's 22nd-story rooftop. Location is everything-the views here (of the downtown skyline and PETCO park) will give you a natural high.

Pacific Beach Bar & Grill (✉ *860 Garnet Ave., Pacific Beach* ☎ *858/272–4745*) is a block away from the beach. The popular nightspot has a huge outdoor patio, so you can enjoy star-filled skies as you party. The lines here on weekends are generally the longest of any club in Pacific Beach. There's plenty to see and do, from billiards and satellite TV sports to an interactive trivia game. The grill takes orders until 1 AM, so it's a great place for a late-night snack.

★ The **W Hotel** (✉ *421 West B St., Downtown* ☎ *619/398–3100*) has three bars, and even after several years on the scene, they continue to lure the young barhopping set. The ground-level Living Room encourages lounging with plush chairs and couches. The scene is always charged at Magnet, adjacent to Rice restaurant. Have a late-night nosh and head for the beach—or, more accurately, Beach, the W's open-air rooftop with private beach cabanas, fire pits, and tons of heated sand covering the floor. On Weekends, get here before 9 PM on weekends to avoid a queue.

JAZZ

★ **Clay's La Jolla** (✉ *7955 La Jolla Shores Dr., La Jolla* ☎ *858/459–0541*), perched on the top floor of the Hotel La Jolla, delivers an ocean view and a lineup of mostly jazz musicians (and the occasional small band) Wednesday through Sunday.

Croce's (✉ *802 5th Ave., Gaslamp Quarter* ☎ *619/233–4355*), the intimate jazz cave of restaurateur Ingrid Croce (widow of singer-songwriter Jim Croce), books superb acoustic-jazz musicians nightly.

Humphrey's by the Bay (✉ *2241 Shelter Island Dr., Shelter Island* ☎ *619/ 224–3577*), surrounded by water, is the summer stomping ground of musicians such as the Cowboy Junkies and Chris Isaak. From June through September this dining and drinking oasis hosts the city's best outdoor jazz, folk, and light-rock concert series presented theater-style. The rest of the year the music moves indoors for some first-rate jazz most Sunday, Monday and Tuesday nights, with piano-bar music on most other nights.

LIVE MUSIC CLUBS

★ **Belly Up Tavern** (✉ *143 S. Cedros Ave., Solana Beach* ☎ *858/481–8140*), a fixture on local "best of" lists, has been drawing crowds of all ages since it opened in the mid-'70s. The "BUT's" longevity attests to the quality of the eclectic entertainment on its stage. Within converted Quonset huts, critically acclaimed artists play everything from reggae and folk to—well, you name it.

★ **'Canes Bar and Grill** (✉ *3105 Oceanfront Walk, Mission Beach* ☎ *858/ 488–1780*) is closer to the ocean than any other music venue in town. Step outside for a walk on the beach, where the sounds of the national rock, reggae, and hip-hop acts onstage create a cacophony with the crashing waves.

Fodor'sChoice **Casbah** (✉ *2501 Kettner Blvd., Middletown* ☎ *619/232–4355*), near
★ the airport, is a small club with a national reputation for showcasing up-and-coming acts. Nirvana, Smashing Pumpkins, and the White Stripes all played the Casbah on their way to stardom. For more than two decades, it's been the unofficial headquarters of the city's indie music scene. You can hear every type of band here—except those that sound like Top 40.

THE ARTS

You can buy half-price tickets to most theater, music, and dance events on the day of performance at **Times Arts Tix** (✉ *Horton Plaza, Gaslamp Quarter* ☎ *619/497–5000*).

DANCE

★ **California Ballet Company** (☎ *858/560–6741*) performs high-quality contemporary and classical works September–May.

MUSIC

Fodor'sChoice **Copley Symphony Hall** (✉ *750 B St., Downtown* ☎ *619/235–0804*) has
★ great acoustics surpassed only by an incredible Spanish Baroque interior. Not just the home of the San Diego Symphony Orchestra, the renovated 2,200-seat 1920s-era theater has also presented such popular musicians as Elvis Costello and Sting.

La Jolla Music Society (☎ *858/459–3728*) presents internationally acclaimed chamber ensembles, orchestras, and soloists at Sherwood

Auditorium, the Civic Theatre, Copley Symphony Hall, and the Stephen and Mary Birch North Park Theatre.

★ **San Diego Opera** (✉ *Civic Theatre, 3rd Ave. and B St., Downtown* ☎ *619/533–7000*) draws international artists. Its season runs January–April. Past performances have included *Die Fledermaus, Faust, Idomeneo,* and *La Bohème,* plus concerts by such talents as the late Luciano Pavarotti.

San Diego Symphony Orchestra (✉ *750 B St., Downtown* ☎ *619/235– 0804*) puts on special events year-round, including classical concerts and summer and winter pops. Concerts are held at Copley Symphony Hall, except the Summer Pops series, which is held on the Embarcadero, beyond the San Diego Convention Center on North Harbor Drive.

★ **Spreckels Organ Pavilion** (✉ *Balboa Park* ☎ *619/702–8138*) holds a giant outdoor pipe organ donated to the city in 1914 by sugar magnates John and Adolph Spreckels. The beautiful Spanish Baroque pavilion hosts concerts by civic organist Carol Williams and guest organists on most Sunday afternoons and on most Monday evenings in summer. Local military bands, gospel groups, and barbershop quartets also perform here. All shows are free.

THEATER

Fodor's Choice
★ **La Jolla Playhouse** (✉ *University of California at San Diego, 2910 La Jolla Village Dr., La Jolla* ☎ *858/550–1010*) crafts exciting and innovative productions under the artistic direction of Christopher Ashley, May through March. Many Broadway shows, such as *Tommy* and *Jersey Boys,* have previewed here before heading for the East Coast. The playhouse has three stages: the Mandell Weiss Theatre has the main stage, the Mandell Weiss Forum is a thrust stage, and the Sheila and Hughes Potiker Theatre is a black-box theater.

★ **Lamb's Players Theatre** (✉ *1142 Orange Ave., Coronado* ☎ *619/437– 0600*) has a regular season of five productions from February through November and stages a musical, *Festival of Christmas,* in December. *An American Christmas* is the company's dinner-theater show at the Hotel Del Coronado.

Fodor's Choice
★ **Old Globe Theatre** (✉ *1363 Old Globe Way, Balboa Park* ☎ *619/234– 5623*) is the oldest professional theater in California, presenting classics, contemporary dramas, and experimental works at the historic Old Globe and its sister theaters, the intimate Cassius Carter Centre Stage and the outdoor Lowell Davies Festival Theater. The Old Globe also mounts a popular Shakespeare Festival every summer at Lowell Davies. The recently opened Conrad Prebys Theatre Center merges the flagship Old Globe Theatre with a new, state-of-the-art multilevel facility.

Spreckels Theatre (✉ *121 Broadway, Downtown* ☎ *619/235–9500*), a landmark theater erected in 1912, hosts comedy, dance, theater, and concerts. Good acoustics and old-time elegance make this a favorite local venue.

SPORTS AND THE OUTDOORS

BASEBALL

Long a favorite spectator sport in San Diego, where games are rarely rained out, baseball gained even more popularity in 2004 with the opening of PETCO Park, a stunning 42,000-seat facility right in the heart of downtown. The **San Diego Padres** (⌧ *100 Park Blvd., Downtown*

Fodor's Choice
★
☎ *619/795–5000 or 877/374–2784* ⊕ *www.sandiegopadres.com*) slug it out for bragging rights in the National League West from April into October. Tickets are usually available on game day, but games with such rivals as the Los Angeles Dodgers and the San Francisco Giants often sell out quickly. For an inexpensive day at the ballpark, go for the $7 ($5 on the day of game) park pass and have a picnic on the grass, while watching the play on one of several giant-screen TVs.

BEACHES

Water temperatures are generally chilly, ranging from 55°F to 65°F from October through June, and 65°F to 73°F from July through September. For a surf and weather report, call ☎ *619/221–8824*. San Diego's beaches are well maintained and very clean during summertime, when rainfall is infrequent. Beaches along San Diego county's northern cities are typically cleaner than ones farther south. Pollution is generally worse near river mouths and storm-drain outlets, especially after heavy rainfall. The weather page of the *San Diego Union-Tribune* includes pollution reports along with listings of surfing and diving conditions.

Lifeguards are stationed at city beaches from Sunset Cliffs up to Black's Beach in the summertime, but coverage in winter is provided by roving patrols only. Pay attention to signs listing illegal activities; undercover police often patrol the beaches. Smoking and alcoholic beverages are completely banned on city beaches. Drinking in beach parking lots, on boardwalks, and in landscaped areas is also illegal. Certain beaches also prohibit skateboarding. Fires are allowed only in fire rings or elevated barbecue grills. Although it may be tempting to take a starfish or some other sea creature as a souvenir from a tide pool, it upsets the delicate ecological balance and is illegal, too.

Finding a parking spot near the ocean can be hard in summer, but for the time being, unmetered parking is at all San Diego city beaches. Del Mar has a pay lot and metered street parking around the 15th Street beach.

Beaches are listed geographically, south to north.

CORONADO

☾ **Silver Strand State Beach.** This quiet Coronado beach is ideal for families. The water is relatively calm, lifeguards and rangers are on duty year-round, and there are places to rollerblade or ride bikes. Three day-use parking lots provide room for more than 1,000 cars. Sites at a state campground ($50 by the beach, $35 inland) for RVs are available by reservation (☎ *800/444–7275*, ⊕ *www.reserveamerica.com*). Foot tunnels under Route 75 lead to a bay-side beach, which affords great views of the San Diego skyline. ⊹ *From San Diego–Coronado Bridge, turn left onto Orange Ave., which becomes Rte. 75, and follow signs, Coronado* ☎ *619/435–5184.*

Ⓒ **Coronado Beach.** With the famous Hotel Del Coronado as a backdrop,
★ this stretch of sandy beach is one of San Diego County's largest and most picturesque. It's perfect for sunbathing, people-watching, or Frisbee. Exercisers include Navy SEAL teams, as well as the occasional Marine Recon unit, who do training runs on the beaches in and around Coronado. Parking can be difficult on the busiest days. There are plenty of restrooms and service facilities, as well as fire rings on the north end. ⊹ *From the San Diego-Coronado bridge, turn left on Orange Ave. and follow signs, Coronado.*

POINT LOMA

Sunset Cliffs. Beneath the jagged cliffs on the west side of the Point Loma peninsula is one of the more secluded beaches in the area. A few miles long, it's popular with surfers and locals. At the south end of the peninsula, near Cabrillo Point, tide pools teeming with small sea creatures are revealed at low tide. Farther north the waves lure surfers and the lonely coves attract sunbathers. Stairs at the foot of Bermuda and Pescadero avenues provide beach access, as do some cliff trails, which are treacherous at points. There are few facilities. A visit here is more enjoyable at low tide; check the local newspaper for tide schedules. ⊹ *Take I–8 west to Sunset Cliffs Blvd. and head west, Point Loma.*

MISSION BAY AND BEACHES

Ocean Beach. Much of this mile-long beach is a haven for volleyball players, sunbathers, and swimmers. The area around the municipal pier at the south end is a hangout for surfers and transients; the pier itself is open to the public 24 hours a day for fishing and walking, and there's a restaurant at the middle. The beach is south of the channel entrance to Mission Bay. You'll find fire rings as well as plenty of casual places to grab a snack on adjoining streets. Swimmers should beware of strong rip currents around the main lifeguard tower. There's a dog beach at the north end where Fido can run leash-free. ⊹ *Take I–8 west to Sunset Cliffs Blvd. and head west. A right turn off Sunset Cliffs Blvd. takes you to the water. Ocean Beach.*

Ⓒ **Mission Beach.** San Diego's most popular beach draws huge crowds
★ on hot summer days, but it's lively year-round. The 2-mi-long stretch extends from the north entrance of Mission Bay to Pacific Beach. A wide boardwalk paralleling the beach is popular with walkers, joggers, roller skaters, bladers, and bicyclists. Surfers, swimmers, and volleyball players congregate at the south end. Scantily clad volleyball players practice on Cohasset Court year-round. Toward its north end, near the Belmont Park roller coaster, the beach narrows and the water becomes rougher. The crowds grow thicker and somewhat rougher as well. For parking, you can try for a spot on the street, but your best bets are the two big lots at Belmont Park. ⊹ *Exit I–5 at Grand Ave. and head west to Mission Blvd. Turn south and look for parking near roller coaster at West Mission Bay Dr., Mission Bay.*

Pacific Beach/North Pacific Beach. The boardwalk of Mission Beach turns into a sidewalk here, but there are still bike paths and picnic tables along the beachfront. Pacific Beach runs from the north end of Mission Beach to Crystal Pier. North Pacific Beach extends from the pier north. The scene here is particularly lively on weekends. There are designated surfing areas, and fire rings are available. Parking can be a challenge, but there are plenty of restrooms, showers, and restaurants in the area. ✛ *Exit I–5 at Grand Ave. and head west to Mission Blvd. Turn north and look for parking, Mission Bay.*

LA JOLLA

Tourmaline Surfing Park. This is one of the area's most popular beaches for surfing and sailboarding year-round. No swimming is allowed, and surfing etiquette is strongly enforced by the locals in and out of the water. There's a 175-space parking lot at the foot of Tourmaline Street that normally fills to capacity by midday. ✛ *Take Mission Blvd. north (it turns into La Jolla Blvd.) and turn west on Tourmaline St.,Mission Bay*

Windansea Beach. The reef break here forms an unusual A-frame wave, making it one of the most popular (and crowded) surf spots in San Diego County. With its incredible views and secluded sunbathing spots set among sandstone rocks, Windansea is also one of the most romantic of West Coast beaches, especially at sunset. ✛ *Take Mission Blvd. north (it turns into La Jolla Blvd.) and turn west on Nautilus St.,La Jolla*

Marine Street Beach. Wide and sandy, this strand often teems with sunbathers, swimmers, walkers, and joggers. The water is known as a great spot for bodysurfing, although the waves break in extremely shallow water and you'll need to watch out for riptides. ✛ *Accessible from Marine St., off La Jolla Blvd.,La Jolla*

Ⓒ
Fodor's Choice
★
La Jolla Cove. This is one of the prettiest spots on the West Coast. A palm-lined park sits on top of cliffs formed by the incessant pounding of the waves. At low tide the tide pools and cliff caves are a destination for explorers. Divers, snorkelers, and kayakers can discover the underwater delights of the San Diego–La Jolla Underwater Park Ecological Reserve. The cove is also a favorite of rough-water swimmers. ✛ *Follow Coast Blvd. north to signs, or take La Jolla Village Dr. Exit from I–5, head west to Torrey Pines Rd., turn left, and drive downhill to Girard Ave. Turn right and follow signs, La Jolla.*

Ⓒ
★
La Jolla Shores. This is one of San Diego's most popular beaches so get here early on summer weekends. The lures are an incredible view of La Jolla peninsula, a wide sandy beach, an adjoining grassy park, and the gentlest waves in San Diego. In fact, several surf schools teach here and kayak rentals are nearby. A concrete boardwalk parallels the beach. Arrive early to get a parking spot in the lot at the foot of Calle Frescota. ✉ *8200 Camino del Oro* ✛ *From I–5 take La Jolla Village Dr. west and turn left onto La Jolla Shores Dr. Head west to Camino del Oro or Vallecitos St. Turn right, La Jolla.*

★
Black's Beach. The powerful waves at this beach, officially known as Torrey Pines City Park Beach, attract world-class surfers, and its relative isolation appeals to nudist nature lovers (although by law nudity is prohibited) as well as gays and lesbians. Access to parts of the shore

Experts and beginners alike head to La Jolla for its excellent surfing.

coincides with very low tide. There are no lifeguards on permanent duty, although they do patrol the area between spring break and mid-October. Strong rip currents are common—only experienced swimmers should take the plunge. Storms have weakened the cliffs in the past few years; they're dangerous to climb and should be avoided. Part of the fun here is watching hang gliders and paragliders ascend from the glider port atop the cliffs. ✢ *Take Genesee Ave. west from I–5 and follow signs to glider port; easier access, via a paved path, available on La Jolla Farms Rd., but parking is limited to 2 hrs, La Jolla.*

DEL MAR

★ **Torrey Pines State Beach and Reserve.** One of San Diego's best beaches encompasses 2,000 acres of bluffs and bird-filled marshes. A network of meandering trails leads to the sandy shoreline below. Along the way enjoy the rare Torrey pine trees, found only here and on Santa Rosa Island, offshore. The large parking lot is rarely full; there are bathrooms, showers, and lifeguards on patrol. Guided tours of the nature preserve here are offered on weekends. Torrey Pines tends to get crowded in summer, but if you head south under the cliffs you'll run into isolated Black's Beach (*above*). ✢ *Take Carmel Valley Rd. Exit west from I–5, turn left on Rte. S21, Del Mar* ☎ *858/755–2063* ⊕ *www.torreypine.org* 🚗 *Parking $10.*

Del Mar Beach. The numbered streets of Del Mar, from 15th north to 29th, end at a wide beach popular with volleyball players, surfers, and sunbathers. Parking can be a problem in town; there's metered parking along the beach, making it challenging to stay for more than a few hours. The portion of Del Mar south of 15th Street is lined with cliffs and rarely crowded. Leashed dogs are permitted on most sections of the beach year-round; from October through May, dogs may run free at Rivermouth, Del Mar's northernmost beach. During the annual summer meeting of the Del Mar Thoroughbred Club, horse bettors sit on the beach in the morning, working on the *Daily Racing Form* before heading across the street to the track. Food, accommodations, and shopping are all within an easy walk of the beach. Because parking is at a premium, it's a great idea to bring a bike to cruise around the city before or after the beach. ✢ *Take Via de la Valle Exit from I–5 west to Rte. S21 (also known as Camino del Mar in Del Mar) and turn left, Del Mar.*

ENCINITAS

★ **Swami's.** Palms and the golden lotus-flower domes of the nearby Self-Realization Center temple and ashram earned this picturesque beach its name. Extreme low tides expose tide pools that harbor anemones, starfish, and other sea life. Remember to look but don't touch; all sea life here is protected. The beach is also a top surfing spot; the only access is by a long stairway leading down from cliff-top Seaside Road-side Park, where there's free parking. On big winter swells, the bluffs are lined with gawkers watching the area's best surfers take on, and be taken down by, some of the best big waves in the county. Offshore, divers do their thing at North County's only underwater park, Encinitas Marine Life Refuge. ✢ *Follow Rte. S21 north from Cardiff, or exit I–5 at Encinitas Blvd., go west to Rte. S21, and turn left, Encinitas.*

BICYCLING

On any given summer day **Route S21** (or Old Highway 101) from La Jolla to Oceanside looks like a freeway for cyclists. It's easily the most popular and scenic bike route around, never straying more than a quarter-mile from the beach. For more leisurely rides, **Mission Bay, San Diego Harbor,** and the **Mission Beach boardwalk** are all flat and scenic. For those who want to take their biking experience to the extreme, the **Kearny BMX** (✉ *3170 Armstrong St., Kearny Mesa* ☎ *619/561–3824* ⊕ *www.kearnybmx.com*) has a dirt track where BMXers rip it up, racing three times a week, with time for practice beforehand.

Bike Tours San Diego (✉ *522 6th Ave., Downtown* ☎ *619/238–2444* ⊕ *www.bike-tours.com*) rents all types of bikes and conducts biking tours in the downtown waterfront and Gaslamp area, to and around Coronado Island, up to Cabrillo National Monument, and elsewhere

★ in the city. **Hike Bike Kayak San Diego** (✉ *2246 Ave. de la Playa, La Jolla* ☎ *858/551–9510 or 866/425–2925* ⊕ *www.hikebikekayak.com*) offers a wide range of guided bike tours, from easy excursions around Mission Bay and Coronado Island to slightly more rigorous trips through coastal La Jolla. Mountain-biking tours are also available, and the company also rents bikes of all types (and can van-deliver them to your hotel).

Cheap Rentals Mission Beach (✉ *3689 Mission Blvd., Mission Beach* ☎ *858/488–9070 or 800/941–7761* ⊕ *www.cheap-rentals.com*) is right on the boardwalk and has good daily and weekly prices for bike rentals, including beach cruisers, tandems, hybrids, and two-wheeled baby carriers.

DIVING

Enthusiasts the world over come to San Diego to snorkel and scuba-dive off La Jolla and Point Loma. At La Jolla Cove you'll find the 6,000-acre ★ **San Diego–La Jolla Underwater Park Ecological Preserve.** Because all sea life is protected here, it's the best place to see large lobster, sea bass, and sculpin (scorpion fish), as well as numerous golden garibaldi, the state marine fish. It's common to see hundreds of beautiful (and harmless) leopard sharks schooling at the north end of the cove, near La Jolla Shores, especially in summer. Farther north, off the south end of Black's Beach, the rim of **Scripps Canyon** lies in about 60 feet of water. The canyon plummets to more than 900 feet in some sections.

The HMCS *Yukon,* a decommissioned Canadian warship, was intentionally sunk off **Mission Beach** to create a diving destination. A mishap caused it to settle on its side, creating a surreal, M. C. Escher–esque diving environment. This is a technical dive and should be attempted by experienced divers only; even diving instructors have become disoriented inside the wreck. Another popular diving spot is **Sunset Cliffs** in Point Loma, where the sea life and flora are relatively close to shore. Strong rip currents make it an area best enjoyed by experienced divers. The *San Diego Union-Tribune* (⊕ *www.signonsandiego.com*) includes diving conditions on its weather page. For recorded diving information, contact the **San Diego City Lifeguard Service** (☎ *619/221–8824).*

Diving Locker (✉ *6167 Balboa Ave., Clairemont Mesa* ☎ *858/292–0547* ⊕ *www.divinglocker.com*) has been a fixture in San Diego since 1958, making it the city's longest-running dive shop. You can rent equipment here, and even take SCUBA lessons. **Scuba San Diego** (✉ *1775 E. Mission Bay Dr., Mission Bay* ☎ *619/260–1880* ⊕ *www.scubasandiego.com*) is well regarded for its top-notch instruction and certification programs, as well as for guided dive tours of La Jolla Cove, night diving at La Jolla Canyon, as well as unguided charter boat trips to Mission Bay's Wreck Alley or to the Coronado Islands (in Mexico, just south of San Diego).

FOOTBALL

The **San Diego Chargers** (✉ *9449 Friars Rd., Mission Valley* ☎ *619/280–2121 or 877/242–7437* ⊕ *www.chargers.com*) of the National Football League fill Qualcomm Stadium from August through December and sometimes as late as January. Games with AFC West rivals the Oakland Raiders are particularly intense.

GOLF

Most public courses in the area provide a list of fees for all San Diego courses. The **Southern California Golf Association** (☎ *818/980–3630* ⊕ *www.scga.org*) publishes an annual directory ($15) with detailed and valuable information on all clubs. Another good resource for golfers is the **Public Links Golf Association of Southern California** (☎ *714/994–4747* ⊕ *www.plga.org*), which details the region's public courses on its Web site.

COURSES

The **Balboa Park Municipal Golf Course** (⊠ *2600 Golf Course Dr., Balboa Park* ☎ *619/235–1184* ⊕ *www.balboaparkgolf.com*), is in the heart of Balboa Park, making it convenient for downtown visitors. Greens fees: $30/$48.

★ **Coronado Municipal Golf Course** (⊠ *2000 Visalia Row, Coronado* ☎ *619/435–3121 Ext. 4* ⊕ *www.golfcoronado.com*) has 18 holes, a driving range and putting green, equipment rentals, and a snack bar and sit-down restaurant. Views of San Diego Bay and the Coronado Bridge from the front 9 make this course popular—but rather difficult to get on unless you reserve a tee time, 8 to 14 days in advance, for an additional $60. Greens fees themselves are $30/$35, plus cart rental if desired.

Fodor's Choice **Four Seasons Aviara Golf Club** (⊠ *7447 Batiquitos Dr., Carlsbad* ☎ *760/*
★ *603–6800* ⊕ *www.fourseasons.com*) is a top-quality course with 18 holes (designed by Arnold Palmer), a driving range, equipment rentals, and views of the protected adjacent Batiquitos Lagoon and the Pacific Ocean. Carts fitted with GPS systems that tell you the distance to the pin, among other features, are included in the cost. Greens fees: $215/$235.

★ **La Costa Resort and Spa** (⊠ *2100 Costa del Mar Rd., Carlsbad* ☎ *760/438–9111* ⊕ *www.lacosta.com*), one of the premier golf resorts in Southern California, has two 18-hole PGA-rated courses, a driving range, a clubhouse, equipment rentals, an excellent golf school, and a pro shop. After a full day on the links you can wind down with a massage, steam bath, and dinner at the exclusive spa resort that shares this verdant property. Greens fees: $195/$205.

★ **Rancho Bernardo Inn and Country Club** (⊠ *17550 Bernardo Oaks Dr., Rancho Bernardo* ☎ *858/675–8470 Ext. 1* ⊕ *www.ranchobernardoinn. com*) has an 18-hole course, driving range, equipment rentals, and a restaurant; the course is managed by JC Golf, which has a golf school as well as several other respected courses throughout Southern California open to guests of Rancho Bernardo Inn. The restaurant here, El Bizcocho, lays out one of the best Sunday brunches in the county. Greens fees: $64/$135.

Fodor's Choice **Torrey Pines Golf Course** (⊠ *11480 N. Torrey Pines Rd., La Jolla* ☎ *858/*
★ *452–3226 or 800/985–4653* ⊕ *www.torreypinesgolfcourse.com*) has a driving range and equipment rentals, and is one of the best public golf courses in the United States. Home to the 2008 U.S. Open and the site of the Buick Invitational since 1968, Torrey Pines has views of the Pacific from many of its 36 holes. The par-72 South Course receives rave reviews from the touring pros. Designed by Rees Jones, it has more length and more challenges than the North Course and, fittingly, commands higher greens fees. Tee times may be booked from eight to 90 days in advance at ☎ *877/581–7171*. A full-day or half-day instructional package includes cart, green fees, and a golf-pro escort for the first 9 holes. Greens fees on the South Course run $58/$218, the North Course $38/$119.

SAILING AND BOATING

★ **Carlsbad Paddle Sports** (✉ *2002 S. Coast Hwy., Oceanside* ☎ *760/434–8686* ⊕ *www.carlsbadpaddle.com*) handles kayak sales, rentals, and instruction for coastal North County. **Harbor Sailboats** (✉ *2040 Harbor Island Dr., Harbor Island* ☎ *619/291–9568 or 800/854–6625* ⊕ *www.harborsailboats.com*) rents sailboats from 22 to 47 feet long for open-ocean adventures. **Seaforth Boat Rentals** (✉ *1715 Strand Way, Coronado* ☎ *619/437–1514 or 888/834–2628* ✉ *1641 Quivira Rd., Mission Bay* ☎ *619/223–1681* ✉ *333 West Harbor Dr., Gate 1, Downtown* ☎ *619/239–2628*) has kayaks, Jet Skis, fishing skiffs, and power boats from 10 feet to 20 feet in length as well as sailboats from 16 to 36 feet. They also can hook you up with a skipper for a deep-sea fishing trip.

SURFING

If you're a beginner, consider paddling in the waves off Mission Beach, Pacific Beach, Tourmaline Surfing Park, La Jolla Shores, Del Mar, or Oceanside. More experienced surfers usually head for Sunset Cliffs, the La Jolla reef breaks, Black's Beach, or Swami's in Encinitas. All necessary equipment is included in the cost of all surfing schools. Beach area Y's offer surf lessons and surf camp in the summer months, and during

★ spring break. **Surf Diva Surf School** (✉ *2160 Avenida de la Playa, La Jolla* ☎ *858/454-8273* ⊕ *www.surfdiva.com*) offers clinics, surf camps, surf trips, and private lessons especially formulated for girls and women. Clinics and trips are for women only, but guys can book private lessons from the nationally recognized staff.

★ Many local surf shops rent both surf and bodyboards. **Cheap Rentals Mission Beach** (✉ *3689 Mission Blvd., Mission Beach* ☎ *858/488–9070 or 800/941–7761* ⊕ *www.cheap-rentals.com*) is right on the boardwalk, just steps from the waves. **Star Surfing Company** (✉ *4652 Mission Blvd., Pacific Beach* ☎ *858/273–7827* ⊕ *www.starsurfingco.com*) can get you out surfing around the Crystal Pier.

Hansen's (✉ *1105 S. Coast Hwy. 101, Encinitas* ☎ *760/753–6595 or 800/480-4754* ⊕ *www.hansensurf.com*) is just a short walk from Swami's beach.

SHOPPING

CORONADO

Fodor'sChoice ★ **Ferry Landing Marketplace.** A staggering view of San Diego's downtown skyline across the bay, a dozen browse-worthy boutiques, and a variety of restaurants provide a delightful place to shop while waiting for a ferry. A farmers' market takes place on Tuesday afternoons from 2:30 to 6 PM. ✉ *1201 1st St., at B Ave.* ☎ *619/435–8895* ⊕ *www.coronadoferrylanding.com*.

DOWNTOWN

Seaport Village. Quintessentially San Diego, this waterfront complex of more than 50 shops and restaurants has sweeping bay views, fresh breezes, and great strolling paths. Horse and carriage rides, an 1895 Looff carousel, and frequent public entertainment are side attractions. The Seaport is within walking distance of hotels, the San Diego Convention Center, and San Diego Trolley, and there's also an easily accessible free parking lot. ⊠ *W. Harbor Dr. at Kettner Blvd.* ☎ *619/235–4014* ⊕ *www.spvillage.com.*

★ **Westfield Horton Plaza.** Within walking distance of most downtown hotels, Horton Plaza is bordered by Broadway, 1st Avenue, G Street, and 4th Avenue. The multilevel shopping, dining, and entertainment complex is an open-air visual delight, with a terra-cotta color scheme and flag-draped facades. There are department stores, including Macy's and Nordstrom; fast-food counters; upscale restaurants; the Lyceum Theater; cinemas; a game arcade; and 130 other stores. Park in the plaza garage and validate your parking ticket at a kiosk inside the mall, good for three free hours. ⊠ *324 Horton Plaza* ☎ *619/238–1596* ⊕ *www. westfield.com/hortonplaza.*

GASLAMP QUARTER

Long a place where fine restaurants and clubs have catered to conventioneers and partying locals, the historic heart of San Diego has recently seen an explosion of specialty shops, art galleries, and boutiques take up residence in the Victorian buildings and renovated warehouses along 4th and 5th avenues. Some stores in this area tend to close early, starting as early as 5 PM. But a trip to the Gaslamp to shop is worth it. Here, you'll find the usual mall denizens as well as hip fashion boutiques and gift shops, even for your pup.

UPTOWN

Located north and northeast of downtown, the Uptown area includes Hillcrest, North Park, South Park, Mission Hills, and University Heights. The boundaries between the neighborhoods tend to blur, but you'll find that each area has unique shops. Hillcrest has a large gay community and boasts many avant-garde apparel shops alongside gift, book, and music stores. North Park, east of Hillcrest, is a retro buff's paradise with many resale shops, trendy boutiques, and stores that sell a mix of old and new. University Avenue offers a mélange of affordably priced furniture, gift, and specialty stores appealing to college students, singles, and young families. South Park's 30th, Juniper, and Fern streets have everything from the hottest new denim lines to baby gear and craft supplies. The shops and art galleries in upscale Mission Hills, west of Hillcrest, have a modern and sophisticated ambience that suits the well-heeled residents just fine.

LA JOLLA

Known as San Diego's Rodeo Drive, La Jolla's chic boutiques, art galleries, and gift shops line narrow twisty streets that are often celebrity-soaked. Prospect Street and Girard Avenue are the primary shopping stretches, and North Prospect is chockablock with art galleries. The Upper Girard Design District stocks home decor accessories and luxury furnishings. Parking is tight in the village and store hours vary widely, so it's wise to call in advance. Most shops on Prospect Street stay open until 10 PM on weeknights to accommodate evening strollers. On the east side of I-5, office buildings surround the Westfield UTC mall, where you'll find department and chain stores.

2

SIDE TRIPS TO NORTH COUNTY

DEL MAR

23 mi north of downtown San Diego on I-5, 9 mi north of La Jolla on Rte. S21.

Del Mar is best known for its quaint old section west of Interstate 5 marked with a glamorous racetrack, half-timber buildings, chic shops, tony restaurants, celebrity visitors, and wide beaches.

The Spanish mission–style **Del Mar Fairgrounds** is the home of the **Del Mar Thoroughbred Club** (☎ *858/755–1141* ⊕ *www.dmtc.com*). Crooner Bing Crosby and his Hollywood buddies—Pat O'Brien, Gary Cooper, and Oliver Hardy, among others—organized the club in the 1930s, primarily because Crosby wanted a track near his Rancho Santa Fe home. Del Mar soon developed into a regular stop for the stars of stage and screen. Even now the racing season here (usually July–September, Wednesday–Monday, post time 2 PM) is one of the most fashionable in California. If you're new to horse racing, stop by the Plaza de Mexico where you'll find staff who can explain how to place a bet on a horse. The track also hosts free Four O'Clock Friday concerts following the races. ⊠ *2260 Jimmy Durante Blvd.* ☎ *858/793–5555* ⊕ *www.sdfair.com*.

WHERE TO EAT

Fodor'sChoice

$$$$

✕ **Addison.** Sophisticated and stylish, Addison's dining room and adjacent bar feel Italian and clubby, with intricately carved dark-wood motifs, heavy arches, and marble and wood floors. The tables, by contrast, are pure white adorned with a single flower. William Bradley, one of San Diego's most acclaimed rising star chefs, serves up explosive flavors in his four-course prix-fixe dinners, such as Prince Edward Island mussels with Champagne sabayon and lemon verbena jus or foie gras de canard with Le Puy lentils, port wine, and smoked bacon mousse. Entrées include spring lamb *persille* with pistachio pâté brisee and caramelized garlic puree or perfectly cooked wild Scottish salmon with sauce *vin jaune,* roasted eggplant stick, and pine nuts. Bradley offer both prix-fixe and à la carte menus. Acclaimed for its extensive wine collection, Addison challenges vino lovers with a 160-page wine list; sommelier Jesse Rodriquez can help you make a selection. ⊠ *5200 Grand Del Mar Way* 🕾 *858/314–1900* ⚓ *Reservations essential* ▭ *AE, D, DC, MC, V* ⊙ *Closed Sun. and Mon. No lunch.*

WHERE TO STAY

$$$$
Fodor's Choice
★

🎦 **Grand Del Mar.** Indulgence in serene surroundings sets the Grand Del Mar apart from any other luxury hotel in the San Diego area. The opulent Mediterranean-style resort, set in a secluded canyon surrounded by 4,100-acre Los Penasquitos Canyon Preserve, is just 12 mi north of urban San Diego. The hotel is drop-dead beautiful, done up in marble, crystal, and gold. Large rooms feature brocaded corner love seats, fine European linens, crystal lamps, and marble bathrooms with separate soaking tubs and showers. Every window, deck, patio, balcony, and lawn affords a view of the surrounding mountains, where you can hike tree-lined trails and dip your toes in streams, fish-filled ponds, or waterfalls. Take advantage of the resort's four cabana-flanked pools and the Tom Fazio–designed golf course. Topping the resort's amenities is complimentary limousine service within 14 mi. **Pros:** ultimate luxury, secluded, on-site golf course. **Cons:** service can be slow, hotel is not on the beach. ⊠ *5200 Grand Del Mar Ct.* 🕾 *858/314–2000 or 888/314–2030* ⊕ *www.thegranddelmar.com* ⟿ *218 rooms, 31 suites* ⚅ *In-room: a/c, safe, refrigerator, DVD, Internet, Wi-Fi. In-hotel: 6 restaurants, room service, bars, golf course, tennis courts, pools, gym, spa, children's programs (ages 5–12), laundry service, Internet terminal, Wi-Fi hotspot, parking (paid), some pets allowed* ▭ *AE, D, DC, MC, V.*

CARLSBAD

6 mi from Encinitas on Rte. S21, 36 mi north of downtown San Diego on I–5.

Once-sleepy Carlsbad, lying astride I–5 at the north end of a string of beach towns extending from San Diego to Oceanside, has long been popular with beach goers and sun seekers. On a clear day in this village you can take in sweeping ocean views that stretch from La Jolla to Oceanside by walking the 2-mi-long seawalk running between the Encina power plant and Pine Street. En route, you'll find several stairways leading to the beach and quite a few benches. More recently, however, much of the attention of visitors to the area has shifted inland, east of I–5, to LEGOLAND California and other attractions in its vicinity.

Fodor's Choice
★

Ⓒ **LEGOLAND California,** the centerpiece of a development that includes resort hotels and a designer discount shopping mall, offers a full day of entertainment with more than 50 rides and attractions for pint-size funseekers and their parents. The mostly outdoor experience is best appreciated by kids ages two to 10, who often beg to ride the mechanical horses around the Royal Joust again and again or to take just one more turn through the popular Volvo Jr. Driving School. Miniland USA, an animated collection of U.S. cities and other areas constructed entirely of Lego blocks, captures the imaginations of all ages. Kids get a chance to dig for buried fossils on Dino Island, which holds the Dig Those Dinos paleontological play area as well as the Coastersaurus, a junior roller coaster. At the Fun Town Fire Academy, families compete at fire fighting

TIP SHEET: LEGOLAND

Who will especially love this park?

LEGOLAND is especially tailored for families with kids 2–12—especially kids who love LEGOs.

What's This Really Gonna Cost?
In addition to tickets, you'll need to pay $12 for parking. Meals range from $3–$20 per person, and there's an extra charge for certain rides. Admission to LEGOLAND's adjacent SEA LIFE Aquarium is $19 for adults, $12 for children, and the Water Park costs $10—unless you purchase Hopper tickets good for admission to both parks ($77 adults; $67 kids and seniors).

Top 5 Attractions:
Lost Kingdom Adventure: Armed with a laser blaster, you'll journey through ancient Egyptian ruins in a desert roadster, scoring points as you hit targets.
Miniland U.S.A: This miniature, animated, interactive collection of U.S. icons was constructed out of 24 million Lego bricks!
Soak-N-Sail: Hundred of gallons of water course through 60

interactive features including a pirate shipwreck–themed area. You'll need your swimsuit for this one....
Dragon Coaster: Little kids love this popular indoor/outdoor steel roller coaster that goes through a castle. Don't let the name frighten you—the motif is more humorous than scary.
Volvo Driving School: Kids 6–13 can drive speed-controlled cars (not on rails) on a miniature road; driver's licenses are awarded after the course. Volvo Junior is the pint-sized version for kids 3–5.

Tips:
Don't Bring the Teens: Kids love LEGOLAND...but your older children will probably find it a bit juvenile.
Get a Hopper Ticket: The best ticket value is one of the Hopper Tickets that give you one admission to LEGOLAND plus Sea Life and the Water Park. These can be used on the same day or on different days.
Go Mid-week: Crowds are much lighter then—one Fodors.com user was able to see everything in four hours on a particularly quiet day!

by racing in a model fire truck and hosing down a simulated burning building. Also in Fun Town, besides the driving school, with miniature cars, is the Skipper School, with miniature boats. In Splash Battle, kids cruise through pirate-infested waters past exploding volcanoes; Treasure Falls, a mini-flume log ride with a 12-foot soaking plunge; and Pirate Shores, water-fight headquarters. Lost Kingdom Adventure, LEGOLAND'S first dark ride (meaning indoors) and part of a new four-ride block, features the adventures of popular LEGO mini-figure Johnny Thunder battling the bad guys in an Egyptian temple with the help of riders using laser blasters to accumulate points and ultimately capture Sam Sinister and find the treasure. Also part of the mix are stage shows and restaurants with kid-friendly buffets. LEGOLAND opened Sea Life, a walk-through aquarium in 2008 and LEGOLAND Water Park in 2010; both have separate admission, although park hopper tickets that include both attractions are available. ⊠ *1 LEGOLAND Dr. Exit I–5 at Cannon Rd. and follow signs east ¼ mi* ☎ *760/918–5346* ⊕ *www.*

A LEGOLAND model worker puts the finishing touches on the San Francisco portion of Miniland U.S.A.

legolandca.com ✉ *$67, additional fees for some rides; $87 Hopper ticket* ⊘ *Hrs vary; Closed Tues.–Wed.; call for information.*

In spring the hillsides are abloom at **Flower Fields at Carlsbad Ranch,** the largest bulb production farm in Southern California. Here, from mid-March through mid-May, you can walk through fields planted with thousands of Giant Tecolote ranunculus—a stunning 50-acre display of color against the backdrop of the blue Pacific Ocean. Also to be seen are the rose gardens—including the miniature rose garden and the Walk of Fame garden, lined with examples of every All-American Rose Selection award-winner since 1940—and demonstration gardens created by artists who normally work with paint and easel. ✉ *5704 Paseo del Norte, east of I–5* ☎ *760/431–0352* ⊕ *www.theflowerfields.com* ✉ *$10* ⊘ *Mar.–May, daily 9–6.*

WHERE TO STAY

$$$$
☺
Fodor'sChoice
★

🏨 **Four Seasons Resort Aviara.** This hilltop resort on 30 acres offers one of the most sublime views in Southern California. Stroll out to the pool overlooking Batiquitos Lagoon, where the panorama stretches endlessly from lagoon to the Pacific. If you watch for a while you may catch sight of one of the 130 species of birds that inhabit the wetland. The quietly elegant Aviara is one of the most luxurious hotels in the San Diego area, with gleaming marble corridors, original artwork, crystal chandeliers, and enormous flower arrangements. Rooms have every possible amenity: oversize closets, private balconies or garden patios, and marble bathrooms with double vanities and deep soaking tubs. The resort is exceptionally family-friendly, providing a wide selection of in-room amenities designed for the younger set. Kids also

DID YOU KNOW?

Escondido's Kit Carson Park is home to psychedelic Queen Califia's Magical Sculpture Garden, by Niki de Saint Phalle. ✉ *Bear Valley Pkwy. and Mary Ln., use Rancho Pkwy. exit from I-15* ⊕ *www. queencalifia.org.*

2

have their own pool—with a water-themed playground—and there are nature walks with wildlife demonstrations. The on-site golf course is considered one of the best in California, and jazz concerts are presented on the lawn on summer Friday evenings. **Pros:** unbeatable location, classy service, excellent restaurant. **Cons:** expensive. ⊠ *7100 Four Seasons Point* ☎ *760/603–6800 or 800/332–3442* ⊕ *www.fourseasons. com/aviara* ↝ *329 rooms, 44 suites* ⚒ *In-room: a/c, safe, refrigerator, DVD (some), Internet, Wi-Fi. In-hotel: 4 restaurants, room service, bars, golf course, tennis courts, pools, gym, spa, children's programs (ages 4–12), laundry service, Internet terminal, Wi-Fi, parking (paid)* ▭ *AE, D, DC, MC, V.*

OCEANSIDE

8 mi north of Carlsbad on Rte. S21, 37 mi north of downtown San Diego on I–5.

🔆 **Mission San Luis Rey,** known as the King of the Missions, was built in
Fodor'sChoice 1798 by Franciscan friars under the direction of Father Fermin Lasuen
★ to help educate and convert local Native Americans. Once a location for filming Disney's *Zorro* TV series, the well-preserved mission, still owned by the Franciscans, was the 18th and largest and most prosperous of California's missions. The *sala* (parlor), the kitchen, a friar's bedroom, a weaving room, and a collection of religious art convey much about early mission life. Retreats are still held here, but a picnic area, a gift shop, and a museum (which has the most extensive collection of old Spanish vestments in the United States) are also on the grounds, as are sunken gardens and the *lavanderia*, the original open-air laundry area. Self-guided and docent-led tours are available. The mission's retreat center has limited, inexpensive dormitory-style overnight accommodations. ⊠ *4050 Mission Ave.* ☎ *760/757–3651* ⊕ *www.sanluisrey.org* 🎫 *$6* ⊘ *Daily 10–4.*

ESCONDIDO

8 mi north of Rancho Bernardo on I–15, 31 mi northeast of downtown San Diego on I–15.

🔆 **San Diego Wild Animal Park** is an extension of the San Diego Zoo, 35
Fodor'sChoice mi to the south. The 1,800-acre preserve in the San Pasqual Valley is
★ designed to protect endangered species from around the world. Exhibit areas have been carved out of the dry, dusty canyons and mesas to represent the animals' natural habitats in various parts of Africa, the Australian rain forest, the Asian swamps, and the Asian plains.

The best way to see these preserves is to take the 45-minute, Journey into Africa bus tour (included in the price of admission). As you pass in front of the large, naturally landscaped enclosures, you can see animals bounding across prairies and mesas as they would in the wild. Predators are separated from prey by deep moats, but only the elephants, tigers, lions and cheetahs are kept in isolation. Lorikeet Landing, simulating the Australian rain forest, holds 75 of the loud and colorful small parrots—you can buy a cup of nectar at the aviary entrance to induce them to land on your hand. The Lion Camp gives you an up-close view of the king of beasts in a slice of African wilderness. As you walk through this exhibit, you can watch the giant cats lounging through a 40-foot-long window. The last stop is a research station where you can see them all around you through glass panels. ⊠ *15500 San Pasqual Valley Rd.* ✛ *Take I–15 north to Via Rancho Pkwy. and follow signs, 6 mi* ☎ *760/747–8702* ⊕ *www.sandiegozoo.org/wap* ⊠ *$37 includes Journey into Africa tour and Conservation Carousel; $70 two-visit pass includes a 1-day pass both to the zoo and WAP or two 1-day passes to either; parking $9* ⊙ *Mid-June–Labor Day, daily 9–8; mid-Sept.–mid-June, daily 9–4* ⊟ *D, MC, V.*

Orange County and Catalina Island

WITH DISNEYLAND AND KNOTT'S BERRY FARM

WORD OF MOUTH

"I'd say either Laguna Beach or Newport Beach . . . these two beaches would have the most action, and the highest possibility of lodging within walking distance. Newport Beach is also close to Newport Harbor, Balboa Island, and Corona Del Mar."
—Wellvis

WELCOME TO ORANGE COUNTY AND CATALINA ISLAND

TOP REASONS TO GO

★ **Disney magic:** Walking down Main Street, U.S.A. with Cinderella's Castle straight ahead, you really will feel like you're in one of the happiest places on earth.

★ **Beautiful beaches:** Surf, swim, sail, or just relax on one of the state's most breathtaking stretches of coastline.

★ **Island Getaways:** Just a short hydrofoil away, Catalina Island feels 1,000 mi away from California. Wander around charming Avalon, or explore the unspoiled beauty of the island's wild interior.

★ **The fine life:** Some of the state's wealthiest communities are in coastal Orange County, so spend at least part of your stay here experiencing how the other half lives.

★ **Family fun:** Spend some quality time with the kids riding roller coasters, eating ice cream, fishing off ocean piers, and bodysurfing.

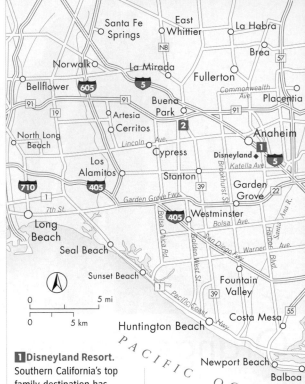

1 Disneyland Resort. Southern California's top family destination has expanded from the humble park of Walt Disney's vision to a megaresort with more attractions spilling over into Disney's California Adventure. But kids still consider it the happiest place on earth!

2 Knott's Berry Farm. Amusement park lovers should check out this Buena Park attraction, with thrill rides, the Peanuts gang, and lots of fried chicken and boysenberry pie.

3 Coastal Orange County. The OC's beach communities may not be quite as glamorous as seen on TV, but coastal spots like Huntington Beach, Newport Harbor, and Laguna Beach are perfect for chilling out in a beachfront hotel.

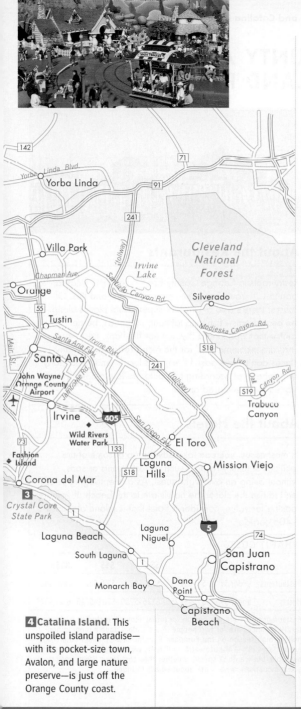

GETTING ORIENTED

Like Los Angeles, Orange County stretches over a large area, lacks a singular focal point, and has limited public transportation. You'll need a car and a sensible game plan to make the most of your visit. Try staying at a midpoint location such as Irvine or Costa Mesa, both equidistant from inland tourist attractions and the coast. These towns are less crowded than Anaheim and less expensive than the beach cities. Of course, if you can afford it, staying at the beach is always recommended.

4 Catalina Island. This unspoiled island paradise—with its pocket-size town, Avalon, and large nature preserve—is just off the Orange County coast.

ORANGE COUNTY AND CATALINA ISLAND PLANNER

Car Travel

The San Diego Freeway (I-405; the coastal route) and the Santa Ana Freeway (I-5; the inland route) run north–south through Orange County. South of Laguna I-405 merges into I-5 (called the San Diego Freeway south from this point). A toll road, Highway 73, runs 15 mi from Newport Beach to San Juan Capistrano; it costs $3 and is usually less jammed than the regular freeways.

Highways 55 and 91 head west to the ocean and east into the mountains and desert. Highway 91, which goes to inland points, has some express lanes for which drivers pay a toll, ostensibly to avoid the worst of rush-hour traffic. If you have three or more people in your car, though, you can use the Highway 91 express lanes most of the day for free (the exception being 4 PM–6 PM on weekdays, when you pay half-fare). Highway 55 leads to Newport Beach. The Pacific Coast Highway (Highway 1) allows easy access to beach communities and is the most scenic route.

Laguna Canyon Road is a beautiful route that winds through a coastal canyon. ■TIP➔ It's quite narrow and is also used by cyclists, so use caution and turn on your headlights even in daytime.

About the Restaurants

Restaurants in Orange County are typically more casual than in L.A. You'll rarely see men in jackets and ties. Of course, there's also a swath of supercasual places along the beachfronts—fish-taco takeout, taquerias, burger joints—that won't mind if you wear flip-flops. Reservations are recommended for the nicest restaurants. Many places don't serve past 11 PM, and locals tend to eat early. Remember that according to California law, smoking is prohibited in all enclosed areas.

About the Hotels

In most cases, you can take advantage of some of the facilities of luxury resorts, such as restaurants or spas, without being an overnight guest. As a rule, lodging prices tend to rise the closer the hotels are to the beach. If you are looking for value, consider a hotel that is inland along the I-405 corridor.

WHAT IT COSTS					
	¢	$	$$	$$$	$$$$
Restaurants	under $7	$7–$12	$13–$22	$23–$32	over $32
Hotels	under $75	$75–$125	$126–$200	$201–$325	over $325

Restaurant prices are per person for a main course, excluding 8.25% sales tax. Hotel prices are for two people in a standard double room in non-holiday high season on the European Plan (no meals) unless otherwise noted. Taxes (9%–14%) are extra. In listings we always name the facilities available, but we don't specify whether they cost extra. When pricing accommodations, always ask about what's included.

3

Updated by
Laura Randall

Few of the citrus groves that gave Orange County its name remain. This region south and east of Los Angeles is now ruled by tourism and high-tech business instead of farmers.

With its tropical flowers and palm trees, the stretch of coast between Seal Beach and San Clemente is often called the California Riviera. Exclusive Newport Beach, artsy Laguna, and the surf town of Huntington Beach are the stars, but lesser-known gems on the glistening coast—such as Corona del Mar—are also worth visiting. Offshore, meanwhile, lies gorgeous Catalina Island, a terrific spot for diving, snorkeling, and hiking. And despite a building boom that began in the 1990s, the area is still a place to find wilderness trails, canyons, greenbelts, and natural parks.

PLANNING

GETTING HERE AND AROUND
AIR TRAVEL
Orange County's main facility is John Wayne Airport Orange County (SNA), which is served by 10 major domestic airlines and three commuter lines. Long Beach Airport (LGB) serves four airlines, including its major player, JetBlue. It's roughly 20–30 minutes by car from Anaheim.

The only transfer service from John Wayne or LAX to Orange County coastal cities is provided by SuperShuttle, which can be expensive. Fares, determined by distance, are for the first person in a party; add $9 for additional persons. You'll pay $18 from John Wayne to Newport Beach and $29 to Laguna Beach. Fares to the same destinations from LAX are $51 and $61 per person, respectively. Airport Bus and Prime Time Airport Shuttle provide transportation from John Wayne and LAX to the Disneyland area of Anaheim. Round-trip fares average about $27 per person from John Wayne and $17 to $32 from LAX.

Airport Information John Wayne Airport Orange County (✉ *MacArthur Blvd. at I–405, Santa Ana* ☎ *949/252–5200* ⊕ *www.ocair.com*). **Long Beach Airport** (✉ *4100 Donald Douglas Dr., Long Beach* ☎ *562/570–2600* ⊕ *www.longbeach. gov/airport*).

Shuttles Airport Bus (☎ *800/938–8933* ⊕ *www.airportbus.com*). **Prime Time Airport Shuttle** (☎ *800/262–7433* ⊕ *www.primetimeshuttle.com*). **SuperShuttle** (☎ *800/258–3826* ⊕ *www.supershuttle.com*).

BUS TRAVEL

The Orange County Transportation Authority will take you virtually anywhere in the county, but it will take time; OCTA buses go from Knott's Berry Farm and Disneyland to Huntington Beach and Newport Beach. Bus 1 travels along the coast; buses 701 and 721 provide express service to Los Angeles. Be aware that there is no weekend service.

Fares for the OCTA local routes are $1.50 per boarding; you can also get a $4 local day pass (valid only on the date of purchase). Day passes can be purchased from bus drivers upon boarding. Express bus fare between Orange County and L.A. is $3.75 a pop, $2.50 if you have a day pass. The bus-fare boxes take coins and dollar bills, but you must use exact change.

Bus Information Greyhound (☎ *714/999–1256 or 800/231–2222* ⊕ *www. greyhound.com*). **Los Angeles MTA** (☎ *213/626–4455* ⊕ *www.mta.net*). **Orange County Transportation Authority (OCTA)** (☎ *714/636–7433* ⊕ *www.octa.net*).

TRAIN TRAVEL

Amtrak makes daily stops in Orange County at Fullerton, Anaheim, Santa Ana, Irvine, San Juan Capistrano, and San Clemente. Metrolink is a weekday commuter train that runs to and from Los Angeles and Orange County, starting as far south as Oceanside and stopping in Laguna Niguel, Tustin, San Juan Capistrano, San Clemente, Irvine, Santa Ana, Orange, Anaheim, and Fullerton. The Metrolink system is divided into a dozen zones; the fare you pay depends on how many zones you cover. Buy tickets from the vending machines at each station. Ticketing is on an honor system.

Train Information Amtrak (☎ *800/872–7245* ⊕ *www.amtrak.com*). **Metrolink** (☎ *800/371–5465* ⊕ *www.metrolinktrains.com*).

VISITOR INFORMATION

Contacts Anaheim-Orange County Visitor and Convention Bureau (✉ *Anaheim Convention Center, 800 W. Katella Ave., Anaheim* ☎ *714/765–8888* ⊕ *www.anaheimoc.org*).

DISNEYLAND RESORT

☾ *26 mi southeast of Los Angeles, via I–5.*

Fodor's Choice ★ The snowcapped Matterhorn, the centerpiece of the Magic Kingdom, punctuates the skyline of **Anaheim**. Since 1955, when Walt Disney chose this once-quiet farming community for the site of his first amusement park, Disneyland has attracted more than 450 million visitors and thousands of workers, and Anaheim has been their host. To understand the symbiotic relationship between Disneyland and Anaheim, you need only look at the $4.2 billion spent in a combined effort by the Walt Disney Company and Anaheim, the latter to revitalize the city's tourist center and run-down areas, the former to expand and renovate the Disney properties into what is known now as **Disneyland Resort.** The resort is a sprawling complex that includes Disney's two amusement parks; three hotels; and Downtown Disney, a shopping, dining, and entertainment promenade. Anaheim's tourist center includes Angel Stadium of Anaheim, home of baseball's World Series Champion Los Angeles Angels of Anaheim; Arrowhead Pond, which hosts concerts and the hockey team the Anaheim Ducks; and the enormous Anaheim Convention Center.

GETTING THERE

Disneyland is about a 30-mi drive from either LAX or downtown. From LAX, follow Sepulveda Boulevard south to the I–105 freeway and drive east 16 mi to the I–605 north exit. Exit at the Santa Ana Freeway (I–5) and continue south for 12 mi to the Disneyland Drive exit. Follow signs to the resort. From downtown, follow I–5 south 28 mi and exit at Disneyland Drive. ⊠ *1313 Harbor Blvd., Anaheim* ☎ *714/781–4565* ⊕ *www.disneyland.com.*

The **Anaheim Orange County Visitor & Convention Bureau** is a good source for maps and news on the area. ⊠ *800 W. Katella Ave., Anaheim* ☎ *714/ 765–8888* ⊕ *www.anaheimoc.org.*

Disneyland Resort Express offers daily nonstop bus service between LAX, John Wayne Airport, and Anaheim. Reservations are not required. The cost is $20 one way for adults, $17 for children. ☎ *714/978–8855* ⊕ *www.airportbus.com.*

TIMING

Disneyland and Disney's California Adventure are open daily, 365 days a year; hours vary, depending on the season, but typically Disneyland opens at 8 AM and Disney's California Adventure at 10 AM. Guests at Disney hotels and those with a multiple-day Park Hopper pass are often allowed in an hour ahead of the official opening time. Disneyland stays open as late as midnight on weekends and in the summer, but it's always a good idea to check the Web site or call ahead.

If you plan to visit for more than a day, you can save money by buying three-, four-, and five-day Park Hopper tickets that grant same-day "hopping" privileges between Disneyland and Disney's California Adventure. You get a discount on the multiple-day passes if you buy online through the Disneyland Web site. A one-day Park Hopper pass costs $97 for anyone 10 or older, $84 for kids ages 3–9. Admission to either park (but not both) is $72 or $62 for kids 3–9; kids under 3 are free. Don't forget to factor in parking costs; $14 for cars, $17 for RVs.

DISNEYLAND

PARK NEIGHBORHOODS

○ MAIN STREET, U.S.A.

Fodor's Choice Walt's hometown of Marceline, Missouri, was the inspiration behind
★ this romanticized image of small-town America, circa 1900. It opens half an hour before the rest of the park, so it's a good place to explore if you're getting an early start to beat the crowds. The sidewalks are lined with a penny arcade and shops that sell everything from tradable pins to Disney-theme clothing and photo supplies. **Main Street Cinema**

offers a cool respite from the crowds and six classic Disney animated shorts, including Steamboat Willie. There's rarely a wait to enter. Board the **Disneyland Railroad** here to save on walking; it tours all the lands, plus offers unique views of Splash Mountain and the Grand Canyon and Primeval World dioramas.

NEW ORLEANS SQUARE

A mini–French Quarter with narrow streets, hidden courtyards, and live street performances, this is home to two iconic attractions and the Cajun-inspired Blue Bayou restaurant. **Pirates of the Caribbean** now features Jack Sparrow and the cursed Captain Barbossa, in a nod to the blockbuster movies of the same name, plus enhanced special effects and battle scenes (complete with cannonball explosions). Nearby **Haunted Mansion** continues to spook guests with its stretching room and "doombuggy" rides (plus there's now an expanded storyline for the beating-heart bride). Its *Nightmare Before Christmas* holiday overlay is an annual tradition. Don't forget to check out the beautiful animation art at **Disney Gallery,** where free tours (no reservation required) are available in the afternoon. This is a good area to get a casual bite to eat; the clam chowder in sourdough bread bowls, sold at the French Market Restaurant and Royal Street Veranda, is a popular choice.

FRONTIERLAND

Located between Adventureland and Fantasyland, Frontierland transports you to the wild, wild West with its rustic buildings, shooting gallery, mountain range, and foot stompin' dance hall. The marquee attraction, **Big Thunder Mountain Railroad,** is a relatively tame roller coaster ride (no steep descents) that takes the form of a runaway mine car as it rumbles past desert canyons and an old mining town. Tour the Rivers of America on the **Mark Twain Riverboat** in the company of a grizzled old river pilot or circumnavigate the globe on the **Sailing Ship Columbia,** though its operating hours are usually limited to weekends. You can also raft over from here to Pirate's Lair on **Tom Sawyer Island,** which now features pirate-theme caves, treasure hunts, and music along with plenty of caves and hills to climb and explore. If you don't mind tight seating, have a snack at the Golden Horseshoe Restaurant while enjoying the always-entertaining comedy and bluegrass show of Billy Hill and the Hillybillies. Children won't want to miss **Big Thunder Ranch,** a small petting zoo of real pigs, goats, and cows beyond Big Thunder Mountain.

CRITTER COUNTRY

Down-home country is the theme in this shady corner of the park, where Winnie the Pooh and Davy Crockett make their homes. So does **Splash Mountain,** a classic flume ride accompanied by music and appearances by Br'er Rabbit and other characters from *Song of the South.* Don't forget to check out your photo (the camera snaps close-ups of each car just before it plunges into the water) on the way out. The patio of the popular Hungry Bear Restaurant has great views of Tom Sawyer's Island and Davy Crockett's Explorer Canoes.

ADVENTURELAND

Modeled after the lands of Africa, Polynesia, and Arabia, this tiny tropical paradise is worth braving the crowds that flock here for the ambience and better-than-average food. Sing along with the animatronic birds and tiki gods in the **Enchanted Tiki Room,** sail the rivers of the world with joke-cracking skippers on **Jungle Cruise,** and climb the Disneyodendron semperflorens (aka always-blooming Disney tree) to **Tarzan's Treehouse,** where you'll walk through scenes, some interactive, from the 1999 animated film. Cap off the visit with a wild jeep ride at **Indiana Jones Adventure,** where the special effects and decipherable hieroglyphics distract you while you're waiting in line. The kebabs at Bengal Barbecue and pineapple whip at Tiki Juice Bar are some of the best fast-food options in the park.

FANTASYLAND

Sleeping Beauty's Castle marks the entrance to Fantasyland, a visual wonderland of princesses, spinning teacups, flying elephants, and other classic storybook characters. Rides and shops (such as the princess-theme Once Upon a Time and Gepetto's Toys and Gifts) take precedence over restaurants in this area of the park, but outdoor carts sell everything from churros to turkey legs. Tots love the **King Arthur Carousel, Casey Jr. Circus Train,** and **Storybook Land Canal Boats.** This is also home to **Mr. Toad's Wild Ride, Peter Pan's Flight,** and **Pinocchio's Daring Journey,** classic, movie-theater-dark rides that immerse riders in Disney fairy tales and appeal to adults and kids alike. The Abominable Snowman pops up on the **Matterhorn Bobsleds,** a roller coaster that twists and turns you up and around a made-to-scale model of the real Swiss mountain. Anchoring the east end of Fantasyland is **It's a Small World,** a smorgasbord of dancing animatronic dolls, cuckoo clock–covered walls, and variations of the song everyone knows by heart. Across the way, little princesses and knights can partake in a coronation ceremony, dancing, and storytelling by a Disney Princess at the **Disney Princess Fantasy Faire.** Check the daily guide for times.

MICKEY'S TOONTOWN

Geared toward small fry, this lopsided cartoonlike downtown, complete with cars and trolleys that invite exploring, is where Mickey, Donald, Goofy, and other classic Disney characters hang their hats. One of the most popular attractions is **Roger Rabbit's Car Toon Spin,** a twisting, turning cab ride through the Toontown of *Who Framed Roger Rabbit?* You can also walk through **Mickey's House** to meet and be photographed with the famous mouse, take a low-key ride on **Gadget's Go Coaster,** or bounce around the fenced-in playground in front of **Goofy's House.**

TOMORROWLAND

This popular section of the park underwent a complete refurbishment in 1998 and continues to tinker with its future with the regular addition of new or enhanced rides. The newest attraction, **Finding Nemo's Submarine Voyage** updates the old Submarine Voyage ride with the exploits of Nemo, Dory, Marlin, and other characters from the Pixar film. Try to visit this popular ride early in the day if you can and be prepared for a wait. The interactive **Buzz Lightyear Astro Blasters** lets

TIP SHEET: DISNEYLAND

Who Will Especially Love This Park?

Disneyland mainly caters to families with young children. That being said, it's pretty difficult to have a bad time in the Magic Kingdom—no matter your age.

What's This Really Gonna Cost?

In addition to tickets, you'll need to pay $12–$16 for parking (unless your hotel has a shuttle or is within walking distance), and meals in the parks and at Downtown Disney range from $10 to $30 per person. Of course, you may end up spending a great deal more if you spring for extras like character dining experiences, souvenirs, etc. If you're staying in a hotel near the park, ask if any discount packages are available when you book.

TOP 5 ATTRACTIONS:

Finding Nemo: Board a submerged yellow submarine and view a 3-D animated adventure featuring characters from the hit film.

Haunted Mansion: A "doombuggy" takes you through a spooky old plantation mansion.

Pirates of the Caribbean: Yaaar! Watch buccaneers wreak havoc in a Caribbean town as you float along in a rowboat.

Space Mountain: This scary-but-thrilling roller coaster is indoors—and much of the ride takes place in the dark.

Matterhorn Bobsleds: It's hard to miss this roller coaster at the center of the Magic Kingdom, which simulates bobsleds racing around the famous mountain.

TIPS:

Avoid the Crowds: Try to see the major attractions at the beginning or end of the day, or during parades. Visit mid-week, if possible.

Be Flexible: Rides occasionally break down or are closed, lines are sometimes quite long, and kids can have meltdowns. Roll with it, and don't hesitate to adjust your plans.

Get a FastPass: These passes allow you to reserve a time to ride popular rides later in the day without waiting in line—using them can save you a ton of time.

Buy Tickets in Advance: Many hotels near the park sell tickets, and you can also buy them online. (Purchasing tickets at the park can take over an hour on busy days.)

Send the Teens Next Door: Disneyland's newer sister park, California Adventure, features more intense rides suitable for older kids (Park Hopper passes include admission to both parks).

you zap your neighbors with laser beams and compete for the highest score. Hurtle through the cosmos on **Space Mountain,** refurbished in 2005, and take a shuttle ride on Endor in **Star Wars.** There are also mainstays like the futuristic **Astro Orbiter** rockets, **Innoventions,** a self-guided tour of the latest toys of tomorrow, and **Honey, I Shrunk the Audience,** a 3-D film featuring Rick Moranis. Disneyland Monorail and Disneyland Railroad both have stations here. There's also a video arcade, and the dancing water fountain makes a perfect playground for kids on hot summer days.

DID YOU KNOW?

Apparently, the plain purple teacup in Disneyland's Mad Tea Party ride spins the fastest—though no one knows why.

OTHER ATTRACTIONS
Besides the eight lands, the daily live-action shows and parades are always crowd pleasers. Fantasmic! is a musical, fireworks, and laser show in which Mickey and friends wage a spellbinding battle against Disneyland's darker characters; and the daytime and nighttime Parade of Dreams features just about every animated Disney character ever drawn. ■TIP→ Arrive early to secure a good view; if there are two shows scheduled for the day, the second one tends to be less crowded. A fireworks display sparks up Friday and Saturday evenings. Brochures with maps, available at the entrance, list show- and parade times.

DISNEY'S CALIFORNIA ADVENTURE

The sprawling 55-acre Disney's California Adventure, right next to Disneyland (their entrances face each other), pays tribute to the Golden State with four theme areas. In an effort to attract more crowds, the park began a major five-year overhaul in late 2007 intended to infuse more of Walt Disney's spirit throughout the park and add a host of new attractions, including a nighttime water-effects show and a 12-acre section called Cars Land based on the Pixar film. The first new attraction, an interactive adventure ride called Toy Story Mania! and hosted by Woody, Buzz Lightyear, and friends opened at Paradise Pier in 2008.

PARK NEIGHBORHOODS
PARADISE PIER
This section re-creates the glory days of California's seaside piers. If you're looking for thrills, the **California Screamin'** roller coaster takes its riders from 0 to 55 MPH in about four seconds and proceeds through scream tunnels, steeply angled drops, and a 360-degree loop. **Sun Wheel,** a giant Ferris wheel, provides a good view of the grounds at a more leisurely pace. **Mulholland Madness** is a fun tribute to L.A.'s crazy traffic cycles. There are also carnival games, a fish-themed carousel, and Ariel's Grotto, where future princesses can dine with the mermaid and her friends (reservations a must).

HOLLYWOOD PICTURES BACKLOT
With a main street modeled after Hollywood Boulevard, a fake blue-sky backdrop, and real soundstages, this area celebrates California's most famous industry. **Walt Disney Imagineering Blue Sky Cellar** gives you an insider's look at the work of animators and how they create characters. **Turtle Talk with Crush** lets kids have an unrehearsed talk with computer-animated Crush, a sea turtle from *Finding Nemo.* The Hyperion theater hosts **Aladdin—A Musical Spectacular,** a 45-minute live performance with terrific visual effects. ■TIP→ Plan on getting in line about half an hour in advance: the show is well worth the wait. On the latest film-inspired ride, **Monsters, Inc. Mike & Sulley to the Rescue,** you climb into taxis and travel the streets of Monstropolis on a mission of safely returning Boo to her bedroom. A major draw for older kids is the looming **Twilight Zone Tower of Terror,** which drops riders 13 floors.

A BUG'S LAND

Inspired by the 1998 film *A Bug's Life,* this section skews its attractions to an insect's point of view. Kids can cool off (or get soaked) in the water jets and giant garden hose of **Princess Dot Puddle Park,** spin around in giant takeout Chinese food boxes on **Flik's Flyers,** and hit the bug-shaped bumper cars on **Tuck and Roll's Drive 'Em Buggies.** The short show *It's Tough to Be a Bug!* gives you a 3-D look at insect life.

GOLDEN STATE

Celebrate California's history and natural beauty with nature trails, a winery, and a tortilla factory (with free samples). The area of Condor Flats has **Soarin' Over California,** a spectacular simulated hang-glider ride over California terrain, and the **Redwood Creek Challenge Trail,** a challenging trek across net ladders and suspension bridges. The film *Golden Dreams* is a sentimental dash through California history narrated by Whoopi Goldberg. **Grizzly River Run** simulates the river rapids of the Sierra Nevadas; be prepared to get soaked. The Wine Country Trattoria is a great place for a relaxing outdoor lunch.

OTHER ATTRACTIONS

Downtown Disney is a 20-acre promenade of dining, shopping, and entertainment that connects the Disneyland Resort hotels and theme parks. Restaurant-nightclubs here include the **House of Blues,** which spices up its Delta-inspired ribs and seafood with various live music acts on an intimate two-story stage. At **Ralph Brennan's Jazz Kitchen** you can dig into New Orleans–style food and music. Sports fans gravitate to **ESPN Zone,** a sports bar–restaurant–entertainment center with American grill food, interactive video games, and 175 video screens telecasting worldwide sports events. There's also an **AMC** multiplex movie theater with stadium-style seating that plays the latest blockbusters and, naturally, a couple of kids' flicks. Promenade shops sell everything from Disney goods to antique jewelry; don't miss **Vault 28,** a hip boutique that sells one-of-kind vintage and couture clothes and accessories from Disney, Betsey Johnson, and other designers. ⊠ *Disneyland Dr. between Ball Rd. and Katella Ave., Anaheim* ☎ *714/300–7800* ⊕ *www. downtowndisney.com* ⏄ *Free* ☉ *Daily 7 AM–2 AM; hrs at shops and restaurants vary.*

WHERE TO EAT AND STAY

An Anaheim Resort Transit (ART) bus can take you around town for $4 a day. The buses run every 10 minutes during peak times, 20 minutes otherwise. They go between major hotels, Disney attractions, the Anaheim Convention Center, and restaurants and shops. See the ART Web site (⊕ *www.rideart.org*) for more information. In addition, many hotels are within walking distance of the Disneyland Resort; some offer shuttle service.

$$$$ ✕ **Anaheim White House.** Several small dining rooms are set with crisp
ITALIAN linens and candles in this flower-filled 1909 mansion. The northern Italian menu includes steak, rack of lamb, and fresh seafood. Try the Gwen Stefani Ravioli, lobster-filled pasta on a bed of ginger and citrus. A three-course prix-fixe "express" lunch, served weekdays, costs $22.

CLOSE UP

Nixon Presidential Library

The **Richard Nixon Presidential Library and Birthplace** (✉ *18001 Yorba Linda Blvd., Yorba Linda* ☎ *714/993-3393* ⊕ *www.nixonlibrary. org* ⌐ *$9.95* ⊙ *Mon.–Sat. 10–5, Sun. 11–5*) is the final resting place of the 37th president and his wife, Pat. Exhibits illustrate the checkered career of Nixon, from heralded leader of the free world to beleaguered resignee. You can listen to the so-called smoking-gun tape from the Watergate days, among other recorded material. Life-size sculptures of foreign world leaders, gifts Nixon received from international heads of state, and a large graffiti-covered section of the Berlin Wall are on display. You can also visit Pat Nixon's tranquil rose garden and tour the small farmhouse where Richard Nixon was born in 1913. Don't miss the bookstore, which sells everything from birdhouses to photos of Nixon with Elvis.

✉ *887 S. Anaheim Blvd., Anaheim* ☎ *714/772–1381* ➡ *AE, MC, V* ⊙ *No lunch weekends.*

$$$
MEDITERRANEAN
⊙

✗ **Catal Restaurant & Uva Bar.** Famed chef Joachim Splichal takes a more casual approach at this bi-level Mediterranean spot—with tapas breaking into the finger-food territory. At the Uva (Spanish for "grape") bar on the ground level you can graze on olives and Spanish ham, choosing from 40 wines by the glass. Upstairs, Catal's fine dining menu spans paella, rotisserie chicken, braised rabbit, and salads. A kids' menu is also available. ✉ *1580 Disneyland Dr., Suite 103, Downtown Disney* ☎ *714/774–4442* ➡ *AE, D, MC, V.*

$$
ITALIAN
⊙

✗ **Luigi's D'Italia.** Despite the simple surroundings—red vinyl booths and plastic checkered tablecloths—Luigi's serves outstanding Italian cuisine: spaghetti marinara, veal Parmesan, homemade pizza, and all the classics. Kids will feel right at home here; there's even a children's menu. It's an easy five-minute drive from Disneyland, but less crowded and expensive than many restaurants adjacent to the park. ✉ *801 S. State College Blvd., Anaheim* ☎ *714/490–0990* ➡ *AE, D, MC, V.*

$$$
MEDITERRANEAN

✗ **Mr. Stox.** Intimate booths and linen tablecloths create a sophisticated, old-school setting at this family-owned restaurant. Prime rib, Maryland crab cakes, and fresh fish specials are excellent; the pasta, bread, and pastries are made in-house; and the wine list is wide-ranging. ✉ *1105 E. Katella Ave., Anaheim* ☎ *714/634–2994* ➡ *AE, D, DC, MC, V* ⊙ *No lunch weekends.*

$$$
AMERICAN
★

✗ **Napa Rose.** In sync with its host hotel, Grand Californian, this restaurant is done in a lovely Arts and Crafts style. The contemporary cuisine here is matched with an extensive wine list (600 bottles on display). For a look into the open kitchen, sit at the counter and watch the chefs as they whip up signature dishes such as scallops in a sauce of lemon, lobster, and vanilla, and grilled filet mignon. A four-course $85 prix-fixe menu changes weekly; add a wine flight for $45. ✉ *Grand Californian Hotel, 1600 S. Disneyland Dr.* ☎ *714/300–7170* ➡ *AE, D, DC, MC, V* ⊙ *No lunch.*

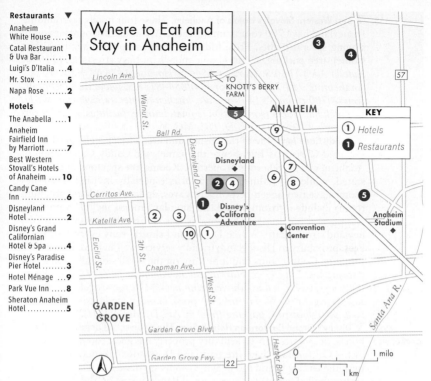

WHERE TO STAY

$$ ☎ **The Anabella.** This Spanish Mission–style hotel on the convention center campus is a good value. The suites are spacious with granite bathrooms and sleeper sofas. The interior rooms (away from Katella Avenue) are quieter. The hotel's Oasis, with a hot tub and pool, plus an adults-only pool, is a perfect place for relaxing. **Pros:** attentive service; landscaped grounds; pet-friendly rooms. **Cons:** some say the room walls are thin; it's a bit removed from the action. ⊠ *1030 W. Katella Ave., Anaheim* ☎ *714/905–1050 or 800/863–4888* ⊕ *www.anabellahotel. com* ➪ *308 rooms, 50 suites* ⚐ *In-room: a/c, safe, refrigerator, Wi-Fi. In-hotel: restaurant, room service, bar, pools, gym, laundry facilities, laundry service, parking (paid)* ☰ *AE, D, DC, MC, V.*

$$ ☎ **Anaheim Fairfield Inn by Marriott.** Attentive service and proximity to Disneyland (a 10-minute walk away) make this high-rise hotel a big draw for families. Most of the spacious rooms come with sleeper sofas as well as beds. **Pros:** proximity to Disneyland; close to many restaurants; the lobby offers fruit-infused drinking water and a TV showing Disney movies. **Cons:** small pool abuts the parking lot; lack of green space. ⊠ *1460 S. Harbor Blvd., Anaheim* ☎ *714/772–6777 or 800/228–2800* ⊕ *www.marriott.com* ➪ *467 rooms* ⚐ *In-room: a/c, refrigerator, Wi-Fi. In-hotel: 2 restaurants, room service, pool, laundry facilities, laundry service, Wi-Fi hotspot, parking (free)* ☰ *AE, D, DC, MC, V.*

$$ ⊡ **Best Western Stovall's Hotels of Anaheim.** These four hotels surrounding Disneyland have 700 rooms among them. Ask about discounts if you're staying several nights. Pros: kids stay free; complimentary breakfast (some); free parking. Cons: simple motels on busy streets. ⊠ *1110 W. Katella Ave.; 1630 S. Harbor; 1544 S. Harbor; 1176 W. Katella Ave., Anaheim* ☎ *714/778–1880 or 800/854–8175* ⊕ *www.stovallshotels. com* ⤳ *700 rooms* ⚏ *In-room: a/c, kitchen (some), refrigerator, Wi-Fi. In-hotel: bar, pools (some), gym (some), laundry facilities, laundry service, parking (free)* ⊟ *AE, D, DC, MC, V.*

$$
★ ⊡ **Candy Cane Inn.** One of the Disneyland area's first hotels (deeds were executed Christmas Eve, hence the name), the Candy Cane is one of Anaheim's most relaxing properties. Rooms are spacious and understated, while the palm-fringed pool is especially inviting. Premium rooms have two queen beds, microwaves, and coffeemakers; premium rooms include in-room breakfasts (standard rooms include a poolside Continental breakfast). The hotel is just around the corner from Disneyland's main gate. A free Disneyland shuttle runs every half hour. Pros: proximity to Disneyland; friendly service; well-lighted, landscaped property. Cons: rooms and lobby are on the small side; all rooms face parking lot. ⊠ *1747 S. Harbor Blvd., Anaheim* ☎ *714/774–5284 or 800/345–7057* ⊕ *www.candycaneinn.net* ⤳ *171 rooms* ⚏ *In-room: a/c, safe, refrigerator, Wi-Fi. In-hotel: pool, laundry facilities, laundry service, Wi-Fi hotspot, parking (free)* ⊟ *AE, D, MC, V* ⦿ *CP.*

$$$$
Fodor'sChoice
★ ⊡ **Disney's Grand Californian Hotel & Spa.** The newest of Disney's Anaheim hotels, this Craftsman-style luxury property has guest rooms with views of the California Adventure park and Downtown Disney. They don't push the Disney brand too heavily; rooms are done in dark woods with amber-shaded lamps and just a small Bambi image on the shower curtain. Restaurants include the Napa Rose dining room and Storytellers Cafe, where Disney characters entertain children at breakfast. Of the three pools, the one shaped like Mickey Mouse is just for kids, plus there's an evening child activity center and portable cribs in every room. The Mandara spa has a couple's suite with Balinese-inspired art and textiles. In 2009 the resort added a new wing with 50 Disney Vacation Club villas, most of which have full kitchens, balconies or patios, and laundry facilities, as well as 200 new rooms. ■TIP→ The spa is open to guests of all three Disney hotels. Pros: gorgeous lobby; supervised evening children's program (ages 5–12); direct access to California Adventure. Cons: self-parking lot is across the street from the hotel; standard rooms are on the small side. ⊠ *1600 S. Disneyland Dr., Disneyland Resort* ☎ *714/956–6425* ⊕ *www.disneyland.com* ⤳ *901 rooms, 44 suites, 50 villas.* ⚏ *In-room: a/c, safe, refrigerator, DVD (some). In-hotel: 2 restaurants, room service, bar, pool, gym, spa, laundry service, laundry facilities, parking (paid)* ⊟ *AE, D, DC, MC, V.*

$$$ ⊡ **Disney's Paradise Pier Hotel.** The Paradise Pier has many of the same Disney touches as the Disneyland Hotel, but it's a bit quieter and tamer. From here you can walk to Disneyland or pick up a shuttle or monorail. SoCal style manifests itself in seafoam-green guest rooms with lamps shaped like lifeguard stands, and surfboard motifs. A wooden roller coaster–inspired waterslide takes adventurers to a high-speed splashdown. **Pros:** first-rate concierge; friendly service. **Cons:** small pool area; it's a 15-minute walk to Disneyland despite its location within the Disney resort area. ✉ *1717 S. Disneyland Dr., Disneyland Resort* ☎ *714/999–0990* ⊕ *www.disneyland.com* ⤳ *489 rooms, 45 suites* ♿ *In-room: a/c, safe, refrigerator, DVD (some) Internet. In-hotel: 2 restaurants, room service, bars, pool, gym, laundry service, parking (paid)* ▭ *AE, D, DC, MC, V.*

$$$ **Disneyland Hotel.** Not surprisingly, the first of Disney's three hotels is
⟳   the one most full of Magic Kingdom magic, with Disney-theme memorabilia and Disney music. Check out the Peter Pan–theme pool, with its wooden bridge, 110-foot waterslide, and relaxing whirlpool. The cove pools' sandy shores are great for sunning and playing volleyball. East-facing rooms in the Sierra Tower have the best views of the park, while west-facing rooms look over gardens. At Goofy's Kitchen, kids can dine with Disney characters. In 2009, the hotel began a three-year multiphase renovation aimed at modernizing the entire facility with wireless Internet, new plumbing, and noise-filtering windows. Updated guest rooms will have flat-screen TVs and new Disney-theme decor such as headboards featuring Sleeping Beauty Castle. ■**TIP→ If you are planning to stay at one of the Disney hotels, ask about packages, which often include lodging discounts, Park Hopper passes, early admission to the parks, and preferred seating at some shows.** **Pros:** Disney theme is everywhere; great kids' activities. **Cons:** uninviting lobby; lots of kids means the noise level is high at all hours. ✉ *1150 Magic Way, Disneyland Resort* ☎ *714/778–6600* ⊕ *www.disneyland.com* ⤳ *909 rooms, 60 suites* ♿ *In-room: a/c, safe, refrigerator, DVD (some), Internet. In-hotel: 5 restaurants, room service, bars, pool, gym, laundry service, Wi-Fi, parking (paid)* ▭ *AE, D, DC, MC, V.*

$ **Hotel Ménage.** Kerry Hotels bought this former Holiday Inn in 2006 and refashioned it into a stylish boutique hotel. All of the rooms in the five-story building have been attractively redecorated in muted browns and whites; most have king beds, plasma TVs, and small sitting areas. Request an upper-floor room facing the pool, and you'll have a front-row view of Disneyland's evening fireworks show. **Pros:** closest hotel to the park; sophisticated decor. **Cons:** located on a busy corner; limited parking. ✉ *1221 S. Harbor Blvd., Anaheim* ☎ *714/758–0900 or 888/462-7275* ⊕ *www.hotelmenage.com* ⤳ *255 rooms, 2 suites* ♿ *In-room: a/c, Wi-Fi. In-hotel: restaurant, room service, bar, pool, laundry facilities, Wi-Fi hotspot, parking (free)* ▭ *AE, D, DC, MC, V.*

$$ **Park Vue Inn.** This bougainvillea-trimmed two-story Spanish-style inn is one of the closest hotels you'll find to Disneyland's main gate. Rooms were renovated in 2007 and most feature two queen beds, desks, and large TVs. **Pros:** easy walk to Disneyland and many restaurants; good value. **Cons:** all rooms face the parking lot; some complain about early-morning street noise. ✉ *1570 S. Harbor Blvd., Anaheim* ☎ *714/772–3691 or 800/334–7021* ⊕ *www.parkvueinn.com* ⤳ *76 rooms, 6 suites* ♿ *In-room: a/c, safe, refrigerator, Wi-Fi. In-hotel: pool, laundry facilities, Wi-Fi hotspot, parking (free)* ▭ *AE, D, DC, MC, V.*

$$ **Sheraton Anaheim Hotel.** If you're hoping to escape from the commer-
★   cial atmosphere of the hotels near Disneyland, consider this sprawling

replica of a Tudor castle. In the flower- and plant-filled lobby you're welcome to sit by the grand fireplace, watching fish swim around in a pond. Rooms are sizable; some first-floor rooms open onto interior gardens and a pool area. A shuttle to Disneyland is available. **Pros:** attractive lobby; spacious rooms with comfortable beds. **Cons:** confusing layout; hotel sits close to a busy freeway and is not within walking distance of Disneyland. ✉ *900 S. Disneyland Dr., Anaheim* ☎ *714/778–1700 or 800/325–3535* ⊕ *www.starwoodhotels.com* ⇨ *460 rooms, 29 suites* ☖ *In-room: a/c, refrigerator, Wi-Fi. In-hotel: restaurant, room service, bar, pool, gym, laundry facilities, laundry service, Wi-Fi hotspot, parking (paid), some pets allowed* ▭ *AE, D, DC, MC, V.*

SPORTS

Pro baseball's **Los Angeles Angels of Anaheim** play at **Angel Stadium Anaheim** (✉ *2000 State College Blvd., East Anaheim* ☎ *714/634–2000* ⊕ *www.angelsbaseball.com*). An "Outfield Extravaganza" celebrates great plays on the field, with fireworks and a geyser exploding over a model evoking the California coast. The National Hockey League's **Anaheim Ducks** play at **Honda Center** (✉ *Formerly Arrowhead Pond, 2695 E. Katella Ave., East Anaheim* ☎ *714/704–2400* ⊕ *www. mightyducks.com*).

KNOTT'S BERRY FARM

☾ *25 mi south of Los Angeles, via I-5, in Buena Park.*

★ The land where the boysenberry was invented (by crossing red raspberry, blackberry, and loganberry bushes) is now occupied by Knott's Berry Farm. In 1934, Cordelia Knott began serving chicken dinners on her wedding china to supplement her family's income. Or so the story goes. The dinners and her boysenberry pies proved more profitable than husband Walter's berry farm, so the two moved first into the restaurant business and then into the entertainment business. The park is now a 160-acre complex with 100-plus rides, dozens of restaurants and shops, and even a brick-by-brick replica of Philadelphia's Independence Hall. While it has some good attractions for small children, the park is best known for its roster of awesome thrill rides. And, yes, you can still get that boysenberry pie (and jam, juice—you name it). ✉ *8039 Beach Blvd., Buena Park* ⊹ *Between La Palma Ave. and Crescent St., 2 blocks south of Hwy. 91* ☎ *714/220–5200* ⊕ *www.knotts.com*

GETTING THERE

Knott's is an easy 10-minute drive from Disneyland or a 30-minute drive from downtown Los Angeles. Take I-5 to Beach Boulevard and head south 3 mi; follow the park entrance signs on the right.

TIMING

The park is open June–mid-Sept., daily 9 AM–midnight; mid-September–May the park usually opens at 10 and closes between 5 and 8 on weekdays, and between 10 and midnight weekends. Call ahead or check Web site to confirm hours. You can see the park in a day, but plan to start early and finish fairly late. Traffic can be heavy, so factor in time for delays.

■ **TIP→** If you think you'll only need a few hours at the main park, you can save money by coming after 4 PM, when admission fees drop to $25. This deal is offered any day the park is open after 6. A full-day pass for adults is $53; Southern California residents pay $43, and children 3–11 are $24. Tickets can be purchased online and printed out ahead of time (with a small discount).

PARK NEIGHBORHOODS

GHOST TOWN

Clusters of authentic old buildings relocated from their original mining-town sites mark this section of the park. You can stroll down the street, stop and chat with a blacksmith, pan for gold (for a fee), crack open a geode, check out the chalkboard of a circa-1875 schoolhouse, and ride an original Butterfield stagecoach. Looming over it all is **GhostRider,** Orange County's first wooden roller coaster. Traveling up to 56 MPH and reaching 118 feet at its highest point, the park's biggest attraction is riddled with sudden dips and curves, subjecting riders to forces up to three times that of gravity. The **Calico Mine** ride descends into a replica of a working gold mine. The **Timber Mountain Log Ride** is a worthwhile flume ride, especially if you're with kids who don't make the height requirements for the flumes at Disneyland. Also found here is the park's newest thrill ride, the Pony Express, a roller coaster that lets riders saddle up on packs of "horses" tethered to a platforms that take off on a series of hairpin turns and travel up to 38 MPH. Don't miss the **Western Trails Museum,** a dusty old gem full of Old West memorabilia, plus menus from the original chicken restaurant, and Mrs. Knott's antique button collection. **Calico Railroad** departs regularly from Ghost Town station for a round-trip tour of the park (bandit holdups notwithstanding).

CAMP SNOOPY

It can get gridlocked on weekends, but small fry love this miniature High Sierra wonderland where the *Peanuts* gang hangs out. They can push and pump their own mini-mining cars on **Huff and Puff,** zip around a pint-size racetrack on **Charlie Brown Speedway,** and hop aboard **Woodstock's Airmail,** a kids' version of the park's Supreme Scream ride. Most of the rides here are geared toward kids only, leaving parents to cheer them on from the sidelines. **Sierra Sidewinder,** a roller coaster near the entrance of Camp Snoopy, is aimed at older children with spinning saucer-type vehicles that go a maximum speed of 37 MPH.

BOARDWALK

Not-for-the-squeamish thrill rides and skill-based games dominate the scene at **Boardwalk.** Go head over heels on the *Boomerang* roller coaster, then do it again—backward. The **Perilous Plunge,** billed as the world's tallest, steepest, and—thanks to its big splash—wettest thrill ride, sends riders down an almost-vertical chute. The 1950s hot rod–theme **Xcelerator** launches you hydraulically into a super-steep U-turn, topping out at 205 feet. On the Western-theme **Silver Bullet,** riders are sent to a height of 146 feet and then back down 109 feet. Riders spiral, corkscrew, fly into a cobra roll, and experience overbanked curves. **Supreme Scream** propels you 254 feet in the air, then plunges

TIP SHEET: KNOTT'S BERRY FARM

Who will especially love this park?

Knott's Berry Farm specializes in spine-tingling roller coasters geared toward older kids, teens, and courageous adults. The park also contains Camp Snoopy, a wonderland for little ones populated by Peanuts characters, miniature mining cars, and a tamer roller coaster.

What's This Really Gonna Cost?

In addition to tickets, you'll need to pay $10 for parking. Meals are about $10–$14 per person. The Laser Tag attraction is an extra $10, and the Big Swing ride is an additional $5.

TOP 5 ATTRACTIONS:

Silver Bullet: Hold on while your legs dangle on this Western-themed roller coaster, which loops and corkscrews around steep curves, rises to 146 feet in the air, and plunges 109 feet.

Supreme Scream: This thrill ride lifts you up 254 feet...then drops you at 50 mph.

Boomerang: Don't eat right before riding this stomach-churning, whiplash-inducing roller coaster.

GhostRider: This classic wooden roller coaster speeds along at 56 mph and reaches a height of 118 feet, with lots of dips, twists, and turns along the way.

Xcelerator: This hydraulically launched roller coaster rockets to 82 mph...in just 2.3 seconds.

TIPS

Look for Web-only Deals: Log onto the park's home page for special discounts.

Arrive Late: After 4 PM, adult admission is only $25.

Cool Off: If it's a hot day, bring your bathing suit—Knott's Soak City water park ($29.99 adults; $19.99 kids and seniors) is just next door.

Avoid Peak Times: Be aware that the park—especially Camp Snoopy—is packed during summer and on holiday weekends. As with most theme parks, visiting off-season and/or during the week is the way to go.

Get your Chicken Dinner to Go: The famous chicken dinners (and boysenberry pie) served at Mrs. Knott's Chicken Dinner Restaurant—just outside the park entrance—are delicious, but the wait for a seat can be long. Order yours as take-out, and have a picnic.

you straight back down again in three terrifying seconds. Boardwalk is also home to a string of test-your-skill games that are fun to watch whether you're playing or not.

FIESTA VILLAGE

Over in **Fiesta Village** are two more musts for adrenaline junkies: **Montezooma's Revenge,** a roller coaster that goes from 0 to 55 MPH in less than five seconds, and **Jaguar!,** which simulates the motions of a cat stalking its prey, twisting, spiraling, and speeding up and slowing down as it takes you on its stomach-dropping course. There's also **Hat Dance,** a version of the spinning teacups but with sombreros, and a 100-year-old **Dentzel Carousel,** complete with an antique organ and menagerie of hand-carved animals.

Many of the buildings in the Ghost Town portion of Knott's Berry Farm are actually authentic structures that were relocated from Old West mining towns.

WILD WATER WILDERNESS

Just like its name implies, this section is home to **Big Foot Rapids**, a splash-fest of white-water river rafting over towering cliffs, cascading waterfalls, and wild rapids. Don't miss the visually stunning show at **Mystery Lodge**, which tells the story of Native Americans in the Pacific Northwest with lights, music, and beautiful images.

Knott's Soak City Water Park is directly across from the main park on 13 acres next to Independence Hall. It has a dozen major water rides; the latest is **Pacific Spin**, an oversize waterslide that drops riders 75 feet into a catch pool. There's also a children's pool, 750,000-gallon wave pool, and funhouse. Soak City is only open late May through late September.

WHERE TO EAT AND STAY

$$–$$$
AMERICAN

✕ **Mrs. Knott's Chicken Dinner Restaurant.** Cordelia Knott's fried chicken and boysenberry pies drew crowds so big that Knott's Berry Farm was built to keep the hungry customers occupied while they waited. The restaurant's current incarnation (outside the park's entrance) still serves crispy fried chicken, along with tangy coleslaw, mashed potatoes, and Mrs. Knott's signature chilled cherry-rhubarb compote. The wait, unfortunately, can be two-plus hours on weekends; another option is to order a bucket of the same tasty chicken from the adjacent takeout counter and have a picnic at the duck pond next to Independence Hall across the street. ⊠ *Knott's Berry Farm, 8039 Beach Blvd., Buena Park* ☎ *714/220–5080* ▤ *AE, D, DC, MC, V.*

$$$$ ✕ Pirate's Dinner Adventure. During this interactive pirate-theme dinner
AMERICAN   show, 150 actors/singers/acrobats (some quite talented) perform on a
☺   galleon while you eat a three-course meal. Food—shrimp, roast chicken,
salad, mixed veggies, and unlimited soda, beer, and wine—is mediocre
and seating is tight, but kids love making a lot of noise to cheer on their
favorite pirate, and the action scenes are breathtaking. ✉ 7600 Beach
Blvd., Buena Park ☎ 866/439–2469 ▭ AE, D, MC, V.

$$ ⌕ Knott's Berry Farm Resort Hotel. The most convenient place to stay if
☺   Knott's is your main destination, this hotel caters to kids. The second-
floor "camp rooms" are decorated in a Camp Snoopy motif and come
with telephone bedtime stories. Shuttle service to Disneyland is avail-
able. Ask about packages that include entry to Knott's Berry Farm. Pros:
easy access to Knott's Berry Farm, great kids' activities. Cons: lobby and
hallways can be noisy and chaotic, hotel occasionally hosts meetings
and conventions. ✉ 7675 Crescent Ave., Buena Park ☎ 714/995–1111
or 866/752–2444 ⊕ www.knottshotel.com ⇗ 320 rooms, 16 suites
⌂ In-room: a/c, safe, Wi-Fi. In-hotel: restaurant, room service, bar, ten-
nis court, pool, gym, laundry facilities, Wi-Fi hotspot, parking (paid)
▭ AE, D, DC, MC, V.

COASTAL ORANGE COUNTY

HUNTINGTON BEACH

*40 mi southeast of Los Angeles, I–5 south to I–605 south to I–405
south to Beach Blvd.*

Once a sleepy residential town with little more than a string of rugged
surf shops, Huntington Beach has transformed itself into a resort des-
tination. The town's appeal is its broad white-sand beaches with often-
towering waves, complemented by a lively pier, shops, and restaurants
on Main Street and the luxurious Hilton Waterfront Beach Resort and
the Hyatt Regency.

ESSENTIALS

Visitor Information Huntington Beach Conference and Visitors Bureau
(✉ 301 Main St., Suite 208, Huntington Beach ☎ 714/969–3492 ⊕ www.
surfcityusa.com).

Huntington Pier stretches 1,800 feet out to sea, well past the powerful
waves that made Huntington Beach reach for the title of America's
"Surf City." A farmers' market is held on Friday; an informal arts fair
sets up most weekends. At the end of the pier sits **Ruby's** (☎ 714/969–
7829 ⊕ www.rubys.com), part of a California chain of 1940s-style
burger joints.

The **Pierside Pavilion** (✉ PCH across from Huntington Pier) has shops,
restaurants, bars with live music, and a theater complex. The best surf-
gear source is **HSS Pierside** (☎ 714/841–4000), next to the pier, staffed
by true surf enthusiasts.

Just up Main Street from the pier, the **International Surfing Museum** pays
tribute to the sport's greats with the Surfing Hall of Fame, which has

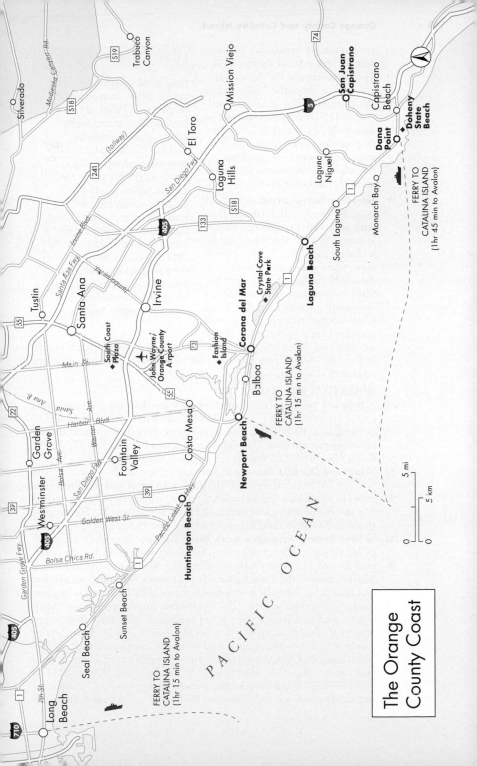

The Orange County Coast

Silverado

Modjeska Canyon Rd.

S19 Trabuco Canyon

S18

El Toro

(tollway)

241

San Diego Fwy.

405

133

S18

Tustin

55

Santa Ana

Santa Ana Fwy.

Irvine Blvd.

MacArthur Blvd.

Irvine

South Coast Plaza

John Wayne/ Orange County Airport

73

Fashion Island

Corona del Mar

Crystal Cove State Park

1

Laguna Beach

Mission Viejo

Laguna Hills

Laguna Niguel

South Laguna

Monarch Bay

74

San Juan Capistrano

5

Capistrano Beach

Doheny State Beach

Dana Point

FERRY TO CATALINA ISLAND (1hr 45 min to Avalon)

Garden Grove

22

Main St.

Santa Ana R.

Harbor Blvd.

Warner Ave.

5E

Balboa

FERRY TO CATALINA ISLAND (1 hr 15 min to Avalon)

Newport Beach

Costa Mesa

Fountain Valley

Westminster

405

Golden West St.

Bolsa Ave.

San Diego Fwy.

39

39

Huntington Beach

Pacific Coast Hwy.

Bolsa Chica Rd.

PACIFIC OCEAN

5 mi

5 km

Garden Grove Fwy.

7th St.

Long Beach

710

1

405

Seal Beach

Sunset Beach

FERRY TO CATALINA ISLAND (1 hr 15 min to Avalon)

an impressive collection of surf-boards and related memorabilia. They've even got the Bolex camera used to shoot the 1966 surfing documentary *The Endless Summer.* ✉ *411 Olive Ave., Huntington Beach* ☎ *714/960–3483* ⊕ *www. surfingmuseum.org* ⧉ *Free,* $1 *suggested donation for students,* $2 *for adults* ⊙ *Year-round weekdays noon–5, weekends 11–6.*

★ **Bolsa Chica Ecological Reserve** beckons wildlife lovers and bird-watchers with an 1,180-acre salt marsh that is home to 200 species of birds, including great blue herons, snowy and great egrets, and brown pelicans. Throughout the reserve are trails for bird-watching, including a comfortable 1½-mi loop. The Bolsa Chica Conservancy operates a small museum here with wetlands exhib-

> **SURF'S UP!**
>
> Many of the world's most famous surfers are represented on the **Surfing Walk of Fame** (✉ *Along Main St. and Pacific Coast Highway, Huntington Beach* ☎ *714/960–3483* ⊕ *www. surfingmuseum.org*), including Robert August, the star of *The Endless Summer;* Corky Carroll, a pioneer surfing promoter; and Mark Richard, winner of the most surfing championships. Supersurfers have been selected since 1994 by a committee representing the surfing industry worldwide. Inductions take place during the annual U.S. Open Surfing event held in Huntington Beach in July.

its; they also offers free guided tours the first Saturday of each month at 9 AM. ✉ *3842 Warner Ave.* ☎ *714/846–1114* ⊕ *www.bolsachica.org* ⧉ *Free* ⊙ *Daily dawn–dusk.*

WHERE TO EAT AND STAY

$$$ ✗ **Duke's.** A perfect people-watching spot overlooking the beach, this
SEAFOOD seafood restaurant has Hawaiian fish including ono and opah, Huli Huli chicken, and salads with a Hawaiian accent. Try crispy coconut shrimp or seven-spice ahi tuna. Duke's mai tai is not to be missed. ✉ *317 Pacific Coast Hwy.* ☎ *714/374–6446* ⊙ *No lunch Sat.* ▭ *AE, D, MC, V.*

$$ ✗ **Lou's Red Oak BBQ.** You won't find any frills at Lou's—just barbecue
ASIAN pork, grilled linguica, rotisserie chicken, and a lot of beef. Try the tri-tip,
★ either as an entrée or on a sandwich served "original style" on a toasted bun smothered with garlic butter. ✉ *21501 Brookhurst St., Huntington Beach* ☎ *714/965–5200* ⊕ *www.lousbbq.com* ▭ *AE, D, DC, MC, V.*

$$$ ☶ **Hyatt Regency Huntington Beach Resort and Spa.** Sprawling along the
☾ PCH, almost every room in this Andalusia-style hotel has an ocean
★ view as well as a private balcony or terrace. With a nod to California's Mission period, the hotel surrounds courtyards with outdoor firepots and fountains. Artwork with a beach theme is by local artists in guest rooms and public spaces. This Hyatt aims to create a village atmosphere, and to a large extent it has succeeded with the village shopping area. Beach access is via a bridge over the PCH. **Pros:** lots of family activities—including a teen program, responsive staff, sunset beach bonfires. **Cons:** partial ocean-view rooms are partial view at best, pesky resort and daily valet fees. ✉ *21500 PCH* ☎ *714/698–1234 or 800/554–9288* ⊕ *www.huntingtonbeach.hyatt.com* ⤳ *517 rooms, 57 suites* ⧉ *In-room: a/c, safe, Internet, Wi-Fi. In-hotel: 5 restaurants, gym,*

spa, water sports, bicycles, children's programs (ages 3–12), laundry service, Wi-Fi hotspot, parking (paid) ☰ *AE, D, MC, V.*

SPORTS AND THE OUTDOORS

BEACHES **Huntington City Beach** (☎ 714/536–5281) stretches for 3 mi north and south of the pier from Bolsa Chica State Beach to Huntington State Beach on the south. The beach is most crowded around the pier; amateur and professional surfers brave the waves daily on its north side. As you continue south, **Huntington State Beach** (☎ 714/536–1454) parallels Pacific Coast Highway. On the state and city beaches there are changing rooms, concessions, lifeguards, Wi-Fi services for park visitors with wireless-enabled laptops and ample parking; the state beach also has barbecue pits. At the northern section of the city, **Bolsa Chica State Beach** (☎ 714/846–3460) has barbecue pits and RV campsites and is usually less crowded than its southern neighbors.

SURFING **Corky Carroll's Surf School** (☎ 714/969–3959 ⊕ *www.surfschool.net*) organizes lessons, weeklong workshops, and surfing trips. You can rent surf- or boogie boards at **Dwight's** (☎ 714/536–8083), one block south of the pier.

NEWPORT BEACH

6 mi south of Huntington Beach, PCH.

Newport Beach has two distinct personalities. There's the island-dotted yacht harbor, where the wealthy play. (Newport is said to have the highest per-capita number of Mercedes-Benzes in the world.) And then there's inland Newport Beach, just southwest of John Wayne Airport, a business and commercial hub that's lined with high-rise office buildings, shopping centers, and hotels.

ESSENTIALS

Visitor Information Newport Beach Conference and Visitors Bureau (✉ *110 Newport Center Dr., Suite 120, Newport Beach* ☎ *800/942–6278* ⊕ *www. visitnewportbeach.com*).

★ **Newport Harbor,** which shelters nearly 10,000 small boats, may seduce even those who don't own a yacht. Spend an afternoon exploring the charming avenues and surrounding alleys.

Within Newport Harbor are eight small islands, including Balboa and Lido. The houses lining the shore may seem modest, but this is some of the most expensive real estate in the world. Marine Avenue, Balboa Island's main street, has shops, restaurants, and places to try the Balboa Bar: a slab of vanilla ice cream that has been dipped first in chocolate and then in a topping of your choice such as hard candy, Oreo crumbs, or peanut butter bark. Sugar & Spice, one of several ice-cream parlors that serve the concoction, claims to have invented it in 1945. As you stroll the perimeters of the island, you can see houses that range in style from Moderne, designed by John Lautner, to the more traditional Cape Cod. Several grassy areas on primarily residential Lido Isle have views of Newport Harbor. In evidence of the upper-crust Orange County mind-set, each is marked PRIVATE COMMUNITY PARK.

Newport Pier, which juts out into the ocean near 20th Street, is the heart of Newport's beach community and a popular fishing spot. Street parking is difficult at the pier, so grab the first space you find and be prepared to walk. A stroll along West Ocean Front reveals much of the town's character. On weekday mornings, head for the beach near the pier, where you're likely to

O SOLE MIO IN THE O.C.

Try a one-hour gondola cruise with the **Gondola Company of Newport** (☎ 949/675–1212, ⊕ www.gondolas.com). It costs $85 for two and is frequently voted as the best place to take a date in Orange County.

encounter dory fishermen hawking their predawn catches, as they've done for generations. On weekends the walk is alive with kids of all ages on in-line skates, skateboards, and bikes dodging pedestrians and whizzing past fast-food joints, shops, and bars.

Newport's best beaches are on **Balboa Peninsula,** where many jetties pave the way to ideal swimming areas. The most intense bodysurfing place in Orange County and arguably on the West Coast, known as the **Wedge,** is at the south end of the peninsula. Created by accident in the 1930s when the Federal Works Progress Administration built a jetty to protect Newport Harbor, the break is pure euphoria for highly skilled bodysurfers. ■**TIP→** Since the waves generally break very close to shore and rip currents are strong, lifeguards strongly discourage visitors from attempting it—but it sure is fun to watch an experienced local ride it.

The **Balboa Pavilion,** on the bay side of the peninsula, was built in 1905 as a bath- and boathouse. Today it houses a restaurant and shops and serves as a departure point for harbor and whale-watching cruises. Look for it on Main Street, off Balboa Boulevard. Adjacent to the pavilion is the three-car ferry that connects the peninsula to Balboa Island. In the blocks around the pavilion you'll find restaurants, beachside shops, and the small **Fun Zone**—a local kiddie hangout with a Ferris wheel and a nautical museum. On the other side of the narrow peninsula is **Balboa Pier.** On its end is the original branch of Ruby's, a 1940s-esque burger-and-shake joint.

Shake the sand out of your shoes to head inland to the ritzy **Fashion Island** outdoor mall, a cluster of arcades and courtyards, complete with koi pond, inside in a sea of parking spaces. Although it doesn't have quite the international-designer clout of South Coast Plaza, it has the luxe department store Neiman Marcus and expensive spots like L'Occitane, Kate Spade, Ligne Roset, and Design Within Reach. Chains, restaurants, and the requisite movie theater fill out the rest. ⊠ *410 Newport Center Dr., between Jamboree and MacArthur Blvds., off PCH, Newport Beach* ☎ *949/721–2000* ⊕ *www.shopfashionisland.com.*

★ The **Orange County Museum of Art** gathers a collection of modernist paintings and sculpture by California artists and cutting-edge, international contemporary works. Works by such key California artists as Richard Diebenkorn, Ed Ruscha, Robert Irwin, and Chris Burden are included in the collection. The museum also displays some of its digital art, Internet-based art, and sound works in the Orange Lounge, a satellite

CLOSE UP

Shop 'til You Drop

South Coast Plaza (⊠ *3333 S. Bristol St., Costa Mesa* ☎ *714/435–2000 or 800/782–8888* ⊕ *www.southcoastplaza.com* ⊗ *Weekdays 10–9, Sat. 10–8, Sun. 11–6:30*). Called Beverly Hills South by the platinum card set, this sprawling shopping complex gets ritzier by the year as international designer boutiques jostle for space. The original section has the densest concentration of shops: Gucci, Armani, Burberry, La Perla, Hermès, Versace, Chloé, and Prada. All the familiar mall names are here, too, from Victoria's Secret to Banana Republic. Major department stores, including Saks and Nordstrom, flank the exterior. A pedestrian bridge crosses Bear Street to the second wing, a smaller offshoot with a huge Crate & Barrel. The complex and adjacent areas hold a collection of trendy restaurants and the **Orange County Performing Arts Center** (⊠ *600 Town Center Dr., east of Bristol St.* ☎ *714/556–2787*) with three venues: the Henry Segerstrom Concert hall, the intimate Founders Hall for chamber music, and the South Coast Repertory Theater.

gallery at South Coast Plaza; free of charge, it's open the same hours as the mall. ⊠ *850 San Clemente Dr., Newport Beach* ☎ *949/759–1122* ⊕ *www.ocma.net* ⊠ *$12* ⊗ *Wed.–Sun. 11–5, Thurs. 11–8.*

The **Newport Harbor Nautical Museum** has exhibits on the history of the harbor as well as of the Pacific as a whole. For lovers of ship models, there are more than $3 million worth, some dating to 1798; one is made entirely of gold and silver. Another fun display is a virtual deep-sea fishing machine. New exhibits include a touch tank holding local sea creatures and a virtual sailing simulator. ⊠ *600 E. Bay Ave., Newport Beach* ☎ *949/675–8915* ⊕ *www.nhnm.org* ⊠ *Free, $5 suggested donation* ⊗ *Wed., Thurs., and Sun. 11–5, Fri. and Sat. 11–6. Closed Mon. and Tues.*

WHERE TO EAT AND STAY

$$$ ✕ **3-Thirty-3.** If there's a nightlife "scene" to be had in Newport Beach,
FRENCH this is it. Swank and stylish, the "small bites, big tastes" menu attracts a convivial crowd—both young and old—for midday, sunset, and late-night dining. Try the lollipop lamb chops as a starter. Hungrier guests may enjoy the Kobe flatiron steak or the potato-crusted halibut. ⊠ *333 Bayside Dr.* ☎ *949/673–8464* ⊕ *www.3thirty3nb.com* ⊟ *AE, D, DC, MC, V.*

$$$ ✕ **The Cannery.** This 1920s cannery building still teems with fish, but
SEAFOOD now they go into dishes on the eclectic Pacific Rim menu rather than
★ being packed into crates. Settle in at the sushi bar, dining room, or patio before choosing between sashimi, oven-roasted Chilean sea bass prepared with a tropical twist. The menu also lists a selection of steaks and ribs. Fodors readers recommend the crème brûlée for dessert. ⊠ *3010 Lafayette Rd., Newport Beach* ☎ *949/566–0060* ⊕ *www.cannerynewport.com* ⊟ *AE, D, MC, V.*

$$$$ ⌂ **Balboa Bay Club and Resort.** For years this ultra-luxe yacht club served as a playground for stars such as Humphrey Bogart, Lauren Bacall,

and the Reagans. They'd cruise into the marina, have lunch at the club's dockside restaurant, and admire each other's boats. The club added a hotel—open to the public—in 2003 for visitors who want to enjoy the great views, pampered service, and celebrity vibe. Rooms, which have either bay or courtyard views, have a beachy decor of rattan furniture, plantation shutters, and tropical-pattern drapes. Duke's Place, a bar named for John Wayne, a former member and club governor, has photos of the star in his mariner-theme films. **Pros:** brunch on the deck amid a sea of yachts; best views in the area; impeccable service. **Cons:** hosts conventions; expensive parking. ✉ *1221 W. Coast Hwy.* ☎ *949/645–5000 or 888/445–7153* ⊕ *www.balboabayclub.com* ↴ *150 rooms, 10 suites* ⊛ *In-room: a/c, safe, refrigerator, DVD, Internet, Wi-Fi. In-hotel: 2 restaurants, room service, bar, gym, spa, water sports, bicycles, laundry service, Wi-Fi hotspot, parking (paid), some pets allowed* ▭ *AE, MC, V.*

$$$ ⌕ **The Island Hotel.** A suitably stylish hotel in a very chic neighborhood
★ (it's across the street from the Fashion Island shopping center), the 20-story tower caters to luxury seekers by offering weekend golf packages in conjunction with the nearby Pelican Hill golf course. Guest rooms have outstanding views, private bars, and original art. The spa does its bit for luxury with a "pearl powder facial." For gustatory richness, try the Pavilion restaurant's contemporary menu, with choices such as potato crusted Chilean sea bass. **Pros:** proximity to Fashion Island; fresh flowers in the bathrooms; first-class spa. **Cons:** steep valet parking prices; some rooms have views of the mall; pricey. ✉ *690 Newport Center Dr., Newport Beach* ☎ *949/759–0808 or 866/554–4620* ⊕ *www.islandhotel.com* ↴ *295 rooms, 83 suites* ⊛ *In-room: a/c, safe, refrigerator, DVD, Internet, Wi-Fi. In-hotel: 2 restaurants, room service, bar, golf course, tennis courts, pool, gym, spa, laundry facilities, laundry service, Internet terminal, Wi-Fi hotspot, some pets allowed* ▭ *AE, D, DC, MC, V.*

SPORTS AND THE OUTDOORS

BOAT RENTALS You can tour Lido and Balboa isles by renting kayaks ($15 an hour), sailboats ($45 an hour), small motorboats ($65 an hour), and electric boats ($75–$90 an hour) at **Balboa Boat Rentals** (✉ *510 E. Edgewater Ave., Newport Beach* ☎ *949/673–7200* ⊕ *www.boats4rent.com*). You must have a driver's license and a credit card, and some knowledge of boating is helpful; rented boats must stay in the bay.

BOAT TOURS **Catalina Passenger Service** (✉ *400 Main St., Newport Beach* ☎ *949/673–5245* ⊕ *www.catalinainfo.com*), at the Balboa Pavilion, operates 90-minute daily round-trip passage to Catalina Island for $68. Call first; winter service is often available only on weekends. **Hornblower Cruises & Events** (✉ *2431 West Coast Hwy., Newport Beach* ☎ *949/646–0155 or 949/631–2469* ⊕ *www.hornblower.com*) books three-hour weekend dinner cruises with dancing for $78; the two-hour Sunday brunch cruise is $55.

GOLF **Newport Beach Golf Course** (✉ *3100 Irvine Ave., Newport Beach* ☎ *949/852–8681* ⊕ *www.npbgolf.com*), a par-59 executive course, is lighted for night play. Rates start at $17. Reservations are accepted up to one week in advance, but walk-ins are accommodated when possible.

SPORTFISHING In addition to a complete tackle shop, **Davey's Locker** (✉ *Balboa Pavilion, 400 Main St., Newport Beach* ☎ *949/673–1434* ⊕ *www.daveyslocker. com*) operates sportfishing trips starting at $40, as well as private charters and, in winter, whale-watching trips for $30.

CORONA DEL MAR

3

2 mi south of Newport Beach, via Hwy. 1.

A small jewel on the Pacific Coast, Corona del Mar (known by locals as "CDM") has exceptional beaches that some say resemble their majestic northern California counterparts.

Corona del Mar State Beach (☎ *949/644–3151* ⊕ *www.parks.ca.gov* ✉ *$8–$15* ⊗ *Daily 6* AM*–10* PM) is actually made up of two beaches, Little Corona and Big Corona, separated by a cliff. Facilities include fire pits, volleyball courts, food stands, restrooms, and parking. ■ TIP➔ Two colorful reefs (and the fact that it's off-limits to boats) make Corona del Mar great for snorkelers and for beachcombers who prefer privacy.

Fodor'sChoice Midway between Corona del Mar and Laguna, stretching along both
★ sides of Pacific Coast Highway, **Crystal Cove State Park** is a favorite of local beachgoers and wilderness trekkers. It encompasses a 3½-mi stretch of unspoiled beach and has some of the best tide-pooling in southern California. Here you can see starfish, crabs, and other sea life on the rocks. The park's 2,400 acres of backcountry are ideal for hiking, horseback riding, and mountain biking, but stay on the trails to preserve the beauty. Environmental camping is allowed in one of the three campgrounds. Bring water, food, and other supplies; there's a pit toilet but no shower. Open fires and pets are forbidden. **Crystal Cove Historic District** holds a collection of 13 handmade historic rental cottages decorated and furnished to reflect the 1935–55 beach culture that flourished here. On the sand above the high tide line and on a bluff above the beach, the cottages offer a funky look at beach life 50 years ago. Cottages, at $165 per night for four people, can be reserved up to six months in advance from **Reserve America** (☎ *800/444–7275* ⊕ *www. reserveamerica.com*).Beach culture also flourishes in the district's two restaurants, the **Beachcomber at Crystal Cove Café** (☎ *949/376–6900* ⊕ *www.thebeachcombercafe.com*)and the Shake Shack. **The Store** (☎ *949/376–8762*), holding works by local plein-air artists and fine art photography, completes the picture. ☎ *949/494–3539* ⊕ *www. crystalcovestatepark.com* ✉ *$10 per car* ⊗ *Daily 6–dusk.*

LAGUNA BEACH

Fodor'sChoice *10 mi south of Newport Beach on Hwy. 1; 60 mi south of Los Angeles,*
★ *I–5 south to Hwy. 133, which turns into Laguna Canyon Rd.*

Even the approach tells you that Laguna Beach is exceptional. Driving into town along Laguna Canyon Road from the I–405 freeway gives you the chance to cruise through a gorgeous coastal canyon, large stretches of which remain undeveloped (⇨ *See the Laguna Coast*

Wilderness Park in Sports and the Outdoors, below). After winding through the canyon, you'll arrive at a glistening wedge of ocean, at the intersection with PCH.

There's a definite creative slant to this tight-knit community. The California plein-air art movement coalesced here in the early 1900s; by 1932 an annual arts festival was established. Art galleries now dot the village streets, and there's usually someone daubing up in Heisler Park, overlooking the beach. The town's main street, Pacific Coast Highway, is referred to as either South Coast or North Coast Highway, depending on the address. From this waterfront, the streets slope up steeply to the residential areas. All along the highway and side streets, you'll find dozens of fine art and crafts galleries, clothing boutiques, and jewelry shops.

ESSENTIALS

Visitor Information Laguna Beach Visitors Bureau (✉ *252 Broadway, Laguna Beach* ☎ *949/497-9229 or 800/877-1115* ⊕ *www.lagunabeachinfo.org*).

Laguna's central beach gives you a perfect slice of local life. A stocky 1920s lifeguard tower marks **Main Beach Park**, at the end of Broadway at South Coast Highway. A wooden boardwalk separates the sand from a strip of lawn. Walk along this, or hang out on one of its benches, to watch people bodysurfing, playing sand volleyball, or scrambling around one of two half-basketball courts. The beach also has children's play equipment, picnic areas, restrooms, and showers. Across the street is a lovely old movie theater.

The **Laguna Art Museum** displays American art, with an emphasis on California artists and works. Special exhibits change quarterly. ■TIP➔ Galleries throughout the area stay open late in coordination with the museum on the first Thursday of each month (visit ⊕ www.firstthursdaysartwalk.com for more information). A free shuttle service runs from the museum to galleries and studios. ✉ *307 Cliff Dr., Laguna Beach* ☎ *949/494-8971* ⊕ *www.lagunaartmuseum.org* ✑ *$12* ⊙ *Daily 11–5.*

WHERE TO EAT AND STAY

$$$$ FRENCH ★ ✕ **Five Feet.** Others have attempted to mimic this restaurant's innovative blend of Chinese and French cooking styles, but Five Feet remains the leader of the pack. Among the standout dishes is the house catfish. The setting is pure Laguna: exposed ceiling, open kitchen, high noise level, and brick walls hung with works by local artists. ✉ *328 Glenneyre St., Laguna Beach* ☎ *949/497-4955* ▭ *AE, D, MC, V* ⊙ *No lunch.*

$$$$ AMERICAN ★ ✕ **Studio.** In a nod to Laguna's art history, Studio has food that entices the eye as well as the palate. You can't beat the location, on a 50-foot bluff overlooking the Pacific Ocean—every table has an ocean view. The menu changes daily to reflect the finest seafood and the freshest local ingredients on hand. You might begin with salmon tartare with caviar, avocado, and tarragon cream, or risotto with lobster and truffles before moving on to rack of lamb or pan-seared John Dory with a curry sauce. The wine list here is bursting, with nearly 2,000 labels. ✉ *Montage Hotel, 30801 S. Coast Hwy.* ☎ *949/715-6420* ⚑ *Reservations essential* ▭ *AE, D, DC, MC, V* ⊙ *Closed Mon. No lunch.*

Laguna Beach's 7 miles of coastline contain some of the nicest stretches of sand in Southern California.

$$$$
Fodor's Choice
★

Montage Resort & Spa. Laguna's connection to the Californian plein-air artists is mined for inspiration at this head-turning, fancy hotel. The Montage uses the local Craftsman style as a touchstone. Shingled buildings ease down a bluff to the cove beaches; inside, works by contemporary and early-20th-century California artists snare your attention. Guest rooms balance ease and refinement; all have ocean views and amenities such as CD/DVD players and extra-deep tubs. Of the restaurants, Studio is the fanciest, with more sweeping Pacific views and a refined contemporary menu. At the oceanfront spa and fitness center, you can indulge in a sea-salt scrub, take a yoga class, or hit the lap pool. **Pros:** top-notch service; central beach location; free fitness classes. **Cons:** priccy; cuisine can be inconsistent. ⊠ *30801 S. Coast Hwy., Laguna Beach* ☎ *949/715–6000 or 888/715–6700* ⊕ *www.montagelagunabeach.com* ⤳ *190 rooms, 60 suites* △ *In-room: a/c, safe, DVD, Internet, Wi-Fi. In-hotel: 3 restaurants, room service, bars, pools, gym, spa, beachfront, children's programs (ages 5–12), laundry service, Internet terminal, Wi-Fi hotspot, some pets allowed, parking (paid)* ⊟ *AE, MC, V.*

$$$$
★

Surf & Sand Resort. One mile south of downtown, this Laguna Beach property has been updated, made over, and is now even more fantastic than longtime locals remember. On an exquisite stretch of beach with thundering waves and gorgeous rocks, this is a getaway for those who want a boutique hotel experience without all the by-the-books formalities. Instead, expect clean white decor in the rooms, private balconies, slumber-worthy beds within earshot of the ocean, and a small, yet full-service spa—all within walking distance of downtown Laguna. The cuisine at Splashes is top-notch, focusing on seasonal California cuisine. **Pros:** easy access to beach; intimate property; new gym facilities. **Cons:** expensive valet parking; the surf is quite loud. ⊠ *1555 S. Coast Hwy., Laguna Beach* ☎ *949/497–4477 or 888/869–7569* ⊕ *www.surfandsandresort.com* ⇨ *155 rooms, 13 suites* ᗖ *In-room: a/c (some), safe, refrigerator (some), DVD, Internet. In-hotel: restaurant, room service, bar, pool, gym, spa, beachfront, water sports, children's programs (ages 5–12), laundry service, Internet terminal, Wi-Fi hotspot, some pets allowed, parking (paid)* ≡ *AE, D, MC, V.*

NIGHTLIFE AND THE ARTS

The **Laguna Playhouse** (⊠ *606 Laguna Canyon Rd., Laguna Beach* ☎ *949/497–2787* ⊕ *www.lagunaplayhouse.com*), dating to the 1920s, mounts a variety of productions, from classics to youth-oriented plays.

SPORTS AND THE OUTDOORS

BEACHES   There are a handful of lovely beaches around town besides the Main Beach.

1,000 Steps Beach, off South Coast Highway at 9th Street, is a hard-to-find locals' spot with great waves. There aren't really 1,000 steps down (it just seems that way). **Woods Cove,** off South Coast Highway at Diamond Street, is especially quiet during the week. Big rock formations hide lurking crabs. Climbing the steps to leave, you can see a Tudor-style mansion that was once the home of Bette Davis.

BICYCLES   Mountain bikes and helmets can be rented at **Rainbow Bicycle Co.** (⊠ *485 N. Coast Hwy., Laguna Beach* ☎ *949/494–5806* ⊕ *www.teamrain.com*).

HIKING   The **Laguna Coast Wilderness Park** (☎ *949/923–2235* ⊕ *www.lagunacanyon.org*) is spread over 19 acres of fragile coastal territory, including the canyon. The trails are great for hiking and mountain biking and are open daily, weather permitting. Docent-led hikes are given regularly; call for information.

WATER SPORTS   Because its entire beach area is a marine preserve, Laguna Beach is ideal for snorkelers. Scuba divers should head to the Marine Life Refuge area, which runs from Seal Rock to Diver's Cove. Rent bodyboards at **Hobie Sports** (⊠ *294 Forest Ave., Laguna Beach* ☎ *949/497–3304* ⊕ *www.hobie.com*).

DANA POINT

10 mi south of Laguna Beach, via PCH.

Dana Point's claim to fame is its small-boat marina tucked into a dramatic natural harbor and surrounded by high bluffs.

LIFE IMITATING ART

An outdoor amphitheater near the mouth of the canyon hosts the annual **Pageant of the Masters** (☎ 949/494–1145 or 800/487–3378 ⊕ www.foapom.com), Laguna's most impressive event. Local participants arrange tableaux vivants, in which live models and carefully orchestrated backgrounds merge in striking mimicry of classical and contemporary paintings. The pageant is part of the **Festival of Arts,** held in July and August; tickets are much in demand, so plan ahead.

Dana Point Harbor (☏ 949/923–2255 ⊕ *www.danapointharbor.com*) was first described more than 100 years ago by its namesake, Richard Henry Dana, in his book *Two Years Before the Mast*. At the marina are docks for small boats, marine-oriented shops, restaurants, and boat and bike rentals. In early March a **whale festival** (☏ 949/472–7888 *or* 888/440–4309 ⊕ *www.festivalofwhales.org*) celebrates the passing gray whale migration with concerts, 40-foot-long balloon whales on parade, films, sports competitions, and a weekend street fair.

At the south end of Dana Point, **Doheny State Beach** (☏ 949/496–6171, 714/433–6400 *water quality information* ⊕ *www.dohenystatebeach.org*) is one of Southern California's top surfing destinations, but there's a lot more to do within this 61-acre area. Divers and anglers hang out at the beach's western end, and during low tide, the tide pools beckon both young and old. You'll also find five indoor tanks and an interpretive center devoted to the wildlife of the Doheny Marine Refuge. There are food stands and shops, picnic facilities, volleyball courts, and a pier for fishing. The beachfront campground here is one of the most popular in the state with 120 no-hookup sites that rent for $30–$35 per night; make essential reservations with Reserve America (☏ 800/444–7275). ■TIP→ Be aware that the waters here periodically do not meet health standards established by California (warning signs are posted if that's the case).

WHERE TO EAT AND STAY

$$
ITALIAN
✗ **Luciana's Ristorante.** This intimate family-owned eatery serves simply prepared, tasty Italian food. Try one of the homemade soups or gnocchi classico—Grandma's homemade potato dumplings with marinara sauce. If you don't have a reservation, be prepared to wait at the bar with a glass of one of the many reasonably priced Italian wines, chatting with the predominantly local clientele. ⊠ *24312 Del Prado Ave., Dana Point* ☏ 949/661–6500 ☰ *AE, MC, V* ☉ *No lunch.*

$$$
AMERICAN
✗ **Wind & Sea.** Set right on the dock and surrounded by water, this is a great place for lunch—and looking out at a sea of boats and on the Pacific beyond might put you in the mood for a retro cocktail like a mai tai. Of the entrées, try the macadamia-crusted mahimahi. On warm days, patio tables beckon you outside. ⊠ *34699 Golden Lantern St., Dana Point* ☏ 949/496–6500 ☰ *AE, MC, V.*

$$$$
Fodor'sChoice
★
▥ **Ritz-Carlton, Laguna Niguel.** Take Ritz-Carlton's top-tier level of service coupled with an unparalleled view of the Pacific and you're in the lap of complete luxury at this opulent resort. Rooms are well-appointed and spacious; tricked out with oversize plasma TVs, private balconies and posh marble bathrooms. Splurge for the Club Level where the list of included extra amenities is long. Service is impeccable for all guests, as every need is anticipated. Dine at Restaurant 162 , where the focus is on California cuisine highlighting fresh fish and seafood, or bone up on your wine knowledge at ENO, the property's wine, cheese, and chocolate tasting room. Beyond the panoramic views of the Pacific and opulent gardens, guests stroll down perfectly manicured trails to pristine white sand. **Pros:** beautiful grounds/views; luxurious bedding; seamless service. **Cons:** some rooms are small; resort and parking fees. ⊠ *1 Ritz-Carlton Dr., Dana Point* ☏ 949/240–2000 *or* 800/240–2000 ⊕ *www.*

ritzcarlton.com ↗ *363 rooms, 30 suites* ↻ *In-room: a/c, safe, refrigerator (some), DVD, Internet, Wi-Fi. In-hotel: 3 restaurants, room service, bar, tennis courts, pools, gym, spa, beachfront, water sports, children's programs (ages 5–12), laundry service, Internet terminal, Wi-Fi hotspot, parking (paid)* ☱ *AE, D, DC, MC, V.*

SPORTS AND THE OUTDOORS

Dana Wharf Sportfishing & Whale Watching (✉ *34675 Golden Lantern St., Dana Point* ☎ *949/496–5794* ⊕ *www.danawharfsportfishing.com*) runs charters and whale-watching excursions from early December to late April. Tickets cost $29; reservations are required.

On **Capt. Dave's Dolphin Safari** (✉ *24440 Dana Point Harbor Dr., Dana Point* ☎ *949/488–2828* ⊕ *www.dolphinsafari.com*), you have a good chance of getting an underwater view of resident dolphins and migrating whales if you take one of these tours on a 35-foot catamaran (portions of which have a clear glass floor). Dave, a marine naturalist–filmmaker, and his wife run the safaris year-round. The endangered blue whale is sometimes seen in summer. Reservations are required for the safaris, which last 2½ hours and cost $55.

SAN JUAN CAPISTRANO

5 mi north of Dana Point, via Hwy. 7; 60 mi north of San Diego, via I–5.

San Juan Capistrano is best known for its historic mission, where the swallows traditionally return each year, migrating from their winter haven in Argentina, but these days they are more likely to choose other local sites for nesting. St. Joseph's Day, March 19, launches a week of fowl festivities. After summering in the arches of the old stone church, the swallows head south on St. John's Day, October 23. Along Camino Capistrano are also antiques stores ranging from pricey to cheap.

If you arrive by train, you'll be dropped off across from the mission at the San Juan Capistrano depot. With its appealing brick café and preserved Santa Fe cars, the depot retains much of the magic of early American railroads. If driving, park near Ortega and Camino Capistrano, the city's main streets.

ESSENTIALS

Visitor Information San Juan Capistrano Chamber of Commerce and Visitors Center (✉ *31421 La Matanza St., San Juan Capistrano* ☎ *949/493–4700* ⊕ *www.sanjuanchamber.com*).

Fodor'sChoice **Mission San Juan Capistrano,** founded in 1776 by Father Junípero Serra,
★ was one of two Roman Catholic outposts between Los Angeles and San Diego. The Great Stone Church, begun in 1797, is the largest structure created by the Spanish in California. Many of the mission's adobe buildings have been preserved to illustrate mission life, with exhibits of an olive millstone, tallow ovens, tanning vats, metalworking furnaces, and the padres' living quarters. The gardens, with their fountains, are a lovely spot in which to wander. The bougainvillea-covered Serra Chapel is believed to be the oldest church still standing in California and is the only building remaining in which Fr. Serra actually led Mass. Mass

takes place daily at 7 AM in the chapel. You can learn all about the mission and explore the gardens on a self-guided audio tour. ✉ *Camino Capistrano and Ortega Hwy., San Juan Capistrano* ☎ *949/234–1300* ⊕ *www.missionsjc.com* ✆ *$9* ☯ *Daily 8:30–5.*

WHERE TO EAT

$$ ✕ **The Ramos House Cafe.** It may be worth hopping the Amtrak for San Juan Capistrano just for the chance to have breakfast or lunch at what many call the restaurant with the best food in Orange County. Here's your chance to visit one of Los Rios Historic District's simple, board and batten homes dating back to 1881. This café sits practically on the railroad tracks across from the depot—nab a table on the patio and dig into a hearty breakfast, such as the mountainous wild-mushroom scramble or the mac 'n' cheese with smoked chicken. The popular weekend prix-fixe brunch has a large selection of items, and everything on the menu illustrates chef-owner John Q. Humphreys' creative hand. ✉ *31752 Los Rios St., San Juan Capistrano* ☎ *949/443–1342* ☷ *AE, D, MC, V* ☯ *Closed Mon. No dinner.*

CATALINA ISLAND

Just 22 mi out from the L.A. coastline, across from Newport Beach and Long Beach, Catalina has unspoiled mountains, canyons, coves, and beaches; best of all, it gives you a glimpse of what undeveloped Southern California once looked like.

Summer, weekends, and holidays, Catalina crawls with thousands of L.A. area boaters, who tie their vessels at protected moorings in Avalon and other coves. Although Catalina is not known for its beaches, sunbathing and water sports are big draws; divers and snorkelers come for the exceptionally clear water surrounding the island. The main town, Avalon, is a charming, old-fashioned beach community, where yachts bob in the crescent-shaped bay.

Although Catalina can be seen in a day, several inviting hotels make it worth extending your stay for one or more nights. A short itinerary might include breakfast along the boardwalk, a tour of the interior, a snorkeling excursion at Casino Point, and dinner in Avalon.

GETTING HERE AND AROUND

Island Express helicopters depart hourly to Catalina Island from San Pedro and Long Beach (8 AM–dusk). The trip takes about 15 minutes and costs $86 one-way, $164 round-trip (plus tax). Reservations a week in advance are recommended.

Two companies offer transportation to Catalina Island via boats with both indoor and outdoor seating and snack bars. Excessive baggage is not allowed, and there are extra fees for bicycles and surfboards. The waters around Santa Catalina can get rough, so if you're prone to seasickness, come prepared.

Catalina Express makes an hour-long run from Long Beach or San Pedro to Avalon and a 90-minute run from Dana Point to Avalon with some stops at Two Harbors. Round-trip fare for the various routes costs $68.50. Service from Newport Beach to Avalon is available through

Catalina Passenger Service. Boats leave from Balboa Pavilion at 9 AM (in season), take 75 minutes to reach the island, and cost $68 round-trip. Return boats leave Catalina at 4:30 PM. Reservations are advised in summer and on weekends for all trips. ■ TIP→ Keep an eye out for dolphins, which sometimes swim alongside the ferries.

Cruise ships sail into Avalon twice a week, depositing thousands of passengers into the town for the day. Smaller boats shuttle between Avalon and Two Harbors, a small isthmus cove on the island's western end. You can also take bus excursions beyond Avalon. Roads are limited and nonresident vehicles prohibited, so hiking (by permit only) and cycling are the only other means of exploring.

Golf carts constitute the island's main form of transportation for sightseeing in the area, but they can't be used on the streets in town. You can rent them along Avalon's Crescent Avenue and Pebbly Beach Road for about $40 per hour with a $30 deposit, payable via cash or traveler's checks only.

LODGING

■ TIP→ Between Memorial Day and Labor Day be sure to make reservations before heading here. After late October, rooms are much easier to find on shorter notice, rates drop dramatically, and many hotels offer packages that include transportation from the mainland and/or sightseeing tours.

TOURS

Santa Catalina Island Company runs the following Discovery Tours: a summer-only coastal cruise to Seal Rocks; the *Flying Fish* boat trip (summer evenings only); a comprehensive inland motor tour (which includes an Arabian horse performance); a tour of Skyline Drive; a Casino tour; a scenic tour of Avalon; a glass-bottom-boat tour, an undersea tour on a semisubmersible vessel; and a tour of the Botanical Garden. Reservations are highly recommended for the inland tours. Tours cost $16 to $99. There are ticket booths on the Green Pleasure Pier, at the Casino, in the plaza, and at the boat landing. Catalina Adventure Tours, which has booths at the boat landing and on the pier, arranges similar excursions at comparable prices.

The Santa Catalina Island Conservancy organizes custom ecotours and hikes of the interior. Naturalist guides drive open Jeeps through some gorgeously untrammeled parts of island. Tours start at $98 per person for a three-hour trip (three-person minimum); you can also book half- and full-day tours. The tours run year-round.

ESSENTIALS

Airline Contacts Island Express (☎ 800/228–2566 ⊕ www.islandexpress.com).

Boat and Ferry Information Catalina Express (☎ 800/481–3470 ⊕ www.catalinaexpress.com). **Catalina Passenger Service** (☎ 949/673–5245 or 800/830–7744 ⊕ www.catalinainfo.com).

Golf Cart Information Island Rentals (✉ 125 Pebbly Beach Rd., Avalon ☎ 310/510–1456).

Visitor and Tour Info Catalina Island Visitors' Bureau (✉ *Green Pleasure Pier, Box 217, Avalon* ☎ *310/510–1520* ⊕ *www.catalina.com*). **Catalina Adventure Tours** (☎ *310/510–2888* ⊕ *www.catalinaadventuretours.com*). **Santa Catalina Island Company** (☎ *310/510–8687 or 800/626–1496* ⊕ *www.scico. com*). **Santa Catalina Island Conservancy** (✉ *3rd and Claressa Sts., Avalon* ☎ *310/510–2595* ⊕ *www.catalinaconservancy.org*).

AVALON

3

A 1- to 2-hr boat ride from Long Beach, Newport Beach, or San Pedro; a 15-min helicopter ride from Long Beach or San Pedro.

Avalon, Catalina's only real town, extends from the shore of its natural harbor to the surrounding hillsides. Most of the city's activity, however, is centered along the pedestrian mall on Crescent Avenue, and most sights are easily reached on foot. Taxis, trams, and shuttles can take you anywhere you need to go, and bicycles and golf carts can be rented from shops along Crescent Avenue.

A walk along **Crescent Avenue** is a nice way to begin a tour of the town. Vivid art-deco tiles adorn the avenue's fountains and planters—fired on the island by the now-defunct Catalina Tile Company, the tiles are a coveted commodity.

★ On the northwest point of Avalon Bay (looking to your right from Green Pleasure Pier) is the majestic landmark **Casino.** This circular white structure is one of the finest examples of art-deco architecture anywhere. Its Spanish-inspired floors and murals gleam with brilliant blue and green Catalina tiles. In this case, *casino,* the Italian word for "gathering place," has nothing to do with gambling. Rather, Casino life revolves around the magnificent ballroom. The same big-band dances that made the Casino famous in the 1930s and '40s still take place several times a year.

Santa Catalina Island Company conducts tours of the Casino, lasting about 55 minutes, for $16. You can also visit the **Catalina Island Museum,** in the lower level of the Casino, which investigates 7,000 years of island history; or stop at the **Casino Art Gallery** to see works by local artists. First-run movies are screened nightly at the **Avalon Theatre,** noteworthy for its classic 1929 theater pipe organ. ✉ *1 Casino Way, Avalon* ☎ *310/510–2414 museum* ⊕ *www.catalina.com/museum.html* ☎ *310/510–0808 art gallery, 310/510–0179 Avalon Theatre* ☑ *Museum $5, art gallery free* ☉ *Museum: daily 10–5. Art gallery: hours vary; call for current information.*

In front of the Casino are the crystal clear waters of the **Casino Point Underwater Park,** a marine preserve protected from watercraft where moray eels, bat rays, spiny lobsters, halibut, and other sea animals cruise around kelp forests and along the sandy bottom. It's a terrific site for scuba diving, with some shallow areas suitable for snorkeling. Scuba and snorkeling equipment can be rented on and near the pier. The shallow waters of **Lover's Cove,** east of the boat landing, are also good for snorkeling.

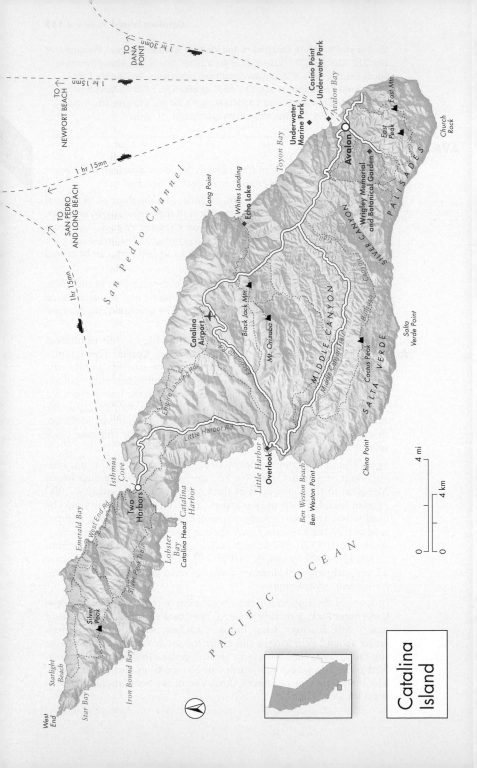

Catalina Island

TO DANA POINT
1 hr 30mn

TO NEWPORT BEACH
1 hr 15mn

TO SAN PEDRO AND LONG BEACH
1 hr 15mn

1 hr 15mn

San Pedro Channel

Casino Point Underwater Park
Underwater Marine Park
Avalon Bay
Avalon
Toyon Bay

Long Point
Whites Landing
Echo Lake

Wrigley Memorial and Botanical Garden

East Mtn.
East Peak
Church Rock

PALISADES

SILVER CANYON

Coyote Canyon

Bulrush Canyon

Catalina Airport

Escondido Rd.

Empire Landing Rd.

Black Jack Mtn.
Mt. Orizaba

MIDDLE CANYON

Middle Canyon Trail

Cactus Peak

SALTA VERDE

Salta Verde Point

Little Harbor Rd.

Little Harbor
Overlook

Ben Weston Beach
Ben Weston Point

China Point

PACIFIC OCEAN

Isthmus Cove

Two Harbors

West End Rd.

Emerald Bay

Silver Peak Trail

Lobster Bay
Catalina Head
Catalina Harbor

Silver Peak

Starlight Beach

West End

Star Bay

Iron Bound Bay

4 mi

4 km

0

0

Two miles south of the bay via Avalon Canyon Road is **Wrigley Memorial and Botanic Garden.** Here you'll find plants native to Southern California, including several that grow only on Catalina Island: Catalina ironwood, wild tomato, and rare Catalina mahogany. The Wrigley family commissioned the garden as well as the monument, which has a grand staircase and a Spanish mausoleum inlaid with colorful Catalina tile. (The mausoleum was never used by the Wrigleys, who are buried in Los Angeles.) Taxi service from Avalon is available, or you can take a tour bus from the downtown Tour Plaza or ferry landing. ⊠ *Avalon Canyon Rd., Avalon* ☎ *310/510–2595* ⊕ *www.catalina.com/memorial. html* ⊡ *$5* ⊙ *Daily 8–5.*

WHERE TO EAT AND STAY

$$$

STEAK HOUSE

✕ **Catalina Country Club.** The spring training clubhouse built for the Chicago Cubs now does duty as a restaurant for surf-and-turf standbys. Much of the fare here is organic, including a wide selection of steaks, plus ahi, duck breast, and carmelized Diver scallops. The adjacent bar is great for an after-dinner drink; it connects to the old Cubs locker room. ⊠ *1 Country Club Dr., Avalon* ☎ *310/510–7404* ⚑ *Reservations essential* ⊟ *AE, D, DC, MC, V.*

$

AMERICAN

✕ **Eric's on the Pier.** This little snack bar has been an Avalon family–run institution since the 1920s. It's a good place to people-watch while munching a breakfast burrito, buffalo burger, or a hot dog. While most of the action is outside, you can sit down at a table inside and dine on a bowl of homemade clam chowder in a baked bread bowl or an order of fish-and-chips. ⊠ *Green Pier No. 2, Avalon* ☎ *310/510–0894* ⊟ *AE, MC, V.*

$$

🏨 **Hotel Villa Portofino.** Steps from the beach and the Pleasure Pier, this hotel strikes a discreet note. Rooms are named after Italian cities, and most are decorated in deep jewel tones. Some ocean-facing rooms have open balconies, fireplaces, and marble baths. Courtyard rooms, opening on a central courtyard, have no exterior windows. You can sunbathe on the private deck, or ask for beach towels and chairs to take to the cove. This hotel offers a variety of packages that include transportation and island tours. **Pros:** romantic; very close to the beach; incredible sundeck. **Cons:** ground-floor rooms can be noisy, although location is quiet in general; some rooms are on the small side. ⊠ *111 Crescent Ave., Avalon* ☎ *310/510–0555 or 800/346–2326* ⊕ *www.hotelvillaportofino. com* ⤳ *35 rooms* ⚏ *In-room: a/c, refrigerator, Wi-Fi. In-hotel: restaurant* ⊟ *AE, D, MC, V* ⦿ *CP.*

$$$$

Fodor'sChoice

★

🏨 **Inn on Mt. Ada.** Staying in the mansion where William Wrigley Jr. once lived gives you all the comforts of a millionaire's home—at a millionaire's prices, beginning at $400 a night in summer. Breakfast, lunch, beverages, snacks, and use of a golf cart are included. The guest rooms are traditional and elegant; some have fireplaces and all have water views. The hilltop view of the curve of the bay is spectacular, and service is discreet. **Pros:** the Windsor room—with views of both the ocean and the bay; heliport and dock shuttle service; cookies and hors d'oeuvres in the evening; first-class service. **Cons:** rooms and bathrooms are on the small side; pricey. ⊠ *398 Wrigley Rd., Avalon* ☎ *310/510–2030 or 800/608–7669* ⊕ *www.innonmtada.com* ⤳ *6 rooms* ⚏ *In-room: no* *phone, no a/c, DVD, Wi-Fi. In-hotel: no kids under 14, Wi-Fi hotspot* ⊟ *MC, V* ⏍ *MAP.*

NIGHTLIFE

El Galleon (⊠ *411 Crescent Ave., Avalon* ☎ *310/510–1188*) has microbrews, bar nibbles, and karaoke. **Luau Larry's** (⊠ *509 Crescent Ave., Avalon* ☎ *310/510–1919*), famous for the potent blue Whicky Whacker cocktail, comes alive with boisterous tourists and locals on summer weekends.

SPORTS AND THE OUTDOORS

BICYCLING Bike rentals are widely available in Avalon starting at $5 per hour and $12 per day. Look for rentals on Crescent Avenue and Pebbly Beach Road such as **Brown's Bikes** (⊠ *107 Pebbly Beach Rd., next to Island Rentals, Avalon* ☎ *310/510–0986* ⊕ *www.catalinabiking.com*). To bike beyond the paved roads of Avalon, you must buy an annual permit from the Catalina Conservancy. Individual passes cost $35; family passes cost $125. You may not ride on hiking paths.

DIVING AND SNORKELING The Casino Point Underwater Park, with its handful of wrecks, is best suited for diving. Lover's Cove is better for snorkeling (no scuba diving allowed, but you'll share the area with glass-bottom boats). Both are protected marine preserves. **Catalina Divers Supply** (⊠ *Green Pleasure Pier* ☎ *310/510–0330* ⊕ *www.catalinadiverssupply.com*) rents equipment, runs guided scuba and snorkel tours, gives certification classes, and more. It has an outpost at Casino Point.

HIKING ■**TIP➜** If you plan to backpack overnight, you'll need a camping reservation. The interior is dry and desertlike; bring plenty of water and sunblock.

Permits from the **Santa Catalina Island Conservancy** (⊠ *3rd and Claressa Sts., Avalon* ☎ *310/510–2595* ⊕ *www.catalinaconservancy.org*) are required for hiking into Catalina Island's interior. The permits are free and can be picked up at the main house of the conservancy or at the airport. You don't need a permit for shorter hikes, such as the one from Avalon to the Botanical Garden. The conservancy has maps of the island's east-end hikes, such as Hermit's Gulch Trail. It's possible to hike between Avalon and Two Harbors, starting at the Hogsback Gate, above Avalon, though the 28-mi journey has an elevation gain of 3,000 feet and is not for the weak. ■**TIP➜** For a pleasant 4-mi hike out of Avalon, take Avalon Canyon Road to Wrigley Gardens and follow the trail to Lone Pine. At the top, you'll have an amazing view of the Palisades cliffs and, beyond them, the sea.

Another hike option is to take the **Airport Shuttle Bus** (☎ *310/510–0143*) from Avalon to the airport for $17 round-trip; the 10-mi hike back to Avalon is mostly downhill.

Los Angeles

WORD OF MOUTH

"One great thing about my trip to L.A. was all of the free guided tours I was able to take (El Pueblo de Los Angeles, Walt Disney Concert Hall, Central Library). There are so many great places to visit without spending a dime. While museum admission can add up, most museums offer free admission on certain days or certain hours."

—yk

WELCOME TO LOS ANGELES

TOP REASONS TO GO

★ **Hollywood magic:** A massive chunk of the world's entertainment is developed, written, filmed, edited, distributed, and sold here; you'll hear people discussing "The Industry" wherever you go.

★ **The beach:** Getting some sand on the floor of your car is practically a requirement here, and the beach is an integral part of the SoCal lifestyle.

★ **Chic shopping:** From Beverly Hills' Rodeo Drive and Downtown's Fashion District to the funky boutiques of Los Feliz, Silver Lake, and Echo Park, L.A. is a shopper's paradise.

★ **Trendy restaurants:** Celebrity is big business here, so it's no accident that the concept of the celebrity chef is a key part of the city's dining scene.

★ **People-watching:** Celeb-spotting in Beverly Hills, trying to get past the velvet rope at hip clubs, hanging out on the Venice Boardwalk . . . there's always something (or someone) interesting to see.

1 Downtown. Spectacular modern architecture, ethnic neighborhoods, and some of the city's key cultural institutions.

2 Hollywood. Catch a flick at Grauman's Chinese Theater, and check out Hollywood and Highland's Kodak Theater, home of the Academy Awards.

3 Wilshire Boulevard, Museum Row, and Farmers Market. Fascinating museums, excellent shopping, great people watching...and a tar pit.

4 Beverly Hills and Century City. Go for the glamour, the restaurants, and the scene. You'll see plastic surgery, scads of sushi spots, a parade of custom cars, and, of course, lots of conspicuous consumption.

5 West Hollywood. Visit this area—home to the Sunset Strip—for urban indulgences: shopping, restaurants, and nightspots.

6 The Westside. Home to some of L.A.'s most exclusive neighborhoods, the Westside is rich in cultural attractions like the dazzling Getty Center.

7 Santa Monica, Venice, and Malibu. These desirable beach communities move from ultrarich,

ultracasual Malibu to bohemian/seedy Venice, with liberal, Mediterranean-style Santa Monica in the middle.

8 The San Fernando Valley. Home of several of the big studios, this is where the movie (and TV) magic happens.

9 Pasadena Area. A separate city, Pasadena is a quiet area with outstanding Arts and Crafts homes, good dining, and a pair of exceptional museums.

10 Long Beach. This port city is home to a nice aquarium and the *Queen Mary*.

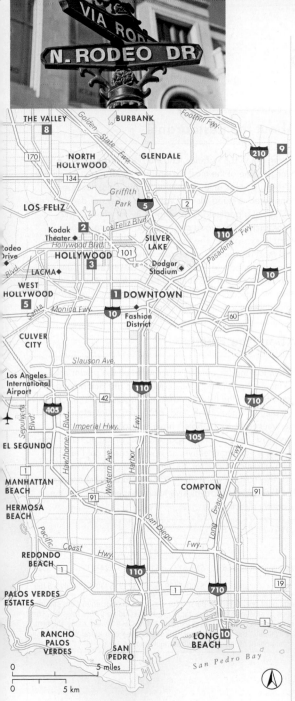

4

GETTING ORIENTED

Looking at a map of sprawling Los Angeles, first-time visitors are sometimes overwhelmed. Where to begin? What to see first? And what about all those freeways? Here's some advice: relax. Begin by setting your priorities—movie and television buffs should first head to Hollywood, Universal Studios, and a taping of a television show. Beach lovers and nature types might start out in Santa Monica or Venice or Malibu, or spend an afternoon in Griffith Park, one of the largest city parks in the country. Culture vultures should make a beeline for the twin Gettys (the center in Brentwood and the villa near Malibu), the Los Angeles County Museum of Art (LACMA), or the Norton Simon Museum. And urban explorers might begin with Downtown Los Angeles.

LOS ANGELES PLANNER

When to Go

Almost any time of the year is the right time to go to Los Angeles; the climate is mild and pleasant year-round. Winter brings crisp, sunny, unusually smogless days from about November to May (expect brief rains from December to April). Los Angeles summers, which are virtually rainless, can lead to air-quality alerts. Prices skyrocket and reservations are a must when tourism peaks from July through early October.

Driving

Most freeways are known by a name and a number; for example, the San Diego Freeway is I-405, the Hollywood Freeway is U.S. 101, the Ventura Freeway is a different stretch of U.S. 101, the Santa Monica Freeway is I-10, and the Harbor Freeway is I-110. It helps, too, to know which direction you're traveling; say, west toward Santa Monica or east toward Downtown Los Angeles. Distance in miles doesn't mean much, depending on the time of day you're traveling: the short 10-mi distance between the San Fernando Valley and Downtown Los Angeles might take an hour to travel during rush hour but only 20 minutes at other times.

About the Restaurants

Dining out in Los Angeles tends to be a casual affair, and even at some of the most expensive restaurants you're likely to see customers in jeans (although this is not necessarily considered in good taste). Despite its veneer of decadence, L.A. is not a particularly late-night city for eating. (The reenergized Hollywood dining scene is emerging as a notable exception.) The peak dinner times are from 7 to 9, and most restaurants won't take reservations after 10 PM. Generally speaking, restaurants are closed either Sunday or Monday; a few are shuttered both days. Most places—even the upscale spots—are open for lunch on weekdays, when Hollywood megadeals are conceived.

About the Hotels

When looking for a hotel, don't write off the pricier establishments immediately. Price categories are determined by "rack rates"—the list price of a hotel room, which is usually discounted. Specials abound, particularly downtown on the weekends. Many hotels have packages that include breakfast, theater tickets, spa services, or exotic rental cars. Pricing is very competitive, so always check out the hotel Web site in advance for current special offers. When making reservations, particularly last-minute ones, check the hotel's Web site for exclusive Internet specials or call the property directly.

WHAT IT COSTS

	¢	$	$$	$$$	$$$$
Restaurants	under $10	$10–$17	$18–$24	$24–$35	over $35
Hotels	under $100	$100–$199	$200–$299	$300–$399	over $400

Restaurant prices are per person for a main course or equivalent combination of smaller plates (e.g., tapas, sushi), excluding 9.75% sales tax. For hotels, taxes (10%–15.5%) are extra. In listings, we always name the facilities available, but we don't specify whether they cost extra. When pricing accommodations, always ask what's included.

4

Updated by Cindy Arora, Tanvi Chheda, Arlene Dawson, Elline Lipkin, Lea Lion, Susan MacCallum-Whitcomb, Laura Randall

Los Angeles is as much a fantasy as it is a physical city. A mecca for face-lifts, film noir, shopping starlets, beach bodies, and mind-numbing traffic, it sprawls across 467 square mi; add in the surrounding five-county metropolitan area, and you've got an area of more than 34,000 square mi.

Contrary to popular myth, however, that doesn't mean you have to spend all your time in a car. In fact, getting out of your car is the only way to really get to know Los Angeles. We've divided the major sightseeing areas into 10 driving and walking tours that take you through the various entertainment-industry-centered, financial, beachfront, wealthy, and fringe neighborhoods and mini-cities that make up the vast L.A. area. But remember, no single locale—whether it be Malibu, Downtown, Beverly Hills, or Burbank—fully embodies Los Angeles. It's in the mix that you'll discover the city's character.

PLANNING

GETTING HERE AND AROUND
AIR TRAVEL
It's generally easier to navigate the secondary airports than to get through sprawling LAX, the city's major gateway. Bob Hope Airport in Burbank is closest to downtown L.A., and domestic flights to it can be cheaper than flights to LAX—it's definitely worth checking out. From Long Beach Airport it's equally convenient to go north to central Los Angeles or south to Orange County. Flights to Orange County's John Wayne Airport are often more expensive than those to the other secondary airports. Parking at the smaller airports is cheaper than at LAX.

Airports Bob Hope Airport (*BUR* ☎ *818/840–8830* ⊕ *www.bobhopeairport. com*). **John Wayne/Orange County Airport** (*SNA* ☎ *949/252–5006* ⊕ *www. ocair.com*). **Long Beach Airport** (*LGB* ☎ *562/570–2600* ⊕ *www.lgb.org*). **Los Angeles International Airport** (*LAX* ☎ *310/646–5252* ⊕ *www.lawa.org*). **Ontario International Airport** (*ONT* ☎ *909/937–2700* ⊕ *www.lawa.org*).

Continued on page 166

HIGHWAY 1: SANTA MONICA TO BIG SUR

Hearst Castle

THE PLAN

Distance: approx. 335 mi

Time: 3-5 days

Good Overnight Options: Malibu, Santa Barbara, Pismo Beach, San Luis Obispo, Cambria, Carmel

For more information on the sights and attractions along this portion of Highway 1, please see chapters 4 and 5.

SANTA MONICA TO MALIBU (approx. 26 mi)

Highway 1 begins in Dana point, but it seems more appropriate to begin a PCH adventure in **Santa Monica.** Be sure to experience the beach culture, then balance the tacky pleasures of Santa Monica's amusement pier with a stylish dinner in a neighborhood restaurant.

MALIBU TO SANTA BARBARA (approx. 70 mi)

The PCH follows the curve of Santa Monica Bay all the way to **Malibu** and **Point Mugu,**

Santa Monica

near **Oxnard.** Chances are you'll experience *déjà vu* driving this 27-mile stretch: mountains on one side, ocean on the other, opulent homes perched on hillsides; you've seen this piece of coast countless times on TV and film. Be sure to walk out on the **Malibu Pier** for a great photo opp, then check out **Surfrider Beach,** with three famous points where perfect waves ignited a worldwide surfing rage in the 1960s.

After Malibu you'll drive through miles of protected, largely unpopulated coastline. Ride a wave at **Zuma Beach,** scout for offshore whales at **Point Dume State Preserve,** or hike the trails at **Point Mugu State Park.** After skirting Point Mugu, Highway 1 merges with U.S. 101 for about 70 mi before reaching **Santa Barbara.** A mini-tour of the city includes a real Mexican lunch at **La Super-Rica,** a visit to the magnificent Spanish **Mission Santa Barbara,** and a walk down hopping **State Street to Stearns Wharf.**

SANTA BARBARA TO SAN SIMEON (approx. 147 mi)

North of Santa Barbara, Highway 1 morphs into the Cabrillo Highway, separating

Santa Barbara

from and then rejoining U.S. 101. The route winds through rolling vineyards and rangeland to **San Luis Obispo,** where any legit road trip includes a photo stop at the wacky, pink **Madonna Inn.** Be sure to also climb the humungous dunes at **Guadalupe-Nipomo Dunes Preserve.**

In downtown San Luis Obispo, the **Mission San Luis Obispo de Tolosa** stands by a tree-shaded creek edged with shops and cafés. Highway 1 continues to **Morro Bay** and up the coast. About 15 mi north of Morro Bay, you'll reach the town of **Harmony** (population 18), a tiny burg with artists' studios, a wedding chapel, shops, and a winery. The road continues through **Cambria** to solitary **Hearst San Simeon State Historical Monument**—the art-filled pleasure palace at **San Simeon.** Just four miles north of the castle, elephant seals grunt and cavort at the

Big Sur

TOP 5 PLACES TO LINGER

- Point Dume State Preserve
- Santa Barbara
- Hearst San Simeon State Historical Monument
- Big Sur/Julia Pfeiffer Burns State Park
- Carmel

Piedras Blancas Elephant Seal Rookery, just off the side of the road.

SAN SIMEON TO CARMEL (approx. 92 mi)

Heading north, you'll drive through **Big Sur,** a place of ancient forests and rugged shoreline stretching 90 mi from San Simeon to **Carmel.** Much of Big Sur lies within several state parks and the 165,000-acre **Ventana Wilderness,** itself part of the **Los Padres National Forest.** This famously scenic stretch of the coastal drive, which twists up and down bluffs above the ocean, can last hours. Take your time.

At **Julia Pfeiffer Burns State Park** one easy but rewarding hike leads to an iconic waterfall off a beachfront cliff. When you reach lovely **Carmel,** stroll around the picture-perfect town's mission, galleries, and shops.

Shuttles Prime Time (☎ *800/733–8267* ⊕ *www.primetimeshuttle.com*).
SuperShuttle (☎ *323/775–6600, 310/782–6600, or 800/258–3826* ⊕ *www. supershuttle.com*). **Xpress Shuttle** (☎ *800/427–7483* ⊕ *www.expressshuttle.com*).

BUS TRAVEL

Inadequate public-transportation systems have been an L.A. problem for decades. That said, many local trips can be made, with time and patience, by bus. In certain cases, it may be your best option; for example, visiting the Getty Center, going to Universal Studios and/or the adjacent CityWalk, or venturing into downtown. The Metropolitan Transit Authority DASH (Downtown Area Short Hop) minibuses cover six different circular routes in Hollywood, Mid-Wilshire, and the downtown area. The buses stop every two blocks or so. The Santa Monica Municipal Bus Line, also known as the Big Blue Bus, is a pleasant and inexpensive way to move around the Westside, where the MTA lines leave off. There's also an express bus to and from downtown L.A., and a shuttle bus, the Tide Shuttle, which runs between Main Street and the Third Street Promenade and stops at hotels along the way. Culver CityBus Lines run six routes through Culver City.

Bus Information California Smart Traveler (☎ *800/266–6883* ⊕ *www.dot. ca.gov/caltrans511*). **Culver CityBus Lines** (☎ *310/253–6500* ⊕ *www.culvercity. org*). **DASH** (☎ *213/626–4455 or 310/808–2273* ⊕ *www.ladottransit.com/dash*). **Greyhound** (☎ *213/629–8405 or 800/231–2222* ⊕ *www.greyhound.com*). **Metropolitan Transit Authority (MTA)** (☎ *213/626–4455* ⊕ *www.mta.net*). **Santa Monica Municipal Bus Line** (☎ *310/451–5444* ⊕ *www.bigbluebus.com*).

CAR TRAVEL

Be aware that a number of major streets have similar-sounding names (Beverly Drive and Beverly Boulevard, or numbered streets north to south downtown and east to west in Hollywood, West Hollywood, and Beverly Hills) or exactly the same name (San Vicente Boulevard in West L.A., Brentwood, Santa Monica, and West Hollywood). Also, some smaller streets seem to exist intermittently for miles, so unless you have good directions, you should use major streets rather than try for an alternative that is actually blocked by a dead end or detours, like the side streets off Sunset Boulevard. Try to get clear directions and stick to them.

If you get discombobulated while on the freeway, remember the rule of thumb: even-numbered freeways run east and west, odd-numbered freeways run north and south.

Major-chain car rental rates in L.A. begin at $35 a day and $110 a week, plus 9.25% sales tax. Luxury and sport utility vehicles start at $69 a day. Open-top convertibles are a popular choice for L.A. visitors wanting to make the most of the sun. Note that the major agencies offer services for travelers with disabilities, such as hand controls, for little or no extra cost.

Information California Highway Patrol (☎ *800/427–7623 in California*). **City of Los Angeles** (⊕ *www.ci.la.ca.us* ⊕ *www.sigalert.com* ⊕ *trafficinfo.lacity.org*).

Emergency Services Freeway Service Patrol (☎ *213/922–2957 general information*).

Local Car Rental Agencies Beverly Hills Budget Car Rental (☎ *310/274–9173 or 800/227–7117* ⊕ *www.budgetbeverlyhills.com*). **Beverly Hills Rent-A-Car** (☎ *310/337–1400 or 800/479–5996* ⊕ *www.bhrentacar.com*). **Enterprise** (☎ *800/736–8222* ⊕ *www.enterprise.com*). **FOX Rental Cars** (☎ *877/387–3682* ⊕ *www.foxrentacar.com*). **Midway Car Rental** (☎ *888/682–0166* ⊕ *www.midwaycarrental.com*). **Rent A Wreck** (☎ *800/995–0994* ⊕ *www.rent-a-wreck.com*). **Town Rent A Car** (☎ *310/973–6815 or 323/934–4780*). **£West Rent a Car** (☎ *310/417–9050 or 877/404–0404* ⊕ *www.atwestcarrental.com*).

METRO RAIL TRAVEL

Metro Rail covers a limited area of L.A.'s vast expanse, but what there is, is helpful and frequent. The underground Red Line runs from Union Station downtown through Mid-Wilshire, Hollywood, and Universal City on its way to North Hollywood, stopping at the most popular tourist destinations along the way. The light commuter rail Green Line stretches from Redondo Beach to Norwalk, while the partially underground Blue Line goes from downtown to the South Bay (Long Beach/San Pedro). The Green and Blue lines are not often used by visitors, though the Green is gaining popularity as an alternative, albeit time-consuming, way to reach LAX. The monorail-like Gold Line begins at Union Station and heads northeast to Pasadena and Sierra Madre. The Orange Line, a 14-mi bus corridor, connects the North Hollywood subway station with the western San Fernando Valley.

The Web site is the best way to get info on Metro Rail.

Metro Rail Information Metropolitan Transit Authority (MTA) (☎ *800/266–6883 or 213/626–4455* ⊕ *www.mta.net*).

TAXI AND LIMOUSINE TRAVEL

Don't even try to hail a cab on the street in Los Angeles. Instead, phone one of the many taxi companies. The metered rate is $2.45 per mile, plus a $2.65 per-fare charge. Taxi rides from LAX have an additional $2.50 surcharge. Be aware that distances between sights in L.A. are vast, so cab fares add up quickly. On the other end of the price spectrum, limousines come equipped with everything from a full bar and telephone to a hot tub. If you open any L.A.–area yellow pages, the number of limo companies will astound you. Most charge by the hour, with a three-hour minimum.

Limo Companies ABC Limousine & Sedan Service (☎ *818/980–6000 or 888/753–7500*). **American Executive** (☎ *213/250–2121 or 800/927–2020*). **Black & White Transportation Services** (☎ *800/924–1624*). **Chauffeur's Unlimited** (☎ *310/645–8711 or 888/546–6019* ⊕ *www.chaufusa.com*). **Dav El Limousine Co.** (☎ *310/550–0070 or 800/922–0343* ⊕ *www.davel.com*). **First Class** (☎ *800/400-9771* ⊕ *www.first-classlimo.com*). **ITS** (☎ *800/487–4255*).

Taxi Companies Beverly Hills Cab Co. (☎ *800/273–6611*). **Checker Cab** (☎ *800/300–5007*). **Independent Cab Co.** (☎ *800/521–8294* ⊕ *www.taxi4u.com*). **United Independent Taxi** (☎ *800/411–0303 or 800/822–8294*). **Yellow Cab/LA Taxi Co-Op** (☎ *800/200–1085 or 800/200–0011*).

TRAIN TRAVEL

Union Station in downtown Los Angeles is one of the great American railroad stations. The interior is well kept and includes comfortable seating, a restaurant, and snack bars. As the city's rail hub, it's the place to catch an Amtrak train. Among Amtrak's Southern California routes are 13 daily trips to San Diego and seven to Santa Barbara. Amtrak's luxury *Coast Starlight* travels along the spectacular coastline from Seattle to Los Angeles in just a day and a half (though it's often a little late). The *Sunset Limited* goes to Los Angeles from Florida (via New Orleans and Texas), and the *Southwest Chief* from Chicago.

Information Amtrak (☎ 800/872–7245 ⊕ www.amtrak.com). **Union Station** (✉ 800 N. Alameda St. ☎ 213/683–6979).

VISITOR INFORMATION

Contacts Beverly Hills Conference and Visitors Bureau (☎ 310/248–1000 or 800/345–2210 ⊕ www.beverlyhillsbehere.com). **California Office of Tourism** (☎ 916/444–4429 or 800/862–2543 ⊕ www.visitcalifornia.com). **Glendale Chamber of Commerce** (☎ 818/240–7870 ⊕ www.glendalechamber. com). **Hollywood Chamber of Commerce Info Center** (☎ 323/469–8311 ⊕ www.hollywoodchamber.net). **L.A. Inc./The Convention and Visitors Bureau** (☎ 213/624–7300 or 800/228–2452 ⊕ discoverlosangeles.com). **Long Beach Area Convention and Visitors Bureau** (☎ 562/436–3645 ⊕ www.visitlongbeach.com). **Pasadena Convention and Visitors Bureau** (☎ 626/795–9311 ⊕ www.pasadenacal.com). **Redondo Beach Visitors Bureau** (☎ 310/374–2171 or 800/282–0333 ⊕ www.redondochamber.com). **Santa Monica Convention & Visitors Bureau** (☎ 310/319–6263 or 800/544–5319 ⊕ www.santamonica.com). **West Hollywood Convention and Visitors Bureau** (☎ 310/289–2525 or 800/368–6020 ⊕ www.visitwesthollywood.com).

EXPLORING LOS ANGELES

DOWNTOWN LOS ANGELES

Once the lively heart of Los Angeles, Downtown has been a glitz-free businessman's domain of high-rises for the past few decades. But if there's one thing Angelinos love, it's a makeover, and now city planners have put the wheels in motion for a dramatic revitalization. Glance in every direction and you'll find construction crews building luxury lofts and retail space in hopes of attracting new high-class residents.

WHAT TO SEE

8 ★ **Bradbury Building.** Stunning wrought-iron railings, ornate moldings, a Victorian-style sky-lighted atrium that rises almost 50 feet, and birdcage elevators that seem to cry out for white-gloved, brass-buttoned operators: it's easy to see why the Bradbury leaves visitors awestruck. Designed in 1893 by a novice architect who drew his inspiration from a science-fiction story and a conversation with his dead brother via a Ouija board, the office building was originally the site of turn-of-the-20th-century sweatshops, but now houses a variety of businesses that try to keep normal working conditions despite the barrage of daily

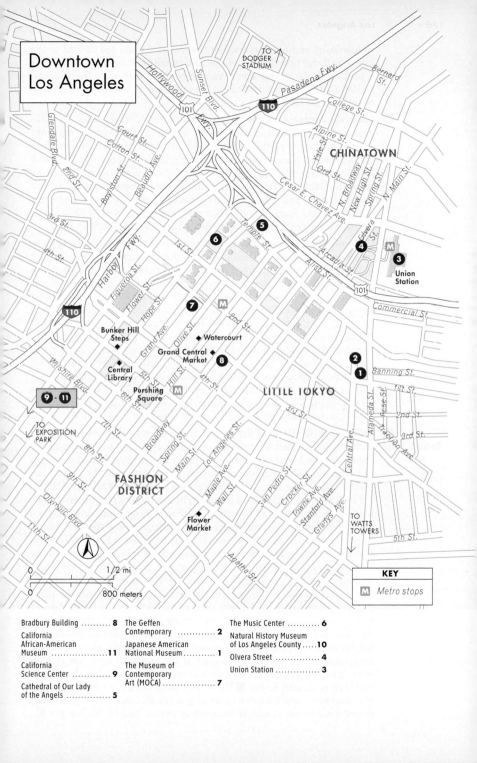

Downtown Los Angeles

CHINATOWN

TO DODGER STADIUM

Pasadena Fwy.

Hollywood Fwy.

Sunset Blvd.

101

110

College St.

Bernard St.

Alpine St.

Ord St.

Cesar E. Chavez Ave.

N. Broadway

New High St.

Spring St.

N. Main St.

Glendale Blvd.

2nd St.

Court St.

Cotton St.

Boylston St.

Beaudry Ave.

3rd St.

4th St.

Harbor Fwy.

Figueroa St.

Flower St.

Hope St.

Grand Ave.

Olive St.

1st St.

Temple St.

2nd St.

Alameda St.

Arcadia St.

Aliso St.

Olvera St.

⑤

❻

④

Ⓜ

③

Union Station

101

Commercial St.

110

Bunker Hill Steps

Central Library

♦ Watercourt

Grand Central Market

Ⓜ

❼

2nd St.

5th St.

Hill St.

Pershing Square

Ⓜ

4th St.

❽

❷
❶

Banning St.

LITTLE TOKYO

Central Ave.

Alameda St.

Jesse St.

Traction Ave.

1st St.

2nd St.

3rd St.

⑨ · ⑪

Wilshire Blvd.

TO EXPOSITION PARK

7th St.

8th St.

9th St.

Olympic Blvd.

11th St.

Broadway

Spring St.

Main St.

Los Angeles St.

Maple Ave.

Wall St.

San Pedro St.

Crocker St.

Towne Ave.

Stanford Ave.

Gladys Ave.

3rd St.

FASHION DISTRICT

Flower Market

Agatha St.

TO WATTS TOWERS

5th St.

0   1/2 mi
0   800 meters

KEY

Ⓜ Metro stops

tourist visits and filmmakers. For that reason, visits are limited to the lobby and the first-floor landing. The building is open daily 9–5 for a peek, as long as you don't wander beyond visitor-approved areas. ✉ *304 S. Broadway, southeast corner Broadway and 3rd St., Downtown* ☎ *213/626–1893.*

⑪ **California African-American Museum.** Works by 20th-century African-American artists and contemporary works of the African diaspora are the backbone of this museum's permanent collection. Its exhibits document the African-American experience from Emancipation and Reconstruction through the 20th century, especially as expressed by artists in California and elsewhere in the West. Special musical as well as educational and cultural events are offered the first Sunday of every month. ✉ *600 State Dr., Exposition Park* ☎ *213/744–7432* ⊕ *www. caamuseum.org* ✎ *Free, parking $8* ☯ *Tues.–Sat. 10–5, Sun. 11–5.*

⑨ **California Science Center.** You're bound to see excited kids running up to
☺ the dozens of interactive exhibits here that illustrate the relevance of science to everyday life, from bacteria to airplanes. Clustered in different "Worlds," this center provides opportunities to examine such topics as structures and communications, where you can be an architect and design your own building and learn how to make it earthquake-proof, to "Life" itself where Tess, the 50-foot animatronic star of the exhibit "Body Works," dramatically demonstrates how the body's organs work together. Air and Space Exhibits show out what it takes to go to outer space with Gemini 11, real capsule flown into space by Pete Conrad and Dick Gordon in September 1966. An IMAX theater shows large-format releases. ✉ *700 State Dr., Exposition Park* ☎ *213/744–7400 or 323/724–3623* ⊕ *www.californiasciencecenter.org* ✎ *Free, except for IMAX, prices vary; parking $8* ☯ *Daily 10–5.*

⑤ **Cathedral of Our Lady of the Angels.** Controversy surrounded Spanish
Fodor's Choice architect José Rafael Moneo's unconventional, costly, austere design for
★ the seat of the Archdiocese of Los Angeles. But judging from the swarms of visitors and the standing-room-only holiday masses, the church has carved out a niche for itself in Downtown's daily life. Opened in 2002, the ocher-concrete cathedral looms up by the Hollywood Freeway. The plaza in front is relatively austere, glaringly bright on sunny days; a children's play garden with bronze animals helps relieve the stark space. Imposing bronze entry doors, designed by local artist Robert Graham, are decorated with multicultural icons and New World images of the Virgin Mary. The canyonlike interior of the church is spare, polished, and airy. By day, sunlight illuminates the sanctuary through translucent curtain walls of thin Spanish alabaster, a departure from the usual stained glass. Artist John Nava used residents from his hometown of Ojai, California, as models for some of the 135 figures in the tapestries that line the nave walls. Make sure to go underground to wander the bright, somewhat incongruous, mazelike white-marble corridors of the mausoleum. Free guided tours start at the entrance fountain at 1 on weekdays. There's plenty of underground visitor parking; the vehicle entrance is on Hill Street. ■ **TIP**➔ The café in the plaza has become one of Downtown's favorite lunch spots, as you can pick up a fresh, reasonably priced meal to eat at one of the outdoor tables. ✉ *555 W. Temple St.,*

Frank Gehry's stunning Walt Disney Concert Hall is the crown jewel of the Music Center, if not all of Downtown Los Angeles.

Downtown ☎ *213/680–5200* ⊕ *www.olacathedral.org* 🖾 *Free, parking $3 every 20 min, $14 maximum* ⊙ *Mon.–Fri. 6:30–6, Sat. 9–6, Sun. 7–6.*

❷ ★ The Geffen Contemporary. Originally opened in 1982 as a temporary exhibit hall while the **Museum of Contemporary Art (MOCA)** was under construction at California Plaza, this large flexible space, designed by architect Frank Gehry, charmed visitors with its antiestablishment character and lively exhibits. Thanks to its hit reception, it remains one of two satellite museums of the MOCA (the other is outside the Pacific Design Center in West Hollywood). Named the Geffen Contemporary, after receiving a $5 million gift from the David Geffen Foundation, this museum houses a sampling of MOCA's permanent collection and usually one or two offbeat exhibits that provoke grins from even the stuffiest museumgoer. Call before you visit as the museum sometimes closes for installations. ✉ *152 N. Central Ave., Downtown* ☎ *213/626–6222* ⊕ *www.moca-la.org* 🖾 *$10, free with MOCA admission on same day and on Thurs.* ⊙ *Mon. 5–8, Fri. 11–5, Thurs. 11–8, weekends 11–6.*

❶ Japanese American National Museum. What was it like to grow up on a sugar plantation in Hawaii? How difficult was life for Japanese-Americans interned in concentration camps during World War II? These questions are addressed by changing exhibits at this museum in Little Tokyo. Insightful volunteer docents are on hand to share their own stories and experiences. The museum occupies an 85,000-square-foot adjacent pavilion as well as its original site in a renovated 1925 Buddhist temple. ✉ *369 E. 1st St., at Central Ave., next to Geffen Contemporary, Downtown* ☎ *213/625–0414* ⊕ *www.janm.org* 🖾 *$8,* *free Thurs. 5–8 and 3rd Thurs. of month* ⊙ *Tues., Wed., and Fri.–Sun. 11–5, Thurs. 11–8.*

❼ **The Museum of Contemporary Art (MOCA).** The MOCA's permanent col-
Fodor'sChoice lection of American and European art from 1940 to the present divides
★ itself between three spaces: this linear red-sandstone building at California Plaza, the **Geffen Contemporary,** in nearby Little Tokyo, and the
satellite gallery at West Hollywood's **Pacific Design Center.** Likewise,
its exhibitions are split between the established and the cutting-edge.
Works by heavy hitters such as Mark Rothko, Franz Kline, Susan Roth-
enberg, Diane Arbus, and Robert Frank are part of the permanent
collection which are rotated into exhibits at different times, while at
least 20 themed shows are featured annually. The museum occasionally closes for exhibit installation. ⊠ *250 S. Grand Ave., Downtown*
☎ *213/626–6222* ⊕ *www.moca.org* ⊠ *$10, free on same day with Gef-
fen Contemporary admission and on Thurs.* ⊙ *Mon. and Fri. 11–5,
Thurs. 11–8, weekends 11–6.*

The Music Center. L.A.'s major performing arts venue since its opening
in 1964, the Music Center is also now Downtown's centerpiece. Home
to the Los Angeles Philharmonic, the Los Angeles Opera, the Center
Theater Group, and the Los Angeles Master Chorale, the Music Center
is also a former site of the Academy Awards. The center's crown jewel
❻ is the **Walt Disney Concert Hall.** Designed by Frank Gehry, the Hall
Fodor'sChoice opened in 2003 and instantly became a stunning icon of the city. The
★ gorgeous stainless-steel-clad structure soars lyrically upward, seeming
to defy the laws of engineering. Free tours of the Music Center are
available by volunteer docents, "the Symphonians," who provide a
wealth of architectural and behind-the-scenes information while escort-
ing you through elaborate, art-punctuated VIP areas. ⊠ *135 N. Grand
Ave., at 1st St., Downtown* ☎ *213/972–7211, 213/972–4399 for tour
information* ⊕ *www.musiccenter.org* ⊠ *Free* ⊙ *Free tours Tues.–Fri.
10–1:30, Sat. 10–noon.*

❿ **Natural History Museum of Los Angeles County.** With more than 35 million
ℭ specimens, this is the third-largest museum of its type in the United
States. Since 1913, the museum has boasted a rich collection of prehistoric fossils and extensive bird, insect, and marine-life exhibits. Brilliant
stones shimmer in the Gem & Mineral Hall. An elaborate diorama
exhibit shows North American and African mammals in detailed repli-
cas of their natural habitats. Exhibits typifying various cultural groups
include pre-Columbian artifacts and a display of crafts from the South
Pacific. The Ralph M. Parsons Discovery Center & Insect Zoo encourages kids to do hands-on exploration of the Museum's collections. The
museum also features its first public paleontological preparation laboratory. This innovative lab features "Thomas," a nearly 70% complete,
65 million-year-old T. rex excavated during field expeditions in southeastern Montana. ■**TIP→** Select exhibits may be temporarily relocated
to different areas as the museum conducts ongoing renovations. ⊠ *900
Exposition Blvd., Exposition Park* ☎ *213/763–3466* ⊕ *www.nhm.org*
⊠ *$9, free 1st Tues. of month* ⊙ *Weekdays 9:30–5, weekends 10–5.*

④ **Olvera Street.** This busy pedestrian block tantalizes with piñatas, mari-
☺ achis, and fragrant Mexican food. As the major draw of the oldest
★ section of the city, known as **El Pueblo de Los Angeles,** Olvera Street
has come to represent the rich Mexican heritage of L.A. It had a close
shave with disintegration in the early 20th century, until the socialite
Christine Sterling walked through in 1926. Jolted by the historic area's
decay, Sterling fought to preserve key buildings and led the transformation of the street into a Mexican-American marketplace. Today this
character remains; vendors sell puppets, leather goods, sandals, serapes
(woolen shawls), and handicrafts from stalls that line the center of the
narrow street. On weekends, the restaurants are packed as musicians
play in the central plaza. The weekends that fall around two Mexican
holidays, Cinco de Mayo (May 5) and Independence Day (September
16), also draw huge crowds. ■TIP→ To see Olvera Street at its quiet-
est, visit late on a weekday afternoon, when long shadows heighten the
romantic feeling of the passageway. For information, stop by the **Olvera
Street Visitors Center** (✉ *622 N. Main St., Downtown* ☎ *213/628-1274*
⊕ *www.olvera-street.com*), in the Sepulveda House, a Victorian built in
1887 as a hotel and boardinghouse. The center is open weekdays and
weekends 9–4. Free hour-long walking tours leave here at 10, 11, and
noon Tuesday–Saturday.

③ **Union Station.** Evoking an era when travel and style went hand in hand,
★ Union Station will transport you to another destination, and another
time. Built in 1939 and designed by City Hall architects John and Donald Parkinson, it combines Spanish colonial revival and art deco styles
that have retained their classic warmth and quality. The waiting hall's
commanding scale and enormous chandeliers have provided the setting
for countless films, TV shows, and music videos. Once the key entry
point into Los Angeles prior to LAX, Union Station is worth a visit
even if you don't plan to go anywhere but merely want to wallow in
the ambience of one of the country's last great rail stations. The indoor
restaurant, **Traxx,** offers a glamorous vintage setting for lunch and dinner. ✉ *800 N. Alameda St., Downtown.*

WILSHIRE BOULEVARD, MUSEUM ROW, AND FARMERS MARKET

The three-block stretch of Wilshire Boulevard known as Museum Row,
east of Fairfax Avenue, racks up five intriguing museums and a prehistoric tar pit to boot. Only a few blocks away are the historic Farmers
Market and The Grove shopping mall, a great place to people-watch
over breakfast. Wilshire Boulevard itself is something of a cultural monument—it begins its grand 16-mi sweep to the sea in Downtown Los
Angeles. ■TIP→ Finding parking along Wilshire Boulevard can present a
challenge any time of the day; you'll find advice on the information phone
lines of most attractions.

WHAT TO SEE

① **Farmers Market and The Grove.** The saying "Meet me at 3rd and Fair-
Fodor'sChoice fax" became a standard line for generations of Angelenos who ate,
★ shopped, and spotted the stars who drifted over from the studios for a

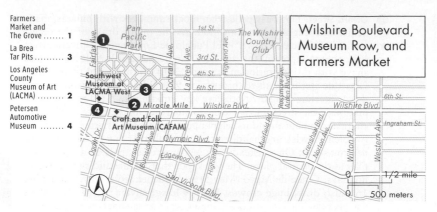

Wilshire Boulevard,
Museum Row, and
Farmers Market

breath of unpretentious air. Starting back in 1934 when two entrepreneurs convinced oil magnate E.B. Gilmore to open a vacant field for a bare-bones market, this spot became a humble shop for farmers selling produce out of their trucks. From this seat-of-the-pants situation grew a European-style open-air market and local institution at the corner of 3rd Street and Fairfax Avenue. Now the market includes 110 stalls and more than 20 counter-order restaurants, plus the landmark 1941 Clock Tower. In 2002 a massive expansion called The Grove opened; this highly conceptualized outdoor mall has a pseudo-European facade, with cobblestones, marble mosaics, and pavilions. Los Angeles history gets a nod with the electric steel-wheeled Red Car trolley, which shuttles two blocks through the Farmers Market and The Grove. If you hate crowds, try visiting The Grove before noon for the most comfortable shopping experience. ■TIP➜ The Grove really dazzles around Christmas, with an enormous Christmas tree and a nightly faux snowfall until New Year's Day. ⊠ Farmers Market, 6333 W. 3rd St.; The Grove, 189 The Grove Dr., Fairfax District ☎ 323/933–9211 Farmers Market; 323/900–8080 The Grove ⊕ www.farmersmarketla.com ☉ Farmers Market weekdays 9–9, Sat. 9–8, Sun. 10–7; The Grove Mon.–Thurs. 10–9, Fri. and Sat. 10–10, Sun. 11–8.

❸ **La Brea Tar Pits.** Do your children have dinos on the brain? Show them
★ where dinosaurs come from by taking them to the stickiest park in town. About 40,000 years ago, deposits of oil rose to the earth's surface, collected in shallow pools, and coagulated into asphalt. In the early 20th century, geologists discovered that all that goo contained the largest collection of Pleistocene, or Ice Age, fossils ever found at one location: more than 600 species of birds, mammals, plants, reptiles, and insects. Roughly 100 tons of fossil bones have been removed in excavations over the last seven decades, making this one of the world's most famous fossil sites. You can see most of the pits through chain-link fences. Pit 91 is the site of ongoing excavation; tours are available, and you can volunteer to help with the excavations in summer. There are several pits scattered around Hancock Park and the surrounding neighborhood; construction in the area has often had to accommodate them, and in nearby streets and along sidewalks, little bits of tar occasionally ooze up, unstoppable.

The nearby **Page Museum at the La Brea Tar Pits** displays fossils from the tar pits. ⊠ *Hancock Park, Miracle Mile* ⊕ *www.tarpits.org* ✉ *$7, free on 1st Tues. of each month.*

2 **Los Angeles County Museum of Art (LACMA).** Serving as the focal point of the museum district along Wilshire Boulevard, LACMA's vast, ency-clopedic collection of more than 100,000 objects dating from ancient times to the present is widely considered one of the most comprehensive in the western United States. Since opening in 1965 the museum has grown from three buildings to seven, stretching across a 20-acre campus. As part of an ambitious 10-year face-lift plan that is becoming a work of art in its own, entitled "Transformation," the museum is on a mission to integrate the seven buildings and outdoor spaces into a coherent whole. Phase one began with the opening of the impressive Broad Contemporary Art Museum (BCAM) in early 2008. With three vast floors, BCAM's purpose is to more fully integrate contemporary art into LACMA's program and explore the interplay art of current times with that of the past.

Fodor'sChoice ★

With rotating displays from its permanent collection, at any time it's possible to see items from LACMA's abundant holdings of works by leading Latin American artists, including Diego Rivera and Frida Kahlo; prominent Southern California artists; collections of Islamic and European art; paintings by Henri Matisse and Rene Magritte; and works by Paul Klee and Wassily Kandinsky, who taught at Germany's Bauhaus school in the 1920s; art representing the ancient civilizations of Egypt, the Near East, Greece, and Rome; plus a vast costume and textiles collection dating back to the 16th century.

The Pavilion for Japanese Art showcases scrolls, screens, drawings, paintings, textiles, and decorative arts from Japan; it's a particularly peaceful space, with natural light and a fountain on the ground floor that fills the building with the sound of flowing water. The Bing Center holds a research library, resource center, and film theater. The Boone's Children's Gallery on the soon-to-be "transformed" LACMA West end maintains an art-making mission through classes, interactive displays, and brightly colored decor. ⚠ Temporary exhibits sometimes require tickets purchased in advance, so check the calendar ahead of time. ⊠ *5905 Wilshire Blvd., Miracle Mile* ☎ *323/857–6000* ⊕ *www.lacma.org* ✉ *$12, free 2nd Tues. of month, after 5 policy: "pay what you wish."* ☉ *Mon., Tues., and Thurs. noon–8, Fri. noon–9, weekends 11–8.*

4 **Petersen Automotive Museum.** You don't have to be a gearhead to appreciate this building full of antique and unusual cars. The Petersen is one of the coolest museums in town, with some of the most unusual creations on wheels and rotating exhibits about the icons who drove them. ⊠ *6060 Wilshire Blvd., Miracle Mile* ☎ *323/930–2277* ⊕ *www.petersen.org* ✉ *$10* ☉ *Tues.–Sun. 10–6.*

Fodor'sChoice ★

WEST HOLLYWOOD

West Hollywood is not a place to see things (like museums or movie studios) as much as it is a place to do things—like go to a nightclub, eat at a world-famous restaurant, or attend an art gallery opening. Also thriving is an important interior-design and art-gallery trade. West Hollywood has always attracted the mavericks and the disenfranchised, and in the 1980s, a coalition of seniors, gays, and lesbians spearheaded a grassroots effort to bring cityhood to West Hollywood, which was still an unincorporated part of Los Angeles County. The coalition succeeded in 1984, and today West Hollywood is one of the most progressive cities in Southern California. It's also one of the most gay-friendly cities anywhere, with one-third of its population estimated to be either gay or lesbian.

WHAT TO SEE

❹ **Avenues of Art and Design.** Established in 1996, the area where Melrose Avenue and Robertson and Beverly boulevards become their own little district creates the Avenues of Art and Design with the distinction of being where fine, decorative, and culinary arts cater to the aesthetically minded. More than 300 businesses including over 30 art galleries; 100 antique, contemporary furniture, and interior design stores; and 40 restaurants are clustered here. While most galleries in this pedestrian-friendly area are very high-end, it doesn't cost anything to window shop. For one Saturday in June, the Avenues of Art and Design hosts the annual Art & Design Walk to give shoppers a chance to let loose in some of the hottest boutiques like John Varvatos, Phyllis Morris, James Perse, and Williams-Sonoma Home. ■TIP→ Periodically, usually on the first Saturday evening of the month, several of the galleries host group-opening receptions, known as Gallery Walks, to premiere new exhibits and artists. Contact the West Hollywood Convention and Visitors Bureau for information. ☎310/289–2525 or 800/368–6020 ⊕ www.avenuesartdesign.com.

❸ **Pacific Design Center.** Cesar Pelli designed these two architecturally intriguing buildings, one sheathed in blue glass (known as the Blue Whale), the other in green (the Green Whale). Together, they house 150 design showrooms, making this the largest interior design complex in the western United States. Though focused on the professional trade (meaning only pro decorators can shop the showrooms), the PDC has become more open over the past few years, with public events and some showroom access. Construction started on the new red building in the fall of 2007, with plans to open sometime at the end of 2010. The Downtown Museum of Contemporary Art has a small satellite **MOCA Gallery** (☎310/289–5233 ⊕ www.moca.org) here that showcases current artists and designers and hosts exhibit-related talks. Three cafés on the premises are also open to the public. ⊠ 8687 Melrose Ave., West Hollywood ☎310/657–0800 ⊕ www.pacificdesigncenter.com ⊙ Weekdays 9–5.

❺ **Sunset Boulevard.** One of the most fabled avenues in the world, Sunset Boulevard began humbly enough in the 18th century as a route from El Pueblo de Los Angeles (today's Downtown L.A.) to the ranches in the west and then to the Pacific Ocean. Now as it winds its way across the L.A. basin to the ocean, it cuts through gritty urban neighborhoods and what used to be the working center of Hollywood's movie industry. In West Hollywood, it becomes the sexy and seductive Sunset Strip, then slips quietly into the tony environs of Beverly Hills and Bel-Air, twisting and winding past gated estates. Continuing on past UCLA in Westwood, through Brentwood and Pacific Palisades, Sunset finally descends to the beach, the edge of the continent, and the setting sun.

6 **Sunset Strip.** For 60 years the Hollywood's night owls have headed for
★ the 1¾-mi stretch of Sunset Boulevard between Crescent Heights Boulevard on the east and Doheny Drive on the west, known as the Sunset Strip. In the 1930s and '40s, stars such as Tyrone Power, Errol Flynn, Norma Shearer, and Rita Hayworth came for wild evenings of dancing and drinking at nightclubs like Trocadero, Ciro's, and Mocambo. By the '60s and '70s, the Strip had become the center of rock and roll for acts like Johnny Rivers, the Byrds, and the Doors. The '80s punk riot gave way to hair metal lead by Mötley Crüe and Guns N' Roses on the stages of the **Whisky A Go-Go** (✉ *8901 Sunset Blvd., West Hollywood* ☎ *310/652–4202* ⊕ *www.whiskyagogo.com*) and **The Roxy** (✉ *9009 Sunset Blvd., West Hollywood* ☎ *310/276–2222* ⊕ *www. theroxyonsunset.com*). Nowadays it's the **Viper Room** (✉ *8852 Sunset Blvd., West Hollywood* ☎ *310/358–1880* ⊕ *www.viperroom.com*), the **House of Blues** (✉ *8430 Sunset Blvd., West Hollywood* ☎ *323/848–5100* ⊕ *www.hob.com*), and the **Key Club** (✉ *9039 Sunset Blvd., West Hollywood* ☎ *310/274–5800* ⊕ *www.keyclub.com*), where you'll find on-the-cusp actors, rock stars, club-hopping regulars, and out-of-towners all mingling over drinks and live music. Parking and traffic around the Strip can be tough on weekends—expect to pay around $10–$25 to park, which can take a bite out of your partying budget—but the time and money may be worth it if you plan to make the rounds. Most clubs are within walking distance of each other.

BEVERLY HILLS AND CENTURY CITY

If you only have a day to see L.A., see Beverly Hills. Love it or hate it, it delivers on a dramatic, cinematic scale of wealth and excess. Beverly Hills is the town's biggest movie star, and she always lets those willing to part with a few bills into her year-round party. Just remember to bring your sunscreen, sunglasses . . . and money for parking. Boutiques and restaurants line the palm tree–fringed sidewalks. People tend to stroll, not rush. Shopping ranges from the accessible and familiar (Pottery Barn) to the unique, expensive, and architecturally stunning (Prada on Rodeo Drive).

A few blocks west on Santa Monica Boulevard is Beverly Hills's buttoned-down brother, Century City. If Beverly Hills is about spending money, Century City is about making it. This collection of glass office towers and a favorite outdoor mall is home to entertainment companies, law firms, and investment corporations. It's a peculiarly precise place, with angular fountains, master-planned boulevards, and pedestrian bridges connecting lawyers to their turkey tahini wraps.

VISITING THE STUDIOS

If you've never been to L.A.—or if you have, and are coming back with your kids—it's hard to resist the allure of being where the magic happens among the cameras, props, and back-lots of Tinseltown's studios.

(above) Go to Universal Studios for a big-bang theme park experience of moviemaking. (lower right) Warner Bros. Studios. (upper right) Paramount Pictures.

Nearly 70 percent of all L.A.'s entertainment productions happen in the Valley. And to really get behind the scenes, studio tours are the best way for mere mortals to get close to where celebs and the industry's crème-de-la-crème work.

Most tours last several hours, and allow you to see where hit television shows are filmed, spot actors on the lot, and visit movie soundstages—some directors even permit visitors on the set while shooting.

Specific sights change daily, so if there's something in particular you're dying to see, it's best to call ahead and ask.

IT'S ALL ABOUT LOCATION

Many L.A. first-timers make the incorrect assumption that because Hollywood is where all the action takes place, it's also where the stars work.

The only studio that's still located in Hollywood is Paramount; Warner Bros., Universal Studios Hollywood, and NBC Television Studios are north of Hollywood, in Universal City and Burbank.

PARAMOUNT PICTURES

BEST FOR
Paramount offers an intimate—8 to 10 people at a time—two-hour tour of its 63-acre lot. It's probably the most authentic studio tour you can take, giving you a real sense of the film industry's history. Paramount is the only studio left in Hollywood—all the others are in Burbank or in Universal City.

TOURING BASICS
Guests primarily visit sets and soundstages that are not in use—though directors occasionally allow visitors during production, so there's a decent chance of seeing a celebrity. Other stops include the New York back-lot and the studio's iconic Bronson Gate.

WHAT'S BEEN FILMED HERE
Chinatown, The Godfather, The Untouchables, Breakfast at Tiffany's, Austin Powers, Cloverfield, Titanic, Star Trek, and the most recent installment of Indiana Jones are just a few of the notable films shot here.

TIPS FOR TOURING
For an inexpensive lunch costing as little as $10, try The Café, the studio's commissary, a buffet where you can grab everything from sandwiches to pizza to Mexican food.

GETTING HERE
From Melrose Avenue, enter on Windsor Boulevard at the main gate. Parking is just north of the gate on the left, and there's additional parking at the lot on the southwest corner of Windsor and Melrose.

VISITOR INFORMATION
Kids must be 12 or older to tour the studio. ⊠ *5555 Melrose Ave., Hollywood* ☎ *323/956–1777* ⊕ *www.paramount. com* ✉ *Tours weekdays by reservation only, $35.*

WARNER BROS. STUDIOS

BEST FOR
If you're looking for an authentic behind-the-scenes look at how films and TV shows are made, head to this major studio center, one of the world's busiest. There aren't many bells and whistles here, but you'll get a much better idea of production work than you will at Universal Studios.

TOURING BASICS
On the VIP Tour, which lasts almost 90 minutes, you'll see the studio from inside an electric cart with 11 others. The specifics of what you'll actually see changes daily but, after viewing a short film on WB movies and shows, you'll be taken by tram to visit sets like the often-recycled Anytown U.S.A.,

(above) Sometimes you can get lucky and meet your favorite stars at Universal Studios.

as well as soundstages and back-lot locations for popular films and shows. The studio's museum has a floor dedicated to *Casablanca* and 85 years of WB history; another belongs exclusively to Harry Potter. The tour ends here, and you can explore it at your leisure.

The Deluxe Tour is a five-hour affair that takes you onto working production sets and includes lunch at the commissary (great stargazing ops).

WHAT'S BEEN FILMED HERE
Without A Trace, *The Mentalist*, *Friends*, the original *Ocean's Eleven*, *Casablanca*, and *Rebel Without a Cause*.

TIPS FOR TOURING
Showing up about 20 minutes before the scheduled time of your tour is recommended. VIP Tours leave continuously throughout the day; the Deluxe Tour leaves daily at 10:20 AM.

GETTING HERE
The studio's Web site (⊕ *www2. warnerbros.com/vipstudiotour*) provides good directions from all parts of the city, including Downtown (take 101 north).

VISITOR INFORMATION
✉ *3400 W. Riverside Dr., Burbank* ☎ *818/972–8687* ⊕ *www.wbsf.com* ⌨ *VIP Tour is $48 per person; the Deluxe Tour is $225 per person* ◷ *Weekdays 8:30–4:30. Children under 8 are not admitted. Advance booking is recommended. Parking is $7 at Gate 6.*

UNIVERSAL STUDIOS HOLLYWOOD

BEST FOR
This studio is more theme park (read lots of roller coasters and thrill rides) than backstage pass, though its studio tour does provide a good firsthand look at familiar TV shows and major movie sets.

TOURING BASICS
The tour lasts about an hour; you'll sit on a tram with nearly 100 other people and pass back-lots, dressing rooms, and production offices.

There's also a VIP Tour where you can explore a historic, working movie studio's back-lot and score a closer view of sets, costumes, and props. It's a full day outing that includes a two-hour studio tour, lunch, valet parking, and front-of-the-line privileges for the theme park's thrill rides.

WHAT'S BEEN FILMED HERE
See the airplane wreckage from *War of the Worlds,* the *Desperate Housewives'* Wisteria Lane, *King Kong* miniatures, *Psycho's* infamous Bates Motel, and the animatronic Great White Shark from *Jaws.*

TIPS FOR TOURING
You may be tempted to get the $109 pass that takes you to the front of the line. Try to resist this splurge. Once inside, you can see that most of the lines move quickly or are nonexistent. Pass on the premium and spend it on a decent lunch outside the park.

GETTING HERE
The park is located in Universal City. From Hollywood, take the 101 Hollywood Freeway north to Universal Studios Boulevard.

VISITOR INFORMATION
✉ *100 Universal City Plaza, Universal City* ☎ *818/622–3801* ⊕ *www.universalstudioshollywood.com* 🎫 *Ticket prices for the studio tour are included in park admission ($69); $239 VIP tour, parking is $14; $10 after 3 PM. Preferred parking is available for $20* ☽ *Contact park for seasonal hrs.*

visit an old broadcast booth, listen to bands rehearsing, view setups for jokes, check out rehearsals, see sets under construction, and visit the prop warehouse and the studios where shows are taped.

WHAT'S FILMED HERE
The Tonight Show with Jay Leno, Days of Our Lives, The Ellen DeGeneres Show, and *Access Hollywood.*

TIPS FOR TOURING
If you decide to take a last-minute studio tour, definitely call ahead; low ticket prices and advance purchase means tickets tend to sell out quickly the day of.

GETTING HERE
The studio is located in Burbank. The best way to get here from Downtown or the Hollywood area is to take the Hollywood Freeway 101 North to Barham Boulevard, which forks off onto West Olive Avenue. Make a right on West Alameda Avenue and then a right on Bob Hope Drive. The studio is on the right.

VISITOR INFORMATION
✉ *3000 W. Alameda Ave., Burbank* ☎ *818/840–3537* 🎫 *Tours $8.50. There's no minimum age requirement for children; those under 4 are free.*

NBC TELEVISION STUDIOS

BEST FOR
In contrast to other studio tours, you get to walk on the set rather than being confined to a tram. It's the only TV studio that offers a behind-the-scenes look at production.

TOURING BASICS
The guided 70-minute tour—a rare opportunity to see the inside of a TV studio—emphasizes the history of the station from its roots in radio. You'll

(below) Jurassic Park—the Ride at Universal Studios

4

WHAT TO SEE

❷ **Paley Center for Media.** Formerly the Museum of Television and Radio,
★ this institution changed its name in 2007 with a look toward a future
that encompasses all media in the ever-evolving world of entertainment
and information. Reruns are taken to a curated level in this sleek stone-
and-glass building, designed by Getty architect Richard Meier. A sister
to the New York location, the Paley Center carries a duplicate of its
collection: more than 100,000 programs spanning eight decades. Search
for your favorite commercials and television shows on easy-to-use computers. A radio program listening room provides cozy seats supplied
with headphones playing snippets of a variety of programming from
a toast to Dean Martin to an interview with John Lennon. Frequent
seminars with movers 'n' shakers from the film, television, and radio
world are big draws, as well as screenings of documentaries and short
films. Free parking is available in the lot off Santa Monica Blvd. ⊠ *465
N. Beverly Dr., Beverly Hills* ☎ *310/786–1000* ⊕ *www.paleycenter.org*
⊙ *Wed.–Sun. noon–5.*

❶ **Rodeo Drive.** The ultimate shopping indulgence—Rodeo Drive is one of
Fodor's Choice   Southern California's bona fide tourist attractions; here you can shop
★ for five-digit jewelry or a $35 handbag. The arts of window-shopping
and window displays play out among the retail elite: Tiffany & Co.,
Gucci, Jimmy Choo, Valentino, Harry Winston, Prada . . . you get the
picture. Several nearby restaurants have patios where you can sip a
drink while watching career shoppers in their size 2 threads saunter
by with shopping bags stuffed with superfluous delights. At the southern end of Rodeo Drive (at Wilshire Boulevard) is **Via Rodeo,** a curvy
cobblestone street designed to resemble a European shopping area or
a Universal Studio backlot—take your pick. The holidays bring a special magic to Rodeo and the surrounding streets with twinkling lights,
swinging music, and colorful banners. ⊠ *Beverly Hills.*

THE WESTSIDE

For some privileged Los Angelenos, the city begins west of La Cienega
Boulevard, where keeping up with the Joneses becomes an epic pur-
suit. Chic, attractive neighborhoods with coveted postal codes—Bel-Air,
Brentwood, Westwood, West Los Angeles, and Pacific Palisades—are
home to power couples pushing power kids in power strollers. Still, the
Westside is rich in culture—and not just entertainment-industry culture.
It's home to UCLA, the monumental Getty Center, and the engrossing
Museum of Tolerance.

WHAT TO SEE

❾ **The Getty Center.** With its curving walls and isolated hilltop perch, the
⊙ Getty Center resembles a pristine fortified city of its own. You may have
Fodor's Choice   been lured up by the beautiful views of L.A. (on a clear day stretching all
★ the way to the Pacific Ocean), but the architecture, uncommon gardens,
and fascinating art collections will be more than enough to capture and
hold your attention. When the sun is out, the complex's rough-cut travertine marble skin seems to soak up the light. You'll need to do some

A mural depicting Hollywood legends like (John Wayne, Elvis Presley, and Marilyn Monroe are pictured here) adorns a wall of West Hollywood's Stella Adler Academy on Highland Avenue.

advance planning, since parking reservations are sometimes required during vacation periods, but the experience is well worth the effort.

Getting to the center involves a bit of anticipatory lead-up. At the base of the hill, a pavilion disguises the underground parking structure. From there you either walk or take a smooth, computer-driven tram up the steep slope, checking out the Bel-Air estates across the humming 405 freeway. The five pavilions that house the museum surround a central courtyard and are bridged by walkways. From the courtyard, plazas, and walkways, you can survey the city from the San Gabriel Mountains to the ocean.

Inside the pavilions are the galleries for the permanent collections of European paintings, drawings, sculpture, illuminated manuscripts, and decorative arts, as well as American and European photographs. The Getty's collection of French furniture and decorative arts, especially from the early years of Louis XIV (1643–1715) to the end of the reign of Louis XVI (1774–92), is renowned for its quality and condition; you can see a pair of completely reconstructed salons. In the paintings galleries, a computerized system of louvered skylights allows natural light to filter in, creating a closer approximation of the conditions in which the artists painted. Notable among the paintings are Rembrandt's *The Abduction of Europa,* Van Gogh's *Irises,* Monet's *Wheatstack, Snow Effects,* and *Morning,* and James Ensor's *Christ's Entry into Brussels.*

If you want to start with a quick overview, pick up the brochure in the entrance hall that guides you to 15 highlights of the collection. There's also an instructive audio tour ($5) with commentaries by art historians. Art information rooms with multimedia computer stations contain

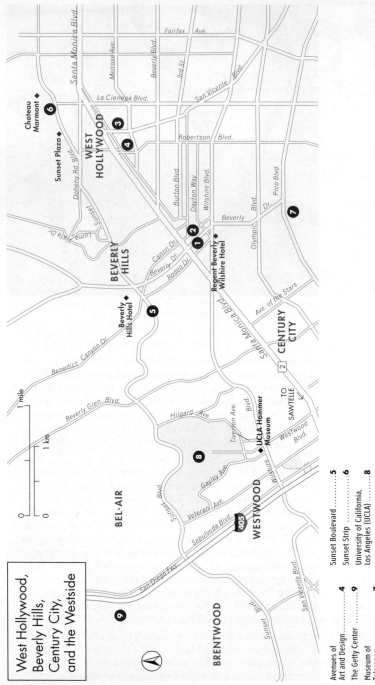

West Hollywood,
Beverly Hills,
Century City,
and the Westside

more details about the collections. The complex includes an upscale restaurant (reservations required) with panoramic window views, and two outdoor coffee bars. ■TIP➔ On-site parking is subject to availability and usually fills up by late afternoon on holidays and summer weekends, so try to come early in the day. You may also take public transportation (MTA Bus 561 or Santa Monica Big Blue Bus 14). ⊠ *1200 Getty Center Dr., Brentwood* ☎ *310/440–7300* ⊕ *www.getty.edu* ✎ *Free, parking $15* ⊗ *Tues.–Fri 10–5:30, Sat. 10–9, Sun. 10–5:30.*

❼ Museum of Tolerance. Using interactive technology, this important museum (part of the Simon Wiesenthal Center) challenges visitors to confront bigotry and racism. One of the most affecting sections covers the Holocaust, with film footage of deportation scenes and simulated sets of concentration camps. Each visitor is issued a "passport" bearing the name of a child whose life was dramatically changed by the German Nazi rule and by World War II; as you go through the exhibit, you learn the fate of that child. Anne Frank artifacts are part of the museum's permanent collection. Interactive exhibits include the "Millennium Machine," which engages visitors in finding solutions to human rights abuses around the world, and the "Point of View Diner," a re-creation of a 1950s diner, red booths and all, that "serves" a menu of controversial topics on video jukeboxes. Recent renovations brought a new youth action floor and revamped 300-seat theater space. To ensure a visit to this popular museum, make reservations in advance (especially for Friday, Sunday, and holidays) and plan to spend at least three hours there. Testimony from Holocaust survivors is offered at specified times. Museum entry stops at least two hours before the actual closing time. A photo ID is required for admission and all visitors must go through a security search. ⊠ *9786 W. Pico Blvd., just south of Beverly Hills* ☎ *310/553–8403* ⊕ *www.museumoftolerance.com* ✎ *$15* ⊗ *Weekdays 10–5, Sun. 11–5, early close at 3 PM Fri. Nov.–Mar.*

❽ University of California, Los Angeles (UCLA). With spectacular buildings such as a Romanesque library, the parklike UCLA campus makes for a fine stroll through one of California's most prestigious universities. In the heart of the north campus, the **Franklin Murphy Sculpture Garden** contains more than 70 works of artists such as Henry Moore and Gaston Lachaise. The **Mildred Mathias Botanic Garden,** which contains some 5,000 species of plants from all over the world in a 7-acre outdoor garden, is in the southeast section of the campus and is accessible from Tiverton Avenue. West of the main-campus bookstore, the **Morgan Center Hall of Fame** displays the sports memorabilia and trophies of the university's athletic departments. Many visitors head straight to the **Fowler Museum at UCLA** (☎ *310/825–4361* ⊕ *www.fowler.ucla.edu*), which presents exhibits on the world's diverse cultures and visual arts, especially those of Africa, Asia, Oceania, and Native and Latin America. Museum admission is free; use parking lot 4 off Sunset Boulevard ($8). It's open Wednesday–Sunday noon–5, Thursday until 8 PM.

Campus maps and information are available at drive-by kiosks at major entrances daily, and free 90-minute walking tours of the campus are given on weekdays at 10:15 and 2:15 and Saturday at 10:15. Call ☎ *310/825–8764* for reservations, which are required several days to two weeks in advance. The campus has cafés, plus bookstores selling UCLA Bruins paraphernalia. The main-entrance gate is on Westwood Boulevard. Campus parking costs $8. ⊠ *Bordered by Le Conte, Hilgard, and Gayley Aves. and Sunset Blvd., Westwood* ⊕ *www.ucla.edu.*

SANTA MONICA, VENICE, AND MALIBU

Hugging the Santa Monica Bay in an arch, the desirable communities of Malibu, Santa Monica, and Venice move from the ultrarich, ultra-casual Malibu to the bohemian/seedy Venice. What they have in common, however, is cleaner air, mild temperatures, horrific traffic, and an emphasis on the beach-focused lifestyle that many people consider the hallmark of Southern California.

WHAT TO SEE

⑤ Getty Villa Malibu. Feeding off the cultures of ancient Rome, Greece, and Etruria, the remodeled Getty Villa opened in 2006 with much fanfare—and some controversy concerning the acquisition and rightful ownership of some of the Italian artifacts on display. The antiquities are astounding, but on a first visit even they take a backseat to their environment. This megamansion sits on some of the most valuable coastal property in the world. Modeled after an Italian country home, the Villa dei Papiri in Herculaneum, the Getty Villa includes beautifully manicured gardens, reflecting pools, and statuary. The largest and most lovely garden, the Outer Peristyle, gives you glorious views over a rectangular reflecting pool and geometric hedges to the Pacific. The new structures blend thoughtfully into the rolling terrain and significantly improve the public spaces, such as the new outdoor amphitheater, gift store, café, and entry arcade. ■**TIP→** An advance timed entry ticket is required for admission. Tickets are free and may be ordered from the Web site or by phone. ⊠ *17985 Pacific Coast Hwy., Pacific Palisades* ☎ *310/440–7300* ⊕ *www.getty.edu* ☞ *Free, reservations required. Parking $15, cash only* ☉ *Wed.–Mon. 10–5.*

④ Malibu Lagoon State Beach. Bird-watchers, take note: in this 5-acre marshy area you could spot egrets, blue herons, avocets, and gulls. (You'll need to stay on the boardwalks so as not to disturb their habitats.) The path leads out to a rocky stretch of beach and makes for a pleasant stroll. You're also likely to spot a variety of marine life. The lagoon is open 24 hours and is particularly enjoyable in the early morning and at sunset. The parking lot has limited hours but street-side parking is usually available at off-peak times. ⊠ *23200 Pacific Coast Hwy., Malibu.*

① Santa Monica Pier. Souvenir shops, a psychic adviser, carnival games, arcades, eateries, and **Pacific Park** are all part of this truncated pier at the foot of Colorado Boulevard below Palisades Park. The pier's trademark 46-horse Looff Carousel, built in 1922, has appeared in several films, including *The Sting.* Free concerts are held on the pier in summer. ⊠ *Colorado Ave. and the ocean, Santa Monica* ☎ *310/458–8900* ⊕ *www.santamonicapier.org* ☞ *Rides $2.50* ☉ *Mon. and Thurs. 11–5, Fri.–Sun. 11–7.*

② Third Street Promenade. Stretch your legs along this pedestrians-only three-block stretch of 3rd Street, just a whiff away from the Pacific, lined with

Fodor'sChoice
★

★

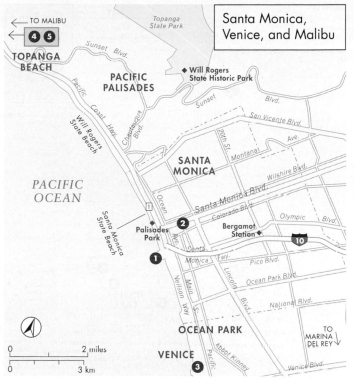

Santa Monica,
Venice, and Malibu

jacaranda trees, ivy-topiary dinosaur fountains, strings of lights, and branches of nearly every major U.S. retail chain. Outdoor cafés, street vendors, movie theaters, and a rich nightlife make this a main gathering spot for locals and visitors, as well as street musicians and performance artists. Plan a night just to take it all in or take an afternoon for a long people-watching stroll. There's plenty of parking in city structures on the streets flanking the promenade. ⊠ *3rd St. between Wilshire Blvd. and Broadway, Santa Monica* ⊕ *www.thirdstreetpromenade.com.*

❸ **Venice Boardwalk.** "Boardwalk" may be something of a misnomer—it's
Fodor's Choice really a five-block section of paved walkway—but this L.A. mainstay
★ delivers year-round action. Bicyclists zip along and bikini-clad roller-bladers attract crowds as they put on impromptu demonstrations, vying for attention with magicians, fortune-tellers, a chain-saw juggler, and sand mermaids. At the adjacent Muscle Beach, bulging bodybuilders with an exhibitionist streak pump iron at an outdoor gym. You can rent in-line skates, roller skates, and bicycles (some with baby seats) at the south end of the boardwalk (officially known as Ocean Front Walk), along Washington Street near the Venice Pier.

THE SAN FERNANDO VALLEY

Some Angelenos swear, with a sneer, that they have never set foot in "the Valley." But without the dreaded Valley, the world would be without Disney, Warner Bros., Universal Studios, NBC, *Seinfeld, Desperate Housewives,* and a large chunk of pornography. In fact, nearly 70% of all entertainment productions in L.A. happen here. That means that some very rich entertainment executives regularly undergo sweltering summer temperatures, smog, and bumper-to-bumper traffic on their trek from their Westside and Malibu compounds to their less glamorous workplaces.

WHAT TO SEE

❸ NBC Television Studios. In the entertainment sector of Burbank, the NBC studios is home to some of TV's most popular talk shows, soap operas, and news broadcasts. An hour-long tour gives you behind-the-scenes access to shows including the *Tonight Show with Jay Leno, Days of Our Lives,* the *Ellen DeGeneres Show, Access Hollywood,* and L.A. studios for the *Today Show* and other news programs. If you'd like to be part of a live studio audience, free tickets are available for tapings of the various NBC shows. ⊠ *3000 W. Alameda Ave., Burbank* ☎ *818/840–3537* ⌨ *Tours $8.50.*

★ **The Ronald Reagan Presidential Library and Museum.** On 100 acres high up in the hills of Simi Valley is the final resting place of President Ronald Reagan along with an extensive museum that chronicles his early days as a Hollywood movie star, the two terms he served as governor of California, and his journey to the presidency. A massive new pavilion shelters the Air Force One plane that flew Reagan and six other presidents from 1973–2001. Give yourself a good three hours to get through it all; a guided tour is your best bet. Don't forget to step outside to take time to enjoy the spectacular views and pay your respects at Reagan's grave site. The library holds more than 50 million pages of presidential papers, photographs, film, video, audio, and books. It takes at least half an hour to drive here from Downtown L.A. ⊠ *40 Presidential Dr., Simi Valley* ☎ *800/410–8354* ⊕ *www.reaganfoundation. org* ⊠ *$12* ⊙ *Daily 10–5.*

4

Santa Monica Mountains National Recreation Area. The line that forms the boundary of the San Fernando Valley is one of the most famous thoroughfares in this vast metropolis. **Mulholland Drive** cuts through the Santa Monica Mountains National Recreation Area, a vast parkland that stretches along the top and west slopes of the Santa Monica Mountains from Hollywood to the Ventura County line. Driving the length of the hilltop road is slow and can be treacherous, but the rewards are sensational views of valley and city on each side and expensive homes along the way. The park incorporates several local and state parks, including Will Rogers and Malibu Lagoon. Large scenic portions of these oak-studded hills were owned at one time by such Hollywood stars as Ronald Reagan and Bob Hope. They provided location sites for many movies; the grassy rolling hillside continues to serve a stand-in for the Wild West. Sets at the **Paramount Ranch** backlot (⊠ *2813 Cornell Rd., Agoura Hills*) have been preserved and continue to be used as location sites. Rangers regularly conduct tours of the Paramount Ranch, where you can see sets used by *M*A*S*H* and *Dr. Quinn, Medicine Woman*. This expansive area provides plenty of hiking and picnicking trails. Pick up a map in the ranger's station. To reach Mulholland Drive from Hollywood, go via Outpost Drive off Franklin Avenue or Cahuenga Boulevard west via Highland Avenue north. Note that it changes from Mulholland Drive to Mulholland Highway when you cross Calabasas. It ends at the coast north of Zuma Beach near Ventura. Keep an eye out for riders on horses as well as deer, raccoons, or a rare mountain lion along the way. Note: The visitor center is located outside of the park area. ⊠ *401 W. Hillcrest Dr., Thousand Oaks, 91360* ☎ *805/370–2301* ⊠ *Free* ⊙ *Daily 9–5.*

❶ **Universal Studios Hollywood.** While most first-time Los Angeles visitors
☾ consider this to be a must-see stop, bear in mind there many other
★ attractions that define Hollywood without the steep prices and tourist traps found here. Despite the amusement park clichés, hard-core sightseeing and entertainment junkies will make this required visiting.
■ **TIP→** If you get here when the park opens, you'll likely save yourself from long waits in line—arriving early pays off.

The first-timer favorite is the tram tour, during which you can experience the parting of the Red Sea; take a trip to old Mexico and Little

TIP SHEET: UNIVERSAL STUDIOS HOLLYWOOD

Who Will Especially Love This Park?

Universal Studios—a theme park and movie studio in one—is geared toward movie lovers of all stripes. Though the park is family oriented, it targets an older crowd; it's best for children 7-and-up and teens.

What's This Really Gonna Cost?

In addition to tickets, you'll need to pay $14 for parking ($10 after 3). For around $25 per person, you can purchase all-you-can-eat passes that allow you eat at select restaurants all day long. The VIP tour is $239 per person.

TOP 5 ATTRACTIONS:

The Simpsons Ride: The Simpson clan comes to life in this motion-sensor-filled attraction that resembles a flight simulator.

Revenge of the Mummy—the Ride: This fast indoor roller coaster runs forward and backward through a tomb as mummy warriors attack.

Shrek 4-D: Shrek and Donkey try to save Fiona in this multi-sensory 3-D movie ride.

Jurassic Park— the Ride: On this water ride, you'll see dinosaurs roaming through swamps and get attacked by a T-rex before dropping 70 feet down a waterfall.

Terminator 2: 3D: This action-packed adventure combines 3-D technology and an interactive show with live actors.

TIPS:

Don't Pay Full Price: Check the park's Web site for special discounts.

Keep Your Visit Short: Universal Studios is totally doable in one full day.

Skip the Standard Tour: Some Fodors.com users complain that the standard tour is touristy and crowded. Film buffs will love the VIP Experience, an actual behind-the-scenes tour of Universal Studios TV and film sets plus front-of-the-line access to theme park attractions—but be aware that it's quite expensive.

Get Ready For Coming Attractions: At this writing, the park was planning a Transformers-themed ride and a new show—Creature From the Black Lagoon, the Musical. Both are expected to open in 2010, along with a rebuilt King Kong attraction.

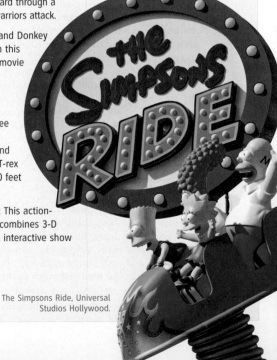

The Simpsons Ride, Universal Studios Hollywood.

Israel; duck from spitting creatures in Jurassic Park; visit *Desperate Housewives* neighborhood and Dr. Seuss's "Whoville"; escape a thunderstorm and flood; see the airplane wreckage of *War of the Worlds*; see the still-creepy *Psycho* house; meet a 30-foot-tall version of King Kong; be attacked by the ravenous killer shark of *Jaws* fame; and survive an all-too-real simulation of an earthquake that measures 8.3 on the Richter scale, complete with collapsing earth. The trams have audiovisual monitors that play video clips of the TV shows and movies shot on the sets you pass by as this guided trip circles the 415-acre complex all day long. ■TIP→ This tram ride is usually the best place to start, since it's on the lower level of the park, which gets really crowded in the afternoon.

Many attractions are based on Universal films and television shows, designed to give you a thrill in one form or another. Take your pick from the bone-rattling roller coaster *Revenge of the Mummy—The Ride* or the virtual world of *Terminator 2: 3D*, visit a jungle full of dinosaurs in *Jurassic Park—The Ride*, which includes an 84-foot water drop, or experience a simulated warehouse fire in *Backdraft* that is so real you can feel the heat.

Shrek 4-D reunites the film's celebrity voices to pick up where the movie left off in a 15-minute trailer of 3-D animation shown in an action simulation theater. *Fear Factor* Live and the House of Horrors are guaranteed to provide screams, while the Animal Actors show provides milder entertainment courtesy of some talented furry friends. The newest attraction based on the *Simpsons* animated series, opened in summer 2008, takes you on a journey like no other through their Springfield neighborhood in a ride that only the beloved, albeit cantankerous, Krusty the Klown could dream up.

Throughout the park you'll wander through prop-style settings of a French Village or travel back in time to the good ol' '50s, as costumed characters mingle with guests and pose for photos. Aside from the park, CityWalk is a separate venue, where you'll find a slew of shops, restaurants, nightclubs, and movie theaters, including IMAX 3-D. ✉ *100 Universal City Plaza, Universal City* ☎ *818/622–3801* ⊕ *www.universalstudioshollywood.com* ✑ *$69, parking $14 ($10 after 3)* ☽ *Contact park for seasonal hrs.*

❷ **Warner Bros. Studios.** If you're looking for a more authentic behind-the-scenes look at how films and TV shows are made, head to this major studio center. There aren't many bells and whistles here, but you'll get a much better idea of production work than you will at Universal Studios. You start with a short film on Warner Bros. movies and TV shows, then hop into a tram for a ride through the sets and soundstages of such favorites as *Friends, Gilmore Girls, ER, Casablanca,* and *Rebel Without A Cause.* You'll see the bungalows where icons such as Marlon Brando and Bette Davis spent time between shots, and the current production offices for Clint Eastwood and George Clooney. You might even spot a celeb or see a shoot in action—tours change from day to day depending on the productions taking place on the lot. Reservations are required. Call at least one week in advance and ask about provisions for people with disabilities; children under 8 are not admitted. Tours are given at least every hour, more frequently from May to September, and last two hours and 15 minutes. A five-hour deluxe tour, $195 including a VIP lunch, allows visitors to spend more time on the sets, with more ops for behind-the-scenes peeks and star spotting. ⊠ *3400 W. Riverside Dr., Burbank* ☎ *818/972–8687* ⊕ *www2.warnerbros.com/vipstudiotour/* 🎫 *$45* ⊘ *Weekdays 8:20–4:30.*

PASADENA AREA

Although seemingly absorbed into the general Los Angeles sprawl, Pasadena is a separate and distinct city. Noted for its Tournament of Roses, seen around the world each New Year's Day, the city brims with noteworthy spots, from its gorgeous Craftsman homes to its exceptional museums, particularly the Norton Simon and the Huntington Library, Art Collections, and Botanical Gardens. Where else can you see a Chaucer manuscript and rare cacti in one place?

WHAT TO SEE

❶ ★ Gamble House. Built by Charles and Henry Greene in 1908, this is a spectacular example of American Arts and Crafts bungalow architecture. The term *bungalow* can be misleading, since the Gamble House is a huge three-story home. To wealthy Easterners such as the Gambles (as in Procter & Gamble), this type of vacation home seemed informal compared with their mansions back home. What makes admirers swoon is the incredible amount of handcraftsmanship, including a teak staircase and cabinetry, Greene & Greene–designed furniture, and an Emil Lange glass door. The dark exterior has broad eaves, with sleeping porches on the second floor. An hour-long, docent-led tour of the Gamble's interior will draw your eye to the exquisite details. If you want to see more Greene & Greene homes, buy a self-guided tour map of the neighborhood in the bookstore. ⊠ *4 Westmoreland Pl., Pasadena* ☎ *626/793-3334* ⊕ *www.gamblehouse.org* 🎫 *$10* ⊘ *Thurs.–Sun. noon–3; tickets go on sale Thurs.–Sat. at 10, Sun. at 11:30. 1-hr tour every 20 min.*

❺ Fodor's Choice ★ Huntington Library, Art Collections, and Botanical Gardens. If you have time for only one stop in the Pasadena area, it should be the Huntington, built in the early 1900s as the home of railroad tycoon Henry E. Huntington. Henry and his wife, Arabella (who was his aunt by marriage), voraciously collected rare books and manuscripts, botanical specimens, and 18th-century British art. The institution they established became one of the most extraordinary cultural complexes in the world. ■ TIP→ Ongoing gallery renovations occasionally require some works from the permanent collection to be shifted to other buildings for display.

Among the highlights are John Constable's intimate *View on the Stour near Dedham* and the monumental *Sarah Siddons as the Tragic Muse,* by Joshua Reynolds. In the Virginia Steele Scott Gallery of American Art you can see paintings by Mary Cassatt, Frederic Remington, and more.

The library contains more than 700,000 books and 4 million manuscripts, including such treasures as a Gutenberg Bible, the Ellesmere manuscript of Chaucer's *Canterbury Tales,* George Washington's genealogy in his own handwriting, scores of works by William Blake, and

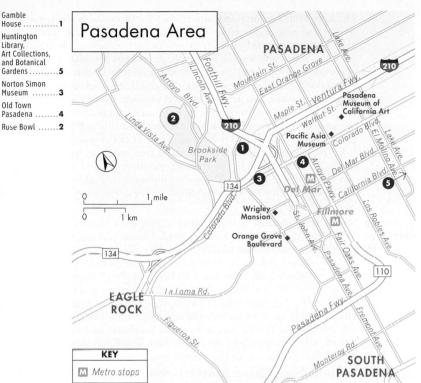

a world-class collection of early editions of Shakespeare. You'll find some of these items in the Library Hall with more than 200 important works on display. In 2006 the library acquired more than 60,000 rare books and reference volumes from the Cambridge, Massachusetts–based Bundy Library, making the Huntington the source of one of the biggest history of science collections in the world.

Although the art collections are increasingly impressive here, don't resist being lured outside into the stunning Botanical Gardens. From the main buildings, lawns and towering trees stretch out toward specialty areas. The 10-acre Desert Garden, for instance, has one of the world's largest groups of mature cacti and other succulents, arranged by continent. Visit this garden on a cool morning or in the late afternoon or a hot midday walk may be a little too authentic. In the Japanese Garden, an arched bridge curves over a pond; the area also has stone ornaments, a Japanese house, a bonsai court, and a Zen rock garden. There are collections of azaleas and 1,500 varieties of camellias. The 3-acre rose garden is displayed chronologically, so the development leading to modern varieties of roses can be observed; on the grounds is the charming **Rose Garden Tea Room,** where traditional afternoon tea is served. There are also herb, palm, and jungle gardens, plus the Shakespeare Garden, which blooms with plants mentioned in Shakespeare's works.

The Rose Hills Foundation Conservatory for Botanical Science, a massive greenhouse-style center with dozens of kid-friendly, hands-on exhibits illustrate plant diversity in various environments. (These rooms are quite warm and humid, especially the central rotunda, which displays rain-forest plants.) The new Bing Children's Garden is a tiny tots wonderland filled with opportunities for children to explore the ancient elements of water, fire, air, and earth. A classical Chinese Garden "Liu Fang Yuan" (or Garden of Flowing Fragrance) opened in spring 2008, the largest of its kind outside China. Work on this will continue for the next several years. A 1¼-hour guided tour of the botanical gardens is led by docents at posted times, and a free brochure with map and highlights is available in the entrance pavilion. ⊠ *1151 Oxford Rd., San Marino* ☎ *626/405–2100* ⊕ *www.huntington.org* ⊡ *$15 weekdays, $20 weekends, free 1st Thurs. of month* ☽ *Tues.–Fri. noon–4:30, weekends 10:30–4:30.*

❸
Fodor's Choice
★

Norton Simon Museum. Long familiar to television viewers of the New Year's Day Rose Parade, this low-profile brown building is more than just a background for the passing floats. It's one of the finest small museums anywhere, with an excellent collection that spans more than 2,000 years of Western and Asian art. It all began in the 1950s when Norton Simon (Hunt-Wesson Foods, McCalls Corporation, and Canada Dry) started collecting the works of Degas, Renoir, Gauguin, and Cézanne. His collection grew to include old masters, impressionists, and modern works from Europe and Indian and Southeast Asian art. After he retired, Simon reorganized the failing Pasadena Art Institute and continued to assemble one of the world's finest collections.

Today the Norton Simon Museum is richest in works by Rembrandt, Goya, Picasso, and, most of all, Degas: this is one of the only two U.S. institutions to hold the complete set of the artist's model bronzes (the other is New York's Metropolitan Museum of Art). Renaissance, baroque, and rococo masterpieces include Raphael's profoundly spiritual *Madonna with Child with Book* (1503), Rembrandt's *Portrait of a Bearded Man in a Wide-Brimmed Hat* (1633), and a magical Tiepolo ceiling, *The Triumph of Virtue and Nobility Over Ignorance* (1740–50). The museum's collections of impressionist (Van Gogh, Matisse, Cézanne, Monet, Renoir) and cubist (Braque, Gris) works are extensive. Several Rodin sculptures are placed throughout the museum. Head down to the bottom floor to see rotating exhibits and phenomenal Southeast Asian and Indian sculptures and artifacts, where graceful pieces like a Ban Chiang blackware vessel date to well before 1000 BC. Don't miss a living artwork outdoors: the garden, conceived by noted Southern California landscape designer Nancy Goslee Power. The tranquil pond was inspired by Monet's gardens at Giverny. ⊠ *411 W. Colorado Blvd., Pasadena* ☎ *626/449–6840* ⊕ *www.nortonsimon.org* ⊡ *$8* ☽ *Wed., Thurs., and Sat.–Mon. noon–6, Fri. noon–9.*

❹
★

Old Town Pasadena. Once the victim of decay, the area was revitalized in the 1990s as a blend of restored 19th-century brick buildings with a contemporary overlay. A phalanx of chain stores has muscled in, but there are still some homegrown shops and plenty of tempting cafés and restaurants. In the evening and on weekends, streets are packed with

people, and Old Town crackles with energy. The 12-block historic district is anchored along Colorado Boulevard between Pasadena Avenue and Arroyo Parkway.

❷ Rose Bowl. With an enormous rose, the city of Pasadena's logo, adorned on its exterior, it's hard to miss this 100,000-seat stadium, host of many Super Bowls and home to the UCLA Bruins. Set in Brookside Park at the wide bottom of an arroyo, the facility is closed except during games and special events such as the monthly Rose Bowl Swap Meet, which is considered the granddaddy of West Coast flea markets. ⊠ *1001 Rose Bowl Dr. at Rosemont Ave., Pasadena* ☎ *626/577–3100* ⊕ *www. rosebowlstadium.com* ☞ *$8 from 9* AM *on, $10 for 8–9* AM *entrance, $15 for 7–8* AM *entrance* ☉ *Flea market 2nd Sun. of month 9–4:30.*

LONG BEACH

Long Beach, long stuck in limbo between Los Angeles and Orange County in the minds of visitors, is steadily rebuilding its place in the Southern California scheme. Founded as a seaside resort in the 19th century, the city boomed in the early 20th century as oil discoveries drew in Midwesterners and Dust Bowlers. Bust followed boom and the city took on a somewhat raw, industrial, neglected feel. But a long-term redevelopment plan begun in the 1970s has finally come to fruition, turning the city back to its resort roots.

WHAT TO SEE

🐚 **Aquarium of the Pacific.** Sea lions, nurse sharks, and octopuses, oh my!—this aquarium focuses primarily on ocean life from the Pacific Ocean, with a detour into Australian birds. The main exhibits include lively sea lions, a crowded tank of various sharks, and ethereal sea dragons, which the aquarium has successfully bred in captivity. Most impressive is the multimedia attraction, *Whales: A Journey with Giants.* This panoramic film shows in the aquarium's Great Hall, and when the entire core of the aquarium goes dark, you suddenly feel as if you're swimming with the giants. Ask for showtimes at the information desk. For a nonaquatic experience, head over to Lorikeet Forest, a walk-in aviary full of the friendliest parrots from down under. Buy a cup of nectar and smile as you become a human bird perch. Since these birds spend most of their day feeding, you're guaranteed a noisy—and possibly messy—encounter. (A sink, soap, and towels are strategically placed at the exhibit exit.) If you're a true animal lover, book an up-close-and-personal Animal Encounters Tour ($90) to learn about and assist in care and feeding of the animals; or find out how the aquarium functions with the extensive Behind the Scenes Tour ($34.95); or just opt for an Overview Tour ($10) for a visit with all the details. ⊠ *100 Aquarium Way, Long Beach* ☎ *562/590–3100* ⊕ *www.aquariumofpacific.org* ☞ *$23.95* ☉ *Daily 9–6.*

Queen Mary. This beautifully preserved ocean liner was launched in 1934 and made 1,001 transatlantic crossings before finally berthing in Long Beach in 1967. It has gone through many periods of renovations since, but in 1993, the RMS Foundation took over ownership and restored its original art deco style. Private investors "Save the Queen" took over in early 2008 with plans to oversee ongoing renovations.

On board, you can take one of five tours, such as the informative Behind the Scenes walk or the downright spooky Ghost and Legends tour. You could stay for dinner at one of the ship's restaurants, partake in the utterly English tradition of afternoon tea ($35–$40, monthly themes, call for reservations ☎ 562/499–1772), or even spend the night in one of the wood-panel rooms. *1126 Queens Hwy., Long Beach ☎ 562/435–3511 ⊕ www.queenmary.com ⏱ Tours $24.95–$31.95, includes a self-guided audio tour ☉ Call for times and frequency of guided tours.*

WHERE TO EAT

4

BEVERLY HILLS, CENTURY CITY, AND HOLLYWOOD

BEVERLY HILLS

$–$$
DELI
✗ **Barney Greengrass.** Unlike your corner lox-and-bagel joint, this haute deli on the fifth floor of Barneys department store has an appropriately runway-ready aesthetic: limestone floors, mahogany furniture, and a wall of windows. On the outdoor terrace, at tables shaded by large umbrellas, you can savor flawless smoked salmon, sturgeon, and whitefish flown in fresh from New York. The deli closes at 6 PM. ⊠ *Barneys, 9570 Wilshire Blvd., Beverly Hills ☎ 310/777–5877* ▬ *AE, DC, MC, V ✛ 1:B3.*

$$$$
STEAK HOUSE
Fodor's Choice
★
✗ **CUT.** In a true collision of artistic titans, celebrity chef Wolfgang Puck presents his take on steak-house cuisine in a space designed by Getty Center architect Richard Meier. Its contemporary lines and cold surfaces recall little of the home comforts of this beloved culinary tradition. And like Meier's design, Puck's fare doesn't dwell much on the past, and a thoroughly modern crab Louis salad is the closest thing to nostalgia on the menu. Playful dishes like bone marrow flan take center stage before delving into a perfect dry-aged hunk of Nebraskan sirloin that proves the Austrian-born superchef understands our quintessentially American love affair. ⊠ *Regent Beverly Wilshire, 9500 Wilshire Blvd., Beverly Hills ☎ 310/276–8500 ⚂ Reservations essential* ▬ *AE, D, DC, MC, V ☉ Closed Sun. No lunch ✛ 1:B3.*

$$–$$$
ITALIAN
✗ **Enoteca Drago.** High-flying Sicilian chef Celestino Drago scores with this sleek but unpretentious version of an *enoteca* (a wine bar serving small snacks). It's an ideal spot for skipping through an Italian wine list—more than 50 wines are available by the glass—and enjoying a menu made up of small plates such as deep-fried olives, an assortment of cheeses and *salumi,* ricotta-stuffed zucchini flowers, or *crudo* (Italy's answer to ceviche) from the raw bar. Although the miniature mushroom-filled ravioli bathed in foie gras–truffle sauce is a bit luxurious for an enoteca, it's one of the city's best pasta dishes. Larger portions and pizzas are also available here, but the essence of an enoteca is preserved. ⊠ *410 N. Cañon Dr., Beverly Hills ☎ 310/786–8236 ⚂ Reservations essential* ▬ *AE, DC, MC, V ✛ 1:B3.*

BEST BETS FOR LOS ANGELES DINING

With thousands of restaurants to choose from, how will you decide where to eat? Fodor's writers and editors have selected their favorite restaurants by price, cuisine, and experience in the lists below. In the first column, Fodor's Choice properties represent the "best of the best" in every price category. You can also search by neighborhood—just peruse the following pages to find specific details about a restaurant in the full reviews later in the chapter.

Fodor's Choice ★

Angelini Osteria $$, p. 202
A.O.C. $$, p. 202
The Apple Pan ¢, p. 209
CUT $$$$, p. 197
The Dining Room $$$$, p. 210
Mélisse $$$$, p. 208
Mimosa $$, p. 203
Mori Sushi $$$, p. 210
Patina $$$$, p. 203
Philippe the Original ¢, p. 206
Pizzeria Mozza $$, p. 201
Providence $$$$, p. 201
Sona $$$$, p. 203
Spago Beverly Hills $$$$, p. 199
Urasawa $$$$, p. 199
Valentino $$$, p. 209
Yujean Kang's Gourmet Chinese Cuisine $$, p. 211

By Price

¢

The Apple Pan, p. 209
Philippe the Original, p. 206

$

Bombay Café, p. 209
La Serenata Gourmet, p. 209

$$

Angelini Osteria, p. 202
A.O.C., p. 202
Mimosa, p. 203
Pizzeria Mozza, p. 201
Traxx, p. 206
Yujean Kang's Gourmet Chinese Cuisine, p. 211

$$$

Campanile, p. 203
La Cachette, p. 199
Lucques, p. 203

Mori Sushi, p. 210
Valentino, p. 209
Water Grill, p. 207

$$$$

CUT, p. 197
The Dining Room, p. 210
Mélisse, p. 208
Patina, p. 203
Providence, p. 201
Sona, p. 203
Spago Beverly Hills, p. 199
Urasawa, p. 199

By Cuisine

AMERICAN

Apple Pan ¢, p. 209
Philippe the Original ¢, p. 206

CHINESE

Yujean Kang's Gourmet Chinese Cuisine $$, p. 211

FRENCH

La Cachette $$$, p. 199
Mélisse $$$$, p. 208
Mimosa $$, p. 203
Patina $$$$, p. 203

INDIAN

Bombay Café $, p. 209

ITALIAN

Angelini Osteria $$, p. 202
Pizzeria Mozza $$, p. 201
Valentino $$$, p. 209

JAPANESE

Mori Sushi $$$, p. 210
Urasawa $$$$, p. 199

MEDITERRANEAN

A.O.C. $$, p. 202
Campanile $$$, p. 203

MEXICAN

La Serenata Gourmet $, p. 209

NEW AMERICAN

The Dining Room $$$$, p. 210
Lucques $$$, p. 203
Sona $$$$, p. 203
Spago Beverly Hills $$$$, p. 199
Traxx $$, p. 206

PIZZA

Pizzeria Mozza $$, p. 201

SEAFOOD

Providence $$$$, p. 201
Water Grill $$$, p. 207

$$$$ ✕ **Spago Beverly Hills.** The famed flagship restaurant of Wolfgang Puck,
MODERN   Mr. Celebrity Chef himself, is justifiably a modern L.A. classic. The
Fodor'sChoice   illustrious restaurant centers on a buzzing outdoor courtyard shaded by
★   100-year-old olive trees. From an elegantly appointed table inside, you
can glimpse the exhibition kitchen and, on rare occasions, the affable
owner greeting his famous friends (these days, compliments to the chef
are directed to Lee Hefter). The people-watching here is worth the price
of admission, but the clientele is surprisingly inclusive, from the biggest
Hollywood stars to Midwestern tourists to foodies more preoccupied
with vintages of Burgundy than with faces from the cover of *People*.
Foie gras has disappeared, but the daily-changing menu might offer a
four-cheese pizza topped with truffles, *côte de boeuf* with Armagnac–
peppercorn sauce, Cantonese-style duck, and some traditional Austrian specialties. Acclaimed pastry chef Sherry Yard works magic with
everything from an ethereal apricot soufflé to Austrian *kaiserschmarrn*
(crème fraîche pancakes with fruit). ⊠ *176 N. Cañon Dr., Beverly Hills*
☎ *310/385–0880* ⚐ *Reservations essential* ▤ *AE, D, DC, MC, V* ⊙ *No
lunch Sun.* ✛ *1:B3.*

$$$$ ✕ **Urasawa.** Shortly after celebrated sushi chef Masa Takayama packed
JAPANESE   his knives for the Big Apple, his soft-spoken protégé Hiroyuki Ura-
Fodor'sChoice   sawa settled into the master's former digs. The understated sushi bar
★   has precious few seats, resulting in incredibly personalized service. At
a minimum of $350 per person for a strictly *omakase* (chef's choice)
meal, Urasawa remains the priciest restaurant in town, but the endless
parade of masterfully crafted, exquisitely presented dishes renders few
regrets. The maple sushi bar, sanded daily to a satinlike finish, is the
scene of a mostly traditional cuisine with magnificent ingredients. You
might be served velvety bluefin toro paired with beluga caviar, slivers
of foie gras to self-cook *shabu-shabu*–style, or egg custard layered with
uni (sea urchin), glittering with gold leaf. This is also the place to come
during *fugu* season, when the legendary, potentially deadly blowfish is
artfully served to adventurous diners. ⊠ *2 Rodeo, 218 N. Rodeo Dr.,
Beverly Hills* ☎ *310/247–8939* ⚐ *Reservations essential* ▤ *AE, DC,
MC, V* ⊙ *Closed Sun. No lunch* ✛ *1:B3.*

CENTURY CITY

$$$–$$$$ ✕ **La Cachette.** Owner-chef Jean-François Meteigner, regarded as one
FRENCH   of the city's top French chefs (he developed a following while cooking
★   at the revered, now-defunct L'Orangerie), continues to pamper a loyal
clientele at La Cachette. Here he combines traditional Gallic fare—
foie gras, Provençal bouillabaisse, rack of lamb—with a lighter, more
modern cuisine reflected in dishes like seared sea scallops in a harissa–
lobster emulsion with couscous. A dressy (well, by L.A. standards)
crowd makes sure that this elegant, flower-filled *cachette* (little hiding
place) doesn't stay hidden. ⊠ *10506 Santa Monica Blvd., Century City*
☎ *310/470–4992* ⚐ *Reservations essential* ▤ *AE, D, DC, MC, V* ⊙ *No
lunch weekends* ✛ *1:A3.*

4

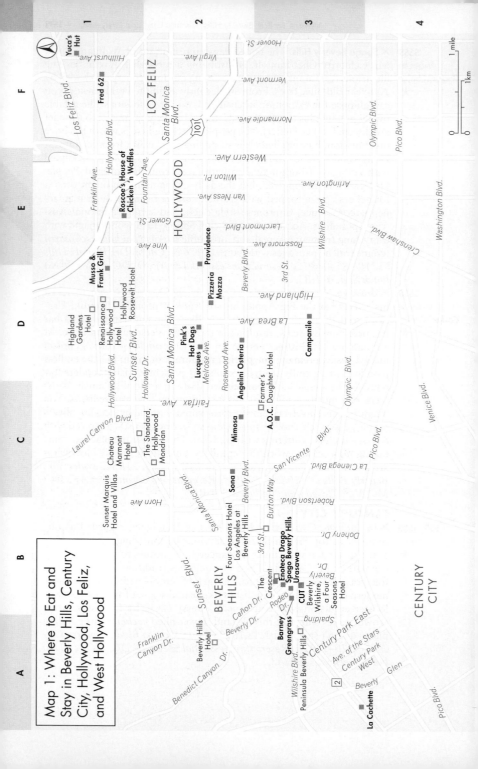

Map 1: Where to Eat and
Stay in Beverly Hills, Century
City, Hollywood, Los Feliz,
and West Hollywood

BEVERLY HILLS

CENTURY CITY

HOLLYWOOD

LOZ FELIZ

Yuca's
Hut

Fred 62

Roscoe's House of
Chicken 'n Waffles

Musso &
Frank Grill

Providence

Pizzeria
Mozza

Highland
Gardens
Hotel

Renaissance
Hollywood
Hotel

Hollywood
Roosevelt Hotel

Pink's
Hot Dogs

Lucques

Campanile

Angelini Osteria

Farmer's
Daughter Hotel

A.O.C.

Chateau
Marmont
Hotel

The Standard,
Hollywood
Mondrian

Mimosa

Sunset Marquis
Hotel and Villas

Sona

Four Seasons Hotel
Los Angeles at
Beverly Hills

Enoteca Drago
Spago Beverly Hills
Urasawa

CUT

Beverly
Wilshire,
a Four
Seasons
Hotel

Barney
Greengrass

The
Crescent

Beverly Hills
Hotel

Peninsula Beverly Hills

La Cachette

Los Feliz Blvd.

Hillhurst Ave.

Hollywood Blvd.

Franklin Ave.

Fountain Ave.

Santa Monica
Blvd.

Virgil Ave.

Hoover St.

Vermont Ave.

Normandie Ave.

Western Ave.

Wilton Pl.

Van Ness Ave.

Larchmont Blvd.

Rossmore Ave.

Beverly Blvd.

3rd St.

Wilshire
Blvd.

Crenshaw Blvd.

Washington Blvd.

Olympic Blvd.

Pico Blvd.

Arlington Ave.

Gower St.

Vine Ave.

Highland Ave.

La Brea Ave.

Rosewood Ave.

Melrose Ave.

Fairfax Ave.

Santa Monica Blvd.

Sunset Blvd.

Holloway Dr.

Hollywood Blvd.

Laurel Canyon Blvd.

Horn Ave.

Santa Monica Blvd.

Sunset Blvd.

Beverly Blvd.

San Vicente
Blvd.

La Cienega Blvd.

Robertson Blvd.

Burton Way

3rd St.

Doheny Dr.

Olympic Blvd.

Pico Blvd.

Venice Blvd.

Cañon Dr.

Beverly Dr.

Rodeo
Dr.

Beverly
Dr.

Spalding

Century Park East

Ave. of the Stars

Century Park
West

Beverly Glen

Pico Blvd.

Wilshire Blvd.

Franklin
Canyon Dr.

Benedict Canyon Dr.

HOLLYWOOD

101

1 mile

1 km

0

0

HOLLYWOOD

$$–$$$$
AMERICAN

✕ **Musso & Frank Grill.** Liver and onions, lamb chops, goulash, shrimp Louis salad, gruff waiters—you'll find all the old favorites here in Hollywood's oldest restaurant. A film-industry hangout since it opened in 1919, Musso & Frank still attracts the working studio set to its maroon faux-leather booths, along with tourists and locals nostalgic for Hollywood's golden era. Great breakfasts are served all day, but the kitchen's famous "flannel cakes" (pancakes) are served only until 3 PM. ✉ 6667 *Hollywood Blvd., Hollywood* ☎ 323/467–7788 ▭ *AE, DC, MC, V* ✪ *Closed Sun. and Mon.* ✛ 1:D1.

¢
AMERICAN
☺

✕ **Pink's Hot Dogs.** Orson Welles ate 18 of these hot dogs in one sitting, and you, too, will be tempted to order more than one. The chili dogs are the main draw, but the menu has expanded to include a Martha Stewart Dog (a 10-inch frank topped with mustard, relish, onions, tomatoes, sauerkraut, bacon, and sour cream). Since 1939 Angelenos and tourists alike have been lining up to plunk down some modest change for one of the greatest guilty pleasures in L.A. Pink's is open until 3 AM on weekends. ✉ 709 *N. La Brea Ave., Beverly–La Brea* ☎ 323/931–4223 ⚑ *Reservations not accepted* ▭ *No credit cards* ✛ 1:D2.

$$
ITALIAN
Fodor's Choice
★

✕ **Pizzeria Mozza.** The more casual half of Nancy Silverton, Mario Batali, and Joseph Bastianich's Mozza partnership gives newfound eminence to the humble "pizza joint." With traditional Mediterranean items like white anchovies, lardo, squash blossoms, and Gorgonzola, Mozza's pies—thin-crusted delights with golden, blistered edges—are much more Campania than California, and virtually every one is a winner. Utterly simple salads sing with vibrant flavors thanks to superb market-fresh ingredients, and daily specials include favorites like lasagna. Like the menu, the wine list is both interesting and affordable. ✉ 641 *N. Highland Ave., Hollywood* ☎ 323/297–0101 ⚑ *Reservations essential* ▭ *AE, MC, V* ✛ 1:D2.

$$$$
SEAFOOD
Fodor's Choice
★

✕ **Providence.** Since its opening in 2005, chef-owner Michael Cimarusti has elevated Providence to the ranks of America's finest seafood restaurants. Activity in the elegant dining room, dappled by subtle nautical accents, is smoothly overseen by co-owner–general manager Donato Poto. Obsessed with quality and freshness, the meticulous chef maintains a network of specialty purveyors, some of whom tip him off to their catch before it even hits the dock. This exquisite seafood then gets the Cimarusti treatment of French technique, traditional American themes, and Asian accents. Pastry chef Adrian Vasquez' exquisite desserts are not to be missed; consider a three- to eight-course dessert tasting menu. ✉ 5955 *Melrose Ave., Hollywood* ☎ 323/460–4170 ▭ *AE, DC, MC, V* ✪ *No lunch Mon.–Thurs. and weekends* ✛ 1:E2.

$–$$
SOUTHERN
☺

✕ **Roscoe's House of Chicken 'n Waffles.** The name of this casual eatery may sound a little weird—but don't be put off. Roscoe's is *the* place for real down-home Southern cooking. Just ask the patrons, who drive from all over L.A. for Roscoe's bargain-price fried chicken, wonderful waffles (which, by the way, turn out to be a great partner for fried chicken), buttery chicken livers, and grits. Although Roscoe's has the intimate feel of a smoky jazz club, those musicians hanging out here are just taking five. ✉ 1514 *N. Gower St., Hollywood* ☎ 323/466–7453 ⚑ *Reservations not accepted* ▭ *AE, D, DC, MC, V* ✛ 1:E1.

4

LOS FELIZ AND SILVER LAKE

$-$$ ✕ **Fred 62.** A tongue-in-cheek take on the American diner created by
ECLECTIC funky L.A. chef-restaurateur Fred Eric. The usual burgers and shakes
ⓒ are joined by choices like grilled salmon, Southern-style brisket, and a
"Poorest Boy" sandwich (crispy fried chicken, onions, and rémoulade
on a French roll). Toasters sit on every table and breakfasts range from
tofu scrambles to "Hunka Hunka Burnin' Love" (pancakes made with
peanut butter, chocolate chips, and banana). Like the neighborhood
itself, nobody is out of place here, with everybody from button-down
businesspeople to tattooed musicians showing up at some point during
its 24/7 cycle. ✉ *1850 N. Vermont Ave., Los Feliz* ☎ *323/667–0062*
♠ *Reservations not accepted* ▤ *AE, DC, MC, V* ✛ *1:F1.*

¢ ✕ **Yuca's Hut.** Blink and you'll miss this place, whose reputation far
MEXICAN exceeds its size (it may be the tiniest place to have ever won a James
Beard award). It's known for carne asada, carnitas, and *cochinita pibil*
(Yucatán-style roasted pork) tacos and burritos. This is a fast-food res-
taurant in the finest tradition—independent, family-owned, and sticking
to what it does best. The liquor store next door sells lots of Coronas to
Hut customers soaking up the sun on the makeshift parking-lot patio.
There's no chance of satisfying a late-night craving, though; it closes at
6 PM. ✉ *2056 N. Hillhurst Ave., Los Feliz* ☎ *323/662–1214* ♠ *Reservations not accepted* ▤ *No credit cards* ◷ *Closed Sun.* ✛ *1:F1.*

WEST HOLLYWOOD

$$-$$$ ✕ **A.O.C.** Since it opened in 2002, this restaurant and wine bar has
MEDITERRANEAN revolutionized dining in L.A., pioneering the small-plate format that has
Fodor's Choice now swept the city. The space is dominated by a long, candle-laden bar
★ serving more than 50 wines by the glass. There's also a charcuterie bar,
an L.A. rarity. The tapaslike menu is perfectly calibrated for the wine
list; you could pick duck confit, fried oysters with celery root rémoulade, an indulgent slab of pork *rillettes* (a sort of pâté), or just plunge
into one of the city's best cheese selections. Named for the acronym for
Appellation d'Origine Contrôlée, the regulatory system that ensures
the quality of local wines and cheeses in France, A.O.C. upholds the
standard of excellence. ✉ *8022 W. 3rd St., south of West Hollywood*
☎ *323/653–6359* ♠ *Reservations essential* ▤ *AE, DC, MC, V* ◷ *No
lunch* ✛ *1:3C.*

$$-$$$ ✕ **Angelini Osteria.** You might not guess it from the modest, rather con-
ITALIAN gested dining room, but this is one of L.A.'s most celebrated Italian
Fodor's Choice restaurants. The key is chef-owner Gino Angelini's thoughtful use of
★ superb ingredients, evident in dishes such as a salad of lobster, apples,
and pomegranate; and pumpkin tortelli with butter, sage, and asparagus.
An awesome lasagna verde, inspired by Angelini's grandmother, is not
to be missed. Whole branzino, crusted in sea salt, and boldly flavored
rustic specials (e.g., tender veal kidneys, rich oxtail stew) consistently
impress. An intelligent selection of mostly Italian wines complements
the menu, and desserts like the open-face marmalade tart are baked
fresh daily. ✉ *7313 Beverly Blvd., Beverly–La Brea* ☎ *323/297–0070*
▤ *AE, MC, V* ◷ *Closed Mon. No lunch weekends* ✛ *1:D2.*

$$$–$$$$
MEDITERRANEAN
★
✕**Campanile.** Chef-owner Mark Peel has mastered the mix of robust Mediterranean flavors with homey Americana. The 1926 building (which once housed the offices of Charlie Chaplin) exudes a lovely Renaissance charm and Campanile is one of L.A.'s most acclaimed and beloved restaurants. Appetizers may include butternut squash risotto topped with white truffles, while pan-seared black cod with white bean-eggplant puree and prime rib with tapenade are likely to appear as entrées. Thursday night, grilled cheese sandwiches are a huge draw, as the beloved five-and-dime classic is morphed into exotic creations. For an ultimate L.A. experience, come for weekend brunch on the enclosed patio. ✉ *624 S. La Brea Ave., Miracle Mile* ☎ *323/938–1447* ♨ *Reservations essential* ▭ *AE, D, DC, MC, V* ◎ *No dinner Sun.* ✛ *1:D3.*

$$$–$$$$
AMERICAN
★
✕**Lucques.** Formerly silent-film star Harold Lloyd's carriage house, this brick building has morphed into a chic restaurant that has elevated chef/co-owner Suzanne Goin to national prominence. In her veggie-intense contemporary American cooking, Goin uses finesse to balance tradition and invention. Consider the Italian heirloom pumpkin soup with sage and chestnut cream, Alaskan cod with acorn squash and chorizo-golden raisin vinaigrette, and short ribs with horseradish cream. Finish with the likes of acacia honey panna cotta with blood orange granita. ✉ *8474 Melrose Ave., West Hollywood* ☎ *323/655–6277* ♨ *Reservations essential* ▭ *AE, MC, V* ◎ *No lunch Sun.* ✛ *1:D2.*

$$–$$$
FRENCH
Fodor'sChoice
★
✕**Mimosa.** If you're craving a perfect Provençal meal, turn to chef Jean-Pierre Bosc's menu. There's *salade Lyonnaise,* served with a poached egg, a nifty tomato tarte Tatin, probably L.A.'s best bouillabaisse, soulful coq au vin, and hearty steak frites. The atmosphere is that of a classic bistro—balanced against a hint of elegance—with mustard walls, cozy banquettes, and crocks of cornichons and olives delivered to every table on arrival. ✉ *8009 Beverly Blvd., West Hollywood* ☎ *323/655–8895* ▭ *AE, DC, MC, V* ◎ *Closed Sun. and Mon. No lunch* ✛ *1:C2.*

$$$$
AMERICAN
Fodor'sChoice
★
✕**Sona.** Young, intense David Myers—one of the city's most exciting and unpredictable chefs—dazzles his fashionable followers here. A slab of polished granite topped with an exquisite orchid arrangement anchors the sleek dining room. If you're willing to spend the money, the prix-fixe tasting menus ($95 for six courses; $145 for nine) are the way to go, since they allow you to try many of Myers's distinctive dishes. An occasional item is too precious, but the successful dishes win out. Highlights might include seared foie gras paired with red plum jam, corn Maine diver scallops with coconut soup, and lobster risotto with shellfish emulsion. ✉ *401 N. La Cienega Blvd., West Hollywood* ☎ *310/659–7708* ♨ *Reservations essential* ▭ *AE, D, DC, MC, V* ◎ *Closed Sun. No lunch* ✛ *1:C2.*

DOWNTOWN

$$$$
FRENCH
Fodor'sChoice
★
✕**Patina.** In a bold move, chef-owner Joachim Splichal moved his flagship restaurant from Hollywood to downtown's striking Frank Gehry–designed Walt Disney Concert Hall. His gamble paid off—the contemporary space, surrounded by a rippled "curtain" of rich walnut, is an elegant, dramatic stage for the acclaimed restaurant's contemporary French cuisine. Specialties include copious amounts of foie

Continued on page 206

SOUTH-OF-THE-BORDER FLAVOR

From Cal-Mex burritos to Mexico City–style tacos, Southern California is a top stateside destination for experiencing Mexico's myriad culinary styles.

Many Americans are surprised to learn that the Mexican menu goes far beyond Tex-Mex (or Cal-Mex) favorites like burritos, chimichangas, enchiladas, fajitas, and nachos—many of which were created or popularized stateside. Indeed, Mexico has rich, regional food styles, like the complex *mole* sauces of Puebla and Oaxaca and the fresh *ceviches* of Veracruz, as well as the trademark snack of Mexico City: tacos.

In Southern California, tacos are an obsession, with numerous blogs and Web sites dedicated to the quest for the perfect taco. They're everywhere—in ramshackle taco stands, roving taco trucks, and strip-mall taquerias. Whether you're looking for a cheap snack or a lunch on-the-go, SoCal's taco selection can't be beat. But be forewarned: there may not be an English menu. Here we've noted unfamiliar taco terms, along with other potentially new-to-you items from the Mexican menu.

THIRST QUENCHERS

Spanish for "fresh water," *agua fresca* is a nonalcoholic Mexican drink made from fruit, rice, or seeds that are blended with sugar and water. Fruit flavors like lemon, lime, and watermelon are common. Other varieties include *agua de Jamaica*, flavored with red hibiscus petals; *agua de horchata*, a cinnamon-scented rice milk; and, *agua de tamarindo*, a bittersweet variety flavored with tamarind. If you're looking for something with a little more kick, try a *Michelada*, a beer that has been enhanced with a mixture of lime juice, chili sauce, and other savory ingredients. It's typically served in a salt-rimmed glass with ice.

DECODING THE MENU

Ceviche—Citrus-marinated seafood appetizer from the Gulf shores of Veracruz. Often eaten with tortilla chips.

Chile relleno—Roasted poblano pepper that is stuffed with ingredients like ground meat or cheese, then dipped in egg batter, fried, and served in tomato sauce.

Clayuda—a Oaxacan dish similar to pizza. Large corn tortillas are baked until hard, then topped with ingredients like refried beans, cheese, and salsa.

Fish taco—a specialty in Southern California, the fish taco is a soft corn tortilla stuffed with grilled or fried white fish (mahi-mahi or wahoo), pico de gallo, and shredded cabbage.

Gordita—"Little fat one" in Spanish, this dish is like a taco, but the cornmeal shell is thicker, similar to pita bread.

Mole—A complex, sweet sauce with Aztec roots made from more than 20 ingredients, including chiles, cinnamon, cumin, anise, black pepper, sesame seeds, and Mexican chocolate. There are many types of mole using various chiles and ingredient combinations, but the most common is *mole poblano* from the Puebla region.

Quesadilla—snack made from a fresh tortilla that is folded over and stuffed with simple fillings like cheese, then toasted on a griddle. Elevated versions of the quesadilla may be stuffed with sautéed

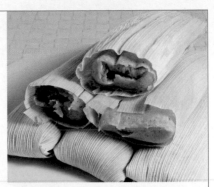

flor de calabaza (squash blossoms) or *huitlacoche* (corn mushrooms).

Salsa—A class of cooked or raw sauces made from chiles, tomatoes, and other ingredients. Popular salsas include *pico de gallo*, a fresh sauce made from chopped tomatoes, onions, chiles, cilantro, and lime; *salsa verde*, made with tomatillos instead of tomatoes; and *salsa roja*, a cooked sauce made with chiles, tomatoes, onion, garlic, and cilantro.

Sopes—small, fried corn cake topped with ingredients like refried beans, shredded chicken, and salsa.

Taco—In Southern California, as in Mexico, tacos are made from soft, palm-sized corn tortillas folded over and filled with meat, chopped onion, cilantro, and salsa. Common taco fillings include *al pastor* (spiced pork), *barbacoa* (braised beef), *carnitas* (roasted pork), *cecina* (chile-coated pork), *carne asada* (roasted, chopped beef), *chorizo* (spicy sausage), *lengua* (beef tongue), *sesos* (cow brain), and *tasajo* (spiced, grilled beef).

Tamales—Sweet or savory corn cakes that are steamed, and may be filled with cheese, roasted chiles, shredded meat, or other fillings.

Torta—A Mexican sandwich served on a crusty sandwich roll. Fillings often include meat, refried beans, and cheese.

A feeling of simple elegance comes through in the food (and décor) at Patina, in Downtown Los Angeles.

gras, butter-poached lobster, and medallions of venison served with lady apples. Finish with a hard-to-match cheese tray (orchestrated by a genuine *maître fromager*) and sensual desserts. ⊠ *Walt Disney Concert Hall, 141 S. Grand Ave., Downtown* ☎ *213/972–3331* ⚿ *Reservations essential* ⊟ *AE, D, DC, MC, V No lunch weekends.* ✛ *2:B2*

¢–$
AMERICAN
☺
Fodor'sChoice
★

✕ **Philippe the Original.** L.A.'s oldest restaurant (1908), Philippe claims the French dip sandwich originated here. You can get one made with beef, pork, ham, lamb, or turkey on a freshly baked roll; the house hot mustard is as famous as the sandwiches. Its reputation is earned by maintaining traditions, from sawdust on the floor to long communal tables where customers debate the Dodgers or local politics. The home cooking—orders are taken at the counter where some of the motherly servers have managed their long lines for decades—includes huge breakfasts, chili, pickled eggs, and an enormous pie selection. The best bargain: a cup of java for just 10¢ including tax. ⊠ *1001 N. Alameda St., Downtown* ☎ *213/628–3781* ⚿ *Reservations not accepted* ⊟ *No credit cards* ✛ *2:D1.*

$$–$$$
AMERICAN
★

✕ **Traxx.** Hidden inside historic Union Station, this intimate restaurant is an art deco delight. Its linen-topped tables spill out onto the main concourse. Chef-owner Tara Thomas's menu gussies up popular favorites; for example, crab cakes come with chipotle rémoulade, while pan-roasted Pacific snapper is paired with black rice and jazzed up with a jalapeño vinaigrette. The jacaranda-shaded courtyard is a local secret. A well-stocked bar, occupying what was originally the station's telephone room, is just across the concourse. ⊠ *Union Station, 800 N. Alameda St., Downtown* ☎ *213/625–1999* ⊟ *AE, D, MC, V* ☾ *Closed Sun. No lunch Sat.* ✛ *2:D1.*

CLOSE UP

Local Chains Worth Stopping For

Cars line up at all hours at **In-N-Out Burger** (many locations), still a family-owned operation (and very possibly America's original drive-through) whose terrific made-to-order burgers are revered by Angelenos. Satisfy your burger fix by ordering something off the "secret" menu, with variations like "Animal style" (mustard-grilled patty with grilled onions and extra spread) or a "4x4" (four burger patties and four cheese slices for heavy eaters). The company's Web site lists explanations for other popular secret menu items (⊕ www.in-n-out.com).

Tommy's sells a delightfully sloppy chili burger; the original location (✉ 2575 Beverly Blvd., Los Angeles ☎ 213/389–9060) is a no-frills culinary landmark. For rotisserie chicken that will make you forget the Colonel forever, head to **Zankou Chicken** (✉ 5065 Sunset Blvd., Hollywood ☎ 323/665–7845), a small chain noted for its golden crispy-skinned birds, potent garlic sauce, and Armenian specialties. Homesick New Yorkers will appreciate **Jerry's Famous Deli** (✉ 10925 Weyburn Ave., Westwood ☎ 310/208–3354), where the massive menu includes all the classic deli favorites. And **Señor Fish** (✉ 422 E. 1st St., Downtown ☎ 213/625–0566) is known for its healthy Mexican seafood specialties, such as scallop burritos and ceviche tostadas.

$$$–$$$$
SEAFOOD
★

✕ **Water Grill.** There's a bustling, enticing rhythm here as platters of glistening shellfish get whisked from the oyster bar to the cozy candlelit booths. Chef David LeFevre's menu shows off his slow cooking skills. Entrées such as olive oil–poached salmon with a mushroom vinaigrette and sumac–coated Australian barramundi with calamari–strewn Israeli couscous and Sicilian olives exemplify his light, sophisticated touch. Excellent desserts and a fine wine list round out this top-notch dining experience. ✉ 544 S. Grand Ave., Downtown ☎ 213/891–0900 ⌲ Reservations essential ☰ AE, D, DC, MC, V ⊗ No lunch weekends ✛ 2:B3.

COASTAL AND WESTERN LOS ANGELES

MALIBU

$$$–$$$$
JAPANESE

✕ **Nobu Malibu.** At famous chef-restaurateur Nobu Matsuhisa's coastal outpost, the casually chic clientele swarm over morsels of the world's finest fish. In addition to stellar sushi, Nobu serves many of the same ingenious specialties offered at his original Matsuhisa in Beverly Hills or glitzy Nobu in West Hollywood. You'll find exotic species of fish artfully accented with equally exotic South American peppers, ultratender Kobe beef, and a broth perfumed with rare matsutake mushrooms. Elaborate omakase dinners start at $90. ✉ 3835 Cross Creek Rd., Malibu ☎ 310/317–9140 ⌲ Reservations essential ☰ AE, DC, MC, V ⊗ No lunch ✛ 3:B1

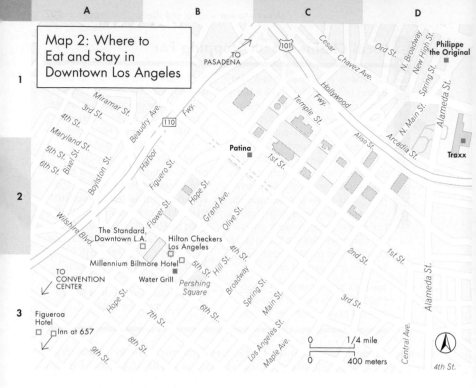

Map 2: Where to
Eat and Stay in
Downtown Los Angeles

A   **B**   **C**   **D**

1

TO
PASADENA

Cesar Chavez Ave.

Ord St.

N. Broadway

New High St.

Spring St.

**Philippe
the Original**

Miramar St.

3rd St.

4th St.

Maryland St.

5th St.

Bixel St.

6th St.

Beaudry Ave.

Boylston St.

Harbor

Figueroa St.

Hope St.

Hollywood

Temple St.

Fwy.

Patina

1st St.

Aliso St.

Arcadia St.

N. Main St.

Alameda St.

Traxx

2

Wilshire Blvd.

Flower St.

Grand Ave.

Olive St.

4th St.

The Standard,
Downtown L.A.

Hilton Checkers
Los Angeles

Millennium Biltmore Hotel

Hill St.

5th St.

Broadway

2nd St.

1st St.

Alameda St.

TO
CONVENTION
CENTER

Water Grill

Pershing
Square

Spring St.

Main St.

3rd St.

3

Figueroa
Hotel

Inn at 657

Hope St.

7th St.

6th St.

8th St.

9th St.

Los Angeles St.

Maple Ave.

0   1/4 mile

0   400 meters

Central Ave.

4th St.

SANTA MONICA

$$$–$$$$
ASIAN

✕ **Chinois on Main.** A once-revolutionary outpost in Wolfgang Puck's repertoire, this is still one of L.A.'s most crowded—and noisy—restaurants. The jazzy interior is just as loud as the clientele. Although the menu has expanded, the restaurant's happy marriage of Asian and French cuisines shows best in its signature dishes such as Chinois chicken salad, Shanghai lobster with spicy ginger-curry sauce, and Cantonese duck with fresh plum sauce. ⊠ *2709 Main St., Santa Monica* ☏ *310/392–9025* ⌔ *Reservations essential* ▤ *AE, D, DC, MC, V* ☾ *No lunch Sat.–Tues.* ✠ *3:B3.*

$$$$
FRENCH
Fodor's Choice
★

✕ **Mélisse.** In a city where informality reigns, this is one of L.A.'s more dressy—but not stuffy—restaurants. A crystal chandelier hangs in the dining room, above well-spaced tables topped with flowers and Limoges china. The garden room loosens up with a stone fountain and a retractable roof. Chef-owner Josiah Citrin enriches his modern French cooking with seasonal California produce. Consider seared sweet corn ravioli in brown butter–truffle froth, lobster bolognese, slow cooked rabbit, or duck confit. The cheese cart is packed with domestic and European selections. ⊠ *1104 Wilshire Blvd., Santa Monica* ☏ *310/395–0881* ⌔ *Reservations essential* ▤ *AE, D, DC, MC, V* ☾ *Closed Sun. and Mon. No lunch* ✠ *3:B2.*

$$$–$$$$
ITALIAN
Fodor's Choice
★

✕ **Valentino.** Renowned as one of the country's top Italian restaurants, Valentino has a truly awe-inspiring wine list. With nearly 2,800 labels consuming 130 pages, backed by a cellar overflowing with 100,000 bottles, this restaurant is nothing short of heaven for serious oenophiles. In the 1970s, suave owner Piero Selvaggio introduced L.A. to his exquisite modern Italian cuisine, and he continues to impress guests with dishes like a timballo of wild mushrooms with rich Parmigiano-Reggiano–*saffron fonduta*, squid ink-tinted risotto with Maine lobster, a memorable osso buco, and sautéed branzino with lemon emulsion. A recent addition to this exalted venue is its more casual V-vin bar for wine tasting, crudo, and carpaccio. ⊠ *3115 Pico Blvd., Santa Monica* ☎ *310/829–4313* ⌂ *Reservations essential* ⊟ *AE, DC, MC, V* ⊘ *Closed Sun. No lunch Sat. and Mon.–Thurs.* ✛ *3:C2.*

$$$–$$$$
AMERICAN

✕ **Wilshire.** The woodsy patio at Wilshire is one of the most coveted spaces on the L.A. dining circuit—its candlelight, firelight, and gurgling fountain reel in a hip crowd beneath a cloud of canvas. A passion for organic market-fresh ingredients in dishes like lobster bisque with lemongrass cream and duck breast with dried cherry chutney. The eclectic wine list is first-rate, and there's a lively bar scene here, too. ⊠ *2454 Wilshire Blvd., Santa Monica* ☎ *310/586–1707* ⌂ *Reservations essential* ⊟ *AE, D, DC, MC, V* ⊘ *Closed Sun. No lunch weekends. Hrs. change in summer* ✛ *3:B2.*

WEST LOS ANGELES

¢
AMERICAN
Fodor's Choice
★

✕ **The Apple Pan.** A burger-insider haunt since 1947, this unassuming joint with a horseshoe-shaped counter—no tables here—turns out one heck of a good burger topped with Tillamook cheddar, plus a hickory burger with barbecue sauce. You'll also find great fries and, of course, an apple pie indulgent enough to christen the restaurant (although many regulars argue that the banana cream deserves the honor). Be prepared to wait, but the veteran countermen turn the stools at a quick pace. ⊠ *10801 W. Pico Blvd., West L.A.* ☎ *310/475–3585* ⌂ *Reservations not accepted* ⊟ *No credit cards* ⊘ *Closed Mon.* ✛ *3:D2.*

$–$$
INDIAN
★

✕ **Bombay Cafe.** Some of the menu items at Bombay Cafe are strictly authentic, others have been lightened up a bit to suit Southern California sensibilities, and a few are truly innovative (e.g., California tandoori salad with lemon-cilantro dressing, green apple-cranberry chutney, ginger margarita). Regulars (and there are many) swear by the chili-laden lamb *frankies* (burritolike snacks sold by vendors on the beaches of Bombay), *sev puri* (wafers topped with onions, potatoes, and chutneys) and Sindhi chicken, a complex poached-then-sautéed recipe with an exotically seasoned crust. ⊠ *12021 Pico Blvd., West L.A.* ☎ *310/473–3388* ⊟ *MC, V* ⊘ *No lunch weekends* ✛ *3:C2.*

$–$$
MEXICAN
★

✕ **La Serenata Gourmet.** With uncomfortable chairs and crowds from the nearby Westside Pavilion boosting decibel levels, this branch of the East L.A. original isn't ideal for leisurely conversation. But the restaurant scores big points for its boldly flavored Mexican cuisine. Pork dishes and moles are delicious, but seafood is the real star—there are chubby gorditas (cornmeal pockets stuffed with shrimp), juicy shrimp enchiladas in tomatillo sauce, and simply grilled fish, with cilantro or garlic sauce, that sings with flavor. If your experience with Mexican food has

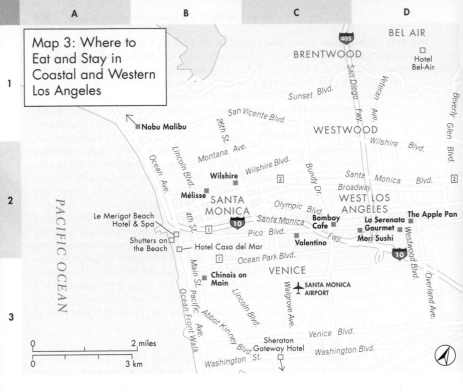

Map 3: Where to Eat and Stay in Coastal and Western Los Angeles

been on the Tex-Mex end of the spectrum, come here to broaden your taste bud horizons. ✉ 10924 W. Pico Blvd., West L.A. ☎ 310/441–9667 ▭ AE, D, DC, MC, V ✛ 3:D2.

$$$–$$$$
JAPANESE
Fodor's Choice
★

✗ **Mori Sushi.** Only a small fish logo identifies the facade of this restaurant, but many consider it the best sushi bar in L.A. and Morihiro Onodera one of the great sushi masters in America. The austere whitewashed space stands in contrast to the chef's artful presentations of pristine morsels of seafood, all served on ceramic plates he makes himself. Allow him to compose an entire meal for you—this can be an expensive proposition—and he'll send out eye-popping presentations of sushi or sashimi accented with touches of rare sea salts, yuzu, and freshly ground wasabi, as well as intricately conceived salads, house-made tofu, and soups. ✉ 11500 Pico Blvd., West L.A. ☎ 310/479–3939 ▭ AE, MC, V ☉ Closed Sun. No lunch Sat. ✛ 3: D2

PASADENA

PASADENA

$$$$
AMERICAN
Fodor's Choice
★

✗ **The Dining Room.** Until the arrival of charismatic chef Michael Voltaggio, there wasn't much to say about this high-price hotel restaurant. But Strong brought with him global inspirations and a culinary finesse beyond his years. A perfectionist (he insists, for instance, on importing butter from Normandy), Strong continually surprises with dishes such as lemongrass-scented spicy coconut milk–Dungeness crab soup, brandade-stuffed squash blossoms, and sautéed duck breast and leg confit with potato-basil mousseline and huckleberry sauce. The chef relishes the opportunity to personalize his cuisine, so consider springing for a customized tasting menu. Langham Hotels, taking over the property from Ritz-Carlton, promises nothing will change at the restaurant. ⊠ *Langham, Huntington Hotel & Spa, 1401 S. Oak Knoll Ave., Pasadena* ☎ *626/577–2867* ▤ *AE, D, DC, MC, V* ☉ *Closed Sun. and Mon. No lunch.*

$$–$$$
CHINESE
Fodor'sChoice
★

✕ **Yujean Kang's Gourmet Chinese Cuisine.** Forget any and all preconceived notions of what Chinese food should look and taste like—Kang's cuisine is nouvelle Chinese. Start with tender slices of veal on a bed of enoki mushrooms, topped with a tangle of quick-fried shoestring yams; or sea bass with kumquats and passion-fruit sauce. Even familiar dishes, such as the crispy sesame beef, result in nearly revelatory culinary experiences. And don't shy away from desserts like sweet bean-curd crepes or delicate mandarin orange cheesecake, which are elegantly light. ⊠ *67 N. Raymond Ave., Pasadena* ☎ *626/585–0855* ▤ *AE, D, DC, MC, V.*

WHERE TO STAY

BEVERLY HILLS, CENTURY CITY, HOLLYWOOD, AND WEST HOLLYWOOD

BEVERLY HILLS AND VICINITY

$$$$
🏨 **Beverly Hills Hotel.** Remarkably still at the top of her game, the "Pink Palace" continues to attract Hollywood's elite after 95 years. Celebrity guests favor the private bungalows; most others come for the "royal" treatment by staff. Standard rooms are also nothing to sniff at, with original artwork, butler service, Frette linens and duvets, walk-in closets, and huge marble bathrooms. Swiss skin-care company La Prairie runs the hotel's swanky day spa, which specializes in de-aging treatments. The Polo Lounge remains an iconic Hollywood meeting place. Bar Nineteen 12 is a most contemporary addition. Canine guests are also pampered here; 24-hour dog-walking service is available. **Pros:** pool, spa, and legendary, retro 20-seat Fountain Coffee room. **Cons:** average and pricey fare at the Polo lounge. ⊠ *9641 Sunset Blvd., Beverly Hills* ☎ *310/276–2251 or 800/283–8885* ⊕ *www.beverlyhillshotel.com* ⊅ *145 rooms, 38 suites, 21 bungalows* ⚭ *In-room: a/c, safe, kitchen (some), refrigerator, DVD, Internet, Wi-Fi. In-hotel: 4 restaurants, room service, bars, tennis courts, pool, gym, spa, laundry service, Wi-Fi hotspot, parking (paid), some pets allowed* ▤ *AE, DC, MC, V* ✛ *1:A2.*

$$$$
Fodor'sChoice
★

🏨 **Beverly Wilshire, a Four Seasons Hotel.** Built in 1928, the Italian Renaissance–style Wilshire wing of this fabled hotel is replete with elegant details: crystal chandeliers, oak paneling, walnut doors, crown moldings, and marble. The contemporary Beverly wing, added in 1971, lacks the Wilshire wing's historic panache. Rodeo Drive beckons outside; a complimentary Rolls-Royce can drive you anywhere within 3 mi of the hotel. Paneled in leather and wood, with soaring ceilings, the Blvd is the hotel's posh dining room. At dinner, Hollywood's elite

BEST BETS FOR LOS ANGELES LODGING

Fodor's offers a selective listing of lodging experiences at every price range. Here, we've compiled our top recommendations by price and experience. The very best properties are designated in the listings with the Fodor's Choice logo.

Fodor's Choice ★

Beverly Wilshire, a Four Seasons Hotel $$$$, p. 211

Four Seasons Hotel Los Angeles at Beverly Hills $$$$, p. 213

Hilton Checkers, p. 218

Hotel Bel-Air $$$$, p. 219

The Langham, Huntington Hotel & Spa $$$$, p. 211

Millennium Biltmore Hotel $$$$, p. 219

Peninsula Beverly Hills $$$$, p. 213

Shutters on the Beach $$$$, p. 221

The Standard, Downtown L.A. $$$, p. 219

Sunset Marquis Hotel & Villas $$$$, p. 216

By Price

$

Farmer's Daughter Hotel, p. 214

$$

Figueroa Hotel, p. 218

$$$

The Crescent, p. 213

Hotel Amarano Burbank, p. 221

Renaissance Hollywood Hotel, p. 215

Sheraton Gateway Hotel, p. 220

The Standard, Downtown L.A., p. 219

$$$$

Beverly Wilshire a Four Seasons Hotel, p. 211

Four Seasons Hotel Los Angeles at Beverly Hills, p. 213

Hilton Checkers, p. 218

Hotel Bel-Air, p. 219

Hotel Casa del Mar, p. 220

The Langham, Huntington Hotel & Spa $$$$, p. 221

Le Merigot Beach Hotel & Spa, p. 220

Millennium Biltmore Hotel, p. 219

Peninsula Beverly Hills, p. 213

Shutters on the Beach, p. 221

Sunset Marquis Hotel & Villas, p. 216

By Experience

BEST DESIGN

Mondrian $$$$, p. 216

The Standard, Downtown L.A. $$$, p. 219

BEST SPAS

Beverly Hills Hotel $$$$, p. 211

Four Seasons Hotel Los Angeles at Beverly Hills $$$$, p. 213

Shutters on the Beach $$$$, p. 221

GREAT POOLS

Beverly Hills Hotel $$$$, p. 211

Millennium Biltmore $$$$, p. 219

The Standard, Hollywood $$, p. 216

HOT SCENE

Beverly Hills Hotel $$$$, p. 211

Hollywood Roosevelt Hotel $$$, p. 214

Mondrian $$$$, p. 216

Standard Downtown L.A. $$$, p. 219

MOST KID-FRIENDLY

Renaissance Hollywood Hotel $$$$, p. 215

Shutters on the Beach $$$$, p. 221

packs the coolly modern steak house CUT featuring steaks and sides by Wolfgang Puck and interiors by architect Richard Meier. Take time to unwind at the hotel's first-rate spa. **Pros:** chic location; top-notch service and refined vibe. **Cons:** small lobby; valet parking backs up at peak times; super-expensive dining choices. ✉ *9500 Wilshire Blvd., Beverly Hills* ☎ *310/275–5200 or 800/427–4354* ⊕ *www.fourseasons.com/beverlywilshire* 🛏 *258 rooms, 137 suites* ⌂ *In-room: a/c, safe, refrigerator, DVD, Internet, Wi-Fi. In-hotel: 2 restaurants, room service, bars, pool, gym, spa, laundry service, Internet terminal, Wi-Fi hotspot, parking (paid), some pets allowed* ▭ *AE, DC, MC, V* ✛ *1:B3.*

$$$
★
🏨 **The Crescent.** Built in 1926 as a dorm for silent film actors, the Crescent is now a sleek boutique hotel within walking distance of the Beverly Hills shopping triangle. Low couches and tables; an indoor-outdoor fireplace; French doors that open to its streetside patio restaurant, boé; and shimmering candlelight at night give the hotel's public areas a welcoming and sophisticated look. Guest rooms are small, but platform beds and built-in furniture maximize the space. Bathrooms are finished in concrete—utilitarian but also coolly cozy. High-tech amenities include flat-screen TVs, in room iPods, and a library of the latest CDs and DVDs. **Pros:** boé's tasty cuisine and convivial happy hour; the lobby is fashionista-central. **Cons:** dorm-size rooms; fee for access to Sports ClubLA gym; no elevator. ✉ *403 N. Crescent Dr., Beverly Hills* ☎ *310/247–0505* ⊕ *www.crescentbh.com* 🛏 *35 rooms* ⌂ *In-room: a/c, refrigerator, Wi-Fi. In-hotel: restaurant, room service, bar, laundry service, Wi-Fi, parking (paid)* ▭ *AE, D, MC, V* ✛ *1:B3.*

$$$$
Fodor's Choice
★
🏨 **Four Seasons Hotel Los Angeles at Beverly Hills.** High hedges and patio gardens make this hotel a secluded retreat that even the hum of traffic can't permeate. It's a favorite of Hollywood's elite, so don't be surprised by a well-known face poolside or in the Windows bar. (Come awards season, expect to spot an Oscar winner or two.) The staff here will make you feel pampered, as will the plush guest rooms, which have beds with Frette linens, soft robes and slippers, and French doors leading to balconies. Extras include 24-hour business services, overnight shoe shine, and a morning newspaper. For a relaxing meal or a healthy smoothie, you can dine poolside on the tropically landscaped terrace. Massages here are among the best. **Pros:** expert concierge; deferential service; celeb magnet. **Cons:** small gym; Hollywood scene in bar and restaurant means rarefied prices. ✉ *300 S. Doheny Dr., Los Angeles* ☎ *310/273–2222 or 800/332–3442* ⊕ *www.fourseasons.com/losangeles* 🛏 *187 rooms, 98 suites* ⌂ *In-room: a/c, safe, kitchen (some), refrigerator, DVD, Internet, Wi-Fi. In-hotel: 2 restaurants, room service, bar, pool, gym, spa, laundry service, Wi-Fi hotspot, parking (paid), some pets allowed* ▭ *AE, DC, MC, V* ✛ *1:B3.*

$$$$
Fodor's Choice
★
🏨 **Peninsula Beverly Hills.** This French Riveria–style palace is a favorite of Hollywood boldface names, but all kinds of visitors consistently describe their stay as near perfect—though very expensive. Rooms overflow with antiques, artwork, and marble; high-tech room amenities and flat-screen TVs are controlled by a bedside panel. Service is exemplary and always discreet. Soak up the sun by the fifth-floor pool with its fully outfitted cabanas or sip afternoon tea in the living room under ornate

chandeliers. Belvedere, the hotel's flower-filled restaurant, is a lunchtime favorite for film business types. A complimentary Rolls-Royce is available for short jaunts in Beverly Hills. **Pros:** central; walkable Beverly Hills location; stunning flowers; one of the best concierges in the city. **Cons:** serious bucks or bank account required to stay here; somewhat stuffy. ✉ *9882 S. Santa Monica Blvd., Beverly Hills* 🕾 *310/551–2888 or 800/462–7899* ⊕ *www.beverlyhills.peninsula.com* ⟿ *142 rooms, 36 suites, 16 villas* ⚿ *In-room: a/c, safe, refrigerator, DVD, Internet, Wi-Fi. In-hotel: restaurant, room service, bar, pool, gym, spa, laundry service, Wi-Fi hotspot, parking (paid), some pets allowed* ⊟ *AE, D, DC, MC, V* ✛ *1:A3.*

HOLLYWOOD AND VICINITY

$–$$ ⊞ **Farmer's Daughter Hotel.** Tongue-in-cheek country style is the name of
★ the game at this motel: rooms are upholstered in blue gingham with denim bedspreads, and farm tools serve as art. A curving blue wall secludes the interior courtyard and the hotel's clapboard-lined restaurant, Tart. Pancakes here are a local favorite. Rooms are snug but outfitted with whimsical original art and amenities such as CD and DVD players. It's a favorite of *The Price Is Right* hopefuls; the TV show tapes at the CBS studios nearby. **Pros:** across from the cheap eats of the Farmers Market and The Grove's shopping/entertainment mix. **Cons:** pricey restaurant; roadside motel-size rooms; shaded pool. ✉ *115 S. Fairfax Ave., Fairfax District* 🕾 *323/937–3930 or 800/334–1658* ⊕ *www.farmersdaughterhotel.com* ⟿ *63 rooms, 2 suites* ⚿ *In-room: a/c, safe, refrigerator, DVD, Internet, Wi-Fi. In-hotel: restaurant, room service, pool, laundry service, Wi-Fi hotspot, parking (paid), some pets allowed* ⊟ *AE, D, DC, MC, V* ✛ *1:C3.*

$ ⊞ **Highland Gardens Hotel.** A large, sparkling pool and a lush, if somewhat overgrown, tropical garden set this hotel apart from other budget lodgings. Spacious but basic units have either two queen-size beds, or a king bed with a queen-size sleeper sofa, plus a desk and sitting area with Formica tables. Rooms facing busy Franklin Avenue are noisy; ask for one facing the courtyard. **Pros:** quick walk to Hollywood and Metro Rail; pet friendly; low price. **Cons:** late '80s decor; street noise; no elevator. ✉ *7047 Franklin Ave., Hollywood* 🕾 *323/850–0536 or 800/404–5472* ⊕ *www.highlandgardenshotel.com* ⟿ *70 rooms, 48 suites* ⚿ *In-room: a/c, kitchen (some), refrigerator, Wi-Fi. In-hotel: pool, laundry facilities, Wi-Fi hotspot, parking (paid), some pets allowed* ⊟ *AE, MC, V* ⎱⎰ *CP* ✛ *1:D1.*

$$$–$$$$ ⊞ **Hollywood Roosevelt Hotel.** Think hip bachelor pad when considering the Roosevelt. Poolside cabana rooms have dark-wood furnishings and mirrored walls; rooms in the main building have contemporary platform beds. Although Hollywood's oldest hotel, a renovation and a pair of hot nightspots have breathed new life into this historic spot. Lobby and poolside socializing is nonstop most weekends. Spanish Colonial Revival details include Spanish tiles, painted ceilings, arches, and fountains that evoke early Hollywood glamour. The David Hockney–painted pool adds to the playful vibe. A Metro stop is one block away. **Pros:** in the heart of Hollywood's action; lively social scene; great burgers at hotel's restaurant, 25 Degrees. **Cons:** noise, attitude, and stiff parking

The Rooftop Bar at The Standard, Downtown L.A., is a swanky place to enjoy a nightcap.

charges. ⊠ *7000 Hollywood Blvd., Hollywood* ☎ *323/466–7000 or 800/950–7667* ⊕ *www.hollywoodroosevelt.com* ⇥ *305 rooms, 18 suites* ⚲ *In-room: a/c, safe, refrigerator, Wi-Fi. In-hotel: 2 restaurants, room service, 3 bars, pool, gym, laundry service, Wi-Fi hotspot, parking (paid)* ▤ *AE, D, DC, MC, V* ✛ *1:D1.*

$$$$ ✺ **Renaissance Hollywood Hotel.** Part of the massive Hollywood & High-
★ land shopping and entertainment complex, this 20-story Renaissance is at the center of Hollywood's action. Contemporary art (notably by L.A. favorites Charles and Ray Eames), retro '60s furniture, terrazzo floors, a Zen rock garden, and wood and aluminum accents greet you in the lobby. Rooms are vibrant: chairs are red, table lamps are molded blue plastic. For the ultimate party pad, book the Panorama Suite, with angled floor-to-ceiling windows, vintage Eames furniture, a grand piano, and a sunken Jacuzzi tub with a view. Spa Luce, the hotel's roof-top spa, was added in 2008. **Pros:** large rooms; blackout shades; Red Line Metro–station adjacent. **Cons:** city hotel = no greenery; large and corporate feeling; very touristy. ⊠ *1755 N. Highland Ave., Hollywood* ☎ *323/856–1200 or 800/769–4774* ⊕ *www.renaissancehollywood.com* ⇥ *604 rooms, 33 suites* ⚲ *In-room: a/c, safe, refrigerator, Internet. In-hotel: restaurant, room service, bars, pool, gym, laundry service, parking (paid)* ▤ *AE, D, DC, MC, V* ✛ *1:D1.*

WEST HOLLYWOOD

$$$$ ✺ **Chateau Marmont Hotel.** The Chateau's swank exterior disguises its lurid place in Hollywood history—many remember it as the scene of John Belushi's fatal overdose in 1982. Celebs like Johnny Depp and Lindsay Lohan appreciate the hotel for its secluded cottages, bungalows, and understated suites and penthouses. For those who don't grace the cover of *Vanity Fair*, service can be frosty. The interior is 1920s style, although some of the decor looks dated rather than vintage. The Wi-Fi throughout the hotel means that you can surf the Net while seated on the hotel's scenic, landscaped terrace with drop-dead sunset views. **Pros:** walking distance to all of Sunset Strip's action; great food and vibe at Bar Marmont; guaranteed celeb spotting. **Cons:** attitude and then some from staff; ancient elevators. ⌧ *8221 Sunset Blvd., West Hollywood* ☎ *323/656–1010 or 800/242–8328* ⊕ *www.chateaumarmont. com* ⌐ *11 rooms, 63 suites* ⌂ *In-room: a/c, safe, refrigerator, DVD, Internet, Wi-Fi. In-hotel: restaurant, room service, bar, pool, gym, laundry service, Wi-Fi hotspot, parking (paid), some pets allowed* ⊟ *AE, DC, MC, V* ⊹ *1:C1.*

$$$$ ⌧ **Mondrian.** A city club attitude pervades at the spendy Mondrian. Socializing begins in the revamped lobby bar and lounge, extends through the all-white Asia de Cuba restaurant, and then moves out onto the sparkly patio to the divans surrounding the pool. Hotel guests gain access to the Sky Bar—still a scene most weekend nights. Designer Benjamin Noriega completely redid the rooms, adding bamboo floors and an oversize mirror that swivels to reveal a flat-screen TV. Bathrooms have a convenient wall of hooks, pocket door, and rain showerhead. Sheer curtains hide the closet. Windows are now double-paned for quiet—a good thing as street noise from Sunset Boulevard is constant to the north and the pool and Sky Bar echo with party people year-round to the south. **Pros:** pool, spa, and nighttime social scene mean never having to leave the property. **Cons:** street noise on Sunset Blvd. side; late-night party scene; inflated prices. ⌧ *8440 Sunset Blvd., West Hollywood* ☎ *323/650–8999 or 800/697–1791* ⊕ *www.mondrianhotel. com* ⌐ *54 rooms, 185 suites* ⌂ *In-room: a/c, safe, kitchen, refrigerator, DVD, Internet, Wi-Fi. In-hotel: restaurant, room service, bars, pool, gym, spa, laundry service, Wi-Fi hotel, parking (paid)* ⊟ *AE, D, DC, MC, V* ⊹ *1:C2.*

$$–$$$ ⌧ **The Standard, Hollywood.** Hotelier André Balazs created this playful Sunset Strip hotel out of a former retirement home. The aesthetic is '70s kitsch: pop art, shag carpets, and ultrasuede sectionals fill the lobby, while the rooms have inflatable sofas, beanbag chairs, surfboard tables, and Warhol poppy-print curtains. After a decade of heavy use, rooms show the wear-and-tear and service issues and staff attitude are commonplace. DJs spin nightly and lobby socializing begins at the front desk and extends to the blue AstroTurfed pool deck outside. **Pros:** on-site, decent 24-hour coffee shop; poolside socializing; live DJs. **Cons:** extended party scene for twentysomethings; staff big on attitude rather than service. ⌧ *8300 Sunset Blvd., West Hollywood* ☎ *323/650–9090* ⊕ *www.standardhotel.com* ⌐ *137 rooms, 2 suites* ⌂ *In-room: a/c, refrigerator, Internet. In-hotel: restaurant, room service, bar, pool, laundry service, Wi-Fi hotspot, parking (paid), some pets allowed* ⊟ *AE, D, DC, MC, V* ⊹ *1:C1.*

$$$$
Fodor's Choice
★
⌧ **Sunset Marquis Hotel and Villas.** If you're in town to cut your new hit single, you'll appreciate the two on-site recording studios here. Many a rocker has called the Sunset Marquis home—check out their oversize

Millennium Biltmore

The Peninsula Beverly Hills

Four Seasons Los Angeles

Beverly Wilshire

The Standard

portraits lining the walls of the hotel's exclusive Bar 1200. But even the musically challenged will appreciate this property on a quiet cul-de-sac just off the Sunset Strip. Suites and ultraprivate villas, which are set amid lush gardens, are roomy and plush (ultrasuede bed throws and flat-screen TVs abound). Windows are as soundproof as they come; blackout curtains ensure total serenity. Forty new villas are lavish with extras: kitchens, fireplaces, room-size bathrooms, and on-call butlers available to handle everything from unpacking to booking spa appointments. **Pros:** superior service; discreet setting just off the Strip; clublike atmosphere. **Cons:** standard suites are somewhat small. ✉ *1200 N. Alta Loma Rd., West Hollywood* ☎ *310/657–1333 or 800/858–9758* ⊕ *www.sunsetmarquishotel.com* ⤴ *102 suites, 52 villas* ⌂ *In-room: a/c, safe, kitchen (some), refrigerator, DVD, Internet, Wi-Fi. In-hotel: 2 restaurants, room service, bars, pools, gym, spa, laundry service, Wi-Fi hotspot, parking (paid)* ═ *AE, D, DC, MC, V* ✛ *1:C1.*

DOWNTOWN

$$
★
⊞ **Figueroa Hotel.** On the outside, it's Spanish Revival; on the inside, this 1926, 12-story hotel is a mix of Southwestern, Mexican, and Mediterranean styles, with earth tones, hand-painted furniture, and wrought-iron beds. You can lounge around the pool and bubbling hot tub surrounded by tropical greenery under the shadow of downtown skyscrapers. (Make it even better with a soothing drink from the back patio bar.) **Pros:** a short walk to Nokia Theatre, LA Live, Convention Center; well-priced, great poolside bar. **Cons:** somewhat funky room decor; small bathrooms; gentrifying neighborhood. ✉ *939 S. Figueroa St., Downtown* ☎ *213/627–8971 or 800/421–9092* ⊕ *www.figueroahotel.com* ⤴ *285 rooms, 2 suites* ⌂ *In-room: a/c, refrigerator, Internet, Wi-Fi. In-hotel: restaurant, bars, pool, laundry facilities, laundry service, Wi-Fi hotspot, parking (paid)* ═ *AE, DC, MC, V* ✛ *2:A3.*

$$
★
⊞ **Inn at 657.** Proprietor Patsy Carter runs a homey, welcoming bed-and-breakfast near the University of Southern California. Rooms in this 1904-built Craftsman have down comforters, Oriental silks on the walls, and needlepoint rugs. The vintage dining room table seats 12; conversation is encouraged. You're also welcome to hang out with the hummingbirds in the private garden. All rooms include a hearty breakfast, homemade cookies, and free local phone calls. **Pros:** vintage home and quiet garden; homemade breakfast; you'll meet the innkeeper. **Cons:** low-tech stay; you'll have to speak to other guests. ✉ *657 W. 23rd St., Downtown* ☎ *213/741–2200 or 800/347–7512* ⊕ *www.patsysinn657.com* ⤴ *11 rooms* ⌂ *In-room: a/c, refrigerator, Internet, Wi-Fi. In-hotel: restaurant, laundry service, Wi-Fi hotspot, parking (paid)* ═ *MC, V* ⦿❘ *BP* ✛ *2:A3.*

$$$$
Fodor's Choice
★
⊞ **Hilton Checkers Los Angeles.** Opened as the Mayflower Hotel in 1927, Checkers retains much of its original character; its various-size rooms all have charming period details, although they also have contemporary luxuries like pillow-top mattresses, coffeemakers, 24-hour room service, and cordless phones. The rooftop pool deck overlooks the L.A. library and nearby office towers. The plush lobby bar and lounge look like they belong in a private club, with comfortable leather chairs and a

large plasma-screen TV. **Pros:** historic charm; business-friendly; rooftop pool and spa. **Cons:** no on-street parking; some rooms very compact; very urban setting. ✉ *535 S. Grand Ave., Downtown* ☎ *213/624–0000 or 800/445–8667* ⊕ *www.hiltoncheckers.com* ⤴ *188 rooms, 9 suites* ♿ *In-room: a/c, Internet, Wi-Fi. In-hotel: restaurant, room service, bar, pool, gym, spa, laundry service, Wi-Fi hotspot, parking (paid)* ▭ *AE, D, DC, MC, V* ✛ *2:B2.*

$$$$ Ⓣ **Millennium Biltmore Hotel.** One of downtown L.A.'s true treasures, the
Fodor'sChoice gilded 1923 beaux-arts masterpiece exudes ambience and history. The
★ lobby (formerly the Music Room) was the local headquarters of JFK's presidential campaign, and the ballroom hosted some of the earliest Academy Awards. These days, the Biltmore hosts business types drawn by its central downtown location, ample meeting spaces, and services such as a well-outfitted business center that stays open 24/7. Some of the guest rooms are small by today's standards, but all have classic, formal furnishings, shuttered windows, and marble bathrooms. Bring your bathing suit for the vintage tiled indoor pool and adjacent steam room. **Pros:** historic character; famed filming location; club-level rooms have many hospitable extras. **Cons:** pricey valet parking; standard rooms truly compact. ✉ *506 S. Grand Ave., Downtown* ☎ *213/624–1011 or 866/866–8086* ⊕ *www.millenniumhotels.com* ⤴ *635 rooms, 48 suites* ♿ *In-room: a/c, Internet. In-hotel: 3 restaurants, room service, bars, pool, gym, laundry service, Internet terminal, Wi-Fi hotspot, parking (paid)* ▭ *AE, D, DC, MC, V* ✛ *2:B3.*

$$$ Ⓣ **The Standard, Downtown L.A.** Built in 1955 as Standard Oil's com-
Fodor'sChoice pany's headquarters, the building was completely revamped under the
★ sharp eye of owner André Balazs. The large guest rooms are practical and funky: all have orange built-in couches; windows that actually open; and platform beds. Bathrooms have extra-large tubs. The indoor–outdoor rooftop lounge has a preening social scene and stunning setting, but be prepared for some attitude at the door. **Pros:** on-site Rudy's barbershop for grooming; 24/7 coffee shop for dining; rooftop pool and lounge for fun. **Cons:** party scene weekends and holidays; street noise; hipper-than-thou attitude at the door. ✉ *550 S. Flower St., Downtown* ☎ *213/892–8080* ⊕ *www.standardhotel.com* ⤴ *171 rooms, 36 suites* ♿ *In-room: a/c, safe, refrigerator, DVD, Internet. In-hotel: restaurant, room service, bars, pool, gym, laundry service, Internet terminal, Wi-Fi hotspot, parking (paid), some pets allowed* ▭ *AE, D, DC, MC, V* ✛ *2:B2.*

COASTAL AND WESTERN LOS ANGELES

BEL-AIR

$$$$ Ⓣ **Hotel Bel-Air.** In a wooded canyon with lush gardens and a swan-filled
Fodor'sChoice lake, the Hotel Bel-Air's fairy-tale luxury and seclusion have made it a
★ favorite of discreet celebs and royalty for decades. Bungalow-style rooms feel like fine homes, with country-French, expensively upholstered furniture in silk or chenille; many have hardwood floors. Several rooms have wood-burning fireplaces (the bell captain will build a fire for you). Eight suites have private outdoor hot tubs. Complimentary tea service greets you upon arrival; enjoy it on the terrace warmed by heated tiles.

A pianist plays nightly in the bar. **Pros:** ultraprivate in-town hideaway; gorgeous restaurant terrace; service par-excellence. **Cons:** very expensive dining. ⊠ *701 Stone Canyon Rd., Bel Air* ☎ *310/472–1211 or 800/648–4097* ⊕ *www.hotelbelair.com* ⌁ *52 rooms, 39 suites* ⌂ *In-room: a/c, safe, refrigerator, DVD, Internet, Wi-Fi. In-hotel: restaurant, room service, bar, pool, gym, laundry service, Internet terminal, Wi-Fi hotspot, parking (paid), some pets allowed* ⊟ *AE, DC, MC, V* ✢ *3:D1.*

LOS ANGELES INTERNATIONAL AIRPORT

$$$
★

🖼 **Sheraton Gateway Hotel.** LAX's coolest-looking hotel is so swank that guests have been known to ask to buy the black-and-white photos hanging behind the front desk. Extras for in-transit visitors include 24-hour room service, a 24-hour fitness center, currency exchange, a business center, and a 24-hour airport shuttle. Rooms are compact but soundproof and have helpful details such as coffeemakers, hooks for hanging garment bags, and oversize work desks. Faux animal-skin headboards and ebonized furniture make the guest rooms feel more sophisticated than corporate. **Pros:** weekend rates significantly lower; free LAX shuttle. **Cons:** convenient to airport but not much else. ⊠ *6101 W. Century Blvd., LAX* ☎ *310/642–1111 or 800/325–3535* ⊕ *www.sheratonlosangeles.com* ⌁ *714 rooms, 88 suites* ⌂ *In-room: a/c, Internet, Wi-Fi. In-hotel: 2 restaurants, room service, bar, pool, gym, laundry service, Internet terminal, Wi-Fi hotspot, parking (paid), some pets allowed* ⊟ *AE, D, DC, MC, V* ✢ *3:C3.*

SANTA MONICA

$$$$
★

🖼 **Hotel Casa del Mar.** In the 1920s it was a posh beach club catering to the city's elite; now the Casa del Mar is one of SoCal's most luxurious and pricey beachfront hotels, with three extravagant two-story penthouses, a raised deck and pool, and an elegant ballroom facing the sand. Guest rooms, designed to evoke the good old days with furnishings like four-poster beds and handsome armoires, are filled with contemporary amenities like flat-screen TVs, iPod docking stations, and supremely comfortable beds with sumptuous white linens. Bathrooms are gorgeous, with sunken whirlpool tubs and glass-enclosed showers. Catch is the hotel's elegant and striking seafood restaurant and sushi bar. **Pros:** excellent dining at Catch; lobby socializing; gorgeous beachfront rooms. **Cons:** no room balconies; without a doubt, one of L.A.'s most pricey stays. ⊠ *1910 Ocean Front Way, Santa Monica* ☎ *310/581–5533 or 800/898–6999* ⊕ *www.hotelcasadelmar.com* ⌁ *113 rooms, 16 suites* ⌂ *In-room: a/c, safe, refrigerator, Internet, Wi-Fi. In-hotel: 2 restaurants, room service, bar, pool, gym, spa, laundry service, Wi-Fi hotspot, parking (paid), some pets allowed* ⊟ *AE, D, DC, MC, V* ✢ *3:B2.*

$$$$
★

🖼 **Le Merigot Beach Hotel & Spa.** Steps from Santa Monica's expansive beach, Le Merigot caters to a corporate clientele. Upper floors have panoramic views of the Santa Monica Pier and the Pacific; many rooms have terraces. The contemporary rooms have featherbeds and fine linens, and bathrooms come with playful bath toys and votive candles. Expect a seashell (not chocolate) at turndown. A checkerboard slate courtyard, including a pool, cabanas, fountains, and outdoor living room, is the center of activity. You can book a massage at the spa for a true attitude adjustment, or enjoy Cal-French fare at the comfortable Cézanne restaurant. **Pros:** steps from the beach and pier; welcoming to international travelers; walk to Third Street Promenade. **Cons:** small shaded pool. ✉ *1740 Ocean Ave., Santa Monica* ☎ *310/395–9700 or 888/539–7899* 🌐 *www.lemerigothotel.com* *160 rooms, 15 suites* *In-room: a/c, safe, refrigerator, Internet. In-hotel: restaurant, room service, bar, pool, gym, spa, beachfront, bicycles, laundry service, Internet terminal, Wi-Fi hotspot, parking (paid), some pets allowed* *AE, D, DC, MC, V* ✣ *3:B2.*

$$$$ Fodor's Choice ★ **Shutters on the Beach.** Set right on the sand, this gray-shingle inn has become synonymous with in-town escapism. Guest rooms have those namesake shutter doors, pillow-top mattresses, and white built-in cabinets filled with art books and curios. Bathrooms are luxe, each with a whirlpool tub, a raft of bath goodies, and a three-nozzle, glass-walled shower. While the hotel's service gets mixed reviews from some readers, the beachfront location and show-house decor make this one of SoCal's most popular luxury hotels. **Pros:** romantic; discreet; residential vibe. **Cons:** service not as good as it should be. ✉ *1 Pico Blvd., Santa Monica* ☎ *310/458–0030 or 800/334–9000* 🌐 *www.shuttersonthebeach.com* *186 rooms, 12 suites* *In-room: a/c, safe, refrigerator, DVD, Internet, Wi-Fi. In-hotel: 2 restaurants, room service, bar, pool, gym, spa, beachfront, bicycles, laundry service, Wi-Fi hotspot, parking (paid)* *AE, D, DC, MC, V* ✣ *3:B2.*

SAN FERNANDO VALLEY

BURBANK

$$$ ★ **Hotel Amarano Burbank.** Close to Burbank's TV and movie studios, the smartly designed Amarano feels like a Beverly Hills boutique hotel. The vibe is residential; the look understated (muted beiges and greens). The lobby is a welcoming living room with glass fireplace and corners for quiet conversation, cocktails or tapas. Feather beds are covered in comfy duvets; thoughtful touches include plush bathrobes and hooks for hanging garment bags. Generous work spaces have state-of-the-art lighting, and bathrooms have granite vanities, makeup mirrors, and shelves for storage. The rooftop sundeck has a brightly striped cabana and view of the nearby hills. **Pros:** boutique style in a Valley location; rooftop gym; pleasant breakfast room. **Cons:** no pool; summertime temperatures; Pass Avenue street noise. ✉ *322 N. Pass Ave., Burbank* ☎ *818/842–8887 or 888/956–1900* 🌐 *www.hotelamarano.com* *91 rooms, 10 suites* *In-room: a/c, safe, kitchen (some), refrigerator, DVD, Internet, Wi-Fi. In-hotel: restaurant, room service, bar, gym, laundry service, Wi-Fi hotspot, parking (paid), some pets allowed* *AE, D, DC, MC, V.*

PASADENA

$$$$ Fodor's Choice ★ **The Langham, Huntington Hotel & Spa.** An azalea-filled Japanese garden and the unusual Picture Bridge, with murals celebrating California's history, are just two of this grande dame's picturesque attributes. Long a mainstay of Pasadena's social history, the hotel first opened in 1907.

The Italianate-style main building, Spanish Revival–style cottages, and lanai building sit on 23 acres fronted by the historic horseshoe garden. In 2008 the hotel was bought by Langham Hotels ending its storied, 15-year stand as Ritz-Carlton. Traditional guest rooms are handsome and sometimes oddly sized; all are in shades of gold and blue. Brocade fabrics are found throughout, as are flat-screen TVs and CD players. The hotel's formal restaurant, The Dining Room, can be counted on for a rarefied contemporary dining experience. Treat yourself and order Chef Michael Voltaggio's multicourse tasting menu. **Pros:** great for romantic escape; excellent restaurant; elegant landscaping and tranquil garden. **Cons:** set in a suburban neighborhood far from local shopping and dining; transition hiccups a possibility. ⊠ *1401 S. Oak Knoll Ave., Pasadena* ☎ *626/568–3900 or 800/591–7481* ⊕ *www.langhamhotels. com* ⬏ *342 rooms, 38 suites* ⬧ *In-room: a/c, safe, refrigerator, Internet, Wi-Fi. In-hotel: 2 restaurants, room service, bar, tennis courts, pool, gym, spa, bicycles, laundry service, Internet terminal, Wi-Fi hotspot, parking (paid), some pets allowed* ▭ *AE, D, DC, MC, V.*

NIGHTLIFE AND THE ARTS

Hollywood and West Hollywood, where hip and happening nightspots liberally dot Sunset and Hollywood boulevards, are the epicenter of L.A. nightlife. The city is one of the best places in the world for seeing soon-to-be-famous rockers as well as top jazz, blues, and classical performers. Movie theaters are naturally well represented here, but the worlds of dance, theater, and opera have flourished in the past few years as well.

For a thorough listing of local events, ⊕ *www.la.com* and *Los Angeles Magazine* are both good sources. The Calendar section of the *Los Angeles Times* (⊕ *www.calendarlive.com*) also lists a wide survey of Los Angeles arts events, especially on Thursday and Sunday, as do the more alternative publications, *LA Weekly* and *Citybeat Los Angeles* (both free, and issued every Thursday). Call ahead to confirm that what you want to see is ongoing.

THE ARTS

CONCERT HALLS

Fodor's Choice

★

Built in 2003 as a grand addition to L.A.'s Music Center, the 2,265-seat **Walt Disney Concert Hall** (⊠ *151 S. Grand Ave., Downtown* ☎ *323/850–2000*) is now the home of the Los Angeles Philharmonic and the Los Angeles Master Chorale. A sculptural monument of gleaming, curved steel, the theater is part of a complex that includes a public park, gardens, and shops as well as two outdoor amphitheaters for children's and preconcert events. ■**TIP**→ **In the main hall, the audience completely surrounds the stage, so it's worth checking the seating chart when buying tickets to gauge your view of the performers.** And the acoustics definitely live up to the hype. Also part of the Music Center, the 3,200-seat **Dorothy Chandler Pavilion** (⊠ *135 N. Grand Ave., Downtown* ☎ *213/972–7211*) is an elegant space with plush red seats and a giant gold curtain. It presents an array of music programs and the L.A. Opera's classics from September through June. Music director Plácido Domingo encourages fresh work. There's also a steady flow of touring ballet and modern ballet companies. In Griffith Park, the open-air auditorium known as the **Greek Theater** (✉ *2700 N. Vermont Ave., Los Feliz* ☎ *323/665–5857*), complete with Doric columns, presents big-name performers in its mainly pop-rock-jazz schedule from June through October.

★ Ever since it opened in 1920, in a park surrounded by mountains, trees, and gardens, the **Hollywood Bowl** (✉ *2301 Highland Ave., Hollywood* ☎ *323/850–2000* ⊕ *www.hollywoodbowl.com*) has been one of the world's largest and most atmospheric outdoor amphitheaters. Its season runs from early July through mid-September; the L.A. Philharmonic spends its summers here. There are performances daily except Monday (and some Sundays); the program ranges from jazz to pop to classical. Concertgoers usually arrive early and bring picnic suppers (picnic tables are available). Additionally, a moderately priced outdoor grill and a more upscale restaurant are among the dining options operated by the Patina Group. ■**TIP→** Be sure to bring a sweater—it gets chilly here in the evening. You might also bring or rent a cushion to apply to the wood seats. Avoid the hassle of parking by taking one of the Park-and-Ride buses, which leave from various locations around town; call the Bowl for information.

Fodor's Choice
★ The jewel in the crown of Hollywood & Highland is the **Kodak Theatre** (✉ *6801 Hollywood Blvd., Hollywood* ☎ *323/308–6363* ⊕ *www.kodaktheatre.com*). Created as the permanent host of the Academy Awards, the lavish 3,500-seat theater is also used for music concerts and ballets. Seeing a show here is worthwhile just to witness the gorgeous, crimson-and-gold interior, with its box seating and glittering chandeliers. Fans wishing to view the red carpet parade outside on Oscar day can register for bleacher seats during the month of September at ⊕ *www.oscars.org*. The one-of-a-kind, 6,300-seat ersatz-Arabic **Shrine Auditorium** (✉ *665 W. Jefferson Blvd., Downtown* ☎ *213/748–5116*), built in 1926 as Al Malaikah Temple, hosts touring companies from all over the world, assorted gospel and choral groups, and other musical acts.High-profile awards shows, including the People's Choice, SAG, and NAACP Image Awards are still televised on-site.

★ Adjacent to Universal Studios, the 6,250-seat **Gibson Amphitheater** (✉ *100 Universal City Plaza, Universal City* ☎ *818/622–4440*) holds more than 100 performances a year, including the Radio City Christmas Spectacular, star-studded benefit concerts, and all-star shindigs for local radio station KROQ 106.7.

FILM

ART AND REVIVAL HOUSES
The **American Cinemathèque Independent Film Series** (✉ *6712 Hollywood Blvd., Hollywood* ☎ *323/466–3456* ⊕ *americancinematheque.com*) screens classics plus recent independent films, sometimes with question-and-answer sessions with the filmmakers. The main venue is the Lloyd E. Rigler Theater, within the 1922 Egyptian Theater, which combines an exterior of pharaoh sculptures and columns with a modern, high-tech design inside. The Cinemathèque also screens movies at the 1940

Aero Theater (✉ *1328 Montana Ave., Santa Monica* ☎ *323/466–3456*).

Fodor's Choice
★

Taking the concept of dinner and a movie to a whole new level, **Cinespace** (✉ *6356 Hollywood Blvd., Hollywood* ☎ *323/817–3456* ⊕ *www.cinespace.info*) is now mostly reserved for private screenings but onspecial occasions such as Valentine's Day you can still catch classics and alternative flicks in its digital theater-restaurant open to the public. Also, the space doubles from time to time as a nightclub with DJ-provided music and a smoking patio that hovers over bustling Hollywood Boulevard and attracts indie lovers and rockers.

Fodor's Choice
★

The **Silent Movie Theatre** (✉ *611 N. Fairfax Ave., Fairfax District* ☎ *323/655–2520* ⊕ *www.silentmovietheatre.com*) is a treasure for both pretalkies and nonsilent films (the artier the better). Live musical accompaniment and shorts precede the films. Each show is made to seem like an event in itself, and it's just about the only theater of its kind. The schedule—which also offers occasional DJ and live music performances—varies, but you can be sure to catch silent screenings every Wednesday.

★

UCLA has two fine film series. The programs of the **Billy Wilder Theater** (✉ *10899 Wilshire Blvd., Westwood* ☎ *310/443–7000* ⊕ *www.cinema.ucla.edu*) might cover the works of major directors, documentaries, children's films, horror movies—just about anything. The **School of Film & Television** (⊕ *www.tft.ucla.edu*) uses **the James Bridges Theater** (✉ *Melnitz Hall, Sunset Blvd. and Hilgard Ave., Westwood* ☎ *310/206–3456*) and has its own program of newer, avant-garde films. Enter the campus at the northeasternmost entrance. Street parking is available on Loring Avenue (a block east of the campus) after 6 PM, or park for a small fee in Lot 3 (go one entrance south to Wyton Drive to pay at the kiosk before 7, after 7 at the lot itself).

THEATER

LA Stage Alliance (⊕ *www.lastagealliance.com*) also gives information on what's playing in Los Angeles, albeit with capsules that are either noncommittal or overly enthusiastic. Its LAStageTIX service allows you to buy tickets online the day of the performance at roughly half price.

Jason Robards and Nick Nolte got their starts at **Geffen Playhouse** (✉ *10886 Le Conte Ave., Westwood* ☎ *310/208–5454* ⊕ *www.geffenplayhouse.com*), an acoustically superior, 498-seat theater that showcases new plays in summer—primarily musicals and comedies. Many of the productions here are on their way to or from Broadway.

In addition to theater performances, lectures, and children's programs, free summer jazz, dance, cabaret, and occasionally Latin and rock

The musical comedy "Minsky's" had its world premier at the Ahmanson Theater in 2009.

★ concerts take place at the **John Anson Ford Amphitheater** (✉ *2580 Cahuenga Blvd. E, Hollywood* ☎ *323/461–3673* ⊕ *www.fordamphitheater.org*), a 1,300-seat outdoor venue in the Hollywood Hills. Winter shows are typically staged at the smaller indoor theater, **Inside the Ford.** There are three theaters in the big downtown complex known as **The Music Center** (✉ *135 N. Grand Ave., Downtown* ☎ *213/972–7211* ⊕ *www. musiccenter.org*) : the 2,140-seat **Ahmanson Theatre** (☎ *213/628–2772* ⊕ *www.taperahmanson.com*) presents both classics and new plays; the 3,200-seat **Dorothy Chandler Pavilion** shows a smattering of plays between the more prevalent musical performances; and the 760-seat **Mark Taper Forum** (☎ *213/628–2772* ⊕ *www.taperahmanson.com*) presents new works that often go on to Broadway, such as Tony Kushner's *Caroline, or Change.*

★ The home of the Academy Awards telecast from 1949 to 1959, the **Pantages Theatre** (✉ *6233 Hollywood Blvd., Hollywood* ☎ *323/468–1770* ⊕ *www.nederlander.com*) is a massive (2,600-seat) and splendid example of high-style Hollywood art deco, presenting large-scale Broadway musicals such as *The Lion King* and *Wicked.* The **Ricardo Montalbán Theatre** (✉ *1615 N. Vine St., Hollywood* ☎ *323/463–0089* ⊕ *www. nosotros.org*) has an intimate feeling despite its 1,038-seat capacity. It presents plays, concerts, seminars, and workshops with an emphasis on Latin culture. The 1,900-seat, art deco **Saban Theatre** (✉ *8440 Wilshire Blvd., Beverly Hills* ☎ *323/655-0111* ⊕ *www.sabantheatre.org*) presents Broadway musicals and occasional concerts.

NIGHTLIFE

Although the ultimate in velvet-roped vampiness and glamour used to be the Sunset Strip, in the past couple of years the glitz has definitely shifted to Hollywood Boulevard and its surrounding streets. The lines are as long as the skirts are short outside the Hollywood club du jour (which changes so fast, it's often hard to keep track). But the Strip still has plenty going for it, with comedy clubs, hard-rock spots, and restaurants. West Hollywood's Santa Monica Boulevard bustles with gay and lesbian bars and clubs. For less conspicuous—and congested—alternatives, check out the events in downtown L.A.'s performance spaces and galleries. Silver Lake and Echo Park are best for boho bars and live music clubs.

Note that parking, especially after 7 PM, is at a premium in Hollywood. In fact, it's restricted on virtually every side street along the "hot zone" of West Hollywood (Sunset Boulevard from Fairfax to Doheny). Posted signs indicate the restrictions, but these are naturally harder to notice at night. Paying $5 to $20 for valet or lot parking is often the easiest way to go.

BARS

HOLLYWOOD

★ The **Beauty Bar** (✉ *1638 Cahuenga Blvd., Hollywood* ☎ *323/464–7676*) offers manicures and makeovers along with the perfect martinis, but the hotties who flock to this retro salon-bar (the little sister of the Beauty Bars in NYC and San Fran) don't really need the cosmetic care—this is where the edgy beautiful people hang.

★ The casually hip **Three Clubs** (✉ *1123 N. Vine St., Hollywood* ☎ *323/462–6441*) is furtively located in a strip mall, beneath the Bargain Clown Mart discount store. The DJs segue through the many faces and phases of rock-and-roll and dance music. With dark-wood paneling, lamp-lighted tables, and even some sofas, you could be in a giant basement rec room from decades past—no fancy dress required, but fashionable looks suggested.

★ A lovely L.A. tradition is to meet at **Yamashiro** (✉ *1999 N. Sycamore Ave., Hollywood* ☎ *323/466–5125*) for cocktails at sunset. In the elegant restaurant, waitresses glide by in kimonos, and entrées can zoom up to $39; on the terrace, a spectacular hilltop view spreads out before you. ■**TIP→** Mandatory valet parking is $7.50.

WEST HOL-
LYWOOD

★ As at so many other nightspots in this neck of the woods, the popularity and clientele of **Bar Marmont** (✉ *8171 Sunset Blvd., West Hollywood* ☎ *323/650–0575*) bulged—and changed—after word got out it was a favorite of celebrities. Lately, it's gotten a second wind thanks to a strong DJ selection and luscious cocktails. The bar is next to the inimitable hotel Chateau Marmont, which boldface names continue to haunt.

★ The **Rainbow Bar & Grill** (✉ *9015 Sunset Blvd., West Hollywood* ☎ *310/278–4232*), in the heart of the Strip and next door to the legendary Roxy, is a landmark in its own right as *the* drinking spot of the '80s hair-metal scene—and it still attracts a music-industry crowd.

A classic Hollywood makeover—formerly a nursing home, this spot in the happening part of Sunset Strip got converted into a smart, brash-
★ looking hotel, the **The Standard, Hollywood** (✉ *8300 Sunset Blvd., West Hollywood* ☎ *323/650–9090*), for the young, hip, and connected. (Check out the live model in the lobby's fish tank.) The hotel and especially the bar here is popular with those in the biz.

ECHO PARK **Cha Cha Lounge** (✉ *2375 Glendale Blvd., Silver Lake* ☎ *323/660–7595*),
AND SILVER Seattle's coolest rock bar, now aims to repeat its success with this col-
LAKE orful, red-lighted space. Think part tiki hut, part tacky Tijuana party
★ palace. The tabletops pay homage to the lounge's former performers; they've got portraits of Latin drag queens.

★ The **Echo** (✉ *1822 Sunset Blvd., Echo Park* ☎ *213/413–8200*) sprang from the people behind the Silver Lake rock joint Spaceland. Most evenings this dark and divey space's tiny dance floor and well-worn booths attract artsy local bands and their followers, but things rev up when DJs spin reggae, rock, and funk. Opened in the club's basement in 2007, **the Echoplex** has a different entrance and books bigger national tours and events.

★ **Tiki Ti** (✉ *4427 W. Sunset Blvd., Silver Lake* ☎ *323/669–9381*) is one of the most charming drinking huts in the city. You can spend hours just looking at the Polynesian artifacts strewn all about the place, but be careful—time flies in this tiny tropical bar, and the colorful drinks can be so potent that you may have to stay marooned for a while.

DOWNTOWN **The Standard, Downtown L.A.** (✉ *550 S. Flower St., Downtown* ☎ *213/892–*
FodorśChoice *8080*) has a groovy lounge with pink sofas and DJs, as well as an
★ all-white restaurant that looks like something out of *2001: A Space Odyssey*. But it's the rooftop bar, with an amazing view of the city's illuminated skyscrapers, a heated swimming pool, and private, podlike water-bed tents, that's worth waiting in line to get into. And wait you probably will, especially on weekends and in summer.

COMEDY

★ A nightly premier comedy showcase, **Comedy Store** (✉ *8433 Sunset Blvd., West Hollywood* ☎ *323/656–6225*) has been going strong for more than two decades, with three stages (with covers ranging from free to $20) to supply the yuks. Famous comedians occasionally make unannounced appearances.

★ More than a quarter century old, **Groundling Theatre** (✉ *7307 Melrose Ave., Hollywood* ☎ *323/934–9700*) has been a breeding ground for *Saturday Night Live* performers; alumni include Lisa Kudrow and *Curb Your Enthusiasm*'s Cheryl Hines. The primarily sketch and improv comedy shows run Wednesday–Sunday, costing $12–$18.

Richard Pryor got his start at the **Improv** (✉ *8162 Melrose Ave., West Hollywood* ☎ *323/651–2583*), a renowned establishment showcasing stand-up comedy. Drew Carey's *Totally Improv* is Thursday night on a semiregular basis. Reservations are recommended. Cover is $15–$20, and there's a two-drink minimum.

FodorśChoice Look for top stand ups—and frequent celeb residents, like Bob Saget,
★ or unannounced drop-ins, like Chris Rock—at **Laugh Factory** (✉ *8001*

Sunset Blvd., West Hollywood ☎ *323/656–1336).* The club has shows Sunday through Thursday nights at 8 PM and 10 PM, plus an additional show on Friday and Saturday at midnight; the cover is $20–$30. New York's **Upright Citizens Brigade** (✉ *5919 Franklin Ave., Hollywood* ☎ *323/908–8702)* marched in with a mix of sketch comedy and wild improvisations skewering pop culture. Members of the L.A. Brigade include VH1 commentator Paul Scheer and *Mad TV*'s Andrew Daly.

DANCE CLUBS

Though the establishments listed below are predominantly dance clubs as opposed to live music venues, there's often some overlap. A given club can vary wildly in genre from night to night, or even on the same night. ■**TIP➔** Gay and promoter-driven theme nights tend to "float" from venue to venue. Call ahead to make sure you don't end up looking for retro '60s music at an industrial bondage celebration (or vice versa). Covers vary according to the night and the DJs.

★ As a bar, **Boardner's** (✉ *1652 N. Cherokee Ave., Hollywood* ☎ *323/462– 9621)* has a multi-decade history (in the '20s it was a speakeasy), but with the adjoining ballroom, which was added a couple of years ago, it's now a state-of-the-art dance club. DJs may be spinning electronica, funk, or something else depending on the night—at the popular Saturday Goth event "Bar Sinister," patrons must wear black or risk not getting in. The cover hovers around $5–$10.

The **Ruby** (✉ *7070 Hollywood Blvd., Hollywood* ☎ *323/467–7070)* is a popular three-room dance venue for young indie-rock and retro-loving twentysomethings. You might find anything from doomy Goth and industrial ("Perversion") to '80s retro ("Beat It") to '60s–'70s Brit pop and soul ("Bang") to trance and techno.

GAY AND LESBIAN CLUBS

Some of the most popular gay and lesbian "clubs" are weekly theme nights at various venues, so read the preceding list of clubs, *LA Weekly* listings, and gay publications such as *Odyssey* in addition to the following recommendations.

★ Nowhere is more gregarious than **Here** (✉ *696 N. Robertson Blvd., West Hollywood* ☎ *310/360–8455)*, where there are hot DJs and an even hotter clientele.

Some weekly highlights include "Truck Stop" on Friday, "Red Hot" on Saturday, and an alcohol-free party on Sunday. A long-running gay-gal fave, the **Palms** (✉ *8572 Santa Monica Blvd., West Hollywood* ☎ *310/652–6188)* continues to thrive thanks to great DJs spinning dance tunes Wednesday–Sunday. There are also an outdoor patio, pool tables, and an occasional live performance. **Rage** (✉ *8911 Santa Monica Blvd., West Hollywood* ☎ *310/652–7055)* is a longtime favorite of the "gym boy" set, with DJs following a different musical theme every night of the week (alternative rock, house, dance remixes, etc.). The cover is free to $10.

Perfect Like Me performs at the Knitting Factory in Hollywood.

ROCK AND OTHER LIVE MUSIC

In addition to the venues listed below, many smaller bars book live music, if less frequently or with less publicity.

The landmark formerly known as the Palace is now the **Avalon** (✉ *1735 N. Vine St., Hollywood* ☎ *323/462–3000*). The multilevel art-deco building opposite Capitol Records has a fabulous sound system, four bars, and a balcony. Big-name rock and pop concerts hit the stage during the week, but on weekends the place becomes a dance club, with the most popular night the DJ-dominated Avaland on Saturday. Upstairs, but with a separate entrance, you'll find celeb hub the **Spider Club,** a Moroccan-style room where celebs and their entourages are frequent visitors. The **Key Club** (✉ *9039 Sunset Blvd., West Hollywood* ☎ *310/274–5800*) is a flashy, multitier rock club with four bars presenting current artists of all genres (some on national tours, others local aspirants). After the concerts, there's often dancing with DJs spinning techno and house.

★   The **Knitting Factory** (✉ *7021 Hollywood Blvd., Hollywood* ☎ *323/463–0204*) is the L.A. offshoot of the Downtown New York club of the same name. The modern, medium-size room seems all the more spacious for its balcony-level seating and sizable stage. Despite its dubious location on Hollywood Boulevard's tourist strip, it's a great setup for the arty, big-name performers it presents. There's live music almost every night in the main room and in the smaller Alter-Knit Lounge. Covers are free to $40.

Musician-producer Jon Brion (Fiona Apple, Aimee Mann, and others) shows off his ability to play virtually any instrument and any song in the rock lexicon—and beyond—as host of a popular evening of music every Friday at **Largo** (✉ *366 N. La Cienega Blvd., Hollywood* ☎ *310/855–0350*). Other nights, low-key rock and singer-songwriter fare is offered at this cozy supper club–bar. And when comedy comes in, about one night a week, it's usually one of the best comedy nights in town, with folks like Margaret Cho. Reservations are required for tables, but bar stools are open.

McCabe's Guitar Shop (✉ *3101 Pico Blvd., Santa Monica* ☎ *310/828–4497, 310/828–4403 for concert information*) is rootsy-retro-central, where all things earnest and (preferably) acoustic are welcome—chiefly folk, blues, bluegrass, and rock. It *is* a guitar shop (so no liquor license), with a room full of folding chairs for concert-style presentations. Make reservations well in advance. The **Roxy** (✉ *9009 Sunset Blvd., West Hollywood* ☎ *310/276–2222*), a Sunset Strip fixture for decades, hosts local and touring rock, alternative, blues, and rockabilly bands. Not the comfiest club around, but it's the site of many memorable shows. Neighborhoody and relaxed, **Silver Lake Lounge** (✉ *2906 Sunset Blvd., Silver Lake* ☎ *323/666–2407*) draws a mixed collegiate and boho crowd. The club is very unmainstream "cool," the booking policy an adventurous mix of local and touring alt-rockers. Bands play three to five nights a week; covers vary but are low.

★ The hottest bands of tomorrow, surprises from yesteryear, and unclassifiable bands of today perform at **Spaceland** (✉ *1717 Silver Lake Blvd., Silver Lake* ☎ *323/661–4380* ⊕ *www.clubspaceland.com*), which has a bar, jukebox, and pool table. Monday is always free, with monthlong gigs by the indie fave du jour. Spaceland has a nice selection of beers, some food if you're hungry, and a hip but relaxed interior. The **Troubadour** (✉ *9081 Santa Monica Blvd., West Hollywood* ☎ *310/276–6168*), one of the best and most comfortable clubs in town, has weathered the test of time since its '60s debut as a folk club. After surviving the '80s heavy-metal scene, this all-ages, wood-panel venue has caught a second (third? fourth?) wind by booking hot alternative rock acts. There's valet parking, but if you don't mind walking up Doheny a block or three, there's usually ample street parking (check the signs carefully).

Actor Johnny Depp sold his share of the infamous **Viper Room** (✉ *8852 Sunset Blvd., West Hollywood* ☎ *310/358–1880*) in 2004, but the place continues to rock with a motley live music lineup, if a less stellar crowd. **Whisky A Go Go** (✉ *8901 Sunset Blvd., West Hollywood* ☎ *310/652–4202*) is the most famous rock-and-roll club on the Strip, where back in the '60s, Johnny Rivers cut hit singles and the Doors, Love, and the Byrds cut their musical eyeteeth. It's still going strong, with up-and-coming alternative, hard rock, and punk bands, though mostly of the unknown variety.

SPORTS AND THE OUTDOORS

BEACHES

Los Angeles County beaches (and state beaches operated by the county) have lifeguards on duty year-round, with expanded forces during the summer. Public parking is usually available, though fees can range anywhere from $8–$20; in some areas, it's possible to find free street and highway parking. Both restrooms and beach access have been brought up to the standards of the Americans with Disabilities Act. Generally, the northernmost beaches are best for surfing, hiking, and fishing, and the wider and sandier southern beaches are better for tanning and relaxing. ■**TIP**➜ Almost all are great for swimming, but beware: pollution in Santa Monica Bay sometimes approaches dangerous levels, particularly after storms. Call ahead for beach conditions (☎ *310/457–9701*) or go to ⊕ *www.watchthewater.com* for specific beach updates. The following beaches are listed in north–south order:

Leo Carrillo State Beach. On the very edge of Ventura County, this narrow beach is better for exploring than for sunning or swimming (watch that strong undertow!). On your own or with a ranger, venture down at low tide to examine the tide pools among the rocks. Sequit Point, a promontory dividing the northwest and southeast halves of the beach, creates secret coves, sea tunnels, and boulders on which you can perch and fish. Generally, anglers stick to the northwest end of the beach; experienced surfers brave the rocks to the southeast. Campgrounds are set back from the beach; call ahead to reserve campsites. ✉ *35000 PCH, Malibu* ☎ *818/880–0350, 800/444–7275 for camping reservations* ☞ *Parking, lifeguard (year-round, except only as needed in winter), restroom, showers, fire pits.*

Fodor'sChoice ★ **Robert H. Meyer Memorial State Beach.** Part of Malibu's most beautiful coastal area, this beach is made up of three minibeaches: El Pescador, La Piedra, and El Matador—all with the same spectacular view. Scramble down the steps to the rocky coves where nude sunbathers sometimes gather—although in recent years, police have been cracking down. "El Mat" has a series of caves, Piedra some nifty rock formations, and Pescador a secluded feel; but they're all picturesque and fairly private. ■**TIP**➜ One warning: watch the incoming tide and don't get trapped between those otherwise scenic boulders. ✉ *32350, 32700, and 32900 PCH, Malibu* ☎ *818/880–0350* ☞ *Parking, 1 roving lifeguard unit, restrooms.*

Zuma Beach Park. Zuma, 2 mi of white sand usually littered with tanning teenagers, has it all: from fishing and diving to swings for the kids to volleyball courts. Beachgoers looking for quiet or privacy should head elsewhere. Stay alert in the water: the surf is rough and inconsistent. ✉ *30050 PCH, Malibu* ☎ *818/880–0350* ☞ *Parking, lifeguard (year-round, except only as needed in winter), restrooms, food concessions, playground.*

Malibu Lagoon State Beach/Surfrider Beach. Steady 3- to 5-foot waves make this beach, just west of Malibu Pier, a surfing paradise. The International

CLOSE UP

Surf City

Nothing captures the laid-back cool of California quite like surfing. Those wanting to sample the surf here should keep a few things in mind before getting wet. First, surfers can be notoriously territorial. Beginners should avoid Palos Verdes and Third Point, at the north end of Malibu Lagoon State Beach, where veterans rule the waves. Once in the water, be as polite and mellow as possible. Give other surfers plenty of space—do *not* cut them off—and avoid swimmers. Beware of rocks and undertows. Surfing calls for caution: that huge piece of flying fiberglass beneath you could kill someone. If you're not a strong swimmer, think twice before jumping in; fighting the surf to where the waves break is a strenuous proposition. The best and safest way to learn is by taking a lesson.

A session with **Malibu Ocean Sports** (✉ 29500 PCH ☎ 310/456–6302) will keep you on the sand for at least 30 minutes explaining the basics. Lessons start at $100; if you don't catch a wave, you get your money back. **Surf Academy** (✉ 302 19th St., Hermosa Beach ☎ 310/372–2790 ⊕ www.surfacademy.org) teaches at El Segundo (Dockweiler), Santa Monica,

and Manhattan Beach, with lessons starting at $45.

Kanoa Aquatics (✉ 302 19th St., Hermosa Beach ☎ 310/308–7264 ⊕ www.kanoaaquatics.com) teaches individuals and groups at Manhattan Beach, Venice, Santa Monica, and Malibu. They also hold highly regarded one- and two-week surf camps for kids ages 5–17. When you hit the surfing hot spots, surf shops with rentals will be in long supply. Competition keeps prices comparable; most rent long and short boards and miniboards (kid-size surfboards) from $20 per day and wet suits from $10 per day (some give discounts for additional days).

Learners should never surf in a busy area; look for somewhere less crowded where you'll catch more waves anyway. Good beaches for beginners are Malibu Lagoon State Beach and Huntington City Beach north of the pier, but you should always check conditions, which change throughout the day, before heading into the water. **L.A. County Lifeguards** (☎ 310/457–9701) has a prerecorded surf-conditions hotline or go to ⊕ www.watchthewater.com for beach reports.

Surfing Contest is held here in September—the surf's premium around that time. Water runoff from Malibu Canyon forms a natural lagoon that's a sanctuary for 250 species of birds. Unfortunately, the lagoon is often polluted and algae filled. If you're leery of going into the water, you can bird-watch, play volleyball, or take a walk on one of the nature trails, which are perfect for romantic sunset strolls. ✉ 23200 PCH, Malibu ☎ 310/305–9503 ☞ Parking, lifeguard (year-round), restrooms, picnic tables.

Will Rogers State Beach. This clean, sandy, 3-mi beach, with a dozen volleyball nets, gymnastics equipment, and playground equipment for kids, is an all-around favorite. The surf is gentle, perfect for swimmers and beginning surfers. However, it's best to avoid the place after a storm,

The Santa Monica Pier is packed with fun diversions and hosts free concerts in summer.

when untreated water flows from storm drains into the sea. ✉ *15100 PCH, 2 mi north of Santa Monica Pier, Pacific Palisades* ☎ *818/880–0350* ✆ *Parking, lifeguard (year-round, except only as needed in winter), restrooms.*

★ **Santa Monica State Beach.** It's the first beach you'll hit after the Santa Monica Freeway (I–10) runs into the PCH, and it's one of L.A.'s best known. Wide and sandy, Santa Monica is *the* place for sunning and socializing: be prepared for a mob scene on summer weekends, when parking becomes an expensive ordeal. Swimming is fine (with the usual poststorm pollution caveat); for surfing, go elsewhere. For a memorable view, climb up the stairway over the PCH to Palisades Park, at the top of the bluffs. Summer-evening concerts are often held here. ✉ *1642 Promenade, PCH at California Incline, Santa Monica* ☎ *310/305–9503* ✆ *Parking, lifeguard (year-round), restrooms, showers.*

Venice City Beach. The surf and sand of Venice are fine, but the main attraction here is the boardwalk scene, which is a cosmos all its own—with fire-eating street performers, vendors hawking everything from cheap sunglasses and aromatherapy oils, and bicep'ed gym rats lifting weights at legendary Muscle Beach. Go on weekend afternoons for the best people-watching experience. There are also swimming, fishing, surfing, basketball (it's the site of some of L.A.'s most hotly contested pickup games), racquetball, handball, and shuffleboard. You can rent a bike or some in-line skates and hit the Strand bike path. ✉ *West of Pacific Ave., Venice* ☎ *310/577–5700* ✆ *Parking, restrooms, food concessions, showers, playground.*

★ **Redondo Beach.** The Redondo Beach Pier marks the starting point of this wide, sandy, busy beach along a heavily developed shoreline community. Restaurants and shops flourish along the pier, excursion boats and privately owned crafts depart from launching ramps, and a reef formed by a sunken ship creates prime fishing and snorkeling conditions. If you're adventurous, you might try to kayak out to the buoys and hobnob with pelicans and sea lions. A series of free rock and jazz concerts takes place at the pier every summer. ⊠ *Torrance Blvd. at Catalina Ave., Redondo Beach* ☎ *310/372–2166* ☞ *Parking, lifeguard (year-round), restrooms, food concessions, showers.*

SPORTS

L.A.'s near-perfect climate allows sports enthusiasts the privilege of being outside year-round. The **City of Los Angeles Department of Recreation and Parks** (⊠ *200 N. Main St., Suite 1350* ☎ *313 from within city limits* ⊕ *www.cityofla.org/rap*) has information on city parks. For information on county parks contact the **Los Angeles County Department of Parks and Recreation** (⊠ *433 S. Vermont Ave.* ☎ *213/738–2961* ⊕ *parks.co.la.ca.us*).

Ticketmaster (☎ *213/480–3232* ⊕ *www.ticketmaster.com*) sells tickets to most sporting events in town.

BASEBALL

You can watch the **Dodgers** take on their National League rivals while you munch on pizza, tacos, or a foot-long "Dodger dog" at one of the game's most comfortable ball parks, **Dodger Stadium** (⊠ *1000 Elysian Park Ave., exit off I–110, Pasadena Fwy.* ☎ *323/224–1448 ticket information* ⊕ *www.dodgers.com*). The **Los Angeles Angels of Anaheim** won the World Series in 2002, the first time since the team formed in 1961. For Angels ticket information, contact **Angel Stadium of Anaheim** (⊠ *2000 Gene Autry Way, Anaheim* ☎ *714/663–9000* ⊕ *www.angelsbaseball.com*). Several colleges in the area also have baseball teams worth watching, especially USC, which has been a perennial source of major-league talent.

BASKETBALL

L.A.'s pro basketball teams play at the Staples Center. The **Los Angeles Lakers** (☎ *310/426–6000* ⊕ *www.nba.com/lakers*) still attract a loyal following that includes celebrity fans like Jack Nicholson, Tyra Banks, and Leonardo DiCaprio. Despite a series of off-the-court conflicts in recent years, the team remains one of the NBA's most successful franchises with 14 NBA championships under its belt. L.A.'s "other" team, the much-maligned but newly revitalized **Clippers** (☎ *888/895–8662* ⊕ *www.nba. com/clippers*), sells tickets that are generally cheaper and easier to get than those for Lakers games. The **Los Angeles Sparks** (☎ *213/929–1300* ⊕ *www.wnba.com/sparks*) have built a WNBA dynasty around former USC star Lisa Leslie.

GOLF

The City Parks and Recreation Department lists seven public 18-hole courses in Los Angeles, and L.A. County runs some good ones, too. **Rancho Park Golf Course** (⊠ *10460 W. Pico Blvd., West L.A.* ☎ *310/838–7373*) is one of the most heavily played links in the country. It's a beautifully designed course, but the towering pines present an obstacle for those who slice or hook. There's a two-level driving range, a 9-hole pitch 'n' putt, a snack bar, and a pro shop where you can rent clubs.

If you want a scenic course, you've got it in spades at the county-run, ★ par-71 **Los Verdes Golf Course** (⊠ *7000 W. Los Verdes Dr., Rancho Palos Verdes* ☎ *310/377–7370*). You get a cliff-top view of the ocean—time it right and you can watch the sun set behind Catalina Island.

Griffith Park has two splendid 18-hole courses along with a challenging 9-hole course. **Harding Municipal Golf Course** and **Wilson Municipal Golf Course** (⊠ *4730 Crystal Springs Dr., Los Feliz* ☎ *323/663–2555*) are about 1½ mi inside the park entrance, at Riverside Drive and Los Feliz Boulevard. Bridle paths surround the outer fairways, and the San Gabriel Mountains make a scenic background. The 9-hole **Roosevelt Municipal Golf Course** (⊠ *2650 N. Vermont Ave., Los Feliz* ☎ *323/665–2011*) can be reached through the park's Vermont Avenue entrance.

SHOPPING

AROUND BEVERLY HILLS

N.Y. has Fifth Avenue, but L.A. has famed **Rodeo Drive.** The triangle, between Santa Monica and Wilshire boulevards and Beverly Drive, is one of the city's biggest tourist attractions and is lined with shops featuring the biggest names in fashion. You'll see well-coifed and -heeled ladies toting multiple packages to their Mercedes and paparazzi staking out street corners. While the dress code in L.A. is considerably laid-back, with residents wearing flip-flops year-round, you might them to be jewel-encrusted on Rodeo. Steep price tags on designer labels make it a "just looking" experience for many residents and tourists alike, but salespeople are used to the ogling and window shopping. In recent years, more mid-range shops have opened up on the strip and surrounding blocks. Keep in mind that some stores are by appointment only. ■ **TIP→** There are several well-marked, free (for two hours) parking lots around the core shopping area.

★ **Beverly Center.** This is one of the more traditional malls you'll find in L.A., with eight levels of stores, including Macy's and Bloomingdale's. Fashion is the biggest draw and there's a little something from everyone, from D&G to H&M, and many shops in the mid-range, including Banana Republic, DKNY, Club Monaco, and Coach. Look for accessories at Jennifer Kaufman, fun fashion at Forever 21, and there's even a destination for the racecar obsessed at the Ferrari Store. For a terrific view of the city, head to the top-floor terrace and rooftop food court. Next door is Loehmann's, which offers a huge selection of discounted designer wear. ⊠ *8500 Beverly Blvd., bounded by Beverly, La Cienega, and San Vicente Blvds. and 3rd St., between Beverly Hills and West Hollywood* ☎ *310/854–0071.*

DOWNTOWN

★ **The Fashion District.** Although this 90-block hub of the West Coast fashion industry is mainly a wholesale market, more than 1,000 independent stores sell to the general public (and some wholesalers do so on Saturday, too, when elbow room is scarce). Bonus: bargaining is expected but note that most sales are cash-only and dressing rooms are scarce. **Santee Alley** (between Santee Street and Maple Avenue, from Olympic Boulevard to 11th Street) is known for back-alley deals on knockoffs of designer sunglasses, jewelry, handbags, shoes, and clothing. Be prepared to haggle, and don't lose sight of your wallet. Visit the fashion district's Web site for maps and tips. ⊠ *Roughly between I–10 and 7th St., San Pedro and Main Sts., Downtown* ⊕ *www.fashiondistrict.org.*

The Jewelry District. This area resembles a slice of Manhattan, with the crowded sidewalks, diverse aromas, and haggling bargain hunters. Expect to save 50% to 70% off retail for everything from wedding bands to sparkling belt buckles. The more upscale stores are along Hill Street between 6th and 7th streets. (There's a parking structure next door on Broadway.) ⊠ *Between Olive St. and Broadway, from 5th to 8th St., Downtown* ⊕ *www.lajd.net.*

Fodor'sChoice **Olvera Street.** Historic buildings line this redbrick walkway overhung
★ with grape vines. At dozens of clapboard stalls you can browse south-of-the-border goods—leather sandals, bright woven blankets, devotional candles, and the like—as well as cheap toys and tchotchkes. With the musicians and cafés providing background noise, the area is constantly lively. ⊠ *Between Cesar Chavez Ave. and Arcadia St., Downtown.*

HOLLYWOOD

Local shops may be a mixed bag, but at least you can read the stars below your feet as you browse along Hollywood Boulevard. Lingerie and movie memorabilia stores predominate here, but there are numerous options in the retail-hotel-dining-entertainment complex Hollywood & Highland. Hollywood impersonators (Michael Jackson, Marilyn Monroe, and, er, Chewbacca) join break-dancers and other street entertainers in keeping tourists entertained on Hollywood Boulevard's sidewalks near the Kodak Theater, home to the Oscars. Along La Brea Avenue, you'll find plenty of trendy, quirky, and hip merchandise, from records to furniture and clothing.

Hollywood & Highland. Dozens of stores, a slew of eateries, and the Kodak Theatre fill this outdoor complex, which mimics cinematic glamour. Find designer shops (Coach, Polo, Ralph Lauren, Louis Vuitton) and chain stores (Victoria's Secret, Planet Funk, Sephora, and the Hard Rock Café). From the upper levels, there's a camera-perfect view of the famous HOLLYWOOD sign. On the second level, next to the Kodak Theatre, is a **Visitor Information Center** (☎ *323/467–6412*) with a multilingual staff, maps, attraction brochures, and information about services. The streets surrounding it provide the setting for the Sunday Hollywood Farmers' Market, where you're likely to spot a celebrity or two picking up fresh produce or stopping to eat breakfast from the food vendors. ✉ *Hollywood Blvd. and Highland Ave., Hollywood* ☎ *323/817–0220.*

LOS FELIZ, SILVER LAKE, AND ECHO PARK

There's a hipster rock-and-roll vibe to this area, which has grown in recent years to add just the slightest shine to its edge. Come for home-grown, funky galleries, vintage shops, and local designers' boutiques. Shopping areas are concentrated along Vermont Avenue and Holly-wood Boulevard in Los Feliz; Sunset Boulevard in both Silver Lake (known as Sunset Junction) and Echo Park; and Echo Park Avenue in Echo Park. ■TIP➔ Keep in mind that things are spread out enough to necessitate a couple of short car trips, and many shops in these neighbor-hoods don't open until noon but stay open later, so grab dinner or drinks at one of the area's über-cool spots after shopping.

WEST HOLLYWOOD AND MELROSE AVENUE

West Hollywood is prime shopping real estate. And as they say with real estate, it's all about location, location, location. Depending on the street address, West Hollywood has everything from upscale art, design, and antiques stores to ladies-who-lunch clothing boutiques to megamusic stores and specialty book vendors. Melrose Avenue, for instance, is part bohemian-punk shopping district (from North Highland to Sweetzer) and part upscale art and design mecca (upper Melrose Avenue and Melrose Place). Discerning locals and celebs haunt the posh boutiques around Sunset Plaza (Sunset Boulevard at Sunset Plaza Drive), on Robertson Boulevard (between Beverly Boulevard and 3rd Street), and along upper Melrose Avenue.

The huge, blue Pacific Design Center, on Melrose at San Vicente Boulevard, is the focal point for this neighborhood's art- and interior design–related stores, including many on nearby Beverly Boulevard. The Beverly–La Brea neighborhood also claims a number of trendy clothing stores. Perched between Beverly Hills and West Hollywood, 3rd Street (between La Cienega and Fairfax) is a magnet for small, friendly designer boutiques. Finally, the Fairfax District, along Fairfax below Melrose, encompasses the flamboyant, historic Farmers Market, at Fairfax Avenue and 3rd Street; the adjacent shopping extravaganza, The Grove; and some excellent galleries around Museum Row at Fairfax Avenue and Wilshire Boulevard.

SANTA MONICA AND VENICE

The breezy beachside communities of Santa Monica and Venice are ideal for leisurely shopping. Scads of tourists (and some locals) gravitate to the Third Street Promenade, a popular pedestrians-only strolling–shopping area that is within walking range of the beach and historic Santa Monica Pier. A number of modern furnishings stores are nearby on 4th and 5th streets. Main Street between Pico Boulevard and Rose Avenue offers upscale chain stores, cafés, and some original shops, while Montana Avenue is a great source for distinctive clothing boutiques and child-friendly shopping, especially between 7th and 17th streets. ■ **TIP→** Parking in Santa Monica is next to impossible on Wednesday, when some streets are blocked off for the farmers' market, but there are several parking structures with free parking for an hour or two. In Venice, Abbot Kinney Boulevard is abuzz with mid-century furniture stores, art galleries and boutiques, and cafés.

★ **Third Street Promenade.** Whimsical dinosaur-shaped, ivy-covered fountains and buskers of every stripe set the scene along this pedestrians-only shopping stretch. Stores are mainly the chain variety (Restoration Hardware, Urban Outfitters, Apple), but there are also Quiksilver and Rip Curl outposts for cool surf attire. Movie theaters, bookstores, pubs, and restaurants ensure that virtually every need is covered. ⊠ *3rd St. between Broadway and Wilshire Blvd.*

The Central Coast

FROM VENTURA TO BIG SUR

WORD OF MOUTH

"I was blown away by the immense outdoor pool at the Hearst Castle. It is huge, and yet incredibly serene in its surroundings. The Castle is situated on top of the hills in the San Simeon area and allows for massive views of nearly 360 degrees around."

—photo by L Vantreight, Fodors.com member

WELCOME TO THE CENTRAL COAST

TOP REASONS TO GO

★ **Incredible nature:** Much of the Central Coast looks as wild and wonderful as it did centuries ago; the area is home to Channel Islands National Park, two national marine sanctuaries, state parks and beaches, and the vast and rugged Los Padres National Forest.

★ **Edible bounty:** Land and sea provide enough fresh regional foods to satisfy even the savviest of foodies—grapes, strawberries, seafood, olive oil . . . the list goes on and on. Get your fill at countless farmers' markets, wineries, and restaurants.

★ **Outdoor activities:** Kick back and revel in the casual California lifestyle. Surf, golf, kayak, hike, play tennis—or just hang out and enjoy the gorgeous scenery.

★ **Small-town charm, big-city culture:** Small, friendly, uncrowded towns offer an amazing array of cultural amenities. With all the art and history museums, theater, music, and festivals, you might start thinking you're in L.A. or San Francisco.

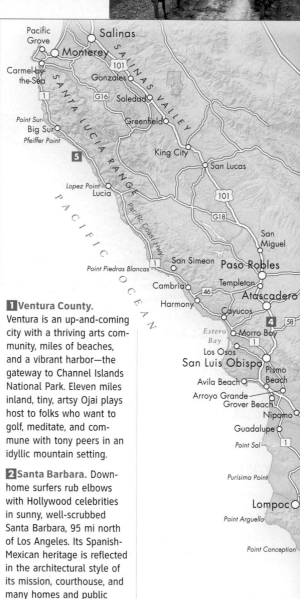

1 Ventura County.
Ventura is an up-and-coming city with a thriving arts community, miles of beaches, and a vibrant harbor—the gateway to Channel Islands National Park. Eleven miles inland, tiny, artsy Ojai plays host to folks who want to golf, meditate, and commune with tony peers in an idyllic mountain setting.

2 Santa Barbara. Down-home surfers rub elbows with Hollywood celebrities in sunny, well-scrubbed Santa Barbara, 95 mi north of Los Angeles. Its Spanish-Mexican heritage is reflected in the architectural style of its mission, courthouse, and many homes and public buildings.

3 **Santa Barbara County.** Wineries, ranches, and small villages dominate the quintessentially Californian landscape here.

4 **San Luis Obispo County.** Friendly college town San Luis Obispo serves as hub of a burgeoning wine region that stretches nearly 100 mi from Pismo Beach north to Paso Robles; the 230-plus wineries here have earned reputations for high-quality vintages that rival those of northern California.

5 **The Big Sur Coastline.** Rugged cliffs meet the Pacific for more than 60 mi—one of the most scenic and dramatic drives in the world.

6 **Channel Islands National Park.** Home to 145 species of plants and animals found nowhere else on Earth, this relatively undiscovered gem of a park encompasses five islands and a mile of surrounding ocean.

GETTING ORIENTED

The Central Coast region begins about 60 mi north of Los Angeles, near the seaside city of Ventura. From there the coastline stretches north about 200 mi, winding through the small cities of Santa Barbara and San Luis Obispo, then north through the small towns of Morro Bay and Cambria to Carmel. The drive through this region, especially the section of Highway 1 from San Simeon to Big Sur, is one of the most scenic in the state.

5

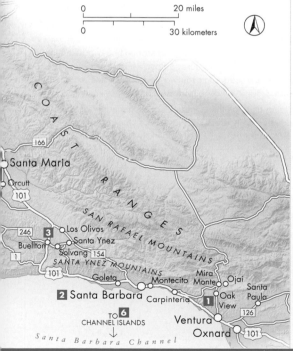

0 ——— 20 miles
0 ——— 30 kilometers

.stopenough

THE CENTRAL COAST PLANNER

When to Go

The Central Coast climate is usually mild throughout the year. If you like to sunbathe and swim in warmer (though still nippy) ocean waters, July and August are the best months to visit. Be aware that this is also high season. Fog often rolls in all along the coastal areas in early summer; you'll need a jacket, especially after sunset, close to the shore. The rains usually come from December through March. From April to early June and in the early fall the weather is almost as fine as in high season, and the pace is less hectic.

Getting Around

Driving is the easiest way to experience the Central Coast. A car gives you the flexibility to stop at scenic vista points along Highway 1, take detours through wine country, and drive to rural lakes and mountains. Traveling north through Ventura County to San Luis Obispo (note that from just south of Ventura up to San Luis Obispo, U.S. 101 and Highway 1 are the same road), you can take in the rolling hills, peaceful valleys, and rugged mountains that stretch for miles along the shore. Amtrak trains link major cities throughout the region.

About the Hotels

There are plenty of lodging options throughout the Central Coast—but expect to pay top dollar for any rooms along the shore, especially in summer. Moderately priced hotels and motels do exist—most just a short drive inland from their higher-price counterparts. Make your reservations as early as possible and take advantage of midweek specials to get the best rates. It's common for hotels to require minimum stays on holidays and some weekends, especially in summer, and to double their rates during festivals and other events.

About the Restaurants

The cuisine in Ventura and Santa Barbara is every bit as eclectic as it is in California's bigger cities; fresh seafood is a standout. The region from Solvang to Big Sur is far enough off the Interstate to ensure that nearly every restaurant or café has its own personality—from chic to down-home and funky. A foodie renaissance has overtaken the entire region from Ventura to Paso Robles, spawning dozens of new restaurants touting nouveau cuisine made with fresh organic produce and meats.

Dining attire on the Central Coast is generally casual, though slightly dressy casual wear is the custom at pricier restaurants.

WHAT IT COSTS

	¢	$	$$	$$$	$$$$
Restaurants	under $10	$10–$15	$16–$22	$23–$30	over $30
Hotels	under $90	$90–$120	$121–$175	$176–$250	over $250

Restaurant prices are for a main course at dinner, excluding sales tax of 7.25%–7.75% (depending on location). Hotel prices are for two people in a standard double room in high season, excluding service charges and 9%–10% tax.

5

Updated by Cheryl Crabtree

Balmy weather, glorious beaches, crystal clear air, and serene landscapes have lured people to the Central Coast since prehistoric times. It's an ideal place to relax, slow down, and appreciate the good things in life.

Along the Pacific coast, the scenic variety is stunning—everything from dramatic cliffs and grass-tufted bluffs to wildlife estuaries and miles of dunes. Offshore, a pristine national park and a vast marine sanctuary protect the wild, wonderful underwater resources of this incredible corner of the planet. But not all of the Central Coast's top attractions are natural: the small cities of Ventura, Santa Barbara, and San Luis Obispo are filled with sparkling examples of Spanish-Mediterranean architecture, bustling shopping districts, and first-rate restaurants showcasing regional foods and wines.

PLANNING

GETTING HERE AND AROUND

BY AIR

Alaska Air, American, Delta, Horizon Air, United, United Express, and US Airways fly to Santa Barbara Municipal Airport, 12 mi from downtown. United Express and US Airways provide service to San Luis Obispo County Regional Airport, 3 mi from downtown San Luis Obispo.

Santa Barbara Airbus shuttles travelers between Santa Barbara and Los Angeles for $48 one-way and $90 round-trip (slight discount with 24-hour notice, larger discount for groups of six or more). Coast Flyer partners with Santa Barbara Airbus to carry travelers between Santa Barbara Airport and Buellton, Santa Maria, Pismo Beach, and San Luis Obispo. The Santa Barbara Metropolitan Transit District Bus 11 ($1.25) runs every 30 minutes from the airport to the downtown transit center. A taxi between the airport and the hotel district runs $18 to $25.

Airport Contacts San Luis Obispo County Regional Airport (✉ 903–5 Airport Dr., San Luis Obispo ☎ 805/781–5205 ⊕ www.sloairport.com). **Santa**

Barbara Airport (✉ *500 Fowler Rd., Santa Barbara* ☎ *805/683–4011* ⊕ *www. flysba.com*).

Airport Transfer Contacts Coast Flyer (☎ *805/545–8400* ⊕ *www.coastflyer. com*). **Santa Barbara Airbus** (☎ *805/964–7759 or 800/733–6354, 800/423– 1618 in CA* ⊕ *www.santabarbaraairbus.com*). **Santa Barbara Metropolitan Transit District** (☎ *805/963–3366* ⊕ *www.sbmtd.gov*).

BY BUS

Greyhound provides service from San Francisco and Los Angeles to San Luis Obispo, Ventura, and Santa Barbara. From Monterey and Carmel, Monterey-Salinas Transit operates buses to Big Sur between May and mid-October. From San Luis Obispo, Central Coast Transit runs buses around Santa Maria and out to the coast. Santa Barbara Metropolitan Transit District provides local service. The Downtown/ State Street and Waterfront shuttles cover their respective sections of Santa Barbara during the day. Gold Coast Transit buses serve the entire Ventura County region.

Bus Contacts Central Coast Transit (☎ *805/781–4472* ⊕ *www.slorta. org*). **Gold Coast Transit** (☎ *805/487–4222 for Oxnard and Port Hueneme, 805/643–3158 for Ojai and Ventura* ⊕ *www.goldcoasttransit.org*). **Greyhound** (☎ *800/231–2222* ⊕ *www.greyhound.com*). **Monterey-Salinas Transit** (☎ *888/678–2871* ⊕ *www.mst.org*). **San Luis Obispo Transit** (☎ *805/781–4472* ⊕ *www.slorta.org*). **Santa Barbara Metropolitan Transit District** (☎ *805/963– 3366* ⊕ *www.sbmtd.gov*).

BY CAR

Highway 1 and U.S. 101 run north–south and more or less parallel along the Central Coast, with Highway 1 hugging the coast and U.S. 101 running inland. The most dramatic section of the Central Coast is the 70 mi between Big Sur and San Simeon. Don't expect to make good time along here: The road is narrow and twisting with a single lane in each direction, making it difficult to pass the many lumbering RVs. In fog or rain the drive can be downright nerve-racking; in wet seasons mudslides can close portions of the road. Once you start south from Carmel, there is no route east from Highway 1 until Highway 46 heads inland from Cambria to connect with U.S. 101. At Morro Bay, Highway 1 turns inland for 13 mi and connects with U.S. 101 at San Luis Obispo. From here south to Pismo Beach the two highways run concurrently. South of Pismo Beach to Las Cruces the roads separate, then run together all the way to Oxnard. Along any stretch where they are separate, U.S. 101 is the quicker route.

U.S. 101 and Highway 1 will get you to the Central Coast from Los Angeles and San Francisco. If you are coming from the east, you can take Highway 46 west from I–5 in the Central Valley (near Bakersfield) to U.S. 101 at Paso Robles, where it continues to the coast, intersecting Highway 1 a few miles south of Cambria. Highway 33 heads south from I–5 at Bakersfield to Ojai. About 60 mi north of Ojai, Highway 166 leaves Highway 33, traveling due west through the Sierra Madre to Santa Maria at U.S. 101 and continuing west to Highway 1 at Guadalupe. South of Carpinteria, Highway 150 winds from Highway 1/U.S.

101 through sparsely populated hills to Ojai. From Highway 1/U.S. 101 at Ventura, Highway 33 leads to Ojai and the Los Padres National Forest. South of Ventura, Highway 126 runs east from Highway 1/U.S. 101 to I–5.

Contacts Caltrans (☎ 800/427–7623 ⊕ www.dot.ca.gov).

BY TRAIN

The Amtrak *Coast Starlight,* which runs between Los Angeles and Seattle via Oakland, stops in Paso Robles, San Luis Obispo, Santa Barbara, and Oxnard. Amtrak runs several *Pacific Surfliner* trains daily between San Luis Obispo, Santa Barbara, Los Angeles, and San Diego. Metrolink Regional Rail Service trains connect Ventura and Oxnard with Los Angeles and points between.

Train Contacts Amtrak (☎ 800/872–7245, 805/963–1015 in Santa Barbara, 805/541–0505 in San Luis Obispo ⊕ www.amtrakcalifornia.com). **Metrolink** (☎ 800/371–5465 ⊕ www.metrolinktrains.com).

TOUR OPTIONS

Cloud Climbers Jeep and Wine Tours offers four types of daily tours: wine-tasting, mountain, sunset, and a discovery tour for families. These trips to the Santa Barbara/Santa Ynez mountains and wine country are conducted in open-air, six-passenger jeeps. Fares range from $89 to $120 per adult. The company also arranges biking, horseback riding, and trap-shooting tours and Paso Robles wine tours by appointment. Wine Edventures operates customized Santa Barbara County tours and narrated North County wine-country tours in 25-passenger minicoaches. Fares for the wine tours are $110 per person. The Grapeline Wine Country Shuttle leads daily wine and vineyard picnic tours with flexible itineraries in San Luis Obispo County and Santa Barbara County wine country; they stop at many area hotels and can provide private custom tours with advance reservations. Fares range from $42 to $85, depending on pickup location and tour choice.

Spencer's Limousine & Tours offers customized tours of the city of Santa Barbara and wine country via sedan, limousine, van, or minibus. A five-hour basic tour with at least four participants costs about $90 per person. Sultan's Limousine Service has a fleet of super stretches; each can take up to eight passengers on Paso Robles and Edna Valley–Arroyo Grande wine tours and tours of the San Luis Obispo County coast. Hiring a limo for a four-hour wine country tour typically costs $400 to $450 with tip. Sustainable Vine Wine Tours' biodiesel-powered vans can take you on a day of eco-friendly wine touring in the Santa Ynez Valley. Trips include door-to-door transportation from your location in the Santa Barbara or Santa Ynez Valley area, tastings at green-minded wineries, and a gourmet organic picnic lunch.

Tour Contacts Cloud Climbers Jeep and Wine Tours (☎ 805/646–3200 ⊕ www.ccjeeps.com). **The Grapeline Wine Country Shuttle** (☎ 805/239–4747 Paso Robles, 805/238–2765 San Luis Obispo, 888/894–6379 Santa Barbara/ Solvang ⊕ www.gogrape.com). **Spencer's Limousine & Tours** (☎ 805/884–9700 ⊕ www.spencerslimo.com). **Sultan's Limousine Service** (☎ 805/466 3167 North SLO County, 805/544–8320 South SLO County, 805/771–0161 coastal SLO County

cities ⊕ *www.sultanslimo.com*). **Sustainable Vine Wine Tours** (☎ *805/698–3911*
⊕ *www.sustainablevine.com*). **Wine Edventures** (✉ *3463 State St., #228, Santa
Barbara* ☎ *805/965–9463* ⊕ *www.welovewines.com*).

VISITOR INFORMATION

Contacts San Luis Obispo County Visitors and Conference Bureau (✉ *811
El Capitan Way #200, San Luis Obispo* ☎ *805/541–8000 or 800/634–1414*
⊕ *www.sanluisobispocounty.com*). **Santa Barbara Conference and Visitors Bureau** (✉ *1601 Anacapa St., Santa Barbara* ☎ *805/966–9222* ⊕ *www.
santabarbaraca.com*).

VENTURA COUNTY

Ventura County was first settled by the Chumash Indians. Spanish missionaries were the first Europeans to arrive, followed by Americans and other Europeans, who established bustling towns, transportation networks, and highly productive farms. Since the 1920s, though, agriculture has been steadily replaced as the area's main industry—first by the oil business, and more recently, by tourism.

VENTURA

60 mi north of Los Angeles on U.S. 101.

Like Los Angeles, the city of Ventura enjoys gorgeous weather and sun-kissed beaches—but without the smog and congestion. The city is filled with classic California buildings, farmers and fish markets, art galleries, and shops. The miles of beautiful beaches attract both athletes—bodysurfers and boogie boarders, runners and bikers—and those who'd rather doze beneath a rented umbrella all day. Ventura Harbor is home to the Channel Islands National Park Visitor Center and myriad fishing boats, restaurants, and water-activity centers where you can rent boats and take harbor cruises. Foodies can get their fix here, too; dozens of upscale cafés and wine and tapas bars have opened in recent years. Ventura is also a magnet for arts and antiques buffs who come to browse the dozens of galleries and shops in the downtown area.

ESSENTIALS

Visitor Information Ventura Visitors and Convention Bureau (✉ *101 S.
California St., Ventura* ☎ *805/648–2075 or 800/483–6214* ⊕ *www.
ventura-usa.com*).

EXPLORING

You can pick up culinary, antiques, and shopping guides downtown at the **visitor center** (✉ *101 S. California St.* ☎ *805/648–2075 or 800/483–
6214* ⊕ *www.ventura-usa.com*) run by the Ventura Visitors and Convention Bureau.

Ventura Oceanfront. Four miles of gorgeous coastline stretch from the county fairgrounds at the northern border of the city of San Buenaventura, through San Buenaventura State Beach, down to Ventura Harbor in the south. The main attraction here is the San Buenaventura City Pier, a historic landmark built in 1872 and restored in 1993. Surfers rip the waves just north of the pier, and sunbathers relax on white-sand beaches on either side. The mile-long promenade and the Omer Rains Bike Trail north of the pier attract scores of joggers, surrey cyclers, and bikers throughout the year. ⊠ *California St., at ocean's edge.*

⏃ Lunker largemouth bass, rainbow trout, crappie, redears, and channel catfish live in the waters at **Lake Casitas Recreation Area**, an impoundment of the Ventura River. The lake is one of the country's best bass-fishing areas, and anglers come from all over the United States to test their luck. The park, nestled below the Santa Ynez Mountains'

> ### TRAFFIC TIMING
>
> The southbound freeway from Santa Barbara to Ventura and L.A. slows from 4 PM to 6 or 7 PM; the reverse is true heading from Ventura to Santa Barbara in the early morning hours. Traffic in the greater Los Angeles region can clog the roads as early as 2 PM. Traveling south, it's best to depart Santa Barbara before 1 PM, or after 6 PM. Heading north, you probably won't encounter many traffic problems until you reach the Salinas/San Jose corridor.

Laguna Ridge, is also a beautiful spot for pitching a tent or having a picnic. The Casitas Water Adventure, which has two water playgrounds and a lazy river for tubing and floating, is a great place to take kids in summer ($12 for an all-day pass; $5 from 5 to 7 PM). The park is 13 mi northwest of Ventura. ⊠ *11311 Santa Ana Rd., off Hwy. 33* ☎ *805/649–2233, 805/649–1122 campground reservations* ⊕ *www. lakecasitas.info* ☞ *$10 per vehicle, $10 per boat* ☉ *Daily.*

The ninth of the 21 California missions, **Mission San Buenaventura** was established in 1782 but burned to the ground in the 1790s. It was rebuilt and rededicated in 1809. A self-guided tour takes you through a small museum, a quiet courtyard, and a chapel with 250-year-old paintings. ⊠ *211 E. Main St.* ☎ *805/643–4318* ⊕ *www.sanbuenaventuramission. org* ☞ *$2* ☉ *Weekdays 10–5, Sat. 9–5, Sun. 10–4.*

WHERE TO EAT

$$$
AMERICAN
✕**Brooks.** Innovative chef Andy Brooks and his wife Jayme—whose grandfather co-owned the famous Chi Chi supper club in Palm Springs in the 1960s—serve some of the town's finest meals in a slick, contemporary downtown dining room. The ever-changing menu centers on seasonal, mostly local, organic ingredients and features a nightly three-course tasting menu, which might include limoncello steamed mussels, cornmeal fried oysters, or free-range chicken breast with sautéed collard greens and goat cheese-potato puree. Ask for the romaine salad dressed in the legendary Chi Chi creamy garlic dressing. Live music and hip martinis and margaritas attract a loyal following after 9 PM on weekends. ⊠ *545 E. Thompson Blvd.* ☎ *805/652–7070* ⊕ *www. restaurantbrooks.com* ▤ *AE, D, MC, V* ☉ *Closed Mon. No lunch.*

$$
SEAFOOD
✕**Brophy Bros.** The Ventura outpost of this wildly popular Santa Barbara restaurant provides the same fresh seafood-oriented meals in a spacious second-story setting overlooking the harbor. Feast on everything from fish and chips and crab cakes to chowder and delectable fish—often straight from the boats moored below. ⊠ *1559 Spinnaker*

5

Ventura and Santa Barbara Counties

Dr., in Ventura Harbor Village ☎ 805/639–0865 ⊕ *www.brophybros. com ⊜ Reservations not accepted ≡ AE, MC, V.*

$ × **Busy Bee Cafe.** A local favorite for decades, this classic 1950s diner has
AMERICAN a jukebox on every table and serves hearty burgers and American comfort food (think meat loaf and mashed potatoes, pot roast, and Cobb
salad). For breakfast, tuck into a huge omelet; for a snack or dessert, be
sure to order a shake or hot fudge sundae from the soda fountain. ✉ *478
E. Main St.* ☎ *805/643–4864* ⊕ *www.busybeecafe.biz* ≡ *MC, V.*

$$ × **Jonathan's at Peirano's.** The main dining room here has a gazebo where
MEDITERRANEAN you can eat surrounded by plants and local art. The menu has dishes
from Spain, Portugal, France, Italy, Greece, and Morocco. Standouts are
the various paellas, the *penne checca* pasta, and the ahi tuna encrusted
with pepper and pistachios. The owners also run an evening tapas bar
next door, which serves exotic martinis. ✉ *204 E. Main St.* ☎ *805/648–
4853* ≡ *AE, D, DC, MC, V.*

WHERE TO STAY

$$ 🏨 **Four Points by Sheraton Ventura Harbor.** The spacious, contemporary
rooms here are still gleaming from a total renovation that was com-
pleted in 2009. An on-site restaurant and a slew of amenities make this
17-acre property (which includes sister hotel Holiday Inn Express) a
popular and practical choice for Channel Islands visitors. The hotel sits

on the edge of the harbor, a few minutes drive from the national park visitor center and concessionaire boat launches. All of the nautical-themed rooms have flat-screen TVs; most have private patios or balconies. (For the best views, request a second-floor marina-facing balcony room.) **Pros:** close to island transportation; mostly quiet; short drive or bus ride to historic downtown Ventura. **Cons:** not in the heart of downtown; noisy seagulls sometimes congregate nearby. ⊠ *1050 Schooner Dr.* ☎ *805/658–1212* ⊕ *www.fourpoints.com/ventura* ⤳ *102 rooms, 4 suites* ⚬ *In-room: a/c, refrigerator, Internet, Wi-Fi. In-hotel: restaurant, room service, bar, pool, gym, laundry service, Internet terminal, Wi-Fi hotspot, some pets allowed* ⊟ *AE, D, DC, MC, V* ⧉ *BP.*

\$\$–\$\$\$ 🏨 **Holiday Inn Express Ventura Harbor.** A favorite among Channel Islands visitors, this quiet, comfortable, lodge-inspired property sits right at the Ventura Harbor entrance. A major renovation in 2006 transformed the guest quarters into spacious, sophisticated retreats with flat-screen TVs and puffy duvets. The south side of the hotel overlooks the marinas; ask for an upper-floor harborside room or suite for the best views. **Pros:** quiet at night; easy access to harbor restaurants and activities; on shuttle bus route to city attractions. **Cons:** busy area on weekends; five minute drive to downtown sights. ⊠ *1080 Navigator Dr.* ☎ *805/856–9533 or 800/315–2621* ⊕ *www.hiexpress.com* ⤳ *68 rooms, 23 suites* ⚬ *In-room: no a/c, kitchen (some), Internet. In-hotel: pool, gym, laundry service, Wi-Fi hotspot* ⊟ *AE, D, DC, MC, V* ⧉ *BP.*

\$\$\$ 🏨 **Pierpont Inn.** Back in 1910, Josephine Pierpont-Ginn built the original Pierpont Inn on a hill overlooking Ventura Beach. Today's renovated complex, which includes an Arts-and-Crafts lobby and English Tudor cottages set amid gardens and gazebos, reflects much of the hotel's original elegance. For a fee you can work out at the neighboring Pierpont Racquet Club, which has indoor and outdoor pools, 15 tennis courts, racquetball courts, spa services, aerobics, and child care. The inn's restaurant has great views of the ocean and harbor. **Pros:** near the beach; lush gardens; Tempur-Pedic mattresses and pillows. **Cons:** near the freeway and train tracks; difficult to walk downtown from here. ⊠ *550 Sanjon Rd.* ☎ *805/643–6144 or 800/285–4667* ⊕ *www.pierpontinn.com* ⤳ *65 rooms, 9 suites, 2 cottages* ⚬ *In-room: no a/c (some), refrigerator, Wi-Fi. In-hotel: restaurant, bar, tennis courts, pool, gym, spa, Internet terminal, Wi-Fi hotspot* ⊟ *AE, D, DC, MC, V* ⧉ *CP (except Sun.).*

\$\$\$ 🏨 **Ventura Beach Marriott.** Spacious, contemporary rooms, a peaceful location just steps from San Buenaventura State Beach, and easy access to historic downtown Ventura's arts and culture district make the Marriott a popular choice for travelers who want to explore Ventura. It's a joy to hang out in the public areas: the marble-tiled lobby doubles as an art gallery with rotating exhibits by local photography students, and waterfalls, lush gardens, and a koi pond with turtles contribute to the tropical theme indoors and out. Ask for a room with a private balcony. **Pros:** walk to beach and biking/jogging trails; a block from historic pier; great value for location. **Cons:** close to highway; near busy intersection. ⊠ *2055 E. Harbor Blvd.* ☎ *805/643–6000 or 800/228–9290* ⊕ *www.marriottventurabeach.com* ⤳ *272 rooms, 12 suites* ⚬ *In-*

room: a/c, Internet, Wi-Fi. In-hotel: restaurant, room service, bar, pool, gym, bicycles, laundry facilities, laundry service, Internet terminal, Wi-Fi hotspot, parking (paid), some pets allowed ⊟AE, D, DC, MC, V ⍩⎮ CP.

SPORTS AND THE OUTDOORS

The most popular outdoor activities in Ventura are beach-going and whale-watching. California gray whales migrate offshore through the Santa Barbara Channel from late December through March; giant blue and humpback whales feed here from mid-June through September. In fact, the channel is teeming with marine life year-round, so tours include more than just whale sightings. A cruise through the Santa Barbara Channel with **Island Packers** (⌧ *1691 Spinnaker Dr., Ventura Harbor* ☎ *805/642–1393* ⊕ *www.islandpackers. com*) will give you the chance to spot dolphins and seals—and sometimes even whales—throughout the year.

> **HOTEL HELP**
>
> **Hot Spots** (☎ *800/793–7666* ⊕ *www.hotspotsusa.com*) provides room reservations and tourist information for destinations in Ventura, Santa Barbara, and San Luis Obispo counties.

OJAI

15 mi north of Ventura, U.S. 101 to Hwy. 33.

The Ojai Valley, which director Frank Capra used as a backdrop for his 1936 film *Lost Horizon,* sizzles in the summer when temperatures routinely reach 90°F. The acres of orange and avocado groves here evoke postcard images of agricultural Southern California from decades ago. This is a lush, slow-moving place, where many artists and celebrities have sought refuge from life in the fast lane.

ESSENTIALS

Visitor Information Ojai Valley Chamber of Commerce (☎ *805/646–8126* ⊕ *www.ojaichamber.org*).

EXPLORING

The town can be easily explored on foot; you can also hop on the **Ojai Valley Trolley** (⊕ *www.ojaitrolley.com* ⍼ *50¢*), which follows two routes around Ojai and neighboring Miramonte between 7:15 and 5:15 on weekdays, 9 and 5 on weekends. If you tell the driver you're a visitor, you'll get an informal guided tour.

Maps and tourist information are available at the **Ojai Valley Chamber of Commerce** (⌧ *201 S. Signal St.* ☎ *805/646–8126* ⊕ *www.ojaichamber. org* ⊙ *Weekdays 9–4*).

The work of local artists is displayed in the Spanish-style shopping arcade along **Ojai Avenue** (Highway 150). Organic and specialty growers sell their produce on Sunday 10–2 (9–1 in summer) at the farmers' market behind the arcade.

The **Ojai Center for the Arts** (⌧ *113 S. Montgomery St.* ☎ *805/646–0117* ⊕ *www.ojaiartcenter.org*) exhibits artwork and presents theater and dance performances.

The **Ojai Valley Museum** (✉ *130 W. Ojai Ave.* ☎ *805/640–1390* ⊕ *www.ojaivalleymuseum.org*) has exhibits on the valley's history and many Native American artifacts.

The 18-mi **Ojai Valley Trail** (✉ *Parallel to Hwy. 33, from Soule Park in Ojai to ocean in Ventura* ☎ *805/654–3951* ⊕ *www.ojaichamber.org*) is open to pedestrians, bikers, joggers, equestrians, and nonmotorized vehicles. You can access it anywhere along its route.

WHERE TO EAT

$$
MEDITERRANEAN

✕**Azu.** Delectable tapas, a full bar, slick furnishings, and piped jazz music lure diners to this popular, artsy Mediterranean bistro. You can also order soups, salads, and bistro fare such as tagine roasted chicken and paella. Save room for the homemade gelato. ✉ *457 E. Ojai Ave.* ☎ *805/640–7987* ⊕ *www.azuojai.com* ▭ *AE, D, MC, V* ⊘ *No lunch Sun. and Mon.*

$
ITALIAN

✕**Boccali's.** Edging a ranch, citrus groves, and a seasonal garden that provides much of the produce for menu items, family-run Boccali's has attracted droves of loyal fans to its modest but cheery restaurant since 1986. In the warmer months, you can dine alfresco in the oak-shaded patio and lawn area and sometimes listen to live music. Best known for their hand-rolled pizzas and homestyle pastas (don't miss the eggplant lasagna), Boccali's also serves a seasonal strawberry shortcake that some patrons drive many miles to savor every year. ✉ *3277 Ojai Ave., about 2 mi east of downtown* ☎ *805/646–6116* ⊕ *www.boccalis.com* ▭ *No credit cards* ⊘ *No lunch Mon. and Tues.*

$$$
AMERICAN
★

✕**The Ranch House.** This elegant yet laid-back eatery—said to be the best in town—has been around for decades, attracting celebrities like Paul Newman. Main dishes such as rack of lamb in an oyster-and-mushroom cream sauce, and grilled diver scallops with curried sweet-corn sauce are not to be missed. The verdant patio is a wonderful place to have Sunday brunch. ✉ *500 S. Lomita Ave.* ☎ *805/646–2360* ⊕ *www.theranchhouse.com* ▭ *AE, D, DC, MC, V* ⊘ *Closed Mon. No lunch.*

$$$
CONTINENTAL

✕**Suzanne's Cuisine.** Peppered filet mignon, linguine with steamed clams, and pan-roasted salmon with a roasted mango sauce are among the offerings at this European-style restaurant. Game, seafood, and vegetarian dishes dominate the dinner menu, and salads and soups star at lunchtime. All the breads and desserts are made on the premises. ✉ *502 W. Ojai Ave.* ☎ *805/640–1961* ⊕ *www.suzannescuisine.com* ▭ *AE, MC, V* ⊘ *Closed Tues.*

WHERE TO STAY

$–$$

⌂ **The Blue Iguana Inn & Cottages.** Artists run this Southwestern-style hotel, and their work (which is for sale) decorates the rooms. The small, cozy main inn is about 2 mi west of downtown. Its sister property, the Emerald Iguana Inn (no children under 14), consists of eight more art nouveau cottages closer to downtown Ojai. Suites and cottages all have kitchenettes. **Pros:** colorful art everywhere; secluded property; breakfast delivered to each room. **Cons:** 2 mi from the heart of Ojai; sits on the main highway to Ventura; small. ✉ *11794 N. Ventura Ave., Hwy. 33* ☎ *805/646–5277* ⊕ *www.blueiguanainn.com* ⇗ *4 rooms, 7 suites, 8* cottages ⟨symbol⟩ In-room: a/c, kitchen (some), refrigerator, Wi-Fi. In-hotel: pool, some pets allowed ⊟ AE, D, DC, MC, V ⟨symbol⟩ CP.

$$$ ⟨symbol⟩ **Oaks at Ojai.** Rejuvenation is the name of the game at this comfortable spa resort. You can work out all day or just lounge by the pool. The fitness package is a great value and includes lodging; use of the spa facilities; a choice of 16 daily exercise classes, hikes, and fitness activities; and three nutritionally balanced, low-calorie meals a day, plus snacks and beverages. Each of the two courtyard suites has a refrigerator and fireplace; seven minisuites include private patios. Nonguests can eat here, too, but it's mainly for the fitness-conscious. Cell-phone use is not allowed in public areas. Bringing kids under age 16 is discouraged. **Pros:** great place to get fit; peaceful retreat; healthy meals. **Cons:** rooms are basic; sits on the main highway through town. ⊠ 122 E. Ojai Ave. ☎ 805/646–5573 or 800/753–6257 ⊕ www.oaksspa.com ⟨symbol⟩ 44 rooms, 2 suites ⟨symbol⟩ ⟨symbol⟩ In-room: a/c, safe (some), refrigerator (some), Wi-Fi. In-hotel: restaurant, pool, gym, spa, laundry facilities, Internet terminal, Wi-Fi hotspot ⊟ D, MC, V ⟨symbol⟩ FAP ⟨symbol⟩ 2-night minimum stay.

$$$$ ⟨symbol⟩ **Ojai Valley Inn & Spa.** This outdoorsy, golf-oriented resort and spa
★ is set on beautifully landscaped grounds, with hillside views in nearly all directions. Though many of the rooms were remodeled in the 21st century, they still reflect the Spanish colonial architecture of the original 1923 resort. If you're a history buff, ask for a room in the original 80-year-old adobe building. The four restaurants tout "Ojai regional cuisine," which incorporates locally grown produce and fresh seasonal meats and seafood. **Pros:** gorgeous grounds; exceptional outdoor activities; romantic yet kid-friendly. **Cons:** expensive; staff isn't always attentive. ⊠ 905 Country Club Rd. ☎ 805/646–1111 or 888/697–8780 ⊕ www.ojairesort.com ⟨symbol⟩ 231 rooms, 77 suites ⟨symbol⟩ In-room: a/c, safe refrigerator, Internet (some), Wi-Fi. In-hotel: 4 restaurants, bar, golf course, tennis courts, pools, spa, bicycles, children's programs (ages 5 and up), Wi-Fi hotspot, some pets allowed ⊟ AE, D, DC, MC, V.

$$$$ ⟨symbol⟩ **Su Nido Inn.** Just a short walk from downtown Ojai sights and restaurants, this posh Mission revival–style inn is nested in a quiet neighborhood a few blocks from Libbey Park. One- and two-bedroom suites, each named after a bird, ring a cobblestone courtyard with fountains and olive trees. All suites have spacious living rooms, private patios, kitchenettes, soaking tubs, fireplaces, and featherbeds. **Pros:** walking distance from downtown; homey feel. **Cons:** no pool; can get hot during summer. ⊠ 301 N. Montgomery St. ☎ 805/646–7080 or 866/646–7080 ⊕ www.sunidoinn.com ⟨symbol⟩ 3 rooms, 9 suites ⟨symbol⟩ In-room: a/c, kitchen (some), refrigerator (some), DVD, Internet, Wi-Fi. In-hotel: Internet terminal, Wi-Fi hotspot ⊟ AE, D, MC, V.

SANTA BARBARA

27 mi northwest of Ventura and 29 mi west of Ojai on U.S. 101.

Santa Barbara has long been an oasis for Los Angelenos seeking respite from hectic big-city life. The attractions begin at the ocean and end in the foothills of the Santa Ynez Mountains. A few miles up the coast—but still very much a part of Santa Barbara—is the exclusive residential district of Hope Ranch. Santa Barbara is on a jog in the coastline, so the ocean is actually to the south, instead of the west; for this reason, directions can be confusing. "Up" the coast toward San Francisco is west, "down" toward Los Angeles is east, and the mountains are north.

GETTING HERE AND AROUND

A car is handy but not essential if you're planning to stay in town. The beaches and downtown are easily explored by bicycle or on foot. You can also hop aboard one of the electric shuttles that cruise the downtown and waterfront every 8 to 15 minutes (25¢ each way) and connect with local buses such as Line 22, which goes to major visitor sights (⊕ www.sbmtd.gov).

A motorized San Francisco–style cable car operated by **Santa Barbara Trolley Co.** (☎ 805/965–0353 ⊕ www.sbtrolley.com) makes 90-minute runs from 10 to 4 past major hotels, shopping areas, and attractions. Get off whenever you like, and pick up another trolley when you're ready to move on (they come every hour). Try to get a seat on the newest vehicle in the fleet, a biodiesel trolley with all seats on the top deck. Trolleys depart from and return to Stearns Wharf. The fare is $19 for the day.

Visit **Santa Barbara Car Free** (⊕ www.santabarbaracarfree.org) for bike route and walking-tour maps and car-free vacation packages with substantial lodging discounts.

ESSENTIALS

Visitor Information Santa Barbara Conference and Visitors Bureau (✉ 1601 Anacapu St., Santa Barbara ☎ 805/966–9222 ⊕ www.santaburbaraca.com). Santa Barbara Chamber of Commerce Visitor Information Center (✉ 1 Garden St., at Cabrillo Blvd. ☎ 805/965–3021 or 805/568–1811 ⊕ www.sbchamber.org).

EXPLORING

Santa Barbara's waterfront is beautiful, with palm-studded promenades and plenty of sand. In the few miles between the beaches and the hills are downtown, the old mission, and the botanic gardens.

⑮ Andree Clark Bird Refuge. This peaceful lagoon and its gardens sit north of East Beach. Bike trails and footpaths, punctuated by signs identifying native and migratory birds, skirt the lagoon. ✉ 1400 E. Cabrillo Blvd. 🎫 Free.

❸ Carriage and Western Art Museum. The country's largest collection of old horse-drawn vehicles—painstakingly restored—is exhibited here. Everything from polished hearses to police buggies to old stagecoaches and circus vehicles is on display. In August the Old Spanish Days Fiesta borrows many of the vehicles for a jaunt about town. This is one of the city's true hidden gems, a wonderful place to help history come alive—especially for children. Docents lead tours the third Sunday of every month from 1 to 4 PM. ✉ 129 Castillo St. ☎ 805/962–2353 ⊕ www.carriagemuseum.org 🎫 Free ⊙ Weekdays 9–3.

❻ El Presidio State Historic Park. Founded in 1782, El Presidio was one of four military strongholds established by the Spanish along the coast of California. The park encompasses much of the original site in the

Continued on page 260

ON A MISSION

Their soul may belong to Spain, their heart to the New World, but the historic missions of California, with their lovely churches, beckon the traveler on a soulful journey back to the very founding of the American West.

by Cheryl Crabtree and Robert I.C. Fisher

California history changed forever in the 18th century when Spanish explorers founded a series of missions along the Pacific coast. Believing they were following God's will, they wanted to spread the gospel and convert as many natives as possible. The process produced a collision between the Hispanic and California Indian cultures, resulting in one of the most striking legacies of Old California: the Spanish mission churches. Rising like mirages in the middle of desert plains and rolling hills, these saintly sites transport you back to the days of the Spanish colonial period.

GOD AND MAN IN CALIFORNIA

The Alta California territory came under pressure around 1750 when Spain feared foreign advances into the territory explorer Juan Rodríguez Cabrillo had claimed for the Spanish crown back in 1542. But how could Spain create a visible and viable presence halfway around the world? They decided to build on the model that had already worked well in Spain's Mexico colony. The plan involved establishing a series of missions, to be operated by the Catholic Church and protected by four of Spain's *presidios* (military outposts). The native Indians—after quick conversion to Christianity—would provide the labor force necessary to build mission towns.

FATHER OF THE MISSIONS

Father Junípero Serra is an icon of the Spanish colonial period. At the behest of the Spanish government, the diminutive padre—then well into his fifties, and despite a chronic leg infection—started out on foot from Baja California to search for suitable mission sites, with a goal of reaching Monterey. In 1769 he helped establish Alta California's first mission in San Diego and continued his travels until his death, in 1784, by which time he had founded eight more missions.

The system ended about a decade after the Mexican government took control of Alta California in the early 1820s and began to secularize the missions. The church lost horses and cattle, as well as vast tracts of land, which the Mexican government in turn granted to private individuals. They also lost laborers, as the Indians were for the most part free to find work and a life beyond the missions. In 1848, the Americans assumed control of the territory, and California became part of the United States. Today, these missions stand as extraordinary monuments to their colorful past.

MISSION ACCOMPLISHED

California's Mission Trail is the best way to follow in the fathers' footsteps. Here, below, are its 21 settlements, north to south.

Amazingly, all 21 Spanish missions in California are still standing—some in their pristine historic state, others with modifications made over the centuries. Many are found on or near the "King's Road"—El Camino Real—which linked these mission outposts. At the height of the mission system the trail was approximately 600 miles long, eventually extending from San Diego to Sonoma. Today the road is commemorated on portions of routes 101 and 82 in the form of roadside bell markers erected by CalTrans every one to two miles between Orange County and San Francisco.

San Francisco Solano, Sonoma (1823; this was the final California mission constructed.)

San Rafael, San Rafael (1817)

San Francisco de Asís (aka Mission Dolores), San Francisco (1776; see Chapter 8). Situated in the heart of San

Mission Santa Clara de Asís

Francisco, these mission grounds and nearby Arroyo de los Dolores (Creek of Sorrows) are home to the oldest intact building in the city.

Santa Clara de Asís, Santa Clara (1777; see Chapter 9). On the campus of Santa Clara University, this beautifully restored mission contains original paintings, statues, a bell, and hundreds of artifacts, as well as a spectacular rose garden.

San José, Fremont (1797)

Santa Cruz, Santa Cruz (1791)

San Juan Bautista, San Juan Bautista (1797; see Chapter 7). Immortalized in Hitchcock's *Vertigo*, this remarkably preserved pueblo contains the largest church of all the California missions, as well as 18th- and 19th-century buildings and a sprawling plaza.

San Carlos Borromeo del Río Carmelo, Carmel (1770;

see Chapter 7).). Carmel Mission was headquarters for the California mission system under Father Serra and the Father Presidents who succeeded him; the on-site museum includes Serra's tiny sleeping quarters (where he died in 1784).

Nuestra Señora de la Soledad, Soledad (1791)

San Antonio de Padua, Jolon (1771)

San Miguel Arcángel, San Miguel (1797; see Chapter 5). San Miguel boasts the only intact original interior work of art in any of the missions, painted in 1821 by Native

Mission San Rafael

Mission Santa Inés

American converts under the direction of Spanish artist Esteban Muras.

San Luis Obispo de Tolosa, San Luis Obispo (1772; see Chapter 5). Bear meat from grizzlies captured here saved the Spaniards from starving, which helped convince Father Serra to establish a mission.

La Purísima Concepción, Lompoc (1787; see Chapter 5). La Purísima is the nation's most completely restored mission complex. It is now a living-history museum with a church and nearly forty craft and residence rooms.

Santa Inés, Solvang (1804; see Chapter 5). Home to one of the most significant pieces of liturgical art created by a California mission Indian.

Santa Bárbara, Santa Barbara (1786; see Chapter 5). The "Queen of the Missions" has twin bell towers, gorgeous gardens with heirloom plant varietals, a massive collection of rare artworks and artifacts, and lovely stonework.

Mission San Fernando Rey de España

San Buenaventura, Ventura (1782; see Chapter 5). This was the last mission founded by Father Serra; it is still an active parish in the Archdiocese of Los Angeles.

San Fernando Rey de España, Mission Hills (1797)

San Gabriel Arcángel, San Gabriel (1771)

San Luis Rey de Francia, Oceanside (1798)

San Juan Capistrano, San Juan Capistrano (1776; see Chapter 3). This mission is famed for its Saint Joseph's Day (March 19) celebration of the return of swallows in the springtime. The mission's adobe walls enclose acres of lush gardens and historic buildings.

San Diego de Alcalá, San Diego (1769). This was the first California missions constructed, although the original was destroyed in 1775.

Mission San Miguel Arcángel

Coalinga
Paso Robles
San Miguel Arcángel
101
McKittrick
San Luis Obispo
San Luis Obispo de Tolosa
Santa Maria
La Purísima Conepción
Lompoc
Santa Inés
Santa Bárbara
Tejon Pass
101
Santa Barbara
Oxnard
Ventura
San Buenaventura
San Fernando Rey de España
Pasadena
1
LOS ANGELES
San Gabriel Arcángel
Huntington Beach
San Luis Rey de Francia
San Juan Capistrano
Oceanside
Julian
101
SAN DIEGO
San Diego de Alcalá
MEXICO

KEY

✝ Mission

0   50 mi
0   50 km

SPANISH MISSION STYLE

(left) Mission San Luis Rey de Francia; (right) Mission San Antonio de Padua

The Spanish mission churches derive much of their strength and enduring power from their extraordinary admixture of styles. They are spectacular examples of the combination of races and cultures that bloomed along Father Serra's road through Alta California.

SPIRIT OF THE PLACE

In building the missions, the Franciscan padres had to rely on available resources. Spanish churches back in Europe boasted marble floors and gilded statues. But here, whitewashed adobe walls gleamed in the sun and floors were often merely packed earth.

However simple the structures, the art within the mission confines continued to glorify the Church. The padres imported much finery to decorate the churches and perform the mass—silver, silk and lovely paintings to teach the life of Christ to the Indians and soldiers and settlers. Serra himself commissioned

fine artists in Mexico to produce custom works using the best materials and according to exact specifications. Sculptures of angels, Mary, Joseph, Jesus and the Franciscan heroes and saints—and of course the Stations of the Cross—adorned all the missions.

AN ENDURING LEGACY

Mission architecture reflects a gorgeous blend of European and New World influences. While naves followed the simple forms of Franciscan Gothic, cloisters (with beautiful arcades) adopted aspects of the Romanesque style, and ornamental touches of the Spanish Renaissance—including red- tiled roofs and wrought-iron grilles—added even more elegance. In the 20th century, the Mission Revival Style had a huge impact on architecture and design in California, as seen in examples ranging from San Diego's Union Station to Stanford University's main quadrangle.

Father Junípero Serra statue at the Mission San Gabriel

FOR WHOM THE BELLS TOLLED

Perhaps the most famous architectural motif of the Spanish Mission churches was the belltower. These took the form of either a campanile—a single tower called a campanario—or, more spectacularly, of an open work espadaña, a perforated adobe wall housing a series of bells (notable examples of this form are at San Miguel Arcángel and San Diego de Alcalá). Bells were essential to maintaining the routines of daily life at the missions.

MISSION LIFE

Morning bells summoned residents to chapel for services; noontime bells introduced the main meal, while the evening bells sounded the alert to gather around 5 pm for mass and dinner. Many of the natives were happy with their new faith, and even enjoyed putting in numerous hours a week working as farmers, soapmakers, weavers, and masons.

Others, however, were less willing to abandon their traditional culture, but were coerced to abide by the new Spanish laws and mission rules. Gated walls and native sleeping quarters were locked at night to prevent escape. Natives were often mistreated by the friars, who used a system of punishments to enforce submission to their teachings.

NATIVE TRAGEDY

In the end, mission life proved extremely destructive to the Native Californian population. European diseases and contaminated water caused the death of nearly a third, with some tribes—notably the Chumash—being virtually decimated. One friar was quoted as noting that the Indians "live well free but as soon as we reduce them to a Christian and community life . . . they fatten, sicken, and die."

Though so native Indians died during the mission era, small numbers of did survive. After the Mexican government secularized the missions in 1833, a majority of the native population was reduced to poverty. Some stayed at the missions, while others went to live in the pueblos, ranchos, and countryside—a tragic end for those whose labor was largely responsible for the magnificent mission churches we see today.

FOR MORE INFORMATION

California Missions Foundation

✉ 4129 Main St., Suite 207 Riverside, CA 92501

☎ 951/369-0440

🌐 www.california missionsfoundation.org

Top, Mission San Gabriel Arcángel
Left, Mission San Miguel Arcángel.

heart of downtown. El Cuartel, the adobe guardhouse, is the oldest building in Santa Barbara and the second oldest in California. ✉ *123 E. Canon Perdido St.* ☎ *805/965-0093* ⊕ *www.sbthp.org* 💲 *$5* ⊗ *Daily 10:30–4:30.*

🔟 **Karpeles Manuscript Library.** Ancient political tracts and old Disney cartoons are among the holdings at this facility, which also houses one of the world's largest privately owned collections of rare manuscripts. Fifty display cases contain a sampling of the archive's million-plus documents. ✉ *21 W. Anapamu St.* ☎ *805/962–5322* ⊕ *www.karpeles.com* 💲 *Free* ⊗ *Daily 10–4.*

> ### SANTA BARBARA STYLE
>
> Why does downtown Santa Barbara look so scrubbed and uniform? After a 1925 earthquake, which demolished many buildings, the city seized a golden opportunity to create a Spanish–Mediterranean look. It established an architectural board of review, which, along with city commissions, created strict architectural codes for the downtown district: red tile roofs, earth-tone facades, arches, wrought-iron embellishments, and height restrictions (about four stories).

⑪ **Mission Santa Barbara.** Widely

Fodor's Choice
★
referred to as the "Queen of Missions," this is one of the most beautiful and frequently photographed buildings in coastal California. Dating to 1786, the architecture evolved from adobe-brick buildings with thatch roofs to more permanent edifices as the mission's population burgeoned. An earthquake in 1812 destroyed the third church built on the site. Its replacement, the present structure, is still a functioning Catholic church. Mission Santa Barbara has a splendid Spanish/Mexican colonial art collection, as well as Chumash sculptures and the only Native American–made altar and tabernacle left in the California missions. A docent-led tour of the adjacent La Huerta Project—a re-creation of the Spanish-era gardens with native and heirloom plants—is available by appointment. ✉ *2201 Laguna St.* ☎ *805/682–4149 or 805/682–4713* ⊕ *www.santabarbaramission.org* 💲 *$5* ⊗ *Daily 9–4:30.*

⑯ **Montecito.** Since the late 1800s the tree-studded hills and valleys of this town have attracted the rich and famous (Hollywood icons, business tycoons, dot-commers who divested before the crash, and old-money families who installed themselves here years ago). Shady roads wind through the community, which consists mostly of gated estates. Swank boutiques line Coast Village Road, where well-heeled residents such as Oprah Winfrey sometimes browse for truffle oil, picture frames, and designer sweats. Residents also hang out in the Upper Village, a chic shopping area with restaurants and cafés at the intersection of San Ysidro and East Valley roads. Montecito is about 3 mi east of Santa Barbara.

Fodor's Choice
★
The 37-acre Montecito estate called **Lotusland** (☎ *805/969–9990* ⊕ *www.lotusland.org* 💲 *$35*) once belonged to Polish opera singer Ganna Walska. Many of the exotic trees and other subtropical flora were planted in 1882 by horticulturist R. Kinton Stevens. On the two-hour guided tour (the only option for visiting), you'll see an outdoor theater, a topiary garden, a huge collection of rare cycads (an unusual

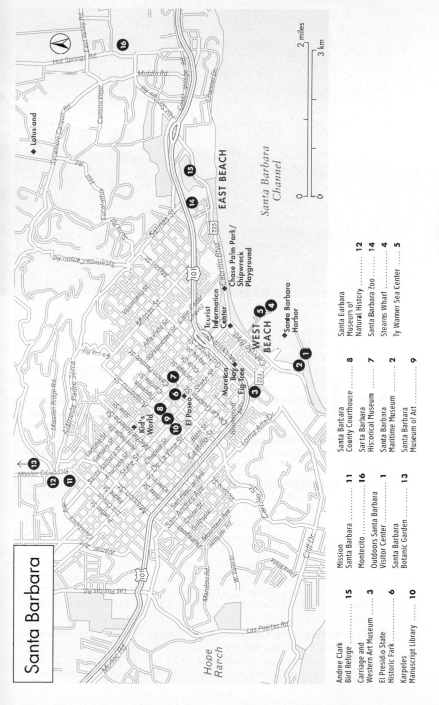

Santa Barbara

5

Santa Barbara's downtown is attractive, but be sure also to visit its beautiful—and uncrowded—beaches.

plant genus that has been around since the time of the dinosaurs), and a lotus pond. Tours are conducted mid-February through mid-November, Wednesday through Saturday at 10 and 1:30. Reservations are required. Child-friendly family tours are available for groups with children under the age of 10; contact Lotusland for scheduling.

① Outdoors Santa Barbara Visitor Center. The small office provides maps and other information about Channel Islands National Park, Channel Islands National Marine Sanctuary, and the Santa Barbara Maritime Museum, which occupies the same building in the harbor. ⊠ *113 Harbor Way* ☎ *805/884–1475* ⊕ *outdoorsb.noaa.gov* ✉ *Free* ☼ *Daily 11–5.*

⑬ Santa Barbara Botanic Garden. Scenic trails meander through the garden's 78 acres of native plants. The Mission Dam, built in 1806, stands just beyond the redwood grove and above the restored aqueduct that once carried water to Mission Santa Barbara. Sadly, the 2009 Jesusita Fire roared through sections of the garden, but thankfully most of it remains intact. All main trails are currently open, and the garden is re-creating several damaged or destroyed items, including an ethnobotanical display that demonstrates how Native Americans used plants to create baskets, clothing, and structures. ⊠ *1212 Mission Canyon Rd.* ☎ *805/682–4726* ⊕ *www.sbbg.org* ✉ *$8* ☼ *Mar.–Oct., daily 9–6; Nov.–Feb., daily 9–5.*

⑧ Santa Barbara County Courthouse. Hand-painted tiles and a spiral staircase
★ infuse the courthouse with the grandeur of a Moorish palace. This magnificent building was completed in 1929, part of a rebuilding process after a 1925 earthquake destroyed many downtown structures. At the

time, Santa Barbara was also in the midst of a cultural awakening, and the trend was toward an architectural style appropriate to the area's climate and history. The result is the harmonious Mediterranean–Spanish look of much of the downtown area, especially the municipal buildings. An elevator rises to an arched observation area in the courthouse tower that provides a panoramic view of the city. The murals in the ceremonial chambers on the courthouse's second floor were painted by an artist who did backdrops for some of Cecil B. DeMille's films. ✉ *1100 block of Anacapa St.* ☎ *805/962–6464* ⊕ *www.santabarbaracourthouse.org* ⊙ *Weekdays 8–4:45, weekends 10–4:30. Free guided tours Mon., Tues., and Fri. at 10:30, Mon.–Sat. at 2.*

LAND SHARK!

Land and Sea Tours (✉ *State St. at Stearns Wharf* ☎ *805/603–7600* ⊕ *www.out2seesb.com* 🎟 *$25* ⊙ *Tours May–Oct., daily noon, 2, and 4; Nov.–Apr., daily noon and 2*) takes visitors on narrated, 90-minute land-and-sea adventures in an amphibious 49-passenger vehicle, nicknamed the Land Shark. Tours begin with a drive through the city and continue with a plunge into the harbor for a cruise along the coast.

5

QUICK BITES
Children and adults can enjoy themselves at **Kids' World** (✉ *Garden St. at Micheltorena St.*), a public playground with a complex, castle-shape maze of fanciful climbing structures, slides, and tunnels built by Santa Barbara parents.

7 **Santa Barbara Historical Museum.** The historical society's museum exhibits decorative and fine arts, furniture, costumes, and documents from the town's past. Adjacent to it is the Gledhill Library, a collection of books, photographs, maps, and manuscripts. ✉ *136 E. De La Guerra St.* ☎ *805/966–1601* ⊕ *www.santabarbaramuseum.com* 🎟 *Museum by donation; library $2–$5 per hr for research* ⊙ *Museum Tues.–Sat. 10–5, Sun. noon–5; library Tues.–Fri. 10–4, 1st Sat. of month 10–1.*

8 **Santa Barbara Maritime Museum.** California's seafaring history is the focus at this museum. High-tech, hands-on exhibits, such as a sportfishing activity that lets you catch a "big one" and a local surfing history retrospective make this a fun stop for families. ✉ *113 Harbor Way* ☎ *805/962–8404* ⊕ *www.sbmm.org* 🎟 *$7* ⊙ *June–Aug., Thurs.–Tues. 10–6; Sept.–May, Thurs.–Tues. 10–5.*

9 **Santa Barbara Museum of Art.** The highlights of this museum's permanent collection include ancient sculpture, Asian art, impressionist paintings, contemporary Latin American art, and American works in several media. ✉ *1130 State St.* ☎ *805/963–4364* ⊕ *www.sbma.net* 🎟 *$9, free on Sun.* ⊙ *Tues.–Sun. 11–5. Free guided tours Tues.–Sun. at noon and 1.*

12 **Santa Barbara Museum of Natural History.** The gigantic skeleton of a blue whale greets you at the entrance of this complex. The major draws include the planetarium, space lab, and a gem and mineral display. A room of dioramas illustrates Chumash Indian history and culture. Startlingly alive-looking stuffed specimens, complete with nests and eggs, roost in the bird diversity room. Many exhibits have interactive components. Outdoors you can stroll on nature trails that wind through the serene oak-studded grounds. Admission is free on the third Sunday of each month. Ask about the Nature Pass, which includes discounted unlimited two-day admission to both the Museum of Natural History and the Ty Warner Sea Center on Stearns Wharf. ⊠ *2559 Puesta del Sol Rd.* ☎ *805/682–4711* ⊕ *www.sbnature.org* ⌷ *$10* ⊙ *Daily 10–5.*

⑭ Santa Barbara Zoo. The grounds of this smallish zoo are so gorgeous
⟳ people book their weddings here long in advance. The palm-studded lawns on a hilltop overlooking the beach are perfect spots for family picnics. The natural settings of the zoo shelter elephants, gorillas, exotic birds like the rare California condor, and big cats such as the rare snow leopard, a thick-furred, high-altitude dweller from Asia. For small children, there's a scenic railroad and barnyard petting zoo. ⊠ *500 Niños Dr.* ☎ *805/962–5339 main line, 805/962–6310 information* ⊕ *www. santabarbarazoo.org* ⌷ *Zoo $12, parking $5* ⊙ *Daily 10–5.*

QUICK BITES The antique carousel, large playground with a nautical theme, picnic areas, and snack bar make the scenic waterfront **Chase Palm Park and Shipwreck Playground** (⊠ *Cabrillo Blvd., between Garden St. and Calle Cesar Chavez*) a favorite destination for kids and parents.

④ Stearns Wharf. Built in 1872, historic Stearns Wharf is Santa Barbara's most visited landmark. Expansive views of the mountains, cityscape, and harbor unfold from every vantage point on the three-block-long pier. Although it's a nice walk from the Cabrillo Boulevard parking areas, you can also park on the pier and then wander through the shops or stop for a meal at one of the wharf's restaurants. ⊠ *Cabrillo Blvd., at foot of State St.* ☎ *805/897–2683 or 805/564–5531* ⊕ *www. stearnswharf.org.*

⑤ Ty Warner Sea Center. A branch of the Santa Barbara Museum of Natural
⟳ History, the Sea Center specializes in Santa Barbara Channel marine life and conservation. In 2005 it reopened in a new $6.5 million facility bearing the name of Ty Warner, Beanie Baby mogul and local resident, whose hefty donation helped the center complete the final stages of construction. The new Sea Center is small compared to aquariums in Monterey and Long Beach, but it's a fascinating, hands-on marine science laboratory that lets you participate in experiments, projects, and exhibits, including touch tanks. Haul up and analyze water samples, learn to identify marine mammals, and check out amazing creatures in the tide-pool lab and animal nursery. The two-story glass walls open to stunning ocean, mountain, and city views. Ask about the Nature Pass, which includes discounted unlimited two-day admission to both the Sea Center and the Museum of Natural History. ⊠ *211 Stearns Wharf* ☎ *805/962–2526* ⊕ *www.sbnature.org* ⌷ *$8* ⊙ *Daily 10–5.*

WHERE TO EAT

$$ ✗**Arigato Sushi.** You might have to wait 45 minutes for a table at this
JAPANESE trendy, two-story restaurant and sushi bar—locals line up early for the hip, casual atmosphere and wildly creative combination rolls. Fans of authentic Japanese food sometimes disagree about the quality of the

seafood, but all dishes are fresh and artfully presented. The menu includes traditional dishes as well as innovative creations such as sushi pizza on seaweed and Hawaiian sashimi salad. ⊠ *1225 State St.* ☎ *805/965–6074* ⚒ *Reservations not accepted* ▤ *AE, MC, V* ☽ *No lunch.*

$$
SEAFOOD

✗ **Brophy Bros**. The outdoor tables at this casual harborside restaurant have perfect views of the marina and mountains. The staff serves enormous, exceptionally fresh fish dishes—don't miss the seafood salad and chowder—and provides you with a pager if there's a long wait for a table. You can stroll along the waterfront until the beep lets you know your table's ready. This place is hugely popular, so it can be crowded and loud, especially on weekend evenings. ⊠ *119 Harbor Way* ☎ *805/966–4418* ⊕ *www.brophybros.com* ▤ *AE, MC, V.*

$$$
AMERICAN

✗ **Elements**. Different sections within this chic, contemporary, restaurant and bar reflect nature's elements: an outdoor porch overlooking the sunken gardens at the Santa Barbara Courthouse across the street (air); the gold-tone main dining room (earth); an intimate corner with sofas for romantic dining (fire); and an often lively, ocean-hue area where professionals unwind over specialty martinis after work at the slick granite bar. The seasonal world-fusion menu, designed around organic and sustainable foods, might include a grilled ahi tuna wrap with wasabi mayonnaise at lunch, or lemongrass and panko-crusted sea bass with curry-coconut sauce and gingered basmati rice for dinner. ⊠ *129 E. Anapamu St.* ☎ *805/884–9218* ⊕ *www.elementsrestaurantandbar. com* ▤ *AE, D, MC, V.*

$$$
SEAFOOD

✗ **The Hungry Cat**. The hip Santa Barbara sibling of a famed Hollywood eatery, run by chefs David Lentz and his wife Suzanne Goin, dishes up savory seafood in a small but lively nook in the downtown arts district. Feast on sea urchin, addictive peel and-eat shrimp, and creative cocktails made from farmers' market fruits and veggies. A busy nightspot on weekends, the Cat also awakens for a popular brunch on Sunday. Night or day, come early or be prepared for a wait. ⊠ *1134 Chapala St.* ☎ *805/884–4701* ⊕ *www.thehungrycat.com* ⚒ *Reservations not accepted* ▤ *AE, D, MC, V* ☽ *Closed Mon.*

¢
MEXICAN
★

✗ **La Super-Rica**. Praised by Julia Child, this food stand with a patio on the east side of town serves some of the spiciest and most authentic Mexican dishes between Los Angeles and San Francisco. Fans drive for miles to fill up on the soft tacos served with yummy spicy or mild sauces and legendary beans. Three daily specials are offered each day. Portions are on the small side; order several dishes and share. ⊠ *622 N. Milpas St., at Alphonse St.* ☎ *805/963–4940* ▤ *No credit cards* ☽ *Closed Wed.*

$$$
ITALIAN

✗ **Olio e Limone**. Sophisticated Italian cuisine (with an emphasis on Sicily) is served at this restaurant near the Arlington Center for the Performing Arts. The juicy veal chop is a popular dish, but surprises abound here; be sure to try unusual dishes such as ribbon pasta with quail and sausage in a mushroom ragout, duck ravioli, or swordfish with Sicilian ratatouille. Tables are placed a bit close together, so this may not be the best spot for intimate conversations. ⊠ *17 W. Victoria St.* ☎ *805/899–2699* ⊕ *www.olioelimone.com* ▤ *AE, D, DC, MC, V* ☽ *No lunch Sun.*

$$$
SOUTHERN

✗**Palace Grill.** Mardi Gras energy, team-style service, lively music, and great food have made the Palace a Santa Barbara icon. Acclaimed for its Cajun and creole dishes such as blackened redfish and jambalaya with dirty rice, the Palace also serves Caribbean fare, including a delicious coconut-shrimp dish. If you're spice-phobic, you can choose pasta, soft-shell crab, or filet mignon. Be prepared to wait as long as 45 minutes for a table on Friday and Saturday night (when reservations are taken for a 5:30 seating only), though the live entertainment and free appetizers, sent out front when the line is long, will whet your appetite for the feast to come. ✉ *8 E. Cota St.* ☎ *805/963–5000* ⊕ *www. palacegrill.com* ⊟ *AE, MC, V.*

> **BEST VIEWS**
>
> Drive along Alameda Padre Serra, a hillside road that begins near the mission and continues to Montecito, to feast your eyes on spectacular views of the city and the Santa Barbara Channel.

$$$
ECLECTIC

✗**Roy.** Owner-chef Leroy Gandy serves a $25 fixed-price dinner (some selections are $20, some $30)—a real bargain—that includes a small salad, fresh soup, homemade organic bread, and a selection from a rotating list of contemporary American main courses. If you're lucky, the entrée choices might include grilled local fish with a mandarin beurre blanc, or bacon-wrapped filet mignon. You can also choose from an à la carte menu of inexpensive appetizers and entrées, plus local wines. Half a block from State Street in the heart of downtown, Roy is a favorite spot for late-night dining (it's open until midnight and has a full bar). ✉ *7 W. Carrillo St.* ☎ *805/966–5636* ⊕ *www.restaurantroy.com* ⊟ *AE, D, DC, MC, V* ☯ *No lunch.*

$$$$
AMERICAN
★

✗**The Stonehouse.** Part of the San Ysidro Ranch resort, this elegantly rustic restaurant, which reopened in 2007 following the resort's $150 million remodeling, is housed in a century-old granite farmhouse. Executive chef John Trotta harvests herbs and veggies from the on-site garden, then adds them to an array of top-quality local ingredients to create outstanding regional cuisine. The menu changes constantly but typically includes favorites such as crab cake with persimmon relish appetizer and local spiny lobster with mascarpone risotto. Dine on the radiant-heated ocean-view deck with stone fireplace, next to a fountain under a canopy of loquat trees, or in the romantic, candlelit dining room overlooking a creek. The Plow & Angel pub, downstairs, offers more casual bistro fare. ✉ *900 San Ysidro La., Montecito* ☎ *805/969–4100* ⊕ *www.sanysidroranch.com* ⌂ *Reservations essential* ⊟ *AE, DC, MC, V* ☯ *No lunch.*

$$$

✗**Wine Cask.** When the Wine Cask closed suddenly in February 2009, the community mourned. So did Doug Margerum, whose family had operated the venerable restaurant, tucked in a romantic courtyard in historic El Paseo, from 1982 to 2007, before selling to an out-of-towner. He teamed up with local restaurateur Mitchel Sjerven to resurrect the Wine Cask, which reopened at year's end. The "new" Wine Cask serves bistro-style meals in a casual, comfortable and classy dining room, with a gold-wood interior and a massive fireplace. The seasonal menu revolves around farmers' market ingredients (just a few blocks away

twice
thank
wine
vint:
yar(
thr(
wi

chandeliers, and vintage black-and-white
were updated in 2008 and now boast
screen high-definition TVs, contempo
microwaves; deluxe and ocean vie
patios. Even if you don't land a
ocean and islands from a table
splurge on a treatment in the
LAX stops here six times
types and rates; walk to
vibe; busy area in su
or 800/643–1994
ments ⌂ In-roo
hotel: restaur
Wi-Fi hotsp
of dow
Sant

\$\$\$\$

\$\$\$\$

ter; som...
or 877/468–3515 🌐 *ww...*
suites ⌂ In-room: a/c, safe, refrigerator, —
restaurant, room service, bar, pool, bicycles, laundry —.
terminal, Wi-Fi hotspot, parking (paid), some pets allowed ▬ AE, D,
DC, MC, V.

\$\$\$\$ ★ **Four Seasons Resort The Biltmore Santa Barbara.** Surrounded by lush,
perfectly manicured gardens and across from the beach, Santa Barbara's
grande dame has long been a favorite for quiet, California-style luxury.
The sumptuous 10,000-square-foot spa near the resort's pool and gardens, which includes 11 treatment rooms, is an oasis for rejuvenation.
Guests also enjoy privileges at the historic, members-only Coral Casino
Beach and Cabana Club across the street. Dining is upscale casual
at the ocean-view Bella Vista Restaurant (\$\$\$–\$\$\$\$), where the sea-
sonal California-contemporary menu changes monthly. **Pros:** first-class
resort; historic Santa Barbara character; personal service; steps from the
beach. **Cons:** back rooms are close to train tracks; expensive. ✉ *1260
Channel Dr.* ☎ *805/969–2261 or 800/332–3442* 🌐 *www.fourseasons.
com/santabarbara* ➦ *181 rooms, 26 suites* ⌂ *In-room: a/c, refrigerator, DVD, Internet, Wi-Fi. In-hotel: restaurant, room service, bar, tennis courts, pool, gym, spa, children's programs (ages 5–12), Internet
terminal, some pets allowed* ▬ *AE, D, DC, MC, V.*

\$\$\$ **Hotel Mar Monte.** A complex of three separate buildings on three land-
scaped acres, plus a neighboring inn and apartment units, the Mar
Monte provides a wide range of value-laden lodging options in a prime
location—right across from East Beach and the Cabrillo Pavilion Bathhouse. The lobby and walkways in the historic main building, constructed in 1931, reflect old Santa Barbara: Spanish tiles, wrought-iron

photos. All rooms and baths
comfy down comforters, flat-
ary furnishings, refrigerators, and
w rooms have private balconies or
oom with a view, you can gaze at the
n the on-site Bistro 1111 Restaurant or
poolside spa. The Santa Barbara Airbus to
day. **Pros:** steps from the beach; many room
the zoo and waterfront shuttle. **Cons:** motelish
mer. ⊠ *1111 E. Cabrillo Blvd.* ☎ *805/963–0744*
⊕ *www.hotelmarmonte.com* ⇥ *218 rooms, 5 apart-*
: *a/c, kitchen (some), refrigerator, Internet, Wi-Fi. In-*
nt, room service, bar, pool, gym, spa, Internet terminal,
ot, parking (free), some pets allowed ⊟ *AE, D, MC, V.*

e **Spanish Garden.** A half block from the Presidio in the heart
ntown, this elegant Spanish-Mediterranean retreat celebrates
Barbara style, from tile floors, wrought-iron balconies, and exotic
nts, to original art by famed local plein-air artists. The luxury rooms
ave private balconies or patios, fireplaces, Frette linens, and deep soaking tubs. In the evening, you can order a glass of wine and relax in the
candlelighted courtyard. This inn is a good choice if you want to park
your car for most of your stay and walk to theaters, restaurants, and
shuttle buses. **Pros:** walking distance from downtown; classic Spanish-
Mediterranean style; caring staff. **Cons:** far from the beach; not much
here for kids. ⊠ *915 Garden St.* ☎ *805/564–4700 or 866/564–4700*
⊕ *www.spanishgardeninn.com* ⇥ *23 rooms* ⌂ *In-room: a/c, refrigera-*
tor, Internet, Wi-Fi. In-hotel: bar, pool, gym, laundry service, parking
(free) ⊟ *AE, D, DC, MC, V* ⦿*I CP.*

$–$$ ⚏ **Motel 6 Santa Barbara Beach.** A half block from East Beach amid fancier
hotels sits this basic but comfortable motel, which was the first Motel
6 in existence. It was also the first in the chain to transform into a contemporary Euro-style abode following a top-to-bottom remodel in 2008.
It's an incredible bargain for the location and fills quickly; book months
in advance if possible. Kids 17 and under stay free. Sister properties
in Goleta and in Carpinteria, 12 mi south of Santa Barbara and 1 mi
from the beach, offer equally comfortable rooms at even lower rates.
Pros: less than a minute's walk from the zoo and beach; friendly staff;
clean and comfortable. **Cons:** no frills; motel-style rooms; no breakfast.
⊠ *443 Corona Del Mar Dr.* ☎ *805/564–1392 or 800/466–8356* ⊕ *www.*
motel6.com ⇥ *51 rooms* ⌂ *In-room: a/c, refrigerator (some), Wi-Fi. In-*
hotel: pool, Wi-Fi hotspot, some pets allowed ⊟ *AE, D, DC, MC, V.*

$$$$ ⚏ **San Ysidro Ranch.** At this romantic hideaway on an historic property
★ in the Montecito foothills—where John and Jackie Kennedy spent their
honeymoon and Oprah sends her out-of-town guests—guest cottages
are scattered among groves of orange trees and flower beds. All have
down comforters and fireplaces, most have private outdoor spas, and
one has its own pool. Seventeen miles of hiking trails crisscross 500
acres of open space surrounding the property. The Stonehouse restaurant ($$–$$$$; *see above*) and Plow & Angel Bistro ($–$$$) are Santa
Barbara institutions. The hotel completed a $150 million restoration

in 2007. **Pros:** ultimate privacy; surrounded by nature; celebrity hangout; pet-friendly. **Cons:** very expensive; too remote for some. ✉ *900 San Ysidro La., Montecito* ☎ *805/565–1700 or 800/368–6788* ⊕ *www. sanysidroranch.com* ↩ *23 rooms, 4 suites, 14 cottages* ⚠ *In-room: a/c, refrigerator, DVD, Internet, Wi-Fi. In-hotel: 2 restaurants, room service, bar, pool, gym, some pets allowed* ▭ *AE, MC, V* ⚲ *2-day minimum stay on weekends, 3 days on holiday weekends.*

$$$$
★
Simpson House Inn. If you're a fan of traditional B&Bs, this property, with its beautifully appointed Victorian main house and acre of lush gardens, is for you. If privacy and luxury are your priority, choose one of the elegant cottages or a room in the century-old barn; each has a wood-burning fireplace, luxurious bedding, and state-of-the-art electronics (several even have whirlpool baths). In-room massages and other spa services are available. Room rates include use of a downtown athletic club. **Pros:** impeccable landscaping; walking distance from everything downtown; ranked among the nation's top B&Bs. **Cons:** some rooms in the main building are small; two-night minimum stay on weekends. ✉ *121 E. Arrellaga St.* ☎ *805/963–7067 or 800/676–1280* ⊕ *www.simpsonhouseinn.com* ↩ *11 rooms, 4 cottages* ⚠ *In-room: a/c, refrigerator (some), DVD, Wi-Fi. In-hotel: bicycles, Wi-Fi hotspot* ▭ *AE, D, MC, V* ⦿ *BP.*

NIGHTLIFE AND THE ARTS

Most major hotels present entertainment nightly during the summer season and on weekends all year. Much of the town's bar, club, and live music scene centers on lower State Street (between the 300 and 800 blocks). The thriving arts district, with theaters, restaurants, and cafés, starts around the 900 block of State Street and continues north to the Arlington Center for the Performing Arts, in the 1300 block. Santa Barbara supports a professional symphony and a chamber orchestra. The proximity to the University of California at Santa Barbara assures an endless stream of visiting artists and performers. To see what's scheduled around town, pick up a copy of the free weekly *Santa Barbara Independent* newspaper or visit their Web site ⊕ *www.independent.com.*

NIGHTLIFE

Rich leather couches, a crackling fire in chilly weather, a cigar balcony, and pool tables draw a fancy Gen-X crowd to **Blue Agave** (✉ *20 E. Cota St.* ☎ *805/899–4694*) for good food and designer martinis. All types of people hang out at **Dargan's** (✉ *18 E. Ortega St.* ☎ *805/568–0702*), a lively pub with four pool tables, a great selection of draft beer and Irish whiskeys, and a full menu of traditional Irish dishes. The **James Joyce** (✉ *513 State St.* ☎ *805/962–2688*), which sometimes plays host to folk and rock performers, is a good place to have a few beers and while away an evening.

Joe's Cafe (✉ *536 State St.* ☎ *805/966–4638*), where steins of beer accompany hearty bar food, is a fun, if occasionally rowdy, collegiate scene. A slick sports bar attached to an upscale steak house owned by the maker of Lucky Brand Dungarees, **Lucky's** (✉ *1279 Coast Village*

Rd., Montecito ☎ *805/565–7540*) attracts a flock of hip, fashionably dressed patrons hoping to see and be seen.

Swank **Milk & Honey** (✉ *30 W. Anapamu St.* ☎ *805/275–4232*) lures trendy crowds with artfully prepared tapas, coconut-mango mojitos, and exotic cocktails—despite high prices and a reputation for inattentive service.

SOhO (✉ *1221 State St.* ☎ *805/962–7776*) —a hip restaurant, bar, and music club—schedules an eclectic mix of live music groups, from jazz to blues to rock, every night of the week.

THE ARTS
Arlington Center for the Performing Arts (✉ *1317 State St.* ☎ *805/963–4408*), a Moorish-style auditorium, is the home of the Santa Barbara Symphony. **Center Stage Theatre** (✉ *700 block of State St., 2nd fl. of Paseo Nuevo* ☎ *805/963–0408*) presents plays, music, dance, and readings. **Ensemble Theatre Company** (✉ *914 Santa Barbara St.* ☎ *805/965–5400*) stages plays by authors ranging from Tennessee Williams and David Mamet to rising contemporary dramatists. Originally opened in 1924, the landmark **Granada Theatre** (✉ *1214 State St.* ☎ *805/899–3000 general info, 805/899–2222 box office*) reopened to great fanfare in 2008 following a $50 million restoration and modernization. The **Lobero Theatre** (✉ *33 E. Canon Perdido St.* ☎ *805/963–0761*), a state landmark, hosts community theater groups and touring professionals. In Montecito, the **Music Academy of the West** (✉ *1070 Fairway Rd.* ☎ *805/969–4726, 805/969–8787 box office*) showcases orchestral, chamber, and operatic works every summer.

SPORTS AND THE OUTDOORS

BEACHES   Santa Barbara's beaches don't have the big surf of the shoreline farther south, but they also don't have the crowds. You can usually find a solitary spot to swim or sunbathe. In June and July, fog often hugs the coast until about noon. The wide swath of sand at the east end of Cabrillo Boulevard on the harbor front is a great spot for people-watching. **East Beach** (✉ *1118 Cabrillo Blvd.* ☎ *805/897–2680*) has sand volleyball courts, summertime lifeguard and sports competitions, and arts-and-crafts shows on Sunday and holidays. You can use showers, a weight room, and lockers (bring your own towel) and rent umbrellas and boogie boards at the Cabrillo Bathhouse. Next door, there's an elaborate jungle-gym play area for kids. The usually gentle surf at **Arroyo Burro County Beach** (✉ *Cliff Dr., at Las Positas Rd.*) makes it ideal for families with young children.

BICYCLING   The level, two-lane, 3-mi **Cabrillo Bike Lane** passes the Santa Barbara Zoo, the Andree Clark Bird Refuge, beaches, and the harbor. There are restaurants along the way, and you can stop for a picnic along the palm-lined path looking out on the Pacific. **Wheel Fun Rentals** (✉ *23 E. Cabrillo Blvd.* ☎ *805/966–2282 or 805/962–2585*) has bikes, quadricycles, and skates; a second outlet around the block rents small electric cars and scooters.

BOATS AND CHARTERS **Captain Don's** (✉ *Stearns Wharf* ☎ *805/969–5217*) operates whale-watching and pirate-theme harbor cruises aboard the 40-foot *Harbour Queen*. **Santa Barbara Sailing Center** (✉ *Santa Barbara Harbor launching ramp* ☎ *805/962–2826 or 800/350–9090*) offers sailing instruction, rents and charters sail boats, and organizes dinner and sunset champagne cruises, island excursions, and whale-watching trips. **Sea Landing** (✉ *Cabrillo Blvd., at Bath St. and breakwater in Santa Barbara Harbor* ☎ *805/965–3564*) operates surface and deep-sea fishing charters year-round. From Sea Landing, the **Condor Express** (☎ *805/963–3564*), a 75-foot high-speed catamaran, whisks up to 149 passengers toward the Channel Islands on dinner cruises, whale-watching excursions, and pelagic-bird trips. **Truth Aquatics** (☎ *805/962–1127*) departs from Sea Landing in the Santa Barbara Harbor to ferry passengers on excursions to the National Marine Sanctuary and Channel Islands National Park. Their three dive boats also take scuba divers on single-day and multiday trips.

> ### BIRTHPLACE OF THE ENVIRONMENTAL MOVEMENT
>
> In 1969, 200,000 gallons of crude oil spilled into the Santa Barbara Channel, causing an immediate outcry from residents, particularly in the UCSB community. The day after the spill, Get Oil Out (GOO) was established; the group helped lead the successful fight for legislation to limit and regulate offshore drilling in California. The Santa Barbara spill also spawned Earth Day, which is still celebrated in communities across the nation today.

GOLF Like Pebble Beach, the 18-hole, par-72 **Sandpiper Golf Club** (✉ *7925 Hollister Ave., 14 mi north of downtown on Hwy. 101* ☎ *805/968–1541*) sits on the ocean bluffs and combines stunning views with a challenging game. Greens fees are $139–$159; a cart (optional) is $16. **Santa Barbara Golf Club** (✉ *Las Positas Rd. and McCaw Ave.* ☎ *805/687–7087*) has an 18-hole, par-70 course. The greens fees are $40–$50; a cart (optional) costs $28 per person.

TENNIS Many hotels in Santa Barbara have courts. The **City of Santa Barbara Parks and Recreation Department** (☎ *805/564–5418*) operates public courts with lighted play until 9 PM weekdays. You can purchase day permits ($6) at the courts, or call the department. **Las Positas Municipal Courts** (✉ *1002 Las Positas Rd.*) has six lighted hard courts open daily. The 12 hard courts at the **Municipal Tennis Center** (✉ *1414 Park Pl., near Salinas St. and U.S. 101*) include an enclosed stadium court and three lighted courts open daily. **Pershing Park** (✉ *100 Castillo St., near Cabrillo Blvd.*) has eight lighted courts available for public play after 5 PM weekdays and all day on weekends and Santa Barbara City College holidays.

SHOPPING

SHOPPING AREAS **State Street**, roughly between Cabrillo Boulevard and Sola Street, is the commercial hub of Santa Barbara and a shopper's paradise. Chic malls, quirky storefronts, antiques emporia, elegant boutiques, and funky thrift shops abound here. **Paseo Nuevo** (✉ *700 and 800 blocks* *of State St.*), an open-air mall anchored by chains such as Nordstrom and Macy's, also contains a few local institutions such as the children's clothier, This Little Piggy. You can do your shopping on foot or by a battery-powered trolley (25¢) that runs between the waterfront and the 1300 block.

Shops, art galleries, and studios share the courtyard and gardens of **El Paseo** (⌧ *Canon Perdido St., between State and Anacapa Sts.*), a historic arcade. Antiques and gift shops are clustered in restored Victorian buildings on **Brinkerhoff Avenue** (⌧ *2 blocks west of State St., at West Cota St.*). Serious antiques hunters can head a few miles south of Santa Barbara to the beach town of **Summerland**, which is full of shops and markets.

CLOTHING   Established in the early 2000s, the original **Blue Bee** (⌧ *911½ State St.* ☎ *805/897–1137*) boutique and its chic line of California clothes and accessories quickly morphed into an empire that now includes a number of specialty shops peddling designer jeans, shoes, jewelry, and clothing for men, women, and kids; most occupy individual spaces in the La Arcada shopping plaza at State and Figueroa streets, across from the Santa Barbara Museum of Art. **Channel Islands Surfboards** (⌧ *36 Anacapa St.* ☎ *805/966–7213*) stocks the latest in California beachwear, sandals, and accessories. **Pierre Lafond–Wendy Foster** (⌧ *833 State St.* ☎ *805/966–2276*) is a casual-chic clothing store for women. **Santa Barbara Outfitters** (⌧ *1200 State St.* ☎ *805/564–1007*) carries stylish, functional clothing, shoes, and accessories for active folks: kayakers, climbers, cyclists, runners, and hikers. **Surf 'N Wear's Beach House** (⌧ *10 State St.* ☎ *805/963–1281*) carries surf clothing, gear, and collectibles; it's also the home of Santa Barbara Surf Shop and the exclusive local dealer of Surfboards by Yater. **Territory Ahead** (⌧ *Main store: 515 State St.* ⌧ *Outlet store: 400 State St.* ☎ *805/962–5558*), a high-quality outdoorsy catalog company, sells fashionably rugged clothing for men and women.

EN
ROUTE   If you choose to drive north via U.S. 101 without detouring to the Solvang/Santa Ynez area, you will drive right past some good beaches. In succession from east to west, **El Capitan, Gaviota, and Refugio state beaches** all have campsites, picnic tables, and fire rings. If you'd like to encounter nature without roughing it, you can try "glamping" (glamorous camping) at **El Capitan Canyon** (⌧ *11560 Calle Real, north side of El Capitan State Beach exit* ☎ *805/685–3887 or 866/352–2729*). The safari tents and cedar cabins here have fresh linens and creature comforts. There are also spacious sites for tent and RV camping at the adjacent **Ocean Mesa Campground** (☎ *805/879–5751 or 866/410–5783*).

SANTA BARBARA COUNTY

Residents refer to the glorious 30-mi stretch of coastline from Carpinteria to Gaviota as the South Coast. The Santa Ynez Mountains divide the county geographically; U.S. 101 passes through a mountain tunnel leading inland. Northern Santa Barbara County used to be known for its sprawling ranches and strawberry and broccoli fields. Today its 100-plus wineries and 22,000 acres of vineyards dominate the landscape from the Santa Ynez Valley in the south to Santa Maria in the north.

WORD OF MOUTH

"California's Central Coast is a popular place for surfers and windsurfers. If you're not up to surfing yourself, spend some time relaxing on the beach and watching the action." —photo by Doreen Miller, Fodors.com member

The hit film *Sideways* was filmed almost entirely in the North County wine country; when the movie won Golden Globe and Oscar awards in 2005, it sparked national and international interest in visits to the region.

ESSENTIALS

Visitor Information Santa Barbara County Vintners' Association (☎ 805/688–0881 ⊕ www.sbcountywines.com).

The Santa Barbara Conference & Visitors Bureau (☎ 805/966–9222 ⊕ www.santabarbaraca.com) created a detailed map highlighting film location spots. Maps can be downloaded from visitor bureau Web sites: ⊕ www.santaynezvalleyvisit.com or www.santabarbaraca.com.

SANTA YNEZ

31 mi north of Goleta via Hwy. 154.

Founded in 1882, the tiny town of Santa Ynez still has many of its original frontier buildings. You can walk through the three-block downtown area in just a few minutes, shop for antiques, and hang around the old-time saloon. At some of the eponymous valley's best restaurants, you just might bump into one of the many celebrities who own nearby ranches.

EXPLORING

Just south of Santa Ynez on the Chumash Indian Reservation lies the sprawling, Las Vegas–style **Chumash Casino Resort** (⊠ 3400 E. Hwy. 246 ☎ 800/248–6274). The casino has 2,000 slot machines, and the property includes three restaurants, a spa, and an upscale hotel ($$$–$$$$).

WHERE TO EAT AND STAY

$$
ITALIAN
★
✕ **Trattoria Grappolo.** Authentic Italian fare, an open kitchen, and festive, family-style seating make this trattoria equally popular with celebrities from Hollywood and ranchers from the Santa Ynez Valley. Italian favorites on the extensive menu range from thin-crust pizza to homemade ravioli, risottos, and seafood linguine to grilled lamb chops in red-wine sauce. The noise level tends to rise in the evening, so this isn't the best spot for a romantic getaway. ⊠ 3687-C Sagunto St. ☎ 805/688–6899 ⊕ www.trattoriagrappolo.com ☰ AE, MC, V ⊗ No lunch Mon.

$$$$
⛆ **Santa Ynez Inn.** This posh two-story Victorian inn in downtown Santa Ynez was built from scratch in 2002. The owners have furnished all the rooms with authentic historical pieces. The inn caters to a discerning crowd with the finest amenities—Frette linens, thermostatically controlled heat and air-conditioning, DVD/CD entertainment systems, and custom-made bathrobes. Most rooms have gas fireplaces, double steam showers, and whirlpool tubs. Rates include a phenomenal evening wine and hors d'oeuvres hour and a full breakfast. **Pros:** near several restaurants; unusual antiques; spacious rooms. **Cons:** high price for location; not in a historic building. ⊠ 3627 Sagunto St. ☎ 805/688–5588 or 800/643–5774 ⊕ www.santaynezinn.com ⇱ 20 rooms, 3 suites ♿ In-room: a/c, safe, refrigerator, DVD, Internet, Wi-Fi. In-hotel: gym, laundry service ☰ AE, D, MC, V ⊚ BP.

LOS OLIVOS

4 mi north of Santa Ynez on Hwy. 154.

This pretty village in the Santa Ynez Valley was once on Spanish-built El Camino Real (Royal Highway) and later a stop on major stagecoach and rail routes. It's so sleepy today, though, that the movie *Return to Mayberry* was filmed here. Tasting rooms, art galleries, antiques stores, and country markets line Grand Avenue and intersecting streets for several blocks.

EXPLORING

Inside the intimate, 99-square-foot **Carhartt Vineyard Tasting Room** (⊠ *2990-A Grand Ave.* ☎ *805/693–5100* ⊕ *www.carharttvineyard. com*), you're likely to meet owners and winemakers Mike and Brooke Carhartt, who pour samples of their small-lot, handcrafted vintages most days.

Historic Heather Cottage, originally an early-1900s doctor's office, houses the **Daniel Gehrs Tasting Room** (⊠ *2939 Grand Ave.* ☎ *805/693– 9686* ⊕ *www.danielgehrswines.com*). Here you can sample Gehrs's various varietals, produced in limited small-lot quantities.

Firestone Vineyard (⊠ *5000 Zaca Station Rd.* ☎ *805/688–3940* ⊕ *www. firestonewine.com*) has been around since 1972. It has daily tours, grassy picnic areas, and hiking trails in the hills overlooking the valley; the views are fantastic.

WHERE TO EAT AND STAY

$$$$
AMERICAN
Fodor's Choice
★

✕ **Brothers Restaurant at Mattei's Tavern.** In the stagecoach days, Mattei's Tavern provided wayfarers with hearty meals and warm beds. Chef-owners and brothers Matt and Jeff Nichols renovated the 1886 building, and while retaining the original character, transformed it into one of the best restaurants in the valley. The casual, unpretentious dining rooms with their red-velvet wallpaper and historic photos reflect the rich history of the tavern. The menu changes every few weeks but often includes house favorites such as spicy fried calamari, prime rib, and salmon, and the locally famous jalapeño corn bread. There's also a full bar and an array of vintages from the custom-built cedar wine cellar. ⊠ *2350 Railway Ave.* ☎ *805/688–4820* ⊕ *www.matteistavern.com* ⚏ *Reservations essential* ☰ AE, D, MC, V ☺ *No lunch.*

$$
AMERICAN

✕ **Los Olivos Cafe.** Site of the scene in *Sideways* where the four main characters dine together and share a few bottles of wine, this down-to-earth restaurant not only provided the setting but served the actors real food from their existing menu during filming. Part wine store and part social hub for locals, the café focuses on wine-friendly fish, pasta, and meat dishes made from local bounty, plus salads, pizzas, and burgers. Don't miss the homemade muffuletta and olive tapenade spreads. Other house favorites include an artisanal cheese plate, baked Brie with honey-roasted hazelnuts, and braised pot roast with whipped potatoes. ⊠ *2879 Grand Ave.* ☎ *805/688–7265 or 888/946–3748* ⊕ *www.losolivoscafe. com* ☰ AE, D, MC, V.

$$$–$$$$

⊡ **The Ballard Inn & Restaurant.** Set among orchards and vineyards in the tiny town of Ballard, 2 mi south of Los Olivos, this inn makes an elegant wine-country escape. Rooms are furnished with antiques and original art. Seven rooms have wood-burning fireplaces; the inn provides room phones and TVs on request. The inn's tasting room serves boutique wines on weekends. At the Ballard Inn Restaurant ($$$), which serves dinner Wednesday through Sunday, owner-chef Budi Kazali creates sumptuous French–Asian dishes in one of the area's most romantic dining rooms. **Pros:** exceptional food; attentive staff; secluded. **Cons:** some baths could use updating; several miles from Los Olivos and Santa Ynez. ☒ *2436 Baseline Ave., Ballard* ☎ *805/688–7770 or 800/638–2466* ⊕ *www.ballardinn.com* ⤴ *15 rooms* ⚥ *In-room: no phone, a/c, no TV, Wi-Fi. In-hotel: restaurant, bicycles, Wi-Fi hotspot* ▤ *AE, MC, V* ⦿ *BP.*

$$$$ ☆ **Fess Parker's Wine Country Inn and Spa.** This luxury inn includes an elegant, tree-shaded French country–style main building and an equally attractive annex across the street with a pool, hot tub, and day spa. The spacious accommodations have fireplaces, seating areas, and wet bars. **Pros:** convenient wine touring base; walking distance from restaurants and galleries; well-appointed rooms. **Cons:** pricey; staff attention is inconsistent. ☒ *2860 Grand Ave.* ☎ *805/688–7788 or 800/446–2455* ⊕ *www.fessparker.com* ⤴ *20 rooms, 1 suite* ⚥ *In-room: a/c, refrigerator, Internet. In-hotel: restaurant, bar, pool, gym, spa, Wi-Fi hotspot, some pets allowed* ▤ *AE, DC, MC, V* ⦿ *BP.*

SOLVANG

⟳   *5 mi south of Los Olivos on Alamo Pintado Rd., Hwy. 246, 3 mi east of U.S. 101.*

You'll know you've reached the town of Solvang when the architecture suddenly changes to half-timber buildings and windmills. This town was settled in 1911 by a group of Danish educators (the flatlands and rolling green hills reminded them of home), and even today, more than two-thirds of the residents are of Danish descent. Although it's attracted tourists for decades, in recent years it has become more sophisticated, with galleries, upscale restaurants, and wine-tasting rooms. Most shops are locally owned; the city has an ordinance prohibiting chain stores. A good way to get your bearings is to park your car in one of the many free public lots and stroll around town. Stop in at one of the visitor centers—at 2nd Street and Copenhagen Drive, or Mission Drive (Highway 246) at 5th Street—for maps and helpful advice on what to see and do. Don't forget to stock up on Danish pastries from the town's excellent bakeries before you leave.

ESSENTIALS

Visitor Information Solvang Conference & Visitors Bureau (☒ *1639 Copenhagen Dr., Solvang* ☎ *805/688–6144 or 800/468–6765* ⊕ *www.solvangusa.com*).

EXPLORING

Just outside Solvang is the **Alma Rosa Winery** (☒ *7250 Santa Rosa Rd.* ☎ *805/688–9090* ⊕ *www.almarosawinery.com*). Owners Richard and Thekla Sanford helped put Santa Barbara County on the international wine map with a 1989 pinot noir. Recently the Sanfords started a new winery, Alma Rosa, with wines made from grapes grown on their 100-plus-acre certified organic vineyards in the Santa Rita Hills. You can taste the current releases at one of the most environmentally sensitive tasting rooms and picnic areas in the valley. All their vineyards are certified organic, and the pinot noirs and chardonnays are exceptional.

Often called the Hidden Gem of the missions, **Mission Santa Inés** (✉ *1760 Mission Dr.* ☎ *805/688–4815* ⊕ *www.missionsantaines.org* ✉ *$4* ⊙ *Daily 9–4:30*) has an impressive collection of paintings, statuary, vestments, and Chumash and Spanish artifacts in a serene bluff-top setting. Take a self-guided tour through the museum, sanctuary, and tranquil gardens.

ON A MISSION

Six important California missions established by Franciscan friars are within the Central Coast region. San Miguel is one of California's best-preserved missions. La Purisima is the most fully restored; Mission Santa Barbara is perhaps the most beautiful in the state; and Mission San Luis Obispo de Tolosa has a fine museum with many Chumash Indian artifacts. Mission Santa Inés is known for its serene gardens and restored artworks, and Mission San Buenaventura has 250-year-old paintings and statuary.

Housed in an 1884 adobe, the **Rideau Vineyard** (✉ *1562 Alamo Pintado Rd.* ☎ *805/688–0717* ⊕ *www.rideauvineyard.com*) tasting room provides simultaneous blasts from the area's ranching past and from its hand-harvested, Rhône-varietal wine-making present.

WHERE TO EAT AND STAY

$$$ ✕ **The Hitching Post II.** You'll find everything from grilled artichokes to
AMERICAN   ostrich at this casual catery just outside of Solvang, but most people come for what is said to be the best Santa Maria–style barbecue in the state. The oak used in the barbecue imparts a wonderful smoky taste. Be sure to try a glass of owner-chef-winemaker Frank Ostini's signature Highliner pinot noir, a star in the 2004 film *Sideways*. ✉ *406 E. Hwy. 246* ☎ *805/688–0676* ⊕ *www.hitchingpost2.com* ▣ *AE, MC, V* ⊙ *No lunch.*

$$$ ✕ **Root 246.** The name of this chic outpost at Hotel Corque is a play
★   on the main route through the Santa Ynez Valley (Highway 246). Chef Bradley Ogden and his team tap local purveyors and shop for organic foods at farmers markets before deciding on the day's menu. Depending on the season, you might feast on local squid with sweet baby prawns, prime rib eye steak grilled over an oak fire and served with root vegetable gratin, or rhubarb and polenta upside-down cake. The attentive wait staff can recommend pairings from the restaurant's 1,800-bottle selection of regional wines. The gorgeous design incorporates wood, stone, tempered glass, and leather elements in several distinct areas, including a slick 47-seat dining room (but jeans and casual wine-touring attire are welcome), a more casual bar with sofas and chairs, and a hip lounge. ✉ *420 Alisal Rd.* ☎ *805/686–8681* ⊕ *www.root-246.com* ▣ *AE, D, MC, V* ⊙ *No lunch weekdays.*

$$$$ ▦ **Alisal Guest Ranch and Resort.** Since 1946 this 10,000-acre ranch has
★   been popular with celebrities and plain folk alike. There are lots of activities to choose from here: horseback riding, golf, fishing, sailing

in the 100-acre spring-fed lake—although you can also just lounge by the pool or book a treatment at the day spa. The ranch-style rooms and suites come with garden views, covered porches, high-beam ceilings, and wood-burning fireplaces, with touches of Spanish tile and fine Western art. A jacket is required at the nightly dinners (which are included in your room rate). **Pros:** Old West atmosphere; tons of activities; ultraprivate. **Cons:** isolated; cut off from the high-tech world; some units are aging. ⊠ *1054 Alisal Rd.* ☎ *805/688–6411 or 800/425–4725* ⊕ *www.alisal.com* ↩ *36 rooms, 37 suites* ♿ *In-room: no phone, no a/c, refrigerator, no TV, Wi-Fi. In-hotel: restaurant, room service, bar, golf courses, tennis courts, pool, gym, spa, bicycles, children's programs (ages 6 and up), Internet terminal, Wi-Fi hotspot* ⊟ *AE, DC, MC, V* ⧖ *MAP.*

$$$–$$$$ ⚿ **Hotel Corque.** Sleek, stunning Hotel Corque—the largest hotel in the
   ★   Santa Ynez Valley—provides a full slate of upscale amenities on the edge of town. The Santa Ynez Band of Chumash Indians bought the aging Royal Scandinavian Inn in 2007, then poured millions into a top-to-bottom renovation. The Chumash popped open the three-story "Corque" in spring 2009, revealing a sophisticated, yet casual resort. Natural elements abound throughout the hotel: mahogany, oak, and maple floors and furnishings, stone tiles, granite countertops, and textured walls and color schemes that reflect the surrounding oak-studded meadows. All guest rooms have super-comfy beds with custom posture-pampering mattresses, 42-inch high-def plasma TVs, and lavish baths with rain showers; ask for one with a private balcony or terrace overlooking the mountains and vineyards. **Pros:** all front desk staff are trained concierges; short walk to shops, tasting rooms and restaurants; smoke-free property. **Cons:** no kitchenettes or laundry facilities; not low-budget. ⊠ *400 Alisal Rd.* ☎ *805/688–8000 or 800/624–5572* ⊕ *www.hotelcorque.com* ↩ *122 rooms, 10 suites* ♿ *In-room: a/c, refrigerator, Wi-Fi. In-hotel: restaurant, bars, pool, laundry service, Internet terminal, Wi-Fi* ⊟ *AE, D, MC, V.*

$$ ⚿ **Solvang Gardens Lodge.** Lush gardens with fountains and waterfalls, friendly staff, and cheery English-country-theme rooms with antiques make for a peaceful retreat just a few blocks—but worlds away—from Solvang's main tourist area. Rooms range from basic to elegant; each has unique character and furnishings, and many have marble showers and baths. **Pros:** homey; family-friendly; colorful gardens. **Cons:** some rooms are tiny; some need upgrades. ⊠ *293 Alisal Rd.* ☎ *805/688–4404 or 888/688–4404* ⊕ *www.solvanggardens.com* ↩ *16 rooms, 8 suites* ♿ *In-room: no phone, a/c, kitchen (some), refrigerator (some), DVD, Wi-Fi. In-hotel: spa, Internet terminal, Wi-Fi hotspot* ⊟ *AE, D, MC, V* ⧖ *CP.*

LOMPOC

20 mi west of Solvang on Hwy. 246.

Known as the flower-seed capital of the world, Lompoc is blanketed with vast fields of brightly colored flowers that bloom from May through August.

EXPLORING

For five days around the last weekend of June, the **Lompoc Valley Flower Festival** (☎ 805/735–8511 ⊕ www.flowerfestival.org) brings a parade, carnival, and crafts show to town.

ⓒ At **La Purisima Mission State Historic Park** you can see Mission La Purisima Concepción, the most fully restored mission in the state. Founded in 1787, it stands in a stark and still remote location and powerfully evokes the lives of California's Spanish settlers. Docents lead tours every afternoon, and displays illustrate the secular and religious activities that were part of mission life. From March through October the mission holds special events, including crafts demonstrations by costumed docents. ⊠ 2295 Purisima Rd., off Hwy. 246 ☎ 805/733–3713 ⊕ www.lapurisimamission.org ⊠ $6 per vehicle ⊗ Daily 9–5; tour daily at 1.

> **VOLCANOES?**
>
> Those funny looking, sawed-off peaks along the drive from Pismo Beach to Morro Bay are the Seven Sisters—a series of ancient volcanic plugs. Morro Rock, the northernmost sibling and a state historic monument, is the most famous and photographed of the clan.

SAN LUIS OBISPO COUNTY

San Luis Obispo County's pristine landscapes and abundant wildlife areas, especially those around Morro Bay and Montaña de Oro State Park, have long attracted nature lovers. In the south, Pismo Beach and other coastal towns have great sand and surf; inland, a booming wine region stretches from the Edna and Arroyo Grande Valleys in the south to Paso Robles in the north. With historical attractions, a photogenic downtown, and busy shops and restaurants, the college town of San Luis Obispo is at the heart of the county.

ESSENTIALS

Visitor Information San Luis Obispo County Visitors and Conference Bureau (⊠ 811 El Capitan Way Suite 200, San Luis Obispo ☎ 805/541–8000 or 800/634–1414 ⊕ www.sanluisobispocounty.com).

PISMO BEACH

U.S. 101/Hwy. 1, about 40 mi north of Lompoc.

About 20 mi of sandy shoreline—nicknamed the Bakersfield Riviera for the throngs of vacationers who come here from the Central Valley—begins at the town of Pismo Beach. The southern end of town runs along sand dunes, some of which are open to cars and off-road vehicles; sheltered by the dunes, a grove of eucalyptus trees attracts thousands of migrating monarch butterflies November through February. A long, broad beach fronts the center of town, where a municipal pier extends into the sea at the foot of shop-lined Pomeroy Street. To the north, hotels and homes perch atop chalky oceanfront cliffs.

Fewer than 10,000 people live in this quintessential surfer haven, but Pismo Beach has a slew of hotels and restaurants with great views of the Pacific Ocean. Still, rooms can sometimes be hard to come by. Each Father's Day weekend the Pismo Beach Classic, one of the West Coast's largest classic-car and street-rod shows, overruns the town. A Dixieland jazz festival in February also draws crowds.

EN ROUTE

The spectacular **Guadalupe-Nipomo Dunes Preserve** stretches 18 mi along the coast south of Pismo Beach. It's the largest and most ecologically diverse dune system in the state, and a habitat for more than 200 species of birds as well as sea otters, black bears, bobcats, coyotes, and deer. The 1,500-foot Mussel Rock is the highest beach dune in the western states. As many as 20 movies have been filmed here, including Cecil B. DeMille's 1923 silent *The Ten Commandments*. The main entrances to the dunes are at Oso Flaco Lake (about 13 mi south of Pismo Beach on U.S. 101/Highway 1, then 3 mi west on Oso Flaco Road) and at the far west end of Highway 166 (Main Street) in Guadalupe. At the **Dunes Center** (⊠ *1055 Guadalupe St., 1 mi north of Hwy. 166* ☎ *805/343–2455* ⊕ *www.dunescenter.org* ⊗ *Wed.–Sun. 10–4*), you can get nature information and view an exhibit about *The Ten Commandments* movie set, which weather and archaeologists are slowly unearthing near Guadalupe Beach. Parking at Oso Flaco Lake is $5 per vehicle.

WHERE TO EAT

$$
SEAFOOD

✕ **Cracked Crab.** This traditional New England–style crab shack imports fresh seafood daily from Australia, Alaska, and the East Coast. Fish is line-caught, much of the produce is organic, and everything is made from scratch. For a real treat, don a bib and chow through a bucket of steamed shellfish with Cajun sausage, potatoes, and corn on the cob, all dumped right onto your table. The menu changes daily. ⊠ *751 Price St.* ☎ *805/773–2722* ⊕ *www.crackedcrab.com* ⚑ *Reservations not accepted* ⊟ *AE, D, MC, V.*

$$
ITALIAN

✕ **Giuseppe's Cucina Italiana.** The classic flavors of southern Italy are highlighted at this lively, warm downtown spot. Most recipes originate from Bari, a seaport on the Adriatic; the menu includes breads and pizzas baked in the wood-burning oven, hearty dishes such as osso buco and lamb, and homemade pastas. The wait for a table can be long at peak dinner hours, but sometimes an accordion player gets the crowd singing. Next door, their bakery sells take-out selections. ⊠ *891 Price St.* ☎ *805/773–2870* ⊕ *www.giuseppesrestaurant.com* ⚑ *Reservations not accepted* ⊟ *AE, D, MC, V* ⊗ *No lunch weekends.*

¢
SEAFOOD

✕ **Splash Café.** Folks line up all the way down the block for clam chowder served in a sourdough bread bowl at this wildly popular seafood stand. You can also order beach food such as fresh steamed clams, burgers, and fried calamari at the counter (no table service)—and many items on the menu are $8 or less. The grimy, cramped, but cheery hole-in-a-wall, a favorite with locals and savvy visitors, is open daily for lunch and dinner (plus a rock-bottom basic breakfast starting at 8 AM), but closes early on weekday evenings during low season. ⊠ *197 Pomeroy St.* ☎ *805/773–4653* ⊕ *www.splashcafe.com* ⊟ *AE, D, MC, V.*

WHERE TO STAY

$$$$ 🏨 **Dolphin Bay.** Perched on grass-covered bluffs overlooking Shell Beach, this luxury resort looks and feels like an exclusive condominium community. Choose among sprawling one- or two-bedroom residences, each with a gourmet kitchen, laundry room with washer and dryer, and contemporary Mission-style furniture. Many have ocean views. Two-bedroom units include either a spa tub or fireplace; penthouse units have both. Rejuvenate at La Bonne Vie day spa, lounge by the infinity pool, or stroll down a short path to the beach to gaze at the sea—this place was made for upscale escape and relaxation. At Lido ($$$–$$$$), the fancy yet casual restaurant (no flip-flops), chef Evan Treadwell presents an impressive menu of California wine country cuisine with an international flair; favorites include Thai-spiced mussels and pulled-pork sliders. **Pros:** lavish apartment units; as upscale as you can get; killer views; walking distance from the beach. **Cons:** hefty price tag; upper-crust vibe. ⊠ *2727 Shell Beach Rd.* ☎ *805/773–4300 or 800/516–0112* ⊕ *www.thedolphinbay.com* ⇄ *63 residences* ⚒ *In-room: a/c, kitchen, DVD, Internet, Wi-Fi. In-hotel: restaurant, room service, bar, pool, gym, spa, Wi-Fi hotspot, some pets allowed* ▭ *AE, D, MC, V.*

$$$$ 🏨 **Pismo Lighthouse Suites.** Each of the well-appointed two-room, two-bath suites at this oceanfront resort has a private balcony or patio. Some suites are suitable for couples, others for families, and all have crisp nautical-style furnishings. Ask for a corner oceanfront suite for the best views. On the central sport court you can play a variety of games, including chess on a life-size board. Sister property Avila Lighthouse Suites, just a few miles north, provides similar comforts and is steps from Avila Beach. **Pros:** lots of space for families and groups; nice pool area. **Cons:** not easy to walk to main attractions; some units are next to busy road. ⊠ *2411 Price St.* ☎ *805/773–2411 or 800/245–2411* ⊕ *www.pismolighthousesuites.com* ➷ *70 suites* ⚴ *In-room: a/c, refrigerator, Internet, Wi-Fi. In-hotel: pool, gym, spa, laundry facilities, Wi-Fi hotspot* ⊟ *AE, D, DC, MC, V* ⦿ *CP.*

$$$ ⊡ **Sea Venture Resort.** The bright, homey rooms at this hotel all have fireplaces and featherbeds; most have balconies with private hot tubs, and some have beautiful ocean views. A breakfast basket is delivered to your room in the morning, and the elegant Sea Venture Restaurant ($$–$$$, no lunch weekdays)—with sweeping ocean vistas from the third floor—features fresh seafood and local wines. **Pros:** on the beach; excellent food; romantic rooms. **Cons:** touristy area; some rooms and facilities are beginning to age; dark hallways. ⊠ *100 Ocean View Ave.* ☎ *805/773–4994 or 800/760–0664* ⊕ *www.seaventure.com* ➷ *50 rooms* ⚴ *In-room: no a/c, refrigerator, Internet, Wi-Fi. In-hotel: restaurant, spa, bicycles, Wi-Fi hotspot* ⊟ *AE, D, DC, MC, V* ⦿ *CP.*

$–$$ ⊡ **Shell Beach Inn.** Just 2½ blocks from the beach, this basic but cozy motor court is a great bargain for the area. Along with a 2005 room remodel, the property upgraded its name from "motel" to "inn." Choose from king, queen, or two-bedded rooms; all have European country-style furnishings and floral details painted on the walls and ceilings. **Pros:** walking distance from the beach; clean rooms; friendly and dependable service. **Cons:** sits on a busy road; small rooms; tiny pool. ⊠ *653 Shell Beach Rd.* ☎ *805/773–4373 or 800/549–4727* ⊕ *www. shellbeachinn.com* ➷ *10 rooms* ⚴ *In-room: no a/c, refrigerator, Wi-Fi. In-hotel: pool, some pets allowed* ⊟ *AE, D, DC, MC, V.*

AVILA BEACH

⟳   *4 mi north of Pismo Beach on U.S. 101/Hwy. 1.*

Because the village of Avila Beach and the sandy, cove-front shoreline for which it's named face south into the Pacific Ocean, they get more sun and less fog than any other stretch of coast in the area. It can be bright and warm here while just beyond the surrounding hills communities shiver under the marine layer. With its fortuitous climate and protected waters, Avila's public beach draws plenty of sunbathers and families; weekends are very busy. Demolished in 1998 to clean up extensive oil seepage from a Unocal tank farm, downtown Avila Beach has sprung back to life. The seaside promenade has been fully restored and shops and hotels have quickly popped up; with mixed results the town has tried to re-create its former offbeat character. For real local color, head to the far end of the cove and watch the commercial fishing boats offload their catch on the old Port San Luis wharf. A few seafood shacks and fish markets do business on the pier while sea lions congregate below. On Fridays from mid-April through mid-September, a fish and farmers' market livens up the beach area with music, fresh local produce and seafood, and children's activities.

WHERE TO EAT AND STAY

$$$
SEAFOOD

✕ **Olde Port Inn.** Locals swear by this old-fashioned fish house at the end of the Port San Luis Pier. Ask for today's fresh catch, or go for the *cioppino* (spicy tomato-based seafood stew) or fish tacos; simplicity is the key to a decent meal here. You can't beat the views, whether you're looking out over the ocean or through the glass surface of your table into the waters below. ⊠ *End of 3rd pier* ☏ *805/595–2515* ⊕ *www. oldeportinn.com* ▭ *AE, D, MC, V.*

$$$$

▥ **Avila La Fonda.** Modeled after a village in early California's Mexican period, Avila La Fonda surrounds guests with rich jewel tones, fountains, and upscale comfort. The facade of the hotel replicates eight different casitas, including several famous historic homes in Mexico. Inside, stained-glass windows and tiled murals celebrate Mexican art and life in Avila Beach. Guests can choose from two types of rooms: a spa room with a huge tub near the king bed, or a great room with gourmet kitchen, queen Murphy bed, and sofa sleeper. You can also combine adjacent rooms to create your own casita. The lavish Owner's Spa Suite includes a sauna and steam shower—it's available to guests when it's not occupied by the owner or special guests. An added bonus: the beach is one block away. **Pros:** one-of-a-kind theme and artwork; flexible room combinations; a block from the beach. **Cons:** pricey; most rooms don't have an ocean view. ⊠ *101 San Miguel St.* ☏ *805/595–1700* ⊕ *www.avilalafondahotel.com* ⇌ *32 rooms, 1 suite* ⌂ *In-room: a/c, kitchen (some), refrigerator, DVD, Internet, Wi-Fi. In-hotel: laundry service, laundry facilities, Wi-Fi hotspot, Internet terminal, some pets allowed* ▭ *AE, D, MC, V.*

$$–$$$

▥ **Sycamore Mineral Springs Resort.** This wellness resort's hot mineral springs bubble up into private outdoor tubs on an oak-and-sycamore-forest hillside. Whether or not you stay here, it's worth coming for a soak—even though the grounds are well within earshot of a busy road. Each room or suite has its own private balcony with a hot tub; about half have mineral water piped in. The spa offers everything from massages and skin care to yoga classes and a variety of integrative healing arts. Creative spa and California cuisine is served in the romantic Gardens of Avila restaurant ($$–$$$). **Pros:** great place to rejuvenate; nice hiking; incredible spa services. **Cons:** rooms vary in quality; 2½ mi from the beach. ⊠ *1215 Avila Beach Dr., San Luis Obispo* ☏ *805/595–7302 or 800/234–5831* ⊕ *www.sycamoresprings.com* ⇌ *26 rooms, 50 suites* ⌂ *In-room: a/c, refrigerator (some), Internet, Wi-Fi. In-hotel: restaurant, room service, bar, pool, spa, Wi-Fi hotspot* ▭ *AE, D, DC, MC, V.*

SAN LUIS OBISPO

8 mi north of Avila Beach on U.S. 101/Hwy. 1.

About halfway between San Francisco and Los Angeles, San Luis Obispo—nicknamed SLO—spreads out below gentle hills and rocky extinct volcanoes. Its main appeal lies in its architecturally diverse and commercially lively downtown, especially several blocks of Higuera

Street. The pedestrian-friendly district bustles with shoppers, restaurant goers, and students from California Polytechnic State University, known as Cal Poly. On Thursday from 6 PM to 9 PM a farmers' market fills Higuera Street with local produce, entertainment, and food stalls. SLO is less a vacation destination than a pleasant stopover along Highway 1; it's a nice place to stay while touring the wine country south of town.

ESSENTIALS

Visitor Information San Luis Obispo Chamber of Commerce (⊠ *1039 Chorro St., San Luis Obispo* ☎ *805/781–2777* ⊕ *www.visitslo.com*). **San Luis Obispo Vintners Association** (☎ *805/541–5868* ⊕ *www.slowine.com*).

EXPLORING

★ Special events often take place on sun-dappled Mission Plaza in front of **Mission San Luis Obispo de Tolosa**, established in 1772. Its small museum exhibits artifacts of the Chumash Indians and early Spanish settlers, and docents sometimes lead tours of the church and grounds. ⊠ *751 Palm St.* ☎ *805/543–6850* ⊕ *www.missionsanluisobispo.org* ⌑ *$3 suggested donation* ⊙ *Apr.–late-Oct., daily 9–5; late Oct.–Mar., daily 9–4.*

Ⓒ The delightful **San Luis Obispo Children's Museum** has 21 indoor and outdoor activities that present a kid-friendly version of the city of San Luis Obispo. Visitors enter through an "imagination-powered" elevator, which transports them to a series of underground caverns beneath the city, while simulated lava and steam sputters from an active volcano. Kids can pick rubber fruit at a farmers' market, clamber up a clockworks tower, race to fight a fire on a fire engine, and learn about solar energy from a 15-foot sunflower. The museum attracts mostly kids under eight; older children may become bored quickly. ⊠ *1010 Nipomo St.* ☎ *805/545–5874* ⊕ *www.slocm.org* ⌑ *$8* ⊙ *Apr.—Sept., Tues.–Fri. 10–4, Sat. 10–5, Sun. and select Mon. holidays 11–5; Oct.–Mar., Tues.–Fri. 10–3, Sat. 10–5, Sun. and select Mon. holidays 1–5.*

Ⓒ Across the street from the old Spanish mission, **San Luis Obispo County Historical Museum** presents rotating exhibits on various aspects of county history—such as Native American life, California ranchos, and the impact of railroads. A separate children's room has theme activities where kids can earn prizes. ⊠ *696 Monterey St.* ☎ *805/543–0638* ⊕ *www.slochs.org* ⌑ *Free* ⊙ *Wed.–Sun. 10–4.*

San Luis Obispo is the commercial center of **Edna Valley/Arroyo Grande Valley wine country,** whose appellations stretch east–west from San Luis Obispo toward the coast and toward Lake Lopez in the inland mountains. Many of the 20 or so wineries line Highway 227 and connecting roads. The region is best known for chardonnay and pinot noir, although many wineries experiment with other varietals and blends. Wine-touring maps are readily available around town; note that many wineries charge a small tasting fee and most tasting rooms close at 5.

For sweeping views of the Edna Valley while you sample estate-grown chardonnay, go to the modern tasting bar at **Edna Valley Vineyard** (⊠ *2585 Biddle Ranch Rd.* ☎ *805/544–5855* ⊕ *www.ednavalleyvineyard.com*).

A refurbished 1909 schoolhouse serves as tasting room for **Baileyana Winery** (⊠ *5828 Orcutt Rd.* ☎ *805/269–8200* ⊕ *www.baileyana.com*), which produces concentrated chardonnays, pinot noirs, and Syrahs. Its sister winery, Tangent, creates alternative white wines and shares the tasting room.

An eco-friendly winery built from straw bales, **Claiborne & Churchill** (✉ 2649 *Carpenter Canyon Rd.* ☎ *805/544–4066* ⊕ *www.claibornechurchill. com*) makes small lots of exceptional Alsatian-style wines such as dry Riesling and Gewürztraminer, plus pinot noir and chardonnay.

While touring Edna Valley wine country, be sure to stop at **Old Edna** (✉ *Hwy. 227, at Price Canyon Rd.* ☎ *805/544–8062* ⊕ *www.oldedna. com*), a peaceful, 2-acre site that once was the town of Edna. Browse for local art, taste wines, pick up sandwiches at the gourmet deli, and stroll along Old Edna Lane.

WHERE TO EAT

$$ ✕ **Big Sky Café.** A popular gathering spot three meals a day, this quintes-
ECLECTIC sentially Californian, family-friendly (and sometimes noisy) café turns
★ local and organically grown ingredients into global dishes. Brazilian churasco chicken breast, Thai catfish, New Mexican *pozole* (hominy stew): just pick your continent. Vegetarians have lots to choose from. ✉ *1121 Broad St.* ☎ *805/545–5401* ⊕ *www.bigskycafe.com* ⚲ *Reservations not accepted* ⊟ *AE, MC, V.*

$$ ✕ **Buona Tavola.** Homemade pasta with river shrimp in a creamy tomato
ITALIAN sauce and porcini-mushroom risotto are among the northern Italian dishes served at this casual spot. Daily fresh fish and salad specials and an impressive wine list attract a steady stream of regulars. In good weather you can dine on the flower-filled patio. The Paso Robles branch is equally enjoyable. ✉ *1037 Monterey St.* ☎ *805/545–8000* ⊕ *www. btslo.com* ✉ *943 Spring St., Paso Robles* ☎ *805/237–0600* ⊟ *AE, D, MC, V* ☉ *No lunch weekends.*

¢ ✕ **Mo's Smokehouse BBQ.** Barbecue joints abound on the Central Coast,
SOUTHERN but this one excels. A variety of Southern-style sauces seasons tender hickory-smoked ribs and shredded meat sandwiches; sides such as baked beans, coleslaw, homemade potato chips, and garlic bread extend the pleasure. ✉ *1005 Monterey St.* ☎ *805/544–6193* ⊕ *www. smokinmosbbq.com* ⊟ *AE, MC, V.*

$ ✕ **Novo Restaurant & Lounge.** In the colorful dining room or on the large
ECLECTIC creek-side deck, this animated downtown eatery will take you on a culinary world tour. The salads, small plates, and entrées come from nearly every continent. The wine and beer list also covers the globe (you can sample various international wines paired with tapas Sunday evenings)—and includes local favorites. Many of the decadent desserts are baked at the restaurant's sister property in Cambria, the French Corner Bakery. ✉ *726 Higuera St.* ☎ *805/543–3986* ⊕ *www. novorestaurant.com* ⊟ *MC, V.*

WHERE TO STAY

$$$–$$$$ ▥ **Apple Farm.** Decorated to the hilt with floral bedspreads and water-
colors by local artists, this Victorian country-style hotel is one of the most popular places to stay in San Luis Obispo. Each room has a gas fireplace and fresh flowers; some have canopy beds and cozy window seats. There's a working gristmill in the courtyard; within the inn are

5

a restaurant serving American food (the hearty breakfasts are best), a gourmet food and wine shop, a bakery, and a gift shop. Smaller, motel-style rooms are also available for a considerably lower price. **Pros:** flowers everywhere; convenient to Cal Poly and Highway 101; creek-side setting. **Cons:** hordes of tourists stop here during the day; too floral for some people's tastes.

> ## DEEP ROOTS
>
> Way back in the 1700s, the Spanish padres who accompanied Father Junípero Serra planted grapevines from Mexico along California's Central Coast, and began using European wine-making techniques to turn the grapes into delectable vintages.

✉ *2015 Monterey St.* ☎ *800/255–2040* ⊕ *www.applefarm.com* ⤵ *104 rooms* ⚄ *In-room: a/c, Internet. In-hotel: restaurant, pool, spa, Wi-Fi hotspot* ⊟ *AE, D, MC, V.*

$$–$$$ 🏨 **Garden Street Inn.** From this fully restored 1887 Italianate Queen Anne, the only lodging in downtown SLO, you can walk to many restaurants and attractions. The individually decorated rooms, each with private bath, are filled with antiques; some have stained-glass windows, fireplaces, and decks. Each evening, wine and hors d'oeuvres are served in the intimate dining room; there's also a lavish homemade breakfast when you rise. **Pros:** classic B&B; walking distance from everywhere downtown; nice wine and cheese reception. **Cons:** city noise filters through some rooms; not a great place for families. ✉ *1212 Garden St.* ☎ *805/545–9802 or 800/488–2045* ⊕ *www.gardenstreetinn.com* ⤵ *9 rooms, 4 suites* ⚄ *In-room: no a/c, no TV (some), Wi-Fi* ⊟ *AE, D, MC, V* ⟐ *BP.*

$$–$$$ 🏨 **Petit Soleil.** A cobblestone courtyard, country-French custom furnishings, and Gallic music piped through the halls evoke a Provençal mood at this cheery inn on upper Monterey Street's motel row. With extensive experience in luxury lodging, the owners are serious about the details: the individually themed rooms, sprinkled with lavender water, have CD players and L'Occitane bath products. Rates include wine and appetizers at cocktail hour and a full homemade breakfast in the sun-filled patio or dining room. **Pros:** French details throughout; scrumptious breakfasts; cozy rooms. **Cons:** sits on a busy avenue; cramped parking. ✉ *1473 Monterey St.* ☎ *805/549–0321 or 800/676–1588* ⊕ *www.psslo. com* ⤵ *15 rooms, 1 suite* ⚄ *In-room: no a/c, Internet, Wi-Fi. In-hotel: Wi-Fi hotspot* ⊟ *AE, MC, V* ⟐ *BP.*

NIGHTLIFE AND THE ARTS

NIGHTLIFE

The club scene in this college town is centered on Higuera Street off Monterey Street. The **Frog and Peach** (✉ *728 Higuera St.* ☎ *805/595–3764*) is a decent spot to nurse an English beer and listen to live music. A trendy urban crowd hangs out at the slick bar at **Koberl at Blue** (✉ *998 Monterey St.* ☎ *805/783–1135*), an upscale wine country restaurant with late-night dining, exotic martinis, and a huge list of local and imported beer and wine. **Linnaea's Cafe** (✉ *1110 Garden St.* ☎ *805/541–5888*), a mellow java joint, sometimes holds poetry readings, as well as blues, jazz, and folk music performances. Chicago style **MoTav** (✉ *725 Higuera St.* ☎ *805/541–8733*) draws crowds with good pub food and live entertainment in a turn-of-the-20th-century setting (complete with antique U.S. flags and a wall-mounted moose head).

THE ARTS

The **Performing Arts Center** (⊠ *1 Grand Ave.* ☎ *805/756–7222, 805/756–2787 for tickets outside CA, 888/233–2787 for tickets in CA* ⊕ *www.pacslo.org*) at Cal Poly hosts live theater, dance, and music performances by artists from around the world. **Festival Mozaic** (☎ *805/781–3008* ⊕ *www. festivalmozaic.com*) celebrates five centuries of classical music and takes place in late July and early August. **San Luis Obispo Art Center** (⊠ *1010 Broad St., at Mission Plaza* ☎ *805/543–8562* ⊕ *www. sloartcenter.org* ۝ *Closed Tues. early Sept.–late June*) displays and sells a mix of traditional work and cutting-edge arts and crafts by Central Coast, national, and international artists.

SPORTS AND THE OUTDOORS

A hilly greenbelt with vast amounts of open space and extensive hiking trails surrounds the city of San Luis Obispo. For information on trailheads, call the city **Parks and Recreation Department** (☎ *805/781–7300* ⊕ *www.slocity.org/parksandrecreation*) or visit its Web site to download a trail map.

EN ROUTE Instead of continuing north on Highway 1 from San Luis Obispo to Morro Bay, consider taking Los Osos Valley Road (off Madonna Road, south of downtown) past farms and ranches to dramatic **Montaña de Oro State Park** (☎ *7 mi south of Los Osos on Pecho Rd.* ☎ *805/528–0513 or 805/772–7434* ⊕ *www.parks.ca.gov*). The park has miles of nature trails along rocky shoreline, wild beaches, and hills overlooking some of California's most spectacular scenery. Check out the tide pools, watch the waves roll into the bluffs, and picnic in the eucalyptus groves.

MORRO BAY

14 mi north of San Luis Obispo on Hwy. 1.

Commercial fishermen slog around Morro Bay in galoshes, and beat-up fishing boats bob in the bay's protected waters.

EXPLORING

At the mouth of Morro Bay, which is both a state and national estuary, stands 576-foot-high **Morro Rock** (⊠ *Northern end of Embarcadero*) one of nine such small volcanic peaks, or morros, in the area. A short walk leads to a breakwater, with the harbor on one side and the crashing waves of the Pacific on the other. You may not climb the rock, where endangered falcons and other birds nest. Sea lions and otters often play in the water at the foot of the peak.

The center of the action on land is the **Embarcadero** (⊠ *On waterfront from Beach St. to Tidelands Park*), where vacationers pour in and out of souvenir shops and seafood restaurants and stroll or bike along the scenic half-mile Harborwalk to Morro Rock. From here, you can get out on the bay in a kayak or tour boat.

۝ ★ South of downtown Morro Bay, interactive exhibits at the spiffy **Morro Bay State Park Museum of Natural History** teach kids and adults about the natural environment and how to preserve it—both in the Morro Bay estuary and on the rest of the planet. ⊠ *State Park Rd.* ☎ *805/772–2694* ⊕ *www.ccnha.org* ⊒ *$3* ⊘ *Daily 10–5.*

WHERE TO EAT AND STAY

$
SOUTHWESTERN
★

✕ **Taco Temple.** The devout stand in line at this family-run diner that serves some of the freshest food around. Seafood anchors a menu of dishes—salmon burritos, superb fish tacos with mango salsa—hailing from somewhere between California and Mexico. Desserts get rave reviews, too. Make an effort to find this gem tucked away in the corner of a supermarket parking lot north of downtown—it's on the frontage road parallel to Highway 1, just north of the Highway 41 junction. ⊠ *2680 Main St., at Elena* ☎ *805/772–4965* ⌂ *Reservations not accepted* ⊟ *No credit cards* ⊘ *Closed Tues.*

$$$
SEAFOOD

✕ **Windows on the Water.** From giant picture windows at this second-floor spot, watch the sun set over the water. Fresh fish and other dishes based on local ingredients emerge from the wood-fired oven in the open kitchen; a variety of oysters on the half shell beckon from the raw bar. About 20 of the wines on the extensive, mostly California list are poured by the glass. ⊠ *699 Embarcadero* ☎ *805/772–0677* ⊟ *AE, D, DC, MC, V* ⊘ *No lunch.*

$$$–$$$$

▦ **Cass House.** The original 1867 home of shipping pioneer Captain James Cass is now a luxurious B&B boasting colorful rose gardens in the heart of Cayucos, a tiny oceanfront enclave about 4 miles north of Morro Bay just west of Highway 1. It reopened in 2007 after a meticulous 14-year restoration that seamlessly blended historic authenticity, eco-friendly operations, and modern conveniences including wireless Internet and high-definition flat-screen TVs with DVD players. Chef Jensen Lorenzen creates sumptuous breakfasts using mostly local, organic ingredients—some of which come from the inn's garden. The intimate dining room ($$$$) also opens to the public for dinner five nights a week. **Pros:** historic property; some ocean views; excellent meals. **Cons:** not near Morro Bay nightlife or tourist attractions; not designed for families. ⊠ *222 N. Ocean Ave., Cayucos* ☎ *805/995–3669* ⊕ *www.casshouseinn.com* ⤙ *5 rooms* ⌂ *In-room: no a/c, Wi-Fi. In-hotel: restaurant, Wi-Fi hotspot* ⊟ *AE, D, DC, MC, V* ◫⦿ *BP.*

$$–$$$

▦ **The Inn at Morro Bay.** Surrounded by eucalyptus trees on the edge of Morro Bay, the inn abuts a heron rookery and Morro Bay State Park. It's a beautiful setting, even though the birds can cause a din (and make a mess of parked cars). Many of the contemporary French Country–style rooms have fireplaces, private decks with spa tubs, and bay views. The most affordable rooms (petite queens) can seem small and dark, but you'll probably be spending much of your time elsewhere: getting a massage at the on-site wellness center, playing a round (fee) at the golf course across the road, or peddling through the state park on a complimentary bicycle. **Pros:** great for wildlife enthusiasts; stellar bay views from restaurant and some rooms. **Cons:** some rooms are cramped and dark; some sections need updating; birds can wake you early. ⊠ *60 State Park Rd.* ☎ *805/772–5651 or 800/321–9566* ⊕ *www.innatmorrobay. com* ⤙ *97 rooms, 1 cottage* ⌂ *In-room: no a/c, refrigerator, Internet. In-hotel: 2 restaurants, room service, bar, spa, bicycles, laundry service* ⊟ *AE, D, DC, MC, V.*

5

SPORTS AND THE OUTDOORS

Kayak Horizons (⊠ *551 Embarcadero* ☎ *805/772–6444* ⊕ *www. kayakhorizons.com*) rents kayaks and gives lessons and guided tours. **Sub-Sea Tours** (⊠ *699 Embarcadero* ☎ *805/772–9463* ⊕ *www.subseatours. com*) operates glass-bottom boat and catamaran cruises, and has kayak and canoe rentals and summer whale-watching cruises. **Virg's Landing** (⊠ *1215 Embarcadero* ☎ *805/772–1222* ⊕ *www.virgs.com*) conducts deep-sea fishing and whale-watching trips.

PASO ROBLES

30 mi north of San Luis Obispo on U.S. 101; 25 mi northwest of Morro Bay via Hwy. 41 and U.S. 101.

In the 1860s tourists began flocking to this dusty ranching outpost to "take the cure" in a luxurious bathhouse fed by underground mineral hot springs. An Old West town, complete with opera house, emerged; grand Victorian homes went up, followed in the 20th century by Craftsman bungalows. A 2003 earthquake demolished or weakened several beloved downtown buildings, but historically faithful reconstruction has proceeded rapidly.

Today the wine industry booms and mile upon mile of vineyards envelop Paso Robles; golfers play the four local courses and spandex-clad bicyclists race along the winding back roads. A mix of down-home and upmarket restaurants, bars, antiques stores, and little shops fills the streets around oak-shaded City Park, where special events of all kinds—custom car shows, an olive festival, Friday night summer concerts—take place on many weekends. Still, Paso (as the locals call it) more or less remains cowboy country: each year in late July and early August, the city throws the two-week California Mid-State Fair, complete with livestock auctions, carnival rides, and corn dogs.

ESSENTIALS

Visitor Information Paso Robles Wine Country Alliance (⊠ *744 Oak St.* ☎ *805/239–8463* ⊕ *www.pasowine.com*). **Paso Robles Chamber of Commerce** (⊠ *1225 Park St., Paso Robles* ☎ *888/988–7276* ⊕ *www.travelpaso.com*).

EXPLORING

Take a look back at California's rural heritage at the **Paso Robles Pioneer Museum**. Displays of historical ranching paraphernalia, horse-drawn vehicles, hot springs artifacts, and photos evoke the town's old days; a one-room schoolhouse is part of the complex. ⊠ *2010 Riverside Ave.* ☎ *805/239–4556* ⊕ *www.pasoroblespioneermuseum.org* 🎟 *Free* ⊙ *Thurs.–Sun. 1–4.*

The lakeside **River Oaks Hot Springs & Spa**, on 240 hilly acres near the intersection of U.S. 101 and Highway 46E, is a great place to relax before and after wine tasting or festival-going. Soak in a private indoor or outdoor hot tub fed by natural mineral springs, or indulge in a massage or facial. ⊠ *800 Clubhouse Dr.* ☎ *805/238–4600* ⊕ *www. riveroakshotsprings.com* 🎟 *Hot tubs $13 to $20 per person per hr* ⊙ *Tues.–Sun. 9–9.*

In **Paso Robles wine country**, nearly 200 wineries and more than 26,000 vineyard acres pepper the wooded hills west of U.S. 101 and blanket the flatter, more open land on the east side. The region's brutally hot summer days and cool nights yield stellar grapes that make noteworthy wines, particularly robust reds such as cabernet sauvignon, merlot, zinfandel, and Rhône varietals such as Syrah. An abundance of exquisite whites also comes out of Paso, including chardonnay and Rhône varietals such as Viognier. Small-town friendliness prevails at most wineries, especially smaller ones, which tend to treat visitors like neighbors. Pick up a regional wine-touring map at lodgings, wineries, and attractions around town. Most tasting rooms close at 5 PM; many charge a small fee.

LAID-BACK WINE COUNTRY

Hundreds of vineyards and wineries dot the hillsides from Paso Robles to San Luis Obispo, through the scenic Edna Valley and south to northern Santa Barbara County. The wineries offer much of the variety of northern California's Napa and Sonoma valleys—without the glitz and crowds. Since the early 1980s the region has developed an international reputation for high-quality wines, most notably pinot noir, chardonnay, and zinfandel. Wineries here tend to be small, but most have tasting rooms (some have tours), and you'll often meet the winemakers themselves.

Most of the local wineries pour at the **Paso Robles Wine Festival**, held mid-May in City Park. The outdoor tasting—the largest such California event—includes live bands and diverse food vendors. Winery open houses and winemaker dinners round out the weekend. ⊠ *Spring St., between 10th and 12th Sts., City Park* ☎ *805/239–8463* ⊕ *www. pasowine.com* ⊠ *$55, designated driver $15.*

Small but swank **Justin Vineyards & Winery** (⊠ *11680 Chimney Rock Rd.* ☎ *805/238–6932 or 800/726–0049* ⊕ *www.justinwine.com*) makes Bordeaux-style blends at the western end of Paso Robles wine country. This reader favorite offers winery, vineyard, and barrel-tasting tours ($15 to $50). In the tasting room there's a deli bar; a tiny high-end restaurant is also part of the complex.

Tucked in the far-west hills of Paso Robles, **Tablas Creek Vineyard** (⊠ *9339 Adelaida Rd.* ☎ *805/237–1231* ⊕ *www.tablascreek.com*) makes some of the area's finest wine by blending organically grown, hand-harvested Rhône varietals such as Syrah, Grenache, Roussanne, and Viognier. Tours include a chance to graft your own grapevine; call to reserve space.

★ While touring the idyllic west side of Paso Robles, take a break from wine by stopping at **Willow Creek Olive Ranch** (⊠ *8530 Vineyard Dr.* ☎ *805/227–0186* ⊕ *www.pasolivo.com*). Find out how they make their Tuscan-style Pasolivo olive oils on a high-tech Italian press, and taste the widely acclaimed results.

In southeastern Paso Robles wine country, **Wild Horse Winery & Vineyards** (⊠ *1137 Wild Horse Winery Ct., Templeton* ☎ *805/434–2541* ⊕ *www. wildhorsewinery.com*) was a pioneer Central Coast producer. You can try delicious, well-priced pinot noir, chardonnay, and merlot in their simple tasting room.

As they say around Paso Robles, it takes a lot of beer to make good wine, and to meet that need the locals turn to **Firestone Walker Fine Ales** (✉ *1400 Ramada Dr.* ☎ *805/238–2556* ⊕ *www.firestonewalker.com*). In the brewery's taproom, sample medal-winning craft beers such as Double Barrel Ale. They close at 7 PM.

Even if you don't drink wine, stop at **Eberle Winery** (✉ *Hwy. 46E, 3½ mi east of U.S. 101* ☎ *805/238–9607* ⊕ *www.eberlewinery.com*) for a fascinating tour of the huge wine caves beneath the east-side Paso Robles vineyard. Gary Eberle, one of Paso wine's founding fathers, is obsessed with cabernet sauvignon.

WHERE TO EAT

$$$
AMERICAN

✗ **Artisan.** Innovative renditions of traditional American comfort foods, a well-chosen list of regional wines, a stylish full bar, and a sophisticated urban vibe lure winemakers, locals, and tourists to this small, family-run American bistro in an art-deco building near the town square. Chris Kobayashi (Chef Koby) uses local, organic, wild-caught ingredients to whip up regional favorites, which might include red abalone with fried green tomatoes and pancetta, scallops with laughing bird prawns, mussels, clams, Spanish chorizo, and saffron, or hanger steak with broccoli, carrots, and potatoes in a Bordelaise sauce. Try to nab a booth facing the open kitchen, and save room for the restaurant's famed homestyle desserts: brownies, peach crumbles, crème brûlée, and the like. ✉ *1401 Park St.* ☎ *805/237–8084* ⊕ *www.artisanpasorobles. com* ▤ *AE, D, MC, V.*

$$$
FRENCH
★

✗ **Bistro Laurent.** Owner-chef Laurent Grangien has created a handsome, welcoming French bistro in an 1890s brick building across from City Park. He focuses on traditional dishes such as osso buco, cassoulet, rack of lamb, goat-cheese tart, and onion soup, but always offers a few updated dishes as daily specials. Wines, sourced from the adjacent wine shop, come from around the world. ✉ *1202 Pine St.* ☎ *805/226–8191* ⊕ *www.bistrolaurent.com* ▤ *MC, V* ⊙ *Closed Sun. and Mon.*

$$$
AMERICAN

✗ **McPhee's Grill.** The grain silos across the street and the floral oilcloths on the tables belie the sophisticated cuisine at this casual chophouse. In an 1860s building in the tiny cow town of Templeton (just south of Paso Robles), the restaurant serves creative, contemporary versions of traditional Western fare—such as oak-grilled filet mignon and cedar-planked salmon. House-label wines, made especially for McPhee's, are quite good. ✉ *416 S. Main St., Templeton* ☎ *805/434–3204* ⊕ *www. mcphees.com* ▤ *AE, D, MC, V.*

$
FRENCH

✗ **Panolivo.** Scrumptious French bistro fare draws a loyal crowd of locals to this cheery downtown café, just a block north of the town square. For breakfast, try a fresh pastry or quiche, or build your own omelet. Lunch choices include traditional French dishes like snails baked in garlic-butter sauce or cassoulet as well as sandwiches, salads, and fresh pastas—including the house-made beef cannelloni. ✉ *1344 Park St.* ☎ *805/239–3366* ▤ *AE, D, MC, V* ⊙ *No dinner Sun.–Thurs.*

$$$
SOUTHWESTERN

✗ **Villa Creek.** With a firm nod to the Southwest, chef Tom Fundero conjures distinctly modern magic with local and sustainable ingredients.

The seasonal menu has included butternut-squash enchiladas and braised rabbit with mole negro, but you might also find duck breast with sweet-potato latkes. Central Coast wines dominate the list, with a smattering of Spanish and French selections. All brick and bare wood, the dining room can get loud when winemakers start passing their bottles from table to table, but it's always festive. For lighter appetites or wallets, the bar serves smaller plates—not to mention a killer margarita. ☒ *1144 Pine St.* ☎ *805/238–3000* ⊕ *www.villacreek.com* ☰ *AE, D, MC, V* ☻ *No lunch.*

WHERE TO STAY

¢–$

Fodor's Choice
★

☷ **Adelaide Inn.** Family-owned and -managed, this clean, friendly oasis with meticulous landscaping offers spacious rooms and everything you need: coffeemaker, iron, hair dryer, and peace and quiet. In the lobby, complimentary muffins and newspapers are set out in the morning; cookies come out in the afternoon. The motel has been around for decades, but nearly half the rooms were built in 2005. It's a tremendous value, so it books out weeks or even months in advance. A short walk from the fairgrounds, the Adelaide is tucked behind a conglomeration of gas stations and fast-food outlets just west of the U.S. 101 and Highway 46E interchange. **Pros:** great bargain; attractive pool area; ideal for families. **Cons:** not a romantic retreat; near a busy intersection and freeway. ☒ *1215 Ysabel Ave.* ☎ *805/238–2770 or 800/549–7276* ⊕ *www.adelaideinn.com* ⟿ *109 rooms* ♻ *In-room: a/c, refrigerator, Internet, Wi-Fi. In-hotel: pool, gym, laundry facilities, laundry service* ☰ *AE, D, DC, MC, V* ☷ *CP.*

5

$$$$

☷ **Hotel Cheval.** Equestrian themes surface throughout this intimate, sophisticated, European-style inn just a half-block from the main square and a short walk to some of Paso's best restaurants. Each of the 16 spacious rooms is named after a famous racehorse (its history and picture hang on the wall) and includes custom European contemporary furnishings, king beds with exquisite linens and comforters, and original works of art. Most rooms have fireplaces and window seats; some have vaulted cedar ceilings. At the on-site Pony Club, you can sip local and international wines and champagne at the horseshoe-shape zinc bar. **Pros:** walking distance from downtown restaurants; European-style facilities; personal service. **Cons:** views aren't great; no pool or hot tub. ☒ *1021 Pine St.* ☎ *805/226–9995 or 866/522–6999* ⊕ *www.hotelcheval.com* ⟿ *16 rooms* ♻ *In-room: a/c, DVD (some), Internet, Wi-Fi. In-hotel: bar, Wi-Fi hotspot* ☰ *AE, D, MC, V* ☷ *CP.*

$$$

☷ **La Bellasera Hotel & Suites.** The swankest full-service hotel for miles around, the La Bellasera, completed in 2008, caters to those looking for luxurious high-tech amenities and close proximity to major Central Coast roadways. The four-story Italianate building rises above vineyards and retail businesses near the intersection of highways 101 and 46 West, just a few miles south of the historic town square. Stone water features, Romanesque columns, marble and granite countertops, and wrought-iron fixtures support an image of elegant opulence throughout the lobby and public areas. Choose among various types of oversize (430 square feet and up) rooms and suites, from a deluxe king with a fireplace or whirlpool to a grand three-room suite with kitchen. All rooms include premium linens, baths with walk-in showers, LCD HDTVs, thin client computers, wet bars with refrigerators, and fully stocked minibars. **Pros:** new property; tons of amenities. **Cons:** far from town square; located at major intersection. ⊠ *206 Alexa Court* ☎ *805/238–2834 or 866/782–9669* ⊕ *www.labellasera.com* ⤳ *35 rooms, 25 suites* ⚒ *In-room: a/c, safe, kitchen (some), refrigerator, Internet, Wi-Fi. In-hotel: restaurant, room service, bar, pool, gym, spa, laundry facilities, laundry service, Internet terminal, Wi-Fi hotspot* ⊟ *AE, D, DC, MC, V.*

$$ ⚏ **Paso Robles Inn.** On the site of a luxurious old spa hotel by the same name, the inn is built around a lush, shady garden with a hot mineral pool. The water is still the reason to stay here, and each deluxe room (new and old) has a spring-fed hot tub in its bathroom or on its balcony. Have breakfast in the circular 1940s coffee shop, and on weekends dance with the ranchers in the Cattlemen's Lounge. **Pros:** private spring-fed hot tubs; historic property; across from park and town square. **Cons:** fronts a busy street; rooms vary in size and quality. ⊠ *1103 Spring St.* ☎ *805/238–2660 or 800/676–1713* ⊕ *www.pasoroblesinn.com* ⤳ *92 rooms, 6 suites* ⚒ *In-room: a/c, refrigerator, Internet. In-hotel: restaurant, bar, pool, Wi-Fi hotspot* ⊟ *AE, D, DC, MC, V.*

CAMBRIA

28 mi west of Paso Robles on Hwy. 46; 20 mi north of Morro Bay on Hwy. 1.

Cambria, set on piney hills above the sea, was settled by Welsh miners in the 1890s. In the 1970s, the gorgeous, isolated setting attracted artists and other independent types; the town now caters to tourists, but it still bears the unmistakable imprint of its bohemian past. Both of Cambria's downtowns, the original East Village and the newer West Village, are packed with art and crafts galleries, antiques shops, cafés, restaurants, and B&Bs. Late-Victorian homes stand along side streets, and the hills are filled with redwood-and-glass residences.

ESSENTIALS

Visitor Information Cambria Chamber of Commerce (☎ *805/927–3624* ⊕ *www.cambriachamber.org*).

EXPLORING

Lined with low-key motels, **Moonstone Beach Drive** runs along a bluff above the ocean. The boardwalk that winds along the beach side of the drive makes a great walk.

Leffingwell's Landing (⊠ *North end of Moonstone Beach Dr.* ☎ *805/927–2070*), a state picnic ground, is a good place for examining tidal pools and watching otters as they frolic in the surf.

Arthur Beal (aka Captain Nit Wit, Der Tinkerpaw) spent 51 years building **Nit Wit Ridge**, a home with terraced rock gardens. For building materials, he used all kinds of collected junk: beer cans, rocks, abalone shells, car parts, TV antennas—you name it. The site, above Cambria's West Village, is a State Historic Landmark. You can drive by and peek in; better yet, call ahead for a guided tour of the house and grounds. ⊠ *881 Hillcrest Dr.* ☎ *805/927–2690* ⚏ *$10* ☉ *Daily by appointment.*

WHERE TO EAT

$$$
AMERICAN ✕ **Black Cat Bistro.** Jazz wafts through the several small rooms of this intimate East Village bistro where leopard-print and other stylish cushions line the banquettes. Start with an order of the fried olives stuffed with Gorgonzola, accompanied by a glass from the eclectic list of local and imported wines. The daily-changing menu is centered on sustainable ingredients and might include roasted rack of elk rubbed in cocoa or breast of pheasant stuffed with caramelized apples. ✉ *1602 Main St.* ☎ *805/927–1600* ⊕ *www.blackcatbistro.com* ⌂ *Reservations essential* ▬ *AE, D, DC, MC, V* ⊘ *Closed Tues. and Wed. No lunch.*

¢
CAFÉ ✕ **French Corner Bakery.** Place your order at the counter and then sit outside to watch the passing East Village scene (if the fog has rolled in, take a seat in the tiny deli). The rich aroma of coffee and fresh breakfast pastries makes mouths water in the morning; for lunch, try a quiche with flaky crust or a sandwich on house-baked bread. ✉ *2214 Main St.* ☎ *805/927–8227* ⌂ *Reservations not accepted* ⊘ *No dinner.*

$$
ECLECTIC ✕ **Robin's.** A truly multiethnic and vegetarian-friendly dining experience awaits you at this East Village cottage filled with country antiques. At dinner, choose from lobster enchiladas, pork osso buco, Thai green chicken curry, and more. Lunchtime's extensive salad and sandwich menu embraces burgers and tempeh alike. Unless it's raining, ask for a table on the secluded (and heated) garden patio. ✉ *4095 Burton Dr.* ☎ *805/927–5007* ▬ *MC, V.*

$$$
SEAFOOD ✕ **The Sea Chest.** By far the best seafood place in town—readers give it a big thumbs-up—this Moonstone Beach restaurant fills soon after it opens at 5:30. Those in the know grab seats at the oyster bar, where they can take in spectacular sunsets while watching the chefs broil fresh halibut and steam garlicky clams. If you can't get there early, play some cribbage or checkers while you wait for a table. ✉ *6216 Moonstone Beach Dr.* ☎ *805/927–4514* ⌂ *Reservations not accepted* ▬ *No credit cards* ⊘ *Closed Tues. mid-Sept.–May. No lunch.*

WHERE TO STAY

¢–$
🛏 **Bluebird Inn.** This sweet motel in Cambria's East Village sits amid beautiful gardens along Santa Rosa Creek. Rooms include simply furnished doubles and nicer creek-side suites with patios, fireplaces, and refrigerators. The Bluebird isn't the fanciest place, but if you don't require beachside accommodations, it's a bargain. **Pros:** excellent value; well-kept gardens; friendly staff. **Cons:** few frills; basic rooms; on Cambria's main drag. ✉ *1880 Main St.* ☎ *805/927–4634 or 800/552–5434* ⊕ *www.bluebirdmotel.com* ⊅ *37 rooms* ⌂ *In-room: a/c, refrigerator (some), Wi-Fi. In-hotel: Wi-Fi hotspot* ▬ *D, MC, V.*

$$–$$$
🛏 **Cambria Pines Lodge.** With lots of recreational facilities and a range of accommodations—from basic state park–style cabins to motel-style standard rooms to large fireplace suites—this 25-acre retreat up the hill from the East Village is a good choice for families. Walls can be thin in buildings dating as far back as the 1940s; a separate cluster of luxury suites and rooms opened in 2006. The lodge is always busy: its extensive gardens are popular with wedding parties; groups and conferences are big business; and bands play light rock, folk, and jazz in the lounge. **Pros:** short walk from downtown; verdant gardens; spacious grounds.

5

Cons: front desk service and housekeeping not always top-quality; some units could use an update. ⊠ *2905 Burton Dr.* ☎ *805/927–4200 or 800/445–6868* ⊕ *www.cambriapineslodge.com* ⤳ *72 rooms, 19 cabins, 62 suites* ⚅ *In-room: a/c, refrigerator (some), Internet. In-hotel: restaurant, room service, bar, pool, spa, Internet terminal, Wi-Fi hotspot, some pets allowed* ▭ *AE, D, DC, MC, V.*

$$–$$$ ⊡ **Moonstone Landing.** Friendly staff, lots of amenities, and reasonable
★   rates make this up-to-date motel a top pick with readers who like to stay right on Moonstone Beach. All rooms have Mission-style furnishings, DVD players, fireplaces, and Internet access. From their balconies or patios, a few of the deluxe rooms, which have marble whirlpool tubs and showers, offer some of the best views in Cambria. **Pros:** sleek furnishings; across from the beach; cheery lounge. **Cons:** narrow property; some rooms overlook a parking lot. ⊠ *6240 Moonstone Beach Dr.* ☎ *805/927–0012 or 800/830–4540* ⊕ *www.moonstonelanding.com* ⤳ *29 rooms* ⚅ *In-room: no a/c, refrigerator, DVD, Wi-Fi. In-hotel: Internet terminal, Wi-Fi hotspot* ▭ *AE, D, MC, V* ⦿ *CP.*

SAN SIMEON

Hwy. 1, 9 mi north of Cambria and 65 mi south of Big Sur.

Whalers founded San Simeon in the 1850s but had virtually abandoned the town by the time Senator George Hearst reestablished it 20 years later. Hearst bought up most of the surrounding ranch land, built a 1,000-foot wharf, and turned San Simeon into a bustling port. His son, William Randolph Hearst, further developed the area during the construction of Hearst Castle. Today the town, 4 mi south of the entrance to Hearst San Simeon State Historical Monument, is basically a strip of gift shops and mediocre motels along Highway 1.

EXPLORING

★   **Hearst Castle,** officially known as "Hearst San Simeon State Historical Monument," sits in solitary splendor atop La Cuesta Encantada (the Enchanted Hill). Its buildings and gardens spread over 127 acres that were the heart of newspaper magnate William Randolph Hearst's 250,000-acre ranch. Hearst devoted nearly 30 years and about $10 million to building this elaborate estate. He commissioned renowned architect Julia Morgan—who also designed buildings at the University of California at Berkeley—but he was very much involved with the final product, a hodgepodge of Italian, Spanish, Moorish, and French styles. The 115-room main building and three huge "cottages" are connected by terraces and staircases and surrounded by pools, gardens, and statuary. In its heyday the castle was a playground for Hearst and his guests, many of them Hollywood celebrities. Construction began in 1919 and was never officially completed. Work was halted in 1947 when Hearst had to leave San Simeon because of failing health. The Hearst family presented the property to the State of California in 1958.

Access to the castle is through the large visitor center at the foot of the hill, which contains a collection of Hearst memorabilia and a giant-screen theater that shows a 40-minute film giving a sanitized version of Hearst's life and of the castle's construction. Buses from the visitor center zigzag up the hillside to the neoclassical extravaganza, where guides conduct four different daytime tours of various parts of the main house and grounds. Tour No. 1 (which includes the movie) provides a good overview of the highlights; the others focus on particular parts of the estate. Daytime tours take about two hours. In spring and fall, docents in period costume portray Hearst's guests and staff for the slightly longer evening tour, which begins at sunset. All tours include a ½-mi walk and between 150 and 400 stairs. Reservations for the tours, which can be made up to eight weeks in advance, are necessary. ⊠ *San Simeon State Park, 750 Hearst Castle Rd.* ☎ *805/927–2020 or 800/444–4445* ⊕ *www.hearstcastle.com* ✉ *Daytime tours $24, evening tours $30* ☉ *Tours daily 8:20–3:20, later in summer; additional tours take place most Fri. and Sat. evenings Mar.–May and Sept.–Dec.* ☐ *AE, D, MC, V.*

☾ A large and growing colony (at last count 15,000 members) of elephant seals gathers every year at **Piedras Blancas Elephant Seal Rookery,** on the beaches near Piedras Blancas Lighthouse. The huge males with their pendulous, trunklike noses typically start appearing on shore in late November, and the females begin to arrive in December to give birth—most babies are born in the last two weeks of January. The newborn pups spend about four weeks nursing before their mothers head out to sea, leaving them on their own; the "weaners" leave the rookery when they are about 3½ months old. The seals return in the spring and summer months to molt or rest, but not en masse as in winter. You can watch them from a boardwalk along the bluffs just a few feet above the beach; do not attempt to approach them, as they are wild animals. Docents are often on hand to give background information and statistics. The rookery is just south of Piedras Blancas Lighthouse (4½ mi north of Hearst San Simeon State Historical Monument); the nonprofit Friends of the Elephant Seal runs a small visitor center and gift shop at their San Simeon office. ⊠ *Friends of the Elephant Seal, 250 San Simeon Ave., Suite 3* ☎ *805/924–1628* ⊕ *www.elephantseal.org.*

WHERE TO STAY

$$ ⌗ **Best Western Cavalier Oceanfront Resort**. Reasonable rates, an ocean-front location, evening bonfires, and well-equipped rooms—some with wood-burning fireplaces and private patios—make this motel one of the best choices in San Simeon. **Pros:** on the bluffs; fantastic views; close to Hearst Castle; bluff bonfires. **Cons:** room amenities and sizes vary; pools are small and sometimes crowded. ⊠ *9415 Hearst Dr.* ☎ *805/927–4688 or 800/826–8168* ⊕ *www.cavalierresort.com* ⌂ *90 rooms* ⌂ *In-room: a/c, refrigerator, DVD, Internet, Wi-Fi (some). In-hotel: 2 restaurants, pools, gym, laundry facilities, Internet terminal, Wi-Fi hotspot, some pets allowed* ☐ *AE, D, DC, MC, V.*

$$–$$$ ⌗ **The Morgan San Simeon**. On the ocean side of Highway 1, near San Simeon restaurants and shops, the Morgan offers a range of motel-style rooming options while paying tribute to famed Hearst Castle architect Julia Morgan. A 2008 head-to-toe remodel transformed the former Orchid Inn into a stylish Asia-inspired complex in two buildings, encompassing six types of guest rooms, some with fireplaces, soaking tubs, and wet bars. Authentic prints of Julia Morgan's design sketches,

juxtaposed with real-life photos, appear in the rooms and throughout the property. **Pros:** fascinating artwork; easy access to Hearst Castle and Highway 1; some ocean views. **Cons:** not right on beach; no fitness room or laundry facilities. ⊠ *9135 Hearst Dr.* ☎ *805/927–3878 or 800/451–9900* ⊕ *www.hotel-morgan.com* ➷ *54 rooms, 1 suite* ⚭ *In-room: a/c, refrigerator (some), DVD (some), Internet (some), Wi-Fi. In-hotel: bar, pool, spa, Wi-Fi hotspot* ⊟ *AE, D, DC, MC, V* ¶⊙¶ *CP.*

BIG SUR COASTLINE

Long a retreat of artists and writers, Big Sur is a place of ancient forests and rugged shoreline, stretching 90 mi from San Simeon to Carmel. Residents have protected it from overdevelopment, and much of the region lies within several state parks and the more than 165,000-acre Ventana Wilderness, itself part of the Los Padres National Forest.

ESSENTIALS

Visitor Information Big Sur Chamber of Commerce (☎ *831/667–2100* ⊕ *www.bigsurcalifornia.org).*

SOUTHERN BIG SUR

Hwy. 1 from San Simeon to Julia Pfeiffer Burns State Park.

This especially rugged stretch of oceanfront is a rocky world of mountains, cliffs, and beaches.

EXPLORING

Fodor's Choice One of California's most spectacular drives, **Highway 1** snakes up the ★ coast north of San Simeon. Numerous pullouts along the way offer tremendous views and photo ops. On some of the beaches, huge elephant seals lounge nonchalantly, seemingly oblivious to the attention of rubberneckers—but keep your distance. In rainy seasons, the southern Big Sur portion of Highway 1 is regularly shut down by mudslides. Contact **CalTrans** (☎ *800/427–7623* ⊕ *www.dot.ca.gov*) for road conditions.

In Los Padres National Forest just north of the town of Gorda is **Jade Cove** (⊠ *Hwy. 1, 34 mi north of San Simeon*), a well-known jade-hunting spot. Rock hunting is allowed on the beach, but you may not remove anything from the walls of the cliffs.

Julia Pfeiffer Burns State Park provides some fine hiking, from an easy ½-mi stroll with marvelous coastal views to a strenuous 6-mi trek through the redwoods. The big attraction here, an 80-foot waterfall that drops into the ocean, gets crowded in summer; still, it's an astounding place to sit and contemplate nature. Migrating whales, as well as harbor seals and sea lions, can sometimes be spotted not far from shore. ⊠ *Hwy. 1, 53 mi north of San Simeon, 15 mi north of Lucia* ☎ *831/667–2315* ⊕ *www.parks.ca.gov* ⊠ *$10* ⊙ *Daily sunrise–sunset.*

WHERE TO STAY

$$–$$$ 🔳 **Ragged Point Inn.** At this cliff-top resort—the only inn and restaurant for miles around—glass walls in most rooms open to awesome, unobstructed ocean views. Though not especially luxurious, some rooms have spa tubs, kitchenettes, and fireplaces. The restaurant ($$–$$$) is a good place for well-made American fare—sandwiches, salads, pastas, and main courses—before or after the winding Highway 1 drive. Even if you're just passing by, stop to stretch your legs on the 14 acres of lush gardens above the sea; you can pick up souvenirs, a burger, or an espresso to go. **Pros:** on the cliffs; great food; idyllic views. **Cons:** busy road stop during the day; often booked for weekend weddings. ✉ *19019 Hwy. 1, 20 mi north of San Simeon, Ragged Point* ☎ *805/927–4502, 805/927–5708 restaurant* ⊕ *www.raggedpointinn.com* ⏎ *30 rooms* ⚒ *In-room: no a/c, no phone, kitchen (some). In-hotel: restaurant, laundry facilities, Wi-Fi hotspot* ☰ *AE, D, DC, MC, V.*

$$–$$$ ⛺ **Treebones Resort.** Perched on a hilltop, surrounded by national forest and stunning, unobstructed ocean views, this yurt resort opened in 2004. The yurts here—circular structures of heavy-duty fabric, on individual platforms with decks—are designed for upscale camping. Each has one or two queen beds with patchwork quilts, wicker furniture, and pine floors. Electricity and hot and cold running water come to you, but you have to walk to squeaky-clean bathhouse and restroom facilities. The sunny main lodge, where breakfast and dinner (not included) are served, has a big fireplace, games, and a well-stocked sundries and gift shop. Younger children have difficulty on the steep paths between buildings. There is a two-night minimum for stays on weekends and between April and October. **Pros:** 360-degree views; spacious pool area; comfortable beds. **Cons:** steep paths; no private bathrooms; more than a mile from the nearest store; not a good place for families with children under six. ✉ *71895 Hwy. 1, Willow Creek Rd., 32 mi north of San Simeon, 1 mi north of Gorda* ☎ *805/927–2390 or 877/424–4787* ⊕ *www.treebonesresort.com* ⏎ *16 yurts, 5 campsites* ⚒ *In-room: no a/c. In-hotel: restaurant, pool, spa, laundry facilities, Internet terminal, some pets allowed* ☰ *AE, MC, V* ⍾ *CP.*

CENTRAL BIG SUR

Hwy. 1, from Partington Cove to Bixby Bridge.

The countercultural spirit of Big Sur—which instead of a conventional town is a loose string of coast-hugging properties along Highway 1—is alive and well today. Its few residents include the very wealthy, the enthusiastically outdoorsy, and the thoroughly evolved: since the 1960s the Esalen Institute, a center for alternative education and East–West philosophical study, has attracted seekers of higher consciousness and devotees of the property's hot springs. Today, posh and rustic resorts hidden among the redwoods cater to visitors drawn from near and far by the extraordinary scenery and serene isolation.

EXPLORING

Through a hole in one of the gigantic boulders at secluded **Pfeiffer Beach**, you can watch the waves break first on the sea side and then on the beach side. Keep a sharp eye out for the unsigned road to the beach: it is the only ungated paved road branching west of Highway 1 between the post office and Pfeiffer Big Sur State Park. The 2-mi, one-lane road

descends sharply. ⊠ *Off Hwy. 1, 1 mi south of Pfeiffer Big Sur State Park* 🍴 *$10 per vehicle per day.*

Among the many hiking trails at **Pfeiffer Big Sur State Park** ($10 per vehicle for day use) a short route through a redwood-filled valley leads to a waterfall. You can double back or continue on the more difficult trail along the valley wall for views over miles of treetops to the sea. Stop in at the Big Sur Station visitor center, off Highway 1, less than ½ mi south of the park entrance, for information about the entire area; it's open 8–4:30. ⊠ *47225 Hwy. 1* 🕿 *831/667–2315* ⊕ *www.parks.ca.gov* 🍴 *$10 per vehicle* ☉ *Daily dawn–dusk.*

★   **Point Sur State Historic Park** is the site of an 1889 lighthouse that still stands watch from atop a large volcanic rock. Four lighthouse keepers lived here with their families until 1974, when the light station became automated. Their homes and working spaces are open to the public only on 2½- to 3-hour ranger-led tours. Considerable walking, including up two stairways, is involved. Strollers are not allowed. ⊠ *Hwy. 1, 7 mi north of Pfeiffer Big Sur State Park* 🕿 *831/625–4419* ⊕ *www.pointsur. org* 🍴 *$10* ☉ *Tours generally Nov.–Mar., weekends at 10; Apr.–Oct., Wed. at 1, Sat. at 10 and 2, Sun. at 10; call to confirm.*

The graceful arc of **Bixby Creek Bridge** (⊠ *Hwy. 1, 6 mi north of Point Sur State Historic Park, 13 mi south of Carmel*) is a photographer's dream. Built in 1932, it spans a deep canyon, more than 100 feet wide at the bottom. From the parking area on the north side you can admire the view or walk across the 550-foot span.

WHERE TO EAT

$$ ✕ **Big Sur Roadhouse**. At this colorful, casual bistro, feast on innovative,
ECLECTIC   well-executed California Latin–fusion fare. Crispy striped bass atop a pillow of carrot-coconut puree, tangy-smoky barbecue chicken breast beneath a julienne of jicama and cilantro: the zesty, balanced flavors wake up your mouth. Emphasizing new-world vintages, the wine list is gently priced. The chocolate-caramel layer cake may bring tears to your eyes. ⊠ *Hwy. 1, 1 mi north of Pfeiffer Big Sur State Park* 🕿 *831/667–2264* ⊕ *www.bigsurroadhouse.com* ☉ *Closed Tues. No lunch.*

$$$ ✕ **Deetjen's Big Sur Inn**. The candlelighted, creaky-floor restaurant in the
AMERICAN   main house at the historic inn of the same name is a Big Sur institution. It serves spicy seafood paella, steak, and rack of lamb for dinner and wonderfully flavorful eggs Benedict for breakfast. The chef procures much of the fish, meats, and produce from purveyors who practice sustainable farming and fishing practices. ⊠ *Hwy. 1, 3½ mi south of Pfeiffer Big Sur State Park* 🕿 *831/667–2377* ⊕ *www.deetjens.com* 🍴 *MC, V* ☉ *No lunch.*

$$$ ✕ **Nepenthe**. It may be that no other restaurant between San Francisco
AMERICAN   and Los Angeles has a better coastal view; no wonder Orson Welles and Rita Hayworth once owned the place. The food and drink are overpriced but good; there are burgers, sandwiches, and salads for lunch, and fresh fish and hormone-free steaks for dinner. For the real show, settle on the terraced deck in the late afternoon, order a glass from the extensive wine list, and watch the sun slip into the Pacific Ocean. The less expensive, outdoor Café Kevah serves brunch and lunch.

✉ *Hwy. 1, 2½ mi south of Big Sur Station* ☎ *831/667–2345* ⊕ *www.
nepenthebigsur.com* ▭ *AE, MC, V.*

$$$$ ✗ **The Restaurant at Ventana.** Closed for remodeling for more than a year
AMERICAN   after a kitchen fire, the Restaurant at Ventana (formerly Cielo) rose
from the ashes in stunning fashion in fall 2009. Redwood, copper, and
cedar elements pay tribute to the historic natural setting, while gleaming
new fixtures and dining accoutrements place the restaurant firmly in the
21st century. Chef Dory Ford's seasonal menu showcases fine California
cuisine, from rabbit loin and California white sea bass to artichokes and
abalone, and a full slate of regional and international wines. Much of
the produce comes from the restaurant's organic vegetable garden. The
restaurant is also open for breakfast and lunch—ask for a table on the
outdoor terrace, where ocean views unfold on clear, sunny days. ✉ *Hwy.
1, 1½ mi south of Pfeiffer Big Sur State Park* ☎ *831/667–2331* ⊕ *www.
ventanainn.com* ⌕ *Reservations essential* ▭ *AE, MC, V.*

$$$$ ✗ **Sierra Mar.** Ocean-view dining doesn't get much better than this.
AMERICAN   Perched at cliff's edge 1,200 feet above the Pacific at the ultra-chic Post
Ranch Inn, Sierra Mar serves cutting-edge American food made from
mostly organic, seasonal ingredients, including a stellar four-course
prix-fixe menu. The restaurant's wine list is one of the most extensive
in the nation. ✉ *Hwy. 1, 1½ mi south of Pfeiffer Big Sur State Park*
☎ *831/667–2800* ⌕ *Reservations essential* ▭ *AE, MC, V.*

WHERE TO STAY

$–$$$ 🛏 **Deetjen's Big Sur Inn.** This historic 1930s Norwegian-style property is
endearingly rustic and charming, especially if you're willing to go with
a camplike flow. The room doors lock only from the inside, and your
neighbors can often be heard through the walls—if you plan to bring
children, you must reserve an entire building. Still, Deetjen's is a special
place. Its village of cabins is nestled in the redwoods, and many of the
very individual rooms have their own fireplaces. **Pros:** surrounded by
Big Sur history; tons of character; wooded grounds. **Cons:** rustic; thin
walls; some rooms don't have private baths. ✉ *Hwy. 1, 3½ mi south
of Pfeiffer Big Sur State Park* ☎ *831/667–2377* ⊕ *www.deetjens.com*
🛏 *20 rooms, 15 with bath* ⌕ *In-room: no phone, no a/c, no TV. In-
hotel: restaurant* ▭ *MC, V.*

$$$$ 🛏 **Post Ranch Inn.** This luxurious retreat, designed exclusively for adult
Fodor's Choice   getaways, has remarkably environmentally conscious architecture. The
★   redwood guesthouses, all of which have views of the sea or the moun-
tains, blend almost invisibly into a wooded cliff 1,200 feet above the
ocean. Each unit has its own fireplace, stereo, private deck, and mas-
sage table. On-site activities include everything from yoga to stargazing.
Pros: world-class resort; spectacular views; gorgeous property with hik-
ing trails. **Cons:** expensive; austere design; not a good choice if you're
scared of heights. ✉ *Hwy. 1, 1½ mi south of Pfeiffer Big Sur State
Park* 🏠 *Hwy. 1, Box 219, 93920* ☎ *831/667–2200 or 800/527–2200*
⊕ *www.postranchinn.com* 🛏 *39 units* ⌕ *In-room: a/c, refrigerator, no
TV (some), Internet (some), Wi-Fi (some). In-hotel: restaurant, bar,
pools, gym, spa, Internet terminal* ▭ *AE, MC, V* ⏀ *BP.*

5

$$$$
Fodor's Choice
★
⊞ **Ventana Inn & Spa.** Hundreds of celebrities, from Oprah Winfrey to Sir Anthony Hopkins, have escaped to Ventana, a romantic resort on 243 tranquil acres 1,200 feet above the Pacific. The activities here are purposely limited. You can sunbathe (one of the pools is clothing-optional), walk or ride horses in the nearby hills, or pamper yourself with mind-and-body treatments at the Spa at Ventana or in your own private quarters. All rooms have walls of natural wood and cool tile floors; some have private hot tubs on their patios. **Pros:** nature trails everywhere; great food; secluded. **Cons:** simple breakfast; some rooms need updating. ⊠ *Hwy. 1, almost 1 mi south of Pfeiffer Big Sur State Park* ☎ *831/667–2331 or 800/628–6500* ⊕ *www.ventanainn.com* ⤳ *25 rooms, 31 suites, 3 houses* ⟑ *In-room: a/c, DVD, Internet, Wi-Fi (some). In-hotel: restaurant, bar, pools, gym, spa* ⊟ *AE, D, DC, MC, V* ⓔ *BP.*

⚠ **Pfeiffer Big Sur State Park.** Redwood trees tower over this large campground. It's often crowded in summer, so reserve a site or a tent cabin as far ahead as possible. There are no hookups, but the park has Wi-Fi. ⟑ *Wi-Fi, flush toilets, dump station, drinking water, guest laundry, showers, fire grates, fire pits, picnic tables, food service, public telephone, general store, ranger station* ⤳ *218 sites* ⊠ *47225 Hwy. 1* ☎ *800/444–7275 reservations* ⊕ *www.parks.ca.gov.*

Channel Islands National Park

WORD OF MOUTH

"Anacapa Island is so small that you could take the boat from Oxnard, hike the entire island on your own, and be back in plenty of time for the return trip. As the boat MIGHT sell out, it's best to reserve in advance. Be aware that you must take EVERYTHING you'll need for the day—including water."

—PaulRabe

WELCOME TO CHANNEL ISLANDS NATIONAL PARK

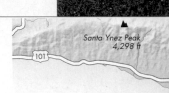

TOP REASONS TO GO

★ **Rare flora and fauna:** The Channel Islands are home to 145 species of terrestrial plants and animals found nowhere else on Earth.

★ **Time travel:** With no cars, phones, or services, these undeveloped islands provide a glimpse of what California was like hundreds of years ago, away from hectic modern life.

★ **Underwater adventures:** The incredibly healthy channel waters rank among the top 10 diving destinations on the planet— but you can also visit the kelp forest virtually via an underwater video program.

★ **Marvelous marine mammals:** More than 30 species of seals, sea lions, whales, and other marine mammals ply the park's waters at various times of year.

★ **Sea-cave kayaking:** Paddle around otherwise inaccessible portions of the park's 175 mi of gorgeous coastline— including one of the world's largest sea caves.

1 Anacapa. Tiny Anacapa is a 5-mi stretch of three islets, with towering cliffs, caves, natural bridges, and rich kelp forests.

2 San Miguel. Isolated, windswept San Miguel, the park's westernmost island, has an ancient caliche forest and hundreds of archaeological sites chronicling the Chumash Indian's 11,000-year history on the island. More than 30,000 pinnipeds (seals and sea lions) hang out on the island's beaches during certain times of year.

3 Santa Barbara. Nearly 6 mi of scenic trails crisscross this tiny island, known for its excellent wildlife viewing and native plants. It's a favorite destination for diving, snorkeling, and kayaking.

Painted Cave

SANTA YNEZ MOUNTAINS

154

Goleta
Point

Goleta

Montecito

Santa
Barbara

Carpinteria

150

33

101

Ventura

Visitor Center

El Rio

126

101

6

Oxnard

Channel

Point
Mugu

Painted Cave

Scorpion
Ranch

San Pedro Point

Summit Peak
936 ft

Prisoners
Harbor

Mount Diablo
2,450 ft

Main Ranch

Central Valley

4

Anacapa Passage

Light Station
& Museum

Santa Cruz
Island

Smugglers
Cove

Anacapa
Island

1

Morse Point

0   10 mi

0   10 km

Santa Barbara Island is
approximately 52 miles southeast
of Santa Cruz Island

**Santa Barbara
Island Light**

3

Santa Barbara
Island

GETTING
ORIENTED

Channel Islands National
Park includes five of the
eight Channel Islands
and the nautical mile of
ocean that surrounds them.
The islands range in size
from 1-square-mi Santa
Barbara to 96-square-mi
Santa Cruz. Together
they form a magnificent
nature preserve with 145
endemic or unique species
of plants and animals. Half
the park lies underwater,
and the 5 mi of surround-
ing channel waters are
teeming with life, including
dolphins, whales, seals,
sea lions, and seabirds.

4 Santa Cruz. The park's
largest island offers some of
the best hikes and kayaking
opportunities, one of the
world's largest and deepest
sea caves, and more species
of flora and fauna than any
other park island.

5 Santa Rosa. Camp-
ers love to stay on Santa
Rosa, with its myriad hiking
opportunities, stunning
white-sand beaches, and
rare grove of Torrey pines.
It's also the only island
accessible by plane.

CHANNEL ISLANDS NATIONAL PARK PLANNER

When to Go

Channel Islands National Park records about 620,000 visitors each year, but many never venture beyond the visitor center. The busiest times are holidays and summer weekends. If you're going then, make your transportation and accommodation arrangements far in advance.

The warm, dry summer months are the best time to go camping. Humpback and blue whales arrive to feed from late June through early fall. The rains usually come from December through March—but this is also the best time to spot gray whales and to get discounts at area hotels. In the late spring, thousands of migratory birds descend on the islands to hatch their young, and wildflowers carpet the slopes. The water temperature is nearly always cool, so bring a wet suit if you plan to spend much time in the ocean, even in the summer. Fog, high winds, and rough seas can happen any time of the year.

AVG. HIGH/LOW TEMPS.

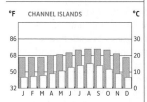

Flora and Fauna

The Channel Islands are home to species found nowhere else on Earth: mammals such as the island fox and the island deer mouse, birds like the island scrub jay, and plants such as the Santa Barbara Island live-forever, on the endangered species list. Thousands of western gulls hatch each summer on Anacapa, then fly off to the mainland where they spend about four years learning all their bad habits. Then they return to the island to roost and have chicks of their own. It all adds up to a living laboratory not unlike the one naturalist Charles Darwin discovered off the coast of South America 200 years ago, which is why the Channel Islands are often called the North American Galapagos.

Getting Here and Around

The visitor center for Channel Islands National Park is on California's mainland, in the town of Ventura, off U.S. 101. From the harbors at Ventura, Santa Barbara, and Oxnard you can board a boat to one of the islands. You also can catch a flight to some of the islands from the Camarillo Airport, near Oxnard, and the Santa Barbara Airport.

If you have your own boat, you can land at any of the islands, but each island has certain closed and restricted areas, so boaters should contact the park ranger on each island for instructions. Private vehicles are not permitted on the islands. Pets are also not allowed in the park.

Several private companies provide transportation by boat or plane to and from the mainland to one of more of the Channel Islands (⇨ *Transportation Options box*).

To reach the Ventura harbor, exit U.S. 101 in Ventura at Seaward Boulevard or Victoria Avenue and follow the signs to Ventura Harbor/Spinnaker Drive. In Santa Barbara, exit U.S. 101 at Castillo Street and head south to Cabrillo Boulevard, then turn right for the harbor entrance. To access Channel Islands Harbor in Oxnard, exit U.S. 101 at Victoria Avenue and head south approximately 7 mi to Channel Islands Boulevard. Amtrak makes stops in Santa Barbara, Ventura, and Oxnard; from the Amtrak station, just take a taxi or waterfront shuttle bus to the harbor.

Updated by Sura Wood and Cheryl Crabtree

On crystal-clear days the craggy peaks of Channel Islands are easy to see from the mainland, jutting from the Pacific in such sharp detail it seems you could reach out and touch them. The islands really aren't that far away—a high-speed boat will whisk you to the closest ones in less than an hour— yet very few people ever visit them. Those fearless, adventurous types who do will experience one of the most splendid land-and-sea wilderness areas on the planet.

6

PARK ESSENTIALS

ADMISSION FEES AND PERMITS
There is no fee to enter Channel Islands National Park, but unless you have your own boat, you will pay $32 or more per person for a ride with a boat operator. The cost of taking a boat to the park varies depending on which operator you choose. Also, there is a $15 per day fee for staying in one of the islands' campgrounds.

ADMISSION HOURS
The islands are open every day of the year. Channel Islands Visitor Center in Ventura is closed on Thanksgiving and Christmas. Channel Islands National Park is located in the Pacific time zone.

EMERGENCIES
In the event of an emergency, contact a park ranger on patrol or call the park dispatch at 805/658–5700 (during business hours) or 911. Boaters can use marine radio channel 16.

PARK CONTACT INFORMATION
Channel Islands Visitor Center ⊠ *1901 Spinnaker Dr., Ventura, CA*
☎ *805/658–5730* ⊕ *www.nps.gov/chis.*

TRANSPORTATION OPTIONS

Channel Islands Aviation (✉ 305 Durley Ave., Camarillo ☎ 805/987–1301 ⊕ www.flycia.com ✈ $160 per person, $300 per person if camping) provides day excursions, surf fishing, and camper transportation year-round, flying from Camarillo Airport, about 10 mi east of Oxnard, to an airstrip on Santa Rosa. The operator will also pick up groups of six or more at Santa Barbara Airport, but no camper transportation is available from Santa Barbara.

Sailing on two high-speed catamarans from Ventura or Oxnard, **Island Packers** (✉ 3600 S. Harbor Blvd., Oxnard ☎ 805/642–1393 ✉ 1691

Spinnaker Dr., Ventura ☎ 805/642–1393 ⊕ www.islandpackers.com ✈ $32–$65) goes to Santa Cruz Island daily most of the year, weather permitting. The boats also go to Anacapa several days a week, and to the other islands three or four times a month, most frequently May through October. **Truth Aquatics** (✉ 301 W. Cabrillo Blvd., Santa Barbara ☎ 805/962–1127 ⊕ www.truthaquatics.com ✈ $120 for scuba day trips, average of $170 per day for all-inclusive trips) departs from Santa Barbara for scuba trips and multiday excursions (where travelers sleep aboard ship) to the islands.

EXPLORING

THE ISLANDS

★ **ANACAPA ISLAND**

Although most people think of it as an island, **Anacapa Island** is actually comprised of three narrow islets. The tips of these volcanic formations nearly touch but are inaccessible from one another except by boat. All three islets have towering cliffs, isolated sea caves, and natural bridges; Arch Rock, on East Anacapa, is one of the best-known symbols of Channel Islands National Park. Wildlife viewing is the reason most people come to East Anacapa—particularly in summer when seagull chicks are newly hatched and sea lions and seals lounge on the beaches. Trips to Middle Anacapa Island require a ranger escort.

SAN MIGUEL ISLAND

The westernmost of the Channel Islands, **San Miguel Island** is frequently battered by storms sweeping across the North Pacific. The 15-square-mi island's wild, windswept landscape is lush with vegetation. Point Bennett, at the western tip, offers one of the world's most spectacular wildlife displays when more than 30,000 pinnipeds hit its beach. Explorer Juan Rodríguez Cabrillo was the first European to visit this island; he claimed it for Spain in 1542. Legend holds that Cabrillo died on one of the Channel Islands—no one knows where he's buried, but there's a memorial to him on a bluff above Cuyler Harbor.

SANTA BARBARA ISLAND

At about 1 square mi, **Santa Barbara Island** is the smallest of the Channel Islands and nearly 35 mi south of the others. Triangular in shape, Santa Barbara's steep cliffs—which offer a perfect nesting spot for the Xantus's murrelet, a rare seabird—are topped by twin peaks. In spring, you can enjoy a brilliant display of yellow coreopsis. Learn about the wildlife on and around the islands at the island's small **museum.** ⊠ *Santa Barbara Island* ☎ *No phone* ☉ *Daily 10–5.*

SANTA CRUZ ISLAND

Five miles west of Anacapa, 96-square-mi **Santa Cruz Island** is the largest of the Channel Islands. The National Park Service manages the easternmost 24% of the island; the rest is owned by the Nature Conservancy, which requires a permit to land. When your boat drops you off on the 70 mi of craggy coastline, you see two rugged mountain ranges with peaks soaring to 2,500 feet and deep canyons traversed by streams. This landscape is the habitat of a remarkable variety of flora and fauna— more than 600 types of plants, 140 kinds of land birds, 11 mammal species, five varieties of reptiles, and three amphibian species live here. Bird-watchers may want to look for the endemic island scrub jay, which is found nowhere else in the world.

★ The largest and deepest sea cave in the world, **Painted Cave,** lies along the northwest coast of Santa Cruz. Named for the colorful lichen and algae that cover its walls, Painted Cave is nearly ¼ mi long and 100 feet wide. In spring a waterfall cascades over the entrance. Kayakers may encounter seals or sea lions cruising alongside their boats inside the cave. The Channel Islands hold some of the richest archeological resources in North America; all artifacts are protected within the park. Remnants of a dozen Chumash villages can be seen on the island. The largest of these villages, at the eastern end of the island, occupied the area now called **Scorpion Ranch.** The Chumash mined extensive chert deposits on the island for tools to produce shell-bead money, which they traded with people on the mainland. Visitors can also explore remnants of the early-1900s ranching era in the restored historic adobe and outbuildings.

SANTA ROSA ISLAND

Set between Santa Cruz and San Miguel, **Santa Rosa Island** is the second largest of the Channel Islands and has a relatively low profile, broken by a central mountain range rising to 1,589 feet. The coastal areas range from broad sandy beaches to sheer cliffs. The island is home to about 500 species of plants, including the rare Torrey pine. Three unusual mammals—the endemic island fox, spotted skunk, and deer mouse—are among those that make their home here. They hardly compare to the mammoths that once roamed the island; a nearly complete skeleton of a 6-foot-tall pygmy mammoth was unearthed here in 1994.

The island was once home to the **Vail & Vickers Ranch,** where sheep and cattle were raised from 1901 to 1998. You can catch a glimpse of what the operation was like when you walk from the landing dock to the campground; the route passes by the historic ranch buildings, barns, equipment, and the wooden pier where cattle were brought onto the island. (Note that these buildings are not accessible to the public.)

VISITOR CENTERS

Channel Islands National Park Robert J. Lagomarsino Visitor Center. The park's main visitor center has a museum, a bookstore, a three-story observation tower with telescopes, and exhibits about the islands. Rangers lead various free public programs describing park resources on weekends and holidays at 11 and 3; they can also give you a detailed map and trip-planning packet if you're interested in visiting the actual islands. ✉ *1901 Spinnaker Dr., Ventura* ☎ *805/658–5730* ⊕ *www.nps.gov/chis* ⊙ *Daily 8:30–5.*

SPORTS AND THE OUTDOORS

DIVING

Some of the best snorkeling and diving in the world can be found in the cool waters surrounding the Channel Islands. The best time to scuba dive is in the summer and fall, when the water is often clear up to a 100-foot depth.

HIKING

The terrain on most of the islands ranges from flat to moderately hilly. There are no services (and no public phones; cell-phone reception is dicey) on the islands—you need to bring all your own food, water, and supplies. To hike on San Miguel, call ☎ *805/658–5711* to be matched up to a ranger, who must accompany you there.

KAYAKING

The most remote parts of the Channel Islands are accessible only by a sea kayak. Some of the best kayaking in the park can be found on Anacapa, Santa Barbara, and the eastern tip of Santa Cruz. It's too far to kayak from the mainland out to the islands, but outfitters have tours that take you to the islands. ⚠ Channel waters can be unpredictable and challenging. Don't venture out alone unless you are an experienced kayaker; guided trips are highly recommended.

WHALE-WATCHING

About a third of the world's cetacean species (27 to be exact) can be seen in the Santa Barbara Channel. In July and August, humpback and blue whales feed off the north shore of Santa Rosa. From late December through March, up to 10,000 gray whales pass through the Santa Barbara Channel on their way from Alaska to Mexico and back again, and on a whale-watching trip during this time frame, you should see one or more of them. Other types of whales, but fewer in number, swim the channel June through August.

WHERE TO STAY

Camping is the best way to experience the natural beauty and isolation of Channel Islands National Park. Campsites are primitive, with no water (except on Santa Rosa and Santa Cruz) or electricity. Campfires are not allowed on the islands, though you may use enclosed camp stoves. Campers must arrange transportation to the islands before reserving a campsite (and yes, park personnel do check). You can get specifics on each campground and reserve a campsite ($15-$25 per night) by contacting the **National Park Service Reservation System** (☎ *877/444–6777* ⊕ *www.recreation.gov*) up to six months in advance.

The Monterey Bay Area

FROM CARMEL TO SANTA CRUZ

WORD OF MOUTH

"To be able to see, up close, the wonders of the ocean, is an amazing experience at the wonderful Monterey Bay Aquarium."

—photo by mellifluous, Fodors.com member

WELCOME TO THE MONTEREY BAY AREA

TOP REASONS TO GO

★ **Marine life:** Monterey Bay is home to the world's third-largest marine sanctuary, home to whales, otters, and other underwater creatures.

★ **Getaway central:** For more than a century, urbanites have come to the Monterey Bay area to unwind, relax, and have fun. It's a great place to browse unique shops and galleries, ride a giant roller coaster, or play a round of golf on a world-class course.

★ **Nature preserves:** More than the sea is protected here—the region boasts nearly 30 state parks, beaches, and preserves, fantastic places for walking, jogging, hiking, and biking.

★ **Wine and dine:** The area's rich agricultural bounty translates to abundant fresh produce, great wines, and fabulous dining. It's no wonder more than 300 culinary events take place here every year.

★ **Small-town vibes:** Even the cities here are friendly, walkable places where you'll feel like a local.

1 Carmel and Pacific Grove. Exclusive Carmel-by-the-Sea and Carmel Valley Village burst with historic charm, fine dining, and unusual boutiques that cater to celebrity residents and well-heeled visitors. Nearby 17-Mile Drive—quite possibly the prettiest stretch of road you'll ever travel—runs between Carmel-by-the-Sea and Victorian-studded Pacific Grove, home to thousands of migrating monarch butterflies between October and February.

2 Monterey. A former Spanish military outpost, Monterey's well-preserved historic district is a hands-on history lesson. Cannery Row, the former center of Monterey's once-thriving sardine industry, has been reborn as a tourist attraction with shops, restaurants, hotels, and the Monterey Bay Aquarium.

3 Around the Bay. Much of California's lettuce, berries, artichokes, and Brussels sprouts come from Salinas and Watsonville. Salinas is also home of the National Steinbeck Center, and Moss Landing and Watsonville encompass pristine wildlife wetlands. Aptos, Capitola, and Soquel are former lumber towns that became popular seaside resorts more than a century ago. Today they're filled with antiques shops, restaurants, and wine-tasting rooms; you'll also find some of the bay's best beaches along the shore here.

4 Santa Cruz. Santa Cruz shows its colors along an old-time beach boardwalk and municipal wharf. A University of California campus imbues the town with arts and culture and a liberal mind-set.

The Forest of
Nisene Marks
State Park

Soquel
Aptos
Capitola
Rio
del Rio
Soquel
Cove
Freedom
3
Watsonville
Pajaro
Las Lomas

M O N T E R E Y   B A Y

Moss Landing
Prunedale
Castroville
Salinas

Marina
S A L I N A S
Salinas
G17
V A L L E Y

Point
Pinos
Seaside
Pacific
Grove
Sand City
Spreckels
Monterey **2**
Del Rey Oaks
Pebble
Beach
Cypress
Point
Carmel
S I E R R A   D E   S A L I N A S
Carmel
Bay
Point
Lobos
Carmel
Highlands
Carmel Valley Rd.
Carmel River
Carmel
Valley
Spanish Bay
17-Mile Dr.
1

GETTING ORIENTED

North of Big Sur the coastline softens into lower
bluffs, windswept dunes,
pristine estuaries, and long,
sandy beaches, bordering
one of the world's most
amazing marine environ-
ments—the Monterey Bay.
On the Monterey Peninsula,
at the southern end of the
bay, are Carmel-by-the-
Sea, Pacific Grove, and
Monterey; Santa Cruz
sits at the northern tip of
the crescent. In between,
Highway 1 cruises along
the coastline, passing windswept beaches piled high
with sand dunes. Along
the route are wetlands,
artichoke and strawberry
fields, and workaday
towns such as Castroville
and Watsonville.

7

THE MONTEREY BAY AREA PLANNER

Timing Your Trip

Summer is peak season; mild weather brings in big crowds. In this coastal region, a cool breeze generally blows and fog often rolls in from offshore; you will frequently need a sweater or windbreaker. Off-season, from November through April, fewer people visit and the mood is mellower. Rainfall is heaviest in January and February, but autumn through spring days are crystal clear more often than in summer.

Helpful Contacts

Bed and Breakfast Inns of Santa Cruz County (⊕ www.santacruzbnb.com), an association of innkeepers, can help you find a bed-and-breakfast. **Monterey County Convention and Visitors Bureau Visitor Services** (☎ 877/666–8373 ⊕ www.montereyinfo.org) operates a lodging referral line and publishes an informational brochure with discount coupons that are good at restaurants, attractions, and shops.

About the Hotels

Monterey-area accommodations range from no-frills motels to luxurious hotels. Pacific Grove, amply endowed with ornate Victorian houses, has quietly turned itself into the region's B&B capital; Carmel also has charming inns in residential areas. Truly lavish resorts, with everything from featherbeds to heated floors, cluster in exclusive Pebble Beach and pastoral Carmel Valley.

High season runs April through October. Rates in winter, especially at the larger hotels, may drop by 50% or more, and B&Bs often offer midweek specials in the off-season. However, special events throughout the year can fill lodgings far in advance. Whatever the month, even the simplest of the area's lodgings are expensive, and many properties require a two-night stay on weekends. ⚠ Many of the fancier accommodations are not suitable for children, so if you're traveling with kids, be sure to ask before you book.

About the Restaurants

Between San Francisco and Los Angeles, some of the finest dining to be found is around Monterey Bay. The surrounding waters are full of fish, wild game roams the foothills, and the inland valleys are some of the most fertile in the country—local chefs draw on this bounty for their fresh, truly California cuisine. Except at beachside stands and inexpensive eateries, where anything goes, casual but neat dress is the norm. Only a few places require formal attire.

WHAT IT COSTS

	¢	$	$$	$$$	$$$$
Restaurants	under $10	$10–$15	$16–$22	$23–$30	over $30
Hotels	under $120	$120–$175	$176–$250	$251–$325	over $325

Restaurant prices are for a main course at dinner, excluding sales tax of 8.25%–9.5% (depending on location). Hotel prices are for two people in a standard double room in high season, excluding service charges and 10%–10.5% tax.

Updated by Cheryl Crabtree

Natural beauty is at the heart of this region's enormous appeal—you sense it everywhere, whether you're exploring one of Monterey Bay's attractive coast-side towns, relaxing at a luxurious resort, or touring the coast on the lookout for marine life.

It's been this way for a long time: an abiding current of plenty runs through the the region's history. Military buffs see it in centuries' worth of battles for control of the rich territory. John Steinbeck saw it in the success of a community built on the elbow grease of farm laborers in the Salinas Valley and fishermen along Cannery Row. Biologists see it in the ocean's potential as a more sustainable source of food.

Downtown Carmel-by-the-Sea and Monterey are walks through history. The bay itself is protected by the Monterey Bay National Marine Sanctuary, the nation's largest undersea canyon—bigger and deeper than the Grand Canyon. And of course, the backdrop of natural beauty is still everywhere to be seen.

PLANNING

GETTING HERE AND AROUND
BY AIR
Monterey Peninsula Airport is 3 mi east of downtown Monterey (take Olmstead Road off Highway 68). It's served by Allegiant Air, American Eagle, Frontier, United, United Express, and US Airways. Taxi service to downtown runs about $15 to $17; to Carmel the fare is $23 to $32. To and from San Jose International Airport and San Francisco International Airport, Monterey Airbus starts at $35 and the Surf City Shuttle runs $69 to $109.

Airport Contact Monterey Peninsula Airport (✉ 200 Fred Kane Dr., Monterey 🕾 831/648–7000 ⊕ www.montereyairport.com).

Taxi Contacts Carmel Taxi (🕾 831/624–3885). **Central Coast Cab Company** (🕾 831/646–8294 or 831/626–3333). **Monterey Airbus** (🕾 831/373–7777

Continued on page 320

HIGHWAY 1: CARMEL TO SAN FRANCISCO

San Francisco

THE PLAN

Distance: approx. 123 mi

Time: 2-4 days

Good Overnight Options: Carmel, Monterey, Santa Cruz, Half Moon Bay, San Francisco

For more information on the sights and attractions along this portion of Highway 1, please see chapters 7, 8, and 9.

CARMEL TO MONTEREY (approx. 4 mi)

Between **Carmel** and **Monterey,** the Highway 1 cuts across the base of the Monterey Peninsula. Pony up the toll and take a brief detour to follow famous **17-Mile Drive,** which traverses a surf-pounded landscape of cypress trees, sea lions, gargantuan estates, and the world famous **Pebble Beach Golf Links.** Take your time here as well, and be sure to allow lots of time for pulling off to enjoy the gorgeous views.

If you have the time, spend a day checking out the sights in **Monterey,** especially the kelp forests and bat rays of the **Monterey Bay Aquarium** and the adobes and artifacts of **Monterey State Historic Park.**

MONTEREY TO SANTA CRUZ (approx. 42 mi)

From Monterey the highway rounds the gentle curve of Monterey Bay, passing through sand dunes and artichoke fields on its way to **Moss Landing** and the **Elkhorn Slough National Estuarine Marine Preserve.** Kayak or walk through the protected wetlands here, or board a pontoon safari boat—don't forget your binoculars. The historic seaside villages of **Aptos, Capitola,** and **Soquel,** just off the highway near the bay's midpoint, are ideal stopovers for beachcombing, antiquing, and hiking through redwoods. In boho **Santa Cruz,** just 7 mi north, walk along the **wharf,** ride the historic roller coaster on the **boardwalk,** and perch on the cliffs to watch surfers peel through tubes at **Steamer Lane.**

SANTA CRUZ TO SAN FRANCISCO (approx. 77 mi)

Highway 1 hugs the ocean's edge once again as it departs Santa Cruz and runs

Davenport cliffs, Devenport

northward past a string of secluded beaches and small towns. Stop and stretch your legs in the tiny, artsy town of **Davenport,** where you can wander through several galleries and enjoy sumptuous views from the bluffs. At **Año Nuevo State Reserve,** walk down to the dunes to view gargantuan elephant

FRIGID WATERS

If you're planning to jump in the ocean in Northern California, wear a wetsuit or prepare to shiver. Even in summer, the water temperatures warm up to just barely tolerable. The fog tends to burn off earlier in the day at relatively sheltered beaches near Monterey Bay's midpoint, near Aptos, Capitola and Santa Cruz. These beaches also tend to attract softer waves than those on the bay's outer edges.

Half Moon Bay

TOP 5 PLACES TO LINGER

- 17 Mile Drive
- Monterey
- Santa Cruz
- Año Nuevo State Reserve
- Half Moon Bay

seals lounging on shore, then break for a meal or snack in **Pescadero** or **Half Moon Bay.**

From Half Moon Bay to **Daly City,** the road includes a number of shoulderless twists and turns that demand slower speeds and nerves of steel. Signs of urban development soon appear: mansions holding fast to Pacific cliffs and then, as the road veers slightly inland to merge with Skyline Boulevard, boxlike houses sprawling across **Daly City** and **South San Francisco.**

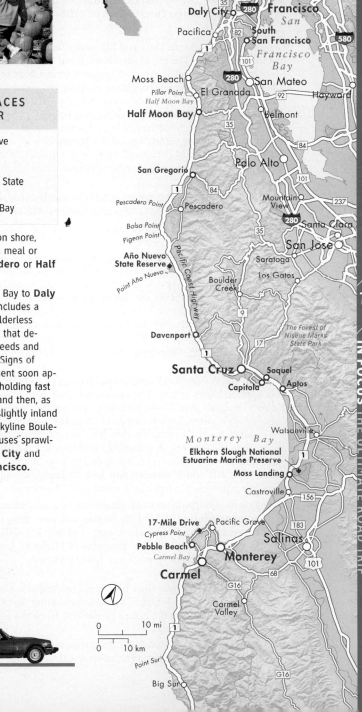

Golden Gate Nat'l. Recreation Area

San Francisco
Daly City
Pacifica
South San Francisco
San Francisco Bay

Moss Beach
Pillar Point
Half Moon Bay
El Granada
Half Moon Bay
San Mateo
Hayward
Belmont

Palo Alto

San Gregorio

Pescadero Point
Pescadero
Mountain View
Santa Clara
Bolsa Point
Pigeon Point
San Jose
Saratoga
Los Gatos
Año Nuevo State Reserve
Point Año Nuevo
Pacific Coast Highway
Boulder Creek

Davenport
The Forest of Nisene Marks State Park

Santa Cruz
Soquel
Capitola
Aptos

Monterey Bay
Watsonville
Elkhorn Slough National Estuarine Marine Preserve
Moss Landing
Castroville

17-Mile Drive
Pacific Grove
Cypress Point
Pebble Beach
Salinas
Carmel Bay
Monterey
Carmel

Carmel Valley

0   10 mi
0   10 km

Point Sur

Big Sur

⊕ *www.montereyairbus.com*). **Surf City Shuttle** (☎ *831/419–2642* ⊕ *www. surfcityshuttle.com*). **Yellow Checker Cabs** (☎ *831/646–1234*).

BY BUS

Greyhound serves Santa Cruz and Monterey from San Francisco three or four times daily. The trips take about 3 and 4½ hours, respectively. Monterey-Salinas Transit provides frequent service between the peninsula's towns and many major sightseeing spots and shopping areas. The base fare is $2.50, with an additional $2.50 for each zone you travel into. A day pass costs $6 to $12, depending on how many zones you'll be traveling through. Monterey-Salinas Transit also runs the MST Trolley, which links major attractions on the Monterey waterfront. The free shuttle operates late May through early September, daily from 10 to 7; from July 5 through early September service is extended weekends and holidays from 10 to 8.

Bus Contacts Greyhound (☎ *800/231–2222* ⊕ *www.greyhound.com*). **Monterey-Salinas Transit** (☎ *831/899–2555 Monterey, 831/424–7695 Salinas, or 888/678–2871* ⊕ *www.mst.org*).

BY CAR

Highway 1 runs south–north along the coast, linking the towns of Carmel-by-the-Sea, Monterey, and Santa Cruz; some sections have only two lanes. The freeway, U.S. 101, lies to the east, roughly parallel to Highway 1. The two roads are connected by Highway 68 from Pacific Grove to Salinas; Highway 156 from Castroville to Prunedale; Highway 152 from Watsonville to Gilroy; and Highway 17 from Santa Cruz to San Jose. Highway 17 crosses the redwood-filled Santa Cruz Mountains. ■**TIP→** Traffic near Santa Cruz can crawl to a standstill during commuter hours.

The drive south from San Francisco to Monterey can be made comfortably in three hours or less. The most scenic way is to follow Highway 1 down the coast past flower, pumpkin, and artichoke fields and small seaside communities. Unless you drive on sunny weekends when locals are heading for the beach, the two-lane coast highway may take no longer than the freeway. A sometimes-faster route is I–280 south from San Francisco to Highway 17, north of San Jose. A third option is to follow U.S. 101 south through San Jose to Prunedale and then take Highway 156 west to Highway 1 south into Monterey.

From Los Angeles the drive to Monterey can be made in five to six hours by heading north on U.S. 101 to Salinas and then west on Highway 68. The spectacular but slow alternative is to take U.S. 101 to San Luis Obispo and then follow the hairpin turns of Highway 1 up the coast. Allow about three extra hours if you take this route.

BY TRAIN

Amtrak's *Coast Starlight* runs between Los Angeles, Oakland, and Seattle. From the train station in Salinas, connecting Amtrak Thruway buses serve Monterey and Carmel-by-the-Sea; from San Jose, connecting buses serve Santa Cruz.

Train Contacts Amtrak (☎ *800/872–7245* ⊕ *www.amtrakcalifornia.com*). **Salinas Amtrak Station** (✉ *11 Station Pl., Salinas* ☎ *831/422–7458*).

TOUR OPTIONS

California Parlor Car Tours operates motor-coach tours from San Francisco that include one or two days in Monterey and Carmel. Ag Venture Tours runs wine-tasting, sightseeing, and agricultural tours in the Monterey, Salinas, Carmel Valley, and Santa Cruz areas.

Tour Contacts Ag Venture Tours (☎ 831/761–8463 ⊕ *www.agventuretours. com*). **California Parlor Car Tours** (☎ 415/474–7500 or 800/227–4250 ⊕ *www. calpartours.com*).

VISITOR INFORMATION

Contacts Monterey County Convention & Visitors Bureau (☎ 877/666–8373 ⊕ *www.seemonterey.com*). **Monterey County Vintners and Growers Association** (☎ 831/375–9400 ⊕ *www.montereywines.org*). **Pajaro Valley Chamber of Commerce & Agriculture** (⊠ 449 Union St., Watsonville ☎ 831/724–3900 ⊕ *www.pajarovalleychamber.com*). **Salinas Valley Chamber of Commerce** (⊠ 119 E. Alisal St., Salinas ☎ 831/751–7725 ⊕ *www.salinaschamber.com*). **San Lorenzo Valley Chamber of Commerce** (⊠ Box 1510, Felton ☎ 831/345–2084 ⊕ *www.slvchamber.org*). **Santa Cruz County Conference and Visitors Council** (⊠ 303 Water St., Santa Cruz ☎ 831/425–1234 or 800/833 3494 ⊕ *www. santacruzcounty.travel*). **Santa Cruz Mountain Winegrowers Association** (⊠ 7605-A Old Dominion Ct., Aptos ☎ 831/685–8463 ⊕ *www.scmwa.com*).

CARMEL AND PACIFIC GROVE

7

CARMEL-BY-THE-SEA

26 mi north of Big Sur on Hwy. 1.

Although the community has grown quickly through the years and its population quadruples with tourists on weekends and in summer, Carmel-by-the-Sea, commonly referred to as Carmel, retains its identity as a quaint village. Self-consciously charming, the town is populated by many celebrities, major and minor, and has more than its share of quirky ordinances. For instance, women wearing high heels do not have the right to pursue legal action if they trip and fall on the cobblestone streets, and drivers who hit a tree and leave the scene are charged with hit-and-run.

Buildings still have no street numbers (street names are written on discreet white posts) and consequently no mail delivery (if you really want to see the locals, go to the post office). Artists started this community, and their legacy is evident in the numerous galleries. Wandering the side streets off Ocean Avenue, where you can poke into hidden courtyards and stop at cafés for tea and crumpets, is a pleasure.

ESSENTIALS

Visitor Information Carmel Chamber of Commerce (⊠ San Carlos, between 5th and 6th, Carmel ☎ 831/624–2522 or 800/550–4333 ⊕ *www. carmelcalifornia.org*).

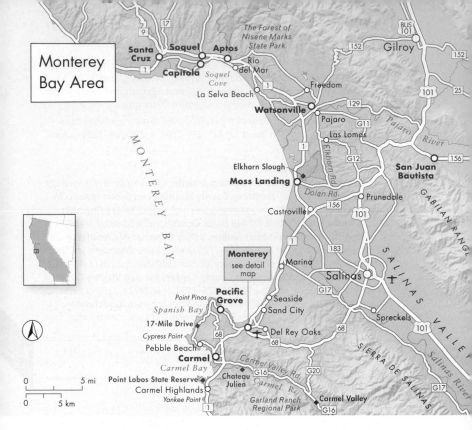

EXPLORING

Downtown Carmel's chief lure is shopping, especially along its main street, **Ocean Avenue**, between Junipero Avenue and Camino Real; the architecture here is a mishmash of ersatz Tudor, Mediterranean, and other styles.

Carmel Plaza (⊠ *Ocean and Junipero Aves.* ☎ *831/624–1385* ⊕ *www. carmelplaza.com*), in the east end of the village proper, holds more than 50 shops and restaurants.

★ Long before it became a shopping and browsing destination, Carmel was an important religious center during the establishment of Spanish California. That heritage is preserved in the Mission San Carlos Borroméo del Rio Carmelo, more commonly known as the **Carmel Mission**. Founded in 1771, it served as headquarters for the mission system in California under Father Junípero Serra. Adjoining the stone church is a tranquil garden planted with California poppies. Museum rooms at the mission include an early kitchen, Serra's spartan sleeping quarters, and the first college library in California. ⊠ *3080 Rio Rd., at Lasuen Dr.* ☎ *831/624–3600* ⊕ *www.carmelmission.org* ☎ *$6.50* ☉ *Mon.–Sat. 9:30–5, Sun. 10:30–5.*

Scattered throughout the pines in Carmel-by-the-Sea are houses and cottages originally built for the writers, artists, and photographers who discovered the area decades ago. Among the most impressive dwellings is **Tor House**, a stone cottage built in 1919 by poet Robinson Jeffers on a craggy knoll overlooking the sea. Portraits, books, and unusual art objects fill the low-ceiling rooms. The highlight of the small estate is Hawk Tower, a detached edifice set with stones from the Carmel coastline—as well as one from the Great Wall of China. The docents who lead tours (six people maximum) are well informed about the poet's work and life. Advance reservations for tours via e-mail at ✎ *thf£torhouse.org* are recommended. ✉ *26304 Ocean View Ave.* ☎ *831/624–1813* ⊕ *www.torhouse.org* 💰 *$7* ⊙ *Tours on hr Fri. and Sat. 10–3* ☞ *No children under 12.*

Carmel-by-the-Sea's greatest attraction is its rugged coastline, with pine and cypress forests and countless inlets. **Carmel Beach** (✉ *End of Ocean Ave.*), an easy walk from downtown shops, has sparkling white sands and magnificent sunsets.

Carmel River State Beach stretches for 106 acres along Carmel Bay. The sugar-white beach is adjacent to a bird sanctuary, where you might spot pelicans, kingfishers, hawks, and sandpipers. ✉ *Off Scenic Rd. south of Carmel Beach* ☎ *831/624–4909 or 831/649–2836* ⊕ *www.parks.ca.gov* 💰 *Free* ⊙ *Daily 8* AM–½ *hr after sunset.*

★ **Point Lobos State Reserve**, a 350-acre headland harboring a wealth of marine life, lies a few miles south of Carmel. The best way to explore the reserve is to walk along one of its many trails. The Cypress Grove Trail leads through a forest of Monterey cypress (one of only two natural groves remaining), which clings to the rocks above an emerald-green cove. Sea Lion Point Trail is a good place to view sea lions. From those and other trails you may also spot otters, harbor seals, and (in winter and spring) migrating whales. An additional 750 acres of the reserve is an undersea marine park open to qualified scuba divers. ■TIP➔ Arrive early (or in late afternoon) to avoid crowds; the parking lots fill up. No pets are allowed. ✉ *Hwy. 1* ☎ *831/624–4909, 831/624–8413 for scuba-diving reservations* ⊕ *www.pointlobos.org* 💰 *$10 per vehicle* ⊙ *Daily 8* AM–½ *hr after sunset.*

WHERE TO EAT

$$$

FRENCH

★

✗ **André's Bouchée.** The food here presents an innovative bistro-style take on local ingredients. A Monterey Bay sea scallop reduction adorns pan-seared veal tenderloin; grilled rib-eye steaks are topped with a shallot—cabernet sauvignon sauce. With its copper wine bar, the dining room feels more urban than most of Carmel; perhaps that's why this is the "cool" place in town to dine. The stellar wine list sources the selection at adjoining Andre's Wine Merchant. ✉ *Mission St., between Ocean and 7th Aves.* ☎ *831/626–7880* ⊕ *www.andresbouchee.com* 🍴 *Reservations essential* ⊟ *AE, MC, V* ⊙ *No lunch Mon. and Tues.*

7

$$$ ✕ **Anton and Michel.** Carefully prepared European cuisine is the draw at
ᴛɪɴᴇɴᴛᴀʟ this airy restaurant. The rack of lamb is carved at the table, the grilled
Halloumi cheese and portobello mushrooms are meticulously stacked
and served with white truffle oil and kalamata olives, and the desserts
are set aflame before your eyes. In summer, you (and your dog!) can
have lunch served in the courtyard; inside, the dining room looks onto a
lighted fountain. ⊠ *Mission St. and 7th Ave.* ☎ *831/624–2406* ⊕ *www.
antonandmichel.com* ⚑ *Reservations essential* ☐ *AE, D, DC, MC, V.*

$$ ✕ **Bahama Billy's.** The energy is electric at this always-bustling Caribbean
CARIBBEAN bar and restaurant. An excellent and diverse menu combined with a
lively crowd makes it a prime spot for fun and good eating in Carmel.
Particularly good is the ahi tuna, which is rolled in Jamaican jerk sea-
soning, seared, and served with aioli. ⊠ *Barnyard Shopping Center,
Hwy. 1 and Carmel Valley Rd.* ☎ *831/626–0430* ⊕ *www.bahamabillys.
com* ⚑ *Reservations essential* ☐ *AE, D, DC, MC, V.*

$$$$ ✕ **Casanova.** Built in a former home, this cozy restaurant inspires Euro-
MEDITERRANEAN pean-style celebration and romance—chairs are painted in all colors,
★ accordions hang from the walls, and tiny party lights dance along the
low ceilings. All entrées include antipasti and your choice of appetizers, which all but insist that you sit back and enjoy a long meal. The
food consists of delectable seasonal dishes from southern France and
northern Italy. Private dining and a special menu are offered at Van
Gogh's Table, a special table imported from France's Auberge Ravoux,
the artist's final residence. ⊠ *5th Ave., between San Carlos and Mission
Sts.* ☎ *831/625–0501* ⊕ *www.casanovarestaurant.com* ⚑ *Reservations
essential* ☐ *AE, MC, V.*

$ ✕ **The Cottage Restaurant.** For the best breakfast in Carmel, look no fur-
AMERICAN ther: The menu here offers six different preparations of eggs Benedict,
and all kinds of sweet and savory crepes. This family-friendly spot
serves sandwiches, pizzas, and homemade soups at lunch and simple
entreés at dinner, but the best meals appear on the breakfast menu
(good thing it's served all day). ⊠ *Lincoln St., between Ocean and 7th
Aves.* ☎ *831/625–6260* ⊕ *www.cottagerestaurant.com* ☐ *MC, V* ☉ *No
dinner Sun.–Wed.*

$$$ ✕ **Flying Fish Grill.** Simple in appearance yet bold with its flavors, this
SEAFOOD Japanese–California seafood restaurant is one of Carmel's most inven-
tive eateries. Among the best entrées is the almond-crusted sea bass
served with Chinese cabbage and rock shrimp stir-fry. The warm,
wood-lined dining room is broken up into very private booths. For
the entrance, go down the steps near the gates to Carmel Plaza. ⊠ *Mis-
sion St., between Ocean and 7th Aves.* ☎ *831/625–1962* ☐ *AE, D, DC,
MC, V* ☉ *No lunch.*

$ ✕ **Jack London's Grill & Taproom.** If anyone's awake after dinner in Carmel,
AMERICAN he's at Jack London's. This publike local hangout is the only Carmel
restaurant to serve food until midnight (Sunday through Thursday until
11). The menu includes everything from nachos to steaks. ⊠ *Su Vecino
Court on Dolores St., between 5th and 6th Aves.* ☎ *831/624–2336*
⊕ *www.jacklondons.com* ☐ *AE, D, DC, MC, V.*

$ ✕ **Katy's Place.** Locals flock to Katy's cozy, country-style eatery to fill
AMERICAN up on hearty eggs Benedict dishes. (There are 16 types to choose from,

Point Lobos Reserve State Park is home to one of the only two natural stands of Monterey Cypress in the world.

each made with three fresh eggs). The huge breakfast menu also includes omelets, pancakes, and eight types of Belgian waffles. An assortment of salads, sandwiches, and burgers is available at lunch—try the grilled calamari burger with melted Monterey Jack cheese. ⊠ *Mission St., between 5th and 6th Aves.* ☎ *831/624–0199* ⊕ *www.katysplacecarmel. com* ⊟ *No credit cards* ☾ *No dinner.*

$$$ ✕ **L'Escargot.** Chef-owner Kericos Loutas personally sees to each plate
FRENCH of food served at this romantic and mercifully unpretentious French restaurant (which also has a full bar). Take his recommendation and order the duck confit in puff pastry or the bone-in steak in truffle butter; or, if you can't decide, choose the three-course prix-fixe dinner. Service is warm and attentive. ⊠ *Mission St., between 4th and 5th Aves.* ☎ *831/620–1942* ⊕ *www.escargot-carmel.com* ✍ *Reservations essential* ⊟ *AE, MC, V* ☾ *No lunch.*

$ ✕ **Tuck Box.** This bright little restaurant is in a cottage right out of a
AMERICAN fairy tale, complete with a stone fireplace that's lighted on rainy days. Handmade scones are the house specialty, and are good for breakfast or afternoon tea. ⊠ *Dolores St., between Ocean and 7th Aves.* ☎ *831/624–6365* ⊟ *No credit cards* ☾ *No dinner.*

WHERE TO STAY

$$ ⌶ **Cypress Inn.** The decorating style here is luxurious but refreshingly simple. Rather than chintz and antiques, there are wrought-iron bed frames, wooden armoires, and rattan armchairs. Some rooms have fireplaces, some hot tubs, and one (Room 215) even has its own sunny veranda that looks out on the ocean. The in-town location makes walking to area attractions easy, and pet owners will be pleased to hear that in the spirit of the dog-loving owner, movie star Doris Day, animal companions are always welcome. **Pros:** luxury without snobbery; popular lounge; traditional British-style afternoon tea. **Cons:** not for the pet-phobic. ⊠ *Lincoln St. and 7th Ave., Box Y* ☎ *831/624–3871 or 800/443–7443* ⊕ *www.cypress-inn.com* ⇦ *39 rooms, 5 suites* ⌂ *In-room: a/c (some), Wi-Fi. In-hotel: restaurant, bar, laundry service, Wi-Fi hotspot, some pets allowed* ⊟ *AE, D, DC, MC, V* ♚ *CP.*

$$$–$$$$ 🏨 **Highlands Inn, A Hyatt Hotel.** High on a hill overlooking the Pacific, this
★   place has superb views. Accommodations include king rooms with fireplaces, suites with personal Jacuzzis, and full town houses with all the perks. The excellent menus at the inn's Pacific's Edge restaurant ($$$$) blend French and California cuisine; the sommelier helps choose the perfect wines. Even if you don't dine here, order a cocktail and appetizers in the ocean-view Sunset Lounge. **Pros:** killer views; romantic getaway; great food. **Cons:** thin walls; must drive to Carmel. ⊠ *120 Highlands Dr.* ☎ *831/620–1234 or 800/682–4811, 831/622–5445 for restaurant* ⊕ *highlandsinn.hyatt.com* ⇦ *46 rooms, 2 suites* ⌂ *In-room: no a/c, safe, kitchen (some), refrigerator, DVD, Internet, Wi-Fi. In-hotel: 2 restaurants, room service, bars, pool, gym, bicycles, laundry facilities, laundry service, Internet terminal, Wi-Fi hotspot* ⊟ *AE, D, DC, MC, V.*

$$$–$$$$ 🏨 **L'Auberge Carmel.** Stepping through the doors of this elegant inn is
Fodor'sChoice   like being transported to a little European village. The rooms are luxuri-
★   ous yet understated, with Italian sheets and huge, classic soaking tubs; sitting in the sun-soaked brick courtyard makes you feel like a movie star. The inn's intimate, 12-table restaurant, Aubergine, epitomizes farm-fresh gourmet dining. **Pros:** in town but off the main drag; four blocks from the beach; full-service luxury. **Cons:** touristy area; not a good choice for families. ⊠ *Monte Verde, at 7th Ave.* ☎ *831/624–8578* ⊕ *www.laubergecarmel.com* ⇦ *20 rooms* ⌂ *In-room: a/c, safe, refrigerator, Wi-Fi. In-hotel: restaurant, room service, bar, Wi-Fi hotspot* ⊟ *AE, MC, V* ♚ *CP.*

$ 🏨 **Mission Ranch.** The property at Mission Ranch is gorgeous and includes a sprawling sheep pasture, bird-filled wetlands, and a sweeping view of the ocean. The ranch is nicely decorated but low-key, with a 19th-century farmhouse as the central building. Other accommodations include rooms in a converted barn, and several cottages, many with fireplaces. Though the ranch belongs to movie star Clint Eastwood, relaxation, not celebrity, is the focus here. **Pros:** farm setting; pastoral views; great for tennis buffs. **Cons:** busy parking lot; must drive to the heart of town. ⊠ *26270 Dolores St.* ☎ *831/624–6436 or 800/538–8221* ⊕ *www.missionranchcarmel.com* ⇦ *31 rooms* ⌂ *In-room: no a/c, refrigerator (some). In-hotel: restaurant, bar, tennis courts, gym, Internet terminal* ⊟ *AE, MC, V* ♚ *CP.*

$$ 🏨 **Sea View Inn.** In a residential area a few hundred feet from the beach, this restored 1905 home has a double parlor with two fireplaces, Oriental rugs, canopy beds, and a spacious front porch. Rooms are individually done in cheery colors and country patterns; taller guests might feel cramped in those tucked up under the eaves. Afternoon tea and evening wine and cheese are offered daily. Because of the fragile furnishings and

quiet atmosphere, families with kids will likely be more comfortable elsewhere. **Pros:** quiet; private; close to the beach. **Cons:** small building; uphill trek to the heart of town. ⊠ *Camino Real, between 11th and 12th Aves.* ☎ *831/624–8778* ⊕ *www.seaviewinncarmel.com* ⟿ *8 rooms, 6 with private bath* ⚏ *In-room: no phone, no a/c, no TV, Wi-Fi. In-hotel: Wi-Fi hotspot* ☰ *AE, MC, V* †⊙† *CP.*

$$$–$$$$ ♜ **Tickle Pink Inn.** Atop a towering cliff, this inn has views of the Big Sur coastline, which you can contemplate from your private balcony. After falling asleep to the sound of surf crashing below, you'll wake to a Continental breakfast and the morning paper in bed. If you prefer the company of fellow travelers, breakfast is also served buffet-style in the lounge, as are complimentary wine and cheese in the afternoon. Many rooms have wood-burning fireplaces, and there are six luxurious spa suites and a private two-bedroom cottage. **Pros:** close to great hiking; intimate; dramatic views. **Cons:** close to a big hotel; lots of traffic during the day. ⊠ *155 Highland Dr.* ☎ *831/624–1244 or 800/635–4774* ⊕ *www.ticklepink.com* ⟿ *23 rooms, 10 suites, 1 cottage* ⚏ *In-room: no a/c, refrigerator, DVD, Wi-Fi. In-hotel: room service, Internet terminal, Wi-Fi hotspot* ☰ *AE, DC, MC, V* †⊙† *CP.*

$$$$ ♜ **Tradewinds Inn.** Its sleek decor inspired by the South Seas, this con-
★ verted motel encircles a courtyard with waterfalls, a meditation garden, and a fire pit. Each room has a tabletop fountain and orchids, to complement antique and custom furniture from Bali and China. Some private balconies afford a view of the bay or the mountains. Treat yourself to a bamboo massage in the soothing spa room; afterward, you'll feel as if you just spent a week unwinding on a tropical beach. The chic boutique hotel, owned by the same family since it opened in 1959, is on a quiet downtown side street. **Pros:** serene; within walking distance of restaurants; friendly service. **Cons:** no pool; long walk to the beach. ⊠ *Mission St., at 3rd Ave.* ☎ *831/624–2776 or 800/624–6665* ⊕ *www.tradewindscarmel.com* ⟿ *25 rooms, 2 suites* ⚏ *In-room: no a/c, safe, refrigerator, DVD (some), Wi-Fi. In-hotel: spa, Wi-Fi hotspot, some pets allowed* ☰ *AE, MC, V* †⊙† *CP.*

SHOPPING

ART GALLERIES **Carmel Art Association** (⊠ *Dolores St., between 5th and 6th Aves.* ☎ *831/ 624–6176* ⊕ *www.carmelart.org*) exhibits the paintings, sculptures, and prints of local artists. **Galerie Plein Aire** (⊠ *Dolores St., between 5th and 6th Aves.* ☎ *831/625–5686* ⊕ *www.galeriepleinaire.com*) showcases oil paintings by a group of local artists. **Masterpiece Gallery** (⊠ *Dolores St. and 6th Ave.* ☎ *831/624–2163* ⊕ *www.masterpiecegallerycarmel. com*) shows early-California-impressionist art. Run by the family of the late Edward Weston, **Weston Gallery** (⊠ *6th Ave., between Dolores and Lincoln Sts.* ☎ *831/624–4453* ⊕ *www.westongallery.com*) is hands down the best photography gallery around, with contemporary color photography complemented by classic black-and-whites.

SPECIALTY **Bittner** (⊠ *Ocean Ave., between Mission and San Carlos Sts.* ☎ *831/626–*
SHOPS *8828 or 888/248–8637*) has a fine selection of collectible and vintage pens from around the world. **Intima** (⊠ *Mission St., between Ocean and 7th Aves.* ☎ *831/625–0599*) is the place to find European lingerie that ranges from lacy to racy. **Jan de Luz** (⊠ *Dolores St., between Ocean and*

7th Aves. ☎*831/622–7621*) monograms and embroiders fine linens (including bathrobes) while you wait. **Madrigal** (✉ *Carmel Plaza and Mission St.* ☎*831/624–3477*) carries sportswear, sweaters, and accessories for women.

☺ **Mischievous Rabbit** (✉ *Lincoln Ave., between 7th and Ocean Aves.* ☎*831/ 624–6854*) sells toys, nursery accessories, books, music boxes, china, and children's clothing, and specializes in Beatrix Potter items.

CARMEL VALLEY

10 mi east of Carmel, Hwy. 1 to Carmel Valley Rd.

Carmel Valley Road, which heads inland from Highway 1 south of Carmel-by-the-Sea, is the main thoroughfare through this valley, a secluded enclave of horse ranchers and other well-heeled residents who prefer the area's sunny climate to the fog and wind on the coast. Once thick with dairy farms, the valley has recently proved itself as a venerable wine appellation. Tiny Carmel Valley Village, about 13 mi southeast of Carmel-by-the-Sea via Carmel Valley Road, has several crafts shops and art galleries, as well as tasting rooms for numerous local wineries.

At **Bernardus Tasting Room**, you can sample many of the wines—including older vintages and reserves—from the nearby Bernardus Winery and Vineyard. ✉ *5 W. Carmel Valley Rd.* ☎*831/659–1900 or 800/223– 2533* ⊕ *www.bernardus.com* ☉ *Daily 11–5.*

Pick up fresh veggies, ready-to-eat meals, gourmet groceries, flowers, and gifts at 32-acre **Earthbound Farm** (✉ *7250 Carmel Valley Rd.* ☎*831/625–6219* ⊕ *www.ebfarm.com* 🖃 *Free* ☉ *Mon.–Sat. 8–6:30, Sun. 9–6*), the world's largest grower of organic produce. You can also take a romp in the kid's garden, cut your own herbs, and stroll through the chamomile aromatherapy labyrinth. On Saturday from April through December the farm offers special events, from bug walks to garlic-braiding workshops.

Garland Ranch Regional Park (✉ *Carmel Valley Rd., 9 mi east of Carmel-by-the-Sea* ☎*831/659–4488*) has hiking trails across nearly 4,500 acres of property that includes meadows, forested hillsides, and creeks.

The extensive **Château Julien** winery, recognized internationally for its chardonnays and merlots, gives weekday tours at 10:30 and 2:30 and weekends at 12:30 and 2:30, all by appointment. The tasting room is open daily. ✉ *8940 Carmel Valley Rd.* ☎*831/624–2600* ⊕ *www. chateaujulien.com* ☉ *Weekdays 8–5, weekends 11–5.*

WHERE TO EAT AND STAY

$ ✕ **Café Rustica.** Italian-inspired country cooking is the focus at this lively
ITALIAN roadhouse. Specialties include roasted meats, pastas, and thin-crust pizzas from the wood-fired oven. Because of the tile floors, it can get quite noisy inside; opt for a table outside if you want a quieter meal. ✉ *10 Delfino Pl.* ☎*831/659–4444* ⊕ *www.caferusticacarmel.com* ⚖ *Reservations essential* ▤ *MC, V* ☉ *Closed Mon.*

¢ ✕ **Wagon Wheel Coffee Shop.** This local hangout decorated with wagon
AMERICAN wheels, cowboy hats, and lassos serves up terrific hearty breakfasts, including date-walnut-cinnamon French toast and a plate of trout and

eggs. The lunch menu includes a dozen different burgers and other sandwiches. ⊠ *Valley Hill Center, Carmel Valley Rd., next to Quail Lodge* ☎ *831/624–8878* ☰ *No credit cards* ⊗ *No dinner.*

$$$ ✕ **Will's Fargo.** On the main street
AMERICAN of Carmel Valley Village since the 1920s, this restaurant calls itself a "dressed-up saloon." Steer horns and gilt-frame paintings adorn the walls of the Victorian-style dining room; you can also eat on the patios. The menu is mainly seafood and steaks, including a 20-ounce porterhouse. ⊠ *16 E. Carmel Valley Rd.* ☎ *831/659–2774* ⊕ *www. bernardus.com* ☰ *AE, DC, MC, V* ⊗ No *lunch.*

> ### WINE TOURING WITH THE MST
>
> Why risk driving while wine tasting when you can hop aboard the Carmel Valley Grapevine Express? This Monterey-Salinas Transit bus travels between downtown Monterey and Carmel Valley Village, with stops near wineries, restaurants, and shopping centers. Buses depart daily every hour from 11 to 6. At $6 for a ride-all-day pass, it's an incredible bargain. For more information, call ☎ *888/678–2871* or visit ⊕ *www. mst.org.*

$$$$ ▥ **Bernardus Lodge.** Even before you check in at this luxury spa resort,
Fodor's Choice the valet hands you a glass of chardonnay. Spacious guest rooms have
★ vaulted ceilings, featherbeds, fireplaces, patios, and bathtubs for two. The restaurant, Marinus ($$$$; jacket recommended), is perhaps the best in the Monterey Bay area, with a menu that changes daily to highlight local meats, seafood, and produce. Reserve the chef's table in the main kitchen and you can talk to the chef as he prepares your meal. **Pros:** exceptional personal service; outstanding food and wine. **Cons:** some guests can seem snooty; pricey. ⊠ *415 Carmel Valley Rd.* ☎ *831/658–3400 or 888/648–9463* ⊕ *www.bernardus.com* ⤳ *55 rooms, 2 suites* ⟁ *In-room: a/c, safe, refrigerator, DVD, Internet, Wi-Fi. In-hotel: 2 restaurants, room service, bar, tennis courts, pool, gym, spa, laundry service, Internet terminal, Wi-Fi hotspot* ☰ *AE, DC, MC, V.*

GOLF

The **Golf Club at Quail Lodge** (⊠ *8000 Valley Greens Dr.* ☎ *831/624–2770*) incorporates several lakes into its course. Depending on the season and day of the week, greens fees range from $150 to $185 for guests and $185 to $210 for nonguests, including cart rental. **Rancho Cañada Golf Club** (⊠ *4860 Carmel Valley Rd., 1 mi east of Hwy. 1* ☎ *831/624–0111 or 800/536–9459*) is a public course with 36 holes, some of them overlooking the Carmel River. Fees range from $35 to $80, plus $38 for cart rental, depending on course and tee time.

17-MILE DRIVE

Fodor's Choice *Off North San Antonio Rd. in Carmel-by-the-Sea or off Sunset Dr. in*
★ *Pacific Grove.*

Primordial nature resides in quiet harmony with palatial late-20th-century estates along 17-Mile Drive, which winds through an 8,400-acre microcosm of the Monterey coastal landscape. Dotting the drive are rare Monterey cypress, trees so gnarled and twisted that Robert

Louis Stevenson described them as "ghosts fleeing before the wind." Some sightseers balk at the $9.25-per-car fee collected at the gates—this is one of only two private toll roads west of the Mississippi—but most find the drive well worth the price. An alternative is to grab a bike. ■TIP➜ Cyclists tour for free.

You can take in views of the impeccable greens at **Pebble Beach Golf Links** (✉ *17-Mile Dr., near Lodge at Pebble Beach* ☎ *800/654–9300* ⊕ *www.pebblebeach.com*) over a drink or lunch at the Lodge at Pebble Beach. The ocean plays a major role in the 18th hole of the famed links. Each February the course is the main site of the AT&T Pebble Beach Pro-Am (formerly the Bing Crosby Pro-Am), where show business celebrities and golf pros team up for one of the nation's most glamorous tournaments.

Many of the stately homes along 17-Mile Drive reflect the classic Monterey or Spanish Mission style typical of the region. A standout is the **Crocker Marble Palace**, about a mile south of the Lone Cypress (⇨ *below*). It's a private waterfront estate inspired by a Byzantine castle, easily identifiable by its dozens of marble arches.

The most-photographed tree along 17-Mile Drive is the weather-sculpted **Lone Cypress**, which grows out of a precipitous outcropping above the waves about 1½ mi up the road from Pebble Beach Golf Links. You can stop for a view of the Lone Cypress at a parking area, but you can't walk out to the tree.

Sea creatures and birds—as well as some very friendly ground squirrels—make use of **Seal Rock**, the largest of a group of islands about 2 mi north of Lone Cypress.

Bird Rock, the largest of several islands at the southern end of the Monterey Peninsula Country Club's golf course, teems with harbor seals, sea lions, cormorants, and pelicans.

WHERE TO STAY

$$$$ 🏨 **Casa Palmero.** This exclusive spa resort evokes a stately Mediterra-
★ nean villa. Rooms are decorated with sumptuous fabrics and fine art; each has a wood-burning fireplace and heated floor, and some have private outdoor patios with in-ground whirlpools. Complimentary cocktail service is offered each evening in the main hall and library. The adjacent Spa at Pebble Beach is state-of-the-art, and you have use of all facilities at the Lodge at Pebble Beach and the Inn at Spanish Bay. **Pros:** ultimate in pampering; more private than sister resorts; right on the golf course. **Cons:** pricey; may be *too* posh for some. ✉ *1518 Cypress Dr., Pebble Beach* ☎ *831/622–6650 or 800/654–9300* ⊕ *www.pebblebeach.com* ↘ *21 rooms, 3 suites* △ *In-room: no a/c, refrigerator, Wi-Fi. In-hotel: room service, bar, golf course, pool, spa, bicycles, laundry service, Wi-Fi hotspot* ═ *AE, D, DC, MC, V.*

$$$$ 🏨 **Inn at Spanish Bay.** This resort sprawls across a breathtaking stretch of shoreline, and has lush, 600-square-foot rooms. Peppoli's restaurant ($$$$), which serves Tuscan cuisine, overlooks the coast and the golf links; Roy's Restaurant ($$$–$$$$) serves more casual and innovative Euro-Asian fare. When you stay here, you're also allowed privileges at the Lodge at Pebble Beach and the Spa at Pebble Beach, which are

under the same management. **Pros:** attentive service; tons of amenities; spectacular views. **Cons:** huge hotel; four miles from other Pebble Beach Resort facilities. ✉ 2700 17-Mile Dr., Pebble Beach ☎ 831/647–7500 or 800/654–9300 ⊕ www.pebblebeach.com ⤳ 252 rooms, 17 suites ♿ In-room: no a/c, refrigerator, Internet, Wi-Fi. In-hotel: 3 restaurants, room service, bar, golf course, tennis courts, pool, gym, beachfront, bicycles, laundry service, Internet terminal ⊟ AE, D, DC, MC, V.

$$$$ ★ 🏨 **Lodge at Pebble Beach.** All rooms have fireplaces and many have wonderful ocean views at this circa 1919 resort. The golf course, tennis club, and equestrian center are posh. Overlooking the 18th green, the intimate Club XIX restaurant ($$$$) serves expertly prepared French cuisine. When staying here, you also have privileges at the Inn at Spanish Bay and the Spa at Pebble Beach. **Pros:** world-class golf; borders the ocean and fairways; fabulous facilities. **Cons:** some rooms are on the small side; very pricey. ✉ 1700 17-Mile Dr., Pebble Beach ☎ 831/624–3811 or 800/654–9300 ⊕ www.pebblebeach.com ⤳ 142 rooms, 19 suites ♿ In-room: no a/c, refrigerator, DVD (some), Internet, Wi-Fi. In-hotel: 3 restaurants, bars, golf course, tennis courts, pool, gym, spa, beachfront, bicycles, laundry service, Internet terminal, Wi-Fi hotspot, some pets allowed ⊟ AE, D, DC, MC, V.

GOLF

The **Links at Spanish Bay** (✉ 17-Mile Dr., north end ☎ 831/624–3811, 831/624–6611, or 800/654–9300), which hugs a choice stretch of shoreline, is designed in the rugged manner of a traditional Scottish course, with sand dunes and coastal marshes interspersed among the greens. The greens fee is $260, plus $35 per person for cart rental (cart is included for resort guests); nonguests can reserve tee times up to two months in advance.

Pebble Beach Golf Links (✉ 17-Mile Dr., near Lodge at Pebble Beach ☎ 831/624–3811, 831/624–6611, or 800/654–9300) attracts golfers from around the world, despite a greens fee of $495, plus $35 per person for an optional cart (complimentary cart for guests of the Pebble Beach and Spanish Bay resorts). Tee times are available to guests who book a minimum two-night stay. Nonguests can reserve a tee time only one day in advance on a space-available basis (up to a year for groups); resort guests can reserve up to 18 months in advance.

Peter Hay (✉ 17-Mile Dr. ☎ 831/622–8723), a 9-hole, par-3 course, charges $25 per person, no reservations necessary.

Poppy Hills (✉ 3200 Lopez Rd., at 17-Mile Dr. ☎ 831/625–2035), a splendid 18-hole course designed in 1986 by Robert Trent Jones Jr., has a greens fee of $200; an optional cart costs $36. Individuals may reserve up to one month in advance, groups up to a year.

Spyglass Hill (✉ Stevenson Dr. and Spyglass Hill Rd. ☎ 831/624–3811, 831/624–6611, or 800/654–9300) is among the most challenging Pebble Beach courses. With the first five holes bordering on the Pacific and the other 13 reaching deep into the Del Monte Forest, the views offer some consolation. The greens fee is $350, and an optional cart costs $35 (the cart is complimentary for resort guests). Reservations are essential and may be made up to one month in advance (18 months for guests).

PACIFIC GROVE

3 mi north of Carmel-by-the-Sea on Hwy. 68.

This picturesque town, which began as a summer retreat for church groups more than a century ago, recalls its prim and proper Victorian heritage in its host of tiny board-and-batten cottages and stately mansions. However, long before the church groups flocked here the area received thousands of annual pilgrims—in the form of bright orange-and-black monarch butterflies. They still come, migrating south from Canada and the Pacific Northwest to take residence in pine and eucalyptus groves from October through March. In Butterfly Town USA, as Pacific Grove is known, the sight of a mass of butterflies hanging from the branches like a long, fluttering veil is unforgettable.

> ## BUTTERFLY SPOTTING
>
> ↺ The **Monarch Grove Sanctuary** (✉ *1073 Lighthouse Ave., at Ridge Rd.* ⊕ *www.pgmuseum. org*) is a fairly reliable spot for viewing the butterflies between October and February. Contact the **Pacific Grove Museum of Natural History** (✉ *165 Forest Ave.* ☎ *831/648–5716* ⊕ *www. pgmuseum.org* ✉ *$3 suggested donation* ⊙ *Tues.–Sun. 10–5*) for the latest information. If you're in Pacific Grove when the monarch butterflies aren't, you can view the well-crafted butterfly tree exhibit at the museum.

A prime way to enjoy Pacific Grove is to walk or bicycle the 3 mi of city-owned shoreline along Ocean View Boulevard, a cliff-top area landscaped with native plants and dotted with benches meant for sitting and gazing at the sea. You can spot many types of birds here, including colonies of web-foot cormorants crowding the massive rocks rising out of the surf.

Among the Victorians of note is the **Pryor House** (✉ *429 Ocean View Blvd.*), a massive, shingled, private residence with a leaded- and beveled-glass doorway.

Green Gables (✉ *5th St. and Ocean View Blvd.* ☎ *831/375–2095* ⊕ *www. greengablesinnpg.com*), a romantic Swiss Gothic–style mansion with peaked gables and stained-glass windows, is a B&B.

↺ The view of the coast is gorgeous from **Lovers Point Park** (☎ *831/648–5730*), on Ocean View Boulevard midway along the waterfront. The park's sheltered beach has a children's pool and picnic area, and the main lawn has a sandy volleyball court and snack bar.

↺ At the 1855-vintage **Point Pinos Lighthouse,** the oldest continuously operating lighthouse on the West Coast, you can learn about the lighting and foghorn operations and wander through a small museum containing U.S. Coast Guard memorabilia. ✉ *Lighthouse Ave., off Asilomar Blvd.* ☎ *831/648–5716* ⊕ *www.pgmuseum.org* ✉ *$2* ⊙ *Thurs.–Mon. 1–4.*

Asilomar State Beach (☎ *831/646–6440* ⊕ *www.parks.ca.gov*), a beautiful coastal area, is on Sunset Drive between Point Pinos and the Del Monte Forest in Pacific Grove. The 100 acres of dunes, tidal pools, and

7

pocket-size beaches form one of the region's richest areas for marine life—including surfers, who migrate here most winter mornings.

WHERE TO EAT

$$
MEDITERRANEAN

✕**Fandango.** The menu here is mostly Mediterranean and southern French, with such dishes as calves' liver and onions and paella served in a skillet. The decor follows suit: stone walls and country furniture give the restaurant the earthy feel of a European farmhouse. This is where locals come when they want to have a big dinner with friends, drink wine, have fun, and generally feel at home. ✉ *223 17th St.* ☎ *831/372-3456* ⊕ *www.fandangorestaurant.com* ▭ *AE, D, DC, MC, V.*

$$
SEAFOOD

✕**Fishwife.** Fresh fish with a Latin accent makes this a favorite of locals for lunch or a casual dinner. Standards are the sea garden salads topped with your choice of fish and the fried seafood plates with fresh veggies. Large appetites appreciate the fisherman's bowls, which feature fresh fish served with rice, black beans, spicy cabbage, salsa, vegetables, and crispy tortilla strips. ✉ *1996½ Sunset Dr., at Asilomar Blvd.* ☎ *831/375-7107* ⊕ *www.fishwife.com* ▭ *AE, D, MC, V.*

$$
ITALIAN

✕**Joe Rombi's.** Pastas, fish, steaks, and chops are the specialties at this modern trattoria, which is the best in town for Italian food. The look is spare and clean, with colorful antique wine posters decorating the white walls. Next door, Joe Rombi's La Piccola Casa serves lunch and early dinner Wednesday through Sunday. ✉ *208 17th St.* ☎ *831/373-2416* ⊕ *www.joerombi.com* ▭ *AE, MC, V* ⊘ *Closed Mon. and Tues. No lunch.*

$$$
NEW AMERICAN
★

✕**Passionfish.** South American artwork and artifacts decorate the room, and Latin and Asian flavors infuse the dishes at Passionfish. Chef Ted Walter—lauded for his commitment to using eco-friendly, sustainable ingredients—shops at local farmers' markets several times a week to find the best produce, fish, and meat available, then pairs it with creative sauces. The ever-changing menu might include crispy squid with spicy orange-cilantro vinaigrette. ✉ *701 Lighthouse Ave.* ☎ *831/655-3311* ⊕ *www.passionfish.net* ▭ *AE, D, MC, V* ⊘ *No lunch.*

$
MEXICAN

✕**Peppers Mexicali Cafe.** A local favorite, this cheerful white-walled storefront serves traditional dishes from Mexico and Latin America, with an emphasis on fresh seafood. Excellent red and green salsas are made throughout the day, and there's a large selection of beers. ✉ *170 Forest Ave.* ☎ *831/373-6892* ⊕ *www.peppersmexicalicafe.com* ▭ *AE, D, DC, MC, V* ⊘ *Closed Tues. No lunch Sun.*

$$
AMERICAN

✕**Red House Café.** When it's nice out, sun pours through the big windows of this cozy restaurant and across tables on the porch; when fog rolls in, the fireplace is lit. The American menu is simple but selective, including grilled lamb fillets atop mashed potatoes for dinner and a huge Dungeness crab cake over salad for lunch. Breakfast on weekends is a local favorite. ✉ *662 Lighthouse Ave.* ☎ *831/643-1060* ⊕ *www.redhousecafe.com* ▭ *AE, D, DC, MC, V* ⊘ *Closed Mon.*

$$
AMERICAN

✕**Taste Café and Bistro.** A favorite of locals, Taste serves hearty European-inspired food in a casual, airy room with high ceilings and an open kitchen. Meats, such as grilled marinated rabbit, roasted half chicken, and filet mignon, are the focus. ✉ *1199 Forest Ave.* ☎ *831/655-0324* ⊕ *www.tastecafebistro.com* ▭ *AE, MC, V* ⊘ *Closed Mon.*

WHERE TO STAY

$$ **Green Gables Inn.** Stained-glass windows and ornate interior details
★ compete with spectacular ocean views at this Queen Anne–style mansion, built by a businessman for his mistress in 1888. Rooms in a carriage house perched on a hill out back are larger, have more modern amenities, and afford more privacy, but rooms in the main house have more charm. Afternoon wine and cheese are served in the parlor. **Pros:** exceptional views; impeccable attention to historic detail. **Cons:** some rooms are small; thin walls. ⊠ *301 Ocean View Blvd.* ☎ *831/375–2095 or 800/722–1774* ⊕ *www.greengablesinnpg.com* ⤶ *10 rooms, 3 with bath; 1 suite* ⚲ *In-room: no a/c, DVD (some), Wi-Fi (some). In-hotel: bicycles, Internet terminal, Wi-Fi hotspot* ▤ *AE, D, MC, V* ⊖ *BP.*

$–$$ **The Inn at 213 Seventeen Mile Drive.** Set in a residential area just past town, this carefully restored 1920s Craftsman-style home and cottage are surrounded by gardens and redwood, cypress, and eucalyptus trees. Spacious, well-appointed rooms have simple, homey furnishings. The innkeepers offer complimentary wine and hors d'oeuvres in the evening and tea and snacks throughout the day. **Pros:** killer gourmet breakfast; historic charm; verdant gardens. **Cons:** far from restaurants and shops; few extra amenities. ⊠ *213 17-Mile Dr., at Lighthouse Dr.* ☎ *831/642–9514 or 800/526–5666* ⊕ *www.innat17.com* ⤶ *14 rooms* ⚲ *In-room: no a/c, Wi-Fi. In-hotel: Wi-Fi hotspot, some pets allowed* ▤ *AE, MC, V* ⊖ *BP.*

$–$$ **Lighthouse Lodge and Resort.** Near the tip of the peninsula, this complex straddles Lighthouse Avenue—the lodge is on one side, the all-suites Lighthouse Resort facility on the other. Suites have fireplaces and whirlpool tubs. Standard rooms are simple, but they're decently sized and much less expensive. ■ TIP→ With daily afternoon barbecues at the lodge, this is a woodsy alternative to downtown Pacific Grove's B&B scene. (The suites do not have a daily barbecue, but instead feature a wine-and-cheese spread.) **Pros:** near lighthouse and 17-Mile Drive; friendly reception; many room options. **Cons:** next to a cemetery; lodge rooms are basic. ⊠ *1150 and 1249 Lighthouse Ave.* ☎ *831/655–2111 or 800/858–1249* ⊕ *www.lhls.com* ⤶ *64 rooms, 31 suites* ⚲ *In-room: no a/c, refrigerator, Wi-Fi. In-hotel: room service, pool, spa, Wi-Fi hotspot, some pets allowed* ▤ *AE, D, DC, MC, V* ⊖ *BP.*

$$–$$$ **Martine Inn.** The glassed-in parlor and many guest rooms at this 1899 Mediterranean-style villa have stunning ocean views. The inn is furnished with exquisite antiques, and the owner's collection of classic race cars is on display in the patio area. In the rooms, thoughtful details such as robes, rocking chairs, and nightly turndown combine in luxuriant comfort. Lavish breakfasts—and winemaker dinners of up to 12 courses—are served on lace-clad tables set with china, crystal, and silver. Because of the fragility of the antiques, the inn is not suitable for children, except in the two-bedroom family suite. **Pros:** romantic; fancy breakfast; ocean views. **Cons:** not child-friendly; sits on a busy thoroughfare. ⊠ *255 Ocean View Blvd.* ☎ *831/373–3388 or 800/852–5588* ⊕ *www.martineinn.com* ⤶ *24 rooms* ⚲ *In-room: no a/c, refrigerator, no TV, Internet, Wi-Fi. In-hotel: Internet terminal, Wi-Fi hotspot* ▤ *AE, D, MC, V* ⊖ *BP.*

7

MONTEREY

2 mi southeast of Pacific Grove via Lighthouse Ave.; 2 mi north of Carmel-by-the-Sea via Hwy. 1.

Early in the 20th century Carmel Martin, the first mayor of the city of Monterey, saw a bright future for his town: "Monterey Bay is the one place where people can live without being disturbed by manufacturing and big factories. I am certain that the day is coming when this will be the most desirable place in the whole state of California." It seems that Mayor Martin was not far off the mark.

ESSENTIALS
Visitor Information Monterey County Convention & Visitors Bureau (☎ 877/666–8373 ⊕ www.seemonterey.com).

EXPLORING

❸ **A Taste of Monterey.** Without driving the back roads, you can taste the wines of up to 70 area vintners while taking in fantastic bay views. Purchase a few bottles and pick up a map and guide to the county's wineries and vineyards. ✉ *700 Cannery Row, Suite KK* ☎ *831/646–5446 or 888/646–5446* ⊕ *www.tastemonterey.com* 🍷 *Wine tastings $10–$15* ☉ *Daily 11–6.*

❽ **California's First Theatre.** This adobe began its life in 1846 as a saloon and lodging house for sailors. Four years later stage curtains were fashioned from army blankets, and some U.S. officers staged plays to the light of whale oil lamps. As of this writing, the building is undergoing restoration and is rarely open. ✉ *Monterey State Historic Park, Scott and Pacific Sts.* ☎ *831/649–7118* ⊕ *www.parks.ca.gov/mshp* 🆓 *Free* ☉ *Call for hrs.*

Cannery Row. When John Steinbeck published the novel *Cannery Row* in 1945, he immortalized a place of rough-edged working people. The waterfront street once was crowded with sardine canneries processing, at their peak, nearly 200,000 tons of the smelly silver fish a year. During the mid-1940s, however, the sardines disappeared from the bay, causing the canneries to close. Through the years the old tin-roof canneries have been converted into restaurants, art galleries, and malls with shops selling T-shirts, fudge, and plastic sea otters. Recent tourist development along the row has been more tasteful, however, and includes several stylish inns and hotels. ✉ *Cannery Row, between Prescott and David Aves.* ⊕ *www.canneryrow.com.*

❷ **Cannery Row IMAX Theatre.** Escape from the hubbub of Cannery Row into wild oceans, mysteries of outer space, and other 3-D adventures at Monterey's 290-seat, super-high-tech movie house, which opened in 2008. The entertainment space also includes a café and art gallery. ✉ *640 Wave St.* ☎ *831/372–4629* ⊕ *www.canneryrowimax.com* 🎟 *$10* ☉ *Films shown approximately every hr 11–9.*

❾ **Casa Soberanes.** A classic low-ceiling adobe structure built in 1842, this was once a Custom House guard's residence. Exhibits at the house survey life in Monterey from the era of Mexican rule to the present.

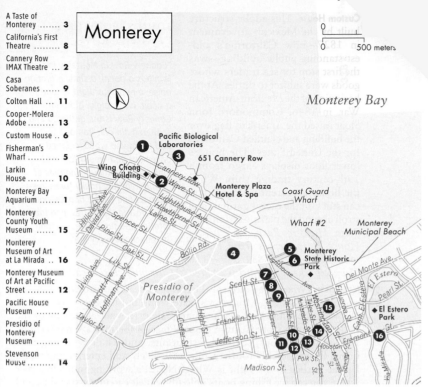

The building is currently closed, but feel free to stop at the peaceful rear garden, which has a lovely rose-covered arbor and sitting benches. ⊠ *Monterey State Historic Park, 336 Pacific St.* ☎ *831/649–7118* ⊕ *www.parks.ca.gov/mshp* ⊠ *Free.*

⓫ Colton Hall. A convention of delegates met in 1849 to draft the first state constitution at California's equivalent of Independence Hall. The stone building, which has served as a school, a courthouse, and the county seat, is a city-run museum furnished as it was during the constitutional convention. The extensive grounds outside the hall surround the Old Monterey Jail. ⊠ *500 block of Pacific St., between Madison and Jefferson Sts.* ☎ *831/646–5648* ⊕ *www.monterey.org/museum/coltonhall. html* ⊠ *Free* ۞ *Daily 10–4.*

⓭ Cooper-Molera Adobe. The restored 2-acre complex includes a house dating from the 1820s, a visitor center, a bookstore, and a large garden enclosed by a high adobe wall. The mostly Victorian-era antiques and memorabilia that fill the house provide a glimpse into the life of a prosperous early sea merchant's family. Although the house is currently closed, you can visit the Cooper Museum visitor center and pick up walking tour maps and walk around the grounds. ⊠ *Monterey State Historic Park, Polk and Munras Sts.* ☎ *831/649 7118 or 831/649– 7111* ⊕ *www.parks.ca.gov/mshp* ⊠ *Free* ۞ *Call for hrs.*

7

buse. This adobe structure
the Mexican government
—now California's old-
ling public building—was
stop for sea traders whose
ere subject to duties. At the
g of the Mexican-American
war, in 1846, Commodore John Sloat raised the American flag over the building and claimed California for the United States. The house's lower floor displays cargo from a 19th-century trading ship. While the house is currently closed, you can still visit the cactus gardens and stroll around the plaza. ⊠ *Monterey State Historic Park, 1 Custom House Plaza, across from Fisherman's Wharf* ☎ *831/649–7118* ⊕ *www.parks.ca.gov/mshp* ⊠ *Free* ☉ *Currently closed; call for hrs.*

JOHN STEINBECK'S CANNERY ROW

"Cannery Row in Monterey in California is a poem, a stink, a grating noise, a quality of light, a tone, a habit, a nostalgia, a dream. Cannery Row is the gathered and scattered, tin and iron and rust and splintered wood, chipped pavement and weedy lots and junk heaps, sardine canneries of corrugated iron, honky tonks, restaurants and whore houses, and little crowded groceries, and laboratories and flophouses." —John Steinbeck, Cannery Row

⑤ **Fisherman's Wharf.** The mournful barking of sea lions provides a steady soundtrack all along Monterey's waterfront, but the best way to actually view the whiskered marine mammals is to walk along one of the two piers across from Custom House Plaza. Fisherman's Wharf is lined with souvenir shops, seafood restaurants, and whale-watching tour boats. It's undeniably touristy, but still a lively and entertaining place. Up the harbor to the right is Wharf No. 2, a working municipal pier where you can see fishing boats unloading their catches to one side, and fishermen casting their lines into the water on the other. The pier has a couple of low-key restaurants, from whose seats lucky customers may spot otters and harbor seals. ⊠ *At end of Calle Principal* ☎ *831/649–6544* ⊕ *www.montereywharf.com.*

⑩ **Larkin House.** A veranda encircles the second floor of this architecturally significant two-story adobe built in 1835, whose design bears witness to the Mexican and New England influences on the Monterey style. The rooms are furnished with period antiques, many of them brought from New Hampshire by the building's namesake, Thomas O. Larkin, an early California statesman. The building is currently closed, but you can stroll the historic gardens and peek in the windows. ⊠ *Monterey State Historic Park, 464 Calle Principal, between Jefferson and Pacific Sts.* ☎ *831/649–7118* ⊕ *www.parks.ca.gov/mshp* ⊠ *Free* ☉ *Currently closed; call for hrs.*

① **Monterey Bay Aquarium.** The minute you hand over your ticket at this extraordinary aquarium you're surrounded by sea creatures; right at the entrance, you can see dozens of them swimming in a three-story-tall, sunlit kelp forest tank. The beauty of the exhibits here is that they are all designed to give a sense of what it's like to be in the water with the animals—sardines swim around your head in a circular tank, and jellyfish drift in and out of view in dramatically lighted spaces that suggest the ocean depths. A petting pool gives you a hands-on experience

Fodor's Choice
★

with bat rays, and the million-gallon Outer Bay tank shows the vast variety of creatures (from sharks to placid-looking turtles) that live in the eastern Pacific. A Splash Zone with 45 interactive bilingual exhibits opened in 2008: here, kids (and kids-at-heart) can commune with sea dragons, potbellied seahorses, and other fascinating creatures. The only drawback to the experience is that it must be shared with the throngs of people that crowd the place daily; most think it's worth it. To avoid the crowds, arrive as soon as the aquarium opens or visit after 2 PM, when field trip groups depart and youngsters head home for their naps. Weekend evenings in summer, the aquarium stays open later and is usually less crowded during the extended hours. ■TIP→ Reserve a lunch table at the aquarium's Portola Café, perched on ocean's edge. Otters and other sea creatures often frolic just outside the floor-to-ceiling windows. ✉ *886 Cannery Row* ☎ *831/648–4888, 866/963–9645 for advance tickets* ⊕ *www.montereybayaquarium.org* ✉ *$30* ☯ *Late May–June and early Sept., daily 9:30–6; July and Aug., weekdays 9:30–6, weekends 9:30–8; early Sept.–late May, daily 10–5.*

⑮ **Monterey County Youth Museum (MY Museum).** Monterey Bay comes to life from a child's perspective in this fun-filled, interactive indoor exploration center that opened in the heart of the historic district in late 2008. The seven exhibit galleries showcase the science and nature of the Big Sur coast, theater arts, Pebble Beach golf, and beaches. There's also a live performance theater, a creation station, a hospital emergency room, and an agriculture corner where kids follow artichokes, strawberries, and other fruits and veggies on their evolution from sprout to harvest to farmers' markets. ✉ *425 Washington St.* ☎ *831/649–6444* ⊕ *www.mymuseum.org* ✉ *$7* ☯ *Mon., Tues, and Thurs.–Sat. 10–5, Sun. noon–5.*

⑯ **Monterey Museum of Art at La Mirada.** Asian and European antiques fill this 19th-century adobe house. A newer 10,000-square-foot gallery space, designed by Charles Moore, houses Asian and California regional art. Outdoors are magnificent rose and rhododendron gardens. A single fee covers admission to the La Mirada and Pacific Street facilities of the Monterey Museum of Art. ✉ *720 Via Mirada, at Fremont St.* ☎ *831/372–3689* ⊕ *www.montereyart.org* ✉ *$5* ☯ *Wed.–Sat. 11–5, Sun. 1–4.*

⑰ **Monterey Museum of Art at Pacific Street.** Photographs by Ansel Adams and Edward Weston, as well as works by other artists who have spent time on the peninsula, are on display here. There's also a colorful collection of international folk art; the pieces range from Kentucky hearth brooms to Tibetan prayer wheels. A single fee covers admission to the Pacific Street and La Mirada facilities of the Monterey Museum of Art. ✉ *559 Pacific St., across from Colton Hall*

7

MONTEREY: FORMER CAPITAL OF CALIFORNIA

In 1602 Spanish explorer Sebastián Vizcaíno stepped ashore on a remote California peninsula. He named it after the viceroy of New Spain—Count de Monte Rey. Soon the Spanish built a military outpost, and the site was the capital of California until the state came under American rule.

Trained "seals" that perform in circuses are actually California sea lions, intelligent, social animals that live (and sleep) close together in groups.

☎ *831/372–5477* ⊕ *www.montereyart.org* ✉ *$5* ☉ *Wed.–Sat. 11–5, Sun. 1–4.*

Monterey State Historic Park. You can glimpse Monterey's early history in the well-preserved adobe buildings scattered along several city blocks. Far from being a hermetic period museum, the park facilities are an integral part of the day-to-day business life of the town—within some of the buildings are a store, a theater, and government offices. At some of the historic houses, the gardens (open daily 10 to 4) are worthy sights themselves. ■**TIP➜ At this writing, many buildings are closed and tours on hiatus due to state park budget cuts. Visit the Web site for up-to-date information.** ✉ *20 Custom House Plaza* ☎ *831/649–7118* ⊕ *www.parks. ca.gov/mshp* ✉ *Free* ☉ *Call for hrs.*

❼ Pacific House Museum. Once a hotel and saloon, this visitor center and museum now commemorates early-California life with gold-rush relics and photographs of old Monterey. The upper floor displays Native American artifacts, including gorgeous baskets and pottery. The museum is currently closed; call for current information. ✉ *Monterey State Historic Park, 10 Custom House Plaza* ☎ *831/649–7118* ⊕ *www. parks.ca.gov/mshp* ✉ *Free.*

❹ Presidio of Monterey Museum. This spot has been significant for centuries as a town, a fort, and the site of several battles, including the skirmish in which the pirate Hipoleto Bruchard conquered the Spanish garrison that stood here. Its first incarnation was as a Native American village for the Rumsien tribe; then it became known as the landing site for explorer Sebastián Vizcaíno in 1602, and father of the California missions, Father Serra, in 1770. The indoor museum tells the stories; the outdoor sites are marked with plaques. ⊠ *Corporal Ewing Rd., Presidio of Monterey* ☎ *831/646–3456* ⊕ *www.monterey.org/museum/pom/* 🔄 *Free* ☉ *Mon. 10–1, Thurs.–Sat. 10–4, Sun. 1–4.*

🄴 **Stevenson House.** This house was named in honor of author Robert Louis Stevenson, who boarded here briefly in a tiny upstairs room. Items from his family's estate furnish Stevenson's room; period-decorated chambers elsewhere in the house include a gallery of the author's memorabilia and a children's nursery stocked with Victorian toys and games. The house is currently closed; visit the Web site for up-to-date information on hours. ⊠ *Monterey State Historic Park, 530 Houston St.* ☎ *831/649–7118* ⊕ *www.parks.ca.gov/mshp* 🔄 *Free* ☉ *Currently closed; call for hrs.*

WHERE TO EAT

$$
SEAFOOD

✕ **Monterey's Fish House.** Casual yet stylish, and removed from the hubbub of the wharf, this always-packed seafood restaurant attracts locals and frequent visitors to the city. If the dining room is full, you can wait at the bar and savor deliciously plump oysters on the half shell. The bartenders and waitstaff will gladly advise you on the perfect wine to go with your poached, blackened, or oak-grilled seafood. ⊠ *2114 Del Monte Ave.* ☎ *831/373–4647* 🔄 *AE, D, MC, V* ☉ *No lunch weekends.*

$$$
AMERICAN
Fodor's Choice
★

✕ **Montrio Bistro.** This quirky, converted firehouse, with its rawhide walls and iron indoor trellises, has a wonderfully sophisticated menu. Chef Tony Baker uses organic produce and meats and sustainably sourced seafood to create imaginative dishes that reflect local agriculture, such as baby artichoke risotto and diver scallops served over a root vegetable puree, smoked bacon, Brussels sprouts, and a shellfish emulsion. Likewise, the wine list draws primarily on California, and many come from the Monterey area. ⊠ *414 Calle Principal* ☎ *831/648–8880* ⊕ *www.montrio.com* ⚱ *Reservations essential* 🔄 *AE, D, DC, MC, V* ☉ *No lunch.*

¢
AMERICAN

✕ **Old Monterey Café.** Breakfast here gets constant local raves. Its fame rests on familiar favorites in many incarnations: a dozen kinds of omelets, and pancakes from blueberry to cinnamon-raisin-pecan. The lunch and dinner menus have good soups, salads, and sandwiches, and this is a great place to relax with an afternoon cappuccino. ⊠ *489 Alvarado St.* ☎ *831/646–1021* ⊕ *www.cafemonterey.com* ⚱ *Reservations not accepted* 🔄 *AE, D, MC, V.*

$$
AMERICAN

✕ **Tarpy's Roadhouse.** Fun, dressed-up American favorites—a little something for everyone—are served in this renovated early-1900s stone farmhouse several miles outside town. The kitchen cranks out everything from Cajun-spiced prawns to meat loaf with marsala-mushroom gravy to grilled ribs and steaks. Eat indoors by a fireplace or outdoors in the courtyard. ⊠ *2999 Monterey–Salinas Hwy., Hwy. 68* ☎ *831/647–1444* ⊕ *www.tarpys.com* 🔄 *AE, D, DC, MC, V.*

WHERE TO STAY

$–$$

🔲 **Best Western Beach Resort Monterey.** With a great waterfront location about 2 mi north of town—with views of the bay and the city skyline—and a surprising array of amenities, this hotel is one of the best

7

values in town. A $5 million renovation transformed the nondescript rooms into modern getaways with platform beds and puffy duvets, flat-screen TVs, and fine linens. The grounds are pleasantly landscaped, and there's a large pool with a sunbathing area. **Pros:** on the beach; great value; family-friendly. **Cons:** several miles from major attractions; big-box mall neighborhood. ⊠ *2600 Sand Dunes Dr.* ☎ *831/394–3321 or 800/242–8627* ⊕ *www.montereybeachresort.com* ⤳ *196 rooms* ♿ *In-room: a/c, safe, refrigerator, Wi-Fi. In-hotel: restaurant, room service, bar, pool, gym, beachfront, laundry service, Internet terminal, Wi-Fi hotspot, parking (paid), some pets allowed* ▭ *AE, D, DC, MC, V.*

$$–$$$ 🏨 **InterContinental The Clement Monterey.** Spectacular bay views, assiduous
☼ service, a slew of upscale amenities, and a superb waterfront location next to the aquarium propelled this full-service luxury hotel to immediate stardom when it opened in 2008. The complex has several buildings on both sides of Cannery Row, with Craftsman-style exteriors and corrugated tin roofs. Natural wood, marble, and glass elements create a feeling of warmth and serenity in the spacious rooms, which include baths with soaking tubs and walk-in showers; many rooms have fireplaces and balconies. The VIP Kids Club provides programs in a well-supervised play space. Unusual artwork abounds in public spaces. **Pros:** a block from the aquarium; fantastic views from some rooms; great for families. **Cons:** a tad formal; not budget-friendly. ⊠ *750 Cannery Row* ☎ *831/375–4500* ⊕ *www.intercontinental.com/montereyic* ⤳ *192 rooms, 16 suites* ♿ *In-room: a/c, safe, refrigerator, Internet, Wi-Fi. In-hotel: restaurant, room service, bar, pool, gym, spa, children's programs (ages 4–12), laundry service, Internet terminal, Wi-Fi hotspot, some pets allowed* ▭ *AE, D, MC, V.*

¢–$ 🏨 **Monterey Bay Lodge.** Location (on the edge of Monterey's El Estero
★ Park) and superior amenities give this cheerful facility an edge over other motels in town. Lots of greenery, indoors and out, views over El Estero Lake, and a secluded courtyard with a heated pool are other pluses. **Pros:** within walking distance of beach and playground; quiet at night; good family choice. **Cons:** near busy boulevard. ⊠ *55 Camino Aguajito* ☎ *831/372–8057 or 800/558–1900* ⊕ *www.montereybaylodge.com* ⤳ *45 rooms, 2 suites* ♿ *In-room: a/c, safe, refrigerator, Internet, Wi-Fi. In-hotel: restaurant, pool, Wi-Fi hotspot, some pets allowed* ▭ *AE, D, DC, MC, V.*

$$$–$$$$ 🏨 **Monterey Plaza Hotel and Spa.** This hotel commands a waterfront location on Cannery Row, where you can see frolicking sea otters from the wide outdoor patio and many room balconies. The architecture blends early California and Mediterranean styles, and also echoes elements of the old cannery design. Meticulously maintained, the property has both simple and luxurious accommodations. On the top floor, the spa offers a full array of treatments, perfect after a workout in the penthouse fitness center. **Pros:** on the ocean; lots of amenities; attentive service. **Cons:** touristy area; heavy traffic. ⊠ *400 Cannery Row* ☎ *831/646–1700 or 800/334–3999* ⊕ *www.montereyplazahotel.com* ⤳ *280 rooms, 10 suites* ♿ *In-room: a/c, refrigerator, DVD, Internet, Wi-Fi. In-hotel: 3 restaurants, room service, bar, gym, spa, laundry service, Internet terminal, Wi-Fi hotspot* ▭ *AE, D, DC, MC, V.*

$$$–$$$$
Fodor's Choice
★
Old Monterey Inn. This three-story manor house was the home of Monterey's first mayor, and today it remains a private enclave within walking distance of downtown. Lush gardens are shaded by huge old trees and bordered by a creek. Rooms are individually decorated with tasteful antiques; many have fireplaces, and all have featherbeds. Those with private entrances have split doors; you can open the top half to let in cool air and the sound of birds. In the spa room, indulge in a massage or wrap in front of the fireplace. The extensive breakfast is delivered to the rooms, and wine, cheese, and cookies are served each afternoon in the parlor. **Pros:** gorgeous gardens; refined luxury; serene. **Cons:** must drive to attractions and sights; fills quickly. ⊠ *500 Martin St.* ☎ *831/375–8284 or 800/350–2344* ⊕ *www.oldmontereyinn.com* ⇆ *6 rooms, 3 suites, 1 cottage* ⚮ *In-room: no a/c, DVD (some), Internet, Wi-Fi. In-hotel: spa, Wi-Fi hotspot* ⊟ *MC, V* ❐ *BP.*

> ### THE FIRST ARTICHOKE QUEEN
>
> Castroville, a tiny town off Highway 1 between Monterey and Watsonville, produces about 95% of U.S. artichokes. Back in 1948, the town chose its first queen to preside during its Artichoke Festival—a beautiful young woman named Norma Jean Mortenson, who later changed her name to Marilyn Monroe.

¢–$
Quality Inn Monterey. This attractive motel has a friendly, country-inn feeling. Rooms are light and airy, some have fireplaces—and the price is right. **Pros:** indoor pool; bargain rates; cheerful innkeepers. **Cons:** street is busy during the day; some rooms are dark. ⊠ *1058 Munras Ave.* ☎ *831/372–3381 or 800/* ⊕ *www.qualityinnmonterey.com* ⇆ *55 rooms* ⚮ *In-room: a/c, refrigerator, Internet, Wi-Fi. In-hotel: pool* ⊟ *AE, D, DC, MC, V* ❐ *BP.*

$$–$$$
Spindrift Inn. This boutique hotel on Cannery Row has beach access and a rooftop garden that overlooks the water. Designed with traditional American style, spacious rooms have sitting areas, hardwood floors, fireplaces, and down comforters, among other pleasures. An afternoon wine and cheese hour takes place in the newly renovated lobby with a soaring four-story ceiling. This property caters to adults and does not welcome children. **Pros:** close to aquarium; steps from the beach; friendly staff. **Cons:** throngs of visitors outside; can be noisy; not good for families. ⊠ *652 Cannery Row* ☎ *831/646–8900 or 800/841–1879* ⊕ *www.spindriftinn.com* ⇆ *45 rooms* ⚮ *In-room: no a/c, refrigerator, DVD, Wi-Fi. In-hotel: Internet terminal, Wi-Fi hotspot* ⊟ *AE, D, DC, MC, V* ❐ *CP.*

THE ARTS

★ **Dixieland Monterey** (☎ *831/675–0298 or 888/349–6879* ⊕ *www. dixieland-monterey.com*), held on the first full weekend of March, presents traditional jazz bands at waterfront venues on the harbor.

The **Monterey Bay Blues Festival** (☎ *831/394–2652* ⊕ *www.montereyblues. com*) draws blues fans to the Monterey Fairgrounds the last weekend in June. The **Monterey Jazz Festival** (☎ *831/373–3366* ⊕ *www.*

montereyjazzfestival.org), the world's oldest, attracts jazz and blues greats from around the world to the Monterey Fairgrounds on the third full weekend of September.

Monterey Bay Theatrefest (☎ *831/622–0100*) presents free outdoor performances at Custom House Plaza on weekend afternoons and evenings from late June to mid-July. The **Bruce Ariss Wharf Theater** (✉ *One Fisherman's Wharf* ☎ *831/372–1373*) focuses on American musicals past and present.

SPORTS AND THE OUTDOORS

Throughout most of the year, the Monterey Bay area is a haven for those who love tennis, golf, surfing, fishing, biking, hiking, scuba diving, and kayaking. In the rainy winter months, when the waves grow larger, adventurous surfers flock to the water. The **Monterey Bay National Marine Sanctuary** (☎ *831/647–4201* ⊕ *montereybay.noaa.gov*), home to mammals, seabirds, fishes, invertebrates, and plants, encompasses a 276-mi shoreline and 5,322 square mi of ocean. Ringed by beaches and campgrounds, it's a place for kayaking, whale-watching, scuba diving, and other water sports.

BICYCLING

For bicycle and surrey rentals, visit **Bay Bikes** (✉ *585 Cannery Row* ☎ *831/655–2453* ⊕ *www.baybikes.com*). **Adventures by the Sea, Inc.** (✉ *299 Cannery Row* ☎ *831/372–1807 or 831/648–7236* ⊕ *www.adventuresbythesea.com*) rents tandem and standard bicycles.

FISHING

Randy's Fishing and Whale Watching Trips (✉ *66 Fisherman's Wharf* ☎ *831/372–7440 or 800/251–7440* ⊕ *www.randysfishingtrips.com*), a small family-run business, has been operating since 1949.

SCUBA DIVING

Monterey Bay waters never warm to the temperatures of their Southern California counterparts (the warmest they get is low 60s), but that's one reason why the marine life here is among the world's most diverse. The staff at **Aquarius Dive Shop** (✉ *2040 Del Monte Ave.* ☎ *831/375–1933, 831/657–1020 diving conditions* ⊕ *www.aquariusdivers.com*) gives diving lessons and tours, and rents equipment. Their scuba-conditions information line is updated daily.

WALKING

From Custom House Plaza, you can walk along the coast in either direction on the 29-mi-long **Monterey Bay Coastal Trail** (☎ *831/372–3196* ⊕ *www.mtycounty.com/pgs-parks/bike-path.html*) for spectacular views of the sea. It runs all the way from north of Monterey to Pacific Grove, with sections continuing around Pebble Beach.

WHALE-WATCHING

Thousands of gray whales pass close by the Monterey Coast on their annual migration between the Bering Sea and Baja California. The gigantic creatures are sometimes visible through binoculars from shore, but a whale-watching cruise is the best way to get a close look at these magnificent mammals. The migration south takes place from December through March; January is prime viewing time. The whales migrate north from March through June. In addition, some 2,000 blue whales and 600 humpbacks pass the coast and are easily spotted in late summer and early fall.

★ **Monterey Bay Whale Watch** (✉ *84 Fisherman's Wharf* ☎ *831/375–4658* ⊕ *www.montereybaywhalewatch.com*), which operates out of the Monterey Bay Whale Watch Center at Fisherman's Wharf, gives three-to five-hour tours led by marine biologists.

Monterey Whale Watching (✉ *96 Fisherman's Wharf #1* ☎ *831/372–2203 or 800/979–3370* ⊕ *www.montereywhalewatching.com*) provides three tours a day on a 150-passenger high-speed cruiser and a large 75-foot boat.

AROUND THE BAY

As Highway 1 follows the curve of the bay between Monterey and Santa Cruz, it passes through a rich agricultural zone. Opening right onto the bay, where the Salinas and Pajaro rivers drain into the Pacific, a broad valley brings together fertile soil, an ideal climate, and a good water supply to create optimum growing conditions for crops such as strawberries, artichokes, Brussels sprouts, and broccoli. Several beautiful beaches line this part of the coast.

MOSS LANDING

17 mi north of Monterey on Hwy. 1.

Moss Landing is not much more than a couple blocks of cafés and antiques shops plus a busy fishing port, but therein lies its charm. It's a fine place to stop for lunch and get a dose of nature.

ESSENTIALS

Visitor Information Monterey County Convention & Visitors Bureau (⬦ *Box 1770, Monterey 93940* ☎ *877/666–8373* ⊕ *www.seemonterey.com*).

EXPLORING

★ In the **Elkhorn Slough National Estuarine Research Reserve** (✉ *1700 Elkhorn Rd., Watsonville* ☎ *831/728–2822* ⊕ *www.elkhornslough.org* ⬦ *$2.50* ☼ *Wed.–Sun. 9–5*), 1,400 acres of tidal flats and salt marshes form a complex environment that supports some 300 species of birds. A walk or a kayak trip along the meandering waterways and wetlands can reveal hawks, white-tailed kites, owls, herons, and egrets. Sea otters, sharks, rays, and many other animals also live or visit here. On weekends guided walks from the visitor center to the heron rookery begin at 10 and 1. Although the reserve lies across the town line in Watsonville, you reach its entrance through Moss Landing.

Aboard a 27-foot pontoon boat operated by **Elkhorn Slough Safari** (✉ *Moss Landing Harbor* ☎ *831/633–5555* ⊕ *www.elkhornslough.com*), a naturalist leads an up-close look at wetlands denizens. Advance reservations are required for the two-hour tours ($32).

7

SALINAS AND JOHN STEINBECK'S LEGACY

Salinas (17 mi east of Monterey), a hard-working city surrounded by vegetable fields, honors the memory and literary legacy of John Steinbeck, its most well-known native, at the modern **National Steinbeck Center** (⊠ *1 Main St., 17 mi east of Monterey via Hwy. 68, Salinas* ☎ *831/796–3833, 831/775–4721 museum store* ⊕ *www.steinbeck. org* ⊠ *$11* ⊘ *Daily 10–5*). Exhibits document the life of the Pulitzer- and Nobel-prize winner and the history of the local communities that inspired Steinbeck novels such as *The Grapes of Wrath*. Highlights include reproductions of the green pickup-camper from *Travels with Charley* and of the bunkroom from *Of Mice and Men*; you can watch actors read from Steinbeck's books on video screens throughout the museum. The museum is the centerpiece of the revival of Old Town Salinas, where handsome turn-of-the-20th-century stone buildings have been renovated and filled with shops and restaurants. Two blocks from the National Steinbeck Center is the author's Victorian birthplace, **Steinbeck House** (⊠ *132 Central Ave.* ☎ *831/424–2735*). It operates as a lunch spot Monday through Saturday and displays some Steinbeck memorabilia.

WHERE TO EAT

$ ✕ **Phil's Fish Market & Eatery.** Exquisitely fresh, simply prepared seafood
SEAFOOD   (try the cioppino) is on the menu at this warehouselike restaurant on the harbor; all kinds of glistening fish are on offer at the market in the front. ■TIP➔ Phil's Snack Shack, a tiny sandwich-and-smoothie joint, serves quicker meals at the north end of town. ⊠ *7600 Sandholdt Rd.* ☎ *831/633–2152* ▤ *AE, D, DC, MC, V.*

WATSONVILLE

7 mi north of Moss Landing on Hwy. 1.

If ever a city was built on strawberries, Watsonville is it. Produce has long driven the economy here, and this is where the county fair takes place each September.

⟳   One feature of the Santa Cruz County Fairgrounds is the **Agricultural History Project,** which preserves the history of farming in the Pajaro Valley. In the Codiga Center and Museum you can examine antique tractors and milking machines, peruse an exhibit on the era when Watsonville was the "frozen food capitol of the West," and watch experts restore farm implements and vehicles. ⊠ *2601 E. Lake Ave.* ☎ *831/724–5898* ⊕ *www.aghistoryproject.org* ⊠ *$2 suggested donation* ⊘ *Thurs.–Sun. noon–4.*

⟳   Every Labor Day weekend, aerial performers execute elaborate aerobatics at the **Watsonville Fly-in & Air Show.** More than 300 classic, experimental, and military aircraft are on display; concerts and other events fill three days. ⊠ *Watsonville Municipal Airport, 100 Aviation Way* ☎ *831/763–5600* ⊕ *www.watsonvilleflyin.org* ⊠ *$15.*

SAN JUAN BAUTISTA

About as close to early-19th-century California as you can get, San Juan Bautista (15 mi east of Watsonville on Highway 156) has been protected from development since 1933, when much of it became a state park. Small antiques shops and restaurants occupy the Old West and art-deco buildings that line 3rd Street.

The wide green plaza of San Juan Bautista State Historic Park is ringed by 18th- and 19th-century buildings, many of them open to the public. The cemetery of the long, low, colonnaded mission church contains the unmarked graves of more than 4,300 Native American converts Nearby is an adobe home furnished with Spanish-colonial antiques, a hotel frozen in the 1860s, a blacksmith shop, a stable, a pioneer cabin, and a jailhouse.

The first Saturday of each month, costumed volunteers engage in quilting bees, tortilla making, and other frontier activities. ⊕ *www.san-juan-bautista.ca.us.*

APTOS

7 mi north of Watsonville on Hwy. 1.

Backed by a redwood forest and facing the sea, downtown Aptos—known as Aptos Village—is a place of wooden walkways and false-fronted shops. Antiques dealers cluster along Trout Gulch Road, off Soquel Drive east of Highway 1.

ESSENTIALS

Visitor Information Aptos Chamber of Commerce (✉ *7605-A Old Dominion Ct., Aptos* ☎ *831/688–1467* ⊕ *www.aptoschamber.com*).

EXPLORING

Sandstone bluffs tower above **Seacliff State Beach** (✉ *201 State Park Dr.* ☎ *831/685–6442* ⊕ *www.parks.ca.gov* 🖘 *$10 per vehicle*), a favorite of locals. You can fish off the pier, which leads out to a sunken World War I tanker ship built of concrete.

WHERE TO EAT AND STAY

$$$
MEDITERRANEAN
★
✕ **Bittersweet Bistro.** A large old tavern with cathedral ceilings houses this popular bistro, where chef-owner Thomas Vinolus draws culinary inspiration from the Mediterranean. The menu changes seasonally, but regular highlights include pan-seared Monterey Bay petrale sole, seafood puttanesca (pasta with a spicy sauce of garlic, tomatoes, anchovies, and olives), and fire-roasted pork tenderloin. The decadent chocolate desserts are not to be missed. You can order many of the entrées in small or regular portions. Lunch is available to go from the express counter. ✉ *787 Rio Del Mar Blvd.* ☎ *831/662–9799* ⊕ *www.bittersweetbistro.com* 🖃 *AE, MC, V.*

$$
🕭
🗓 **Best Western Seacliff Inn.** A favorite lair of families and business travelers, this 6-acre Best Western near Seacliff State Beach is more resort than motel. Six two-story lodge buildings encircle a large pool and lush gardens with a koi pond and waterfall—ask for a room in a building away from the busy restaurant and bar, which can get noisy at night. The

decent-size rooms sport a fresh—if somewhat generic—contemporary look. **Pros:** walking distance from the beach; family-friendly; includes full breakfast. **Cons:** close to the freeway; occasional nighttime bar noise. ⊠ *7500 Old Dominion Ct.* ☎ *831/688–7300 or 800/367–2003* ⊕ *www.seacliffinn.com* ↷ *139 rooms, 10 suites* ♧ *In-room: a/c, refrigerator, Internet. In-hotel: restaurant, room service, bar, pool, gym, laundry facilities, laundry service, Wi-Fi hotspot* ⊟ *AE, D, MC, V* ⏏⏐ *BP.*

$$ ⊡ **Flora Vista.** Multicolor fields of flowers, strawberries, and veggies unfold in every direction at this luxury neo-Georgian inn set on two serene acres in a rural community just south of Aptos; Sand Dollar Beach is just a short walk away. Innkeepers Deanna and Ed Boos transformed the 1867 home, a replica of Abe Lincoln's Springfield farmhouse, adding modern conveniences like Wi-Fi and spa tubs while retaining the house's original redwood floors and country charm. Guests wake to a full breakfast—which might include the neighbor's strawberries—and enjoy a wine and cheese spread in the late afternoon. Stroll through the eclectic gardens (something's always in bloom) or play tennis on one of the two courts. The inn is on the Pacific Coast Bike Route and welcomes cyclists. **Pros:** super-private; near the beach; flowers everywhere. **Cons:** no restaurants or nightlife within walking distance; not a good place for kids. ⊠ *1258 San Andreas Rd., La Selva Beach* ☎ *831/724–8663 or 877/753–5672* ⊕ *www.floravistainn.com* ↷ *5 rooms* ♧ *In-room: no a/c, Wi-Fi. In-hotel: tennis courts, Wi-Fi hotspot* ⊟ *AE, MC, V* ⏏⏐ *BP.*

$$$$ ⊡ **Seascape Beach Resort.** On a bluff overlooking Monterey Bay, Seascape is a full-fledged resort that makes it easy to unwind. The spacious suites sleep from two to six people; each has a kitchenette and fireplace, and many have ocean-view patios with barbecue grills. Treat yourself to an in-room manicure, facial, or massage, or a bonfire with s'mores on the beach. **Pros:** time-share-style apartments; access to miles of beachfront; superb views. **Cons:** far from city life; most bathrooms are small. ⊠ *1 Seascape Resort Dr.* ☎ *831/688–6800 or 800/929–7727* ⊕ *www.seascaperesort.com* ↷ *285 suites* ♧ *In-room: no a/c, kitchen (some), DVD, Internet, Wi-Fi. In-hotel: restaurant, room service, pools, gym, spa, beachfront, children's programs (ages 5–10), laundry service, Internet terminal, Wi-Fi hotspot* ⊟ *AE, D, DC, MC, V.*

CAPITOLA AND SOQUEL

4 mi northwest of Aptos on Hwy. 1.

On the National Register of Historic places as California's first seaside resort town, the village of Capitola has been in a holiday mood since the late 1800s. Its walkable downtown is jam-packed with casual eateries, surf shops, and ice-cream parlors. Inland, across Highway 1, antiques shops line Soquel Drive in the town of Soquel. Wineries dot the Santa Cruz Mountains beyond.

ESSENTIALS

Visitor Information Capitola-Soquel Chamber of Commerce (⊠ *716-G Capitola Ave., Capitola* ☎ *831/475–6522* ⊕ *www.capitolachamber.com*).

EXPLORING

New Brighton State Beach (✉ *1500 State Park Dr.* ☎ *831/464–6330* ⊕ *www.parks.ca.gov* 🖃 *$10 per vehicle*), once the site of a Chinese fishing village, is now a popular surfing and camping spot. Its Pacific Migrations Visitor Center traces the history of the Chinese and other peoples who settled around Monterey Bay, as well as the migratory patterns of the area's wildlife, such as monarch butterflies and gray whales. ■**TIP→** New Brighton Beach connects with Seacliff Beach, and at low tide you can walk or run along this scenic stretch of sand for nearly 16 mi south (you might have to wade through a few creeks). The 1½-mi stroll from New Brighton to Seacliff's cement ship is a local favorite.

WHERE TO EAT AND STAY

¢
SEAFOOD
☺
✗ **Carpo's.** Locals line up in droves at Carpo's counter, hankering for mouthwatering, casual family meals. The menu leans heavily toward seafood, but also includes burgers, salads, and steaks. Favorites include the fishermen's baskets of fresh battered snapper, calamari and prawns, seafood kabobs, and homemade olallieberry pie. Nearly everything here costs less than $10. Go early to beat the crowds, or be prepared to wait for a table. ✉ *2400 Porter St.* ☎ *831/476–6260* ⊕ *www.carposrestaurant.com* ▭ *D, MC, V.*

¢
CAFÉ
☺
✗ **Gayle's Bakery & Rosticceria.** Whether you're in the mood for an orange-olallieberry muffin, a wild rice and chicken salad, or tri-tip on garlic toast, this bakery-cum-deli's varied menu is likely to satisfy. Munch your chocolate macaroon on the shady patio or dig into the daily blue-plate dinner—there's a junior blue plate for the kids—amid the whirl inside. ✉ *504 Bay Ave.* ☎ *831/462–1200* ⊕ *www.gaylesbakery.com* ▭ *AE, MC, V.*

$$
AMERICAN
✗ **Michael's on Main.** Classic comfort food with a creative gourmet twist, reasonable prices, and attentive service draw a lively crowd of locals to this upscale-but-casual creek-side eatery. Chef Michael Clark's commitment to locally sustainable fisheries and farmers has earned him community accolades and infuses dishes with the inimitable taste that comes from using fresh local ingredients. The menu changes seasonally, but you can always count on finding such home-style dishes as house-smoked baby back pork ribs and garlic fries as well as unusual entrées like pistachio-crusted salmon with mint vinaigrette. For a quiet conversation spot, ask for a table on the romantic patio overlooking the creek. The busy bar area hosts Wednesday karaoke nights and live music Thursday through Saturday. ✉ *2591 Main St.* ☎ *831/479–9777* ⊕ *www.michaelsonmain.net* ▭ *AE, D, MC, V* ☾ *Closed Mon.*

$$$ ✕ **Shadowbrook**. To get to this romantic spot overlooking Soquel Creek,
CONTINENTAL you can take a cable car or walk the stairs down a steep, fern-lined bank beside a running waterfall. Dining room options include the rooftop Redwood Room, the wood-paneled Wine Cellar, and the airy, glass-enclosed Garden Room. Prime rib and grilled seafood are the stars of the simple menu. A cheaper menu of light entrées is available in the lounge. ✉ *1750 Wharf Rd.* ☎ *831/475–1511 or 800/975–1511* ⊕ *www.shadowbrook-capitola.com* ▭ *AE, D, DC, MC, V* ☺ *No lunch.*

$$$–$$$$ 📷 **Inn at Depot Hill**. This inventively designed B&B in a former rail depot sees itself as a link to the era of luxury train travel. Each double room or suite, complete with fireplace and featherbeds, is inspired by a different destination—Italy's Portofino, France's Côte d'Azur, Japan's Kyoto. One suite is decorated like a Pullman car for a railroad baron. Some accommodations have private patios with hot tubs. This is a great place for an adults-only weekend. **Pros:** short walk to beach and village; historic charm; excellent service. **Cons:** fills quickly; hot tub conversation on the patio may irk second-floor guests. ✉ *250 Monterey Ave.* ☎ *831/462–3376 or 800/572–2632* ⊕ *www.innatdepothill.com* ⇝ *8 rooms, 4 suites* ⚲ *In-room: no a/c, Wi-Fi. In-hotel: Wi-Fi hotspot* ▭ *AE, D, MC, V.*

SANTA CRUZ

5 mi west of Capitola on Hwy. 1; 48 mi north of Monterey on Hwy. 1.

The big city on this stretch of the California coast, Santa Cruz (pop. 57,500) is less manicured than Carmel or Monterey. Long known for its surfing and its amusement-filled beach boardwalk, the town is a mix of grand Victorian-era homes and rinky-dink motels. The opening of the University of California campus in the 1960s swung the town sharply to the left, and the counterculture more or less lives on here. At the same time, the revitalized downtown and an insane real-estate market reflect the city's proximity to Silicon Valley and to a growing wine country in the surrounding mountains.

ESSENTIALS

Visitor Information Santa Cruz County Conference and Visitors Council (✉ *303 Water St. Santa Cruz* ☎ *831/425–1234 or 800/833–3494* ⊕ *www.santacruzcounty.travel*).

EXPLORING

🕭 Santa Cruz has been a seaside resort since the mid-19th century. Along one end of the broad, south-facing beach, the **Santa Cruz Beach Boardwalk** has entertained holidaymakers for almost as long—it celebrated its 100th anniversary in 2007. Its Looff carousel and classic wooden Giant Dipper roller coaster, both dating from the early 1900s, are surrounded by high-tech thrill rides and easygoing kiddie rides with ocean views. Video and arcade games, a mini-golf course, and a laser-tag arena pack one gigantic building, which is open daily even if the rides aren't running. You have to pay to play, but you can wander the entire boardwalk for free while sampling delicacies such as corn dogs and chowder fries.

✉ *Along Beach St.* ☎ *831/423–5590 or 831/426–7433* ⊕ *www. beachboardwalk.com* 💲 *$30 day pass for unlimited rides, or pay per ride* ☉ *Apr.–early Sept., daily; early Sept.–late May, weekends, weather permitting; call for hrs.*

☾ Jutting half a mile into the ocean near one end of the Santa Cruz Beach Boardwalk, the **Santa Cruz Municipal Wharf** (✉ *Beach St., at Pacific Ave.* ☎ *831/420–6025* ⊕ *www.santacruzwharf.com*) is topped with seafood restaurants; souvenir shops; and outfitters offering bay cruises, fishing trips, and boat rentals. A salty sound track drifts up from under the wharf, where barking sea lions lounge in heaps on crossbeams.

West Cliff Drive winds along the top of an oceanfront bluff from the municipal wharf to Natural Bridges State Beach. It's a spectacular drive, but it's much more fun to walk, blade, or bike the paved path that parallels the road. Groups of surfers bob and swoosh in Monterey Bay at several points near the foot of the bluff, especially at a break known as Steamer Lane. Named for a surfer who died here in 1965, nearby Mark Abbott Memorial Lighthouse stands at Point Santa Cruz, the cliff's major promontory. From here you can watch pinnipeds hang out, sunbathe, and frolic on Seal Rock.

★ The **Santa Cruz Surfing Museum**, inside the Mark Abbott Memorial Lighthouse, traces local surfing history back to the early 20th century. Historical photographs show old-time surfers, and a display of boards includes rarities such as a heavy redwood plank predating the fiberglass era and the remains of a modern board chomped by a great white shark. Surfer-docents are on site to talk about the old days. ✉ *701 W. Cliff Dr.* ☎ *831/420–6289* ⊕ *www.santacruzsurfingmuseum.org* 💲 *$2 suggested donation* ☉ *Sept.–June, Thurs.–Mon. noon–4; July and Aug., Weds.–Mon. 10–5.*

☾ At the end of West Cliff Drive lies **Natural Bridges State Beach**, a stretch of soft sand edged with tide pools and sea-sculpted rock bridges. ■TIP→ From October to early March a colony of monarch butterflies roosts in a eucalyptus grove. ✉ *2531 W. Cliff Dr.* ☎ *831/423–4609* ⊕ *www. parks.ca.gov* 💲 *Beach free, parking $10* ☉ *Daily 8 AM–sunset. Visitor center Oct.–Feb., daily 10–4; Mar.–Sept., weekends 10–4.*

☾ **Seymour Marine Discovery Center**, part of Long Marine Laboratory at UCSC's Institute of Marine Sciences, looks more like a research facility than a slick aquarium. Interactive exhibits demonstrate how scientists study the ocean, and the aquarium displays creatures of particular interest to marine biologists. The 87-foot blue whale skeleton is one of the world's largest. ✉ *100 Shaffer Rd., off Delaware St. west of Natural Bridges State Beach* ☎ *831/459–3800* ⊕ *seymourcenter.ucsc.edu* 💲 *$6* ☉ *Tues.–Sat. 10–5, Sun. noon–5.*

7

In the Cultural Preserve of **Wilder Ranch State Park** you can visit the homes, barns, workshops, and bunkhouse of a 19th-century dairy farm. Nature has reclaimed most of the ranch land, and native plants and wildlife have returned to the 7,000 acres of forest, grassland, canyons, estuaries, and beaches. Hike, bike, or ride horseback on miles of ocean-view trails. ⊠ *Hwy. 1, 1 mi north of Santa Cruz* ☎ *831/426–0505 Interpretive Center, 831/423–9703 trail information* ⊕ *www.parks.ca.gov* ⊠ *Parking $10* ☉ *Daily 8* AM*–sunset.*

When you've had your fill of the city's beaches and waters, take a stroll in downtown Santa Cruz, especially on **Pacific Avenue** between Laurel and Water streets. Vintage boutiques and mountain sports stores, sushi bars and Mexican restaurants, day spas, and nightclubs keep the main drag and the surrounding streets hopping mid-morning until late evening.

On the northern fringes of downtown, **Santa Cruz Mission State Historic Park** preserves the site of California's 12th Spanish mission, built in the 1790s and destroyed by an earthquake in 1857. A museum in a restored 1791 adobe and a half-scale replica of the mission church are part of the complex. ⊠ *144 School St.* ☎ *831/425–5849* ⊕ *www.parks.ca.gov* ⊠ *Free* ☉ *Thurs.–Sat. 10–4.*

Hokey tourist trap or genuine scientific enigma? Since 1940, curious throngs baffled by the **Mystery Spot** have made it one of the most visited attractions in Santa Cruz. The laws of gravity and physics don't appear to apply in this tiny patch of redwood forest, where balls roll uphill and people stand on a slant. Advance online tickets ($6) are recommended for weekend and holiday visits. ⊠ *465 Mystery Spot Rd.* ☎ *831/423–8897* ⊕ *www.mysteryspot.com* ⊠ *$5 on site, $6 in advance, parking $5* ☉ *Late May–early Sept., daily 9–7, early Sept.–late May, weekdays 10–5, weekends 9–5.*

The modern 2,000-acre campus of the **University of California at Santa Cruz** nestles in the forested hills above town. Its sylvan setting, sweeping ocean vistas, and redwood architecture make the university worth a visit. Campus tours, offered several times daily (reserve in advance), offer a glimpse of college life and campus highlights. They run about an hour and 45 minutes and combine moderate walking with shuttle transport. Half a mile beyond the main campus entrance, the **UCSC Arboretum** (⊠ *1156 High St.* ☎ *831/427–2998* ⊕ *www2.ucsc.edu/ arboretum* ⊠ *$5* ☉ *Daily 9–5, guided tours Sat. at 11*) is a stellar collection of gardens arranged by geography. A walking path leads through areas dedicated to the plants of California, Australia, New Zealand, and South Africa. ⊠ *Main entrance at Bay and High Sts.* ☎ *831/459–0111* ⊕ *www.ucsc.edu.*

OFF THE
BEATEN
PATH

★ **Santa Cruz Mountains.** Highway 9 heads northeast from Santa Cruz into hills densely timbered with massive coastal redwoods. The road winds through the lush San Lorenzo Valley, past hamlets consisting of a few cafés, antiques shops, and old-style tourist cabins. Here, residents of the hunting-and-fishing persuasion coexist with hardcore flower-power survivors and wannabes. Along Highway 9 and its side roads are about a dozen **wineries,** most notably Bonny Doon Vineyard, Organic

Wineworks, and David Bruce Winery. ■ **TIP→** The Santa Cruz Mountains Winegrowers Association (⊕ www.scmwa.com) distributes a wine-touring map at many lodgings and attractions around Santa Cruz.

WHERE TO EAT

$–$$ ✕ **Crow's Nest.** A local favorite since 1969, this classic California beach-

SEAFOOD side eatery sits right on the water in Santa Cruz Harbor. Vintage surf-

★ boards and local surf photography line the walls in the main dining room; nearly every table overlooks the sand and surf. Seafood and steaks, served with local veggies, dominate the menu; favorite appetizers include the chilled shrimp-stuffed artichoke and crispy tempura prawns, served with rice pilaf. No need to pile high on your first trip to the endless salad bar—you can return as often as you like. For sweeping ocean views and more casual fare (think fish tacos and burgers), head upstairs to the Breakwater Bar & Grill. Live entertainment several days a week makes for a dynamic atmosphere year-round. ⊠ *2218 E. Cliff Dr.* ☎ *831/476–4560* ⊕ *www.crowsnest-santacruz.com* ▭ *AE, D, DC, MC, V.*

$$ ✕ **Gabriella Café.** The work of local artists hangs on the walls of this

ITALIAN petite, romantic café in a tile-roof cottage. Featuring organic produce from area farms, the seasonal Italian menu has offered steamed mussels, braised lamb shank, and grilled portobello mushrooms. ⊠ *910 Cedar St.* ☎ *831/457–1677* ⊕ *www.gabriellacafe.com* ▭ *AE, D, MC, V.*

$$$ ✕ **La Posta.** Locals and tourists alike cram into La Posta's cozy, modern-

ITALIAN rustic dining room, lured by authentic Italian fare made with fresh local produce. Near everything is house-made, from pizzas and breads baked in the brick oven to pasta and vanilla bean gelato (eggs come from a chicken coop out back). The seasonal menu changes often, but always includes flavorful dishes with a Santa Cruz flair, like fried artichokes, ravioli filled with crab, chicken with Brussels sprouts, or sautéed fish, caught sustainably from local waters. Come Sunday for a lively, family-style, fixed-price dinner—four courses for just $30. ⊠ *538 Seabright Ave.* ☎ *831/457–2782* ▭ *AE, MC, V* ☉ *Closed Mon. No lunch.*

$$$ ✕ **Oswald.** Sophisticated yet unpretentious European-inspired Califor-

CONTINENTAL nia cooking is the order of the day at this intimate and stylish bistro.

★ The menu changes seasonally, but might include such items as perfectly prepared sherry-steamed mussels or sautéed duck breast. Sit at the slick marble bar and order a creative concoction like bourbon mixed with local apple and lemon juices or gin with cucumber and ginger beer, or choose from a range of wines and spirits. ⊠ *121 Soquel Ave., at Front St.* ☎ *831/423–7427* ⊕ *www.oswaldrestaurant.com* ▭ *AE, D, DC, MC, V* ☉ *Closed Mon. No lunch weekends.*

$ ✕ **Seabright Brewery.** Great burgers, big salads, and stellar microbrews

AMERICAN make this a favorite hangout in the youthful Seabright neighborhood east of downtown. Sit outside on the large patio or inside at a comfortable, spacious booth; both are popular with families. ⊠ *519 Seabright Ave.* ☎ *831/426–2739* ⊕ *www.seabrightbrewery.com* ▭ *AE, MC, V.*

$$ ✕ **Soif.** Wine reigns at this sleek bistro and wine shop that takes its name

MEDITERRANEAN from the French word for thirst. The lengthy list includes selections from near and far, dozens of which you can order by the taste or glass.

7

Infused with the tastes of the Mediterranean, small plates and mains are served at the copper-top bar, the big communal table, and private tables. A jazz combo or solo pianist play some evenings. ⊠ *105 Walnut Ave.* ☏ *831/423–2020* ⊕ *www.soifwine.com* ⊟ *AE, MC, V* ⊘ *No lunch.*

¢   ✗ **Zachary's.** This noisy café filled with students and families defines

AMERICAN   the funky essence of Santa Cruz. It also dishes up great breakfasts: stay simple with sourdough pancakes, or go for Mike's Mess—eggs scrambled with bacon, mushrooms, and home fries, then topped with sour cream, melted cheese, and fresh tomatoes. ■**TIP**➜ If you arrive after 9 AM, expect a long wait for a table; lunch is a shade calmer, but closing time is 2:30 PM. ⊠ *819 Pacific Ave.* ☏ *831/427–0646* ⟡ *Reservations not accepted* ⊟ *D, MC, V* ⊘ *Closed Mon. No dinner.*

WHERE TO STAY

$$ ⊞ **Babbling Brook Inn.** Though it's smack in the middle of Santa Cruz, this B&B has lush gardens, a running stream, and tall trees that make you feel like you're in a secluded wood. All rooms have fireplaces (though a few are electric) and featherbeds; most have private patios. Complimentary wine, cheese, and fresh-baked cookies are available in the afternoon. **Pros:** close to UCSC; walking distance from downtown shops; woodsy feel. **Cons:** near a high school; some rooms are close to a busy street. ⊠ *1025 Laurel St.* ☏ *831/427–2437 or 800/866–1131* ⊕ *www. babblingbrookinn.com* ⟲ *11 rooms, 2 suites* ⟐ *In-room: no a/c, Wi-Fi. In-hotel: Wi-Fi hotspot* ⊟ *AE, D, DC, MC, V* ⊠⊙ *BP.*

$$–$$$ ⊞ **Chaminade Resort & Spa.** A full-on renovation of the entire property, completed in 2009, sharpened this hilltop resort's look, enhanced its amenities, and qualified it for regional green certification. Secluded on 300 acres of redwood and eucalyptus forest with hiking trails, the mission-style complex commands expansive views of Monterey Bay. Guest rooms are furnished in a modern Spanish style, with dark wood, deep colors, and patterned fabrics; some have private patios or decks. The spa employs all-natural products in its complete menu of body and beauty treatments. **Pros:** far from city life; spectacular property; ideal spot for romance and rejuvenation. **Cons:** must drive to attractions and sights; near major hospital. ⊠ *1 Chaminade La.* ☏ *800/283–6569* ⊕ *www.chaminade.com* ⟲ *112 rooms, 44 suites* ⟐ *In-room: a/c, safe, refrigerator (some), Internet, Wi-Fi. In-hotel: 2 restaurants, bar, room service, tennis courts, pool, gym, spa, laundry service, Internet terminal, Wi-Fi hotspot, some pets allowed* ⊟ *AE, D, DC, MC, V.*

¢   ⊞ **Harbor Inn.** Family-run, friendly, and funky, this basic but sparkling-clean lodge offers exceptional value just a few blocks from Santa Cruz Harbor and Twin Lakes Beach. Rooms come in an array of sizes, shapes, and configurations in two separate buildings—most have armoires and fans, and some have cozy breakfast nooks and writing areas. When booking a particular room, ask about the bath situation—some have tubs, while others have just showers, and three rooms in the main building share a single bath. Owner/innkeepers Chris and Clare Finelli furnished each room with unusual tables and other pieces acquired over two decades. **Pros:** affordable; free Wi-Fi; park your car and walk to the beach. **Cons:** not fancy; wall heaters can be noisy. ⊠ *645 7th Ave.*

☎ *831/479–9731* ⊕ *www.harborinn.info* ➶ *17 rooms, 2 suites* ♿ *In-room: no a/c, refrigerator, Wi-Fi. In-hotel: Wi-Fi hotspot, some pets allowed* ☰ *AE, D, MC, V.*

$$ ▥ **Pacific Blue Inn.** Green themes reign in this three-story, eco-friendly B&B, built from scratch in 2009 on a sliver of prime property on the outer edge of Pacific Avenue, downtown Santa Cruz's main drag. Much of the building was constructed with nontoxic wood and paints and recycled, reused, or reclaimed materials. All rooms include bamboo flooring, electric fireplaces, and pillowtop king beds, piled high with hypoallergenic comforters and pillows. All rooms are wheelchair friendly. Outdoors, you can relax around the fire pit in a secluded courtyard garden. The stellar breakfast typically includes a series of delectable, cooked-to-order dishes, including melt-in-your-mouth popovers. **Pros:** free bicycles; five-minute walk to boardwalk and wharf; right in downtown. **Cons:** tiny property; not suitable for children. ✉ *636 Pacific Ave.* ☎ *831/600–8880* ⊕ *www.pacificblueinn.com* ➶ *9 rooms* ♿ *In-room: DVD, Wi-Fi. In-hotel: bicycles, Wi-Fi hotspot, some pets allowed* ☰ *AE, D, MC, V* ⍣ *BP*

$$$ ▥ **Pleasure Point Inn.** Tucked in a residential neighborhood at the east end of town, this modern Mediterranean-style B&B sits right across the street from the ocean and a popular surfing beach (where surfing lessons are available). The rooms are handsomely furnished and include such deluxe amenities as fireplaces and private patios. You have use of the large rooftop sundeck and hot tub, which overlook the Pacific. Because this is a popular romantic getaway spot, it's best not to bring kids. **Pros:** fantastic views; ideal for checking the swells, quirky neighborhood. **Cons:** few rooms; several miles from major attractions. ✉ *2–3665 E. Cliff Dr.* ☎ *831/475–4657* ⊕ *www.pleasurepointinn.com* ➶ *4 rooms* ♿ *In-room: no a/c, safe, refrigerator, DVD, Wi-Fi. In-hotel: beachfront, Wi-Fi hotspot* ☰ *MC, V* ⍣ *CP.*

$$$–$$$$ ▥ **Santa Cruz Dream Inn.** Just a short stroll from the boardwalk and
★ wharf, this full-service luxury hotel is the only lodging in Santa Cruz directly on the beach. All rooms have private balconies or patios overlooking Monterey Bay. New owners completed a top-to-bottom remodel of the hotel in 2008; rooms now sparkle with contemporary furnishings, bold colors, and upscale linens—but the main draw here is having the ocean at your doorstep. Have the valet store your surfboard or bike for free, then take in the Pacific sunset from the poolside bar or the on-site restaurant, Aquarius, with sweeping southfacing views of Monterey Bay. **Pros:** directly on the beach; easy parking; walk to boardwalk and downtown. **Cons:** expensive; area gets congested on busy weekends. ✉ *175 W. Cliff Dr.* ☎ *831/426–4330 or 866/774–7735* 🖷 *831/427–2025* ⊕ *www.jdvhotels.com* ➶ *149 rooms, 16 suites* ♿ *In-room: a/c, safe, refrigerator, Wi-Fi. In-hotel: restaurant, room service, bars, pool, beachfront, laundry service, Internet terminal, Wi-Fi hotspot* ☰ *AE, D, DC, MC, V.*

$$$–$$$$ ▥ **West Cliff Inn.** Perched on the bluffs across from Cowell Beach, this
★ posh nautical-theme inn commands sweeping views of the boardwalk and Monterey Bay. Built in 1877, the Italianate three-story Victorian has classic California-beach style with color schemes that hint of ocean,

sky, and reflecting light. All rooms have a comfy king bed, fireplace, and fancy marble tile bathroom, many with spa tubs and some with sitting areas; rooms facing the bay have the best views. For the ultimate in privacy, ask for the room that has a private patio and hot tub. In the morning, enjoy a lavish breakfast in the elegant dining room and watch the surfers and seals catching the waves below. **Pros:** killer views; walking distance from the beach; close to downtown. **Cons:** boardwalk noise; street traffic. ⊠ *174 West Cliff Dr.* ☎ *800/979–0910* ⊕ *www.westcliffinn.com* ↰ *7 rooms, 2 suites, 1 cottage* ♿ *In-room: a/c, DVD, Wi-Fi. In-hotel: bicycles, Internet terminal, Wi-Fi hotspot* ▤ *AE, D, MC, V* ❙◎❙ *BP.*

NIGHTLIFE AND THE ARTS

NIGHTLIFE

★ Dance with the crowds at the **Catalyst** (⊠ *1011 Pacific Ave.* ☎ *831/423–1338* ⊕ *www.catalystclub.com*), a huge, grimy downtown club that has regularly featured big names, from Neil Young to Nirvana to Ice T.

Renowned in the international jazz community, and drawing performers such as Herbie Hancock, Pat Metheny, and Charlie Hunter, the nonprofit **Kuumbwa Jazz Center** (⊠ *320–2 Cedar St.* ☎ *831/427–2227* ⊕ *www.kuumbwajazz.org*) bops with live music most nights; the café serves meals an hour before most shows. Blues, salsa, reggae, funk: you name it, **Moe's Alley** (⊠ *1535 Commercial Way* ☎ *831/479–1854* ⊕ *www.moesalley.com*) has it all, six nights a week.

THE ARTS

Each August, the **Cabrillo Festival of Contemporary Music** (☎ *831/426–6966, 831/420–5260 box office* ⊕ *www.cabrillomusic.org*) brings some of the world's finest artists to the Santa Cruz Civic Auditorium to play groundbreaking symphonic music, including major world premieres. Using period and reproduction instruments, the **Santa Cruz Baroque Festival** (☎ *831/457–9693* ⊕ *www.scbaroque.org*) presents a wide range of classical music at various venues throughout the year. As the name suggests, the focus is on 17th- and 18th-century composers such as Bach and Handel.

Shakespeare Santa Cruz (⊠ *SSC/UCSC Theater Arts Center, 1156 High St.* ☎ *831/459–2121, 831/459–2159 tickets* ⊕ *www.shakespearesantacruz. org*) stages a six-week Shakespeare festival in July and August that may also include the occasional modern dramatic performance. Most performances are outdoors under the redwoods. A holiday program takes place in December.

SPORTS AND THE OUTDOORS

BICYCLING

Mountain bikers should head to **Another Bike Shop** (⊠ *2361 Mission St.* ☎ *831/427–2232* ⊕ *www.anotherbikeshop.com*) for tips on the best trails around and a look at cutting-edge gear made and tested locally. Park the car and rent a beach cruiser at **Bicycle Shop Santa Cruz** (⊠ *1325 Mission St.* ☎ *831/454–0909* ⊕ *www.thebicycleshopsantacruz.com*).

CLOSE UP

O'Neill: A Santa Cruz Icon

O'Neill wet suits and beachwear weren't exactly born in Santa Cruz, but as far as most of the world is concerned, the O'Neill brand is synonymous with Santa Cruz and surfing legend.

The O'Neill wet suit story began in 1952, when Jack O'Neill and his brother Robert opened their first Surf Shop in a garage across from San Francisco's Ocean Beach. While shaping balsa surfboards and selling accessories, the O'Neills experimented with solutions to a common surfer problem: frigid waters. Tired of being forced back to shore, blue-lipped and shivering, after just 20 or 30 minutes riding the waves, they played with various materials and eventually designed a neoprene vest.

In 1959 Jack moved his Surf Shop 90 miles south to Cowell Beach in Santa Cruz. It quickly became a popular surf hangout, and O'Neill's new wet suits began to sell like hotcakes. In the early 1960s the company opened a warehouse for manufacturing on a larger scale. Santa Cruz soon became a major surf city, attracting wave-riders to prime breaks at Steamer Lane, Pleasure Point, and The Hook. In 1965 O'Neill pioneered the first wet-suit boots, and in 1971 Jack's son invented the surf leash. By 1980, O'Neill stood at the top of the world wet-suit market.

O'Neill operates two flagship stores, one downtown and one close to Jack O'Neill's home on Pleasure Point. Check out the latest versions, along with casual beachwear and surfing gear. You can also pop into a smaller outlet on the Santa Cruz Wharf.

O'Neill Surf Shop. ⊠ 110 Cooper St. ☎ 831/469–4377 ⊠ 1115 41st Ave. Capitola ☎ 831/475–4151 ⊕ www. oneill.com.

7

BOATS AND CHARTERS

Chardonnay Sailing Charters (☎ 831/423–1213 ⊕ www.chardonnay.com) cruises Monterey Bay year-round on a variety of trips, such as whale-watching, astronomy, and winemaker sails. The 70-foot *Chardonnay II* leaves from the yacht harbor in Santa Cruz. Food and drink are served on many of their cruises. Reservations are essential. **Stagnaro Sport Fishing** (⊠ June–Aug., Santa Cruz Municipal Wharf; Sept.–May, Santa Cruz West Harbor ☎ 831/427–2334 ⊕ www.stagnaros.com) operates salmon, albacore, and rock-cod fishing expeditions; the fees ($50 to $75) include bait. The company also runs whale-watching, dolphin, and sealife cruises ($43) year-round.

GOLF

Designed by famed golf architect Dr. Alister MacKenzie in 1929, semi-private **Pasatiempo Golf Club** (⊠ 20 Clubhouse Rd. ☎ 831/459–9155 ⊕ www.pasatiempo.com), set amid undulating hills just above the city, often ranks among the nation's top championship courses in annual polls. Golfers rave about the spectacular views and challenging terrain. The greens fee is $220; an electric cart is $30 per player.

KAYAKING

In March, April, and May paddle out in the bay to mingle with gray whales and their calves on their northward journey to Alaska with **Kayak Connection** (✉ *413 Lake Ave. #3, Santa Cruz Harbor* ☎ *831/479-1121* ⊕ *www.kayakconnection.com*). Kayak Connection also guides other tours around Monterey, including Natural Bridges State Beach, Capitola, and Elkhorn Slough.

Explore hidden coves and kelp forests with **Venture Quest Kayaking** (✉ *#2 Santa Cruz Wharf* ☎ *831/427–2267 or 831/425–8445* ⊕ *www.kayaksantacruz.com*). The company's guided nature tours depart from Santa Cruz Wharf or Harbor, depending on the season. A two-hour kayak nature tour and introductory lesson costs $55. A three-hour kayak rental is $30 and includes wet suit and gear. Venture Quest also arranges tours at other Monterey Bay destinations, including Capitola and Elkhorn Slough.

SURFING

Surfers gather for spectacular waves and sunsets at **Pleasure Point** (✉ *E. Cliff and Pleasure Point Drs.*). **Steamer Lane**, near the lighthouse on West Cliff Drive, has a decent break. The area plays host to several competitions in summer.

Find out what all the fun is about at **Club-Ed Surf School and Camps** (✉ *Cowell Beach, at Santa Cruz Dream Inn* ☎ *831/464–0177* ⊕ *www.club-ed.com*). Your first private or group lesson ($85 and up) includes all equipment. The most welcoming place in town to buy or rent surf gear is **Paradise Surf Shop** (✉ *3961 Portola Dr.* ☎ *831/462–3880* ⊕ *www.paradisesurf.com*). The shop is owned and run by women who aim to help everyone feel comfortable on the water. **Cowell's Beach Surf Shop** (✉ *30 Front St.* ☎ *831/427–2355* ⊕ *www.cowellssurfshop.com*) sells bikinis, rents surfboards and wet suits, and offers lessons.

San Francisco

WORD OF MOUTH

"The part I was really looking forward to was walking down [Telegraph Hill] and looking for parrots. I'd seen the movie The Wild Parrots of Telegraph Hill, and the neighborhood was one of the things that meant 'San Francisco' to me. The neighborhood itself was beautiful, and we did indeed see parrots."

—sunny16

WELCOME TO SAN FRANCISCO

TOP REASONS TO GO

★ **The bay:** It's hard not to gasp as you catch sight of sunlight dancing on the water when you crest a hill, or watch the Golden Gate Bridge vanish and reemerge in the summer fog.

★ **The food:** San Franciscans are serious about what they eat, and with good reason. Home to some of the nation's best chefs, top restaurants, and finest local produce, it's hard not to eat well here.

★ **The shopping:** Shopaholics visiting the city will not be disappointed: San Francisco is packed with browsing destinations, everything from quirky boutiques to massive malls.

★ **The good life:** A laid-back atmosphere, beautiful surroundings, and oodles of cultural, culinary, and aesthetic pleasures . . . if you spend too much time here, you might not leave!

★ **The great outdoors:** From Golden Gate Park to sidewalk cafés in North Beach, San Franciscans relish their outdoor spaces.

1 Union Square and Chinatown. Union Square has hotels, public transportation, and shopping; walking through Chinatown is like visiting another country.

2 SoMa and Civic Center. SoMa is anchored by SFMOMA and Yerba Buena Gardens; the city's performing arts venues are in Civic Center.

3 Nob Hill and Russian Hill. Nob Hill is old money San Francisco; Russian Hill's steep streets have excellent eateries and shopping.

4 North Beach. This small Italian neighborhood is a great place to enjoy an espresso.

5 On the Waterfront. Head here to visit the exquisitely restored Ferry Building, Fisherman's Wharf, Pier 39, and Ghirardelli Square.

6 The Marina and the Presidio. The Marina has trendy boutiques, restaurants, and cafés; the wooded Presidio offers great views of the Golden Gate Bridge.

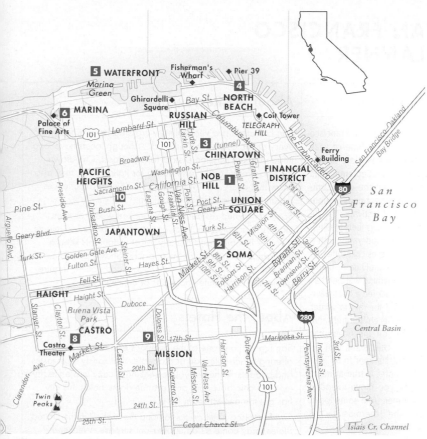

5 WATERFRONT
Fisherman's Wharf
Pier 39
Marina Green
Ghirardelli Square
Bay St.
4 NORTH BEACH
6 MARINA
Palace of Fine Arts
101
Lombard St.
RUSSIAN HILL
Hyde St.
Larkin St.
Columbus Ave.
Coit Tower
TELEGRAPH HILL
The Embarcadero
Broadway
101
(tunnel)
3 CHINATOWN
Grant Ave.
Ferry Building
PACIFIC HEIGHTS
Washington St.
Sacramento St.
California St.
NOB HILL 1
Powell St.
Post St.
Geary St.
FINANCIAL DISTRICT
80
San Francisco Bay
Presidio Ave.
Pine St.
10
Divisadero St.
Bush St.
Van Ness Ave.
Franklin St.
Gough St.
Laguna St.
Polk St.
UNION SQUARE
2nd St.
3rd St.
San Francisco–Oakland Bay Bridge
Arguello Ave.
Geary Blvd.
JAPANTOWN
Steiner St.
Golden Gate Ave.
Fulton St.
Turk St.
Turk St.
Hayes St.
Market St.
8th St.
9th St.
10th St.
Mission St.
4th St.
5th St.
6th St.
Folsom St.
Harrison St.
2 SOMA
Bryant St.
Brannan St.
Townsend St.
Berry St.
7th St.
280
Central Basin
Fell St.
HAIGHT
Haight St.
Stanyan St.
Claytor St.
Buena Vista Park
Duboce
Dolores St.
CASTRO
Castro Theater
8
Market St.
9
17th St.
Castro St.
MISSION
Harrison St.
Potrero Ave.
Mariposa St.
Pennsylvania Ave.
Indiana St.
3rd St.
Clarendon Ave.
Twin Peaks
20th St.
Guerrero St.
Mission St.
Van Ness Ave.
101
24th St.
25th St.
Cesar Chavez St.
Islais Cr. Channel

8

7 Golden Gate Park and the Western Shoreline. San Francisco's 1,000-acre backyard has sports fields, windmills, museums, and gardens; the windswept Western Shoreline stretches for miles.

8 The Haight, the Castro, and Noe Valley. After you've seen the blockbuster sights, come to these neighborhoods to see where the city's heart beats.

9 The Mission. This Latino neighborhood has destination restaurants, bargain ethnic eateries, and a hip bar scene.

10 Pacific Heights and Japantown. Pacific Heights has some of the city's most opulent real estate; Japantown is packed with authentic Japanese shops and restaurants.

GETTING ORIENTED

San Francisco is a compact city; just 46½ square mi. Essentially a tightly packed cluster of extremely diverse neighborhoods, the city dearly rewards walking. The areas that most visitors cover are easy (and safe) to reach on foot, but many have steep—make that *steep*—hills.

SAN FRANCISCO PLANNER

When to Go

You can visit San Francisco comfortably any time of year. Possibly the best time to visit San Francisco is September and October, when the city's summerlike weather brings outdoor concerts and festivals. The climate here always feels Mediterranean and moderate—with a foggy, sometimes chilly bite. The temperature rarely drops below 40°F, and anything warmer than 80°F is considered a heat wave. Be prepared for rain in winter, especially December and January. Winds off the ocean can add to the chill factor. That old joke about summer in SF feeling like winter is true at heart, but once you move inland, it gets warmer. (And some locals swear the thermostat has inched up in recent years.)

About the Restaurants

San Francisco is a vital culinary crossroads, with nearly every ethnic cuisine represented. Although locals have long headed to the Mission District for Latin food, Chinatown for Asian food, and North Beach for Italian food, they also know that every part of the city offers dining experiences beyond the neighborhood tradition.

Some renowned restaurants are booked weeks or even months in advance. But you can get lucky at the last minute if you're flexible—and friendly. Most restaurants keep a few tables open for walk-ins and VIPs. Show up for dinner early (5:30 PM) or late (after 9 PM) and politely inquire about any last-minute vacancies or cancellations.

About the Hotels

San Francisco is one of the country's best hotel towns, offering a rich selection of properties that satisfy most tastes and budgets. Whether you're seeking a cozy inn, a kitschy motel, a chic boutique, or a grande dame hotel, this city has got the perfect room for you.

San Francisco hotel prices, among the highest in the United States, may come as an unpleasant surprise. Weekend rates for double rooms in high season average about $132 a night citywide. Rates may vary according to room availability; always inquire about special rates and packages when making reservations; call the property directly, but also check its Web site and try Internet booking agencies.

WHAT IT COSTS

	¢	$	$$	$$$	$$$$
Restaurants	under $10	$10–$14	$15–$22	$23–$30	over $30
Hotels	under $90	$90–$149	$150–$199	$200–$250	over $250

Dining prices are per person for a typical main course. Note: if a restaurant offers only prix-fixe (set-price) meals, it has been given the price category that reflects the full prix-fixe price. Lodging prices are for two people in a standard double room in high season, excluding 14% tax.

Updated by Denise M. Leto, Fiona G. Parrott, Natasha Sarkisian, Sharon Silva, Sharron Wood, Sura Wood

"You could live in San Francisco a month and ask no greater entertainment than walking through it," wrote Inez Hayes Irwin, author of *The Californiacs*, an effusive 1921 homage to the Golden State and the City by the Bay. Follow in her footsteps, and you'll find that her claim still rings true today: simply wandering around this beautiful metropolis on foot is the best way to experience all of its diverse wonders.

Snuggling on a 46½-square-mi strip of land between San Francisco Bay and the Pacific Ocean, San Francisco is a relatively small city of about 750,000 residents. San Franciscans cherish their city for the same reasons visitors do: the proximity to the Bay and its pleasures, rows of Victorian homes clinging precariously to the hillsides, the sun setting behind the Golden Gate Bridge. But the city's attraction goes much deeper, from the diversity of its neighborhoods to the progressive free spirit here. Take all these things together, and you'll begin to understand why many San Franciscans can't imagine calling anyplace else home—despite the dizzying cost of living.

San Francisco's charms are great and small. You won't want to miss Golden Gate Park, the Palace of Fine Arts, The Golden Gate Bridge, or a cable-car ride over Nob Hill. But a walk down the Filbert Street Steps or through Macondray Lane or an hour gazing at murals in the Mission or the thundering Pacific from the cliffs of Lincoln Park can be equally inspiring.

PLANNING

GETTING HERE AND AROUND
AIR TRAVEL
The major gateway to San Francisco is San Francisco International Airport (SFO), 15 mi south of the city. It's off U.S. 101 near Millbrae and San Bruno. Oakland International Airport (OAK) is across the bay, not much farther away from downtown San Francisco (via I–80 east and I–880 south), but rush-hour traffic on the Bay Bridge may lengthen

Continued on page 366

HIGHWAY 1: SAN FRANCISCO TO FORT BRAGG

Mendocino Coast Botanical Garden

Point Reyes National Seashore

THE PLAN

Distance: 177 mi

Time: 2-4 days

Good Overnight Options: San Francisco, Olema, Bodega Bay, Gualala, Mendocino, Fort Bragg

For more information on the sights and attractions along this portion of Highway 1, please see chapters 8, 9, and 11.

SAN FRANCISCO

The official Highway 1 heads straight through **San Francisco** along 19th Avenue through **Golden Gate Park** and the **Presidio** toward the **Golden Gate Bridge.** For a more scenic tour, watch for signs announcing exits for 35 North/Skyline Boulevard, then Ocean Beach/The Great Highway (past Lake Merced). The Great Highway follows the coast along the western border of San Francisco; you'll cruise past entrances to the **San Francisco Zoo, Golden Gate Park,** and the **Cliff**

House. Hike out to **Point Lobos** or **Land's End** for awesome vistas, then drive through **Lincoln Park** and the **Palace of the Legion of Honor** and follow El Camino de Mar/Lincoln Boulevard all the way to the Golden Gate Bridge.

The best way to see San Francisco is on foot and public transportation. A **Union Square** stroll—complete with people-watching, window-shopping, and architecture-viewing—is a good first stop. In **Chinatown,** department stores give way to storefront temples, open-air markets, and delightful dim-sum shops. After lunch in one, catch a **Powell Street cable car** to the end of the line and get off to see the bay views and the antique arcade games at **Musée Mécanique** (the gem of otherwise mindless **Fisherman's Wharf**). For dinner and live music, try cosmopolitan **North Beach.**

SAN FRANCISCO TO OLEMA (approx. 37 mi)

Leaving the city the next day, your drive across the Golden Gate Bridge and a stop at a **Marin Headlands** overlook will yield memorable views (if fog hasn't socked in the bay). So will a hike in **Point Reyes National Seashore,** farther up Highway 1 (now

called Shoreline Highway). On this wild swath of coast you'll likely be able to claim an unspoiled beach for yourself. You should expect company, however, around the lighthouse at the tip of Point Reyes because year-round views—and seasonal elephant seal– and whale-watching—draw crowds. If you have time, poke around tiny **Olema,** which has some excellent restaurants, and **Inverness,** home to the famous Manka's Inverness Lodge.

OLEMA TO MENDOCINO (approx. 131 mi)

Passing only a few minuscule towns, this next stretch of Highway 1 showcases the northern coast in all its rugged glory. The reconstructed compound of eerily foreign buildings at **Fort Ross State Historic Park** recalls the era of Russian fur trading in California. Pull into **Gualala** for an espresso, a sandwich,

Point Reyes National Seashore

TOP 5 PLACES TO LINGER

- San Francisco
- Marin Headlands
- Point Reyes National Seashore
- Fort Ross State Historic Park
- Mendocino

and a little human contact before rolling onward. After another 50 mi of tranquil state beaches and parks you'll return to civilization in **Mendocino.**

MENDOCINO TO FORT BRAGG (approx. 9 mi)

Exploring Mendocino you may feel like you've fallen through a rabbit hole: the weather screams Northern California, but the 19th-century buildings—erected by homesick Yankee loggers—definitely say New England. Once you've browsed around the artsy shops, continue on to the **Mendocino Coast Botanical Gardens;** then travel back in time on the **Skunk Train,** which follows an old logging route from **Fort Bragg** deep into the redwood forest.

travel times considerably. San Jose International Airport (SJC) is about 40 mi south of San Francisco; travel time depends largely on traffic flow, but plan on an hour and a half with moderate traffic.

Airports San Francisco International Airport (*SFO* ☎ *800/435–9736* ⊕ *www. flysfo.com*). **Oakland International Airport** (*OAK* ☎ *510/563–3300* ⊕ *www. flyoakland.com*). **San Jose International Airport** (*SJC* ☎ *408/277–4759* ⊕ *www.sjc.org*).

Airport Transfers American Airporter (☎ *415/202–0733* ⊕ *www. americanairporter.com*). **BayPorter Express** (☎ *415/467–1800* ⊕ *www. bayporter.com*). **Caltrain** (☎ *800/660–4287* ⊕ *www.caltrain.com*). **East Bay Express Airporter** (☎ *877/526–0304* ⊕ *www.eastbaytransportation.com*). **Lorrie's Airport Service** (☎ *415/334–9000* ⊕ *www.gosfovan.com*). **Marin Airporter** (☎ *415/461–4222* ⊕ *www.marinairporter.com*). **Marin Door to Door** (☎ *415/457–2717* ⊕ *www.marindoortodoor.com*). **SamTrans** (☎ *800/660–4287* ⊕ *www.samtrans.com*). **South & East Bay Airport Shuttle** (☎ *800/548–4664* ⊕ *www.southandeastbayairportshuttle.com*). **SuperShuttle** (☎ *415/558–8500* or *800/258–3826* ⊕ *www.supershuttle.com*). **VIP Airport Shuttle** (☎ *408/986– 6000* or *800/235–8847* ⊕ *www.yourairportride.com*).

BART TRAVEL

Bay Area Rapid Transit (BART) trains, which run until midnight, travel under the bay via tunnel to connect San Francisco with Oakland, Berkeley, Pittsburgh/Bay Point, Richmond, Fremont, Dublin/Pleasanton, and other small cities and towns in between. Within San Francisco, stations are limited to downtown, the Mission, and a couple of outlying neighborhoods.

Trains travel frequently from early morning until evening on weekdays. After 8 PM weekdays and on weekends there's often a 20-minute wait between trains on the same line. Trains also travel south from San Francisco as far as Millbrae. BART trains connect downtown San Francisco to San Francisco International Airport; a ride is $8.10.

Intracity San Francisco fares are $1.75; intercity fares are $3.10 to $5.95. BART bases its ticket prices on miles traveled and does not offer price breaks by zone. A discounted pass, called a Smart Card, is available for $45 and can be used on BART and on all Muni lines (including cable cars) within city limits.

Contact Bay Area Rapid Transit (*BART* ☎ *415/989–2278* or *650/992–2278* ⊕ *www.bart.gov*).

BOAT AND FERRY TRAVEL

Several ferry lines run out of San Francisco. Blue & Gold Fleet operates a number of routes, including service to Sausalito ($11 one-way) and Tiburon ($11 one-way). Tickets are sold at Pier 41 (between Fisherman's Wharf and Pier 39), where the boats depart. There are also weekday Blue & Gold commuter ferries to Tiburon ($11) and Vallejo ($13) from the San Francisco Ferry Building. Alcatraz Cruises, owned by Hornblower Yachts, operates the ferries to Alcatraz Island ($26 including audio tour and National Park Service ranger-led programs) from Pier 33, about a half-mile east of Fisherman's Wharf ($3 shuttle buses serve several area hotels and other locations). Boats leave 10 times a day (14 times a day in summer) and the journey itself is 30 minutes. Allow roughly 2½ hours for a round-trip jaunt. Golden Gate Ferry runs daily to and from Sausalito and Lark-spur (each costs $7.85 one-way), leaving from Pier 1, behind the San Francisco Ferry Building. The Alameda/Oakland Ferry operates daily between Alameda's Main Street Ferry Building, Oakland's Jack London Square, and San Francisco's Pier 41 and the Ferry Building ($6.25 one-way); some ferries go only to Pier 41 or the Ferry Building, so ask when you board. Purchase tickets onboard.

Ferry Lines Alameda/Oakland Ferry (☎ 510/522–3300 ⊕ www.eastbayferry. com). **Alcatraz Cruises** (☎ 415/981–7625 ⊕ www.alcatrazcruises.com). **Blue & Gold Fleet** (☎ 415/705–5555 or 415/705–8200 ⊕ www.blueandgoldfleet.com). **Golden Gate Ferry** (☎ 415/923–2000 ⊕ www.goldengateferry.org).

Ferry Terminal San Francisco Ferry Building (✉ 1 Ferry Bldg., at foot of Market St. on Embarcadero).

CABLE CAR TRAVEL

The fare (for one direction) is $5 (Muni Passport holders pay a $1 supplement). You can buy tickets onboard (exact change isn't necessary) or at the kiosks at the cable car turnarounds at Hyde and Beach streets and at Powell and Market streets.

The heavily traveled Powell–Mason and Powell–Hyde lines begin at Powell and Market streets near Union Square and terminate at Fisherman's Wharf; lines for these routes can be long, especially in summer. The California Street line runs east and west from Market and California streets to Van Ness Avenue; there is often no wait to board this route.

CAR TRAVEL

Driving in San Francisco can be a challenge because of the one-way streets, snarly traffic, and steep hills. The first two elements can be frustrating enough, but those hills are tough for unfamiliar drivers. ■TIP➔ Remember to curb your wheels when parking on hills—turn wheels away from the curb when facing uphill, toward the curb when facing downhill. You can get a ticket if you don't do this.

MUNI TRAVEL

The San Francisco Municipal Railway, or Muni, operates light-rail vehicles, the historic F-line streetcars along Fisherman's Wharf and Market Street, trolley buses, and the world-famous cable cars. Light rail travels along Market Street to the Mission District and Noe Valley (J line), the Ingleside District (K line), and the Sunset District (L, M, and N lines); during peak hours (Monday through Friday, 6 AM–9 AM and 3 PM–7 PM) the J line continues around the Embarcadero to the Caltrain station at 4th and King streets. The new T line light rail runs from the Castro, down Market Street, around the Embarcadero, and south past Hunters Point and Monster Park to Sunnydale Avenue and Bayshore Boulevard. Muni provides 24-hour service on select lines to all areas of the city.

On buses and streetcars the fare is $2. Exact change is required, and dollar bills are accepted in the fare boxes. For all Muni vehicles other than cable cars, 90-minute transfers are issued free upon request at the time the fare is paid. These are valid for two additional transfers in any direction. Cable cars cost $5 and include no transfers (see Cable Car Travel, above).

One-day ($13), three-day ($20), and seven-day ($26) Passports valid on the entire Muni system can be purchased at several outlets, including the cable-car ticket booth at Powell and Market streets and the visitor information center downstairs in Hallidie Plaza. A monthly ticket, called a Fast Pass, is available for $70 and can be used on all Muni lines (including cable cars) and on BART within city limits. The San Francisco CityPass, a discount ticket booklet to several major city attractions, also covers all Muni travel for seven consecutive days.

The San Francisco Municipal Transit and Street Map ($3) is a useful guide to the extensive transportation system. You can buy the map at most bookstores and at the San Francisco Visitor Information Center, on the lower level of Hallidie Plaza at Powell and Market streets.

Outside the city, AC Transit serves the East Bay, and Golden Gate Transit serves Marin and Sonoma counties.

Bus Lines AC Transit (☎ *510/839–2882* ⊕ *www.actransit.org*). **Golden Gate Transit** (☎ *415/923–2000* ⊕ *www.goldengate.org*). **San Francisco Municipal Railway System** (*Muni* ☎ *415/673–6864* ⊕ *www.sfmuni.com*).

TAXI TRAVEL

Taxi service is notoriously bad in San Francisco, and hailing a cab can be frustratingly difficult in some parts of the city, especially on weekends. Popular nightspots such as the Mission, SoMa, North Beach, the Haight, and the Castro have a lot of cabs but a lot of people looking for taxis, too. Midweek, and during the day, you shouldn't have much of a problem—unless it's raining. In a pinch, hotel taxi stands are an option, as is calling for a pickup. But be forewarned: taxi companies frequently don't answer the phone in peak periods. The absolute worst time to find a taxi is Friday afternoon and evening; plan well ahead, and if you're going to the airport, make a reservation or book a shuttle instead. Most taxi companies take advance reservations for airport and out-of-town runs but not in-town transfers.

Taxis in San Francisco charge $3.10 for the first 1/5 mi (one of the highest base rates in the United States), 45¢ for each additional 1/5 mi, and 45¢ per minute in stalled traffic. There is no charge for additional passengers; there is no surcharge for luggage. For trips outside city limits, multiply the metered rate by 1.5.

Taxi Companies DeSoto Cab (☎ *415/970–1300*). **Luxor Cab** (☎ *415/282–4141*). **Veteran's Taxicab** (☎ *415/648–1313*). **Yellow Cab** (☎ *415/626–2345*).

Taxi Complaints San Francisco Police Department Taxi Detail (☎ *415/553–1447*).

TRAIN TRAVEL

Amtrak trains travel to the Bay Area from some cities in California and the United States. The *Coast Starlight* travels north from Los Angeles to Seattle, passing the Bay Area along the way, but contrary to its name, the train runs inland through the Central Valley for much of its route through Northern California; the most scenic stretch is in Southern California, between San Luis Obispo and Los Angeles. Amtrak also has several routes between San Jose, Oakland, and Sacramento. The *California Zephyr* travels from Chicago to the Bay Area and has spectacular alpine vistas as it crosses the Sierra Nevada mountains. San Francisco doesn't have an Amtrak train station but does have an Amtrak bus station, at the Ferry Building, which provides service to trains in Emeryville, just over the Bay Bridge. Shuttle buses also connect the Emeryville train station with downtown Oakland, the Caltrain station, and other points in downtown San Francisco.

Caltrain connects San Francisco to Palo Alto, San Jose, Santa Clara, and many smaller cities en route. In San Francisco, trains leave from the main depot, at 4th and Townsend streets, and a rail-side stop at 22nd and Pennsylvania streets. One-way fares are $2.50 to $11.25, depending on the number of zones through which your travel tickets are valid for four hours after purchase time. A ticket is $6 from San Francisco to Palo Alto, at least $7.75 to San Jose. You can also buy a day pass ($5–$22.50) for unlimited travel in a 24-hour period. Trips last 1 to 1¾ hours; it's worth waiting for an express train. On weekdays, trains depart three or four times per hour during the morning and evening, twice per hour during daytime non-commute hours, and as little as once per hour in the evening. Weekend trains run once per hour. The system shuts down at midnight. There are no onboard ticket sales. You must buy tickets before boarding the train or risk paying a $250 fine for fare evasion.

Train Lines Amtrak (☎ 800/872–7245 ⊕ www.amtrak.com). **Caltrain** (☎ 800/660–4287 ⊕ www.caltrain.com).

Train Depot San Francisco Caltrain station (✉ 700 4th St., at King St. ☎ 800/660–4287).

VISITOR INFORMATION

The San Francisco Convention and Visitors Bureau can mail you brochures, maps, and festivals and events listings. Once you're in town, you can stop by their info center near Union Square. Information about the Wine Country, redwood groves, and northwestern California is available at the California Welcome Center on Pier 39.

Contacts San Francisco Convention and Visitors Bureau (✉ 201 3rd St., Suite 900, San Francisco ☎ 415/391–2000, 415/392–0328 TDD ⊕ www. onlyinsanfrancisco.com). **San Francisco Visitor Information Center** (✉ Hallidie Plaza, lower level, 900 Market St., Union Sq. ☎ 415/391–2000, 415/392–0328 TDD ⊕ www.onlyinsanfrancisco.com).

EXPLORING SAN FRANCISCO

UNION SQUARE AND CHINATOWN

The Union Square area bristles with big-city bravado, while just a stone's throw away is a place that feels like a city unto itself, Chinatown. The two areas share a strong commercial streak, although manifested very differently. In Union Square, the crowds zigzag among international brands, trailing glossy shopping bags. A few blocks north, people dash between small neighborhood stores, their arms draped with plastic totes filled with groceries or souvenirs.

EXPLORING IN UNION SQUARE

④ Maiden Lane. Known as Morton Street in the raffish Barbary Coast era, this former red-light district reported at least one murder a week during the late 19th century. Things cooled down after the 1906 fire destroyed the brothels, and these days Maiden Lane is a chic, boutique-lined pedestrian mall stretching two blocks, between Stockton and Kearny streets. Wrought-iron gates close the street to traffic most days between 11 and 5, when the lane becomes a patchwork of umbrella-shaded tables.

> ### CABLE CAR TERMINUS
>
> Two of the three cable car lines begin and end their runs at Powell and Market streets, a couple of blocks south of Union Square. These two lines are the most scenic, and both pass near Fisherman's Wharf, so they're usually clogged with first-time sightseers. The wait to board a cable car at this intersection is longer than at any other stop in the system. If you'd rather avoid the mob, board the less-touristy California line at the bottom of Market Street, at Drumm Street.

At **140 Maiden Lane** you can see the only Frank Lloyd Wright building in San Francisco. Walking through the brick archway and recessed entry feels a bit like entering a glowing cave. The interior's graceful, curving ramp and skylights are said to have been his model for the Guggenheim Museum in New York. Xanadu Tribal Arts, a gallery showcasing Baltic, Latin-American, and African folk art, now occupies the space. ⊠ *Between Stockton and Kearny Sts., Union Square.*

① San Francisco Visitor Information Center. A multilingual staff operates this facility below the cable car terminus. Staffers answer questions and provide maps and pamphlets. You can also pick up discount coupons—the savings can be significant, especially for families—and hotel brochures here. If you're planning to hit the big-ticket stops like the California Academy of Sciences, the Exploratorium, and SFMOMA, and ride the cable cars, consider picking up a CityPass here (or at any of the attractions it covers). ■TIP➜ The CityPass ($59, $39 ages 5–12), good for nine days including seven days of transit, will save you about 50%. Also buy your Muni Passport here. ⊠ *Hallidie Plaza, lower level, Powell and Market Sts., Union Square* ☎ *415/391–2000 or 415/283–0177* ⊕ *www. onlyinsanfrancisco.com* ⊗ *Weekdays 9–5, Sat. 9–3; also Sun. 9–3 in May–Oct.*

③ Union Square. The heart of San Francisco's downtown since 1850, a 2½-acre square surrounded by department stores and the St. Francis Hotel, is about the only place you can sit for free in this part of town. The public responded to Union Square's 2002 redesign with a resounding shrug. With its pretty landscaping, easier street access, and the addition of a café (welcome, but nothing special), it's certainly an improvement over the old concrete wasteland, but no one's beating a path downtown to hang out here. Four globular lamp sculptures by the artist R. M. Fischer preside over the space; there's also an open-air stage, a visitor information booth, and a front-row seat to the cable car tracks. And there's a familiar kaleidoscope of characters: office workers

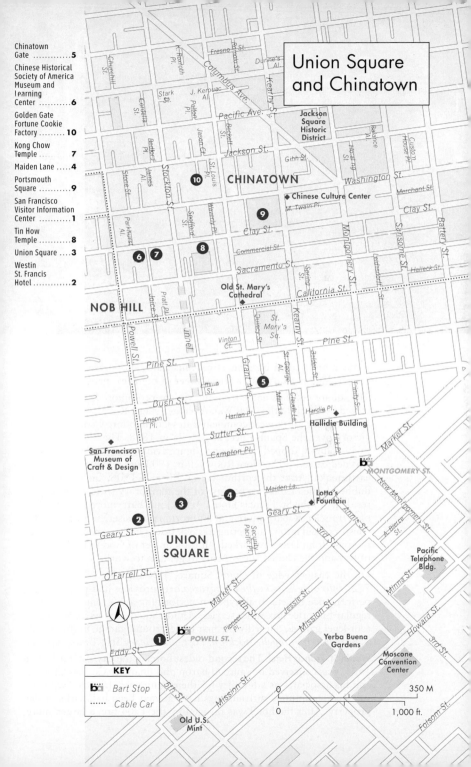

Union Square and Chinatown

Jackson
Square
Historic
District

CHINATOWN

◆ Chinese Culture Center

M. Twain Pl.

❿

❾

NOB HILL

Old St. Mary's
Cathedral

St.
Mary's
Sq.

❻ ❼

❽

❺

Hallidie Building

San Francisco
Museum of
Craft & Design

❸

❹

Maiden La.

◆ Lotta's
Fountain

❷

**UNION
SQUARE**

❶

Pacific
Telephone
Bldg.

Yerba Buena
Gardens

Moscone
Convention
Center

Old U.S.
Mint

Streets (labels): K. Rexroth Pl., Fresno St., Dunne's Al., Churchill St., Columbus Ave., Kearny St., Stark St., J. Kerouac Al., Pacific Ave., Balance Al., Custom House Pl., Cordelia St., Patton Pl., Beckett St., Jason Ct., Jackson St., Hotaling St., Gibb St., Washington St., Merchant St., Bertha Pl., Vernon Al., St. Louis Pl., Clay St., Battery St., Parkhurst Al., Waverly Pl., Spofford, Commercial St., Montgomery St., Leidesdorff St., Sansome St., Halleck St., Sacramento St., Spring St., California St., Pratt Pl., Joice St., Vinton Ct., Pine St., Jones St., Powell St., Joice St., Pine St., Emma St., Grant Ave., St. George Al., St. Mary's Ct., Quincy St., Jessie St., Bush St., Anson Pl., Harlan Pl., Mark La., Claude La., Hardie Pl., Trinity Pl., Sutter St., Campton Pl., Market St., New Montgomery St., Geary St., Security Pacific Pl., Annie's St., A. Bierce St., Howard St., O'Farrell St., Minna St., Eddy St., Pioneer Pl., Mission St., Jessie St., 3rd St., 4th St., Folsom St.

MONTGOMERY ST.

POWELL ST.

0   350 M

0   1,000 ft.

Chinatown bursts into color and light on Chinese New Year's.

sunning and brown-bagging, street musicians, shoppers taking a rest, kids chasing pigeons, and a fair number of homeless people.

The square takes its name from the violent pro-union demonstrations staged here before the Civil War. At center stage, Robert Ingersoll Aitken's *Victory Monument* commemorates Commodore George Dewey's victory over the Spanish fleet at Manila in 1898. The 97-foot Corinthian column, topped by a bronze figure symbolizing naval conquest, was dedicated by Theodore Roosevelt in 1903 and withstood the 1906 earthquake. After the earthquake and fire of 1906, the square was dubbed Little St. Francis because of the temporary shelter erected for residents of the St. Francis Hotel. Actor John Barrymore (grandfather of actress Drew Barrymore and a notorious carouser) was among the guests pressed into volunteering to stack bricks in the square. His uncle, thespian John Drew, remarked, "It took an act of God to get John out of bed and the United States Army to get him to work."

On the eastern edge of Union Square, **TIX Bay Area** (☎ 415/433–7827 *info only* ⊕ *www.theatrebayarea.org*) provides half-price day-of-performance tickets to all types of performing-arts events, as well as regular full-price box-office services. Union Square covers a convenient four-level garage, allegedly the first underground garage in the world. ⊠ *Bordered by Powell, Stockton, Post, and Geary Sts., Union Square.*

❷ Westin St. Francis Hotel. The second-oldest hotel in the city, established in 1904, was conceived by railroad baron and financier Charles Crocker and his associates as a hostelry for their millionaire friends. Swift service and sumptuous surroundings have always been hallmarks of the property. After the hotel was ravaged by the 1906 fire, a larger, more luxurious Italian Renaissance–style residence was opened in 1907 to attract loyal clients from among the world's rich and powerful. The hotel's checkered past includes the ill-fated 1921 bash in the suite of the silent-film comedian Fatty Arbuckle, at which a woman became ill and later died. Arbuckle endured three sensational trials for rape and murder before being acquitted, by which time his career was kaput. In 1975 Sara Jane Moore, standing among a crowd outside the hotel, attempted to shoot then-president Gerald Ford. As might be imagined, no plaques in the lobby commemorate these events. ■TIP→ One of the best views in the city is from the glass elevators here—and best of all, a ride is free. Zip up to the 32nd floor for a bird's-eye view; the lights of the nighttime cityscape are particularly lovely. Don't be shy if you're not a guest: some visitors make this a stop every time they're in town. Every November the hotel's pastry chef creates a spectacular, rotating 12-foot gingerbread castle, on display in the grand lobby—a fun holiday treat for families. ⊠ *335 Powell St., at Geary St., Union Square* ☎ *415/397–7000* ⊕ *www. westinstfrancis.com.*

> **LOOK UP!**
>
> When wandering around Chinatown, don't forget to look up! Above the chintziest souvenir shop might loom an ornate balcony or a curly pagoda roof. The best examples are on the 900 block of Grant Avenue (at Washington Street) and at Waverly Place.

EXPLORING IN CHINATOWN

5 **Chinatown Gate.** This is the official entrance to Chinatown. Stone lions flank the base of the pagoda-topped gate; the lions, dragons, and fish up top symbolize wealth, prosperity, and other good things. The four Chinese characters immediately beneath the pagoda represent the philosophy of Sun Yat-sen (1866–1925), the leader who unified China in the early 20th century. Sun Yat-sen, who lived in exile in San Francisco for a few years, promoted the notion of friendship and peace among all nations based on equality, justice, and goodwill. The vertical characters under the left pagoda read "peace" and "trust," the ones under the right pagoda "respect" and "love." The whole shebang usually telegraphs the internationally understood message of "photo op." ⊠ *Grant Ave. at Bush St., Chinatown.*

6 **Chinese Historical Society of America Museum and Learning Center.** This airy, light-filled gallery has displays about the Chinese-American experience from 19th-century agriculture to 21st-century food and fashion trends, including a poignant collection of racist games and toys. A separate room hosts rotating exhibits by contemporary Chinese-American artists. ⊠ *965 Clay St., Chinatown* ☎ *415/391–1188* ⊕ *www.chsa.org* ⊠ *$3, free 1st Thurs. of month* ☉ *Tues.–Fri. noon–5.*

10 **Golden Gate Fortune Cookie Factory.** Follow your nose down Ross Alley to this tiny but fragrant cookie factory. Workers sit at circular motorized griddles and wait for dollops of batter to drop onto a tiny metal plate, which rotates into an oven. A few moments later out comes a cookie that's pliable and ready for folding. It's easy to peek in for a moment, and hard to leave without a few free samples. A bagful of cookies—with mildly racy "adult" fortunes or more-benign ones—costs about $3. You can also purchase the cookies "fortuneless" in their waferlike unfolded state, which makes snacking that much more efficient. Being allowed to photograph the cookie makers at work will set you back 50¢. ⊠ 56 *Ross Alley, west of and parallel to Grant Ave., between Washington and Jackson Sts., Chinatown* ☎ 415/781–3956 ☑ *Free* ☉ *Daily 9–8.*

❼ **Kong Chow Temple.** This ornate temple sets a somber, spiritual tone right away with a sign warning visitors not to touch *anything.* The god to whom the members of this temple pray represents honesty and trust. Chinese stores and restaurants often display his image because he's thought to bring good luck in business. Chinese immigrants established the temple in 1851; its congregation moved to this building in 1977. Take the elevator up to the fourth floor, where incense fills the air. You can show respect by placing a dollar or two in the donation box and by leaving your camera in its case. Amid the statuary, flowers, and richly colored altars (red wards off evil spirits and signifies virility, green symbolizes longevity, and gold connotes majesty), a couple of plaques announce that MRS. HARRY S. TRUMAN CAME TO THIS TEMPLE IN JUNE 1948 FOR A PREDICTION ON THE OUTCOME OF THE ELECTION . . . THIS FORTUNE CAME TRUE. The temple's balcony has a good view of Chinatown. ⊠ *855 Stockton St., Chinatown* ☎ *No phone* ☑ *Free* ☉ *Mon.–Sat. 9–4.*

❾ **Portsmouth Square.** Chinatown's living room buzzes with activity. The square, with its pagoda-shape structures, is a favorite spot for morning tai chi; by noon dozens of men huddle around Chinese chess tables, engaged in not-always-legal competition. Kids scamper about the square's two grungy playgrounds (warning: the bathrooms are sketchy). Back in the late 19th century this land was near the waterfront and Robert Louis Stevenson, the author of *Treasure Island,* often dropped by, chatting up the sailors who hung out here. Some of the information he gleaned about life at sea found its way into his fiction. A bronze galleon sculpture, a tribute to Stevenson, is anchored in a corner of the square. ⊠ *Bordered by Walter Lum Pl. and Kearny, Washington, and Clay Sts., Chinatown.*

❽ **Tin How Temple.** Duck into the inconspicuous doorway, climb three flights of stairs—on the second floor is a mah-jongg parlor whose patrons hope the spirits above will favor them—and be assaulted by the aroma of incense in this tiny, altar-filled room. Day Ju, one of the first three Chinese to arrive in San Francisco, dedicated this temple to the Queen of the Heavens and the Goddess of the Seven Seas in 1852. In the temple's entryway, elderly ladies can often be seen preparing "money" to be burned as offerings to various Buddhist gods or as funds for ancestors to use in the afterlife. Hundreds of red-and-gold lanterns cover the ceiling; the larger the lamp, the larger its donor's contribution to the temple. Gifts of oranges, dim sum, and money left by the faithful, who kneel mumbling prayers, rest on altars to various gods. Tin How presides over the middle back of the temple, flanked by one red and one green lesser god. Take a good look around, since taking photographs is not allowed. ⊠ *125 Waverly Pl., Chinatown* ☎ *No phone* ☑ *Free, donations accepted* ☉ *Daily 9–4.*

Continued on page 381

CHINATOWN

8

Chinatown's streets flood the senses. Incense and cigarette smoke mingle with the scents of briny fish and sweet vanilla. Rooflines flare outward, pagoda-style. Loud Cantonese bargaining and honking car horns rise above the sharp clack of mah-jongg tiles and the eternally humming cables beneath the street.

Most Chinatown visitors march down Grant Avenue, buy a few trinkets, and call it a day. Do yourself a favor and dig deeper. This is one of the largest Chinese communities outside Asia, and there is far more to it than buying a back-scratcher near Chinatown Gate. To get a real feel for the neighborhood, wander off the main drag. Step into a temple or an herb shop and wander down a flag-draped alley. And don't be shy: residents welcome guests warmly, though rarely in English.

Whatever you do, don't leave without eating something. Noodle houses, bakeries, tea houses, and dim sum shops seem to occupy every other storefront. There's a feast for your eyes as well: in the market windows on Stockton and Grant, you'll see hanging whole roast ducks, fish, and shellfish swimming in tanks, and strips of shiny, pink-glazed Chinese-style barbecued pork.

CHINATOWN'S HISTORY

Sam Brannan's 1848 cry of "Gold!" didn't take long to reach across the world to China. Struggling with famine, drought, and political upheaval at home, thousands of Chinese jumped at the chance to try their luck in California. Most came from the Pearl River Delta region, in the Guangdong province, and spoke Cantonese dialects. From the start, Chinese businesses circled around Portsmouth Square, which was conveniently central. Bachelor rooming houses sprang up, since the vast majority of new arrivals were men. By 1853, the area was called Chinatown.

The Street of Gamblers (Ross Alley), 1898 (top). The first Chinese telephone operator in Chinatown (bottom).

COLD WELCOME
The Chinese faced discrimination from the get-go. Harrassment became outright hostility as first the gold rush, then the work on the Transcontinental Railroad petered out. Special taxes were imposed to shoulder aside competing "coolie labor." Laws forbidding the Chinese from moving outside Chinatown kept the residents packed in like sardines,

with nowhere to go but up and down—thus the many basement establishments in the neighborhood. State and federal laws passed in the 1870s deterred Chinese women from immigrating, deeming them prostitutes. In the late 1870s, looting and arson attacks on Chinatown businesses soared.

The coup de grace, though, was the Chinese Exclusion Act, passed by the U.S.

Chinatown's Grant Avenue.

Women and children flooded into the neighborhood after the Great Quake.

Congress in 1882, which slammed the doors to America for "Asiatics." This was the country's first significant restriction on immigration. The law also prevented the existing Chinese residents, including American-born children, from becoming naturalized citizens. With a society of mostly men (forbidden, of course, from marrying white women), San Francisco hoped that Chinatown would simply die out.

OUT OF THE ASHES

When the devastating 1906 earthquake and fire hit, city fathers thought they'd seize the opportunity to kick the Chinese out of Chinatown and get their hands on that desirable piece of downtown real estate. Then Chinatown businessman Look Tin Eli had a brainstorm of Disneyesque proportions.

He proposed that Chinatown be rebuilt, but in a tourist-friendly, stylized, "Oriental" way. Anglo-American architects would design new buildings with pagoda roofs and dragon-covered columns. Chinatown would attract more tourists—the curious had been visiting on the sly for decades—and add more tax money to the city's coffers. Ka-ching: the sales pitch worked.

PAPER SONS

For the Chinese, the 1906 earthquake turned the virtual "no entry" sign into a flashing neon "welcome!" All the city's immigration records went up in smoke, and the Chinese quickly began to apply for passports as U.S. citizens, claiming their old ones were lost in the fire. Not only did thousands of Chinese become legal overnight, but so did their sons in China, or "sons," if they weren't really related. Whole families in Chinatown had passports in names that weren't their own; these "paper sons" were not only a windfall but also an uncomfortable neighborhood conspiracy. The city caught on eventually and set up an immigration center on Angel Island in 1910. Immigrants spent weeks or months being inspected and interrogated while their papers were checked. Roughly 250,000 people made it through. With this influx, including women and children, Chinatown finally became a more complete community.

A GREAT WALK THROUGH CHINATOWN

■ Start at the Chinatown Gate and walk ahead on Grant Avenue, entering the souvenir gauntlet. (You'll also pass Old St. Mary's Cathedral.)

■ Make a right on Clay Street and walk to Portsmouth Square. Sometimes it feels like the whole neighborhood's here, playing chess and exercising.

■ Head up Washington Street to the elaborately pagodaed Old Chinese Telephone Exchange building, now the Bank of Canton. Across Grant, look left for Waverly Place. Here Republic of China flags flap over some of the neighborhood's most striking buildings, including Tin How Temple.

■ At the Sacramento Street end of Waverly Place stands the oddly beautiful brick First Chinese Baptist Church of 1908. Just across the way, the Clarion Music Center is chock-full of unusual instruments, as well as exquisite lion-dance sets.

■ Head back to Washington Street and check out the herb shops, like the Superior Trading Company (No. 839) and the Great China Herb Co. (No. 857).

■ Follow the scent of vanilla from Washington Street down Ross Alley (entrance across

from Superior Trading Company) to the Golden Gate Fortune Cookie Factory. Then head across the alley to Sam Bo Trading Co., where religious items are stacked chockablock in the narrow space. Tell the friendly owners your troubles and they'll prepare a package of joss papers, joss sticks, and candles, and tell you how and when to offer them up.

■ Turn left on Jackson Street; ahead is the real Chinatown's main artery, Stockton Street. This is where most residents do their grocery shopping; if it's Saturday, get ready for throngs (and their elbows). Look toward the back of stores for Buddhist altars with offerings of oranges and grapefruit. From here you can loop one block east back to Grant.

ALL THE TEA IN CHINATOWN

Preparing a perfect brew at Red Blossom Tea.

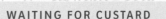

San Francisco's close ties to Asia have always made it more tea-conscious than other American burgs, but these days the city is in the throes of a tea renaissance, with new tasting rooms popping up in every neighborhood. Below are our favorite Chinatown spots for every tea under the sun.

Red Blossom Tea. A light and modern shop—the staff really know their stuff. It's a favorite among younger tea enthusiasts, who swear by its excellent bang-for-the-buck value. While Red Blossom doesn't do formal tastings or sell tea by the cup, they'll gladly brew up perfect samples of the teas you're interested in. ⊠ *831 Grant Ave.* ☎ *415/395–0868.*

Vital Tea Leaf. Tastings here work like those for wine—one of the gregarious, knowledgeable servers chooses the teas and describes them as you sample. It's a great spot for tea newbies to get their feet wet without a hard sell, but local connoisseurs grumble about the high prices and the self-promotion. ⊠ *1044 Grant Ave.* ☎ *415/981–2388.*

Imperial Tea Court. If you want to visit the most respected of traditional tea purveyors, you'll need to venture outside of Chinatown. Imperial Tea Court's serene Powell Street oasis closed unexpectedly in 2007, but you'll find the same great selection and expertise at their fancy new digs in the Ferry Building. ☎ *415/544–9830.*

WAITING FOR CUSTARD

As you're strolling down Grant Avenue, past the plastic Buddhas and yin/yang balls, be sure to stop at the **Golden Gate Bakery** (No. 1029) for some delicious eggy *dan tat* (custard tarts). These flaky-crusted treats are heaven for just a buck. There's often a line, but it's worth the wait.

DON'T-MISS SHOPS

Locals snap up flowers from an outdoor vendor.

If you're in the market for a pair of chirping metal crickets (oh you'll hear them, trust us), you can duck into any of the obvious souvenir-stuffed storefronts. But if you're looking for something special, head for these tempting sources. ■TIP→ Fierce neighborhood competition keeps prices within reason, but for popular wares like jade, it pays to shop around before making a serious investment. Many stores accept cash only.

Chinatown Kite Shop. Family-run shop selling bright, fun-shaped kites—dragons, butterflies, sharks—since the 1960s. ⊠ *717 Grant Ave.* ☎ *415/989–5182.*

Dragon House. A veritable museum: the store sells authentic, centuries-old antiques like ivory carvings. ⊠ *455 Grant Ave.* ☎ *415/421–3693.*

Jade Galore. Not the cheapest place to pick up jade figures and jewelry, but locals trust its quality and adore its

wide selection of Chinese bling. ⊠ *1000 Stockton St.* ☎ *415/982–4863.*

Old Shanghai. One of the largest selections of hand-painted robes, formal dresses, and jackets in Chinatown, plus chic Asian-inspired pieces. ⊠ *645 Grant Ave.* ☎ *415/986–1222.*

CHINATOWN WITH KIDS

It can be tough for the little ones to keep their hands to themselves, especially when all sorts of curios spill out onto the sidewalk at just the right height. To burn off some steam (in them) and relieve some stress (in you), take them to the small but spruce playground directly behind Old St. Mary's at Grant Avenue and California Street. If that setting's too tranquil, head to the more boisterous Willie Wong Playground, on Sacramento Street at Waverly Place.

SOMA AND CIVIC CENTER

To a newcomer, SoMa (short for "south of Market") and Civic Center may look like cheek-by-jowl neighbors—they're divided by Market Street. To locals, though, these areas are firmly separate entities, especially since Market Street itself is considered such a strong demarcation line. SoMa is less a neighborhood than it is a sprawling area of wide, traffic-heavy boulevards lined with office high-rises and pricey live-work lofts. Across Market Street from the western edge of SoMa is Civic Center, with San Francisco's eye-catching, gold-domed City Hall. Tickets to a show at one of the neighborhood's grand performance halls are the main reason to venture here.

EXPLORING SOMA

7 California Historical Society. If you're not a history buff, the CHS might seem like an obvious skip—who wants to look at fading old photographs and musty artifacts? If the answer is an indignant "I do!" or if you're just curious, these airy galleries are well worth a stop. A rotating selection draws from the society's vast repository of Californiana—hundreds of thousands of photographs, publications, paintings, and gold-rush paraphernalia. ■TIP➔ From out front, take a look across the street: this is the best view of MoAD's three-story photo mosaic. ✉ *678 Mission St., SoMa* ☎ *415/357–1848* ⊕ *www.californiahistoricalsociety.org* ⛶ *$3* ☾ *Wed.–Sat. noon–4:30; galleries close between exhibitions.*

6 Cartoon Art Museum. Krazy Kat, Zippy the Pinhead, Batman, and other colorful cartoon icons greet you at the Cartoon Art Museum, established with an endowment from cartoonist icon Charles M. Schulz. The museum's strength is its changing exhibits, which explore such topics as America from the perspective of international political cartoons, and the output of women and African-American cartoonists. Serious fans of cartoons—especially those on the quirky underground side—will likely enjoy the exhibits; those with a casual interest may be disappointed. The museum store carries lots of cool books. ✉ *655 Mission St., SoMa* ☎ *415/227–8666* ⊕ *www.cartoonart.org* ⛶ *$6, pay what you wish 1st Tues. of month* ☾ *Tues.–Sun. 11–5.*

1 Contemporary Jewish Museum. Opened in 2008, this Daniel Liebeskind–designed CJM is a real coup for SoMa. It's impossible to ignore that diagonal blue cube. The all-new addition jutting into a painstakingly restored power substation is a physical manifestation of the Hebrew phrase *l'chaim* (to life). And even if the architectural philosophy behind the design seems a bit esoteric, the blue, steel-clad cube—one of the most striking structures in town—creates a unique, light-filled space that merits a stroll through the lobby even if current exhibits don't entice you into the galleries. Be sure to check out the seam where old building meets new. ■TIP➔ "Seeing Gertrude Stein," an exhibit examining this cultural giant's role in 20th-century arts, is set to open in mid-2011. ✉ *736 Mission St., between 3rd and 4th Sts., SoMa* ☎ *415/655–7800* ⊕ *www.thejcm.org* ⛶ *$10, $5 Thurs. after 5 PM* ☾ *Thurs. 1–8, Fri.–Tues. 11–5.*

4 Museum of the African Diaspora (*MoAD*). Dedicated to the influence that people of African descent have had all over the world, MoAD provokes

8

discussion from the get-go with the question, "When did you discover you are African?" painted on the wall at the entrance. With no permanent collection, the museum is light on displays and heavy on interactive exhibits. For instance, you can sit in a darkened theater and listen to the moving life stories of slaves; hear snippets of music that helped create genres from gospel to hip-hop; and see videos about the Civil Rights movement or the Haitian Revolution. Some grumble that sweeping generalities replace specific information, but almost everyone can appreciate the museum's most striking exhibit, in the front window. The three-story mosaic, made from thousands of photographs, forms the image of a little girl's face. Walk up the stairs inside the museum and view the photographs up close—Malcolm X is there, Muhammad Ali, too, along with everyday folks—but the best view is from across the street. ⊠ *685 Mission St., SoMa* ☎ *415/358–7200* ⊕ *www.moadsf. org* ⊠ *$10* ⊙ *Wed.–Sat. 11–6, Sun. noon–5.*

❺ San Francisco Museum of Modern Art (SFMOMA). With its brick facade and
Fodor's Choice a striped central tower lopped at a lipstick-like angle, architect Mario
★ Botta's SFMOMA building fairly screams "modern-art museum." Indeed it is. The stripes continue inside, from the black marble and gray granite of the floors right up the imposing staircase to the wooden slats on the ceiling.

■**TIP→** Taking in all of SFMOMA's four exhibit floors can be overwhelming, so having a plan is helpful. Keep in mind that the museum's heavy hitters are on floors 2 and 3. Floor 2 gets the big-name traveling exhibits and collection highlights such as Matisse's *Woman with the Hat,* Diego Rivera's *The Flower Carrier,* and Georgia O'Keeffe's *Black Place 1.* Photography buffs should hustle up to floor 3, with its works by Ansel Adams and Alfred Stieglitz. The large-scale contemporary exhibits on floors 4 and 5 can usually be seen quickly (or skipped). If it's on display, don't miss sculptor Jeff Koons' memorably creepy, life-size gilded porcelain *Michael Jackson and Bubbles,* on the fifth floor at the end of the Turret Bridge, a vertiginous catwalk dangling under the central tower. In 2009, the museum's new fifth-floor, garage-top sculpture garden opened.

Seating in the museum can be scarce, so luckily Caffè Museo, accessible from the street, provides a refuge for quite good, reasonably priced drinks and light meals. It's easy to drop a fortune at the museum's large store, chockablock with fun gadgets, artsy doodads of all kinds, very modern furniture, and possibly the best selection of kids' books in town. ■**TIP→** No ticket is required to visit the lobby, so if it's the architecture you're interested in, save yourself the admission and have a gander for free. ⊠ *151 3rd St., SoMa* ☎ *415/357–4000* ⊕ *www.sfmoma.org* ⊠ *$15, free 1st Tues. of month, ½ price Thurs. 6–9* ⊙ *Labor Day–Memorial Day, Fri.–Tues. 11–5:45, Thurs. 11–8:45; Memorial Day–Labor Day, Fri.–Tues. 10–5:45, Thurs. 10–8:45.*

❸ Yerba Buena Center for the Arts. If MOMA's for your parents, the Center is for you. You never know what's going to be on at this facility in the Yerba Buena Gardens, but whether it's an exhibit of Mexican street graphics (graffiti to laypeople), innovative modern dance, or baffling video installations, it's likely to be memorable. The productions here

Light streams in through the skylight atop the bold striped cylinder of the San Francisco Museum of Modern Art (SFMOMA).

tend to draw a young, energetic crowd and lean hard toward the cutting edge. ✉ *701 Mission St., SoMa* ☎ *415/978–2787* ⊕ *www.ybca. org* 🎟 *Galleries $7, free 1st Tues. of month* 🕙 *Thurs. and Fri. 2–8, Sat. noon–8, Sun. noon–6, 1st Tues. of the month noon–8.*

❷ Yerba Buena Gardens. There's not much south of Market that encourages lingering outdoors, or indeed walking at all, with this notable exception. These two blocks encompass the **Center for the Arts, Metreon, Moscone Convention Center,** and the convention center's rooftop **Zeum,** but the gardens themselves are the everyday draw. Office workers escape to the green swath of the East Garden. The memorial to Martin Luther King Jr. is the focal point here. Powerful streams of water surge over large, jagged stone columns, mirroring the enduring force of King's words that are carved on the stone walls and on glass blocks behind the waterfall. Moscone North is behind the memorial, and an overhead walkway leads to Moscone South and its rooftop attractions. ■TIP→ The gardens are liveliest during the week and especially during the Yerba Buena Gardens Festival (May–October, ⊕ www.ybgf.org), when free performances run from Latin music to Balinese dance.

Atop the Moscone Convention Center perch a few lures for kids. The historic **Looff carousel** ($3 for two rides) twirls daily 11–6. South of the carousel is **Zeum** (☎ *415/820–3320* ⊕ *www.zeum.org*), a high-tech, interactive arts-and-technology center (adults, $10; kids 3–18, $8) geared to children ages eight and over. Kids can make Claymation videos, work in a computer lab, and view exhibits and performances. Zeum is open 1–5 Wednesday through Friday and 11–5 weekends during the school year and Tuesday through Sunday 11–5 when school's out.

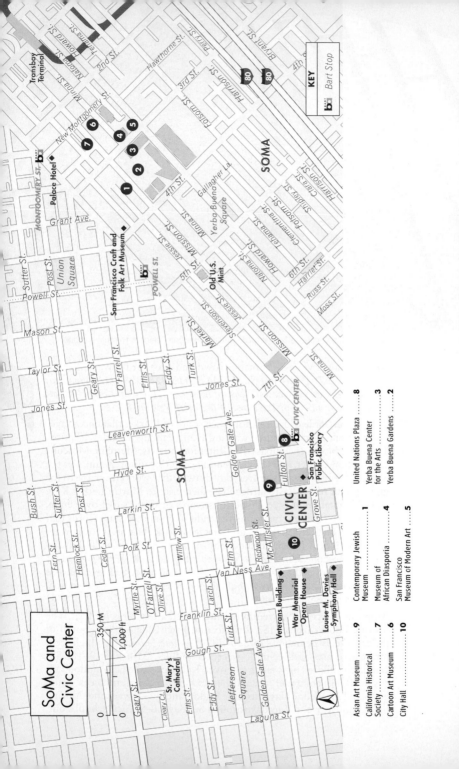

SoMa and Civic Center

Asian Art Museum 9
California Historical Society 7
Cartoon Art Museum 6
City Hall 10

Contemporary Jewish Museum 1
Museum of African Diaspora 4
San Francisco Museum of Modern Art 5

United Nations Plaza 8
Yerba Buena Center for the Arts 3
Yerba Buena Gardens 2

KEY

b⃝ Bart Stop

Also part of the rooftop complex are gardens, an ice-skating rink, and a bowling alley. ⊠ *Bordered by 3rd, 4th, Mission, and Folsom Sts., SoMa* ☎ *No phone* ⊕ *www.yerbabuena.org* ⊠ *Free* ⊙ *Daily sunrise–10 PM.*

EXPLORING CIVIC CENTER

9 ⓩ **Asian Art Museum.** Expecting a building full of Buddhas and jade? Well, yeah, you can find plenty of that here. Happily, though, you don't have to be a connoisseur of Asian art to appreciate a visit to this splendidly renovated museum, whose monumental exterior conceals a light, open, and welcoming space. The fraction of the museum's items on display (about 2,500 pieces from a 15,000-plus-piece collection) is laid out thematically and by region, making it easy to follow developments.

HAYES VALLEY

Hayes Valley, right next door to the Civic Center, is an offbeat neighborhood with terrific eateries, cool watering holes, and great browsing in its funky clothing and home decor boutiques. Swing down main drag Hayes Street, between Franklin and Laguna, and you can hit the highlights, including two very popular restaurants, Absinthe and Suppenküche. Comfy Place Pigalle (at Hayes and Octavia streets) is also a favorite for its living-room atmosphere, wines, and microbrews. Locals love this quarter, but without any big-name draws, it remains off the radar for most visitors.

Begin on the third floor, where highlights of Buddhist art in Southeast Asia and early China include a large, jewel-encrusted, exquisitely painted 19th-century Burmese Buddha and clothed rod puppets from Java. On the second floor you can find later Chinese works, as well as pieces from Korea and Japan. Look for a cobalt tiger jauntily smoking a pipe on a whimsical Korean jar and delicate Japanese tea implements. The ground floor displays rotating exhibits, including contemporary and traveling shows. ■**TIP➔** If you'd like to attend one of the occasional tea ceremonies and tastings at the Japanese Teahouse, call ahead, since preregistration is required. ⊠ *200 Larkin St., between McAllister and Fulton Sts., Civic Center* ☎ *415/581–3500* ⊕ *www.asianart.org* ⊠ *$12, free 1st Sun. of month; $5 Thurs. 5–9; tea ceremony $20, includes museum* ⊙ *Tues., Wed., and Fri.–Sun. 10–5, Thurs. 10–9.*

10 **City Hall.** This imposing 1915 structure with its massive gold-leaf dome—higher than the U.S. Capitol's—is about as close to a palace as you're going to get in San Francisco. (The metal detectors take something away from the grandeur, though.) The classic granite-and-marble behemoth was modeled after St. Peter's Cathedral in Rome. Architect Arthur Brown Jr., who also designed Coit Tower and the War Memorial Opera House, designed an interior with grand columns and a sweeping central staircase. San Franciscans were thrilled, and probably a bit surprised, when his firm built City Hall in just a few years. The building it replaced, dubbed "the new City Hall ruin," had lined the pockets of corrupt builders and politicians during its 27 years of construction. That 1899 structure collapsed in about 27 seconds in the 1906 earthquake, revealing trash and newspapers mixed into the building materials.

City Hall was spruced up and seismically retrofitted in the late 1990s, but the sense of history remains palpable. Some noteworthy events that have taken place here include the marriage of Marilyn Monroe and Joe DiMaggio (1954); the hosing—down the central staircase—of civil-rights and freedom-of-speech protesters (1960); the murders of Mayor George Moscone and openly gay supervisor Harvey Milk (1978); the torching of the lobby by angry members of the gay community in response to the light sentence given to the former supervisor who killed both men (1979); and the registrations of scores of gay couples in celebration of the passage of San Francisco's Domestic Partners Act (1991). February 2004 has come to be known as the Winter of Love: thousands of gay and lesbian couples responded to Mayor Gavin Newsom's decision to issue marriage licenses to same-sex partners, turning City Hall into the site of raucous celebration and joyful nuptials for a month before the state Supreme Court ordered the practice stopped. That celebratory scene replayed during 2008, when scores of couples were wed between the court's June ruling that everyone enjoys the civil right to marry and the November passage of California's ballot proposition banning same-sex marriage. (Stay tuned . . .) Free tours are offered weekdays at 10, noon, and 2.

❽ United Nations Plaza. Locals know this plaza for two things: its Wednesday and Sunday farmers' market—cheap and earthy to the Ferry Building's pricey and beautiful—and its homeless population, which seems to return no matter how many times the city tries to shunt them aside. Brick pillars listing various nations and the dates of their admittance into the United Nations line the plaza, and its floor is inscribed with the goals and philosophy of the United Nations charter, which was signed at the War Memorial Opera House in 1945. ⊠ *Fulton St. between Hyde and Market Sts., Civic Center.*

NOB HILL AND RUSSIAN HILL

In place of the quirky charm and cultural diversity that mark other San Francisco neighborhoods, Nob Hill exudes history and good breeding. Topped with some of the city's most elegant hotels, Gothic Grace Cathedral, and private blue-blood clubs, it's the pinnacle of privilege. One hill over, across Pacific Avenue, is another old-family bastion, Russian Hill. It may not be quite as wealthy as Nob Hill, but it's no slouch—and it's known for its jaw-dropping views.

Nob Hill was officially dubbed during the 1870s when "the Big Four"—Charles Crocker, Leland Stanford, Mark Hopkins, and Collis Huntington, who were involved in the construction of the transcontinental railroad—built their hilltop estates. The lingo is thick from this era: those on the hilltop were referred to as "nabobs" (originally meaning a provincial governor from India) and "swells," and the hill itself was called Snob Hill, a term that survives to this day. By 1882 so many estates had sprung up on Nob Hill that Robert Louis Stevenson called it "the hill of palaces." But the 1906 earthquake and fire destroyed all the palatial mansions, except for portions of the Flood brownstone.

Nob Hill and Russian Hill

History buffs may choose to linger here, but for most visitors, a casual glimpse from a cable car will be enough.

Essentially a tony residential neighborhood of spiffy pieds-à-terre, Victorian flats, Edwardian cottages, and boxlike condos, Russian Hill also has some of the city's loveliest stairway walks, hidden garden ways, and steepest streets—brave drivers can really have some fun here—not to mention those bay views. Several stories explain the origin of Russian Hill's name. One legend has it that Russian farmers raised vegetables here for Farallon Islands seal hunters; another attributes the name to a Russian sailor of prodigious drinking habits who drowned when he fell into a well on the hill. A plaque at the top of the Vallejo Steps gives credence to the version that says sailors of the Russian-American company were buried here in the 1840s. Be sure to visit the sign for yourself—its location offers perhaps the finest vantage point on the hill.

EXPLORING NOB HILL

2 **Grace Cathedral.** Not many churches can boast a Keith Haring sculpture and not one but two labyrinths. The seat of the Episcopal Church in San Francisco, this soaring Gothic-style structure, erected on the site of Charles Crocker's mansion, took 53 years to build, wrapping up in 1964. The gilded bronze doors at the east entrance were taken from casts of Lorenzo Ghiberti's incredible Gates of Paradise, which are on the baptistery in Florence, Italy. A black-and-bronze stone sculpture of St. Francis by Beniamino Bufano greets you as you enter.

The 35-foot-wide labyrinth, a large, purplish rug with a looping pattern, is a replica of the 13th-century stone maze on the floor of Chartres Cathedral. All are encouraged to walk the ¼-mi-long labyrinth, a ritual based on the tradition of meditative walking. There's also a terrazzo outdoor labyrinth on the church's north side. The AIDS Interfaith Chapel, to the right as you enter Grace, contains a metal tryptich sculpture by the late artist Keith Haring and panels from the AIDS Memorial Quilt. ■TIP→ Especially dramatic times to view the cathedral are during Thursday-night evensong (5:15) and during special holiday programs. ✉ 1100 California St., at Taylor St., Nob Hill ☎ 415/749–6300 ⊕ www.gracecathedral.org ⊙ Weekdays 7–6, Sat. 8–6, Sun. 7–7.

❶ Pacific Union Club. The former home of silver baron James Flood cost a whopping $1.5 million in 1886, when even a stylish Victorian like the Haas-Lilienthal House cost less than $20,000. All that cash did buy some structural stability. The Flood residence (to be precise, its shell) was the only Nob Hill mansion to survive the 1906 earthquake and fire. The Pacific Union Club, a bastion of the wealthy and powerful, purchased the house in 1907 and commissioned Willis Polk to redesign it; the architect added the semicircular wings and third floor. (The ornate fence design dates from the mansion's construction.) West of the house, Huntington Park is the site of the Huntington mansion, destroyed in 1906. Mrs. Huntington donated the land to the city for use as a park; the Crockers purchased the Fountain of the Tortoises, based on the original in Rome. ■TIP→ The benches around the fountain offer a welcome break after climbing Nob Hill. It's hard to get the skinny on the club itself; its 700 or so members allegedly follow the directive "no women, no Democrats, no reporters." Those who join usually spend decades on the waiting list and undergo a stringent vetting process, the rigors of which might embarrass the NSA. Needless to say, the club is closed to the public. ✉ 1000 California St., Nob Hill.

EXPLORING RUSSIAN HILL

❹ Feusier House. Octagonal houses were once thought to make the best use of space and enhance the physical and mental well-being of their occupants. A brief mid-19th-century craze inspired the construction of several in San Francisco. Only the Feusier House, built in 1857, and the Octagon House in Pacific Heights remain standing. A private residence, the Feusier House is easy to overlook unless you look closely— it's dwarfed by the large-scale apartments around it. Across from the Feusier House is the **1907 Firehouse** (✉ 1088 Green St., Russian Hill). Louise M. Davies, the local art patron for whom symphony hall is named, bought it from the city in 1957. The firehouse is closed to the public, but it's worth taking in the exterior. ✉ 1067 Green St., Russian Hill.

❸ Ina Coolbrith Park. ★ If you make it all the way up here, you may have the place all to yourself, or at least feel like you do. The park's terraces are carved from a hill so steep that it's difficult to see if anyone else is there or not. Locals love this park because it feels like a secret no one else

Continued on page 393

CABLE CARS

The moment it dawns on you that you severely underestimated the steepness of the San Francisco hills will likely be the same moment you look down and realize those tracks aren't just for show—or just for tourists.

Sure, locals rarely use the cable cars for commuting these days. (That's partially due to the recent fare hikes—hear that, Muni?) So you'll likely be packed in with plenty of fellow sightseers. You may even be approaching cable-car fatigue after seeing its image on so many souvenirs. But if you fear the magic is gone, simply climb on board, and those jaded thoughts will dissolve. Grab the pole and gawk at the view as the car clanks down an insanely steep grade toward the bay. Listen to the humming cable, the clang of the bell, and the occasional quip from the gripman. It's an experience you shouldn't pass up, whether on your first trip or your fiftieth.

HOW CABLE CARS WORK

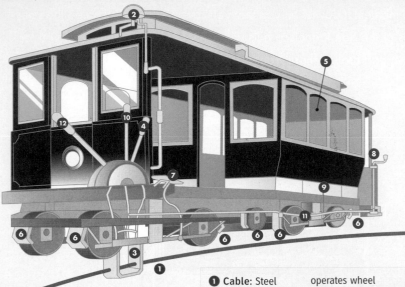

The mechanics are pretty simple: cable cars grab a moving subterranean cable with a "grip" to go. To stop, they release the grip and apply one or more types of brakes. Four cables, totaling 9 miles, power the city's three lines. If the gripman doesn't adjust the grip just right when going up a steep hill, the cable will start to slip and the car will have to back down the hill and try again. This is an extremely rare occurrence—imagine the ribbing the gripman gets back at the cable car barn!

Gripman: Stands in front and operates the grip, brakes, and bell. Favorite joke, especially at the peak of a steep hill: "This is my first day on the job folks…"

Conductor: Moves around the car, deals with tickets, alerts the grip about what's coming up, and operates the rear wheel brakes.

❶ **Cable:** Steel wrapped around flexible sisal core; 2 inches thick; runs at a constant 9½ mph.

❷ **Bells:** Used for crew communication; alerts other drivers and pedestrians.

❸ **Grip:** Vice-like lever extends through the center slot in the track to grab or release the cable.

❹ **Grip Lever:** Left-hand lever; operates grip.

❺ **Car:** Entire car weighs 8 tons.

❻ **Wheel Brake:** Steel brake pads on each wheel.

❼ **Wheel Brake Lever:** Foot pedal; operates wheel brakes.

❽ **Rear Wheel Brake Lever:** Applied for extra traction on hills.

❾ **Track Brake:** 2-foot long sections of Monterey pine push down against the track to help stop the car.

❿ **Track Brake Lever:** Middle lever; operates track brakes.

⓫ **Emergency Brake:** 18-inch steel wedge, jams into street slot to bring car to an immediate stop.

⓬ **Emergency Brake Lever:** Right-hand lever, red; operates emergency brake.

ROUTES

Cars run at least every 15 minutes, from around 6 AM to about 1 AM.

Powell–Hyde line: Most scenic, with classic Bay views. Begins at Powell and Market streets, then crosses Nob Hill and Russian Hill before a white-knuckle descent down Hyde Street, ending near the Hyde Street Pier.

Powell–Mason line: Also begins at Powell and Market streets, but winds through North Beach to Bay and Taylor streets, a few blocks from Fisherman's Wharf.

California line: Runs from the foot of Market Street, at Drumm Street, up Nob Hill and back. Great views (and aromas and sounds) of Chinatown on the way up. Sit in back to catch glimpses of the Bay. ■ **TIP→** Take the California line if it's just the cable-car experience you're after—the lines are shorter, and the grips and conductors say it's friendlier and has a slower pace.

RULES OF THE RIDE

Tickets. A whopping $5 each way. There are ticket booths at all three turnarounds, or you can pay the conductor after you board (they can make change). Try not to grumble about the price—they're embarrassed enough as it is.

■ **TIP→** If you're planning to use public transit a few times, or if you'd like to ride back and forth on the cable car without worrying about the price, consider a one-day Muni passport ($11). You can get passports online, at the Powell Street turnaround, the TIX booth on Union Square, or the Fisherman's Wharf cable-car ticket booth at Beach and Hyde streets.

All Aboard. You can board on either side of the cable car. It's legal to stand on the running boards and hang on to the pole, but keep your ears open for the gripman's warnings. ■ **TIP→** Grab a seat on the outside bench for the best views.

Most people wait (and wait) in line at one of the cable car turnarounds, but you can also hop on along the route. Board wherever you see a white sign showing a figure climbing aboard a brown cable car; wave to the approaching driver, and wait until the car stops.

Riding on the running boards can be part of the thrill.

CABLE CAR HISTORY

HALLIDIE FREES THE HORSES

In the 1850s and '60s, San Francisco's streetcars were drawn by horses. Legend has it that the horrible sight of a car dragging a team of horses downhill to their deaths roused Andrew Smith Hallidie to action. The English immigrant had invented the "Hallidie Ropeway," essentially a cable car for mined ore, and he was convinced that his invention could also move people. In 1873, Hallidie and his intrepid crew prepared to test the first cable car high on Russian Hill. The anxious engineer peered down into the foggy darkness, failed to see the bottom of the hill, and promptly turned the controls over to Hallidie. Needless to say, the thing worked . . . but rides were free for the first two days because people were afraid to get on.

SEE IT FOR YOURSELF

The **Cable Car Museum** is one of the city's best free offerings and an absolute must for kids. (You can even ride a cable car there, since all three lines stop between Russian Hill and Nob Hill.) The museum, which is inside the city's last cable-car barn, takes the top off the system to let you see how it all works.

Eternally humming and squealing, the massive powerhouse cable wheels steal the show. You can also climb aboard a vintage car and take the grip, let the kids ring a cable-car bell (briefly), and check out vintage gear dating from 1873.

✉ *1201 Mason St., at Washington St., Nob Hill* ☎ *415/474–1887* ⊕ *www.cablecarmuseum.com* 🖃 *Free* ☺ *Oct.–Mar., daily 10–5; Apr.–Sept., daily 10–6*

■**TIP➔** The gift shop sells cable car paraphernalia, including an authentic gripman's bell for $600 (it'll sound like Powell Street in your house every day). For significantly less, you can pick up a key chain made from a piece of worn-out cable.

CHAMPION OF THE CABLE CAR BELL

Each June the city's best and brightest come together to crown a bell-ringing champion at Union Square. The crowd cheers gripmen and conductors as they stomp, shake, and riff with the rope. But it's not a popularity contest; the ringers are judged by former bell-ringing champions who take each ping and gong very seriously.

knows about—one of the city's magic hidden gardens, with a meditative setting and spectacular views of the bay peeking out from among the trees. A poet, Oakland librarian, and niece of Mormon prophet Joseph Smith, Ina Coolbrith (1842–1928) introduced Jack London and Isadora Duncan to the world of books. For years she entertained literary greats in her Macondray Lane home near the park. In 1915 she was named poet laureate of California. ⊠ *Vallejo St. between Mason and Taylor Sts., Russian Hill.*

6 **Lombard Street.** The block-long "Crookedest Street in the World" makes eight switchbacks down the east face of Russian Hill between Hyde and Leavenworth streets. Residents bemoan the traffic jam outside their front doors, and occasionally the city attempts to discourage drivers by posting a traffic cop near the top of the hill, but the determined can find a way around. If no one is standing guard, join the line of cars waiting to drive down the steep hill, or avoid the whole mess and walk down the steps on either side of Lombard. You take in super views of North Beach and Coit Tower whether you walk or drive—though if you're the one behind the wheel, you'd better keep your eye on the road lest you become yet another of the many folks who ram the garden barriers. ■**TIP**→ Can't stand the throngs? Thrill seekers of a different stripe may want to head two blocks south of Lombard to Filbert Street. At a gradient of 31.5%, the hair-raising descent between Hyde and Leavenworth streets is the city's steepest. Go slowly! ⊠ *Lombard St. between Hyde and Leavenworth Sts., Russian Hill.*

5 **Macondray Lane.** San Francisco has no shortage of impressive, grand homes, but it's the tiny fairy-tale lanes that make most folks want to move here, and Macondray Lane is the quintessential hidden garden. Enter under a lovely wooden trellis and proceed down a quiet, cobbled pedestrian lane lined with Edwardian cottages and flowering plants and trees. ■**TIP**→ Watch your step—the cobblestones are quite uneven in spots. A flight of steep wooden stairs at the end of the lane leads to Taylor Street—on the way down you can't miss the bay views. If you've read any of Armistead Maupin's *Tales of the City* books, you may find the lane vaguely familiar. It's the thinly disguised setting for part of the series' action. ⊠ *Between Jones and Taylor Sts., and Union and Green Sts., Russian Hill.*

Fodor's Choice
★

7 **San Francisco Art Institute.** A Moorish-tile fountain in a tree-shaded courtyard draws the eye as soon as you enter the institute. The number-one reason for a visit is Mexican master Diego Rivera's *Making of a Fresco Showing the Building of a City* (1931), in the student gallery to your immediate left inside the entrance. Rivera himself is in the fresco—his broad behind is to the viewer—and he's surrounded by his assistants. They in turn are surrounded by a construction scene, laborers, and city notables such as sculptor Robert Stackpole and architect Timothy Pflueger. *The Making of a Fresco* is one of three San Francisco murals painted by Rivera. The number-two reason to come here is the café, or more precisely the eye-popping, panoramic view from the café, which serves surprisingly decent food for a song.

★

8

The older portions of the Art Institute, including the lovely Mission-style bell tower, were erected in 1926. To this day, otherwise pragmatic people claim that ghostly footsteps can be heard in the tower at night. Ansel Adams created the school's fine-arts photography department in 1946, and school directors established the country's first fine-arts film program. Notable faculty and alumni have included painter Richard Diebenkorn and photographers Dorothea Lange, Edward Weston, and Annie Leibovitz. The **Walter & McBean Galleries** (☎ 415/749–4563 ⊙ Tues.–Sat. 11–6) exhibit the often provocative works of established artists. ⊠ 800 Chestnut St., North Beach ☎ 415/771–7020 ⊕ www.sfai. edu ☒ Galleries free ⊙ Student gallery daily 8:30–8:30.

NORTH BEACH

San Francisco novelist Herbert Gold calls North Beach "the longest-running, most glorious American bohemian operetta outside Greenwich Village." Indeed, to anyone who's spent some time in its eccentric old bars and cafés, North Beach evokes everything from the Barbary Coast days to the no-less-rowdy beatnik era. Italian bakeries appear frozen in time, homages to Jack Kerouac and Allen Ginsberg pop up everywhere, and the modern equivalent of the Barbary Coast's "houses of ill repute," strip joints, do business on Broadway. With its outdoor café tables, throngs of tourists, and holiday vibe, this is probably the part of town Europeans are thinking of when they say San Francisco is the most European city in America.

EXPLORING NORTH BEACH

❻ ★ City Lights Bookstore. Take a look at the exterior of the store: the replica of a revolutionary mural destroyed in Chiapas, Mexico, by military forces; the poetry in the windows; and the sign that says "Turn your sell [sic] phone off. Be here now." This place isn't just doling out best sellers. Designated a city landmark, the hangout of Beat-era writers—Allen Ginsberg and store founder Lawrence Ferlinghetti among them—remains a vital part of San Francisco's literary scene. Browse the three levels of sometimes haphazardly arranged poetry, philosophy, politics, fiction, history, and local 'zines, to the tune of creaking wood floors. ■TIP→ Be sure to check their calendar of literary events.

Back in the day, the basement was a kind of literary living room, where writers like Ginsberg and Kerouac would read and even receive mail. Ferlinghetti cemented City Lights' place in history by publishing Ginsberg's *Howl and Other Poems* in 1956. The small volume was ignored in the mainstream . . . until Ferlinghetti and the bookstore manager were arrested for corruption of youth and obscenity. In the landmark First Amendment trial that followed, the judge exonerated both, saying a work that has "redeeming social significance" can't be obscene. *Howl* went on to become a classic.

Kerouac Alley, branching off Columbus Avenue next to City Lights, was rehabbed in 2007. Embedded in the pavement are quotes from Lawrence Ferlinghetti, Maya Angelou, Confucius, John Steinbeck, and of course, the namesake himself. ⊠ 261 Columbus Ave., North Beach ☎ 415/362–8193 ⊕ www.citylights.com ⊙ Daily 10 AM–midnight.

8 **Coit Tower.** Whether you think it resembles a fire hose or something
★ more, ahem, adult, this 210-foot tower is among San Francisco's most
distinctive skyline sights. Although the monument wasn't intended as a
tribute to firemen, it's often considered as such because of the donor's
special attachment to the local fire company. As the story goes, a young
gold rush–era girl, Lillie Hitchcock Coit (known as Miss Lil), was a
fervent admirer of her local fire company—so much so that she once
deserted a wedding party and chased down the street after her favorite engine, Knickerbocker No. 5, while clad in her bridesmaid finery.
She became the Knickerbocker Company's mascot and always signed
her name "Lillie Coit 5." When Lillie died in 1929 she left the city
$125,000 to "expend in an appropriate manner . . . to the beauty of
San Francisco."

You can ride the elevator to the top of the tower—the only thing you
have to pay for here—to enjoy the view of the Bay Bridge and the
Golden Gate Bridge; due north is Alcatraz Island. ■TIP➜ The views
from the base of the tower are also expansive—and free. Parking at Coit
Tower is limited; in fact, you may have to wait (and wait) for a space. Save
yourself some frustration and take the 39 bus which goes all the way up to
the tower's base or, if you're in good shape, hike up. ⇨ *For more details on
the lovely stairway walk, see Telegraph Hill, below.*

Inside the tower, 19 Depression-era murals depict California's economic
and political life. The federal government commissioned the paintings
from 25 local artists, and ended up funding quite a controversy. The
radical Mexican painter Diego Rivera inspired the murals' socialist-
realist style, with its biting cultural commentary, particularly about the
exploitation of workers. At the time the murals were painted, clashes
between management and labor along the waterfront and elsewhere in
San Francisco were widespread. ⊠ *Telegraph Hill Blvd. at Greenwich
St. or Lombard St., North Beach* ☎ *415/362–0808* ⊛ *Free; elevator to
top $5* ☉ *Daily 10–6.*

7 **Telegraph Hill.** Hill residents have some of the best views in the city, as
Fodor's Choice well as the most difficult ascents to their aeries. The hill rises from the
★ east end of Lombard Street to a height of 284 feet and is capped by
Coit Tower (*see above*). Imagine lugging your groceries up that! If you
brave the slope, though, you can be rewarded with a "secret treasure"
SF moment. Filbert Street starts up the hill, then becomes the Filbert
Steps when the going gets too steep. You can cut between the Filbert
Steps and another flight, the Greenwich Steps, on up to the hilltop. As
you climb, you can pass some of the city's oldest houses and be surrounded by beautiful, flowering private gardens. In some places the
trees grow over the stairs so they feel like a green tunnel; elsewhere,
you'll have wide-open views of the bay. And the telegraphic name? It
comes from the hill's status as the first Morse code signal station back
in 1853. ⊠ *Bordered by Lombard, Filbert, Kearny, and Sansome Sts.,
North Beach.*

5 **Washington Square.** Once the daytime social heart of Little Italy, this
grassy patch has changed character numerous times over the years. The
Beats hung out in the 1950s, hippies camped out in the 1960s and early

North Beach and On the Waterfront

East Harbor

Mexican Museum

Fort Mason

Aquatic Park

San Francisco Bay

⑬

⑪

⑫

Pier 45

Pier 47

The Cannery at Del Monte Square

⑩

Pier 41

NORTH BEACH

⑨

Bay St.

Francisco St.

Chestnut St.

Russian Hill Park

North Point St.

Francisco St.

Chestnut St.

Lombard St.

Greenwich St.

Filbert St.

Union St.

Jefferson St.

Taylor St.

Mason St.

Powell St.

Stockton St.

Beach St.

North Point St.

Bay St.

Pier 35

Pier 33

Pier 31

Pier 29

Pier 27

Van Ness Ave.

Larkin St.

Polk St.

Hyde St.

Leavenworth St.

Jones St.

Broadway

RUSSIAN HILL

Green St.

Vallejo St.

Broadway

Pacific Ave.

Jackson St.

Washington St.

Clay St.

Taylor St.

Mason St.

Washington Square

⑤

Columbus Ave.

Grant Ave.

Kearny St.

⑦

⑧

Lombard St.

Chestnut St.

Levi Strauss Headquarters

Pier 23

Pier 19

Pier 17

Pier 15

Pier 9

Hotaling Pl.

Sonoma St.

Vallejo St.

Union St.

Green St.

Montgomery St.

Sansome St.

Battery St.

Front St.

Davis St.

The Embarcadero

⑥

Cable Car Museum

Huntington Park

NOB HILL

Taylor St.

Mason St.

Powell St.

Bush St. Tunnel

St. Mary's Sq.

④

③

Jackson St.

Washington St.

Clay St.

Sacramento St.

California St.

Pine St.

Dupont St.

Pier 7

Pier 5

Pier 3

Pier 1

Wells Fargo Bank History Museum

DOWNTOWN

Union Square

Sutter St.

Post St.

Justin Herman Plaza

MONTGOMERY ST.

Market St.

EMBARCADERO

New Montgomery St.

Annie St.

Jessie St.

Mission St.

Minna St.

Natoma St.

Tehama St.

Clementina St.

Folsom St.

Taber Pl.

Hawthorne St.

1st St.

2nd St.

Essex St.

Ecker St.

Elim St.

Fremont St.

Beale St.

Main St.

Spear St.

Steuart St.

Hyatt Regency Hotel

②

①

Mission St.

Audiffred Building

CITY FRONT

Howard St.

Harrison St.

80

San Francisco - Oakland Bay Bridge

Pier 26

Bryant St.

Yerba Buena Gardens

KEY

b   *Bart Stop*

······   *Cable Car*

0   350 meters

0   1,000 ft

The Birds

While on Telegraph Hill, you might be startled by a chorus of piercing squawks and a rushing sound of wings. No, you're not about to have a Hitchcock bird-attack moment. These small, vivid green parrots with cherry-red heads number in the hundreds; they're descendants of former pets that escaped or were released by their owners. (The birds dislike cages and they bite if bothered...must've been some disillusioned owners along the way.)

The parrots like to roost high in the aging cypress trees on the hill, chattering and fluttering, sometimes taking wing en masse. They're not popular with most residents, but they did find a champion in local bohemian Mark Bittner, a former street musician. Bittner began chronicling their habits, publishing a book and battling the homeowners who wanted to cut down the cypresses. A documentary, *The Wild Parrots of Telegraph Hill*, made the issue a cause célèbre. In 2007, City Hall, which recognizes a golden goose when it sees one, stepped in and brokered a solution to keep the celebrity birds in town. The city will cover the homeowners' insurance worries and plant new trees for the next generation of wild parrots.

—Denise M. Leto

'70s, and nowadays you're just as likely to see kids of Southeast Asian descent tossing a Frisbee as Italian men or women chat about their children and the old country. In the morning elderly Asians perform the motions of tai chi, but by mid-morning groups of conservatively dressed Italian men in their 70s and 80s begin to arrive. Any time of day, the park may attract a number of homeless people, who stretch out to rest on the benches and grass, and young locals sunbathing or running their dogs. Lillie Hitchcock Coit, in yet another show of affection for San Francisco's firefighters, donated the statue of two firemen with a child they rescued. ■TIP➔ The North Beach Festival, the city's oldest street fair, celebrates the area's Italian culture here each June. ⊠ *Bordered by Columbus Ave. and Stockton, Filbert, and Union Sts., North Beach.*

ON THE WATERFRONT

San Francisco's waterfront neighborhoods have fabulous views and utterly different personalities. Kitschy, overpriced Fisherman's Wharf struggles to maintain the last shreds of its existence as a working wharf, while Pier 39 is a full-fledged consumer circus. The Ferry Building draws well-heeled locals with its culinary pleasures, firmly reconnecting the Embarcadero to downtown. Between the Ferry Building and Pier 39, a former maritime no-man's land is filling in a bit—especially near Pier 33, where the perpetually booked Alcatraz cruises depart—with a waterfront restaurant here and a restored pedestrian-friendly pier there.

Today's shoreline was once Yerba Buena Cove, filled in during the latter half of the 19th century when San Francisco was a brawling, extravagant gold-rush town. Jackson Square, now a genteel and upscale corner of the inland Financial District, was the heart of the Barbary Coast, bordering some of the roughest wharves in the world. Below Montgomery Street (in today's Financial District), between California Street and Broadway, lies a remnant of these wild days: more than 100 ships abandoned by frantic crews and passengers caught up in gold fever lie under the foundations of buildings here.

EXPLORING THE WATERFRONT

⑬ **Alcatraz.** Thousands of visitors a
Fodor'sChoice day take the 15-minute ferry ride to
★ "the Rock" to walk in the footsteps of Alcatraz's notorious criminals. Definitely take the splendid audio tour; gravelly voiced former inmates and hardened guards bring one of America's most notorious penal colonies to life. Plan your schedule to allow at least three hours for the visit and boat rides combined, and buy tickets in advance, even in the off-season. ⊠ *Pier 33, Fisherman's Wharf* 🕾 *415/981–7625* ⊕ *www.nps.gov/alca, www.parkconservancy.org/visit/alcatraz, www.alcatrazcruises.com* 🎟 *$26, including audio tour; $33 evening tour, including audio* ⊗ *Ferry departs every 30–45 mins Sept.– late May, daily 9:30–3:20, 4:20 for evening tour Thurs.–Mon. only; late May–Aug., daily 9–4, 5:55 and 6:45 for evening tour.*

❷ **Ferry Building.** Renovated in 2003, the Ferry Building is the jewel of the
Fodor'sChoice Embarcadero. The beacon of the port area, erected in 1896, has a 230-
★ foot clock tower modeled after the campanile of the cathedral in Seville, Spain. On the morning of April 18, 1906, the tower's four clock faces, powered by the swinging of a 14-foot pendulum, stopped at 5:17—the moment the great earthquake struck—and stayed still for 12 months.

Today San Franciscans flock to the street-level Market Hall, stocking up on supplies from local favorites such as Acme Bread, Scharffen Berger Chocolate, and Cowgirl Creamery. Lucky diners claim a coveted table at Slanted Door, the city's beloved high-end Vietnamese restaurant. The seafood bars at Hog Island Oyster Company and Ferry Plaza Seafood have fantastic city panoramas—or you can take your purchases around to the building's bay side, where benches face views of the Bay Bridge. Saturday mornings the plaza in front of the building buzzes with an upscale, celebrity-chef-studded farmers' market. Extending from the piers on the north side of the building south to the Bay Bridge, the waterfront promenade is a favorite among joggers and picnickers, with a front-row view of the sailboats slipping by. The Ferry Building also serves actual ferries: from behind the building they sail to Sausalito, Larkspur, Tiburon, and the East Bay. ⊠ *Embarcadero at foot of Market St., Embarcadero* ⊕ *www.ferrybuildingmarketplace.com.*

F-LINE TROLLEYS

The F-line, the city's system of vintage electric trolleys, gives the cable cars a run for their money as San Francisco's best-loved mode of transportation. These beautifully restored streetcars— some dating from the 19th century—run from the Castro all the way down Market Street to the Embarcadero, then north to Fisherman's Wharf. Each car is unique, restored to the colors of its city of origin, from New Orleans and Philadelphia to Moscow and Milan. Purchase tickets on board; exact change is required. ⊕ *www.streetcar.org* 🎟 *$2.*

Thousands of visitors take ferries to Alcatraz each day to walk in the footsteps of the notorious criminals who were held on "The Rock."

QUICK BITES

Even locals love the cheery **Buena Vista Café** (✉ *2765 Hyde St., Fisherman's Wharf* ☎ *415/474–5044*), which claims to be the first place in the United States to have served Irish coffee. The café opens at 9 AM weekdays (8 AM weekends) and dishes up a great breakfast. They serve about 2,000 Irish coffees a day, so it's always crowded; try for a table overlooking nostalgic Victorian Park and its cable-car turntable.

⑩ Fisherman's Wharf. It may be one of the city's best-known attractions, but the wharf is a no-go zone for most locals, who shy away from the difficult parking, overpriced food, and cheesy shops at third-rate shopping centers like the Cannery at Del Monte Square. If you just can't resist a visit here, come early to avoid the crowds and get a sense of the wharf's functional role—it's not just an amusement park replica.

Most of the entertainment at the wharf is schlocky and overpriced, with one notable exception: the splendid **Musée Mécanique** (☎ *415/346–2000* ⏱ *Weekdays 10–7, weekends 10–8*), a time-warped arcade with antique mechanical contrivances, including peep shows and nickelodeons. Some favorites are the giant and rather creepy "Laffing Sal" (you enter the museum through his gaping mouth), an arm-wrestling machine, the world's only steam-powered motorcycle, and mechanical fortune-telling figures that speak from their curtained boxes. Note the depictions of race that betray the prejudices of the time: stoned Chinese figures in the "Opium-Den" and clown-faced African-Americans eating watermelon in the "Mechanical Farm." Admission is free, but you'll need quarters to bring the machines to life.

Among the two floors of exhibits at **Ripley's Believe It or Not! Museum** (✉ *175 Jefferson St., Fisherman's Wharf* ☎ *415/771–6188* ⊕ *www. ripleysf.com* ⊠ *$14.99* ⊙ *Late June–Labor Day, Sun.–Thurs. 9* AM–*11* PM, *Fri. and Sat. 9* AM–*midnight; Labor Day–early June, Sun.–Thurs. 10–10, Fri. and Sat., 10* AM–*midnight*) is a tribute to San Francisco—an 8-foot-long scale model of a cable car, made entirely of matchsticks. Notables from local boy Robin Williams to Jesus await at the **Wax Museum** (✉ *145 Jefferson St., Fisherman's Wharf* ☎ *415/202–0400 or 800/439–4305* ⊕ *www.waxmuseum.com*), open weekdays 10–9, weekends 9 AM–11 PM. Admission is $14.

The USS *Pampanito* (✉ *Pier 45, Fisherman's Wharf* ☎ *415/775–1943* ⊕ *www.maritime.org/pamphome.htm* ⊙ *Oct.–Memorial Day, Sun.– Thurs. 9–6, Fri. and Sat. 9–8; Memorial Day–Sept., Thurs.–Tues. 9–8, Wed. 9–6*) provides an intriguing if mildly claustrophobic glimpse into life on a submarine during World War II. The sub sank six Japanese warships and damaged four others. Admission is $10; the family pass is a great deal at $20 for two adults and up to four kids. ✉ *Jefferson St. between Leavenworth St. and Pier 39, Fisherman's Wharf.*

⑫ Ghirardelli Square. Most of the redbrick buildings in this early-20th-century complex were once part of the Ghirardelli factory. Now tourists come here to pick up the famous chocolate, but you can purchase it all over town and save yourself a trip to what is essentially a mall. (If you're a shopaholic, though, it definitely beats the Cannery.) There are no fewer than three Ghirardelli stores here, as well as gift shops and a couple of restaurants—including Ana Mandara—that even locals love. Fairmont recently opened an upscale urban time-share directly on the square. Placards throughout the square describe the factory's history. ✉ *900 N. Point St., Fisherman's Wharf* ☎ *415/775–5500* ⊕ *www. ghirardellisq.com.*

⑪ Hyde Street Pier. Cotton candy and souvenirs are all well and good, but
Ⓒ if you want to get to the heart of the Wharf—boats—there's no bet-
★ ter place to do it than at this pier, by far one of the Wharf area's best bargains. Depending on the time of day, you might see boat builders at work or children pretending to man an early-1900s ship.

Don't pass up the centerpiece collection of historic vessels, part of the **San Francisco Maritime National Historic Park,** almost all of which can be boarded. The newly restored *Balclutha,* an 1886 full-rigged three-masted sailing vessel that's more than 250 feet long, sailed around Cape Horn 17 times; kids especially love the *Eureka,* a side-wheel passenger and car ferry, for her onboard collection of vintage cars; the *Hercules* is a steam-powered tugboat. The *C. A. Thayer,* a three-masted schooner, recently underwent a painstaking restoration and is back on display. Across the street from the pier and almost a museum in itself is the San Francisco Maritime National Historic Park's **Visitor Center** (✉ *499 Jefferson St., at Hyde St., Fisherman's Wharf* ☎ *415/447– 5000* ⊙ *Memorial Day–Sept., daily 9:30–6; Oct.–Memorial Day, daily 9:30–5*), happily free of mind-numbing, text-heavy displays. Instead, fun, large-scale exhibits, such as a huge First Order Fresnel lighthouse lens and a shipwrecked boat, make this an engaging and relatively quick stop. ⊠ *Hyde and Jefferson Sts., Fisherman's Wharf* ☎ *415/561–7100* ⊕ *www.nps.gov/safr* ⊠ *Ships $5* ⊗ *Memorial Day–Sept., daily 9:30–6; Oct.–Memorial Day, daily 9:30–5.*

❹ **Jackson Square.** This was the heart of the Barbary Coast of the Gay '90s (the 1890s, that is). Although most of the red-light district was destroyed in the fire that followed the 1906 earthquake, old redbrick buildings and narrow alleys recall the romance and rowdiness of San Francisco's early days. The days of

> **WHISKEY RHYME**
>
> The Italianate Hotaling building survived the disastrous 1906 quake and fire—a miracle considering the thousands of barrels of inflammable liquid inside. A plaque on the side of the structure repeats a famous query: IF, AS THEY SAY, GOD SPANKED THE TOWN FOR BEING OVER FRISKY, WHY DID HE BURN THE CHURCHES DOWN AND SAVE HOTALING'S WHISKEY?

brothels and bar fights are long gone—now Jackson Square is a genteel, quiet corner of the Financial District. It's of interest to the historically inclined and antiques-shop browsers, but otherwise safely skipped.

Some of the city's first business buildings, survivors of the 1906 quake, still stand between Montgomery and Sansome streets. After a few decades of neglect, these old-timers were adopted by preservation-minded interior designers and wholesale-furniture dealers for use as showrooms. In 1972 the city officially designated the area—bordered by Columbus Avenue on the west, Broadway and Pacific Avenue on the north, Washington Street on the south, and Sansome Street on the east—San Francisco's first historic district. When property values soared, many of the fabric and furniture outlets fled to Potrero Hill. Advertising agencies, attorneys, and antiques dealers now occupy the Jackson Square–area structures. Restored 19th-century brick buildings line Hotaling Place, which connects Washington and Jackson streets. The lane is named for the head of the **A. P. Hotaling Company whiskey distillery** (⊠ *451 Jackson St., at Hotaling Pl.*), which was the largest liquor repository on the West Coast in its day. (Hotaling whiskey is still made in the city, by the way; look for their single malts for a sip of truly local flavor.) *Jackson Sq. district bordered by Broadway and Washington, Kearny, and Sansome Sts., Financial District.*

❾ **Pier 39.** The city's most popular waterfront attraction draws millions of visitors each year who come to browse through its vertiginous array of shops and concessions hawking every conceivable form of souvenir. The pier can be quite crowded, and the numerous street performers may leave you feeling more harassed than entertained. Arriving early in the morning ensures you a front-row view of the sea lions, but if you're here to shop—and make no mistake about it, Pier 39 wants your money—be aware that most stores don't open until 9:30 or 10 (later in winter).

Pick up a buckwheat hull–filled otter neck wrap or a plush sea lion to snuggle at the **Marine Mammal Store** (☎ *415/289–7373*), whose proceeds benefit Sausalito's respected wild-animal hospital, the Marine Mammal Center. Sales of the excellent books, maps, and collectibles—including a series of gorgeous, distinctive art-deco posters for Alcatraz, the Presidio,

Fort Point, and the other members of the Golden Gate National Recreation Area—at the **National Park Store** (☎ 415/433-7221) help to support the National Park Service. Brilliant colors enliven the double-decker **San Francisco Carousel** (☑ $3 per ride), decorated with images of such city landmarks as the Golden Gate Bridge and Lombard Street. Follow the sound of barking to the northwest side of the pier to view the sea lions that remain after the majority of them migrated. At **Aquarium of the Bay** (☎ 415/623-5300 or 888/732-3483 ⊕ www.aquariumofthebay. org ☑ $15.95) moving walkways transport you through a space surrounded on three sides by water filled with indigenous San Francisco Bay marine life, from fish and plankton to sharks. Many find the aquarium overpriced; if you can, take advantage of the family rate ($39.95 for two adults and two kids under 12). The aquarium is open June through September daily 9–8; during the rest of the year it's open Monday through Thursday 10–6 and Friday through Sunday 10–7.

The **California Welcome Center** (☎ 415/981-1280 ⊕ www.visitcwc. com ⊗ Daily 10–6), on Pier 39's second level, includes an Internet café. Parking (free with validation from a Pier 39 restaurant) is at the Pier 39 Garage, off Powell Street at the Embarcadero. ⊠ Beach St. at Embarcadero, Fisherman's Wharf ⊕ www.pier39.com.

❶ San Francisco Railway Museum. A labor of love brought to you by the
Ⓒ same vintage-transit enthusiasts responsible for the F-line's revival, this one-room museum and store celebrates the city's storied streetcars and cable cars with photographs, models, and artifacts. Kids can explore the (replicated) end of a streetcar with a working cab, operate a cool, antique Wiley birdcage traffic signal, and view (but not touch) models and display cases. Right on the F-line track, just across from the Ferry Building, this is a great quick stop. ⊠ 77 Steuart St., Embarcadero ☎ 415/974-1948 ⊕ www.streetcar.org ☑ Free ⊗ Tues.–Sun. 10–6.

❸ Transamerica Pyramid. It's neither owned by Transamerica nor is it a pyramid, but this 853-foot-tall obelisk *is* the most photographed of the city's high-rises. Excoriated in the design stages as "the world's largest architectural folly," the icon was quickly hailed as a masterpiece when it opened in 1972. Today it's probably the city's most recognized structure after the Golden Gate Bridge. A fragrant redwood grove along the east side of the building, replete with benches and a cheerful fountain, is a placid patch in which to unwind. ⊠ 600 Montgomery St., Financial District ⊕ www.transamerica.com.

THE MARINA AND THE PRESIDIO

Yachts bob at their moorings, satisfied-looking folks jog along the Marina Green, and multimillion-dollar homes overlook the bay in this picturesque, if somewhat sterile, neighborhood. Does it all seem a bit too perfect? Well, it got this way after the hard knock of Loma Prieta— the current pretty face was put on after hundreds of homes collapsed in the 1989 earthquake. Just west of this waterfront area is a more natural beauty: the Presidio. Once a military base, this beautiful, sprawling park is mostly green space, with hills, woods, and the marshlands of Crissy Field.

EXPLORING THE MARINA

3
🙂
★
Exploratorium. Walking into this fascinating "museum of science, art, and human perception" is like visiting a mad scientist's laboratory. Most of the exhibits are supersize, and you can play with everything. You can feel like Alice in Wonderland in the distortion room, where you seem to shrink and grow as you walk across the slanted, checkered floor. In the shadow room, a powerful flash freezes an image of your shadow on the wall; jumping is a favorite pose. "Pushover" demonstrates cow-tipping, but for people: stand on one foot and try to keep your balance while a friend swings a striped panel in front of you (trust us, you're going to fall).

More than 650 other exhibits focus on sea and insect life, computers, electricity, patterns and light, language, the weather, and much more. "Explainers"—usually high-school students on their days off—demonstrate cool scientific tools and procedures, like DNA sample-collection and cow-eye dissection. One surefire hit is the pitch-black, touchy-feely Tactile Dome. In this geodesic dome strewn with textured objects, you crawl through a course of ladders, slides, and tunnels, relying solely on your sense of touch. Not surprisingly, lovey-dovey couples sometimes linger in the "grope dome," but be forewarned: the staff will turn on the lights if they have to. ■ **TIP→** Reservations are required for the Tactile Dome and will get you 75 minutes of access. You have to be at least seven years old to go through the dome, and the space is not for the claustrophobic. ⊠ *3601 Lyon St., at Marina Blvd., Marina* 🕾 *415/561–0360 general information, 415/561–0362 Tactile Dome reservations* ⊕ *www.exploratorium.edu* 🖪 *$14, free 1st Wed. of month; Tactile Dome $3 extra* ⊙ *Tues.–Sun. 10–5.*

4
Fodor's Choice
★
Palace of Fine Arts. At first glance this stunning, rosy rococo palace seems to be from another world, and indeed, it's the sole survivor of the many tinted-plaster structures (a temporary classical city of sorts) built for the 1915 Panama-Pacific International Exposition, the world's fair that celebrated San Francisco's recovery from the 1906 earthquake and fire. The expo buildings originally extended about a mile along the shore. Bernard Maybeck designed this faux–Roman Classic beauty, which was reconstructed in concrete and reopened in 1967.

A victim of the elements, the Palace completed a piece-by-piece renovation in 2008, though the pseudo-Latin language adorning the exterior urns continues to stump scholars. The massive columns (each topped with four "weeping maidens"), great rotunda, and swan-filled lagoon have been used in countless fashion layouts, films, and wedding photo shoots. After admiring the lagoon, look across the street to the house at 3460 Baker Street. If the maidens out front look familiar, they should—they're original casts of the lovely "garland ladies" you can see in the Palace's colonnade. The house was on the market in 2007; if you'd had a cool $8 million, it could've been yours. ⊠ *Baker and Beach Sts., Marina* 🕾 *415/561–0364 Palace history tours* ⊕ *www.exploratorium.edu/palace* 🖪 *Free* ⊙ *Daily 24 hrs.*

8

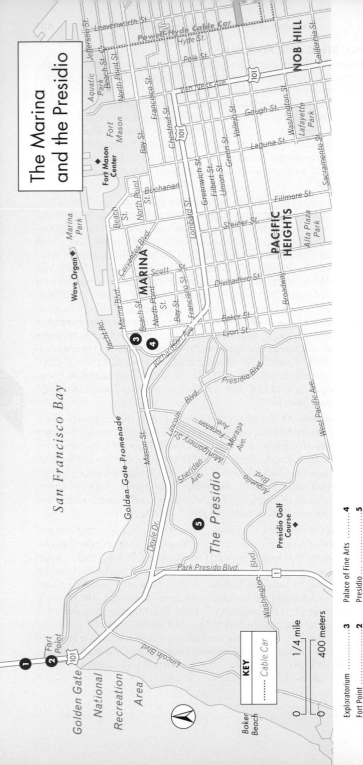

The Marina
and the Presidio

Leavenworth St.
Jefferson St.
Powell-Hyde Cable Car
Hyde St.
Polk St.
Van Ness Ave.
Beach St.
North Point St.
Aquatic
NOB HILL
Francisco St.
California St.
Bay St.
Chestnut St.
Gough St.
Washington St.
Lafayette
Park
Laguna St.
Valleio St.
Green St.
Union St.
Filbert St.
Greenwich St.
Sacramento St.
Fort Mason
Fort Mason Center
Buchanan
North Point St.
Lombard St.
Fillmore St.
Steiner St.
PACIFIC HEIGHTS
Alta Plaza Park
Broadway
Divisadero St.
Marina Park
Wave Organ
Marina Blvd.
Beach St.
Cervantes Blvd.
Scott
MARINA
North Point St.
Baker St.
Lyon St.
Bay St.
Francisco St.
Yacht Rd.
Richardson Ave.
Presidio Blvd.
West Pacific Ave.
San Francisco Bay
Golden Gate Promenade
Mason St.
Blvd.
Lincoln
Funston Ave.
Montgomery St.
Moraga Ave.
Arguello Blvd.
Sheridan Ave.
The Presidio
Doyle Dr.
Presidio Golf Course
Park Presidio Blvd.
Washington
Golden Gate National Recreation Area
Fort Point
Lincoln Blvd.
Baker Beach

KEY
········· Cable Car

0 ___ 1/4 mile
0 ___ 400 meters

EXPLORING THE PRESIDIO

❷ Fort Point. Dwarfed today by the Golden Gate Bridge, this brick fortress constructed between 1853 and 1861 was designed to protect San Francisco from a Civil War sea attack that never materialized. It was also used as a coastal-defense fortification post during World War II, when soldiers stood watch here. This National Historic Site is now a sprawling museum filled with military memorabilia, surrounding a lonely, windswept courtyard. The building has a gloomy air and is suitably atmospheric. (It's usually chilly and windy, too, so bring a jacket.) On days when Fort Point is staffed, guided group tours and cannon drills take place. The top floor affords a unique angle on the bay. ■ TIP→ Take care when walking along the front side of the building, as it's slippery and the waves have a dizzying effect. The fort's popular guided candlelight tours, available only in winter, sell out in advance, so be sure to book ahead. Southeast of this structure is the **Fort Point Mine Depot,** an army facility that functioned as the headquarters for underwater mining operations throughout World War II. Today it's the Warming Hut, a National Park Service café and bookstore. ✉ *Marine Dr. off Lincoln Blvd., Presidio* ☎ *415/556–1693* ⊕ *www.nps.gov/fopo* 💲 *Free* ☉ *Fri.–Sun. 10–5.*

❶ Golden Gate Bridge. The suspension bridge that connects San Francisco with Marin County has long wowed sightseers with its simple but powerful art-deco design. Completed in 1937 after four years of construction, the 2-mi span and its 750-foot towers were built to withstand winds of more than 100 mph. It's also not a bad place to be in an earthquake: designed to sway up to 27.7 feet, the Golden Gate Bridge, unlike the Bay Bridge, was undamaged by the 1989 Loma Prieta quake. (If you're on the bridge when it's windy, stand still and you can feel it swaying a bit.) Though it's frequently gusty and misty—always bring a jacket, no matter what the weather's like—the bridge provides unparalleled views of the Bay Area. Muni buses 28 and 29 make stops at the Golden Gate Bridge toll plaza, on the San Francisco side. However, drive to fully appreciate the bridge from multiple vantage points in and around the Presidio; you'll be able to park at designated areas.

From the bridge's eastern-side walkway—the only side pedestrians are allowed on—you can take in the San Francisco skyline and the bay islands; look west for the wild hills of the Marin Headlands, the curving coast south to Land's End, and the Pacific Ocean. On sunny days, sailboats dot the water, and brave windsurfers test the often-treacherous tides beneath the bridge. ■ TIP→ A vista point on the Marin side gives you a spectacular city panorama.

But there's a well-known, darker side to the bridge's story, too. The bridge is perhaps the world's most popular suicide platform, with an average of about 20 jumpers per year. (The first leaped just three months after the bridge's completion, and the official count was stopped in 1995 as the 1,000th jump approached.) Signs along the bridge read "There is hope. Make the call," referring the disconsolate to the special telephones on the bridge. Bridge officers, who patrol the walkway and watch by security camera to spot potential jumpers, successfully talk down two-thirds to three-quarters of them each year. Documentary filmmaker Eric

Fodor's Choice
★

8

Steel's controversial 2006 movie *The Bridge* once again put pressure on the Golden Gate Bridge Highway and Transportation District to install a suicide barrier; various options are being considered, with most locals supporting an unobtrusive net. ✉ *Lincoln Blvd. near Doyle Dr. and Fort Point, Presidio* ☎ *415/921–5858* ⊕ *www.goldengatebridge.org* ☉ *Pedestrians Mar.–Oct., daily 5 AM–9 PM; Nov.–Feb., daily 5 AM–6 PM; hrs change with daylight saving time. Bicyclists daily 24 hrs.*

❺ **Presidio.** When San Franciscans want to spend a day in the woods, they
★ head here. The Presidio has 1,400 acres of hills and majestic woods, two small beaches, and—the one thing Golden Gate Park doesn't have— stunning views of the bay, the Golden Gate Bridge, and Marin County. Famed environmental artist Andy Goldsworthy's new sculpture greets visitors at the Arguello Gate entrance. Erected at the end of 2008, the 100-plus-foot *Spire*, made of 37 cypress logs reclaimed from the Presidio, looks like a rough, natural version of a church spire. ■**TIP→** The best lookout points lie along Washington Boulevard, which meanders through the park.

Part of the **Golden Gate National Recreation Area,** the Presidio was a military post for more than 200 years. Don Juan Bautista de Anza and a band of Spanish settlers first claimed the area in 1776. It became a Mexican garrison in 1822, when Mexico gained its independence from Spain; U.S. troops forcibly occupied the Presidio in 1846. The U.S. Sixth Army was stationed here until October 1994, when the coveted space was transferred into civilian hands.

Today the area is being transformed into a self-sustaining national park with a combination of public, commercial, and residential projects. In 2005 Bay Area filmmaker George Lucas opened the **Letterman Digital Arts Center,** his 23-acre digital studio "campus," along the eastern edge of the land. Seventeen of those acres are exquisitely landscaped and open to the public, but not even landscaping this perfect can compete with the wilds of the Presidio.

The battle over the fate of the rest of the Presidio is ongoing. Many older buildings have been reconstructed; the issue now is how to fill them. The original plan described a nexus for arts, education, and environmental groups. Since the Presidio's overseeing trust must make the park financially self-sufficient by 2013, which means generating enough revenue to keep afloat without the federal government's monthly $20 million checks, many fear that money will trump culture. The Asian-theme SenSpa and a new Walt Disney museum have opened, and a lodge at the Main Post is in the planning stages. With old military housing now repurposed as apartments and homes with rents up to $10,000 a month, there's some concern that the Presidio will become an incoherent mix of pricey real estate. Still, the $6 million that Lucas shells out annually for rent does plant a lot of saplings. . . .

The Presidio also has two beaches, a golf course, a visitor center, and picnic sites; the views from the many overlooks are sublime.

☾ Especially popular is **Crissy Field,** a stretch of restored marshlands along
★ the sand of the bay. Kids on bikes, folks walking dogs, and joggers share the paved path along the shore, often winding up at the Warming Hut,

Armed with only helmets, safety harnesses, and painting equipment, a full-time crew of 38 painters keeps the Golden Gate Bridge clad in International Orange.

a combination café and fun gift store at the end of the path, for a hot chocolate in the shadow of the Golden Gate Bridge. Midway along the Golden Gate Promenade that winds along the shore is the Gulf of the Farallones National Marine Sanctuary Visitor Center, where kids can get a close-up view of small sea creatures and learn about the rich ecosystem offshore. Toward the promenade's eastern end, Crissy Field Center offers great children's programs and has cool science displays. West of the Golden Gate Bridge is sandy **Baker Beach,** beloved for its spectacular views and laid-back vibe (read: you'll see naked people here). This is one of those places locals like to show off to visitors. ⊠ *Between Marina and Lincoln Park, Presidio* ⊕ *www.nps.gov/prsf and www.presidio.gov.*

GOLDEN GATE PARK AND THE WESTERN SHORELINE

More than 1,000 acres, stretching from the Haight all the way to the windy Pacific coast, Golden Gate Park is a vast patchwork of woods, trails, lakes, lush gardens, sports facilities, museums—even a herd of buffalo. There's more natural beauty beyond the park's borders, along San Francisco's wild Western Shoreline.

EXPLORING GOLDEN GATE PARK

⑤ Botanical Garden at Strybing Arboretum. One of the best picnic spots in a very picnic-friendly park, this 55-acre arboretum specializes in plants from areas with climates similar to that of the Bay Area. Walk the newly updated Eastern Australian garden to see tough, pokey shrubs and plants with cartoon-like names, such as the hilly-pilly tree. Kids gravitate toward the large shallow fountain and the pond with ducks, turtles,

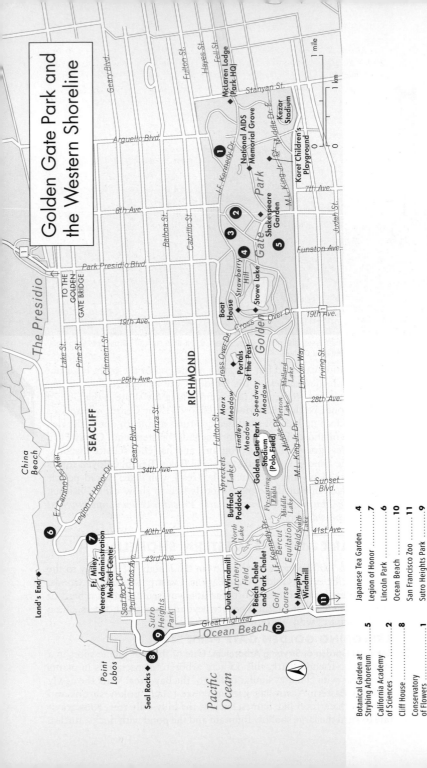

Golden Gate Park and the Western Shoreline

Pacific Ocean

The Presidio

TO THE GOLDEN GATE BRIDGE

SEACLIFF

RICHMOND

China Beach

Land's End

Point Lobos

Seal Rocks

Golden Gate Park

McLaren Lodge (Park HQ)

National AIDS Memorial Grove

Shakespeare Garden

Kezer Stadium

Koret Children's Playground

Boat House

Strawberry Hill

Stowe Lake

Portals of the Post

Marx Meadow

Speedway Meadow

Lindley Meadow

Golden Gate Park Stadium (Polo Field)

Buffalo Paddock

Spreckels Lake

North Lake

Middle Lake

Watson Lake

Mallard Lake

South Lake

Casting Pools

Equitation Field

Golf Course

Dutch Windmill

Archery Field

Beach Chalet and Park Chalet

Murphy Windmill

Ft. Miley

Veteran's Administration Medical Center

Ocean Beach

Sutro Heights Park

Geary Blvd.
Fulton St.
Hayes St.
Fell St.
Stanyan St.
Arguello Blvd.
8th Ave.
Balboa St.
Cabrillo St.
Park Presidio Blvd.
19th Ave.
Park Presidio Blvd.
Lake St.
Pine St.
Clement St.
25th Ave.
Anza St.
Geary Blvd.
34th Ave.
40th Ave.
43rd Ave.
41st Ave.
28th Ave.
Irving St.
Judah St.
Funston Ave.
7th Ave.
Sunset Blvd.
Lincoln Way
M.L. King Jr. Dr.
J.F. Kennedy Dr.
Cross Over Dr.
Middle Dr.
Over Dr.
19th Ave.
Great Highway
El Camino Del Mar
Legion of Honor Dr.
Seal Rock Dr.
Point Lobos Ave.
Stowe Lake Dr.
M.L. King Jr. Dr.
Middle Dr. E.

1 mile
1 km

and egrets. Another favorite is an area devoted to aromatic plants; take a deep sniff of lemon verbena or lavender. The bookstore is also a great resource. Maps are available at the main and Eugene L. Friend entrances. ⊠ *Enter the park at 9th Ave. at Lincoln Way, Golden Gate Park* ☎ *415/661–1316* ⊕ *www.sfbotanicalgarden.org* ⊠ *Free* ⊙ *Weekdays 8–4:30, weekends 10–5.*

❶ **Conservatory of Flowers.** Whatever you do, be sure to at least drive by the Conservatory of Flowers—it's just too darn pretty to miss. The gorgeous, white-framed 1878 glass structure is topped with a 14-ton glass dome. Stepping inside the giant greenhouse is like taking a quick trip to the rain forest; it's humid, warm, and smells earthy. The undeniable highlight is the Aquatic Plants section, where lily pads float and carnivorous plants dine on bugs to the sounds of rushing water. On the east side of the conservatory (to the right as you face the building), cypress, pine, and redwood trees surround the Dahlia Garden, which blooms in summer and fall. To the west is the Rhododendron Dell, which contains 850 varieties, more than any other garden in the country. It's a favorite local Mother's Day picnic spot. ⊠ *John F. Kennedy Dr. at Conservatory Dr., Golden Gate Park* ☎ *415/666–7001* ⊕ *www. conservatoryofflowers.org* ⊠ *$5, free 1st Tues. of month* ⊙ *Tues.–Sun. 9–5, last entry at 4:30.*

❸ **de Young Museum.** It seems that everyone in town has a strong opinion about the new museum, unveiled in 2005. Some adore the striking copper facade, while others grimace and hope that the green patina of age will mellow the effect. Most maligned is the 144-foot tower, but the view from its ninth-story observation room, ringed by floor-to-ceiling windows, is worth the price of admission alone. The building almost overshadows the de Young's respected collection of American, African, and Oceanic art. Works by Wayne Thiebaud, John Singer Sargent, Winslow Homer, and Richard Diebenkorn are the painting collection's highlights. Your ticket here is also good for same day admission to the Legion of Honor. ⊠ *50 Hagiwara Tea Garden Dr., Golden Gate Park* ☎ *415/863–3330* ⊕ *www.deyoungmuseum.org* ⊠ *$10, free 1st Tues. of month* ⊙ *Tues.–Sun. 9:30–5:15, Fri. until 8:45.*

❹ **Japanese Tea Garden.** As you amble through the manicured landscape, past Japanese sculptures and perfect miniature pagodas, over ponds of carp that have been here since before the 1906 quake, you may be transported to a more peaceful plane. Or maybe the shrieks of kids clambering over the almost vertical "humpback" bridges will keep you firmly in the here and now. Either way, this garden is one of those tourist spots that are truly worth a stop (a half-hour will do). And at 5 acres, it's large enough that you'll always be able to find a bit of serenity, even when the tour buses drop by. The garden is especially lovely in April, when the cherry blossoms are in bloom. ⊠ *Hagiwara Tea Garden Dr., off John F. Kennedy Dr., Golden Gate Park* ☎ *415/752–4227* ⊠ *$7, free Mon., Wed., and Fri. 9 AM–10 AM* ⊙ *Mar.–Sept., daily 9–6; Oct.– Feb., daily 9–4:45.*

❷ **California Academy of Sciences.** Renzo Piano's audacious, prescient design for this natural history museum—which opened in 2008—complements

8

the dramatic transformation of Golden Gate Park's Music Concourse. An eco-friendly, energy-efficient adventure in biodiversity and green architecture, the museum is equipped with a rain forest, a planetarium, and a retractable ceiling over the central courtyard—but its most dramatic feature is a "living roof" that's covered with native plants. ⊠ *55 Music Concourse Dr., Golden Gate Park* ☎ *415/379–8000* ⊕ *www. calacademy.org* ⊠ *$24.95* ☉ *Mon.–Sat. 9:30–5, Sun. 11–5.*

EXPLORING THE WESTERN SHORELINE

8 **Cliff House.** A meal at the Cliff House isn't about the food—the spectacular ocean view is what brings folks here. The vistas, which include offshore Seal Rock (the barking marine mammals who reside there are actually sea lions), can be 30 mi or more on a clear day—or less than a mile on foggy days. ■ TIP→ Come for drinks just before sunset; then head back into town for dinner.

Three buildings have occupied this site since 1863. The current building dates from 1909; a 2004 renovation has left a strikingly attractive restaurant and a squat concrete viewing platform out back. The complex, owned by the National Park Service, includes a gift shop.

Sitting on the observation deck is the **Giant Camera,** a cute yellow-painted wooden model of an old-fashioned camera with its lens pointing skyward. Built in the 1940s and threatened many times with demolition, it's now on the National Register of Historic Places. Step into the dark, tiny room inside (for a rather steep $5 fee); a fascinating 360-degree image of the surrounding area—which rotates as the "lens" on the roof rotates—is projected on a large, circular table. ■ TIP→ In winter and spring, you may also glimpse migrating gray whales from the observation deck.

To the north of the Cliff House are the ruins of the once-grand glass-roof **Sutro Baths,** which you can explore on your own (they look a bit like water-storage receptacles). Adolf Sutro, eccentric onetime San Francisco mayor and Cliff House owner, built the bath complex, including a train out to the site, in 1896, so that everyday folks could enjoy the benefits of swimming. Six enormous baths (some freshwater and some seawater), more than 500 dressing rooms, and several restaurants covered 3 acres north of the Cliff House and accommodated 25,000 bathers. Likened to Roman baths in a European glass palace, the baths were for decades the favorite destination of San Franciscans in search of entertainment. The complex fell into disuse after World War II, was closed in 1952, and burned down (under officially questionable circumstances, wink wink) during demolition in 1966. ⊠ *1090 Point Lobos Ave., Outer Richmond* ☎ *415/386–3330* ⊕ *www.cliffhouse.com* ⊠ *Free* ☉ *Weekdays 9 AM–9:30 PM, weekends 9 AM–10 PM.*

7 **Legion of Honor.** The old adage of real estate—location, location, location—is at full force here. You can't beat the spot of this museum of European art—situated on cliffs overlooking the ocean, the Golden Gate Bridge, and the Marin Headlands. A pyramidal glass skylight in the entrance court illuminates the lower-level galleries, which exhibit prints and drawings, English and European porcelain, and ancient Assyrian, Greek, Roman, and Egyptian art. The 20-plus galleries on

Fodor's Choice
★

the upper level display the permanent collection of European art (paintings, sculpture, decorative arts, and tapestries) from the 14th century to the present day.

The noteworthy Auguste Rodin collection includes two galleries devoted to the master and a third with works by Rodin and other 19th-century sculptors. An original cast of Rodin's *The Thinker* welcomes you as you walk through the courtyard. As fine as the museum is, the setting and view outshine the collection and make a trip here worthwhile.

The **Legion Café,** on the lower level, serves tasty light meals (soup, sandwiches, grilled chicken) inside and on a garden terrace. (Unfortunately, there's no view.) Just north of the museum's parking lot is George Segal's *The Holocaust,* a stark white installation that evokes life in concentration camps during World War II. It's haunting at night, when backlighted by lights in the Legion's parking lot. ■**TIP**➔ Admission to the Legion also counts as same-day admission to the de Young Museum. ✉ *34th Ave. at Clement St., Outer Richmond* ☎ *415/750–3600* ⊕ *www.thinker.org* ✑ *$10, $2 off with Muni transfer, free 1st Tues. of month* ☿ *Tues.–Sun. 9:30–5:15.*

❻ **Lincoln Park.** Although many of the city's green spaces are gentle and ★ welcoming, Lincoln Park is a wild 275-acre park with windswept cliffs and panoramic views. The newly renovated Coastal Trail, the park's most dramatic, leads out to **Lands End**; pick it up west of the Legion of Honor (at the end of El Camino del Mar) or from the parking lot at Point Lobos and El Camino del Mar. Time your hike to hit Mile Rock at low tide, and you might catch a glimpse of two wrecked ships peeking up from their watery graves. ⚠ Do be careful if you hike here; landslides are frequent, and many people have fallen into the sea by standing too close to the edge of a crumbling bluff top.

On the tamer side, large Monterey cypresses line the fairways at Lincoln Park's 18-hole golf course, near the Legion of Honor. At one time this land was the Golden Gate Cemetery, where the dead were segregated by nationality; most were indigent and interred without ceremony in the potter's field. In 1900 the Board of Supervisors voted to ban burials within city limits, and all but two city cemeteries (at Mission Dolores and the Presidio) were moved to Colma, a small town just south of San Francisco. When digging has to be done in the park, bones occasionally surface again. ✉ *Entrance at 34th Ave. at Clement St., Outer Richmond.*

❿ **Ocean Beach.** Stretching 3 mi along the western side of the city from the Richmond to the Sunset, this sandy swath of the Pacific coast is good for jogging or walking the dog—but not for swimming. The water is so cold that surfers wear wet suits year-round, and riptides are strong. As for sunbathing, it's rarely warm enough here; think meditative walking instead of sun worshipping.

Paths on both sides of the Great Highway lead from Lincoln Way to Sloat Boulevard (near the zoo); the beachside path winds through landscaped sand dunes, and the paved path across the highway is good for biking and in-line skating. (Though you have to rent bikes elsewhere.) The **Beach Chalet** restaurant and brewpub is across the Great Highway

8

from Ocean Beach, about five blocks south of the Cliff House. ⊠ *Along Great Hwy. from Cliff House to Sloat Blvd. and beyond.*

⓫ **San Francisco Zoo.** Awash in bad press since one of its tigers escaped its
☾ enclosure and killed a visitor on Christmas day 2007, the zoo is touting its metamorphosis into the "New Zoo," a wildlife-focused recreation center that inspires visitors to become conservationists. Integrated exhibits group different species of animals from the same geographic areas together in enclosures that don't look like cages. The zoo's superstar exhibit is **Grizzly Gulch,** where orphaned sisters Kachina and Kiona enchant visitors with their frolicking and swimming. The **Lemur Forest** has five varieties of the bug-eyed, long-tailed primates from Madagascar, and **Gorilla Preserve is** one of the largest and most natural gorilla habitats of any zoo in the world. The **Children's Zoo** includes an insect zoo, a meerkat and prairie-dog exhibit, a restored 1921 Dentzel carousel, and a mini–steam train. ⊠ *Sloat Blvd. and 47th Ave., Sunset* ✛ *Muni L–Taraval streetcar from downtown* ☎ *415/753–7080* ⊕ *www. sfzoo.org* 🖃 *$15, $1 off with Muni transfer* ☉ *Daily 10–5. Children's zoo 10–4:30.*

❾ **Sutro Heights Park.** Crows and other large birds battle the heady breezes at this cliff-top park on what were once the grounds of the home of Adolph Sutro, an eccentric mining engineer and former San Francisco mayor. An extremely wealthy man, Sutro may have owned about 10% of San Francisco at one point, but he couldn't buy good taste: a few remnants of his gaudy, faux-classical statue collection still stand (including the lions at what was the main gate). Monterey cypresses and Canary Island palms dot the park, and photos on placards depict what things looked like before the house burned down in 1896, from the greenhouse to the ornate carpet-bed designs.

All that remains of the main house is its foundation. Climb up for a sweeping view of the Pacific Ocean and the Cliff House below (which Sutro owned), and try to imagine what the perspective might have been like from one of the upper floors. San Francisco City Guides (☎ 415/557–4266) runs a free Saturday tour of the park that starts at 2 (meet at the lion statue at 48th and Point Lobos avenues). ⊠ *Point Lobos and 48th Aves., Outer Richmond.*

THE HAIGHT, THE CASTRO, AND NOE VALLEY

Once you've seen the blockbuster sights and you're getting curious about the neighborhoods where the city's soul resides, come out to these three areas. They wear their personalities large and proud, and all are perfect for just strolling around. You can move from the Haight's residue of 1960s counterculture to the Castro's connection to 1970s and '80s gay life to 1990s gentrification in Noe Valley. Although history thrust the Haight and the Castro onto the international stage, both are anything but stagnant—they're still dynamic areas well worth exploring. Noe Valley may lack the headlines, but a mellow morning walk here will make you feel like a local.

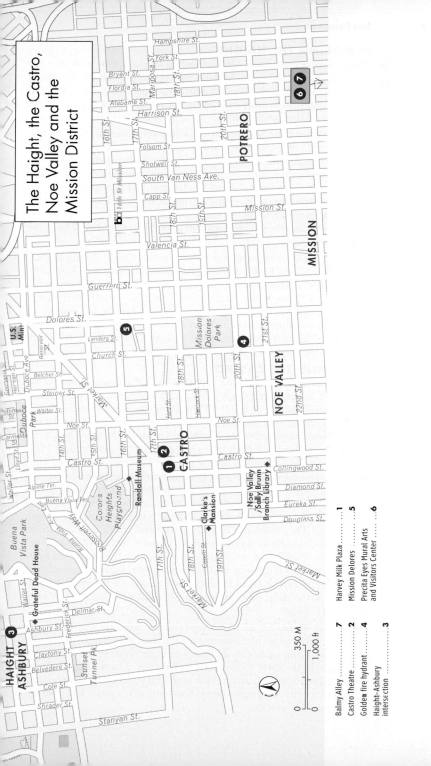

The Haight, the Castro, Noe Valley and the Mission District

Hampshire St.
York St.
Mariposa St.
Bryant St.
Flordia St.
18th St.
Alabama St.
Harrison St.
16th St.
17th St.
Folsom St.
20th St.
Shotwell St.
South Van Ness Ave.
Capp St.
Mission St.
18th St.
19th St.
Valencia St.
16th St Mission

POTRERO

6 7

MISSION

Guerrero St.

Dolores St.

U.S. Mint

Reservoir St.

Landers St.

5

Church St.

Mission Dolores Park

21st St.

4

20th St.

Belcher St.

Steiner St.

Market St.

Duboce Ave.

Herman St.

Sanchez St.

Fort St.

Hancock St.

22nd St.

Noe St.

NOE VALLEY

Noe St.

14th St.

15th St.

Castro St.

16th St.

17th St.

CASTRO

1 2

Castro St.

Collingwood St.

Noe Valley /Sally Brum Branch Library

Diamond St.

Eureka St.

Douglass St.

Randall Museum

Corona Heights Playground

Clarke's Mansion

Caselli St.

18th St.

19th St.

Market St.

Roosevelt Way

Buena Vista Ave.

Alpine Ter.

Buena Vista Ter.

Waller St.

Buena Vista Park

Grateful Dead House

Castro St.

Carmelita St.

Lloyd St.

Pierce St.

Scott St.

Ord St.

HAIGHT ASHBURY 3

Delmar St.

Ashbury St.

Frederick St.

Claytony St.

Belvedere St.

Cole St.

Sunset Tunnel Pk.

Shrader St.

Stanyan St.

350 M

0

1,000 ft

0

EXPLORING THE HAIGHT

❸ Haight-Ashbury intersection. On October 6, 1967, hippies took over the intersection of Haight and Ashbury streets to proclaim the "Death of Hip." If they thought hip was dead then, they'd find absolute confirmation of it today, what with the only tie-dye in sight on the Ben & Jerry's storefront on the famed corner.

Everyone knows the Summer of Love had something to do with free love and LSD, but the drugs and other excesses of that period have tended to obscure the residents' serious attempts to create an America that was more spiritually oriented, more environmentally aware, and less caught up in commercialism. The Diggers, a radical group of actors and populist agitators, for example, operated a free shop a few blocks off Haight Street. Everything really was free at the free shop; people brought in things they didn't need and took things they did. (The group also coined immortal phrases like "Do your own thing.")

Among the folks who hung out in or near the Haight during the late 1960s were writers Richard Brautigan, Allen Ginsberg, Ken Kesey, and Gary Snyder; anarchist Abbie Hoffman; rock performers Marty Balin, Jerry Garcia, Janis Joplin, and Grace Slick; LSD champion Timothy Leary; and filmmaker Kenneth Anger. If you're keen to feel something resembling the hippie spirit these days, there's always Hippie Hill, just inside the Haight Street entrance of Golden Gate Park. Think drum circles, guitar players, and whiffs of pot smoke.

EXPLORING THE CASTRO

❷ Castro Theatre.
★ Here's a classic way to join in the Castro community: grab some popcorn and catch a flick at this gorgeous, 1,500-seat art-deco theater; opened in 1922, it's the grandest of San Francisco's few remaining movie palaces. The neon marquee, which stands at the top of the Castro strip, is the neighborhood's great landmark. The Castro was the fitting host of 2008's red-carpet preview of Gus Van Sant's film *Milk*, starring Sean Penn as openly gay San Francisco supervisor Harvey Milk. The theater's elaborate Spanish baroque interior is fairly well preserved. Before many shows the theater's pipe organ rises from the orchestra pit and an organist plays pop and movie tunes, usually ending with the Jeanette McDonald standard "San Francisco" (go ahead, sing along). The crowd can be enthusiastic and vocal, talking back to the screen as loudly as it talks to them. Classics such as *Who's Afraid of Virginia Woolf?* take on a whole new life, with the assembled beating the actors to the punch and fashioning even snappier comebacks for Elizabeth Taylor. Head here to catch classics, a Fellini film retrospective, or the latest take on same-sex love. ⊠ *429 Castro St., Castro* ☏ *415/621–6120.*

❶ Harvey Milk Plaza. An 18-foot-long rainbow flag, the symbol of gay pride, flies above this plaza named for the man who electrified the city in 1977 by being elected to its Board of Supervisors as an openly gay candidate. In the early 1970s, Milk had opened a camera store on the block of Castro Street between 18th and 19th streets. The store became the center for his campaign to open San Francisco's social and political life to gays and lesbians.

A colorful mosaic mural in the Castro.

The liberal Milk hadn't served a full year of his term before he and Mayor George Moscone, also a liberal, were shot in November 1978 at City Hall. The murderer was a conservative ex-supervisor named Dan White, who had recently resigned his post and then became enraged when Moscone wouldn't reinstate him. Milk and White had often been at odds on the board, and White thought Milk had been part of a cabal to keep him from returning to his post. Milk's assassination shocked the gay community, which became infuriated when the infamous "Twinkie defense"—that junk food had led to diminished mental capacity—resulted in a manslaughter verdict for White. During the so-called White Night Riot of May 21, 1979, gays and their sympathizers stormed City Hall, torching its lobby and several police cars.

Milk, who had feared assassination, left behind a tape recording in which he urged the community to continue the work he had begun. His legacy is the high visibility of gay people throughout city government; a bust of him was unveiled at City Hall on his birthday in 2008, and the 2008 film *Milk* gives insight into his life. A plaque at the base of the flagpole lists the names of past and present openly gay and lesbian state and local officials. ⊠ *Southwest corner of Castro and Market Sts., Castro.*

EXPLORING NOE VALLEY

④ **Golden fire hydrant.** When all the other fire hydrants went dry during the fire that followed the 1906 earthquake, this one kept pumping. Noe Valley and the Mission District were thus spared the devastation wrought elsewhere in the city, which explains the large number of pre-quake homes here. Every year on April 18 (the anniversary of the quake) the famous hydrant gets a fresh coat of gold paint. ⊠ *Church and 20th Sts., southeast corner, across from Dolores Park, Noe Valley.*

CASTRO AND NOE WALK

The Castro and Noe Valley are both neighborhoods that beg to be walked—or ambled through, really, without time pressure or an absolute destination. Hit the Castro first, beginning at **Harvey Milk Plaza** under the gigantic rainbow flag. If you're going on to Noe Valley, first head east down **Market Street** for the cafés, bistros, and shops, then go back to **Castro Street** and head south, past the glorious art-deco **Castro Theatre**, checking out boutiques and cafés along the way (Cliff's Variety, at 479 Castro Street, is a must). To tour Noe Valley, go east down **18th Street** to Church (at Dolores Park), and then either strap on your hiking boots and head south over the hill or hop the J–Church to **24th Street**, the center of this rambling neighborhood.

MISSION DISTRICT

The Mission has a number of distinct personalities: it's the Latino neighborhood, where working-class folks raise their families and where gangs occasionally clash; it's the hipster hood, where tattooed and pierced twenty- and thirtysomethings hold court in the coolest cafés and bars in town; it's a culinary epicenter, with the strongest concentration of destination restaurants and affordable ethnic cuisine; and it's the artists' quarter, where murals adorn literally blocks of walls. It's also the city's equivalent of the Sunshine State—this neighborhood's always the last to succumb to fog.

EXPLORING THE MISSION DISTRICT

⑦ Balmy Alley. Mission District artists have transformed the walls of their neighborhood with paintings, and Balmy Alley is one of the best-executed examples. Murals fill the one-block alley, with newer ones continually filling in the blank spaces. Local children working with adults started the project in 1971. Since then dozens of artists have steadily added to it, with the aim of promoting peace in Central America, as well as community spirit and AIDS awareness. ■TIP➔ Be alert here: the 25th Street end of the alley adjoins a somewhat dangerous area. ⊠ *24th St. between and parallel to Harrison and Treat Sts., alley runs south to 25th St., Mission.*

⑤ Mission Dolores. Two churches stand side by side at this mission, including the small adobe **Mission San Francisco de Asís**, the oldest standing ★ structure in San Francisco. Completed in 1791, it's the sixth of the 21 California missions founded by Father Junípero Serra in the 18th and early 19th centuries. Its ceiling depicts original Ohlone Indian basket designs, executed in vegetable dyes. The tiny chapel includes frescoes and a hand-painted wooden altar. There's a hidden treasure here, too. In 2004 an archaeologist and an artist crawling along the ceiling's rafters opened a trapdoor behind the altar and rediscovered the mission's original mural, painted with natural dyes by Native Americans in 1791. The centuries have taken their toll, so the team photographed the 20-by-22-foot mural and began digitally restoring the photographic version.

Among the images is a dagger-pierced Sacred Heart of Jesus. There's a small museum covering the mission's founding and history, and the pretty little mission cemetery (made famous by a scene in Alfred Hitchcock's *Vertigo*) maintains the graves of mid-19th-century European immigrants. (The remains of an estimated 5,000 Native Americans lie in unmarked graves.) Services are held in both the Mission San Francisco de Asís and next door in the handsome multi-dome basilica. ✉ *Dolores and 16th Sts., Mission* 🕾 *415/621–8203* ⊕ *www.missiondolores. org* 🖭 *$5 donation, audio tour $7* 🕙 *Nov.–Apr., daily 9–4; May–Oct., daily 9–4:30.*

❻ Precita Eyes Mural Arts and Visitors Center. Founded by muralists, this nonprofit arts organization designs and creates murals. The artists themselves lead informative guided walks of murals in the area. Most tours start with a 45-minute slide presentation. The bike and walking trips, which take between one and three hours, pass several dozen murals. May is Mural Awareness Month, with visits to murals-in-progress and presentations by artists. You can pick up a map of 24th Street's murals at the center and buy art supplies, T-shirts, postcards, and other mural-related items. Bike tours are available by appointment; Saturday's 11 AM walking tour meets at Cafe Venice, at 24th and Mission streets. (All other tours meet at the center.) ✉ *2981 24th St., Mission* 🕾 *415/285– 2287* ⊕ *www.precitaeyes.org* 🖭 *Center free, tours $10–$12* 🕙 *Center weekdays 10–5, Sat. 10–4, Sun. noon–4; walks weekends at 11 and 1:30 or by appointment.*

PACIFIC HEIGHTS AND JAPANTOWN

8

Pacific Heights and Japantown are something of an odd couple: privileged, old-school San Francisco and the workaday commercial center of Japanese-American life in the city, stacked virtually on top of each other. The sprawling, extravagant mansions of Pacific Heights gradually give way to the more modest Victorians and unassuming housing tracts of Japantown. The cool boutiques and cafés of northern Fillmore Street fade into salons and pizzerias farther south. The most interesting spots in Japantown huddle in the Japan Center, the neighborhood's two-block centerpiece, and along Post Street. You can find plenty of authentic Japanese treats in the shops and restaurants, but unless you have a special interest in these, the area likely won't make it onto your must-see list.

▪**TIP→** Japantown is a relatively safe area, but the Western Addition, south of Geary Boulevard, can be dangerous even during the daytime. Avoid going too far west of Fillmore Street on either side of Geary.

EXPLORING PACIFIC HEIGHTS

❷ Alta Plaza Park. Golden Gate Park's fierce longtime superintendent, John ♻ McLaren, designed Alta Plaza in 1910, modeling its terracing on that of the Grand Casino in Monte Carlo, Monaco. From the top you can see Marin to the north, downtown to the east, Twin Peaks to the south, and Golden Gate Park to the west. Kids love the many play structures at the large, enclosed playground at the top; everywhere else is dog territory. ✉ *Bordered by Clay, Steiner, Jackson, and Scott Sts., Pacific Heights.*

⑤ Franklin Street buildings. What at first looks like a stone facade on the **Golden Gate Church** (✉ *1901 Franklin St., Pacific Heights*) is actually redwood painted white. A Georgian-style residence built in the early 1900s for a coffee merchant sits at 1735 Franklin. On the northeast corner of Franklin and California streets is a **Christian Science church**; built in the Tuscan revival style, it's noteworthy for its terra-cotta detailing. The **Coleman House** (✉ *1701 Franklin St., Pacific Heights*) is an impressive twin-turret Queen Anne mansion that was built for a gold-rush mining and lumber baron. Don't miss the large, brilliant-purple stained-glass window on the house's north side. ✉ *Franklin St. between Washington and California Sts., Pacific Heights.*

④ Haas-Lilienthal House. A small display of photographs on the bottom floor of this elaborate, gray 1886 Queen Anne house makes clear that despite its lofty stature and striking, round third-story tower, the house was modest compared with some of the giants that fell victim to the 1906 earthquake and fire. The Foundation for San Francisco's Architectural Heritage operates the home, whose carefully kept rooms provide an intriguing glimpse into late-19th-century life through period furniture, authentic details (antique dishes in the kitchen built-in), and photos of the family who occupied the house until 1972. Volunteers conduct one-hour house tours three days a week and informative two-hour walking tours ($8) of the Civic Center, Broadway, and Union Street areas on Saturday afternoon, and of the eastern portion of Pacific Heights on Sunday afternoon (call or check Web site for schedule). ✉ *2007 Franklin St., between Washington and Jackson Sts., Pacific Heights* ☎ *415/441–3004* ⊕ *www.sfheritage.org* ✉ *Entry $8* ⊙ *1-hr tour Wed. and Sat. noon–3, Sun. 11–4; 2-hr tour Sun. at 12:30.*

⑥ Noteworthy Victorians. Two **Italianate Victorians** (✉ *1818 and 1834 California St., Pacific Heights*) stand out on the 1800 block of California. A block farther is the Victorian-era **Atherton House** (✉ *1990 California St., Pacific Heights*), whose mildly daffy design incorporates Queen Anne, Stick-Eastlake, and other architectural elements. Many claim the house—now apartments—is haunted by the ghosts of its 19th-century residents, who regularly whisper, glow, and generally cause a mild fuss. The oft-photographed **Laguna Street Victorians,** on the west side of the 1800 block of Laguna Street, cost between $2,000 and $2,600 when they were built in the 1870s. No bright colors here though—most of the paint jobs are in soft beiges or pastels. ✉ *California St. between Franklin and Octavia Sts., and Laguna St. between Pine and Bush Sts., Pacific Heights.*

① Octagon House. This eight-sided home sits across the street from its original site on Gough Street; it's one of two remaining octagonal houses in the city (the other is on Russian Hill), and the only one open to the public. White quoins accent each of the eight corners of the pretty blue-gray exterior, and a colonial-style garden completes the picture. Inside, it's full of antique American furniture, decorative arts (paintings, silver, rugs), and documents from the 18th and 19th centuries. A deck of Revolutionary-era hand-painted playing cards takes an antimonarchist position: in place of kings, queens, and jacks, the American upstarts substituted American statesmen, Roman goddesses, and Indian chiefs.

DID YOU KNOW?

These soft-colored Victorian homes in Pacific Heights are closer to the original hues sported back in the 1900s. It wasn't until the 1960s that the bold, electric colors now seen around SF gained popularity. Before that, the most typical house paint color was a standard gray.

✉ *2645 Gough St., Pacific Heights* ☎ *415/441–7512* 🎫 *Free, donations encouraged* ☾ *Feb.–Dec., 2nd Sun. and 2nd and 4th Thurs. of month noon–3; group tours weekdays by appointment.*

❸ **Spreckels Mansion.** Shrouded behind tall juniper hedges at the corner of lovely winding, brick Octavia Street, overlooking Lafayette Park, the estate was built for sugar heir Adolph Spreckels and his wife Alma. Mrs. Spreckels was so pleased with her house that she commissioned George Applegarth to design another building in a similar vein: the Legion of Honor. One of the city's great iconoclasts, Alma Spreckels was the model for the bronze figure atop the Victory Monument in Union Square. Today this house belongs to prolific romance novelist Danielle Steel. ✉ *2080 Washington St., at Octavia St., Pacific Heights.*

EXPLORING JAPANTOWN

❼ **Japan Center.** Cool and curious trinkets, noodle houses and sushi joints,
★ a destination bookstore, and a peek at Japanese culture high and low await at this 5-acre complex, designed in 1968 by noted American architect Minoru Yamasaki. Architecturally, the development hasn't aged well, and its Peace Plaza, where seasonal festivals are held, is an unwelcoming sea of cement. The Japan Center includes the shop- and restaurant-filled Kintetsu and Kinokuniya buildings; the excellent

Kabuki Springs & Spa; the Hotel Kabuki; and the Sundance Kabuki, Robert Redford's fancy, reserved-seating cinema/restaurant complex.

The Kinokuniya Bookstores, in the Kinokuniya Building, has an extensive selection of Japanese-language books, *manga* (graphic novels), books on design, and English-language translations and books on Japanese topics. Just outside, follow the Japanese teenagers to Pika Pika, where you and your friends can step into a photo booth and then use special effects and stickers to decorate your creation. On the bridge connecting the center's two buildings, check out Shige Antiques for *yukata* (lightweight cotton kimonos) for kids and lovely silk kimonos, and Asakichi and its tiny incense shop for tinkling wind chimes and display-worthy teakettles. Continue into the Kintetsu Building for a selection of Japanese restaurants.

Between the Miyako Mall and Kintetsu Building are the five-tier, 100-foot-tall **Peace Pagoda** and the Peace Plaza. The pagoda, which draws on the 1,200-year-old tradition of miniature round pagodas dedicated to eternal peace, was designed in the late 1960s by Yoshiro Taniguchi to convey the "friendship and goodwill" of the Japanese people to the people of the United States. The plaza itself is a shadeless, unwelcoming stretch of cement with little seating. Continue into the Miyako Mall to Ichiban Kan, a Japanese dollar store where you can pick up fun Japanese kitchenware, tote bags decorated with hedgehogs, and erasers shaped like food. ⊠ *Bordered by Geary Blvd. and Fillmore, Post, and Laguna Sts., Japantown* ✆ *No phone.*

8 **Japan Center Mall.** The buildings lining this open-air mall are of the shoji school of architecture. The mall's many good restaurants draw a lively crowd of nearby workers for lunch, but the atmosphere remains weirdly hushed. The shops are geared more toward locals—travel agencies, electronics shops—but there are some fun Japanese-goods stores. Arrive early in the day and you may score some fabulous *mochi* (a soft, sweet Japanese rice treat) at **Benkyodo** (⊠ *1747 Buchanan St., Japantown* ✆ *415/922–1244*). It's easy to spend hours among the fabulous origami and craft papers at **Paper Tree** (⊠ *1743 Buchanan St., Japantown* ✆ *415/921–7100*), open since the 1960s. Be sure to swing around the corner, just off the mall, to **Super 7** (⊠ *1628 Post St., Japantown* ✆ *415/409–4700*), home of many large plastic Godzillas, glow-in-the-dark robots, and cool graphic tees. You can have a seat on local artist Ruth Asawa's twin origami-style fountains, which sit in the middle of the mall; they're squat circular structures made of fieldstone, with three levels for sitting and a brick floor. ⊠ *Buchanan St. between Post and Sutter Sts., Japantown* ✆ *No phone.*

9 ★ **Kabuki Springs & Spa.** This serene spa is one Japantown destination that draws locals from all over town, from hipster to grandma, Japanese-American or not. Balinese urns decorate the communal bath area of this house of tranquillity, and you're just as likely to hear soothing flute or classical music as you are Kitaro.

The massage palette has also expanded well beyond traditional Shiatsu technique. The experience is no less relaxing, however, and the treatment regimen includes facials, salt scrubs, and mud and seaweed wraps. You can take your massage in a private room with a bath or in a curtained-off area. The communal baths ($22 weekdays, $25 weekends) contain hot and cold tubs, a large Japanese-style bath, a sauna, a steam room, and showers. Bang the gong for quiet if your fellow bathers are speaking too loudly.

The clothing-optional baths are open for men only on Monday, Thursday, and Saturday; women bathe on Wednesday, Friday, and Sunday. Bathing suits are required on Tuesday, when the baths are coed. Men and women can reserve private rooms daily. An 80-minute massage-and-bath package with a private room costs $130; a package that includes a 50-minute massage and the use of the communal baths costs $100. ⊠ *1750 Geary Blvd., Japantown* ☎ *415/922–6000* ⊕ *www.kabukisprings.com* ☉ *Daily 10–10.*

WHERE TO EAT

You can find just about any food in San Francisco, a place where trends are set and culinary diversity rules. Since the 1849 gold rush flooded the city with foreign flavors, residents' appetites for exotic eats haven't diminished by even one bite.

UNION SQUARE

$$$
AMERICAN

✕ **Canteen.** Blink and you'll miss this place. Chef-owner Dennis Leary has transformed this narrow coffee shop into one of the most sought-after dinner reservations in town. The homey place has just 20 counter seats and a quartet of wooden booths. But that's all Leary, with a modest open kitchen and a single assistant, can handle. The dinner menu, which changes often, offers only four first courses, four mains, and three or four desserts. A typical meal might start with mussels soup spiked with chili paste, followed by bulgur-crusted sole or stuffed breast of guinea hen with a confit leg and lentils, and then a dreamy vanilla soufflé or pistachio tart. On Tuesday night a three-course prix-fixe menu is in force (no choices within each course) for $35. Because this is a one-man band, your food arrives at a leisurely pace. If a dinner reservation is elusive, try for lunch on weekdays or weekend brunch. ⊠ *Commodore Hotel, 817 Sutter St., Union Square* ☎ *415/928–8870* ⌂ *Reservations essential* ⊟ *AE, MC, V* ☉ *Closed Mon. No lunch Tues. or weekends* ✛ *D4.*

$$$$
NEW AMERICAN
Fodor's Choice
★

✕ **Michael Mina.** Decorated in celadon and ivory with stately columns and a vaulted ceiling, this elegant space, inside the Westin St. Francis Hotel, is a match for chef Michael Mina's highly refined fare. His three-course prix-fixe (multiple choices for each course) includes a trio of tastes on each plate—for example, three preparations of pork for a first (terrine with foie gras, belly pork with frisée and quail egg, short ribs bourguignon with forest mushrooms), or of chocolate for a dessert (white chocolate and rose panna cotta, s'mores, chocolate ice cream with lavender and shortbread). Folks who prefer one taste rather than triple bites can opt for one of Mina's signature dishes, such as black mussel soufflé or lobster potpie. Deep-pocketed diners can splurge on

Continued on page 426

BEST BETS FOR SAN FRANCISO DINING

With thousands of restaurants to choose from, how will you decide where to eat? Fodor's writers and editors have selected their favorite restaurants by price, cuisine, and experience in the Best Bets lists below. In the first column, Fodor's Choice designations represent the "best of the best" in every price category. You can also search by neighborhood for excellent eats—just peruse the following pages.

Fodor'sChoice ★

A16, $$$, p. 434
Boulevard, $$$$, p. 427
Coi, $$$$, p. 429
Delfina, $$$, p. 435
Gary Danko, $$$$, p. 434
Jardinière, $$$$, p. 433
L'Osteria del Forno, $, p. 429
Michael Mina, $$$$, p. 422
Swan Oyster Depot, $, p. 432
Zuni Café, $$$, p. 433

By Price

$

L'Osteria del Forno, p. 429
Swan Oyster Depot, p. 432

$$

Nopa, p. 437

$$$

A16, p. 434
Canteen, p. 422
Delfina, p. 435
Zuni Café, p. 433

$$$$

Boulevard, p. 427
Gary Danko, p. 434
Jardinière, p. 433
Michael Mina, p. 422

By Cuisine

AMERICAN

Canteen, $$$, p. 422
Nopa, $$, p. 437

CHINESE

R&G Lounge, $$, p. 428
Yank Sing, $$, p. 426

FRENCH

Masa's, $$$$, p. 429

INDIAN

Indian Oven, $$, p. 437

ITALIAN

A16, $$$, p. 434
Delfina, $$$, p. 435

JAPANESE

Mifune, $, p. 433

LATIN AMERICAN

La Mar Cebicheria Peruana, $$, p. 428

MEDITERRANEAN

Zuni Café, $$$, p. 433

MEXICAN

Los Jarritos, $, p. 435

SEAFOOD

Hog Island Oyster Company, $$, p. 427
Plouf, $$, p. 426
Swan Oyster Depot, $, p. 432

VIETNAMESE

Slanted Door, $$$, p. 428

By Experience

BAY VIEWS

Slanted Door, $$$, p. 428

BRUNCH

Rose's Café, $$, p. 434

BUSINESS DINING

Boulevard, $$$$, p. 427

CHILD-FRIENDLY

Yank Sing, $$, p. 426

COMMUNAL TABLE

Bocadillos, $$, p. 426
Nopa, $$, p. 437

HISTORIC INTEREST

Boulevard, $$$$, p. 427
Swan Oyster Depot, $, p. 432

HOT SPOTS

A16, $$$, p. 434
Nopa, $$, p. 437
Spruce, $$$$, p. 432

SMALL PLATES

Bocadillos, $$, p. 426
Laïola, $$, p. 434

8

NORCAL'S LOCAVORE FOOD MOVEMENT

Organic, local, and sustainable are buzzwords in Northern California, home to hundreds of small family farmers, sustainable ranchers, and artisan producers are leading the country's back-to-the-earth food movement.

When Alice Waters opened Chez Panisse in Berkeley in 1971, she sparked a culinary revolution that continues today. Initially called California cuisine, the cooking style showcased local, seasonal ingredients in fresh preparations. It also marked a new willingness by American chefs to experiment with international influences. As the movement spread, it became known as New American cooking. This "eat local, think global" ethos has lead to a resurgence of artisanal producers across the country.

The *locavore* (focused on sustainable, local foods) movement's epicenter is still Northern California. At the Ferry Plaza Farmers Market in San Francisco alone, farmers bring over 1,200 varieties of fruits and vegetables to market every year. Chefs proudly call out their purveyors on menus and Web sites, elevating humble vegetable growers to starring culinary roles.

FARMERS MARKETS

One of the best ways to taste Northern California's bounty is by stopping by the Ferry Plaza Farmers Market, held outside of the Ferry Building on the Embarcadero, at Market Street. Held on Tuesday and Saturday mornings, the market offers produce, meats, fish, and flowers from small regional farmers and ranchers, many of whom are certified organic.

It is also a great place to pick up items for a picnic. Prepared foods like tamales and pasta are available, as are specialties like jams, breads, and cheeses from local artisan producers.

Check ⊕ *www.cuesa.org* for hours.

FRUIT

Northern California's diverse climate makes it an ideal place to grow all types of fruit, from berries to stone fruit. Farmers markets and restaurants abound with a staggering selection of produce: Blossom Bluff Orchards, south of San Francisco, offers more than 150 varieties of stone fruits, like apricots, nectarines, and peaches. North of the city, The Apple Farm grows 80 varieties of apples, pears, persimmons, quince, and French plums. The Bay Area is also one of the best places in the country to find rare fruit varieties like aprium, cherimoya, cactus pear, jujube, and loquat; California's famous Meyer lemons—sweeter and less acidic than common lemons—are celebrated in restaurant desserts.

VEGETABLES

Some chefs give top billing to their produce purveyors, like a recently observed menu touting a salad of Star Route Farm field greens with Picholine olives, sweet herbs, and goat cheese. Along with these tantalizing items, be on the lookout for locally grown artichokes, Asian vegetables, multi-hued beets and carrots, and heirloom varieties of tomatoes, squash, and beans.

MEAT

Family-owned ranches and farms are prominent in the region, with many raising organic or "humane certified" beef, pork, lamb, and poultry. Upscale

Bay Area restaurants are fervent about recognizing their high-quality protein producers. From recent menus at two well-known San Francisco restaurants: Wolfe Ranch quail and foie gras crostini with Murcott mandarins, smoked bacon and bok choy, and vanilla gastrique; and Prather Ranch lamb with fava greens, cranberry beans, crispy artichokes, and salsa verde.

FISH

Diners and shoppers will find myriad seafood from local waters, from farm-raised scallops to line-caught California salmon. On menus, look for Hog Island Oysters, a local producer that raises more than three million oysters a year in Tomales Bay. Sardines netted in Monterey Bay are popular in preparations like mesquite-grilled sardines with fava beans, French radish and fennel salad, and preserved Meyer lemon.

CHEESE

Restaurant cheese plates, often served before—or in lieu of—dessert, are great way to experience the region's excellent local cheeses. Look for selections from Cypress Grove Chevre, popular for its artisan goat cheeses, and Cowgirl Creamery, a renowned local producer of fresh and aged cow's milk cheeses. Additionally, some shops and bakeries offer fresh local butter and cheeses.

8

a six-course tasting menu. Diners who want to taste Mina's food but not squander next month's rent can stop in at the swanky Clock Bar, across the lobby, where the same kitchen turns out lobster corn dogs, lamb panini, and black truffle popcorn, all nicely partnered with some of the best cocktails in town. ✉ *Westin St. Francis Hotel, 335 Powell St., Union Square* ☎ *415/397–9222* ☖ *Reservations essential* ▬ *AE, D, DC, MC, V* ☯ *Closed Sun. and Mon. No lunch* ✛ *E4.*

FINANCIAL DISTRICT

$$ ✕ **Bocadillos.** The name means "sandwiches," but that's only half the
SPANISH   story here. You'll find 11 bocadillos at lunchtime: plump rolls filled with everything from serrano ham to Catalan sausage with arugula to a memorable lamb burger. But at night chef-owner Gerald Hirigoyen, who also owns the high-profile Piperade, focuses on tapas, offering some two-dozen choices, including a delicious grilled quail, an equally superb pig's trotters with herbs, and calamari with *romesco* sauce (a thick combination of red pepper, tomato, almonds, and garlic). His wine list is well matched to the food. A youngish crowd typically piles into the modern, red-brick-wall dining space, so be prepared to wait for a seat. A large communal table is a good perch for singles. If you're in the neighborhood at breakfast time, there is plenty here to keep you happy, including a scrambled eggs and cheese bocadillo or house-made chorizo and eggs. ✉ *710 Montgomery St., Financial District* ☎ *415/982–2622* ☖ *Reservations not accepted* ▬ *AE, D, DC, MC, V* ☯ *Closed Sun. No lunch Sat.* ✛ *F3.*

$$ ✕ **Plouf.** This French-friendly spot is a gold mine for mussel lovers, with
SEAFOOD   six preparations to choose from, plus a mussels and clams combo, all at a modest price. Among the best are *marinière* (white wine, garlic, and parsley) and one combining coconut milk, lime juice, and chili. Add a side of the skinny fries and that's all most appetites need. The menu changes seasonally and includes grilled rack of lamb and roasted duck to satisfy any unrepentant carnivores. Many of the appetizers—oysters on the half shell, calamari with fennel tempura, tuna tartare—stick to seafood, as well. The tables are squeezed together in the bright, lively dining room, so you might overhear neighboring conversations. On temperate days and nights, try for one of the outdoor tables. ✉ *40 Belden Pl., Financial District* ☎ *415/986–6491* ▬ *AE, MC, V* ☯ *Closed Sun. No lunch Sat.* ✛ *F2.*

$$ ✕ **Yank Sing.** This is the granddaddy of the city's dim sum teahouses. It
CHINESE   opened in a plain-Jane storefront in Chinatown in 1959, but left its Can-
☉   tonese neighbors behind for the high-rises of downtown by the 1970s.
Multiple   This brightly decorated location on quiet Stevenson Street (there's also a
Locations   big, brassy branch in the Rincon Center) serves some of San Francisco's best dim sum to office workers—bosses and clerks alike—on weekdays and to big, boisterous families on weekends. The kitchen cooks up some 100 varieties of dim sum on a rotating basis, offering 60 different types daily. These include both the classic (steamed pork buns, shrimp dumplings, egg custard tartlets) and the creative (scallion-skewered prawns tied with bacon, lobster and tobiko roe dumplings, basil seafood dumplings). A take-out counter makes a meal on the run a satisfying and

penny-wise compromise when office duties—or touring—won't wait. ⊠ *49 Stevenson St., Financial District* ☎ *415/541–4949* ☰ *AE, DC, MC, V* ☺ *No dinner* ⊠ *1 Rincon Center, 101 Spear St., Embarcadero* ☎ *415/957–9300* ☰ *AE, D, DC, MC, V* ☺ *No dinner* ✥ *F4, G4.*

SOMA

$$$

ITALIAN

✕ **Ducca.** Nowadays some of the city's best restaurants are in hotel dining rooms, and Ducca, resting smartly in a busy neighborhood of museums, movie houses, and theater spaces, is part of that welcome trend. Start off right with an aperitif and little fried rice balls concealing truffled cheese, or a handful of fried green olives stuffed with Gorgonzola. Follow that up with chef Richard Corbo's dreamy lobster *sformato* (a custardy soufflé) or rustic—and delicious—whole-wheat pasta tossed with sardines and caramelized fennel. Mains are split nearly evenly between meats and fish, including chicken riding alongside polenta flecked with chanterelles and peas. Alas, service is unforgivably ragged at times. Just looking to rest your feet? Join the after-work crowd in the handsome alfresco bar (wisely heated) for a drink and a snack. ⊠ *Westin San Francisco Market Street, 50 3rd St., SoMa* ☎ *415/977–0271* ☰ *AE, D, DC, MC, V* ✥ *F5.*

EMBARCADERO

$$$$

AMERICAN

Fodor's Choice

★

✕ **Boulevard.** Two of San Francisco's top restaurant celebrities—chef Nancy Oakes and designer Pat Kuleto—are responsible for this high-profile, high-priced eatery in the magnificent 1889 Audiffred Building, a Parisian look-alike and one of the few downtown structures to survive the 1906 earthquake. Kuleto's Belle Époque interior and Oakes's sophisticated American food with a French accent attract well-dressed locals and flush out-of-towners. The menu changes seasonally, but count on generous portions of dishes like roasted quail stuffed with sweetbreads, chanterelle bisque with pan-seared ricotta gnocchi, and wood-grilled extra-thick pork chop with roasted Lady apples. Save room (and calories) for one of the dynamite desserts, such as butterscotch-almond apple tart Tatin with cinnamon ice cream. There's counter seating for folks too hungry to wait for a table, and a Kobe beef burger at lunchtime that lets you eat with the swells without raiding your piggy bank. ⊠ *1 Mission St., Embarcadero* ☎ *415/543–6084* ⚠ *Reservations essential* ☰ *AE, D, DC, MC, V* ☺ *No lunch weekends* ✥ *G4.*

$$

SEAFOOD

✕ **Hog Island Oyster Company.** Hog Island, a thriving oyster farm in Tomales Bay, north of San Francisco, serves up its harvest at this attractive raw bar and retail shop in the busy Ferry Building. The U-shape counter and a handful of tables seat no more than three-dozen diners, who come here for impeccably fresh oysters (from Hog Island and elsewhere) or clams (from Hog Island) on the half shell. Other mollusk-centered options include a first-rate oyster stew, clam chowder, and Manila clams with white beans. The bar also turns out what is arguably the best grilled-cheese sandwich (with three artisanal cheeses on artisanal bread) this side of Wisconsin. You need to eat early, however, as the bar closes at 8 on weekdays and 6 on weekends. Happy hour,

8

5 to 7 on Monday and Thursday, is an oyster lover's dream and jam-packed: sweetwaters for a buck apiece and beer for $3.50. ✉ *Ferry Bldg., Embarcadero at Market St., Embarcadero* ☎ *415/391–7177* ▭ *AE, MC, V* ⊘ *Closed Sun.* ✛ *H3.*

$$ ╳ **La Mar Cebicheria Peruana.** This casually chic restaurant, set right on
LATIN AMERICAN the water's edge, is divided into three areas: a lounge with a long ceviche bar where diners watch chefs put together their plates; the savvy Pisco Bar facing the Embarcadero, where mixologists make a dozen different cocktails based on Peru's famed Pisco brandy; and a bright blue and whitewashed dining room overlooking an outdoor patio and the bay. The waiter starts you out with a pile of potato and plantain chips with three dipping sauces, but then you're on your own, choosing from a long list of ceviches, *causas* (cubed potatoes topped with a choice of fish, shellfish, or vegetable salads), and everything from crisp, light deep-fried fish and shellfish to soups and stews and rice dishes. The original La Mar is in Lima, Peru. San Francisco is the first stop in its campaign to open a string of cebicherias across the United States and Latin America. ✉ *Pier 1½ between Washington and Jackson Sts., Embarcadero* ☎ *415/397–8880* ▭ *AE, D, MC, V* ✛ *H3.*

$$$ ╳ **Slanted Door.** If you're looking for homey Vietnamese food served in a
VIETNAMESE down-to-earth dining room at a decent price, *don't* stop here. Celebrated chef-owner Charles Phan has mastered the upmarket, Western-accented Vietnamese menu. To showcase his cuisine, he chose a big space with sleek wooden tables and chairs, white marble floors, a cocktail lounge, a bar, and an enviable bay view. Among his popular dishes are green papaya salad, cellophane crab noodles, chicken clay pot, and shaking beef (tender beef cubes with garlic and onion). Alas, the crush of fame means that no one speaking in a normal voice can be heard. To avoid the midday and evening crowds (and to save some bucks), stop in for the afternoon-tea menu (spring rolls, grilled pork over rice noodles), or visit Out the Door, Phan's take-out counter around the corner from the restaurant. A second Out the Door, complete with table service, is in the Westfield Centre downtown, and a third one, again with table service, is now open in Lower Pacific Heights. ✉ *Ferry Bldg., Embarcadero at Market St., Embarcadero* ☎ *415/861–8032* ✎ *Reservations essential* ▭ *AE, MC, V* ✛ *G3.*

CHINATOWN

$$ ╳ **R&G Lounge.** The name conjures up an image of a dark, smoky bar
CHINESE with a piano player, but this Cantonese restaurant is actually as bright
☺ as a new penny. On the lower level (entrance on Kearny Street) is a no-tablecloth dining room that's packed at lunch and dinner. The classy upstairs space (entrance on Commercial Street) is a favorite stop for Chinese businessmen on expense accounts and special-occasion banquets. The street-level room on Kearny is a comfortable spot to wait for a table to open. A menu with photographs helps you pick from the many wonderful, sometimes pricey, always authentic dishes, such as salt-and-pepper Dungeness crab, roast squab, and shrimp-stuffed tofu. You can sip a lychee- or watermelon-flavor martini while wait-

ing for your table. ✉ *631 Kearny St., Chinatown* ☎ *415/982–7877 or
415/982–3811* ▤ *AE, D, DC, MC, V* ✛ *F3.*

NORTH BEACH

$$$$ ✕**Coi.** Daniel Patterson, who has made a name for himself both as a
NEW AMERICAN chef and as a pundit on contemporary restaurant trends, has had a
Fodor's Choice restless career, but seems to have settled in at this intriguing 50-seat
★ spot on the gritty end of Broadway. Coi (pronounced *kwa*) is really
two restaurants. One is a 30-seat formal dining room—ascetic gold-
taupe banquettes on two walls—that offers an 11-course tasting menu
($120). The food matches the space in sophistication, with such inspired
dishes as chilled piquillo pepper soup, smoked and seared bone marrow
with pomegranate and Asian pear, seared bison with gold turnips, and
Monterey Bay abalone with escarole. The menu in the more casual—
and more casually priced—lounge is à la carte, with less than a dozen
items, including a crisp-skinned roast chicken, a bowl of udon noodles,
and a grilled Gruyère cheese sandwich. ✉ *373 Broadway, North Beach*
☎ *415/393–9000* ⬠ *Reservations not accepted for lounge* ▤ *AE, MC,
V* ✹ *Closed Sun. and Mon. No lunch* ✛ *F2.*

$ ✕**L'Osteria del Forno.** A staff chattering in Italian and seductive aromas
ITALIAN drifting from the open kitchen make customers who pass through the
☺ door of this modest storefront, with its sunny yellow walls and friendly
Fodor's Choice waitstaff, feel as if they've stumbled into a homey trattoria in Italy.
★ Each day the kitchen produces small plates of simply cooked vegetables
(grilled radicchio, roasted carrots and fennel), a few pastas, a daily
special or two, milk-braised pork, a roast of the day, creamy polenta,
and thin-crust pizzas—including a memorable "white" pie topped with
porcini mushrooms and mozzarella. Wine drinkers will find a good
match for any dish they order on the all-Italian list, which showcases
gems from limited-production vineyards. At lunch try one of North
Beach's best focaccia sandwiches. ✉ *519 Columbus Ave., North Beach*
☎ *415/982–1124* ▤ *No credit cards* ✹ *Closed Tues.* ✛ *E2.*

NOB HILL

$$$$ ✕**Masa's.** Although the toque has been passed to several chefs since
FRENCH the death of founding chef Masataka Kobayashi, this 25-year-old restaurant, with its chocolate-brown walls, white fabric ceiling, and red-
silk-shaded lanterns, is still one of the country's most celebrated food
temples. Chef Gregory Short, who worked alongside Thomas Keller at
the famed French Laundry for seven years, is at the helm these days, and
his tasting menus of six and nine courses, including a vegetarian option,
are pleasing both diners and critics. The fare is dubbed New French, and
all the dishes are laced with fancy ingredients, leaving diners struggling
to choose between foie gras au torchon with poached Seckel pears and
foie gras *en sous vide* with Agen prunes. In fall, when northern Italy's
exquisite white truffles are in season, Short typically puts together a tasting menu that tucks them into every course, including dessert, which in
a past season featured white-truffle ice cream perched next to an apple
tartlet. Wine drinkers are bound to find something that suits them, with

8

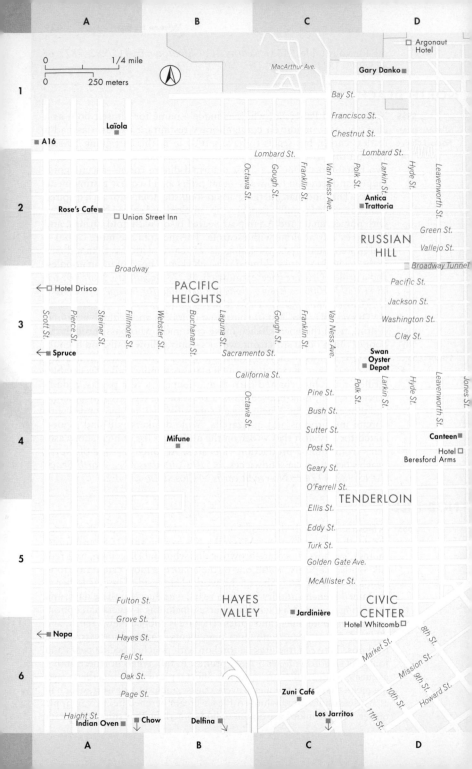

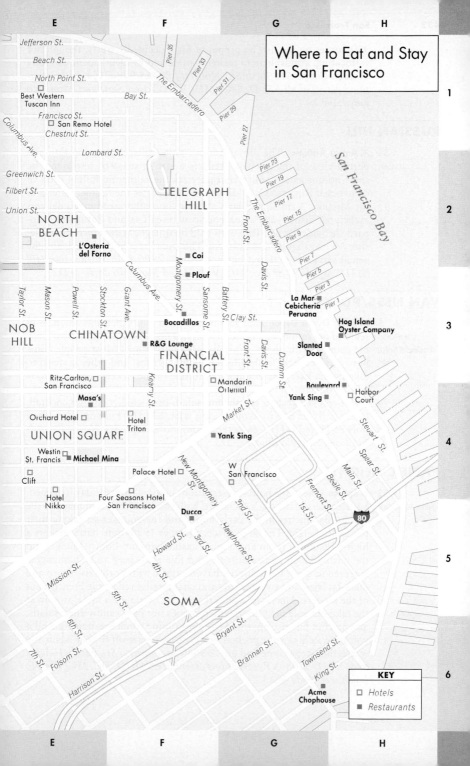

Where to Eat and Stay in San Francisco

KEY
□ Hotels
■ Restaurants

900 bottles on the list. Be prepared for a decidedly stuffy, though not suffocating, atmosphere (a jacket is preferred for gentlemen). ⊠ *Hotel Vintage Court, 648 Bush St., Nob Hill* ☎ *415/989–7154* ⌕ *Reservations essential* ▤ *AE, D, DC, MC, V* ⊙ *Closed Sun. and Mon. No lunch* ✛ *E4.*

RUSSIAN HILL

$$
ITALIAN

✕ **Antica Trattoria.** The dining room—pale walls, dark-wood floors, a partial view of the kitchen—reflects a strong sense of restraint. The same no-nonsense quality characterizes the authentic Italian food of owner-chef Ruggero Gadaldi, who also operates the flashier Beretta in the Mission. A small, regularly shifting, honestly priced menu delivers archetypal dishes such as carpaccio with capers and Parmesan, pappardelle (wide flat noodles) with wild boar, *tagliata di manzo* (beef fillet slices) with arugula, and tiramisu. The wine list is fairly priced, and the genial service is polished but not stiff. ⊠ *2400 Polk St., Russian Hill* ☎ *415/928–5797* ▤ *DC, MC, V* ⊙ *Closed Mon. No lunch* ✛ *D2.*

VAN NESS/POLK

$
SEAFOOD
Fodor's Choice
★

✕ **Swan Oyster Depot.** Half fish market and half diner, this small, slim seafood operation, open since 1912, has no tables, only a narrow marble counter with about a dozen-and-a-half stools. Most people come in to buy perfectly fresh salmon, halibut, crabs, and other seafood to take home. Everyone else hops onto one of the rickety stools to enjoy a bowl of clam chowder—the only hot food served—a dozen oysters, half a cracked crab, a big shrimp salad, or a smaller shrimp cocktail. Come early or late to avoid a long wait. ⊠ *1517 Polk St., Van Ness/Polk* ☎ *415/673–1101* ⌕ *Reservations not accepted* ▤ *No credit cards* ⊙ *Closed Sun. No dinner* ✛ *D3.*

PACIFIC HEIGHTS

$$$$
NEW AMERICAN

✕ **Spruce.** One of the hottest reservations in town from the day it opened, Spruce caters to the city's social set, with the older crowd sliding into the mohair banquettes in the early hours and the younger set taking their places after eight. The large space, a former 1930s auto barn, shelters a high-style dining room and a more casual bar-cum-library lounge, and the menu, which boasts burgers and foie gras, beer and Champagne, is served in both. Charcuterie, bavette steak with bordelaise sauce and duck-fat fries, and sweetbreads and chanterelles reflect the French slant of the modern American menu. If you can't wrangle a table, stop in at the take-out café next door, which carries not only sandwiches, salads, and pastries but also anything from the dining room menu to go. And if you are watching your pocketbook, you can graze off the bar menu and watch the swells come and go. ⊠ *3640 Sacramento St., Pacific Heights* ☎ *415/931–5100* ⌕ *Reservations essential* ▤ *AE, D, DC, MC, V* ⊙ *No lunch weekends* ✛ *A3.*

JAPANTOWN

$ ✕**Mifune.** Thin brown soba and thick white udon are the stars at this

JAPANESE long-popular North American outpost of an Osaka-based noodle

☺ empire. A line regularly snakes out the door, but the house-made noodles, served both hot and cold and with a score of toppings, are worth the wait. Seating is at wooden tables, where diners of every age can be heard slurping down big bowls of such traditional Japanese combinations as *nabeyaki udon,* wheat noodles topped with tempura, chicken, and fish cake; and *tenzaru,* cold noodles and hot tempura with gingery dipping sauce served on lacquered trays. The noodle-phobic can choose from a few rice dishes. ⊠ *Japan Center, Kintetsu Bldg., 1737 Post St., Japantown* ☎ *415/922–0337* ▱ *AE, D, MC, V* ✢ *B4.*

HAYES VALLEY

$$$$ ✕**Jardinière.** A special anniversary? An important business dinner? A

NEW AMERICAN fat tax refund? These are the reasons you book a table at Jardinière.

Fodor's Choice The restaurant takes its name from its chef-owner, Traci Des Jardins,

★ and the sophisticated interior, with its eye-catching oval atrium and curving staircase, fills nightly with locals and out-of-towners alike. The equally sophisticated French-cum-Californian dining-room menu, served upstairs in the atrium, changes daily but regularly includes such high-priced adornments as caviar, foie gras, and truffles. Downstairs, the lounge menu, with smaller plates and smaller prices ($8 to $25), is ideal for when you want to eat light while visiting with friends or tame your hunger before or after the nearby opera or symphony. Cheese lovers will appreciate the wide variety of choices—both Old World and New—housed in the glassed-in cheese-aging chamber in the rear of the restaurant. ⊠ *300 Grove St., Hayes Valley* ☎ *415/861–5555* ⌂ *Reservations essential* ▱ *AE, DC, MC, V* ⊗ *No lunch* ✢ *C5.*

$$$ ✕**Zuni Café.** After one bite of chef Judy Rodgers' succulent brick-oven-

MEDITERRANEAN roasted whole chicken with Tuscan bread salad, you'll understand

Fodor's Choice why she's a national star. Food is served here on two floors; the rabbit

★ warren of rooms on the second level includes a balcony overlooking the main dining room. The crowd is a disparate mix that reflects the makeup of the city: casual and dressy, young and old, hip and staid. At the long copper bar, trays of briny-fresh oysters on the half shell are dispensed along with cocktails and wine. The southern French–Italian menu changes daily (though the signature chicken, prepared for two, is a fixture). Rotating dishes include house-cured anchovies with Parmigiano-Reggiano, deep-fried squid and lemons, nettle and onion soup with a poached egg, and brick-oven squab with polenta. Desserts are simple and satisfying, and include crumbly crusted tarts and an addictive cream-laced coffee granita. The lunchtime burger on rosemary focaccia with a side of shoestring potatoes is a favorite with locals. ⊠ *1658 Market St., Hayes Valley* ☎ *415/552–2522* ▱ *AE, MC, V* ⊗ *Closed Mon.* ✢ *C6.*

8

FISHERMAN'S WHARF

$$$$
NEW AMERICAN
Fodor's Choice
★

✕**Gary Danko.** Be prepared to wait your turn for a table behind chef Gary Danko's legion of loyal fans, who typically keep the reservation book chock-full here (plan on reserving two months in advance). The cost of a meal ($66–$98) is pegged to the number of courses, from three to five. The menu, which changes seasonally, may include pancetta-wrapped frogs' legs, seared foie gras with Fuji apples, shellfish with Thai red curry, and quail stuffed with foie gras and pine nuts. A diet-destroying chocolate soufflé with two sauces is usually among the desserts. So, too, is a "no-cholesterol" Grand Marnier soufflé with raspberry sorbet, perfect for diners with a conscience or a heart problem. The wine list is the size of a small-town phone book, and the banquette-lined room, with beautiful wood floors and stunning (but restrained) floral arrangements, is as memorable as the food. ⊠ *800 N. Point St., Fisherman's Wharf* ☎ *415/749–2060* ⌲ *Reservations essential* ▤ *D, DC, MC, V* ⊗ *No lunch* ✛ *D1.*

COW HOLLOW

$$
ITALIAN
☾

✕**Rose's Café.** Sleepy-headed locals turn up at Rose's for the breakfast pizza of ham, eggs, and fontina; house-baked pastries and breads; poached eggs with Yukon Gold potatoes and chanterelles, or soft polenta with mascarpone and jam. Midday is time for a roasted chicken and fontina sandwich; pizza with mushrooms, feta, and thyme; or pasta with clams. Evening hours find customers eating their way through more pizza and pasta if they are on a budget, and sirloin steak and roasted sea bass if they aren't. The ingredients are top-notch, the service is friendly, and the seating is in comfortable booths, at tables, and at a counter. At the outside tables, overhead heaters keep you toasty when the temperature dips. Expect long lines for Sunday brunch. ⊠ *2298 Union St., Cow Hollow* ☎ *415/775–2200* ▤ *AE, D, DC, MC, V* ✛ *A2.*

MARINA

$$$
ITALIAN
Fodor's Choice
★

✕**A16.** Marina residents—and, judging from the crowds, everybody else—gravitate to this lively trattoria, named for the autostrada that winds through Italy's sunny south. The kitchen serves the food of Naples and surrounding Campania, such as *burrata* (cream-filled mozzarella) with olive oil and crostini and crisp-crust pizzas, including a classic Neapolitan Margherita (mozzarella, tomato, and basil). Among the regularly changing mains are chicken meatballs with fennel and *salsa verde* (green sauce) and rock cod, scallops, and clams in *acqua pazza* (literally, "crazy water"). A big wine list of primarily southern Italian with some California wines suits the fare perfectly. The long space includes an animated bar scene near the door; ask for a table in the quieter alcove at the far end. Reservations are easier to snag midweek. ⊠ *2355 Chestnut St., Marina* ☎ *415/771–2216* ▤ *AE, MC, V* ⊗ *No lunch Sat.–Tues.* ✛ *A1.*

$$
SPANISH

✕**Laïola.** San Franciscans never seem to tire of tapas, as the crowds—mostly young—at this smart, compact Marina outpost of Spanish small plates prove. Try for a seat at the long copper-top bar or at a window table, and then contemplate the seasonally shifting menu that boasts some two dozen tempting tapas, such as braised pork meatballs, Brussels sprouts flecked with bacon, potatoes with pepper-spiked aioli, chickpea croquettes, and slow-roasted piglet. Most regulars seem to skip the four large plates but save room for a creamy chocolate pudding sprinkled with sea salt and olive oil. On Monday nights you can fill up on a big plate of chicken and seafood paella, churros and hot chocolate, and a glass of wine for just $30. If you are hard of hearing or don't want to speak in a raised voice, this is not the restaurant for you, unless you go on a very slow weeknight. ⊠ *2031 Chestnut St., Marina* ☎ *415/346–5641* ⊟ *AE, D, MC, V* ⊘ *No lunch* ✛ *A1.*

THE MISSION

$$$
ITALIAN
Fodor'sChoice
★

✕ **Delfina.** "Irresistible." That's how countless die-hard fans describe Craig and Anne Stoll's Delfina. Such wild enthusiasm has made patience the critical virtue for anyone wanting a reservation here. The interior is comfortable, with hardwood floors, aluminum-top tables, a tile bar, and a casual, friendly atmosphere. The menu changes daily, and among the usual offerings are salt cod *mantecato* (whipped with olive oil) with fennel flatbread and grilled squid with warm white bean salad. If Piedmontese fresh white truffles have made their way to San Francisco, you are likely to find hand-cut tagliarini dressed with butter, cream, and the pricey aromatic fungus on the menu alongside dishes built on more prosaic ingredients. On warm nights, try for a table on the outdoor heated patio. The storefront next door is home to pint-size Pizzeria Delfina. And for folks who can't get to the Mission, the Stolls have opened a second pizzeria on California Street in lively Lower Pacific Heights. ⊠ *3621 18th St., Mission* ☎ *415/552–4055* ⌕ *Reservations essential* ⊟ *MC, V* ⊘ *No lunch* ✛ *B6.*

$
MEXICAN
☾

✕ **Los Jarritos.** A *jarrito* is an earthenware cup used for drinking tequila and other beverages in Mexico. You'll see plenty of these small traditional mugs hanging from the ceiling and decorating the walls in this old-time, sun-filled, family-run restaurant. At brunch try the hearty *chilaquiles*, made from day-old tortillas cut into strips and cooked with cheese, eggs, chilies, and sauce. Or order eggs scrambled with cactus or with *chicharrones* (crisp pork skins) and served with freshly made tortillas. Soup offerings change daily, with Tuesday's *albondigás* (meatballs) comfort food at its best. On weekend evenings adventurous eaters may opt for *birria,* a spicy goat stew, or *menudo,* a tongue-searing soup made from tripe, calf's foot, and hominy. The latter is a time-honored hangover cure. Bring plenty of change for the jukebox loaded with Latin hits. ⊠ *901 S. Van Ness Ave., Mission* ☎ *415/648–8383* ⊟ *AE, MC, V* ✛ *C6.*

THE CASTRO

$
AMERICAN
☾

✕ **Chow.** Wildly popular and consciously unpretentious, Chow is a funky yet savvy diner where soporific standards like hamburgers, pizzas, and spaghetti and meatballs are treated with culinary respect. A

8

CLOSE UP

Eating with Kids

Kids can be fussy eaters, but parents can be, too, so picking places that will satisfy both is important. Fortunately, there are plenty of excellent possibilities all over town.

If you're downtown for breakfast, stop at the venerable **Sears Fine Foods** (✉ 439 Powell St., near Post St. ☎ 415/986–0700), home of "the world-famous Swedish pancakes." Eighteen of the silver-dollar-size beauties cost less than a movie ticket. Nearby in Chinatown, **City View Restaurant** (✉ 662 Commercial St., near Kearny St. ☎ 415/398–2838) serves a varied selection of dim sum, with tasty pork buns for kids and more exotic fare for adults.

If you found yourself dragging the kids through SFMOMA, you can win them back with lunch at the nearby **Crêpe O Chocolate** (✉ 75 O'Farrell St., between Stockton St. and Grant Ave. ☎ 415/362–0255), where they can fill up on a turkey and cheese sandwich and a crepe filled with peanut butter and chocolate—and you can, too. Try **Pluto's** (✉ 627 Irving St., between 7th and 8th Sts. ☎ 415/753–8867) after a visit to Golden Gate Park. Small kids love the chicken nuggets, which arrive with good-for-you carrot and celery sticks, whereas bigger kids will likely opt for one of the two-fisted sandwiches. Everyone will want a double fudge brownie for dessert. **Barney's Gourmet Burgers** (✉ 3344 Steiner St., near Union St. ☎ 415/563–0307), not far from Fort Mason and the Exploratorium, caters to older kids and their parents with mile-high burgers and giant salads. But Barney's doesn't forget "kids under 8," who have their own menu featuring a burger, an all-beef frank, chicken strips with ranch dressing, and more.

Nearly everybody loves pasta, and **Pasta Pomodoro** (✉ 655 Union St., near Powell St. ☎ 415/399–0300), in North Beach offers a kids'-only menu that lets youngsters match up any one of three pasta shapes with five different sauces.

The Mission has dozens of no-frills taco-and-burrito parlors; especially worthy is the bustling **La Corneta** (✉ 2731 Mission St., between 23rd and 24th Sts. ☎ 415/252–9560), which has a baby burrito. Banana splits and hot fudge sundaes are what **St. Francis Fountain** (✉ 2801 24th St., at York St. ☎ 415/826–4200) is known for, along with its vintage decor. Opened in 1918, it recalls the early 1950s, and the menu, with its burgers, BLT, grilled-cheese sandwich, and chili with corn bread, is timeless. In Lower Haight, the small **Rosamunde Sausage Grill** (✉ 545 Haight St., between Steiner and Fillmore Sts. ☎ 415/437–6851) serves just that—a slew of different sausages, from Polish to duck to Weisswurst (Bavarian veal). Grilled onions, sauerkraut, and chili are extra, and since there are only six stools, plan on takeout. Hint: head to nearby Duboce Park, with its cute playground.

Finally, both kids and adults love to be by the ocean, and the **Park Chalet** (✉ 1000 Great Hwy., at Fulton St. ☎ 415/386–8439), hidden behind the two-story Beach Chalet, offers pizza, a juicy burger, sticky ribs, a big banana split, and, on sunny days, outdoor tables and a wide expanse of lawn where kids can play.

—Sharon Silva

magnet for penny-pinchers, the restaurant has built its top-notch reputation on honest fare made with fresh local ingredients priced to sell. Salads, pastas, and mains come in two sizes to accommodate big and small appetites, there's a daily sandwich special, and kids can peruse their mini-menu. Because reservations are restricted to large parties, folks hoping to snag seats usually surround the doorway. Come early (before 6:30) or late (after 10) to reduce the wait, and don't even think about leaving without trying the ginger cake with caramel sauce. ⊠ *215 Church St., Castro* ☎ *415/552–2469* ▭ *MC, V* ✛ *A6.*

THE HAIGHT

$$ ✕**Indian Oven.** This Victorian storefront draws diners from all over
INDIAN the city who come for the tandoori specialties—chicken, lamb, breads. The *saag paneer* (spinach with Indian cheese), *aloo gobbi* (potato, cauliflower, and spices), and *bengan bartha* (roasted eggplant with onions and spices) are also excellent. The chef wants to keep his clientele around for the long haul, too, and puts a little "heart healthy" icon next to some of the menu items. On Friday and Saturday nights famished patrons overflow onto the sidewalk as they wait for open tables. If you try to linger over a mango *lassi* or an order of the excellent *kheer* (rice pudding) on one of these nights, you'll probably be hurried along by a waiter. For better service, come on a slower weeknight. ⊠ *233 Fillmore St., Lower Haight* ☎ *415/626–1628* ▭ *AE, D, DC, MC, V* ⊙ *No lunch* ✛ *A6.*

$$ ✕**Nopa.** In the mid-2000s, North of the Panhandle became the city's
AMERICAN newest talked-about neighborhood in part because of the big, bustling Nopa, which is cleverly named after it. This casual space, with its high ceilings, concrete floor, long bar, and sea of tables, suits the high-energy crowd of young suits and neighborhood residents that fills it every night. They come primarily for the rustic fare, like an irresistible flatbread topped with fennel sausage and chanterelles; creamy cauliflower soup with almonds and mint; smoky, crisp-skinned rotisserie chicken; a juicy grass-fed hamburger with thick-cut fries; and dark ginger cake with caramelized pears and cream. But they also love the lively spirit of the place. Unfortunately, that buzz sometimes means that raised voices are the only way to communicate with fellow diners. A big community table eases the way for anyone dining out on his or her own. ⊠ *560 Divisadero St., Haight* ☎ *415/864–8643* ▭ *AE, MC, V* ⊙ *No lunch* ✛ *A6.*

8

WHERE TO STAY

San Francisco is one of the country's best hotel towns, offering a rich selection of properties that satisfy most tastes and budgets. Whether you're seeking a cozy inn, a kitschy motel, a chic boutique, or a grande dame hotel, this city has got the perfect room for you.

BEST BETS FOR SAN FRANCISCO LODGING

Fodor's offers a selective listing of quality lodging experiences at every price range, from the city's best budget motel to its most sophisticated luxury hotel. Here we've compiled our top recommendations by price and experience. The very best properties—in other words, those that provide a particularly remarkable experience in their price range—are designated in the listings with the Fodor's Choice logo.

Fodor'sChoice ★

Argonaut Hotel, $$$, p. 442

Four Seasons, $$$$, p. 444

Hotel Drisco, $$$–$$$$, p. 443

Hotel Nikko, $$$$, p. 446

Mandarin Oriental, $$$$, p. 439

Orchard Hotel, $$$–$$$$, p. 447

Palace Hotel, $$$$, p. 444

Ritz-Carlton, $$$$, p. 443

San Remo Hotel, ¢, p. 442

Union Street Inn, $$$–$$$$, p. 443

By Price

¢

San Remo Hotel, p. 442

$

Beresford Arms, p. 446

$$

Harbor Court, p. 444

$$$

Hotel Drisco, p. 443

Orchard Hotel, p. 447

$$$$

Hotel Nikko, p. 446

Mandarin Oriental, p. 439

Ritz-Carlton, p. 443

By Experience

BUSINESS TRAVELERS

Four Seasons, p. 444

Hotel Nikko, p. 446

GREAT CONCIERGE

Hotel Triton, p. 447

Ritz-Carlton, p. 443

HISTORICAL FLAVOR

Hotel Whitcomb, p. 439

Palace Hotel, p. 444

Westin St. Francis, p. 448

JET-SETTING CLIENTELE

Clift, p. 446

Hotel Triton, p. 447

W San Francisco, p. 445

MOST KID-FRIENDLY

Argonaut Hotel, p. 442

Beresford Arms, p. 446

Four Seasons, p. 444

W San Francisco, p. 445

MOST ROMANTIC

Hotel Drisco, p. 443

Palace Hotel, p. 444

TOP B&BS

Hotel Drisco, p. 443

TOP SPAS

Mandarin Oriental, p. 439

CIVIC CENTER/VAN NESS

$–$$ ⊞ **Hotel Whitcomb.** Built in 1910, this historic hotel (formerly the Ramada Plaza) was the temporary seat of city government from 1912 to 1915 before becoming a hotel in 1916. (What was once the mayor's office now serves as the hotel's administrative offices, and the jail cells are still intact in the hotel basement.) The expansive, well-appointed lobby boasts marble balustrades and columns, carved wooden ceilings, rare Janesero paneling, Austrian crystal chandeliers, Tiffany stained glass, and a ballroom with one of the largest parquet dance floors in the city. Broad halls lead to spacious, newly refurbished rooms with flat-screen TVs and baths. Northeast corner suites offer views of Market Street and the gold-encrusted dome of City Hall. Stroll out the front door to find the Civic Center Muni and BART stations and the main public library; the Asian Art Museum, Opera House, Davies Symphony Hall, and Westfield Centre are close by. **Pros:** good location; rich architectural and historical legacy; opulent lobby; spacious rooms; airport shuttle. **Cons:** difficult to find street parking; area can be dodgy at night. ⊠ *1231 Market St., Civic Center* ☎ *415/626–8000 or 800/227–4747* ⊕ *www. hotelwhitcomb.com* ⤳ *447 rooms, 12 suites* ⚴ *In room: a/c, Wi-Fi. In hotel: restaurant, room service, bar, gym, laundry service, Wi-Fi hotspot, parking (paid)* ▤ *AE, D, DC, MC, V* ✛ *D6.*

FINANCIAL DISTRICT

$$$$
Fodor's Choice
★
⊞ **Mandarin Oriental, San Francisco.** Two towers connected by glass-enclosed sky bridges compose the top 11 floors of one of San Francisco's tallest buildings. Spectacular panoramas grace every room, and windows open so you can hear that trademark San Francisco sound: the "ding ding" of the cable cars some 40 floors below. The rooms, corridors, and lobby areas are decorated in rich hues of red, gold, and chocolate-brown. The Mandarin Rooms have extra-deep tubs next to picture windows, enabling guests to literally and figuratively soak up what one reader called "unbelievable views from the Golden Gate to the Bay Bridge and everything in between." Pamper yourself with luxurious Egyptian-cotton sheets, two kinds of robes (terry and waffle-weave), and cozy slippers. A lovely complimentary tea-and-cookie tray delivered to your room upon your arrival is one among many illustrations of the hotel's commitment to service. The pricey mezzanine-level restaurant, Silks, earns rave reviews for innovative American cuisine with an Asian flair. Special rate plans for families are available. Several top-floor suites have been recently revamped, as has the Mandarin Lounge. **Pros:** spectacular "bridge-to-bridge" views; attentive service. **Cons:** located in a business area that's quiet on weekends; restaurant is excellent but expensive (as is the hotel). ⊠ *222 Sansome St., Financial District* ☎ *415/276–9600 or 800/622–0404* ⊕ *www.mandarinoriental. com/sanfrancisco* ⤳ *151 rooms, 7 suites* ⚴ *In-room: a/c, safe, DVD, Wi-Fi. In-hotel: restaurant, room service, bar, gym, laundry service, Internet terminal, Wi-Fi hotspot, parking (paid), some pets allowed* ▤ *AE, D, DC, MC, V* ✛ *F4.*

8

Mandarin Oriental

Argonaut Hotel

Hotel Drisco

Palace Hotel

Union Street Inn

Four Seasons Hotel

Orchard Hotel

Hotel Nikko

The Ritz-Calton

FISHERMAN'S WHARF/NORTH BEACH

$$$–$$$$
⟳
Fodor's Choice
★

⊞ Argonaut Hotel. When the four-story Haslett Warehouse was a fruit-and-vegetable canning complex in 1907, boats docked right up against the building. Today it's a hotel with a nautical decor—think anchors, ropes, compasses, and a row of cruise-ship deck chairs in the lobby—that reflects its unique partnership with the San Francisco Maritime National Historical Park. Spacious rooms, many with a sofa bed in the sitting area, have exposed-brick walls, wood-beam ceilings, and whitewashed wooden furniture reminiscent of a summer beach house. Windows open to the sea air and the sounds of the waterfront, and many rooms have views of Alcatraz and the Golden Gate Bridge. Suites come with extra-deep whirlpool tubs and telescopes for close-up views of passing ships. **Pros:** bay views; clean rooms; near Hyde Street cable car; sofa beds; toys for the kids. **Cons:** nautical theme isn't for everyone; cramped public areas; service can be hit or miss; location is a bit of a hike from other parts of town. ⊠ *495 Jefferson St., at Hyde St., Fisherman's Wharf* ☎ *415/563–0800 or 866/415–0704* ⊕ *www.argonauthotel.com* ⟳ *239 rooms, 13 suites* ⚒ *In-room: a/c, safe, refrigerator, Internet, Wi-Fi. In-hotel: restaurant, room service, bar, gym, laundry service, Wi-Fi terminal, parking (paid), some pets allowed* ▭ *AE, D, DC, MC, V* ✛ *D1.*

$$–$$$
⊞

⊞ Best Western Tuscan Inn. Described by some Fodors.com users as a "hidden treasure," this hotel's redbrick facade barely hints at the Tuscan country villa that lies within. Each small, Italianate room has white-pine furniture, floral bedspreads and curtains, a completely mirrored wall, and a refurbished bathroom. Complimentary beverages and biscotti are laid out mornings near the fireplace in the oak-panel lobby, where a convivial wine hour is held nightly. There's free morning limousine service to the Financial District. Café Pescatore, the Italian seafood restaurant off the lobby, provides room service for breakfast. **Pros:** wine/beer hour; down-home feeling. **Cons:** congested touristy area; small rooms. ⊠ *425 N. Point St., at Mason St., Fisherman's Wharf* ☎ *415/561–1100 or 800/648–4626* ⊕ *www.tuscaninn.com* ⟳ *209 rooms, 12 suites* ⚒ *In-room: a/c, Wi-Fi. In-hotel: restaurant, room service, bar, laundry service, Internet terminal, parking (paid), some pets allowed* ▭ *AE, D, DC, MC, V* ✛ *E1.*

¢
Fodor's Choice
★

⊞ San Remo Hotel. A few blocks from Fisherman's Wharf, this three-story 1906 Italianate Victorian—once home to longshoremen and Beat poets—has a narrow stairway from the street leading to the front desk and labyrinthine hallways. Rooms are small but charming, with lace curtains, forest-green-painted wood floors, brass beds, and other antique furnishings. The top floor is brighter, because it's closer to the skylights that provide sunshine to the thriving population of potted plants that line the brass-banistered hallways. About a third of the rooms have sinks, and all share spotless black-and-white-tile bathroom facilities with pull-chain toilets. A rooftop suite must be reserved three to six months in advance. Fior D'Italia, "America's Oldest Italian Restaurant," occupies the building's entire first floor. **Pros:** inexpensive. **Cons:** some rooms are dark; no private bath; spartan amenities. ⊠ *2237 Mason St., North Beach* ☎ *415/776–8688 or 800/352–7366* ⊕ *www.*

sanremohotel.com ⤴ 64 rooms with shared baths, 1 suite ⚑ In-room: no phone, no a/c, no TV, Wi-Fi. In-hotel: laundry facilities, Wi-Fi hotspot, parking (paid), no-smoking rooms ⊟ AE, D, MC, V ⚓ E1.

NOB HILL

$$$$

Fodor's Choice

★

Ritz-Carlton, San Francisco. A preferred destination for travel-industry honchos, movie stars, and visitors alike, this hotel—a stunning tribute to beauty and attentive, professional service—completed a $12.5-million renovation of its guest rooms and meeting spaces in 2006. Ionic columns grace the neoclassical facade; crystal chandeliers illuminate Georgian antiques and museum-quality 18th- and 19th-century paintings in the lobby. All rooms have flat-screen TVs, featherbeds with 300-thread-count Egyptian cotton Frette sheets, and down comforters. Club Level rooms include use of the upgraded Club Lounge, which has a dedicated concierge and several elaborate complimentary food presentations daily. The Dining Room has a seasonal menu with modern French accents. The delightful afternoon tea service in the Lobby Lounge, which overlooks the beautifully landscaped Terrace courtyard, is a San Francisco institution. **Pros:** terrific service; all-day food service on club level; beautiful surroundings. **Cons:** expensive; hilly location. ⊠ *600 Stockton St., at California St., Nob Hill* ☎ *415/296–7465* ⊕ *www.ritzcarlton.com* ⤴ *276 rooms, 60 suites ⚑ In-room: a/c, safe, refrigerator, DVD, Wi-Fi. In-hotel: 2 restaurants, room service, bars, pool, gym, laundry service, Internet terminal, parking (paid), some pets allowed ⊟ AE, D, DC, MC, V ⚓ E3.*

PACIFIC HEIGHTS/COW HOLLOW

$$$–$$$$

Fodor's Choice

★

Hotel Drisco. Pretend you're a resident of one of the wealthiest and most beautiful residential neighborhoods in San Francisco at this understated, elegant 1903 Edwardian hotel. The quiet haven, which feels like a secluded B&B, serves as a celebrity hideaway for the likes of Ethan Hawke and Ashley Judd. Genteel furnishings and luxurious amenities like flat-screen TVs grace pale yellow-and-white rooms, some of which have sweeping city views. Morning newspaper, plush robes, slippers, and nightly turndown service are included. A free breakfast is offered in a sunny, spacious room; wine is set out each evening in a lovely area off the lobby. Guests have commented on the helpful and incredibly friendly staff. Recent renovations added flat-screen TVs and new carpeting, furnishings, and bedding to the guest rooms. **Pros:** great service; comfortable rooms; quiet residential retreat. **Cons:** small rooms; far from downtown. ⊠ *2901 Pacific Ave., Pacific Heights* ☎ *415/346–2880 or 800/634–7277* ⊕ *www.hoteldrisco.com* ⤴ *29 rooms, 19 suites ⚑ In-room: no a/c, safe, refrigerator, DVD. In-hotel: laundry service, Internet terminal* ⊟ *AE, D, DC, MC, V* ⦿ *CP* ⚓ *A3.*

$$$–$$$$

Fodor's Choice

★

Union Street Inn. Precious family antiques and unique artwork helped British innkeepers Jane Bertorelli and David Coyle (former chef for the Duke and Duchess of Bedford) transform this green-and-cream 1902 Edwardian into a delightful B&B. Equipped with candles, fresh flowers, wineglasses, and fine linens, rooms are popular with honeymooners and

8

those looking for a romantic getaway. The newly renovated Carriage House, separated from the main house by an old-fashioned English garden planted with lemon trees, is equipped with a double Jacuzzi, refinished hardwood floors, and upgraded bathrooms. An elaborate breakfast, which many guests rave about, is included, as are afternoon tea and evening hors d'oeuvres. **Pros:** personal service; excellent full breakfast; romantic setting. **Cons:** congested neighborhood; no a/c; no elevator. ✉ *2229 Union St., Cow Hollow* ☎ *415/346–0424* ⊕ *www.unionstreetinn.com* ↙ *6 rooms* ☼ *In-room: no a/c, Wi-Fi. In-hotel: parking (paid)* ☰ *AE, D, MC, V* ⚭*BP* ♧ *A2.*

SOMA

$$$$

☼

Fodor'sChoice

★

🖵 **Four Seasons Hotel San Francisco.** Occupying floors 5 through 17 of a skyscraper, this luxurious hotel, designated as the "heart of the city," is sandwiched between multimillion-dollar condos, elite shops, and a premier sports-and-fitness complex. Elegant rooms with contemporary artwork and fine linens have floor-to-ceiling windows overlooking either Yerba Buena Gardens or the historic downtown. All have deep soaking tubs, glass-enclosed showers, and flat-screen TVs. From the contemporary street-level lobby, take the elevator to the vast Sports Club/LA, where you have free access to the junior Olympic pool, full-size indoor basketball court, and the rest of the magnificent facilities, classes, and spa services. Seasons restaurant serves high-end California cuisine, with a strong focus on seasonal and local ingredients. Various packages offer focuses on art, shopping, and cooking. **Pros:** near museums, galleries, restaurants, and clubs; terrific fitness facilities. **Cons:** pricey. ✉ *757 Market St., SoMa* ☎ *415/633–3000, 800/332–3442, or 800/819–5053* ⊕ *www.fourseasons.com/sanfrancisco* ↙ *231 rooms, 46 suites* ☼ *In-room: a/c, safe, DVD, Internet, Wi-Fi. In-hotel: restaurant, room service, bar, pool, gym, spa, laundry service, Internet terminal, parking (paid), some pets allowed* ☰ *AE, D, DC, MC, V* ♧ *F4.*

$$–$$$

🖵 **Harbor Court.** Exemplary service and a friendly staff earn high marks for this cozy hotel, which overlooks the Embarcadero and is within shouting distance of the Bay Bridge. Guest rooms are on the small side, but have double sets of soundproof windows and include nice touches such as wall-mounted 27-inch flat-screen TVs. Brightly colored throw pillows adorn beds with 320-thread-count sheets, and tub-showers have curved shower-curtain rods for more elbow room. Some rooms have views of the Bay Bridge and the Ferry Building. Complimentary evening wine and late-night cookies and milk are served in the lounge, where coffee and tea are available mornings. The hotel provides free use of the adjacent YMCA. **Pros:** convenient location; quiet, friendly service; cozy. **Cons:** small rooms. ✉ *165 Steuart St., SoMa* ☎ *415/882–1300 or 866/792–6283* ⊕ *www.harborcourthotel.com* ↙ *130 rooms, 1 suite* ☼ *In-room: a/c, Wi-Fi. In-hotel: bar, laundry service, Internet terminal, Wi-Fi hotspot, parking (paid), some pets allowed* ☰ *AE, D, DC, MC, V* ♧ *H4.*

$$$$

Fodor'sChoice

★

🖵 **Palace Hotel.** "Majestic" is the word that best sums up this landmark hotel, which was the world's largest and most luxurious when it opened in 1875. It was completely rebuilt after the 1906 earthquake and fire, and the carriage entrance reemerged as the grand Garden Court restaurant. Today the hotel is still graced with architectural details that recall a bygone era, like chandeliers; tall, mirrored glass doors; and eight pairs of turn-of-the-century, bronze-filigreed marble columns supporting a magnificent dome ceiling filtering natural light; it's a refined environment ideally suited for the high tea served on weekends and daily during holiday periods. Rooms, with twice-daily maid service and nightly turndown, have soaring 14-foot ceilings, traditional mahogany furnishings, flat-screen TVs, and marble bathrooms. The wood-panel Pied Piper Bar is named after the delightful 1909 Maxfield Parrish mural behind the bar. **Pros:** gracious service; close to Union Square; near BART. **Cons:** older design; small rooms with even smaller baths; many nearby establishments closed on weekends; west-facing rooms can be warm and stuffy. ⊠ *2 New Montgomery St., SoMa* ☎ *415/512–1111 or 888/627–7196* ⊕ *www.sfpalace.com* ⊃ *518 rooms, 34 suites* ⬧ *In-room: a/c, safe, refrigerator, Internet. In-hotel: 3 restaurants, room service, bar, pool, gym, laundry service, Wi-Fi hotspot, parking (paid)* ▭ *AE, D, DC, MC, V* ✛ *F4.*

$$$–$$$$

W San Francisco. The epitome of cool urban chic and fashion forward in design and clientele, this swanky 31-story Starwood hotel owes some of its cachet to a prime location next door to the San Francisco Museum of Modern Art. The hotel is infused with hip energy: techno-pop pulses in the lobby and café, and otherworldly mobiles (which change with the seasons) hang overhead; add the mauve leather ottomans and blue velvet sofas to the mix, and you have a cross between a fashion-show runway and a stage set. Compact guest rooms, some of which have upholstered window seats, come with flat-screen TVs, luxurious beds, comfy pillow-top mattresses, and goose-down comforters and pillows. Sleek baths sport green glass countertops and shiny steel sinks. The glass-roof pool and hot-tub area, next to Bliss Spa, is open 24/7, as is the Whatever/Whenever concierge desk in the lobby. In the evening there's a lively bar scene, and the lobby, lit by candlelight, sets the mood for XYZ, the hotel's signature restaurant, an "in spot" which attracts celebs such as Sharon Stone and Kanye West. Upper floors boast excellent views of the Museum of Modern Art, Yerba Buena Gardens, and/or the Bay Bridge. During the week the majority of the clientele is businesspeople, but on weekends the hotel is kid-friendly, and pets are always welcome. The accommodating staff will help parents arrange for babysitting and will take your pup for a walk. Fragrances waft throughout the hotel and guest rooms, so sensitive noses should call ahead to request special preparations. **Pros:** hip energy; mod, sophisticated digs; in the heart of the cultural district. **Cons:** three blocks from BART; hotel's signature scents could pose a problem for sensitive noses. ⊠ *181 3rd St., SoMa* ☎ *415/777–5300* ⊕ *www.whotels.com/sf* ⊃ *404 rooms, 9 suites* ⬧ *In-room: a/c, safe, refrigerator, DVD, Internet, Wi-Fi. In-hotel: restaurant, room service, bar, pool, gym, spa, laundry service, Internet terminal, Wi-Fi hotspot, parking (paid), some pets allowed* ▭ *AE, D, DC, MC, V* ✛ *G4.*

8

UNION SQUARE/DOWNTOWN

$$$$ ⊡ **Clift.** A favorite of hipsters, music industry types, and celebrities flee-ing the media onslaught—security discreetly keeps photographers and other heat-seekers away—this sexy hotel, whose entrance is so nonde-script you can walk right past it without a hint of what's inside, is the brainchild of entrepreneur Ian Schrager and artist-designer Philippe Starck, known for his collection of eccentric chairs. The moody, dra-matically illuminated lobby is dominated by a gigantic Napoleonic chair that could accommodate Shrek, with room to spare. This theatrical staging is enhanced by surreal seating options like a leather love seat with buffalo tusks and a miniature "drink me" chair, all surrounding a floor-to-ceiling, pitch-black fireplace. Spacious rooms—as light as the lobby is darkly intriguing—have translucent orange Plexiglas tables, high ceilings, flat-screen TVs, and two huge "infinity" wall mirrors. Some visitors have remarked on the thin walls and advise booking a room on an upper-level floor to avoid street noise. The art-deco Red-wood Room bar, paneled with wood from a 2,000-year-old tree, is known for its "beautiful people." Asia de Cuba restaurant prepares an artful fusion of Asian and Latino cuisines. **Pros:** good rates compared to similar top-tier hotels in SF; surreal moody interior design; ideal loca-tion for shopping and theaters; close to public transportation; discreet and helpful staff. **Cons:** some guests note thin walls; street noise. ⊠ *495 Geary St., Union Square* ☎ *415/775–4700 or 800/606–6090* ⊕ *www. clifthotel.com* ➷ *337 rooms, 26 suites* ⌕ *In-room: a/c, safe, Internet, Wi-Fi. In-hotel: restaurant, room service, bar, gym, laundry service, Internet terminal, parking (paid), some pets allowed (paid)* ⊟ *AE, D, DC, MC, V* ✛ *E4.*

$–$$ ⊡ **Hotel Beresford Arms.** Surrounded by fancy molding and 10-foot-tall
🌣 windows, the red-carpet lobby of this ornate brick Victorian explains why the building is on the National Register of Historic Places. Rooms with dark-wood antique-reproduction furniture vary in size and setup: junior suites have sitting areas and either a wet bar or kitchenette; full suites have two queen beds, a Murphy bed, and a kitchen. All suites have a bidet in the bathroom. Continental breakfast, afternoon tea, and wine are served beneath a crystal chandelier in the lobby. **Pros:** moderately priced; suites with kitchenettes and Murphy beds are a plus for families with kids. **Cons:** no a/c. ⊠ *701 Post St., Union Square* ☎ *415/673–2600 or 800/533–6533* ⊕ *www.beresford.com* ➷ *83 rooms, 12 suites* ⌕ *In-room: no a/c, kitchen (some), refrigerator, Wi-Fi. In-hotel: laundry service, Internet terminal, Wi-Fi hotspot, parking (paid), some pets allowed* ⊟ *AE, D, DC, MC, V* ⏀⍟ *CP* ✛ *D4.*

$$$$ ⊡ **Hotel Nikko.** The vast gray-flecked white marble and gurgling foun-
Fodor's Choice tains in the neoclassical lobby of this business traveler hotel have the
★ sterility of an airport. Crisply designed rooms in muted tones have flat-screen TVs, modern bathrooms with sinks that sit on top of black vani-ties, and "in-vogue" separate showers and tubs. Some higher-end rooms come with complimentary breakfast. The excellent, 10,000-square-foot Club Nikko fitness facility has traditional *ofuros* (Japanese soak-ing tubs), his-and-her *kamaburso* (Japanese meditation rooms), and a glass-enclosed 16-meter rooftop pool and a whirlpool. The Rrazz

Room, San Francisco's only cabaret theater, located on the lobby level, is a venue for national talent and nostalgia acts most evenings. **Pros:** friendly multilingual staff; some rooms have ultramodern baths; very clean. **Cons:** rooms and antiseptic lobby lack color; some may find the atmosphere cold; expensive parking. ⊠ *222 Mason St., Union Square* ☎ *415/394–1111 or 800/248–3308* ⊕ *www.hotelnikkosf.com* ⤴ *510 rooms, 22 suites* ☆ *In-room: a/c, refrigerator, Internet, Wi-Fi. In-hotel: restaurant, room service, bar, pool, gym, laundry service, Internet terminal, Wi-Fi hotspot, parking (paid), some pets allowed* ☰ *AE, D, DC, MC, V* ✛ *E4.*

$$$–$$$$ 🛏 **Hotel Triton.** The spirit of fun has taken up full-time residence in this Kimpton property, which has a youngish, super-friendly staff; pink and blue neon elevators; and a colorful psychedelic lobby mural depicting the San Francisco art and music scene—think flower power mixed with Andy Warhol. Playful furniture includes a green-and-gold metallic couch and striped carpeting, a whimsical and far-out setting for free morning coffee and tea, fresh afternoon cookies, evening wine events, and the on-call tarot reader. Smallish rooms are painted silvergray and tomato-soup red and come with ergonomic desk chairs, flatscreen TVs, and oddball light fixtures; sinks are positioned outside the bathrooms, European style. Twenty-four "environmentally sensitive" rooms have water- and air-filtration systems and biodegradable soap. A 24-hour yoga channel will help you find that elusive path to inner peace. **Pros:** attentive service; refreshingly funky atmosphere; hip arty environs; good location. **Cons:** rooms and baths are on the small side. ⊠ *342 Grant Ave., Union Square* ☎ *415/394–0500 or 800/433–6611* ⊕ *www.hoteltriton.com* ⤴ *133 rooms, 7 suites* ☆ *In-room: a/c, refrigerator, Wi-Fi. In-hotel: gym, laundry service, parking (paid), some pets allowed* ☰ *AE, D, DC, MC, V* ✛ *F4.*

$$$–$$$$
Fodor's Choice
★
🛏 **Orchard Hotel.** Unlike most other boutique hotels in the area, which sometimes occupy century-old buildings, the strictly-21st-century Orchard was built in 2000. The 104-room hotel embraces state-of-the-art technology—from CD and DVD players in each room to Wi-Fi access throughout the building—mixing cutting-edge Silicon Valley chic with classic European touches. The hotel's marble lobby, where the bronze statue *Spring Awakening* greets visitors, previews the dramatic architectural embellishments, like arched openings, vaulted ceilings, and stone floors that are found throughout the hotel. With just 12 rooms per floor, the hotel feels quite intimate; some guests have compared it to a cozy (decidedly upscale) mountain inn. Rooms, sizable by boutique hotel standards, are done in a soft palette of relaxing colors, a balm for harried shoppers returning from a busy day of retail therapy in Union Square. The hotel's restaurant, Daffodil, serves seasonal California fare for breakfast and dinner. Like its "green sister," the Orchard Garden, this hotel has also received LEED certification (the only one in SF) giving SF visitors yet another eco-friendly option. **Pros:** cutting-edge technology. **Cons:** can be a bit pricey. ⊠ *665 Bush St., Union Square* ☎ *415/362–8878 or 888/717–2881* ⊕ *www.theorchardhotel.com* ⤴ *104 rooms, 9 suites* ☆ *In-room: a/c, safe, DVD, Wi-Fi. In-hotel: restaurant, room service, laundry service, parking (paid), some pets allowed* ☰ *AE, D, DC, MC, V* ✛ *E4.*

8

$$$–$$$$ 🖼 **Westin St. Francis.** The site of sensational, banner headline scandals, this hotel's past is shrouded in as much infamy as stardust. This is the place where Sara Jane Moore tried to assassinate Gerald Ford, where Al Jolson died playing poker; Suite 1219–1221 was the scene of a massive scandal, which erupted when a 30-year-old aspiring actress died after a night of heavy boozing in the close company of silent film comedian Fatty Arbuckle. The hotel is comprised of the original building (Empire-style furnishings, Victorian moldings) and a modern 32-story tower (Asian-inspired lacquered furniture, glass elevators); guests are divided when it comes to the virtues of the modern addition vs. the historic building. In 2009, the hotel completed a $40-million renovation—the most extensive in its history—of all guest rooms and common areas. Now Wi-Fi is available throughout the hotel. Adding to the air of upscale sophistication is the cool chic of Michael Mina's classy restaurant and his new cocktail lounge, the Clock Bar, as well as the venerable Oak Room Restaurant and Lounge. **Pros:** fantastic beds; prime location; spacious rooms, some with great views. **Cons:** some guests comment on the long wait at check-in; rooms in original building can be small; glass elevators are not for the faint of heart. ✉ *335 Powell St., Union Square* ☎ *415/397–7000 or 800/917–7458* ⊕ *www.westinstfrancis.com* ⤳ *1,157 rooms, 38 suites* ⚓ *In-room: a/c, safe, refrigerator (some), Internet, Wi-Fi. In-hotel: 3 restaurants, room service, bars, spa, laundry service, Internet terminal, Wi-Fi hotspot, parking (paid), some pets allowed* ▭ *AE, D, DC, MC, V* ✛ *E4.*

NIGHTLIFE

This small city packs the punch of a much larger metropolis after dark. Sophisticated, trendy, relaxed, quirky, and downright outrageous could all be used to describe San Francisco's diverse and vibrant collection of bars, clubs, and performance venues.

THE 4-1-1

Entertainment information is printed in the pink Sunday "Datebook" section (⊕ *www.sfgate.com/datebook*) and the more calendar-based Thursday "96 Hours" section (⊕ *www.sfgate.com/96hours*) in the *San Francisco Chronicle*. Also consult any of the free alternative weeklies, notably the *SF Weekly* (⊕ *www.sfweekly.com*), which blurbs nightclubs and music, and the *San Francisco Bay Guardian* (⊕ *www.sfbg.com*), which lists neighborhood, avant-garde, and budget events. SF Station (⊕ *www.sfstation.com*; online only) has an up-to-date calendar of entertainment goings-on.

BARS AND LOUNGES

★ **Cliff House.** A bit classier than the Beach Chalet, with a more impressive, sweeping view of Ocean Beach, the Cliff House is our pick if you must choose just one oceanfront restaurant/bar. Sure, it's the site of many high-school prom dates, and you could argue that the food and drinks are overpriced, and some say the sleek facade looks like a mausoleum— but the views are terrific. The best window seats are reserved for diners, but there's a small upstairs lounge where you can watch gulls sail high above the vast blue Pacific. Come before sunset. ⊠ *1090 Point Lobos, at Great Hwy., Lincoln Park* ☎ *415/386–3330* ⊕ *www.cliffhouse.com.*

Eos Restaurant and Wine Bar. Though it's just a few blocks away, Cole Valley is a world apart from funky, grungy Haight Street. Eos, along with the handful of restaurants and bars that line this part of Cole Street, manages to be both sophisticated and unpretentious—and truly fantastic. This narrow and romantically lighted space, with more than 400 wines by the bottle and 40-plus by the glass, offers two different wine flights—one red and one white—every month. The adjoining restaurant's excellent East-meets-West cuisine is available at the bar. ⊠ *901 Cole St., at Carl St., Haight* ☎ *415/566–3063* ⊕ *www.eossf.com.*

★ **Hôtel Biron.** Sharing an alleylike block with the backs of Market Street restaurants, this tiny, cavelike (in a good way) spot displays rotating artwork of the Mission School aesthetic on its brick walls. The clientele is well-behaved twenty- to thirtysomethings who enjoy the cramped quarters, good range of wines and prices, off-the-beaten path location, soft lighting, and hip music. If it's too crowded, CAV is just around the corner. ⊠ *45 Rose St., off Market St., Hayes Valley* ☎ *415/703–0403* ⊕ *www.hotelbiron.com.*

MatrixFillmore. Don a pair of Diesel jeans and a Michael Kors sweater and sip cosmos or Cabernet with the Marina's bon vivants. This is the premier spot in the "Triangle" (short for Bermuda Triangle, named for all of the singles who disappear in the bars clustered at Greenwich and Fillmore streets). Although there's a small dance floor where some folks bump and grind to high-energy DJ-spun dance tracks, the majority of the clientele usually vies for the plush seats near the central open fireplace, flirts at the bar, or huddles for romantic tête-à-têtes in the back. The singles scene can be overwhelming on weekends. ⊠ *3138 Fillmore St., between Greenwich and Filbert Sts., Marina* ☎ *415/563–4180* ⊕ *www.matrixfillmore.com.*

Park Chalet. You'll feel like you're in a cabin in the woods as you relax in an Adirondack chair under a heat lamp, enclosed by the greenery of Golden Gate Park. In addition to serving pub food such as burgers, salads, steaks, and fish-and-chips, the brewery churns out its own beer. The Park Chalet shares a building with the Beach Chalet *(see below)*—but it isn't waterside, so you won't freeze if it's overcast. ⊠ *1000 Great Hwy., near Martin Luther King Jr. Dr., Golden Gate Park* ☎ *415/386–8439* ⊕ *www.beachchalet.com.*

Redwood Room. Opened in 1933 and updated by über-hip designer Philippe Starck in 2001, the Redwood Room at the Clift Hotel is a San Francisco icon. The entire room, floor to ceiling, is paneled with the wood from a single redwood tree, giving the place a rich, monochromatic look. The gorgeous original art-deco sconces and chandeliers still hang, but bizarre video installations on plasma screens also adorn the walls. It's packed on weekend evenings after 10, when young scenesters swarm the hotel; for maximum glamour, visit on a weeknight. ⊠ *Clift Hotel, 495 Geary St., at Taylor St., Union Square* ☎ *415/929–2372 for table reservations, 415/775–4700 for hotel.*

8

Tonga Room. Since 1947 the Tonga Room has given San Francisco a taste of high Polynesian kitsch. Fake palm trees, grass huts, a lagoon (three-piece combos play pop standards on a floating barge), and faux monsoons—courtesy of sprinkler-system rain and simulated thunder and lightning—grow more surreal as you quaff more fruity cocktails. ✉ *Fairmont San Francisco, 950 Mason St., at California St., Nob Hill* ☎ *415/772–5278.*

Vesuvio Café. If you're only hitting one bar in North Beach, it should be this one. The low-ceiling second floor of this raucous boho hangout, little altered since its 1960s heyday (when Jack Kerouac frequented the place), is a fine vantage point for watching the colorful Broadway and Columbus Avenue intersection. Another part of Vesuvio's appeal is its diverse, always-mixed clientele (20s to 60s), from neighborhood regulars and young couples to Bacchanalian posses of friends. ✉ *255 Columbus Ave., at Broadway, North Beach* ☎ *415/362–3370* ⊕ *www. vesuvio.com.*

GAY AND LESBIAN NIGHTLIFE

The *Bay Area Reporter* (☎ *415/861–5019* ⊕ *www.ebar.com*), a biweekly newspaper, lists gay and lesbian events in its calendar. The biweekly *San Francisco Bay Times* (☎ *415/626–0260* ⊕ *www.sfbaytimes.com*) is aimed at gay and lesbian readers.

GAY MALE BARS

Eagle Tavern. Bikers are courted with endless drink specials and, increasingly, live rock music at this humongous indoor-outdoor leather bar, one of the few SoMa bars remaining from the days before AIDS and gentrification. The Sunday-afternoon "Beer Busts" (3–6 PM) are a social high point and benefit charitable organizations. It's a surprisingly welcoming place for people from all walks of life. ✉ *398 12th St., at Harrison St., SoMa* ☎ *415/626–0880* ⊕ *www.sfeagle.com.*

★ **Martuni's.** A mixed crowd enjoys cocktails in the semi-refined environment of this elegant bar at the intersection of the Castro, the Mission, and Hayes Valley; variations on the martini are a specialty. In the intimate back room, a pianist plays nightly and patrons take turns singing show tunes. It's a favorite post-theater spot—especially after the symphony or opera, which are within walking distance. ✉ *4 Valencia St., at Market St., Mission* ☎ *415/241–0205.*

The Stud. Mingle with glam trannies, tight-teed pretty boys, ladies and their ladies, and a handful of straight onlookers who dance to the live DJ and watch world-class drag performers on the small stage. The entertainment is often campy, pee-your-pants funny, and downright talented. Each night's music is different—from funk, soul, and hip-hop to '80s tunes and disco favorites. The club is sometimes closed Sunday. ✉ *399 9th St., at Harrison St., SoMa* ☎ *415/863–6623* ⊕ *www.studsf.com.*

LESBIAN BARS

Lexington Club. According to its slogan, "every night is ladies' night" at this all-girl club geared to urban alterna-dykes in their 20s and 30s (think piercings and tattoos, not lipstick). Catfights are not uncommon.

■ **TIP →** **The women's room has awesome graffiti.** ⊠ *3464 19th St., at Lexington St., Mission* ☎ *415/863–2052* ⊕ *www.lexingtonclub.com.*

JAZZ CLUBS

★ **Yoshi's.** The city's outpost of the legendary Oakland club that has pulled in some of the world's best jazz musicians—Pat Martino, Betty Carter, and Dizzy Gillespie, to name just a few—has terrific acoustics, a 9-foot Steinway grand piano (broken in by Chick Corea), and seating for 411; it's been hailed as "simply the best jazz club in the city." Yoshi's also serves Japanese food in an adjoining restaurant; you can also order food at café tables in the club. And yes, the coupling of sushi and jazz *is* as elegant as it sounds. Sightlines are good from just about any vantage point, including the back balcony. Be advised, the strip where the club is located is part of a new city redevelopment project—it's on a tough block in an even tougher neighborhood; so, take advantage of the valet parking. ⊠ *1330 Fillmore St., at Eddy St., Japantown* ☎ *415/655–5600* ⊕ *www.yoshis.com.*

ROCK, POP, HIP-HOP, FOLK, AND BLUES CLUBS

Bimbo's 365 Club. The plush main room and adjacent lounge of this club, here since 1951, retain a retro vibe perfect for the "Cocktail Nation" programming that keeps the crowds entertained. For a taste of the old-school San Francisco nightclub scene, you can't beat this place. Indie low-fi and pop bands like Stephen Malkmus and the Jicks and Camera Obscura fill the bill. ⊠ *1025 Columbus Ave., at Chestnut St., North Beach* ☎ *415/474–0365* ⊕ *www.bimbos365club.com.*

Fodor'sChoice ★ **BooM BooM RooM.** John Lee Hooker's old haunt has been an old-school blues haven for years, attracting top-notch acts from all around the country. Luck out with legendary masters like James "Super Chikan" Johnson, or discover new blues and funk artists. ⊠ *1601 Fillmore St., at Geary Blvd., Japantown* ☎ *415/673–8000* ⊕ *www.boomboomblues.com.*

★ **Bottom of the Hill.** This is a great live-music dive—in the best sense of the word—and truly the epicenter for independent rock in the Bay Area. The club has hosted some great acts over the years, including the Strokes and the Throwing Muses. Rap and hip-hop acts occasionally make it to the stage. ⊠ *1233 17th St., at Texas St., Potrero Hill* ☎ *415/621–4455* ⊕ *www.bottomofthehill.com.*

The Fillmore. This is *the* club that all the big names, from Coldplay to Clapton, want to play. San Francisco's most famous rock-music hall serves up a varied menu of national and local acts: rock, reggae, grunge, jazz, folk, acid house, and more. Most tickets cost $20–$30, and some shows are open to all ages. ■ **TIP →** **Avoid steep service charges by buying tickets at the Fillmore box office on Sunday (10–4).** ⊠ *1805 Geary Blvd., at Fillmore St., Western Addition* ☎ *415/346–6000* ⊕ *www.thefillmore.com.*

Fodor'sChoice ★ **Great American Music Hall.** You can find top-drawer entertainment at this great, eclectic nightclub. Acts range from the best in blues, folk, and jazz to up-and-coming college-radio and American-roots artists to of-the-

8

moment indie rock stars (OK Go, Mates of State) and the establishment (Cowboy Junkies). The colorful marble-pillared emporium (built in 1907 as a bordello) also accommodates dancing at some shows. Pub grub is available most nights. ✉ *859 O'Farrell St., between Polk and Larkin Sts., Tenderloin* ☎ *415/885–0750* ⊕ *www.gamh.com.*

THE ARTS

San Francisco's symphony, opera, and ballet all perform in the Civic Center area, also home to the 928-seat Herbst Theatre, which hosts many fine soloists and ensembles. **San Francisco Performances** (✉ *500 Sutter St., Suite 710* ☎ *415/398–6449* ⊕ *www.performances.org*) brings an eclectic array of topflight global music and dance talents to various venues—mostly the Yerba Buena Center for the Arts, Davies Symphony Hall, and Herbst Theatre. Artists have included the Los Angeles Guitar Quartet, Edgar Meyer, the Paul Taylor Dance Company, and Midori.

TICKETS

City Box Office (✉ *180 Redwood St., Suite 100, off Van Ness Ave. between Golden Gate Ave. and McAllister St., Civic Center* ☎ *415/392–4400* ⊕ *www.cityboxoffice.com*), a charge-by-phone service, offers tickets for many performances and lectures. You can buy tickets in person at its downtown location weekdays 9:30–5:30. You can charge tickets for everything from jazz concerts to Giants games by phone or online through **Tickets.com** (☎ *800/955–5566* ⊕ *www.tickets.com*). Half-price, same-day tickets for many local and touring stage shows go on sale (cash only) at 11 AM Tuesday through Saturday at the **TIX Bay Area** (✉ *Powell St. between Geary and Post Sts., Union Square* ☎ *415/433–7827* ⊕ *www.tixbayarea.com*) booth on Union Square. TIX is also a full-service ticket agency for theater and music events around the Bay Area, open Tuesday through Friday 11 to 6, Saturday 10 to 6, and Sunday 10 to 3.

THE 4-1-1

The best guide to the arts is the Sunday "Datebook" section (⊕ *www. sfgate.com/datebook*), printed on pink paper, in the *San Francisco Chronicle*. The four-day entertainment supplement "96 Hours" (⊕ *www.sfgate.com/96hours*) is in the Thursday *Chronicle*. Also be sure to check out the city's free alternative weeklies, including *SF Weekly* (⊕ *www.sfweekly.com*) and the more avant-garde *San Francisco Bay Guardian* (⊕ *www.sfbg.com*).

Online, SF Station (⊕ *www.sfstation.com*) has a frequently updated arts and nightlife calendar. San Francisco Arts Monthly (⊕ *www.sfarts. org*), which is published at the end of the month, has arts features and events, plus a helpful "Visiting San Francisco?" section. For offbeat, emerging artist performances, consult CounterPULSE (⊕ *www. counterpulse.org*).

DANCE

★ **San Francisco Ballet.** Under artistic director Helgi Tomasson, the San Francisco Ballet's works—both classical and contemporary—have won admiring reviews. The primary season runs from February through May. Its repertoire includes full-length ballets such as *Don Quixote* and *Sleeping Beauty*; the December presentation of the *Nutcracker* is one of the most spectacular in the nation. The company also performs bold new dances from star choreographers such as William Forsythe and Mark Morris, alongside modern classics by George Balanchine and Jerome Robbins. Tickets and information are available at the **War Memorial Opera House.** ⊠ *War Memorial Opera House, 301 Van Ness Ave., Civic Center* ☎ *415/865–2000* ⊕ *www.sfballet.org* ☉ *Weekdays 10–4.*

MUSIC

★ **San Francisco Symphony.** One of America's top orchestras, the San Francisco Symphony performs from September through May, with additional summer performances of light classical music and show tunes; visiting artists perform here the rest of the year. Michael Tilson Thomas, who is known for his innovative programming of 20th-century American works (most notably his Grammy Award–winning Mahler cycle), is the music director, and he and his orchestra often perform with soloists of the caliber of Andre Watts, Gil Shaham, and Renée Fleming. Just to illustrate the more adventuresome side of the organization, this symphony once collaborated with the heavy-metal group Metallica. David Byrne has performed here, as well. Tickets run about $15–$100. ⊠ *Davies Symphony Hall, 201 Van Ness Ave., at Grove St., Civic Center* ☎ *415/864–6000* ⊕ *www.sfsymphony.org.*

MUSIC FESTIVALS

☾ **Stern Grove Festival.** The nation's oldest continual free summer music Fodor'sChoice festival hosts Sunday-afternoon performances of symphony, opera, jazz, ★ pop music, and dance. The amphitheater is in a beautiful eucalyptus grove below street level, perfect for picnicking before the show. (Dress for cool weather.) ⊠ *Sloat Blvd. at 19th Ave., Sunset* ☎ *415/252–6252* ⊕ *www.sterngrove.org.*

OPERA

★ **San Francisco Opera.** Founded in 1923, this world-renowned company has resided in the Civic Center's War Memorial Opera House since the building's completion in 1932. Over its split season—September through January and June through July—the opera presents about 70 performances of 10 to 12 operas. Translations are projected above the stage during almost all non-English operas. Long considered a major international company and the most important operatic organization in the United States outside New York, the opera frequently embarks on productions with European opera companies. Ticket prices can range from $25 to $195. The full-time box office (Monday 10–5, Tuesday–Friday 10–6) is at 199 Grove Street, at Van Ness Avenue. ⊠ *War*

8

Built as a bordello in 1907, the Great American Music Hall now pulls in top-tier performers.

Memorial Opera House, 301 Van Ness Ave., at Grove St., Civic Center ☎ 415/864–3330 tickets ⊕ www.sfopera.com.

THEATER

★ **American Conservatory Theater.** Not long after its founding in the mid-1960s, the city's major nonprofit theater company became one of the nation's leading regional theaters. During its season, which runs from early fall to late spring, ACT presents approximately eight plays, from classics to contemporary works, often in rotating repertory. In December ACT stages a much-loved version of Charles Dickens's *A Christmas Carol.* The **ACT ticket office** (⊠ *405 Geary St., Union Square* ☎ 415/749–2228) is next door to **Geary Theater,** the company's home. ⊠ *Geary Theater, 425 Geary St., Union Square* ⊕ *www.act-sf.org.*

Fodor's Choice ★ **Teatro ZinZanni.** Contortionists, chanteuses, jugglers, illusionists, and circus performers ply the audience as you're served a surprisingly good five-course dinner in a fabulous antique Belgian traveling-dance-hall tent. Be ready to laugh, and arrive early for a front-and-center table. Reservations are essential; tickets are $125 to $150. Dress fancy. ⊠ *Pier 29, Embarcadero at Battery St., Embarcadero* ☎ 415/438–2668 ⊕ *www.zinzanni.org.*

SPORTS AND THE OUTDOORS

BASEBALL

       The **San Francisco Giants** (⊠ *AT&T Park, 24 Willie Mays Plaza, between*
Fodor's Choice *2nd and 3rd Sts., SoMa* ☎ *415/972–2000 or 800/734–4268* ⊕ *sanfran-*
★ *cisco.giants.mlb.com*) play in beautiful, classic AT&T Park. **Tickets.
com** (☎ *877/473–4849* ⊕ *www.tickets.com*) sells game tickets over the
phone and charges a per-ticket fee of $2–$10, plus a per-call processing fee of up to $5. The **Giants Dugout** (⊠ *AT&T Park, 24 Willie
Mays Plaza, SoMa* ☎ *415/972–2000 or 800/734–4268* ⊠ *4 Embarcadero Center, Embarcadero* ☎ *415/951–8888*) sells tickets in any of its
stores (check the Web site, ⊕ *sanfrancisco.giants.mlb.com/sf/ballpark/
dugout_stores.jsp*, for all locations); a surcharge is added at all but the
ballpark store.

BICYCLING

The **San Francisco Bicycle Coalition** (☎ *415/431–2453* ⊕ *www.sfbike.org*)
has extensive information about the policies and politics of riding a
bicycle in the city and lists local events for cyclists on its Web site. You
can also download (but not print) a PDF version of the *San Francisco
Bike Map and Walking Guide*.

WHERE TO RENT

Bike and Roll. You can rent bikes here for $7 per hour or $28 per day;
discounted weekly rates are available. They have three locations and
also have complimentary maps. ⊠ *899 Columbus Ave., North Beach*
⊠ *353 Jefferson St. between Jones and Leavenworth Sts., Fisherman's
Wharf* ⊠ *Leavenworth St. between Jefferson and Beach Sts., Fisherman's Wharf* ☎ *415/229–2000 or 888/245–3929* ⊕ *www.bicyclerental.
com*.

Bike Hut. Known for its mom-and-pop–style service, the Hut is a
small rental, repair, and used-bike shop. Hourly rentals go for $6,
daily rentals for $22. ⊠ *Pier 40,
SoMa* ☎ *415/543–4335* ⊕ *www.
thebikehut.com* ⊗ *Closed Mon.
and Tues.*

Blazing Saddles. This outfitter rents
bikes for $7 to $11 an hour, depending on the type of bike, or $28 to $68
a day, and shares tips on sights to see
along the paths. ⊠ *2715 Hyde St.,
Fisherman's Wharf* ⊠ *465 Jefferson
St., at Hyde St., Fisherman's Wharf*
⊠ *Pier 43½ near Taylor St., Fisherman's Wharf* ⊠ *Pier 41 at Powell St.,
Fisherman's Wharf* ⊠ *1095 Columbus, North Beach* ☎ *415/202–8888*
⊕ *www.blazingsaddles.com*.

8

NO UPHILL BATTLE

Don't want to get stuck slogging
up 30-degree inclines? Then be
sure to pick up a copy of the
foldout *San Francisco Bike Map
and Walking Guide* ($3), which
indicates street grades by color
and delineates bike routes that
avoid major hills and heavy traffic.
You can pick up a copy in bicycle
shops, select bookstores, or at the
San Francisco Bicycle Coalition's
Web site (⊕ *www.bikesf.org*).

San Francisco Cyclery. Rent a bike for $15 for one to two hours, $20 for two to four hours, or $30 for eight hours. ⊠ *672 Stanyan St., between Page and Haight Sts., Haight* ☎ *415/379–3870* ⊕ *www. sanfranciscocyclery.com* ⊗ *Wed.–Mon. 10–6.*

SHOPPING

MAJOR SHOPPING DISTRICTS

THE CASTRO AND NOE VALLEY

The Castro, often called the gay capital of the world, is also a major shopping destination for all travelers. It's filled with men's clothing boutiques and home-accessories stores geared to the neighborhood's fairly wealthy demographic. Of course, there are plenty of places hawking kitsch, too, and if you're looking for something to shock your Aunt Martha back home, you've come to the right place. Just south of the Castro on 24th Street, largely residential Noe Valley is an enclave of fancy-food stores, bookshops, women's clothing boutiques, and specialty gift stores.

CHINATOWN

The intersection of Grant Avenue and Bush Street marks the gateway to Chinatown. The area's 24 blocks of shops, restaurants, and markets are a nonstop tide of activity. Dominating the exotic cityscape are the sights and smells of food: crates of bok choy, tanks of live crabs, cages of live partridges, and hanging whole chickens. Racks of Chinese silks, colorful pottery, baskets, and carved figurines are displayed chockablock on the sidewalks, alongside fragrant herb shops where your bill might be tallied on an abacus. And if you need to knock off souvenir shopping for the kids and office-mates in your life, the dense and multiple selections of toys, T-shirts, mugs, magnets, decorative boxes, and countless other trinkets make it a quick, easy, and inexpensive proposition.

FISHERMAN'S WHARF

A constant throng of sightseers crowds Fisherman's Wharf, and with good reason: Pier 39, the Anchorage, Ghirardelli Square, and the Cannery are all here, each with shops and restaurants, as well as outdoor entertainment—musicians, mimes, and magicians. Best of all are the Wharf's view of the bay and its proximity to cable-car lines, which can shuttle shoppers directly to Union Square. Many of the tourist-oriented shops border on tacky, peddling the requisite Golden Gate tees, taffy, and baskets of shells, but tucked into the mix are a few fine galleries, clothing shops, and groceries that even locals will deign to visit.

THE HAIGHT

Haight Street is a perennial attraction for visitors, if only to see the sign at Haight and Ashbury streets—the geographic center of the Flower Power movement during the 1960s, so it can be a bummer to find this famous intersection is now the turf for Gap and Ben & Jerry's. Don't be discouraged; it's still possible to find high-quality vintage clothing, funky shoes, folk art from around the world, and used records and CDs galore in this always-busy neighborhood.

The beat movement of the 1950s was born in San Francisco's most famous bookstore, City Lights.

HAYES VALLEY

A community park called Hayes Green breaks up a crowd of cool shops just west of the Civic Center. Here you can find everything from hip housewares to art galleries to handcrafted jewelry. The density of unique stores—as well as the lack of chains anywhere in sight—makes it a favorite destination for many San Francisco shoppers.

JAPANTOWN

Unlike the ethnic enclaves of Chinatown, North Beach, and the Mission, the 5-acre **Japan Center** (⊠ *Bordered by Laguna, Fillmore, and Post Sts. and Geary Blvd.* ☎ *No phone*) is under one roof. The three-block complex includes a reasonably priced public garage and three shop-filled buildings. Especially worthwhile are the Kintetsu and Kinokuniya buildings, where shops sell things like bonsai trees, tapes and records, jewelry, antique kimonos, *tansu* (Japanese chests), electronics, and colorful glazed dinnerware and teapots.

THE MARINA DISTRICT

With the city's highest density of (mostly) non-chain stores, the Marina is an outstanding shopping nexus. But it's nobody's secret—those with plenty of cash and style to burn flood the boutiques to snap up luxe accessories and housewares. Union Street and Chestnut Street in particular cater to the shopping whims of the grown-up sorority sisters and frat boys who live in the surrounding pastel Victorians.

THE MISSION

The aesthetic of the resident Pabst Blue Ribbon–downing hipsters and starving-artist types contributes to the affordability and individuality of shopping here. These night owls keep the city's best thrift stores, vintage-furniture shops, alternative bookstores, and, increasingly, small clothing boutiques afloat. As the Mission gentrifies, though, bargain hunters find themselves trekking the long blocks in search of truly local flavor. Thankfully, many of the city's best bakeries and cafés are sprinkled throughout the area.

NORTH BEACH

Although it's sometimes compared to New York City's Greenwich Village, North Beach is only a fraction of the size, clustered tightly around Washington Square and Columbus Avenue. Most of its businesses are small eateries, cafés, and shops selling clothing, antiques, and vintage wares. Once the center of the Beat movement, North Beach still has a bohemian spirit that's especially apparent at the rambling City Lights Bookstore, where Beat poetry lives on.

PACIFIC HEIGHTS

The rest of the city likes to deprecate its wealthiest neighborhood, but no one has any qualms about weaving through the mansions to come to Fillmore and Sacramento streets to shop. With grocery and hardware stores sitting alongside local clothing ateliers and international designer outposts, these streets manage to mix small-town America with big-city glitz. After you've splurged on a cashmere sweater or a handblown glass vase, snag an outdoor seat at Peet's or Coffee Bean; it's the perfect way to pass an afternoon watching the parade of Old Money, dogs, and strollers.

UNION SQUARE

Serious shoppers head straight to Union Square, San Francisco's main shopping area and the site of most of its department stores, including Macy's, Neiman Marcus, and Saks Fifth Avenue. Nearby are such platinum-card international boutiques as Yves Saint Laurent, Cartier, Emporio Armani, Gucci, Hermès of Paris, Louis Vuitton, Gianni Versace, and Barneys CO-OP, with high, urban fashion on seven exquisitely appointed floors.

One major arrival is the **Westfield San Francisco Shopping Centre** (⊠ *865 Market St., between 4th and 5th Sts., Union Square* ☎ *415/495–5656*), anchored by Bloomingdale's and Nordstrom. Besides the sheer scale of this mammoth mall, it's notable for its gorgeous atriums and its topnotch dining options (no typical food courts here—instead you'll find branches of a few top local restaurants).

The Bay Area

WITH MARIN COUNTY, BERKELEY, OAKLAND, AND THE COASTAL PENINSULA

WORD OF MOUTH

"We . . . caught the ferry over to Sausalito. A stroll along the sheltered waterfront and a close-quarters view of Alcatraz on the way back rounded out a perfect stay in the City by the Bay."

—kiwi_rob

WELCOME TO THE BAY AREA

TOP REASONS TO GO

★ **Great outdoors:**
A wealth of wild land lies right outside San Francisco's borders, including the beaches, forests, and meadows of the Golden Gate National Recreation Area; Point Reyes National Seashore; Big Basin Redwoods State Park; and numerous state beaches.

★ **Wining and dining:** Some of the best restaurants and markets in California (and in the country) are in the greater Bay Area, most notably Chez Panisse in Berkeley.

★ **Two-wheeling:** Whether you're cycling through the countryside or bombing down a mountain-side single track, great cycling opportunities are everywhere here in the birthplace of mountain biking.

★ **Café culture:** While away your day over a latte. Coffeehouses, tea-rooms, and bookstore cafés abound, especially in the East Bay.

★ **On the water:** The Bay itself is a place to explore, by sailboat, kayak, or ferry.

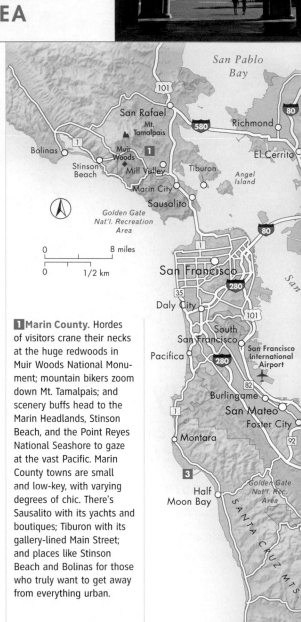

1 Marin County. Hordes of visitors crane their necks at the huge redwoods in Muir Woods National Monument; mountain bikers zoom down Mt. Tamalpais; and scenery buffs head to the Marin Headlands, Stinson Beach, and the Point Reyes National Seashore to gaze at the vast Pacific. Marin County towns are small and low-key, with varying degrees of chic. There's Sausalito with its yachts and boutiques; Tiburon with its gallery-lined Main Street; and places like Stinson Beach and Bolinas for those who truly want to get away from everything urban.

2 The East Bay. When San Franciscans refer to it, the East Bay often means nothing more than what you can see across the bay from the city—mainly Oakland and Berkeley. Oakland is gritty and diverse, home to a buzzing arts scene, Jack London Square, and famous jazz joint Yoshi's. Berkeley, defined by its University of California campus and liberal-to-radical politics, is a place of renegade spirits, bursting bookstores, and creature comforts like Alice Waters's Chez Panisse.

3 The Coastal Peninsula. The coastal towns between Santa Cruz and San Francisco have long been agricultural outposts, supplying food for the missions and the towns that succeeded them. Today artichokes and other cool-weather crops still grow in coastal fields, but the big attraction here is the beaches. The shoreline is nearly all public and varies widely from long, sandy stretches to tide pool–covered flats.

GETTING ORIENTED

Cross the Golden Gate Bridge and head north to reach Marin County's rolling hills and green expanses, where residents enjoy an haute-suburban lifestyle. East of the city, across the San Francisco Bay, are Berkeley and Oakland, which most Bay Area residents refer to as the East Bay. Life here feels more relaxed than in the city—but every bit as vibrant. To the south of San Francisco lies the peninsula; which part you see depends on your route: Highway 1 passes through a sparsely populated landscape along the coast, while inland a tangle of freeways leads to bustling Silicon Valley.

9

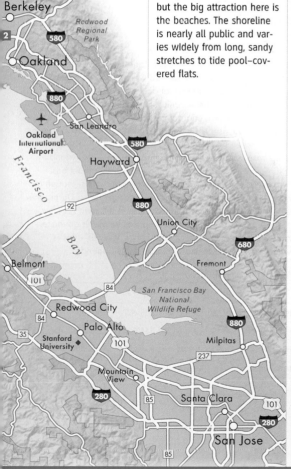

THE BAY AREA PLANNER

When to Go

For such a small place, the Bay Area has a surprisingly varied climate. The rainy season runs from about November through March, and temperatures in the 50s and 60s are generally constant across the region. But on any given day between April and November, 10 different local cities can have 10 different forecasts. Some things hold constant: protected from the fog, inland areas stay warm and dry, while coastal areas seesaw between sun and fog (and rarely get truly hot). The East Bay is usually warmer and sunnier than points west, though when the fog rolls in hard it can hit here, too.

Getting Around

Getting around the Bay Area can be challenging. Rush hour on the highways is maddening, and in some neighborhoods looking for a parking space can feel like punishment. Public transit options—trains, subways, buses, and ferries—are abundant, but this is only a good option if you're traveling between the city and major destinations like Oakland, Berkeley, Sausalito, Tiburon, and Palo Alto.

About the Restaurants

The Bay Area is home to some of the most popular and innovative restaurants in the country, including Berkeley's famous Chez Panisse Café & Restaurant. Expect an emphasis on locally grown produce, hormone-free meats, and California wine—and not just in the finest dining rooms. Even casual spots like Fish, in Sausalito, serve memorable meals.

About the Hotels

There aren't many hotels in Berkeley or Oakland, but Marin is a destination where hotels package themselves as cozy retreats. Summer is often booked well in advance, despite weather that is often mercurial and sometimes downright chilly. Along the coastal peninsula, accommodations tend to have homegrown character and cater to San Franciscans and weekend visitors here for a romantic getaway. Because of the weekend demand on the coast you'd be wise to make reservations as far in advance as possible. Inland Peninsula and South Bay lodgings generally attract business travelers—most are chain motels and hotels, though a handful of B&Bs have popped up in recent years. During the week, when business conventions are in full swing, many of these hotels are fully booked up two weeks in advance. However, some are nearly empty on weekends—this is when rates plummet and package deals abound.

WHAT IT COSTS

	¢	$	$$	$$$	$$$$
Restaurants	under $10	$10–$14	$15–$22	$23–$30	over $30
Hotels	under $90	$90–$149	$150–$199	$200–$250	over $250

Restaurant prices are for a main course at dinner, excluding sales tax of 8.25% (depending on location). Hotel prices are for two people in a standard double room in high season, excluding service charges and 10% tax.

Updated by
Lisa M. Hamil-
ton and Fiona
G. Parrott

It's rare for a metropolis to compete with its suburbs for visitors, but the view from any of San Francisco's hilltops shows
that the Bay Area's temptations extend far beyond the city
limits.

To the north is Marin County, the beauty queen: small but chic villages
like Tiburon and Mill Valley plus dramatic coastal scenery. East of town
are two energetic urban centers, Berkeley and Oakland. Formerly radical Berkeley is getting more glam, while Oakland is slowly shaking off
its image as San Francisco's ugly stepsister. Along the peninsula south
of San Francisco you'll find a largely undeveloped coastline dotted with
small towns and wild beaches—a place so peaceful it's hard to believe
that behind the rolling green hills lies Silicon Valley.

MARIN COUNTY

9

Marin is quite simply a knockout—some go so far as to call it spectacular and wild. This isn't an extravagant claim, since more than 40% of
the county (180,000 acres), including the majority of the coastline, is
parkland. The territory ranges from chaparral, grassland, and coastal
scrub to broadleaf and evergreen forest, redwood, salt marsh, and rocky
shoreline.

Adrenaline junkies mountain bike down Mt. Tamalpais, and those who
want solitude take a walk on one of Point Reyes's many empty beaches.
Cosmopolitan Sausalito is just over the Golden Gate Bridge from San
Francisco; across an inlet are Tiburon and Belvedere, lined with grand
homes that regularly appear on fund-raising circuits.

West Marin is about as far as you can get from the big city, both physically and ideologically. Separated from the inland county by the slopes
and ridges of giant Mt. Tamalpais, this territory beckons to mavericks,
artists, ocean lovers, and other free spirits. Stinson Beach has tempered its isolationist attitude to accommodate out-of-towners, as have
Inverness and Point Reyes Station. Bolinas, on the other hand, would
prefer you not know its location.

PLANNING

GETTING HERE AND AROUND

BOAT AND FERRY TRAVEL

The Golden Gate Ferry crosses the bay to Sausalito from the south wing of San Francisco's Ferry Building (at Market Street and the Embarcadero). Blue & Gold Fleet ferries depart daily for Sausalito and Tiburon from Pier 41 at Fisherman's Wharf; weekday commuter ferries leave from the Ferry Building for Tiburon. The trip to Sausalito takes 30 minutes; to Tiburon, it takes 20 minutes. Seas can be choppy, but the ride is not long. Expect more crowds on weekends and during peak commute times.

The Angel Island–Tiburon Ferry sails across the strait to the island daily April through September and weekends the rest of the year.

Boat and Ferry Lines Angel Island–Tiburon Ferry (☎ 415/435–2131 ⊕ www.angelislandferry.com). **Blue & Gold Fleet** (☎ 415/705–8200 ⊕ www. blueandgoldfleet.com). **Golden Gate Ferry** (☎ 415/455–2000 ⊕ www. goldengateferry.org).

BUS TRAVEL

Golden Gate Transit buses travel to Sausalito, Tiburon, and Mill Valley from 1st and Mission streets as well as from other points in San Francisco. For Mt. Tamalpais State Park, take Bus 10, 70, or 80 to Marin City; in Marin City transfer to Golden Gate Transit Bus 63 (weekends and holidays, mid-March through early December only). To reach points in West Marin (e.g., Bolinas, Point Reyes Station, and the edge of Mt. Tamalpais State Park) on weekdays only, take West Marin Stagecoach vans from Marin City; call for routes and schedules. San Francisco MuniBus 76 runs hourly from 4th and Townsend streets to the Marin Headlands Visitor Center on Sunday and major holidays only. The trip takes roughly 45 minutes.

Bus Lines Golden Gate Transit (☎ 415/455–2000 ⊕ www.goldengate.org). **San Francisco Muni** (☎ 415/701–2311 ⊕ www.sfmuni.com). **West Marin Stagecoach** (☎ 415/526–3239 ⊕ www.marin-stagecoach.org).

CAR TRAVEL

To cross the Golden Gate Bridge, take U.S. 101 north. For Sausalito, take the first exit, Alexander Avenue, just past Vista Point; after winding all the way down the hill to the water, the road becomes Bridgeway. Continue north on Bridgeway to the municipal parking lot near the center of town—but expect the lot to be full on weekends, in which case you should continue north and hunt for street spots. For Tiburon, exit at Tiburon Boulevard. For Mill Valley, exit at East Blithedale, continue west on East Blithedale to Throckmorton Avenue, and turn left to reach Lytton Square. All three trips take 20 to 45 minutes one-way, depending on traffic.

The Marin Headlands are a logical stop en route to Sausalito, but reaching them can be tricky. After exiting on Alexander Avenue, take the first left (signs read SAN FRANCISCO/U.S. 101 SOUTH), pass through a tunnel under the freeway, and make a hard right up the steep hill just before the road merges back on to the bridge toward San Francisco. You

Marin
County

should see a small sign that says FORTS BARRY AND CRONKHITE. Conzelman Road follows the cliffs that face the ocean and becomes one-way before a spectacular drop toward Point Bonita; Bunker Road is a less spectacular inland route through Rodeo to the forts.

For Muir Woods and Mt. Tamalpais, take the Route 1–Stinson Beach exit off U.S. 101 and follow Route 1 west and then north. Both trips may take from 30 minutes to more than an hour, depending on traffic; allow plenty of extra time on summer weekends.

SIGHTSEEING GUIDES

Blue & Gold Fleet has a one-hour narrated tour of the San Francisco Bay, for $24, with frequent daily departures from Pier 39 in San Francisco. Super Sightseeing offers a four-hour bus tour of Muir Woods. The tour, which stops in Sausalito en route, leaves at 9 AM and 2 PM daily from North Point and Taylor Street at Fisherman's Wharf and costs $46 ($45 senior citizens, $24 ages 5–11); 24-hour advance reservations are recommended. Great Pacific Tour Co. runs four-hour morning and afternoon tours of Muir Woods and Sausalito for $49 ($47 senior citizens, $39 ages 5–11), with hotel pickup in 14-passenger vans with excellent interpretation.

By Bus and Van Blue & Gold Fleet (☎ 415/705–8200 ⊕ www. blueandgoldfleet.com). **Great Pacific Tour Co.** (☎ 415/626–4499 ⊕ www.

greatpacifictour.com). **Super Sightseeing** (📞 *415/777–2288* ⊕ *www. supersightseeing.com*).

VISITOR INFORMATION

Contact Marin County Visitors Bureau (✉ *1013 Larkspur Landing Circle, Larkspur* 📞 *866/925–2060* ⊕ *www.visitmarin.org*).

SAUSALITO

2 mi north of Golden Gate Bridge.

Bougainvillea-covered hillsides and an expansive yacht harbor give Sausalito the feel of an Adriatic resort. The town sits on the northwestern edge of San Francisco Bay, where it's sheltered from the ocean by the Marin Headlands; the mostly mild weather here is perfect for strolling and outdoor dining. Nevertheless, morning fog and afternoon winds can roll over the hills without warning, funneling through the central part of Sausalito once known as Hurricane Gulch.

South on **Bridgeway** (toward San Francisco), which snakes between the bay and the hills, a waterside esplanade is lined with restaurants on piers that lure diners with good seafood and even better views. Stairs along the west side of Bridgeway climb the hill to wooded neighborhoods filled with both rustic and opulent homes. As you amble along Bridgeway past boutiques, gift shops, and galleries, you'll notice the absence of basic services. If you need an aspirin or some groceries (or if you want to see the locals), you'll have to head to Caledonia Street, which runs parallel to Bridgeway, north of the ferry terminus and inland a couple of blocks. The streets closest to the ferry landing flaunt their fair share of shops selling T-shirts and kitschy souvenirs. Venture into some of the side streets or narrow alleyways to catch a bit more of the town's taste for eccentric jewelry and handmade crafts.

■TIP→ The ferry is the best way to get to Sausalito from San Francisco; you get more romance (and less traffic) and disembark in the heart of downtown.

ESSENTIALS

Visitor Information Sausalito Chamber of Commerce (✉ *780 Bridgeway* 📞 *415/332–0505 or 415/331–7262* ⊕ *www.sausalito.org*).

Get your bearings and find out what's happening in town at the **Sausalito Visitors Center and Historical Exhibit** (✉ *780 Bridgeway* 📞 *415/332–0505*), operated by the town's historical society. It's closed Monday.

EXPLORING

The landmark **Plaza Viña del Mar** (✉ *Bridgeway and Park St.*), named for Sausalito's sister city in Chile, marks the center of town. Flanked by two 14-foot-tall elephant statues (created in 1915 for the Panama-Pacific International Exposition), the fountain is a great setting for snapshots and people-watching.

On the waterfront between the Hotel Sausalito and the Sausalito Yacht Club is an unusual historic landmark—a **drinking fountain.** It's inscribed with HAVE A DRINK ON SALLY in remembrance of Sally Stanford, the former San Francisco madam who later became the town's mayor in the

The rolling hills of Marin County are a serene backdrop for the crowded piers of the Sausalito waterfront.

1970s. Sassy Sally, as they called her, would have appreciated the fountain's eccentric custom attachment: a knee-level basin that reads HAVE A DRINK ON LELAND, in memory of her beloved dog.

QUICK BITES

Judging by the crowds gathered outside **Hamburgers** (⊠ *737 Bridgeway* ☎ *415/332–9471*), you'd think someone was juggling flaming torches out front. They're really gaping at the juicy hand-formed beef patties sizzling on a rotating grill. Brave the line (it moves fast), get your food to go, and head for the esplanade to enjoy the sweeping views. Hours are 11 AM to 5 PM.

🔆 An anonymous-looking World War II shipyard building holds one of Sausalito's great treasures: the sprawling (more than 1½ acres) **Bay Model** of the entire San Francisco Bay and the San Joaquin–Sacramento River delta, complete with flowing water. The U.S. Army Corps of Engineers uses the model to reproduce the rise and fall of tides, the flow of currents, and the other physical forces at work on the bay. *2100 Bridgeway, at Marinship Way* ☎ *415/332–3870 recorded information, 415/332–3871 operator assistance* ⊕ *www.spn.usace.army.mil/bmvc* ⊠ *Free* ☉ *Memorial Day–Labor Day, Tues.–Fri. 9–4, weekends 10–5; Labor Day–Memorial Day, Tues.–Sat. 9–4.*

🔆 The **Bay Area Discovery Museum** fills five former military buildings with entertaining and enlightening hands-on exhibits related to science and the arts. Kids and their families can fish from a boat at the indoor wharf, imagine themselves as marine biologists in the Wave Workshop, and play outdoors at Lookout Cove, a 2½-acre bay-in-miniature made up of scaled-down sea caves, tidal pools, and even a re-created shipwreck. At Tot Zone, toddlers and preschoolers can play in an indoor-outdoor interactive area. From San Francisco, take the Alexander Avenue exit from U.S. 101 and follow signs to East Fort Baker. ⊠ *557 McReynolds Rd., at East Fort Baker* ☎ *415/339–3900* ⊕ *www.baykidsmuseum.org* 🖙 *$10; children under 1 free* ⊘ *Tues.–Fri. 9–4, weekends 10–5.*

WHERE TO EAT

$–$$
SEAFOOD
🖑
Fodor's Choice
★

✕**Fish.** If you're wondering where the locals go, this is the place. For fresh seafood you can't beat this gleaming dockside fish house a mile north of downtown. Order at the counter, and then grab a seat by the floor-to-ceiling windows or at a picnic table on the pier, overlooking the yachts and fishing boats. Most of the sustainably caught fish is hauled in from the owner's boats, right at the dock outside. Try the ceviche, crab Louis, cioppino, barbecue oysters, or anything fresh that day that's being grilled over the oak-wood fire. Outside, kids can doodle with sidewalk chalk on the pier. ⊠ *350 Harbor Dr.* ☎ *415/331–3474* ⚞ *Reservations not accepted* ⊟ *No credit cards.*

$$–$$$
ITALIAN

✕**Poggio.** One of the few restaurants in Sausalito to attract both food-savvy locals and tourists, Poggio serves modern Tuscan cuisine in a handsome, open-wall space that spills onto the street. Expect dishes such as grilled lamb chops with roasted eggplant, braised artichokes with polenta, feather-light gnocchi, and pizzas from the open kitchen's wood-fired oven. ⊠ *777 Bridgeway* ☎ *415/332–7771* ⚞ *Reservations essential* ⊟ *AE, D, MC, V.*

$$–$$$
JAPANESE
★

✕**Sushi Ran.** Sushi aficionados swear this is the Bay Area's best for raw fish, but don't overlook the excellent Pacific Rim fusions, a result of Japanese ingredients and French cooking techniques, served up in unusual presentations. Because Sushi Ran is so highly ranked among area foodies, book two to seven days in advance for dinner. Otherwise, expect a long wait, which you can soften by sipping one of the 45 by-the-glass sakes from the outstanding wine-and-sake bar. ■**TIP→** If you wander in after a day of sightseeing and can't get a table, you can sup in the noisy bar. ⊠ *107 Caledonia St.* ☎ *415/332–3620* ⊟ *AE, D, MC, V* ⊘ *No lunch weekends.*

WHERE TO STAY

$$$$

🏨**Cavallo Point.** Set in Golden Gate National Park, this luxury hotel and resort's location is truly one of a kind. A former Army post, it features turn-of-the-century buildings converted into well-appointed yet eco-friendly rooms. Both historic and contemporary guest rooms are scattered around the property, most overlooking a massive lawn with stunning views of the Golden Gate Bridge and San Francisco Bay. The staff is accommodating and helpful. Murray Circle, the notable on-site restaurant with a Michelin-starred chef, serves top-notch California ingredients and features an impressive wine cellar. The neighboring casual bar offers food and drink on a large porch. **Pros:** numerous activities: a cooking school, yoga classes, and nature walks; spa with a tea bar; art gallery. **Cons:** landscaping feels incomplete; some staff act a bit informal. ⊠ *601 Murray Circle, Fort Baker, Sausalito* ☎ *415/339–4700* ⊕ *www.cavallopoint.com* ⇌ *68 historic and 74 contemporary guest rooms* ⚭ *In-room: a/c (some), safe, refrigerator, Internet, Wi-Fi. In hotel: 2 restaurants, room service, bar, pool, gym, spa, water sports, laundry service, parking (paid), some pets allowed* ⊟ *AE, D, DC, MC, V.*

$$$$ ⊞ **The Inn Above Tide.** This is the only hotel in the Bay Area with balconies literally hanging over the water, and each of its rooms has a perfect-10 view that takes in wild Angel Island as well as the city lights across the bay. In the corner Vista Suite (the most expensive room here, at nearly triple the standard-room rate), you can even watch San Francisco twinkle from the king-size bed. Lovely touches—gardenias by the sink, large tubs, binoculars in every room, complimentary California wine and imported cheese—abound, and most rooms have wood-burning or gas fireplaces. Although it's set in the middle of town, this place is tranquil. **Pros:** great complimentary breakfast; minutes from restaurants/attractions; free in-room binoculars let you indulge in the incredible views. **Cons:** costly parking; some rooms are on the small side; no room service. ⊠ *30 El Portal* ☎ *415/332–9535 or 800/893–8433* ⊕ *www.innabovetide.com* ⏎ *29 rooms, 2 suites* ⚭ *In-room: a/c, DVD, Wi-Fi. In-hotel: laundry service* ▭ *AE, DC, MC, V* ⊠⍟ *CP.*

SPORTS AND THE OUTDOORS

Specializing in sea kayaking, **Sea Trek Ocean Kayaking Center** (⊠ *Schoonmaker Point Marina, off Libertyship Way* ☎ *415/488–1000* ⊕ *www.seatrekkayak.com*) offers guided half-day trips underneath the Golden Gate Bridge and full- and half-day trips to Angel Island, both for beginners. Starlight and full-moon paddles are particularly popular. Trips for experienced kayakers, classes, and rentals also are available. Prices start at $20 per hour for rentals; $65 for a three-hour guided trip.

SHOPPING

Something/Anything Gallery. Tucked away where Broadway ends and curves toward the dock, this gallery has a huge array of jewelry and gifts, from unique watches to humorous pendants. With friendly service and carefully crafted mementos of Sausalito, it's easy to find an inexpensive souvenir. ⊠ *20 Princess St., Sausalito* ☎ *415/339–8831.*

9

TIBURON

2 mi north of Sausalito; 7 mi north of Golden Gate Bridge.

On a peninsula that was called Punta de Tiburon (Shark Point) by the Spanish explorers, this beautiful Marin County community retains the feel of a village, despite the encroachment of commercial establishments from the downtown area. The harbor faces Angel Island across Raccoon Strait, and San Francisco is directly south across the bay—which makes the views from the decks of harbor restaurants a major attraction. Tiburon is slightly more low-key than Sausalito, and the community favors Sunday brunch and cocktail hour. Since its incarnation, in 1884, when ferries from San Francisco connected the point with a railroad to San Rafael, the town has centered on the waterfront. ■**TIP→** The ferry is the most relaxing (and fastest) way to get here whenever the weather is pleasant, particularly in summer, allowing you to skip traffic and parking problems. Think about avoiding a midweek visit to Tiburon. Although there will be fewer strollers on the street, most shops close either Tuesday or Wednesday, or both.

ESSENTIALS

Visitor Information Tiburon Peninsula Chamber of Commerce (✉ 96-B Main St. ☎ 415/435–5633 ⊕ www. tiburonchamber.org).

EXPLORING

Tiburon's narrow **Main Street** is on the bay side; you can browse the shops and galleries or relax on a restaurant's deck jutting out over the harbor.

Past the pink-brick bank building, Main Street is known as **Ark Row** (⊕ www.landmarks-society.org) and has a tree-shaded walk lined with antiques and specialty stores. Look closely and you can see that some of the buildings are actually old houseboats. They floated in Belvedere Cove before being beached and transformed into stores. If you're curious about architectural history, the Tiburon Heritage & Arts Commission prints a self-guided walking-tour map, which you can pick up at local businesses.

The stark-white **Old St. Hilary's Landmark and Wildflower Preserve,** an 1886 Carpenter Gothic church barged over from Strawberry Point in 1957, overlooks the town and the bay from its hillside perch. ■**TIP→** The church is surrounded by a wildflower preserve that is spectacular in May and June, when the rare black jewel flower blooms. Expect a steep walk uphill to reach the preserve. ✉ 201 Esperanza St., off Mar West St. ☎ 415/435–1853 ⊕ www.landmarks-society.org ✍ $2 suggested donation ◷ Apr.–Oct., Wed. and Sun. 1–4 and by appointment.

WHERE TO EAT

$–$$ ✕ **Rooney's.** Beloved by locals, this is a Tiburon favorite. A friendly
AMERICAN greeting will make you feel as if you're at home, as will the lanterns and polished wood floors (head inside over dining dockside). Comfort food anchors the lunch menu with choices like "New York–style" sandwiches, salads, and a few surprises such as African chicken. For dinner, choose from fresh Dungeness crab, rib-eye steak, or seasonal specials. Last orders are taken at 9 PM except on Friday and Saturday, when you have an extra half-hour. ✉ 38 Main St. ☎ 415/435–1911 ▤ MC, V ◷ No dinner Mon. or Tues.

$$–$$$ ✕ **Sam's Anchor Cafe.** Open since 1921, this casual dockside restaurant
AMERICAN with mahogany wainscoting is the town's most famous eatery. Today most people flock here for the deck, where out-of-towners and old salts sit shoulder to shoulder for bay views, beer, seafood, and Ramos fizzes. The lunch menu is nothing special—burgers, sandwiches, salads, fried fish with tartar sauce—and you'll sit on plastic chairs at tables covered with blue-and-white-checked oilcloths. At night you can find standard seafood dishes with vegetarian and meat options. Expect a wait for outside tables on weekends (there are no reservations for deck seating or weekend lunch). Mind the seagulls; they know no restraint. ✉ 27 Main St. ☎ 415/435–4527 ▤ AE, D, DC, MC, V.

WHERE TO STAY

$$–$$$ ⚉ **Waters Edge Hotel.** Checking into this spacious and elegant hotel feels
★ like tucking away into a cozy retreat by the water. The views are stunning, the lighting perfect. Most rooms have a gas fireplace, and many
have balconies with bay views at this stylish small hotel in downtown
Tiburon. Furnishings are chic and modern in cocoa and cream colors; down comforters and high-thread-count linens make the beds
deliciously comfortable. High-vaulted ceilings show off the carefully
placed, Asian-influenced objects, which line the hallways and front living room area. ■TIP➔ In the morning, breakfast is delivered to your door,
but take your coffee outside to the giant communal sundeck over the water;
the south-facing views of San Francisco Bay are incredible. **Pros:** complimentary wine and cheese for guests every evening; restaurants/sights are
minutes away. **Cons:** no room service; extra charge for Wi-Fi access; not
a great place to bring small children. ⊠ *25 Main St.* ☎ *415/789–5999 or
877/789–5999* ⊕ *www.marinhotels.com* ⤴ *23 rooms* ⚲ *In-room: a/c,
DVD, Wi-Fi. In-hotel: laundry service* ▭ *AE, D, DC, MC, V* ⦿|*CP.*

THE MARIN HEADLANDS

★ The term "Golden Gate" may now be synonymous with the world-
famous bridge, but it originally referred to the grassy, poppy-strewn
hills flanking the passageway into San Francisco Bay. To the north of
the gate lie the **Marin Headlands,** part of the Golden Gate National Recreation Area (GGNRA) and the most dramatic scenery in these parts.
The raw beauty of the headlands, which consist of several small but
steep bluffs, is particularly striking if you've just come from the enclosed
silence of the nearby redwood groves. Windswept hills plunge down to
the ocean, and creek-fed thickets shelter swaying wildflowers.

The headlands stretch from the Golden Gate Bridge to Muir Beach. Photographers flock to the southern headlands for shots of the city, with the
Golden Gate Bridge in the foreground and the skyline on the horizon.
Equally remarkable are the views north along the coast and out to sea,
where the Farallon Islands are visible on clear days. ■TIP➔ Almost any
of the roads, all very windy, offer great coast views, especially as you drive
at higher elevations. You'll see copious markers for scenic spots.

The headlands' strategic position at the mouth of San Francisco Bay
made them a logical site for World War II military installations. Today
you can explore the crumbling concrete batteries where naval guns
protected the approaches from the sea; kids especially love climbing on
these structures. The headlands' main attractions are centered on Forts
Barry and Cronkhite, which lie just across Rodeo Lagoon from each
other. Fronting the lagoon is Rodeo Beach, a dark stretch of sand that
attracts sand-castle builders and dog owners.

⚠ Note: The beaches at the Marin Headlands are not safe for swimming.
The giant cliffs are steep and unstable, so hiking down them can be dangerous. Stay on trails. Head farther north, to Muir Beach and beyond, for
better ocean access.

EXPLORING

The **Marin Headlands Visitor Center** (✉ *Fort Barry, Field and Bunker Rds., Bldg. 948* ☎ *415/331–1540* ⊕ *www.nps.gov/goga/marin-headlands. htm*), open daily 9:30-4:30, sells a useful guide to historic sites and wildlife and has exhibits on the area's history and ecology. Pick up the park newspaper, which lists a calendar of events, including a schedule of guided walks. Kids will enjoy the "please touch" educational sites and small play area inside.

☺
★   At the end of Conzelman Road, in the southern headlands, is the **Point Bonita Lighthouse,** a restored beauty that still guides ships to safety with its original 1855 refractory lens. Half the fun of a visit is the steep ½-mi walk from the parking area down to the lighthouse, which takes you through a rock tunnel and across a suspension bridge. Signposts along the way detail the bravado of surfmen, as the early lifeguards were called, and the tenacity of the "wickies," the first keepers of the light. ✉ *End of Conzelman Rd.* ☎ *Free* ☼ *Sat.–Mon. 12:30–3:30.*

If you're an art lover, stop by the **Headlands Center for the Arts** (✉ *944 Fort Barry* ☎ *415/331–2787* ⊕ *www.headlands.org* ☼ *Weekdays 10–5, Sun. noon–5*), where you can see contemporary art in a rustic natural setting. All but one of the center's nine converted military buildings are usually closed to the public, but you can visit the main building (the former barracks) to see several changing installations. The downstairs "archive room" features an odd assortment of objects found and created by residents, such as natural rocks, interesting glass bottles filled with collected items, and unusual masks. Stop by the industrial gallery space, two flights up, to see what the resident visual artists are up to—most of the work is quite contemporary. The center also hosts biweekly public programs, from artist talks to open studios. Call for current schedules.

☺   Small but scenic, **Muir Beach,** a rocky patch of shoreline off Route 1 in the northern headlands, is a good place to stretch your legs and gaze out at the Pacific. Locals often walk their dogs here, and anglers and boogie boarders share the gentle surf. Families and cuddling couples come for picnicking and sunbathing. At one end of the sand is a cluster of waterfront homes, and at the other are the bluffs of Golden Gate National Recreation Area.

WHERE TO STAY

¢ ⚏ **Marin Headlands Hostel.** As hostels go, it's hard to beat this beautifully located, well-maintained property in a valley on the north side of the headlands. This is also the only lodging in the GGNRA that isn't a campsite. Accommodations, inside the old military infirmary, consist of private rooms with space for up to five, or shared dorm-style rooms that sleep six to 22 people in bunk beds. Cook your own food in the communal kitchen and eat at a table in the giant common area near the woodstove; big windows look out onto stands of pine and eucalyptus. Couples can share rooms in a separate two-story house made cozy with couches in some rooms, comfortable wooden tables, and forest views. Don't miss the map of the world, which reaches over a corner and across two walls in the main house. **Pros:** plenty of peace

Shutterbugs rejoice in catching a scenic Muir Beach sunset.

and quiet; great prices; lovely setting. **Cons:** no Wi-Fi; difficult to get to without a car or bike; far from restaurants and shops. ✉ *941 Fort Barry* ☎ *415/331–2777* ⊕ *www.norcalhostels.org/marin* ⌕ *1 private rooms, 8 dormitory rooms; all with shared bath ⌂ In room: no phone, no a/c, no TV. In-hotel: laundry facilities* ⊟ *D, MC, V.*

$$$–$$$$ 🛏 **Pelican Inn.** From its slate roof to its whitewashed plaster walls, this inn looks so Tudor that it's hard to believe it was built in the 1970s. The Pelican is English to the core, with its smallish guest rooms upstairs (no elevator), high half-tester beds draped in heavy fabrics, and bangers and grilled tomatoes for breakfast. Downstairs, the little pub pours ales and ports, and "the snug" is a private fireplace lounge for overnight guests. At dinner in the tavernlike or solarium dining rooms ($$–$$$), keep it simple with fish-and-chips, roasted hen, or prime rib and focus on the well-crafted wine list. Lunch is served, too . . . a good thing, since your nearest alternatives are miles away via slow, winding roads. **Pros:** 5-minute walk to beach; great bar and restaurant; peaceful setting. **Cons:** 20-minute drive to nearby attractions; no Wi-Fi or wheelchair access to bedrooms. ✉ *10 Pacific Way, off Rte. 1, Muir Beach* ☎ *415/383–6000* ⊕ *www.pelicaninn.com* ⌕ *7 rooms ⌂ In-room: no phone, no a/c, no TV. In-hotel: restaurant, bar* ⊟ *MC, V* ⊙ *BP.*

MUIR WOODS NATIONAL MONUMENT

12 mi northwest of the Golden Gate Bridge.

One hundred fifty million years ago, ancestors of redwood and sequoia trees grew throughout the United States. Today the *Sequoia sempervirens* can be found only in a narrow, cool coastal belt from Monterey to Oregon. The 550 acres of Muir Woods National Monument contain some of the most majestic redwoods in the world—some nearly 250 feet tall and 1,000 years old. The stand was saved from destruction in 1905, when it was purchased by a couple who donated it to the federal government. Three years later it was named after naturalist John Muir, whose environmental campaigns helped to establish the national park system. His response: "This is the best tree lover's monument that could be found in all of the forests of the world. Saving these woods from the ax and saw is in many ways the most notable service to God and man I have heard of since my forest wandering began."

Fodor's Choice ★

Muir Woods, part of the Golden Gate National Recreation Area, is a pedestrian's park. The trails vary in difficulty and distance. Beginning from the park headquarters, a 2-mi, wheelchair-accessible **loop trail** crosses streams and passes ferns and azaleas, as well as magnificent redwood groves. Among the most famous are **Bohemian Grove** and the circular formation called **Cathedral Grove.** On summer weekends visitors oohing and aahing in a dozen languages line the trail. If you prefer a little more serenity, consider the challenging **Dipsea Trail,** which climbs west from the forest floor to soothing views of the ocean and the Golden Gate Bridge. For a complete list of trails, check with rangers, who can also help you pick the best one for your ability level.

■ TIP→ The weather in Muir Woods is usually cool and often wet, so wear warm clothes and shoes appropriate for damp trails. Picnicking and camping aren't allowed, and pets aren't permitted. Parking can be difficult here—the lots are small and the crowds are large—so try to come early in the morning or late in the afternoon. The **Muir Woods Visitor Center** has a wide selection of books and exhibits on redwood trees and the history of Muir Woods.

To get here from San Francisco, take U.S. 101 north across the Golden Gate Bridge to the Mill Valley/Stinson Beach exit and then follow signs to Highway 1 north. On weekends, Memorial Day through Labor Day, Golden Gate Transit operates a free shuttle from Mill Valley every half hour. Park in Marin City at the Gateway Shopping Center (look for lighted signs directing you from U.S. 101) or at the Manzanita Park-and-Ride, at the Highway 1 exit off U.S. 101 (look for the lot under the elevated freeway), or take connecting bus service from San Francisco with Golden Gate Transit. At this writing, there were plans to expand the service to year-round operation; call ahead. ⊠ *Panoramic*

DID YOU KNOW?

The gorgeous old-growth redwood trees in Muir Woods are often enveloped in fog, a useful dampness for the trees, especially to counteract the dry summers.

Hwy. off Hwy. 1, approximately 12 mi north of Golden Gate Bridge, ☏ *415/388–2595 park information, 415/925–4501 shuttle information* ⊕ *www.nps.gov/muwo* ⊠ *$5* ⊙ *Daily 8* AM*–sunset.*

MT. TAMALPAIS STATE PARK

16 mi northwest of Golden Gate Bridge.

Although the summit of Mt. Tamalpais is only 2,571 feet high, the mountain rises practically from sea level, dominating the topography of Marin County. Adjacent to Muir Woods National Monument, Mt. Tamalpais State Park affords views of the entire Bay Area and the Pacific Ocean to the west. The mountain was sacred to Native Americans, who saw in its profile—as you can see today—the silhouette of a sleeping Indian maiden. Locals fondly refer to it as the "Sleeping Lady." For years the 6,300-acre park has been a favorite destination for hikers. There are more than 200 mi of trails, some rugged but many developed for easy walking through meadows, grasslands, and forests and along creeks. Mt. Tam, as it's called by locals, is also the birthplace (in the 1970s) of mountain biking, and today many spandex-clad bikers whiz down the park's winding roads.

The park's major thoroughfare, the Panoramic Highway, snakes its way up from U.S. 101 to the **Pantoll Ranger Station** (⊠ *3801 Panoramic Hwy., at Pantoll Rd.* ☏ *415/388–2070* ⊕ *www.parks.ca.gov*). The office is staffed sporadically, depending on funding, but if you leave a phone message, a ranger will call you back (within several days) during business hours. From the ranger station, the Panoramic Highway drops down to the town of Stinson Beach. Pantoll Road branches off the highway at the station, connecting up with Ridgecrest Boulevard. Along these roads are numerous parking areas, picnic spots, scenic overlooks, and trailheads. Parking is free along the roadside, but there's a fee at the ranger station and at some of the other parking lots.

STINSON BEACH

ⓒ *20 mi northwest of Golden Gate Bridge.*

Stinson Beach is the most expansive stretch of sand in Marin County. It's as close (when the fog hasn't rolled in) as you can get to the stereotypical feel of a Southern California beach. ⚠ Swimming here is recommended only from early May through September, when lifeguards are on duty, because the undertow can be strong and shark sightings, although infrequent, aren't unusual. There are several clothing-optional areas (such as Red Rock Beach). On any hot summer weekend every road to Stinson Beach is jam-packed, so factor this into your plans. The town itself is very down to earth—like tonier Mill Valley, but more relaxed.

WHERE TO EAT AND STAY

$$–$$$

AMERICAN

✕ **Parkside Cafe.** Most people know the Parkside for its beachfront snack bar (cash only), but inside is the best restaurant in Stinson Beach. The food is classic Cal cuisine, with appetizers such as day-boat scallops, ceviche, and mains such as lamb with goat-cheese-stuffed red peppers.

Breakfast, a favorite among locals, is served until 2 PM. Eat on the sunny patio, which is sheltered from the wind by creeping vines, or by the fire in the contemporary dining room. ✉ *43 Arenal Ave.* ☎ *415/868–1272* ☐ *MC, V.*

$–$$ ✕ **Sand Dollar.** The town's oldest restaurant still attracts all the old salts
AMERICAN   from Muir Beach to Bolinas, but these days they sip whiskey over an up-to-date bar or beneath market umbrellas on the spiffy deck. The food is good—try the panfried sand dabs (small flatfish) and pear salad with blue cheese—but the big draw is the lively atmosphere. Musicians play weekends in summer, and on sunny afternoons the deck gets so packed that people sit on the fence rails, sipping beer. ✉ *3458 Rte. 1* ☎ *415/868–0434* ☐ *AE, MC, V* ⊘ *No lunch Tues. Nov.–Mar.*

$–$$ ▣ **Stinson Beach Motel.** Built in the 1930s, this motel surrounds three courtyards that burst with flowering greenery. Rooms are immaculate, simple, and summery, with freshly painted walls, good mattresses, and some kitchenettes. The motel is on the main drag, so it's convenient to everything in town, but it can get loud on busy summer weekend days. ■**TIP**➔ Room 3 has the most privacy, though all rooms face a central courtyard, not the street. Weekday room rates ($90–$150) are a bargain for the north coast. **Pros:** minutes from the beach; cozy, unpretentious rooms. **Cons:** no Wi-Fi; not much to do once the sun sets. ✉ *3416 Hwy. 1* ☎ *415/868 1712* ⊕ *www.stinsonbeachmotel.com* ⊅ *7 rooms* ⚴ *In room: no phone, no a/c, kitchen (some).* ☐ *D, MC, V.*

BOLINAS

7 mi north of Stinson Beach.

The tiny town of Bolinas wears its 1960s idealism on its sleeve, attracting potters, poets, and peace lovers to its quiet streets. With a funky gallery, a general store selling organic produce, a café, and an offbeat saloon, the main thoroughfare, Wharf Road, looks like a hippie-fied version of Main Street USA. Although privacy-seeking locals openly dislike tourism and have torn down signs to the town, Bolinas isn't difficult to find: heading north from Stinson Beach on Route 1, make a left at the first road just past the Bolinas Lagoon (Bolinas Olema Road), and then turn left at the stop sign. ■**TIP**➔ The road dead-ends smack-dab in the middle of the tiny town, so drive slowly lest you find yourself in a confrontation with an angry local.

9

POINT REYES NATIONAL SEASHORE

Fodor'sChoice   *Bear Valley Visitor Center is 12 mi north of Bolinas.*
★   One of the Bay Area's most spectacular treasures and the only national seashore on the West Coast, the 66,500-acre **Point Reyes National Seashore** (⊕ *www.nps.gov/pore*) encompasses hiking trails, secluded beaches, and rugged grasslands as well as **Point Reyes**, a triangular peninsula that juts into the Pacific. The town itself is a quaint, one-main-drag affair, with a charming bakery, some good gift shops with imported goods, and a few places to eat. It's nothing fancy, but that's part of its relaxed charm.

ESSENTIALS

Visitor Information West Marin Chamber of Commerce (☎ *415/663–9232* ⊕ *www.pointreyes.org*).

EXPLORING

The **Bear Valley Visitor Center** (⊠ *Bear Valley Rd. west of Rte. 1* ☎ *415/ 464–5100*), open weekdays 9–5 and weekends 8–5, has informative exhibits about the park wildlife. Rangers here dispense information about beaches, whale-watching, hiking trails, and camping The infamous San Andreas Fault runs along the eastern edge of the park and up the center of Tomales Bay; take the short **Earthquake Trail** from the visitor center to see the impact near the epicenter of the 1906 earthquake that devastated San Francisco.

Drive past Inverness on **Sir Francis Drake Boulevard** to reach the heart of the park: a 20-mi-long road through rolling hills spotted with cattle ranches and dairy farms. There are turnoffs to several beaches along the way; those on the western side compose a 10-mi-long beach that has reliably dramatic surf and gorgeous dunes. At Drakes Beach the water is usually calmer (often even swimmable), and there's a visitor center. Drakes also has an excellent café (☎ *415/669–1297* ⊙ *Closed Tues. and Wed., no lunch weekdays*) that serves hamburgers from beef raised on the surrounding ranches; on Friday and Saturday nights it transforms into the most romantic restaurant on the coast, serving a four-course, prix-fixe dinner (reservations required).

★   The **Point Reyes Lighthouse** (⊠ *Western end of Sir Francis Drake Blvd.* ☎ *415/669–1534* ⊙ *Thurs.–Mon. 10–4:30; weather lens room 2:30–4, except during very windy weather*), in operation since December 1, 1870, is one of the premier attractions of the Point Reyes National Seashore. It occupies the tip of Point Reyes, 22 mi from the Bear Valley Visitor Center, a scenic 45-minute drive over hills scattered with old cattle ranches. The lighthouse originally cast a rotating beam lighted by four wicks that burned lard oil. Keeping the wicks lighted and the lens soot-free in Point Reyes's perpetually foggy climate was a constant struggle that reputedly drove the early attendants to alcoholism and insanity. On busy whale-watching weekends (late December through mid-April), parking at the forged-iron-plate lighthouse may be restricted by park staff; on these days buses shuttle visitors from the Drakes Beach lot to the top of the stairs leading down to the lighthouse (bus $5, admission free). Once there, consider whether you have it in you to walk down— and up—the 308 steps to the lighthouse. The view from the bottom is worth the effort, but the whales are visible from the cliffs above the lighthouse. ■TIP➔ In late winter and spring, wildlife enthusiasts should make a stop at Chimney Rock, just before the lighthouse, and take the short walk to the Elephant Seal Overlook. Even from up on the cliff, the males look enormous as they spar for the resident females.

WHERE TO EAT

¢–$ ✕**Pine Cone Diner.** For California country-kitchen cooking, you can't
AMERICAN   beat the Pine Cone. A block off the main drag, this oh-so-cute diner serves great traditional breakfasts as well as Mexican specialties such as huevos rancheros. At lunch expect hearty homemade soups, fresh

DID YOU KNOW?

Majestic Point Reyes National Seashore offers a variety of attractions for nature-lovers: hiking, bird-watching, camping, or whale-watching depending on the season. But flower picking isn't an approved activity; the wild flowers here are protected.

salads, and thick sandwiches, all made with local, organic ingredients. The dinner menu has a good selection of comfort food. ■TIP→ Kids love the outdoor picnic tables. ✉ 60 4th St., Point Reyes Station ☎ 415/663–1536 ▭ No credit cards ⊘ No dinner.

$$
AMERICAN

✕ **Station House Cafe.** In good weather hikers fresh from the park fill the garden to enjoy alfresco dining, and on weekends there's not a spare seat on the banquettes in the wide-open dining room. The focus is on traditional American food—fresh popovers hit the table as soon as you arrive—and there's a little of everything on the menu. Grilled salmon, barbecued oysters, and burgers are all predictable hits. The place is also open for breakfast, and there's a full bar, too. ✉ 11180 Rte. 1, Point Reyes Station ☎ 415/663–1515 ▭ AE, D, MC, V ⊘ Closed Wed.

¢–$
AMERICAN
★

✕ **Tomales Bay Foods.** A renovated hay barn off the main drag houses this collection of food shops, a favorite stopover among Bay Area foodies. Watch workers making Cowgirl Creamery cheese; then buy some at a counter that sells exquisite artisanal cheeses from around the world. Tomales Bay Foods showcases local organic fruits and vegetables and premium packaged foods, and the kitchen turns the best ingredients into creative sandwiches, salads, and soups. You can eat at a small café table or on the lawn, or take it away for a picnic. The shops are open until 6 PM. ✉ 80 4th St., Point Reyes Station ☎ 415/663–9335 cheese shop, 415/663–8478 deli ▭ MC, V ⊘ Closed Mon. and Tues.

WHERE TO STAY

$$$–$$$$

🏨 **Blackthorne Inn.** There's no other inn quite like the Blackthorne, a combination of whimsy and sophistication tucked on a hill in the woods. The giant tree-house-like structure has spiral staircases, a 3,500-square-foot deck, and a fireman's pole. The solarium was made with timbers from San Francisco wharves, and the outer walls are salvaged doors from a railway station. The best room is aptly named the Eagle's Nest, perched as it is in the glass-sheathed octagonal tower that crowns the inn. **Pros:** great views; quiet atmosphere. **Cons:** not a good place for kids; steep spaces. ✉ 266 Vallejo Ave., Inverness Park ☎ 415/663–8621 ⊕ www.blackthorneinn.com ⇆ 3 rooms, 1 suite ⚥ In-room: no phone, no a/c, no TV. In-hotel: restaurant, no kids under 14 ▭ MC, V ⦿ BP.

$$

🏨 **Olema Inn & Restaurant.** Built in 1876, the inn retains all its 19th-century architectural charm but has been decorated in a sophisticated, uncluttered style. The spartan, understated rooms have antique armoires and sumptuous beds with crisp linens; the white-tile baths have gleaming fixtures. But the main attraction is the top-notch Northern California cooking served in the restaurant ($$$, reservations essential). The preparations of organic, local, and free-range ingredients include fresh oysters, pork chops with apple-cider glaze, and house-made ricotta gnocchi. ■TIP→ Come on Monday, locals' night, when the place hops with live music and you can browse through a delectable small-plates menu. **Pros:** great restaurant; magnificent scenery. **Cons:** extremely remote; sporadic cell phone reception. ✉ 10000 Sir Francis Drake Blvd., Olema ☎ 415/663–9559 ⊕ www.theolemainn.com ⇆ 6 rooms ⚥ In-room: no phone, no a/c. In-hotel: some pets allowed ▭ AE, MC, V ⊘ Closed Tues. No lunch weekdays.

MARSHALL

13 mi north of Point Reyes National Seashore on Hwy. 1.

The northern side of Point Reyes National Seashore is divided from the mainland by Tomales Bay, a finger of water 15 mi long and only 1 mi wide at most points. Heading north from Point Reyes Station, Highway 1 follows the eastern edge of the bay through the tiny town of Marshall. Nearly every building here hugs the strip of land between the highway and the bay, which means pretty much anywhere you go there's a great view of the water and the park beyond.

EXPLORING

In the past Marshall was known for its dairy farming, but these days it's famous for oysters, which you can buy throughout town. **Tomales Bay Oyster Company** (⊠ *15479 Hwy. 1, Marshall* ☎ *415/663–1242* ⊕ *www.tomalesbayoysters.com* ☉ *Daily 8–6*) has farmed oysters since 1909. Today, visitors buy them by the dozen and eat at the picnic tables, usually barbecuing the bivalves on the grills. Bring your shucking knife, fixings, and charcoal.

Known as the growers of the Bay Area's most gourmet bivalves, **Hog Island Oyster Company** (⊠ *20215 Hwy. 1, Marshall* ☎ *415/663–9218* ⊕ *www.hogislandoysters.com* ☉ *Daily 9–5*) is so popular it must charge for picnicking. For a table and grill on the water, the weekend fee is $8 per person with a reservation, $10 for walk-ins; during the week it's first-come, first-served, fee $5. (The oysters are not included.) Most people supplement by bringing drinks and (often elaborate) picnics. The **Marshall Store** (⊠ *19225 Hwy. 1, Marshall* ☎ *415/663–1339* ⊕ *www.themarshallstore.com* ☉ *Weekdays 10–4, weekends 10–5. Closed Tues.*) offers oysters raw, grilled and Rockefeller-style, along with food from a full deli and wine market. Seats and tables line the waterfront.

WHERE TO EAT AND STAY

¢–$

SEAFOOD

✗ **Tony's Seafood.** Giant barbecued and fried oysters are the specialty at this friendly joint, family-owned and -operated since it opened in 1948. For those who think bivalves are slimy, there are good, cheap hamburgers as well. ⊠ *18663 Hwy. 1, Marshall* ☎ *415/663–1107* ▭ *No credit cards* ☉ *Fri.–Sun. noon–8.*

$$$–$$$$

▥ **Nick's Cove.** Long famous as a settlement of funky cabins surrounding a greasy spoon restaurant, Nick's Cove has been transformed into the area's premier "rustic chic" spot. The unique cottages are like deluxe hunting cabins, with cushy king-size beds, wood-burning stoves, and minibars stocked with top-shelf tequila and gin. As the fog sets in the five cabins with decks over the water become particularly sublime. The wood-paneled restaurant ($$–$$$) tips its hat to a former life with deer trophies and a long bar decorated with fishing rope, but the food is decidedly 21st-century California: mostly organic, with excellent local seafood and meats. **Pros:** cozy; quiet; a place to indulge. **Cons:** noise from the road can sometimes break the quiet. ⊠ *23240 Hwy. 1* ☎ *415/663–1033* ⊕ *www.nickscove.com* ⇴ *12 cottages* ☖ *In-room: no a/c, refrigerator, Wi-Fi. In-hotel: restaurant, room service, Wi-Fi hotspot, some pets allowed* ▭ *AE, D, MC, V.*

9

SPORTS AND THE OUTDOORS

Blue Waters Kayaking (✉ *19225 Hwy. 1* ☎ *415/669–2600* ⊕ *www. bwkayak.com*) provides guided morning, full-day, sunset, full-moon, and overnight camping paddles out of their launches in Marshall and Inverness. They also rent out kayaks and offer beginner through advanced lessons. Best to make a reservation in summer, especially on weekends.

THE EAST BAY

To San Franciscans, the East Bay is shorthand for Berkeley and Oakland, both across the Bay Bridge from the city. Berkeley is defined by its University of California campus and its liberal-to-radical politics. Ever since the Free Speech Movement ignited at the Cal campus in the 1960s, Berkeley has been the place for renegade spirits, bursting bookstores, and caffeine-fueled debates. It's not all intellectual-politico jargon, though; there are plenty of creature comforts too. Most famously, there's Chez Panisse, the restaurant that embodies seasonal, simple, local cooking—but there are countless tasty treasures to be sampled in Berkeley's Gourmet Ghetto. Or you could shop for indie tracks at Amoeba Music, obscure tomes at Moe's Books, or the perfect bottle of Sancerre at Kermit Lynch Wine Merchant.

Oakland is grittier and even more diverse, with a buzzing arts scene. Small pockets of the city are pretty dodgy, so it's important to know where you're going. Old Oakland has a concentration of evocative Victorian buildings, now full of cafés and shops; the Rockridge neighborhood is home to lovely Market Hall, a European-style market. Jack London Square may be the best place to get a sense of Oakland's role as a major port, but it feels pretty sterile. Head to a jazz joint like Yoshi's or a gallery-bar like Café van Kleef, though, and you'll feel the city's indomitable energy.

PLANNING

GETTING HERE AND AROUND

BOAT AND FERRY TRAVEL

The Alameda/Oakland Ferry runs several times daily between San Francisco's Ferry Building or Pier 39, Alameda, and the Clay Street dock near Oakland's Jack London Square; one-way tickets are $6.25. The trip lasts 30 to 45 minutes, depending on your departure point, and leads to the heart of Oakland's gentrified shopping and restaurant district. Arriving in Oakland by boat conveys a historic sense of the city's heyday as a World War II–era shipbuilding center. Purchase tickets on board.

Contacts Alameda/Oakland Ferry (☎ *510/522–3300* ⊕ *www.eastbayferry.com*).

BUS TRAVEL

Although Bay Area Rapid Transit (BART) travel is often cheaper and more convenient, buses run frequently between San Francisco's Trans-Bay Terminal (at 1st and Mission streets) and the East Bay. AC Transit's F and FS lines stop near the university and 4th Street shopping in

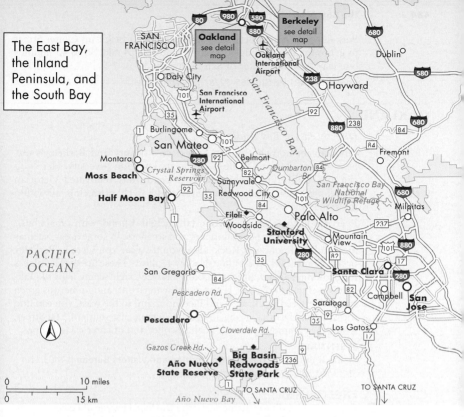

The East Bay, the Inland Peninsula, and the South Bay

Berkeley. Lines C and P travel to Piedmont in Oakland. The O bus stops at the edge of Chinatown near downtown Oakland.

Contacts AC Transit (☎ 817–1717 after any Bay Area area code ⊕ www.actransit.org).

CAR TRAVEL

From San Francisco, take I–80 east across the Bay Bridge. For most of Berkeley, take the University Avenue exit through downtown Berkeley to the campus or take the Ashby Avenue exit and turn left on Telegraph Avenue to the traditional campus entrance; there's a parking garage on Channing Way. For Oakland, take I–580 off the Bay Bridge to the Grand Avenue exit for Lake Merritt. To reach downtown and the waterfront, take I–980 from I–580 and exit at 12th Street. Both trips take about 30 minutes, unless it's rush hour or a weekend afternoon, when you should count on an hour.

TRAIN TRAVEL

BART (Bay Area Rapid Transit, formally) trains make stops in downtown Berkeley and in several parts of Oakland, including Rockridge. Use the Lake Merritt Station for the Oakland Museum and southern Lake Merritt; the Oakland City Center–12th Street Station for downtown, Chinatown, and Old Oakland; and the 19th Street Station for the Paramount Theatre and the north side of Lake Merritt. From the

Berkeley (not North Berkeley) Station, walk a block up Center Street to get to the western edge of campus. Both trips take 30 to 45 minutes one way from the center of San Francisco.

Contacts BART (☎ 510/465–2278 ⊕ www.bart.gov).

OAKLAND

Directly east of Bay Bridge.

Often overshadowed by San Francisco's beauty and Berkeley's off-beat antics, Oakland's allure lies in its amazing diversity. Here you can find a Nigerian clothing store, a beautifully renovated Victorian home, a Buddhist meditation center, and a lively salsa club, all within the same block.

Everyday life here revolves around the neighborhood, with a main business strip attracting both shoppers and strollers. In some areas, such as high-end Piedmont and Rockridge, you'd swear you were in Berkeley or San Francisco's Noe Valley or Cow Hollow. These are perfect places for browsing, eating, or just relaxing between sightseeing trips to Oakland's architectural gems, rejuvenated waterfront, and numerous green spaces. Between Rockridge and Piedmont and to the west, you can find the Temescal District, along Telegraph Avenue just south of 51st Street, which is beginning to attract a small collection of eateries and shops.

ESSENTIALS

Visitor Information Oakland Convention and Visitors Bureau (⊠ 463 11th St. ☎ 510/839–9000 ⊕ www.oaklandcvb.com).

EXPLORING

❷ One of Oakland's top attractions, the **Oakland Museum of California** is an
☺ excellent introduction to a tour of California, and its detailed exhibits
★ on the state's art, history, and natural wonders can help fill the gaps on a brief visit. You can travel through the state's myriad ecosystems in the Natural Sciences Gallery, from the sand dunes of the Pacific to the coyotes and brush of the Nevada border. Kids love the lifelike wild-animal exhibits, especially the snarling wolverine, big-eyed harbor seal, and trove of hidden creatures. The rambling Cowell Hall of California History includes everything from Spanish-era armor to a small but impressive collection of vintage vehicles, including a gorgeous, candy-apple-red "Mystery" car from the 1960s and a gleaming red, gold, and silver fire engine that battled the flames in San Francisco in 1906. The Gallery of California Art holds an eclectic collection of modern works and early landscapes. Of particular interest are paintings by Richard Diebenkorn, Joan Brown, Elmer Bischoff, and David Park, all members of the Bay Area Figurative School, which flourished here after World War II. Fans of Dorothea Lange won't want to miss the gallery's comprehensive collection of her work. The museum also has a sculpture garden with a view of the Oakland and Berkeley hills in the distance. ⊠ 1000 Oak St., at 10th St. ☎ 510/238–2200 ⊕ www.museumca.org ☞ $8, free 2nd Sun. of month ☉ Wed.–Sat. 10–5, until 9 1st Fri. of month, Sun. noon–5.

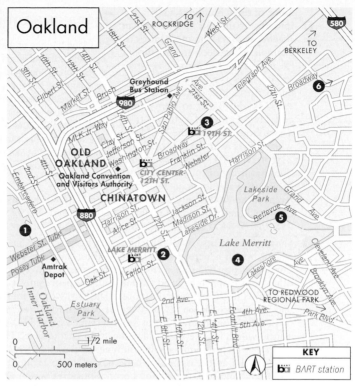

4 The 155-acre **Lake Merritt** (⊠ *Bordered by Lakeshore Ave. on the south, Lakeside Dr. on the west, Harrison St. on the north, and Bellevue Ave. on the east*), a natural saltwater lake, sits in the middle of downtown Oakland. Joggers and power-walkers charge along the 3-mi path that encircles the lake, crew teams often glide across the water, and boatmen guide snuggling couples in authentic Venetian gondolas. **California gondoliers** (⊠ *568 Bellevue Ave., Lake Merritt* ☎ *866/737–8494* ⊕ *www. gondolaservizio.com*) is by the sign that says "Sailboat House, Gondola Servizio." Fares start at $45 per couple for 30 minutes.

5 **Lakeside Park,** which surrounds the north side of Lake Merritt, has several outdoor attractions, including a children's park. The **Rotary Nature Center and Waterfowl Refuge** is the nesting site of herons, egrets, geese, and ducks in spring and summer. Migrating birds pass through from September through February, and you can watch the birds being fed daily at 3:30 (year-round). ⊠ *600 Bellevue Ave.* ☎ *510/238–7275* ⊕ *www.oaklandnet. com/parks/facilities/points_lakeside_park.asp* ✉ *Free* ⊙ *Daily 10–5.*

Given Oakland's reputation for Victorian and Craftsman homes, newcomers are generally surprised by the profusion of art-deco architecture in the downtown neighborhood around the 19th Street BART station.

9

❸
★
Some of these buildings have fallen into disrepair, but the **Paramount Theatre,** perhaps the most glorious example of art-deco architecture in the city, if not the entire Bay Area, still operates as a venue for concerts and performances of all kinds, from the Oakland Ballet to Tom Waits and Elvis Costello. You can take a two-hour tour of the building, which starts near the box office on 21st Street at 10 AM on the first and third Saturday of each month. Just behind the Paramount on Telegraph

WORD OF MOUTH

"Oakland has one of the most beautiful urban drives in the USA: Skyline Drive/Boulevard. It's a winding drive, bordering the Oakland/Berkeley Hills. From it, you have absolutely stunning views of the entire Bay. One advantage of a view from Oakland is that you are looking at San Francisco's famous landmarks." —CaliNurse

Avenue, the Fox Theater, another art-deco landmark, was saved from the wrecking ball and is being lovingly restored. ⊠ *2025 Broadway* ☎ *510/465–6400* ⊕ *www.paramounttheatre.com* ☜ *Tour $5.*

❶ Shops, restaurants, small museums, and historic sites line **Jack London Square,** which is named after one of California's best-known authors; London wrote *The Call of the Wild* and *The Sea Wolf,* among many other books. When he lived in Oakland, he spent many a day boozing and brawling in the waterfront area. The tiny, wonderful **Heinold's First and Last Chance Saloon** (⊠ *48 Webster St.* ☎ *510/839–6761*) was one of London's old haunts. It has been serving since 1883, although it's a little worse for the wear since the 1906 earthquake. The Klondike cabin in which London spent a summer in the late 1890s was moved from Alaska and reassembled here, next door to Heinold's saloon, in 1970. The square also contains a bronze bust of London. ■TIP→ Since it's on the waterfront, the square is an obvious spot for tourists to visit and is worth a peek if you take a ferry that docks here; to really get a feel for Oakland, though, you're better off browsing downtown, or at least in Rockridge. ⊠ *Embarcadero at Broadway* ☎ *866/295–9853* ⊕ *www. jacklondonsquare.com.*

Bordered by 7th, 10th, Clay, and Washington streets in the shadow of the convention center and towering downtown hotels, **Old Oakland** was once a booming business district. Today the restored Victorian storefronts lining these four blocks house restaurants, cafés, shops, galleries, and a lively three-block farmers' market, which takes place Friday morning. Architectural consistency distinguishes the area from surrounding streets and lends it a distinct neighborhood feel. **Ratto's International Market** (⊠ *827 Washington St.* ☎ *510/832–6503*), the Italian grocer that's been dishing up meat, cheese, imported sweets, and liquor to the neighborhood since 1897, has fresh deli sandwiches. **Pacific Coast Brewing Company** (⊠ *906 Washington St.* ☎ *510/836–2739*) is a homey place for some pub grub and a microbrew. The block-long Swan's Marketplace houses shops and the **Housewives Market** (⊠ *907 Washington St.*), an old-fashioned market with stalls for meat, seafood, and even a sausage maker.

Across Broadway from Old Oakland but worlds apart, **Chinatown** is a densely packed, bustling neighborhood. Unlike its San Francisco

A fun place to wet your whistle, Heinold's First and Last Chance Saloon.

counterpart, Oakland's Chinatown makes no concessions to tourists; you won't find baskets of trinkets lining the sidewalk and souvenir displays in the shop windows. Supermarkets such as **Yuen Hop Noodle Company and Asian Food Products** (✉ *824 Webster St.*), open since 1931, overflow with goodies. The line for sweets, breads, and towering cakes snakes out the door of **Napoleon Super Bakery** (✉ *810 Franklin St.*).

9

The upscale neighborhood of **Rockridge** is one of Oakland's most desirable places to live. Explore the tree-lined streets that radiate out from College Avenue just north and south of the Rockridge BART station for a look at California bungalow architecture at its finest.

❻ **College Avenue** is the main shopping drag in Rockridge. By day it's crowded with shoppers buying fresh flowers, used books, and clothing; by night the same folks are back for dinner and locally brewed ales in the numerous restaurants and pubs. The hub of College Avenue life in Rockridge is **Market Hall** (✉ *5655 College Ave.* ☎ *510/250–6000* ⊕ *www.rockridgemarkethall.com*), an airy European-style marketplace with pricey specialty-food shops. The avenue ends at the California College of the Arts campus.

WHERE TO EAT

$ ✕ **À Côté.** This is the place for Mediterranean food in the East Bay. It's all

MEDITERRANEAN   about small plates, cozy tables, and family-style eating here—and truly excellent food. The butternut-squash ravioli, Alsatian goose sausage, and pear-and-walnut flatbread are all lovely choices. And you won't find a better plate of pommes frites anywhere. The restaurant offers over 40 wines by the glass from an extensive, ever-changing wine list.

Desserts here are tempting: try the warm crème-fraîche pound cake with apple confit, vanilla ice cream, and huckleberry sauce or a tangy pomegranate sorbet. The heavy wooden tables, cool tiles, and natural light make this a coveted destination for students, families, couples, and after-work crowds. ✉ *5478 College Ave., Rockridge* ☎ *510/655–6469* ♨ *Reservations not accepted* ☱ *AE, MC, V* ⊘ *No lunch.*

$$　　✕ **Camino.** This first solo venture from chef-owner Russell Moore (a
AMERICAN　　Chez Panisse alum of 21 years) and co-owner Allison Hopelain was quite the labor of love. Many of the menu's simple, seasonal, and straightforward dishes emerge from the enormous crackling *camino* (Italian for "fireplace"). Everything is made with top-notch ingredients, including local sardines; grilled lamb and sausage with shell beans; and grilled white sea bass with green beans and new potatoes. The menu of approximately eight dishes rotates nightly, with vegetarian options such as eggplant gratin available as well. The restaurant is decorated in a craftsman-meets-refectory style, with brick walls and two long redwood communal tables filled with East Bay couples and friends. Seasonally inspired cocktails from the small bar are not to be missed; the gin-based drink with house-made cherry and hibiscus bitters is notably delicious. ✉ *3917 Grand Ave., Oakland* ☎ *510/547–5035* ☱ *AE, MC, V* ⊘ *Closed Tues. No lunch.*

$$　　✕ **Doña Tomás.** A neighborhood favorite, this spot in Oakland's up-and-
MEXICAN　　coming Temescal District serves seasonal Mexican fare to a hip but low-key crowd. Mexican textiles and art adorn walls in two long rooms; there's also a vine-covered patio. Banish all images of taquería grub and tuck into starters such as quesadillas filled with butternut squash and goat cheese and entrées such as *albondigas en sopa de zanahoria* (pork-and-beef meatballs in carrot puree). A fine selection of tequilas rounds out the offerings. ✉ *5004 Telegraph Ave.* ☎ *510/450–0522* ☱ *AE, MC, V* ⊘ *Closed Sun. and Mon. No lunch.*

$–$$　　✕ **Luka's Taproom & Lounge.** Luka's is a real taste of downtown Oakland:
FRENCH　　hip and urban, with an unpretentious vibe. Diners nibble on *frites* any Belgian would be proud of and entrées like *choucroute garni* (sauer-kraut with duck confit, ham hock, and pork shoulder). The brews draw 'em in, too—you'd be hard pressed to find a larger selection of Belgian beer this side of the pond—and the DJs in the adjacent lounge keep the scene going late. ✉ *2221 Broadway, at West Grand Ave.* ☎ *510/451–4677* ☱ *AE, MC, V* ⊘ *No lunch Sat.*

WHERE TO STAY

$–$$　　▦ **Washington Inn Hotel.** This stylish four-story brick hotel sits across the street from the convention center, in the heart of Old Oakland. In operation since 1905, the hotel has up-to-the-minute decor. Red couches brighten the spacious lobby, which has Wi-Fi access. Elegant touches include intricately molded ceiling tiles and a wrought-iron elevator, a relic of the building's early days. Guest rooms are chic but on the small side. Rooms overlooking the atrium lobby are the quietest (and small-est); corner rooms get the most sunlight. **Pros:** central location; good restaurant. **Cons:** rooms are small; parking is pricey. ✉ *495 10th St., at Washington St.* ☎ *510/452–1776* ⊕ *www.thewashingtoninn.com* ⇔ *47 rooms, 6 suites* ♨ *In-room: a/c, safe, DVD, Wi-Fi. In-hotel: restaurant,* *bar, gym, laundry service, Wi-Fi hotspot, parking (paid)* $\equiv$ *AE, D, DC, MC, V* |O| *CP.*

$$–$$$ **Waterfront Plaza Hotel.** One of Oakland's more appealing neighborhoods is home to this thoroughly modern waterfront hotel. Rooms in the hotel's five-story section overlook Jack London Square and have shared balconies; those in the three-story building each have a private balcony facing the water. Some rooms have fireplaces. **Pros:** great location; dog friendly ($35 per day); newly remodeled rooms. **Cons:** pricey; service can be spotty. $\boxtimes$ *10 Washington St., Jack London Sq.* $\textcircled{a}$ *510/836–3800 or 800/729–3638* $\oplus$ *www.waterfrontplaza.com* $\rightleftharpoons$ *143 rooms* $\triangle$ *In-room: a/c, safe, Wi-Fi. In-hotel: restaurant, room service, bar, pool, gym, laundry service, Wi-Fi hotspot, parking (paid)* $\equiv$ *AE, D, DC, MC, V.*

NIGHTLIFE AND THE ARTS

Oakland is where practicing artists have turned to for cheaper rent and loft spaces. Oakland's underground arts scene—visual arts, indie music, spoken word, film—is definitely buzzing.

Fodor's Choice ★ **Café van Kleef.** When Dutch artist Peter van Kleef first opened his gallery in this downtown space, the booze flowed freely—and free, for lack of a liquor license. That gallery has morphed into this candle-strewn, funky café-bar that crackles with creative energy. Van Kleef has a lot to do with the convivial atmosphere; the garrulous owner loves sharing tales about his quirky, floor-to-ceiling collection of mementos, including what he claims are Cassius Clay's boxing gloves and Dorothy's ruby slippers. The café also has a consistently solid calendar of live music, heavy on the jazz side. And the drinks may not be free anymore, but they're quite possibly the stiffest in town. $\boxtimes$ *1621 Telegraph Ave., between 16th and 17th Sts.* $\textcircled{a}$ *510/763–7711* $\oplus$ *www.cafevankleef.com.*

Mama Buzz Café. At this well-worn café-gallery, a kind of living room for the indie arts crowd, you can get the lowdown on one of the most diverse arts communities around. In addition to coffee and light fare, the calendar includes poetry readings, live-music events, art exhibits, and hard-to-categorize events such as Punk Rock Haircut Night (get a new 'do, cheap), the Knitty Gritty knitting circle, and the Left-Wing Letter Bee. The owners publish the 'zine *Kitchen Sink.* $\boxtimes$ *2318 Telegraph Ave.* $\textcircled{a}$ *510/465–4073* $\oplus$ *www.mamabuzzcafe.com.*

Fodor's Choice ★ **Yoshi's.** Oma Sosa and Charlie Hunter are among the musicians who play at Yoshi's, one of the area's best jazz venues. Monday through Saturday shows start at 8 PM and 10 PM; Sunday shows usually start at 2 PM and 8 PM. The cover runs from $10 to $30. $\boxtimes$ *510 Embarcadero St., between Washington and Clay Sts.* $\textcircled{a}$ *510/238–9200* $\oplus$ *www.yoshis.com.*

SPORTS AND THE OUTDOORS

BASEBALL The American League's **Oakland A's** ($\boxtimes$ *McAfee Coliseum, 7000 Coliseum Way, off I–880, north of Hegenberger Rd.* $\textcircled{a}$ *510/638–4900* $\oplus$ *oakland.athletics.mlb.com*), formally the Oakland Athletics, play at

9

the **McAfee Coliseum.** Same-day tickets usually can be purchased at the stadium box office (Gate D), but advance purchase is recommended. On Wednesday, entry is a bargain at $2, and you can buy a hot dog for a dollar. To get to the game, take a BART train to the Coliseum/ Oakland Airport Station.

SHOPPING

College Avenue is great for upscale strolling, shopping, and people-watching. The streets around Lake Merritt and the Grand Lake have more casual fare and smaller boutiques.

Diesel. Wandering bibliophiles collect armfuls of the latest fiction and nonfiction here. The loftlike space, with its high ceilings and spare design, encourages airy contemplation, and on chilly days (a rarity) there's a fire going in the hearth. Keep an eye out for their excellent reading series. ✉ *5433 College Ave., Oakland* ☎ *510/653–9965.*

Maison d'Etre. Close to the Rockridge BART station, this store crystal-lizes the funky-chic shopping scene of Rockridge. Look for impulse buys like whimsical watches, imported fruit tea blends, and a bas-ket of funky slippers near the back. ✉ *5640 College Ave., Oakland* ☎ *510/658–2801.*

BERKELEY

2 mi northeast of Bay Bridge.

The birthplace of the Free Speech Movement, the radical hub of the 1960s, the home of arguably the nation's top public university, and the city whose government condemned the bombing of Afghanistan— Berkeley is all of those things. The city of 100,000 facing San Francisco across the bay is also culturally diverse, a breeding ground for social trends, a bastion of the counterculture, and an important center for Bay Area writers, artists, and musicians. Berkeley residents, students, and faculty spend hours nursing various coffee concoctions while they read, discuss, and debate at any of the dozens of cafés that surround the campus. Oakland may have Berkeley beat when it comes to cutting-edge arts, and the city may have forfeited some of its renegade 1960s spirit, as some residents say, but unless a guy in a hot-pink satin body suit, skull cap, and cape rides a unicycle around *your* town, you'll likely find that Berkeley remains plenty offbeat.

It's the quintessential university town, and many who graduated years ago still bask in daily intellectual conversation, great weather, and good food. Residents will walk out of their way to go to the perfect bread shop or consult with their favorite wine merchant. And every September, residents gently lampoon themselves during the annual "How Berkeley Can You Be?" parade and festival where they celebrate their tie-dyed past and consider its new incarnations.

ESSENTIALS

Visitor Information Berkeley Convention and Visitors Bureau (✉ *2015 Cen-ter St.* ☎ *510/549–7040* ⊕ *www.visitberkeley.com*).

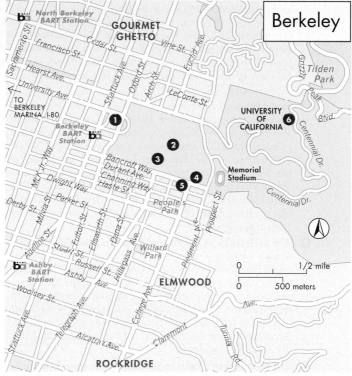

Berkeley

EXPLORING

The state legislature chartered the **University of California** (⊕ *www. berkeley.edu*) in 1868 as the founding campus of the state university system, and established it five years later on a rising plain of oak trees split by Strawberry Creek. Frederick Law Olmsted, who designed New York City's Central Park, proposed the first campus plan. University architects over the years have included Bernard Maybeck as well as Julia Morgan, who designed Hearst Castle at San Simeon. The central campus occupies 178 acres, bounded by Bancroft Way to the south, Hearst Avenue to the north, Oxford Street to the west, and Gayley Road to the east. With more than 30,000 students and a full-time faculty of 1,400, the university, known simply as "Cal," is one of the leading intellectual centers in the United States and a major site for scientific research.

❶ The **Berkeley Visitor Information Center** (⊠ *University Hall, Room 101, 2200 University Ave., at Oxford St.* ☎ *510/642–5215* ☉ *Weekdays 8:30–4:30*) is the starting point for the free, student-guided tours of the campus, which last 1½ hours and start at 10 on weekdays. (Weekend tours depart from Sather Tower, *see below.*)

❷ Student-guided campus tours leave from **Sather Tower,** the campus landmark popularly known as the Campanile, at 10 on Saturday and 1 on Sunday. The 307-foot structure, modeled on St. Mark's Tower in Venice and completed in 1914, can be seen for miles. The carillon is played daily at 7:50 AM, noon, and 6 PM and for an extended 45-minute concert Sunday at 2. Take the elevator up 175 feet; then walk another 38 steps to the observation deck for a view of the campus and a close-up look at the iron bells, each of which weighs up to 10,500 pounds. ✉ *South of University Dr.* ☜ *$2* ☉ *Weekdays 10–4, Sat. 10–5, Sun. 10–1:30 and 3–5.*

❸ **Sproul Plaza** (✉ *Telegraph Ave. and Bancroft Way*), just inside the U.C. Berkeley campus border on Bancroft Way, was the site of several free-speech and civil-rights protests in the 1960s. Today a lively panorama of political and social activists, musicians, and students show off Berkeley's flair for the bizarre. Preachers orate atop milk crates, amateur entertainers bang on makeshift drum sets, and protesters distribute leaflets about everything from marijuana to the Middle East. No matter what the combination, on weekdays when school is in swing, it always feels like a carnival. ■ TIP→ **Walk through at noon for the liveliest show of student spirit.**

❹ The collection of the **Phoebe A. Hearst Museum of Anthropology** counts almost 4 million artifacts, of which fewer than 1% are on display at any time. The Native Californian Cultures gallery showcases items related to the native peoples of California. Changing exhibits may cover the archaeology of ancient America or spotlight the museum's especially strong ancient Egyptian holdings. Mood music enhances the experience. ✉ *Kroeber Hall, Bancroft Way, at end of College Ave.* ☎ *510/642–3682* ⊕ *hearstmuseum.berkeley.edu* ☜ *Free; guided tour $5* ☉ *Wed.–Sat. 10–4:30, Sun. noon–4.*

❺ The **University of California, Berkeley Art Museum & Pacific Film Archive** has an interesting collection of works that spans five centuries. Changing exhibits line the spiral ramps and balcony galleries. Look for the museum's enormous orange-red statue of a man hammering, which can be seen from the outside when strolling by its floor-to-ceiling windows. Don't miss the museum's series of vibrant paintings by abstract expressionist Hans Hofmann. On the ground floor, the Pacific Film Archive has a library and hosts programs about historic and contemporary films, but the exhibition theater is across the street at 2575 Bancroft Way, near Bowditch Street. The downstairs galleries, which house rotating exhibits, are always free. The museum's raw foods café is famous, and you can also find some cooked options, too. ✉ *2626 Bancroft Way, entrance to theater at 2575 Bancroft Way, between College and Telegraph* ☎ *510/642–0808, 510/642–1124 film-program information* ⊕ *www. bampfa.berkeley.edu* ☜ *$8* ☉ *Wed. and Fri.–Sun. 11–5, Thurs. 11–7.*

❻ At the fortresslike **Lawrence Hall of Science**, a dazzling hands-on science center, kids can look at insects under microscopes, solve crimes using chemical forensics, and explore the physics of baseball. On weekends there are special lectures, demonstrations, and planetarium shows. The museum runs a popular (and free) stargazing program, which is held on the first and third Saturday of each month, weather permitting. (Call for times.) ✉ *Centennial Dr. near Grizzly Peak Blvd.* ☎ *510/642–5132* ⊕ *www.lawrencehallofscience.org* ☜ *$12* ☉ *Daily 10–5.*

South of campus, along College Avenue between Ashby Avenue and Claremont, shops and cafés pack the area known as **Elmwood,** a local favorite for browsing. **Nabolom Bakery** (✉ *2708 Russell St.* ☎ *510/845–2253*), which has been around since 1976, is a workers' collective where politics and delicious pastries collide. Shingled houses line tree-shaded streets nearby.

Telegraph Avenue is Berkeley's student-oriented thoroughfare and the best place to get a dose of the city's famed counterculture. On any given day you might encounter a troop of chanting Hare Krishnas or a drumming band of Rastafarians. First and foremost, however, Telegraph is a place for socializing and shopping, the only uniquely Berkeley shopping experience in town and a definite don't-miss. ■TIP➔ Take care when wandering the street at night, things can feel a bit edgy. Nearby People's Park, mostly harmless by day, is best avoided at night. Cafés, bookstores, poster shops, and street vendors line the avenue. T-shirt vendors and tarot-card readers come and go on a whim, but a few establishments—**Rasputin Music** (No. 2401), **Amoeba Music** (No. 2455), and **Moe's Books** (No. 2476)—are neighborhood landmarks. Allen Ginsberg wrote his acclaimed poem "Howl" at **Caffe Mediterraneum** (No. 2475), a relic of 1960s-era café culture.

An industrial area on **4th Street** north of University Avenue has been converted into a pleasant shopping stretch with popular eateries and shops selling handcrafted and eco-conscious goods. About six blocks long, this compact area is busiest on bright weekend afternoons. Popular destinations are the Stained Glass Garden, Hear Music, and the Crate and Barrel Outlet, along with a mini-slew of upscale boutiques and wonderful paper stores.

Northwest of the U.C. Berkeley campus, **Walnut Square,** at Walnut and Vine streets, has coffee shops and an eclectic assortment of boutiques proffering such goodies as holistic products for your pet, African masks, and French children's clothing. Around the corner on Shattuck Avenue is Chez Panisse Café & Restaurant, at the heart of what is locally known as the **Gourmet Ghetto,** a three-block stretch of specialty shops and eateries. Your senses will immediately perk up as you enter the upscale market **Epicurious Garden** (✉ *1509–1513 Shattuck Ave.*), which has everything from impeccable sushi to gelato. Outside, you can find a terraced garden—the only place to sit—that winds up four levels and ends at the Imperial Tea Court. The restaurant Taste anchors this zone; it offers a rechargeable wine-tasting card that guests use to help themselves to one-ounce automated pours from new wine selections.

9

QUICK
BITES

With a jazz combo playing in the storefront and a long line snaking down the block, Cheeseboard Pizza (✉ *151 Shattuck Ave.* ☎ *510/549–3055* ⊙ *Tues.–Fri. 11:30–2 and 4:30–7, Sat. 11:30–3*) counts out the pulse of the Gourmet Ghetto. This cooperatively owned take-out spot draws devoted customers with the smell of just-baked garlic, fresh vegetables, and perfect sauces. Next door at the bakery–cheese shop, customers take a playing card instead of a number and are served in suites.

Vine Street is another culinary destination. In a historic building **Vintage Berkeley** (✉ *2113 Vine St.* ☎ *510/665–8600*) gathers locals in its large front garden for nightly wine-tastings of California wines from smaller vineyards. Take the stairs up to the top floor of Walnut Square to find **Love at First Bite** (✉ *1510 Walnut St., Suite G* ☎ *510/848–5727*) a cup-cakery showcasing scrumptious confections. **Twig & Fig** (✉ *210 Vine St., Suite B* ☎ *510/848–5599*) invites you in for a peek at its three rhythmi-cally clacking letterpresses. Stop in for one-of-a-kind papery gifts and publications such as *Inside the Brambles*, a local's guide to Tilden Park. Of all the coffeehouses in caffeine-crazed Berkeley, the one that deserves a pilgrimage is **Peet's** (✉ *2124 Vine St.* ☎ *510/841–0564*). When this, the original, opened at Vine and Walnut streets in 1966, the unparalleled coffee was roasted in the store and brewed by the cup. Named after the Dutch last name of the founder, Peet's has since expanded, but this isn't a café where you can sit on sofas or order quiche. It's strictly cof-fee, tea, and sweets to go.

WHERE TO EAT

Dining in Berkeley is a low-key affair; even in the finest restaurants—and some are quite fine—most folks dress casually. Late diners be fore-warned: Berkeley is an "early to bed" kind of town. For inexpensive lodging, investigate University Avenue, west of campus. The area is noisy, congested, and somewhat dilapidated but does include a few decent motels and chain properties. All Berkeley lodgings, except for the swanky Claremont, are strictly mid-range.

$$$–$$$$
AMERICAN

✕ **Café Rouge.** You can recover from 4th Street shopping in this spacious two-story bistro, complete with zinc bar, skylights, and festive lanterns. The short, seasonal menu ranges from the sophisticated, such as rack of lamb and juniper-berry-cured pork chops, to the homey, such as spit-roasted chicken or pork loin, or cheddar-topped burgers. If you visit by day, be certain to peek at the meat market in the back. ✉ *1782 4th St.* ☎ *510/525–1440* ▬ *MC, V* ☺ *No dinner Mon.*

$$$–$$$$
AMERICAN
Fodor's Choice
★

✕ **Chez Panisse Café & Restaurant.** At Chez Panisse even humble pizza is reincarnated, with innovative toppings of the freshest local ingredients. The downstairs portion of Alice Waters's legendary eatery is noted for its formality and personal service. The daily-changing multicourse dinners are prix-fixe ($$$$), with the cost slightly lower on weekdays. Upstairs, in the informal café, the crowd is livelier, the prices are lower ($$–$$$$), and the ever-changing menu is à la carte. The food is sim-pler, too: penne with new potatoes, arugula, and sheep's-milk cheese; fresh figs with Parmigiano-Reggiano cheese and arugula; and grilled tuna with Savoy cabbage, for example. Legions of loyal fans insist Chez Panisse lives up to its reputation and delivers a dining experience well worth the price. Visiting foodies won't want to miss a meal here; be sure to make reservations a few weeks ahead of time. ✉ *1517 Shattuck Ave., north of University Ave.* ☎ *510/548–5525 restaurant, 510/548–5049 café* ⚏ *Reservations essential* ▬ *AE, D, DC, MC, V* ☺ *Closed Sun. No lunch in restaurant.*

$$–$$$
MEDITERRANEAN
★

✕ **Lalime's.** The food served in this charming, flower-covered house reflects the entire Mediterranean region. The menu, constantly chang-ing and unfailingly great, depends on the availability of fresh seasonal

The trailblazing restaurant Chez Panisse focuses on seasonal local ingredients.

ingredients. Choices might include grilled ahi tuna or creamy Italian risotto. The light colors of the dining room, which has two levels, help to create a cheerful mood. A star in its own right, Lalime's is a good second choice if Chez Panisse is booked. ⊠ *1329 Gilman St.* ☎ *510/527–9838* ⚛ *Reservations essential* ⊟ *AE, DC, MC, V* ⊘ *No lunch.*

¢–$
MEXICAN

✗ **Picante Cocina Mexicana.** A barnlike space full of cheerful Mexican tiles and folk-art masks, Picante is a find for anyone seeking good Mexican food for a song. The *masa* (flour) is freshly ground for the tortillas and tamales, the salsas are complex, and the combinations are inventive. Try tamales filled with butternut squash and chilies or a simple taco of roasted poblanos and sautéed onions; we challenge you to finish a plate of super nachos. ⊠ *1328 6th St.* ☎ *510/525–3121* ⚛ *Reservations not accepted* ⊟ *MC, V.*

¢–$$
AMERICAN

✗ **Rick & Ann's.** Haute comfort food is the signature here. The brunches are legendary for quality and value, and customers line up outside the door before the restaurant opens on the weekend. If you come during prime brunch time, expect a long wait, but their soft-style eggs are worth it. Pancakes, waffles, and French toast are more flavorful than usual with variations such as potato-cheese and orange-rice pancakes. Lunch and dinner offer burgers, favorites such as Mom's macaroni and cheese, and chicken potpie, but always with a festive twist. Reservations are accepted 48 hours in advance for dinner and for lunch parties of six or more, but you can't reserve a table for brunch. ⊠ *2922 Domingo Ave.* ☎ *510/649–8568* ⊟ *MC, V* ⊘ *No dinner Mon.*

WHERE TO STAY

$$$$

Fodor's Choice

★

🏨 **Claremont Resort and Spa.** Straddling the Oakland–Berkeley border, the hotel beckons like a gleaming white castle in the hills. Traveling executives come for the business amenities, including T-1 Internet connections, guest e-mail addresses, and oversize desks. The Claremont also draws honeymooners and leisure travelers with its luxurious suites, therapeutic massages, and personalized yoga workouts at the on-site spa. The rooms on the spa side of the hotel glow with new fixtures and furniture. Some offer spa tubs and, if you're high enough up, spectacular bay views. ■TIP➜ Another advantage: the scents wafting upward from the spa treatment rooms. **Pros:** amazing spa; supervised child care; some rooms have great views of the bay. **Cons:** parking is pricey; the hotel can be busy with weddings; so-so lobby. ⊠ *41 Tunnel Rd., at Ashby and Domingo Aves.* ☎ *510/843–3000 or 800/551–7266* ⊕ *www.claremontresort.com* ⤷ *249 rooms, 30 suites* 🛏 *In-room: a/c, safe, refrigerator (some), Wi-Fi. In-hotel: 2 restaurants, bars, tennis courts, pools, gym, spa, children's programs (ages 6 wks–10 yrs), laundry service, Wi-Fi hotspot, parking (paid)* ▤ *AE, D, DC, MC, V.*

$

🏨 **French Hotel.** The only hotel in north Berkeley, one of the best walking neighborhoods in town, this three-level brick structure has a certain *pensione* feel—guests check in at a counter at the back of the café, and the only public space in the hotel is the hallway to the elevator. Rooms have pastel or brick walls and cherrywood armoires and writing tables. Balconies make the rooms seem larger than their modest dimensions. The bedspreads and decor are '70s-chic, but you couldn't ask for a more central location. A ground-floor café, serving arguably the best latte in town, buzzes day and night with overflow from the Gourmet Ghetto (Chez Panisse is across the street). **Pros:** great location; affordable. **Cons:** don't expect a lot of peace and quiet; rear rooms are small and dark. ⊠ *1538 Shattuck Ave.* ☎ *510/548–9930* 🖷 *510/548–9930* ⤷ *18 rooms* 🛏 *In-room: no a/c. In-hotel: restaurant, Wi-Fi hotspot, parking (free)* ▤ *AE, D, MC, V.*

$

🏨 **Holiday Inn Express.** Convenient to the freeway and 4th Street shopping, this inviting, peach-and-beige-hue hotel offers lots of bang for the buck. The two-story property is surprisingly elegant; high ceilings lend the lobby and rooms an airy quality. Each room has a small kitchen area with a refrigerator, microwave, sink, and cabinets. The hotel also offers a free breakfast bar, a small but well-equipped gym, and free access to a business center. **Pros:** spacious rooms; central location. **Cons:** gets packed during graduation season; area can get noisy and congested with traffic. ⊠ *1175 University Ave.* ☎ *510/548–1700 or 866/548–1700* ⊕ *www.hiexberkeley.com* ⤷ *69 rooms, 3 suites with spas* 🛏 *In-room: a/c, refrigerator, Wi-Fi. In-hotel: gym, laundry facilities, laundry service, parking (free)* ▤ *AE, D, DC, MC, V* ⎮◎⎮ *CP.*

$$

🏨 **Hotel Durant.** This newly renovated boutique hotel has long been the mainstay of parents visiting their children at U.C. Berkeley; it's also a good option for those who want to be a short walk from Telegraph Avenue. The rooms, updated in 2006 with new bathrooms and dark wood set against deep jewel tones, are small without feeling cramped. The historic photos of Berkeley highlight the hotel's storied past, and the central location is perfect for the car-less. This hotel is also eco-conscious, using nonchemical, all-natural cleaning products. ■TIP→ Guests receive free passes to the extensive Cal Recreational Sports Facility, known as RSF. **Pros:** blackout shades; organic bathrobes; fantastic attention to detail. **Cons:** downstairs bar can get a little noisy during Cal games; pricey parking. ⊠ *2600 Durant Ave.* ☎ *510/845–8981* ⊕ *www.hoteldurant.com* ⤴ *139 rooms, 5 suites* ⚹ *In-room: no a/c, safe, refrigerator. In-hotel: restaurant, room service, bar, laundry service, Wi-Fi, parking (paid)* ☰ *AE, D, DC, MC, V.*

NIGHTLIFE AND THE ARTS

Berkeley Repertory Theatre. One of the region's highly respected resident professional companies and a Tony Award winner for Outstanding Regional Theatre (in 1997), the theater performs classic and contemporary plays from autumn to spring. Well-known pieces such as *Mother Courage* and *Oliver Twist* mix with edgier fare. The theater's complex is near BART's Downtown Berkeley Station. ⊠ *2025 Addison St.* ☎ *510/845–4700* ⊕ *www.berkeleyrep.org.*

Berkeley Symphony Orchestra. The ensemble has risen to considerable prominence under artistic director Kent Nagano. The works of 20th-century composers are a focus, but traditional pieces are also performed. The orchestra plays a handful of concerts each year, in Zellerbach Hall and other locations. ⊠ *1942 University Ave., Suite 207* ☎ *510/841–2800* ⊕ *www.berkeleysymphony.org.*

★ **Cal Performances.** The series, running from September through May at various U.C. Berkeley venues, offers the Bay Area's most varied bill of internationally acclaimed artists in all disciplines, from classical soloists to the latest jazz, world-music, theater, and dance ensembles. Look for frequent campus colloquia or preshow talks featuring Berkeley's professors. ⊠ *University of California, Zellerbach Hall, Telegraph Ave. and Bancroft Way* ☎ *510/642–9988* ⊕ *www.calperfs.berkeley.edu.*

Fodor's Choice ★ **Freight & Salvage Coffee House.** Some of the most talented practitioners of folk, blues, Cajun, and bluegrass perform in this alcohol-free space, one of the finest folk houses in the country. Most tickets are less than $20. ⊠ *2020 Addison St.* ☎ *510/548–1761* ⊕ *www.thefreight.org.*

SHOPPING

Fodor's Choice ★ **Amoeba Music.** Heaven for audiophiles, this legendary Berkeley favorite is *the* place to go for new and used CDs, records, cassettes, and DVDs. The dazzling stock includes thousands of titles for all music tastes—no matter what you're looking for, you can probably find it here. The store even has its own record label. There are now branches in San Francisco and Hollywood, but this is the original. ⊠ *2455 Telegraph Ave., at Haste St.* ☎ *510/549–1125.*

Body Time. The local chain, founded in Berkeley in 1970, emphasizes the premium-quality ingredients it uses in its natural perfumes and skin-care and aromatherapy products. Sustainably harvested essential oils that you can combine and dilute to create your own personal fragrances are the specialty. Its distinct Citrus, Lavender-Mint, and China Rain scents are all popular. ⊠ *1942 Shattuck Ave.* ☎ *510/841–5818.*

Kermit Lynch Wine Merchant. Kermit Lynch's friendly salespeople can direct you to the latest French bargains. Lynch's newsletters describing

9

his finds are legendary, as is his friendship with Alice Waters of Chez Panisse. Responsible for taking American appreciation of French wine to another level, the shop is a great place to peruse as you educate your palate. ⊠ *1605 San Pablo Ave., at Dwight Way* ☎ *510/524–1524.*

Moe's Books. The spirit of Moe—the cantankerous, cigar-smoking late proprietor—lives on in this four-story house of books. Students and professors come here for used books, including large sections of literary and cultural criticism, art books, and literature in foreign languages. ■TIP→ Wear good shoes and eat lunch first; you won't want to come out for hours. ⊠ *2476 Telegraph Ave., near Haste St.* ☎ *510/849–2087.*

Rasputin Music. A huge selection of new music for every taste draws crowds. In any other town, its stock of used CDs and vinyl would certainly be unsurpassed. ⊠ *2401 Telegraph Ave., at Channing Way* ☎ *800/350–8700 or 510/848–9004.*

THE COASTAL PENINSULA

Bookended by San Francisco and Silicon Valley are some surprisingly low-key and unspoiled natural treasures. The vistas here are the Pacific and rolling hills, making it easy to forget the hustle and bustle that's just out of sight.

PLANNING

GETTING HERE AND AROUND

BY AIR

All the major airlines serve San Francisco International Airport, and most of them fly to San Jose International Airport.

BY BUS

SamTrans buses travel to Moss Beach and Half Moon Bay from the Daly City BART (Bay Area Rapid Transit) station. Another bus connects Half Moon Bay with Pescadero. Each trip takes approximately one hour. Call for schedules, because departures are infrequent.

Contacts **SamTrans** (☎ *800/660–4287* ⊕ *www.samtrans.org*).

BY CAR

Public transportation to coastal areas is limited (and you'll likely want a car to get around once you arrive), so it's probably best to drive. To get to Moss Beach or Half Moon Bay, take Highway 1, also known as the Coast Highway, south along the length of the San Mateo coast. When coastal traffic is heavy, you can also reach Half Moon Bay via I–280, the Junipero Serra Freeway; follow it south as far as Route 92, where you can turn west toward the coast. To get to Pescadero, drive south 16 mi on Highway 1 from Half Moon Bay. For Año Nuevo continue south on Highway 1 another 12 mi.

VISITOR INFORMATION

Contact **California State Parks** (☎ *800/777–0369* ⊕ *www.parks.ca.gov*). **Half Moon Bay Chamber of Commerce** (⊠ *235 Main St., Half Moon Bay* ☎ *650/726–8380* ⊕ *www.halfmoonbaychamber.org*).

BIG BASIN REDWOODS STATE PARK

17 mi north of Santa Cruz on Hwy. 1.

California's oldest state park is the best place to see old-growth redwoods without going north of San Francisco (and it's far less crowded than Muir Woods and other famous spots). The parkland ranges from sea level up to 2,000 feet in elevation, which means the landscape changes often, from dark redwood groves to oak pastures that are deep green in winter and bleached nearly white in summer. The mountain setting also makes for countless waterfalls, most visible during the winter rains. The visitor center is inland, at park headquarters in Boulder Creek. Staffing is spotty, but there are always park information and camping check-in available at a self-service kiosk.

Coming from the coast, you'll access the park at Waddell Creek (Highway 1, 17 mi north of Santa Cruz), where a confluence of waterways pours out of the redwoods and into the ocean.

A short walk on the Marsh Trail leads to the **Rancho Del Oso Nature Center** (☎ *831/427–2288* ☉ *Weekends noon–4*), which has natural-history exhibits and is the starting point for several self-guided nature walks.

Mountain bikers, horseback riders, and hikers can take the nearly level Canyon Road (a dirt fire road) back up the creek and into the woods. Hikers looking for solitude might consider a more strenuous, uphill climb on Clark Connection to Westridge Trail, which rewards hard work with spectacular views of the ocean. Those who don't want to go anywhere can just stay on the windswept beach, where the main attraction is watching kite surfers get huge air on the windy shoreline waves. ✉ *21600 Big Basin Way, Boulder Creek* ☎ *831/338–8860* ☑ *$10 parking fee.*

AÑO NUEVO STATE RESERVE

21 mi north of Santa Cruz on Hwy. 1.

At the height of mating season, upward of 4,000 elephant seals congregate at Año Nuevo, the world's only approachable mainland rookery. The seals are both vocal and spectacularly big (especially the males, which can weigh up to 2½ tons), and some are in residence year-round. An easy, 1½-hour round-trip walk takes you to the dunes, from which you can look down onto the animals lounging on the shoreline. Note that during mating season (mid-December through March), visitors may do the hike only as part of a 2½-hour guided tour, for which reservations must be made well in advance. The area's visitor center has a fascinating film about the seals and some natural-history exhibits (including a sea otter's pelt that you can touch). Dogs are not allowed, even in cars in the parking lot. ✉ *Hwy. 1, 13 mi south of Pescadero* ☎ *650/879–2025, 800/444–4445 for tour reservations* ☑ *Tour $7, parking $10* ☉ *Guided tours leave every 15 min, mid-Dec.–Mar., daily 8:45–3.*

9

PESCADERO

12 mi north of Año Nuevo State Reserve on Hwy. 1.

As you walk down Stage Road, Pescadero's main street, it's hard to believe you're only 30 minutes from Silicon Valley. If you could block out the throngs of weekend cyclists, the downtown area could almost serve as the backdrop for a western movie. (In fact, with few changes, Duarte's Tavern could fill in as the requisite saloon.) This is a good place to stop for a bite or to browse for antiques. The real attractions, though, are the spectacular beaches and hiking in the area.

If a quarantine is not in effect (watch for signs), from November through April you can look for mussels amid tidal pools and rocky outcroppings at **Pescadero State Beach,** then roast them at the barbecue pits. Any time of year is good for exploring the beach, the north side of which has several secluded spots along sandstone cliffs. Across U.S. 101, the **Pescadero Marsh Natural Preserve** has hiking trails that cover 600 acres of marshland. Early spring and fall are the best times to come, when there are lots of migrating birds and other wildlife to see. ⊠ *14½ mi south of Half Moon Bay on Hwy. 1* ☏ *650/879–2170* 🎟 *Free, parking $8* ⊗ *Daily 8 AM–sunset.*

WHERE TO EAT

$–$$ ✕ **Duarte's Tavern.** Though it has been noted by national press, this

AMERICAN 19th-century roadhouse continues to serve simple American fare with a modest, hometown attitude. The restaurant's bar, for instance, is a great place to sip a whiskey; but it's also the town's liquor store, which means some locals take their orders to go. The no-frills dining room offers a solid menu based on locally grown vegetables and fresh fish. House specialties include abalone ($40), artichoke soup, and old-fashioned olallieberry pie à la mode (which *Life* magazine once named best in the United States). ⊠ *202 Stage Rd.* ☏ *650/879–0464* ⊕ *www. duartestavern.com* ▭ *AE, MC, V.*

HALF MOON BAY

16 mi north of Pescadero on Hwy. 1.

It may be the largest and most visited of the coastal communities, but Half Moon Bay is still by all measures a small town. Looking from the highway you'd hardly even know it was there. Turn onto Main Street, though, and you'll find five blocks of galleries, shops, and cafés, many of which occupy renovated 19th-century buildings. While traditionally this was an agricultural center for local growers of artichokes and other coastal crops, in recent years it has also come to be a haven for Bay Area retirees.

ESSENTIALS

Visitor Information Half Moon Bay Chamber of Commerce (⊠ *235 Main St., Half Moon Bay* ☏ *650/726–8380* ⊕ *www.halfmoonbaychamber.org*).

The town comes to life on the third weekend in October, when 250,000 people gather for the **Half Moon Bay Art and Pumpkin Festival** (☏ *650/726–9652*). Highlights include a parade, pie-eating contests, street performers and a "weigh-off" of giant pumpkins, some as big as 1,200 pounds.

The 4-mi stretch of **Half Moon Bay State Beach** (✉ *Hwy. 1, west of Main St.* ☎ *650/726–8819*) is perfect for long walks, kite flying, and picnic lunches, though the 50°F water and dangerous currents make swimming inadvisable. There are three access points, one in Half Moon Bay and two south of town off the highway. To find them, look for road signs that have a picture of footsteps.

WHERE TO EAT

$$$–$$$$

MEDITERRANEAN

★

✕ **Cetrella.** This is the coast at its most dressed up. The restaurant is all polished wood and pressed tablecloths, and hits every gourmet mark—adventurous wine list, sumptuous cheese course, and live jazz on Friday and Saturday nights. The creative menu (which changes daily) pairs regional produce and fish with choice imported ingredients, like tangy Italian *Burrata di Bufala* cheese. What results is sophisticated but not stuffy, for instance the Catalonian shellfish stew, which has a tomato, almond, and saffron broth and comes with a lobster cracker and extra napkins. The café has a smaller and cheaper but no less delectable menu. ✉ *845 Main St.* ☎ *650/726–4090* ⊕ *www.cetrella.com* ▤ *AE, D, DC, MC, V* ☺ *No lunch.*

$$–$$$

ITALIAN

★

✕ **Pasta Moon.** As one of the best restaurants on the coast between San Francisco and Monterey, Pasta Moon boasts a friendly, laid-back staff and fun, jovial crowd. Local produce flavors the seasonal menu, which includes such highlights as wood-fired pizzas and grilled quail. Beware: the dining room can get slightly noisy on weekend nights. ✉ *315 Main St.* ☎ *650/726–5125* ⊕ *www.pastamoon.com* ▤ *AE, D, DC, MC, V.*

WHERE TO STAY

$$–$$$

🏨 **Old Thyme Inn.** The owners of this 1898 Princess Anne Victorian love herbs and flowers. If you have a green thumb of your own, this is the place for you. The gardens alongside the house burst with blossoms year-round, guest rooms are filled with fragrant bouquets, and each room is named after an herb and decorated in its colors. Down comforters and luxury linens make the beds here especially wonderful. **Pros:** pretty; laid-back; comfortable. **Cons:** close quarters when the inn is full. ✉ *779 Main St.* ☎ *650/726–1616 or 800/720–4277* ⊕ *www. oldthymeinn.com* ⮡ *7 rooms* ♿ *In-room: no a/c, Internet, Wi-Fi. In-hotel: Wi-Fi hotspot* ▤ *AE, D, MC, V* ⦿ *BP.*

$$$$

★

🏨 **The Ritz-Carlton.** With its enormous and elegantly decorated rooms, secluded oceanfront property, and a staff that waits on guests hand and foot, this golf and spa resort defines opulence. Attention to detail is remarkable, right down to the silver service, china, and 300-thread-count Egyptian cotton sheets. During cocktail hour, view the ocean from the plush Conservatory bar, or from under a heavy blanket on an Adirondack chair on the lawn. The main restaurant, Navio ($$$–$$$$), is suitably decadent, with a kitchen that turns local fish and produce into dishes like squid tagliatelle with arugula and Meyer lemon, and carrot cake with carrot sorbet and cream cheese ice cream. **Pros:** four-star service; total luxury; ocean views. **Cons:** formal; not within walking distance of anything. ✉ *1 Miramontes Point Rd.* ☎ *650/712–7000 or*

9

800/241–3333 ⊕ www.ritzcarlton.com ⇆ 239 rooms, 22 suites ♁ In-room: a/c, safe, DVD, Internet, Wi-Fi. In-hotel: 2 restaurants, room service, bars, golf courses, tennis courts, gym, spa, bicycles, children's programs (ages 5–12), laundry service, Internet terminal, Wi-Fi hotspot, some pets allowed ▭ AE, D, DC, MC, V.

SPORTS

The **Bike Works** (✉ *520 Kelly St.* ☎ *650/726–6708*) rents bikes and can provide information on organized rides up and down the coast. If you prefer to go it alone, try the 3-mi bike trail that leads from Kelly Avenue in Half Moon Bay to Mirada Road in Miramar.

MOSS BEACH

7 mi north of Half Moon Bay on Hwy. 1; 20 mi south of San Francisco on Hwy. 1.

Moss Beach was a busy outpost during Prohibition, when regular shipments of liquid contraband from Canada were unloaded at the secluded beach and hauled off to San Francisco. The town stayed under the radar out of necessity, with only one local hotel and bar (now the Distillery) where Bay Area politicians and gangsters could go for a drink while waiting for their shipments. Today, although it has grown into a cheerful surfing town with charming inns and restaurants, it is still all but invisible from the highway—a good hideaway for those allergic to crowds.

The biggest Moss Beach attraction is the **Fitzgerald Marine Reserve** (✉ *California and North Lake Sts.* ☎ *650/728–3584*), a 3-mi stretch of bluffs and tide pools. Since the reserve was protected in 1969, scientists have discovered 25 new aquatic species here; depending on the tide, you'll most likely find shells, anemones, or starfish.

Just off the coast at Moss Beach is **Mavericks**. When there's a big swell, it's one of the biggest surfing breaks in the world. Waves here have reportedly reached 60 feet in height, and surfers get towed out to them by Jet Skis. The break is a mile offshore, so seeing it from the coast can be tough and requires a challenging hike.

The intrepid can get photocopied directions at the Distillery restaurant, then drive 3 mi south for the trail out of **Pillar Point Harbor**. Even if you're not hunting for waves, the harbor is a nice place to wander, with its laid-back restaurants and waters full of fishing boats and sea lions.

Built in 1928 after two horrible shipwrecks on the point, the **Point Montara Lighthouse** still has its original light keeper's quarters from the late 1800s. Gray whales pass this point during their migration from November through April, so bring your binoculars. Visiting hours coincide with morning and afternoon check-in and check-out times at the adjoining youth hostel ($23 to $28 dorm beds, $64 to $78 private room). ✉ *16th St., at Hwy. 1, Montara* ☎ *650/728–7177* ⊕ *www.norcalhostels.org* ⊙ *Daily 8 AM–sunset.*

The Inland Peninsula

Driving south of San Francisco along the San Mateo coast, it's hard to believe that inland, behind the rolling hills, is Silicon Valley. And while the high-tech hub is known more for its semiconductors and Fortune 500 companies than its sightseeing, it does have a few highlights worth stopping for—especially if you're already driving through on I-280.

Adorable Palo Alto and it's intellectual neighbor, **Stanford University** (✉ 450 Serra Mall, Stanford ☎ 650/723–2300 ⊕ www.stanford.edu), are about 35 mi south of San Francisco. Stanford's gorgeous grounds are home to a primordial-looking cactus garden, a stone sculpture by Scottish artist Andy Goldsworthy, aboriginal artworks from Papua New Guinea, and an excellent art museum—The Iris and B. Gerald Cantor Center for Visual Arts—whose lawn is planted with bronzes works by Rodin. Free one-hour walking tours of the campus leave daily at 11 and 3:15 from the visitor center in the front hall of Memorial Auditorium.

In the center of Santa Clara University's campus is the **Mission Santa Clara de Asis**. Roof tiles of the current building, a reproduction of the original, were salvaged from earlier structures, which dated from the 1790s and 1820s. Early adobe walls and a spectacular garden with 4,500 roses remain intact as well. ✉ 500 El Camino Real ☎ 408/554–4023

⊕ www.scu.edu/visitors/mission ⛨ Free ⊘ Self guided tours daily 1–sundown.

At the southern end of Silicon Valley, San Jose is home to several good museums. The permanent collection at the **San Jose Museum of Art** (✉ 110 S. Market St., San Jose ☎ 408/294–2787 ⊕ www.sjmusart.org ⛨ $8 ⊘ Tues.–Sun. 11–5) focuses on cutting-edge California and Latino artists. The **Tech Museum of Innovation** (✉ 201 S. Market St., San Jose ☎ 408/294–8324 ⊕ www.thetech.org ⛨ $8 ⊘ Daily 10–5) is a hands-on, high-tech children's museum. The **Rosicrucian Egyptian Museum** (✉ 1342 Naglee Ave., San Jose ☎ 408/947–3635 ⊕ www.egyptianmuseum.org ⛨ $9 ⊘ Mon., Wed., and Fri. 10–5, Thurs. 10–8, weekends 11–6) showcases an exquisite collection of Egyptian and Babalonian antiquities.

Southwest of San Jose are the pretty village of Saratoga and the ritzy town of Los Gatos, nestled in the foothills of the Coastal Range. Los Gatos is also home to one of the finest restaurants in the country, **Manresa** (✉ 320 Village La., Los Gatos ☎ 408/354–4330 ⊕ www.manresarestaurant.com ▭ AE, MC, V ⊘ Closed Mon. and Tues. No lunch), which runs its own farm to produce ingredients for its French-Catalan cuisine.

9

WHERE TO EAT

$$–$$$
MEDITERRANEAN
★

✕ **Cafe Gibraltar.** While the cuisine here is broadly called Mediterranean, in the kitchen of chef-owner Jose Luiz Ugalde that term can mean sweet crab dumplings with sumac butter and Turkish spices, or Sardinian shellfish cassoula with garlic aioli. The imaginative dishes are served in a warm, pretty dining room; peach walls are lighted by flickering candles, and the booths are adorned with curtains and pillows. Two miles south of Moss Beach on the east side of the highway, the restaurant is a bit hard to find—but definitely worth the hunt. At signs for Pillar Point Harbor, turn inland onto Capistrano, then right onto Alhambra. ⊠ *425 Ave. Alhambra, at Palma Ave., El Granada* ☎ *650/560–9039* ⊕ *www. cafegibraltar.com* ▤ *AE, D, DC, MC, V* ☺ *Closed Mon. No lunch.*

$$–$$$
SEAFOOD

✕ **Sam's Chowder House.** An East Coast–style seafood joint in the Bay Area? This waterfront restaurant isn't textbook Cape Cod, but that's OK—dine here, and you'll get the best of both coasts: true New England–style clam chowder and lump crab cakes and ahi tuna poke with sesame oil and scallions or local halibut with mango salsa. Indoor seats are in one of several long dining rooms; outdoor seats are warmed by gas fire pits and heaters on chilly days; and every seat in the house looks out to the water. The attached market sells fresh fish and picnic food. ⊠ *4210 N. Hwy. 1* ☎ *650/712–0245* ⊕ *www.samschowderhouse. com* ▤ *AE, D, DC, MC, V.*

The Wine Country

WORD OF MOUTH

"I specifically wanted to visit Sonoma on this trip in order to compare to Napa. . . . Sonoma is quieter, more rural and spread out. Napa is a bit glitzier and the wineries seem more densely packed. . . . Both areas are a really nice experience though; the scenery was lovely with the rolling vineyards."

—Miramar

WELCOME TO WINE COUNTRY

TOP REASONS TO GO

★ **Touring the Wineries:** Sure, the landscape is lovely and the food is delicious, but the main reason you're here is to sip your way through the region while exploring the diverse wineries.

★ **Biking:** Cycling is one of the best ways to see the Wine Country—the Russian River and Dry Creek valleys are particularly beautiful.

★ **Browsing the farmers' markets:** Almost every town in Napa and Sonoma has a seasonal farmers' market, each rounding up an amazing variety of local produce.

★ **Canoeing on the Russian River:** Trade in your car keys for a paddle and glide down the Russian River. May through October is the best time to be on the water.

★ **Cocktails at Cyrus:** At the bar of Healdsburg's well-loved restaurant, the bartenders mix superb, inventive drinks with house-made infused syrups and seasonal ingredients like local Meyer lemons.

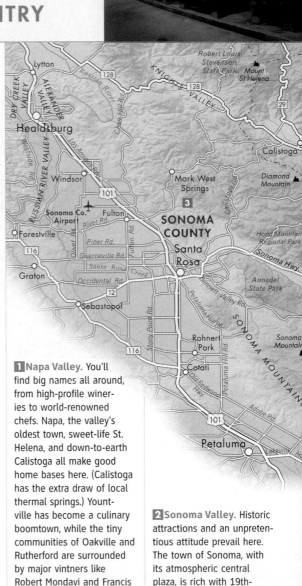

1 Napa Valley. You'll find big names all around, from high-profile wineries to world-renowned chefs. Napa, the valley's oldest town, sweet-life St. Helena, and down-to-earth Calistoga all make good home bases here. (Calistoga has the extra draw of local thermal springs.) Yountville has become a culinary boomtown, while the tiny communities of Oakville and Rutherford are surrounded by major vintners like Robert Mondavi and Francis Ford Coppola. Rutherford in particular is the source for outstanding cabernet sauvignon.

2 Sonoma Valley. Historic attractions and an unpretentious attitude prevail here. The town of Sonoma, with its atmospheric central plaza, is rich with 19th-century buildings. Glen Ellen, meanwhile, has a special connection with author Jack London.

GETTING ORIENTED

The Napa and Sonoma valleys run roughly parallel, northwest to southeast, and are separated by the Mayacamas Mountains. Northwest of the Sonoma Valley are several more important viticultural areas in Sonoma County, including the Dry Creek, Alexander, and Russian River valleys. The Carneros region, which spans southern Sonoma and Napa counties, is just north of San Pablo Bay, and the closest of all these wine regions to San Francisco.

10

3 Elsewhere in Sonoma.
The winding, rural roads here feel a world away from Napa's main drag. The lovely Russian River, Dry Creek, and Alexander valleys are all excellent places to seek out pinot noir, zinfandel, and chardonnay. The small town of Healdsburg gets lots of attention, thanks to its terrific restaurants, bed-and-breakfasts, and chic boutiques.

WINE COUNTRY PLANNER

Getting Around

Driving your own car is by far the best way to explore the Wine Country. Well-maintained roads zip through the centers of the Napa and Sonoma valleys, while scenic routes thread through the backcountry. Distances between towns are fairly short, and you can sometimes drive from one end of the Napa or Sonoma Valley to the other in less than an hour—if there's no significant traffic. (However, it's not quite as easy as you might think to get between the two valleys, since they're divided by the Mayacamas Mountains.) This may be a relatively rural area, but the usual rush hours still apply, and high-season weekend traffic can be excruciatingly slow, especially on Route 29. ■TIP→ If you're wine-tasting, either select a designated driver or be very careful of your wine intake. Local cops are quick with DUIs.

Timing

"Crush," the term used to indicate the season when grapes are picked and crushed, usually takes place in September or October, depending on the weather. From September until November the entire Wine Country celebrates its bounty with street fairs and festivals. The Sonoma County Harvest Fair, with its famous grape stomp, is held the first weekend in October. Golf tournaments, wine auctions, and art and food fairs occur throughout the fall.

In season (April through November), Napa Valley draws crowds of tourists, and traffic along Route 29 from St. Helena to Calistoga is often backed up on weekends. The Sonoma Valley, Santa Rosa, and Healdsburg are less crowded. In season and over holiday weekends it's best to book lodging, restaurant, and winery reservations at least a month in advance. Many wineries give tours at specified times and require appointments.

To avoid crowds, visit the Wine Country during the week and get an early start (most wineries open around 10). Because many wineries close as early as 4 or 4:30—and almost none are open past 5—you'll need to get a reasonably early start if you want to fit in more than one or two, especially if you're going to enjoy the leisurely lunch customary in the Wine Country. Summer is usually hot and dry, and autumn can be even hotter, so dress appropriately if you go during these times.

About the Hotels

Napa and Sonoma know the tourism ropes well; their inns and hotels range from low key to utterly luxurious, and generally maintain high standards. Most of the bed-and-breakfasts are in historic Victorian and Spanish buildings and the breakfast part of the equation often involves fresh local produce. The newer hotels tend to have a more modern, streamlined aesthetic and elaborate, spalike bathrooms. Many hotels and B&Bs have excellent restaurants on their grounds, and those that don't are still just a short car ride away from gastronomic bliss.

However, all of this comes with a hefty price tag. As the cost of vineyards and grapes has risen, so have lodging rates. Santa Rosa, the largest population center in the area, has the widest selection of moderately priced rooms. Try there if you've failed to reserve in advance or have a limited budget. In general, all accommodations in the area often have lower rates on weeknights, and prices are about 20% lower in winter.

On weekends, two- or even three-night minimum stays are commonly required, especially at smaller inns and B&Bs. If you'd prefer to stay a single night, though, innkeepers are usually more flexible in winter. Many B&Bs book up long in advance of the summer and fall seasons, and many of them aren't suitable for children.

WHAT IT COSTS

	¢	$	$$	$$$	$$$$
Restaurants	under $10	$10–$14	$15–$22	$23–$30	over $30
Hotels		under $200	$200–$250	$251–$300	$301–$400	over $400

Restaurant prices are per person for a main course at dinner, or for a prix fixe if a set menu is the only option. Hotel prices are for two people in a standard double room in high season

About the Restaurants

Star chefs from around the world have come into the Wine Country's orbit, drawn by the area's phenomenal produce, artisanal foods, and wines. These days, many visitors come to Napa and Sonoma as much for the restaurants' tasting menus as for the wineries' tasting rooms.

Although excellent meals can be found virtually everywhere in the region, the small town of Yountville has become a culinary crossroads under the influence of chef Thomas Keller. If a table at Keller's famed French Laundry is out of reach, keep in mind that he's also behind a number of more modest restaurants in town. And the buzzed-about restaurants in Sonoma County, including Cyrus and Farmhouse Inn, offer plenty of mouthwatering options.

Inexpensive eateries include high-end delis serve superb picnic fare, and brunch is a cost-effective strategy at pricey restaurants, as is sitting at the bar and ordering a few appetizers instead of sitting down to a full-blown meal.

With few exceptions (which are noted in individual restaurant listings), dress is informal. Where reservations are indicated as essential, you may need to make them a week or more ahead. In summer and early fall you may need to book several weeks ahead.

10

Updated by
Sharron Wood

Life is good in the California Wine Country. Eating and, above all, drinking are cultivated as high arts. Have you been daydreaming about driving through vineyards, stopping here and there for a wine tasting or a picnic? Well, that fantasy is a common reality here.

It's little wonder that so many visitors to San Francisco take a day or two—or five or six—to unwind in the Napa and Sonoma valleys. They join the locals in the tasting rooms, from serious wine collectors making their annual pilgrimages to wine newbies who don't know the difference between a merlot and mourvèdre but are eager to learn.

The state's wine industry is booming, and the Napa and Sonoma valleys have long led the field. For instance, in 1975 Napa Valley had no more than 20 wineries; today there are more than 275. A recent up-and-comer is the Carneros region, which overlaps Napa and Sonoma counties at the head of the San Francisco Bay. (Chardonnay and pinot noir grapes thrive on its cool, windy hillsides.)

Great dining and wine go hand in hand, and the local viticulture has naturally encouraged a robust passion for food. Several outstanding chefs have taken root here, sealing the area's reputation as one of the best restaurant destinations in the country. The lust for fine food doesn't stop at the doors of the bistros, either. Whether you visit an artisanal olive-oil producer, nibble locally made cheese, or browse the fresh vegetables in the farmers' markets, you'll soon see why Napa and Sonoma are a food-lover's paradise.

Napa and Sonoma counties are also rich in history. In the town of Sonoma, for example, you can explore buildings from California's Spanish and Mexican past. Some wineries, such as Napa Valley's Beringer, have cellars or tasting rooms dating to the late 1800s. The town of Calistoga is a flurry of Steamboat Gothic architecture, gussied up with the fretwork favored by late-19th-century spa goers. Modern architecture is the exception rather than the rule, but one standout example is the postmodern extravaganza of Clos Pegase winery in Calistoga.

Binding all these temptations together is the sheer scenic beauty of the place. Much of Napa Valley's landscape unspools in orderly, densely planted rows of vines. Sonoma's vistas are broken by rolling hills or stands of ancient oak and madrone trees. Even the climate cooperates, as the warm summer days and refreshingly cool evenings that make the area one of the world's best grape-growing regions make perfect weather for traveling, too. If you're inspired to dig further into the Wine Country, grab a copy of *California Wine Country* or the in-depth *Compass American Guide: California Wine Country*.

PLANNING

GETTING HERE AND AROUND

AIR TRAVEL

If you'd like to bypass San Francisco or Oakland, you can fly directly to the small Charles M. Schulz Sonoma County Airport (STS) in Santa Rosa on Horizon Air, which has direct flights from Los Angeles, Portland, Las Vegas, and Seattle. Rental cars are available from Avis, Enterprise, and Hertz at the airport.

BUS TRAVEL

Bus travel is an inconvenient way to explore the Wine Country. Service is infrequent and buses from San Francisco can only get you to Santa Rosa or the town of Vallejo, south of Napa—neither of which is close to the vineyards. Sonoma County Transit offers daily bus service to points all over the county. VINE (Valley Intracity Neighborhood Express) provides bus service within the city of Napa and between other Napa Valley towns.

Bus Lines Greyhound (☎ 800/231–2222). **Sonoma County Transit** (☎ 707/576–7433 or 800/345–7433). **VINE** (☎ 707/251–2800).

CAR TRAVEL

Five major roads cut through the Napa and Sonoma valleys. U.S. 101 and Routes 12 and 121 travel through Sonoma County. Route 29 heads north from Napa. The 25-mi Silverado Trail, which runs parallel to Route 29 north from Napa to Calistoga, is Napa Valley's more scenic, less-crowded alternative to Route 29.

■ TIP➔ Remember, if you're wine-tasting, either select a designated driver or be careful of your wine intake. (When you're taking just a sip or two of any given wine, it can be hard to keep track of how much you're drinking.) Also, keep in mind that you'll likely be sharing the road with cyclists; keep a close eye on the shoulder.

When calculating the time it will take you to drive between the Napa and Sonoma valleys, remember that the Mayacamas Mountains are between the two. If it's not too far out of your way, you might want to travel between the two valleys along Highway 12/121 to the south, or along Highway 128 to the north, to avoid the slow, winding drive on the Oakville Grade, which connects Oakville, in Napa, and Glen Ellen, in Sonoma.

From San Francisco to Napa: Cross the Golden Gate Bridge, then go north on U.S. 101. Next go east on Route 37 toward Vallejo, then north on

10

Route 121, also called the Carneros Highway. Turn left (north) when Route 121 runs into Route 29. This should take about 1½ hours when traffic is light.

From San Francisco to Sonoma: Cross the Golden Gate Bridge, then go north on U.S. 101, east on Route 37 toward Vallejo, and north on Route 121, aka the Carneros Highway. When you reach Route 12, take it north. If you're going to any of the Sonoma County destinations north of the valley, take U.S. 101 all the way north through Santa Rosa to Healdsburg. This should take about an hour, not counting substantial traffic.

From Berkeley and other East Bay towns: Take Interstate 80 north to Route 37 west, then on to Route 29 north. To head up the Napa Valley, continue on Route 29; to reach Sonoma County, turn off Route 29 onto Route 121 heading north. Getting from Berkeley to Napa will take at least 45 minutes, from Berkeley to Sonoma at least an hour.

BED-AND-BREAKFAST ASSOCIATIONS

Bed & Breakfast Association of Sonoma Valley ☎ 800/969–4667 ⊕ www.sonomabb.com). **The Wine Country Inns of Sonoma County** (☎ 800/946–3268 ⊕ www.winecountryinns.com).

TOURS

Full-day guided tours of the Wine Country generally include lunch and cost about $60–$100 per person. Reservations are usually required.

Beau Wine Tours (✉ 21707 8th St. E, Sonoma ☎ 707/938–8001 or 800/387–2328 ⊕ www.beauwinetours.com) organizes personalized tours of Napa and Sonoma in their limos, vans, and shuttle buses. **Gray Line** (✉ Pier 43½, Embarcadero, San Francisco ☎ 415/434–8687 or 888/428–6937 ⊕ www.grayline.com) has a tour that covers both the southern Napa and Sonoma valleys in a single day, with a stop for lunch in Yountville. **Great Pacific Tour Co.** (✉ 518 Octavia St., Hayes Valley, San Francisco ☎ 415/626–4499 ⊕ www.greatpacifictour.com) operates full-day tours of Napa and Sonoma, including a restaurant or picnic lunch, in passenger vans that seat 14. In addition to renting bikes by the day, **Wine Country Bikes** (✉ 61 Front St., Healdsburg ☎ 707/473–0610 ⊕ www.winecountrybikes.com) organizes both one-day and multiday trips throughout Sonoma County.

THE NAPA VALLEY

When it comes to wine production in the United States, Napa Valley rules the roost, with more than 275 wineries and many of the biggest brands in the business. Vastly diverse soils and microclimates give Napa winemakers the chance to make a tremendous variety of wines. But what's the area like beyond the glossy advertising and boldface names?

The handful of small towns strung along Highway 29 are where wine industry workers live, and they're also where most of the area lodging is. Napa—the valley's largest town—lures with its few cultural attractions and accommodations that are (relatively) reasonably priced. A few miles farther north, compact Yountville is a culinary boomtown, densely packed with top-notch restaurants and hotels, including a few luxury properties. Continuing north, St. Helena teems with elegant boutiques and restaurants; mellow Calistoga, known for spas and hot springs, feels a bit like an Old West frontier town and has a more casual attitude than many Wine Country towns.

ESSENTIALS

Contacts Napa Valley Conference and Visitors Bureau (✉ *1310 Napa Town Center, Napa* ☎ *707/226-7459* ⊕ *www.napavalley.org*).

NAPA

46 mi from San Francisco via I–80 east and north, Rte. 37 west, and Rte. 29 north.

The town of Napa is the valley's largest, and visitors who get a glimpse of the strip malls and big-box stores from Highway 29 often speed right past on the way to the smaller and more seductive Yountville or St. Helena. But Napa doesn't entirely deserve its dowdy reputation. After many years as a blue-collar town that more or less turned its back on the Wine Country scene, Napa has spent the last few years attempting to increase its appeal to visitors, with somewhat mixed results. A walkway that follows the river through town, completed in 2008, makes the city more pedestrian-friendly, and new restaurants and hotels are continually popping up (there are even plans to open a Ritz-Carlton on the river's banks in 2011). But you'll still find a handful of empty storefronts among the wine bars, bookstores, and restaurants, and Napa's biggest tourist attraction, a food-and-wine-theme museum and educational center, closed in late 2008.

Many visitors choose to stay in Napa after experiencing hotel sticker shock; prices in Napa are marginally more reasonable than elsewhere. If you set up your home base here, you'll undoubtedly want to spend some time getting out of town and into the beautiful countryside, but don't neglect taking a stroll to see what Napa's least pretentious town has to offer.

★ The majestic château of **Domaine Carneros** looks for all the world like it belongs in France, and in fact it does: it's modeled after the Château de la Marquetterie, an 18th-century mansion owned by the Taittinger family near Epernay, France. Carved into the hillside beneath the winery, Domaine Carneros's cellars produce delicate sparkling wines reminiscent of those made by Taittinger, using only grapes grown locally in the Carneros wine district. The winery sells full glasses, flights, and bottles of their wines, which also include still wines like a handful of pinot noirs and a merlot, and serves them with cheese plates or caviar to those seated in the Louis XV–inspired salon or on the terrace overlooking the vineyards. Though this makes a visit here a tad more expensive than some stops on a winery tour, it's also one of the most opulent ways to enjoy the Carneros District, especially on fair days, when the views over the vineyards are spectacular. ✉ *1240 Duhig Rd., Napa* ☎ *707/257-0101* ⊕ *www.domainecarneros.com* ☎ *Tasting $6.50–$25, tour $25* ☉ *Daily 10–6; tour daily at 11, 1, and 3.*

10

Continued on page 522

WINE
TASTING *in*
NAPA *and*
SONOMA

VISITING WINERIES

Napa and Sonoma are outstanding destinations for both wine newcomers and serious wine buffs. Tasting rooms range from modest to swanky, offering everything from a casual conversation over a few sips of wine to in-depth tours of winemaking facilities and vineyards. And there's a tremendous variety of wines to taste. The one constant is a deep, shared pleasure in the experience of wine tasting.

Wineries in Napa and Sonoma range from faux châteaux with vast gift shops to rustic converted barns where you might have to step over the vintner's dog in the doorway. Many are regularly open to the public, usually daily from around 10 AM to 5 PM. Others require advance reservations to visit, and still others are closed to the public entirely. When in doubt, call ahead.

There are many, many more wineries in Napa and Sonoma than we could possibly include here. Free maps pinpointing most of them are widely available, though; ask the staff at the tasting rooms you visit or look for the ubiquitous free tourist magazines.

The tantalizing pop of a cork. Roads unspooling through hypnotically even rows of vines. Sun glinting through a glass of sparkling wine or ruby colored cabernet. If these are your daydreams, you won't be disappointed when you get to Napa and Sonoma. The vineyard-blanketed hills, shady town squares, and ivy-draped wineries—not to mention the luxurious restaurants, hotels, and spas—really *are* that captivating.

Pick a designated driver before setting out for the day. Although wineries rarely advertise it, many will provide a free nonalcoholic drink for the designated driver; it never hurts to ask.

Fees. In the past few years, tasting fees have skyrocketed. Most Napa wineries charge $10 to $20 to taste four or so wines, though $30 or even $40 fees aren't unheard of. Sonoma wineries are often a bit cheaper, in the $5 to $15 range, and you'll still find the occasional freebie.

Some winery tours are free, in which case you're usually required to pay a separate fee if you want to taste the wine. If you've paid a fee for the tour—often $10 to $30—your wine tasting is usually included in that price.

(opposite page) Carneros vineyards in autumn, Napa Valley. (top) Pinot Gris grapes (bottom) Bottles from Far Niente winery.

MAKING THE MOST OF YOUR TIME

(top) Sipping and swirling in the De Loach tasting room. (bottom) Learning about barrel aging at Robert Mondavi Winery.

■ **Call ahead.** Some wineries require reservations to visit or tour. If you have your heart set on visiting a specific place, double-check their availability.

■ **Come on weekdays,** especially if you're visiting during high season (May to November), to avoid traffic-clogged roads and crowded tasting rooms. For more info on the best times of year to visit, see this chapter's Planner.

■ **Get an early start.** Tasting rooms are often deserted before 11 AM or so, when most visitors are still lingering over a second cup of coffee. If you come early, you'll have the staff's undivided attention. You'll usually encounter the largest crowds between 3 and 5 PM.

■ **Consider skipping Napa.** If you've got less than two days to spend in the Wine Country, dip into the Carneros area or the Sonoma Valley rather than Napa Valley or northern Sonoma County. Though you might find fewer big-name wineries and critically acclaimed restaurants, these regions are only about an hour and half away from the city . . . if you don't hit traffic.

■ **Divide your attention.** If you're lucky enough to have three nights or more here, split your overnights between Napa and Sonoma to easily see the best that both counties have to offer.

A tasting at Heitz Cellar.

AT THE BAR

In most tasting rooms, you'll be handed a list of the wines available that day. The wines will be listed in a suggested tasting order, starting with the lightest-bodied whites, progressing to the most intense reds, and ending with dessert wines. If you can't decide which wines to choose, tell the server what types of wines you usually like and ask for a recommendation.

The server will pour you an ounce or so of each wine you select. As you taste it, feel free to take notes or ask questions. Don't be shy—the staff are there to educate you about their wine. If you don't like a wine, or you've simply tasted enough, feel free to pour the rest into one of the dump buckets on the bar.

TOURS

Tours tend to be the most exciting (and the most crowded) in September and October, when the harvest and crush-ing are underway. Tours typically last from 30 minutes to an hour and give you a brief overview of the winemaking process. At some of the older wineries, the tour guide might focus on the history of the property.

■ **TIP→** If you plan to take any tours, wear comfortable shoes, since you might be walking on wet floors or dirt or gravel pathways or stepping over hoses or other equipment.

MONEY-SAVING TIPS

■ Many hotels and B&Bs distribute coupons for free or discounted tastings to their guests—don't forget to ask.

■ If you and your travel partner don't mind sharing a glass, servers are happy to let you split a tasting.

■ Some wineries will refund all or part of the tasting fee if you buy a bottle, making it so much easier to rationalize buying that $80 bottle of cabernet.

■ Almost all wineries will also waive the fee if you join their wine club program. However, this typically commits you to buying a certain number of bottles of their wine for a period of time, so be sure you really like their wines before signing up.

Preston Vineyards bottles only estate-grown grapes.

TOP 2-DAY ITINERARIES

First-Timer's Napa Tour

Start: Oxbow Public market, Napa. Get underway by browsing the shops selling wines, spices, locally grown produce, and other fine foods, for a taste of what the Wine Country has to offer.

Rubicon Estate, Rutherford. The tour here is a particularly fun way to learn about the

history of Napa wine-making—and you can see the old, atmospheric, ivy-covered château.

Frog's Leap, Rutherford. Friendly, unpretentious, and knowledgeable staff makes this place great for wine newbies. (Make sure

you get that advance reservation lined up.)

Dinner and Overnight: St. Helena. Spluge at Meadowood Resort with dinner at

Domaine Carneros

di Rosa Preserve

Old Sonoma Rd.

121

12

Oxbow Public Market
Napa
29

NAPA COUNTY

Rober Monda

Far Niente

Yountville

Oakville

KEY
First-Timer's Napa Tour
Wine Buff's Tour

Silverado Trail

Stag's Leap Wine Cellars

Wine Buff's Tour

Start: Stag's Leap Wine Cellars, Yountville. Famed for its cabernet sauvignon and Bordeaux blends.

Beaulieu Vineyard, Rutherford. Pony up the extra fee to visit the reserve tasting room to try their flagship cabernet sauvignon.

Caymus Vineyards, Rutherford. The low-key tasting room is a great place to learn more about Rutherford and Napa cabernet artistry. Reserve in advance.

Dinner and Overnight: Yountville. Have dinner at one of the Thomas Keller restaurants. Splurge

at the Villagio Inn & Spa; save at Maison Fleurie.

Next Day: Robert Mondavi, Oakville. Spring for the reserve room tasting so you can sip the top-of-the-line wines, especially the stellar cabernet. Head across Highway 29 to the Oakville Grocery

to pick up a picnic lunch.

Terra. Save at El Bonita Motel with dinner at Taylor's.

Next Day: Poke around St. Helena's shops, then drive to Yountville for lunch.

di Rosa, Napa. Call ahead to book a one- or two-hour tour of the acres of gardens and galleries, which are chock-full of thousands of works of art.

Domaine Carneros, Napa. Toast your trip with a glass of outstanding bubbly.

Sonoma Backroads

Start: Iron Horse Vineyards, Russian River Valley.
Soak up a view of vine-covered hills and Mount St. Helena while sipping a sparkling wine or pinot noir at this beautifully rustic spot.

Hartford Family Winery, Russian River Valley.
A terrific source for pinot noir and chardonnay, the stars of this valley.

Dinner and Overnight: Forestville. Splurge at the Applewood Inn and its cozy restaurant, or go all out with a stay at the Farmhouse Inn, whose Michelin-starred restaurant is one of the best in all of Sonoma.

Next Day: Westside Road, Russian River Valley.
This scenic route, which follows the river, is crowded with worthwhile wineries like Gary Farrell and Rochioli—but it's not crowded with visitors. Pinot fans will find a lot to love. Picnic at Rochioli and enjoy the lovely view.

Matanzas Creek Winery, near Santa Rosa.
End on an especially relaxed note with a walk through their lavender fields (best in June).

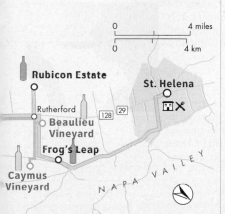

Far Niente, Oakville. You have to reserve in advance and the fee for the tasting and tour is steep, but the

payoff is an especially intimate winery experience. You'll taste excellent cabernet and chardonnay, then end your trip on a sweet note with a dessert wine.

10

WINE TASTING 101

TAKE A GOOD LOOK.

Hold your glass by the stem, raise it to the light, and take a close look at the wine. Check for clarity and color. (This is easiest to do if you can hold the glass in front of a white background.) Any tinge of brown usually means that the wine is over the hill or has gone bad.

BREATHE DEEP.

1. Sniff the wine once or twice to see if you can identify any smells.

2. Swirl the wine gently in the glass. Aerating the wine this way releases more of its aromas. (It's called "volatilizing the esters," if you're trying to impress someone.)

3. Take another long sniff. You might notice that experienced wine tasters spend more time sniffing the wine than drinking it. This is because this step is where the magic happens. The number of scents you might detect is almost endless, from berries, apricots, honey, and wildflowers to leather, cedar, or even tar. Does the wine smell good to you? Do you detect any "off" flavors, like wet dog or sulfur?

AT LAST! TAKE A SIP.

1. Swirl the wine around your mouth so that it makes contact with all your taste buds and releases more of its aromas. Think about the way the wine feels in your mouth. Is it watery or rich? Is it crisp or silky? Does it have a bold flavor, or is it subtle? The weight and intensity of a wine are called its body.

2. Hold the wine in your mouth for a few seconds and see if you can identify any developing flavors. More complex wines will reveal many different flavors as you drink them.

SPIT OR SWALLOW.

The pros typically spit, since they want to preserve their palate (and sobriety!) for the wines to come, but you'll find that swallowers far outnumber the spitters in the winery tasting rooms. Whether you spit or swallow, notice the flavor that remains after the wine is gone (the finish).

Swirl

Sniff

Sip

DODGE THE CROWDS

To avoid bumping elbows in the tasting rooms, look for wineries off the main drags of Highway 29 in Napa and Highway 12 in Sonoma. The back roads of the Russian River, Dry Creek, and Alexander valleys, all in Sonoma, are excellent places to explore. In Napa, try the northern end. Also look for wineries that are open by appointment only; they tend to schedule visitors carefully to avoid a big crush at any one time.

HOW WINE IS MADE

1. CRUSHING
Harvested grapes go into a stemmer-crusher, which separates stems from fruit and crushes the grapes to release "free-run" juice.

2. PRESSING
Remaining juice is gently extracted from grapes. Usually done by pressing grapes against the walls of a tank with an inflatable bladder.

3. FERMENTING
Extracted juice (and also grape skins and pulp, when making red wine) goes into stainless-steel tanks or oak barrels to ferment. During fermentation, sugars convert to alcohol.

4. AGING
Wine is stored in stainless-steel or oak casks or barrels to develop flavors.

5. RACKING
Wine is transferred to clean barrels; sediment is removed. Wine may be filtered and fined (clarified) to improve its clarity, color, and sometimes flavor.

6. BOTTLING
Wine is bottled either at the winery or at a special facility, then stored again for bottle-aging.

WHAT'S AN APPELLATION?

A specific region with a particular set of grape-growing conditions, such as soil type, climate, and elevation, is called an appellation. What makes things a little confusing is that appellations, which are defined by the Alcohol and Tobacco Tax and Trade Bureau, often overlap. California is an appellation, for example, but so is the Napa Valley. Napa and Sonoma counties are each county appellations, but they, too, are divided into even smaller regions, usually called subappellations or AVAs (American Viticultural Areas). You'll hear a lot about these AVAs from the staff in the tasting rooms; they might explain, for example, why the Russian River Valley AVA is such an excellent place to grow pinot noir grapes. By law, if the label on a bottle of wine lists the name of an appellation, then at least 85% of the grapes in that wine must come from that appellation.

Wine and contemporary art find a home at the di Rosa.

★ While you're driving along the Carneros Highway on your way to Napa from San Francisco, it would be easy to zip by one of the region's best-kept secrets: **di Rosa.** Metal sculptures of sheep grazing in the grass mark the entrance to this sprawling, art-stuffed property. Thousands of 20th-century artworks by hundreds of Northern California artists crop up everywhere—in galleries, in the former di Rosa residence, on every lawn, in every courtyard, and even on the lake. Some of the works were commissioned especially for the preserve, such as Paul Kos's meditative *Chartres Bleu,* a video installation in a chapel-like setting that replicates a stained-glass window of the cathedral in Chartres, France. If you stop by without a reservation, you'll only gain access to the Gatehouse Gallery, where there's a small collection of riotously colorful figurative and abstract sculpture and painting. ■**TIP→**To see the rest of the property and artwork, you'll have to sign up for one of the various tours of the grounds (from 1 to 2½ hours). Reservations for the tours are recommended, but they can sometimes accommodate walk-ins. ⊠ *5200 Sonoma Hwy./Carneros Hwy., Napa* ☎ *707/226–5991* ⊕ *www.dirosaart.org* ✉ *Free, tour $10–$15* ⊙ *Wed.–Fri. 9:30–3; Sat. by reservation; call for tour times.*

With its modern, minimalist look in the tasting room, which is dug into a Carneros hilltop, and contemporary sculptures and fountains on the property, **Artesa Vineyards & Winery** is a far cry from the many faux French châteaus and rustic Italian-style villas in the region. Although the Spanish owners once made only sparkling wines, now they produce primarily still wines, mostly chardonnay and pinot noir, but also cabernet sauvignon and a smattering of other limited-release wines such as syrah and albariño. Call ahead to reserve a spot on one of the specialty tours, such as a wine-and-cheese pairing or the walk through the vineyard ($40). ✉ *1345 Henry Rd., north off Old Sonoma Rd. and Dealy La., Napa* ☎ *707/224–1668* ⊕ *www.artesawinery.com* 🍷 *Tasting $10–$15, tour $20* ⊙ *Daily 10–5; tour daily at 11 and 2.*

Though it's not terribly large, **Oxbow Public Market,** a collection of about 20 small shops, wine bars, and artisanal food producers, is a fun place to begin your introduction to the wealth of food and wine available in the Napa Valley. Swoon over the decadent charcuterie at the Fatted Calf, slurp down some oysters on the half shell at Hog Island Oyster Company, sample a large variety of local olive oils at the Olive Press, or get a whiff of the hard-to-find seasonings at the Whole Spice Company before sitting down to a glass of wine at one of the two wine bars. A branch of the retro fast-food joint Gott's Roadside Tray Gourmet tempts those who prefer hamburgers to duck-liver mousse. ✉ *610 and 644 1st St., Napa* ☎ *No phone* ⊕ *www.oxbowpublicmarket.com* 🍷 *Free* ⊙ *Generally weekdays 9–7, weekends 10–6, though hrs of some merchants vary.*

Luna Vineyards was established in 1995 by veterans of the Napa wine industry intent on making less-conventional wines, particularly Italian varieties such as sangiovese and pinot grigio. Though these days you're just as likely to taste a merlot or a cabernet blend, it's still well worth visiting its Tuscan-style tasting room with a coffered ceiling, especially for a nip of late-harvest pinto grigio dessert wine called Mille Baci ("a thousand kisses" in Italian). ✉ *2921 Silverado Trail, Napa* ☎ *707/255–5862* ⊕ *www.lunavineyards.com* 🍷 *Tasting $15–$25* ⊙ *Sun.–Thurs. 10–5, Fri. and Sat. 10–6.*

Austere **Clos du Val** doesn't seduce you with dramatic architecture or lush grounds, but it doesn't have to: the wines, crafted by winemaker John Clews, have a wide following, especially among those who are patient enough to cellar the wines for a number of years. Though Clews's team makes great pinot noir and chardonnay (grown in the nearby Carneros region), the real claim to fame is the intense reserve cabernet, made with fruit from the Stags Leap District. The few picnic tables fill up early on summer weekends, and anyone is welcome to try a hand at the boccie-style French game of pétanque. ✉ *5330 Silverado Trail, Napa* ☎ *707/259–2200* ⊕ *www.closduval.com* 🍷 *Tasting $10–$20* ⊙ *Daily 10–5; tour by appointment.*

10

Fodor'sChoice
★

The **Hess Collection Winery and Vineyards** is a delightful discovery on Mt. Veeder, 9 mi northwest of the city of Napa. (Don't give up; the road leading to the winery is long and winding.) The simple limestone structure, rustic from the outside but modern and airy within, contains Swiss owner Donald Hess's personal art collection, including mostly large-scale works by such contemporary European and American artists as Robert Motherwell, Andy Goldsworthy, and Frank Stella. Cabernet sauvignon is the real strength here, though Hess also produces some fine chardonnays. Self-guided tours of the art collection and guided tours of the winery's production facilities are both free. ✉ *4411 Redwood Rd., west of Rte. 29, Napa* ☎ *707/255–1144* ⊕ *www.hesscollection.*

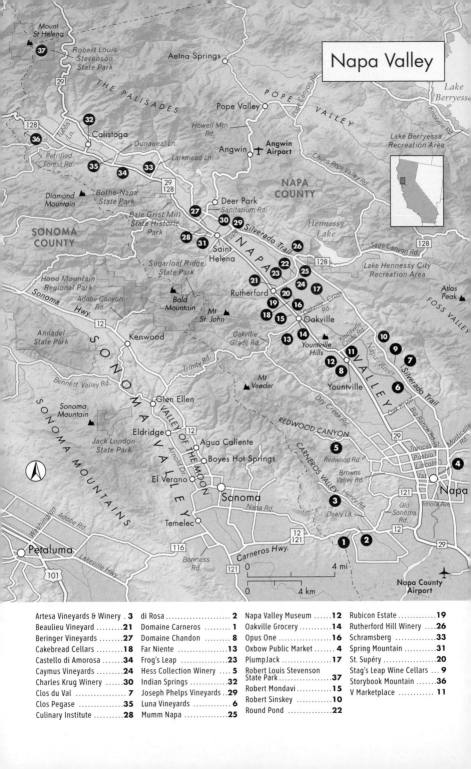

Napa Valley

Mount St Helena 37

Robert Louis Stevenson State Park

THE PALISADES

Aetna Springs

POPE VALLEY

Lake Berryessa

128
36

32 Calistoga

Dunaweal Ln.

Petrified Forest Rd.

35

34

33

Larkmead Ln.

Pope Valley

Howell Mtn Rd.

Angwin · Angwin Airport

Lake Berryessa Recreation Area

Knoxville Rd.

Chiles Pope Valley Rd.

NAPA COUNTY

29
128

Diamond Mountain

Bothe-Napa State Park

Bale Grist Mill State Historic Park

27

30 29 Silverado Trail

Deer Park
Sanitarium Rd.

Hennessy Lake

Sage Canyon Rd.

128

SONOMA COUNTY

28

31

Saint Helena

26

Lake Hennessy City Recreation Area

Atlas Peak

Sugarloaf Ridge State Park

22
23
25

FOSS VALLEY

Hood Mountain Regional Park

Bald Mountain

Mt St. John

21 Rutherford
20
19
18 15

24 17

16

Oakville Cross Rd.

Adobe Canyon Rd.

Sonoma Hwy.

12

Kenwood

Annadel State Park

Oakville Grade Rd.

13

Oakville

14 Yountville Hills

Yountville Cross Rd.

10
9
7
6

Silverado Trail

Oak Knoll

Napa River

Trinity Rd.

Mt Veeder

12
8 Yountville

11

Big Ranch Rd.

Bennett Valley Rd.

Glen Ellen

SONOMA MOUNTAINS

Sonoma Mountain

Eldridge

12

Jack London State Park

VALLEY OF THE MOON

Agua Caliente

Boyes Hot Springs

El Verano

Arnold Dr.

Dry Creek Rd.

REDWOOD CANYON

CARNEROS VALLEY

Redwood Rd.

Browns Valley Rd.

29

5

Henry Rd.

Old Sonoma Rd.

121

Trancas St.
Pueblo
Lincoln

4 Napa

Temelec

Sonoma

Napa Rd.

3

Dealy La.

12

Imola Ave.

Washington

Adobe Rd.

Lakeville Hwy.

116

Bonness Rd.

Carneros Hwy.

121

12
121

1 2

0   4 mi

0   4 km

Napa County Airport

101

Petaluma

Winery Index

Artesa Vineyards & Winery . **3**
Beaulieu Vineyard **21**
Beringer Vineyards **27**
Cakebread Cellars **18**
Castello di Amorosa **34**
Caymus Vineyards **24**
Charles Krug Winery **30**
Clos du Val **7**
Clos Pegase **35**
Culinary Institute **28**

di Rosa **2**
Domaine Carneros **1**
Domaine Chandon **8**
Far Niente **13**
Frog's Leap **23**
Hess Collection Winery ... **5**
Indian Springs **32**
Joseph Phelps Vineyards .**29**
Luna Vineyards **6**
Mumm Napa **25**

Napa Valley Museum ...**12**
Oakville Grocery **14**
Opus One **16**
Oxbow Public Market **4**
PlumpJack **17**
Robert Louis Stevenson
State Park **37**
Robert Mondavi...........**15**
Robert Sinskey **10**
Round Pond **22**

Rubicon Estate **19**
Rutherford Hill Winery **26**
Schramsberg **33**
Spring Mountain **31**
St. Supéry **20**
Stag's Leap Wine Cellars .. **9**
Storybook Mountain **36**
V Marketplace **11**

Climbing ivy and lily pads decorate the Hess Collection's rustic exterior.

com ✉ *Tasting $10–$30* ⊙ *Daily 10–5:30; guided tours daily, hourly 10:30–3:30.*

WHERE TO EAT

$$$
FRENCH
✕ **Angèle.** An 1890s boathouse with a vaulted wood-beam ceiling sets the scene for romance at this cozy French bistro. Though the style is casual—tables are close together, and the warm, crusty bread is plunked right down on the paper-top tables—the food is always well executed. Look for classic French dishes like beef bourguignonne, a rib-eye steak with red wine sauce and french fries, or a starter of *ris de veau* (veal sweetbreads). In fair weather, ask for one of the charming outdoor tables. ✉ *540 Main St.* ☎ *707/252–8115* ⊕ *www.angelerestaurant.com* ▤ *AE, D, DC, MC, V.*

$
AMERICAN
✕ **BarBersQ.** Hardly a down-home ramshackle barbecue shack, this temple to meat in the middle of a shopping center has a clean, modern aesthetic, with the black-and-white photos on the wall and brushed aluminum chairs. The menu of barbecue favorites includes a half or full rack of smoked baby back ribs and a Memphis-style pulled pork sandwich, all served with your choice of three different sauces. The supremely juicy fried chicken, made with free-range chicken and served with mashed potatoes and vinegary collard greens, is also popular. If you can save any room, the root-beer float or sweet potato–pecan pie is a fitting end to a homey meal. Outside seating (on a patio facing the parking lot) is available on fair days. ✉ *3900D Bel Aire Plaza* ☎ *707/224–6600* ⊕ *www.barbersqu.com* ▤ *AE, MC, V.*

10

Where to Eat and Stay in Napa Valley

$$$
ITALIAN
★
X **Bistro Don Giovanni.** At this lively bistro, the Cal-Italian food is simultaneously inventive and comforting: an excellent fritto misto of onions, fennel, calamari, and plump rock shrimp; risotto with scallops and wild mushrooms; pizza with caramelized onions and Gorgonzola; and tender braised lamb on a bed on fried polenta. Dishes roasted in the wood-burning oven are a specialty. Children are unusually welcome here, catered to with crayons and paper-topped tables and a menu with items like pizza topped with cheese, french fries, and "no green stuff." Fodors.com Forum users suggest snagging a table on the covered patio for a "more intimate and quiet" experience. ⊠ *4110 Howard La./Rte. 29* ☎ *707/224–3300* ⊕ *www.bistrodongiovanni.com* ☰ *AE, D, DC, MC, V.*

$$
AMERICAN
★
X **Bounty Hunter.** A triple threat, Bounty Hunter is a wine store, wine bar, and restaurant in one. You can stop by for just a glass of wine from their impressive list—a frequently changing list with 40 available by the glass in both 2- and 5-ounce pours, and 400 by the bottle—but it's best to come with an appetite. A miniscule kitchen means the menu is also small, but every dish is a standout, including the pulled pork and beef brisket sandwiches served with three types of barbecue sauce, the signature beer-can chicken, and meltingly tender St. Louis–style ribs. The space is whimsically rustic, with stuffed game trophies mounted on the wall and leather saddles standing in for seats at a couple of tables. ■**TIP**➔ It's open until midnight on Friday and Saturday, making it a popular spot among locals for a late-night bite. At this writing, plans to expand into the space next door were in the works. ⊠ *975 1st St.* ☎ *707/226–3976* ⊕ *www.bountyhunterwinebar.com* ⚏ *Reservations not accepted* ☰ *AE, MC, V.*

$$$
SPANISH
X **ZuZu.** Ocher-color walls, a weathered wood bar, a faded tile floor, and hammered-tin ceiling panels set the scene for a menu composed almost entirely of tapas. These little dishes, so perfect for sharing, and Latin jazz on the stereo help make this place a popular spot for festive get-togethers. Diners down *cava* (Spanish sparkling wine) or sangria with dishes such as white anchovies with endive, ratatouille, and salt cod with garlic croutons. Reservations aren't accepted, so expect a wait on weekends, when local young adults flood the zone. The *bocadillos* (Spanish-style sandwiches) and empanadas available at lunch make it an inexpensive stop for a midday snack. ⊠ *829 Main St.* ☎ *707/224–8555* ⊕ *www.zuzunapa.com* ⚏ *Reservations not accepted* ☰ *AE, MC, V* ⊘ *No lunch weekends.*

WHERE TO STAY

$–$$
🏠 **Blackbird Inn.** Arts and Crafts style infuses this 1905 building, from the lobby's enormous fieldstone fireplace to the lamps that cast a warm glow over the impressive wooden staircase. The style is continued in the attractive guest rooms, with sturdy turn-of-the-20th-century oak beds and matching night tables, which nonetheless are updated with spacious, modern bathrooms, most with spa bathtubs. The inn is within walking distance of Napa's historic, restaurant-rich downtown area. It tends to book up quickly, so reserve well in advance. **Pros:** gorgeous architecture and period furnishings; convenient to downtown Napa; free DVD library. **Cons:** must be booked well in advance; some rooms

10

are on the small side. ✉ *1755 1st St.* ☎ *707/226–2450 or 888/567–9811* ⊕ *www.blackbirdinnnapa.com* ⤢ *8 rooms* ♿ *In-room: a/c, DVD, Wi-Fi. In-hotel: some pets allowed* ⊟ *AE, D, DC, MC, V* ⦿ *CP.*

$$$$
Fodor's Choice
★

🏠 **Carneros Inn.** Freestanding board-and-batten cottages with rocking chairs on each porch are simultaneously rustic and chic at this luxurious property. Inside, each cottage is flooded with natural light but still manages to maintain privacy, with windows and French doors leading to a private garden. (The suites are actually two-cottage clusters.) Wood-burning fireplaces, ethereal beds topped with Italian linens and pristine white down comforters, and spacious bathrooms with heated slate floors and large indoor-outdoor showers may make it difficult to summon the will to leave the cottage and enjoy the hilltop infinity swimming pool and hot tub. The Hilltop Dining Room, with views of the neighboring vineyards, is open to guests only for breakfast and lunch, but Boon Fly Cafe and FARM, their public restaurants, are popular with visitors throughout the Wine Country. **Pros:** cottages have lots of privacy; beautiful views from the hilltop pool and hot tub; heaters on each private patio encourage lounging outside in the evening. **Cons:** a long drive from destinations up-valley; smallish rooms with limited seating options. ✉ *4048 Sonoma Hwy.* ☎ *707/299–4900* ⊕ *www. thecarnerosinn.com* ⤢ *76 cottages, 10 suites* ♿ *In-room: a/c, refrigerator, DVD, Internet. In-hotel: 3 restaurants, room service, bar, pool, gym, spa, laundry service* ⊟ *AE, D, DC, MC, V.*

$$$$

🏠 **Milliken Creek Inn.** Wine and cheese at sunset set a romantic mood in the intimate lobby, with its terrace overlooking the Napa River and a lush lawn. The chic rooms take a page from the stylebook of British-colonial Asia, with a khaki-and-cream color scheme and gauzy canopies over the beds in some rooms, alongside hydrotherapy spa tubs and some of the fluffiest beds in the Wine Country. All but one have a gas-burning fireplace. A tiny deck overlooking the river is the spot for massages and private yoga classes. In the serene spa, all the treatment rooms, including one used for popular couple's treatments, have river views. **Pros:** soft-as-clouds beds; serene hotel-guests-only spa; breakfast delivered to your room (or wherever you'd like to eat on the grounds); gratuities are not accepted (except at the spa). **Cons:** expensive; road noise can be heard from the admittedly beautiful outdoor areas. ✉ *1815 Silverado Trail* ☎ *707/255–1197 or 800/835–6112* ⊕ *www.millikencreekinn.com* ⤢ *12 rooms* ♿ *In-room: a/c, safe, refrigerator, DVD, Wi-Fi. In-hotel: spa, no kids under 18* ⊟ *AE, D, DC, MC, V* ⦿ *CP.*

$$–$$$

🏠 **Napa River Inn.** Almost everything's close here: this waterfront inn is part of a complex of restaurants, shops, a gallery, and a spa, all within easy walking distance of downtown Napa. Guest rooms spread through three neighboring buildings. Those in the 1884 Hatt Building, in Victorian style, are arguably the most romantic, with deep-red walls, original architectural details such as maple hardwood floors, and old-fashioned slipper tubs. Brighter colors dominate in the rooms of the Plaza and Embarcadero buildings; many of the rooms have river views. Baked goods from the neighboring bakery are delivered to your door for breakfast. **Pros:** a pedestrian walkway connects the hotel to downtown Napa; unusual pet-friendly policy; wide range of room sizes and prices.

Cons: river views could be more scenic; some rooms get noise from nearby restaurants. ⊠ *500 Main St.* ☎ *707/251–8500 or 877/251–8500* ⊕ *www.napariverinn.com* ⋑ *65 rooms, 1 suite* ⚫ *In-room: a/c, safe, refrigerator, DVD (some), Wi-Fi. In-hotel: 4 restaurants, bar, gym, spa, bicycles, laundry service, Internet terminal, some pets allowed* ⊟ *AE, D, DC, MC, V* ⏏◎⏐*CP.*

\$\$\$–\$\$\$\$ 🏨 **Westin Verasa.** Across the street from the Wine Train depot and just behind the Oxbow Public Market is this spacious hotel-condo complex, which considerably expanded the city's once-limited options for full-service hotels when it opened in 2008. Although its style is hardly cutting-edge, its look is sophisticated and soothing, all pristine white bedding and furniture in warm earth tones. Gadgets like Xbox 360s, iPod docking stations, and 32-inch flat-screen televisions are a convenient perk for the technologically inclined, while the heated saltwater pool and hot tub and boccie court are there for those who want to unplug. The attached restaurant, Ken Frank's acclaimed La Toque, is one of the best in town. It's open for dinner only, but a more casual café and wine bar is also open for breakfast and lunch. **Pros:** centrally located in downtown Napa; well-equipped kitchenettes; spacious double-headed showers. **Cons:** \$20 "amenities fee" charged in addition to room rate. ⊠ *1314 Mckinstry St.* ☎ *707/257–1800* ⊕ *www.westin. com/napa* ⋑ *130 rooms, 50 suites* ⚫ *In-room: a/c, safe, kitchen (some), refrigerator (some), DVD, Internet, Wi-Fi. In-hotel: 2 restaurants, room service, bar, pool, gym, laundry service, some pets allowed* ⊟ *AE, D, DC, MC, V.*

> ### MAKING TRACKS IN NAPA
>
> Turn the driving over to someone else—a train conductor. The **Napa Valley Wine Train** (⊠ *1275 McKinstry St.* ☎ *707/253–2111 or 800/427–4124* ⊕ *www.winetrain. com*) runs a scenic route between Napa and St. Helena with several restored 1915–17 Pullman railroad cars. The ride often includes a meal, such as brunch or dinner. While it's no bargain (starting at around \$90 for lunch, \$100 for dinner) and can feel a bit hokey, the train gives you a chance to enjoy the vineyard views without any driving worries.

10

NIGHTLIFE AND THE ARTS

The interior of the 1879 Italianate Victorian **Napa Valley Opera House** isn't quite as majestic as the facade, but the intimate 500-seat venue is still an excellent place to see all sorts of performances, from Pat Metheny and Mandy Patinkin to various dance and theater companies and, yes, even the occasional opera. ⊠ *1030 Main St.* ☎ *707/226–7372* ⊕ *www.napavalleyoperahouse.org.*

SPORTS AND THE OUTDOORS

BICYCLING   Thanks to the scenic country roads that wind through the region, bicycling is a practically perfect way to get around the Wine Country. And whether you're interested in an easy spin to a few wineries or a strenuous haul up a mountainside, there's a way to make it happen. ■ **TIP→** There are almost no designated bike lanes in the Wine Country, though, so be sure to pay attention to traffic.

Napa Valley Bike Tours (✉ *6488 Washington St., Yountville* ☎ *707/944–2953*) will deliver the bikes, which go for $30 to $70 a day, to many hotels in the Napa Valley if you're renting at least two bikes for a full day. One-day guided winery tours are $149.

YOUNTVILLE

13 mi north of the town of Napa on Rte. 29.

These days Yountville is something like Disneyland for food-lovers. It all started with Thomas Keller's French Laundry, one of the best restaurants in the United States. Now Keller is also behind two more casual restaurants a few blocks from his mother ship—and that's only the tip of the iceberg. You could stay here for a week and not exhaust all the options in this tiny town with a big culinary reputation.

Yountville is full of small inns and high-end hotels that cater to those who prefer to walk (not drive) after an extravagant meal. It's also well located for excursions to many big-name Napa wineries, especially those in the Stags Leap District, where big, bold cabernet sauvignons helped put the Napa Valley on the wine-making map.

In between bouts of eating and drinking, you might stop by **V Marketplace** (✉ *6525 Washington St.* ☎ *707/944–2451*). The vine-covered brick complex, which once housed a winery, livery stable, and distillery, contains a smattering of clothing boutiques, art galleries, and gift stores. NapaStyle, a large store, deli, and wine bar, sells cookbooks, luxury food items, and kitchenware, as well as an assortment of prepared foods perfect for picnics. The complex's signature restaurant, Bottega, features the food of celebrity chef Michael Chiarello.

Although it's not worth a long detour, if you need a break from wine tasting you can visit the **Napa Valley Museum** (✉ *55 Presidents Circle* ☎ *707/944–0500* ⊕ *www.napavalleymuseum.org* 🎫 *$4.50* ☉ *Wed.–Mon. 10–5*), next to Domaine Chandon on the grounds of the town's Veterans Home. Downstairs you'll find exhibits on local history, from the Wappo Indians through the pioneer period to modern wine making, while upstairs are rotating art exhibits.

French-owned **Domaine Chandon** claims one of Yountville's prime pieces of real estate, on a knoll west of downtown where whimsical sculptures sprout out of the lawn and ancient oaks shade the winery. Basic tours of the sleek, modern facilities are available for $12 (not including a tasting), but other tours ($30 each), which focusing on various topics (food-and-wine pairing or pinot production, for example), end with a seated tasting. The top-quality sparklers are made using the laborious *méthode champenoise*. To complete the experience, you can order hors d'oeuvres to accompany the wines in the tasting room, which can be ordered either by tasting flights or by the glass. Although Chandon is best known for its bubblies, still wines like their chardonnay, pinot noir, and roséare also worth a try. ✉ *1 California Dr., west of Rte. 29* ☎ *707/944–2280* ⊕ *www.chandon.com* 🎫 *Tasting $5.50–$25 by the glass, $16–$22 by the flight* ☉ *Daily 10–6; tours daily at 11, 1, and 3.*

CLOSE UP

Winespeak

Like any activity, wine making and wine tasting have specialized vocabularies, and most of the terms are actually quite helpful, once you have them down. Here are some core terms to know:

American Viticultural Area (AVA). More commonly termed an "appellation," this is a region with unique soil, climate, and other grape-growing conditions. When a label lists an appellation—Napa Valley or Mt. Veeder, for example—at least 75% of the grapes used to make the wine must come from that region.

Aroma and bouquet. Aroma is the fruit-derived scent of young wine. It diminishes with fermentation and becomes a more complex **bouquet** as the wine ages.

Corked. Describes wine that is flawed by the musty, wet-cardboard flavor imparted by cork mold.

Estate bottled. A wine entirely made by one winery at a single facility. The grapes must come from the winery's own vineyards within the same appellation (which must be printed on the label).

Horizontal tasting. A tasting of several different wines of the same vintage.

Library wine. An older vintage that the winery has put aside to sell at a later date.

Méthode champenoise. The traditional, time-consuming method of making sparkling wines that are fermented in individual bottles.

Oaky. A vanilla-woody flavor that develops when wine is aged in oak barrels. Too much overpowers the other flavors.

Reserve wine. Fuzzy term applied by vintners to indicate that a wine is better in some way (through aging, source of the grapes, etc.) than others from their winery.

Table wine. Any wine that has at least 7% but not more than 14% alcohol by volume. The term doesn't necessarily imply anything about the wine's quality or price—both super-premium and jug wines can be labeled as table wine.

Tannins. These natural grape compounds produce a sensation of drying or astringency in the mouth and throat.

Terroir. French for "soil." Typically used to describe the soil and climate conditions that influence the quality and characteristics of grapes and wine.

Varietal. A wine that takes its name from the grape variety from which it is predominantly made. California wines that qualify are almost always labeled with the variety of the source grape.

Vertical tasting. A tasting of several wines of different vintages.

Vinification. Wine making, the process by which grapes are made into wine.

Vintage. The grape harvest of a given year, and the year in which the grapes are harvested. A vintage date on a bottle indicates the year in which the grapes were harvested rather than the year in which the wine was bottled.

Viticulture. The cultivation of grapes.

10

It was the 1973 cabernet sauvignon produced by **Stag's Leap Wine Cellars** that put the winery—and the California wine industry—on the map by placing first in the famous Paris tasting of 1976. A visit to the winery is a no-frills affair; visitors in the tasting room are clearly serious about tasting wine and aren't interested in distractions like a gift shop. It costs $30 to taste the top-of-the-line wines, including their limited-production estate-grown cabernets, a few of which sell for well over $100. If you're interested in more modestly priced wines, try the $15 tasting, which usually includes a sauvignon blanc, chardonnay, merlot, and cabernet. ⊠ *5766 Silverado Trail, Napa* ☎ *707/265–2441* ⊕ *www.cask23.com* 🖃 *Tasting $15–$30, tour $40* ⊙ *Daily 10–4:30; tour by appointment.*

Robert Sinskey Vineyards makes well-regarded cabernet blends from their all-organic, certified biodynamic vineyards, as well as a dry, refreshing pinot gris, gewürztraminer, Riesling, and pinot blanc blend. However, it's best known for its intense, brambly pinot noirs, grown in the cooler Carneros District, where the grape thrives. The influence of Robert's wife, Maria Helm Sinskey—a chef and cookbook author—is evident during the tastings, which come with a few bites of food paired with each wine (her books and other culinary items are also available in the gift shop, next to the open kitchen). But for the best sense of how Sinskey wines pair with food, reserve a spot on the culinary tour, which ends with local cheeses and charcuterie served with the wines. ⊠ *6320 Silverado Trail, Napa* ☎ *707/944–9090* ⊕ *www.robertsinskey.com* 🖃 *Tasting $25, tour $30–$50* ⊙ *Daily 10–4:30; tour by appointment.*

WHERE TO EAT

$$$$
AMERICAN
Fodor's Choice
★

✕ **Ad Hoc.** When superstar chef Thomas Keller opened this relatively casual spot in 2006, he meant to run it for only six months until he opened a burger joint in the same space—but locals were so charmed by the homey food that they clamored for the stopgap to stay. Now a single, seasonal fixed-price menu ($49) is served nightly, with a slightly less expensive menu but equally hearty meal served for Sunday brunch. The selection might include a juicy pork loin and buttery polenta, served family style, or a delicate *panna cotta* with a citrus glaze. The dining room is warmly low-key, with zinc-top tables, wine served in tumblers, and rock and jazz on the stereo. If you just can't wait to know what's going be served before you visit, you can call a day in advance for the menu. ⊠ *6476 Washington St.* ☎ *707/944–2487* ⊕ *www.adhocrestaurant.com* ▭ *AE, MC, V* ⊙ *No lunch Mon.–Sat.; no dinner Tues. and Wed.*

$$$
ITALIAN
Fodor's Choice
★

✕ **Bottega.** At this lively trattoria, the menu is simultaneously soulful and inventive, transforming local ingredients into regional Italian dishes with a twist. The antipasti in particular shine: you can order olives grown on chef Michael Chiarello's own property in St. Helena, house-made charcuterie, or a creamy *burrata,* mozzarella cheese wrapped around a creamy center, which is served with meaty mushrooms and topped with beads of "caviar" made from balsamic vinegar. Potato gnocchi might be served with duck and a chestnut ragù, and hearty main courses like braised short ribs may come on a bed of spinach prepared with preserved lemons. The vibe is more festival than formal, with exposed brick walls, an open kitchen, and paper-topped tables, but service is spot on, and the reasonably priced wine list offers lots of interesting choices from both Italy and California. ⊠ *6525 Washington St.* ☎ *707/945–1050* ⊕ *www.botteganapavalley.com* ▤ *AE, MC, V* ⊙ *No lunch Mon.*

$$$
FRENCH
✕ **Bouchon.** The team that brought French Laundry to its current pinnacle is also behind this place, where everything—the lively and crowded zinc bar, the elbow-to-elbow seating, the traditional French onion soup—could have come straight from a Parisian bistro. Roast chicken with mustard greens and fingerling potatoes and steamed mussels served with crispy, addictive *frites* (french fries) are among the hearty dishes served in the high-ceilinged room. ■**TIP→** Late-night meals from a limited menu are served until 12:30 AM—a rarity in the Wine Country, where it's often difficult to find a place to eat after 10. ⊠ *6534 Washington St.* ☎ *707/944–8037* ⊕ *www.bouchonbistro.com* ▤ *AE, MC, V.*

$$$
AMERICAN
✕ **Étoile.** Housed at Domaine Chandon, this quietly elegant stunner seems built for romance, with delicate orchids on each table and views of the beautiful wooded winery grounds from the large windows. After a few years of being off the radar of many local critics, the restaurant has gotten more attention lately under the young chef Perry Hoffman, who turns out sophisticated California cuisine. Starters like poached lobster with radishes, Asian pear, and pearl barley play with a variety of textures, and luxe ingredients like shavings of black truffle dress up a perfectly cooked beef tenderloin. Four- and six-course tasting menus can be ordered with or without wine pairings. The wine list naturally features plenty of Domaine Chandon sparklers, but it's strong in wines from throughout California as well. ⊠ *1 California Dr.* ☎ *888/242–6366* ⊕ *www.chandon.com/etoile-restaurant* ▤ *AE, D, MC, V* ⊙ *Closed Tues. and Wed. and Jan.*

$$$$
AMERICAN
Fodor's Choice
★
✕ **French Laundry.** An old stone building laced with ivy houses the most acclaimed restaurant in Napa Valley—and, indeed, one of the most highly regarded in the country. The restaurant's two prix-fixe menus (both $240), one of which is vegetarian, vary, but "oysters and pearls," a silky dish of pearl tapioca with oysters and white sturgeon caviar, is a signature starter. Some courses rely on luxe ingredients like foie gras, while others take humble foods like fava beans and elevate them to art. Reservations at French Laundry are hard-won, and not accepted more than two months in advance. ■**TIP→** Call two months ahead to the day at 10 AM on the dot. Didn't get a reservation? Call on the day you'd like to dine here to be considered if there's a cancellation. ⊠ *6640 Washington St.* ☎ *707/944–2380* ⌕ *Reservations essential, jacket required* ⊕ *www. frenchlaundry.com* ▤ *AE, MC, V* ⊙ *Closed 1st 2 or 3 wks in Jan. No lunch Mon.–Thurs.*

10

$$
AMERICAN
✕ **Mustards Grill.** There's not an ounce of pretension at Cindy Pawlcyn's longtime Napa favorite, despite the fact that it's filled every day and night with fans of her hearty cuisine. The menu mixes updated renditions of traditional American dishes, such as baby back pork ribs and a lemon-lime tart piled high with browned meringue, with innovative choices such as sweet corn tamales with tomatillo-avocado salsa and pumpkin seeds. A black-and-white marble tile floor and upbeat

artwork set a scene that one Fodors.com reader describes as "pure fun, if not fancy." ⊠ *7399 St. Helena Hwy./Rte. 29, 1 mi north of town* ☎ *707/944–2424* ⊕ *www.mustardsgrill.com* ⌕ *Reservations essential* ⊟ *AE, D, DC, MC, V.*

WHERE TO STAY

$$$$ ⊞ **Bardessono.** Although Bardessono bills itself as the "greenest luxury hotel in America," there's nothing spartan about its large, spare rooms, arranged around four landscaped courtyards, which have luxurious organic white bedding, gas fireplaces, and huge bathrooms with walnut floors. It's got all the high-tech touches you'd expect for a property that opened in 2009—speakers for your iPhone, a flat-panel TV, and fancy spa tubs—and a few you wouldn't, like motion sensors that detect when you're gone and adjust the blinds for energy efficiency. Service is smooth, from the valet who takes your car to those who staff the 75-foot-long rooftop lap pool area April through October, serving food and drinks to those lounging in the cabanas. At the hotel's restaurant, chef Sean O'Toole uses largely local ingredients (some grown by the hotel itself) to concoct a seasonal menu of California fare with an adventurous twist. **Pros:** large rooftop lap pool; exciting restaurant on-site; polished service. **Cons:** expensive. ⊠ *6526 Yount St.* ☎ *707/204–6000* ⊕ *www. bardessono.com* ↰ *50 rooms, 12 suites* ⌕ *In-room: a/c, safe, Internet, Wi-Fi. In-hotel: restaurant, room service, bar, pool, spa, bicycles, laundry service, some pets allowed* ⊟ *AE, D, DC, MC, V.*

$$$–$$$$ ⊞ **Hotel Luca.** Although this 20-room newcomer to Yountville just opened in December 2009, the property embodies a rustic Tuscan style through and through, with dark wood furniture and soothing decor in brown and sage. Rooms are clustered around a courtyard, which is warmed by a fireplace when the weather demands it. Uncommonly spacious bathrooms with large tubs and separate showers, warmed by radiant floor heating, invite lingering in the fluffy robes and slippers. A wide variety of spa services are available in the small spa or in your room. The hotel's excellent restaurant, Cantinetta Piero, serves soul-warming Tuscan fare, such as pastas, house-made preserved meats, and thin-crust pizzas from a wood-burning oven. **Pros:** extremely comfortable beds; attentive service; breakfast, included in rates, is served in the restaurant or delivered to your room. **Cons:** rooms are soundproofed, but outdoor areas get some traffic noise. ⊠ *6774 Washington St.* ☎ *707/944–8080* ⊕ *www.hotellucanapa.com* ↰ *20 rooms* ⌕ *In-room: a/c, refrigerator, safe, Wi-Fi. In-hotel: restaurant, room service, bar, pool, spa, gym, laundry service* ⊟ *AE, D, MC, V.* ⦿ *BP.*

$–$$ ⊞ **Maison Fleurie.** If you'd like to be within easy walking distance of most
★ of Yountville's best restaurants, and possibly score a great bargain, look into this casual, comfortable inn. Rooms share a French country style (picture toile bedspreads, wooden armoires, and trompe-l'oeil paintings on the walls) but vary dramatically in size and amenities. The largest have a private entrance, deck, fireplace, and jetted bathtub big enough for two. ■**TIP→** For a much lower rate, however, you can get one of the tiny but well-kept rooms with a small shower but no bathtub—and save for a French Laundry meal instead. **Pros:** smallest rooms are some of the most affordable in town; free bike rental; refrigerator stocked with free soda.

Cons: breakfast room can be crowded at peak times; bedding could be nicer. ✉ *6529 Yount St.* ☎ *800/788–0369* 🌐 *www.maisonfleurienapa.com* ⇨ *13 rooms* ♨ *In-room: a/c, refrigerator (some), DVD (some), no TV (some), Wi-Fi. In-hotel: pool, bicycles* ▭ *AE, D, MC, V* ꟾ◎ꟾ *CP.*

¢ **Napa Valley Railway Inn.** Budget minded travelers and those with kids appreciate these basic accommodations just steps away from most of Yountville's best restaurants. Actual railcars, more than a hundred years old, house nine long, narrow rooms that have a bit more charm than your average motel. Most have armoires or other turn-of-the-20th-century furniture, as well as small flat-panel TVs and sparkling-clean bathrooms. A coffee shop in an adjacent railcar sells beverages and pastries. **Pros:** central Yountville location; guests have access to adjacent gym. **Cons:** minimal service, since the office is often unstaffed; rooms on the parking-lot side get some noise. ✉ *6523 Washington St.* ☎ *707/944–2000* 🌐 *www.napavalleyrailwayinn.com* ⇨ *9 rooms* ♨ *In-room: no phone, a/c, refrigerator, Wi-Fi* ▭ *AE, MC, V.*

$$$–$$$$ ★ **Villagio Inn & Spa.** The luxury here is quiet and refined, not flashy. Stroll past the fountains and clusters of low buildings to reach the pool, where automated misters cool the sunbathers. Streamlined furnishings, subdued color schemes, and high ceilings enhance a sense of spaciousness in the guest rooms. Each room also has a fireplace and, beyond louvered doors, a balcony or patio. The spa has huge "suites" big enough for small groups, as well as individual treatment rooms, spread out over 13,000 square feet. Rates include afternoon tea, a bottle of wine, and a generous buffet breakfast—and as the hotel is near the town center, you'll be right next to all those outstanding restaurants. **Pros:** amazing buffet breakfast; no extra charge for hotel guests to use the spa facilities; steps away from Yountville's best restaurants. **Cons:** can be bustling with large groups; you can hear the highway from many of the room's balconies or patios. ✉ *6481 Washington St.* ☎ *707/944–8877 or 800/351–1133* 🌐 *www.villagio.com* ⇨ *86 rooms, 26 suites* ♨ *In-room: a/c, refrigerator, DVD, Internet, Wi-Fi. In-hotel: room service, bar, tennis courts, pool, spa, bicycles, laundry service,* ▭ *AE, D, DC, MC, V* ꟾ◎ꟾ *CP.*

$$$–$$$$ **Vintage Inn.** Rooms in this lavish inn are housed in two-story villas scattered around a lush, landscaped 3½-acre property. French fabrics and plump upholstered chairs outfit the spacious, airy guest rooms. Those on the second floor have vaulted beam ceilings, and all have a private patio or balcony, a fireplace, and a whirlpool tub in the bathroom. Some private patios have vineyard views. Rates include a bottle of wine, a buffet breakfast, and afternoon tea and scones. **Pros:** spacious bathrooms with spa tubs; lavish breakfast buffet; luscious bedding. **Cons:** some exterior rooms get highway noise; pool area is smaller than the one at its sister property, the Villagio Inn & Spa. ✉ *6541 Washington St.* ☎ *707/944–1112 or 800/351–1133* 🌐 *www.vintageinn.com* ⇨ *68 rooms, 12 suites* ♨ *In-room: a/c, refrigerator, DVD, Internet, Wi-Fi. In-hotel: room service, bar, tennis courts, pool, bicycles, laundry service, some pets allowed* ▭ *AE, D, DC, MC, V* ꟾ◎ꟾ *CP.*

OAKVILLE

2 mi west of Yountville on Rte. 29.

There are three reasons to visit the town of Oakville: its gourmet grocery store; its scenic mountain road; and its magnificent, highly exclusive wineries.

The **Oakville Grocery** (✉ *7856 St. Helena Hwy./Rte. 29* ☎ *707/944–8802*), built in 1881 as a general store, now carries a surprisingly wide range of unusual and chichi groceries and prepared foods. Unbearable crowds pack the narrow aisles on weekends, but it's still a fine place to sit on a bench out front and sip an espresso between winery visits.

Along the mountain range that divides Napa and Sonoma, the **Oakville Grade** (✉ *West of Rte. 29*) is a twisting half-hour route with breathtaking views of both valleys. Although the surface of the road is good, it can be difficult to negotiate at night, and the continual curves mean that it's not ideal for those who suffer from motion sickness.

The combined venture of the late California winemaker Robert Mondavi and the late French baron Philippe de Rothschild, **Opus One** produces only one wine: a big, inky Bordeaux blend that was the first of Napa's ultra-premium wines, fetching unheard-of prices before it was overtaken by cult wines like Screaming Eagle. The winery's futuristic limestone-clad structure, built into the hillside, seems to be pushing itself out of the earth. Although the tour, which focuses on why it costs so much to produce this exceptional wine, can come off as "stuffy" (in the words of one Fodors.com reader), the facilities are undoubtedly impressive, with gilded mirrors, exotic orchids, and a large semicircular cellar modeled on the Château Mouton Rothschild winery in France. You can also taste the current vintage without the tour ($30), as long as you've called ahead for a reservation. ■ TIP→ Take your glass up to the rooftop terrace if you want to appreciate the views out over the vineyards. ✉ *7900 St. Helena Hwy./Rte. 29* ☎ *707/944–9442* ⊕ *www.opusonewinery.com* 🍷 *Tour $35* ☉ *Daily 10–4; tasting and tour by appointment.*

The arch at the center of the sprawling Mission-style building at **Robert Mondavi** perfectly frames the lawn and the vineyard behind, inviting a stroll under the lovely arcades. If you've never been on a winery tour before, the comprehensive 70- to 90-minute tour ($25), followed by a seated tasting, is a good way to learn about enology, as well as the late Robert Mondavi's role in California wine making (shorter tours are also available). You can also head straight for one of the two tasting rooms. Serious wine lovers should definitely consider springing for the $30 reserve-room tasting, where you can enjoy four tastes of Mondavi's top-of-the-line wines, including both the current vintage and several previous vintages of the reserve cabernet that cemented the winery's reputation. Concerts, mostly jazz and R&B, take place in summer on the lawn; call ahead for tickets. ✉ *7801 St. Helena Hwy./Rte. 29* ☎ *888/766–6328* ⊕ *www.robertmondaviwinery.com* 🍷 *Tasting $15–$30, tour $15–$50* ☉ *Daily 10–5; tour times vary.*

Fodor's Choice
★ Though the fee for the combined tour and tasting is at the high end, **Far Niente** is especially worth visiting if you're tired of elbowing your way

Far Niente's wine cellars have a touch of ballroom elegance.

through crowded tasting rooms and are looking for a more personal experience. Here you're welcomed by name and treated to a glimpse of one of the most beautiful Napa properties. Small groups are shepherded through the historic 1885 stone winery, including some of the 40,000 square feet of caves, for a lesson on the labor-intensive method for making Far Niente's two wines, a cabernet blend and a chardonnay. (The latter is made without undergoing malolactic fermentation, so it doesn't have that buttery taste that's characteristic of many California chards.) The next stop is the Carriage House, where you can see the founder's gleaming collection of classic cars. The tour ends with a seated tasting of wines and cheeses, capped by a sip of the spectacular Dolce, a late-harvest dessert wine made by Far Niente's sister winery. ⊠ *1350 Acacia Dr.* ☎ *707/944–2861* ⊕ *www.farniente.com* ✉ *$50* ☉ *Tasting and tour by appointment.*

In contrast to its snootier neighbors, **PlumpJack** is fun, casual, and sporty. With its metal chandelier and wall hangings, the tasting room looks like it could be the stage set for a modern Shakespeare production. (The name "PlumpJack" is a nod to Shakespeare's Falstaff.) The reserve chardonnay has a good balance of baked fruit and fresh citrus flavors, while a merlot is blended with a bit of cabernet sauvignon, giving the wine enough tannins to ensure it can be aged for another five years or more. If the tasting room is crowded, take a breather under the shady arbor on the back patio, where you can enjoy a close-up view of the vines. ⊠ *620 Oakville Cross Rd.* ☎ *707/945–1220* ⊕ *www.plumpjack. com* ✉ *Tasting $10* ☉ *Daily 10–4.*

RUTHERFORD

2 mi northwest of Oakville on Rte. 29.

From a fast-moving car, Rutherford is a quick blur of vineyards and a rustic barn or two, but don't speed by this tiny hamlet. With its singular microclimate and soil, this is an important viticultural center, with more big-name wineries than you can shake a corkscrew at. Cabernet sauvignon is king here. The well-drained, loamy soil is ideal for those vines, and since this part of the valley gets plenty of sun, the grapes develop exceptionally intense flavors. The late, great winemaker André Tchelistcheff claimed that "it takes Rutherford dust to grow great cabernet."

★ It's not all grapevines here—you can switch your fruit focus to olives at **Round Pond.** This small farm grows five varieties of Italian olives and three types of Spanish olives. Within an hour of being handpicked, the olives are crushed in the mill on the property to produce pungent, peppery oils that are later blended and sold. Call at least a day or two in advance to arrange a tour of the mill followed by an informative tasting, during which you can sample several types of oil, both alone and with Round Pond's own red-wine vinegars and other tasty foods. ■TIP→ If you can arrange to visit between mid-November and the end of December, you might be lucky enough to see the mill in action. ⊠ *877 Rutherford Rd.* ☎ *888/302–2575* ⊕ *www.roundpond.com* ☒ *Tour $25* ☉ *Tour by appointment.*

Jack and Dolores Cakebread snapped up the property at **Cakebread Cellars** in 1973, after Jack fell in love with the area while visiting on a photography assignment. Since then, they've been making luscious chardonnays, as well as merlot, a great sauvignon blanc, and a beautifully complex cabernet sauvignon. You must make an appointment for a tasting, which might take place during a stroll through the winery's barrel room and crush pad and past Dolores's kitchen garden, or it could be a seated event in the winery's modern wing, where an elevator is crafted out of a stainless-steel fermentation tank and the ceiling is lined with thousands of corks. ⊠ *8300 St. Helena Hwy.* ☎ *707/963–5221* ⊕ *www. cakebread.com* ☒ *Tasting $10–$30, tour $25* ☉ *Daily 10–4:30; tasting and tour by appointment.*

It's the house *The Godfather* built. Filmmaker Francis Ford Coppola began his wine-making career in 1975, when he bought part of the historic, renowned Inglenook estate. He eventually reunited the original Inglenook land and snagged the ivy-covered 19th-century château to boot. In 2006 he renamed the property **Rubicon Estate,** intending to focus on his premium wines, including the namesake cabernet sauvignon–based blend. (The less expensive wines are showcased at the Francis Ford Coppola Winery in Sonoma County's Geyserville.) The many tours cover topics that include the history of the estate, the Rutherford climate and geology, and food-and-wine pairings, but many just come to taste in the opulent, high-ceilinged tasting room. ⊠ *1991 St. Helena Hwy./Rte. 29* ☎ *707/963–9099* ⊕ *www.rubiconestate.com* ☒ *$15–$50* ☉ *Daily 10–5; call for tour times.*

Your instinct may be to enter the beautifully restored 1882 Queen Anne Victorian at **St. Supéry** looking for the tasting room; actually the

Frog's Leap's picturesque country charm extends all the way to the white picket fence.

wines are being poured in the building behind it, a bland, unappealing, officelike structure. But you'll likely forgive the atmospheric lapse once you taste their fine sauvignon blancs, merlots, and chardonnays, as well as a couple of unusual wines that are made primarily of either cabernet franc or petit verdot, both of which are usually used for blending with cabernet sauvignon. An excellent, free self-guided tour also allows you a peek at the barrel and fermentation rooms, as well as a gallery of rotating art exhibits. At the "Smell-a-Vision" station you can test your ability to identify different smells that might be present in wine. ⊠ 8440 St. Helena Hwy. S/Rte. 29 ☎ 707/963–4507 ⊕ www.stsupery. com ✎ Tasting $15–$25 ☉ Daily 10–5.

10

The cabernet sauvignon produced at the ivy-covered **Beaulieu Vineyard** is a benchmark of the Napa Valley. The legendary André Tchelistcheff, who helped define the California style of wine making, worked his magic here from 1938 until his death in 1973. This helps explain why Beaulieu's flagship, the Georges de Latour Private Reserve Cabernet Sauvignon, still garners high marks from major wine publications. The zinfandels, merlots, and chardonnays being poured in the main tasting room are notably good. Still, it's worth paying the extra money to taste that special cabernet in the more luxe, less-crowded reserve tasting room. ⊠ 1960 St. Helena Hwy./Rte. 29 ☎ 707/967–5200 ⊕ www. bvwines.com ✎ Tasting $10–$30 ☉ Daily 10–5.

♺
Fodor's Choice
★

Frog's Leap is the perfect place for wine novices to begin their education. The owner, John Williams, maintains a goofy sense of humor about wine that translates into an entertaining yet informative experience. You'll also find some fine zinfandel, cabernet sauvignon, merlot, chardonnay, sauvignon blanc, rosé, and also their take on the German dessert wine Trockenbeerenauslese. The winery includes a red barn built in 1884, 5 acres of organic gardens, an ecofriendly visitor center, and, naturally, a frog pond topped with lily pads. Tastings accompanied by the highly recommended tour are free, but if you just want a seated tasting of their wines (on a porch overlooking the garden, weather permitting), you pay $15. ⊠ *8815 Conn Creek Rd.* ☎ *707/963–4704* ⊕ *www. frogsleap.com* ☜ *Tasting and tour free; tasting alone, $15* ☉ *Mon.–Sat. 10–4; tour by appointment.*

Caymus Vineyards is run by wine master Chuck Wagner, who started making wine on the property in 1972. His family, however, had been farming in the valley since 1906. Though they make a fine zinfandel and sauvignon blanc, cabernet is the winery's claim to fame, a ripe, powerful wine that's known for its consistently high quality. ■**TIP→ There's no tour and you have to reserve to taste, but it's still worth planning ahead to visit, because the low-key seated tasting (limited to 10 guests) is a great opportunity to learn about the valley's cabernet artistry.** ⊠ *8700 Conn Creek Rd.* ☎ *707/967–3010* ⊕ *www.caymus.com* ☜ *Tasting $25* ☉ *Sales daily 10–4; tasting by appointment.*

Mumm Napa is one of California's best-known sparkling-wine producers. But enjoying the bubbly from the light-filled tasting room—available in either single flutes ($8–$15) or by the flight ($16–$20)—isn't the only reason to visit. There's also an excellent photography gallery with 30 Ansel Adams prints and rotating exhibits. You can even take that glass of wonderfully crisp Brut Rosé with you as wander. For a leisurely tasting of a flight of their library wines while seated on their outdoor terrace ($30), reserve in advance. ⊠ *8445 Silverado Trail* ☎ *707/967–7700* ⊕ *www.mummnapa.com* ☜ *Tasting $8–$30, tour free–$20* ☉ *Daily 10–5; tour daily at 10 (free; tasting not included), 11, 1, and 3 ($20, tasting included).*

Rutherford Hill Winery is a merlot lover's paradise in a cabernet sauvignon world. When the winery's founders were deciding what grapes to plant, they discovered that the climate and soil conditions of their vineyards resembled those of Pomerol, a region of Bordeaux where merlot is king. The wine caves here are some of the most extensive of any California winery—nearly a mile of tunnels and passageways. You can get a glimpse of the tunnels and the 8,000 barrels inside on the tours, then cap your visit with a picnic in their oak, olive, or madrone groves. With views over the valley from a perch high on a hill, the picnic grounds are more charming than many others in Napa, which tend to be rather close to one of the busy thoroughfares. ⊠ *200 Rutherford Hill Rd., east of Silverado Trail* ☎ *707/963–1871* ⊕ *www.rutherfordhill.com* ☜ *Tasting $15–$30, tour $20* ☉ *Daily 10–5; tour weekdays at 11:30, 1:30, and 3:30, weekends at 11:30, 12:30, 1:30, 2:30, and 3:30.*

WHERE TO STAY

$$$$ 🏨 **Auberge du Soleil.** Taking a cue from the olive-tree-studded landscape,
★ this renowned hotel cultivates a Mediterranean look. It's luxury as simplicity: earth-tone tile floors, heavy wood furniture, and terra-cotta colors. This spare style is backed with lavish amenities, though, such

as private terraces and truly grand bathrooms. The Auberge du Soleil restaurant has an impressive wine list and serves a Mediterranean-inflected menu that relies largely on local produce. **Pros:** stunning views over the valley; spectacular pool and spa areas; the most expensive suites are fit for a superstar. **Cons:** stratospheric prices; the two least expensive rooms (in the main house) get some noise from the bar and restaurant. ⊠ *180 Rutherford Hill Rd., off Silverado Trail north of Rte. 128* ☎ *707/963–1211 or 800/348–5406* ⊕ *www.aubergedusoleil.com* ⤴ *31 rooms, 21 suites* ⬧ *In-room: a/c, safe, refrigerator, DVD, Internet, Wi-Fi. In-hotel: 2 restaurants, room service, bar, tennis court, pool, gym, spa, laundry service* ⊟ *AE, D, DC, MC, V* ⓘ *BP.*

WORD OF MOUTH

"For wineries to visit, Napa is Cab Country. Mondavi, BV, Inglenook (now Rubicon) and Heitz helped put the Napa Valley on the world's wine map. Others now include Silver Oak, Clos du Val, Stag's Leap, Opus One, Groth, and Caymus.... You should take a tour somewhere. Both Mondavi and Groth give good tours about cabernet production." —Otis_B_Driftwood

ST. HELENA

2 mi northwest of Oakville on Rte. 29.

Downtown St. Helena is a symbol of how well life can be lived in the Wine Country. Sycamore trees arch over Main Street (Route 29), a funnel of outstanding restaurants and tempting boutiques. At the north end of town looms the hulking stone building of the Culinary Institute of America. Weathered stone and brick buildings from the late 1800s give off that gratifying whiff of history.

By the time pioneer winemaker Charles Krug planted grapes in St. Helena around 1860, quite a few vineyards already existed in the area. Today the town is hemmed in by wineries, and you could easily spend days visiting vintners within a few miles.

The West Coast headquarters of the **Culinary Institute of America,** the country's leading school for chefs, are in the **Greystone Winery,** an imposing building that was the largest stone winery in the world when it was built in 1889. The upper floors are reserved for students and teachers, but on the ground floor you can check out the quirky corkscrew display and shop at a well-stocked culinary store that tempts aspiring chefs with gleaming gadgets and an impressive selection of cookbooks. One-hour cooking demonstrations take place regularly, usually twice a day on weekends and occasionally more often; call or visit the Web site for times and reservations. ⊠ *2555 Main St.* ☎ *707/967–1100* ⊕ *www. ciachef.edu* ⤴ *Free, demonstrations $15* ⊙ *Restaurant Sun.–Thurs. 11:30–9, Fri. and Sat. 11:30–10; store and museum daily 10–6.*

Fodor's Choice
★

Although an appointment is required to taste at **Joseph Phelps Vineyards,** it's worth the trouble. In fair weather the casual, self-paced wine tastings are held on the terrace of a huge, modern barnlike building with stunning views down the slopes over oak trees and orderly vines. Though the sauvignon blanc and viognier are good, the blockbuster wines are reds.

10

✉ *200 Taplin Rd.* ☎ *707/963–2745* ⊕ *www.jpvwines.com* 🍷 *Tasting $20* ⊙ *Weekdays 9–5, weekends 9–4; tasting by appointment.*

Arguably the most beautiful winery in Napa Valley, the 1876 **Beringer Vineyards** is also the oldest continuously operating property. In 1884 Frederick and Jacob Beringer built the Rhine House Mansion to serve as Frederick's family home. Today it serves as the reserve tasting room, where you can sample four wines amid the Belgian art-nouveau hand-carved oak and walnut furniture and stained-glass windows, choosing from among wines such as a limited-release chardonnay, a few big but very drinkable cabernets, and a luscious white dessert wine named Nightingale. Another, less expensive tasting takes place in the less atmospheric but also historic original stone winery. ■ **TIP→** If you're looking for an undiscovered gem, pass this one by, but first-time visitors to the valley will learn a lot about the history of wine making in the region on the introductory tour. Longer tours, which might pass through a demonstration vineyard or end with a seated tasting in the wine-aging tunnels, are also offered a few times a day. ✉ *2000 Main St./Rte. 29* ☎ *707/963–4812* ⊕ *www.beringer.com* 🍷 *Tasting $15–$25, tour $15–$40* ⊙ *May 30–Oct. 23, daily 10–6; Oct. 24–May 29, daily 10–5; call for tour times.*

The first winery founded in the Napa Valley, **Charles Krug Winery,** opened in 1861 when Count Haraszthy lent Krug a small cider press. Today the Peter Mondavi family runs it. At this writing, tours have been suspended indefinitely because a major earthquake retrofit project is in the works, but you can still come for tastings. Though the tasting room is fairly modest, the knowledgeable and friendly servers ensure a relaxed visit. The winery is best known for its lush red Bordeaux blends, but its zinfandel is also good—or go for something unusual with the New Zealand–style sauvignon blanc. Its zingy flavor of citrus and tropical fruit is rare in wines from this area. ✉ *2800 N. Main St.* ☎ *707/963–5057* ⊕ *www.charleskrug.com* 🍷 *Tasting $10–$20* ⊙ *Daily 10:30–5.*

★ Hidden off a winding road behind a security gate, **Spring Mountain Vineyard** has the feeling of a private estate in the countryside, even though it's only a few miles from downtown St. Helena. Though some sauvignon blanc, pinot noir, and syrah is produced, the calling card here is cabernet—big, chewy wines that demand some time in the bottle but promise great things. Tours meander through the beautiful property, from the cellars to the beautifully preserved 1885 mansion. If you're interested in finding out what their wines taste like after years in the bottle, set aside at least an hour and a half for your visit and spring for the $50 reserve tasting, when they'll pour wines of various vintages while you're seated in the mansion's dining room. ✉ *2805 Spring Mountain Rd.* ☎ *707/967–4188* ⊕ *www.springmtn.com* 🍷 *Tour and tasting $25–$50* ⊙ *Tour and tasting by appointment.*

WHERE TO EAT

$$ ✗ **Go Fish.** Prolific restaurateur Cindy Pawlcyn is the big name behind
SEAFOOD one of the few restaurants in the Wine Country to specialize in sea-
★ food. You can either sit at the long marble bar and watch the chefs whip up inventive sushi rolls and raw-bar bites, or head into the dining

room to study the mouthwatering menu, with listings that include a French-inflected sole almondine and Asian-inspired dishes like miso-marinated black cod. Hearty sandwiches like the bigeye tuna Reuben are popular at lunch. The large, lively space works a modern-chic look, with stainless-steel lamps and comfortable banquettes. ⊠ *641 Main St.* ☎ *707/963–0700* ⊕ *www.gofishrestaurant.net* ⊟ *AE, D, DC, MC, V.*

¢–$

AMERICAN

★

✕ **Gott's Roadside Tray Gourmet.** A slick 1950s-style outdoor hamburger stand goes upscale at this hugely popular spot, where locals are willing to brave long lines to order juicy burgers, root-beer floats, and garlic fries. There are also plenty of choices you wouldn't have found 50 years ago, such as the ahi tuna burger and chicken club with pesto mayo. Try to get here early or late for lunch, or all the shaded picnic tables on the lawn might be filled with happy throngs. Lines are usually shorter at the Gott's in downtown Napa's Oxbow Public Market. ⊠ *933 Main St.* ☎ *707/963–3486* ⊕ *www.gottsroadside.com* ⊟ *AE, MC, V.*

$$$$

AMERICAN

✕ **Martini House.** Beautiful and boisterous, St. Helena's most stylish restaurant fills a converted 1923 Craftsman-style home, where earthy colors are made even warmer by the glow of three fireplaces. Woodsy ingredients such as chanterelles or juniper berries might accompany braised veal sweetbreads or a hearty grilled loin of venison. Inventive salads and delicate desserts such as the blood-orange sorbet demonstrate chef-owner Todd Humphries's range. In warm weather, angle for a table on the patio, where lights sparkle in the trees. If you don't have a reservation, ask for a seat at the bar downstairs, where you can order from either the small (but much less expensive) bar menu or the full menu. ⊠ *1245 Spring St.* ☎ *707/963–2233* ⊕ *www.martinihouse. com* ⊟ *AE, DC, MC, V* ☺ *No lunch Mon.–Thurs.*

$$$$

AMERICAN

Fodor'sChoice

★

✕ **The Restaurant at Meadowood.** Chef Christopher Kostow has garnered rave reviews (and two Michelin stars) for transforming seasonal local products (some grown right on the property) into elaborate, elegant fare. The "composition of carrots," constructed of the tiniest carrots imaginable accompanied by delicate shavings of chocolate, foie gras, and candied tangerine (it sounds odd, but it works) is just one example of Kostow's inventiveness and playfulness. The slow-cooked black cod with chorizo and lamb demonstrates an earthier approach. The chef's menu ($155, $260 with wine pairings), composed of eight or so courses, is the best way to appreciate the experience, but the gracious and well-trained servers provide some of the best service in the valley even if you're ordering a less extravagant three-, four-, or five-course menu. ⊠ *900 Meadowood La.* ☎ *707/967–1205* ⊕ *www.meadowood. com* ⊟ *AE, D, DC, MC, V* ☺ *Closed Sun. No lunch.*

$$$$

MEDITERRANEAN

★

✕ **Terra.** St. Helena may have newer, flashier, and more dramatic restaurants, but for old-school romance and service, many diners return year after year to this quiet favorite in an 1884 fieldstone building. Since 1988, chef Hiro Sone has been giving unexpected twists to Italian and southern-French cuisine in dishes such as the mussel soup with caramelized onions and garlic croutons, heavily perfumed with the scent of saffron. A few, like the signature sake-marinated black cod in a *shiso* broth, draw on Sone's Japanese background. Inventive desserts, courtesy of Sone's wife, Lissa Doumani, might include a maple

10

bread pudding served in a baked apple. The gracious staff unobtrusively attends to every dropped fork or half-full water glass. ✉ *1345 Railroad Ave.* ☎ *707/963–8931* ⊕ *www.terrarestaurant.com* ⌖ *Reservations essential* ▤ *AE, DC, MC, V* ⊘ *Closed Tues. and 1st 2 wks in Jan. No lunch.*

$$$
MEDITERRANEAN
✕ **Wine Spectator Greystone Restaurant.** The Culinary Institute of America runs this place in the handsome old Christian Brothers Winery. Century-old stone walls house a spacious restaurant that bustles at both lunch and dinner, with several cooking stations in full view. On busy nights you might find the hard-at-work chefs (who, incidentally, are generally full-fledged chefs rather than mere students) more entertaining than your dinner partner. On fair days the tables on the terrace, shaded by red umbrellas, are away from the action, but equally appealing. The menu has a Mediterranean spirit and emphasizes locally grown produce. Typical main courses include pan-roasted scallops with spinach and shiitake mushrooms and house-made pasta with a sherry-thyme cream sauce. ✉ *2555 Main St.* ☎ *707/967–1010* ⊕ *www.ciachef.edu* ▤ *AE, D, DC, MC, V.*

WHERE TO STAY

¢–$
🛏 **El Bonita Motel.** Only in St. Helena would a basic room in a road-side motel cost around $200 a night in high season. Still, for budget-minded travelers the tidy rooms here are pleasant enough, and the landscaped grounds and picnic tables elevate the property over similar places. There's even a small sauna next to the hot tub and swimming pool, which is heated year-round. ■**TIP→** Family-friendly pluses include roll-away beds and cribs for a modest charge. Its location right on Route 29 makes it convenient, but light sleepers should ask for rooms farthest from the road. **Pros:** cheerful rooms; hot tub; microwaves and mini-refrigerators. **Cons:** road noise is a problem in some rooms. ✉ *195 Main St./Rte. 29* ☎ *707/963–3216 or 800/541–3284* ⊕ *www.elbonita.com* ⬎ *38 rooms, 4 suites* ⌖ *In-room: a/c, refrigerator, Wi-Fi. In-hotel: pool, Internet terminal, some pets allowed* ▤ *AE, D, DC, MC, V* ⫽⊙ *CP.*

$$$$
Fodor's Choice
★
🛏 **Meadowood Resort.** Everything at Meadowood seems to run seamlessly, starting with the gatehouse staff who alert the front desk to arrivals, so that a receptionist is ready for each guest. A rambling lodge and several gray clapboard bungalows are scattered across the sprawling property, giving it the air of an exclusive New England retreat. Guest rooms have views over these wooded grounds from expansive windows. The supremely comfortable beds defy you to get up and pursue the golf, tennis, hiking, croquet, or other activities on offer. In recent years the elegant but unstuffy dining room has won rave reviews, becoming a destination restaurant (*see above*). **Pros:** site of one of Napa's best restaurants; lovely hiking trail on the property; the most gracious service in all of Napa. **Cons:** very expensive; most bathrooms are not as extravagant as at other similarly priced resorts. ✉ *900 Meadowood La.* ☎ *707/963–3646 or 800/458–8080* ⊕ *www.meadowood.com* ⬎ *40 rooms, 45 suites* ⌖ *In-room: a/c, refrigerator, DVD, Internet, Wi-Fi. In-hotel: 2 restaurants, room service, bar, golf course, tennis courts, pools, gym, children's programs (ages 6–12, summer only)* ▤ *AE, D, DC, MC, V.*

$$$–$$$$ ⊞ **Wine Country Inn.** A pastoral landscape of vine-covered hills surrounds this retreat, which was styled after the traditional New England inns its owners liked to visit in the 1970s. Rooms are comfortably done with homey furniture like four-poster beds topped with quilts, and many have a wood-burning or gas fireplace, a large jetted tub, and a patio or balcony overlooking the vineyards. A hearty breakfast is served buffet-style in the sun-splashed common room, and wine and appetizers are available in the afternoon next to the wood-burning cast-iron stove. Though it's not the most stylish lodging in the area, the thoughtful staff and the vineyard views from several rooms encourage many people to return year after year. **Pros:** free shuttle to some restaurants (reserve early); lovely grounds; swimming pool is heated year-round. **Cons:** some rooms let in noise from neighbors; some areas could use updating. ⊠ *1152 Lodi La., east of Rte. 29* ☎ *707/963–7077* ⊕ *www. winecountryinn.com* ⤺ *24 rooms, 5 suites* ⚿ *In-room: a/c, refrigerator (some), no TV, Wi-Fi. In-hotel: pool* ⊟ *MC, V* �ⓞ| *BP.*

SHOPPING

Dean & Deluca (⊠ *607 St. Helena Hwy. S/Rte. 29* ☎ *707/967–9980*), a branch of the famous Manhattan store, is crammed with everything you need in the kitchen—including terrific produce and deli items—as well as a large wine selection. The **Spice Islands Marketplace** (⊠ *Culinary Institute of America, 2555 Main St.* ☎ *888/424–2433*) is the place to shop for cookbooks, kitchenwares, and everything else related to cooking and preparing food. Elaborate confections handmade on the premises are displayed like miniature works of art at **Woodhouse Chocolate** (⊠ *1367 Main St.* ☎ *707/963–8413*), a lovely shop that resembles an 18th-century Parisian salon.

CALISTOGA

3 mi northwest of St. Helena on Rte. 29.

With false-fronted/Old West–style shops, 19th-century hotels, and unpretentious cafés lining Lincoln Avenue, the town's main drag, Calistoga has a slightly rough-and-tumble feel that's unique in the Napa Valley. It comes across as more down-to-earth than some of the polished towns to the south. And it's easier to find a bargain here, making it a handy home base for exploring the surrounding vineyards and back roads.

Ironically, Calistoga was developed as a swell, tourist-oriented getaway. In 1859, maverick entrepreneur Sam Brannan snapped up 2,000 acres of prime property and laid out a resort, intending to use the area's natural hot springs as the main attraction. Brannan's gamble didn't pay off as he'd hoped, but the hotels and bathhouses won a local following. Many of them are still going, and you can come for an old-school experience of a mud bath or a dip in a warm spring-fed pool.

Indian Springs has welcomed clients to mud baths, mineral pools, and steam rooms, all supplied with mineral water from its three geysers, since 1871. You can choose from the various spa treatments and volcanic-ash mud baths, or soak in the Olympic-size mineral-water pool (kept at 92°F in summer, and a toasty 102°F in winter). Those who visit

10

Floor-to-ceiling stacked bottles are no exaggeration in Schramsberg's cellars.

the spa also get access to a small Zen-inspired garden out back, where you can relax after your treatment. If you're planning several sessions, you might want to overnight in one of the lodge rooms or bungalows ($–$$$). Reservations are recommended for spa treatments. ✉ *1712 Lincoln Ave./Rte. 29* ☎ *707/942–4913* ⊕ *www.indianspringscalistoga. com* ⊙ *Daily 9–8.*

Fodor's Choice
★

Schramsberg, hidden on the hillside near Route 29, is one of Napa's oldest wineries. Founded in the 1860s, it now produces a variety of bubblies made using the traditional *méthode champenoise* process (which means, among other things, that the wine undergoes a second fermentation in the bottle before being "riddled," or turned every few days over a period of weeks, to nudge the sediment into the neck of the bottle). If you want to taste, you must tour first, but what a tour: in addition to getting a glimpse of the winery's historic architecture, you get to tour the cellars dug in the late 19th century by Chinese laborers, where a mind-boggling 2.5 million bottles are stacked in gravity-defying configurations. The tour fee includes generous pours of several very different sparkling wines. ✉ *1400 Schramsberg Rd.* ☎ *707/942–4558* ⊕ *www.schramsberg.com* 🍷 *Tasting and tour $40* ⊙ *Tasting and tour by appointment.*

Designed by postmodern architect Michael Graves, the **Clos Pegase** winery is a one-of-a-kind "temple to wine and art" packed with unusual art objects from the collection of owner and publishing entrepreneur Jan Shrem. After tasting the wines, which include a bright sauvignon blanc, fruity chardonnays, and mellow pinot noir, merlot, and cabernet (they're made in a soft, approachable style and meant to be drunk somewhat young), be sure to check out the surrealist paintings near the main tasting room, which include a Jean Dubuffet painting you may have seen on one of their labels. Better yet, bring a picnic and have lunch in the courtyard, where a curvaceous Henry Moore sculpture is one of about two dozen works of art. ⊠ *1060 Dunaweal La.* ☎ *707/942–4981* ⊕ *www.clospegase.com* ☜ *Tasting $15, tour free* ☉ *Daily 10:30–5; tour daily at 11:30 and 2.*

Tucked into a rock face in the Mayacamas range, **Storybook Mountain Vineyards** is one of the more beautiful wineries in Napa, with vines rising steeply from the winery in dramatic tiers. Zinfandel is king here, and they even make a Zin Gris, an unusual dry rosé of zinfandel grapes. (In Burgundy, *vin gris*—pale rosé—is made from pinot noir grapes.) Tastings are preceded by a low-key tour, during which you take a short walk up the hillside into the picture-perfect vineyard and then visit the atmospheric tunnels, parts of which have the same rough-hewn look as they did when Chinese laborers painstakingly dug them around 1888. ⊠ *3835 Hwy. 128* ☎ *707/942–5310* ⊕ *www.storybookwines.com* ☜ *Free* ☉ *Tour and tasting by appointment.*

Robert Louis Stevenson State Park encompasses the summit of **Mt. St. Helena.** It was here, in the summer of 1880, in an abandoned bunkhouse of the Silverado Mine, that Stevenson and his bride, Fanny Osbourne, spent their honeymoon. This stay inspired the writer's travel memoir *The Silverado Squatters*, and Spyglass Hill in *Treasure Island* is thought to be a portrait of Mt. St. Helena. The park's approximately 3,600 acres are mostly undeveloped except for a trail leading to the site of the bunkhouse—which is marked with a marble memorial in the form of an open book on top of a pedestal—and a fire trail to the summit beyond. ■TIP→ If you're planning on attempting the hike to the top, a 10-mi round-trip, bring plenty of water and dress appropriately: the trail is steep and lacks shade in spots, but the summit is often cool and breezy. ⊠ *Rte. 29, 7 mi north of Calistoga* ☎ *707/942–4575* ⊕ *www.parks.ca.gov* ☜ *Free* ☉ *Daily sunrise–sunset.*

★ Possibly the most astounding sight in Napa Valley is your first glimpse of the **Castello di Amorosa,** which looks for all the world like a medieval castle, complete with drawbridge and moat, chapel, stables, and secret passageways. Some of the 107 rooms contain replicas of 13th-century frescoes, and the dungeon has an actual iron maiden from Nuremberg, Germany. You must pay for the tour to see the most of the extensive eight-level property, though paying for a tasting allows you access to a small portion of the astounding complex, as well as taste several of their excellent Italian-style wines. ■TIP→ Prices for tastings and tours are $5 higher on Fridays and weekends (a rarity in the Wine Country), so schedule this stop for a weekday, if possible. ⊠ *4045 N. Saint Helena Hwy.* ☎ *707/967–6272* ⊕ *www.castellodiamorosa.com* ☜ *Tasting $10–$27, tour $25–$42* ☉ *Mar.–Nov., daily 9:30–6; Dec.–Feb., daily 9:30–5; tour by appointment.*

10

☾ The **Petrified Forest** contains the remains of the volcanic eruptions of Mt. St. Helena 3.4 million years ago: petrified giant redwoods. Pick up a brochure before starting off on the leisurely 15-minute walk around the property, which takes you by the largest specimen, "The Queen of the Forest," a 65-by-8-foot petrified log. The site isn't worth a long detour unless you're a geology buff. For the best experience, consider taking a meadow hike, which leads through the woodland until you have a view of Mt. St. Helena. The 45-minute excursion, led by a naturalist, is offered on Sunday at 11 AM and by appointment, weather permitting. ✉ *4100 Petrified Forest Rd., 5 mi west of Calistoga* ☎ *707/942–6667* ⊕ *www.petrifiedforest.org* ⊟ *$8* ⊙ *Mid-Apr.–mid-Sept., daily 9–7; mid-Sept.–mid-Apr., daily 9–5.*

WHERE TO EAT

$$
FRENCH
✕ **All Seasons Bistro.** Bistro cuisine takes a California spin in this cheerful sun-filled space, where tables topped with flowers stand on an old-fashioned black-and-white checkerboard floor. The seasonal menu might include seared scallops with a cauliflower puree or fettuccine puttanesca. Homey desserts include crème brûlée and rum-raisin bread pudding. You can order reasonably priced wines from their extensive list, or buy a bottle at the attached wineshop and have it poured at your table. Attentive service contributes to the welcoming atmosphere. ✉ *1400 Lincoln Ave.* ☎ *707/942–9111* ⊕ *www.allseasonsnapavalley. net* ⊟ *AE, D, MC, V* ⊙ *Closed Mon.*

$$
ITALIAN
✕ **Barolo.** With red-leather seats, artsy light fixtures, and a marble bar indoors and café seating out, this Italian-inflected wine bar is a stylish, modern spot for a glass of wine, with many from small producers you probably haven't heard of. Small plates that could have come straight from Tuscany—fried calamari, risotto croquettes, a selection of *salumi*—are great for sharing. A handful of well-executed large plates, like the pappardelle with shrimp and veal scaloppine, round out the menu. ✉ *Mount View Hotel, 1457 Lincoln Ave.* ☎ *707/942–9900* ⊕ *www.barolocalistoga.com* ⊟ *AE, MC, V* ⊙ *No lunch.*

$$$
AMERICAN
✕ **Calistoga Inn Restaurant and Brewery.** On pleasant days this riverside restaurant and its sprawling, tree-shaded patio come into their own. At lunchtime, casual plates like a grilled-turkey-and-Brie sandwich or a Chinese chicken salad are light enough to leave some energy for an afternoon of wine tasting. And at night, when there's often live jazz played on the patio during the warm months, you'll find heartier dishes such as braised lamb shank or grilled Sonoma duck breast with a fennel-and-Parmesan stuffing. Service can be a bit lackadaisical, so order one of the house-made brews and enjoy the atmosphere while you're waiting. ✉ *1250 Lincoln Ave.* ☎ *707/942–4101* ⊕ *www.calistogainn.com* ⊟ *AE, MC, V.*

WHERE TO STAY

¢–$
🛏 **Brannan Cottage Inn.** The pristine Victorian house with lacy white fretwork, large windows, and a shady porch is the only one of Sam Brannan's 1860 resort cottages still standing on its original site. Each room has individual touches, such as a four-poster bed, a claw-foot tub, or a velvet settee. **Pros:** innkeepers go the extra mile; most rooms have fireplaces; a five-minute walk from most of Calistoga's restaurants. **Cons:** owners' dog may be a problem for those with allergies; beds may be too firm for some. ✉ *109 Wapoo Ave.* ☎ *707/942–4200* ⊕ *www.*

All it needs is a fair maiden: Castello di Amorosa's recreated castle.

brannancottageinn.com ⤵ *6 rooms* ⚓ *In-room: no phone, a/c, no TV (some), Wi-Fi. In-hotel: some pets allowed* ▭ *AE, MC, V* ⦿ *BP*.

$$$$ ★ ⚍ **Calistoga Ranch.** Spacious cedar-shingle bungalows throughout this posh, wooded property have outdoor living areas, and even the restaurant, spa, and reception area have outdoor seating areas and fireplaces. Though it feels casual and ranchlike, the lodges are still supremely luxurious, with large bathrooms; a large, romantic outdoor shower; beds dressed with down bedding; and a minibar stocked with free drinks and snacks. **Pros:** almost half the cottages have private hot tubs on the deck; lovely hiking trails on the property; guests have reciprocal privileges at Auberge du Soleil. **Cons:** very expensive; innovative indoor-outdoor organization works better in fair weather than in rain or cold; staff, though friendly, sometimes seems inexperienced. ✉ *580 Lommel Rd.* ☎ *707/254–2800 or 800/942–4220* ⊕ *www.calistogaranch.com* ⤵ *46 rooms* ⚓ *In-room: a/c, safe, refrigerator, DVD, Internet, Wi-Fi. In-hotel: restaurant, room service, bar, pool, gym, spa, bicycles, laundry service, some pets allowed* ▭ *AE, D, MC, V.*

$$$ ⚍ **Cottage Grove Inn.** A long driveway lined with 16 freestanding cottages, each shaded by elm trees and with rocking chairs on the porch, looks a bit like Main Street, U.S.A., but inside the sky-lighted buildings are all the perks you could want for a romantic weekend away. There are overstuffed chairs in front of a wood-burning fireplace, flat-panel TVs, and an extra-deep two-person whirlpool tub. Each cottage also has its own variation on the overall comfy-rustic look, with telltale names like Fly Fishing Cottage and Provence. Spas and restaurants are within walking distance. Rates include afternoon wine and cheese. **Pros:** bicycles available for loan; freestanding cottages offer lots of privacy;

10

CLOSE UP

Best Wine Country Spas

Spas in Napa and Sonoma have two special angles. First, there are the local mud baths and mineral-water sources, concentrated particularly around Calistoga. Admittedly, no one loves dipping into a thick, muddy paste. But once you've had a few minutes to get used to the intense heat and peaty smell, you may never want to leave. Second, there are all those grapes: their seeds, skins, and vines are credited with all sorts of antioxidant and other healthful properties by those who use them in scrubs, lotions, and other spa products.

Below are some of the best spas of the bunch.

■ **Dr. Wilkinson's.** The oldest spa in Calistoga. Although it's the least chic of the bunch, it's still well loved for its reasonable prices and its friendly, unpretentious vibe. Their mud baths are a mix of volcanic ash and peat moss. ⊠ *1507 Lincoln Ave., Calistoga* ☎ *707/942–4102* ⊕ *www.drwilkinson. com.*

■ **Fairmont Sonoma Mission Inn & Spa.** The largest such destination in

the Wine Country. The vast complex covers every amenity you could want in a spa, including several pools and Jacuzzis fed by local thermal mineral springs. ⊠ *100 Boyes Blvd./Rte. 12, Boyes Hot Springs* ☎ *707/938–9000* ⊕ *www.fairmont.com/sonoma.*

■ **Kenwood Inn & Spa.** The prettiest spa setting in the Wine Country, thanks to the vineyards across the road and the Mediterranean style of the inn. The "wine wrap" body wrap is followed by a slathering of lotion made from various grape-seed oils and red-wine extract. ⊠ *10400 Sonoma Hwy./Rte. 12, Kenwood* ☎ *707/833–1293* ⊕ *www.kenwoodinn. com.*

■ **Spa at Villagio.** This 13,000-square-foot spa with fieldstone walls and a Mediterranean theme has all the latest gadgets, including men's and women's outdoor hot tubs and showers with an extravagant number of showerheads. Huge spa suites—complete with flat-panel TV screens and wet bars—are perfect for couples and groups. ⊠ *6481 Washington St., Yountville* ☎ *707/948–5050.*

bathtubs so big you could swim in them. **Cons:** no pool; decor may seem a bit frumpy for some. ⊠ *1711 Lincoln Ave.* ☎ *707/942–8400 or 800/799–2284* ⊕ *www.cottagegrove.com* ⬄ *16 rooms* ⚬ *In-room: a/c, safe, refrigerator, DVD, Internet, Wi-Fi. In-hotel: bicycles, Internet terminal* ⊟ *AE, D, DC, MC, V* ⚬⎮ *CP.*

$–$$ ★ ⊡ **Indian Springs.** Since 1871, this old-time spa has welcomed clients to its mud baths, mineral pool, and steam room, all of them supplied with mineral water from its four geysers. Rooms in the lodge, though quite small, are beautifully done up a simple Zen style, with Asian-inspired furnishings, Frette linens on the bed, and flat-panel televisions. The cottages dotted around the property have anything from a small kitchenette to a fully equipped kitchen, encouraging longer stays (book well in advance for these). A boccie ball court, shuffleboard, and croquet lawn outside your door provide entertainment when you're not indulging in various spa treatments and volcanic-ash mud baths, or soaking in the toasty Olympic-size mineral-water pool. **Pros:** lovely grounds with outdoor seating areas; stylish for the price; enormous mineral pool. **Cons:** lodge rooms are small; oddly uncomfortable pillows. ⊠ *1712 Lincoln Ave.* ☎ *707/942–4913* ⊕ *www.indianspringscalistoga.com* ➵ *24 rooms, 17 suites* ⚒ *In room: no phone, a/c, kitchen (some), refrigerator (some), Wi-Fi. In-hotel: tennis court, pool, spa* ⊟ *D, MC, V.*

$–$$ ⊞ **Meadowlark Country House.** Twenty hillside acres just north of down-
Fodor's Choice   town Calistoga surround this decidedly laid-back but sophisticated inn.
★   Rooms in the main house and guest wing each have their own charms: one has a deep whirlpool tub looking onto a green hillside, and others have a deck with a view of the mountains. Many rooms have fireplaces, and all but one have whirlpool tubs large enough for two. A spacious two-story guesthouse opens directly onto the clothing-optional pool, hot tub, and sauna area, which is open to all guests and enjoyed by a diverse crowd (the inn is welcoming to all, gay and straight). Fodors. com readers point out that "Kurt and Richard are delightful, helpful hosts." **Pros:** sauna next to the pool and hot tub; welcoming vibe attracts diverse guests; some of the most gracious innkeepers in Napa. **Cons:** clothing-optional pool policy isn't for everyone. ⊠ *601 Petrified Forest Rd.* ☎ *707/942–5651 or 800/942–5651* ⊕ *www.meadowlarkinn. com* ➵ *5 rooms, 5 suites* ⚒ *In-room: no phone, a/c, kitchen (some), refrigerator (some), DVD (some), Wi-Fi. In-hotel: pool, Internet terminal, some pets allowed* ⊟ *AE, MC, V* ⎮⚭⎮ *BP.*

$–$$ ⊞ **Mount View Hotel & Spa.** A National Historic Landmark built in 1917 in the Mission revival style, the Mount View nevertheless feels up-to-date, after renovations in 2008 resulted in repainted rooms (some are a dramatic red and black), feather duvets, and high tech touches like iPod alarm clocks. A full-service spa provides state-of-the-art pampering, and three cottages are each equipped with a private redwood deck, whirlpool tub, and wet bar. The hotel's location on Calistoga's main drag, plus the two excellent restaurants off the lobby, mean you won't need to go far if your spa treatment has left you too indolent to drive. **Pros:** convenient location; excellent spa treatments. **Cons:** ground-floor rooms dark; mediocre Continental breakfast; some bathrooms could use updating. ⊠ *1457 Lincoln Ave.* ☎ *707/942–6877 or 800/816–6877* ⊕ *www.mountviewhotel.com* ➵ *18 rooms, 13 suites* ⚒ *In-room: a/c, refrigerator (some), DVD, Wi-Fi. In-hotel: restaurant, bar, pool, spa* ⊟ *AE, D, MC, V* ⎮⚭⎮ *CP.*

$$$$ ⊞ **Solage.** A resort for sociable sorts who like to lounge at the bar overlooking the large pool or play a game of boccie after lunch at the excellent indoor-outdoor restaurant, this Calistoga newcomer sprawls over 22 acres. The cottages don't look particularly luxurious from the outside, but inside they flaunt a Napa-Valley-barn-meets-San-Francisco-loft aesthetic, with high ceilings, polished concrete floors, recycled walnut furniture, and all-natural fabrics in soothing muted colors. Sports and fitness are a high priority here: in addition to a large, well-equipped spa and "mud bar," where you can indulge in mud-bath variations, there's a packed schedule of fitness activities that include yoga, Pilates, and biking and hiking excursions. ■**TIP**➜ **If you want to be in the middle of the action, ask for a room facing the pool. For more seclusion, ask for one of the quieter rooms near the oak grove.** **Pros:** great service; bike cruisers parked

10

at every cottage for guests' use; separate pools for kids and adults. **Cons:** new landscaping looks a little bleak; some rooms don't have tubs. ⊠ *755 Silverado Trail* ☎ *866/942–7442* ⊕ *www.solagecalistoga. com* ⇥ *89 rooms* ♿ *In-room: a/c, safe, refrigerator, DVD, Wi-Fi. In-hotel: restaurant, room service, bar, pools, gym, spa, bicycles, laundry service* ⊟ *AE, D, DC, MC, V.*

SPORTS AND THE OUTDOORS

Calistoga Bikeshop (⊠ *1318 Lincoln Ave.* ☎ *707/942–9687*) offers a self-guided Calistoga Cool Wine Tour package ($79), which includes free tastings at a number of small wineries. Best of all, they'll pick up any wine you purchase along the way if you've bought more than will fit in the handy bottle carrier on your bike.

SHOPPING

Enoteca Wine Shop (⊠ *1348B Lincoln Ave.* ☎ *707/942–1117*), on Calistoga's main drag, displays almost all of their wines with extensive tasting notes. This makes it easier to choose from among this unusually fine collection, which includes both hard-to-find bottles from Napa and Sonoma and many rare French wines. The **Wine Garage** (⊠ *1020 Hwy. 29* ☎ *707/942–5332*) is the stop for bargain hunters, since all their bottles go for $25 or less. It's a great way to discover the work of smaller wineries producing undervalued wines. The unusually helpful staffers are happy to share information on all the wines they stock.

THE SONOMA VALLEY

Although the Sonoma Valley may not have quite the cachet of the neighboring Napa Valley, wineries here entice with their unpretentious attitude and smaller crowds. The Napa-style glitzy tasting rooms with enormous gift shops and $25 tasting fees are the exception here. Sonoma's landscape seduces, too, its roads gently climbing and descending on their way to wineries hidden from the road by trees.

The scenic valley, bounded by the Mayacamas Mountains on the east and Sonoma Mountain on the west, extends north from San Pablo Bay nearly 20 mi to the eastern outskirts of Santa Rosa. The varied terrain, soils, and climate (cooler in the south because of the bay influence and hotter toward the north) allow grape growers to raise cool-weather varietals such as chardonnay and pinot noir as well as merlot, cabernet sauvignon, and other heat-seeking vines. The valley is home to dozens of wineries, many of them on or near Route 12, which runs the length of the valley.

ESSENTIALS

Contacts Sonoma County Tourism Bureau (⊠ *3637 Westwind Blvd., Santa Rosa* ☎ *707/522–5800 or 800/576–6662* ⊕ *www.sonomacounty.com*). **Sonoma Valley Visitors Bureau** (⊠ *453 1st St. E, Sonoma* ☎ *707/996–1090 or 866/996–1090* ⊕ *www.sonomavalley.com*).

SONOMA

14 mi west of Napa on Rte. 12; 45 mi from San Francisco, north on U.S. 101, east on Rte. 37, and north on Rte. 121/12.

Founded in the early 1800s, Sonoma is the oldest town in the Wine Country, and one of the few where you can find some attractions not related to food and wine. The central **Sonoma Plaza** dates from the Mission era; surrounding it are 19th-century adobes, atmospheric hotels, and the swooping marquee of the 1930s Sebastiani Theatre. On summer days the plaza is a hive of activity, with children blowing off steam in the playground while their folks stock up on picnic supplies and browse the boutiques surrounding the square.

On your way into town from the south, you pass through the Carneros wine district, which straddles the southern sections of Sonoma and Napa counties.

A tree-lined driveway leads to **Lachryma Montis,** which General Mariano G. Vallejo, the last Mexican governor of California, built for his large family in 1852. The Victorian Gothic house, insulated with adobe, represents a blend of Mexican and American cultures. Opulent furnishings, including white-marble fireplaces and a French rosewood piano, are particularly noteworthy. Free tours are occasionally conducted by docents on weekends. ✉ *W. Spain St. near 3rd St. W* ☎ *707/938–9559* ✉ *$3, tour free* ⊘ *Fri.–Wed. 10–5.*

Reminiscent of a Tuscan villa, with ocher-color buildings surrounded by olive trees and colorful flower beds, sprawling **Viansa** focuses on Italian varietals such as sangiovese, nebbiolo, and tocai friulano. Fodor's readers are generally split when summing up the charms of the winery. Some love the market on the premises that sells sandwiches and deli foods to complement the Italian-style wines, as well as a large selection of dinnerware, cookbooks, and condiments. Others find the crowds that tend to congregate here off-putting (it's popular for large parties and weddings). Regardless, the many picnic tables, some of which overlook a wetland preserve below, are a fine place to enjoy a glass of wine while bird-watching (only food and wines sold on the premises are permitted). ✉ *25200 Arnold Dr.* ☎ *707/935–4700* ⊕ *www.viansa. com* ✉ *Tasting $5–$20, tour $10 (tasting fee additional)* ⊘ *Daily 10–5; tour daily at 11, 2, and 3.*

The **Robledo Family Winery,** founded by Reynaldo Robledo Sr., a former migrant worker from Michoacán, Mexico, is truly a family affair. You're likely to encounter one of the charming Robledo sons in the tasting room, where he'll proudly tell you the story of the immigrant family while pouring tastes of their sauvignon blanc, pinot noir, merlot, cabernet sauvignon, and other wines, including a chardonnay that comes from the vineyard right outside the tasting room's door. All seven Robledo sons and two Robledo daughters, as well as matriarch Maria, are involved in the winery operations. If you don't run into them on your visit to the winery, you'll see their names and pictures on the bottles of wine, such as the Dos Hermanas late-harvest dessert wine, or one of the ports dedicated to Maria Robledo. ✉ *21901 Bonness Rd.*

☎ *707/939–6903* ⊕ *www.robledofamilywinery.com* 🍷 *Tasting $5–$10* 🕐 *Mon.–Sat. 10–5, Sun. 11–4.*

Although many Carneros wineries specialize in pinot noir and chardonnay, **Cline Cellars** goes its own way by focusing on Rhône varietals, such as syrah, roussanne, and viognier, all grown here in Carneros, as well as mourvèdre and carignane, which are cultivated in Contra Costa County. They're also known for their Ancient Vines Zinfandel, produced from vines that are around 100 years old. The 1850s farmhouse that houses the tasting room has a pleasant wraparound porch for enjoying the weeping willows, ponds, fountains, and thousands of rosebushes on the property. Pack a picnic and plan to stay for a while, if you have the time. ✉ *24737 Hwy. 121/Arnold Dr.* ☎ *707/940–4030* ⊕ *www.clinecellars.com* 🍷 *Tasting free–$1 per reserve wine, tour free* 🕐 *Daily 10–6; tour daily at 11, 1, and 3.*

★ Just far enough off the beaten track to feel like a real find, **DeLoach Vineyards** produces a variety of Russian River Valley old-vine zinfandels, chardonnays, and handful of other varietals, but it is best for known for its pinot noir, some of which is made using open-top wood fermentation vats that are uncommon in Sonoma but have been used in France for centuries. (Some think that they intensify a wine's flavor.) Tours focus on the estate vineyards outside the tasting room door, where you can learn about the labor-intensive biodynamic and organic farming methods used here, and take you through their culinary garden. ✉ *1791 Olivet Rd.* ☎ *707/526–9111* ⊕ *www.deloachvineyards.com* 🍷 *Tasting $10, tour free* 🕐 *Daily 10–5; tour daily by appointment.*

Buena Vista Carneros Winery is the oldest continually operating winery in California. It was here, in 1857, that Count Agoston Haraszthy de Mokcsa laid the basis for modern California wine making, bucking the conventional wisdom that vines should be planted on well-watered ground by instead planting on well-drained hillsides. Chinese laborers dug tunnels 100 feet into the hillside, and the limestone they extracted was used to build the main house, which is now surrounded by redwood and eucalyptus trees and a picnic area. Their best wines are their chardonnay, pinot noir, syrah, and merlot grown in the Ramal Vineyard in the Carneros District. If you're a bit peckish, reserve ahead for a seated tasting of five wines paired with cheeses or other nibbles. ✉ *18000 Old Winery Rd., off Napa Rd.* ☎ *800/678–8504* ⊕ *buenavistacarneros.com* 🍷 *Tasting $10–$20* 🕐 *Daily 10–5.*

Ravenswood, whose tasting room is housed in a stone building covered in climbing vines, has a punchy mission statement: "no wimpy wines." They generally succeed, especially with their signature big, bold zinfandels, which are sometimes blended with petit syrah, carignane, or other varietals. Be sure to taste the syrah, early-harvest gewürztraminer, and lightly sparkling moscato, too. Tours that focus on their viticultural practices ($15), held 10:30 daily, include a barrel tasting of wines in progress in the cellar. Another tour, at 11:30 on weekdays from mid-May through September, concludes with wine-and-cheese pairings ($25). Tour reservations are recommended for the former and required for the latter. ✉ *18701 Gehricke Rd., off E. Spain St.* ☎ *707/938–1960*

⊕ *www.ravenswood-wine.com* 🍷 *Tasting $10–$15, tour $15–$25* ⊙ *Daily 10–4:30; call for tour times.*

Fodor's Choice ★ Although **Bartholomew Park Winery** was founded only in 1994, grapes were grown in some of its vineyards as early as the 1830s. The emphasis here is on handcrafted, single-varietal wines—cabernet, merlot, zinfandel, syrah, and sauvignon blanc. The wines themselves, available only at the winery, make a stop worth it, but another reason to visit is its small museum, with vivid exhibits about the history of the winery and the Sonoma region. Another plus is the beautiful, slightly off-the-beaten-path location in a 375-acre private park about 2 mi from downtown Sonoma. Pack a picnic to enjoy on the woodsy grounds. ⊠ *1000 Vineyard La.* ☎ *707/939–3026* ⊕ *www.bartholomewparkwinery.com* 🍷 *Tasting $5* ⊙ *Daily 11–4:30.*

WHERE TO EAT

$$ ✕ **Cafe La Haye.** In a postage-stamp-size open kitchen, skillful chefs turn out about half a dozen main courses that star on a small but worthwhile seasonal menu emphasizing local ingredients. Chicken, beef, pasta, and fish get deluxe treatment without fuss or fanfare. The chicken roasted with rosemary, for instance, and the daily risotto special is always good. Butterscotch pudding is a homey signature dessert. The dining room is also compact, but the friendly owner, who is often there to greet diners, gives it a particularly welcoming vibe. ⊠ *140 E. Napa St.* ☎ *707/935–5994* ⊕ *www.cafelahaye.com* ▤ *MC, V* ⊙ *Closed Sun. and Mon. No lunch.*

AMERICAN ★

$ ✕ **Della Santina's.** This longtime favorite, with a charming heated brick patio out back, serves the most authentic Italian food in town. (The Della Santina family, which has been running the restaurant since 1990, hails from Lucca, Italy.) Daily fish and veal specials join classic northern Italian pastas such as linguine with pesto and lasagna Bolognese. Of special note are the roasted meat dishes and, when available, petrale sole and sand dabs (both are types of flounder). ⊠ *133 E. Napa St.* ☎ *707/935–0576* ⊕ *www.dellasantinas.com* ▤ *AE, D, MC, V.*

ITALIAN

$$ ✕ **The Girl & the Fig.** Chef Sondra Bernstein has turned the historic barroom of the Sonoma Hotel into a hot spot for inventive French cooking. You can always find something with the signature figs in it here, whether it's a fig-and-arugula salad or an aperitif of sparkling wine with a fig liqueur. Also look for duck confit with French lentils, a burger with matchstick fries, or wild boar braised in red wine. The wine list is notable for its emphasis on Rhône varietals, and a counter in the bar area sells artisanal cheese platters for eating here as well as cheese by the pound to go. Sunday brunch brings rib-sticking dishes such as steak and eggs and a Basque frittata with potatoes, onions, and tomatoes. ⊠ *Sonoma Hotel, Sonoma Plaza, 110 W. Spain St.* ☎ *707/938–3634* ⊕ *www.thegirlandthefig.com* ▤ *D, MC, V.*

FRENCH

10

$$ ✕ **Harvest Moon Cafe.** It's easy to feel like one of the family at this little restaurant with an odd, zigzagging layout. Diners seated at one of the two tiny bars chat with the servers like old friends, but the husband-and-wife team in the kitchen is serious about the food, much of which relies on local produce. The daily menu sticks to homey dishes like half a grilled chicken served with polenta and tapenade, rib-eye steak with

AMERICAN ★

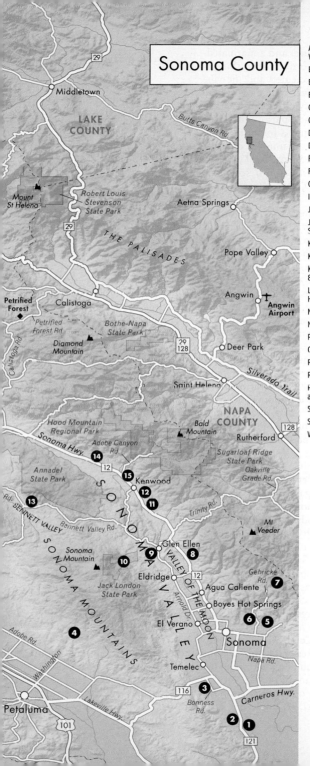

Sonoma County

a red wine sauce, and a marinated-beet-and-leek salad. Everything is so perfectly executed and the vibe so genuinely warm that a visit here is deeply satisfying. In fair weather, a spacious back patio, with seats arranged around a fountain, more than doubles the number of seats. ⊠ *487 W. 1st St.* ☎ *707/933–8160* ⊕ *www.harvestmooncafesonoma. com* ▤ *AE, D, MC, V* ☺ *No lunch Mon.–Sat.*

\$ ✕ **La Casa.** Terra cotta–color tile
MEXICAN floors and ceramics on the walls evoke Old Mexico at this spot that has been at the edge of Sonoma's plaza for more than four decades. There's bar seating, a patio, and large menu of traditional Mexican favorites, like enchiladas *suizas* (chicken enchiladas with a tomatillo salsa), burritos, and fish tacos. Though the food is fairly standard, the casual, festive atmosphere and margaritas sold by the glass or pitcher make it a popular stop, especially during happy hour (weekdays 4–7). ⊠ *121 E. Spain St.* ☎ *707/996–3406* ⊕ *www.lacasarestaurant.com* ▤ *AE, D, DC, MC, V.*

\$\$ ✕ **LaSalette.** Chef-owner Manuel Azevedo, born in the Azores and raised
PORTUGUESE in Sonoma, serves dishes inspired by his native Portugal in this warmly decorated spot, where the best seats are on the patio, along a pedestrian alleyway off of Sonoma's plaza. Boldly flavored dishes such as *pork tenderloin recheado,* stuffed with olives and almonds and topped with a port sauce, or one of the daily seafood specials might be followed by a dish of rice pudding with Madeira-braised figs or a port from the varied list. ⊠ *452 E. 1st St.* ☎ *707/938–1927* ⊕ *www.lasalette-restaurant. com* ▤ *AE, MC, V.*

\$\$\$\$ ✕ **Santé.** Under the leadership of chef de cuisine Andrew Cain, this
AMERICAN elegant dining room in the Sonoma Mission Inn has gained a reputation
Fodor's Choice as a destination restaurant through its focus on seasonal and locally
★ sourced ingredients. The room is understated, with drapes in rich earth tones and softly lighted chandeliers, but the food is anything but. Dishes on the frequently changing menu, such as a roasted Sonoma duck breast with braised Swiss chard and duck confit, are complex without being fussy, while some dishes, like the butter-poached Maine lobster with flageolet beans and lardons, are pure decadence. ⊠ *Fairmont Sonoma Mission Inn & Spa, 100 Boyes Blvd./Rte. 12, at Boyes Blvd., 2 mi north of Sonoma, Boyes Hot Springs* ☎ *707/939–2415* ▤ *AE, D, DC, MC, V* ☺ *No lunch.*

\$ ✕ **Sunflower Caffé.** Although you wouldn't realize it as you walk by,
AMERICAN this casual breakfast-and-lunch-only café has one of Sonoma's prettiest patios. Equipped with both heating lamps and plenty of shade, it's comfortable in all but the most inclement weather. The menu, composed mostly of salads and sandwiches (as well as omelets and waffles for breakfast), is simple but satisfying, and it relies largely on local

CLOSE UP

Who's Who in the Grape World

Well more than 50 varieties of grapes are grown in the California Wine Country. Although you don't need to be on a first-name basis with them all, you'll see the following dozen again and again as you visit the wineries.

WHITES

■ **Chardonnay.** Now as firmly associated with California wine making as it is with Burgundy, where it's used extensively. California chardonnays spent many years chasing big, buttery flavor, but the current trend is toward more restrained wines.

■ **Gewürztraminer.** Cooler California climes such as the Russian River Valley are great for growing this German-Alsatian grape, which is turned into a boldly perfumed, fruity wine.

■ **Riesling.** Also called Johannisberg Riesling or White Riesling, this cool-climate German grape has a sweet rep in America. When made in a dry style, as it more and more often is, it can be crisply refreshing, with lush aromas.

■ **Sauvignon Blanc.** Hails from Bordeaux and the Loire Valley. Wines made from this grape vary widely, from herbaceous to tropical-fruity.

■ **Viognier.** Once rarely planted outside of France's Rhône Valley, it's one of the hottest white-wine varietals in California today. The best viogniers have an intense fruity or floral bouquet; they're usually dry.

REDS

■ **Cabernet Franc.** Most often used in blends, often to add complexity to cabernet sauvignon, this French grape can produce aromatic, soft, and subtle wine.

■ **Cabernet Sauvignon.** The king of California reds, this Bordeaux grape grows best in austere, well-drained soils. At its best, the California version is dark, bold, and tannic, with black-currant notes. It's often blended with cabernet franc, merlot, and other red varieties to soften the resulting wine and make it ready for earlier drinking.

■ **Merlot.** A blue-black Bordeaux variety that in California makes soft, full-bodied wine. Was well on its way to being the most popular red until anti-merlot jokes in the movie *Sideways* and elsewhere damaged its rep ... for now.

■ **Pinot Noir.** The darling of grape growers in cooler parts of Napa and Sonoma, such as the Carneros region and the Russian River Valley. At its best it has a subtle but addictive earthy quality.

■ **Sangiovese.** The main red grape of Italy's Chianti District and of much of central Italy. It can be made into vibrant, light- to medium-bodied wines, as well as into long-lived, very complex reds. Increasingly planted in California.

■ **Syrah.** A big red from France's Rhône Valley. With good tannins it can become a full-bodied beauty, but without them it can be flabby and forgettable. Also known as shiraz, particularly when it's grown in Australia.

■ **Zinfandel.** A quintessential California grape. Rich, jammy, and often spicy, zinfandel wines can be quite high in alcohol.

10

Where to Eat and Stay in Sonoma County

ingredients. It's also a comfortable spot to take a quick break with an excellent coffee drink or something from the well-stocked outdoor wine bar. ⊠ *421 W. 1st St.* ☎ *707/996–6645* ⊕ *www.sonomasunflower.com* ♨ *Reservations not accepted* ☰ *AE, MC, V* ⊘ *No dinner.*

WHERE TO STAY

¢   ⌐ **El Dorado Hotel.** Rooms in this remodeled 1843 building strike a spare, modern pose, with rectilinear four-poster beds and pristine white bedding, but the Mexican-tile floors hint at Sonoma's Mission-era past. Rooms are small, but high-tech features like flat-panel TVs and iPod alarm clocks are a nice touch, and each has a small balcony that overlooks the street or the courtyard or El Dorado Kitchen. Though its position (right on Sonoma's plaza and on top of a bustling restaurant and bar) is considered a boon by some, earplugs are advised for all but the hardiest sleepers. **Pros:** stylish for the price; hip restaurant downstairs; central location. **Cons:** rooms could use better lighting; noisy. ⊠ *405 1st St. W* ☎ *707/996–3030* ⊕ *www.eldoradosonoma.com* ⟳ *27 rooms* ♿ *In-room: a/c, refrigerator, DVD, Wi-Fi. In-hotel: restaurant, bar, pool* ☰ *AE, MC, V.*

\$\$\$–\$\$\$\$ ⌐ **The Fairmont Sonoma Mission Inn & Spa.** The real draw at this Mission-style resort is the extensive, swanky spa, easily the biggest in Sonoma. There's a vast array of massages and treatments, some using locally sourced grape and lavender products. (It's a coed spa, and there are several treatments designed for couples.) The focus on fitness and rejuvenation extends to a 7,087-yard golf course winding through trees and vineyards, a changing schedule of fitness classes, and guided hiking and biking excursions each morning. The guest rooms aren't terribly large but are supremely comfortable; some have fireplaces and patios or balconies. The staff stays on top of every detail. **Pros:** enormous spa; excellent Michelin-starred restaurant on-site; free shuttle to downtown. **Cons:** not as intimate as some similarly priced places. ⊠ *100 Boyes Blvd./Rte. 12, 2 mi north of Sonoma, Boyes Hot Springs* ☎ *707/938–9000* ⊕ *www.fairmont.com/sonoma* ⟳ *168 rooms, 60 suites* ♿ *In-room: a/c, safe, refrigerator, Internet, Wi-Fi. In-hotel: 2 restaurants, room service, bars, golf course, tennis courts, pools, gym, spa, bicycles, laundry service, some pets allowed* ☰ *AE, D, DC, MC, V.*

¢   ⌐ **Sonoma Creek Inn.** The small but cheerful rooms at this roadside inn with a sunny yellow exterior are individually decorated with painted wooden armoires, cozy quilts, and brightly colored contemporary artwork, elevating this bargain option well above your average motel. Most rooms even have vaulted ceilings, and many have small patios with a little fountain. Free roll-away beds for kids and an independently owned diner attached to the property make it an especially family-friendly option. **Pros:** clean, well-lighted bathrooms; a lot of charm for the low price. **Cons:** office not staffed 24 hours a day; slightly out-of-the-way location (about a 10-minute drive from Sonoma's Plaza). ⊠ *239 Boyes Blvd.* ☎ *707/939–9463* ⊕ *www.sonomacreekinn.com* ⟳ *16 rooms* ♿ *In-room: a/c, Wi-Fi. In-hotel: restaurant, some pets allowed* ☰ *AE, D, MC, V.*

NIGHTLIFE AND THE ARTS

The **Sebastiani Theatre** (⌧ 476 1st St. E ☎ 707/996–2020), built on Sonoma's plaza in 1934 by Italian immigrant and entrepreneur Samuele Sebastiani, schedules first-run films, as well as the occasional musical or theatrical performance.

Hit the **Swiss Hotel**'s bar (⌧ 18 W. Spain St. ☎ 707/938–2884) to sip a Glariffee, a cold and potent cousin to Irish coffee that's unique to this 19th-century spot.

SHOPPING

Sonoma Plaza is the town's main shopping magnet, with tempting boutiques and specialty food purveyors facing the square or just a block or two away. **Sign of the Bear** (⌧ Sonoma Plaza, 435 1st St. W ☎ 707/996–3722) sells the latest and greatest in kitchenware and cookware, as well as a few Wine Country–theme items, like lazy Susans made from wine barrels.

The **Sonoma Cheese Factory and Deli** (⌧ Sonoma Plaza, 2 Spain St. ☎ 707/996–1931), run by the same family for four generations, makes Sonoma Jack cheese and the tangy Sonoma Teleme. It has everything you need for a picnic.

A block east of Sonoma Plaza, the **Vella Cheese Company** (⌧ 315 2nd St. E ☎ 707/938–3232) has been making superb cheeses, such as raw-milk cheddars and several varieties of jack, since 1931.

GLEN ELLEN

7 mi north of Sonoma on Rte. 12.

Craggy Glen Ellen embodies the difference between the Napa and Sonoma valleys. In small Napa towns such as St. Helena well-groomed sidewalks are lined with upscale boutiques and restaurants, but in Glen Ellen the crooked streets are shaded with stands of old oak trees and occasionally bisected by the Sonoma and Calabasas creeks.

Jack London, who represents Glen Ellen's rugged spirit, lived in the area for many years; the town commemorates him with place-names and nostalgic establishments.

In the Jack London Village complex, **Figone's Olive Oil Co.** (⌧ 14301 Arnold Dr. ☎ 707/938–3164) not only carries many local olive oils, serving bowls, books, and dining accessories, but also presses olives for a number of local growers, usually in late fall. You can taste a selection of olive oils that have surprisingly different flavors.

Built in 1905, the **Jack London Saloon** (⌧ 13740 Arnold Dr. ☎ 707/996–3100 ⊕ www.jacklondonlodge.com) is decorated with photos of London and other London memorabilia.

In the hills above Glen Ellen—known as the Valley of the Moon—lies **Jack London State Historic Park,** where you could easily spend the

10

afternoon hiking along the edge of vineyards and through stands of oak trees. Several of the author's manuscripts and a handful of personal effects are on view at the House of Happy Walls museum, once the home of London's widow. A short hike away from Happy Walls are the ruins of Wolf House. Designed by London, it mysteriously burned down just before he was to move in. Also open to the public are a few restored farm outbuildings. London is buried on the property. ⊠ *2400 London Ranch Rd.* ☎ *707/938–5216* 🖾 *Parking $8, admission to buildings free* ⊙ *Park Sat.–Wed. 10–5. Museum weekends 10–5, Mon.–Wed. 10–4.*

Arrowood Vineyards & Winery is neither as old nor as famous as some of its neighbors (they made their first wines in 1986), but winemakers and critics are quite familiar with the wines produced here by Richard Arrowood, especially the chardonnays, syrahs, and age-worthy cabernets. A wraparound porch with wicker chairs invites you to linger outside the tasting room, built to resemble a New England farmhouse. Tours, offered twice daily by appointment, conclude with a seated tasting. An unusually kid-friendly destination, the winery has a small toy box in the tasting room, and will offer a tasting of nonalcoholic drinks on their tour, if you give them advance notice. ■ TIP➔ If you're doing a reserve tasting on a weekend, and you're interested in discovering what Arrowood wines taste like after several years in the bottle, ask if they happen to have any library wines open they can pour. ⊠ *14347 Sonoma Hwy./Rte. 12* ☎ *707/935–2600* ⊕ *www.arrowoodvineyards.com* 🖾 *Tasting $5–$10, tour $25* ⊙ *Daily 10–4:30; tour by appointment.*

★ One of the best-known local wineries is **Benziger Family Winery,** on a sprawling estate in a bowl with 360-degree sun exposure. Benziger is noted for its merlot, cabernet sauvignon, chardonnay, and sauvignon blanc. The tram tours here are especially interesting (they're first come, first served). On a ride through the vineyards, guides explain the regional microclimates and geography and give you a glimpse of the extensive cave system. Tours depart several times a day, weather permitting, but are sometimes fully booked during the high season. Reservations are needed for smaller tours that conclude with a seated tasting ($40). ■ TIP➔ Arrive before lunch for the best shot at joining a tour—and bring a picnic, since the grounds here are lovely. ⊠ *1883 London Ranch Rd.* ☎ *707/935–3000* ⊕ *www.benziger.com* 🖾 *Tasting $10–$15, tour $15–$40* ⊙ *Daily 10–5.*

WHERE TO EAT

$$
FRENCH
Fodor's Choice
★

✕ **The Fig Cafe.** Pale sage walls, a high, sloping ceiling, and casual but very warm service set a sunny mood in this little bistro that's run by the same team behind Sonoma's The Girl & the Fig. The restaurant's eponymous fruit shows up in all sorts of places—not only in salads and desserts, but also on thin-crust pizzas piled high with arugula. The small menu focuses on California and French comfort food, like steamed mussels served with terrific crispy fries, and a braised pot roast served with seasonal vegetables. Don't forget to look on the chalkboard for frequently changing desserts, such as butterscotch pots de crème. ■ TIP➔ The unusual no-corkage-fee policy makes it a great place to drink the wine you just discovered down the road. ⊠ *13690 Arnold*

Dr. ☎ *707/938–2130* ⊕ *www.thegirlandthefig.com* ⚓ *Reservations not accepted* ▤ *D, MC, V* ⊘ *No lunch weekdays.*

$$
ECLECTIC
✕ **Glen Ellen Inn Oyster Grill & Martini Bar.** This cozy restaurant in a creek-side 1940s cottage exudes romance, especially if you snag a seat in the shady garden or on the patio strung with tiny lights. After taking the edge off your hunger with some oysters on the half shell and an ice-cold martini (or one of their 25 or so variations on the theme), order from the eclectic, frequently changing menu that plucks elements from California, French, and occasionally Asian cuisines. For instance, you might try Dungeness crab pot stickers or a filet mignon with cambozola cheese and wild mushrooms. Desserts tend toward the indulgent; witness the warm pecan bread pudding with a chocolate center that sits in a puddle of brandy sauce. ⊠ *13670 Arnold Dr.* ☎ *707/996–6409* ⊕ *www.glenelleninn.com* ▤ *AE, MC, V* ⊘ *No lunch Wed. or Thurs.*

WHERE TO STAY

¢–$
★
🛏 **Beltane Ranch.** On a slope of the Mayacamas range a few miles from Glen Ellen, this 1892 ranch house stands in the shade of magnificent oak trees. The charmingly old-fashioned rooms, each individually decorated with antiques and thick old-fashioned bedcovers, have exterior entrances, and some open onto a wraparound balcony ideal for whiling away lazy afternoons. A bountiful breakfast, included in the price, incorporates produce from the gardens here, when it's in season, as well as eggs from their chickens. **Pros:** casual, friendly atmosphere; reasonably priced; beautiful grounds with ancient oak trees. **Cons:** downstairs rooms get some noise from upstairs rooms; cooled with ceiling fans instead of air-conditioning. ⊠ *11775 Sonoma Hwy./Rte. 12* ☎ *707/996–6501* ⊕ *www.beltaneranch.com* ⇆ *3 rooms, 3 suites* ⚹ *In room: no phone, a/c, no TV, Wi-Fi. In-hotel: tennis court* ▤ *MC, V* ◉ *BP.*

$$$–$$$$
Fodor's Choice
★
🛏 **Gaige House.** Gorgeous Asian objets d'art and leather club chairs cozied up to the fireplace in the lobby are just a few of the graceful touches in this luxurious but understated B&B. Rooms in the main house, an 1890 Queen Anne, are mostly done in pale colors, and each has its advantages. One upstairs room has wraparound windows to let in floods of light, for instance, while the lavish creek-side cottages feel Japanese, with massive granite soaking tubs overlooking private atriums. Magnolia trees shade the backyard, where there's a small but idyllic swimming pool and hot tub. Though the staffers are helpful, service never seems fussy, and there's a bottomless jar of cookies in the common area. Although a Continental breakfast is included, you can pay a bit more for a full breakfast. **Pros:** beautiful lounge areas; cottages are very private. **Cons:** sound carries in the main house; the least expensive rooms are on the small side. ⊠ *13540 Arnold Dr.* ☎ *707/935–0237 or 800/935–0237* ⊕ *www.gaige.com* ⇆ *10 rooms, 13 suites* ⚹ *In-room: a/c, safe, refrigerator (some), DVD, Wi-Fi. In-hotel: pool, spa, no kids under 12* ▤ *AE, D, DC, MC, V.*

¢
🛏 **Glenelly Inn and Cottages.** On a quiet side street a few blocks from the town center, this sunny little establishment has a long history as a getaway. It was built as an inn in 1916, and the rooms, each individually decorated, tend toward a simple country style. Many have four-poster beds and touches such as a wood-burning stove or antique oak dresser;

10

some have whirlpool tubs. All have puffy down comforters. Breakfast is served in front of the common room's fireplace, as are cookies or other snacks in the afternoon. ■TIP→ **Innkeeper Kristi Hallamore Jeppesen has two children of her own, so this is an unusually kid-friendly inn.** **Pros:** children are welcome; quiet location; hot tub in a pretty garden. **Cons:** some may not appreciate the presence of children; less expensive rooms are on the small side. ⊠ *5131 Warm Springs Rd.* ☎ *707/996–6720* ⊕ *www. glenellyinn.com* ⋑ *8 rooms, 2 suites* ⚹ *In-room: no phone (some), a/c (some), refrigerator (some), DVD, Wi-Fi. In-hotel: laundry facilities, some pets allowed* ⊟ *AE, D, MC, V* ⁏◎⁏ *BP.*

KENWOOD

3 mi north of Glen Ellen on Rte. 12.

Blink and you might miss tiny Kenwood, which consists of little more than a few restaurants and shops and a historic train depot, now used for private events. But hidden in this pretty landscape of meadows and woods at the north end of Sonoma Valley are several good wineries, most just off the Sonoma Highway.

Many wineries around the Kenwood area are small, so tiny that they don't have tasting rooms of their own. At **Family Wineries** you can sample the output of several such spots. Though the lineup of participating wineries occasionally changes, look for sweet flavored sparklers produced by SL Cellars and still wines from Sonoma producers such as David Noyes and Collier Falls. ⊠ *9380 Sonoma Hwy.* ☎ *888/433–6555* ⊕ *www.familywines.com* ⊠ *Tasting $5* ☉ *Daily 10:30–5.*

On your way into **Kunde Estate Winery & Vineyards** you pass a terrace flanked with fountains, virtually coaxing you to stay for a picnic with views over the vineyard. The tour of the grounds includes its extensive caves, some of which stretch 175 feet below a syrah vineyard. Kunde is perhaps best known for its toasty chardonnays, although tastings might include sauvignon blanc, cabernet sauvignon, and zinfandel as well. If you skip the tour, take a few minutes to wander around the demonstration vineyard outside the tasting room. In the months before crush (usually in September), you can taste the different grapes on the vines and see if you can taste the similarities between the grapes and wines you just tasted. ⊠ *9825 Sonoma Hwy./Rte. 12* ☎ *707/833–5501* ⊕ *www.kunde.com* ⊠ *Tasting $10–$20, tour free* ☉ *Daily 10:30–4:30; tours weekdays at 11, weekends on the hr 11–3.*

Kenwood Vineyards makes some good value-priced red and white wines, as well as some showier cabernet sauvignons, zinfandels, and merlots, many of which are poured in the tasting room housed in one of the original barns on the property. The best of these come from Jack London's old vineyard, in the Sonoma Mountain appellation, above the fog belt of the Sonoma Valley (Kenwood has an exclusive lease). But the crisp sauvignon blanc is what keeps wine connoisseurs coming back for more. ⊠ *9592 Sonoma Hwy./Rte. 12* ☎ *707/833–5891* ⊕ *www. kenwoodvineyards.com* ⊠ *Tasting $5* ☉ *Daily 10–4:30.*

★ Named for St. Francis of Assisi, founder of the Franciscan order, which established missions and vineyards throughout California, **St. Francis**

Winery has one of the most scenic locations in Sonoma, nestled at the foot of Mt. Hood. The visitor center beautifully replicates the California Mission style, with its red tile roof and dramatic bell tower (a plaque explains that the bell was actually blessed in the Basilica di San Francesco in Assisi, Italy). Out back, a slate patio overlooks vineyards, lavender gardens, and hummingbirds flitting about the flower beds. The charm of the surroundings is matched by the wines, most of them red. Consider paying a bit more ($30) to taste wines paired with artisanal cheeses and charcuterie, served either on the patio or seated in the dining room. ✉ *100 Pythian Rd.* ☎ *800/543–7713* ⊕ *www.stfranciswinery. com* 🍷 *Tasting $10–$15* ☉ *Daily 10–5.*

WHERE TO EAT AND STAY

$

ITALIAN

✗ **Café Citti.** Opera tunes in the background and a friendly staff (as well as a roaring fire when the weather's cold) keep this no-frills roadside café from feeling too spartan. Order dishes such as roast chicken and slabs of tiramisu from the counter and they're delivered to your table, a few of which are on an outdoor patio. An ample array of prepared salads and sandwiches means they do a brisk business in takeout for picnic packers, but you can also choose pasta made to order, mixing and matching linguine, penne, and other pastas with sauces like pesto or marinara. ✉ *9049 Sonoma Hwy./Rte. 12* ☎ *707/833–2690* ⊕ *www. cafecitti.com* 💳 *MC, V.*

$$$$

★

🏨 **Kenwood Inn and Spa.** Buildings resembling graceful old haciendas and mature fruit trees shading the courtyards make it seem like this inn has been here for more than a century (it was actually built in 1990). French doors opening onto terraces or balconies, fluffy featherbeds, and wood-burning fireplaces give the uncommonly spacious guest rooms, many with tile floors, a particularly romantic air. A swimming pool, Jacuzzis, and saunas pepper three atmospheric courtyards, and you could easily spend an afternoon padding from one to another in your robe and slippers. The spa is intimate but well equipped. **Pros:** large rooms; lavish furnishings; extremely romantic. **Cons:** Wi-Fi can be spotty in some areas; the expensive restaurant isn't quite up to the level of the inn. ✉ *10400 Sonoma Hwy.* ☎ *707/833–1293* ⊕ *www.kenwoodinn.com* 🛏 *29 rooms* & *In-room: a/c, no TV, Internet, Wi-Fi. In-hotel: restaurant, bar, pool, spa, laundry service, no kids under 18.* 💳 *AE, MC, V.*

10

ELSEWHERE IN SONOMA COUNTY

At nearly 1,598 square mi, there's much more to Sonoma County than the day-tripper favorites of Sonoma, Glen Ellen, and Kenwood. To the north is Healdsburg, a lovely small town with a rapidly rising buzz. The national media have latched onto it for its swank hotels and remarkable restaurants, and many Fodors.com readers recommend it as an ideal home base for wine tasting.

Within easy striking distance of Healdsburg are some of the Wine Country's most scenic vineyards, in the Alexander, Dry Creek, and Russian River valleys. And these lookers also happen to produce some of the country's best pinot noir, cabernet sauvignon, zinfandel, and sauvignon blanc. Though these regions are hardly unknown names, their quiet, narrow roads feel a world away from Highway 29 in Napa.

The western stretches of Sonoma County, which reach all the way to the Pacific Ocean, are sparsely populated in comparison to the above destinations, with only the occasional vineyard popping up in between isolated ranches. Guerneville, a popular destination for weekending San Franciscans, who come to canoe down the Russian River, is a convenient place for picking up River Road, then Westside Road, which passes through pinot noir paradise on its way to Healdsburg.

SANTA ROSA

8 mi northwest of Kenwood on Rte. 12.

Santa Rosa, the Wine Country's largest city, isn't likely to charm you with its office buildings, department stores, and frequent snarls of traffic along U.S. 101. It is, however, home to a couple of interesting cultural offerings. Its chain motels and hotels are also handy if you're finding that everything else is booked up, especially since Santa Rosa is roughly equidistant from Sonoma, Healdsburg, and the Russian River Valley, three of the most popular wine-tasting destinations.

The **Luther Burbank Home and Gardens** commemorates the great botanist who lived and worked on these grounds and single-handedly developed the modern techniques of hybridization. The 1.6-acre garden and a greenhouse show the results of some of Burbank's experiments to develop spineless cactus, fruit trees, and flowers such as the Shasta daisy. In the music room of his house, a modified Greek Revival structure that was Burbank's home from 1884 to 1906, a dictionary lies open to a page on which the verb "burbank" is defined as "to modify and improve plant life." (To see the house, you'll need to join one of the docent-led tours, which leave from the gift shop every half hour.) ⊠ *Santa Rosa and Sonoma Aves.* ☎ *707/524–5445* ⊕ *www.lutherburbank.org* ⊠ *Gardens free, tour $7* ☉ *Gardens daily 8–dusk; museum and gift shop Apr.–Oct., Tues.–Sun. 10–4.*

Fans of Snoopy and Charlie Brown should head to the **Charles M. Schulz Museum,** dedicated to the cartoonist who lived in Santa Rosa for the last 30 years of his life, until his death in 2000. Permanent installations such as a re-creation of the artist's studio share the space with temporary exhibits, which often focus on a particular theme in Schulz's work. Both children and adults can try their hand at creating cartoons in the Education Room or wander through the labyrinth in the form of Snoopy's head. Check the Web site or call for information about occasional kid-friendly workshops and events. ⊠ *2301 Hardies La.* ☎ *707/579–4452* ⊕ *www.schulzmuseum.org* ⊠ *$10* ☉ *Labor Day–Memorial Day, Wed.–Fri. and Mon. 11–5, weekends 10–5; Memorial Day–Labor Day, weekdays 11–5, weekends 10–5.*

Fodor's Choice
★ The visitor center at beautiful **Matanzas Creek Winery** sets itself apart with an understated Japanese aesthetic, with a tranquil fountain and a koi pond. Best of all, huge windows overlook a vast field of lavender plants. ■ TIP➔ The ideal time to visit is in May and June, when the lavender

blooms and perfumes the air. The winery specializes in sauvignon blanc, merlot, and chardonnay, although they also produce a popular dry rosé as well as some syrah, pinot noir, and cabernet. Guided tours range from an hour-long intro to the Bennett Valley, the tiny AVA where the winery is located, to a more expensive one that concludes with a taste of limited-production and library wines paired with artisanal cheeses. ⊠ *6097 Bennett Valley Rd.* ☎ *707/528–6464 or 800/590–6464* ⊕ *www. matanzascreek.com* 🖃 *Tasting $5–$10, tour $10–$35* ☉ *Daily 10–4:30; tour by appointment.*

WHERE TO EAT

$$$
Fodor'sChoice
★

✕ **Zazu.** A low wooden ceiling, rustic copper tables, and rock music on the stereo create a casual vibe at this roadhouse. It's a few miles from downtown Santa Rosa, but the hearty, soulful cooking of owners Duskie Estes and John Stewart brings passionate fans from all over the Wine Country. Some of the produce for the salads comes from their own garden, and the meats are house-cured, so the antipasto plate or a pizza with house-made pepperoni are both excellent choices. The small seasonal menu—a mix of Italian-influenced dishes and updated American classics—tends toward rich flavors, with choices like rabbit braised in red wine and served with a mushroom risotto. ⊠ *3535 Guerneville Rd.* ☎ *707/523–4814* ⊕ *www.zazurestaurant.com* ▭ *MC, V.*

RUSSIAN RIVER VALLEY

10 mi northwest of Santa Rosa.

The Russian River flows all the way from Mendocino to the Pacific Ocean, but in terms of wine making, the Russian River Valley is centered on a triangle with points at Healdsburg, Guerneville, and Sebastopol. Tall redwoods shade many of the two-lane roads that access this scenic area, where, thanks to the cooling marine influence, pinot noir and chardonnay are the king and queen of grapes.

ESSENTIALS

Contacts Russian River Wine Road (⊠ *Box 46, Healdsburg* ☎ *707/433–4335 or 800/723–6336* ⊕ *www.wineroad.com*).

10

At the **J Vineyards and Winery**, behind the bar in the tasting room is a dramatic steel sculpture studded with illuminated chunks of glass that suggests a bottle of bubbly. It's a big clue to what's most important here. The dry sparkling wines, made from pinot noir and chardonnay grapes planted in Russian River vineyards, have wonderfully complex fruit and floral aromas and good acidity. Still best known for its sparklers, J has also begun to make a larger number of fine still wines, often from pinot and chardonnay grapes but also from pinot gris, viognier, and zinfandel. Although you can sample wines on their own at the tasting bar, for a truly indulgent experience make a reservation for the Bubble Room, where you should set aside a couple of hours for a selection of top-end still and sparkling wines served with different foods. Tours are offered twice daily by appointment. ⊠ *11447 Old Redwood Hwy. Healdsburg* ☎ *707/431–3646* ⊕ *www.jwine.com* 🖃 *Tasting $20–$60* ☉ *Daily 11–5; Bubble Room hrs vary.*

Fodor's Choice
★

Iron Horse Vineyards makes a wide variety of sparkling wines, from the bright and austere to the rich and toasty, as well as estate chardonnays and pinot noirs. Three hundred acres of rolling, vine-covered hills, barn-like winery buildings, and a beautifully rustic outdoor tasting area with a view of Mt. St. Helena set it apart from stuffier spots. (Instead of providing buckets for you to dump out the wine you don't want to finish, they ask you to toss it into the grass behind you.) Tours are available by appointment on weekdays at 10 AM. ⊠ *9786 Ross Station Rd., Sebastopol* ☎ *707/887–1507* ⊕ *www.ironhorsevineyards.com* 🗔 *Tasting $10, tour free* ⊘ *Daily 10–3:30; tour weekdays at 10 by appointment.*

Rochioli Vineyards and Winery claims one of the prettiest picnic sites in the area, with tables overlooking vineyards, which are also visible from the airy little tasting room hung with modern artwork. Production is small—about 12,000 or 13,000 cases annually—and fans on the winery's mailing list snap up most of the bottles, but the wines are still worth a stop. Because of the cool growing conditions in the Russian River Valley, the flavors of their chardonnay and sauvignon blanc are intense and complex. It's their pinot, though, that is largely responsible for the winery's stellar reputation; it helped cement the Russian River's status as a pinot powerhouse. ■TIP➔ Though Rochioli typically pours only a couple of wines for visitors, it's one of the few wineries of its stature that doesn't charge for a tasting. ⊠ *6192 Westside Rd., Healdsburg* ☎ *707/433–2305* ⊕ *www.rochioliwinery.com* 🗔 *Tasting free* ⊘ *Thurs.–Mon. 11–4, Tues. and Wed. by appointment; closed mid-Dec.–early Jan.*

Fans of pinot noir will surely want to stop at **Hartford Family Winery,** a surprisingly opulent winery off a meandering country road in Forestville. Here grapes from the cooler areas of the Russian River Valley, Sonoma Coast, and other regions are turned into crisp chardonnays, old-vine zinfandels, and a wide variety of pinots, many of which are single-vineyard wines. ⊠ *8075 Martinelli Rd. Forestville* ☎ *707/887–1756* ⊕ *www.hartfordwines.com* 🗔 *Tasting $5–$15* ⊘ *Daily 10–4:30.*

Pass through an impressive metal gate and wind your way up a steep hill to reach **Gary Farrell Winery,** a spot with knockout views over the rolling hills and vineyards below. Although the winery has changed hands a few times since Farrell sold it in 2004, it has managed to continue producing well-regarded bottles under Susan Reed, who worked alongside him. Though their earthy, full-bodied zinfandels are winners, the winery has built its reputation on its pinot noirs. They also make a fine sauvignon blanc and chardonnay. ⊠ *10701 Westside Rd. Healdsburg* ☎ *707/473–2900* ⊕ *www.garyfarrellwines.com* 🗔 *Tasting $10–$15, tour $20* ⊘ *Daily 10:30–4:30; tour by appointment.*

**OFF THE
BEATEN
PATH**

Korbel Champagne Cellars produces several tasty, reasonably priced bubblies and still wines, as well as its own brandy. The wine tour clearly explains the process of making sparkling wine and takes you through the winery's ivy-covered 19th-century buildings. If you've already had the process of wine making explained to you one too many times, a tour of the rose garden, where there are more than 250 varieties of roses, may be a welcome break. Garden tours are given a few times daily

Annual barrel tasting along Russian River's wine road.

Tuesday through Sunday, mid-April through mid-October. ✉ *13250 River Rd., Guerneville* ☎ *707/824–7000* ⊕ *www.korbel.com* 🍷 *Tasting and tour free* ☯ *Daily 10–4:30; call for tour times.*

WHERE TO EAT

$$$$

FRENCH

Fodor'sChoice

★

✕ **The Farmhouse Inn.** From the personable sommelier who arrives at the table to help you pick wines from the excellent list to the servers who lovingly describe the provenance of the black truffles shaved over your pasta stuffed with salt-roasted pears and Parmesan, the staff match the quality of the outstanding French-inspired cuisine. The signature dish, "rabbit, rabbit, rabbit," a rich trio of confit of leg, rabbit loin wrapped in applewood-smoked bacon, and roasted rack of rabbit with a whole-grain mustard sauce, is typical of the dishes that are both rustic and refined, and the starters often include a seared Sonoma foie gras served with an apple cider sauce. ■**TIP**→ The inn's a favorite of local foodies in the wine industry, who also know that their head sommelier is one of only about a hundred Master Sommeliers working in the United States, so reserve well in advance. ✉ *7871 River Rd., Forestville* ☎ *707/887–3300 or 800/464–6642* ⊕ *www.farmhouseinn.com* ⌦ *Reservations essential* ▭ *AE, D, DC, MC, V* ☯ *Closed Tues. and Wed. No lunch.*

WHERE TO STAY

$$–$$$

★

▣ **Applewood Inn & Restaurant.** On a knoll in the shelter of towering redwoods, this romantic inn has two distinct types of accommodations. The original Belden House, built in 1922, has a river-rock fireplace that encourages loitering in the reception area. Its rooms are smaller than those in the newer buildings, but have charming touches, such as an exposed-brick wall in one or a view of a stand of redwood trees from

10

another. Most of the rooms in the newer buildings are larger and airier, decorated in sage-green and terra-cotta tones. Readers rave about the stellar service, soothing atmosphere, and the earthy Cal-Italian cuisine that's served in the restaurant ($$$), built to recall a French barn. At this writing, new owners had plans for redecorating, adding a small spa, and instituting regional Italian cooking classes, so call ahead or check their Web site for the latest. **Pros:** quiet, secluded location; friendly, homey service. **Cons:** planned improvements may cause some disruption; sounds can carry in the Belden House. ⊠ *13555 Rte. 116, Guerneville* ☎ *707/869–9093 or 800/555–8509* ⊕ *www.applewoodinn.com* ⟳ *19 rooms* ⚲ *In-room: a/c (some), Wi-Fi. In-hotel: restaurant, pool, spa* ▭ *AE, D, MC, V* ⊚| *BP.*

$$$–$$$$ | **The Farmhouse Inn.** This pale yellow 1873 farmhouse and adjacent
Fodor's Choice | cottages offer individually decorated rooms with comfortable touches
★ | such as down comforters and whirlpool tubs. Most of the cottages have wood-burning fireplaces and even their own private saunas, which make this place especially inviting during the rainy months. The most romantic (and expensive) rooms are those in the newest building, finished in 2009 and built to resemble an old barn that was once on the property. With a chic rustic-farmhouse-meets-modern-loft aesthetic, the spacious rooms have king-size four-poster beds, spa tubs, and patios or balconies overlooking the hillside. It's worth leaving your supremely comfortable bed for the sumptuous breakfasts here. **Pros:** one of Sonoma's best restaurants is on-site; free snacks, games, and movies available; extremely comfortable beds. **Cons:** rooms closest to the street get a bit of road noise. ⊠ *7871 River Rd., Forestville* ☎ *707/887–3300 or 800/464–6642* ⊕ *www.farmhouseinn.com* ⟳ *12 rooms, 6 suites* ⚲ *In-room: a/c, refrigerator, DVD, Wi-Fi. In-hotel: restaurant, pool, spa* ▭ *AE, D, DC, MC, V* ⊚| *BP.*

¢ | **Sebastopol Inn.** Simple but cheerful rooms, freshly painted a sunny yellow and equipped with blue-and-white striped curtains, have a spare California country style at this reasonably priced inn. Rooms clustered around a pleasant courtyard are also steps away from an old train station that has been converted into a cluster of cafés and shops. Some of the rooms have microwaves, some have small balconies or patios, and the uncommonly spacious suites (which also have jetted tubs) offer plenty of room for families. **Pros:** friendly staff; just steps from a café, wine bar, and spa. **Cons:** at least a 30-minute drive from most Russian River wineries; some will find the beds too firm. ⊠ *6751 Sebastopol Ave., Sebastopol* ☎ *707/829–2500* ⊕ *www.sebastopolinn.com* ⟳ *29 rooms, 2 suites* ⚲ *In-room: refrigerator, Wi-Fi. In-hotel: restaurant, pool, laundry facilities* ▭ *AE, D, DC, MC, V.*

HEALDSBURG

17 mi north of Santa Rosa on U.S. 101.

Just when it seems that the buzz about Healdsburg couldn't get any bigger, there's another article published in a glossy food or wine magazine about posh properties like the restaurant Cyrus and the ultra-luxe Hôtel Les Mars. But you don't have to be a tycoon to stay here and enjoy the town. For every ritzy restaurant there's a great bakery or relatively modest B&B. A whitewashed bandstand on Healdsburg's plaza hosts free summer concerts, where you might hear anything from bluegrass to Sousa marches. Add to that the fragrant magnolia trees shading the square and the bright flower beds, and the whole thing is as pretty as a Norman Rockwell painting.

The countryside around Healdsburg is the sort you dream about when you're planning a Wine Country vacation. Alongside the relatively untrafficked roads, country stores offer just-plucked fruits and vine-ripened tomatoes. The wineries here are barely visible, since they're tucked behind groves of eucalyptus or hidden high on fog-shrouded hills.

WHERE TO EAT

$$$
AMERICAN

✕ **Barndiva.** This hip joint abandons the homey vibe of so many Wine Country spots for a younger, more urban feel. Electronic music plays quietly in the background while hipster servers ferry inventive seasonal cocktails. The food is as stylish as the well-dressed couples cozying up next to one another on the banquette seats. Make a light meal out of starters like goat-cheese croquettes or "The Works," a bountiful plate of cheeses and charcuterie, or settle in for the evening with crispy lamb cheeks or risotto with seasonal vegetables. During warm weather the patio is the place to be. ⊠ *231 Center St.* ☎ *707/431–0100* ⊕ *www. barndiva.com* ⊟ *AE, MC, V* ⊘ *Closed Mon. and Tues.*

$
ITALIAN

✕ **Bovolo.** Husband-and-wife team John Stewart and Duskie Estes serve what they call "slow food . . . fast." Though you might pop into this casual café at the back of Copperfield's Books for half an hour, the staff will have spent hours curing the meats that star in the menu of salads, pizzas, pastas, and sandwiches. For instance, the Salumist's Salad mixes a variety of cured meats with greens, white beans, and a tangy vinaigrette; and a thin-crust pizza might come topped with house-made Italian pork sausage and roasted peppers. House-made gelato served with a dark chocolate sauce or *zeppole* (Italian donuts) are a simply perfect ending to a meal. ⊠ *106 Matheson St.* ☎ *707/431–2962* ⊕ *www. bovolorestaurant.com* ⊛ *Reservations not accepted* ⊟ *MC, V.*

$$$$
AMERICAN
Fodor's Choice
★

✕ **Cyrus.** Hailed as the best thing to hit the Wine Country since French Laundry, Cyrus has collected lots of awards and many raves from guests. From the moment you're seated to the minute your dessert plates are whisked away, you'll be carefully tended by gracious servers and an expert sommelier. The formal dining room, with its vaulted Venetian-plaster ceiling, is a suitably plush setting for chef Douglas Keane's creative, subtle cuisine. Each night, diners have their choice of four set menus: five- and eight-course extravaganzas ($102 and $130), for both omnivores and vegetarians. Set aside three hours to work your way from savory starters like the terrine of foie gras with curried apple compote, through fragrant dishes like the truffled wine risotto with Parmesan broth, to desserts such as the hazelnut *dacquoise* (layers of hazelnut and buttercream). If you've failed to make reservations, you can order à la carte at the bar, which also has the best collection of cocktails and spirits in all of the Wine Country. ⊠ *29 North St., Healdsburg*

10

☎ 707/433–3311 ⊕ *www.cyrusrestaurant.com* ⟨ *Reservations essential* ⊟ *AE, DC, MC, V* ☉ *Closed Tues. and Wed. in winter. No lunch.*

$$ ✕ **Scopa.** At this tiny eatery chef Ari Rosen cooks up rustic Italian spe-
ITALIAN   cialties such as house-made ravioli stuffed with ricotta cheese, braised
chicken with greens and polenta, and *polpette Calabrese* (spicy meat-
balls served with smoked mozzarella in a tomato sauce). Simple thin-
crust pizzas are worth ordering, too. Locals love the restaurant for
its lack of pretension: wine is served in juice glasses, and the friendly
hostess visits guests frequently to make sure all are satisfied. You'll be
packed in elbow-to-elbow with your fellow diners, but for a convivial
evening over a bottle of nebbiolo, there's no better choice. ⊠ *109A
Plaza St.* ☎ 707/433–5282 ⊕ *www.scopahealdsburg.com* ⊟ *AE, MC,
V* ☉ *Closed Mon. No lunch.*

$$ ✕ **Zin Restaurant and Wine Bar.** Concrete walls and floors and large can-
AMERICAN   vases on the walls make the restaurant casual, industrial, and slightly
artsy. The American cuisine—such as smoked pork chop with homemade applesauce or the lamb sirloin with mint jelly—is hearty and
highly seasoned. Portions are large, so consider sharing if you hope to
save room for desserts like the brownie sundae with Kahlua chocolate
sauce. As you might have guessed, zinfandel is the drink of choice
here: the varietal makes up roughly half of the 100 or so bottles on
the wine list. ⊠ *344 Center St.* ☎ 707/473–0946 ⊟ *AE, MC, V* ☉ *No
lunch weekends.*

WHERE TO STAY

¢–$ ⊡ **Camellia Inn.** In a well-preserved Victorian constructed in 1869, this
colorful B&B is on a quiet residential street a block from the town's
main square. The parlors downstairs are chockablock with ceramics
and other decorative items, while rooms are individually decorated with
antiques. Each room has its own charms, like a canopy bed, a claw-foot
tub, or a whirlpool bath. ■TIP➔ Those on a budget should ask about
the cozy (and popular) budget room with a full-size bed and large private
bath across the hall. **Pros:** reasonable rates for the neighborhood; a rare
family-friendly inn; within easy walking distance of dozens of restaurants. **Cons:** a few rooms have a shower but no bath; the only TV on the
property is in the common sunroom. ⊠ *211 North St.* ☎ 707/433–8182
or 800/727–8182 ⊕ *www.camelliainn.com* ⇝ *8 rooms, 1 suite* ⚭ *In-
room: no phone, a/c, no TV, Wi-Fi. In-hotel: pool, some pets allowed*
⊟ *AE, D, MC, V* ❉⌷ *BP.*

$$$ ⊡ **The Honor Mansion.** Each room is unique at this photogenic 1883
★ Italianate Victorian. Rooms in the main house preserve a sense of the
building's heritage, while the larger suites are comparatively under-
stated. Luxurious touches such as antiques and decanters of sherry are
found in every room, and suites have the advantage of a deck; some even
have private outdoor hot tubs. Fodors.com readers rave about the atten-
tive staff, who "think of things you don't even know you want." **Pros:**
spacious grounds with boccie and tennis courts, a putting green, and
half-court for basketball; homemade sweets available at all hours; spa
pavilions by pool available for massages in fair weather. **Cons:** almost
a mile from Healdsburg's plaza; on a moderately busy street. ⊠ *14891
Grove St.* ☎ 707/433–4277 *or 800/554–4667* ⊕ *www.honormansion.*

com 🛏*5 rooms, 8 suites* 🛁 *In-room: a/c, safe (some), refrigerator (some), DVD (some), Wi-Fi. In-hotel: tennis court, pool, Internet terminal* ☰ *AE, MC, V* ☺ *Closed 1 wk around Christmas* ⦿*BP.*

$$$–$$$$ 🏨 **Hotel Healdsburg.** Across the street from Healdsburg's tidy town plaza, this spare, sophisticated hotel caters to travelers with an urban sensibility. Unadorned olive-green walls, dark hardwood floors, and clean-line furniture fill the guest rooms; the beds are some of the most comfortable you can find. Spacious bathrooms continue the sleek style with monochromatic tiles and deep soaking tubs that are all right angles. The attached restaurant, Dry Creek Kitchen ($$$$), is one of the best in Healdsburg. Celebrity chef Charlie Palmer is the man behind seasonal dishes that largely rely on local ingredients, like a spice-crusted Sonoma duck breast or seared Sonoma foie gras, plus a wine list covering the best Sonoma vintners. **Pros:** several rooms overlook the town plaza; free valet parking; extremely comfortable beds. **Cons:** least expensive rooms are small; exterior rooms get some street noise. ⊠ *25 Matheson St.* ☎ *707/431–2800 or 800/889–7188* ⊕ *www.hotelhealdsburg.com* 🛏*45 rooms, 10 suites* 🛁 *In-room: a/c, safe, refrigerator, DVD, Internet, Wi-Fi. In-hotel: restaurant, room service, bar, pool, gym, spa, laundry service, some pets allowed* ☰ *AE, MC, V* ⦿*CP.*

$$$$ 🏨 **Hôtel Les Mars.** In 2005, posh Healdsburg got even more chichi with the opening of this opulent Relais & Châteaux hotel. Guest rooms are spacious and elegant enough for French nobility, with 18th- and 19th-century antiques and reproductions, canopied beds, and gas burning fireplaces. Most of the gleaming, white-marble bathrooms have spa tubs in addition to enormous showers. Rooms on the third floor have soaring 20-foot ceilings that make them feel particularly large, while the second-floor rooms have a slightly more understated style. Wine and cheese are served every evening in the library, which is sumptuously paneled with hand-carved black walnut, and a Continental breakfast is delivered to your room each morning. **Pros:** large rooms; just off Healdsburg's plaza; impeccable service; Bulgari bath products. **Cons:** very expensive. ⊠ *27 North St.* ☎ *707/433–4211* ⊕ *www.lesmarshotel. com* 🛏 *16 rooms* 🛁 *In-room: a/c, safe, DVD, Internet, Wi-Fi. In-hotel: restaurant, bar, pool, gym, laundry service* ☰ *AE, MC, V* ⦿*CP.*

$$$–$$$$ 🏨 **Madrona Manor.** The oldest continuously operating inn in the area, this 1881 Victorian mansion is surrounded by 8 acres of wooded and landscaped grounds. Rooms in the three-story mansion, the carriage house, and the three separate cottages are splendidly ornate, with mirrors in gilt frames and paintings covering every wall. Much of the furniture is even original to the 19th-century house. Candlelight dinners are served in the formal dining rooms nightly except Monday and Tuesday. Chef Jesse Mallgren has earned much praise for his elaborate three-, four-, and five-course menus ($$$$), where luxuries like the a Périgord truffle risotto might precede a bacon-wrapped rabbit loin and a warm chocolate soufflé. ■ **TIP→ For a ridiculously romantic experience, ask for Room 203 or 204. They both have huge balconies that overlook the hotel grounds and beyond. Pros:** old-fashioned and romantic; pretty veranda perfect for a cocktail. **Cons:** pool heated May through October only; decor might be too fussy for some. ⊠ *1001 Westside Rd., central Healdsburg exit*

10

off U.S. 101, then left on Mill St.
☎ *707/433–4231 or 800/258–4003*
⊕ *www.madronamanor.com* ⤴ *17*
rooms, 5 suites & *In-room: a/c, no*
TV, Wi-Fi. In-hotel: restaurant, bar,
pool ☱ *AE, MC, V* ⧀ *BP.*

SHOPPING
Oakville Grocery (⊠ *124 Matheson*
St. ☎ *707/433–3200*) has a bustling
Healdsburg branch filled with wine,
condiments, and deli items. A terrace with ample seating makes a
good place for an impromptu picnic, but you might want to lunch
early or late to avoid the worst
crowds. You'll have to get in your
car to head north on Healdsburg

> ### FARMERS MARKET
>
> During two weekly **Healdsburg farmers' markets** you can buy locally made goat cheese, fragrant lavender, and olive oil in addition to the usual produce. On Saturday from May through November the market takes place one block west of the town plaza, at the corner of North and Vine streets, from 9 AM to noon. The Tuesday market, which runs from June through October, takes place on the plaza itself from 4 to 6:30 PM.

Avenue to **Tip Top Liquor Warehouse** (⊠ *90 Dry Creek Rd., Healdsburg*
☎ *707/431–0841*), a nondescript spot that stocks an interesting selection of wines and spirits at fair prices. Though it's strongest in bottles
from Sonoma, you'll also find a few Napa wines, including some rare
cult cabernets.

DRY CREEK AND ALEXANDER VALLEYS

On the west side of U.S. 101, Dry Creek Valley remains one of the least-
developed appellations in Sonoma. Zinfandel grapes flourish on the
benchlands, whereas the gravelly, well-drained soil of the valley floor is
better known for chardonnay and, in the north, sauvignon blanc. The
wineries in this region tend to be smaller, which makes them a good
bet on summer weekends, when larger spots and those along the main
thoroughfares fill up with tourists.

The Alexander Valley, which lies northeast of Healdsburg, is similarly
rustic, and you can see as many folks cycling along Highway 128 here
as you can behind the wheel of a car. The largely family-owned wineries
often produce zinfandel and chardonnay.

★ Inside the tasting room at **Stryker Sonoma**, vaulted ceilings and seemingly
endless walls of windows onto the vineyards suggest you've entered
a cathedral to wine. The wines are almost as impressive as the architecture: most of their bottles are single varietals, such as chardonnay,
merlot, zinfandel, and cabernet sauvignon. An exception, however, are
a few Bordeaux-style blends, including the powerful E1K, which, unfortunately, is not usually poured in the tasting room (though it never hurts
to ask whether they have a bottle open). The picnic tables are a particularly lovely way to enjoy the quiet countryside of the Alexander Valley.
⊠ *5110 Hwy. 28, Geyserville* ☎ *707/433–1944* ⊕ *www.strykersonoma.*
com ⤴ *Tasting free–$10* ☉ *Daily 10:30–5.*

In 2006, filmmaker-winemaker-publisher-hotelier Francis Ford Coppola snapped up a majestic French-style château, formerly Château

Best Wine Country Festivals

■ **Napa Valley Mustard Festival, Feb.–Mar.** When Napa is at its least crowded, and wild mustard blooms in between the vines, locals celebrate wine, food, and art with exhibitions, auctions, dinners, and cooking competitions. (☎ 707/938–1133 ⊕ www. mustardfestival.org)

■ **Wine Road Barrel Tasting Weekends, Mar.** For two weekends in March more than 100 wineries in the Russian River, Dry Creek, and Alexander valleys open their cellars to visitors who want to taste the wine in the barrels, getting a preview of what's to come. (☎ 707/433–4335 or 800/723–6336 ⊕ www.wineroad.com)

■ **Hospice du Rhône, early May** This three-day event in Paso Robles is the largest celebration of Rhône varietals in the world. (☎ 805/784–9543 ⊕ hospicedurhone.org)

■ **Sonoma Jazz + Festival, late May** Headlining jazz, rock, and world music performers play in a 3,800-person tent in downtown Sonoma, while smaller music, food, and wine events take place around town. (☎ 866/468–8355 ⊕ www.sonomajazz.org)

■ **Auction Napa Valley, early June** The world's biggest charity wine auction is one of Napa's glitziest nights. Events hosted by various wineries culminate in an opulent dinner and auction. (☎ 707/963–3388 ⊕ www. napavintners.com)

■ **Sonoma County Harvest Fair, early Oct.** This festival celebrates agriculture in Sonoma County, with wine tastings, cooking demos, livestock shows, crafts, carnival rides, and local entertainers filling the Sonoma County Fairgrounds in Santa Rosa. (☎ 707/545–4203 ⊕ www.harvestfair. org)

Souverain and now called **Francis Ford Coppola Winery,** to showcase his less-expensive wines. (His Napa winery, Rubicon Estate, focuses on the high-end vintages). It's still very much a work in progress: at this writing, the property was in full renovation mode, and wines were being poured in a makeshift tasting room. After all the dust settles, however, the winery intends to have a full-service restaurant, a café, and an area for viewing Coppola memorabilia (the desk from *The Godfather* and costumes from *Bram Stoker's Dracula*, for example) that were once housed at Rubicon. Fans of Coppola's wines or movies should check the Web site or call ahead for the latest. ✉ *300 Via Archimedes (formerly Souverain Rd.), Geyserville* ☎ *707/433–8282* ⊕ *www. franciscoppolawinery.com* ✉ *Tasting free–$8* ☉ *Daily 11–5.*

At **Dry Creek Vineyard** fumé blanc is king. Dry Creek also makes well-regarded zinfandels, a zesty dry chenin blanc, a pinot noir, and a handful of cabernet sauvignon blends. Since many of their quality wines go for less than $20 or $30 a bottle, it's a popular stop for those who want to stock their cellars for a reasonable price. After picking up a bottle you might want to picnic on the lawn, next to the flowering magnolia tree. Conveniently, a general store and deli with plenty of picnic fixings is just steps down the road. ✉ *3770 Lambert Bridge Rd., Healdsburg*

☎ 707/433–1000 ⊕ www.drycreekvineyard.com ☞ Tasting $5–$10 ⊙ Daily 10:30–4:30.

An unassuming winery in a modern wooden barn topped by solar panels, **Quivira** produces some of the most interesting wines in Dry Creek Valley. It's known for its dangerously drinkable reds, including a petite syrah, and a few hearty zinfandel blends. The excellent tour provides information about their biodynamic farming practices and also offers a glimpse of the chickens and goats kept on the property. Redwood and olive trees shade the picnic area. ✉ 4900 W. Dry Creek Rd., Healdsburg ☎ 707/431–8333 ⊕ www.quivirawine.com ☞ Tasting $5, tour $15 ⊙ Daily 11–5; tour by appointment.

Fodor's Choice
★ Down a narrow road at the westernmost edge of the Dry Creek Valley, **Michel-Schlumberger** is one of Sonoma's finest producers of cabernet sauvignon, aptly described by the winery's tour guide as a "full, rich big mouthful of wine." The tour is unusually casual and friendly. Weather permitting, you'll wander up a hill on a gravel pathway to the edge of their lovely terraced vineyards before swinging through the barrel room in the California Mission–style building that once served as the home of the winery's founder, Jean-Jacques Michel. To taste older vintages of their cabernet and learn what their wines will taste like after 10 or so years in the bottle, reserve in advance for a vertical tasting. ✉ 4155 Wine Creek Rd., Healdsburg ☎ 707/433–7427 or 800/447–3060 ⊕ www.michelschlumberger.com ☞ Tasting $25, tour $15 ⊙ Tours at 11 and 2, by appointment; tasting by appointment.

Fodor's Choice
★ Once you wind your way down **Preston Vineyards'** long driveway, flanked by vineyards and punctuated by the occasional olive tree, you'll be welcomed by the sight of a few farmhouses encircling a shady yard prowled by several friendly cats. In summer a small selection of organic produce grown in their gardens is sold from an impromptu stand on the front porch, and house-made bread and olive oil are available year-round. Their down-home style is particularly in evidence on Sunday, the only day of the week that tasting-room staffers sell a 3-liter bottle of Guadagni Red, a primarily zinfandel blend filled from the barrel right in front of you. Owners Lou and Susan Preston are committed to organic growing techniques, and use only estate-grown grapes in their wines. ✉ 9282 W. Dry Creek Rd., Healdsburg ☎ 707/433–3372 ⊕ www.prestonvineyards.com ☞ $5 ⊙ Daily 11–4:30.

The North Coast

FROM THE SONOMA COAST TO REDWOOD NATIONAL PARK

WORD OF MOUTH

"Steep stairs leads to an historic lighthouse at Point Reyes National Seashore. Whales are visible from this point a few months out of the year."

—photo by spirobulldog, Fodors.com member

WELCOME TO THE NORTH COAST

TOP REASONS TO GO

★ **Scenic coastal drives:** There's hardly a road here that *isn't* scenic.

★ **Wild beaches:** This stretch of California is one of nature's masterpieces. Revel in the unbridled, rugged coastline, without a building in sight.

★ **Dinnertime:** When you're done hiking the beach, refuel with delectable food; you'll find everything from burritos to bouillabaisse.

★ **Romance:** Here you can end almost every day with a perfect sunset.

★ **Wildlife:** Sea lions and otters and deer, oh my!

1 The Sonoma Coast. Heading up through northwestern Marin into Sonoma County, Highway 1 traverses gently rolling pastureland. North of Bodega Bay dramatic shoreline scenery takes over. The road snakes up, down, and around sheer cliffs and steep inclines—some without guardrails—where cows seem to cling precariously. Stunning vistas (or cottony fog) and hairpin turns make this one of the most exhilarating drives north of San Francisco.

2 The Mendocino Coast. The timber industry gave birth to most of the small towns strung along this stretch of the California coastline. Although tourism now drives the economy, the region has retained much of its old-fashioned charm. The beauty of the coastal landscape, of course, has not changed.

3 Redwood Country. There's a different state of mind in Humboldt County. Here, instead of spas, there are old-time hotels. Instead of wineries, there are breweries. The landscape is primarily thick redwood forest, which gets snow in winter and sizzles in summer while the coast sits covered in fog. Until as late as 1924, there was no road that went north of Willits; the coastal towns were reachable only by sea. That legacy is apparent in the communities here today: Eureka and Arcata are sizeable (both formerly ports), but otherwise towns are tiny and tucked away into the woods, and people have an independent spirit that recalls the original homesteaders. Coming from the south, Garberville is a good place to stop for picnic provisions and stretch your legs.

4 Redwood National Park. For a pristine encounter with giant redwoods, make the trek to this seldom-visited park where even casual visitors have easy access to the trees. *(See Chapter 12, Redwood National Park.)*

GETTING ORIENTED

It's all but impossible to explore the northern California coast without a car. Indeed, you wouldn't want to—driving here is half the fun. The main road is Highway 1, two lanes that twist and turn (sometimes 180 degrees) up cliffs and down through valleys. Towns appear every so often, but this is mostly a land of green pasture, dense forest, and natural, undeveloped coastline. Pace yourself: Most drivers stop frequently to appreciate the views (and you can't drive faster than 20–40 MPH on many portions of the highway), so don't plan to drive too far in one day.

THE NORTH COAST PLANNER

Getting Here and Around

Although there are excellent services along U.S. 101, long, lonesome stretches separate towns (with their gas stations and mechanics) along Highway 1, and services are even fewer and farther between on the smaller roads. ■TIP→ If you're running low on fuel and see a gas station, stop for a refill. Driving directly to Mendocino from San Francisco is quicker if, instead of driving up the coast on Highway 1, you take U.S. 101 north to Highway 128 west (from Cloverdale) to Highway 1 north. The quickest way to the far North Coast from the Bay Area is a straight shot up U.S. 101, which runs inland all the way until Eureka.

Weather

The coastal climate is quite similar to San Francisco's, although with greater extremes: winter nights are colder than in the city, and in July and August thick fog can drop temperatures to the high 50s. If you do get caught in the summer fog, fear not! You need only drive inland to find temperatures that are often 20 degrees higher.

Restaurants

A few restaurants with national reputations, plus several more of regional note, entertain palates on the North Coast. Even the workaday local spots take advantage of the abundant fresh seafood and locally grown vegetables and herbs. Attire is usually informal, though at the pricier establishments dressy casual (somewhere between flip-flops and high heels) is the norm. As in many rural areas, plan to dine early: the majority of kitchens close at 8 or 8:30 and virtually no one serves past 9:30. Also note that many restaurants in the northern part of this region close for a winter break in January.

Hotels

Restored Victorians, rustic lodges, country inns, and vintage motels are among the accommodations available here. Hardly any have air-conditioning (the ocean breezes make it unnecessary), and many have no phones or TVs in the rooms. Although several towns have only one or two places to spend the night, some of these lodgings are destinations in themselves. Budget accommodations are rare, but in winter you're likely to find reduced rates and nearly empty inns and B&Bs. In summer and on the weekends, though, make bed-and-breakfast reservations as far ahead as possible—rooms at the best inns often sell out months in advance.

WHAT IT COSTS

	¢	$	$$	$$$	$$$$
Restaurants	under $10	$10–$15	$16–$22	$23–$30	over $30
Hotels	under $90	$90–$120	$121–$175	$176–$250	over $250

Restaurant prices are for a main course at dinner, excluding sales tax of 8.5%–9.25% (depending on location). Hotel prices are for two people in a standard double room in high season, excluding service charges and 8%–10% tax.

11

Updated
by Lisa M.
Hamilton

The spectacular coastline between Marin County and the Oregon border defies what most people expect of California. The landscape is defined by the Pacific Ocean, but instead of boardwalks and bikinis there are ragged cliffs and pounding waves—and the sunbathers are mostly sea lions. Instead of strip malls and freeways, there are small towns that tuck in around sundown and a single-lane road that follows the fickle shoreline. And that's exactly why many Californians, especially those from the Bay Area, come here to escape daily life.

This stretch of Highway 1 is made up of numerous little worlds, each different from the next. From Point Reyes toward Bodega Bay, the land spreads out into green, rolling pastures and sandy beaches. The road climbs higher and higher as it heads north through Sonoma County, where cows graze on precipitous cliffs and the ocean views are breathtaking. In Mendocino the coastline follows the ins and outs of lush valleys where rivers pour down from the forests and into the ocean. At Humboldt County the highway heads inland to the redwoods, then returns to the shoreline at the tidal flats surrounding the ports of Eureka and Arcata. Heading north to the Oregon border, the coast is increasingly wild and lined with redwood trees.

Although the towns along the way vary from deluxe spa town to hippie hideaway, all are reliably sleepy. Most communities have fewer than 1,000 inhabitants, and most main streets are shuttered by 9 PM. Exceptions are Mendocino and Eureka, but even they are loved best by those who want to cozy up in bed rather than paint the town.

PLANNING

GETTING HERE AND AROUND

BY AIR

The only North Coast airport with commercial air service, Arcata/Eureka Airport (ACV) receives flights on United Express, Delta, and Horizon Airlines. The airport is in McKinleyville, which is 16 mi from Eureka.

A taxi to Eureka costs about $40 and takes roughly 20 minutes. Door-to-door airport shuttles cost $19 to Arcata and Trinidad, $23 to Eureka, and $50 to Ferndale. All prices are for the first person, and go up only $5 total for each additional person.

Airport Contact Arcata/Eureka Airport (✉ *3561 Boeing Ave., McKinleyville* ☎ *707/839–5401*).

Shuttle Contact Door to Door Airport Shuttle (☎ *888/338–5497* ⊕ *www.doortodoorairporter.com*).

BY BUS

Greyhound buses travel along U.S. 101 from San Francisco to Seattle, with regular stops in Eureka and Arcata. Bus drivers will stop in other towns along the route if you specify your destination when you board. Humboldt Transit Authority connects Eureka, Arcata, and Trinidad.

Bus Contacts Greyhound (☎ *800/231–2222* ⊕ *www.greyhound.com*). **Humboldt Transit Authority** (☎ *707/443–0826* ⊕ *www.hta.org*).

BY CAR

Although there are excellent services along U.S. 101, long, lonesome stretches separate towns (with their gas stations and mechanics) along Highway 1, and services are even fewer and farther between on the smaller roads. ■TIP➔ If you're running low on fuel and see a gas station, stop for a refill. Driving directly to Mendocino from San Francisco is quicker if, instead of driving up the coast on Highway 1, you take U.S. 101 north to Highway 128 west (from Cloverdale) to Highway 1 north. The quickest way to the far North Coast from the Bay Area is a straight shot up U.S. 101, which runs inland all way until Eureka. Weather sometimes forces closure of parts of Highway 1, but it's rare. For information on the condition of roads in northern California, call the Caltrans Highway Information Network's voice-activated system.

Road Conditions Caltrans Highway Information Network (☎ *800/427–7623* ⊕ *www.dot.ca.gov*).

HEALTH AND SAFETY

In an emergency dial 911. In state and national parks, park rangers serve as police officers and will help you in any emergency. Bigger towns along the coast have hospitals, but for major medical emergencies you will need to go to San Francisco. Note that cell phones don't work along large swaths of the North Coast.

VISITOR INFORMATION

Information **Sonoma County Tourism Bureau** (⊠ *420 Aviation Blvd., Suite 106, Santa Rosa* ☎ *707/522–5800 or 800/576–6662* ⊕ *www.sonomacounty. com*). **Redwood Coast Chamber of Commerce** (✆ *Box 199, Gualala 95445* ☎ *707/884–1080 or 800/778–5252* ⊕ *www.redwoodcoastchamber.com*). **Visit Mendocino County** (⊠ *525 S. Main St., Ukiah 95482* ☎ *707/462–7417 or 866/466–3636* ⊕ *www.gomendo.com*). **Fort Bragg–Mendocino Coast Chamber of Commerce** (⊠ *217 S. Main St., Fort Bragg 95437* ☎ *707/961–6300* ⊕ *www.mendocinocoast.com*). **Humboldt County Convention and Visitors Bureau** (⊠ *1034 2nd St., Eureka 95501* ☎ *707/443–5097 or 800/346–3482* ⊕ *www.redwoods.info*).

THE SONOMA COAST

BODEGA BAY

21 mi north of Marshall on Hwy. 1.

From the busy harbor here, commercial boats pursue fish and Dungeness crab. There's nothing cutesy about this working town without a center—it's just a string of businesses along several miles of Highway 1. But some tourists still come to see where Alfred Hitchcock shot *The Birds* in 1962. The buildings in the movie are gone, but in nearby Bodega you can find Potter Schoolhouse and the Tides Wharf complex, which was a major, if now unrecognizable, location for the movie.

WHERE TO EAT AND STAY

$$
SEAFOOD

✕ **Sandpiper Restaurant**. A local favorite for breakfast, this friendly café on the marina does a good job for a fair price. Peruse the board for the day's fresh catches or order a menu regular such as crab stew or wasabi tuna; clam chowder is the house specialty. There's often live jazz Friday and Saturday evenings. ⊠ *1410 Bay Flat Rd.* ☎ *707/875–2278* ⊕ *www. sandpiperrestaurant.com* ▭ *MC, V.*

$$$–$$$$

🏨 **Bodega Bay Lodge**. Looking out to the ocean across a wetland, a group of shingle-and-river-rock buildings houses Bodega Bay's finest accommodations. Capacious rooms are appointed with high-quality bedding, fireplaces, and patios or balconies; some have vaulted ceilings and jetted tubs. In the health complex, state-of-the-art fitness equipment sparkles and the spa provides a full roster of pampering treatments. The quiet Duck Club restaurant ($$$–$$$$; no lunch), a notch or two above most places in town, hits more than it misses; try the Dungeness crab cakes with tomato-ginger chutney. **Pros:** pampering; ocean views. **Cons:** on the highway. ⊠ *103 Hwy. 1* ☎ *707/875–3525 or 888/875–2250* ⊕ *www. bodegabaylodge.com* ⤴ *77 rooms, 6 suites* ☙ *In-room: a/c, refrigerator, Wi-Fi. In-hotel: restaurant, room service, pool, gym, laundry facilities, Internet terminal, Wi-Fi hotspot* ▭ *AE, D, DC, MC, V.*

SPORTS AND THE OUTDOORS

Bodega Bay Sportfishing (⊠ *1410 B Bay Flat Rd.* ☎ *707/875–3344* ⊕ *www. bodegabaysportfishing.com*) charters ocean fishing boats and rents equipment. They also offer whale-watching trips mid-winter through

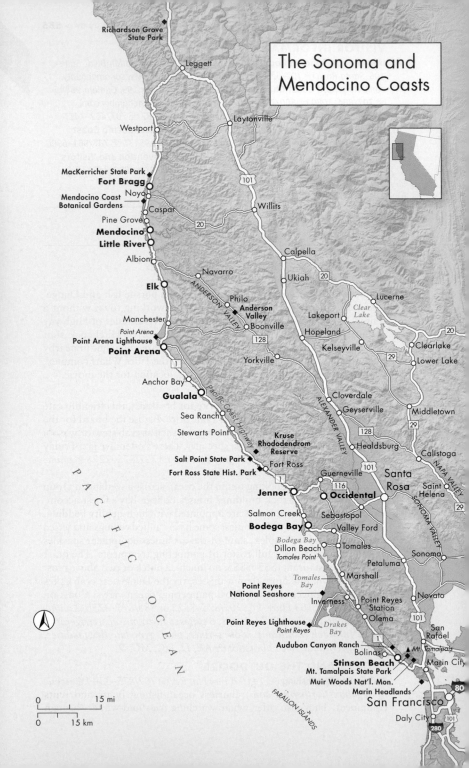

The Sonoma and Mendocino Coasts

Richardson Grove State Park

Leggett

Westport

Laytonville

MacKerricher State Park
Fort Bragg
Noyo
Mendocino Coast
Botanical Gardens
Caspar
Pine Grove
Mendocino
Little River
Albion

Willits

Calpella

Ukiah

Navarro
Philo
Anderson Valley
Boonville

ANDERSON VALLEY

Elk

Lucerne
Clear Lake
Lakeport
Hopeland
Kelseyville
Clearlake
Lower Lake

Manchester
Point Arena
Point Arena Lighthouse
Point Arena

Yorkville

Anchor Bay

Gualala

Pacific Coast Highway

Sea Ranch
Stewarts Point

Kruse Rhododendrom Reserve
Salt Point State Park
Fort Ross State Hist. Park
Fort Ross

Cloverdale
Geyserville

ALEXANDER VALLEY

Healdsburg

Middletown

Calistoga

PACIFIC OCEAN

Jenner

Salmon Creek

Bodega Bay

Bodega Bay
Dillon Beach
Tomales Point

Point Reyes
National Seashore

Point Reyes Lighthouse
Point Reyes

Audubon Canyon Ranch
Bolinas
Stinson Beach
Mt. Tamalpais State Park
Muir Woods Nat'l. Mon.
Marin Headlands

Guerneville

Occidental

Sebastopol
Valley Ford
Tomales

Tomales Bay
Marshall

Inverness
Olema

Drakes Bay

Santa Rosa
Saint Helena

NAPA VALLEY

SONOMA VALLEY

Petaluma
Sonoma

Point Reyes Station

Novato

San Rafael

Mt. Tamalpais
Marin City

San Francisco

Daly City

FARALLON ISLANDS

0   15 mi

0   15 km

spring. **Sonoma Villa Horse Rental** (✉ *16702 Hwy. 1* ☎ *707/876–3374* ⊕ *www.scvilla.com*) at the Sonoma Coast Villa & Spa, offers guided horseback trail rides, some along the beach. At the incredibly scenic oceanfront **Links at Bodega Harbour** (✉ *21301 Heron Dr.* ☎ *707/875–3538 or 800/503–8158* ⊕ *www.bodegaharbourgolf.com*) you can play an 18-hole Robert Trent Jones–designed course.

OCCIDENTAL

14 mi northeast of Bodega Bay on Bohemian Hwy.

A village surrounded by redwood forests, orchards, and vineyards, Occidental is a former logging hub with a bohemian feel. The 19th-century downtown offers a top-notch B&B, good food, and a handful of art galleries and boutiques. The neighboring town of Freestone offers much of the same, but on a smaller scale. To reach Occidental, take Highway 12 (Bodega Highway) east 5 mi from Highway 1. Take a left onto Bohemian Highway, where you'll find Freestone; another 3½ mi and you'll be in Occidental.

EXPLORING

A traditional Japanese detoxifying treatment awaits you at **Osmosis–The Enzyme Bath Spa,** which claims to be the only such facility in America. Your bath is a deep redwood tub of damp cedar shavings and rice bran, naturally heated to 140°F by the action of enzymes. Serene attendants bury you up to the neck and during the 20-minute treatment bring you sips of water and place cool cloths on your forehead. After a shower, lie down and listen to brain-balancing music through headphones or have a massage, perhaps in one of the creek-side pagodas. A treatment and access to the gardens costs $85 per person (less for parties of two or more people); reservations are recommended. ✉ *209 Bohemian Hwy., Freestone* ☎ *707/823–8231* ⊕ *www.osmosis.com* ▤ *AE, MC, V* ⊙ *Daily 9–8.*

Once a month, usually on Friday or Saturday evenings, **chamber music concerts** featuring notable musicians from California and around the country are held at the Occidental Community Church. ✉ *2nd and Church Sts.* ☎ *707/874–1124* ⊕ *www.redwoodarts.org* ▤ *AE, MC, V.*

WHERE TO EAT AND STAY

¢ ✕ **Wild Flour Bread.** There are no appliances at this bakery, which occupies a renovated barn. Dough is kneaded by hand, and baked in a wood-fired oven. The result: delectable breads both savory and sweet (don't miss the sticky bun bread). ✉ *140 Bohemian Hwy., Freestone* ☎ *707/874–2938* ⊕ *www.wildflourbread.com* ▤ *No credit cards* ⊙ *Closed Tues.–Thurs.*

CAFÉ

$$$$ ☖ **The Inn at Occidental.** Quilts, folk

★ art, and original paintings and

> **SCENIC STOP**
>
> The gorgeous sandy coves of **Sonoma Coast State Beach** (☎ *707/875-3483* ✉ *$8 per vehicle*) stretch along the shoreline from Bodega Head to a point several miles north of Jenner. Rock Point, Duncan's Landing, and Wright's Beach, clustered at about the halfway mark, have picnic areas. Wright's Beach and Bodega Dunes have developed campsites.

photographs fill this colorful and friendly inn. Some rooms—such as the Cirque du Sonoma Room, with a bright yellow-and-red color scheme—brim with personality and others are more sedate; all are comfortable and have fireplaces. Most guest rooms are spacious and have private decks and jetted tubs. An air of relaxed refinement prevails amid the whimsical antiques and fine Asian rugs in the ground-floor living room, where guests gather for evening hors d'oeuvres and wine. The two-bedroom Sonoma Cottage (which allows pets for an additional fee), goes for $689 a night. **Pros:** colorful; luxurious; friendly. **Cons:** not for those with minimalist tastes; not for kids. ⊠ *3657 Church St.* ☐ *Box 857, Occidental, CA 95465* ☎ *707/874–1047 or 800/522–6324* ⊕ *www. innatoccidental.com* ⇨ *13 rooms, 3 suites, 1 cottage* ♨ *In-room: no a/c, refrigerator (some), no TV (some), Wi-Fi. In-hotel: Wi-Fi hotspot, no kids under 10* ⊟ *AE, MC, V* ⦿ *BP.*

JENNER

10 mi north of Bodega Bay on Hwy. 1.

The broad, lazy Russian River empties into the Pacific Ocean at Jenner, a wide spot in the road where houses are sprinkled up a mountainside high above the sea. Facing south, the village looks across the river's mouth to **Goat Rock State Beach,** home to a colony of sea lions for most of the year; pupping season is March through June. The beach, accessed for free off Highway 1 a couple of miles south of town, is open daily from 8 AM to sunset. Bring binoculars and walk north from the parking lot to view the sea lions.

WHERE TO EAT

$$$–$$$$
NEW AMERICAN

✗ **River's End.** A magnificent ocean view makes lunch or an evening here memorable. Come for cocktails and Hog Island oysters on the half shell and hope for a splashy sunset. If you stay for dinner, choose from elaborate entrées such as grilled wild king salmon on cucumber noodles or elk with a red-wine-poached pear and Gorgonzola. The execution may not always justify the prices and the dining room is plain-Jane, but just look at that view. Open hours sometimes vary, so call to confirm. River's End also rents out a few ocean-view rooms and cabins ($$–$$$). ⊠ *11048 Hwy. 1* ☎ *707/865–2484* ⊕ *www.ilovesunsets.com* ⊟ *D, MC, V* ⊗ *Closed mid-week fall through spring.*

FORT ROSS STATE HISTORIC PARK

☺ *12 mi north of Jenner on Hwy. 1.*

Fort Ross, established in 1812, became Russia's major outpost in California, meant to produce crops and other supplies for northerly fur-trading operations. The Russians brought Aleut sea-otter hunters down from Alaska. By 1841 the area was depleted of seals and otters, and the Russians sold their post to John Sutter, later of gold-rush fame. After a local Anglo rebellion against the Mexicans, the land fell under U.S. domain, becoming part of California in 1850. The state park service has reconstructed Fort Ross, including its Russian Orthodox chapel, a redwood stockade, the officers' barracks, and a blockhouse. The

Surfers check out the waves near Bodega Bay on the Sonoma Coast.

excellent museum here documents the history of the fort and this part of the North Coast. ✉ *19005 Hwy. 1* ☎ *707/847–3286* 🏷 *$8 per vehicle* 🕙 *Fri.–Sun., sunrise–sunset; visitor center Fri.–Sun. 10–4:30* ☞ *No dogs allowed past parking lot and picnic area.*

SALT POINT STATE PARK

6 mi north of Fort Ross on Hwy. 1.

For 5 mi, Highway 1 winds through this park, 6,000 acres of forest, meadows, and rocky shoreline. Heading north, the first park entrance (on the right) leads to forest hiking trails and several campgrounds. The next entrance—the park's main road—winds through meadows and along the wave-splashed coastline (a great place to stop so the kids can let off steam). This is also the route to the visitor center (open April to October, weekends 10–3) and Gerstle Cove, a favorite spot for abalone divers and sunbathing seals. Next along the highway is Stump Beach Cove, with picnic tables, toilets, and a ¼-mi walk to the sandy beach. The park's final entrance is at Fisk Mill Cove, where centuries of wind and rain erosion have carved unusual honeycomb patterns in the sandstone called "tafonis." A five-minute walk uphill from the parking lot leads to a dramatic view of Sentinel Rock, an excellent spot for sunsets. Just up the highway, narrow, unpaved Kruse Ranch Road leads to the **Kruse Rhododendron State Reserve** (☎ *707/847–3221* 🏷 *Free* 🕙 *Daily sunrise–sunset*), where each May thousands of rhododendrons bloom within a quiet forest of redwoods and tan oaks. ✉ *20705 Hwy. 1* ☎ *707/847–3221* 🏷 *$8 per vehicle* 🕙 *Daily sunrise–sunset.*

THE MENDOCINO COAST

GUALALA

16 mi north of Salt Point State Park on Hwy. 1.

This former lumber port on the Gualala River has become a headquarters for exploring the coast. The busiest town between Bodega Bay and Mendocino, it has all the basic services plus a number of galleries and gift shops.

EXPLORING

Gualala Point Regional Park (✉ *1 mi south of Gualala on Hwy. 1* ☎ *707/ 785–2377* ☉ *Daily 8 AM–sunset*) has a long, sandy beach, picnic areas ($6 day-use fee) and is an excellent whale-watching spot December through April. Along the river, shaded by redwoods, are two dozen campsites.

WHERE TO EAT AND STAY

$$$–$$$$
NEW AMERICAN
✕ **Pangaea.** Some of Gualala's best food is prepared in the artsy jewel-color dining rooms of this little log cabin. The well-traveled chef serves imaginative dishes based on ingredients from local farms and fisheries, such as wild salmon with truffled golden beets, and lamb kebabs with blood oranges and asparagus. Cheeses from Sonoma County and throughout northern California are available for dessert. Intelligent and well priced, the wine list balances local and European selections. ✉ *39165 Hwy. 1* ☎ *707/884–9669* ⊕ *www.pangaeacafe.com* ⊟ *MC, V* ☉ *Closed Mon.–Thurs. No lunch.*

$$–$$$
🏨 **Mar Vista Cottages.** The dozen 1930s cottages at Mar Vista have been beautifully restored. Intentionally slim on modern gadgetry (no TV, phone, radio, or even a clock), the thoughtfully appointed and sparkling clean, one-story cottages are big on retro charm: windows are hung with embroidered drapes, coffee percolates on a white enamel stove in the full, if diminutive, kitchen, and straw sun hats hang from hooks. Outside, where benches overlook the blustery coastline, you can harvest greens, eggs, and flowers from the organic garden for your supper or take a path to Fish Rock Beach. Smoking is not allowed anywhere on the property, and there's a two-night minimum stay. **Pros:** charming, peaceful retreat. **Cons:** no other businesses in walking distance. ✉ *35101 S. Hwy 1, 5 mi north of Gualala,* ☎ *707/884–3522 or 877/855–3522* ⊕ *www.marvistamendocino.com* 🛏 *8 1-bedroom cottages, 4 2-bedroom cottages* ♿ *In-room: no phone, no a/c, kitchen, refrigerator, no TV, Wi-Fi. In-hotel: Wi-Fi hotspot, some pets allowed* ⊟ *MC, V.*

$$
🏨 **Seacliff on the Bluff.** Wedged behind a downtown shopping center, it's not much to look at. The interiors are motel standard, but you'll spend your time here staring at the Pacific panorama. Surprising extras ice the cake: take the binoculars out to your balcony or patio; stay in and watch the sunset from your jetted tub; snuggle into a robe and pop that complimentary champagne in front of your gas fireplace. Upstairs rooms have cathedral ceilings; Wi-Fi is available throughout for a fee. **Pros:** budget choice; great views. **Cons:** less-than-scenic setting. ✉ *39140*

Hwy. 1 ☎ 707/884–1213 or 800/400–5053 ⊕ www.seacliffmotel.com
⇨ 16 rooms ♨ In-room: a/c, refrigerator, Wi-Fi. In-hotel: Wi-Fi hotspot
🖹 MC, V.

11

POINT ARENA

★ *14 mi north of Gualala on Hwy. 1.*

Occupied by an odd mixture of long-time locals and long-haired surfers, this former timber town is partly New Age, partly rowdy—and always sleepy. The one road going west out of downtown will lead you to the harbor, where fishing boats unload urchins and salmon and there's almost always someone riding the waves.

EXPLORING

For an outstanding view of the ocean and, in winter, migrating whales, take the marked road off Highway 1 north of town to the 115-foot **Point Arena Lighthouse.** The lighthouse is open for tours daily from 10 until 3:30; admission is $7.50. It's possible to stay out here, in one of four cottages ($$–$$$), all of which have full kitchens (on weekends there's a two-night minimum). ⊠ *6300 S. Hwy. 1* ☎ *707/882–2777* ⊕ *www.pointarenalighthouse.com.*

As you continue north on Highway 1 toward Elk, you'll pass several beaches. Most notable is the one at **Manchester State Park,** 3 mi north of Point Arena, which has 5 mi of sandy, usually empty shoreline and lots of trails through the dunes.

WHERE TO EAT AND STAY

¢ **✕ Arena Market.** The simple café at this all-organic grocery store offers
CAFÉ hot soups, good sandwiches, and an ample salad bar. Picnickers can stock up on cheese, bread, and other good stuff in the market, which specializes in food from local farms. ⊠ *265 Main St.* ☎ *707/882–3663* 🖹 *MC, V.*

¢ **✕ Franny's Cup and Saucer.** Aided by her mother, Barbara, a former pastry
CAFÉ chef at Chez Panisse, Franny turns out baked goods that are sophisticated and inventive. Take the coffee crunch cake: vanilla chiffon cake layered with coffee whipped cream, topped with chocolate ganache and puffs of coffee caramel "seafoam." More familiar options include berry tarts and strawberry-apricot crisp. While normally closed on Sunday, once a month during spring and summer they open for a decadent brunch. ⊠ *213 Main St.* ☎ *707/882–2500* ⊕ *www.frannyscupandsaucer.com* 🖹 *No credit cards* ⊗ *Closed Sun.–Tues. No dinner.*

$$$–$$$$ **🖻 Inn at Victorian Gardens.** Set amid 100 acres of meadows and trees,
★ this Victorian is exquisite. The original house dates to 1904, but owner-architect Pauline Zamboni has updated and expanded it seamlessly over the past 17 years—skylights open up bathrooms with original hardwood floors, and peaked alcoves frame windows that look out onto lush gardens. Furnishings are crisp and tasteful—nothing knickknacky here—and multiple sitting rooms and patios offer plenty of room to spread out (indeed, many guests never leave the property during their stays). **Pros:** total relaxation; total quiet; total elegance. **Cons:** 6 mi from the nearest town. ⊠ *14409 S. Hwy. 1* ☎ *707/882–3606* ⊕ *www.*

innatvictoriangardens.com ➥ *4 rooms* ✆ *In-room: no phone, no a/c, no TV. In-hotel: no kids under 12* ▭ *AE, MC, V* ⭐ *BP.*

ELK

33 mi north of Gualala on Hwy. 1.

This quiet town is arranged on the cliff above Greenwood Cove, and just about every spot has a view of the rocky coastline and stunning Pacific sunsets. Beyond walking the beach there's little here for visitors, aside from a handful of restaurants and inns—and that's exactly why people come. Families don't tend to stay here, perhaps because it's such a romantic place.

WHERE TO EAT AND STAY

¢–$ ✕ **Queenie's Roadhouse Cafe.** The chrome and patent-leather diner-style
AMERICAN chairs here are usually occupied by locals, as it's a good bet for big breakfasts (served all day) and casual lunches (the cheeseburgers are highly recommended). On sunny days, grab one of the two picnic tables out front. ✉ *6061 S. Hwy. 1* ☎ *707/877–3285* ▭ *AE, MC, V* ⊙ *Closed Tues. and Wed. No dinner. Closed Jan.*

$$$–$$$$ ⌂ **Elk Cove Inn & Spa.** Perched on a bluff above pounding surf and a driftwood-strewn beach, this property has stunning views from most rooms. The most romantic accommodations here are in the pretty, antiquey cottage buildings, where each room is unique but all have peaked ceilings and hardwood floors. A newer Arts-and-Crafts-style building houses suites ($375–$395) with a more modern feel (including Jacuzzi tubs). All rooms include a lavish breakfast in the main house as well as afternoon hors d'oeuvres with wine and cocktails. Spa treatments take place one at a time in a private building with a view of the ocean. If you want a massage, book early; the calendar is often full. **Pros:** steps to the beach; gorgeous views; great breakfast. **Cons:** rooms in main house are smallish and within earshot of common TV. ✉ *6300 S. Hwy. 1* ☎ *707/877–3321 or 800/275–2967* ⊕ *www.elkcoveinn.com* ➥ *7 rooms, 4 suites, 4 cottages* ✆ *In-room: no phone, no a/c, refrigerator (some), no TV, Wi-Fi. In-hotel: spa, beachfront, Wi-Fi hotspot* ▭ *AE, D, MC, V* ⭐ *BP.*

$$$$ ⌂ **Harbor House.** Constructed in 1916, this redwood Craftsman-style house is as elegant as its location is rugged. Rooms in the main house are decorated with antiques and have gas fireplaces. The newer cottages are luxurious; each has a fireplace and deck, and three have ocean-view claw-foot bathtubs. Room rates include breakfast and a four-course dinner (except on weeknights during January and February, when the rates drop drastically). The ocean-view restaurant ($$$$; reservations essential) serves California cuisine on a prix-fixe menu; seating for nonguests is limited. **Pros:** luxurious; romantic. **Cons:** not a place for kids. ✉ *5600 S. Hwy. 1* ☎ *707/877–3203 or 800/720–7474* ⊕ *www.theharborhouseinn.com* ➥ *6 rooms, 4 cottages* ✆ *In-room: no a/c, no phone, no TV, Wi-Fi. In-hotel: restaurant, laundry service, Wi-Fi hotspot, some pets allowed* ▭ *AE, MC, V* ⭐ *MAP.*

ANDERSON VALLEY

6 mi north of Elk on Hwy. 101, then 22 mi southeast on Hwy. 128.

At the town of Albion, Highway 128 leads southeast into the Anderson Valley, whose hot summer weather might lure those tired of coastal fog. Most of the first 13 mi wind through redwood forest along the Navarro River, then the road opens up to reveal farms and vineyards. While the community here is anchored in ranching, in the past few decades a progressive, gourmet minded counterculture has taken root and that is what defines most visitors' experience. In the towns of Philo and Boonville you'll find B&Bs with classic Victorian style as well as small eateries.

Anderson Valley is best known to outsiders for its wineries. Tasting rooms here are more low-key than in Napa; most are in farmhouses and are more likely to play reggae than classical music. That said, Anderson Valley wineries produce world-class wines, particularly pinot noirs and gewürztraminers, whose grapes thrive in the cool, coastal climate. All the wineries are along Highway 128, mostly in Philo with a few east of Boonville. The following are our favorites and are listed here from west to east.

EXPLORING

The valley's oldest winery, **Husch** (⊠ *4400 Hwy. 128* ☎ *800/554–8724* ⊗ *Tasting room daily 10–5*), has a cozy tasting room next to sheep pastures and picnic tables under a grapevine-covered arbor.

Roederer (⊠ *4501 Hwy. 128* ☎ *707/895–2288* ⊗ *Tasting room daily 11–5*) pours its famed sparkling wines in a grand tasting room amid vineyards.

Look closely on the north side of Highway 128 for a rust-color sign reading LCV, and if the gate is open, drive the winding road through oak forest to **Lazy Creek Vineyards** (⊠ *4741 Hwy. 128* ☎ *707/895–3623*). Gregarious owner and chef Josh Chandler offers unique wines, such as his Rosé of Pinot Noir, and has a bountiful rose garden where chickens run loose.

White Riesling is the specialty of **Greenwood Ridge Vineyards** (⊠ *5501 Hwy. 128* ☎ *707/895–2002* ⊗ *Tasting room daily 10–5*), where awards line the walls and you can picnic at tables on a dock in the middle of a pond.

★ Family-run **Navarro** (⊠ *5601 Hwy. 128* ☎ *707/895–3686* ⊗ *Tasting room daily 10–5*) focuses on Alsatian varietals and offers a wide range of wines (pouring up to 15 at a time in the tasting room). The tasting room sells cheese and charcuterie for picnickers, and walking tours of the organic vineyard and winery are given daily at 10:30 AM and 3 PM (call in advance to make an appointment).

The aptly named **Navarro River Redwoods State Park** (⊠ *Hwy. 128, Navarro* ☎ *707/937–5804*) is great for walks in the second-growth redwood forest and for swimming in the gentle Navarro River. There's also fishing and kayaking in the late winter and spring, when the river is higher. The two campgrounds (one on the river "beach") are quiet and clean.

You'll find excellent vintages and great places to taste wine in the Anderson Valley—but it's much more laid back than Napa.

WHERE TO EAT AND STAY

¢–$
CAFÉ
✗ **The Boonville General Store**. The café menu here is nothing surprising, but the exacting attention paid to ingredients elevates each dish above the ordinary. Sandwiches are served on fresh-baked bread, the beet salad comes with roasted pecans and local blue cheese. Even the macaroni and cheese—freshly made—is noteworthy. For breakfast there are granola and pastries, made in-house. ✉ *14077A Hwy. 128, Boonville* ☎ *707/895–9477* 🖃 *D, DC, MC, V* ☽ *No dinner.*

$$–$$$
🏨 **Boonville Hotel**. From the street it looks a little rusty, but inside this hotel's decor is straight out of Martha Stewart—artful linens, perfectly weathered tiles, walls painted tangerine and lime. Rooms upstairs are breezy and bright, and the luxurious bungalow in the garden includes a private porch with hammock. Equally of note is the restaurant ($$–$$$; closed Tues. and Wed.; no lunch), where owner John Schmitt uses local ingredients (including some from his kitchen garden, behind the hotel) to create simple, delicious dishes like braised oxtails with shiitake mushrooms and mashed potatoes, or strawberry-rhubarb shortcake. **Pros:** stylish; simple; building is the town's main hub. **Cons:** less-expensive rooms are small. ✉ *Hwy. 128, Boonville* ☎ *707/895–2210* ⊕ *www. boonvillehotel.com* 🖃 *8 rooms, 2 suites* 🖘 *In-room: no phone, no a/c, refrigerator (some), no TV, Wi-Fi. In-hotel: restaurant, bar, Wi-Fi hotspot, some pets allowed* 🖃 *MC, V.*

$$$
🏨 **The Philo Apple Farm**. Set in an orchard of organic, heirloom apples, the three cottages and one guest room here are tasteful, spare, and inspired by the surrounding landscape. It all feels very Provençal, from the elegant country linens to the deep soaking tubs and dried flowers adorning the walls. On most weekends the cottages are reserved

for people attending the highly respected cooking school here (two of the owners founded the renowned restaurant the French Laundry, in Napa), but midweek there is nearly always a room available. The farm stand, similarly refined, is also worth a stop. **Pros:** pretty; quiet; country feel. **Cons:** hard to get a reservation on weekends; occasionally hot in summer. ✉ *18501 Greenwood Rd., Philo* ☎ *707/895–2333* ⊕ *www. philoapplefarm.com* ➪ *1 room, 3 cottages* ♿ *In-room: no phone, no a/c, no TV* ▭ *MC, V* ⑩ *CP.*

LITTLE RIVER

14 mi north of Elk on Hwy. 1.

The town of Little River is not much more than a post office and a convenience store; Albion, its neighbor to the south, is even smaller. Along the winding road, though, you'll find numerous inns and restaurants, all of them quiet and focused on the breathtaking ocean.

EXPLORING

Van Damme State Park is best known for its beach and for being a prime abalone diving spot. Upland trails lead through lush riparian habitat and the bizarre **Pygmy Forest,** where acidic soil and poor drainage have produced mature cypress and pine trees that are no taller than a person. The visitor center has displays on ocean life and Native American history. There's an $8 day-use fee. ✉ *Hwy. 1* ☎ *707/937–4016 visitor center* ⊕ *www.parks.ca.gov.*

WHERE TO EAT AND STAY

$$$–$$$$

FRENCH

★

✕ **Ledford House.** The only thing separating this bluff-top wood-and-glass restaurant from the Pacific Ocean is a great view. Entrées evoke the flavors of southern France and include hearty bistro dishes—stews, cassoulets, and pastas—and large portions of grilled meats and freshly caught fish (though it also is vegetarian friendly). The long bar, with its unobstructed water view, is a scenic spot for a sunset aperitif. ✉ *3000 N. Hwy. 1* ☎ *707/937–0282* ⊕ *www.ledfordhouse.com* ▭ *AE, DC, MC, V* ☉ *Closed Mon. and Tues. No lunch.*

$$$–$$$$

🏨 **Albion River Inn.** Contemporary New England–style cottages at this inn overlook the dramatic bridge and seascape where the Albion River empties into the Pacific. All but two have decks facing the ocean, and one is wheelchair accessible. Six have spa tubs with ocean views; all have fireplaces. The traditional, homey rooms are filled with antiques; at the glassed-in restaurant ($$$–$$$$), the grilled meats and fresh seafood are as captivating as the views. **Pros:** great views; great bathtubs. **Cons:** newer buildings aren't as quaint as they could be. ✉ *3790 N. Hwy. 1* ☎ *707/937–1919 or 800/479–7944* ⊕ *www.albionriverinn.com* ➪ *18 rooms, 4 cottages* ♿ *In-room: a/c, refrigerator, no TV (some), Wi-Fi. In-hotel: restaurant, bar, Wi-Fi hotspot* ▭ *AE, D, MC, V* ⑩ *BP.*

$$$–$$$$

★

🏨 **Glendeven Inn.** If Mendocino is the New England village of the West Coast, then Glendeven is the local country manor. The main house was built in 1867 and is surrounded by acres of gardens, complete with llamas and chickens. Inside are five guest rooms, three with fireplaces. A converted barn holds an art gallery and a wine bar that are open to the public daily. The 1986 Stevenscroft building, with its high gabled roof, contains four rooms with fireplaces. The carriage-house suite makes for a romantic retreat, and an additional two-story loft in the barn accommodates groups of up to six people (and children). The inn is on the road, so ask for a room on the far side of the property. **Pros:** picture-book pretty; elegant; romantic. **Cons:** not within walking distance of town; on the road. ⊠ *8205 N. Hwy. 1* ☎ *707/937–0083 or 800/822–4536* ⊕ *www.glendeven.com* ⋑ *6 rooms, 4 suites* ♿ *In-room: no phone (some), no a/c, no TV (some), Wi-Fi. In-hotel: Wi-Fi hotspot, no kids under 17* ▭ *AE, D, MC, V* ⦿⦿ *BP.*

MENDOCINO

3 mi north of Little River on Hwy. 1; 153 mi from San Francisco, north on U.S. 101, west on Hwy. 128, and north on Hwy. 1.

Many of Mendocino's original settlers came from the Northeast and built houses in the New England style. Thanks to the logging boom the town flourished for most of the second half of the 19th century. As the timber industry declined, many residents left, but the town's setting was too beautiful to be ignored. Artists and craftspeople began flocking here in the 1950s, and Elia Kazan chose Mendocino as the backdrop for his 1955 film adaptation of John Steinbeck's *East of Eden,* starring James Dean. As the arts community thrived, restaurants, cafés, and inns started to open. Today, the small downtown area consists almost entirely of places to eat and shop.

EXPLORING

The restored **Ford House**, built in 1854, serves as the visitor center for Mendocino Headlands State Park. The house has a scale model of Mendocino as it looked in 1890, when the town had 34 water towers and a 12-seat public outhouse. From the museum, you can head out on a 3-mi trail across the spectacular seaside cliffs that border the town. ⊠ *Main St., west of Lansing St.* ☎ *707/937–5397* ⋑ *$2 suggested donation* ⊙ *Daily 11–4.*

An 1861 structure holds the **Kelley House Museum**, whose artifacts include Victorian-era furniture and historical photographs of Mendocino's logging days. ⊠ *45007 Albion St.* ☎ *707/937–5791* ⊕ *www.kelleyhousemuseum.org* ⋑ *$2* ⊙ *June–Sept., Thurs.–Tues. 11–3; Oct.–May, Fri.–Mon. 11–3.*

The **Mendocino Art Center** (⊠ *45200 Little Lake St.* ☎ *707/937–5818 or 800/653–3328* ⊕ *www.mendocinoartcenter.org*), which has an extensive program of workshops, also mounts rotating exhibits in its galleries and is the home of the Mendocino Theatre Company.

WHERE TO EAT AND STAY

$$$–$$$$ ✕ **Cafe Beaujolais**. The Victorian cottage that houses this popular res-
AMERICAN taurant is surrounded by a garden of heirloom and exotic plantings. A commitment to the freshest possible organic, local, and hormone-free ingredients guides the chef here. The menu is eclectic and ever-evolving, but often includes free-range fowl, line-caught fish, and edible flowers. The bakery turns out several delicious varieties of bread from a wood-

fired oven. ⊠ *961 Ukiah St.* ☎ *707/937–5614* ⊕ *www.cafebeaujolais. com* ➡ *AE, D, DC, MC, V* ⊙ *No lunch Mon. and Tues.*

$$$$ ★ **Brewery Gulch Inn.** This tasteful inn gives a modern twist to the elegance of Mendocino. Furnishings are redwood and leather, beds are plush, and all rooms but two have whirlpool tubs with views. The luxury is in tune with the surrounding nature: Large windows frame views of the 10-acre property, bird-filled trees, and winding paths that lead through native plant gardens. Organic vegetable and herb gardens provide ingredients for the sumptuous breakfast menu. **Pros:** stylish; peaceful; intimate. **Cons:** must drive to town. ⊠ *9401 Hwy. 1, 1 mi south of Mendocino* ☎ *707/937–4752 or 800/578–4454* ⊕ *www. brewerygulchinn.com* ➧ *10 rooms* ⚴ *In-room: a/c, DVD, Wi-Fi. In-hotel: Internet terminal, Wi-Fi hotspot* ➡ *AE, MC, V* ⊡ *BP.*

$$$–$$$$ Fodor'sChoice ★ **MacCallum House.** Set on two flower-filled acres in the middle of town, this inn is a perfect mix of Victorian charm and modern luxury. Rosebushes planted by the original owner in the late 1800s still bloom in the garden, but inside the rooms have private saunas and spa tubs. Rooms in the main house and renovated barn feel genteel and romantic, while the cottages are bright and honeymoon-y. The water tower is unforgettable—with a living room on the first floor, a sauna on the second, and a huge view of the ocean from the bed on the third. Don't miss the outstanding restaurant ($$$$), where the chef hand selects the best local ingredients—foraging for some of them himself—and everything from ice cream to mozzarella is prepared daily from scratch. **Pros:** best B&B around; excellent breakfast; great in-town location. **Cons:** new luxury suites on a separate property are less charming. ⊠ *45020 Albion St., Box 206 95460* ☎ *707/937–0289 or 800/609–0492* ⊕ *www.maccallumhouse.com* ➧ *10 rooms, 2 suites, 7 cottages* ⚴ *In-room: a/c, refrigerator, DVD, Internet, Wi-Fi. In-hotel: restaurant, bar, bicycles, Internet terminal, Wi-Fi hotspot, some pets allowed* ➡ *AE, D, MC, V* ⊡ *BP.*

NIGHTLIFE AND THE ARTS

Mendocino Theatre Company (⊠ *Mendocino Art Center, 42500 Little Lake St.* ☎ *707/937–4477* ⊕ *mendocinotheatre.org*) has been around for more than three decades. Their repertoire ranges all over the contemporary map, including works by David Mamet, Neil Simon, and local playwrights. Performances take place Thursday through Saturday evenings, with some weekend matinees.

SPORTS AND THE OUTDOORS

Catch-A-Canoe and Bicycles Too (⊠ *Stanford Inn by the Sea, Comptche-Ukiah Rd., off Hwy. 1* ☎ *707/937–0273*) rents kayaks and regular and outrigger canoes as well as mountain and suspension bicycles.

FORT BRAGG

10 mi north of Mendocino on Hwy. 1.

The commercial center of Mendocino County, Fort Bragg is a working-class town that many feel is the most authentic place around; it's certainly less expensive across the board than towns to the south. The declining timber industry has been steadily replaced by booming tourism, but the city maintains a local feel since most people who work at the area hotels and restaurants live here, as do many local artists. A stroll down Franklin Street (one block east of Highway 1) takes you past numerous bookstores, antiques shops, and boutiques.

EXPLORING

★ The **Mendocino Coast Botanical Gardens** has something for nature lovers in every season. Even in winter, heather and camellias bloom. Along 2 mi of trails with ocean views and observation points for whale-watching is a splendid profusion of flowers. The rhododendrons are at their peak from April through June, and the dahlias are spectacular in August. ⊠ *18220 N. Hwy. 1, 1 mi south of Fort Bragg* ☎ *707/964–4352* ⊕ *www.gardenbythesea.org* ⊠ *$10* ☉ *Mar.–Oct., daily 9–5; Nov.–Feb., daily 9–4.*

Back in the 1920s, a fume-spewing gas-powered train car shuttled passengers along a rail line dating from the logging days of the 1880s. Ↄ Nicknamed the **Skunk Train**, it traversed redwood forests inaccessible to automobiles. The reproduction that you can ride today travels the same route, making a 3½-hour round-trip between Fort Bragg and the town of Northspur, 21 mi inland. The schedule varies depending on the season and in summer includes evening barbecue excursions and wine parties. ⊠ *Foot of Laurel St., west of Main St.* ☎ *707/964–6371 or 866/457–5865* ⊕ *www.skunktrain.com* ⊠ *$47–$70.*

MacKerricher State Park includes 9 mi of sandy beach and several square miles of dunes. The headland is a good place for whale-watching from December to mid-April. Fishing (at a freshwater lake stocked with trout), canoeing, hiking, jogging, bicycling, beachcombing, camping, and harbor seal watching at Laguna Point are among the popular activities, many of which are accessible to the mobility-impaired. Rangers lead nature hikes in summer. ⊠ *Hwy. 1, 3 mi north of Fort Bragg* ☎ *707/964–9112* ⊠ *$8 per vehicle.*

The ocean is not visible from most of Fort Bragg, but go three blocks west of Main Street and a flat, dirt path leads to wild coastline where you can walk for miles in either direction along the bluffs. The sandy coves in the area you first reach from the road are called **Glass Beach** (⊠ *Elm St. and Glass Beach Dr.*) because this used to be the dumping ground for the city. That history is still apparent—in a good way. Look closely at the sand and you'll find the top layer is comprised almost entirely of sea glass, likely more than you've ever seen in one place before.

An unexpected nod to Fort Bragg's rough-and-tumble past is the **Museum in the Triangle Tattoo Parlor** (⊠ *356-B N. Main St.* ☎ *707/964–8814* ⊠ *Free* ☉ *Daily noon–6*). The two-room display shows a wonderful collection of tattoo memorabilia, including pictures of astonishing tattoos from around the world, early 20th-century Burmese tattooing instruments, and a small shrine to sword-swallowing sideshow king Captain Don Leslie.

The north coast is famous for its locally caught Dungeness crab; be sure to try some during your visit.

WHERE TO EAT AND STAY

$–$$
ITALIAN

✕ **Piaci.** The seats are stools and your elbows might bang a neighbor's, but nobody seems to mind at this cozy little spot—this is hands down the most popular casual restaurant around. The food is simple, mostly pizza and calzones, but everything is given careful attention and comes out tasty. Alongside the selective list of wines is a distinctive beer list that has been given equal respect; noted are the origin, brewmaster, and alcohol content for each brew. Dogs and their owners are welcome at the tables outside. ⊠ *120 W. Redwood Ave.* ☎ *707/961–1133* ⊕ *www. piacipizza.com* ⊟ *MC, V* ✆ *No lunch weekends.*

$$$–$$$$
FRENCH
★

✕ **Rendezvous Inn.** Applying sophisticated European technique to fresh seasonal ingredients, chef Kim Badenhop turns out a northern California interpretation of country French cooking. To start you might try Dungeness crab bisque finished with brandy, then follow with pheasant pot-au-feu with black chanterelles and glazed root vegetables. A sense of well-being prevails in the redwood-panel dining room, where service is never rushed. ⊠ *647 N. Main St.* ☎ *707/964–8142 or 800/491–8142* ⊕ *www.rendezvousinn.com* ⊟ *D, MC, V* ✆ *Closed Mon. and Tues. No lunch.*

$$–$$$

⌂ **Weller House Inn.** It's hard to believe that when Ted and Eva Kidwell found this house in 1994, it was abandoned and slated for demolition. She is an artist and he a craftsman; together they have hammered and quilted this into the loveliest Victorian in Fort Bragg. Each of the nine guest rooms is colorful and tasteful, with hand-painted ceilings and deep, claw-foot tubs. The water tower—the tallest structure in town—offers ocean views from its second-floor hot tub and rooftop viewing deck. The stunning redwood-panel ballroom is the location for breakfast in the morning and spirited tango dancing events on some weekends. **Pros:** handcrafted details; homey; friendly innkeepers. **Cons:** some may find it too old-fashioned. ✉ *524 Stewart St.* ☎ *707/964–4415 or 877/893–5537* ⊕ *www.wellerhouse.com* ⤴ *10 rooms* ⚭ *In-room: no phone, no a/c, refrigerator (some), no TV (some), Wi-Fi. In-hotel: bicycles, Wi-Fi hotspot* ▤ *AE, D, DC, MC, V* ⍩ *BP.*

SPORTS AND THE OUTDOORS

All Aboard Adventures (✉ *32400 N. Harbor Dr.* ☎ *707/964–1881* ⊕ *www.allaboardadventures.com*) operates whale-watching trips from December through mid-April, as well as fishing excursions all year. **Ricochet Ridge Ranch** (✉ *24201 N. Hwy. 1* ☎ *707/964–7669 or 888/873–5777* ⊕ *www.horse-vacation.com*) guides private and group trail rides through redwood forest and on the beach.

REDWOOD COUNTRY

HUMBOLDT REDWOODS STATE PARK

20 mi north of Garberville on U.S. 101.

The **Avenue of the Giants** (Highway 254) traverses the park south–north, branching off U.S. 101 about 7 mi north of Garberville and more or less paralleling that road for 33 mi north to Pepperwood. Some of the tallest trees on the planet tower over the stretch of two-lane blacktop that follows the south fork of the Eel River. At the **Humboldt Redwoods State Park Visitor Center** you can pick up information about the redwoods, waterways, and recreational activities in the 53,000-acre park. One brochure describes a self-guided auto tour of the park, with short and long hikes into redwood groves. ✉ *Ave. of the Giants, 2 mi south of Weott* ☎ *707/946–2263 visitor center* ⊕ *www.humboldtredwoods. org* ⌦ *Free; $8 day-use fee for parking and facilities in Williams Grove* ⊙ *Park daily; visitor center Apr–Oct., daily 9–5; Nov.–Mar., daily 10–4.*

Reached via a ½-mi trail off Avenue of the Giants is **Founders Grove** (✉ *Hwy. 254, 4 mi north of Humboldt Redwoods State Park Visitor Center*). One of the most impressive trees here—the 362-foot-long Dyerville Giant—fell to the ground in 1991; its root base points skyward 35 feet. **Rockefeller Forest** (✉ *Mattole Rd., 6 mi north of Humboldt Redwoods State Park Visitor Center*) is the largest remaining coastal redwood forest. It contains 40 of the 100 tallest trees in the world.

FERNDALE

35 mi northwest of Weott; 57 mi northwest of Garberville via U.S. 101 north to Hwy. 211 west.

Gift shops and ice-cream stores make up a fair share of the businesses here, but at its core, Ferndale miraculously remains a working small town. There's a butcher, a small grocery, and a local saloon (the westernmost in the contiguous United States), and descendants of the Portuguese and Scandinavian dairy farmers who settled this town continue

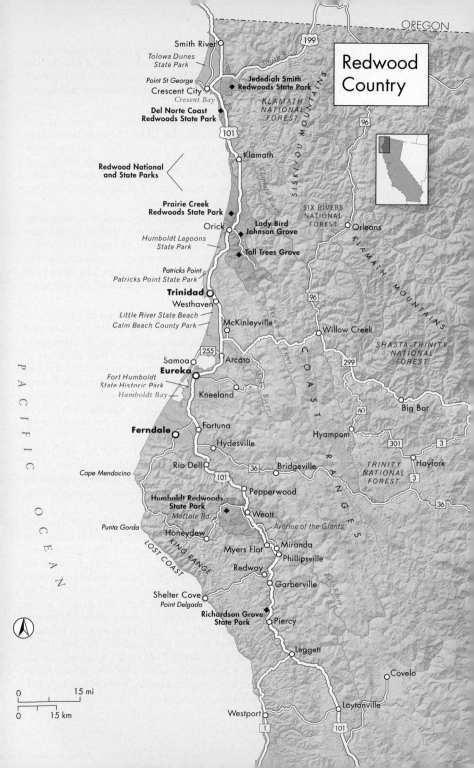

OREGON

199

Redwood Country

Smith River

Tolowa Dunes State Park

Point St George
Crescent City
Cresent Bay

Del Norte Coast Redwoods State Park

Jedediah Smith Redwoods State Park

KLAMATH NATIONAL FOREST

96

101

Klamath

Klamath River

SISKIYOU MOUNTAINS

Redwood National and State Parks

SIX RIVERS NATIONAL FOREST

Prairie Creek Redwoods State Park

Orick

Lady Bird Johnson Grove

Humboldt Lagoons State Park

Tall Trees Grove

Orleans

KLAMATH MOUNTAINS

Patricks Point
Patricks Point State Park

Trinidad
Westhaven

96

Little River State Beach
Calm Beach County Park

McKinleyville

Willow Creek

Redwood Creek

COAST

SHASTA-TRINITY NATIONAL FOREST

299

255

Samoa
Eureka

Arcata

Mad River

Fort Humboldt State Historic Park
Humboldt Bay

Kneeland

60

Big Bar

RANGES

Ferndale

Fortuna

Hydesville

Hyampom

301

3

Cape Mendocino

Rio Dell

36

Bridgeville

Hayfork

3

101

TRINITY NATIONAL FOREST

Pepperwood

36

Humboldt Redwoods State Park
Mottole Rd.

Weott

Avenue of the Giants

Punta Gorda

Honeydew

Myers Flat
Miranda
Phillipsville

KING RANGE

Redway

Eel River

Garberville

Shelter Cove
Point Delgada

Richardson Grove State Park

Piercy

LOST COAST

Leggett

Covelo

0 ___ 15 mi

0 ___ 15 km

Westport

1

Laytonville

101

to raise dairy cows on the pastures surrounding town. Ferndale is best known for its colorful Victorian architecture, the queen of which is the Gingerbread Mansion, built in 1899. Many shops carry a self-guided tour map that shows the town's most interesting historical buildings.

EXPLORING

The main building of the **Ferndale Museum** exhibits Victoriana and historical photographs and has a display of an old-style barbershop and another of Wiyot Indian baskets. In the annex are a horse-drawn buggy, a re-created blacksmith's shop, and antique farming, fishing, and dairy equipment. ⊠ *515 Shaw Ave.* ☎ *707/786–4466* ⊕ *www.ferndale-museum.org* ⊠ *$1* ⊙ *June–Sept., Tues.–Sat. 11–4, Sun. 1–4; Oct.–Dec. and Feb.–May, Wed.–Sat. 11–4, Sun. 1–4.*

A walk through **Ferndale Historic Cemetery** on the east side of town gives interesting insight into the hard, often short lives of the European immigrants who cultivated this area of California in the mid-18th century. The gravestones are worn, lovely, and sometimes imaginative, one in the shape of a nubbly redwood log. The cemetery is lined by forest, and from the top of the hill here there's a nice view of town, the surrounding farms, and the ocean.

Memorial Day weekend's annual **Kinetic Sculpture Race** has artists and engineers (and plenty of hacks) building moving sculptures from used bicycle parts and other scraps, which they race from Arcata to the finish line in Ferndale. Contestants are judged as much on their creativity as on their ability to cross the finish line, which makes for sculptures like the past Albino Rhino and a 93-foot-long fish. The **Ferndale Kinetic Museum** (⊠ *580 Main St.* ☎ *No phone*) has a display of "vehicles, costumes, awards, and bribes" from past races. The museum is open 10–5 weekdays and 10–4 Sunday. Admission is free but donations are encouraged.

Eel River Delta Tours (⊠ *285 Morgan Slough Rd.* ☎ *707/786–4902*) conducts two-hour boat trips that examine the wildlife and history of the Eel River's estuary and salt marsh. (Don't be surprised if you get an informal answering machine when you inquire—this is laid-back Humboldt, and you will get a call back.)

WHERE TO STAY

$$–$$$ 🏨 **Gingerbread Mansion.** This beautifully restored Victorian is dazzling enough to rival San Francisco's "painted ladies." The exterior has detailed spindle work, turrets, and gables; inside, the guest rooms are decorated in plush, flowery period splendor. Some rooms have views of the mansion's English garden; one has side-by-side bathtubs. One particularly posh suite is the Veneto, which has hand-painted scenes of Venice on the walls and ceiling as well as marble floors. Afternoon tea and breakfast are both served with style. **Pros:** elegant; relaxing; friendly. **Cons:** some may find it a bit gaudy. ⊠ *400 Berding St., off Brown St.* ☎ *707/786–4000 or 800/952–4136* ⊕ *www.gingerbread-mansion.com* ⊃ *7 rooms, 4 suites* ⌂ *In-room: no phone, no a/c, Wi-Fi. In-hotel: water sports, bicycles, laundry service, Wi-Fi hotspot, no kids under 12* ⊟ *AE, MC, V* ⊙❘*BP.*

EUREKA

18 mi north of Ferndale; 66 mi north of Garberville on U.S. 101.

With a population of 26,381, Eureka is the North Coast's largest city. Over the past century, it has gone through several cycles of boom and bust—first with mining and later with timber and fishing—but these days, tourism is becoming a healthy industry. The town's nearly 100 Victorian buildings have caused some to dub it "the Williamsburg of the West." Shops draw people to the renovated downtown, and a walking pier reaches into the harbor.

EXPLORING

At the **Eureka Chamber of Commerce** you can pick up maps with self-guided driving tours of Eureka's Victorian architecture, and also learn about organized tours. ⊠ *2112 Broadway* ☎ *707/442–3738 or 800/356–6381* ⊕ *www.eurekachamber.com* ☉ *May–Oct., weekdays 8:30–5, Sat. 10–4; Nov.–Apr., Mon.–Thurs. 8:30–5, Fri. 8:30–4.*

The Native American Wing of the **Clarke Memorial Museum** contains a beautiful collection of northwestern California basketry. Artifacts from Eureka's Victorian, logging, and maritime eras fill the rest of the museum. ⊠ *240 E St.* ☎ *707/443–1947* ⊕ *www.clarkemuseum.org* ⊠ *Donations accepted* ☉ *Wed.–Sat. 11–4.*

The structure that gave **Fort Humboldt State Historic Park** its name was built in response to conflicts between white settlers and Native Americans. It no longer stands, but on its grounds are some reconstructed buildings, fort and logging museums, and old logging locomotives. Demonstrators steam up the machines on the third Saturday of the month, April through September. The park is a good place for a picnic. ⊠ *3431 Fort Ave.* ☎ *707/445–6567* ⊕ *www.parks.ca.gov* ⊠ *Free* ☉ *Daily 8–5, museum and fort 8–4.*

Blue Ox Millworks is one of only a handful of woodshops in the country that specialize in Victorian-era architecture, but what makes it truly unique is that it uses antique tools to do the work. The most modern tool here is a 1948 band saw. Lucky for curious craftspeople and history buffs, the shop doubles as a dusty historical park. Visitors can watch craftsmen use printing presses, lathes, and even a mill that pares down whole redwood logs into the ornate fixtures for Victorians like those around town. The museum is less interesting on Saturday, when the craftspeople mostly take the day off. ⊠ *1 X St.* ☎ *707/444–3437 or 800/248–4259* ⊕ *www.blueoxmill.com* ⊠ *$7.50* ☉ *Weekdays 9–5, Sat. 9–4.*

WHERE TO EAT AND STAY

$$–$$$

AMERICAN

Fodor's Choice

★

✕ **Restaurant 301.** Eureka's most elegant restaurant, housed in the lovely Carter House, uses ingredients hand selected from the farmers' market, local cheese makers and ranchers, and the on-site gardens. Dishes are prepared with a delicate hand and a sensuous imagination—the ever-changing menu has featured sturgeon with house-made mushroom pasta, braised fennel, and white wine sauce. The extensive wine list has over 3,800 selections. ⊠ *301 L St.* ☎ *707/444–8062 or 800/404–1390* ⊕ *www.carterhouse.com* ⊟ *AE, D, DC, MC, V* ☉ *No lunch.*

$
AMERICAN
☺

✕ **Samoa Cookhouse**. Originally a cafeteria that fed 500 local mill workers, the cookhouse became a public restaurant in the 1950s—though not much but the clientele has changed. Take a seat at one of the long, communal tables, and waiters will bring bottomless, family-style bowls of whatever is being served at that meal. For breakfast that means eggs, sausage, biscuits and gravy, and the like. Lunch and

dinner usually feature soup, potatoes, salad, and pie, plus daily changing entrées such as pot roast and pork loin. A back room contains a museum of logging culture, but really the whole place is a tribute to the rough-and-tumble life and hard work that tamed this wild land. Dieters and vegetarians should look elsewhere for sustenance. ☒ *Cookhouse Rd.; from U.S. 101 cross Samoa Bridge, turn left onto Samoa Rd., then left 1 block later onto Cookhouse Rd.* ☎ *707/442–1659* ⊕ *www. samoacookhouse.net* ☰ *AE, MC, V.*

$$–$$$

🏠 **Abigail's Elegant Victorian Mansion**. Lodging at this 1890 Victorian mansion is not a passive experience. Innkeepers Doug and Lily Vieyra have devoted themselves to honoring this National Historic Landmark (once home to the town's millionaire real-estate sultan) by decorating it with authentic, Victorian-era opulence. It seems that every square inch is covered in brocade, antique wallpaper, or redwood paneling, and from every possible surface hangs a painting with gilt frame, or a historical costume. The Vieyras want their visitors not to just flop into bed, but to pretend they are the current inhabitants—drink tea in the parlor, play croquet on the lawn, select one of hundreds of period movies and watch it while the innkeepers wait on you in the sitting room. If you're ready, don your top hat or corset and embrace what Doug calls his "interactive living history museum." **Pros:** unique; lots of character; fun innkeepers. **Cons:** downtown is not within walking distance; bedrooms are a bit worn. ☒ *1406 C St.* ☎ *707/444–3144* ⊕ *www.eureka-california.com* 🛏 *4 rooms, 2 with shared bath* ⚐ *In-room: a/c, Wi-Fi. In-hotel: tennis court, bicycles, laundry service, Internet terminal, Wi-Fi hotspot* ☰ *MC, V.*

$$–$$$
Fodor's Choice
★

🏠 **Carter House**. According to owner Mark Carter, his staff has been trained always to say yes. Whether it's breakfast in bed or an in-room massage, someone here will make sure you get what you want. Richly painted and aglow with wood detailing, rooms blend modern and antique furnishings in two main buildings and several cottages. **Pros:** elegant; every detail in place; excellent dining at Restaurant 301. **Cons:** while kids are allowed, it's better for grown-ups. ☒ *301 L St.* ☎ *707/444–8062 or 800/404–1390* ⊕ *www.carterhouse.com* 🛏 *22 rooms, 8 suites, 1 cottage* ⚐ *In-room: a/c, kitchen (some), DVD, Wi-Fi. In-hotel: restaurant, bar, laundry service, Internet terminal, Wi-Fi hotspot, some pets allowed* ☰ *AE, D, DC, MC, V* ⊚❘ *BP.*

SPORTS AND THE OUTDOORS

Hum-Boats (✉ *A Dock, Woodley Island Marina* ☎ *707/443–5157* ⊕ *www. humboats.com*) provides kayak rental and lessons. They also offer a variety of group kayak tours, including popular whale-watching trips ($65, December–June) that get you close enough to get good photos of migrating gray whales and resident humpback whales.

SHOPPING

Eureka has several art galleries and numerous antiques stores in the district running from C to I streets between 2nd and 3rd streets. Best for contemporary art is **First Street Gallery** (✉ *422 1st St.* ☎ *707/443–6363*), run by Humboldt State University, which showcases sophisticated work by local artists.

Eureka Books (✉ *126 2nd St.* ☎ *707/444–9593*) has an exceptional collection of used books on all topics.

TRINIDAD

21 mi north of Eureka on U.S. 101.

Trinidad got its name from the Spanish mariners who entered the bay on Trinity Sunday, June 9, 1775. The town became a principal trading post for the mining camps along the Klamath and Trinity rivers. Mining and whaling have faded from the scene, and now Trinidad is a quiet and genuinely charming community with enough sights and activities to entertain low-key visitors.

EXPLORING

On a forested plateau almost 200 feet above the surf, **Patrick's Point State Park** (✉ *5 mi north of Trinidad on U.S. 101* ☎ *707/677-3570* 🖃 *$8 per vehicle*) has stunning views of the Pacific, great whale- and sea lion–watching in season, picnic areas, bike paths, and hiking trails through old-growth spruce forest. There are also tidal pools at Agate Beach, a re-created Yurok Indian village, and a small museum with natural-history exhibits. Because the park is far from major tourist hubs, there are few visitors (most are local surfers), which leaves the land sublimely quiet. In spruce and alder forest above the ocean, the park's three **campgrounds** (☎ *800/444-7275* 🖃 *$35*) have all amenities except RV hookups. In summer it's best to reserve in advance.

🐾 Together, **Clam Beach County Park and Little River State Beach** (✉ *6½ mi south of Trinidad, on Hwy. 1* ☎ *707/445-7651* ☽ *5 AM–midnight*) make a park that stretches from Trinidad to as far as one can see south. The sandy beach here is exceptionally wide, perfect for kids who need to get out of the car and burn off some energy. It's also the rare sort of beach where vehicles are allowed, so those with four-wheel-drive can drive to a perfect fishing spot or tailgate on the sand.

WHERE TO EAT AND STAY

¢–$ ✕ **Katy's Smokehouse.** Purchase delectable picnic fixings at this tiny
SEAFOOD shop that has been doing things the same way since the 1940s, curing day-boat, line-caught fish with its original smokers. Salmon cured with brown sugar, albacore jerky, and smoked scallops are popular. Buy bread and drinks in town and walk to the waterside for alfresco

snacking. Katy's closes at 6 PM. ⊠ *740 Edwards St.* ☎ *707/677–0151*
⊕ *www.katyssmokehouse.com* ⊟ *MC, V.*

$$$ ✗ **Larrupin' Cafe.** Locals consider this restaurant one of the best places to
AMERICAN   eat on the North Coast. Set in a two-story house on a quiet country road
north of town, it's often thronged with people enjoying fresh seafood,
Cornish game hen, or mesquite-grilled ribs. While the garden setting
and candlelight stir thoughts of romance, service is sometimes rather
rushed. ⊠ *1658 Patrick's Point Dr.* ☎ *707/677–0230* ⊕ *www.larrupin.*
com ⚭ *Reservations essential* ⊟ *No credit cards* ⊙ *Closed Tues. and*
Wed. No lunch.

$$$–$$$$ ⊞ **Trinidad Bay Bed and Breakfast Inn.** Staying at this small Cape Cod–
style inn perched above Trinidad Bay is like spending the weekend at
a friend's vacation house. Every room has a downy, king-size bed and
softly colored, beachy furnishings. There are as many windows as the
walls will allow providing a view that starts at the harbor and stretches
for miles south down the coastline. The nicest room is also the largest;
called Tidepool, it has overstuffed chairs in front of a gas fireplace, as
well as two entire walls of windows. **Pros:** great location above bay;
lots of light. **Cons:** if all rooms are full, the main house can feel a bit
crowded. ⊠ *560 Edwards St., Box 84995570* ☎ *707/677–0840* ⊕ *www.*
trinidadbaybnb.com ⇝ *4 rooms* ⚭ *In-room: no a/c, refrigerator (some),*
no TV, Wi-Fi. In-hotel: Wi-Fi hotspot ⊟ *AE, MC, V* ◉| *BP.*

$$$$ ⊞ **Turtle Rocks Oceanfront Inn.** This comfortable inn has the best view
in Trinidad, and the builders have made the most of it. Each room's
private, glassed-in deck overlooks the ocean and rocks where sea lions
lie sunning. Interiors are spare and contemporary, and all rooms have
wonderfully comfortable king-size beds. The surrounding landscape has
been left wild and natural; tucked among the low bushes are sundecks
for winter whale watching and summer catnaps. Patrick's Point State
Park is a short walk away. **Pros:** great ocean views; comfy king beds.
Cons: no businesses within walking distance; not as deluxe as the price.
⊠ *3392 Patrick's Point Dr., 4½ mi north of town* ☎ *707/677–3707*
⊕ *www.turtlerocksinn.com* ⇝ *5 rooms, 1 suite* ⚭ *In-room: no a/c, DVD*
(some), Wi-Fi. In-hotel: Wi-Fi hotspot ⊟ *AE, D, MC, V* ◉| *BP.*

Redwood National Park

WORD OF MOUTH

"I thought that Stout Grove and the drive through was fantastic in Jedediah Smith area of the Redwoods. It is easy to get confused about the Redwoods as certain groves are within certain state parks within the national park itself."

—spirobulldog

WELCOME TO REDWOOD NATIONAL PARK

TOP REASONS TO GO

★ **Giant trees:** These mature coastal redwoods are the tallest trees in the world.

★ **Hiking to the sea:** The park's trails wind between majestic redwood groves, and many connect to the Coastal Trail running along the western edge of the park.

★ **Rare wildlife:** Mighty Roosevelt elk favor the park's flat prairie and open lands; seldom-seen black bears roam the backcountry; trout and salmon leap through streams, and Pacific gray whales swim along the coast during their biannual migrations.

★ **Stepping back in time:** Hike Fern Canyon Trail, which weaves through a prehistoric scene of lush vegetation and giant ferns.

★ **Cheeps, not beeps:** Amid the majestic redwoods you're out of range for cell-phone service—and in range for the soothing sounds of warblers and burbling creeks.

1 Del Norte Coast Redwoods State Park. The rugged terrain of this far northwest corner of California combines stretches of treacherous surf, steep cliffs, and forested ridges. On a clear day it's postcard-perfect; with fog, it's mysteriously mesmerizing.

2 Jedediah Smith Redwoods State Park. Gargantuan old growth redwoods dominate the scenery here. The Smith River cuts through canyons and splits across boulders, carrying salmon to the inland creeks where they spawn.

3 Prairie Creek Redwoods State Park. The forests here give way to spacious, grassy plains where abundant wildlife thrives. Roosevelt elk are a common sight in the meadows and down to Gold Bluffs Beach.

4 Orick Area. The highlight of the southern portion of Redwood National Park is the Tall Trees Grove. It's difficult to reach and requires a special pass, but it's worth the hassle—this section has the tallest coast redwood trees, with a new record holder discovered in 2006.

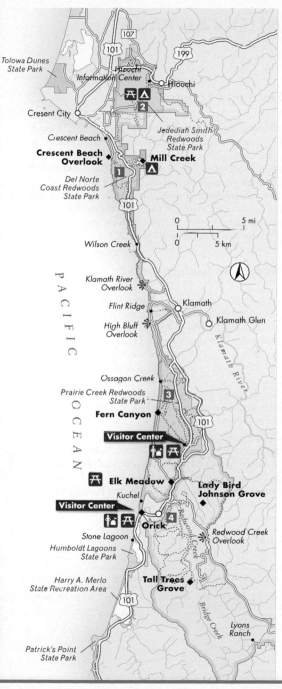

12

GETTING ORIENTED

U.S. 101 weaves through the southern portion of the park, skirts around the center, and then slips back through redwoods in the north and on to Crescent City. Kuchel Visitor Center, Prairie Creek Redwoods State Park and Visitor Center, Tall Trees Grove, Fern Canyon, and Lady Bird Johnson Grove are all in the park's southern section. The graveled Coastal Drive curves along ocean vistas and dips down to the Klamath River in the park's central section. To the north you'll find Mill Creek Trail, Enderts Beach, and Crescent Beach Overlook in Del Norte Coast Redwoods State Park as well as Jedediah Smith Redwoods State Park, Stout Grove, Little Bald Hills, and Simpson-Reed Grove.

REDWOOD NATIONAL PARK PLANNER

Getting Here and Around

U.S. 101 runs north–south along the park, and Highway 199 cuts east–west through its northern portion. Access routes off 101 include Bald Hills Road, Davison Road, Newton B. Drury Scenic Parkway, Coastal Drive, Requa Road, and Enderts Beach Road. From 199 take South Fork Road to Howland Hill Road. Many of the park's roads aren't paved, and winter rains can turn them into obstacle courses; sometimes they're closed completely. RVs and trailers aren't permitted on some routes.

WHEN TO GO

Campers and hikers flock to the park from mid-June to early September. Crowds disappear in winter, but you'll have to contend with frequent rains and nasty potholes on side roads. Temperatures fluctuate widely throughout the park: the foggy coastal lowland is much cooler than the higher-altitude interior. The average annual rainfall here is 90 to 100 inches.

AVG. HIGH/LOW TEMPS.

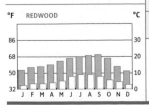

Flora and Fauna

A healthy redwood forest is diverse and includes Douglas firs, western hemlocks, tan oaks, and madrone trees. In the park's backcountry, you might spot mountain lions, black bears, black-tailed deer, river otters, beavers, and minks. Roosevelt elk roam the flatlands, and the rivers and streams teem with salmon and trout. Gray whales, seals, and sea lions cavort near the coastline. And thanks to the area's location along the Pacific Flyway, an amazing 402 species of birds have been sighted here.

About the Campgrounds

Within a 30-minute drive of Redwood National and State parks there are nearly 60 public and private camping facilities. None of the four primitive areas in Redwood—DeMartin, Flint Ridge, Little Bald Hills, and Nickel Creek—is a drive-in site. Although you don't need a permit at these four hike-in sites, stop at a ranger station to inquire about availability. You will need to get a permit from a ranger station for camping along Redwood Creek in the backcountry. Bring your own water, since drinking water isn't available in any of these sites.

If you'd rather drive than hike in, Redwood has four developed campgrounds—Elk Prairie, Gold Bluffs Beach, Jedediah Smith, and Mill Creek—that are within the state park boundaries. None has RV hookups, and some length restrictions apply. Fees are $35 in state park campgrounds. For details and reservations, call ☎ *800/444–7275* or check ⊕ *www.reserveamerica.com*.

WHAT IT COSTS				
¢	$	$$	$$$	$$$$
Campgrounds under $10	$10–$17	$18–$35	$36–$49	over $50
Camping prices are for a standard (no hookups, pit toilets, fire grates, picnic tables) campsite per night.				

12

Updated by
Sura Wood
and Christine
Vovakes

Soaring to more than 300 feet, the coastal redwoods that give this park its name are miracles of efficiency—some have survived hundreds of years (a few live for more than 2,000 years). These massive trees glean nutrients from the rich alluvial flats at their feet and from the moisture and nitrogen trapped in their uneven canopy. Their huge, thick-barked trunks can hold thousands of gallons of water, reservoirs that have helped them withstand centuries of firestorms.

PARK ESSENTIALS

ADMISSION FEES AND PERMITS

Admission to Redwood National Park is free. There's a $8 day-use fee to enter one or all of Redwood's state parks; for camping at these state parks it's an additional $35. To visit Tall Trees Grove, you must get a free permit at the Kuchel Information Center in Orick. Permits also are needed to camp in Redwood Creek backcountry.

ADMISSION HOURS

The park is open year-round, 24 hours a day.

PARK CONTACT INFORMATION

Redwood National Park ✉ *1111 2nd St., Crescent City, CA* ☎ *707/465–7306* ⊕ *www.nps.gov/redw.*

SCENIC DRIVES

★ **Coastal Drive.** This 8-mi, partially paved road is closed to trailers and RVs and takes about one hour to drive one way. The slow pace alongside stands of redwoods offers close-up views of the Klamath River and expansive panoramas of the Pacific. From here you'll find access to the Flint Ridge section of the Coastal Trail.

EXPLORING

SCENIC STOPS

Crescent Beach Overlook. The scenery here includes ocean views and, in the distance, Crescent City and its working harbor; in balmy weather this is a great place for a picnic. From the overlook you can spot migrating gray whales November through December and March through April. ⊠ *2 mi south of Crescent City off Enderts Beach Rd.*

★ **Fern Canyon.** Enter another world and be surrounded by 30-foot canyon walls covered with sword, maidenhair, and five-finger ferns. Allow an hour to explore the ¼-mi long vertical garden along a 0.7-mi loop. From the north end of Gold Bluffs Beach it's an easy walk, although you'll have to wade across a small stream several times (in addition to driving across streams on the way to the parking area). But the lush surroundings are otherworldly, and worth a visit when creeks aren't running too high. Be aware that RVs longer than 24 feet and all trailers are not allowed here. ⊠ *10 mi northwest of Prairie Creek Visitor Center, via Davison Rd. off U.S. 101.*

Lady Bird Johnson Grove. This section of the park was dedicated by, and named for, the former first lady. A 1-mi, wheelchair-accessible nature loop follows an old logging road through a mature redwood forest. Allow 45 minutes to complete the trail. ⊠ *5 mi east of Kuchel Visitor Center, along U.S. 101 and Bald Hills Rd.*

★ **Tall Trees Grove.** From the Kuchel Visitor Center, you can get a free permit to make the drive up the steep 17-mi Tall Trees Access Road (the last 6 mi are gravel) to the grove's trailhead (trailers and RVs not allowed). Access to the popular grove is first-come, first-served, and a maximum of 50 permits are handed out each day. ⊠ *Access road is 10 mi drive east of Kuchel Visitor Center, via U.S. 101 and Bald Hills Rd.*

VISITOR CENTERS

Crescent City Information Center. As the park's headquarters, this center is the main information stop if you're approaching the redwoods from the north. A gift shop and picnic area are here. ⊠ *Off U.S. 101 at 2nd and K Sts., Crescent City* ☎ *707/465–7306* ⊕ *www.nps.gov/redw* ⊙ *Mid-May–mid-Oct., daily 9–6; mid-Oct.–mid-May, daily 9–4.*

Hiouchi Information Center. Located in Jedediah Smith Redwoods State Park, 2 mi west of Hiouchi and 9 mi east of Crescent City off U.S. 199, this center has a bookstore, film, and exhibits about the flora and fauna in the park. It's also a starting point for seasonal ranger programs. ⊠ *Hiouchi Information Center, Hwy. 199, Hiouchi* ☎ *707/458–3294* ⊕ *www.nps.gov/redw* ⊙ *Late May–mid-Sept., daily 9–6.*

Jedediah Smith Visitor Center. Located off U.S. 199, this center has information about ranger-led walks and evening campfire programs in the summer in Jedediah Smith Redwoods State Park. Also here are nature and history exhibits, a gift shop, a pay phone, and a picnic area. ⊠ *Off U.S. 199, Hiouchi* ☎ *707/465–2144* ⊕ *www.parks.ca.gov* ⊙ *Late May–late Sept., daily 9–5; late Sept.–late May, Fri.–Sun. 10–6.*

★ **Prairie Creek Visitor Center.** This center, housed in a redwood lodge, has wildlife displays and a massive stone fireplace that was built in

12

1933. Several trailheads begin here. Stretch your legs with an easy stroll along Revelation Trail, a short loop behind the lodge. Pick up information about summer programs in Prairie Creek Redwoods State Park. There's a pay phone, nature museum, gift shop, picnic area, and exhibits on flora and fauna. ✉ *Off southern end of Newton B. Drury Scenic Pkwy., Orick* ☎ *707/465–7354* ⊕ *www.parks.ca.gov* ⊙ *Late May–early Sept., daily 9–6; early Sept.–late May, daily 9–5.*

★ **Thomas H. Kuchel Visitor Center.** Here you can get brochures, advice, and a free permit to drive up the access road to Tall Trees Grove. Whale-watchers will find the deck of the visitor center an excellent observation point, and bird-watchers will enjoy the nearby Freshwater Lagoon, a popular layover for migrating waterfowl. ✉ *Off U.S. 101, Orick* ☎ *707/465-7765* ⊕ *www.nps.gov/redw* ⊙ *Late May–early Sept., daily 9–6; early Sept.–late May, daily 9–5.*

OUTFITTERS

Coast True Value (✉ *900 Northcrest Dr., Crescent City* ☎ *707/464–3535*) is a good place to get fishing licenses (valid for both river and ocean fishing; $41.50 annual fee or $20.75 two-day fee for California residents; two-day and 10-day licenses for $20.75 and $41.20 can also be purchased by nonresidents).

You can rent hard-shell kayaks at **Adventure's Edge** (✉ *650 10th St., Arcata* ☎ *707/822–4673* ⊙ *Mon.–Sat. 9–6, Sun. 10–5*) for $40 a day. In business since 1970, this Arcata outfitter also rents camping equipment and tents.

SPORTS AND THE OUTDOORS

FISHING

Both deep-sea and freshwater fishing are popular here. Anglers often stake out sections of the Klamath and Smith rivers in their search for salmon and trout. (A single fishing license covers both ocean and river fishing.) Less serious anglers go crabbing and clamming on the coast, but check the tides carefully: rip currents and sneaker waves are deadly.

HIKING

★ **Coastal Trail.** Although this easy-to-difficult trail runs along most of the park's length, smaller sections—of varying degrees of difficulty—are accessible via frequent, well-marked trailheads. The moderate to difficult DeMartin section leads past 5 mi of old growth redwoods and through prairie. If you're up for a real workout, you'll be well rewarded with the brutally difficult but stunning Flint Ridge section, a 4.5-mi stretch of steep grades and numerous switchbacks that leads past redwoods and Marshall Pond. The moderate 4-mi-long Hidden Beach section connects the Lagoon Creek picnic area with Klamath Overlook and provides coastal views and whale-watching opportunities. ✉ *Flint Ridge trailhead: Douglas Bridge parking area, north end of Coastal Dr.*

KAYAKING

With many miles of often-shallow rivers and streams in the area, kayaking is a popular pastime in the park.

WHALE-WATCHING

Good vantage points for whale-watching include Crescent Beach Over-look, the Kuchel Visitor Center in Orick, points along the Coastal Drive, and the Klamath River Overlook. Late November through January are the best months to see their southward migrations; February through April they return and generally pass closer to shore.

WHERE TO STAY

$	⚠ **Gold Bluffs Beach Campground.** You can camp in tents or RVs right
Fodor's Choice	on the beach at this Prairie Creek Redwoods State Park campground
★	near Fern Canyon. Keep your eyes open for Roosevelt elk. Note that RVs must be less than 24 feet long and 8 feet wide, and trailers aren't allowed on the access road. You pay the fee at the campground. **Pros:** gorgeous setting. **Cons:** no reservations. ⊠ *At end of Davison Rd., 5 mi north of Redwood Information Center off U.S. 101* ☎ *707/465–7354* ⚠ *26 tent/RV sites* ♿ *Flush toilets, drinking water, showers, fire pits, picnic tables* ⊟ *No credit cards.*

$$	⚠ **Jedediah Smith Campground.** This is one of the few places to camp—in tents or RVs—within groves of old-growth redwood forest. The length limit on RVs is 36 feet; for trailers it's 31 feet. **Pros:** family friendly, only campground with swimming. **Cons:** can get crowded. ⊠ *8 mi north-east of Crescent City on U.S. 199* ☎ *800/444–7275* ⚠ *86 tent/RV sites* ♿ *Flush toilets, dump station, drinking water, bear boxes, fire pits, picnic tables, public telephone, play area, ranger station, swimming (river)* ⊟ *AE, D, MC, V.*

$$	⚠ **Mill Creek Campground.** Mill Creek is the largest of the state park campgrounds. **Pros:** good family campground. **Cons:** open only in summer. ⊠ *West of U.S. 101, 7 mi southeast of Crescent City* ☎ *800/444– 7275* ⚠ *145 tent/RV sites* ♿ *Flush toilets, dump station, drinking water, showers, bear boxes, fire pits, picnic tables* ⊟ *AE, D, MC, V* ☉ *Closed Day after Labor Day–April.*

The Inland Empire

EAST OF LOS ANGELES TO THE SAN JACINTO MOUNTAINS

WORD OF MOUTH

"We stayed overnight at the Lake Arrowhead resort and loved it. We hiked around the lake and hung out on the hotel's 'beach.' Felt like we were in a luxury hunting lodge in the Alps. Instant and AFFORDABLE getaway."

—ArleneW

WELCOME TO THE INLAND EMPIRE

TOP REASONS TO GO

★ **Wine country:** The Temecula Valley is a mélange of rolling hills, faint ocean breezes, beautiful and funky wineries, lovely lodging options, and gourmet restaurants.

★ **The Mission Inn:** One of the most unique hotels in America, Riverside's rambling, eclectic Mission Inn feels like a small Hearst Castle.

★ **Apple country:** Oak Glen is one of Southern California's largest apple-growing regions. Attend an old-fashioned hoedown, take a wagon ride, and sample Mile High apple pies and homemade ciders.

★ **Soothing spas:** The lushly landscaped grounds, bubbling hot springs, and playful mud baths of Glen Ivy are ideal spots to unwind, while Kelly's Spa at the historic Mission Inn provides a Tuscan-style retreat.

★ **Alpine escapes:** Breathe in the clean mountain air or cozy up in a rustic cabin at one of the Inland Empire's great mountain hideaways: Lake Arrowhead, Big Bear, and Idyllwild.

1 The Western Inland Empire. At the foot of 10,000-foot-high Mt. Baldy in the San Gabriel Mountains, the tree-lined communities of Pomona and Claremont are known for their prestigious colleges: California State Polytechnic University–Pomona and the seven-school Claremont college complex. Pomona is urban and industrial, but Claremont is a classic tree-shaded, lively college town where you can generally find interesting conversation in any café.

2 Riverside Area. In the late 1700s, Mexican settlers called this now-suburban region Valle de Paraiso. Citrus-growing here began in 1873, when homesteader Eliza Tibbets planted two navel-orange trees in her yard. The area's biggest draws are the majestic Mission Inn, with its fine restaurants and unique history and architecture, and Glen Ivy Hot Springs in nearby Corona.

GETTING ORIENTED

13

Several major freeways provide access to the Inland Empire from the L.A. and San Diego areas. Ontario, Corona, and Temecula line up along I–15, and I–215; and Highway 91 leads to Riverside and San Bernardino. The area's popularity as a bedroom community for Los Angeles has created some nasty freeway congestion on Highway 60, I–10, and I–15, so try to avoid driving during rush hour, usually 6 to 8 AM and 4 to 7 PM.

3 San Bernardino Mountains. Lake Arrowhead and always-sunny Big Bear are the recreational centers of this area. Though the two are geographically close, they're distinct in appeal—smaller, but similar to Lake Tahoe, say visitors. Lake Arrowhead, with its cool mountain air, trail-threaded woods, and brilliant lake, draws a summertime crowd—a well-heeled one, if the prices in its shops and restaurants are any indication. Big Bear's ski and snowboarding slopes, cross-country trails, and cheerful lodges come alive in winter. Even if you're not interested in the resorts themselves, the Rim of the World Scenic Byway (Highway 18), which connects the two at an elevation of 8,000 feet, is a magnificent drive; on a clear day, you'll feel like you can see forever.

4 The Southern Inland Empire. Life is quieter in the southern portion of the Inland Empire than it is to the north. In this corner of Riverside County, towns such as Idyllwild and Temecula are oases of the good life for locals and visitors alike.

THE INLAND EMPIRE PLANNER

How's the Weather?

The climate varies greatly depending on what part of the Inland Empire you're visiting. Summer temperatures in the mountains and in Temecula, 20 mi from the coast, usually hover around 80°F, though it's not uncommon for Riverside to reach temperatures over 100°F. From September to March this area is subject to increasingly high Santa Ana winds, sometimes strong enough to overturn trucks on the freeway. In winter, temperatures in the mountains and in Temecula usually range from 30°F to 55°F, and in the Riverside area 40°F to 60°F. Most of the ski areas open when the first natural snow falls (usually in November) and close in mid-March.

About the Restaurants

Inland Empire residents no longer have to travel to L.A. or Orange County for a good meal. Downtown Riverside is home to some ambitious restaurants, along with the chains you can find in most areas. The college towns of Claremont and Redlands showcase creative vegetarian cuisine. In Temecula, the choices expand to wine-country cooking, with many vintners showcasing their products alongside California–French dishes. Your options are limited in the smaller mountain communities; typically each town supports a single upscale restaurant, along with fast-food outlets, steak-and-potatoes family spots, and perhaps an Italian or Mexican eatery. Universally, dining out is casual.

About the Hotels

In the San Gabriel and San Bernardino mountains, most accommodations are bed-and-breakfasts or rustic cabins, though Lake Arrowhead offers more luxurious resort lodging. Rates for Big Bear lodgings fluctuate widely, depending on the season. When winter snow brings droves of Angelenos to the mountains for skiing, expect to pay sky-high prices for any kind of room. Most establishments require a two-night stay on weekends. In Riverside, you might enjoy a stay at the landmark Mission Inn, a rambling Spanish-style hotel with elaborate courtyards, fountains, and a mixture of ornate Mission revival–, Spanish baroque–, Renaissance revival–, and Asian-architecture styles. In the wine country, lodgings can be found at wineries, golf resorts, and chain hotels.

WHAT IT COSTS

	¢	$	$$	$$$	$$$$
Restaurants	under $10	$10–$15	$16–$22	$23–$30	over $30
Hotels	under $90	$90–$120	$121–$175	$176–$250	over $250

Restaurant prices are for a main course at dinner, excluding sales tax of 7.75%. Hotel prices are for two people in a standard double room in high season, excluding service charges and 7.75% tax.

13

Updated by
Bobbi Zane

The Inland Empire, an area often overlooked by visitors because of its tangled freeways and suburban sprawl, does have its charms. No more than a few hours' drive from metropolitan Los Angeles, you can ski a 7,000-foot mountain overlooking a crystal blue lake or go wine tasting at a vineyard cooled by ocean breezes.

At the heart of this desert and mountain region is Riverside, the birthplace of California's multimillion-dollar navel-orange industry—established in 1875—and home of the University of California at Riverside. The tree that started it all still flourishes on Magnolia Avenue. Today the streets of downtown buzz with people on their way to shop for antiques, eat in exciting restaurants, and listen to live jazz.

The scene is completely different northeast of Riverside, in the San Bernardino Mountains. There Big Bear Lake and Lake Arrowhead are set like bowls surrounded by wooded mountain peaks. To the south, in the San Jacinto Mountains just west of Palm Springs, Idyllwild is a popular year-round getaway with romantic cottages, an impressive collection of art galleries, and cozy restaurants. In the southernmost reaches of the Inland Empire, on the way from Riverside to San Diego, is what is known as the Southern California Wine Country around Temecula, a hip and trendy destination for oenophiles. This is also prime territory for hot-air ballooning, golfing, fine dining, and—of course—vineyard tours and wine tasting.

PLANNING

GETTING HERE AND AROUND
BY AIR
Aero Mexico, Alaska, American, Continental, Delta, Southwest, United, US Airways, and Great Lakes Airlines serve LA/Ontario International Airport.

Airport Contacts LA/Ontario International Airport (✉ *Airport Dr., Archibald Ave. exit off I-10, Ontario* ☎ *909/937-2700* ⊕ *www.lawa.org*).

BY BUS

Greyhound serves Claremont, Riverside, San Bernardino, and Temecula. Most stations are open daily during business hours; some are open 24 hours.

The Foothill Transit Bus Line serves Pomona, Claremont, and Montclair, with stops at Cal Poly and the Fairplex. Riverside Transit Authority (RTA) serves Riverside and some outlying communities, as does OmniTrans.

Bus Contacts Foothill Transit (☎ 800/743–3463 ⊕ www.foothilltransit. org). **OmniTrans** (☎ 800/966–6428 ⊕ www.omnitrans.org). **Riverside Transit Authority** (☎ 800/800–7821 ⊕ www.rrta.com).

BY CAR

Avoid Highway 91 if possible; it's almost always backed up from Corona through Orange County.

Car Contact California Highway Patrol 24-hour road info (☎ 800/427–7623 ⊕ www.dot.ca.gov/hq/roadinfo).

BY TRAIN

■ TIP→ Many locals use the Metrolink to get around, which is clean and quick, and generally a much nicer way to travel than by bus.

Metrolink has several Inland Empire stations on its Inter-County, San Bernardino, and Riverside rail lines. The Riverside Line connects downtown Riverside, Pedley, East Ontario, and downtown Pomona with City of Industry, Montebello/City of Commerce, and Union Station in Los Angeles. The Inland Empire Orange County Line connects San Bernardino, downtown Riverside, Riverside La Sierra, and West Corona with San Juan Capistrano and other Orange County destinations. Metrolink's busiest train, the San Bernardino Line, connects Pomona, Claremont, Montclair, and San Bernardino with the San Gabriel Valley and downtown Los Angeles. Bus service extends the reach of train service, to spots including L.A./Ontario Airport, the Claremont colleges, and the Fairplex at Pomona. You can buy tickets and passes at the ticket vending machine at each station, or by telephone. A recorded message announces Metrolink schedules 24 hours a day.

Train Contact Metrolink (☎ 800/371–5465 ⊕ www.metrolinktrains.com).

HEALTH AND SAFETY

In an emergency dial 911.

Emergency Services Big Bear Lake Sheriff /(☎ 909/866–0100).**Parkview Community Hospital** (✉ 3865 Jackson St., Riverside ☎ 951/688–2211). **Rancho Springs Medical Center** (✉ 25500 Medical Center Dr., Murrieta ☎ 951/696–6000). **Riverside Community Hospital** (✉ 4445 Magnolia Ave., Riverside ☎ 951/788–3000). **St. Bernardine Medical Center** (✉ 2101 N. Waterman Ave., San Bernardino ☎ 909/883–8711).

THE WESTERN INLAND EMPIRE

POMONA

13

23 mi north of Anaheim on Hwy. 57; 27 mi east of Pasadena on I–210.

The green hills of Pomona, dotted with horses and houses, are perhaps best known as the site of the Los Angeles County Fair and of California State Polytechnic University–Pomona. Named for the Roman goddess of fruit, the city has a rich citrus-growing heritage.

ESSENTIALS

Visitor Information Pomona Chamber of Commerce (✉ *101 W. Mission Blvd., #223, Pomona* ☎ *909/622–1256* ⊕ *www.pomonachamber.org*).

EXPLORING

California Polytechnic University at Pomona (✉ *3801 W. Temple, Pomona* ☎ *909/869–7659* ⊕ *www.csupomona.edu*) occupies 1,438 acres of the Kellogg Ranch, originally the winter home of cereal magnate W.K. Kellogg. The university specializes in teaching agriculture, and you can find lush grounds here: rose gardens, avocado groves, lots of farm animals, and a working Arabian Horse Ranch. You can sample the best that California agriculture has to offer at the Farm Store (✉ *4102 University Dr. S.* ☎ *909/869–4906*), where you can find locally grown seasonal fruit and vegetables, campus-grown pork and beef, cheeses and other deli items, gift baskets, and plants grown in the university nursery.

On the Cal Poly campus, **Kellogg House** (✉ *3801 W. Temple Ave.* ☎ *909/869–2280* ⊕ *www.kellogghousepomona.com* 🎟 *Free* ☉ *Oct.–June, open house 1st Sun. of every month, noon–2, otherwise access by group tour only*) was the scenic hilltop winter estate of cereal magnate Will Keith Kellogg. The circa-1925 home was designed by Myron Hunt (of Rose Bowl and Huntington Library fame) and has a blend of Islamic, Spanish, and Italian architecture. You can stroll the courtyard and gardens (both open to the public year-round), landscaped by Charles Gibbs Adams of Hearst Castle fame, then head inside for a look at the grand tapestries, hardwood floors, and intricately detailed ceilings.

The classic **Arabian Horse Shows** (✉ *3801 W. Temple Ave.* ☎ *909/869–2224* 🎟 *$3*), started by Kellogg in 1926, are still a tradition on the CSU–Pomona campus. More than 85 of the purebreds still call Kellogg's ranch home, and the university offers exhibitions of the equines in English and Western tack every first Sunday at 2 PM from October through May; tours of the stables are available by appointment only.

Site of the Los Angeles County Fair (ninth-largest in the United States), the **Fairplex** exposition center has a 9,500-seat grandstand, an outdoor exhibit area, and nine exhibit buildings. The venue is the site of open-air markets, antiques shows, historical train and model train exhibits, a track for Thoroughbred racing during the fair, and the annual International Wine and Spirits competition. Fairplex houses the **Wally Parks NHRA Motorsports Museum** (☎ *909/622–2133* 🎟 *$7* ☉ *Wed.–Sun. 10–5*), dedicated to the history of American motor sports with exhibits of vintage racing vehicles. ⊠ *1101 W. McKinley Ave.* ☎ *909/623–3111* ⊕ *www.fairplex.com* ⊘ *Call for current show listings and admission prices.*

WHERE TO EAT

$$$
AMERICAN
✕ **Pomona Valley Mining Company**. Perched on a hilltop near an old mining site, this rustic steak-and-seafood restaurant provides a great view of the city at night. The decor reflects the local mining heritage—authentic gold-rush pieces and 1800s memorabilia hang on the walls, and old lanterns are the centerpiece of each table. The food is well prepared, with a special nod to steak and prime rib, and be sure to try the Pickin's Combo, an hors d'oeuvre and more comprised of coconut beer shrimp, calamari and Buffalo wings. Service is friendly. During May book early—this is a favorite spot on prom nights. ⊠ *1777 Gillette Rd.* ☎ *909/623–3515* ⊕ *www.pomonavalleyminingco.com* ☰ *AE, D, MC, V* ⊘ *No lunch.*

$$
🏨 **Sheraton Suites Fairplex**. County-fair murals and whimsical carousel animals welcome you to this all-suites hotel at the entrance to Pomona's Fairplex. Contemporary in style, rooms are done in neutral tans and blues and have coffeemakers and wet bars. Most have balconies. It's about the only lodging in Pomona you should consider staying at, say locals and visitors alike, who rave about its comfort and cleanliness. The hotel books many groups throughout the year, so be sure to book in advance. McKinley's Grill serves steak and seafood, and Mountain Meadows Golf Course is adjacent. **Pros:** close to Fairplex; clean rooms; comfortable beds; signature dog beds. **Cons:** parts of the hotel feel dated; not close to many restaurants. ⊠ *601 W. McKinley Ave.* ☎ *888/627–8074* ⊕ *www.sheraton.com* ↩ *247 suites* � *In-room: a/c, refrigerator, Internet, Wi-Fi. In-hotel: restaurant, room service, bar, pool, gym, laundry service, Wi-Fi hotspot, parking (paid), some pets allowed* ☰ *AE, D, MC, V.*

CLAREMONT

4 mi north of Pomona along Gary Ave., then 2 mi east on Foothill Blvd.

Nicknamed "Oxford in the Orange Belt," the seven Claremont colleges are among the most prestigious in California. The campuses are all laid out cheek-by-jowl; as you wander from one leafy street to the next, you won't be able to tell where one college ends and the next begins.

Claremont was originally the home of the Sunkist citrus growers cooperative movement. Today, Claremont Village harks back to the 1950s with its walkable tree-shaded streets named for Ivy League colleges. The downtown district is a beautiful place to visit, with Victorian, Craftsman, and Spanish-colonial buildings.

ESSENTIALS

Visitor Information Claremont Chamber of Commerce (⊠ *205 Yale Ave., Claremont* ☎ *909/624–1681* ⊕ *www.claremontchamber.org*).

EXPLORING

Pomona College Museum of Art (⊠ *330 N. College Way, Claremont* ☎ *909/621–8283* ⊕ *www.pomona. edu/museum* ☐ *Free* ⊙ *Tues.–Fri. noon–5, weekends 1–5; closed between exhibits*), a small museum on the campus of Pomona College,

holds a significant collection of contemporary art, works by old masters, and examples of Native American arts and artifacts. Highlights include the first mural painted by Mexican artist Jose Clemente Orozco in North America, a collection of first-edition etchings by Goya dating back to the 18th century, and the Kress collection of 15th- and 16th-century Italian panel paintings.

College walking tours, a downtown tour, and historic home tours are conducted throughout the year by **Claremont Heritage** (☎ *909/621–0848* ⊕ *www.claremontheritage.org* ☐ *$8*). On the first Saturday of each month the organization gives walking tours of the village.

QUICK BITES

Bert & Rocky's Cream Company (⊠ *242 Yale Ave.* ☎ *909/625–1852*). This independent ice-cream store is known for its innovative and simply sinful concoctions. The champagne and merlot sorbets are hot items, as are the vanilla ice cream, chocolate raspberry swirl ice cream, and cheesecake ice cream. For a real treat, ask for a scoop of chocolate ice cream topped with a splash of red wine from Rancho Cucamonga winery.

★ Founded in 1927 by Susanna Bixby Bryant, a wealthy landowner and conservationist, **Rancho Santa Ana Botanic Garden** is a living museum and research center dedicated to the conservation of more than 2,800 native California plant species. Meandering trails on 86 acres of ponds and greenery guide visitors past such fragrant specimens as California wild lilacs (ceanothus), big berry manzanita, and four-needled piñon. Countless birds also make their homes here. Before you start your tour, pick up a native-bird field guide at the gift shop. ⊠ *1500 N. College Ave.* ☎ *909/625–8767* ⊕ *www.rsabg.org* ☐ *$8* ⊙ *Daily 8–5.*

WHERE TO EAT

$$$
ITALIAN

✕ **Tutti Mangia Italian Grill.** College students have their parents take them to Tutti Mangia when they're in town visiting. Filling a corner storefront, the dining room with tables well spaced feels warm and cozy. The menu offers lots of choices including herb-crusted Atlantic salmon, grilled thick-cut pork chops, and veal shank. The Sunday night prime rib special comes with soup or salad. ⊠ *102 Harvard Ave., Claremont* ☎ *909/625–4669* ▭ *AE, D, MC, V* ⊙ *No lunch Sun.*

NIGHTLIFE

Being a college town, Claremont has lots of bars and cafés, some of which showcase bands. Most of the best venues are a few miles east of the village in Upland. Karaoke and British fare are popular at the **British Bulldog Pub and Restaurant** (⊠ *1667 N. Mountain Ave., Upland* ☎ *909/946–6614*). Both college kids and old-timers appreciate the

Buffalo Inn (⊠ *1814 W. Foothill Blvd., Upland* ☎ *909/981–5515*), a rustic bar and hamburger joint along historic Route 66. Recent reviews have complained about service.

SPORTS AND THE OUTDOORS

SKIING The 10,064-foot mountain's real name is Mt. San Antonio, but **Mt. Baldy Ski Resort**—the oldest ski area in Southern California—takes its name from the treeless slopes. It's known for its steep triple-diamond runs, though the facilities could use some updating. ■ **TIP→** If you are an experienced skier, the runs here probably will not challenge you.

The Mt. Baldy base lies at 6,500 feet, and four chairlifts ascend to 8,600 feet. There are 26 runs; the longest is 2,100 vertical feet. Whenever abundant fresh snow falls, there's a danger of avalanche in out-of-bounds areas. Backcountry skiing is available via shuttle in the spring, and there's a kiddie school on weekends for children ages five to 12. Winter or summer, you can take a scenic chairlift ride ($15) to the Top of the Notch restaurant, and hiking and mountain-biking trails. ⊠ *From E. Foothill Blvd., about ½ mi north on N. Claremont Blvd., then 3 mi north on Monte Vista Ave. and 7 mi east on Mount Baldy Rd.* ☎ *909/981–3344* ⊕ *www.mtbaldy.com* ☒ *Full day $54–$64, half day $44–$54* ☉ *Snow season Nov.–Apr., weekdays 8–4:30, weekends 7:30–4:30; summer season May–Oct., weekends 9–4:30.*

ONTARIO

Junction of I–10 and I–15, 6 mi east of Pomona.

Ontario has a rich agricultural and industrial heritage. The valley's warm climate once supported vineyards that produced Mediterranean-grape varietals such as grenache, mourvèdre, and zinfandel. Today almost all of the vineyards have been replaced by housing tracts and shopping malls. But the LA/Ontario International Airport is here, so you may well find yourself passing through Ontario.

ESSENTIALS

Visitor Information Ontario Convention & Visitors Bureau (⊠ *2000 E. Convention Center Way, Ontario* ☎ *909/937–3000* ⊕ *www.ontariocvb.com*).

EXPLORING

Ontario's oldest existing business, **Graber Olive House**, opened in 1894 when, at the urging of family and friends, C.C. Graber bottled his meaty, tree-ripened olives and started selling them; they are still sold throughout the United States. Stop by the gourmet shop for a jar, then have a picnic on the shaded grounds. Free tours are conducted year-round; in fall you can watch workers grade, cure, and can the olives. ⊠ *315 E. 4th St.* ☎ *800/996–5483* ⊕ *www.graberolives.com* ☒ *Free* ☉ *Daily 9–5:30.*

WHERE TO STAY

$$ ☒ **Doubletree Hotel Ontario Airport.** A beautifully landscaped court-
Ⓒ yard greets you at this exceptional chain, the only full-service hotel
★ in Ontario. Rooms here are spacious, and decorated in jewel tones and dark wood; the business center has printers, a copier, and laptop hookups as well as a computer with Internet access. While this

is a business-oriented hotel, the welcome mat is out for kids. **Pros:** well-landscaped grounds; clean, large rooms; complimentary shuttle to Ontario Mills Mall. **Cons:** some airport noise; some rooms feel dated. ⊠ *222 N. Vineyard Ave.* ☎ *909/937–0900 or 800/222–8733* ⊕ *www. doubletree.com* ⟿ *184 rooms, 22 suites* ☖ *In-room: a/c, refrigerator, Internet, Wi-Fi. In-hotel: 2 restaurants, room service, bars, pool, gym, laundry service, Wi-Fi hotspot, parking (free), some pets allowed* ⊟ *AE, D, MC, V* ⦿| *CP.*

SHOPPING

☺ The gargantuan **Ontario Mills Mall** is California's largest, packing in more than 200 outlet stores, a 30-screen movie theater, and the Improv comedy theater. Also in the mall are two entertainment complexes: Dave & Buster's pool hall–restaurant–arcade, and GameWorks video-game center. Dining options include the kid-friendly jungle-theme Rainforest Cafe (complete with audio-animatronic elephants and simulated thunderstorms), the Cheesecake Factory, and a 1,000-seat food court. ⊠ *1 Mills Circle, 4th St. and I–15* ☎ *909/484–8300* ⊕ *www.ontariomills. com* ⊙ *Mon.–Sat. 10–9, Sun. 11–8.*

RANCHO CUCAMONGA

5 mi north of Ontario on I–15.

Once a thriving wine-making area with more than 50,000 acres of wine grapes, Rancho Cucamonga—the oldest wine district in California— lost most of its pastoral charm after real-estate developers bought up the land for a megamall and affordable housing. Most of it is now a squeaky-clean planned community, but the wine-making tradition still thrives at the Joseph Filippi Winery.

EXPLORING

J.P. and Gino Filippi continue the family tradition that was started in 1922 at the **Joseph Filippi Winery**. They produce handcrafted wines from cabernet, Sangiovese, and zinfandel grapes, among other varieties. You can taste up to five wines for $5, and take the free, guided tour that's given at 1 PM, Wednesday through Sunday. The winery holds a small museum chronicling the history of wine making in the Cucamonga area. ⊠ *12467 Base Line Rd.* ☎ *909/899–5755* ⊕ *www.josephfilippiwinery. com* ⊠ *Free* ⊙ *Mon.–Sat. 10–6, Sun. 11–5.*

☺
★ **Victoria Gardens** feels a lot like downtown Disneyland with its vintage signs, antique lampposts, and colorful California-theme murals along its 12 city blocks. At this shopping, dining, and entertainment complex, such stores as Banana Republic, Abercrombie & Fitch, Williams-Sonoma, and Pottery Barn are flanked by a Macy's and a 12-screen AMC movie theater. After you're finished shopping, grab an ice cream at the Ben & Jerry's shop and linger in the 1920s-style Town Square, a relaxing little park with fountains, grass, and an old-fashioned trolley ($2 per ride). Restaurants such as the Cheesecake Factory, Lucille's Smokehouse Bar-B-Que, P.F. Chang's China Bistro, and the Yard House often have lines out the door. The Victoria Gardens Cultural Center has a library and a 540-seat performing-arts center. ⊠ *12505 N. Mainstreet*

☎ *909/463–2829 general information, 909/477–2775 Cultural Center* ⊕ *www.victoriagardensie.com* ☕ *Free* ☉ *Mon.–Thurs. 10–9, Fri. and Sat. 10–10, Sun. 11–7.*

WHERE TO EAT

$$$$
AMERICAN

★

✕ **The Sycamore Inn.** Flickering gas lamps and a glowing fireplace greet you at this rustic inn. Built in 1921, the restaurant stands on the site of a pre-statehood stagecoach stop on historic Route 66; it's one of the oldest buildings in town. The inn specializes in USDA prime steak—portion sizes range from 8 to 22 ounces—but the menu also offers sushi-quality ahi, surf and turf, and Colorado rack of lamb. The wine list is impressive; by the glass, you can choose from more than 40 vintages from the Central Coast, Napa Valley, and such nearby wineries as Joseph Filippi and Temecula. ⊠ *8318 Foothill Blvd.* ☎ *909/982–1104* ⊕ *www.thesycamoreinn.com* ☱ *AE, D, MC, V* ☉ *No lunch.*

RIVERSIDE AREA

CORONA

13 mi south of Ontario on I–15.

Corona's Temescal Canyon is named for the dome-shape mud saunas that the Luiseno Indians built around the artesian hot springs in the early 19th century. Starting in 1860, weary Overland Stage Company passengers stopped to relax in the soothing mineral springs. In 1890 Mr. and Mrs. W.G. Steers turned the springs into a resort whose popularity has yet to fade.

EXPLORING

Fodor'sChoice

★

Presidents Herbert Hoover and Ronald Reagan are among the thousands of guests who have soaked their toes at the very relaxing and beautiful **Glen Ivy Hot Springs.** Colorful bougainvillea and birds-of-paradise surround the secluded canyon day spa, which offers a full range of facials, manicures, pedicures, body wraps, and massages; some treatments are performed in underground granite spa chambers known collectively as the Grotto, highly recommended by readers. In 2007 the spa added several new pools, renovated its treatment rooms, and opened its Under the Oaks treatment center, a cluster of eight open-air massage rooms surrounded by waterfalls and ancient oak trees. Don't bring your best bikini if you plan to dive into the red clay (brought in daily from a local mine) of Club Mud. Children under 16 are not permitted at the spa except on three family days: Memorial Day, July 4, and Labor Day. ⊠ *25000 Glen Ivy Rd., Corona* ☎ *888/453–6486* ⊕ *www.glenivy.com* ☕ *Mon.–Thurs. $38, Fri.–Sun. $49* ☉ *Apr.–Oct., daily 9:30–6; Nov.–Mar., daily 9:30–5.*

♻ Opened as a produce stand along I–15 in 1974, **Tom's Farms** has grown to include a hamburger stand, furniture showroom, and sweet shop. You can still buy produce here, but the big draw is various attractions for the kiddies on weekends: a duck pond, a petting zoo, a children's train, a pony ride, free magic shows, face painting, and an old-style

It's OK to get a little dirty at Glen Ivy Hot Springs, which offers a wide variety of treatments at its famous spa—including the red clay pool at Club Mud.

carousel. Of interest for adults is the wine-and-cheese shop, which has more than 600 varieties of wine, including many from nearby Temecula Valley; wine tasting ($1 for three samples) takes place daily 11 to 6. ⊠ *23900 Temescal Canyon Rd.* ☏ *951/277–4422* ⊕ *www.tomsfarms. com* ☜ *Free* ⊘ *Daily 8–8.*

RIVERSIDE

14 mi north of Corona on Rte. 91; 34 mi from Anaheim on Rte. 91.

By 1882 Riverside was home to more than half of California's citrus groves, making it the state's wealthiest city per capita in 1895. The prosperity produced a downtown area of opulent architecture, which is well preserved today. Main Street's pedestrian strip is lined with antiques and gift stores, art galleries, salons, and the UCR/California Museum of Photography.

ESSENTIALS

Visitor Information Riverside Convention and Visitors Bureau (⊠ *3750 University Ave., #175, Riverside* ☏ *888/748–7733 or 951/222–4700*).

EXPLORING

Fodor'sChoice ★ The crown jewel of Riverside is the **Mission Inn**, a remarkable Spanish-revival hotel whose elaborate turrets, clock tower, mission bells, and flying buttresses rise above downtown. The inn was designed in 1902 by Arthur B. Benton and Myron Hunt; the team took its cues from the Spanish missions in San Gabriel and Carmel. You can climb to the top of the Rotunda Wing's five-story spiral stairway, or linger awhile in the Courtyard of the Birds, where a tinkling fountain and

CLOSE UP

Good As Gold

In 1873 a woman named Eliza Tibbets changed the course of California history when she planted two Brazilian navel-orange trees in her Riverside garden.

The trees (which were called Washington Navels in honor of America's first president) flourished in the area's warm climate and rich soil—and before long, Tibbett's garden was producing the sweetest seedless oranges anyone had ever tasted. After winning awards at several major exhibitions, Tibbets realized she could make a profit from her trees. She sold buds to the increasing droves of citrus farmers

flocking to the Inland Empire, and by 1882, almost 250,000 citrus trees had been planted in Riverside alone. California's citrus industry had been born.

Today, Riverside still celebrates its citrus-growing heritage. The downtown Marketplace district contains several restored packing houses, and the Riverside Municipal Museum is home to a permanent exhibit of historic tools and machinery once used in the industry. The University of California at Riverside still remains at the forefront of citrus research; its Citrus Variety Collection includes 900 different fruit trees from around the world.

---

shady trees invite meditation. You can also peek inside the St. Francis Chapel, where celebrities such as Bette Davis, Humphrey Bogart, and Richard and Pat Nixon tied the knot before the Mexican cedar altar. ■TIP→ Docent-led walking tours focusing on the history, architecture, and celebrity guests of the inn are available weekdays. Reservations are recommended (📞 951/788-9556).

The Presidential Lounge, a dark, wood-panel bar, has been patronized by eight U.S. presidents. ✉ *3649 Mission Inn Ave.* 📞 *951/784–0300 or 800/843–7755* ⊕ *www.missioninn.com.*

★ In the 1990s downtown Riverside resurrected itself as an arts community. You can browse several commercial art galleries and stop in at the **UCR/California Museum of Photography.** On display is a collection of 10,000 cameras and viewing devices, along with the world's largest assemblage of vintage stereographs. In the Collection Department, on view by appointment Tuesday–Friday 10–4:30, you can see works by Will Connell, Ansel Adams, Harry Pidgeon, and Olindo Ceccarini. ✉ *3824 Main St.* 📞 *951/827–4787* ⊕ *www.cmp.ucr.edu* 💳 *$3* ⊙ *Tues.–Sat. 11–5.*

The **Riverside Art Museum,** designed by Hearst Castle architect Julia Morgan, houses a fine collection of paintings by Southern California landscape artists, including William Keith, Robert Wood, and Ralph Love. Major temporary exhibitions are mounted year-round. ✉ *3425 Mission Inn Ave.* 📞 *951/684–7111* ⊕ *www.riversideartmuseum.org* 💳 *$5* ⊙ *Mon.–Sat. 10–4.*

WHERE TO EAT AND STAY

$$$
ITALIAN
Fodor'sChoice
★

✕ **Mario's Place.** The clientele is as beautiful as the food at this intimate jazz and supper club just across the street from the Mission Inn. The northern Italian cuisine is first-rate, as are the bands that perform Friday and Saturday at 10 PM. Try the pear-and-Gorgonzola wood-fired pizza, followed by the caramelized banana napoleon (made with hazelnut phyllo, vanilla mascarpone, and coffee sauce). ✉ *3646 Mission Inn Ave.* ☎ *951/684–7755* ⊕ *www.mariosplace.com* ▭ *AE, D, MC, V* ⊘ *Closed Sun. No lunch Fri.*

¢ ✕ **Simple Simon's.** Expect to wait in line at this little sandwich shop
AMERICAN on the pedestrian-only shopping strip outside the Mission Inn. Traditional salads, soups, and sandwiches on house-baked breads are served; standout specialties include the chicken-apple sausage sandwich and the roast lamb sandwich topped with grilled eggplant, red peppers, and tomato-fennel-olive sauce. ✉ *3636 Main St.* ☎ *951/369–6030* ▭ *MC, V* ⊘ *Closed Sun. No dinner.*

$$$–$$$$ 🏨 **Mission Inn and Spa.** This grand Spanish colonial–style hotel was des-
Fodor'sChoice ignated a National Historic Landmark in 1977. Most standard rooms
★ have an early Spanish-California look, with Mission-style artwork and dark wooden headboards. Those on the Writer's Walk were occupied by famous writers at one time; each is unique, but all have lots of stained glass and quirky cubbies. Dining is a rewarding experience, whether you choose the grand Duane's Prime Steak & Seafood ($$–$$$$); Las Campanas ($–$$), where Mexican-style *carnitas* (shredded pork) are served in a pool of mole *negro* (a savory chili-and-chocolate-based sauce); the Mission Inn Restaurant ($–$$), where you can relax next to a bubbling fountain on the Spanish patio; or the Bella Trattoria ($–$$), which serves southern Italian fare like wood-fired pizzas and grilled Panini. ■ TIP➔ Sunday brunch here is excellent, though pricey, say locals. Kelly's Spa, is a tranquil Tuscan-style relaxation destination, with hand-painted frescoes, Venetian chandeliers, and barrel vaulted ceilings, there are six treatment rooms and two private villas with outdoor teak rain showers, marble encased aromatherapy baths, and flat-screen TVs. **Pros:** fascinating historical site; clean rooms; great restaurants; family friendly. **Cons:** train noise can be deafening at night. ✉ *3649 Mission Inn Ave., Riverside* ☎ *951/784–0300 or 800/843–7755* ⊕ *www.missioninn.com* 🛏 *239 rooms, 28 suites* ⌂ *In-room: a/c, safe (some), Internet. In-hotel: 4 restaurants, room service, bars, pool, gym, spa, laundry service, Wi-Fi hotspot* ▭ *AE, D, MC, V.*

NIGHTLIFE AND THE ARTS

NIGHTLIFE Savor tapas and sangria at **Cafe Sevilla** (✉ *3252 Mission Inn Ave.* ☎ *91/ 778–0611* ⊕ *www.cafesevilla.com*) while enjoying nightly live flamenco, salsa, and rumba music Thursday through Sunday. Dance lessons are offered Thursday nights. On weekend nights, the restaurant plays host to a Latin-Euro Top 40 dance club.

REDLANDS

15 mi northeast of Riverside via I–215 north and I–10 east.

Redlands lies at the center of what once was the largest navel-orange-producing region in the world. Orange groves are still plentiful throughout the area. You can glimpse Redlands' origins in several fine examples of California Victorian residential architecture.

ESSENTIALS

Visitor Information Redlands Chamber of Commerce (✉ *1 E. Redlands Blvd., Redlands* ☎ *909/793-2546* ⊕ *www.redlandschamber.org*).

EXPLORING

In 1897 Cornelia A. Hill built **Kimberly Crest House and Gardens** to mimic the châteaus of France's Loire Valley. Surrounded by orange groves, lily ponds, and terraced Italian gardens, the mansion has a French-revival parlor, a mahogany staircase, a glass mosaic fireplace, and a bubbling fountain in the form of Venus rising from the sea. In 1905 the property was purchased by Alfred and Helen Kimberly, founders of the Kimberly-Clark Paper Company. Their daughter, Mary, lived in the house until 1979. Almost all of the home's 22 rooms are in original condition. ✉ *1325 Prospect Dr.* ☎ *909/792-2111* ⊕ *www.kimberlycrest.org* ▧ *$7* ◷ *Sept.–July, Thurs.–Sun. 1–4.*

To learn more about Southern California's shaky history, head to the **San Bernardino County Museum**, where you can watch a working seismometer or check out a display about the San Andreas Fault. Specializing in the natural and regional history of Southern California, the museum is big on birds, eggs, dinosaurs, and mammals. Afterward, go for a light lunch at the Garden Café, open Tuesday through Sunday 11 to 2. ✉ *2024 Orange Tree La.* ☎ *909/307-2669* ⊕ *www.sbcounty.gov/museum* ▧ *$8* ◷ *Tues.–Sun. 9–5.*

The **Lincoln Memorial Shrine** houses the largest collection of Abraham Lincoln artifacts on the West Coast. You can view a marble bust of Lincoln by sculptor George Grey Barnard, along with more than a dozen letters and rare pamphlets. The gift shop sells many books, toys, and reproductions pertaining to the Civil War. ✉ *125 W. Vine St.* ☎ *909/798-7636 or 909/798-7632* ⊕ *www.lincolnshrine.org* ▧ *Free* ◷ *Tues.–Sun. 1–5.*

After the Franciscan Fathers of Mission San Gabriel built it in 1830, the **Asistencia Mission de San Gabriel** functioned as a mission only for a few years. In 1834 it became part of a Spanish-colonial rancho; later the mission served as a school and a factory and was finally purchased by the county, which restored it in 1937. The landscaped courtyard contains an old Spanish mission bell; one building holds a small museum. ✉ *26930 Barton Rd.* ☎ *909/793-5402* ⊕ *www.sbcounty.gov/museum* ▧ *$2* ◷ *Tues.–Sat. 10–3.*

WHERE TO EAT

$$$ ✕ **Joe Greensleeves.** Housed in the 19th-century brick Board of Trade
ITALIAN building, this classic restaurant is homey and inviting. Locals consider one of the best in the region. Wood-grilled steaks, chicken, and fish take up most of the menu, which leans toward Italian. There's a long list of pastas and risottos lobster ravioli chocolate fettuccini, and risotto with asparagus and saffron. ✉ *220 N. Orange St., Redlands* ☎ *909/792-6969* ⊕ *www.joegreensleevesrestaurant.com* ◷ *No lunch weekends* ▭ *D, MC, V.*

OAK GLEN

★ *17 mi east of Redlands via I–10 and Live Oak Canyon Rd.*

More than 60 varieties of apples are grown in Oak Glen. This rustic village, tucked in the foothills above Yucaipa, is home to acres of farms, produce stands, country shops, and homey cafés. The town really comes alive during the fall harvest (September through December), which is celebrated with piglet races, live entertainment, and other events.

13

Most farms also grow berries and stone fruit, which is available during the summer months. You'll find most of the apple farms along Oak Glen Road. Many of the ranches host school groups during the week, when they present historical and educational programs.

ESSENTIALS

Visitor Information Oak Glen Apple Growers Association (✉ *39610 Oak Glen Rd., Yucaipa* ☎ *909/797–6833* ⊕ *www.oakglen.net*).

EXPLORING

Los Rios Rancho (✉ *39611 S. Oak Glen Rd., Oak Glen* ⊕ *www.losriosrancho.com*) has 50 acres of apple trees. This massive farm, open daily during apple season from 9 to 5, has a fantastic country store where you can stock up on jams, cookbooks, syrups, and candied apples. Head into the bakery for a hot tri-tip sandwich (thinly cut seasoned beef served hot on a hoagie roll, usually with grilled onions and bell peppers) and apple streusel pie before going outside to the picnic grounds for lunch. During the fall, you can pick your own apples and pumpkins, jump on a wagon ride, or enjoy live bluegrass music. On the grounds of Los Rios Rancho, the **Wildlands Conservancy** is home to 400 acres of preserved nature trails open weekends from 8:30 AM to 4:30 PM. Guided night walks are offered on the third Saturday of each month, April through December.

Oak Glen's informal information center is at **Mom's Country Orchards** (✉ *38695 Oak Glen Rd., Oak Glen* ☎ *909/797–4249* ⊕ *www.momscountryorchards.com*), where you can belly up to the bar and learn about the nuances of apple tasting, or warm up with a hot cider heated on an antique stove. Organic produce, local honey, apple butter, and salsa are also specialties here.

Employees dress in period costumes at **Riley's Farm** (✉ *12261 S. Oak Glen Rd., Oak Glen* ☎ *909/797–7534* ⊕ *www.rileysfarm.com*), one of the most interactive and kid-friendly ranches in apple country. Here, you can hop on a hay ride, take part in a barn dance, pick your own apples, press some cider, or throw a tomahawk while enjoying living-history performances throughout the orchard. The farm is also home to Colonial Chesterfield, a gorgeous replica New England–style estate where costumed 18th-century reenactors offer lessons in cider pressing, candle dipping, and colonial games and etiquette. The four-hour living history Revolutionary War Adventures are especially popular. Afterward, head into the Public House for a bite of colonial specialties. The warm apple pies—made from the farm's fresh-cut apples—are unforgettable.

🄲 Don't miss **Oak Tree Village** (✉ *38480 Oak Glen Rd.* ☎ *909/797–4020* ⊕ *www.oaktreevillageonline.com* ✆ *$3* ⊙ *Daily 10–5*), a 14-acre children's park with miniature train rides, trout fishing, gold panning, exotic animal exhibits, and a petting zoo.

WHERE TO EAT

$$ ✕ **Apple Annie's.** You won't leave hungry from this country-western
AMERICAN diner, known for its 5-pound apple pies and family-style seven-course dinners. The decor is comfortable and rustic; old guns and handcuffs hang on the walls alongside pictures of cowboys, trail wagons, and outlaws. Standout dishes include the tuna melt and the Annie deluxe burger. ✉ *38480 Oak Glen Rd.* ☎ *909/797–7371* ▭ *AE, D, MC, V* ⊙ *Daily 8–8.*

$ ✕ **Law's Oak Glen Coffee Shop.** Since 1953, this old-fashioned coffee shop
AMERICAN has been serving up hot coffee, hearty breakfasts, and famous apple pies to hungry and grateful customers. Service has been known to be slow, so if you're in a hurry, look elsewhere. ✉ *38392 Oak Glen Rd.* ☎ *909/797–1642* ▭ *MC, V* ⊙ *Wed. and Thurs. 8–3, Fri.–Sun. 8–5.*

SAN BERNARDINO MOUNTAINS

LAKE ARROWHEAD

37 mi northeast of Riverside via I–215 north, to I–10 east, to Hwy. 30 north, join Hwy. 330 north, to Hwy. 18 west.

Lake Arrowhead Village is an alpine community with offices, shops, outlet stores, and eateries that descend the hill to the lake. Outside the village, access to the lake and its beaches is limited to area residents and their guests.

ESSENTIALS
Visitor Information Lake Arrowhead Communities Chamber of Commerce and Visitor Center (✉ *28200 Hwy. 189, Bldg. F, Suite 290, Lake Arrowhead* ☎ *909/337–3715* ⊕ *www.lakearrowhead.net*).

EXPLORING
You can take a 45-minute cruise on the *Arrowhead Queen,* operated daily by **LeRoy Sports** (☎ *909/336–6992*) from the waterfront marina in Lake Arrowhead Village. Tickets are available on a first-come, first-served basis and cost $16. Call for departure times.

🄲 The **Ice Castle** is an international-size rink and former training center for
★ Olympic medalist Michelle Kwan. The facility offers classes, individual and group lessons as well as recreational skating. Skate rentals cost $2 per person. ✉ *401 Burnt Mill Rd.* ☎ *909/337–5283* ⊕ *www.icecastle.us* ✆ *$8* ⊙ *Tues. and Fri. 7:30 PM–9 PM, Sat. 2:30–4:30, Sun. noon–2.*

WHERE TO EAT AND STAY

$ ✕ **Belgian Waffle Works.** This dockside eatery, just steps from the Arrow-
CAFÉ head Queen, is quaint and homey, with country decor and beautiful
views of the lake. Don't miss their namesake waffles, crisp on the outside and moist on the inside, topped with fresh berries and cream. Lunch
is also delicious, with choices that include basic burgers, tuna melts,
chili, meat loaf, chicken, and salads. The restaurant gets crowded during lunch on the weekend, so get there early to snag a table with a view.
✉ *28200 Hwy. 189, Bldg. E140, Lake Arrowhead* ☎ *909/337–5222*
▭ *AE, DC, MC, V* ⊘ *No dinner.*

$$$$ ✕ **Casual Elegance.** Just a few miles outside Arrowhead Village, this inti-
AMERICAN mate 1939 house has been charming locals and guests for more than
15 years. Owner-chef Kathleen Kirk's specialties include rack of lamb
prepared with herb crust, crusted filet mignon with Stilton, and steak au
poivre. Featured menu items change weekly. Dine by the fireplace for a
particularly cozy experience. ✉ *26848 Hwy. 189, Blue Jay* ☎ *909/337–
8932* ▭ *AE, D, MC, V* ⊘ *Closed Mon. and Tues. No lunch.*

$$$ ▦ **Lake Arrowhead Resort and Spa.** This lakeside lodge completed
★ a $12-million renovation in 2007. Most rooms have water- or for-
est views from private patios or balconies, down comforters, granite
counters, and flat-screen TVs. The on-premises Spa of the Pines offers
facials, massages, and other body treatments. BIN189 restaurant, with
its granite-and-pine decor and private wine-tasting room, serves up
a homey menu of international and American specialties including
Diver scallops in a grape reduction, and braised short ribs with lob-
ster mashed potatoes. **Pros:** beautiful lake views; delicious on-site din-
ing; children's programs. **Cons:** some rooms have thin walls. ✉ *27984
Hwy. 189, Lake Arrowhead Village* ☎ *909/336–1511 or 800/800–6792*
⊕ *www.lakearrowheadresort.com* ⤴ *162 rooms, 11 suites* ♿ *In-room:
a/c, Wi-Fi. In-hotel: 2 restaurants, room service, bar, pool, gym, spa,
beachfront, children's programs (ages 4–12), Wi-Fi hotspot, parking
(paid), some pets allowed* ▭ *AE, D, DC, MC, V.*

SPORTS AND THE OUTDOORS

Waterskiing and wakeboarding lessons are available on Lake Arrow-
head in summer at **McKenzie Waterski School** (☎☎ *909/337–3814*).

BIG BEAR LAKE

24 mi east of Lake Arrowhead on Hwy. 18 (Rim of the World Hwy.).

The town of Big Bear Lake, on the lake's south shore, has a classic
Western Alpine style; you'll spot the occasional chalet like building
here. Big Bear City, at the east end of Big Bear Lake, has restaurants,
motels, and a small airport.

ESSENTIALS

Visitor Information Big Bear Lake Resort Association (✉ *630 Bartlett Rd.,
Big Bear Lake* ☎ *909/866–7000 or 800/424–4232* ⊕ *www.bigbearinfo.com*).

13

EXPLORING

From April through Labor Day, the paddle wheeler *Big Bear Queen* departs daily at 2 and 4 from **Big Bear Marina** (✉ *500 Paine Rd., Big Bear Lake* ☎ *909/866–3218* ⊕ *www.bigbearmarina.com/queen.html*) for 90-minute tours of the lake; the cost is $16.

🌀 Kids will enjoy a cruise on the **Time Bandit Pirate Ship,** which is a small-scale replica of a 17th-century English galleon. The ship, which was featured in Terry Gilliam's 1981 movie, *Time Bandits,* is also the centerpiece attraction at the annual Big Bear Pirate Faire, held in June (⊕ *www.bigbearrenfair.com/pirate*). During the event, Captain John's Harbor in Fawnskin is transformed into a 17th-century Buccaneer Village, complete with ship-to-shore pirate battles, a treasure hunt, and cold grog. ✉ *398 Edgemoor Rd., Big Bear Lake* ☎ *909/878–4040* ⊕ *www.800bigbear.com/water/pirateship* 🎟 *$19* ⊙ *Tours daily at 2 in warm weather; call for schedule.*

🌀 **Moonridge Animal Park,** a rescue and rehabilitation center, specializes in animals native to the San Bernardino Mountains. Among its residents are black and (nonnative) grizzly bears, bald eagles, coyote, beavers, snow leopard, and bobcats. You can catch an educational presentation at noon and feeding tour at 3. At this writing, the facility was planning to move in 2010, so call ahead before visiting. ✉ *43285 Goldmine Dr.* ☎ *909/584–1171* ⊕ *www.moonridgezoo.org* 🎟 *$9* ⊙ *June–Sept., daily 10–5; Sept.–June, weekdays 10–4, weekends 10–5.*

🌀 Take a ride down a twisting bobsled course in winter, or beat the summer heat on a dual waterslide at **Alpine Slide at Magic Mountain.** Miniature golf and go-carts add to the fun. ✉ *800 Wildrose La.* ☎ *909/866–4626* ⊕ *www.alpineslidebigbear.com* 🎟 *$4 single rides, $18 5-ride pass* ⊙ *Daily 11–4.*

🌀 **Big Bear Discovery Center.** Operated by the forest service, this nature center
Fodor's Choice   is the place to sign up for a canoe ride through Grout Bay, or naturalist-
★   led Discovery Tours, including visits to bald eagle roosts, wildflower fields, and historic gold mines. The popular Bald Eagle Tours, which run January through March, take you to the winter nesting grounds of these magnificent birds. You can also participate in a winter bird count. The center also has rotating flora and fauna exhibits, and a nature-oriented gift shop. ✉ *North Shore Dr., Hwy. 38, between Fawnskin and Stanfield Cutoff* ☎ *909/866–3437* ⊕ *www.bigbeardiscoverycenter.com* 🎟 *Free* ⊙ *Daily 8:30–4:30; closed Wed. and Thurs. in winter.*

WHERE TO EAT

$$$$ ✕ **Evergreen International.** This rustic-style steak house—with sweeping
STEAK   views of Big Bear Lake—is a good place to go for fine dining. In winter you can stay warm in the comfortable dining room, which has dark paneling and exposed beams; in summer head out to the deck to enjoy a glass of wine while you watch the sun set. Lunch and dinner choices include grilled chicken topped with passion-fruit sauce, pepper-crusted ahi tuna, or prime rib with king crab legs. ✉ *40771 Lakeview Dr.* ☎ *909/878–5588* ▤ *AE, D, MC, V.*

$$ ✕ **Madlon's.** The menu at this gingerbread-style cottage includes sophisti-
FRENCH   cated dishes such as lamb chops with port wine reduction, cream of

jalapeño soup, and filet mignon with Drambuie sauce. Reservations are essential on weekends. ✉ *829 W. Big Bear Blvd., Big Bear City* ☎ *909/585–3762* ▤ *AE, D, MC, V* ⊘ *Closed Tues.*

$$ ╳ **Mandoline Bistro.** Locals looking to impress out-of-town guests make
ECLECTIC   reservations at this Cal-fusion restaurant, known for its flavorful combinations of Mexican, Thai, Asian, and Island cuisine. The mountain-chic bistro, accented with stark black-and-white linens and antler chandeliers, serves up fusion cuisine like tempura avocados with raspberry rémoulade, roasted duck salad with sweet walnuts and Gorgonzola cheese, or Caribbean salmon with sticky rice and grilled bananas. On Friday and Saturday nights, the Loft Bar offers live jazz. ✉ *40701 Village Dr.* ☎ *909/866–4200* ▤ *AE, MC, V* ⊘ *No lunch Mon. and Tues.*

WHERE TO STAY

$$$ 🛏 **Apples Bed & Breakfast Inn.** Despite its location on a busy road to the
★   ski lifts, the Apples Inn feels remote and peaceful, thanks to the surrounding pine trees. The colorful rooms have names such as Golden Delicious, Royal Gala, and Sweet Bough; all have gas fireplaces, and four have Jacuzzis. A common room has a wood-burning stove, baby grand piano, game table, and library loft. A full breakfast, afternoon refreshments, and evening dessert are included. **Pros:** large rooms; clean; free snacks and movies; delicious big breakfast. **Cons:** some traffic noise; sometimes feels very busy. ✉ *42430 Moonridge Rd.* ☎ *909/866–0903* ⊕ *www.applesbigbear.com* ➴ *19 rooms* ⟁ *In-room: no phone, no a/c, DVD, Wi-Fi. In-hotel: Wi-Fi hotspot* ▤ *AE, D, MC, V* ⦿❙ *BP.*

$$$ 🛏 **Gold Mountain Manor.** This restored log mansion, originally built in 1928, has a wide porch under wooden eaves and an Adirondack-style swing set on the lawn. Each room has its own theme; the Clark Gable room, for example, contains the old Franklin stove that once graced Gable's and Carole Lombard's honeymoon suite. All rooms have fireplaces, and some have log beds original to the house. The common area has a TV, a VCR, and a collection of videos. Afternoon hors d'oeuvres and wine are included. **Pros:** gracious hosts; gourmet food; cozy and comfortable rooms. **Cons:** somewhat thin walls; 10-minute drive to the village, one room has detached bathroom. ✉ *1117 Anita Ave., Big Bear City* ☎ *909/585–6997 or 800/509–2604* ⊕ *www.goldmountainmanor. com* ➴ *4 rooms, 3 suites* ⟁ *In-room: no phone, no a/c, no TV, Wi-Fi. In-hotel: Wi-Fi hotspot* ▤ *AE, MC, V* ⦿❙ *BP.*

$$$ 🛏 **Northwoods Resort.** A giant log cabin with the amenities of a resort, Northwoods has a lobby that resembles a 1930s hunting lodge: canoes, antlers, fishing poles, and a grand stone fireplace all decorate the walls. Rooms are large but cozy. The decor is rustic with knotty pine paneling and lodgepole furnishings; some have fireplaces and whirlpool tubs. Stillwells Restaurant, next to the lobby, serves hearty American fare. Ski packages are available. **Pros:** within walking distance of shops and restaurants; good central Big Bear location. **Cons:** parts of the hotel are showing their age; rooms can be noisy at night; rates fluctuate depending on whether there is snow. ✉ *40650 Village Dr.* ☎ *909/866–3121 or 800/866–3121* ⊕ *www.northwoodsresort.com* ➴ *140 rooms, 7 suites* ⟁ *In-room: a/c, refrigerators (some), Wi-Fi. In-hotel: 2 restaurants, room service, bar, pool, gym, Wi-Fi hotspot, parking (free)* ▤ *AE, D, MC, V.*

$$$ ⊡ **Robinhood Resort.** Across the street from the Pine Knot Marina, this family-oriented motel has rooms with fireplaces and some with whirlpool tubs or kitchenettes. Also available are several condos just feet from Snow Summit ski resort and deluxe spa rooms with in-room hot tubs, DVD players, and fireplaces. **Pros:** short walk from the marina; near shops and restaurants; good on-site restaurant. **Cons:** no a/c in some rooms; parts of motel are showing their age. ✉ *40797 Lakeview Dr.* ☎ *909/866–4643 or 800/990–9956* ⊕ *www.robinhoodresort.info* ↩ *60 rooms, 10 condos* ☐ *In-room: a/c (some), kitchen (some), Wi-Fi. In-hotel: restaurant, bar, Wi-Fi hotspot* ☐ *AE, D, MC, V.*

SPORTS AND THE OUTDOORS

Looking for adventure? For $40, you can ride a horse through the snowcovered forest at **Baldwin Lake Stables** (☎ *909/585–6482* ⊕ *www. baldwinlakestables.com*). If you want to get out on the lake for a day, stop at **Big Bear Parasail and Water Sports** (✉ *439 Pine Knot Ave., Big Bear Lake* ☎ *909/866–4359*) for water-skiing, tubing, and parasailing.

Jet Ski, water-ski, fishing boat, and equipment rentals are available from **Big Bear Marina** (✉ *Paine Rd.* ☎ *909/866–3218*). **Pine Knot Landing** (✉ *439 Pine Knot* ☎ *909/866–2628*) rents fishing boats and sells bait, ice, and snacks.

SKIING **Big Bear Mountain Resorts** is Southern California's largest winter resort, and the only one that will challenge skilled skiers. Here you can board more than 200 freestyle terrain features at Bear Mountain's massive snowboard terrain park, then shuttle 1 mi down the road to Snow Summit for its open skiing terrain and special area designed for kids. The megaresort offers 430 skiable acres, 55 runs, and 23 chairlifts, including four high-speed quads. An all-day lift ticket includes admission and shuttle rides at both resorts. On busy winter weekends and holidays it's best to reserve tickets before heading to either mountain.

You don't have to be a mountain biker to enjoy Bear Mountain's Scenic Sky Chair. The lift takes you to the mountain's 8,400-foot peak, where you can lunch at View Haus (¢), a casual outdoor restaurant with breathtaking views of the lake and San Gorgonio mountain. Fare includes barbecued-chicken sandwiches, hot dogs, and burgers, along with cold beer and wine. ✉ *Big Bear, 43101 Goldmine Dr., off Moonridge Rd.* ✉ *Snow Summit, 880 Summit Blvd., off Big Bear Blvd.* ☎ *909/866–5766* ⊕ *www.bigbearmountainresorts.com* ☐ *$53–$66.*

THE SOUTHERN INLAND EMPIRE

IDYLLWILD

44 mi east of Riverside via State Hwy. 60 and I–10 to State Hwy. 243

Famous as a serene hideaway and artists' colony, the low-key and relaxed community of Idyllwild also has great rock climbing, hiking, and shopping.

ESSENTIALS

Visitor Information Idyllwild Chamber of Commerce (⊠ *54325 N. Circle Dr., Idyllwild* ☎ *951/659–3259 or 888/659–3259* ⊕ *www.idyllwildchamber.com*).

EXPLORING

☻ At the **Idyllwild Nature Center**, you can learn about the area's Native American history, try your hand at astronomy, and listen to traditional storytellers. Outside there are 3 mi of hiking trails, plus picnic areas. Native-plant lectures and wildflower walks are offered every Memorial Day weekend during the center's Wildflower Show. ⊠ *25225 Hwy. 243* ☎ *951/659–3850* ⊕ *www.idyllwildnaturecenter.com* ☜ *$2* ☉ *9–4:30, closed Mon.*

WHERE TO EAT AND STAY

$$$
FRENCH
★

✗ **Restaurant Gastrognome.** Elegant and dimly lighted, with wood paneling, lace curtains, and an often-glowing fireplace, "The Gnome" is where locals go for a romantic dinner with great food, a full bar, and nice ambience. The French onion soup is a standout appetizer; the roast duck with orange sauce and Southwest-style grilled pork are excellent entrées. The crème brûlée makes for a sweet finale. ⊠ *54381 Ridgeview Dr.* ☎ *951/659–5055* ⊕ *www.gastrognome.com* ▭ *AE, D, MC, V.*

THE ARTS

In August, Idyllwild is host of the two-day **Jazz in the Pines** (⊕ *www.idyllwildjazz.com*) festival, drawing smooth-jazz greats such as David Benoit. The **Idyllwild Arts Academy** (☎ *951/659–2171* ⊕ *www.idyllwildarts.org*) is a summer camp offering more than 60 workshops in dance, music, Native American arts, theater, visual arts, and writing. There are free summer concerts and theater productions featuring students and professional performers.

SPORTS AND THE OUTDOORS

FISHING **Lake Fulmor** (⊠ *Hwy. 243, 10 mi north of Idyllwild* ☎ *951/659–2117*) is stocked with rainbow trout, largemouth bass, catfish, and bluegill. To fish here you'll need a California fishing license and a National Forest Adventure Pass ($5 per vehicle per day). Adventure Passes are available at the **Idyllwild Ranger Station** (⊠ *Pine Crest Ave., off Hwy. 243* ☎ *951/659–2117*).

HIKING Hike the 2.6-mi Ernie Maxwell Scenic Trail at **Humber Park** (⊠ *At top of Fern Valley Rd.* ☎ *951/659–2117*). Along the way you'll have views of Little Tahquitz Creek, Marion Mountain, and Suicide Rock. A permit is not required to hike this trail. The **Pacific Crest Trail** is accessible at Highway 74, 1 mi east of Highway 371; or via the Fuller Ridge Trail at Black Mountain Road, 15 mi north of Idyllwild. Permits ($5 per day) are required for camping and day hikes in San Jacinto Wilderness. They are available through the **Idyllwild Ranger Station** (⊠ *Pine Crest Ave., off Hwy. 243* ☎ *951/659–2117*).

EN
ROUTE

If you're headed for Temecula via Route 74 east from Idyllwild, make a detour to **Winchester Cheese Company** for a taste of Jules Wesselink's famous goudas, made from the raw milk of his Holstein cows. Take a tour, or sample one of four varieties, including a spicy jalapeño, in

WINERY TOURS

If you plan to visit several wineries (and taste a lot of wine), catch the **Grapeline Wine Country Shuttle** (✉ *Ridge Park Dr. #204* ☎ *951/693–5755 or 888/894–6379* ⊕ *www.gogrape.com* 🎫 *$42 transportation only*), which operates daily with pick up at Temecula and San Diego hotels. The Vineyard Picnic Tour, at $88 ($108 Saturday), includes transportation, a winemaking demonstration, free tastings at four wineries, and a gourmet picnic lunch catered by Creekside Grill at Wilson Creek Winery.

Many limousine services offer wine-tasting tours, including **Sterling** **Rose Limo** (☎ *800/649–6463* ⊕ *www.sterlingroselimo.com*), which offers packages that include four to five tasting tickets and a gourmet picnic lunch or winery restaurant lunch. Per-passenger rates, which start at $95, are cheapest for groups of 13.

Destination Temecula (☎ *877/305-0501* ⊕ *www.destem.com*) runs daily four-hour tours of wine country, departing from Old Town Temecula at 11:30. For $89 you're taken around the perimeter of Temecula Valley before stopping for lunch in the barrel room at Frangipani Winery.

the tasting room. ✉ *32605 Holland Rd., Winchester* ☎ *951/926–4239* ⊕ *www.winchestercheese.com* 🎫 *Free* ⊙ *Weekdays 10–5, weekends 10–4.*

TEMECULA

Fodor's Choice
★ *43 mi south of Riverside on I–15; 60 mi north of San Diego on I–15; 90 mi southeast of Los Angeles via I–10 and I–15.*

Temecula, with its rolling green vineyards, comfy country inns, and first-rate restaurants, is a fine alternative to Napa Valley if you can't make it up to Northern California. Now billing itself the "Southern California Wine Country," the valley is home to more than 36 wineries, several of which offer fine dining, luxury lodging, and spas in addition to appealing boutiques, charming picnic areas, and, of course, award-winning vintages.

The name Temecula comes from a Luiseno Indian word meaning "where the sun shines through the mist"—ideal conditions for growing wine grapes. Intense afternoon sun and cool nighttime temperatures, complemented by ocean breezes that flow through the Rainbow and Santa Margarita gaps in the coastal range, help grapevines flourish in the area's granite soil. Best known for chardonnay, Temecula Valley winemakers are moving in new directions, producing viognier, syrah, old vine zinfandel, and pinot gris varietals. Most wineries charge a small fee ($5 to $15) for a tasting that includes several wines. Most of the wineries are strung out along Rancho California Rd., east of I–15; a few newer ones lie along the eastern portion of De Portola Rd. For a map of the area's wineries, visit ⊕ *www.temeculawines.org.*

ESSENTIALS

Visitor Information Temecula Valley Convention and Visitors Bureau (⊠ *26790 Ynez Ct., Temecula* ☎ *951/491–6085 or 888/363–2852* ⊕ *www. temeculacvb.com*).

EXPLORING

Temecula is more than just vineyards and tasting rooms. For a bit of old-fashioned fun, head to **Old Town Temecula** (⊠ *Front St., between Rancho California Rd. and Hwy. 79* ☎ *888/363–2852*), a turn-of-the-20th-century-style cluster of storefronts and boardwalks that holds more than 640 antiques stores, boutiques, and art galleries. A farmers' market is held here every Saturday from 8 to noon.

☾ If you have the kids along, check out the **Imagination Workshop**, the fictional 7,500-square-foot home of Professor Phineas T. Pennypickle, PhD. This elaborately decorated children's museum is filled with secret passageways, machines, wacky contraptions, and time-travel inventions, making it an imaginative way to spend the afternoon. ⊠ *42081 Main St.* ☎ *951/308–6376* ⊕ *www.pennypickles.org* ⊠ *$4.50* ☉ *Tues.– Sat. 10–5, Sun. 12:30–5.*

WINERIES

Baily Vineyard & Winery has grown to include an 8,000-square-foot winemaking facility with 50,000 gallons of wine tanks. The restaurant here, Carol's, is locally popular. In the tasting room, browse the gourmet gift shop before sampling the cabernet, Riesling, and Muscat Blanc. ⊠ *33440 La Serena Way* ☎ *951/676–9463* ⊕ *www.baily.com* ⊠ *Winery free, tastings $10* ☉ *Sun.–Fri. 11–5, Sat. 10–5.*

Briar Rose Winery is run out of an English cottage that was once the home of a Disney set designer. The lush grounds include a rose garden, rustic stone walls, and an olive tree; the small, casual tasting room has copper walls and a river rock fireplace. Try the 2005 Estate Zinfandel, which is aged in American oak for 14 months. ⊠ *41720 Calle Cabrillo Rd.* ☎ *951/308–1098* ⊕ *www.briarrosewinery.com* ⊠ *Winery free, tastings $10–$15* ⚠ *Reservations essential* ☉ *By appointment.*

Established in 1969, **Callaway Coastal Vineyards** is well known for chardonnays and merlots by winemaker Craig Larson. Complimentary tours are offered weekdays at 11, 1, and 3, and on weekends 11 to 4 on the hour. The Meritage Restaurant, perched on a hill overlooking the vineyards, is open for prix-fixe lunch ($$) daily and dinner ($$$) Friday and Saturday. ⊠ *32720 Rancho California Rd.* ☎ *951/676–4001* ⊕ *www. callawaywinery.com* ⊠ *Free; $10 tastings* ☉ *Daily 10–5.*

Falkner Winery's big Western-style barn with its wraparound deck overlooking the vineyards is a great spot to enjoy Temecula's cool breezes. Falkner has garnered great word-of-mouth, especially for their red Tuscan Amante. Winemaker Steve Hagata is also known for his viognier, chardonnay, and Riesling. Packaged snacks, along with a huge variety of gourmet gifts, are available in the shop. The winery's Pinnacle Restaurant is open for lunch daily. Tours are given at 11 AM and 2 PM on weekends. Coupons are on the Web site. ⊠ *40620 Calle Contento Rd.* ☎ *951/676–8231* ⊕ *www.falknerwinery.com* ⊠ *Winery free, tours $10, tastings $10–$15* ☉ *Daily 10–5.*

Fodor's Choice
★

With Mediterranean varietals grown on 11 acres of vineyards in Temecula, **Hart Family Winery** is known for producing some of the best red wines in Temecula Valley. Joe Hart, one of the area's pioneer winemakers, creates small lots of big, hearty zinfandels, cabernet

UP, UP, AND AWAY

Temecula holds its annual **Balloon and Wine Festival** (☎ 951/676-6713 ⊕ www.tvbwf. com) each June.

13

sauvignon, and sangiovese, and the winery's purple tasting room is decked out with ribbons, medals, and awards. ✉ 41300 Avenida Biona ☎ 951/676-6300 ⊕ www.thehartfamilywinery.com ✉ Winery free, tastings $5–$10 ⊙ Daily 9–4:30.

Don't be surprised to come upon a barbecue or equestrian event at **Keyways Vineyard & Winery**, which has an Old West feel. Terri Pebley Delhamer—the only woman winery owner in the Temecula Valley—has created an appealing tasting room decorated with antiques and a roaring fireplace, where you can listen to country music while sampling tasty reds such as the zinfandel or cabernet franc. ✉ 37338 De Portola Rd. ☎ 951/302-7888 ⊕ www.keywayswine.com ✉ Winery free, tastings $10 ⊙, Daily 10–6.

Leonesse Cellars is a casual farmhouse style winery with a stone turret overlooking 20 acres of cabernet sauvignon grapes. The basic tasting includes a chocolate truffle served alongside their port. The winery offers a selection of hosted private tours (reservations required) that include rides through the vineyards, tasting seven or eight varietals, wine and cheese pairings, and a bit of chocolate with dessert wines. ✉ 38311 DePortola Rd. ☎ 951/302-7601 ⊕ www.leonessecellars.com ✉ Winery free, tours $16 to $55 per person ⊙ Daily 11–5.

Perched on a hilltop, **Miramonte Winery** may be Temecula's hippest, thanks to the vision of owner Cane Vanderhoof, whose wines have earned 36 medals in recent years. Listen to Spanish-guitar recordings while sampling the Opulente Meritage, a supple sauvignon blanc, or the sultry blanc de noir. On Friday and Saturday nights from 5 to 9, the winery turns into a hot spot with signature wines ($6 to $10), live music, and dancing that spills out into the vineyards. ✉ 33410 Rancho California Rd. ☎ 951/506-5500 ⊕ www.miramontewinery.com ✉ Winery free, tastings $10 ⊙ Tastings Sun. to Thurs. 11–6, Fri. and Sat. 11–10.

Opened in 1969, **Mount Palomar Winery** was one of the original wineries in Temecula Valley, and the first to introduce Sangiovese grapes to Temecula. (The varietal has proven perfectly suited to the region's soil and climate.) The winery's tasting room is in a Spanish colonial–style building, an excellent setting for sampling red meritage, white cortese, and a cream sherry that is to die for. Tours are available on weekends. If you want to picnic on the grounds, stop by the deli for top-notch potato salad and Italian-style sandwiches. ✉ 33820 Rancho California Rd. ☎ 951/676-5047 ⊕ www.mountpalomar.com ✉ Winery free, tastings $10 ⊙ Mon.–Thurs. 10–5, Fri.–Sun. 11–6.

There's no more relaxing way to enjoy Temecula's wine country than by taking a peaceful hot-air balloon ride over the vineyards.

★ Lush gardens and 350 acres of vineyards welcome you onto **Ponte Family Estates**, a rustic winery that fills a beautiful new barn. In the open-beam tasting room, you can sample six different varietals, including cabernet, syrah (recommended by readers), viognier, and chardonnay. One area is devoted to an eye-popping marketplace selling artisan ceramics, specialty foods, and wine-country gift baskets. The winery's outdoor Smokehouse Cafe serves wood-fired pizza and rustic fare at lunch. ⊠ *35053 Rancho California Rd.* ☎ *951/694–8855* ⊕ *www. pontewinery.com* ✉ *Winery free; tastings $10 Mon.–Thurs., $12 Fri.– Sun.* ☉ *Daily 10–5.*

Fodor's Choice A rambling French Mediterranean–style stone building houses **Thornton**
★ **Winery**, a producer best known for its sparkling wine. You can taste winemaker Don Reha's outstanding brut reserve and Cuvée Rouge at a table in the lounge, or along with some food at Café Champagne. Readers rave about the pinot blanc. On the weekend, take a free tour of the grounds and the wine cave. Summer smooth-jazz concerts (admission is charged) and elaborate winemaker dinners ($100 to $125) make this a fun place to spend an afternoon or evening. ⊠ *32575 Rancho California Rd.* ☎ *951/699–0099* ⊕ *www.thorntonwine.com* ✉ *Winery free, tastings $10–$17* ☉ *Daily 10–5, winery tours weekends only.*

A small stream winds through flower gardens and vineyards at peaceful, parklike **Wilson Creek Winery & Vineyard**. In the huge tasting room you can find a little bit of heaven in the "Decadencia" chocolate port and the almond Oh-My-Gosh sparkling wine, much loved by Fodor's readers. Their Creekside Grill Restaurant serves sandwiches, salads, and entrées such as gluten-free vegetable potpie and Mexican white sea bass. ⊠ *35960 Rancho California Rd.* ☏ *951/699–9463* ⊕ *www. wilsoncreekwinery.com* 🍷 *Winery free, tastings $10 weekdays, $12 weekends* ⊙ *Daily 10–5, restaurant daily 11–5.*

WHERE TO EAT AND STAY

$$$

AMERICAN

✕ **Baily's Fine Dining and Front Street Bar & Grill.** These are two restaurants owned by the Baily family that also owns the Baily Winery. Fine dining (dinner only) is upstairs, casual dining is street side at the Front Street Bar & Grill, which also offers entertainment. Locals rave about chef Neftali Torres's well-executed cuisine, which changes weekly according to his creative whims. The menu may include chicken schnitzel drizzled in lemon-caper-wine sauce or salmon Wellington. The wine list includes more than 100 bottles, most from Temecula Valley. Call ahead to find out about upcoming winemaker dinners. ⊠ *28699 Front St.* ☏ *951/676–9567* ⊕ *www.oldtowndining.com* ▭ *AE, MC, V* ⊙ *No lunch at Baily's Fine Dining.*

$$$$

ECLECTIC

Fodor's Choice

★

✕ **Café Champagne.** The spacious patio, with its bubbling fountain, flowering trellises, and views of Thornton Winery's vineyards, is the perfect place to lunch on a sunny day. Inside, the dining room is decked out in French-country style, and the kitchen turns out such dishes as braised boneless beef short ribs and seafood cioppino. The eclectic menu is complemented by a reasonably priced wine list featuring Italian, French, and California wines—including, of course, Thornton sparklers. ⊠ *32575 Rancho California Rd.* ☏ *951/699–0088* ⊕ *www.thorntonwine.com/ cafe.html* ▭ *AE, D, MC, V.*

$$$

Fodor's Choice

★

▦ **South Coast Winery Resort and Spa.** This luxurious resort combines lovely accommodations, an excellent restaurant, a spa, and a working winery in one location. Locals and readers highly recommend its vineyard villas, which are spacious and very private with opulent marble bathrooms, secluded patios, and flickering fireplaces. Readers particularly appreciate that there are no common walls between the villas, making their stay quieter than at most resorts. The Grapeseed spa has 13 treatment rooms, featuring such services as Merlot Masks and Grapeseed Body Scrubs plus a saltwater pool. The on-site Vineyard Rose Restaurant is a huge room and quite suitable for families. Fare ranges from comfort to sophisticated. The winery produces quality wines that regularly earn prizes; tours and tastings are available to resort guests. **Pros:** good wine-country location; quiet private villas; beautiful grounds. **Cons:** service can be hit-or-miss; it's a large property requiring quite a bit of walking; $15 resort fee. ⊠ *34843 Rancho California Rd.* ☏ *951/587–9463* ⊕ *www.wineresort.com* ⤴ *76 villas* ⑁ *In-room: a/c, refrigerator, DVD (some), Internet, Wi-Fi. In-hotel: restaurant, room service, bar, pool, gym, spa, laundry service, Internet terminal, Wi-Fi hotspot, parking (free),* ▭ *AE, D, MC, V.*

$$

▦ **Temecula Creek Inn.** If you want the relaxation of the wine country and the challenge of hitting the links on a championship golf course, this is the place for you. Each room has a private patio or balcony overlooking the course and is decorated in soothing earth tones with a Southwestern theme. The on-site restaurant, Temet Grill ($$$) serves regional fare and local wines. Try the marinated Colorado rack of lamb with mascarpone polenta or the herbed roasted chicken breast with warm basil vinaigrette drizzle. **Pros:** beautiful grounds; great restaurant; clean and comfortable rooms. **Cons:** resort is a bit isolated from Old Town and wineries; some parts feel dated. ⊠ *44501 Rainbow Canyon Rd.* ☎ *951/694–1000 or 800/962–7335* ⊕ *www.temeculacreekinn.com* ⊃ *130 rooms, 1 guesthouse* ☆ *In-room: a/c, refrigerator, Internet, Wi-Fi. In-hotel: restaurant, bar, golf course, pool, gym, laundry service, Internet, Wi-Fi hotspot, parking (paid)* ⊟ *AE, D, DC, MC, V.*

SPORTS AND THE OUTDOORS

GOLF   Temecula has seven championship golf courses cooled by the valley's ocean breezes.

Redhawk Golf Club (⊠ *45100 Redhawk Pkwy.* ☎ *951/302–3850* ⊕ *www. redhawkgolfcourse.com*) has an 18-hole championship course designed by Ron Fream. For a special treat, head to the **Temecula Creek Inn Golf Resort** (⊠ *44501 Rainbow Canyon Rd.* ☎ *951/675–8470* ⊕ *www. temeculacreekinn.com*), whose 27-hole course was designed by Ted Robinson and Dick Rossen.

The public is welcome on the Robinson-designed 18-hole championship course at **Temeku Golf Club** (⊠ *41487 Temeku Dr.* ☎ *951/694–9998* ⊕ *www.temekuhills.com*).

Palm Springs

AND THE DESERT RESORTS

WORD OF MOUTH

"We were in PS in November and had a great time. We did the aerial tram up Mt. San Jacinto. . . . We also had a historic inn guide from the visitor's bureau and did our own little tour of some of the vintage motels."

—MichelleY

WELCOME TO PALM SPRINGS

TOP REASONS TO GO

★ **Fun in the sun:** The Palm Springs area has 350 days of sun each year, and the weather's usually perfect for playing one of the area's more than 100 golf courses.

★ **Spa under the stars:** Many resorts and small hotels now offer after-dark spa services, including outdoor soaks and treatments you can savor while sipping wine under the clear, starry sky.

★ **Personal pampering:** The resorts here have it all: beautifully appointed rooms packed with amenities, professional staffs, sublime spas, and delicious dining options.

★ **Devine desert scenery:** You'll probably spend a lot of your time here taking in the gorgeous 360-degree natural panorama, a flat desert floor surrounded by 10,000-foot mountains rising into a brilliant blue sky.

★ **The Hollywood connection:** The Palm Springs area has more celebrity ties than any other resort community. So keep your eyes open for your favorite star.

1 The Desert Resorts. Around the desert resorts, privacy is the watchword. Celebrities flock to the desert from Los Angeles, and many communities are walled and guarded. Still, you might spot Hollywood stars, sports personalities, politicians, and other high-profile types in restaurants, out on the town, at the weekly Villagefest, or on a golf course. For the most part, the desert's social, sports, shopping, and entertainment scenes center on Palm Springs, Palm Desert, and (increasingly) La Quinta.

2 Along Twentynine Palms Highway. The towns of Yucca Valley and Twentynine Palms punctuate Twentynine Palms Highway (Highway 62)—the northern highway from the desert resorts to Joshua Tree National Park (⇨ see Chapter 15)—and provide visitor information, lodging, and other services to park visitors.

3 Anza-Borrego Desert. If you're looking for a break from the action, you'll find sublime solitude in this 600,000-acre desert landscape.

4 Joshua Tree National Park. This is desert scenery at its best and most abundant. Tiptoe through fields of wildflowers in spring, scramble on and around giant boulders, and check out the park's bizarre namesake trees (⇨ see Chapter 15).

14

GETTING ORIENTED

The Palm Springs resort area lies within the Colorado Desert, on the western edge of the Coachella Valley. The area holds seven cities that are strung out along Highway 111, with Palm Springs at the northwestern end of this strip and Indio at the southeastern end. North of Palm Springs, between Interstate 10 and Highway 62, is Desert Hot Springs. Northeast of Palm Springs, the towns of the Morongo Valley lie along Twentynine Palms Highway (Highway 62), which leads to Joshua Tree National Park (⇨ *see Chapter 15*). Head south on Highway 86 from Indio to reach Anza-Borrego State Park and the Salton Sea. All of the area's attractions are easy day trips from Palm Springs.

PALM SPRINGS PLANNER

When to Go

Desert weather is best between January and April, the height of the visitor season. The fall months are nearly as lovely, but less crowded and less expensive (although autumn draws a lot of conventions and business travelers). In summer, an increasingly popular time for European visitors, daytime temperatures may rise above 110°F (though evenings cool to the mid-70s); some attractions and restaurants close or reduce their hours during this time.

Nightlife

Desert nightlife is casual. It's concentrated and abundant in Palm Springs, where there are many straight and gay bars and clubs. The Fabulous Palm Springs Follies—a vaudeville-style revue starring retired professional performers—is a must-see. Arts festivals occur on a regular basis, especially in winter and spring. The "Desert Guide" section of *Palm Springs Life* magazine (available at hotels and visitor information centers) has nightlife listings, as does the "Weekender" pull-out in the Friday edition of the *Desert Sun* newspaper. The gay scene is covered in the *Bottom Line* and in the *Gay Guide to Palm Springs*, published by the Desert Gay Tourism Guild.

About the Restaurants

Dining in the desert is casual and low-key. Expect to find many good, but not stellar, dining experiences. Fare, once limited to Italian and a smattering of French choices, now includes fresh seafood, contemporary Californian, Asian, vegetarian, and steaks; you can find Mexican food everywhere. Restaurants that remain open in July and August frequently discount deeply; others close in July and August or offer limited service.

About the Hotels

In general you can find the widest choice of lodgings in Palm Springs, rangnig from tiny B&Bs and chain motels to business and resort hotels. All-inclusive resorts dominate in down-valley communities. In 2009 many hotels in the area reduced their prices by 10% to 15%.

You can stay in the desert for as little as $80 or spend more than $1,000 a night. Rates vary widely by season. Hotel/resort prices are frequently 50% less in summer and fall than in winter and early spring. January through May prices soar, and lodgings book up far in advance. Most resort hotels charge a resort fee that is not included in the room rate; be sure to ask about extra fees when you book.

Small boutique hotels and bed-and-breakfasts have historic character and offer good value; discounts are sometimes given for extended stays. Casino hotels can also offer good deals on lodging. Take care when considering budget lodgings; other than reliable chains, they may not be up to par.

WHAT IT COSTS	¢	$	$$	$$$	$$$$
Restaurants	under $10	$10–$15	$16–$22	$23–$30	over $30
Hotels	under $90	$90–$120	$121–$175	$176–$250	over $250

Restaurant prices are for a main course at dinner, excluding sales tax of 8.75 %. Hotel prices are for a standard double room in high season, excluding service charges, resort fees, and 9%–13.5% tax. Most hotels add a resort fee of $15 to $35 per day for parking, newspaper, spa admission, in-room Wi-Fi, and other incidentals. Some charge up to $50 per day for pets (in addition to a security deposit).

14

Updated by
Bobbi Zane

Many millions of years ago, the Southern Desert was the bottom of a vast sea. By 10 million years ago, the waters had receded and the climate was hospitable to prehistoric mastodons, zebras, and camels. The first human inhabitants of record were the Agua Caliente, part of the Cahuilla people, who settled in and around the Coachella Valley about 1,000 years ago.

Lake Cahuilla dried up about 300 years ago, but by then the Agua Caliente had discovered the area's hot springs and were making use of their healing properties during winter visits to the desert. The springs became a tourist attraction in 1871, when the tribe built a bathhouse (on a site near the current Spa Resort Casino in Palm Springs) to serve passengers on a pioneer stage highway. The Agua Caliente still own about 32,000 acres of desert, 6,700 of which lie within the city limits of Palm Springs.

In the last half of the 19th century, farmers established a date-growing industry at the southern end of the Coachella Valley. By 1900 word had spread about the health benefits of the area's dry climate, inspiring the gentry of the northern United States to winter under the warm desert sun. Growth hit the Coachella Valley in the 1970s, when developers began to construct the fabulous golf courses, country clubs, and residential communities that would draw celebrities, tycoons, and politicians. Communities sprang up south and east of what is now Palm Springs, creating a sprawl of tract houses and strip malls and forcing nature lovers to push farther south into the sparsely settled Anza-Borrego Desert.

PLANNING

GETTING HERE AND AROUND

BY AIR

Palm Springs International Airport is the major airport serving California's desert communities. Alaska, American, Continental, Delta, United, and US Airways all fly to Palm Springs year-round. A Valley Cabousine has taxis serving the Palm Springs airport.

Airport Information Palm Springs International Airport (☎ 760/318–3800 ⊕ www.palmspringsairport.com).

Airport Transfers A Valley Cabousine (☎ 760/340–5845).

BY BUS

Greyhound provides service to the Palm Springs depot. SunBus, operated by the SunLine Transit Agency, serves the entire Coachella Valley, from Desert Hot Springs to Mecca.

Bus Contacts Greyhound (☎ 800/231–2222 ⊕ www.greyhound.com). **Palm Springs Depot** (✉ 311 N. Indian Canyon Dr.). **SunLine Transit** (☎ 800/347–8628 ⊕ www.sunline.org).

BY CAR

The desert resort communities occupy a 20-mi stretch between I–10, to the east, and Palm Canyon Drive (Highway 111), to the west. The area is about a two-hour drive east of Los Angeles and a three-hour drive northeast of San Diego. It can take twice as long to make the trip from Los Angeles to the desert on winter and spring weekends because of heavy traffic. From Los Angeles take the San Bernardino Freeway (I–10) east to Highway 111. From San Diego I–15 heading north connects with the Pomona Freeway (Highway 60), leading to the San Bernardino Freeway (I–10) east.

To reach Borrego Springs from Los Angeles, take I–10 east past the desert resorts area to Highway 86 south, and follow it to the Borrego Salton Seaway (Highway S22). Drive west on S22 to Borrego Springs. You can reach the Borrego area from San Diego via I–8 to Highway 79 through Cuyamaca State Park. This will take you to Highway 78 in Julian, which you follow east to Yaqui Pass Road (S3) into Borrego Springs.

BY TAXI

A Valley Cabousine serves Palm Desert and goes to the Palm Springs airport. Mirage Taxi serves the Coachella Valley and the Los Angeles and Ontario International airports. Fares in the Coachella Valley run about $2.96 per mi and up to $375 one-way to LAX.

Taxi Contacts A Valley Cabousine (☎ 760/340–5845). **Mirage Taxi** (☎ 760/322–2008).

BY TRAIN

The Amtrak *Sunset Limited,* which runs between Florida and Los Angeles, stops in Palm Springs.

Train Contact Amtrak (☎ 800/872–7245 ⊕ www.amtrakcalifornia.com).

The Desert
Resorts

HEALTH AND SAFETY

Never travel alone in the desert. Let someone know your trip route, destination, and estimated time and date of return. Before setting out, make sure your vehicle is in good condition. Carry a jack, tools, and towrope or chain. Fill up your tank whenever you see a gas pump. Stay on main roads, and watch out for horses and range cattle.

Drink at least a gallon of water a day (three gallons if you're hiking or otherwise exerting yourself). Dress in layered clothing and wear comfortable, sturdy shoes and a hat. Keep snacks, sunscreen, and a first-aid kit on hand. If you suddenly have a headache or feel dizzy or nauseous, you could be suffering from dehydration. Get out of the sun immediately and drink plenty of water. Dampen your clothing to lower your body temperature.

Do not enter mine tunnels or shafts. Avoid canyons during rainstorms. Never place your hands or feet where you can't see them. Rattlesnakes, scorpions, and black widow spiders may be hiding there.

Emergency Services Borrego Medical Center (✉ 4343 Yaqui Pass Rd., Borrego Springs ☎ 760/767–5051). **Desert Regional Medical Center** (✉ 1150 N. Indian Canyon Dr., Palm Springs ☎ 760/323–6511).

The green revolution is proudly on display in many parts of the Palm Springs area.

TOUR OPTIONS

Desert Adventures takes to the wilds with two- to four-hour red Jeep tours ($109 to $159) on private land along the canyons and palm oases above the San Andreas earthquake fault. Their other public tours include Indian Cultural Adventure, Pioneer Adventure, and Joshua Tree National Park (⇨ *see Chapter 15*). Groups are small and guides are knowledgeable. Departures are from Palm Springs and La Quinta; hotel pickups are available. Elite Land Tours gives two- to five-hour luxurious treks via Hummer and helicopter led by knowledgeable guides who take you to the San Andreas Fault, Joshua Tree National Park (⇨ *see Chapter 15*), Indian Canyons, Pioneertown, Old Indian Pueblo in Desert Hot Springs, and the Salton Sea. Tours include hotel pickup, lunch, snacks, and beverages. The company also offers VIP tours to Los Angeles and San Diego including a one-night stay.

Palm Springs Celebrity Tours conducts 2½-hour tours that cover Palm Springs–area history, points of interest, and celebrity homes. Desert Safari Guides conducts tours of various lengths through the Indian Canyons, moonlight hiking in the Palm Springs area, and daytime excursions to Joshua Tree National Park (⇨ *see Chapter 15*). Transportation from most area hotels is included.

The city of Palm Desert offers four self-guided tours of its 150-piece Art in Public Places collection. Each tour is walkable or drivable: The El Paseo tour features sculptures installed along the grassy median strip that runs the length of the street; the Fred Waring Corridor Tour includes sculptures of bighorn sheep, komodo dragons, and mountain lions along the street named for the bandleader; the City Tour encompasses several large pieces of art ringing the Desert Willow Golf Resort; and the Civic Center Park walk includes a massive water feature and plantings of 68 varieties of roses. Maps are available at the Palm Desert Visitor Center.

Palm Springs holds one of the largest collections of homes and public buildings designed by the famed Desert Moderne architects of the 1950s, Albert Frey, Richard Neutra, and William F. Cody. You can see many of these beauties on tours assembled by the cities of Palm Springs and Palm Desert; the Palm Springs Visitor Center also offers three-hour tours to these mid-century landmarks (you can also pick up a copy of *Palm Springs: Brief History and Architectural Guide* here). If you'd rather go it alone, pick up a map and guide to more than 40 distinctive mid-century buildings at the Palm Desert Visitor Center.

14

Tour Contacts Desert Adventures (✉ 74-794 Lennon Pl., Suite A, Palm Desert ☎ 760/340–2345 ⊕ www.red-jeep.com). **Desert Safari Guides** (☎ 760/861–6292 ⊕ www.palmspringshiking.com). **Elite Land Tours** (✉ 540 S. Vella Rd., Palm Springs ☎ 760/318-1200 ⊕ www.elitelandtours.com). **Palm Desert Visitor Center** (✉ 72–567 Hwy. 111, Palm Desert ☎ 760/568–1441 ⊕ www.palm-desert.org). **Palm Springs Celebrity Tours** (✉ 4751 E. Palm Canyon Dr., Palm Springs ☎ 760/770–2700).

THE DESERT RESORTS

PALM SPRINGS

90 mi southeast of Los Angeles on I–10.

A tourist destination since the late 19th century, Palm Springs had already caught Hollywood's eye by the time of the Great Depression. It was an ideal hideaway: Celebrities could slip into town, play a few sets of tennis, lounge around the pool, attend a party or two, and, unless things got out of hand, remain safely beyond the reach of gossip columnists. But it took a pair of tennis-playing celebrities to put Palm Springs on the map. In the 1930s actors Charlie Farrell and Ralph Bellamy bought 200 acres of land for $30 an acre and opened the Palm Springs Racquet Club, which soon listed Ginger Rogers, Humphrey Bogart, and Clark Gable among its members.

During its slow, steady growth period from the 1930s to 1970s, the Palm Springs area drew some of the world's most famous architects to design homes for the rich and famous. The collected works, inspired by the mountains and desert sands and notable for the use of glass and indoor–outdoor space, became known as Palm Springs Modernism. The city lost some of its luster in the 1970s as the wealthy moved to newer down-valley, golf-oriented communities. But Palm Springs reinvented itself starting in the 1990s, restoring the bright and airy old houses and hotels, and cultivating a welcoming atmosphere for well-heeled gay visitors.

You'll find reminders of the city's glamorous past in its unique architecture and renovated hotels; change and progress are evidenced by trendy

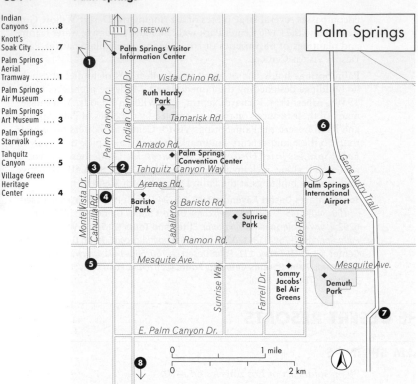

restaurants and upscale shops. Formerly exclusive Palm Canyon Drive is now a lively avenue filled with coffeehouses, outdoor cafés, and bars.

■ TIP→ Tahquitz Canyon Way marks the division between north and south on major streets (e.g., North and South Palm Canyon Drive).

ESSENTIALS

Visitor Information Palm Springs Desert Resorts Convention and Visitors Authority (✉ 70-100 Hwy. 111, Rancho Mirage ☎ 760/770–9000 or 800/967–3767 ⊕ www.palmsprings usa.com). **Palm Springs Visitor Information Center** (✉ 2901 N. Palm Canyon Dr., Palm Springs ☎ 760/778–8418 or 800/347–7746 ⊕ www.palm-springs.org).

EXPLORING

❶ A trip on the **Palm Springs Aerial Tramway** provides a 360-degree view
☾ of the desert through the picture windows of rotating tramcars. The
★ 2½-mi ascent through Chino Canyon, the steepest vertical cable ride in the United States, brings you to an elevation of 8,516 feet in less than 20 minutes. On clear days, which are common, the view stretches 75 mi— from the peak of Mt. San Gorgonio in the north, to the Salton Sea in the southeast. Stepping out into the snow at the summit is a winter treat. At the top, a bit below the summit of Mt. San Jacinto, are several diversions. Mountain Station has an observation deck, two restaurants, a cocktail lounge, apparel and gift shops, picnic facilities, a small wildlife

14

LOVE ME TENDER

Elvis's Honeymoon Hideaway—where the King and Priscilla lived during the first year of their marriage—is perched on a hilltop right up against the mountains in Palm Springs. The house, which is opened for tours, is a stunning example of Palm Springs Mid-Century Modern; it's rich in Elvis lore, photos, and furnishings. Docents describe the fabulous parties, celebrities, and some local legends. You can see some home movies of the loving couple, sit on the King's sofa, and strum one of his guitars. The house, built in 1962 by one of Palm Spring's largest developers, consists of four perfect circles, each set on a different level. At the time, *Look* magazine described it as the "house of tomorrow." (And indeed many features, like the huge kitchen with circular island, are standard in today's homes.) Tours are offered daily by appointment only; they're $25 during the week and $35 on weekends. Call ☎ *760/322-1192* or visit ⊕ *www.elvishoneymoon.com* for reservations.

exhibit, and a theater that screens a worthwhile 22-minute film on the history of the tramway. Take advantage of free guided and self-guided nature walks through the adjacent Mount San Jacinto State Park and Wilderness, or if there's snow on the ground, rent skis, snowshoes, or snow tubes (inner tubes or similar contraptions for sliding down hills). The tramway generally closes for maintenance in mid-September. ■TIP→ Ride-and-dine packages are available in late afternoon. The tram is a popular attraction; to avoid a two-hour or longer wait, arrive before the first car leaves in the morning. ✉ *1 Tramway Rd.* ☎ *760/325-1391* or *888/515-8726* ⊕ *www.pstramway.com* ✆ *$22.95, ride-and-dine package $35.50* ☉ *Tramcars depart at least every 30 mins from 10* AM *weekdays and 8* AM *weekends; last car up leaves at 8* PM, *last car down leaves Mountain Station at 9:45* PM.

② A stroll down shop-lined Palm Canyon Drive will take you along the **Palm Springs Starwalk** (✉ *Palm Canyon Dr., around Tahquitz Canyon Way, and Tahquitz Canyon Way, between Palm Canyon and Indian Canyon Drs.*), where nearly 200 bronze stars are embedded in the sidewalk (à la Hollywood Walk of Fame). Most of the names, all with a Palm Springs connection, are ones you'll recognize (such as Elvis Presley, Marilyn Monroe, Lauren Bacall, Lucille Ball, and Liberace). Others are local celebrities.

③
★ The **Palm Springs Art Museum** and its grounds hold several wide-ranging collections of contemporary and traditional art displayed in bright, open galleries, with daylight streaming through huge skylights. The permanent collection includes a shimmering display of contemporary studio glass, highlighted by works by Dale Chihuly, Ginny Ruffner, and William Morris. You'll also find handcrafted furniture by the late actor George Montgomery, an array of enormous Native American baskets, and works by artists like Allen Houser, Arlo Naminigha, and Fritz Scholder; the museum also displays significant works of 20th century sculpture by Henry Moore, Marino Marina, Deborah Butterfield, and Mark Di Suvero. The Annenberg Theater presents plays,

concerts, lectures, operas, and other cultural events. ✉ *101 Museum Dr.* ☎ *760/322–4800* ⊕ *www.psmuseum.org* ☞ *$12.50, free Thurs. 4–8 during Villagefest* ⊙ *Tues., Wed., and Fri.–Sun. 10–5, Thurs. noon–8.*

❹ Three small museums at the **Village Green Heritage Center** illustrate pioneer life in Palm Springs. The **Agua Caliente Cultural Museum** traces the culture and history of the Cahuilla tribe with several exhibits. The **McCallum Adobe** holds the collection of the Palm Springs Historical Society. **Rudy's General Store Museum** is a re-creation of a 1930s general store. ✉ *221 S. Palm Canyon Dr.* ☎ *760/327–2156* ☞ *Agua Caliente Cultural Museum free, McCallum Adobe $2, Rudy's General Store 95¢* ⊙ *Call for hrs.*

❺ Ranger-led tours of **Tahquitz Canyon** take you into a secluded canyon on the Agua Caliente Reservation. Within the canyon are a spectacular 60-foot waterfall, rock art, ancient irrigation systems, and native wildlife and plants. Tours are conducted several times daily; participants must be able to navigate 100 steep steps. (You can also take a self-guided tour of the 1.8-mi trail.) A visitor center at the canyon entrance shows a video tour, displays artifacts, and sells maps. ✉ *500 W. Mesquite Ave.* ☎ *760/416–7044* ⊕ *www.tahquitzcanyon.com* ☞ *$12.50* ⊙ *Oct.– June, daily 7:30–5; July–Sept., Fri.–Sun. 7:30–5.*

❻ The **Palm Springs Air Museum** showcases 26 World War II aircraft, ⟳ including a B-17 Flying Fortress bomber, a P-51 Mustang, a Lockheed P-38, and a Grumman TBF Avenger. Cool exhibits include a Grumman Goose into which kids can crawl, model warships, and a Pearl Harbor diorama. Flight demonstrations are scheduled regularly. ✉ *745 N. Gene Autry Trail* ☎ *760/778–6262* ⊕ *www.air-museum.org* ☞ *$12* ⊙ *Daily 10–5.*

❼ For a break from the desert heat, head to **Knott's Soak City**. You'll find ⟳ 1950s-theme ambience complete with Woodies (antique station wagons from the 1950s), 13 waterslides, a huge wave pool, an arcade, and other fun family attractions. The park also contains the full-service Fitness Point Health Club, where you can take exercise classes—including water aerobics and yoga—use the weight room, or swim; day passes are $11. ✉ *1500 S. Gene Autry Trail* ☎ *760/327–0499, 760/325–8155 Fitness Point Health Club* ⊕ *www.knotts.com* ☞ *$30, $20 after 3 PM, $11 health club day pass* ⊙ *Mid-March–early Sept., daily; early Sept.– Oct., weekends. Opens at 10 AM, closing times vary.*

❽ The **Indian Canyons** are the ancestral home of the Agua Caliente, part of ⟳ the Cahuilla people. You can see remnants of their ancient life, including rock art, house pits and foundations, irrigation ditches, bedrock mortars, pictographs, and stone houses and shelters built atop high cliff walls. Short, easy walks through the canyons reveal palm oases, waterfalls, and spring wildflowers. Tree-shaded picnic areas are abundant. The attraction includes three canyons open for touring: Palm Canyon, noted for its stand of Washingtonia palms; Murray Canyon, home of Peninsula bighorn sheep and a herd of wild ponies; and Andreas Canyon, where a stand of fan palms contrasts with sharp rock formations. Ranger-led hikes to Palm and Andreas canyons are offered daily for an additional charge. The trading post at the entrance to Palm Canyon has hiking maps and refreshments, as well as Native American art, jewelry, and weavings. ⊠ *38520 S. Palm Canyon Dr.* ☎ *760/323–6018* ⊕ *www. indian-canyons.com* 🖾 *$8, ranger hikes $3* ☉ *Oct.–June, daily 8–5; July–Sept., Fri.–Sun. 8–5.*

WHERE TO EAT

$$$
AMERICAN
✕ **Copley's on Palm Canyon.** Chef Manion Copley is cooking up some of the most innovative cuisine in the desert in a setting that's straight out of Hollywood—a hacienda once owned by Cary Grant. Dine in the clubby house or under the stars in the garden. Start with such appetizers as roasted beet and warm goat cheese salad or a vanilla-poached shrimp martini. Oh My Lobster Pot Pie is the biggest hit on an entrée menu that also features an elegant rack of lamb crusted with parsley and lavender. And save room for Copley's sweet and savory servings of herb ice cream. Service is pleasant and friendly. ⊠ *621 N. Palm Canyon Dr.* ☎ *760/327–9555* ⊕ *www.copleyspalmsprings.com* ▭ *AE, D, DC, MC, V* ☉ *Closed Mon. No lunch.*

$$$$
STEAK HOUSE
✕ **The Falls Steak House.** A mile-long martini menu lures a chic, moneyed crowd to this steak house with an inside waterfall tucked into an upstairs corner overlooking the Palm Canyon Drive action. Reserve well in advance for one of the outdoor balcony tables to get the best view. While this eatery specializes in aged beef, you can also get seafood and chops; there's a separate vegetarian menu. Steaks and chops are prepared your way with a selection of sides that includes mac and cheese with apple bacon served in a brioche crust and steamed asparagus with hollandaise sauce. Go early for the nightly happy hour (between 5 and 7) when everything on the bar menu is half price—or hang around late to savor the action at the Martini Dome bar. ⊠ *155 S. Palm Canyon Dr.* ☎ *760/416–8664* ⊕ *www.thefallsprimesteakhouse.com* ⚭ *Reservations essential* ▭ *AE, D, MC, V* ☉ *No lunch.*

$$$$
FRENCH
★
✕ **Le Vallauris.** Le Vallauris, in the historic Roberson House, is popular with ladies who lunch, all of whom get a hug from the maître d'. The menu changes daily, and each day it's handwritten on a white board. Lunch entrées may include perfectly rare tuna niçoise salad, or grilled whitefish with Dijon mustard sauce. Dinner might bring a sublime smoked salmon, sautéed calves' liver, roasted quail with orange sauce, or rack of lamb. Service is beyond attentive. The restaurant has a lovely tree-shaded garden. On cool winter evenings, request a table by the fireplace. ⊠ *385 W. Tahquitz Canyon Way* ☎ *760/325–5059* ⊕ *www.levallauris.com* ⚭ *Reservations essential* ▭ *AE, D, DC, MC, V* ☉ *Closed July and Aug.*

$$
ITALIAN
✕ **Matchbox Vintage Pizza Bistro.** The name says pizza, but this bistro offers much more: you'll find interesting salads topped with grilled tuna, and a selection of sandwiches with fillings like chicken with portobello mushrooms or Angus beef with Gorgonzola. The pizzas are made just about any way you'd like, including vegetarian. This is the place to go for cocktails, small plates, and cigars after work. The bistro has an upstairs location in Mercado Plaza, and overlooks the nightly action on Palm Canyon Drive. ⊠ *155 S. Palm Canyon Dr.* ☎ *760/778–6000* ⊕ *www.matchboxpalmsprings.com* ▭ *AE, D, MC, V* ☉ *No lunch.*

14

$$$
MEDITERRANEAN
★

✕ **Purple Palm.** The hottest tables in Palm Springs are those that surround the pool at the Colony Palms Hotel, where the hip and elite pay homage to Purple Gang mobster Al Wertheimer, who reportedly built the hotel in the mid-1930s. Now it's a casual, convivial place where you can dine alfresco surrounded by a tropical garden. Start with spicy macaroni and cheese with chipotle and sun-dried tomatoes. Main courses range from grilled hanger steak with frites to garlic- and herb-crusted lamb loin with beluga lentils. An impressive wine list roams the globe. ■ TIP➔ A visit to the ladies room is a must for Paul Newman fans. The loo holds a fabulous black and white image of a very young Newman. ⊠ *572 N. Indian Canyon Dr.* ☎ *800/557–2187* ⊕ *www.colonypalmshotel. com* ♙ *Reservations essential* ⊟ *AE, D, DC, MC, V.*

> ### SINATRA AND THE DESERT
>
> Old Blue Eyes probably had more haunts in the Palm Springs area than any other celebrity. He owned two homes here, one of them a mid-century modern jewel built in 1947 (Twin Palms Estate at ⊠ *1148 E. Alejo Road*), and called the landscape home for more than 50 years. He frequented Melvyn's Restaurant and Lounge at the Ingleside Hotel (⊠ *200 W. Ramon Road*)—ask Melvyn to tell you about Sinatra's pre-wedding dinner with Barbara Marx in 1976—as well as Riccio's (⊠ *1900 E. Palm Canyon Drive*) and Lord Fletcher's (⊠ *70–385 Highway 111*).

$$$
NEW AMERICAN

✕ **The Tropicale.** Tucked onto a side-street corner, the Tropicale offers a mid-century–style watering hole with a contemporary vibe. The bar and main dining room hold cozy leather booths while flowers and water features brighten the outdoor area. The menu roams the world with small and large plates, from saffron linguini with ginger prawns and mango tandoori pizza to barbecue meat loaf and an Angus burger with onion rings. ⊠ *330 E. Amado Rd.* ☎ *760/866–1952* ⊕ *www.thetropicale.com* ♙ *Reservations essential* ☽ *AE, DC, M, V* ☽ *No lunch.*

$$
MEDITERRANEAN

✕ **Zini Café Med.** One of the best people-watching spots in Palm Springs, this sidewalk café is a delightful choice before or after seeing the Follies. The lunch and dinner menus feature a wide selection of small plates in addition to hearty items such as pasta, pizza, *pollo alla diavolo* (macadamia-crusted chicken breast), and veal scaloppini. On a separate tapas menu you can find some surprises: spicy chickpeas with Mediterranean chicken sausage, layered grilled artichoke, asparagus topped with a fried egg, or spicy lime drizzled shrimp. Service is pleasant and personal. ⊠ *140 S. Palm Canyon Dr.* ☎ *760/325–9464* ⊕ *www. zinicafemed.com* ⊟ *AE, MC, V.*

WHERE TO STAY
HOTELS AND RESORTS

$$
⌂ **Ace Hotel and Swim Club.** Take a trip back to the 1960s at the Ace. With the hotel's vintage feel and hippie-chic decor, it would be no surprise to find the Grateful Dead playing in the bar. Guests gather around cozy communal fire pits enjoying the feel-good vibe. Rooms, on two floors of the former Howard Johnson's, are spacious; those on the ground floor have patios with fireplaces. Vintage appointments are simple, and everything inside and out is immaculate. King's Highway

restaurant, occupying the old Denny's, gets rave reviews from locals for its contemporary menu. The hotel is dog-friendly, with its own dog park. The Ace's weekend events draw locals and enhance the party atmosphere. **Pros:** happy hour at the Amigo Room; poolside stargazing deck; cozy fire pits. **Cons:** party atmosphere not for everyone; limited amenities; casual staff and service. ⊠ *701 E. Palm Canyon Dr.* ☎ *760/325–9900* ⊕ *www.acehotel. com/palmsprings* ⟿ *180 rooms, 8 suites* ⬥ *In-room: a/c, refrigerator, DVD, Wi-Fi. In-hotel: restaurant, room service, bar, pools, gym, spa, bicycles, laundry facilities, laundry service, Internet terminal, Wi-Fi hotspot, parking (free) some pets allowed* ⊟ *AE, D, DC, MC, V.*

> **TRIBAL WEALTH**
>
> The Agua Caliente band of Cahuilla Indians owns nearly half the land in the Palm Springs area. Wanting to encourage the railroad to bring their trains through the desert, Congress granted half the land to the railroad and the other half to the Native Americans. The Cahuilla were granted all the even-numbered one-square-mi sections—but they were unable to develop the land for years due to litigation. The resulting patchwork of developed and vacant land can still be seen today (though the Cahuilla are making up for lost time by opening new hotels and casinos).

14

$$ **Colony Palms Hotel.** Detroit's Purple Gang mobsters, Hollywood's starlets and leading men, and Sea Biscuit all cast a long shadow over the Colony Palms. The hotel has been the hip place to go since the 1930s, when gangster Al Wertheimer built it to front his casino, bar, and brothel. It became the Howard Hotel, owned by Hollywood luminaries Robert Leeds and Andrea Howard (who also owned the race horse). They hosted young Frank Sinatra, Elizabeth Taylor, and Liberace. Fast-forward to now. The hotel is still hot with a nice youthful vibe. The rooms, created by A-list designer Martyn Lawrence Bullard, are quasi-Moroccan with brilliantly colored mosaic tiles and fabrics, rich woods, and black-and-white vintage movie star photos everywhere. Mature gardens throughout the property provide privacy, even though rooms open to a central courtyard holding the pool. When you go, ask to visit the speakeasy beneath the bar. **Pros:** glam with a swagger; attentive staff; all that history. **Cons:** high noise level outside; not for families with young children. ⊠ *572 N. Indian Canyon Dr., Palm Springs* ☎ *760/969–1800 or 800/577–2187* ⊕ *www.colonypalmshotel. com* ⟿ *43 rooms, 3 suites, 8 casitas* ⬥ *In-room: a/c, Internet, Wi-Fi. In-hotel: restaurant, room service, bar, pool, gym, spa, bicycles, laundry service, Wi-Fi hotspot, parking (free), some pets allowed* ⊟ *AE, D, DC, MC, V.*

$$$ **Hyatt Regency Suites Palm Springs.** Totally renovated in 2009, the Hyatt is the best-situated downtown hotel in Palm Springs. You can watch the sun rise over the city or set behind the mountains from the balcony of your spacious one- or two-bedroom suite. Now boasting a streamlined mid-century look, suites feature spacious living rooms with sofa beds and large flat-screen TVs. Poolside rooms open onto private cabanas, where you can entertain or hide out. Guests have golf privileges at Rancho Mirage Country Club and four other area courses. **Pros:**

underground parking; no resort fees; walking distance from restaurants. **Cons:** lots of business travelers, some street noise. ✉ *285 N. Palm Canyon Dr.* ☎ *760/322–9000 or 800/633–7313* ⊕ *www.hyattpalmsprings. com* ⤙ *197 suites* ☾ *In-room: a/c, Wi-Fi. In-hotel: restaurant, room service, bar, pool, gym, spa, laundry service, Internet terminal, Wi-Fi hotspot, parking (paid), some pets allowed* ⊟ *AE, D, DC, MC, V.*

$$$$ ⊡ **The Parker Palm Springs.** A cacophony of color, flashing lights, and
★ over-the-top contemporary art assembled by New York designer Jonathan Adler, this is the hippest hotel in the desert, appealing to a young L.A.-based clientele. When you arrive, a greeter will whisk you from your car to your room to complete registration; the stroll takes you through a brilliant desert garden. You can find relaxation around the pools, if nowhere else—pulsating music fills the air throughout the resort. Rooms have textured sisal floor coverings, exotic woven fabrics in bright reds and browns, and leather seating. All have private balconies or patios (with hammocks) that are secluded behind tall shrubs. The clubby restaurant, Mister Parker's ($$$$), will delight any well-heeled carnivore. **Pros:** fun in the sun; celebrity clientele; high jinks at the Palm Springs Yacht Club Spa. **Cons:** pricey drinks and wine; confused service; long walks in the hot sun to get anywhere. ✉ *4200 E. Palm Canyon Dr.* ☎ *760/770–5000 or 800/543–4300* ⊕ *www.theparkerpalmsprings. com* ⤙ *131 rooms, 13 suites* ☾ *In-room: a/c, refrigerator, DVD, Wi-Fi. In-hotel: 4 restaurants, room service, bar, tennis courts, pools, gym, spa, bicycles, laundry service, Wi-Fi hotspot, parking (free)* ⊟ *AE, D, DC, MC, V.*

$$ ⊡ **Riviera Resort & Spa.** This mid-century hotel—built in 1958 and reopened in 2008 following an extensive renovation—is beyond bling. It's emerged as a party place that attracts young well-heeled bikini-clad guests who hang out around the pool by day and the Bikini Bar by night. Spacious rooms fill a collection of two-story buildings that circle a huge free-form pool, with a restaurant and a couple of bars tucked into corners. That's where you'll find the action. You can watch from your balcony, or reach out and join the fun from your ground floor patio. Although adorned with huge and tiny mirrors everywhere, rooms are nicely done in an Age of Aquarius style palette of orange, brown, and green. There are oversized mid-century lamps, chandeliers dripping with baubles and mirrors, and ample bathrooms with marble counters and floors, many holding whirlpool or soaking tubs and fireplaces. All rooms have jack packs where you can plug in MP3 players, DVD players, or computers. **Pros:** personal beachy fire pits throughout the property; hip vibe; sublime spa. **Cons:** high noise level outdoors; party atmosphere; location at north end of Palm Springs. ✉ *1600 N. Indian Canyon Dr., Palm Springs* ☎ *760/327–8311* ⊕ *www.psriviera.com* ⤙ *406 rooms, 45 suites* ☾ *In-room: a/c, refrigerator, Internet, Wi-Fi. In-hotel: restaurant, room service, bars, tennis courts, pools, gym, spa, Wi-Fi hotspot, parking (free), some pets allowed* ⊟ *AE, D, MC, V.*

$$$$ ⊡ **Smoke Tree Ranch.** A world apart from Palm Springs' pulsating urban
☾ village, the area's most exclusive resort occupies 400 pristine desert
★ acres, surrounded by mountains and unspoiled vistas. A laid-back genteel retreat since the mid-1930s for some of the world's foremost

families, including Walt Disney's, it still provides a quietly luxurious experience reminiscent of the Old West. A collection of simple mid-century cottages is spread among manicured desert gardens and shaded by smoke trees. Most have fireplaces and private patios. A large rambling ranch house right out of a western movie, with gleaming paneled walls and picture windows framing desert scenery, holds a dining room where three meals are served daily. Two optional meal plans are offered: full American plan at $82 per day per person, and breakfast plan at $16 per day per person. **Pros:** priceless privacy; simple luxury; many recreation choices include horseback riding, lawn bowling, hiking, and jogging. **Cons:** no glitz or glamour; limited entertainment options; family atmosphere. ✉ *1850 Smoke Tree La.* ☎ *760/327–1221 or 800/787–3922* ⊕ *www.smoketreeranch.com* ⌁ *49 cottages* ♿ *In-room: a/c, refrigerator, DVD, Wi-Fi. In-hotel: restaurant, bar, tennis courts, pool, gym, bicycles, children's programs (ages 5–12), laundry facilities, Internet terminal, Wi-Fi hotspot, parking (free), some pets allowed* ▭ *AE, D, MC, V* ☯ *Closed Apr.–late Oct.*

14

¢ 🖵 **Vagabond Inn.** Rooms are smallish at this centrally located motel, but they're clean, comfortable, and a good value. Continental breakfast and daily newspaper are included in the price. BJ's Snack Shoppe has sandwiches and deli items. **Pros:** quiet; inexpensive; breakfast included. **Cons:** limited amenities, facilities, and service. ✉ *1699 S. Palm Canyon Dr.* ☎ *760/325–7211 or 800/522–1555* ⊕ *www.vagabondinn.com* ⌁ *117 rooms* ♿ *In-room: a/c, refrigerator, Internet, Wi-Fi (some). In-hotel: restaurant, pool, parking (free), some pets allowed* ▭ *AE, D, DC, MC, V* ⧉ *CP.*

$$ 🖵 **The Viceroy Palm Springs.** The first thing that strikes you at the Viceroy
★ is its bright, sunny white-and-yellow ambience, reminiscent of a sun-filled desert day. Guest rooms for two and villas for three or more (some with fireplaces and private patios) are spread out over four tree-shaded acres, where secluded nooks and blue-and-white-striped cabanas beg chic bikini-clad guests to hole up with a good book and a glass of the inn's delicious iced tea. The tranquil inn, just a short walk from Palm Canyon Drive, is home to the stylish eatery Citron ($$–$$$), where you can dine indoors or poolside on perfectly prepared comfort food. The inn is exceptionally canine friendly—they even offer dog-walking and -sitting services. The on-site Estrella Spa is one of the most luxurious in Palm Springs. **Pros:** poolside cabanas; celebrity clientele; pet friendly. **Cons:** uneven service; popular wedding site. ✉ *415 S. Belardo Rd.* ☎ *760/320–4117 or 800/327–3687* ⊕ *www.viceroypalmsprings. com* ⌁ *43 rooms, 16 suites* ♿ *In-room: a/c, safe, kitchen (some), refrigerator, Internet, Wi-Fi. In-hotel: restaurant, room service, bar, pools, gym, spa, bicycles, Internet terminal, Wi-Fi hotspot, parking (paid), some pets allowed* ▭ *AE, D, MC, V.*

SMALL HOTELS AND BED-AND-BREAKFASTS

$$$ 🖵 **Calla Lily Inn.** This tranquil palm-shaded oasis one block from Palm Canyon Drive has spacious rooms decorated in a vaguely tropical style. Furnishings are contemporary wicker, and an image of a calla lily adorns every room. Rooms surround the pool, and there is an on-site hair stylist and massage therapist. **Pros:** lush tropical gardens; gracious

CLOSE UP

Palm Springs Modernism

Some of the world's most forward-looking architects designed and constructed buildings around Palm Springs between 1940 and 1970, and modernism, also popular elsewhere in California in the years after World War II, became an ideal fit for desert living, because it minimizes the separation between indoors and outdoors. See-through houses with glass exterior walls are common. Oversize flat roofs provide shade from the sun, and many buildings' sculptural forms reflect nearby landforms. The style is notable for elegant informality, clean lines, and simple landscaping. Emblematic structures in Palm Springs include public buildings, hotels, stores, banks, and private residences.

Most obvious to visitors are three buildings that are part of the Palm Springs Aerial Tramway complex, built in the 1960s. Albert Frey, a Swiss-born architect, designed the soaring A-frame Tramway Gas Station, visually echoing the pointed peaks behind it. Frey also created the glass-walled Valley Station, from which you get your initial view of the Coachella Valley before you board the tram to the Mountain Station, designed by E. Stewart Williams.

Frey, a Palm Springs resident for more than 60 years, also designed the indoor–outdoor City Hall, Fire Station #1, and numerous houses. You can see his second home, perched atop stilts on the hillside above the Desert Museum; it affords a sweeping view of the Coachella Valley through glass walls. The classy Movie Colony Hotel, one of the first buildings Frey designed in the desert, may seem like a typical 1950s motel with rooms surrounding a swimming pool now, but when it was built in 1935, it was years ahead of its time.

Donald Wexler, who honed his vision with Los Angeles architect Richard Neutra, brought new ideas about the use of materials to the desert, where he teamed up with William Cody on a number of projects, including the terminal at the Palm Springs airport. Many of Wexler's buildings have soaring overhanging roofs, designed to provide shade from the blazing desert sun. Wexler also experimented with steel framing back in 1961, but the metal proved too expensive. Seven of his steel-frame houses can be seen in a neighborhood off Indian Canyon and Frances drives.

The Palm Springs Modern Committee is protecting these period structures, occasionally protesting projected demolition projects. The committee also publishes a map and driving guide to 52 historic buildings, which is available for $5 at the Palm Springs Visitor Information Center or at ⊕ www.psmodcom.com.

---

hosts; within walking distance of everything. **Cons:** small property; rooms are close to the pool. ⊠ 350 S. Belardo Rd. ☎ 760/323–3654 or 888/888–5787 ⊕ www.callalilypalmsprings.com 🛏9 rooms ⌂ In-room: a/c, kitchen (some), refrigerator, DVD, Internet, Wi-Fi. In-hotel: pool, bicycles, parking (free) ⊟ AE, D, MC, V.

$$$ 🔅 **East Canyon Resort & Spa.** This classy resort, which serves a primarily gay clientele, is the only one in the desert with an in-house, full-service spa exclusively for men. Large rooms, each individually decorated, surround a sparkling pool; they have carefully coordinated dark colors,

Frette linens, and ample bathrooms. The club room has a giant TV, plus a library well stocked with videos and books. The vibe here is social, presided over by the resort's gracious hosts. **Pros:** elegant laid-back feel; attentive service; weekend cocktail gatherings. **Cons:** spa is for men only. ✉ *288 E. Camino Monte Vista* ☎ *760/320–1928 or 877/324–6835* ⊕ *www.eastcanyonps.com* ⇔ *15 rooms, 1 suite* ⚒ *In-room: a/c, refrigerator, DVD, Wi-Fi. In-hotel: pool, spa, Wi-Fi hotspot, parking (free)* ▭ *AE, MC, V* ⦿ *CP.*

$$$$

★ ⊞ **Movie Colony Hotel.** This intimate hotel, designed in 1935 by Albert Frey, evokes mid-century minimalist ambience. Its sparkling, white, two-story buildings, flanked with balconies and porthole windows, evoke the image of a luxury yacht. Rooms are elegantly appointed with soft desert colors accented by bright reds and yellows; many features, including tiny showers, are authentic to the period. A cool vibe prevails in late afternoon, as sophisticated young guests share experiences during the wine hour and again over morning coffee and a sumptuous Continental breakfast served in the flower-decked courtyard. **Pros:** architectural icon; Dean Martinis at happy hour; cruiser bikes. **Cons:** close quarters; off the beaten path; staff not available 24 hours. ✉ *726 N. Indian Canyon Dr.* ☎ *760/320–6340 or 888/953–5700* ⊕ *www.moviecolonyhotel. com* ⇔ *13 rooms, 3 suites* ⚒ *In-room: a/c, refrigerator, DVD, Internet, Wi-Fi (some). In-hotel: bar, pools, bicycles, Internet terminal, Wi-Fi hotspot, parking (free), no kids under 21* ▭ *AE, MC, V* ⦿ *CP.*

$$$

⊞ **Orbit In Hotel.** Step back to 1957 at this hip inn, located on a quiet back street downtown. The architectural roots here date back to the late 1940s and '50s—nearly flat roofs, wide overhangs, glass everywhere—with the ambience to match. Rooms are appointed with mid-century modern furnishings by such designers as Eames, Noguchi, and Breuer. Some have private patios; all have lava lamps, chrome Crosley reproduction record players (that will take your CDs), plus a few Melmac dishes tucked here and there. An outside shower, vintage cruiser bikes, books, games, and videos are available for guest use. A lively atmosphere prevails poolside, where a complimentary breakfast is served daily. **Pros:** saltwater pool; in-room spa services; Orbitini cocktail hour. **Cons:** best for couples; not to everyone's taste; staff not available 24 hours. ✉ *562 W. Arenas Rd.* ☎ *760/323–3585 or 877/996–7248* ⊕ *www.orbitin.com* ⇔ *9 rooms* ⚒ *In-room: a/c, safe, kitchen (some), refrigerator, DVD, Internet, Wi-Fi. In-hotel: pool, bicycles, Internet terminal, Wi-Fi hotspot, parking (free), no kids under 21* ▭ *AE, D, MC, V* ⦿ *CP.*

$$$$

★ ⊞ **Willows Historic Palm Springs Inn.** This luxurious hillside B&B is within walking distance of many village attractions. An opulent Mediterranean-style mansion built in the 1920s, it has gleaming hardwood and slate floors, stone fireplaces, frescoed ceilings, hand-painted tiles, iron balconies, antiques throughout, and a 50-foot waterfall that splashes into a pool outside the dining room. There's even a private hillside garden planted with native flora, with one of the best views in the area. Guest rooms are decorated to recall the movies of Hollywood's golden era. **Pros:** luxurious; sublime service; La Vallauris provides room service. **Cons:** noisy hardwood floors; pricey. ✉ *412 W. Tahquitz Canyon Way*

14

Palm Springs is a golfer's paradise: the area is home to more than 125 courses.

☎ 760/320–0771 or 800/966–9597 ⊕ *www.thewillowspalmsprings. com* ⌂ 8 rooms ⌂ In-room: a/c, refrigerator, DVD, Internet, Wi-Fi. In-hotel: room service, pool, Wi-Fi hotspot, parking (free) ☰ AE, D, DC, MC, V ⧫ BP.

NIGHTLIFE AND THE ARTS

NIGHTLIFE **Hair of the Dog English Pub** (✉ 238 N. Palm Canyon Dr. ☎ 760/323–9890) is a lively bar popular with a young crowd that likes to tip back English ales and ciders. **Village Pub** (✉ 266 S. Palm Canyon Dr. ☎ 760/323–3265) is a popular but loud sports bar with friendly service that caters to a young crowd. **Zelda's** (✉ 169 N. Indian Canyon Dr. ☎ 760/325–2375) has two rooms, one featuring Latin sounds and another with Top 40 dance music and a male dance revue. It's closed Sunday and Monday.

Casino Morongo (✉ Cabazon off-ramp, I–10 ☎ 800/252–4499), about 20 minutes west of Palm Springs, has 2,000 slot machines plus Vegas-style shows. The classy **Spa Resort Casino** (✉ 401 E. Amado Rd. ☎ 888/999–1995) holds 1,000 slot machines, blackjack tables, a high-limit room, four restaurants, two bars, and a lounge with entertainment.

GAY AND **Confessions** (✉ 611 S. Palm Canyon Dr. ☎ 760/416–0950) is a multitier LESBIAN dance club catering to a mixed gay clientele. **Hunter's Video Bar** (✉ 302 E. Arenas Rd. ☎ 760/323–0700) is a popular bar with dancing that draws a young crowd. **Toucans** (✉ 2100 N. Palm Canyon Dr. ☎ 760/416–7584), a friendly place with a tropical jungle in a rain-forest setting, serves festive drinks and has live entertainment and theme nights.

In late March, when the world's finest female golfers hit the links for the Annual LPGA Kraft Nabisco Championship in Rancho Mirage, thousands of lesbians converge on Palm Springs for a four-day party popularly known as **Dinah Shore Weekend–Palm Springs** (☎ *888/923– 4624* ✆ *www.clubskirts.com*). The **White Party** (✆ *jeffreysanker.com*), held on Easter weekend, draws tens of thousands of gay men from around the country to the Palm Springs area for a round of parties and gala events.

THE ARTS At the Palm Springs Art Museum, the **Annenberg Theater** (✉ *101 Museum Dr.* ☎ *760/325–4490* ✆ *www.psmuseum.org*) is the site of Broadway shows, opera, lectures, Sunday-afternoon chamber concerts, and other events. In mid-January the **Palm Springs International Film Festival** (☎ *760/ 322–2930 or 800/898–7256* ✆ *www.psfilmfest.org*) brings stars and more than 150 feature films from 25 countries, plus panel discussions, short films, and documentaries, to the McCallum and other venues.

The Spanish-style **Historic Plaza Theatre** (✉ *128 S. Palm Canyon Dr.* ☎ *760/327–0225*) opened in 1936 with a glittering premiere of the MGM film *Camille*. In the '40s and '50s, it presented some of Hollywood's biggest stars, including Bob Hope, Bing Crosby, and Frank Sinatra. Today it plays host to the hottest ticket in the desert, the **Fabulous Palm Springs Follies** (✆ *www.palmspringsfollies.com*), which mounts 10 weekly sell-out performances November through May. The vaudeville-style revue, about half of which focuses on mid-century nostalgia, stars extravagantly costumed, retired (but very fit) showgirls, singers, and dancers. Tickets are $59 to $92. In addition to the Follies, the theater is home to the Palm Springs International Film Festival in January and is favored by fans of old-time radio even in the off-season.

SPORTS AND THE OUTDOORS

BICYCLING Many hotels and resorts have bicycles available for guest use. **Big Wheel Tours** (☎ *760/802–2236* ✆ *www.bwbtours.com*) rents cruisers, performance road bikes, and mountain bikes in Palm Springs and offers road tours to La Quinta Loop, Joshua Tree National Park (⇨ *see chapter 15*), and the San Andreas fault. Off-road tours are also available. The company doesn't have a retail outlet but will pick up and deliver bikes to your hotel and supply you with area maps. **Palm Springs Recreation Division** (✉ *401 S. Pavilion Way* ☎ *760/323–8272* ☉ *Weekdays 7:30–6*) can provide you with maps of city bike trails.

GOLF Palm Springs is host to more than 100 golf tournaments annually. The **Palm Springs Desert Resorts Convention and Visitors Bureau** lists events on its Web site (✆ *www.palmspringsusa.com*). **Palm Springs TeeTimes** (✆ *www. palmspringsteetimes.com*) can match golfers with courses and arrange tee times. If you know which course you want to play, you can book tee times online up to 60 days in advance.

Indian Canyons Golf Resort (✉ *1097 E. Murray Canyon Dr.* ☎ *760/327– 6550* ✆ *www.indiancanyonsgolf.com*), an 18-hole course designed by Casey O'Callaghan and Amy Alcott and operated by the Aqua Caliente tribe, is at the base of the mountains. **Tahquitz Creek Palm Springs Golf Resort** (✉ *1885 Golf Club Dr.* ☎ *760/328–1005* ✆ *www. tahquitzgolfresort.com*) has two 18-hole, par-72 courses and a 50-space driving range. Greens fees, including cart, run $65 to $110, depending on the course and day of the week. **Tommy Jacobs' Bel Air Greens Country**

Club (✉ *1001 S. El Cielo Rd.* ☎ *760/322–6062*) has a 9-hole executive course. The greens fee is $20 ($10 for replay).

SPAS   Taking the Waters at the **Spa Resort Casino** (✉ *100 N. Indian Canyon Dr.* ☎ *760/778–1772* ⊕ *www.sparesortcasino.com*) is an indulgent pleasure. You can spend a full day enjoying a five-step, wet-and-dry treatment program that includes a mineral bath, steam, sauna, and eucalyptus inhalation. The program allows you to take fitness classes and use the gym and, for an extra charge, add massage or body treatments. During the week, the spa admission rate is $40 for a full day, less for hotel guests or if you combine it with a treatment; on weekends you cannot purchase a day pass without booking a treatment.

SHOPPING

The main **North Palm Canyon Drive shopping district** (✉ *Between Alejo and Ramon Rds.*) is the commercial core of Palm Springs. **Villagefest** (✉ *Palm Canyon Dr., between Tahquitz Canyon Way and Baristo Rd.* ☎ *760/327–3781* ⊕ *www.palmspringsvillagefest.com*) fills the drive with street musicians, a farmers' market, and stalls with food, crafts, art, and antiques every Thursday evening. It's a great place for celebrity spotting.

Extending north of the main shopping area, the **Uptown Heritage Galleries & Antiques District** (✉ *N. Palm Canyon Dr., between Amado Rd. and Tachevah Dr.* ☎ *760/318–7227* ⊕ *www.palmcanyondrive.org*) is a loose-knit collection of consignment and secondhand shops, galleries, and restaurants whose theme is decidedly retro. Many shops and galleries offer mid-century modern furniture and decorator items, and others carry consignment clothing and estate jewelry.

East Palm Canyon Drive can be a source of great bargains. **Estate Sale Co.** (✉ *4185 E. Palm Canyon Dr.* ☎ *760/321–7628*) is the biggest consignment store in the desert, with a warehouse of furniture, fine art, china and crystal, accessories, jewelry, movie memorabilia, and exercise equipment. Prices are set to keep merchandise moving. It's closed Monday and Tuesday.

About 20 mi west of Palm Springs at the Cabazon exit of I–10 lies **Desert Hills Premium Outlets** (✉ *48400 Seminole Rd., Cabazon* ☎ *951/849–6641* ⊕ *www.premiumoutlets.com*), an outlet center with more than 130 brand-name discount fashion shops, among them J. Crew, Giorgio Armani, Gucci, and Prada.

CATHEDRAL CITY

2 mi southeast of Palm Springs on Hwy. 111.

One of the fastest-growing communities in the desert, Cathedral City is more residential than tourist-oriented. However, the city has a number of good restaurants and entertainment venues with moderate prices.

EXPLORING

Pickford Salon, a small museum inside the Mary Pickford Theater, showcases the life of the famed actress. On display is a selection of personal items contributed by family members, including her 1976 Oscar for contributions to the film industry, a gown she wore in the 1927 film

Dorothy Vernon of Haddon Hall, and dinnerware from Pickfair, Pickford's storied Beverly Hills mansion. One of the two biographical video presentations was produced by Mary herself. ⊠ *36-850 Pickfair St.* ☎ *760/328–7100* 🖘 *Free* ⊙ *Daily 10:30* AM*–midnight.*

☼ At **Boomers Camelot Park** you can play miniature golf, drive bumper boats, climb a rock wall, drive a go-kart, swing in the batting cages, test your skill in an arcade, and play video games. ⊠ *67–700 E. Palm Canyon Dr.* ☎ *760/770–7522* 🖘 *$5–$8 per activity, $28 day passes* ⊙ *Mon.–Thurs. noon–8, Fri. noon–10, Sat. 10–10, Sun. 10–8.*

WHERE TO EAT AND STAY

$$$

ITALIAN

✕ **Trilussa.** Locals gather at this San Francisco–style storefront restaurant for delicious food, big drinks, and a friendly welcome. The congenial bar is busy during happy hour (Monday to Thursday), after which diners drift to their nicely spaced tables indoors and out. The long menu changes daily, but staples include homemade pasta, risotto, veal, and fish. All come with an Italian accent. ⊠ *68718 Hwy. 111* ☎ *760/328– 2300* 🖃 *AE, D, DC, MC, V.*

¢ 🖫 **Quality Inn & Suites Date Palm.** This chain motel is about as close as you can get to Rancho Mirage without paying sky-high prices. Public areas are spacious, modern, and attractively appointed. Some accommodations here are cramped and appear well used, even though most are one- or two-bedroom suites. Noise can be a problem, because the motel is on busy Highway 111. **Pros:** good value; barbecues for guest use; suites. **Cons:** highway noise; low light levels. ⊠ *69–151 E. Palm Canyon Dr.* ☎ *760/324–5939 or 800/862–5085* ⊕ *www.choicehotels. com* 🖘 *21 rooms, 77 suites* ⌂ *In-room: a/c, kitchen (some), refrigerator, Wi-Fi. In-hotel: pool, laundry facilities, Wi-Fi hotspot, parking (free), some pets allowed* 🖃 *AE, D, DC, MC, V* ⍃◻⍄ *CP.*

DESERT HOT SPRINGS

9 mi north of Palm Springs on Gene Autry Trail.

Desert Hot Springs' famous hot mineral waters, thought by some to have curative powers, bubble up at temperatures of 90°F to 148°F and flow into the wells of more than 40 hotel spas.

WHERE TO STAY

$$$ 🖫 **The Spring.** This serious spa—designed for those who want to detox, lose weight, or take special treatments—caters to guests seeking quiet and personal service. Simply furnished rooms have modern decor; most open onto the pool and colorful flower gardens. In addition to the typical wraps, scrubs, and massages, the inn's spa menu offers treatments like the Splurge Back Facial, the 90-minute Spring Buff, and the Cranial Dreamwork massage. Spa packages, which include two nights' accommodations, Continental breakfast, and three hours of treatment, start at $715; day spa services, with two treatments, start at $110. **Pros:** European massage; colorful gardens; multiday fasting/cleansing retreats available. **Cons:** far from everything; dinner not available; adults only. ⊠ *12699 Reposo Way* ☎ *760/251–6700 or 877/200–2110* ⊕ *www.the-spring.com* 🖘 *12 rooms* ⌂ *In-room: a/c, no phone, kitchen (some),*

refrigerator, no TV, Wi-Fi. In-hotel: pool, spa, Wi-Fi hotspot, no kids under 18 ⊟ AE, D, MC, V.

RANCHO MIRAGE

4 mi southeast of Cathedral City on Hwy. 111.

Much of the scenery in exclusive Rancho Mirage is concealed behind the walls of gated communities and country clubs. The rich and famous live in estates and patronize elegant resorts and expensive restaurants. The city's golf courses host many high-profile tournaments. When the excesses of the luxe life become too much, the area's residents can check themselves into the Betty Ford Center, the famous drug-and-alcohol rehab center.

You can find some of the swankiest resorts in the desert here—plus great golf, and plenty of peace and quiet.

EXPLORING

The **Children's Discovery Museum of the Desert** contains instructive hands-on exhibits—a miniature rock-climbing area, a magnetic sculpture wall, make-it-and-take-it-apart projects, a rope maze—and an area for toddlers. Kids can paint a VW Bug, work as chefs in the museum's pizza parlor, and build pies out of arts and crafts supplies. ⊠ 71–701 Gerald Ford Dr. ☎ 760/321–0602 ⊕ www.cdmod.org ⊠ $8 ⊙ Jan.–Apr., daily 10–5; May–Dec., Tues.–Sun. 10–5.

WHERE TO EAT AND STAY

$$ X **Las Casuelas Nuevas.** Hundreds of artifacts from Guadalajara, Mexico,
MEXICAN lend festive charm to this casual restaurant, which has an expansive garden patio. Tamales and shellfish dishes are among the specialties. A special tequila menu lists dozens of aged and reserve selections, served by the shot or incorporated into one of the eatery's margaritas. There's live entertainment nightly. ⊠ 70-050 Hwy. 111 ☎ 760/328–8844 ⊕ www.lascasuelasnuevas.com ⊟ AE, D, MC, V.

$$ ☷ **Agua Caliente Casino, Resort & Spa.** This sparkling resort completes the Agua Caliente casino complex. Done in Las Vegas style, the casino is in the lobby. Once you get into the spacious, beautifully appointed rooms, all of the cacophony at the entrance is forgotten. Decor is a contemporary take on Arts and Crafts, with lots of white offset by dark wood. Niches hold original art, and high ceilings and wall-to-wall windows frame mountain views. Bathrooms have marble everywhere, flat-screen TVs, and oversize sunken tubs. There are two entertainment venues—a lounge and a showroom presenting headliners. Poolside cabanas push the concept to the limit; each has Wi-Fi, a phone, a TV, misters, ceiling fans, a mini-refrigerator, and available food and beverage service. **Pros:** gorgeous; excellent service; value priced. **Cons:** casino ambience; not appropriate for kids. ⊠ 32-250 Bob Hope Dr. ☎ 888/999–1995 ⊕ www.hotwatercasino.com ⋫ 340 rooms, 26 suites ⌂ In-room: a/c, refrigerator, DVD, Wi-Fi. In-hotel: 6 restaurants, room service, bars, pool, gym, spa, bicycles, laundry service, Internet terminal, Wi-Fi hotspot, parking (free) ⊟ AE, D, DC, MC, V.

$$$$ 🏨 **Rancho Las Palmas Resort & Spa.** This is the most family-friendly resort in the desert in the wake of a $35-million renovation that upgraded the entire 240-acre property, freshened rooms and public areas, and added Splashtopia. Kids and their parents can spend an entire day cruising the lazy river, crashing down two waterslides, and building sand castles on a beach. Rooms are in two-story Spanish-style buildings that surround courtyards and gardens; one section is primarily for families. French doors lead to balconies or patios where you can take in the mountain views or watch ducks cruising a pond in the fairway. The new spa has 26 treatment rooms as well as a private courtyard with a sanctuary pool. **Pros:** Kidtopia camp for kids; trails for hiking and jogging; nightly entertainment. **Cons:** second-floor rooms accessed by very steep stairs; golf course surrounds rooms; resort hosts conventions. ✉ *41-000 Bob Hope Dr.* ☎ *760/568–2727 or 866/423–1195* ⊕ *www.rancholaspalmas. com* ⏎ *422 room, 22 suites* ♿ *In-room: a/c, safe, refrigerator, Internet, Wi-Fi. In-hotel: 5 restaurants, room service, bar, golf course, tennis courts, pools, gym, spa, children's programs (ages 4–12), laundry service, Internet terminal, Wi-Fi hotspot, parking (free), some pets allowed* ▤ *AE, D, DC, MC, V.*

14

$$$ 🏨 **Westin Mission Hills Resort.** A sprawling resort on 360 acres, the Westin is surrounded by fairways, putting greens, and a collection of time-share accommodations. Rooms, in two-story buildings amid patios and fountains, have a stylish Arts-and-Crafts look with sleek, dark, mahogany furnishings accented with sand-color upholstery and crisp white linens. All have private patios or balconies. In the cool early morning, enjoy a walk or jog on the property's many paths, which wind past bougainvillea covered walls, beds planted with blue salvia and pink petunias, families of ducks, and a koi pond. There's also a lagoon-style swimming pool with a waterslide that's several stories high. **Pros:** gorgeous grounds; first-class golf facilities; excellent for families. **Cons:** lots of dogs; rooms are spread out. ✉ *71333 Dinah Shore Dr.* ☎ *760/328–5955 or 800/544–0287* ⊕ *www.westin.com* ⏎ *472 rooms, 30 suites* ♿ *In-room: a/c, safe, refrigerator (some), Internet, Wi-Fi. In-hotel: restaurants, room service, bar, golf courses, tennis courts, pools, gym, spa, children's programs (ages 5–12), Wi-Fi hotspot, parking (free), some pets allowed* ▤ *AE, D, MC, V.*

NIGHTLIFE

The elegant and surprisingly quiet **Agua Caliente Casino** (✉ *32–250 Bob Hope Dr.* ☎ *760/321–2000*) contains 1,600 slot machines, 48 table games, a high-limit room, and a no-smoking area, plus six restaurants and a food court. The Show, the resort's concert theater, features such headliners as Matchbox Twenty, Martina McBride, Tony Bennett, Jay Leno, as well as live sporting events.

SPORTS AND THE OUTDOORS

The best female golfers in the world compete in the LPGA **Kraft Nabisco Championship** (✉ *Mission Hills Country Club* ☎ *760/324–4546* ⊕ *www. kncgolf.com*) held in late March.

★ Of the two golf courses at the **Westin Mission Hills Resort Golf Club** (✉ *71–501 Dinah Shore Dr.* ☎ *760/328–3198* ⊕ *www.troongolf.com*), the

18-hole, par-70 Pete Dye course is especially noteworthy. The club plays host to a number of major tournaments, is a member of the Troon Golf Institute, and has several teaching facilities, including the Westin Mission Hills Resort Golf Academy and the *Golf Digest* Golf School. Greens fees are $145 during peak season, including a mandatory cart; off-season promotional packages sometimes run as low as $35.

SHOPPING

The **River at Rancho Mirage** (✉ *71-800 Hwy. 111* ☎ *760/341–2711*) is a shopping-dining-entertainment complex with a collection of 20 high-end shops. Bang & Olufsen, Borders Books & Music, Cohiba Cigar Lounge, Tulip Hill Winery tasting room, and other shops front a faux river with cascading waterfalls. The complex includes a 12-screen cinema, an outdoor amphitheater, and seven restaurants, including Flemings Prime Steakhouse and P.F. Chang's.

PALM DESERT

2 mi southeast of Rancho Mirage on Hwy. 111.

Palm Desert is a thriving retail and business community, with some of the desert's most popular restaurants, private and public golf courses, and premium shopping.

EXPLORING

★ West of and parallel to Highway 111, **El Paseo** (✉ *Between Monterey and Portola Aves.* ☎ *877/735–7273* ⊕ *www.elpaseo.com*) is a mile-long Mediterranean-style avenue with fountains and courtyards, French and Italian fashion boutiques, shoe salons, jewelry stores, children's shops, 23 restaurants, and nearly 20 art galleries. The pretty strip is a pleasant place to stroll, window-shop, people-watch, and exercise your credit cards. Each October, the **Palm Desert Golf Cart Parade** (☎ *760/346–6111* ⊕ *www.golfcartparade.com*) launches the "season" with a procession of 100 golf carts decked out as floats buzzing up and down El Paseo.

☾ Come eyeball-to-eyeball with wolves, coyotes, mountain lions, chee-
★ tahs, bighorn sheep, golden eagles, warthogs, and owls at the **Living Desert**. Easy to challenging scenic trails traverse 1,200 acres of desert preserve populated with plants of the Mojave, Colorado, and Sonoran deserts in 11 habitats. But in recent years, the park has expanded its vision to Africa. At the 3-acre African WaTuTu village, there's a traditional marketplace as well as camels, leopards, hyenas, and other African animals. Children can pet African domestic animals, including goats and guinea fowl, in a petting kraal. Gecko Gulch is a children's playground with crawl-through underground tunnels and climb-on snake sculptures. Yet another exhibit demonstrates the path of the San Andreas Fault across the Coachella Valley. The Tennity Amphitheater stages daily wildlife shows, and "Wildlights," an evening light show, takes place during the winter holidays. ■TIP➔ A garden center sells native desert flora, much of which is unavailable elsewhere. ✉ *47-900 Portola Ave.* ☎ *760/346–5694* ⊕ *www.livingdesert.org* ☙ *Mid-June–*

Aug. $9.50, Sept.–mid-June $12.50
⊘ Mid-June–Aug., daily 8–1:30;
Sept.–mid-June, daily 9–5.

The **Santa Rosa Mountains/San Jacinto National Monument**, administered by the Bureau of Land Management, protects Peninsula bighorn sheep and other wildlife on 272,000 acres of desert habitat. For an introduction to the site, stop by the visitor center—staffed by knowledgeable volunteers—for a look at exhibits illustrating the natural history of the desert. A landscaped garden displays native plants and frames a sweeping view. ⊠ *51-500 Hwy. 74* ☎ *760/862–9984* ⊕ *www.ca.blm. gov/palmsprings* 🎫 *Free* ⊘ *Daily 9–4.*

WHERE TO EAT AND STAY

$$$$
FRENCH
★
✕ **Cuistot.** The creation of chef-owner Bernard Dervieux, Cuistot is a big, bright, airy reproduction of a rustic French farmhouse on El Paseo's west end. The menu lists quail stuffed with sweetbreads, along with such signature dishes as skillet-roasted veal chop with mushrooms and roasted garlic, fresh Dover sole with hazelnut-lemon sauce, and Mediterranean vegetable tajine. Fashion shows are presented nearly every afternoon at lunchtime. ⊠ *72-595 El Paseo* ☎ *760/340–1000* ⊕ *www. cuistotrestaurant.com* ⟍ *Reservations essential* ☰ *AE, D, MC, V* ⊘ *Closed Mon. and July and Aug. No lunch Sun.*

$$$
SEAFOOD
✕ **Pacifica Seafood.** Sublime seafood, rooftop dining, and reduced-price sunset dinners draw locals to this busy restaurant tucked into a second-floor corner of the Gardens of El Paseo. The stars of such dishes as honey-glazed Chilean sea bass, black tiger shrimp, and swordfish arrive daily from San Diego; a small selection of beef and chicken rounds out the menu. Preparations feature sauces such as orange-cumin glaze, Szechuan peppercorn butter, and green curry-coconut. Servers are pleasant and knowledgeable. ⊠ *73505 El Paseo* ☎ *760/674–8666* ⊕ *www.pacificaseafoodrestaurant.com* ⟍ *Reservations essential* ☰ *AE, D, MC, V.*

$$$$
🏨 **Desert Springs J. W. Marriott Resort and Spa.** This sprawling convention-oriented hotel set on 450 landscaped acres has a dramatic U-shape design. The building wraps around the desert's largest private lake, into which an indoor, stair-stepped waterfall flows. Rooms in the main building wrap around the lobby; some have lake or Santa Rosa Mountains views, balconies, and oversize bathrooms. It's a long walk from the lobby to the rooms; if you're driving, you might want to request a room close to the parking lot. **Pros:** gondola rides to restaurants; caters to families; lobby bar is a popular watering hole. **Cons:** crowded in season; rooms and facilities are spread out; business traveler vibe. ⊠ *74-855 Country Club Dr.* ☎ *760/341–2211 or 800/331–3112* ⊕ *www.*

desertspringsresort.com ⟲ *833 rooms, 51 suites* ♨ *In-room: a/c, safe, refrigerator, Internet, Wi-Fi. In-hotel: 4 restaurants, room service, bars, golf courses, tennis courts, pools, gym, spa, children's programs (ages 4–12), laundry service, Wi-Fi hotspot, parking (paid)* ▤ *AE, D, DC, MC, V.*

THE ARTS

McCallum Theatre (⊠ *73-000 Fred Waring Dr.* ☎ *760/340–2787* ⊕ *www. mccallumtheatre.com*), the principal cultural venue in the desert, presents film, classical and popular music, opera, ballet, and theater.

SPORTS AND THE OUTDOORS

BALLOONING **Fantasy Balloon Flights** (⊠ *74-181 Parosella St.* ☎ *760/568–0997* ⊕ *www. fantasyballoonflights.com*) operates sunrise excursions over the southern end of the Coachella Valley. Flights ($185 per person) run from an hour to an hour and a half, followed by a traditional champagne toast.

BICYCLING **Big Wheel Bike Tours** (☎ *760/779–1837* ⊕ *www.bwbtours.com*) delivers rental mountain, three-speed, and tandem bikes to area hotels. The company also conducts full- and half-day escorted on- and off-road bike tours throughout the area, starting at about $75 per person.

GOLF **Desert Willow Golf Resort** (⊠ *38-500 Portola Ave.* ☎ *760/346–7060* ⊕ *www.desertwillow.com*) has been praised for its environmentally smart design, which features pesticide-free and water-thrifty turf grasses. The clubhouse holds a display of contemporary art, including an original blown glass chandelier by Dale Chihuly. The public course, managed by the City of Palm Desert, has two challenging 18-hole links. The greens fee is $145, including cart.

INDIAN WELLS

5 mi east of Palm Desert on Hwy. 111.

For the most part a quiet residential community, Indian Wells is the site of golf and tennis tournaments throughout the year, including the BNP Paribus Open tennis tournament. The city has three hotels that share access to city-owned championship golf and tennis facilities.

WHERE TO EAT AND STAY

$$$$ ✕**Sirocco.** This family-run restaurant in the Renaissance Esmeralda
ITALIAN hotel is one of the best in the desert, a local choice for special occa-
★ sions or entertaining important clients. "If you don't see what you want on the menu, just ask for it," urges chef-owner Livio Massignani, who offers to set up customized tasting menus from the extensive Italian list that includes Dungeness crab cakes, aged prime beef carpaccio, lamb marsala, and stuffed veal chop. An extensive wine list offers a wide selection of hard-to-find Italian vintages and selections from the best California wineries. The dining room has floor-to-ceiling windows that reveal a view of fountains rising alongside the building against a golf course background. ⊠ *44-400 Indian Wells La.* ☎ *760/773–4444* ♨ *Reservations essential* ▤ *AE, D, DC, MC, V* ☉ *No lunch.*

$$$ ⊞ **Hyatt Grand Champions Resort.** This stark-white resort on 34 acres is one of the grandest in the desert. Standard rooms, large even by local standards, come with furnished patios or balconies and separate living

and sleeping areas; they're decorated in soft sea grass and white. Private villas have secluded garden courtyards with outdoor whirlpool tubs, living rooms with fireplaces, dining rooms, and private butlers who attend to your every whim. There are 16 pools on the property, including an adults-only pool and one designed especially for families. Despite all of its resorty trappings, the Hyatt actually caters to business travelers, not vacationers. **Pros:** spacious rooms; excellent business services. **Cons:** big and impersonal; spread out over many acres; noisy public areas. ⊠ *44-600 Indian Wells La.* ☎ *760/341–1000 or 800/552–4386* ⊕ *www. grandchampions.hyatt.com* 🛏 *426 rooms, 54 suites* ♿ *In-room: a/c, safe, refrigerator, Wi-Fi. In-hotel: 4 restaurants, room service, bars, golf courses, tennis courts, pools, gym, spa, bicycles, children's programs (ages 3–12), laundry service, parking (free)* ▭ *AE, D, DC, MC, V.*

$$$$ 🏨 **Miramonte Resort & Spa.** A warm bit of Tuscany against a backdrop
★ of the Santa Rosa Mountains characterizes the smallest, most intimate, and most opulent of the Indian Wells hotels. Guest rooms, with lavish appointments (especially in the bathrooms) are in red-roofed villas on 11 acres of bougainvillea-filled gardens. Many have private patios or balconies with views of perfectly manicured, brilliantly colored gardens. Reading nooks and hammocks are tucked into secluded corners. The resort holds one of the best spas in the desert: although small, The Well offers guests intimate indulgence and tranquillity in relaxation suites, mud bars, and river benches. Guests may use facilities at the Indian Wells Golf and Tennis Center. **Pros:** romantic intimacy; gorgeous gardens; discreet service. **Cons:** adult-oriented; limited resort facilities on-site. ⊠ *45-000 Indian Wells La.* ☎ *760/341–2200* ⊕ *www. miramonteresort.com* 🛏 *215 rooms* ♿ *In-room: a/c, safe, refrigerator, DVD (some), Wi-Fi. In-hotel: 2 restaurants, room service, bars, golf course, tennis courts, pools, gym, spa, bicycles, laundry service, Wi-Fi hotspot, parking (free), some pets allowed* ▭ *AE, D, DC, MC, V.*

$$$$ 🏨 **Renaissance Esmeralda Resort and Spa.** The centerpiece of this luxuri-
☾ ous resort is an eight-story atrium lobby, to which most rooms open. There's soothing water everywhere: pools, ponds, lakes, fountains, and streams. Rooms are bright and airy, with ample balconies affording pool or mountain views. They're decorated in dark wood and sand tones, furnished with work desks, chaise lounges, and oversize marble bathrooms with clear glass showers. Although the hotel is popular with business travelers, it's also very family friendly. One of the pools has a sandy beach that kids love. **Pros:** balcony views; adjacent to golf-tennis complex; bicycles. **Cons:** higher noise level in rooms surrounding pool; somewhat impersonal ambience. ⊠ *44-400 Indian Wells La.* ☎ *760/773–4444 or 800/214–5540* ⊕ *www.renaissanceesmeralda.com* 🛏 *538 rooms, 22 suites* ♿ *In-room: a/c, safe, refrigerator, Internet, Wi-Fi. In-hotel: 5 restaurants, room service, bars, golf courses, tennis courts, pools, gym, spa, bicycles, children's programs (ages 5–12), laundry service, Wi-Fi hotspot, parking (free)* ▭ *AE, D, DC, MC, V.*

SPORTS AND THE OUTDOORS

GOLF Adjacent to the Hyatt Grand Champions Resort, the **Golf Resort at Indian Wells** (⊠ *44-500 Indian Wells La.* ☎ *760/346–4653*) has two 18-hole Ted Robinson–designed championship courses: the 6,500-yard West

Course and the 6,700-yard East Course. A public course, it has been named one of the country's top 10 resorts by *Golf Magazine*. Monday through Thursday the green fee is $145; Friday through Sunday it's $155 (fees may be deeply discounted in summer). The resort also offers instruction through the Indian Wells Golf School.

TENNIS The **BNP Paribas Open** (☎ *800/999–1585 for tickets* ⊕ *www.bnpparibasopen.org*) tennis tournament draws 200 of the world's top players to the Indian Wells Tennis Garden for two weeks in March. With more than 16,000 seats, the stadium is the second largest in the nation.

LA QUINTA

4 mi south of Indian Wells via Washington St.

The desert became a Hollywood hideout in the 1920s, when La Quinta Hotel (now La Quinta Resort) opened, introducing the Coachella Valley's first golf course. The opening of Old Town La Quinta in 2004 changed the once-quiet atmosphere of this community. A popular attraction, the complex holds dining spots, shops, and galleries.

WHERE TO EAT AND STAY

$$$ ✗ **Arnold Palmer's.** From the photos on the walls to the trophy-filled dis-
AMERICAN play cases to the putting green for diners awaiting a table, Arnie's image fills this restaurant. It's a big, clubby place where families gather for birthdays and Sunday dinners, and the service is attentive and knowledgeable. Don't eat too many of the addictive house-made potato chips with blue cheese sauce before you dive into the barbecued pork ribs, fillet with béarnaise sauce, certified Angus beef, or seared scallops. And save room for the splendid desserts, which range from Coachella date bread pudding to grasshopper ice-cream sandwiches. Arnie's Pub offers a more limited menu of burgers, fish and chips, and shrimp tacos. There's entertainment most nights. ⊠ *78-164 Ave. 52* ☎ *760/771–4653* ⊕ *arnoldparlmers.net* ⌂ *Reservations essential* ⊟ *AE, D, MC, V* ⊘ *No lunch.*

$$$ ✗ **Hog's Breath Inn.** Clint Eastwood watches over this replica of his Hog's
AMERICAN Breath restaurant in Carmel, his presence felt in the larger-than-life photos that fill the walls of its bright dining room. The menu lists a large selection of American comfort food ranging from barbecued baby back ribs to sole stuffed with crab and shrimp to the Dirty Harry dinner: chopped sirloin with capers and mashed potatoes. ⊠ *78-065 Main St.* ☎ *760/564–5556 or 866/464–7888* ⊟ *AE, D, MC, V.*

$$$ 🗈 **La Quinta Resort and Club.** Opened in 1926 (and now a member of the Waldorf-Astoria Collection), the desert's oldest resort is a lush green oasis set on 45 acres. Broad expanses of lawn separate the adobe casitas that house some historic rooms; other rooms, decorated in early-California style with wrought iron, tile, and dark woods, are in newer two-story units surrounding individual swimming pools and hot tubs amid brilliant gardens. Fireplaces, stocked refrigerators, and fruit-laden orange trees contribute to a luxurious ambience. A premium is placed on privacy, which accounts for La Quinta's continuing popularity with Hollywood celebrities. You can play on the championship golf courses either at La Quinta or at the adjacent PGA West. The tennis stadium holds 23 courts. Celebrity chef Jimmy Schmidt opened Morgan's in

the Desert here in 2009, offering locally grown produce on a small- and large-plate menu that drew raves at the Rattlesnake Club. **Pros:** individual swimming pools; gorgeous gardens; best golf courses in the desert. **Cons:** a party atmosphere sometimes prevails; spotty housekeeping/maintenance. ⊠ 49-499 Eisenhower Dr. ☎ 760/564–4111 or 800/598–3828 ⊕ www.laquintaresort.com ☞ 640 rooms, 244 suites ◊ In-room: a/c, safe, refrigerator (some), Internet. In-hotel: 7 restaurants, room service, bar, golf courses, tennis courts, pools, gym, spa, Wi-Fi hotspot, parking (free), some pets allowed ☰ AE, D, DC, MC, V.

THE FIRST CELEBRITY HOTEL

Frank Capra probably started the trend when he booked a casita at the then-new, very remote La Quinta Hotel (now Resort) to write the script for the movie *It Happened One Night*. The movie went on to earn an Academy Award, and Capra continued to book that room whenever he had some writing to do. A long line of Hollywood stars followed Capra's example over the years; the current list includes Oprah Winfrey, Adam Sandler, and Christina Aguilera.

14

SPORTS AND THE OUTDOORS

★ **PGA West** (⊠ 49-499 Eisenhower Dr. ☎ 760/564–5729 for tee times ⊕ www.pgawest.com) operates three 18-hole, par-72 championship courses and provides instruction and golf clinics. Greens fees (which include a mandatory cart) range from $50 on weekdays in summer to $235 on weekends in February and March. Bookings are accepted 30 days in advance, but prices are lower when you book close to the date you need.

INDIO

5 mi east of Indian Wells on Hwy. 111.

Indio is the home of the date shake, which is exactly what it sounds like: a delicious, extremely thick milk shake made with dates. The city and surrounding countryside generate 95% of the dates grown and harvested in the United States. If you take a hot-air balloon ride, you will likely drift over the tops of date palm trees.

EXPLORING

Displays at the **Coachella Valley History Museum**, in a former farmhouse, explain how dates are harvested and how the desert is irrigated for date farming. On the grounds you'll find a restored 1909 schoolhouse and displays depicting Native American and pioneer life. ⊠ 82-616 Miles Ave. ☎ 760/342–6651 ☞ $3 ☼ Oct.–May, Thurs.–Sat. 10–4, Sun. 1–4.

You can learn about date production at the 175-acre palm arboretum and orchard at **Oasis Date Gardens**. Discover how dates are pollinated, grown, sorted, stored, and packed for shipping. ⊠ 59-111 Grapefruit Blvd., Thermal ☎ 800/827–8017 ⊕ oasisdategardens.com ☞ Free ☼ Presentations daily 10:30 and 2:30.

Indio celebrates its raison d'être each February at the **National Date Festival and Riverside County Fair.** The midmonth festivities include an Arabian Nights pageant, camel and ostrich races, and exhibits of local dates. Admission includes camel rides. ✉ *Riverside County Fairgrounds, 46-350 Arabia St.* ☎ *800/811–3247* ⊕ *www.datefest. org* 🖾 *$8.*

WHERE TO EAT AND STAY

$$

ITALIAN

✗ **Ciro's Ristorante and Pizzeria.** This popular casual restaurant has been serving pizza and pasta since the 1970s. The menu lists some unusual pizzas, such as cashew with three cheeses. Daily pasta specials vary but might include red- or white-clam sauce or scallops with parsley and red wine. ✉ *81-963 Hwy. 111* ☎ *760/347–6503* ⊕ *www.cirospasta.com* 🖃 *AE, D, MC, V* ⊗ *No lunch Sun.*

$$$

🖾 **Fantasy Springs Resort Casino.** This family-oriented resort casino, operated by the Cabazon Band of Mission Indians, is the tallest building in the Coachella Valley, affording mountain views from most rooms and the rooftop bar. Rooms are appointed in dark-wood Arts-and-Crafts style. Many have balconies overlooking the pool area, which has not only a free-form pool with a sandy beach at one end but also fountains and waterfalls adjacent to a grassy area where families are welcome to picnic. The casino provides Las Vegas–style gaming and has an outpost of the Improv comedy club. The casual Pom restaurant offers Tuesday night barbecue. **Pros:** big-name entertainment; great views from the rooftop bar; bowling alley. **Cons:** in the middle of nowhere; average service. ✉ *84-245 Indio Springs Pkwy.* ☎ *760/342–5000 or 800/827–2946* ⊕ *www.fantasyspringsresort.com* ⇨ *240 rooms, 11 suites* ⚒ *In-room: a/c, safe, refrigerator (some), DVD (some), Wi-Fi. In-hotel: 7 restaurants, room service, bars, golf course, pools, gym, parking (free), Wi-Fi hotspot* 🖃 *AE, D, MC, V.*

EN ROUTE For a glimpse of how the desert appeared before development, head northeast from Palm Springs to **Coachella Valley Preserve** (✉ *From Ramon Rd. exit off I–10, drive east to Thousand Palm Canyon Dr., turn north, and continue 2 mi*). The preserve has a system of sand dunes and several palm oases that were formed because the San Andreas Fault lines here allow water flowing underground to rise to the surface. A mile-long walk along Thousand Palms Oasis reveals pools supporting the tiny endangered desert pupfish and more than 183 bird species. Managed by the Nature Conservancy, the preserve has a visitor center, nature and equestrian trails, restrooms, and picnic facilities. Note that it is exceptionally hot in summer. **Covered Wagon Tours** (✉ *East end of Ramon Rd.* ☎ *760/347–2161 or 800/367–2161* ⊕ *www.coveredwagontours. com*) can take you on a two- or four-hour tour of the Coachella Valley

---

ROCKIN' AT COACHELLA

The Coachella Valley Music and Arts Festival, one of the biggest parties in SoCal, draws hundreds of thousands of rock music fans to Indio for three days of live concerts and dancing each April. Hundreds of bands show up, including headliners such as Jack Johnson, the Raconteurs, Portishead, Roger Waters, and My Morning Jacket. Everybody camps at the Polo Grounds. Visit ⊕ *www.coachella. com* for details and tickets.

Preserve via mule-drawn covered wagon October through May. Schedule your visit with or without a cookout and entertainment at the end of the journey.

ALONG TWENTYNINE PALMS HIGHWAY

YUCCA VALLEY

30 mi northeast of Palm Springs on Hwy. 62, Twentynine Palms Hwy.

One of the fastest-growing cities in the high desert, Yucca Valley is emerging as a bedroom community for people who work as far away as Ontario, 85 mi to the west. In this sprawling suburb you can shop for necessities, get your car serviced, and chow down at the fast-food outlets.

EXPLORING

The **Hi-Desert Nature Museum** has a small live-animal display containing creatures that make their homes in Joshua Tree National Park (⇨ *see Chapter 15*), including scorpions, snakes, ground squirrels, and chuckwallas, a type of lizard. There are also a collection of rocks, minerals, and fossils from the Paleozoic era, a collection of Native American artifacts, and a children's room. ⊠ *57-116 Twentynine Palms Hwy.* ☎ *760/369-7212* ⊕ *www.highdesertnaturemuseum.org* ⊠ *Free* ☉ *Tues.–Sun. 10–5.*

In 1946 Roy Rogers, Gene Autry, the Sons of the Pioneers (the music group for whom the town is named), and Russ Hayden built **Pioneertown** (⊠ *Pioneertown Rd., 4 mi north of Yucca Valley* ⊕ *www.pioneertown. com*), an 1880s-style Wild West movie set complete with hitching posts, saloon, and an OK Corral. Today 250 people call the place home, even as film crews continue shooting. You can stroll past wooden and adobe storefronts and feel like you're back in the Old West. The owners of Pappy & Harriet's have an outdoor concert venue for about 500 people where they present popular bands and singers. Gunfights are staged April through October, weekends at 2:30.

WHERE TO EAT AND STAY

$$ ✕**Pappy & Harriet's Pioneertown Palace.** Smack in the middle of a Western-movie-set town is this Western-movie-set saloon where you can
AMERICAN have dinner, dance to live country-and-western music, or just relax with a drink at the bar. The food ranges from Tex-Mex to Santa Maria barbecue to steak and burgers—no surprises but plenty of fun. ■TIP➔ Pappy & Harriet's may be in the middle of nowhere, but you'll need reservations for dinner on weekends. ⊠ *53688 Pioneertown Rd., Pioneertown* ☎ *760/365-5956* ⊕ *www.pappyandharriets.com* ⊟ *AE, D, MC, V* ☉ *Closed Tues. and Wed.*

$ ⊞ **Best Western Yucca Valley Hotel & Suites.** Opened in 2008, this hotel is a welcome addition to the slim pickings near Joshua Tree National Park (⇨ *see Chapter 15*). Rooms are spacious, nicely appointed, and decorated in soft desert colors. There are two sections: one is exclusively extended-stay while the other is for short-term guests. Continental breakfast, served in the parlor, is included in the price. **Pros:** convenient to Joshua Tree NP; pleasant lounge. **Cons:** location on busy highway; limited service. ✉ *56525 Twentynine Palms Hwy.* ☎ *760/365–3555* ⊕ *www.bestwestern.com* ↻ *95 rooms* ⚇ *In-room: a/c, safe, kitchen (some), refrigerator (some), Wi-Fi. In-hotel: pool, gym, laundry facilities, Internet terminal, Wi-Fi hotspot, parking (free)* ☰ *AE, D, DC, MC, V* ◎ *CP.*

TWENTYNINE PALMS

24 mi east of Yucca Valley on Hwy. 62, Twentynine Palms Hwy.

The main gateway town to Joshua Tree National Park (⇨ *see Chapter 15*), Twentynine Palms is also the location of the U.S. Marine Air Ground Task Force Training Center. You can find services, supplies, and limited lodgings in town.

ESSENTIALS

Visitor Information Twentynine Palms Chamber of Commerce and Visitor Center (✉ *73491 Twentynine Palms Hwy., Twentynine Palms* ☎ *760/367–3445* ⊕ *www.visit29.org*).

The history and current life of Twentynine Palms is depicted in **Oasis of Murals,** a collection of 20 murals painted on the sides of buildings. If you drive around town, you can't miss the murals, but you can also pick up a free map from the Twentynine Palms Chamber of Commerce. **29 Palms Art Gallery** (✉ *74055 Cottonwood Dr.* ☎ *760/367–7819* ⊕ *www.29palmsartgallery.com* ☉ *Wed.–Sun. noon–3*) features work by local painters, sculptors, and jewelry makers who find inspiration in the desert landscape.

WHERE TO STAY

$$ 🏨 **29 Palms Inn.** The funky 29 Palms is the lodging closest to the entrance to Joshua Tree National Park (⇨ *see Chapter 15*). The collection of adobe and wood-frame cottages, some dating back to the 1920s and 1930s, is scattered over 70 acres of grounds that are popular with birds and bird-watchers year-round. Innkeeper Jane Smith's warm, personal service more than makes up for the cottages' rustic qualities. Ranging from pasta to seafood, the contemporary fare at the inn's convivial restaurant ($$) is more sophisticated than its Old West appearance might suggest. **Pros:** gracious hospitality; exceptional bird-watching; popular with artists. **Cons:** rustic accommodations; limited amenities. ✉ *73-950 Inn Ave.* ☎ *760/367–3505* ⊕ *www.29palmsinn.com* ↻ *18 rooms, 5 suites* ⚇ *In-room: no phone, a/c (some). In-hotel: restaurant, pool, Wi-Fi hotspot, some pets allowed, parking (free)* ☰ *AE, D, MC, V* ◎ *CP.*

$$ 🏨 **Roughley Manor.** To the wealthy pioneer who erected the stone man-
★ sion now occupied by this B&B, expense was no object. A 50-foot-long planked maple floor is the pride of the great room, the carpentry on the walls throughout is intricate, and huge stone fireplaces warm the house on the rare cold night. Original fixtures still gleam in the bathrooms, and bedrooms hold pencil and canopy beds and some fireplaces. The innkeepers serve afternoon tea and evening dessert. An acre of gardens shaded by Washingtonia palms surrounds the house. **Pros:** elegant

rooms and public spaces; good stargazing in the gazebo; great horned owls on property. **Cons:** somewhat isolated location; three-story main building doesn't have an elevator. ✉ *74-744 Joe Davis Rd.* ☎ *760/367–3238* ⊕ *www.roughleymanor.com* ⤴ *2 suites, 7 cottages* ♿ *In-room: no phone, a/c, kitchen (some), refrigerator. In-hotel: pool, Wi-Fi hotspot, some pets allowed* ⊟ *DC, MC, V* ⊣◎⊢ *BP.*

ANZA-BORREGO DESERT

Largely uninhabited, the Anza-Borrego Desert is popular with those who love solitude, silence, space, starry nights, light, and sweeping vistas. The desert lies south of the Palm Springs area, stretching along the western shore of the Salton Sea down toward Interstate 8 along the Mexican border. Isolated from the rest of California by mile-high mountains to the north and west, most of this desert falls within the borders of Anza-Borrego Desert State Park, which at more than 600,000 acres is the largest state park in the contiguous United States. This is a place where you can escape the cares of the human world.

For thousands of years Native Americans of the Cahuilla and Kumeyaay people inhabited this area, spending their winters on the warm desert floor and their summers in the mountains. The first Europeans—a party led by Spanish explorer Juan Baptiste de Anza—crossed this desert in 1776. Anza, for whom the desert is named, made the trip through here twice. Roadside signs along highways 86, 78, and S2 mark the route of the Anza expedition, which spent Christmas Eve 1776 in what is now Anza-Borrego Desert State Park. Seventy-five years later thousands of immigrants on their way to the goldfields up north crossed the desert on the Southern Immigrant Trail, remnants of which remain along Highway S2. Permanent settlers arrived early in the 20th century, and by the 1930s the first adobe resort cottage had been built.

BORREGO SPRINGS

59 mi south of Indio via Hwys. 86 and S22.

The permanent population of Borrego Springs, set squarely in the middle of Anza-Borrego Desert State Park, hovers around 2,500. Long a quiet town, it's emerging as a laid-back destination for desert lovers. September through June, when temperatures stay in the 80s and 90s, you can engage in outdoor activities such as hiking, nature study, golf, tennis, horseback riding, and mountain biking. If winter rains cooperate, Borrego Springs puts on some of the best wildflower displays in the low desert. In some years the desert floor is carpeted with color: yellow dandelions and sunflowers, pink primrose, purple sand verbena, and blue phacelia. The bloom generally runs from late February through April. For current information on wildflowers around Borrego Springs, call Anza-Borrego Desert State Park's wildflower hotline (☎ 760/767–4684).

If you think the desert is just a sandy wasteland, the stark beauty of the Anza-Borrego Desert will shock you.

ESSENTIALS
EXPLORING
Visitor Information Borrego Springs Chamber of Commerce (✉ *786 Palm Canyon Dr., Borrego Springs* ☎ *760/767–5555 or 800/559–5524* ⊕ *www. borregosprings.org*).

Flowers aren't the only thing popping up from the earth in Borrego Springs. At **Galleta Meadows** (✉ *Borrego Springs Rd. from Christmas Circle to Henderson Canyon* ☎ *760/767–5555* ⊕ *www.galletameadows. com* ☒ *Free*) camels, llamas, sabre-toothed tigers, tortoises, and monumental gomphotherium (a sort of ancient elephant) appear to roam the earth again. These life-size bronze figures are of prehistoric animals whose fossils can be found in the Borrego Badlands. The collection, currently more than 50 sets of animals and growing, is the project of a wealthy Borrego Springs resident who is installing the works of art on property he owns for the entertainment of locals and visitors. Maps are available from Borrego Springs Chamber of Commerce.

★ One of the richest living natural-history museums in the nation, **Anza-Borrego Desert State Park** is a vast, nearly uninhabited wilderness where you can step through a field of wildflowers, cool off in a palm-shaded oasis, count zillions of stars in the black night sky, and listen to coyotes howl at dusk. The landscape, largely undisturbed by humans, reveals a rich natural history. There's evidence of a vast inland sea in the piles of oyster beds near Split Mountain and of the power of natural forces such as earthquakes and flash floods. In addition, recent scientific work has confirmed that the Borrego Badlands, with more than 6,000 meters of exposed fossil-bearing sediments, is likely the richest such deposit in

North America, telling the story of 7 million years of climate change, upheaval, and prehistoric animals. They've found evidence of saber-tooth cats, flamingos, zebras, and the largest flying bird in the northern hemisphere beneath the now-parched sand. Today the desert's most treasured inhabitants are the herds of elusive and endangered native bighorn sheep, or *borrego*, for which the park is named. Among the strange desert plants you may observe are the gnarly elephant trees. As these are endangered, rangers don't encourage visitors to seek out the secluded grove at Fish Creek, but there are a few examples at the visitor center garden. After a wet winter you can see a short-lived but stunning display of cacti, succulents, and desert wildflowers in bloom.

Anza-Borrego Desert State Park is unusually accessible to visitors. Admission to the park is free, and few areas are off-limits. Unlike most parks in the country, Anza-Borrego lets you camp anywhere; just follow the trails and pitch a tent wherever you like. There are more than 500 mi of dirt roads, two huge wilderness areas, and 110 mi of riding and hiking trails. Many of the park's sites can be seen from paved roads, but some require driving on dirt roads, for which rangers recommend you use a four-wheel-drive vehicle. When you do leave the pavement, carry the appropriate supplies: a cell phone (which may be unreliable in some areas), a shovel and other tools, flares, blankets, and plenty of water. The canyons are susceptible to flash flooding, so inquire about weather conditions (even on sunny days) before entering.

To get oriented and obtain information on weather and wildlife conditions, stop by the **Visitors Information Center.** Designed to keep cool during the desert's blazing hot summers, the center is built underground, beneath a demonstration desert garden. A nature trail here takes you through a garden containing examples of most of the native flora and a little pupfish pond. ■**TIP➔** Borrego resorts, restaurants, and the state park have Wi-Fi, but the service is spotty at best. If you need to talk to someone in the area, it's best to find a phone with a landline. ⊠ *200 Palm Canyon Dr., Hwy. S22* ☎ *760/767–5311, 760/767–4684 wildflower hotline* ⊕ *www.parks.ca.gov* ⊠ *Free* ☉ *Thurs.–Mon. 9–5.*

At **Borrego Palm Canyon** (⊠ *Palm Canyon Dr., Hwy. S22, about 1 mi west of the Visitors Information Center*), a 1.5-mi trail leads to one of the few native palm groves in North America. There are more than 1,000 native fan palms in the grove, and a stream and waterfall greet you at trail's end. The moderate hike is the most popular in the park.

Yaqui Well Nature Trail (⊠ *Hwy. 78, across from Tamarisk Campground*) takes you along a path to a desert water hole where birds and wildlife are abundant. It's also a good place to look for wildflowers in spring.

Coyote Canyon (⊠ *Off DiGiorgio Rd., 4½ mi north of Borrego Springs*) has a year-round stream and lush plant life, making it one of the best places to see and photograph spring wildflowers. Portions of the canyon road follow a section of the old Anza Trail. The canyon is closed between June 15 and September 15 to allow native bighorn sheep undisturbed use of the water. The dirt road that gives access to the canyon may be sandy enough to require a four-wheel-drive vehicle.

The late-afternoon vista of the Borrego badlands from **Font's Point** (⊠ *Off Borrego Salton Seaway, Hwy. S22, 13 mi east of Borrego Springs*) is one of the most breathtaking views seen in the desert, especially when the setting sun casts a golden glow in high relief on the eroded mountain slopes. The road from the Font's Point turnoff can be rough enough to make using a four-wheel-drive vehicle advisable; inquire about its condition at the visitor center before starting out. Even if you can't make it out on the paved road, you can see some of the view from the highway.

Narrows Earth Trail (⊠ *Off Hwy. 78, 13 mi west of Borrego Springs*) is a short walk off the road east of Tamarisk Grove campground. Along the way you can see evidence of the many geologic processes involved in forming the canyons of the desert, such as a contact zone between two earthquake faults, and sedimentary layers of metamorphic and igneous rock.

Geology students from all over the world visit the Fish Creek area of Anza-Borrego to explore a canyon known as **Split Mountain** (⊠ *Split Mountain Rd., 9 mi south of Hwy. 78, at Ocotillo Wells*). The narrow gorge with 600-foot walls was formed by an ancient stream. Fossils in this area indicate that a sea once covered the desert floor.

The easy, mostly flat **Pictograph/Smuggler's Canyon Trail** (⊠ *Blair Valley, Hwy. S2, 6 mi southeast of Hwy. 78, at Scissors Crossing intersection*) traverses a boulder-strewn trail. At the end is a collection of rocks covered with muted red and yellow pictographs painted within the last hundred years or so by Native Americans. Walk about ½ mi beyond the pictures to reach Smuggler's Canyon, where an overlook provides views of the Vallecito Valley. The hike is 2 to 3 mi round-trip.

Just a few steps off the paved road, **Carrizo Badlands Overlook** (⊠ *Off Hwy. S2, 40 mi south of Scissors Crossing [intersection of Hwys. S2 and 78]*) offers a view of eroded and twisted sedimentary rock that obscures the fossils of the mastodons, saber-tooths, zebras, and camels that roamed this region a million years ago. The route to the overlook through Earthquake Valley and Blair Valley parallels the Southern Emigrant Trail.

WHERE TO EAT AND STAY

$$
AMERICAN
✕ **The Arches.** Set right on the edge of the Borrego Springs Golf Course, beneath a canopy of grapefruit trees this is one of the most pleasant dining options in the area. You'll find abundant options at every meal starting with the breakfast buffet. Dinner selections range from prime rib to salmon and shellfish, plus some entrée-size composed salads and chicken potpie. ⊠ *1112 Tilting T Dr.* ☎ *760/767–5700* ▭ *AE, MC, V* ⊙ *Summer hrs vary; call ahead.*

$
MEXICAN
✕ **Carmelita's Mexican Grill and Cantina.** A friendly, family-run eatery tucked into a back corner of what is called "The Mall," Carmelita's draws locals and visitors all day whether it's for a hearty breakfast, a cooked-to-order enchilada or burrito, or to tip back a brew at the bar. The menu lists typical combination plates (enchiladas, burritos, tamales, and tacos). Salsas have a bit of zing, and the *masas* (corn dough used to

make tortillas and tamales) are tasty and tender. ✉ *575 Palm Canyon Dr.* ☎ *760/767–5666* 🖃 *AE, MC, V.*

$$ 🛏 **Borrego Springs Resort and Country Club**. This quiet resort is a good value compared to other Borrego Springs lodgings. Large rooms in a collection of two-story buildings surrounding the swimming pool are nicely kept and appointed with simple oak furnishings. All have shaded balconies or patios with pleasant desert views. In spring, desert gardens surrounding the property burst into colorful bloom. **Pros:** golf and tennis on-site; most rooms have good desert views. **Cons:** limited amenities; average service. ✉ *1112 Tilting T Dr.* ☎ *760/767–5700 or 888/826–7734* ⊕ *www.borregospringsresort.com* 🛏 *66 rooms, 34 suites* ♿ *In-room: a/c, kitchen (some), refrigerator, Wi-Fi (some). In-hotel: 2 restaurants, bar, golf courses, tennis courts, pools, gym, laundry facilities, Wi-Fi hotspot, parking (free), some pets allowed* 🖃 *AE, D, MC, V.*

SPORTS AND THE OUTDOORS

The 27 holes of golf at **Borrego Springs Resort and Country Club** (✉ *1112 Tilting T Dr.* ☎ *760/767–3330* ⊕ *www.borregospringsresort.com*) are open to the public. Three 9-hole courses, with natural desert landscaping and mature date palms, can be played individually or in any combination. Greens fees are $55 to $65, depending on the course and the day of the week, and include a cart and range balls. **Roadrunner Club** (✉ *1010 Palm Canyon Dr.* ☎ *760/767–5373* ⊕ *www.roadrunnerclub.com*) has an 18-hole golf course. The greens fee is $30. **Springs at Borrego** (✉ *2255 DiGiorgio Rd.* ☎ *760/767–2004* ⊕ *www.springsatborrego.com*) is part of an RV park complex. There is one 18-hole course; greens fees are $45 to $50, not including cart fees.

You can select from a variety of equine encounters at **Smoketree Institute and Ranch** (☎ *760/767–5850* ⊕ *www.smoketreearabianranch.com*), which gives desert horseback rides on Arabian or quarter horses, pony rides for kids, and a nonriding human-to-horse communication experience similar to horse-whispering.

SALTON SEA

★ *30 mi southeast of Indio via Hwy. 86 on western shore and via Hwy. 111 on eastern shore; 29 mi east of Borrego Springs via Hwy. S22.*

The Salton Sea, barely 100 years old, is the product of both natural and artificial forces. The sea occupies the Salton Basin, a remnant of prehistoric Lake Cahuilla. Over the centuries the Colorado River flooded the basin and the water drained into the Gulf of California. In 1905 a flood once again filled the Salton Basin, but the exit to the gulf was blocked by sediment. The floodwaters remained in the basin, creating a saline lake 228 feet below sea level, about 35 mi long and 15 mi wide, with a surface area of nearly 380 square mi. The sea, which lies along the Pacific Flyway, supports 400 species of birds. Four sport fish inhabit the Salton Sea: corvina, sargo, Gulf croaker, and tilapia. Fishing, boating, camping, and bird-watching are popular activities year-round.

EXPLORING

On the north shore of the sea, the huge **Salton Sea State Recreation Area** draws thousands each year to its playgrounds, hiking trails, fishing spots, boat launches, and swimming areas. The Headquarters Visitor Center contains exhibits and shows a short film on the history of the Salton Sea. Because of budget constraints, the following beaches were closed: Bombay, Corvina, and Mecca, at this writing. ⊠ *100-225 State Park Rd., North Shore* ☎ *760/393-3052* ⊕ *www.parks.ca.gov* ✉ *$8* ☉ *Park daily 8–sunset; visitor center Oct.–Apr., daily 8–sunset, May– Sept., weekends 8–sunset.*

The 1,785-acre **Sonny Bono Salton Sea National Wildlife Refuge**, on the Pacific Flyway, is a wonderful spot for viewing migratory birds. You might see eared grebes, burrowing owls, great blue herons, ospreys, yellow-footed gulls, white and brown pelicans, and snow geese heading south from Canada. ⊠ *906 W. Sinclair Rd., Calipatria* ☎ *760/348-5278* ⊕ *www.fws.gov/saltonsea* ✉ *Free* ☉ *Sept.–June, daily sunrise–sunset (visitor center weekdays 7–3); June–Sept., weekends 8–4:30.*

Joshua Tree National Park

WORD OF MOUTH

"The roads in the park are very well marked. . . . There is a good-size parking lot as [Keys View] is a very popular stop in Joshua Tree NP. We had a very clear day and you could see all the way to Mexico in the south, snowcapped mountains to the north, and all of the Coachella Valley."

—joeyi

WELCOME TO JOSHUA TREE NATIONAL PARK

TOP REASONS TO GO

★ **Rock climbing:** Joshua Tree is a world-class site with challenges for climbers of just about every skill level.

★ **Peace and quiet:** Savor the solitude of one of the last great wildernesses in America.

★ **Stargazing:** You'll be mesmerized by the Milky Way flowing across the dark night sky. For spectacular natural fireworks, visit in mid-August during the Perseid meteor shower and watch shooting stars streak overhead.

★ **Wildflowers:** In spring, the hillsides explode in a patchwork of yellow, blue, pink, and white.

★ **Sunsets:** Twilight is a special time here, especially during the winter, when the setting sun casts a golden glow on the mountains.

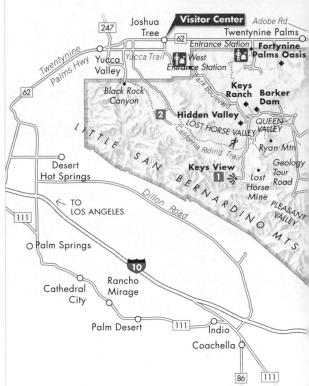

1 Keys View. This is the most dramatic overlook in the park—on clear days you can see Signal Mountain in Mexico.

2 Hidden Valley. Crawl between the big rocks and you'll understand why this boulder-strewn area was once a cattle rustlers' hideout.

3 Cholla Cactus Garden. Come here in the late afternoon, when the spiky stalks of the bigelow (jumping) cholla cactus are backlit against an intense blue sky.

4 Oasis of Mara. Walk the nature trail around this desert oasis, which the first settlers, the Serrano, dubbed "the place of little springs and much grass."

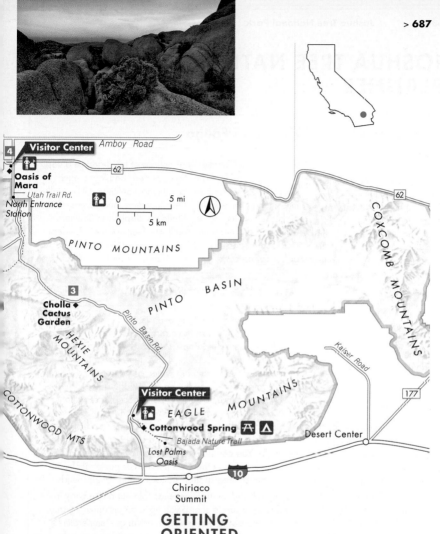

GETTING
ORIENTED

Daggerlike tufts grace the branches of the namesake of Joshua Tree National Park in southeastern California, where the arid Mojave Desert meets the sparsely vegetated Colorado Desert (part of the Sonoran Desert, which lies within California and Northern Mexico).

Passenger cars are fine for paved areas, but you'll need four-wheel drive for many of the rugged backcountry roadways. At the park's most popular sites, parking is limited. Joshua Tree does not have public transportation.

JOSHUA TREE NATIONAL PARK PLANNER

Getting Here and Around

Joshua Tree National Park is within a short drive of 11 million Southern California residents. Most visitors, in fact, make the two-hour drive from the Los Angeles area. The urban sprawl of Palm Springs (home to the nearest airport) is 45 mi away, but gateway towns Joshua Tree, Yucca Valley, and Twentynine Palms are just north of the park. If you're staying in the Palm Springs area, you can enjoy the highlights of the park in one day, including a stop for a picnic at a scenic spot.

WHEN TO GO

October through May, when the desert is cooler, is when most visitors arrive. Daytime temperatures range from the mid-70s in December and January to mid-90s in October and May. Lows can dip to near freezing in mid-winter. Summers can be torrid, with daytime temperatures reaching 110°F.

AVG. HIGH/LOW TEMPS.

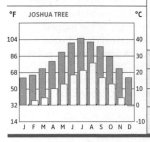

Flora and Fauna

Joshua Tree will shatter your notions of the desert as a vast wasteland. Life flourishes here, as flora and fauna have adapted to heat and drought. In most areas you'll be walking among native Joshua trees, ocotillos, and yuccas. One of the best spring desert wildflower displays in Southern California blooms here. You'll see plenty of animals—reptiles such as nocturnal sidewinders, birds like golden eagles or burrowing owls, and mammals like coyotes and bobcats.

About the Campgrounds

Camping is the best way to experience the stark beauty of Joshua Tree. You'll also have a rare opportunity to sleep outside in a semi-wilderness setting. The campgrounds, set at elevations from 3,000 to 4,500 feet, have only primitive facilities; few have drinking water. Black Rock and Indian Cove campgrounds, on the northern edge of the park (but not on a road that transits the park) accept reservations up to six months in advance (☎ 877/444–6777 ⊕ www. recreation.gov). Campsites elsewhere are on a first-come, first-served basis. Camping fees are $10 to $25 per site per night. You can pay with your credit card (AE, MC, V) at a visitor center; otherwise it's cash or personal check only at the self-registration stations at the campgrounds.

During fall and spring weekends, plan to arrive early in the day to ensure a site; if you have an organized group, reserve one of the group sites in advance. Temperatures can drop at night year-round—bring a sweater or light jacket. If you plan to camp in late winter or early spring, be prepared for the gusty Santa Ana winds. Backcountry camping is permitted in certain wilderness areas of Joshua Tree. You must sign in at a backcountry register board if you plan to stay overnight. For more information, stop at the visitor centers or ranger stations.

WHAT IT COSTS

	¢	$	$$	$$$	$$$$
Campgrounds	under $10	$10–$17	$18–$35	$36–$49	over $50

Camping prices are for a standard (no hookups, pit toilets, fire grates, picnic tables) campsite per night.

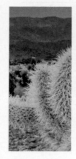

Updated by
Sura Wood
and Bobbi
Zane

Ruggedly beautiful desert scenery attracts nearly 2 million visitors each year to Joshua Tree National Park, one of the last great wildernesses in the continental United States. Its mountains support mounds of enormous boulders and jagged rock; natural cactus gardens and lush oases shaded by tall fan palms mark the meeting place of the Mojave (high) and Sonora (low) deserts. Extensive stands of Joshua trees gave the park its name; the plants (members of the Yucca family of shrubs) reminded early white settlers of the biblical Joshua, with their thick, stubby branches representing the prophet raising his arms toward heaven.

15

PARK ESSENTIALS

ADMISSION FEES AND PERMITS
Park admission is $15 per car, $5 per person on foot. The Joshua Tree Pass, good for one year, is $30. Free permits—available at all visitor centers—are required for rock climbing.

ADMISSION HOURS
The park is open every day, around the clock. The park is in the Pacific time zone.

EMERGENCIES
Emergency assistance within Joshua Tree is limited. Emergency-only phones are at Intersection Rock at the entrance to Hidden Valley Campground and Indian Cove Campground; call San Bernardino Dispatch at ☎ 909/383–5651, or dial 911.

PARK CONTACT INFORMATION
Joshua Tree National Park ✉ 74485 National Park Dr., Twentynine Palms, CA ☎ 760/367–5500 ⊕ www.nps.gov/jotr.

SCENIC DRIVES

★ **Park Boulevard.** Traversing the most scenic portions of Joshua Tree, this well-paved road connects the north and west entrances in the park's high desert section. Along with some sweeping desert views, you'll see jumbles of splendid boulder formations, stands of Joshua trees, and Hidden Valley and Barker Dam, remnants of the area's wild and woolly past. From the Oasis Visitor Center, drive south. After about 5 mi, the road forks; turn right and head west toward Jumbo Rocks (clearly marked with a road sign).

EXPLORING

HISTORIC SITES

Hidden Valley. This legendary cattle-rustlers hideout is set among big boulders, which kids love to scramble over and around. ⊠ *Park Blvd., 14 mi south of West Entrance.*

★ **Keys Ranch.** This 150-acre ranch that once belonged to William and Frances Keys illustrates one of the area's most successful attempts at homesteading. The couple raised five children under extreme desert conditions. Most of the original buildings, including the house, school, store, and workshop, have been restored to the way it was when William died in 1969. The only way to see the ranch is on one of the 60-minute, ranger-led walking tours, offered weekdays October–May; tour reservations are essential. ⊠ *2 mi north of Barker Dam Rd.* ☎ *760/367–5555* 🖾 *$5* ☉ *Oct.–May, tours weekdays and weekends at 10 and 1.*

SCENIC STOPS

Cholla Cactus Garden. This stand of bigelow cholla (sometimes called jumping cholla, since its hooked spines seem to jump at you) is best seen and photographed in late afternoon, when the backlit spiky stalks stand out against a colorful sky. ⊠ *Pinto Basin Rd., 20 mi north of Cottonwood Visitor Center.*

Cottonwood Spring. Home to the native Cahuilla people for centuries, this spring provided water for travelers and early prospectors. The area, which supports a large stand of fan palms, is a stop for migrating birds and a winter water source for bighorn sheep. A number of gold mills were located here, and the area still has some remains, including an *arrastra* (gold-mining tool) and concrete pillars. You can access the site via a 1-mi paved trail that begins at sites 13A and 13B of the Cottonwood Campground. ⊠ *Cottonwood Visitor Center.*

Fortynine Palms Oasis. A short drive off Highway 62, this site is a bit if a preview of what the park's interior has to offer: stands of fan palms, interesting petroglyphs, and evidence of fires built by early American Indians. Since animals frequent this area, you may spot a coyote, bobcat, or roadrunner. ⊠ *End of Canyon Rd., 4 mi west of Twentynine Palms.*

★ **Keys View.** At 5,185 feet, this point affords a sweeping view of the Santa Rosa Mountains and Coachella Valley, the mountains of the San Bernardino National Forest, the Salton Sea, San Andreas Fault, and—on a rare clear day—Signal Mountain in Mexico. Sunrise and sunset are magical times, when the light throws rocks and trees into high relief before bathing the hills in brilliant shades of red, orange, and gold. ✉ *Keys View Rd., 21 mi south of west entrance.*

Lost Palms Oasis. More than 100 fan palms comprise the largest group of the exotic plants in the park. A spring bubbles from between the rocks, but disappears into the sandy, boulder-strewn canyon. As you hike along the 4-mi trail, you might spot bighorn sheep. ✉ *Cottonwood Visitor Center.*

> ## LOOK, DON'T TOUCH—REALLY
>
> Some cactus needles, like those on the cholla, can become embedded in your skin with just the slightest touch. If you do get zapped, use tweezers to gently pull it out.

VISITOR CENTERS

Cottonwood Visitor Center. Exhibits in this small center, staffed by rangers and volunteers, illustrate the region's natural history. ✉ *Pinto Basin Rd.* ☎ *No phone* ⊕ *www.nps.gov/jotr* ☉ *Daily 8–4.*

Joshua Tree Visitor Center. This visitor center, opened in 2006, holds exhibits illustrating park geology, cultural and historic sites, and hiking and rock-climbing activities. There's also a small bookstore. ✉ *6554 Park Blvd. Joshua Tree* ☎ *760/367–5500* ⊕ *www.nps.gov/jotr* ☉ *Daily 8–5.*

Oasis Visitor Center. Exhibits here illustrate how Joshua Tree was formed, reveal the differences between the two types of desert within the park, and demonstrate how plants and animals eke out an existence in this arid climate. Take the ½-mi nature walk through the nearby Oasis of Mara, which is alive with cottonwood trees, palm trees, and mesquite shrubs. ✉ *74485 National Park Dr., Twentynine Palms* ☎ *760/367–5500* ⊕ *www.nps.gov/jotr* ☉ *Daily 8–4:30.*

15

SPORTS AND THE OUTDOORS

HIKING

There are more than 191 mi of hiking trails in Joshua Tree, ranging from quarter-of-a-mile nature trails to 35-mi treks. Some connect with each other, so you can design your own desert maze. Remember that drinking water is hard to come by—you won't find water in the park except at the entrances. Bring along at least a gallon per person for all but the shortest hikes, more if the weather is hot. Before striking out on a hike or apparent nature trail, check out the signage. Roadside signage identifies hiking- and rock-climbing routes.

EASY

Cap Rock. This ½-mi wheelchair-accessible loop—named after a boulder that sits atop a huge rock formation like a cap—winds through fascinating rock formations and has signs that explain the geology of the Mojave Desert. ✉ *Trailhead at junction of Park Blvd. and Keys View Rd.*

MODERATE

Fodor's Choice ★ **Ryan Mountain Trail.** The payoff for hiking to the top of 5,461-foot Ryan Mountain is one of the best panoramic views of Joshua Tree. From here you can see Mt. San Jacinto, Mt. San Gorgonio, Lost Horse Valley, and the Pinto Basin. You'll need two to three hours to complete the

3-mi round-trip. ⊠ *Trailhead at Ryan Mountain parking area, 16 mi southeast of park's west entrance or Sheep Pass, 16 mi southwest of Oasis Visitor Center.*

DIFFICULT

★ **Mastodon Peak Trail.** Some boulder scrambling is required on this 3-mi hike up 3,371-foot Mastodon Peak, but the journey rewards you with stunning views of the Salton Sea. The trail passes through a region where gold was mined from 1919 to 1932, so be on the lookout for open mines. The peak draws its name from a large rock formation that early miners believed looked like the head of a prehistoric behemoth. ⊠ *Trailhead at Cottonwood Spring Oasis.*

ROCK CLIMBING

Fodor'sChoice
★ With an abundance of weathered igneous boulder outcroppings, Joshua Tree is one of the nation's top winter climbing destinations and offers a full menu of climbing experiences—from bouldering for beginners in the Wonderland of Rocks to multiple-pitch climbs at Echo Rock and Saddle Rock. The best-known climb in the park is Hidden Valley's Sports Challenge Rock. A map inside the *Joshua Tree Guide* shows locations of selected wilderness and nonwilderness climbs.

OUTFIT-
TERS AND
EXPEDITIONS
Joshua Tree Rock Climbing School offers several programs, from one-day introductory classes to multiday programs for experienced climbers. The school provides all needed equipment. Beginning classes are limited to six people age 13 or older. ⊡ *Box 3034, Joshua Tree, CA 92252* ☎ *760/366–4745 or 800/890–4745* ⊕ *www.joshuatreerockclimbing. com* ⌨ *$125 for beginner class.*

WHERE TO STAY

$ ⚠ **Black Rock Canyon Campground.** Set among juniper bushes, cholla cacti, and other desert shrubs, Black Rock Canyon is one of the prettiest campgrounds in Joshua Tree. South of Yucca Valley, it's the closest campground to most of the desert communities. Located on the California Riding and Hiking Trail, it has facilities for horses and mules. **Pros:** reservations available; good choice for RVs; ranger talks. **Cons:** fills up early; outside the main park. ⊠ *Joshua La., south of Hwy. 62 and Hwy. 247* ☎ *760/367–5500, 877/444–6777 for reservations* ⊕ *www. recreation.gov* ⚠ *100 tent/RV sites* ⚐ *Flush toilets, dump station, drinking water, fire pits, picnic tables, ranger station* ⊟ *AE, D, MC, V.*

$ ⚠ **Jumbo Rocks.** Each campsite at this well-regarded campground tucked among giant boulders has a bit of privacy. It's a good home base for visiting many of Joshua Tree's attractions, including Geology Tour Road. Sites are first-come, first-served. **Pros:** good stargazing. **Cons:** crowded in spring; some small sites. ⊠ *Park Blvd., 11 mi from Oasis of Mara* ☎ *760/367–5500* ⊕ *www.nps.gov/jotr* ⚠ *125 tent/RV sites* ⚐ *Pit toilets, fire pits, picnic tables* ⊟ *No credit cards.*

The Mojave Desert

WITH OWENS VALLEY

WORD OF MOUTH

"We detoured from Hwy 15 at Baker, taking the Kelbaker Road through the Mojave National Preserve (no fee). The road passes through scenery with Joshua Trees, lava beds and cinder cones, the restored 1924 Kelso Depot visitor center, and the impressive Kelso Dunes."

—mlgb

WELCOME TO THE MOJAVE DESERT

TOP REASONS TO GO

★ **Nostalgia:** Old neon signs, historic motels, and restored Harvey House rail stations abound across this desert landscape. Don't miss some of the classic eateries along the way, including Bagdad Café in Newberry Springs, Emma Jean's Hollandburger Cafe in Victorville, and Summit Inn on the Cajon Pass.

★ **Death Valley wonders:** Visit this strange landscape to tour some of the most breathtaking desert terrain in the world. (⇨ Chapter 17, Death Valley National Park.)

★ **Great ghost towns:** California's gold rush brought miners to the Mojave, and each of the towns they left behind has its own unique charms.

★ **Cool down in Sierra country:** Head up Highway 395 toward Bishop to visit the High Sierra, home to majestic Mt. Whitney.

★ **Explore ancient history:** The Mojave Desert is replete with rare petroglyphs, some dating back almost 16,000 years.

1 The Western Mojave. Stretching from the town of Ridgecrest to the base of the San Gabriel Mountains, the western Mojave is a varied landscape of ancient Native American petroglyphs, tufa towers, and hillsides covered in bright orange poppies.

2 The Eastern Mojave. Like the western Mojave, the east has plenty of flat, open land dotted with Joshua trees and rock-strewn mountains. It also has more greenery and regular stretches of cool weather. Much of this area is uninhabited, so be cautious when driving the back roads, where towns and services are few and far between.

3 Owens Valley. Lying in the shadow of the eastern Sierra Nevada, the Owens Valley stretches along U.S. 395 from the Mono–Inyo county line, in the north, to the town of Olancha, in the south. This stretch of highway is dotted with tiny towns, some containing only a minimart and a gas station. If you're traveling between Yosemite National Park and Death Valley National Park or are headed from Lake Tahoe or Mammoth to the desert, U.S. 395 is your corridor.

4 **Death Valley National Park.** This arid desert landscape is one of the hottest, lowest, and driest places in North America. Here, among the beautiful canyons and wide-open spaces, you'll find some quirky bits of Americana, including the elaborate Scotty's Castle and eclectic Amargosa Opera House. (⇨ *Chapter 17, Death Valley National Park*)

GETTING ORIENTED

The Mojave Desert, once part of an ancient inland sea, is one of the largest swaths of open land in Southern California. Its boundaries to the south include the San Gabriel and San Bernardino mountain ranges; the areas of Palmdale and Ridgecrest to the west; Death Valley (⇨ *Chapter 17*) to the north; and Needles and the Nevada towns of Lake Havasu and Primm to the east. The area is instantly distinguishable by its wide-open sandy spaces, peppered with creosote bushes, Joshua trees, and abandoned homesteads. You can access the Mojave via interstates 40 and 15, and highways 14, 95, and 395.

16

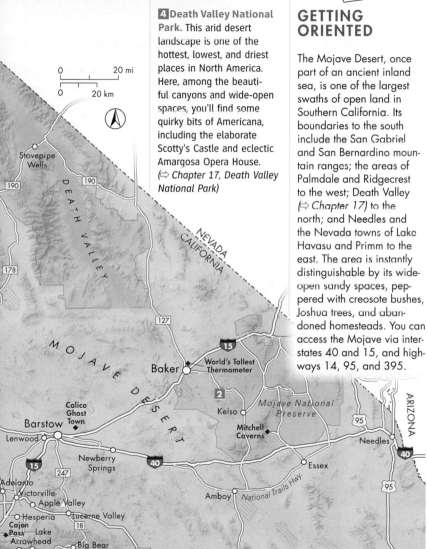

THE MOJAVE DESERT PLANNER

Warnings

Believe everything you've ever heard about desert heat: It can be brutal. You need sunglasses, sunblock, a hat, clothing that blocks the sun's rays and the wind, and plenty of water. Because this region is vast and the weather is unpredictable, you'll also need to make careful driving plans. Facilities such as gas stations and supermarkets are few, so be sure to fill your gas tank often and check your vehicle's fluids and tire pressure frequently. Shut off your car's air-conditioning on steep grades to avoid engine overheating. At the start of each day load the car with three gallons of water per person, plus additional radiator water, and a cooler stocked with extra food. Be sure to bring reliable maps; signage can be limited. It's a good idea to have a compass and a cell phone (though the signal may fade in remote areas).

Timing

Spring and fall are the best seasons to tour the desert and Owens Valley. Winters are generally mild, but summers can be cruel. If you're on a budget, keep in mind that room rates drop as the temperatures rise.

Hours of Operation

Early morning is the best time to visit sights and avoid crowds, but some museums and visitor centers don't open until 10. If you schedule your town arrivals for late afternoon, you can drop by the visitor centers just before closing hours to line up an itinerary for the next day.

About the Restaurants

Throughout the desert and the eastern Sierra, dining is a fairly simple affair. Owens Valley is home to many mom-and-pop eateries, as well as a few fast-food chains. The restaurants in Death Valley (⇨ Chapter 17) range from coffee shops to upscale cafés. In the Mojave there are chain establishments in Ridgecrest, Victorville, and Barstow, as well as some ethnic eateries.

About the Hotels

Hotel chains and roadside motels make up most of the lodging options in the desert. The tourist season runs through the summer months, from late May through September, when many travelers are heading out of California on Interstate 15. Reservations are never a problem: you're almost always guaranteed a room. But if your plans take you to the most luxurious resort in the entire desert—the Furnace Creek Inn, in Death Valley—be sure to book in advance for the winter season.

WHAT IT COSTS

	¢	$	$$	$$$	$$$$
Restaurants	under $10	$10–$15	$16–$22	$23–$30	over $30
Hotels	under $90	$90–$120	$121–$175	$176–$250	over $250

Restaurant prices are for a main course at dinner, excluding sales tax of 7.75%. Hotel prices are for two people in a standard double room in high season, excluding service charges and 7.25% tax.

Updated by
Reed Parsell

Dust and desolation, tumbleweeds and rattlesnakes, barren landscapes—these are the bleak images that come to mind when most people hear the word *desert*. But east of the Sierra Nevada, where the land quickly flattens and the rain seldom falls, the desert is anything but a wasteland.

16

The topography here is extreme; whereas Death Valley (⇨ *Chapter 17, Death Valley National Park*) drops to almost 300 feet below sea level and contains the lowest (and hottest) spot in the Western Hemisphere, the Mojave Desert, which lies to the south, has elevations ranging from 3,000 to 5,000 feet. These remote regions (which are known, respectively, as low desert and high desert) possess a singular beauty found nowhere else in California: there are vast open spaces populated with spiky Joshua trees, undulating sand dunes, faulted mountains, and dramatic rock formations. Owens Valley is where the desert meets the mountains; its 80-mi width separates the depths of Death Valley from Mt. Whitney, the highest mountain in the continental United States.

PLANNING

GETTING HERE AND AROUND
BY AIR
Inyokern Airport, near Ridgecrest, is served by United Express from Los Angeles. McCarran International Airport, in Las Vegas, Nevada, served by dozens of major airlines, is about as close as Inyokern Airport to Furnace Creek, in Death Valley National Park (⇨ *Chapter 17*). Needles Airport serves small, private planes, as does Furnace Creek's 3,000-foot airstrip in Death Valley.

Contacts Inyokern Airport (✉ *Inyokern Rd., Hwy. 178, 9 mi west of Ridgecrest, Inyokern* ☎ *760/377–5844* ⊕ *www.inyokernairport.com*). **McCarran International Airport** (✉ *5757 Wayne Newton Blvd., Las Vegas, NV* ☎ *702/261–5733* ⊕ *www.mccarran.com*). **Needles Airport** (✉ *711 Airport Rd., Needles* ☎ *760/326–5263*).

BY CAR

Much of the desert can be seen from the comfort of an air-conditioned car. You can approach Death Valley (⇨ *Chapter 17*) from the west or the southeast. Whether you've come south from Bishop or north from Ridgecrest, head east from U.S. 395 on Highway 190 or 178.

NOT SOUVENIRS

You may spot fossils at some of the archaeological sites in the desert. If you do, leave them where they are; it's against the law to remove them.

To enter Death Valley from the southeast, take Highway 127 north from Interstate 15 in Baker and link up with Highway 178, which travels west into the valley and then cuts north toward Highway 190 at Furnace Creek.

The major north–south route through the western Mojave is U.S. 395, which intersects with I–15 between Cajon Pass and Victorville. U.S. 395 travels north into the Owens Valley, passing such dusty little stops as Lone Pine, Independence, Big Pine, and Bishop. Farther west, Highway 14 runs north–south between Inyokern (near Ridgecrest) and Palmdale. Two major east–west routes travel through the Mojave: to the north, I–15 between Barstow and Las Vegas, Nevada; to the south, I–40 between Barstow and Needles. At the intersection of the two interstates, in Barstow, I–15 veers south toward Victorville and Los Angeles, and I–40 gives way to Highway 58 toward Bakersfield.

Contact California Highway Patrol 24-hour road info (☎ *800/427-7623* ⊕ *www.dot.ca.gov/cgi-bin/roads.cgi*).

BY TRAIN

Amtrak makes stops in Victorville, Barstow, and Needles, but the stations are not staffed and do not have phone numbers, so you'll have to purchase your tickets in advance and handle your own baggage. You can travel west to connect with the *Coast Starlight* in Los Angeles or the *Pacific Surfliner* in Fullerton. The *Southwest Chief* stops twice a day at the above cities on its route from Los Angeles to Chicago and back. The Barstow station is served daily by Amtrak California motor coaches that travel between San Joaquin, Bakersfield, and Las Vegas.

Contact Amtrak (☎ *800/872-7245* ⊕ *www.amtrakcalifornia.com*).

EMERGENCIES

In an emergency dial 911.

Let someone know your trip route, destination, and estimated time of return. Before setting out, make sure your vehicle is in good condition. Carry a jack, tools, and towrope or chain. Fill up your tank whenever you see a gas pump. Stay on main roads, and watch out for wild burros, horses, and cattle.

Drink at least a gallon of water a day (three gallons if you're hiking or otherwise exerting yourself). Dress in layered clothing and wear comfortable, sturdy shoes and a hat. Keep snacks, sunscreen, and a first-aid kit on hand. If you have a headache or feel dizzy or nauseous, you could be suffering from dehydration. Get out of the sun immediately and drink plenty of water. Dampen your clothing to lower your body temperature.

Do not enter mine tunnels or shafts. The structures may be unstable, and there may be hidden dangers such as pockets of bad air. Avoid canyons during rainstorms. Floodwaters can quickly fill up dry riverbeds and cover or wash away roads. Never place your hands or feet where you can't see them. Rattlesnakes, scorpions, and black widow spiders may be hiding there.

Contacts BLM Rangers (✆ 760/255–8700). **Community Hospital** (✉ Barstow ✆ 760/256–1761). **Northern Inyo Hospital** (✉ 150 Pioneer La., Bishop ✆ 760/873–5811). **San Bernardino County Sheriff** (✆ 760/256–1796 in Barstow, 760/733–4448 in Baker).

TOUR OPTIONS

The Mojave Group of the Sierra Club regularly organizes field trips to interesting spots, and the San Gorgonio Sierra Club chapter also conducts desert excursions.

Contact Sierra Club (✉ 3345 Wilshire Blvd., Suite 508, Los Angeles ✆ 213/387–4287, 951/684–6203 for San Gorgonio chapter ⊕ www.sierraclub.com).

VISITOR INFORMATION

Contacts Bureau of Land Management (✉ California Desert District Office, 6221 Box Springs Blvd., Riverside ✆ 909/697–5200 ⊕ www.ca.blm.gov). **California Welcome Center** (✉ 2796 Tanger Way, Barstow ✆ 760/253–4782 ⊕ www.visitcwc.com). **Death Valley Chamber of Commerce** (✉ 118 Hwy. 127, Shoshone ✆ 760/852–4524 ⊕ www.deathvalleychamber.com). **San Bernardino County Regional Parks Department** (✉ 777 E. Rialto Ave., San Bernardino ✆ 909/387–2594 ⊕ www.co.san-bernardino.ca.us/parks).

16

THE WESTERN MOJAVE

PALMDALE

60 mi north of Los Angeles on Hwy. 14.

Before calling itself the aerospace capital of the world, the desert town of Palmdale was an agricultural community. Swiss and German descendants, moving west from Nebraska, settled here in 1886. Most residents made their living as farmers, growing alfalfa, pears, and apples. After World War II, with the creation of Edwards Air Force Base and U.S. Air Force Plant 42, the area turned into a center for aerospace and defense, with such big companies as McDonnell Douglas, Rockwell, Northrop, and Lockheed establishing factories here. Until the housing crisis and most recent recession struck, it was one of the fastest-growing cities in Southern California.

EXPLORING

A mile from the San Andreas Fault, the namesake of the **Devil's Punchbowl Natural Area** is a natural bowl-shape depression in the earth, framed by 300-foot rock walls. At the bottom is a stream, which you can reach via a moderately strenuous 1-mi hike. You also can veer off on a short nature trail; at the top an interpretive center has displays of native flora and fauna, including live animals such as snakes, lizards, and birds of prey. ⊠ *28000 Devil's Punchbowl Rd., south of Hwy. 138, Pearblossom* ☎ *661/944–2743* ▣ *Free* ☉ *Park daily sunrise–sunset, center daily 8–4.*

The Benedictine monastery **St. Andrew's Abbey** stands on 760 acres of lush greenery and natural springs. A big draw here is the property's ceramics studio, established in 1969; St. Andrew's Ceramics sells handmade tile saints, angels, and plaques designed by Father Maur van Doorslaer, a monk from Sint Andries in Bruges, Belgium, whose work is collected across the United States and Canada. Don't miss the abbey's fall festival, where you can sample tasty dishes and enjoy entertainment that includes singing nuns and dancing monks. ⊠ *31101 N. Valyermo Rd., south of Hwy. 138, Valyermo* ☎ *888/454–5411, 661/944–1047 ceramics studio* ⊕ *www.saintsandangels.org* ▣ *Free* ☉ *Weekdays 9–12:30 and 1:30–4:30, weekends 9–11:45 and 12:30–4:30.*

Adventure-seekers will enjoy flying over the scenic San Gabriel mountain pines, across the jagged San Andreas Fault, and over the sandy soil of El Mirage Dry Lake at **Southern California Soaring Academy**, the only place near Los Angeles that offers sailplane rides (no engines!). You'll be accompanied by an FAA-certified instructor, who will teach you the basics of airspeed control, straight flight, and turns before letting you handle the craft on your own. Basic flights range from $96 to $176. Advance reservations are required. ⊠ *32810 165th St. E, Llano* ☎ *661/944–1090* ⊕ *www.soaringacademy.org* ☉ *Fri.–Mon. 10–6, Tues.–Thurs. by appointment.*

You can take ultralight (very small two-seater planes that can be flown without a pilot's license) lessons at the **Brian Ranch Airport**, which offers 15-minute ($40), half-hour ($60), and hour-long ($95) rides across the Mojave. The airport is also known for its annual "World's Smallest Air Show" every Memorial Day weekend, which draws aviation enthusiasts from around the country. ⊠ *34180 Largo Vista Rd., Llano* ☎ *661/261–3216* ⊕ *www.brianranch.com.*

The closest you'll get to an African safari near Los Angeles is **Shambala Preserve**, an 80-acre wildlife preserve run by actress Tippi Hedren. Afternoon safaris, held twice a month (during one weekend) by advance reservation only, get you as close as a foot away from 70 rescued wildcats and an African elephant. ⊠ *6867 Soledad Canyon, Acton* ☎ *661/268–0380* ⊕ *www.shambala.org* ▣ *$40 minimum donation.*

WHERE TO STAY

$$ ▦ **Best Western John Jay Inn & Suites.** Antique furnishings decorate the rooms and suites at this modern hotel. Each room has a large desk with ergonomic chair. Suites have balconies, fireplaces, wet bars, and Jacuzzis. Buffet breakfast and a *USA Today* newspaper are included in your room rate. **Pros:** clean; good rates; spacious rooms. **Cons:** no on-site restaurant; rather corporate. ⊠ *600 W. Palmdale Blvd.* ☎ *661/575–9322* ⊕ *www.bestwestern.com* ⇆ *54 rooms, 13 suites* ⌂ *In-room: a/c, refrigerator. In-hotel: pool, gym, laundry service, Wi-Fi hotspot* ▤ *AE, D, DC, MC, V* ⦿ *CP.*

Mojave Desert

LANCASTER

8 mi north of Palmdale via Hwy. 14.

Lancaster was founded in 1876, when the Southern Pacific Railroad arrived. Before that it was inhabited by Native American tribes: Kawaiisu, Kitanemuk, Serrano, Tataviam, and Chemehuevi. Descendants of some of these tribes still live in the surrounding mountains. Points of interest around Lancaster are far from the downtown area, some in neighboring communities.

EXPLORING

★ California's state flower, the California poppy, can be spotted just about anywhere in the state, but the densest concentration is in the **Antelope Valley Poppy Reserve.** Seven miles of trails (parts of which are paved, but inclines are too steep for wheelchairs) lead you through 1,745 acres of hills carpeted with poppies and other wildflowers as far as the eye can see. Peak blooming time is usually March through May, though you're free to hike the grounds year-round. The visitor center has books and information about the reserve and other desert areas. ⌧ *Ave. I, between 110th and 170th Sts.* W ☎ *661/724–1180 or 661/942–0662* ⊕ *www. parks.ca.gov* ⌧ *$8 per vehicle* ⊙ *Visitor center mid-Mar.–mid-May, daily 9–5.*

Desert Tortoise Natural Area. Between mid-March and mid-June, this natural habitat of the elusive desert tortoise blazes with desert candles, primroses, lupine, and other wildflowers. Get there bright and early to spot the state reptile, while it grazes on fresh flowers and grass shoots. It's also a great spot to see desert kit fox, red-tailed hawks, cactus wrens, and Mojave rattlesnakes. ⌧ *8 mi northeast of California City via Randsburg Mojave Rd.* ☎ *951/683–3872* ⊕ *www.tortoise-tracks. org* ⌧ *Free* ⊙ *Daily.*

OFF THE BEATEN PATH

Ȼ Thirteen species of wildcats, from the weasel-size jaguarundi to leopards, tigers, and jaguars, inhabit the **Exotic Feline Breeding Compound & Feline Conservation Center.** You can see the cats (behind barrier fences) in the parklike public zoo and research center. The center supplies city zoos with wild cats and does a few rescues. The on-site museum's taxidermied cats all died of old age. ⌧ *Off Mojave-Tropico Rd., Rosamond* ☎ *661/256–3793* ⊕ *www.cathouse-fcc.org.*

A winery in the middle of the desert? Only in California could you find a place like **Antelope Valley Winery and Buffalo Company.** Industry scoffing hasn't stopped Cecil W. McLester, a graduate of UC Davis's renowned wine-making and viticulture program, from crafting a decent batch of wines, including the award-winning AV Burgundy (a house red) and Paloma Blanca (a Riesling-style blend of French Colombard, chenin blanc, and muscat grapes). The winery is also home to the Antelope Valley Buffalo Company, a producer of fine buffalo steaks, patties, and jerky, made from its roaming herd in the Leona Valley. ⌧ *42041 20th St.* W ☎ *661/722–0145* ⊕ *www.avwinery.com* ⌧ *Winery free, wine tasting $6* ⊙ *Wed.–Sun. 11–6.*

RED ROCK CANYON STATE PARK

48 mi north of Lancaster via Hwy. 14; 17 mi west of U.S. 395 via Red Rock–Randsburg Rd.

A geological feast for the eyes with its layers of pink, white, red, and brown rock, Red Rock Canyon State Park is also a region of fascinating biological diversity—the ecosystems of the Sierra Nevada, the Mojave Desert, and the Basin Range all converge here. Entering the park from the south on Red Rock–Randsburg Road, you pass through a steep-walled gorge to a wide bowl tinted pink by volcanic ash. Native Americans known as the Old People lived here some 20,000 years ago; later, Mojave Indians roamed the land for centuries. Gold-rush fever hit the region in the mid-1800s, and you can still see remains of mining operations in the park. In the 20th century, Hollywood invaded the canyon, shooting westerns, TV shows, commercials, music videos, and movies such as *Jurassic Park* here. Be sure to check out the Red Cliffs Preserve on Highway 14, across from the entrance to the Red Rock campground. ⊠ *Ranger station: Abbott Dr. off Hwy. 14* ☎ *661/942–0662* ⊕ *www. parks.ca.gov* ✉ *$6 per vehicle* ☉ *Visitor center Fri.–Sun. 10–4.*

LIQUID REFRESHMENT

After driving through the hot desert, you'll surely appreciate a cold one at **Indian Wells Brewing Company** (⊠ *2565 N. Hwy. 14, Inyokern* ✛ *2 mi west of Hwy. 395* ☎ *760/377–5989* ☉ *Daily 9:30–5*), where master brewer Rick Lovett lovingly crafts his Desert Pale Ale, Eastern Sierra Lager, Mojave Gold, and Sidewinder Missile Ales. If you have the kids along, grab a six-pack of his specialty root beer, black cherry, orange, or cream sodas.

RIDGECREST

28 mi northeast of Red Rock Canyon State Park via Hwy. 14; 77 mi south of Lone Pine via U.S. 395.

A military town that serves the U.S. Naval Weapons Center to its north, Ridgecrest has dozens of stores, restaurants, and hotels. It's a good base for exploring the northwestern Mojave, because it's the last big city you'll hit along U.S. 395 before you enter the desert.

ESSENTIALS

Visitor Information Ridgecrest Area Convention and Visitors Bureau (⊠ *100 W. California Ave., Ridgecrest* ☎ *760/375–8202 or 800/847–4830* ⊕ *www.visitdeserts.com*).

EXPLORING

The **Maturango Museum** also has a small bookstore and serves as a visitor information center. Small but informative exhibits detail the natural and cultural history of the northern Mojave. Outside there's a short but creative nature trail. The museum runs wildflower tours in March and April. ⊠ *100 E. Las Flores Ave.* ☎ *760/375–6900* ⊕ *www.maturango. org* ✉ *$5* ☉ *Daily 10–5.*

Fodor's Choice
★

Guided tours conducted by the Maturango Museum are the only way
to see **Petroglyph Canyons**, among
the desert's most amazing specta-
cles. The two canyons, commonly
called Big Petroglyph and Little
Petroglyph, are in the Coso Mountain Range on the million-acre U.S.
Naval Weapons Center at China
Lake. Each of the canyons holds a
superlative concentration of ancient
rock art, the largest of its kind in the
Northern Hemisphere. Thousands
of well-preserved images of animals and humans—some more than
16,000 years old—are scratched or
pecked into dark basaltic rocks.
The tour takes you through 3 mi
of sandy washes and boulders, so
wear comfortable walking shoes.

> ### FORMER BOOMTOWNS
>
> The towns of Randsburg, Red
> Mountain, and Johannesburg
> make up the **Rand Mining Dis-**
> **trict** (⊠ *U.S. 395, 20 mi south of*
> *Ridgecrest*), which first boomed
> with the discovery of gold in
> the Rand Mountains in 1895.
> Rich tungsten ore, used in World
> War I to make steel alloy, was
> discovered in 1907, and silver
> was found in 1919. The boom has
> gone bust, but the area still has
> a few residents, a dozen antiques
> shops, and plenty of character.
> Johannesburg is overlooked by an
> archetypal Old West cemetery in
> the hills above town.

16

■TIP➔ At an elevation of 5,000 feet,
weather conditions can be quite extreme, so dress in layers and bring plenty of
drinking water (none is available at the site) and snacks. Children under 10
are not allowed on the tour. The military requires everyone to produce
a valid driver's license, Social Security number, passport, and vehicle
registration before the trip (nondrivers must provide a birth certificate).
⊠ *Tours depart from Maturango Museum* ☎ *760/375–6900* ⊕ *www.*
maturango.org ☞ *$35* ☉ *Museum daily 10–5. Tours Feb.–June and Sept.*
or Oct.–early Dec.; call for tour times.

☝ Rounded up by the Bureau of Land Management on public lands
throughout the Southwest, the animals at the **Wild Horse and Burro Cor-**
rals are available for adoption. You can bring along an apple or carrot
to feed the horses, but the burros are usually too wild to approach.
Individual and group tours are available. ⊠ *Off Hwy. 178, 3 mi east*
of Ridgecrest ☎ *760/384–5765* ⊕ *www.blm.gov* ☞ *Free* ☉ *Weekdays*
7:30–4.

It's worth the effort (especially for sci-fi buffs, who will recognize the
landscape from the film *Star Trek V*) to seek out **Trona Pinnacles National**
Natural Landmark. These fantastic-looking formations of calcium carbonate, known as tufa, are were formed underwater along fault lines in the
bed of what is now Searles Dry Lake. The dirt road from Highway 178
is decaying, so proceed slowly. The main parking lot has an outhouse,
but that's it for man-made touches other than a few interpretive signs.
There's no formal trail; walk wherever you'd like, but beware of sharp,
coral-like rocks underfoot. Prime photography times are in early morning and just before sunset. ⊠ *5 mi south of Hwy. 178, 18 mi east of*
Ridgecrest ☎ *760/384–5400 Ridgecrest BLM office* ⊕ *www.blm.gov/*
ca/st/en/fo/ridgecrest/trona.3.html.

WHERE TO STAY

$$ ⊞ **Carriage Inn.** All the rooms at this large hotel are roomy and well kept, but the poolside cabanas are a bit cozier. The hotel has a long list of amenities, some of which are definitely not standard: a mister cools off sunbathers during the hot summer months. Café Potpourri serves a mix of American, Italian, and Southwestern specials. Charlie's Pub & Grill ($) serves burgers and sandwiches, which go nicely with the custom home-brewed ale from Indian Wells Valley Brewery. **Pros:** full complimentary breakfast; nice outdoor pool. **Cons:** old decor; some rooms could use an update. ✉ *901 N. China Lake Blvd.* ☎ *760/446–7910 or 800/772–8527* ⊕ *www.carriageinn.biz* ⤸ *152 rooms, 8 suites, 2 cabanas* ৬ *In-room: a/c, refrigerator. In-hotel: 2 restaurants, room service, bar, pool, gym, Wi-Fi hotspot* ⊟ *AE, D, DC, MC, V* ⎮◯⎮ *MAP.*

$ ⊞ **Heritage Inn and Suites.** This well-appointed and popular establishment is geared to business travelers, but the staff is equally attentive to tourists' concerns. Victoria's Restaurant ($), with an American-casual menu, is a favorite fine-dining spot for locals. **Pros:** spacious rooms; full complimentary breakfast. **Cons:** some walls are thin. ✉ *1050 N. Norma St.* ☎ *760/446–6543 or 800/843–0693* ⊕ *www.heritageinnsuites.com* ⤸ *123 rooms, 46 suites* ৬ *In-room: a/c, refrigerator, Internet. In-hotel: restaurant, room service, bar, pools, gym, laundry facilities, Wi-Fi hotspot, some pets allowed* ⊟ *AE, D, DC, MC, V* ⎮◯⎮ *BP.*

> ## SPOOKY SIDE TRIP
>
> The dusty **Ballarat Ghost Town** saw its heyday between 1897 and 1917. Don't miss the saloon, assay office, and small graveyard, where wooden crosses mark the graves of forgotten prospectors. Ballarat's more infamous draw is Barker Ranch, accessible by four-wheel-drive vehicle, where convicted murderer Charles Manson and his "family" were captured after a 1969 murder spree. From Highway 395, take exit SR-178 and travel 45 mi to the historic marker; Ballarat is 3½ mi from the end of the pavement.

THE EASTERN MOJAVE

VICTORVILLE

87 mi south of Ridgecrest on U.S. 395. Turn east onto Bear Valley Rd. and travel 2 mi to town center.

At the southwest corner of the Mojave is the sprawling town of Victorville, a town rich in Route 66 heritage. Victorville was named for Santa Fe Railroad pioneer Jacob Nash Victor, who drove the first locomotive through the Cajon Pass here in 1885. Once home to Native Americans, the town later became a rest stop for Mormons and missionaries. In 1941 George Air Force Base (which now serves as an airport and storage area) brought scores of military families to the area, many of which have stayed on to raise families of their own. February is one of the best times to visit, when the city holds its annual Roy Rogers and Dale Evans Western Film Festival and Adelanto Grand Prix, the largest motorcycle and quad off-road event in the country.

ESSENTIALS

Visitor Information Victorville Chamber of Commerce (⊠ *14174 Green Tree Blvd., Victorville* ☎ *760/245-6506* ⊕ *www.vvchamber.com*).

EXPLORING

Fans of the Mother Road can visit the **California Route 66 Museum**, whose exhibits chronicle the history of America's most famous highway. At the museum you can pick up a book that details a self-guided tour of the old Sagebrush Route from Oro Grande to Helendale. The road passes Route 66 icons such as Potapov's Gas and Service Station (where the words BILL'S SERVICE are still legible) and the once-rowdy Sagebrush Inn, now a private residence. ⊠ *16825 D St., Rte. 66* ☎ *760/951-0436* ⊕ *www.califrt66museum.org* 🎫 *Free* ⊘ *Thurs., Fri., and Mon. 10-4, Sun. 11-3.*

☺ The California high desert's only zoo, the small-scale **Hesperia Zoo** houses animals that have retired from or are still working in the entertainment industry. Among the residents are a lion, a tiger, and a baboon; performing-animal shows are sometimes held. You can visit the zoo on a regularly scheduled tour or by appointment. ⊠ *19038 Willow St., Hesperia* ☎ *760/948-9430* ⊕ *www.thehesperiazoo.com* 🎫 *$6* ⊘ *Tours weekends 10-4.*

Forested **Silverwood Lake State Recreation Area** lies at the base of the San Bernardino Mountains, 10 mi east of Cajon Pass. One of the desert's most popular boating and fishing areas, 1,000-acre Silverwood Lake also has a beach with a lifeguard. You can fish for trout, largemouth bass, crappie, and catfish; hike and bike the trails; or come in winter to count bald eagles, which nest in the tall Jeffrey pines by the shore. Campgrounds accommodate tents and RVs. At the marina, you can rent pontoon and fishing boats as well as paddleboats, kayaks, and Wave-Runners. Campfire programs are offered in summer, and public Wi-Fi is available in the park. ⊠ *14651 Cedar Cir., Hesperia* ☎ *760/389-2303* ⊕ *www.parks.ca.gov* 🎫 *$10 per car, $8 per boat* ⊘ *May–Sept., daily 6 AM–9 PM; Oct.–Apr., daily 7–7.*

WHERE TO EAT

¢–$
AMERICAN
★
✕ **Emma Jean's Holland Burger Cafe.** This circa-1940s diner sits right on U.S. Historic Route 66 and is favored by locals for its generous portions and old-fashioned home cooking. Try the biscuits and gravy, chicken-fried steak, or the famous Trucker's Sandwich, chock-full of roast beef, bacon, chilies, and cheese. ⊠ *17143 D St.* ☎ *760/243-9938* ⊕ *www.hollandburger.com/home* 🍴 *AE, MC, V* ⊘ *Closed Sun. No dinner.*

¢–$
AMERICAN
✕ **Summit Inn.** Elvis Presley is one of many famous customers who passed through this kitschy diner perched atop the Cajon Pass. Open since 1951, the restaurant is filled with Route 66 novelty items, a gift shop, and vintage jukebox, which plays oldies from the 1960s. The food isn't anything special, unless you have a hankering for ostrich, but the funky decor and historic significance make it worth a stop. ⊠ *6000 Mariposa Rd., Oak Hills* ☎ *760/949-8688* 🍴 *MC, V.*

16

Many of the buildings in the popular Calico Ghost Town are authentic.

BARSTOW

32 mi northeast of Victorville on I–15.

In 1886, when a subsidiary of the Atchison, Topeka, and Santa Fe Railway began construction of a depot and hotel here, Barstow was born. Today outlet stores, chain restaurants, and motels define the landscape, though old-time neon signs light up the town's main street.

ESSENTIALS

Visitor Information Barstow Area Chamber of Commerce and Visitors Bureau (✉ *681 N. 1st Ave., Barstow* ☎ *760/256–8617* ⊕ *www.barstowchamber.com*).

EXPLORING

When the sun sets in the Mojave, check out a bit of surviving Americana at the **Skyline Drive-In Theatre,** where you can watch the latest Hollywood flicks among the Joshua trees and starry night sky in good old-fashioned stereo FM sound. ✉ *31175 Old Hwy. 58* ☎ *760/256–3333* 💲 *$6* ☉ *Shows Wed.–Sun. at 7:30; closed Mon. and Tues.*

The **California Welcome Center** has exhibits about desert ecology, wildflowers, and wildlife, as well as general visitor information for the state of California. ✉ *2796 Tanger Way* ☎ *760/253–4782* ⊕ *www.visitcwc. com* ☉ *Daily 9–6.*

★ The earliest-known Americans fashioned the artifacts buried in the walls and floors of the pits at **Calico Early Man Archaeological Site.** Nearly 12,000 stone tools—used for scraping, cutting, and gouging—have been excavated here. The apparent age of some of these items (said to be as much as 200,000 years old) contradicts the dominant archaeological theory that humans populated North America only 13,000 years ago. Noted archaeologist Louis Leakey was so impressed with the Calico site that he became its director in 1963 and served in that capacity until his death in 1972. His old camp is now a visitor center and museum. The only way into the site is by guided tour (call ahead, as scheduled tours sometimes don't take place). ☒ *Off I–15, Minneola Rd. exit, 15 mi northeast of Barstow* ☎ *760/254–2248* ⊕ *www.blm.gov/ca/st/en/fo/ barstow/calico.html* ☒ *$5* ☉ *Visitor center Wed. 12:30–4:30, Thurs.– Sun. 9–4:30; tours Wed. 1:30 and 3:30, Thurs.–Sun. 9:30, 11:30, 1:30, and 3:30.*

☾ **Fodor's Choice** ★ **Calico Ghost Town** was once a wild and wealthy mining town. In 1881 prospectors found a rich deposit of silver in the area, and by 1886 more than $85 million worth of silver, gold, and other precious metals had been harvested from the surrounding hills. Once the price of silver fell, though, the town slipped into decline. Many buildings here are authentic, but the restoration has created a theme-park version of the 1880s. You can stroll the wooden sidewalks of Main Street, browse shops filled with Western goods, roam the tunnels of Maggie's Mine, and take a ride on the Calico-Odessa Railroad. Festivals in March, May, October, and November celebrate Calico's Wild West theme. ☒ *Ghost Town Rd., 3 mi north of I–15, 5 mi east of Barstow* ☎ *760/254–2122* ⊕ *www.calicotown.com* ☒ *$6* ☉ *Daily 9–5.*

16

A Spanish-named spot meaning "house of the desert," the **Casa Del Desierto Harvey House** was one of many hotel and restaurant depots opened by Santa Fe railroad guru Fred Harvey in the early 20th century. The location where Judy Garland's film *The Harvey Girls* was shot, the building is now completely restored. Inside the Casa Del Desierto is the Route 66 Mother Road Museum and Gift Shop. ☒ *681 N. 1st Ave.* ☎ *760/255–1890* ⊕ *www.route66museum.org* ☒ *Free* ☉ *Apr.– Oct., Fri.–Sun. 10–4; Mar.–Nov., Fri.–Sun. 11–4. Guided tours by appointment.*

☾ Stop by the **Desert Discovery Center** to see exhibits of fossils, plants, and local animals. The main attraction here is Old Woman, the second-largest iron meteorite ever found in the United States. It was discovered in 1976 about 50 mi from Barstow in the Old Woman Mountains. The center also has visitor information for the Mojave Desert. ☒ *831 Barstow Rd.* ☎ *760/252–6060* ⊕ *www.discoverytrails.org* ☒ *Free* ☉ *Tues.– Sat. 11–4.*

One of the world's largest natural Native American art galleries, **Inscription Canyon**, 42 mi northwest of Barstow in the Black Mountains, has nearly 10,000 petroglyphs and pictographs of bighorn sheep and other Mojave wildlife. ☒ *EF373, off Copper City Rd., 10 mi west of Fort Irwin Rd.* ☎ *760/252–6000* ☉ *Weekdays 7:45–4:30.*

★ Many science-fiction movies set on Mars have been filmed at **Rainbow Basin National Natural Landmark,** 8 mi north of Barstow. Huge slabs of mildly red, orange, white, and green stone tilt at crazy angles like ships about to capsize; hike the washes, and you'll likely see the fossilized remains of creatures (such as mastodons and bear-dogs), which roamed the basin up to 16 million years ago. You can camp here, at Owl

Canyon Campground, on the east side of Rainbow Basin. Be aware that the dirt roads to—and especially within—the site are in poor condition. ✉ *Fossil Bed Rd., 3 mi west of Fort Irwin Rd.* ☎ *760/252–6000* ⊕ *www. blm.gov/ca/barstow/basin.html.*

Ȼ If you're a railroad buff, then you'll love the **Western American Rail Museum.** It houses memorabilia from Barstow's early railroad days, as well as interactive and historic displays on railroad history. Be sure to check out the old locomotives and cabooses for a truly nostalgic experience. ✉ *685 N. 1st St.* ☎ *760/256–9276* ⊕ *www.barstowrailmuseum. org* ✍ *Free* ☉ *Fri.–Sun. 11–4.*

Ȼ If you've seen Jodie Foster's movie *Contact,* about intelligent signals from outer space, then you'll probably enjoy visiting the **Goldstone Deep Space Communications Complex** on the Fort Irwin Military Base near Barstow. By appointment, the staff offers guided tours of the 53-square-mi complex, including its large antennas, which search for signs of otherworldly life. Start out at the Goldstone Museum, with its exhibits dedicated to current missions, past missions, and Deep Space Network history, or take the kids into the hands-on room for a lesson about the universe. ✉ *35 mi north of Barstow on Ft. Irwin Military Base* ☎ *760/255–8687 or 760/255–8688* ⊕ *deepspace.jpl.nasa.gov/dsn/features/goldstonetours. html* ✍ *Free* ☉ *Guided tours by appointment only.*

WHERE TO EAT AND STAY

¢–$　AMERICAN　★　× **Bagdad Café.** Tourists from all over the world flock to the site where the 1988 film of the same name was shot. Built in the 1940s, this Route 66 eatery serves a home-style menu of burgers, chicken-fried steak, and seafood. An old Airstream trailer from the movie sits outside the café. ✉ *46548 National Trails Hwy., Newberry Springs* ☎ *760/257–3101* ⊟ *AE, MC, V.*

$$–$$$　AMERICAN　★　× **Idle Spurs Steakhouse.** Since the 1950s this roadside ranch has been a Barstow dining staple. Covered in cacti outside and Christmas lights inside, it's a colorful, cheerful place with a big wooden bar. The menu features prime cuts of meat, ribs, and lobster, and there's a great microbrew list. ✉ *690 Hwy. 58* ☎ *760/256–8888* ⊕ *www.idlespurssteakhouse. com* ⊟ *AE, D, MC, V* ☉ *No lunch weekends.*

¢–$　SOUTHERN　× **Slash X Ranch Cafe.** If you have a craving for cold beer, burgers, and chili-cheese fries, look no further than this Wild West watering hole, a Barstow favorite since 1954. Named for the cattle ranch that preceded it, the café lures a mix of visitors and locals, who relish its rowdy atmosphere, hearty portions, and friendly service. Shuffleboard tables and horseshoe pits add to the fun. ✉ *28040 Barstow Rd.* ☎ *760/252–1197* ⊟ *AE, D, MC, V* ☉ *Closed weekdays.*

¢–$　🏨 **Ramada Inn.** Though this large property is slightly more expensive than others lining Main Street, it also has more amenities (which is why it tends to attract business travelers). The modern rooms have a desert theme and are decorated in browns and pinks that evoke the surrounding landscape. **Pros:** clean; large rooms. **Cons:** some rooms feel dated; occasional nighttime train noise. ✉ *1511 E. Main St.* ☎ *760/256–5673* ⊕ *www.ramada.com* ↩ *148 rooms* ♿ *In-hotel: restaurant, room service, pool, laundry service, Wi-Fi hotspot, some pets allowed* ⊟ *AE, D, DC, MC, V* ⧠*BP.*

BAKER

63 mi northeast of Barstow on I–15; 84 mi south of Death Valley Junction via Hwy. 127.

The small town of Baker is Death Valley's gateway to the western Mojave. There are several gas stations and restaurants (many of them fast-food outlets), a few motels, and a general store (that for many years has claimed to sell the most winning Lotto tickets in California).

■TIP➔ While you're driving through the Mojave, tune in to the Highway Stations (98.1 FM near Barstow, 98.9 FM near Essex, and 99.7 FM near Baker) for the latest Mojave traffic and weather. The stations cover 40,000 square mi of the desert, making it an important source of information on the area. Traffic can be especially troublesome Friday through Sunday, when scores of harried Angelenos head to Las Vegas for a bit of R&R.

AFTON CANYON

Because of its colorful, steep walls, **Afton Canyon** (⊠ *Off Afton Canyon Rd., 36 mi northeast of Barstow via I–15*) is often called the Grand Canyon of the Mojave. It was carved over thousands of years by the rushing waters of the Mojave River, which makes one of its few aboveground appearances here. The dirt road that leads to the canyon is ungraded in spots, so you are best off driving it in an all-terrain vehicle.

16

EXPLORING

You can't help but notice Baker's 134-foot-tall **thermometer** (⊠ *72157 Baker Blvd.*), whose world-record height in feet pays homage to the record-high U.S. temperature: 134°F, recorded in Death Valley on July 10, 1913.

PRIMM, NV

52 mi northeast of Baker, via I–15; 118 mi east of Death Valley, via Hwy. 160 and I–15; 114 mi north of Barstow, via I–15.

Amid the rugged beauty of the Mojave's landscapes, this bustling mecca for gamblers and theme-park lovers has sprung up on the border between California and southern Nevada. The casino resorts here are the first to greet you on the lonely stretch of road connecting Los Angeles with Las Vegas—and increasingly, visitors are simply stopping and spending their gambling vacations here.

EXPLORING

One of Primm's greatest claims to fame is its 24-hour **Bonnie and Clyde Gangster Exhibit.** Here, you'll find the bullet-riddled Ford car in which the 1930s duo perished in a hailstorm of gunfire in Louisiana on May 3, 1934. There are also other Bonnie and Clyde memorabilia, such as newspaper clippings and items owned by the couple, and a restored 1931 armored Lincoln belonging to gangsters Al Capone and Dutch Schultz. The exhibits are free to view in the rotunda connecting Primm Valley Resort and Casino with the Fashion Outlet Mall. ⊠ *32100 Las Vegas Blvd. S* ☎ *702/874–1400 Ext. 7073.*

Though there are plenty of family-friendly activities in Primm (such as shopping at the mall, hitting the waterslide at Whiskey Pete's, or the amusement park at Buffalo Bill's), guests under 21 are not allowed on the casino floors, and children under 13 may not be left unattended. Each of the casinos has a video arcade, which may provide some solace for the teenage set.

WHERE TO STAY

$–$$ ⛺ **Buffalo Bill's Resort and Casino.** Decorated in the style of a Western frontier town, this hotel is the biggest and most popular in Primm. Its buffalo-shape swimming pool and a large amusement park—which features several roller coasters and other rides—make the property a hit with families. The casino itself is enormous (46,000 square feet), and rooms here are bright and cheery and decorated with lodge-style furniture. Among the resort's several restaurants, Tony Roma's ($–$$) is a favorite. **Pros:** on-site restaurants and shops; casino. **Cons:** roller coaster noise at night; basic rooms seem a little worn. ⊠ *31700 Las Vegas Blvd. S* ☎ *702/386–7867 or 800/386–7867* ⊕ *www.primmvalleyresorts.com* ⤣ *1,193 rooms, 49 suites* ♿ *In-room: a/c, kitchen (some), refrigerator (some). In-hotel: 8 restaurants, bars, pool, Wi-Fi hotspot* ⊟ *AE, D, DC, MC, V.*

¢–$ ⛺ **Primm Valley Resort and Casino.** This elegant resort, which evokes a 1930s country club, is conveniently near the Primm Valley Conference Center. Rooms are decorated in warm tones, with dark-wood furniture. If you feel like splurging, check into one of the 640-square-foot Jacuzzi suites. GP's ($–$$), one of the on-site restaurants, is the fanciest in town, and popular for its aged prime rib and veal cordon bleu. **Pros:** on-site restaurants and shops; casino. **Cons:** basic rooms seem a little worn. ⊠ *31900 Las Vegas Blvd. S* ☎ *702/386–7867 or 800/386–7867* ⊕ *www.primmvalleyresorts.com* ⤣ *592 rooms, 31 suites* ♿ *In-room: a/c, kitchen (some), refrigerator (some). In-hotel: 3 restaurants, room service, bars, pool, Wi-Fi hotspot* ⊟ *AE, D, DC, MC, V.*

¢–$ ⛺ **Whiskey Pete's Hotel and Casino.** Opened in 1977, this castle-inspired property is the oldest of the three casinos in Primm. Rooms are decorated in mahogany and have Spanish tile floors; each of the 725-square-foot Jacuzzi suites has a four-person hot tub in the living room and a full bar. If you're visiting in summer, the tropical-theme pool with its shade trees and waterslide is a cool retreat. The Silver Spur Steakhouse ($–$$) serves excellent prime rib and chateaubriand. **Pros:** nice pool; cheap rooms. **Cons:** kind of cramped; bathrooms could use a remodel. ⊠ *100 W. Primm Blvd.* ☎ *702/386–7867 or 800/386–7867* ⊕ *www.primmvalleyresorts.com* ⤣ *765 rooms, 12 suites* ♿ *In-room: a/c, kitchen (some), refrigerator (some). In-hotel: 4 restaurants, room service, bars, pool, gym, Wi-Fi hotspot* ⊟ *AE, D, DC, MC, V.*

SPORTS AND THE OUTDOORS

All hotel guests have privileges at the **Primm Valley Golf Club** (☎ *888/847–2757*), which has two 18-hole courses designed by Tom Fazio that rank among the top 100 in the nation. Two putting greens and a pro shop complete the club, which is 4 mi south of Primm Valley Resort.

MOJAVE NATIONAL PRESERVE

Between I–15 and I–40, roughly east of Baker and Ludlow to the California/Nevada border.

The 1.4 million acres of the Mojave National Preserve hold a surprising abundance of plant and animal life—especially considering their elevation (nearly 8,000 feet in some areas). There are traces of human history here as well, including abandoned army posts and vestiges of mining and ranching towns. The town of Cima still has a small functioning store.

EXPLORING

Created millions of years ago by volcanic activity, **Hole-in-the-Wall** formed when gases were trapped between layers of deposited ash, rock, and lava; the gas bubbles left holes in the solidified material. The area was named by Bob Hollimon, a member of the Butch Cassidy gang, because it reminded him of his former hideout in Wyoming. To hike the canyon, you first must make your way down Rings Trail, a narrow 200-foot vertical chute. To make the rather strenuous descent you must grasp a series of metal rings embedded in the rock. The trail drops you into Banshee Canyon, where you are surrounded by steep, pockmarked walls and small caverns. You can explore the length of the canyon, but climbing the walls is not recommended, as the rock is soft and crumbles easily. Keep your eyes open for native lizards such as the chuckwalla. The Hole-in-the-Wall ranger station has docents who can answer questions about the area. ⊠ *Black Canyon Rd., 9 mi north of Mitchell Caverns* ☎ *760/928–2572* ⊕ *www.nps.gov/moja* ☉ *Fri.–Sun. 9–4.*

16

★ As you enter the preserve from the south, you'll pass miles of open scrub brush, Joshua trees, and beautiful red-black cinder cones before encountering the **Kelso Dunes** (⊠ *Kelbaker Rd., 90 mi east of I–15 and 14 mi north of I–40* ☎ *760/928–2572 or 760/252–6100* ⊕ *www.nps. gov/moja*). These golden, fine-sand slopes cover 70 square mi, reaching heights of 600 feet. You can reach them via a ½-mi walk from the main parking area, but be prepared for a serious workout. When you reach the top of a dune, kick a little bit of sand down the lee side and listen to the sand "sing." North of the dunes, in the town of Kelso, is the Mission revival–style **Kelso Depot Information Center**, flanked by five swaying palm trees. The building, which dates to 1923, was extensively renovated in 2005 and contains several rooms of desert- and train-themed exhibits. The Depot's restaurant, which has an early- to mid-20th-century diner look, is worth a gander even if you don't order anything.

☾ The National Park Service administers most of the Mojave preserve,
★ but **Providence Mountains State Recreation Area** is under the jurisdiction of the California Department of Parks. The visitor center has views of mountain peaks, dunes, buttes, crags, and desert valleys. At **Mitchell Caverns Natural Preserve** (⊡ *$6*) you have a rare opportunity to see all three types of cave formations—dripstone, flowstone, and erratics—in one place. The year-round 65°F temperature provides a break from the desert heat. Tours, the only way to see the caverns, are given daily at 1:30. Reservations must be made by mail and at least three weeks in advance; call first to check availability. ⊠ *Essex Rd., 16 mi*

north of I–40 ☎ *760/928–2586* ⊕ *www.parks.ca.gov* ☾ *Visitor center May–Sept., weekends 9–4.*

NEEDLES

I–40, 150 mi east of Barstow.

On Route 66 and the Colorado River, Needles is a good base for exploring many desert attractions, including Mojave National Preserve. Founded in 1883, the town of Needles, named for the jagged mountain peaks that overlook the city, served as a stop along the Santa Fe Railroad. One of its crown jewels was the elegant El Garces Harvey House Train Depot, which at this writing was being renovated through 2010. Today, Needles is a thriving community and a popular getaway for California residents who want to enjoy the river a little closer to home.

ESSENTIALS

Visitor Information Needles Chamber of Commerce (⊠ *100 G St., Needles* ☎ *760/326–2050* ⊕ *www.needleschamber.com*).

EXPLORING

Don't miss the historic 1908 **El Garces Harvey House Train Depot** (⊠ *900 Front St.* ☎ *760/326–5678*), one of the many restaurant-boardinghouses built by the Fred Harvey company.

Mystic Maze (⊠ *Park Moabi Rd., off I–40, 11 mi southeast of Needles* ☎ *760/326–5678*) is an unexplained geological site of spiritual significance to Pipa Aha Macav (Fort Mojave) Indians. The maze consists of several rows of rocks and mounds of dirt in different patterns.

    ☺
Fodor's Choice
★

In 1941, after the construction of Parker Dam, President Franklin D. Roosevelt set aside **Havasu National Wildlife Refuge**, a 24-mi stretch of land along the Colorado River between Needles and Lake Havasu City. Best seen by boat, this beautiful waterway is punctuated with isolated coves, sandy beaches, and Topock Marsh, a favorite nesting site of herons, egrets, and other waterbirds. You can see wonderful petroglyphs on the rocky red canyon cliffs of Topock Gorge. The park has 11 access points, including boat launches at Catfish Paradise, Five Mile Landing, and Pintail Slough. There's camping below Castle Rock. ⊠ *Off I–40, 13 mi southeast of Needles* ☎ *760/326–3853* ⊕ *www.fws.gov/ southwest/refuges/arizona/havasu.*

Moabi Regional Park, on the banks of the Colorado River, is a good place for swimming, boating, picnicking, horseback riding, and fishing. Bass, bluegill, and trout are plentiful in the river. There are 600 campsites with full amenities, including RV hookups, laundry and showers, and grills. ⊠ *Park Moabi Rd., off I–40, 11 mi southeast of Needles* ☎ *760/326–3831* 🗫 *Day use $10, camping $15–$35.*

WHERE TO EAT AND STAY

$–$$
PIZZA

✕**River City Pizza.** It's slim pickins in Needles when it comes to finding good grub, but this little pizza place is a local favorite. The restaurant is clean and simple, and the walls are covered with vibrant hand-painted scenes of Route 66 and the Colorado River. Try the Teriyaki Chicken

Pizza with a mug of cold lager or a glass of wine. ✉ *819 Broadway* ☎ *760/326–9191* ▤ *AE, D, MC, V.*

$–$$ ▦ **Best Western Colorado River Inn**. The country-western style rooms at this reliable chain are spartan, but they're decorated in rich colors. The property is right off Interstate 40. Expect the standard Best Western amenities, including free local calls and complimentary coffee in the lobby each morning. **Pros:** good rates; clean rooms. **Cons:** occasional nighttime train noise. ✉ *2371 Needles Hwy.* ☎ *760/326–4552 or 800/780–7234* ⊕ *www.bestwestern.com* ⇲ *63 rooms* ᐟ *In-room: a/c, refrigerator (some), Internet (some). In-hotel: pool, laundry facilities, Wi-Fi hotspot, some pets allowed* ▤ *AE, DC, MC, V* ꙮ *BP.*

¢–$ ▦ **Fender's River Road Resort**. This funky little 1960s-era motel is one of
☺ the best-kept secrets in Needles. The rooms are clean and well kept, many decorated with such whimsical accents as fish and stars. On a calm section of the Colorado River, this resort caters to families with a grassy play area shaded with trees and an area with grills and picnic tables. Camping is $44 a night. **Pros:** on the river; clean rooms. **Cons:** bare-bones amenities. ✉ *3396 Needles Hwy.* ☎ *760/326–3423* ⊕ *www. fendersriverroadresort.com* ⇲ *10 rooms, 27 campsites with full hookups* ᐟ *In-room: a/c, kitchen, refrigerator. In-hotel: beachfront, laundry facilities* ▤ *D, MC, V.*

16

LAKE HAVASU CITY, AZ

Hwy. 95, 43 mi southeast of Needles in Arizona.

In summer Angelenos throng to Lake Havasu. This wide spot in the Colorado River, which has backed up behind Parker Dam, is accessed from its eastern shore in Arizona. Here you can swim; zip around on a Jet Ski; paddle a kayak; fish for trout, bass, or bluegill; or boat beneath the London Bridge, one of the desert's oddest sights. During sunset the views are breathtaking.

Once home to the Mohave Indians, this riverfront community (which means "blue water") was settled in the 1930s with the construction of Parker Dam.

WHERE TO EAT

$$–$$$ ✕ **Shugrue's**. This lakefront restau-
AMERICAN   rant, a favorite of locals and tour-
★   ists, serves up beautiful views of London Bridge and the English Village. Heavy on fresh seafood, steak, and lobster, the restaurant is also known for such specials as Bombay chicken and shrimp, served with spicy yogurt sauce and mango chutney. ✉ *1425 McCulloch Blvd.* ☎ *928/453–1400* ⊕ *www.shugrues. com/lhc* ▤ *AE, D, DC, V.*

LONDON, ARIZONA?

What really put this town on the map was the piece-by-piece reconstruction in 1971 of **London Bridge** by town founder Robert P. McCulloch. Today the circa-1831 bridge, designed by John Rennie, connects the city to a small island and is the center of a town including numerous restaurants, hotels, RV parks, and a reconstructed English village. ☎ *928/855–4115* ⊕ *www.havasuchamber.com* 🎫 *Free* ☉ *Daily 24 hrs.*

SPORTS AND THE OUTDOORS

Ⓒ Docked at the London Bridge, the *Dixie Bell* (☎ *928/453–6776* ☐ *$15*) offers a leisurely way to spend an afternoon. The two-story, old-fashioned paddle-wheel boat, with air-conditioning and a cocktail lounge, takes guests on a one-hour narrated tour around the island. Tours are given daily at noon and 1:30. Right on the beach, **London Bridge Watercraft Tours & Rentals** (✉ *1534 Beachcomber Blvd., Crazy Horse Campground* ☎ *928/453–8883* ⊕ *www.londonbridgewatercraft.com*) rents personal watercraft such as Jet Skis and Sea-Doos.

OWENS VALLEY

Along U.S. 395 east of the Sierra Nevada.

LONE PINE

30 mi west of Panamint Valley via Hwy. 190.

Mt. Whitney towers majestically over this tiny community, which supplied nearby gold- and silver-mining outposts in the 1860s. In more recent decades—especially the 1950s and '60s—the town has been touched by Hollywood glamour: more than 300 movies, TV shows, and commercials have been filmed here. The Lone Pine Film Festival now takes place here every October.

ESSENTIALS

Visitor Information Lone Pine Chamber of Commerce (✉ *126 S. Main St., Lone Pine* ☎ *760/876–4444 or 877/253–8981* ⊕ *www.lonepinechamber.org*).

EXPLORING

Drop by the Lone Pine Visitor Center for a map of the **Alabama Hills** and take a drive up Whitney Portal Road (turn west at the light) to this wonderland of granite boulders. Erosion has worn the rocks smooth; some have been chiseled to leave arches and other formations. The hills have become a popular location for rock climbing. There are three campgrounds among the rocks, each with a stream for fishing. ✉ *Whitney Portal Rd., 4½ mi west of Lone Pine.*

★ Straddling the border of Sequoia National Park and Inyo National Forest–John Muir Wilderness, **Mt. Whitney** (14,496 feet) is the highest mountain in the continental United States. A favorite game for travelers passing through Lone Pine is trying to guess which peak is Mt. Whitney. Almost no one gets it right because Mt. Whitney is hidden behind other mountains. There is no road that ascends the peak, but you can catch a glimpse of the mountain by driving curvy Whitney Portal Road west from Lone Pine into the mountains. The pavement ends at the trailhead to the top of the mountain, which is also the start of the 211-mi John Muir Trail from Mt. Whitney to Yosemite National Park. At the portal, a restaurant (known for its pancakes) and a small store mostly cater to hikers and campers staying at Whitney Portal Campground. You can see a waterfall from the parking lot and go fishing in a small trout pond. The portal area is closed from mid-October to early May; the road closes when snow conditions require.

WHERE TO EAT AND STAY

¢–$ ✗ **Alabama Hills Café & Bakery.** Locals flock to this breakfast and lunch
AMERICAN   eatery just off the main drag. The extensive menu includes many vegetarian items. Portions are huge, which is good news for anyone who
is fueling up for a walk in the Sierra range looming to the west. ✉ *111
W. Post St.* ☎ *760/876–4675* ▭ *DC, MC, V* ☉ *Closed Tues.*

$$–$$$ ✗ **Seasons Restaurant.** This inviting, country-style diner serves all kinds of
AMERICAN   upscale American fare. For a special treat, try the medallions of Cervena
venison, smothered in port wine, dried cranberries, and toasted walnuts;
finish with the Baileys Irish Cream cheesecake or the lemon crème brûlée
for dessert. Children's items include a mini–sirloin steak. ✉ *206 S. Main
St.* ☎ *760/876–8927* ▭ *AE, D, MC, V* ☉ *No lunch. Closed Mon.*

$–$$ ⌨ **Dow Villa Motel and Hotel.** Built in 1923 to cater to the film industry,
Dow Villa is in the center of Lone Pine. Some rooms have views of the
mountains; both buildings are within walking distance of just about
everything in town. Pets are allowed only in the motel rooms. Many
units have an Old West feel, and are decorated with antique furniture
and pictures of John Wayne or Mt. Whitney. Wayne, who stayed here
in 1935, was here again (Room 20) in 1978 to film a TV commercial,
his last acting gig. **Pros:** historic property; recently updated; nice views.
Cons: feels a bit dated; road noise. ✉ *310 S. Main St.* ☎ *760/876–5521
or 800/824–9317* ⊕ *www.dowvillamotel.com* ↰ *91 rooms* ♿ *In-room:
a/c, refrigerator, DVD. In-hotel: pool, spa, Wi-Fi hotspot* ▭ *AE, D,
DC, MC, V.*

16

MANZANAR NATIONAL HISTORIC SITE

U.S. 395, 11 mi north of Lone Pine.

A reminder of an ugly episode in U.S. history, the remnants of the
Manzanar War Relocation Center have been designated the Manzanar
National Historic Site. This is where some 10,000 Japanese-Americans
were confined behind barbed-wire fences between 1942 and 1945. Manzanar was the first of 10 such internment camps erected by the federal
government following Japan's attack on Pearl Harbor in 1941. In the
name of national security, American citizens of Japanese descent were
forcibly relocated to these camps, many of them losing their homes,
businesses, and most of their possessions in the process. Today not much
remains of Manzanar but a guard post, the auditorium, and some concrete foundations. But you can stop at the entrance station, pick up a
brochure, and drive the one-way dirt road past the ruins to a small cemetery, where a monument stands as a reminder of what took place here.
Signs mark where structures such as the barracks, a hospital, school,
and fire station once stood. An outstanding 8,000-square-foot interpretive center has exhibits and a 15-minute film. ☐ *Manzanar Information,
c/o Superintendent: Death Valley National Park, Death Valley 92398*
☎ *760/878–2932* ⊕ *www.nps.gov/manz* ▣ *Free* ☉ *Park daily dawn–
dusk. Center Apr.–Nov., daily 9–5:30; Nov.–Apr., daily 9–4:30.*

CERRO GORDO GHOST TOWN

20 mi east of Lone Pine.

★ Discovered by Mexican miner Pablo Flores in 1865, Cerro Gordo was California's biggest producer of silver and lead, raking in almost $13 million before it shut down in 1959. Today it's a ghost town, home to many original buildings, including the circa-1871 American Hotel, the fully restored 1904 bunkhouse, the 1868 Belshaw House, a bullet-riddled saloon, and Union Mine and General Store, which now serves as a museum and outlook point over the majestic Sierra mountains and Owens Dry Lake.

The Sarsaparilla Saloon inside the hotel serves up its own Cerro Gordo Freighting Company Root Beer, bottled in nearby Indian Wells (proceeds go back to restoring and maintaining the ghost town). You'll have to time your visit for summer (usually early June through mid-November), as its 8,300-foot elevation means that the steep road into the town is impassable in winter. A four-wheel-drive vehicle is recommended at all times. A day pass is $5 per person, which includes a tour if arranged in advance. Guests are forbidden to take artifacts from the area or explore nearby mines. ⌂ *Box 221, Keeler 93530* ☎ *760/876–5030* ⊕ *www.cerrogordo.us.*

INDEPENDENCE

U.S. 395, 5 mi north of Manzanar National Historic Site.

Named for a military outpost that was established near here in 1862, Independence is small and sleepy. But the town has some wonderful historic buildings and is certainly worth a stop on your way from the Sierra Nevada to Death Valley (⇨ *Chapter 17*).

ESSENTIALS

Visitor Information Independence Chamber of Commerce (✉ *139 N. Edwards, Independence* ☎ *760/878–0084* ⊕ *www.independence-ca.com*).

EXPLORING

As you approach Independence from the north, you'll pass the **Mt. Whitney Fish Hatchery**, a delightful place for a family picnic. The hatchery's lakes were full of hefty, always-hungry breeder trout until a devastating mudslide in July 2008 prompted an expensive and extensive rebuilding project that took a year to complete. Built in 1915, the hatchery was one of the first trout farms in California, and today it produces fish that stock lakes throughout the state. ✉ *Fish Hatchery Rd., 1 mi north of Independence* ☎ *760/878–2272* ▦ *Free* ⊙ *Daily 9–4.*

The **Eastern California Museum** provides a glimpse of Inyo County's history. Highlights include a fine collection of Paiute and Shoshone Indian basketry, an exhibit about the Manzanar internment camp, and a yard full of agricultural implements used by early area miners and farmers. ✉ *155 N. Grant St.* ☎ *760/878–0364* ⊕ *www.inyocounty.us/ecmuseum* ▦ *Donations accepted* ⊙ *Daily 10–5.*

A memorial honors the 10,000 Japanese-Americans who were held at the Manzanar War Relocations Center during World War II.

WHERE TO STAY

¢–$ **Winnedumah Hotel Bed & Breakfast.** This 1927 B&B has the best—and most famous—digs in town: celebrities such as Roy Rogers, John Wayne, and Bing Crosby all stayed here while filming nearby. Outfitted in an eclectic mix of Wild West chic and modern bric-a-brac, the rooms are simple yet comfortable. There are also hostel rooms. Breakfast is usually a hearty affair of bacon, eggs, waffles, and fresh fruit. **Pros:** historic property; clean rooms. **Cons:** no television. ✉ *211 N. Edwards St.* ☎ *760/878–2040* 🌐 *www.winnedumah.com* *24 rooms, 14 with bath* *In-room: a/c, no phone (some), no TV. In-hotel: Wi-Fi hotspot, some pets allowed* *AE, D, DC, MC, V* *BP.*

BISHOP

U.S. 395, 43 mi north of Independence.

One of the biggest towns along U.S. 395, Bishop has views of the Sierra Nevada and the White and Inyo mountains. First settled by the Northern Paiute Indians, the area was named in 1861 for cattle rancher Samuel Bishop, who established a camp here. Paiute and Shoshone people reside on four reservations in the area.

ESSENTIALS

Visitor Information Bishop Chamber of Commerce (✉ *690 N. Main St., Bishop* ☎ *760/873–8405* 🌐 *www.bishopvisitor.com*).

EXPLORING

🕲 The **Laws Railroad Museum** is a complex of historic buildings and train cars from the Carson and Colorado Railroad Company, which set up a narrow-gauge railroad yard here in 1883. Among the exhibits are a self-propelled car from the Death Valley Railroad and a full village of rescued buildings, including a post office, an 1883 train depot, the 1909 North Inyo Schoolhouse, and a restored 1900 ranch house. ⊠ *U.S. 6, 3 mi north of U.S. 395* ☎ *760/873–5950* ⊕ *www.lawsmuseum.org* ⊠ *$5 suggested donation* ☉ *Daily 10–4.*

WHERE TO EAT AND STAY

¢-$
SCANDINAVIAN
✕ **Erick Schat's Bakerÿ.** A popular stop for motorists traveling to and from Mammoth Lakes, this shop is chock-full of delicious pastries, cookies, rolls, and other baked goods. But the biggest draw here is the sheepherder bread, a hand-shape and stone hearth–baked sourdough that was introduced during the gold rush by immigrant Basque sheepherders in 1907. In addition to the bakery, Schat's has a gift shop and a sandwich bar. ⊠ *763 N. Main St.* ☎ *760/873–7156* ⊕ *www. erickschatsbakery.com* ▤ *AE, MC, V.*

$$-$$$
AMERICAN
★
✕ **Whiskey Creek.** Since 1924, this Wild West–style saloon, restaurant, and gift shop has been serving crisp salads, warm soups, and juicy barbecued steaks to locals and tourists. Warm days are perfect for sitting on the shaded deck and enjoying one of the many available microbrews. ⊠ *524 N. Main St.* ☎ *760/873–7174* ⊕ *www.whiskeycreekbishop.com* ▤ *AE, MC, V.*

$-$$
🏨 **Best Western Creekside Inn.** The nicest spot to stay in Bishop, this clean and comfortable mountain-style hotel is a good base from which to explore the town or go skiing and trout fishing nearby. Rooms are elegantly furnished with cherrywood armoires and beds; the ranch-style lobby has a wonderfully large brick hearth. In summer you can sit on the patio near a trickling creek. **Pros:** nice pool; spacious and modern rooms; all rooms are nonsmoking. **Cons:** pets not allowed. ⊠ *725 N. Main St.* ☎ *760/872–3044 or 800/273–3550* ⊕ *www.bishopcreekside. com* ⤳ *89 rooms* ⚼ *In-room: a/c, kitchen (some), refrigerator (some), Internet. In-hotel: pool, Wi-Fi hotspot* ▤ *AE, MC, V* �🍽 *CP.*

SPORTS AND THE OUTDOORS

Sierra Mountain Center (⊠ *174 W. Line St.* ☎ *760/873–8526* ⊕ *www. sierramountaincenter.com*) provides instruction and guided hiking, skiing, snowshoeing, rock-climbing, and mountain-biking trips for all levels of expertise.

FISHING
The Owens Valley is trout country; its glistening alpine lakes and streams are brimming with feisty rainbow, brown, brook, and golden trout. Popular spots include Owens River, the Owens River gorge, and Pleasant Valley Reservoir. Although you can fish year-round here, some fishing is catch-and-release. Bishop is the site of fishing derbies throughout the year, including the popular Blake Jones Blind Bogey Trout Derby, in March. Whether you want to take a fly-fishing class or a guided wade trip, **Brock's Flyfishing Specialists and Tackle Experts** (⊠ *100 N. Main St.* ☎ *760/872–3581 or 888/619–3581* ⊕ *www.brocksflyfish. com*) is a valuable resource.

Death Valley National Park

WORD OF MOUTH

"DV is worth more than one day trip. The drive down into it is fantastic. We usually drive north on 95 to Beatty and then go west over the hump and down into the valley, stopping at Rhyolite if we're with someone who hasn't been to a ghost town."

—emalloy

WELCOME TO DEATH VALLEY NATIONAL PARK

TOP REASONS TO GO

★ **Weird science:** Death Valley's Racetrack is home to a moving boulder, an unexplained phenomenon that has scientists baffled.

★ **Lowest spot on the continent:** Stand on the lowest spot on the continent at Badwater, 282 feet below sea level.

★ **Wildflower explosion:** During the spring, this desert landscape is ablaze with greenery and colorful flowers, especially between Badwater and Ashford Mill.

★ **Ghost towns:** Death Valley is renowned for its Wild West heritage and is home to dozens of crumbling settlements including Ballarat, Cerro Gordo, Chloride City, Greenwater, Harrisburg, Keeler, Leadfield, Panamint City, Rhyolite, and Skidoo.

★ **Natural wonders:** From canyons to sand dunes to salt flats and dry lake beds, Death Valley serves up plenty of geological treasures.

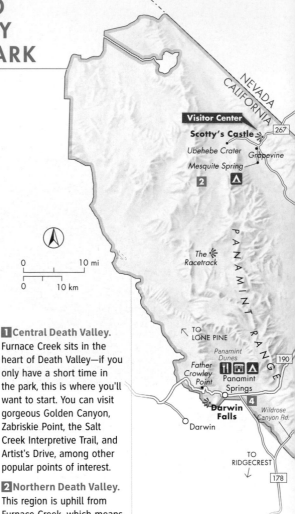

1 Central Death Valley. Furnace Creek sits in the heart of Death Valley—if you only have a short time in the park, this is where you'll want to start. You can visit gorgeous Golden Canyon, Zabriskie Point, the Salt Creek Interpretive Trail, and Artist's Drive, among other popular points of interest.

2 Northern Death Valley. This region is uphill from Furnace Creek, which means marginally cooler temperatures. Be sure to stop by Rhyolite Ghost Town on Highway 374 before entering the park and exploring Moorish Scotty's Castle, colorful Titus Canyon, crumbling Keane Wonder Mine, and jaw-dropping Ubehebe Crater.

3 Southern Death Valley. This is a desolate area, but there are plenty of sights that help convey Death Valley's rich history. Don't miss the Dublin Gulch Caves, or the famous Amargosa Opera House, where aging ballerina Marta Becket still wows the crowds.

4 Western Death Valley. Panamint Springs Resort is a nice place to grab a meal and get your bearings before moving on to quaint Darwin Falls, smooth rolling sand dunes, beehive-shaped Wildrose Charcoal Kilns, and historic Stovepipe Wells Village. On the way in, stop at Cerro Gordo Ghost Town, where you can view restored buildings dating back to 1867.

GETTING ORIENTED

Death Valley National Park covers 5,310 square mi, ranges from 6 to 60 mi wide, and measures 140 mi north to south. Within the park, the Panamint Range parallels Death Valley to the west, the Amargosa Range to the east. Nearly all of the park lies in southeastern California, with a small eastern portion crossing over into Nevada.

17

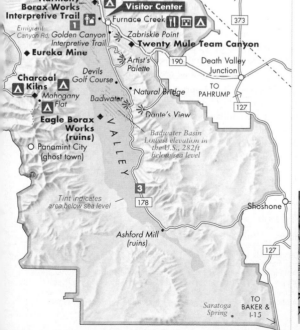

DEATH VALLEY NATIONAL PARK PLANNER

When to Go

Most of the park's one million annual visitors still come between late fall and early spring, taking advantage of moderate temperatures and the lack of rainfall. During these cooler months you will need to book a room in advance, but don't worry: the park never feels crowded. If you visit during summer, believe everything you've ever heard about desert heat—it can be brutal, with temperatures often topping 120°F. The dry air wicks moisture from the body without causing a sweat, so drink plenty of water. Bring sunglasses, a hat, and sufficient clothing to block the sun's rays and the wind. Flash floods are common; sections of roadway can be flooded or washed away. The wettest month is February, when the park receives an average of 0.3 inch of rain.

AVG. HIGH/LOW TEMPS.

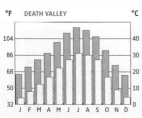

Getting Here and Around

It can take more than three hours to cross from one side of the park to another, so it's important to choose an entrance point that makes sense for what you want to see. If you're driving from Los Angeles, enter through the western portion along Highway 395; enter from the north at Beatty, Nevada, or via the central entrance at Death Valley Junction if you're coming from Las Vegas. Travelers from Orange County, San Diego, and the Inland Empire should access the park via I–15 North at Baker.

Much of the park can be toured on regularly scheduled bus tours, but these often don't allow time for hikes to sites not seen from the road, such as Salt Creek, Golden Canyon, and Natural Bridge. The best option is to drive to a number of the sites, get out of the car, and walk.

When driving in Death Valley, reliable maps are a must, as signage is often limited. Other important accessories include a compass, a mobile phone (though these don't always work in remote areas), and extra food and water (3 gallons per person per day is recommended, plus additional radiator water). If you're able to take a four-wheel-drive vehicle, bring it: many of Death Valley's most spectacular canyons are otherwise inaccessible.

The **California State Department of Transportation Hotline** (☎ 916/445–7623 or 800/427–7623 ⊕ www.dot.ca.gov) has updates on Death Valley road conditions. The **California Highway Patrol** (☎ 760/ 255-8750 near Barstow, 760/872–5900 near Bishop ⊕ cad.chp.ca.gov) offers the latest traffic incident information.

WHAT IT COSTS

	¢	$	$$	$$$	$$$$
Restaurants	under $8	$8–$12	$13–$20	$21–$30	over $30
Hotels	under $50	$50–$100	$101–$150	$151–$200	over $200
Campgrounds	under $10	$10–$17	$18–$35	$36–$49	over $50

Restaurant prices are per person for a main course at dinner. Hotel prices are per night for two people in a standard double room in high season, excluding taxes and service charges. Camping prices are for a standard (no hookups, pit toilets, fire grates, picnic tables) campsite per night.

Updated by Sura Wood and Reed Parsell

The desert is no Disneyland. With its scorching summer heat and vast, sparsely populated tracts of land, it's not often at the top of the list when most people plan their California vacations. But the natural riches of Death Valley—the largest national park outside Alaska—are overwhelming: rolling waves of sand dunes, black cinder cones thrusting up hundreds of feet from a blistered desert floor, riotous sheets of wildflowers, bizarrely shaped Joshua trees basking in the orange glow of a sunset, tiny pupfish that enthrall youngsters, and a silence that is both dramatic and startling.

17

PARK ESSENTIALS

ADMISSION FEES AND PERMITS
The entrance fee is $20 per vehicle and $10 for those entering on foot, bus, bike, or motorcycle. The payment, valid for seven consecutive days, is collected at the park's entrance stations and at the visitor center at Furnace Creek. (If you enter the park on Highway 190, there is no entrance station; remember to stop by the visitor center to pay the fee.) Annual park passes, valid only at Death Valley, are $40.

A permit is not required for groups of 14 or fewer, but if you're planning an overnight visit to the backcountry, complete a registration form at the Furnace Creek Visitor Center. Backcountry camping is allowed in areas that are at least 2 mi from maintained campgrounds and the main paved or unpaved roads, and ¼ mi from water sources. Most abandoned mining areas are restricted to day use.

ADMISSION HOURS
Most facilities within the park remain open year-round, daily 8–5.

EMERGENCIES
For all emergencies, call 911. Note that cell phones don't work in many parts of the park.

PARK CONTACT INFORMATION
Death Valley National Park ☐ *P.O. Box 579, Death Valley 92328* ☎ *760/786– 2331* ⊕ *www.nps.gov/deva.*

EXPLORING

HISTORIC SITES

Fodor'sChoice ★ **Keane Wonder Mine.** The tram towers and cables from the old mill used to process gold from Keane Wonder Mine are still here, leading up to the crumbling mine, which is a steep 1-mi hike up the mountain. A nearby path leads north to Keane Wonder Spring. ⊠ *Access road off Beatty Cutoff Rd., 17½ mi north of Furnace Creek.*

⟳ ★ **Scotty's Castle.** This Moorish-style mansion, begun in 1924 and never completed, takes its name from Walter Scott, better known as Death Valley Scotty. An ex-cowboy, prospector, and performer in Buffalo Bill's Wild West Show, Scotty always told people the castle was his, financed by gold from a secret mine. In reality, there was no mine, and the house belonged to a Chicago millionaire named Albert Johnson, whom Scott had finagled into investing in the fictitious mine. Despite the con, Johnson and Scott became great friends. The house functioned for a while as a hotel and still contains works of art, imported carpets, handmade European furniture, and a tremendous pipe organ. Costumed rangers, to varying degrees of enthusiasm, re-create life at the castle circa 1939. Check out the Underground Mysteries Tour, which takes you through a ¼-mile tunnel in the castle basement. ⊠ *Scotty's Castle Rd. (Hwy. 267), 53 mi north of Furnace Creek Interpretive Trail* ☎ *760/786–2392* ⊕ *www.nps.gov/deva* ☑ *$11* ⊙ *Winter: Daily 8:30–5:30; Summer: 9-4:30, tours daily 9–5.*

SCENIC STOPS

★ **Artist's Palette.** So called for the contrasting colors of its volcanic deposits, this is one of signature sights of Death Valley. Artist's Drive, the approach to the area, is one way heading north off Badwater Road, so if you're visiting Badwater, come here on the way back. The drive winds through foothills of sedimentary and volcanic rocks. About 4 mi into the drive, a short side road veers right to a parking lot that's a few hundred feet before the "palette," whose natural colors include shades of green, gold, and pink. ⊠ *11 mi south of Furnace Creek, off Badwater Rd.*

★ **Badwater.** At 282 feet below sea level, Badwater is the lowest spot on land in the Western Hemisphere—and also one of the hottest. Stairs and wheelchair ramps descend from the parking lot to a wooden platform that overlooks a sodium chloride pool, a small but remarkably persistent reminder that the valley floor used to contain a lake. You can continue past the platform on a broad, white path that peters out after a half-mile or so. Badwater is one of the most popular and easily accessible sites within the park. From this lowest point, be sure to look across to Telescope Peak, which towers more than 2 mi above the valley floor. ⊠ *Badwater Rd., 19 mi south of Furnace Creek.*

Fodor'sChoice **Dante's View.** This lookout is more than 5,000 feet up in the Black
★ Mountains. In the dry desert air you can see across most of 110-mi-wide Death Valley. The view is astounding. Take a 10-minute, mildly strenuous walk from the parking lot toward a series of rocky overlooks, where with binoculars you can spot some of Death Valley's signature sites. A few interpretive signs point out the highlights below in the valley and across, in the Sierra. Getting here from Furnace Creek takes an hour—time well invested. ⊠ *Dante's View Rd., off Hwy. 190, 35 mi from Badwater, 20 mi south of Twenty Mule Team Canyon.*

Devil's Golf Course. Thousands of miniature salt pinnacles carved into surreal shapes by the desert wind dot this wildly varied landscape. The salt was pushed up to the earth's surface by pressure created as underground salt- and water-bearing gravel crystallized. Get out of your vehicle and take a closer look; you'll see perfectly round holes descending into the ground. ⊠ *Badwater Rd., 13 mi south of Furnace Creek. Turn right onto dirt road and drive 1 mi.*

★ **Racetrack.** Getting here involves a 27-mi journey over a rough and almost nonexistent dirt road, but the trip is well worth the reward. Where else in the world do rocks move on their own? This phenomenon has baffled scientists for years. No one has actually seen the rocks in motion, but theory has it that when it rains, the hard-packed lake bed becomes slippery enough that gusty winds push the rocks along—sometimes for several hundred yards. When the mud dries, a telltale trail remains. The trek to the Racetrack can be made in a passenger vehicle, but high clearance is suggested. ⊠ *27 mi west of Ubehebe Crater via dirt road.*

Sand Dunes at Mesquite Flat. These dunes, made up of minute pieces of quartz and other rock, are ever-changing products of the wind-rippled hills, with curving crests and a sun-bleached hue. The dunes are the most photographed destination in the park, and you can see them at their best at sunrise and sunset. Keep your eyes open for animal tracks—you may even spot a coyote or fox. Bring plenty of water, and note where you parked your car: it's easy to become disoriented in this ocean of sand. If you lose your bearings, climb to the top of a dune and scan the horizon for the parking lot. ⊠ *19 mi north of Hwy. 190, northeast of Stovepipe Wells Village.*

★ **Titus Canyon.** Titus Canyon is a popular 28-mi drive from Beatty south along Scotty's Castle Road. Along the way you'll pass Leadville Ghost Town, petroglyphs at Klare Spring, and spectacular limestone and dolomite narrows at the end of the canyon. Toward the end, a two-section of gravel road will lead you into the mouth of the canyon. ⊠ *Access road off Scotty's Castle Rd., 33 mi northwest of Furnace Creek.*

★ **Zabriskie Point.** Although only about 710 feet in elevation, this is one of Death Valley National Park's most scenic spots, overlooking a striking panorama of wrinkled, multicolor hills. It's a great place to watch the sunrise, but it can be bustling any time of day. Pair it with a drive out to magnificent Dante's View. ⊠ *Hwy. 190, 5 mi south of Furnace Creek.*

17

DID YOU KNOW?

One of the best ways to experience Artist's Palate— a beautiful landscape of colorful volcanic deposits—is by following Artist's Drive, a 9-mi one-way road through the area.

Flora and Fauna

There's a general misconception that Death Valley National Park consists of mile upon endless mile of flat desert sands, scattered cacti, and an occasional cow skull. Many people don't realize that across the valley floor from Badwater—the lowest point in the Western Hemisphere—Telescope Peak towers at 11,049 feet above sea level. The extreme topography of Death Valley is a lesson in geology. Two hundred million years ago seas covered the area, depositing layers of sediment and fossils. Between 3.5 million and 5 million years ago faults in the Earth's crust and volcanic activity pushed and folded the ground, causing mountain ranges to rise and the valley floor to drop. The valley was then filled periodically by lakes, which eroded the surrounding rocks into fantastic formations and deposited the salts that now cover the floor of the basin.

Most animal life in Death Valley (51 mammal, 36 reptile, 307 bird, and 3 amphibian species) is found near the limited sources of water. The bighorn sheep spend most of their time in the secluded upper reaches of the park's rugged canyons and ridges. Coyotes can often be seen lazing in the shade next to the golf course and have been known to run onto the fairways to steal a golf ball. The only native fish in the park is the pupfish, which grows to slightly longer than 1 inch. In winter, when the water is cold, the fish lie dormant in the bottom mud, becoming active again in spring. Because they are wary of large moving shapes, you must stand quietly over a pool at Salt Creek to see them.

Botanists say there are more than 1,000 species of plants here (21 exist nowhere else in the world), though many annual plants lie dormant as seeds for all but a few months in spring, when rains trigger a bloom. The rest congregate around limited sources of water. Most of the low-elevation vegetation grows around the oases at Furnace Creek and Scotty's Castle, where oleanders, palms, and salt cedar grow. At higher elevations you will find pinyon, juniper, and bristlecone pine.

VISITOR CENTERS

Furnace Creek Visitor Center and Museum. The exhibits and artifacts here provide a broad overview of how Death Valley formed; you can pick up maps at the bookstore run by the Death Valley Natural History Association. This is also the place to sign up for ranger-led walks (available November through April) or check out a live presentation about the valley's cultural and natural history. The center offers 12-minute slide shows about the park every 30 minutes. Your children are likely to receive plenty of individual attention from the enthusiastic rangers. ✉ *Hwy. 190, 30 mi northwest of Death Valley Junction* ☎ *760/786–3200* ⊕ *www.nps.gov/deva* ☉ *Daily 8–5.*

Scotty's Castle Visitor Center and Museum. If you visit Death Valley, you'll likely make a stop here at the main ticket center for Scotty's Castle living-history tours. Here you'll also find a nice display of exhibits, books, self-guided tour pamphlets, and displays about the castle's creators, Death Valley Scotty and Albert M. Johnson. Fuel up with gasoline, sandwiches, or souvenirs before heading back out to the park. ⊠ *Rte. 267, 53 mi northwest of Furnace Creek and 45 mi northwest of Stovepipe Wells Village* ☎ *760/786–2392* ⊕ *www.nps.gov/deva* ⊙ *Daily 7:30–5.*

SPORTS AND THE OUTDOORS

BIRD-WATCHING

Approximately 350 bird species have been identified in Death Valley. The best place to see the park's birds is along the Salt Creek Interpretive Trail, where you can spot ravens, common snipes, killdeer, spotted sandpipers, and great blue herons. Along the fairways at Furnace Creek Golf Club, you can see kingfishers, peregrine falcons, hawks, Canada geese, yellow warblers, and the occasional golden eagle—just remember to stay off the greens. Scotty's Castle attracts wintering birds from around the globe who are attracted to its running water, shady trees, and shrubs. Other good spots to find birds are at Saratoga Springs, Mesquite Springs, Travertine Springs, and Grimshaw Lake near Tecopa. You can download a complete park bird checklist, divided by season, at ⊕ *www.nps.gov/deva/naturescience/birds.htm.* Rangers at Furnace Creek Visitor Center often lead birding walks through Salt Creek between November and March.

FOUR-WHEELING

Maps and SUV guidebooks for four-wheel-drive and other backcountry roads (including the popular Cottonwood/Marble canyons, Racetrack, Eureka Dunes, Saratoga Springs, Warm Springs Canyon) are offered at the Furnace Creek Visitor Center. Remember: never travel alone and be sure to pack plenty of water and snacks. Driving off established roads is strictly prohibited in the park.

HIKING

Plan to hike before or after midday in the spring, summer, or fall, unless you're in the mood for a masochistic baking. Carry plenty of water, wear protective clothing, and keep an eye out for tarantulas, black widows, scorpions, snakes, and other potentially dangerous creatures. Some of the best trails are unmarked; if the opportunity arises, ask for directions.

EASY

Fodor's Choice ★

Darwin Falls. This lovely 2-mi round-trip hike rewards you with a refreshing waterfall surrounded by thick vegetation and a rocky gorge. No swimming or bathing is allowed, but it's a beautiful place for a picnic. Adventurous hikers can scramble higher toward more rewarding views of the falls. ⊠ *Access the 2-mi graded dirt road and parking area off Hwy. 190, 1 mi west of Panamint Springs Resort.*

Natural Bridge Canyon. A 2-mi access road with potholes that could swallow basketballs leads to a parking lot. From there, set off to see interesting geological features in addition to the bridge, which is ¼-mi away. The one-way trail continues for a few hundred meters, but scenic returns diminish quickly and eventually you're confronted with

17

climbing boulders. ⊠ *Access road off Badwater Rd., 15 mi south of Furnace Creek.*

Ⓒ **Salt Creek Interpretive Trail.** This trail, a ½-mi boardwalk circuit, loops through a spring-fed wash. The nearby hills are brown and gray, but the floor of the wash is alive with aquatic plants such as pickerelweed and salt grass. The stream and ponds here are among the few places in the park to see the rare pupfish, the only native fish species in Death Valley. Animals such as bobcats, fox, coyotes, and snakes visit the spring, and you may also see ravens, common snipes, killdeer, and great blue herons. ⊠ *Off Hwy. 190, 14 mi north of Furnace Creek.*

★ **Titus Canyon.** The narrow floor of Titus Canyon is made of hard-packed gravel and dirt, and it's a constant, moderate uphill walk. Klare Spring and some petroglyphs are 5½ mi from the mouth of the canyon, but you can get a feeling for the area on a shorter walk.

MODERATE

Ⓒ **Mosaic Canyon.** A gradual uphill trail (4 mi round-trip) winds through the smoothly polished walls of this narrow canyon. There are dry falls to climb at the upper end. ⊠ *Access road off Hwy. 190, ½ mi west of Stovepipe Wells Village.*

DIFFICULT

Fodor'sChoice **Keane Wonder Mine.** Allow two hours for the 2-mi round-trip trail that
★ follows an out-of-service aerial tramway to this mine. The way is steep, but the views of the valley are spectacular. Do not enter the tunnels or hike beyond the top of the tramway—it's dangerous. The trailhead is 2 mi down an unpaved and bumpy access road. ⊠ *Access road off Beatty Cutoff Rd., 17½ mi north of Furnace Creek.*

Telescope Peak Trail. The 14-mi round-trip begins at Mahogany Flat Campground, which is accessible by a very rough dirt road. The steep and at some points treacherous trail winds through pinyon, juniper, and bristlecone pines, with excellent views of Death Valley and Panamint Valley. Ice axes and crampons may be necessary in winter—check at the Furnace Creek Visitor Center. It takes a minimum of eight hours to hike to the top of the 11,049-foot peak and then return. Getting to the peak is a strenuous endeavor; take plenty of water and only attempt it in fall unless you're an experienced hiker. ⊠ *Off Wildrose Rd., south of Charcoal Kilns.*

EDUCATIONAL OFFERINGS

GUIDED TOURS

Death Valley Explorer Tour. This 11-hour luxury motor-coach tour of the park passes through its most famous landmarks. Tours include lunch and hotel pickup from designated Las Vegas–area hotels. ☎ *800/719–3768 Death Valley Tours, 800/566–5868 or 702/233–1627 Look Tours* ▥ *$173.99* ◷ *Tues., Fri., and Sun. at 7 AM.*

Furnace Creek Visitor Center tours. This center has the most tour options, including a weekly 2-mi Harmony Borax Walk and guided hikes to Keane Wonder Mine, Mosaic Canyon, and Golden Canyon. Less strenuous options include wildflower walks, birding walks, geology walks, and a Furnace Creek Inn historical tour. The Furnace Creek Visitor Center is where you hop aboard a distinctive, pink four-wheel-drive vehicle with **Pink Jeep Tours Las Vegas** (☎ 702/895–6777 *www.pinkjeep. com*), to visit places—the Charcola Kilns, the Racetrack, and Titus Canyon among them—that your own vehicle might not be able to handle. Pink Jeep tours last two to six hours and cost $65 to $165. The visitor center also offers orientation programs every half hour, daily from 8 to 6. ✉ *Furnace Creek Visitor Center, Rte. 190, 30 mi northwest of Death Valley Junction* ☎ 760/786–2331.

Gadabout Tours. Take multiday trips through Death Valley from Ontario, California, in February, March, and November. ✉ *Sheraton Ontario Airport, 428 N. Vineyard Ave., Ontario* ✆ *1801 E. Tahquitz Canyon Way, Palm Springs 92262* ☎ 760/325–5556 *or* 800/952–5068 ⊕ *www. gadabouttours.com.*

ENTERTAINMENT

Marta Becket's Amargosa Opera House. An artist and dancer from New York, Becket first visited the former railway town of Amargosa while on tour in 1964. Three years later she returned to town and bought a boarded-up theater that sat amid a group of run-down mock–Spanish colonial buildings. To compensate for the sparse audiences in the early days, Becket painted a Renaissance-era Spanish crowd on the walls and ceiling, turning the theater into a trompe l'oeil masterpiece. Now in her late 70s, Becket performs her blend of ballet, mime, and 19th-century melodrama to sellout crowds. After the show you can meet her in the adjacent gallery, where she sells her paintings and autographs her books. There are no performances mid-May through September. Reservations are required. ✉ *Rte. 127,608 Death Valley Junction 92328* ☎ 760/852–4441 ⊕ *www.amargosa-opera-house.com* 🎫 *$15* ☉ *Oct.– May (through Mother's Day weekend).*

17

WHERE TO EAT

$$ ✕ **Forty-Niner Cafe.** This casual coffee shop serves typical American fare
CAFÉ for breakfast, lunch, and dinner. It's done up in a rustic mining style
☺ with whitewashed pine walls, vintage map-covered tables, and prospector-branded chairs. Past menus and old photographs decorate the walls. ✉ *Furnace Creek Ranch, Hwy. 190, Furnace Creek* ☎ 760/786–2345 ⊕ *www.furnacecreekresort.com* ⊟ *AE, D, DC, MC, V.*

$$$–$$$$ ✕ **Furnace Creek Inn Dining Room.** Fireplaces, beamed ceilings, and spec-
AMERICAN tacular views provide a visual feast to match the inn's ambitious menu.
Fodor's Choice Dishes may include such desert-theme items as rattlesnake empanadas
★ and crispy cactus, and simpler fare such as salmon, free-range chicken, and lamb chops. For vegetarians, there's squash lasagna and polenta. An evening dress code (no jeans, T-shirts, or shorts) is enforced. Lunch is served October–May only, but you can always have afternoon tea, an inn tradition since 1927. Breakfast and Sunday brunch are also served. ✉ *Furnace Creek Inn Resort, Hwy. 190, Furnace Creek* ☎ 760/786–2345 ⊕ *www.furnacecreekresort.com* 🍴 *Reservations essential* ⊟ *AE, D, DC, MC, V* ☉ *No lunch June–Sept.*

"I'd always wanted to photograph this remote location, and on my drive into Death Valley I was rewarded at Zabriskie Point with this amazing view." —photo by Rodney Ee, Fodors.com member

$$–$$$ ✕**Toll Road Restaurant.** There are wagon wheels in the yard and Old West
AMERICAN artifacts on the interior walls at this restaurant in the Stovepipe Wells
Village hotel. A stone fireplace heats the dining room. A full menu, with
steaks, chicken, fish, and pasta, is served October–mid-May; breakfast
and dinner buffets are laid out during summer. Quench your thirst in
the full-service saloon. ⊠ *Hwy. 190, Stovepipe Wells* ☎ *760/786–2604*
▭ *AE, D, DC, MC, V* ☺ *No lunch mid-May–Oct.*

WHERE TO STAY

During the busy season (November–March) you should make reservations for lodgings within the park at least one month in advance.

$$$$ ⊞ **Furnace Creek Inn.** This is Death Valley's most luxurious accommoda-
Fodor'sChoice tions, going so far as to have valet parking. Built in 1927, this adobe-
★ brick-and-stone lodge is nestled in one of the park's greenest oases. A
warm mineral stream gurgles across the property, and its 85°F waters
feed into a swimming pool. The rooms are decorated in earth tones,
with tasteful furnishings. The top-notch Furnace Creek Inn Dining
Room ($$$) serves desert-theme dishes such as rattlesnake empanadas
and crispy cactus, as well as less exotic fare such as cumin-lime shrimp,
lamb, and New York strip steak. Afternoon tea has been a tradition
since 1927. **Pros:** refined; comfortable; great views. **Cons:** a far cry from
roughing it; expensive. ⊠ *Furnace Creek Village, near intersection of
Hwy. 190 and Badwater Rd.* ⊕ *P.O. Box 190, Death Valley 92328*
☎ *760/786–2345* ⊕ *www.furnacecreekresort.com* ➘ *66 rooms* ⚒ *In-*

OUTFITTERS AND EXPEDITIONS

Reserve well in advance for all tours.

FOUR-WHEELING

The 10-hour **Death Valley SUV Tour** (*Death Valley Tours* ☎ *800/719–3768* ⊕ *www.deathvalleytours.net*) departs from Las Vegas and takes you on a fully narrated whirl through Death Valley in a four-wheel-drive Jeep. Tours ($255.95 per person; slightly less if booked through the Internet) departs daily, Sept. through May at 7:45 AM and include free pickup from designated hotels. Bottled water and snacks are provided, and camera rentals, tripods, and film are available for an additional fee.

HIKING

Join an experienced guide and spend six days exploring Death Valley's most popular sights with **Death Valley National Park and Red Rock Hiker** (*Escape Adventures* ☎ *800/596–2953 or 702/596–2953* ⊕ *www.escapeadventures.com*). The tour ($1, 290), offered October and

February–April, also spends two days in Red Rock Canyon National Conservation Area. For an additional fee, you can rent, tents, sleeping bags, ground pad, and pillow in a kit for $90, The price includes a night in the Bonnie Springs Inn.

HORSEBACK AND CARRIAGE RIDES

Set off on a one- or two-hour guided horseback or carriage ride ($30–$65) from **Furnace Creek Stables** (⊠ *Hwy. 190, Furnace Creek* ☎ *760/786–2345 Ext. 339* ⊕ *www. furnacecreekstables.net*). The rides traverse trails with views of the surrounding mountains, where multi-color volcanic rock and alluvial fans form a background for date palms and other vegetation. Evening carriage rides take passengers around the golf course and Furnace Creek Ranch. Cocktail rides, with champagne, margaritas, and hot spiced wine, are available. The stables are open October–May only.

17

room: Internet. In-hotel: restaurant, room service, bar, tennis courts, pool ⊟ AE, D, DC, MC, V ⊗ Closed mid-May–mid-Oct.

$ 🍴 **Panamint Springs Resort.** Ten miles inside the west entrance of the park, this low-key resort overlooks the sand dunes and peculiar geological formations of the Panamint Valley. It's a modest mom-and-pop-style operation with a wraparound porch and rustic furnishings. One room has a king-size bed, and two of the rooms accommodate up to six people. A pay phone, a gas pump, and a grocery store are on the premises. The resort uses satellite telephones to link to the outside world, so it is sometimes difficult to reach the property via phone. **Pros:** slow-paced; friendly; there's a glorious amount of peace and quiet after sundown. **Cons:** far from the park's main attractions. ⊠ Hwy. 190, 28 mi west of Stovepipe Wells ☎ P.O. Box 395, Ridgecrest, 93556 ☎ 775/482–7680 ⊕ www.deathvalley.com/psr ⇆ 14 rooms, 1 cabin ☒ In-room: a/c (some), no phone, no TV. In-hotel: restaurant, bar, Wi-Fi hotspot, some pets allowed ⊟ AE, D, MC, V.

$$ 🍴 **Stovepipe Wells Village.** If you prefer quiet nights and an unfettered view of the night sky and nearby sand dunes, this property is for you. No telephones break the silence here, and only the deluxe rooms have

televisions and some refrigerators. Rooms are simple yet comfortable and provide wide-open desert vistas. The Toll Road Restaurant serves American breakfast, lunch, and dinner favorites, from omelets and sandwiches to burgers and steaks. RV campsites with full hookups ($30) are available on a first-come, first-served basis. **Pros:** intimate, relaxed; no big-time partying; authentic desert community ambience. **Cons:** isolated; a bit dated; can feel a bit dodgy after dark. ⊠ *Hwy. 190, Stovepipe Wells* ⌑ *P.O. Box187, Death Valley 92328* ☎ *760/786–2387* ⊕ *www.stovepipewells.com* ⌇ *83 rooms* ⌂ *In-room: no phone, refrigerator (some), no TV (some). In-hotel: restaurant, bar, pool, Wi-Fi hotspot, some pets allowed* ⊟ *AE, D, MC, V.*

CAMPING
$$

⚠ **Furnace Creek.** This campground, 196 feet below sea level, has some shaded tent sites. Pay showers, a laundry, and a swimming pool are at nearby Furnace Creek Ranch. Reservations are accepted for stays between mid-October and mid-April; at other times sites are available on a first-come, first-served basis. Two group campsites can accommodate 40 people each. **Pros:** inexpensive; central to park's main attractions; many tent-only sites have trees for limited shade. **Cons:** the campground often is full or parts of it are closed; tent-only sites are hard and pebbly; RV spots have no shade. ⊠ *Hwy. 190, Furnace Creek* ☎ *301/722–1257, 800/365–2267 reservations* ⌇ *136 tent/RV sites* ⌂ *Flush toilets, dump station, drinking water, fire grates, picnic tables, public telephone, ranger station* ⊟ *AE, DC, MC, V (credit cards accepted for reservations only).*

$–$$

⚠ **Panamint Springs Resort.** Part of a complex that includes a motel and cabin, this campground is surrounded by cottonwoods. The daily fee includes use of the showers and restrooms. **Pros:** at an elevation of 1,000 feet, it's cooler than the valley floor; has water and electricity. **Cons:** road to it has many potholes; some reports of rude hosts. ⊠ *Hwy. 190, 28 mi west of Stovepipe Wells* ☎ *775/482–7680* ⌇ *11 RV sites, 26 tent sites, 30 water-only RV sites* ⌂ *Flush toilets, full hookups, partial hookups (water), dump station, drinking water, showers, fire grates, picnic tables, public telephone, general store, service station (gas only)* ⊟ *AE, D, MC, V.*

$–$$

⚠ **Stovepipe Wells Village.** This is the second-largest campground in the park. This area is little more than a giant parking lot, but pay showers and laundry facilities are available at the adjacent motel. It's first-come, first-served. **Pros:** creature comforts are nearby, including a saloon; near the sand dunes; lots of socializing possibilities. **Cons:** nothing special as a camping experience, as there's no shade or frills inside the campground. ⊠ *Hwy. 190, Stovepipe Wells* ☎ *760/786–2387* ⌇ *190 tent sites, 14 RV sites* ⌂ *Flush toilets, full hookups, dump station, drinking water, public telephone, general store, swimming (pool)* ⊟ *No credit cards for tent sites* ⊙ *Mid-Oct.–mid-Apr.*

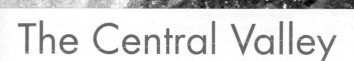

The Central Valley

HIGHWAY 99 FROM BAKERSFIELD TO LODI

WORD OF MOUTH

"We have many rivers that can be rafted. The closest river to Southern California and one of the best is the Upper Kern near Bakersfield. This was a fun day in June!"

—photo by Kim Brogan, Fodors.com member

WELCOME TO THE CENTRAL VALLEY

TOP REASONS TO GO

★ **Down under:** Forestiere Underground Gardens is not the flashiest tourist attraction in California, but it is one of the strangest— and oddly inspirational.

★ **Grape escape:** In the past decade, Lodi's wineries have grown enough in stature for the charming little town to become a must-sip destination.

★ **Port with authority:** Stockton has long been a hub for merchandise that is being transferred from roadway to waterway— or vice versa. Watch some of that commotion in commerce from the riverfront downtown area.

★ **Go with the flow:** White-water rafting will get your blood pumping, and maybe your clothes wet, on the Stanislaus River near Oakdale.

★ **Hee haw!:** Kick up your heels and break out your drawl at Buck Owens' Crystal Palace in Bakersfield, a city some believe is the heart of country music.

1 Southern Central Valley. When gold was discovered in Kern County in the 1860s, settlers flocked to the southern end of the Central Valley. Black gold— oil—is now the area's most valuable commodity; the county provides 64% of California's oil production. Kern is also among the country's five most productive agricultural counties. From the flat plains around Bakersfield, the landscape grows gently hilly and then graduates to mountains as it nears Kernville, which lies in the Kern River valley.

2 Mid-Central Valley. The Mid-Central Valley extends over three counties—Tulare, Kings, and Fresno. Historic Hanford and bustling Visalia are off the tourist-traffic radar but have their charms. From Visalia, Highway 198 winds east 35 mi to Generals Highway, which passes through Sequoia and Kings Canyon national parks (⇨ *see Chapter 21*). Highway 180 snakes east 55 mi to Sequoia and Kings Canyon. From Fresno, Highway 41 leads north 95 mi to Yosemite National Park (⇨ *see Chapter 20*).

3 North Central Valley. The northern section of the valley cuts through Merced, Madera, Stanislaus, and San Joaquin counties, from the flat, abundantly fertile terrain between Merced and Modesto north to the edges of the Sacramento River delta and the fringes of the Gold Country. If you're heading to Yosemite National Park (⇨ *see Chapter 20*) from northern California, chances are you'll pass through (or very near) at least one of several small gateway communities, which include Mariposa and Oakdale.

GETTING ORIENTED

California has a diversity of delicious vacation possibilities. Among its many outstanding regions, however, the Central Valley is arguably the least inviting. This flat landscape, sometimes blistery hot and smelly, contains no famous attractions and cannot honestly be touted as a can't-miss. For many vacationers, it is a region to drive through as quickly as possible on the way to fabulous Sequoia, Kings Canyon, and Yosemite national parks (⇨ see Chapters 20 and 21). For those who have an extra day or two, whose tourism tastes don't demand Disneyland-level excitement, it can represent a pleasant diversion and provide insights into an enormous agricultural region. The valley is the vast geographical center of California, if not quite its proverbial heart.

18

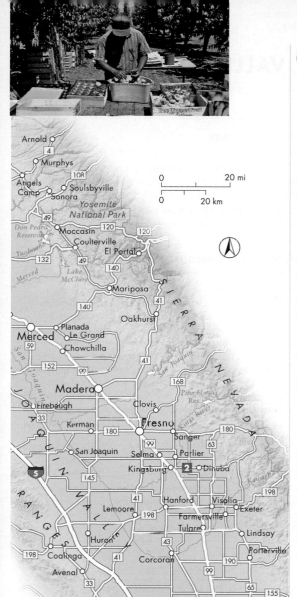

THE CENTRAL VALLEY PLANNER

Exploring the Central Valley

The 225-mi Central Valley cuts through Kern, Tulare, Kings, Fresno, Madera, Merced, Stanislaus, and San Joaquin counties. It's bounded on the east by the mighty Sierra Nevada and on the west by the smaller coastal ranges. Interstate 5 runs south–north through the valley, as does Highway 99.

When to Go

Spring, when wildflowers are in bloom and the scent of fruit blossoms is in the air, and fall, when the air is brisk and leaves turn red and gold, are the best times to visit. Many of the valley's biggest festivals take place during these seasons. (If you suffer from allergies, though, beware of spring, when stone-fruit trees blossom.) Summer, when temperatures often top 100°F, can be oppressive. June through August, though, are the months to visit area water parks and lakes or to take in the air-conditioned museums. Many attractions close in winter, which can get dreary. Thick, ground-hugging fog is a common driving hazard November through February.

Tour Options

Central Valley Tours provides general and customized tours of the Fresno area and the valley, with special emphasis on the fruit harvests and Blossom Trail.

Contacts Central Valley Tours (☎ 559/276–4479 ⊕ www. angelfire.com/poetry/inc/valleytours.html).

About the Restaurants

Fast-food places and chain restaurants dominate valley highways, but away from the main drag, independent and family-owned eateries will awaken your taste buds. Many bistros and fine restaurants take advantage of the local produce and locally raised meats that are the cornerstone of California cuisine. Even simple restaurants produce hearty, tasty fare that often reflects the valley's ethnic mix. Some of the nation's best Mexican restaurants call the valley home. Chinese, Italian, Armenian, and Basque restaurants also are abundant; many serve massive, several-course meals.

About the Hotels

The Central Valley has many chain motels and hotels, but independently owned hotels and bed-and-breakfasts also can be found. There's a large selection of upscale lodgings, Victorian-style B&Bs, and places that are simply utilitarian but clean and comfortable.

WHAT IT COSTS

	¢	$	$$	$$$	$$$$
Restaurants	under $10	$10–$15	$16–$22	$23–$30	over $30
Hotels	under $90	$90–$120	$121–$175	$176–$250	over $250

Restaurant prices are for a main course at dinner, excluding sales tax of 8.25%–9.5% (depending on location). Hotel prices are for two people in a standard double room in high season, excluding service charges and 8%–13% tax.

Updated by
Reed Parsell

Among the world's most fertile working lands, the Central Valley is important due to the scale of its food production but, to be honest, it lacks substantial appeal for visitors. For most people, the Central Valley is simply a place to pass through on the way to greater attractions in the north, south, east, or west. For those willing to invest a little effort, however, California's heartland can be rewarding.

The agriculturally rich area is home to a diversity of wildlife. Many telephone posts are crowned by a hawk or kestrel hunting the land below. Vineyards, especially in the northern valley around Lodi, and almond orchards whose white blossoms make February a brighter month are pleasant sights out motorists' windows. In the towns, historical societies display artifacts of the valley's eccentric past; concert halls and restored theaters showcase samplings of contemporary culture; and museums provide a blend of both. Restaurants can be very good, whether they be fancy or mom-and-pop. For fruit lovers, roadside stands can be treasure troves. Country-music enthusiasts will find a lot to appreciate on the radio and on stages, especially in the Bakersfield area. Summer nights spent at one of the valley's minor-league baseball parks—Bakersfield, Fresno, Modesto, Stockton, and Visalia have teams—can be a relaxing experience. Whether on back roads or main streets, people are not only friendly but proud to help outsiders explore the Central Valley.

GETTING HERE AND AROUND

Fresno Yosemite International Airport is serviced by Alaska, Allegiant, American and American Eagle, Delta, Horizon, Mexicana, United, United Express, and US Airways. Kern County Airport at Meadows Field is serviced by United Express and US Airways. United Express flies from Los Angeles and San Francisco to Modesto City-County Airport, and US Airways flies from Las Vegas to Visalia Municipal Airport.

Greyhound provides service among major valley cities. Orange Belt Stages provides bus service, including Amtrak connections, to many valley locations.

18

Amtrak's daily *San Joaquin* travels among Bakersfield, San Jose, and Oakland, stopping in Hanford, Fresno, Madera, Merced, Turlock, Modesto, and Stockton. Highway 99 is the main route between the valley's major cities and towns. I–5 runs roughly parallel to it to the west but misses the major population centers; its main use is for quick access from San Francisco or Los Angeles. Major roads that connect I–5 with Highway 99 are Highways 58 (to Bakersfield), 198 (to Hanford and Visalia), 152 (to Chowchilla, via Los Banos), 140 (to Merced), 132 (to Modesto), and 120 (to Manteca).

ESSENTIALS

Airport Contacts Kern County Airport at Meadows Field (⊠ *1401 Skyway Dr., Bakersfield* ☎ *661/391-1800* ⊕ *www.meadowsfield.com*).

Bus Contact Greyhound (☎ *800/231-2222* ⊕ *www.greyhound.com*). **Orange Belt Stages** (☎ *800/266-7433* ⊕ *www.orangebelt.com*).

Road Conditions California Department of Transportation hotline (☎ *800/266-6883 or 916/445-1534*).

Train Contact Amtrak (☎ *800/872-7245* ⊕ *www.amtrakcalifornia.com*).

SOUTHERN CENTRAL VALLEY

BAKERSFIELD

110 mi north of Los Angeles via I–5 and Hwy. 99; 110 mi west of Ridgecrest via Hwy. 14 south and Hwy. 58 west.

Bakersfield's founder, Colonel Thomas Baker, arrived with the discovery of gold in the nearby Kern River valley in 1851. Now Kern County's biggest city (it has a population of 334,000, which includes the largest Basque community in the United States), Bakersfield probably is best known as Nashville West, a country-music haven closely affiliated with performers Buck Owens (who died here in 2006) and Merle Haggard (who was born here in 1937). It also has a symphony orchestra and two good museums.

ESSENTIALS

Bus Contact Orange Belt Stages (☎ *800/266-7433* ⊕ *www.orangebelt.com*).

Visitor Information Greater Bakersfield Convention & Visitors Bureau (⊠ *515 Truxton Ave., Bakersfield* ☎ *661/325-5051 or 866/425-7353* ⊕ *www. bakersfieldcvb.org*). **Kern County Board of Trade** (⊠ *2101 Oak St., Bakersfield* ☎ *661/500-5376 or 800/500-5376* ⊕ *www.visitkern.com*).

EXPLORING

At the **California Living Museum**, a combination zoo, botanical garden, and natural-history museum, the emphasis is on the zoo. All animal and plant species displayed are native to the state. Within the reptile house lives every species of rattlesnake found in California. The landscaped grounds—in the hills about a 20-minute drive northeast of Bakersfield—also shelter captive bald eagles, tortoises, coyotes, black bears,

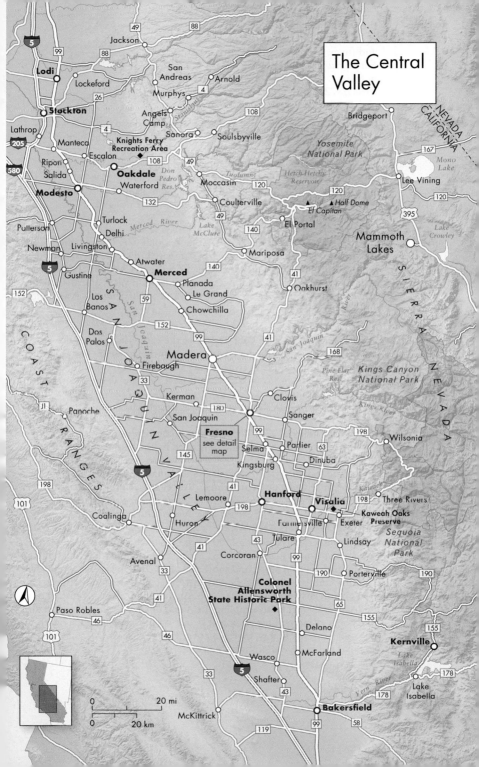

The Central Valley

NEVADA
CALIFORNIA

Jackson
San Andreas
Arnold
Lodi
Lockeford
Murphys
Stockton
Angels Camp
Sonora
Soulsbyville
Bridgeport
Lathrop
Manteca
Knights Ferry Recreation Area
Waterford
Moccasin
Escalon
Oakdale
Ripon
Salida
Modesto
Turlock
Delhi
Merced River
Lake McClure
Coulterville
El Capitan
Half Dome
Lee Vining
Mono Lake
Patterson
Newman
Livingston
Atwater
Merced
Planada
Le Grand
El Portal
Mammoth Lakes
Lake Crowley
Gustine
Los Banos
Dos Palos
Chowchilla
Oakhurst
San Joaquin
Madera
Firebaugh
Panoche
Kerman
San Joaquin
Clovis
Sanger
Pine Flat Res.
Kings Canyon National Park
Kings River
Fresno
see detail map
Selma
Parlier
Dinuba
Wilsonia
Kingsburg
Lemoore
Huron
Hanford
Visalia
Three Rivers
Kaweah Oaks Preserve
Coalinga
Farmersville
Exeter
Sequoia National Park
Avenal
Tulare
Lindsay
Corcoran
Porterville
Paso Robles
Colonel Allensworth State Historic Park
Delano
Kernville
Lake Isabella
Wasco
McFarland
Shafter
Lake Isabella
McKittrick
Bakersfield
Kern River

Yosemite National Park
Hetch-Hetchy Reservoir
Tuolumne

SIERRA NEVADA

COAST RANGES

SAN JOAQUIN VALLEY

0   20 mi
0   20 km

and foxes. ✉ *10500 Alfred Harrell Hwy.; Hwy. 178 east, then 3½ mi northwest on Alfred Harrell Hwy.* ☎ *661/872–2256* ⊕ *www.calmzoo. org* 💲*$7* ⊙ *Mar.–Oct., daily 9–5; Nov.–Feb., daily 9–4.*

☺ The 16-acre **Kern County Museum and**
★ **Lori Brock Children's Discovery Center** form one of the Central Valley's top museum complexes. The indoor-outdoor Kern County Museum is set up as an open-air, walk-through historic village with more than 55 restored or re-created buildings dating from the 1860s to the 1940s. "Black Gold: The Oil Experience," a permanent exhibit, shows how oil is created, discovered, extracted, and transformed for various uses. The Lori Brock Children's Discovery Center, for ages eight and younger, has hands-on displays and an indoor playground. ✉ *3801 Chester Ave.* ☎ *661/852–5000* ⊕ *www.kcmuseum. org* 💲*$10* ⊙ *Mon.–Sat. 10–5, Sun. noon–5.*

> **LOCAL LITERARY LEGENDS**
>
> The Central Valley's cultural diversity and agricultural roots have woven a textured social fabric that has been chronicled by some of the country's finest writers, including Fresno native William Saroyan, Stockton native Maxine Hong Kingston, and *Grapes of Wrath* author John Steinbeck.

WHERE TO EAT

$ ✕ **Jake's Original Tex Mex Cafe.** Don't let the cafeteria-style service fool
MEXICAN you; this is probably the best lunch place in Bakersfield. The chicken burritos and the chili fries (with meaty chili ladled on top) are superb; the coleslaw draws raves, too. For dessert, try the Texas sheet cake. It's open for dinner, too. ✉ *1710 Oak St.* ☎ *661/322–6380* ⊕ *www. jakestexmex.com* ⚖ *Reservations not accepted* ⊟ *AE, D, MC, V* ⊙ *Closed Sun.*

$–$$ ✕ **Uricchio's Trattoria.** This downtown restaurant draws everyone from
ITALIAN office workers to oil barons—all attracted by the tasty food and casual atmosphere. *Panini* (Italian pressed sandwiches, served at lunch only), pasta, and Italian-style chicken dishes dominate the menu; the chicken piccata outsells all other offerings. Reservations are recommended. ✉ *1400 17th St.* ☎ *661/326–8870* ⊕ *www.uricchios-trattoria.com* ⊟ *AE, D, DC, MC, V* ⊙ *Closed Sun. No lunch Sat.*

NIGHTLIFE AND THE ARTS

★ **Buck Owens' Crystal Palace** (✉ *2800 Buck Owens Blvd.* ☎ *661/328–7560* ⊕ *www.buckowens.com* ⊙ *Closed Mon.*) is a combination nightclub, restaurant, souvenir store, and showcase of country-music memorabilia. Country-and-western singers perform here, as Owens did countless times before his death in March 2006. A dance floor beckons customers who can still twirl after sampling the menu of steaks, burgers, nachos, and gooey desserts. Entertainment is free on most weeknights; on Friday and Saturday nights, there's a cover charge (usually $8 to $15) for some of the more well-known entertainers.

KERNVILLE

50 mi northeast of Bakersfield, via Hwys. 178 and 155.

The wild and scenic Kern River, which flows through Kernville en route from Mt. Whitney to Bakersfield, delivers some of the most exciting white-water rafting in the state. Kernville (population 1,700) rests in a mountain valley on both banks of the river and also at the northern tip of Lake Isabella (a dammed portion of the river used as a reservoir and for recreation). By far the most scenic town described in this chapter, Kernville has lodgings, restaurants, and antiques shops. The main streets are lined with Old West–style buildings, reflecting Kernville's heritage as a rough-and-tumble gold-mining town once known as Whiskey Flat. (Present-day Kernville dates from the 1950s, when it was moved upriver to make room for Lake Isabella.) The road from Bakersfield includes stretches where the rushing river is on one side and granite cliffs are on the other.

ESSENTIALS

Visitor Information Kern County Board of Trade (✉ *2101 Oak St., Bakersfield* ☎ *661/500–5376 or 800/500–5376* ⊕ *www.visitkern.com*).

WHERE TO EAT AND STAY

$–$$
ITALIAN
✕ **That's Italian.** For northern Italian cuisine in a typical trattoria, this is the spot. Try the braised lamb shanks in a Chianti wine sauce or the linguine with clams, mussels, calamari, and shrimp in a white-wine clam sauce. ✉ *9 Big Blue Rd.* ☎ *760/376–6020* ▤ *AE, D, MC, V.*

$$–$$$
▦ **Whispering Pines Lodge Bed & Breakfast.** Perched on the banks of the Kern River, this 8-acre property gives you a variety of overnight options. Units are motel-style or in duplex bungalows and all have fireplaces, coffeemakers, and king-size beds. Some have full kitchens, queen-size sleepers, and whirlpool tubs. **Pros:** rustic setting; big breakfasts; great views; very clean. **Cons:** bungalows are pricey; town is a bit remote. ✉ *13745 Sierra Way* ☎ *760/376–3733 or 877/241–4100* ⊕ *www.kernvalley.com/whisperingpines* ⤲ *17 rooms* ⚘ *In-room: a/c, kitchen (some), refrigerator (some). In-hotel: pool* ▤ *AE, D, MC, V* ⎟◑ *BP.*

SPORTS AND THE OUTDOORS

BOATING AND
WINDSURFING
The Lower Kern River, which extends from Lake Isabella to Bakersfield and beyond, is open for fishing year-round. Catches include rainbow trout, catfish, smallmouth bass, crappie, and bluegill. Lake Isabella is popular with anglers, water-skiers, sailors, and windsurfers. Its shoreline marinas have boats for rent, bait and tackle, and moorings. **North Fork Marina** (☎ *760/376–1812*) is in Wofford Heights, on the lake's north shore. **French Gulch Marina** (☎ *760/379–8774*) is near the dam on Lake Isabella's west shore.

WHITE-WATER
RAFTING
The three sections of the Kern River—known as the Lower Kern, Upper Kern, and the Forks—add up to nearly 50 mi of white water, ranging from Class I (easy) to Class V (expert). The Lower and Upper Kern are the most popular and accessible sections. Organized trips can last from one hour (for as little as $35) to more than two days. Rafting season usually runs from late spring until the end of summer. **Kern River Tours** (☎ *800/844–7238* ⊕ *www.kernrivertours.com*) leads several rafting

18

tours from half-day trips to three days of navigating Class V rapids, and also arranges for mountain-bike trips.

Mountain & River Adventures (☎ 760/376–6553 or 800/861–6553 ⊕ *www. mtnriver.com*) gives calm-water kayaking tours as well as white-water rafting trips, plus leads mountain bike excursions and has a campground. In the wintertime, M&R has snowshoe and cross-country ski rentals. Half-day Class II and III white-water rafting trips are emphasized at **Sierra South** (☎ 760/376–3745 or 800/457–2082 ⊕ *www.sierrasouth. com*), which also offers kayaking classes and calm-water excursions.

MID-CENTRAL VALLEY

COLONEL ALLENSWORTH STATE HISTORIC PARK

45 mi north of Bakersfield on Hwy. 43.

★ A former slave who became the country's highest-ranking black military officer of his time founded Allensworth—the only California town settled, governed, and financed by African-Americans—in 1908. After enjoying early prosperity, the town was plagued by hardships and eventually was deserted. Its scattering of rebuilt buildings reflects the few years in which it thrived. Festivities each October commemorate the town's rededication. Amtrak stops here (group travel with advanced reservations), which makes the park a potential side trip for those taking the train between Los Angeles and San Francisco. At this writing the park was closed to cars except Friday through Sunday, but accessible to visitors on foot daily; call for the latest information. ⊠ 4129 Palmer Ave. ☎ 661/849–3433 ⊕ *www.cal-parks.ca.gov* ⊠ *$6 per car* ☉ *Daily sunrise–sunset, visitor center open on request, buildings open by appointment.*

VISALIA

40 mi north of Colonel Allensworth State Historic Park on Hwy. 99 and east on Hwy. 198; 75 mi north of Bakersfield via Hwy. 99 north and Hwy. 198 east.

Visalia's combination of a reliable agricultural economy and civic pride has yielded the most vibrant downtown in the Central Valley (not that competition in the category is too fierce). A clear day's view of the Sierra from Main Street is spectacular, if sadly rare due to smog and dust, and even Sunday night can find the streets bustling with pedestrians.

ESSENTIALS

Airport Contacts Visalia Municipal Airport (⊠ *9501 W. Airport Dr., Visalia* ☎ *559/713–4201* ⊕ *www.flyvisalia.com*).

Bus Contact Orange Belt Stages (☎ *800/266–7433* ⊕ *www.orangebelt.com*).

Visitor Information Visalia Chamber of Commerce and Visitors Bureau (⊠ *220 N. Santa Fe St., Visalia* ☎ *559/334–0141* ⊕ *www.visaliachamber.org*).

Each spring the fruit orchards along the Blossom Trail, near Fresno, burst into bloom.

EXPLORING

Founded in 1852, the town contains many historic homes; ask for a free guide at the **visitor center** (✉ 220 N. Santa Fe St. ☎ 559/734–5876 ⊙ Mon. 10–5, Tues.–Fri. 8:30–5).

The **Chinese Cultural Center**, housed in a pagoda-style building, mounts exhibits about Asian art and culture and documents the influx of Chinese workers to central California during the gold rush. ✉ 500 S. Akers Rd., at Hwy. 198 ☎ 559/625–4545 ☛ Free ⊙ By appointment only.

☼ In oak-shaded **Mooney Grove Park** you can picnic alongside duck ponds, rent a boat for a ride around the lagoon, and view a replica of the famous End of the Trail statue. The original, designed by James Earl Fraser for the 1915 Panama-Pacific International Exposition, is now in the Cowboy Hall of Fame in Oklahoma. ✉ 27000 S. Mooney Blvd., 5 mi south of downtown ☎ 559/733–6291 ☛ $7 per car, free in winter (dates vary) ⊙ Late May–early Sept., weekdays 8–7, weekends 8 AM– 9 PM; early Sept.–Oct. and Mar.–late May, Mon., Thurs., and Fri. 8–5, weekends 8–7; Nov.–Feb., Thurs.–Mon. 8–5.

The indoor-outdoor **Tulare County Museum** contains several re-created environments from the pioneer era. Also on display are Yokuts tribal artifacts (basketry, arrowheads, clamshell-necklace currency) as well as saddles, guns, dolls, quilts, and gowns. A $1.45 million replacement building opened in 2009. ✉ Mooney Grove Park, 27000 S. Mooney Blvd., 5 mi south of downtown ☎ 559/733–6616 ☛ Free with park entrance fee of $7 ⊙ Weekdays 10–4, weekends 1–4.

Trails at the 324-acre **Kaweah Oaks Preserve**, a wildlife sanctuary off the main road to Sequoia National Park (⇨ see chapter 21), lead past majestic valley oak, sycamore, cottonwood, and willow trees. Among the 134 bird species you might spot are hawks, hummingbirds, and great blue herons. Lizards, coyotes, and cottontails also live here. ⊠ *Follow Hwy. 198 for 7 mi east of Visalia, turn north on Rd. 182, and proceed ½ mi to gate on left side* ☎ *559/738–0211* ⊕ *www.sequoiariverlands. org* ▣ *Free* ☉ *Daily sunrise–sunset.*

WHERE TO EAT

$–$$ | ✕ **Henry Salazar's.** Traditional Mexican food with a contemporary twist
MEXICAN | is served at this restaurant that uses fresh ingredients from local farms. Bring your appetite if you expect to finish the Burrito Fantastico, a large flour tortilla stuffed with your choice of meat, beans, and chili sauce, and smothered with melted Monterey Jack cheese. Another signature dish is grilled salmon with lemon-butter sauce. Colorfully painted walls, soft reflections from candles in wall niches, and color-coordinated tablecloths and napkins make the atmosphere cozy and restful. ⊠ *123 W. Main St.* ☎ *559/741–7060* ⊕ *www.henrysalazars.com* ▭ *AE, D, MC, V.*

$$$–$$$$ | ✕ **The Vintage Press.** Built in 1966, the Vintage Press is the best restau-
CONTINENTAL | rant in the Central Valley. Cut-glass doors and bar fixtures decorate the
Fodor's Choice | artfully designed rooms. The California–Continental cuisine includes
★ | dishes such as crispy veal sweetbreads with a port-wine sauce, and a bacon-wrapped filet mignon stuffed with mushrooms. The chocolate Grand Marnier cake is a standout among the homemade desserts and ice creams. The wine list has more than 900 selections. ⊠ *216 N. Willis St.* ☎ *559/733–3033* ⊕ *www.thevintagepress.com* ▭ *AE, DC, MC, V.*

HANFORD

★ *20 mi west of Visalia on Hwy. 198; 43 mi north of Colonel Allensworth State Historic Park on Hwy. 43.*

Founded in 1877 as a Southern Pacific Railroad stop, Hanford had one of California's largest Chinatowns—the Chinese came to help build the railroads and stayed on to farm.

ESSENTIALS

Bus Contact Orange Belt Stages (☎ *800/266–7433* ⊕ www.orangebelt.com).

Visitor Information Hanford Visitor Agency (⊠ *200 Santa Fe Ave., Suite D, Hanford* ☎ *559/582–5024* ⊕ www.visithanford.com).

EXPLORING

You can take a self-guided walking tour with the help of a free brochure, or take a driving tour in a restored 1930s Studebaker fire truck ($35 for up to 15 people) through the **Hanford Conference & Visitors Agency** (☎ *559/582–5024* ⊕ *www.visithanford.com*). One tour explores the restored buildings of Courthouse Square, whose art-deco Hanford Auditorium is a visual standout; another heads to narrow China Alley. If you have specific interests, a tour can also be designed for you.

The **Hanford Carnegie Museum** displays fashions, furnishings, toys, and military artifacts that tell the region's story. The living-history museum is inside the former Carnegie Library, a Romanesque building dating from 1905 that is on the U.S. National Register of Historic Places.

✉ *108 E. 8th St.* ☎ *559/584–1367*
📷 *$1* ⊙ *Wed.–Sat. 10–2.*

A first-floor museum in the 1893
Taoist Temple displays photos, furnishings, and kitchenware from
Hanford's once-bustling Chinatown. The second-floor temple,
largely unchanged for a century,
contains altars, carvings, and ceremonial staves. You can visit as
part of a guided tour at noon on
the first Saturday of the month, or
by appointment. ✉ *12 China Alley*
☎ *559/582–4508* 📷 *Free; donations
welcome.*

WHERE TO EAT AND STAY

¢–$ ✕ **La Fiesta Spanish Kitchen.** Mexican-

MEXICAN American families, farmworkers,
and farmers all eat here, polishing
off traditional Mexican dishes such
as enchiladas and tacos. The Fiesta

BLOSSOM TRAIL

The 62-mi self-guided **Blossom
Trail** driving tour takes in Fresno-
area orchards, citrus groves, and
vineyards during spring blossom
season. Pick up a route map at
the **Fresno City & County Convention and Visitors Bureau**
(✉ *848 M St., Fresno* ☎ *559/233–
0836 or 800/788–0836* ⊕ *www.
gofresnocounty.com*). The Blossom
Trail passes through small towns
and past rivers, lakes, and canals.
The most colorful and aromatic
time to go is from late February to
mid-March, when almond, plum,
apple, apricot, and peach blossoms shower the landscape with
shades of white, pink, and red.

Special—for two or more—includes nachos, garlic shrimp, shrimp in a
spicy red sauce, clams, and two pieces of top sirloin. ✉ *106 N. Green
St.* ☎ *559/583–8775* 💳 *AE, D, MC, V.*

$$–$$$ ✕ **The Purple Potato.** This locally owned, colorful restaurant—with purple

AMERICAN walls, not surprisingly—has become what locals say is the best restaurant in town. The broad menu, which includes steaks, pasta, and
poultry, draws raves for its shrimp scampi and pan-seared scallops. The
wine list is extensive. ✉ *A few blocks west of downtown, 601 W. 7th St.*
☎ *559/587–4568* 💳 *AE, D, MC, V* ⊙ *No lunch weekends.*

$–$$ 🏨 **Irwin Street Inn.** This inn is one of the few lodgings in the valley that
★ warrants a detour. Four tree-shaded, restored Victorian homes have
been converted into spacious accommodations with comfortable rooms
and suites. Most have antique armoires, dark-wood detailing, lead-
glass windows, and four-poster beds; bathrooms have old-fashioned
tubs, brass fixtures, and marble basins. **Pros:** big rooms and bathrooms;
funky decor; very unlike chain hotels. **Cons:** mattresses can be uncomfortable; not much to do in town. ✉ *522 N. Irwin St.* ☎ *559/583–8000*
⊕ *www.irwinstreet.com* 🛏 *24 rooms, 3 suites* ⚹ *In-room: a/c. In-hotel:
restaurant, pool* 💳 *AE, D, DC, MC, V* 🍽 *CP.*

FRESNO

35 mi north of Hanford via Hwys. 43 and 99 north.

Sprawling Fresno, with more than 470,000 people, is the center of
the richest agricultural county in the United States. Cotton, grapes,
and oranges are among the major crops; poultry and milk are also
important. About 75 ethnic groups, including Armenians, Laotians,
and Indians, call Fresno home. The city has a vibrant arts scene, several
public parks, and an abundance of low-price restaurants. The Tower

18

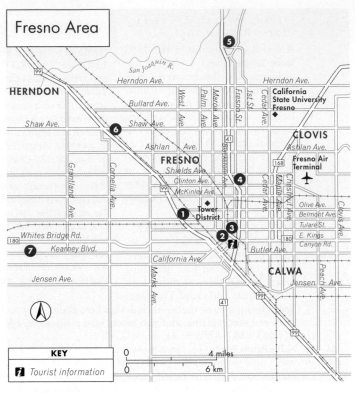

District—with its chic restaurants, coffeehouses, and boutiques—is the trendy spot (though even it can look drab on a cloudy day). Pulitzer Prize–winning playwright and novelist William Saroyan (*The Time of Your Life, The Human Comedy*) was born here in 1908.

ESSENTIALS

Airport Contacts Fresno Yosemite International Airport (✉ 4995 E. Clinton Way, Fresno ☎ 559/621–4500 ⊕ www.fresno.gov/discoverfresno/airports).

Visitor Information Fresno City & County Convention and Visitors Bureau (✉ 848 M St., Fresno ☎ 559/445–8300 or 800/788–0836 ⊕ www.fresnocvb.org).

EXPLORING

① Tree-shaded **Roeding Park** is a place of respite on hot summer days; it has picnic areas, playgrounds, tennis courts, horseshoe pits, and a zoo. The most striking exhibit at **Chaffee Zoological Gardens** (☎ 559/498–2671 ⊕ www.chaffeezoo.org ☎ $7 ☉ Feb.–Oct., daily 9–4; Nov.–Jan., daily 10–3) is the tropical rain forest, where you'll encounter exotic birds along the paths and bridges. Elsewhere on the grounds you'll find tigers, grizzly bears, sea lions, tule elk, camels, elephants, and hooting siamangs. Also here are a high-tech reptile house and a petting zoo. A train, little race cars, paddleboats, and other rides for kids are among the amusements that operate March through November at **Playland** (☎ 559/233–3980 ☉ Wed.–Fri. 11–5, weekends 10–6). Children can explore attractions with fairy-tale themes at **Rotary Storyland** (☎ 559/264–2235 ☉ Weekdays 11–5, weekends 10–6), which is also open March through November. ✉ Olive and Belmont Aves. ☎ 559/498–1551 ☜ $1 per vehicle at park entrance, Playland rides require tokens, Storyland $4.

❷ The **Legion of Valor Museum** is a real find for military-history buffs of all ages. It has German bayonets and daggers, a Japanese Namby pistol, a Gatling gun, and an extensive collection of Japanese, German, and American uniforms. The staff is extremely enthusiastic. ✉ 2425 Fresno St. ☎ 559/498–0510 ⊕ www.legionofvalor.com ☜ Free ☉ Mon.–Sat. 10–3.

❸ Inside a restored 1889 Victorian, the **Meux Home Museum** displays furnishings typical of an upper-class household in early Fresno (Thomas Richard Meux was a doctor for the Confederate army during the Civil War, and subsequently was a family practitioner out West). Guided tours proceed from the front parlor to the backyard carriage house. ✉ Tulare and R Sts. ☎ 559/233–8007 ⊕ www.meux.mus.ca.us ☜ $5 ☉ Fri.–Sun. noon–3:30.

❹ The **Fresno Art Museum** exhibits American, Mexican, and French art; highlights of the permanent collection include pre-Columbian works and graphic art from the postimpressionist period. The 152-seat Bonner Auditorium is the site of lectures, films, and concerts. ✉ Radio Park, 2233 N. 1st St. ☎ 559/441–4221 ⊕ www.fresnoartmuseum.org ☜ $5; free Sun. ☉ Tues., Wed., and Fri. Sun. 11–5, Thurs. 11–8.

❺ **Woodward Park,** the Central Valley's largest urban park with 300 acres
★ of jogging trails, picnic areas, and playgrounds in the northern reaches of the city, is especially pretty in spring, when plum and cherry trees, magnolias, and camellias bloom. Outdoor concerts take place in summer. The **Shinzen Friendship Garden** has a teahouse, a koi pond, arched bridges, a waterfall, and Japanese art. ✉ Audubon Dr. and Friant Rd. ☎ 559/621–2900 ☜ $3 per car Feb.–Oct.; additional $3 for Shinzen Garden ☉ Apr.–Oct., daily 7 AM–10 PM; Nov.–Mar., daily 7–7.

❻ Sicilian immigrant Baldasare Forestiere spent four decades (1906–46)
☾ carving out the **Forestiere Underground Gardens,** a subterranean realm of
★ rooms, tunnels, grottoes, alcoves, and arched passageways that once extended for more than 10 acres between Highway 99 and busy, mall-pocked Shaw Avenue. Only a fraction of Forestiere's prodigious output is on view, but you can tour his underground living quarters, including bedrooms (one with a fireplace), the kitchen, living room, and bath, as well as a fishpond and auto tunnel. Skylights allow exotic full-grown fruit trees, including one that bears seven kinds of citrus as a result of grafting, to flourish more than 20 feet belowground. The gardens are renovated each year. ✉ 5021 W. Shaw Ave., 2 blocks east of Hwy. 99 ☎ 559/271–0734 ⊕ www.undergroundgardens.info ☜ $12 ☉ Tours weekends 11–2 Mar–Nov.; also Fri. in summer. Call for other tour times.

❼ The drive along palm-lined Kearney Boulevard is one of the best reasons to visit the **Kearney Mansion Museum,** which stands in shaded 225-acre **Kearney Park.** The century-old home of M. Theo Kearney, Fresno's

18

onetime "raisin king," is accessible only by taking a guided 45-minute tour. ✉ *7160 W. Kearney Blvd., 6 mi west of Fresno* ☎ *559/441–0862* ✉ *Museum $5; park entry $5 (waived for museum visitors)* ⊙ *Park 7 AM–10 PM; museum tours Fri.–Sun. at 1, 2, and 3.*

WHERE TO EAT AND STAY

$$-$$$ ✗ **La Rocca's Ristorante Italiano.** The
ITALIAN   sauces that top these pasta and meat dishes will make your taste buds sing. The rich tomato sauce, which comes with or without meat, is fresh and tangy. The marsala sauce—served on either chicken or veal—is rich but not overpowering. Typical red-sauce dishes such as spaghetti, rigatoni, and lasagna are offered here, but you'll also be happily surprised with more adventurous offerings such as the bow-tie pasta with cream, peas, bacon, tomato sauce, and olive oil. Pizzas also are served. ✉ *6735 N. 1st St.* ☎ *559/431–1278* ⊟ *AE, MC, V* ⊙ *No lunch weekends.*

$$-$$$ ✗ **Tahoe Joe's.** This restaurant is known for its steaks—rib eye, strip,
STEAK HOUSE   or filet mignon. Other selections include the slow-roasted prime rib, center-cut pork chops, and chicken breast served with a whiskey-peppercorn sauce. The baked potato that accompanies almost every dish is loaded table-side with your choice of butter, sour cream, chives, and bacon bits. Tahoe Joe's has two Fresno locations. ✉ *7006 N. Cedar Ave.* ☎ *559/299–9740* ✉ *2700 W. Shaw Ave.* ☎ *559/277–8028* ⊕ *www.tahoejoes.com* ⚖ *Reservations not accepted* ⊟ *AE, D, MC, V* ⊙ *No lunch.*

$$ ⊡ **Piccadilly Inn Shaw.** This two-story property has 7½ attractively landscaped acres and a big swimming pool. The sizeable rooms have king- and queen-size beds, robes, ironing boards, and coffeemakers; some have fireplaces. **Pros:** big rooms; nice pool; best lodging option in town. **Cons:** some rooms are showing mild wear; neighborhood is somewhat sketchy. ✉ *2305 W. Shaw Ave.* ☎ *559/226–3850* 📠 *559/226–2448* ⊕ *www.piccadillyinn.com* ↪ *194 rooms, 5 suites* ⚲ *In-room: a/c, refrigerator, Internet. In-hotel: restaurant, pool, gym, laundry facilities, laundry service* ⊟ *AE, D, DC, MC, V.*

NIGHTLIFE AND THE ARTS

The **Tower Theatre for the Performing Arts** (✉ *815 E. Olive Ave.* ☎ *559/485–9050* ⊕ *www.towertheatrefresno.org*) has given its name to the trendy Tower District of theaters, clubs, restaurants, and cafés. The restored 1930s art-deco movie house presents theater, ballet, concerts, and other cultural events year-round.

SPORTS AND THE OUTDOORS

Kings River Expeditions (✉ *211 N. Van Ness Ave.* ☎ *559/233–4881 or 800/846–3674* ⊕ *www.kingsriver.com*) arranges one- and two-day white-water rafting trips on the Kings River. **Wild Water Adventures** (✉ *11413*

OLD TOWN CLOVIS

Old Town Clovis (✉ *Upper Clovis Ave., Clovis*) is an area of restored brick buildings with numerous antiques shops and art galleries (along with restaurants and saloons). Be warned, though—not much here is open on Sunday. To get here, head east on Fresno's Herndon Avenue about 10 mi, and then turn right onto Clovis Avenue.

E. Shaw Ave., Clovis ☎ *559/299–9453 or 800/564–9453* ⊕ *www. wildwater.net* ⌂ *$26, $17 after 3* PM), a 52-acre water park about 10 mi east of Fresno, is open from late May to early September.

NORTH CENTRAL VALLEY

MERCED

50 mi north of Fresno on Hwy. 99.

Thanks to a branch of the University of California opening in 2005 and an aggressive community redevelopment plan, the downtown of county seat Merced is coming back to life. The transformation is not yet complete, but there are promising signs: a brewpub, several boutiques, a multiplex, the restoration of numerous historic buildings, and foot traffic won back from outlying strip malls.

ESSENTIALS

Visitor Information Merced Conference and Visitors Bureau (⊠ *710 W. 16th St., Merced* ☎ *209/384–2791 or 800/446–5353* ⊕ *www.yosemite-gateway.org*).

EXPLORING

Even if you don't go inside, be sure to swing by the **Merced County Courthouse Museum.** The three-story former courthouse, built in 1875, is a striking example of Victorian Italianate style. The upper two floors are a museum of early Merced history. Highlights include ornate restored courtrooms and an 1870 Chinese temple with carved redwood altars. ⊠ *21st and N Sts.* ☎ *209/723–2401* ⊕ *www.mercedmuseum.org* ⌂ *Free* ⊙ *Wed.–Sun. 1–4.*

The **Merced Multicultural Arts Center** displays paintings, sculpture, and photography. The Big Valley Arts & Culture Festival, which celebrates the area's ethnic diversity and children's creativity, is held here in late September or early October. ⊠ *645 W. Main St.* ☎ *209/388–1090* ⊕ *www.artsmerced.org* ⌂ *Free* ⊙ *Weekdays 9–5, Sat. 10–2.*

WHERE TO EAT AND STAY

$$–$$$
STEAK HOUSE

✕ **The Branding Iron.** Beef is what this restaurant is all about. It's a favorite among farmers and ranchers looking for a place to refuel as they travel through cattle country. Try the juicy cut of prime rib paired with potato and Parmesan-cheese bread. California cattle brands decorate the walls, and when the weather is nice, cooling breezes refresh diners on the outdoor patio. ⊠ *640 W. 16th St.* ☎ *209/722–1822* ⊕ *www. thebrandingiron-merced.com* ⊟ *AE, MC, V* ⊙ *No lunch weekends.*

$$–$$$
ITALIAN
★

✕ **DeAngelo's.** This restaurant isn't just the best in Merced—it's one of the best in the Central Valley. Chef Vincent DeAngelo, a graduate of the Culinary Institute of America, brings his considerable skill to everything from basic ravioli to calamari steak topped with two prawns. Half the restaurant is occupied by Bellini's, a bar-bistro with its own menu, which includes brick-oven pizza. The delicious crusty bread comes from the Golden Sheath bakery, in Watsonville. ⊠ *350 W. Main St.* ☎ *209/383–3020* ⊕ *www.deangelosrestaurant.com* ⊟ *AE, D, MC, V* ⊙ *No lunch weekends.*

18

$$ ⊡ **Hooper House Bear Creek Inn.** This 1931 neocolonial home stands regally at the corner of M Street. The immaculately landscaped 1½-acre property has fruit trees and grapevines, and the house is appointed in well-chosen antiques and big, soft beds. Breakfast (which can be served in your room) is hearty and imaginative, featuring locally grown foods such as fried sweet potatoes and black walnuts. Across the street is a walking–bicycling trail that runs for a few miles beside the creek. **Pros:** historic charm; friendly staff; good breakfast. **Cons:** front rooms can be noisy. ⊠ *575 W. N. Bear Creek Dr., at M St.* ☎ *209/723–3991* ⊕ *www. hooperhouse.com* ↪ *3 rooms, 1 cottage* ✑ *In-room: a/c, Internet* ⊟ *AE, D, MC, V* ⊠ *BP.*

SPORTS AND THE OUTDOORS

At **Lake Yosemite Regional Park** (⊠ *N. Lake Rd. off Yosemite Ave., 5 mi northeast of Merced* ☎ *209/385–7426* ⊠ *$6 per car late May–early Sept.*), you can boat, swim, windsurf, water-ski, and fish on a 387-acre reservoir. Paddleboat rentals and picnic areas are available.

MODESTO

38 mi north of Merced on Hwy. 99.

Modesto, a gateway to Yosemite (⇨ *see Chapter 20*) and the southern reaches of the Gold Country, was founded in 1870 to serve the Central Pacific Railroad. The frontier town was originally to be named Ralston, after a railroad baron, but as the story goes, he modestly declined— thus the name Modesto. The Stanislaus County seat, a tree-lined city of 207,000, is perhaps best known as the site of the annual Modesto Invitational Track Meet and Relays and birthplace of film producer-director George Lucas, creator of the *Star Wars* film series.

ESSENTIALS

Airport Contacts Modesto City-County Airport (⊠ *617 Airport Way, Modesto* ☎ *209/577–5319* ⊕ *www.modairport.com*).

Visitor Information Modesto Convention and Visitors Bureau (⊠ *1150 9th St., Suite C, Modesto* ☎ *209/526–5588 or 888/640–8467* ⊕ *www.visitmodesto.com*).

EXPLORING

The **Modesto Arch** (⊠ *9th and I Sts.*) bears the city's motto: WATER, WEALTH, CONTENTMENT, HEALTH.

The prosperity that water brought to Modesto has attracted people from all over the world. The city holds a well-attended **International Heritage Festival** (☎ *209/521–3852* ⊕ *www.internationalfestivalmodesto. org*) in early October that celebrates the cultures, crafts, and cuisines of many nationalities.

You can witness the everyday abundance of the Modesto area at the **Blue Diamond Growers Store** (⊠ *4800 Sisk Rd.* ☎ *209/545–3222*), which offers free samples, shows a film about almond growing, and sells many roasts and flavors of almonds, as well as other nuts.

★   A rancher and banker built the 1883 **McHenry Mansion**, the city's sole surviving original Victorian home. The Italianate mansion has been decorated to reflect Modesto life in the late 19th century. Its period-

The Central Valley is California's agricultural powerhouse.

appropriate wallpaper is especially impressive. ✉ *15th and I Sts.* ☏ *209/ 577-5341* ⊕ *www.mchenrymuseum.org* ✉ *Free* ⊗ *Tours Sun.–Thurs. 12:30–4.*

The **McHenry Museum** is a repository of early Modesto and Stanislaus County memorabilia, including re-creations of an old-time dentist's office, a blacksmith's shop, a one room schoolhouse, an extensive doll collection, and a general store stocked with period goods such as hair crimpers and corsets. ✉ *1402 I St.* ☏ *209/577-5366* ⊕ *www. mchenrymuseum.org* ✉ *Free* ⊗ *Tues.–Sun. noon–4.*

WHERE TO EAT AND STAY

$–$$
AMERICAN
✕ **Hero's Sports Lounge & Pizza Co.** Modesto's renowned microbrewery makes Hero's (formerly St. Stan's) beers. The 14 on tap include the delicious Whistle Stop pale ale and Red Sky ale. The restaurant is casual and serves good corned-beef sandwiches loaded with sauerkraut as well as a tasty beer-sausage nibbler. ✉ *821 L St.* ☏ *209/524-2337* ⊟ *AE, MC, V* ⊗ *Closed Sun.*

$$$
AMERICAN
✕ **Tresetti's World Caffe.** An intimate setting with white tablecloths and contemporary art draws diners to this eatery—part wineshop (with 500-plus selections), part restaurant—with a seasonally changing menu. For a small supplemental fee, the staff will uncork any wine you select from the shop. The Cajun-style crab cakes, served for lunch year-round, are outstanding. ✉ *927 11th St.* ☏ *209/572-2990* ⊕ *www.tresetti.com* ⊟ *AE, D, DC, MC, V* ⊗ *Closed Sun.*

¢
🏨 **Best Western Town House Lodge.** The downtown location is the primary draw for this hotel. The county's historical library is across the street, and the McHenry Mansion and the McHenry Museum are nearby.

All rooms come equipped with a coffeemaker, hair dryer, and iron. **Pros:** perfect location; updated. **Cons:** staff's knowledge of town is sometimes limited. ⊠ *909 16th St.* ☎ *209/524–7261 or 800/772–7261* ⊕ *www.bestwesterncalifornia.com* ↪ *59 rooms* ⚗ *In-room: a/c, refrigerator. In-hotel: pool, Wi-Fi hotspot, parking (free)* ⊟ *AE, D, DC, MC, V* †⦿† *CP.*

OAKDALE

15 mi northeast of Modesto on Hwy. 108.

Oakdale was founded as an orchard community and, in a real stretch, calls itself the Cowboy Capital of the World.

EXPLORING

You can sample the wares at **Oakdale Cheese & Specialties** (⊠ *10040 Hwy. 120* ☎ *209/848–3139* ⊕ *www.oakdalecheese.com*), which has tastings (try the aged Gouda) and cheese-making tours. There's a picnic area and a petting zoo.

If you're in Oakdale—formerly home of a Hershey's chocolate factory—the third weekend in May, check out the **Oakdale Chocolate Festival** (☎ *209/847–2244* ▨ *$4*), which attracts 50,000 to 60,000 people each year. The event's main attraction is Chocolate Avenue, where vendors proffer cakes, cookies, ice cream, fudge, and cheesecake.

Ⓒ ★ The featured attraction at the **Knights Ferry Recreation Area** is the 355-foot-long Knights Ferry covered bridge. The beautiful and haunting structure, built in 1863, crosses the Stanislaus River near the ruins of an old gristmill. The park has camping, picnic, and barbecue areas along the riverbanks, as well as three campgrounds accessible only by boat. You can hike, fish, canoe, and raft on 4 mi of rapids. ⊠ *Corps of Engineers Park, 17968 Covered Bridge Rd., Knights Ferry, 12 mi east of Oakdale via Hwy. 108* ☎ *209/881–3517* ▨ *Free* ☾ *Daily dawn–dusk.*

SPORTS AND THE OUTDOORS

Rafting on the Stanislaus River is a popular activity near Oakdale. **River Journey** (⊠ *14842 Orange Blossom Rd.* ☎ *209/847–4671 or 800/292–2938* ⊕ *www.riverjourney.com*) will take you out for a few hours of fun. To satisfy your white-water or flat-water cravings, contact **Sunshine River Adventures** (☎ *209/848–4800 or 800/829–7238* ⊕ *www.raftadventure.com*).

STOCKTON

29 mi north of Modesto on Hwy. 99.

California's first inland port—connected since 1933 to San Francisco via a 60-mi-long deepwater channel—is wedged between I–5 and Highway 99, on the eastern end of the Sacramento River delta. Stockton, founded during the gold rush as a way station for miners traveling from San Francisco to the Mother Lode and now a city of 290,000, is where many of the valley's agricultural products begin their journey to other parts of the world. In recent years, the city has made significant strides in sprucing up its riverfront area downtown, including a spiffy minor-league baseball park for the Stockton Ports.

ESSENTIALS

Visitor Information Stockton Visitors Bureau (⊠ *46 W. Fremont St., Stockton* ☎ *209/547–2770 or 888/778–6256* ⊕ *www.visitstockton.org*).

EXPLORING

★ The **Haggin Museum**, in pretty Victory Park, has one of the Central Valley's finest art collections. Highlights include landscapes by Albert Bierstadt and Thomas Moran, a still life by Paul Gauguin, a Native American gallery, and an Egyptian mummy. ⊠ *1201 N. Pershing Ave.* ☎ *209/940–6300* ⊕ *www.hagginmuseum.org* 🏛 *$5* ⊙ *Wed.–Sun. 1:30–5; open until 9 on 1st and 3rd Thurs.*

> ### ASPARAGUS FEST
>
> If you're here in late April, don't miss the **Stockton Asparagus Festival** (☎ *209/644–3740* ⊕ *www.asparagusfest.com*), at the Downtown Stockton Waterfront. The highlight of the festival is the food, with more than 500 vendor booths; organizers try to prove that almost any dish can be made with asparagus.

WHERE TO EAT

$$$–$$$$
CONTINENTAL
✕ **Le Bistro.** This upscale restaurant serves modern interpretations of classic French cuisine—steak tartare, Grand Marnier soufflé—and warms hearts with a romantic atmosphere. ⊠ *Marina Center Mall, 3121 W. Benjamin Holt Dr., off I–5, behind Lyon's* ☎ *209/951–0885* ⊕ *www.lebistrostockton.com* ⊟ *AE, D, DC, MC, V* ⊙ *No lunch weekends.*

¢–$
CHINESE
✕ **On Lock Sam.** This Stockton landmark (it's been operating since 1898) is in a modern pagoda-style building with framed Chinese prints on the walls, a garden outside one window, and a sparkling bar area. One touch of old-time Chinatown remains: a few booths have curtains that can be drawn for complete privacy. A change in ownership in late 2009 provoked disgruntlement among some longtime patrons. ⊠ *333 S. Sutter St.* ☎ *209/466–4561* ⊟ *AE, D, MC, V.*

SPORTS AND THE OUTDOORS

Several companies rent houseboats (of various sizes, usually for three, four, or seven days) on the Sacramento River delta waterways near Stockton. **Herman & Helen's Marina** (⊠ *15135 W. 8 Mile Rd.* ☎ *209/951–4634*) rents houseboats with hot tubs and fireplaces. **Paradise Point Marina** (⊠ *8095 Rio Blanco Rd.* ☎ *209/952–1000*) rents a variety of watercraft, including patio boats.

18

LODI

13 mi north of Stockton and 34 mi south of Sacramento on Hwy. 99.

Founded on agriculture, Lodi was once the watermelon capital of the country. Today it's surrounded by fields of asparagus, pumpkins, beans, safflowers, sunflowers, kiwis, melons, squashes, peaches, and cherries. It also has become a wine-grape capital of sorts, producing zinfandel, merlot, cabernet sauvignon, chardonnay, and sauvignon blanc grapes. For years California wineries have built their reputations on the juice of grapes grown around Lodi. Now the area that includes Lodi, Lockeford, and Woodbridge is a wine destination in itself, boasting about

40 wineries, many offering tours and tastings. Lodi still retains an old rural charm, despite its population of nearly 70,000. You can stroll downtown or visit a wildlife refuge, all the while benefiting from a Sacramento River delta breeze that keeps this microclimate cooler in summer than anyplace else in the area.

ESSENTIALS

Visitor Information Lodi Conference and Visitors Bureau (⊠ *2545 W. Turner Dr., Lodi* 🕾 *209/365–1195 or 800/798–1810* ⊕ *www.visitlodi.com*).

EXPLORING

☉ The 258-acre **Micke Grove Regional Park**, an oak-shaded county park 5 mi north of Stockton off Highway 99, includes a Japanese tea garden, picnic areas, children's play areas, softball fields, an agricultural museum, and a water-play feature. (Micke Grove Golf Links, an 18-hole course, is next to the park.) Geckos and frogs, black-and-white ruffed lemurs, and hissing cockroaches found only on Madagascar inhabit "An Island Lost in Time," an exhibit at the **Micke Grove Zoo** (🕾 *209/953–8840* ⊕ *www.mgzoo.com* 🖾 *$2* ☉ *Daily 10–5*). California sea lions, Chinese alligators and a walk-through Mediterranean aviary are among the highlights of this compact facility. Most rides and attractions at the park's **Fun Town at Micke Grove** (🕾 *209/369–7330* ☉ *Mid-May– Labor Day, daily 11–dusk*), a family-oriented amusement park, are geared toward children. ⊠ *11793 N. Micke Grove Rd.* 🕾 *209/953– 8800* 🖾 *Parking $5.*

Stop by the **Lodi Wine & Visitor Center** (⊠ *2545 W. Turner Rd.* 🕾 *209/365– 0621* ⊕ *www.lodiwine.com*) to see exhibits on Lodi's viticultural history, pick up a map of area wineries, and even buy wine.

★ One of the standout wineries in the area is **Jessie's Grove** (⊠ *1973 W. Turner Rd.* 🕾 *209/368–0880* ⊕ *www.jgwinery.com* ☉ *Daily 11–5*), a wooded horse ranch and vineyard that has been in the same family since 1863. In addition to producing outstanding old-vine zinfandels, it presents blues concerts on various Saturdays June through October.

At the **Woodbridge Winery** (⊠ *5950 E. Woodbridge Rd., Acampo* 🕾 *209/ 365–8139* ⊕ *www.woodbridgewines.com* ☉ *Tues.–Sun. 10:30–4:30*), you can take a free 30-minute tour of the vineyard and barrel room. The label's legendary founder, Robert Mondavi, died in 2008 at age 94.

At its homey facility, kid-friendly **Phillips Farms Michael-David Winery** (⊠ *4580 W. Hwy. 12* 🕾 *209/368–7384* ⊕ *www.lodivineyards.com*) offers tastings from its affordable Michael-David vineyard. You can also cut flowers from the garden, eat breakfast or lunch at the café, and buy Phillips' and other local produce.

WHERE TO EAT AND STAY

$ ✕ **Habañero Hots**. If your mouth can handle the heat promised by the res-

MEXICAN   taurant's name, try the tamales. If you want to take it easy on your taste buds, stick with the rest of the menu. ⊠ *1024 E. Victor Rd.* 🕾 *209/369– 3791* ⊕ *www.habanerohots.com* ▭ *AE, MC, V.*

$$–$$$ ✕ **Rosewood Bar & Grill**. In downtown Lodi, Rosewood offers fine dining

AMERICAN   without formality. Operated by the folks at Wine & Roses Hotel and

Lodi Lake Park is a great place to escape the Central Valley heat in summer.

Restaurant, this low-key spot serves American fare with a twist, such as meat loaf wrapped in bacon, and daily seafood specials. The bar has a full-service menu, and live music on Friday and Saturday. ⊠ *28 S. School St.* ☎ *209/369–0470* ⊕ *www.rosewoodbarandgrill.com* ⊟ *AE, D, DC, MC, V* ☺ *No lunch.*

$$ 🛏 **The Inn at Locke House.** Built in 1865, this B&B was a pioneer doctor's
★ family home and is on the National Register of Historic Places. Airy rooms with garden views are filled with Locke family antique furnishings, and all have fireplaces and private bathrooms. The centerpiece of the three-level Water Tower Suite is a queen canopy bed; it also has a deck and a private sitting room at the top of the tower. Refreshments are served in the parlor, where there's also an old pump organ. Breakfasts made with local organic products are served in the carriageway. **Pros:** friendly; quiet; lovely. **Cons:** remote; can be hard to find. ⊠ *19960 N. Elliott Rd., Lockeford* ☎ *209/727–5715* ⊕ *www.theinnatlockehouse. com* ➥ *4 rooms, 1 suite* ⚐ *In-room: a/c, no TV. In-hotel: Wi-Fi hotspot* ⊟ *AE, D, DC, MC, V* ❧| *BP.*

$$–$$$ 🛏 **Wine & Roses Hotel and Restaurant.** Set on 7 acres amid a tapestry
★ of informal gardens, this hotel has cultivated a sense of refinement typically associated with Napa or Carmel. Rooms are decorated in rich earth tones, and linens are imported from Italy. Some rooms have fireplaces; all have coffeemakers, irons, and hair dryers. Some of the bathrooms even have TVs. The restaurant ($$–$$$) is *the* place to eat in Lodi. The Sunday buffet champagne brunch includes ham, prime rib, and made-to-order crepes and omelets. Afterward, consider heading to the spa for a facial or herbal body scrub. **Pros:** luxurious; relaxing; quiet. **Cons:** expensive; isolated; some guests have said the walls are

thin. ⊠ *2505 W. Turner Rd.* ☎ *209/334–6988* ⊕ *www.winerose.com*
↩ *47 rooms, 4 suites* ⚬ *In-room: a/c, refrigerator. In-hotel: restaurant,*
room service, bar, spa, laundry service, Wi-Fi hotspot ⊟ *AE, D, DC,*
MC, V ⏪ *CP.*

SPORTS AND THE OUTDOORS

Even locals need respite from the heat of Central Valley summers, and
Lodi Lake Park (⊠ *1101 W. Turner Rd.* ☎ *209/333–6742* ⊠ *$5*) is where
they find it. The banks, shaded by grand old elms and oaks, are much
cooler than other spots in town. Swimming, bird-watching, and picnicking are possibilities, as is renting a kayak, canoe, or pedal boat ($2
to $4 per half hour, Tuesday through Sunday, late May through early
September only).

The Southern Sierra

AROUND SEQUOIA, KINGS CANYON, AND YOSEMITE NATIONAL PARKS

WORD OF MOUTH

"Sitting on the edge of [the] Sierra Nevada Mountains, Mono Lake is an ancient saline lake. It is home to trillions of brine shrimp and alkali flies. You can see many limestone formations known as Tufa Towers, such as this, rising from the water's surface. Mono Lake is visited by millions of migratory birds each year."
—photo by Randall Pugh, Fodors.com member

WELCOME TO THE SOUTHERN SIERRA

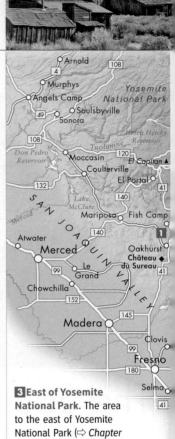

TOP REASONS TO GO

★ **Take a hike:** Whether you walk the paved loops in the national parks (⇨ *Chapter 20, Yosemite National Park, and Chapter 21, Sequoia and Kings Canyon National Parks*) or head off the beaten path into the backcountry, a hike through groves and meadows or alongside streams and waterfalls will allow you to see, smell, and feel nature up close.

★ **Hit the slopes:** Famous for its incredible snowpack—some of the deepest in the North American continent—the Sierra Nevada has something for every winter-sports fan.

★ **Mammoth fun:** Mammoth Lakes is eastern California's most exciting resort area.

★ **Old-world charm:** Tucked in the hills south of Oakhurst, the elegant Château du Sureau will make you feel as if you've stepped into a fairy tale.

★ **Go with the flow:** Three Rivers, the gateway to Sequoia National Park, is the launching pad for white-water trips down the Kaweah River.

1 South of Yosemite National Park. Several gateway towns to the south and west of Yosemite National Park (⇨ *Chapter 20*), most within an hour's drive of Yosemite Valley, have food, lodging, and other services.

2 Mammoth Lakes. A jewel in the vast eastern Sierra Nevada, the Mammoth Lakes area lies just east of the Sierra crest, on the back side of Yosemite and the Ansel Adams Wilderness. It's a place of rugged beauty, where giant sawtooth mountains drop into the vast deserts of the Great Basin. In winter, 11,053-foot-high Mammoth Mountain provides the finest skiing and snowboarding in California—sometimes as late as June or even July. Once the snows melt, Mammoth transforms itself into a warm-weather playground, with fishing, mountain biking, golfing, hiking, and horseback riding. Nine deep-blue lakes are spread through the Mammoth Lakes Basin, and another 100 lakes dot the surrounding countryside.

3 East of Yosemite National Park. The area to the east of Yosemite National Park (⇨ *Chapter 20*) includes some ruggedly handsome, albeit desolate, terrain, most notably around Mono Lake. The area is best visited by car, as distances are great and public transportation is negligible. U.S. 395 is the main north–south road on the eastern side of the Sierra Nevada, the western edge of the Great Basin. It's one of California's most beautiful highways; plan to snap pictures at roadside pullouts.

GETTING ORIENTED

The transition between the Central Valley and the rugged Southern Sierra may be the most dramatic in California sightseeing; as you head into the mountains, your temptation to stop the car and gawk will increase with every foot gained in elevation. While you should spend most of your time here in the national parks (⇨ *Chapter 20, Yosemite National Park,* and *Chapter 21, Sequoia and Kings Canyon National Parks*), be sure to check out some of the mountain towns on the parks' fringes—in addition to being great places to stock up on supplies, they have a variety of worthy attractions, restaurants, and lodging options.

19

4 South of Sequoia and Kings Canyon: Three Rivers. Scenic Three Rivers is the main gateway for Sequoia and Kings Canyon National Parks (⇨ *Chapter 21*).

THE SOUTHERN SIERRA PLANNER

Getting Here and Around

Fresno Yosemite International Airport (FYI) is the nearest airport to the national parks; Reno–Tahoe is the closest major airport to Mammoth Lakes.

Airports Fresno Yosemite International Airport (⊠ 5175 E. Clinton Ave., Fresno ☎ 559/621–4500 or 559/498–4095 ⊕ www.flyfresno.org). **Reno–Tahoe International Airport** (⊠ U.S. 395, Exit 65B, Reno, NV ☎ 775/328–6400 ⊕ www.renoairport.com).

From San Francisco, interstates 80 and 580 are the fastest routes to the central Sierra Nevada. Through the Central Valley, Interstate 5 and Highway 99 are the fastest north–south routes; the latter is narrower and has heavy farm-truck traffic.

To get to Mammoth Lakes in summer and early fall (or whenever snows aren't blocking Tioga Road), you can travel via Highway 120 (to U.S. 395 south) through the Yosemite high country; the quickest route in winter is Interstate 80 to U.S. 50 to Highway 207 (Kingsbury Grade) to U.S. 395 south; either route takes about seven hours.

Contacts California Road Conditions (☎ 800/427–7623 ⊕ www.dot.ca.gov/hq/roadinfo).

About the Restaurants

Most small towns in the Sierra Nevada have at least one restaurant; with few exceptions, dress is casual. You'll most likely be spending a lot of time in the car while you're exploring the area, so pick up snacks and drinks to keep with you. With picnic supplies on hand, you'll be able to enjoy an impromptu meal under giant trees.

About the Hotels

If you're planning to stay on the Sierra's western side, book your hotel in advance—especially in summer. Otherwise, you may end up driving pretty far to find a place to sleep. Thanks to the surge in hotel development in Mammoth Lakes, making an advance reservation is not as critical on the Sierra's less-traveled eastern side. Wherever you visit, however, be prepared for sticker shock—rural and rustic does not mean inexpensive here.

Booking a Room

If you'd like assistance booking your lodgings, try the following agencies: **Mammoth Lakes Visitors Bureau Lodging Referral** (☎ 760/934–2712 or 888/466–2666 ⊕ www.visitmammoth.com). **Mammoth Reservations** (☎ 800/223–3032 ⊕ www.mammothreservations.com). **Three Rivers Reservation Center** (☎ 866/561–0410 or 559/561–0410 ⊕ www.rescentre.com).

WHAT IT COSTS

	¢	$	$$	$$$	$$$$
Restaurants	under $10	$10–$15	$16–$22	$23–$30	over $30
Hotels	under $90	$90–$120	$121–$175	$176–$250	over $250

Restaurant prices are for a main course at dinner, excluding sales tax of 7.25%–7.75% (depending on location). Hotel prices are for two people in a standard double room in high season, excluding service charges and 9%–10% tax.

Updated by
Reed Parsell

Vast granite peaks and giant sequoias are among the mind-boggling natural wonders of the Southern Sierra, many of which are protected in three national parks (⇨ *Chapter 20, Yosemite National Park, and Chapter 21, Sequoia and Kings Canyon National Parks*).

Outside the parks, pristine lakes, superb skiing, rolling hills, and small towns complete the picture of the Southern Sierra. Heading up Highway 395, on the Sierra's eastern side, you'll be rewarded with outstanding vistas of dramatic mountain peaks, including Mt. Whitney, the highest point in the contiguous United States, and Mono Lake, a vast but slowly vanishing expanse of deep blue—one of the most-photographed natural attractions in California.

SOUTH OF YOSEMITE NATIONAL PARK

19

OAKHURST

40 mi north of Fresno and 23 mi south of Yosemite National Park's south entrance on Hwy. 41.

Motels, restaurants, gas stations, and small businesses line both sides of Highway 41 as it cuts through Oakhurst. This is the last sizeable community before Yosemite (⇨ *Chapter 20*) and a good spot to find provisions. There are two major grocery stores near the intersection of highways 41 and 49. Three miles north of town, then 6 mi east, honky-tonky Bass Lake is a popular spot in summer with motorboaters, Jet Skiers, and families looking to cool off in the reservoir.

ESSENTIALS

Visitor Information Yosemite Sierra Visitors Bureau (⌂ *41969 Hwy. 41, Box 1998, Oakhurst 93644* 🕾 *559/683–4636* ⊕ *www.yosemitethisyear.com*).

WHERE TO EAT AND STAY

$$$$
CONTINENTAL
Fodor'sChoice
★

✕ **Erna's Elderberry House.** Austrian-born Erna Kubin-Clanin, the grande dame of Château du Sureau, has created a culinary oasis, stunning for its elegance, gorgeous setting, and impeccable service. Crimson walls and dark beams accent the dining room's high ceilings, and arched windows reflect the glow of candles. The seasonal six-course prix-fixe dinner can be paired with superb wines, a must-do for oenophiles. When the waitstaff places all the plates on the table in perfect synchronicity, you know this will be a meal to remember. Premeal drinks are served in the former wine cellar. ⊠ *48688 Victoria La.* ☎ *559/683–6800* ⊕ *www.elderberryhouse.com* ♙ *Reservations essential* ⊟ *AE, D, MC, V* ⊗ *No lunch Mon.–Sat.*

DRIVING TIPS

Keep your tank full. Distances between gas stations can be long, and there's no fuel available in Yosemite Valley, Sequoia, or Kings Canyon (⇨ *Chapters 20 and 21*). If you're traveling from October through April, rain on the coast can mean heavy snow in the mountains. Carry tire chains, know how to put them on (on Interstate 80 and U.S. 50 you can pay a chain installer $20 to do it for you, but on other routes you'll have to do it yourself), and always check road conditions before you leave. Traffic in national parks in summer can be heavy, and there are sometimes travel restrictions.

$
AMERICAN

✕ **Yosemite Fork Mountain House.** Bypass Oakhurst's greasy spoons and instead head to this family restaurant, 3 mi north of the Highway 49/Highway 41 intersection, with an open-beam ceiling and a canoe in the rafters. Portions are huge. Expect standard American fare: bacon and eggs at breakfast, sandwiches at lunch, and pastas and steaks at dinner. ⊠ *Hwy. 41, at Bass Lake turnoff* ☎ *559/683–5191* ⊕ *www.yosemiteforkmountainhouse.com* ♙ *Reservations not accepted* ⊟ *D, MC, V.*

$$$$
Fodor'sChoice
★

☷ **Château du Sureau.** This romantic inn, adjacent to Erna's Elderberry House, is straight out of one of Grimm's fairy tales. From the moment you drive through the wrought-iron gates and up to the enchanting castle, you feel pampered. Every room is impeccably styled with European antiques, sumptuous fabrics, fresh-cut flowers, and oversize soaking tubs. Fall asleep by the glow of a crackling fire amid feather-light goose-down pillows and Italian linens, awaken to a hearty European breakfast in the dining room, then relax with a game of chess in the grand salon beneath an exquisite mural—or play chess on the giant board amid tall pine trees off the impeccably landscaped garden trail. Cable TV is available by request only. In 2006 the Château added a stunning spa. **Pros:** luxurious; spectacular property. **Cons:** you'll need to take out a second mortgage to stay here. ⊠ *48688 Victoria La.* ☎ *559/683–6860* ⊕ *www.elderberryhouse.com* ♫ *10 rooms, 1 villa* ♿ *In-room: a/c. In-hotel: restaurant, bar, pool, spa, laundry service, Wi-Fi hotspot, no kids under 8* ⊟ *AE, MC, V* ℍℍ *BP.*

$$$–$$$$
★

☷ **Homestead Cottages.** If you're looking for peace and quiet, this is the place. Serenity is the order of the day at this secluded getaway in Ahwahnee, 6 mi west of Oakhurst. On 160 acres of rolling hills that once held a Miwok village, these cottages have gas fireplaces, living rooms, fully equipped kitchens, and queen-size beds; the largest sleeps six. The cottages, hand-built by the owners out of real adobe bricks, are stocked with soft robes, oversize towels, and paperback books. **Pros:** remote; quiet; friendly owners. **Cons:** remote; some urbanites might find it *too* quiet. ⊠*41110 Rd. 600, 2½ mi off Hwy. 49, Ahwahnee* ☎*559/683– 0495 or 800/483–0495* ⊕*www.homesteadcottages.com* ⟳*5 cottages, 1 loft* ⚭ *In-room: no phone, a/c, kitchen* ☰ *AE, D, MC, V.*

FISH CAMP

57 mi north of Fresno and 4 mi south of Yosemite National Park's south entrance.

As you climb in elevation along Highway 41 northbound, you see nothing but trees until you get to the small settlement of Fish Camp, where there's a post office and general store, but no gasoline (for gas, head 10 mi north to Wawona, in the park, or 17 mi south to Oakhurst).

ℭ The **Yosemite Mountain Sugar Pine Railroad** has a narrow-gauge steam train that chugs through the forest. It follows 4 mi of the route the Madera Sugar Pine Lumber Company cut through the forest in 1899 to harvest timber. The steam train, as well as Jenny railcars, run year-round on fluctuating schedules; call for details. On Saturday (and Wednesday in summer), the Moonlight Special dinner excursion (reservations essential) includes a picnic with toe-tappin' music by the Sugar Pine Singers, followed by a sunset steam-train ride. ⊠*56001 Hwy. 41* ☎*559/683– 7273* ⊕*www.ymsprr.com* ☒*$17.50 steam train; Jenny railcar $13.50; Moonlight Special $46* ☉ *Mar.–Oct., daily.*

WHERE TO STAY

$-$$$ ☷ **Narrow Gauge Inn.** All of the rooms at this well-tended, family-owned
★   property have balconies (some shared) and great views of the surrounding woods and mountains. For maximum atmosphere, book a room overlooking the brook; for quiet, choose a lower-level room on the edge of the forest. All of the recently renovated rooms are comfortably furnished with old-fashioned accents. Reserve way ahead. The restaurant ($$–$$$$; open April–October, Wednesday–Sunday), which is festooned with moose, bison, and other wildlife trophies, specializes in steaks and American fare, and merits a special trip. **Pros:** close to Yosemite's south entrance; well-appointed; wonderful balconies. **Cons:** rooms can feel a bit dark; dining options are limited (especially for vegetarians). ⊠*48571 Hwy. 41* ☎*559/683–7720 or 888/644–9050* ⊕*www.narrowgaugeinn.com* ⟳*26 rooms, 1 suite* ⚭ *In-room: no a/c (some), Internet, Wi-Fi (some). In-hotel: restaurant, bar, pool, some pets allowed* ☰*D, MC, V* ⟊*CP.*

$$$$ ☷ **Tenaya Lodge.** One of the region's largest hotels, the Tenaya Lodge is
★   ideal for people who enjoy wilderness treks by day but prefer creature comforts at night. The hulking prefab buildings and giant parking lot look out of place in the woods, but inside, the rooms have the amenities of a modern, full-service hotel. The ample regular rooms are decorated in pleasant earth tones, deluxe rooms have minibars and other extras, and the suites have balconies. Off-season rates can be as low as $100. The Sierra Restaurant ($$$), with its high ceilings and giant

19

fireplace, serves Continental cuisine. The more casual Jackalopes Bar and Grill ($) has burgers, salads, and sandwiches. **Pros:** rustic setting with modern comforts; good off-season deals. **Cons:** so big it can seem impersonal; few dining options. ✉ *1122 Hwy. 41* ✆ *Box 159, 93623* ☎ *559/683–6555 or 888/514–2167* ⊕ *www.tenayalodge.com* ⤳ *244 rooms, 6 suites* ♿ *In-room: a/c, refrigerator. In-hotel: 2 restaurants, room service, bar, pool, gym, bicycles, children's programs (ages 5–12), laundry service, Wi-Fi hotspot* ☰ *AE, D, DC, MC, V.*

EL PORTAL

14 mi west of Yosemite Valley on Hwy. 140.

The market in town is a good place to pick up provisions before you get to Yosemite (⇨ *Chapter 20*). There's also a post office and a gas station, but not much else.

WHERE TO STAY

$$–$$$ ☎ **Yosemite View Lodge.** The Yosemite View Lodge's motel-like design aesthetic is ameliorated by its location right on the banks of the boulder-strewn Merced River and its proximity to the park entrance 2 mi east. Many rooms have whirlpool baths, fireplaces, kitchenettes, and balconies or decks. The motel complex is on the public bus route to the park, near fishing and river rafting. Ask for a river-view room. The lodge's sister property, the Cedar Lodge, sits 6 mi farther west and has similar, less expensive rooms without river views. **Pros:** huge spa baths; great views; friendly service. **Cons:** air-conditioning inconsistent; restaurant can get crowded; can be pricey. ✉ *11136 Hwy. 140* ☎ *209/379–2681 or 888/742–4371* ⊕ *www.yosemiteresorts.us* ⤳ *335 rooms* ♿ *In-room: a/c, kitchen (some). In-hotel: restaurant, bar, pools, laundry facilities, some pets allowed* ☰ *AE, MC, V.*

MAMMOTH LAKES

30 mi south of eastern edge of Yosemite National Park on U.S. 395.

Much of the architecture in Mammoth Lakes (elevation 7,800 feet) is of the faux-alpine variety. You'll find increasingly sophisticated dining and lodging options here. International real-estate developers joined forces with Mammoth Mountain Ski Area and have worked hard to transform the once sleepy town into a chic ski destination. The Village at Mammoth (⇨ *below*) is the epicenter of all the recent development. Winter is high season at Mammoth; in summer room rates plummet. Highway 203 heads west from U.S. 395, becoming Main Street as it passes through the town of Mammoth Lakes, and later Minaret Road (which makes a right turn) as it continues west to the Mammoth Mountain ski area and Devils Postpile National Monument.

ESSENTIALS

Visitor Information Mammoth Lakes Visitors Bureau (✉ *Along Hwy. 203, Main St., near Sawmill Cutoff Rd., Box 48, Mammoth Lakes* ☎ *760/934–2712 or 888/466–2666* ⊕ *www.visitmammoth.com*).

Twin Lakes, in the Mammoth Lakes region, is a great place to unwind.

EXPLORING

The lakes of the **Mammoth Lakes Basin**, reached by Lake Mary Road off Highway 203 southwest of town, are popular for fishing and boating in summer. First comes Twin Lakes, at the far end of which is Twin Falls, where water cascades 300 feet over a shelf of volcanic rock. Also popular are Lake Mary, the largest lake in the basin; Lake Mamie; and Lake George. Horseshoe Lake is the only lake in which you can swim.

The glacier-carved sawtooth spires of the Minarets, the remains of an ancient lava flow, are best viewed from the **Minaret Vista**, off Highway 203 west of Mammoth Lakes.

Ⓒ Even if you don't ski, ride the **Panorama Gondola** to see Mammoth Mountain, the aptly named dormant volcano that gives Mammoth Lakes its name. Gondolas serve skiers in winter and mountain bikers and sightseers in summer. The high-speed, eight-passenger gondolas whisk you from the chalet to the summit, where you can read about the area's volcanic history and take in top-of-the-world views. Standing high above the tree line atop this dormant volcano, you can look west 150 mi across the state to the Coastal Range; to the east are the highest peaks of Nevada and the Great Basin beyond. You won't find a better view of the Sierra High Country without climbing. Remember, though, that the air is thin at the 11,053-foot summit; carry water, and don't overexert yourself. The boarding area is at the Main Lodge. ⊠ *Off Hwy. 203* ☎ *760/934–2571 Ext. 2400 information, Ext. 3850 gondola station* 🎫 *$18 in summer* ☻ *July 4–Oct., daily 9–4:30; Nov.– July 3, daily 8:30–4.*

Fodor'sChoice
★

The overwhelming popularity of Mammoth Mountain has generated a real-estate boom, and a huge new complex of shops, restaurants, and luxury accommodations, called the **Village at Mammoth**, has become the town's tourist center. Parking can be tricky. There's a lot across the street on Minaret Road; pay attention to time limits.

WHERE TO EAT

$$$
AMERICAN

✕ **Petra's Bistro & Wine Bar.** Other restaurateurs speak highly of Petra's as the most convivial restaurant in town. Its lovely ambience—quiet, dark, and warm—complements the carefully prepared meat main dishes and seasonal sides, and the more than two dozen California wines from behind the bar. The service is top-notch. Downstairs, the Clocktower Cellar bar provides a late-night, rowdy alternative—or chaser. ✉ 6080 Minaret Rd. ☎ 760/934–3500 ⊕ www.petrasbistro.com ⚱ Reservations essential ⊟ AE, D, DC, MC, V ☯ No lunch.

$$$–$$$$
AMERICAN
★

✕ **Restaurant at Convict Lake.** Tucked in a tiny valley ringed by mile-high peaks, Convict Lake is one of the most spectacular spots in the eastern Sierra. Thank heaven the food lives up to the view. The chef's specialties include beef Wellington, rack of lamb, and pan-seared local trout, all beautifully prepared. The woodsy room has a vaulted knotty-pine ceiling and a copper-chimney fireplace that roars on cold nights. Natural light abounds in the daytime, but if it's summer, opt for a table outdoors under the white-barked aspens. Service is so good that if you forget your glasses, the waiter will provide a pair. The wine list is exceptional with reasonably priced European and California varietals. ✉ 2 mi off U.S. 395, 4 mi south of Mammoth Lakes ☎ 760/934–3803 ⚱ Reservations essential ⊟ AE, D, MC, V ☯ No lunch early Sept.–July 4.

$$$–$$$$
FRENCH
★

✕ **Restaurant LuLu.** LuLu imports the sunny, sensual, and assertive flavors of Provençale cooking—think olive tapenade, aioli, and lemony vinaigrettes—to Mammoth Lakes. At this outpost of the famous San Francisco restaurant, the formula remains the same: small plates of southern French cooking served family-style in a spare, modern, and sexy dining room. Standouts include rotisserie meats, succulent roasted mussels, homemade gnocchi, and a fantastic wine list, with 50 vintages available in 2-ounce pours. Outside, the sidewalk café includes a fire pit where kids will love do-it-themselves s'mores. LuLu's only drawback is price, but if you can swing it, it's worth every penny. The waiters wear jeans, so you can, too. ✉ Village at Mammoth, 1111 Forest Trail, Unit 201 ☎ 760/924–8781 ⊕ www.restaurantlulu.com ⚱ Reservations essential ⊟ AE, D, MC, V.

¢–$
CAFÉ

✕ **Side Door Café.** Half wine bar, half café, this is a laid-back spot for an easy lunch or a long, lingering afternoon. The café serves grilled panini sandwiches, sweet and savory crepes, and espresso. At the wine bar, order cheese plates and charcuterie platters, designed to pair with the 25 wines (fewer in summertime) available by the glass. If you're lucky, a winemaker will show up and hold court at the bar. ✉ Village at Mammoth, 1111 Forest Trail, Unit 229 ☎ 760/934–5200 ⊟ AE, D, MC, V.

$–$$ ✕ **The Stove.** A longtime family favorite for down-to-ear⟨
AMERICAN   ing, The Stove is the kind of place you take the family t⟨
⟨   long car ride. The omelets, pancakes, huevos rancheros
won't win any awards, but they're tasty. The room is cut⟨
curtains and pinewood booths, and service is friendly.
lunch are the best bets here. ⊠ *644 Old Mammoth Ra.* ☎ */60/934–
2821* ⚠ *Reservations not accepted* ▭ *AE, MC, V.*

WHERE TO STAY

$–$$ ⊞ **Alpenhof Lodge.** The owners of the Alpenhof lucked out when devel-
opers built the fancy-schmancy Village at Mammoth right across the
street from their mom-and-pop motel. The place remains a simple, mid-
budget motel, with basic comforts and a few niceties like attractive pine
furniture. Rooms are dark and the foam pillows thin, but the damask
bedspreads are pretty and the low-pile carpeting clean, and best of all
you can walk to restaurants and shops. Downstairs there's a lively, fun
pub; if you want quiet, request a room that's not above it. Some rooms
have fireplaces and kitchens. In winter the Village Gondola is across the
street, a major plus for skiers. **Pros:** convenient for skiers; good price.
Cons: could use an update; rooms above the pub can be noisy. ⊠ *6080
Minaret Rd., Box 1157* ☎ *760/934–6330 or 800/828–0371* ⊕ *www.
alpenhof-lodge.com* ↻ *54 rooms, 3 cabins* ⚹ *In-room: no a/c, kitchen
(some), refrigerator (some). In-hotel: restaurant, bar, pool, laundry
facilities* ▭ *AE, D, MC, V.*

$–$$ ⊞ **Cinnamon Bear Inn Bed and Breakfast.** In a business district off Main
Street, this bed-and-breakfast feels more like a small motel, with nicely
decorated rooms, many with four-poster beds. Suites have pull-out
sofas, good for families; some have full kitchens. The exterior is weathered, but not at all derelict. For skiers looking for an alternative to a
motel, this is a solid choice. Year-round, it's comparatively quiet due
to its being a block from the main drag. Rates include a made-to-order
breakfast and wine and cheese in the afternoon. **Pros:** quiet; affordable; friendly. **Cons:** a bit tricky to find; limited parking. ⊠ *113 Center
St.* ✎ *Box 3338, 93546* ☎ *760/934–2873 or 800/845–2873* ⊕ *www.
cinnamonbearinn.com* ↻ *22 rooms* ⚹ *In-room: no a/c, kitchen (some).
In-hotel: bar, Wi-Fi hotspot* ▭ *AE, D, DC, MC, V* ⦿|*BP.*

$$$–$$$$ ⊞ **Double Eagle Resort and Spa.** You won't find a better spa retreat in
the eastern Sierra than the Double Eagle. Dwarfed by towering, craggy
peaks, the resort is in a spectacularly beautiful spot along a creek,
near June Lake, 20 minutes north of Mammoth Lakes. Accommoda-
tions are in comfortable knotty-pine two-bedroom cabins that sleep
up to six, or in cabin suites with efficiency kitchens; all come fully
equipped with modern amenities. If you don't want to cook, the Eagles
Landing Restaurant serves three meals a day, but the quality is erratic.
Spa services and treatments are available for nonguests by reservation.
The small, uncrowded June Mountain Ski Area is 1½ mi away. **Pros:**
pretty setting; generous breakfast; good for families. **Cons:** expensive,
remote. ⊠ *5587 Hwy. 158, Box 736, June Lake* ☎ *760/648–7004 or
877/648–7004* ⊕ *www.doubleeagleresort.com* ↻ *16 2-bedroom cabins,
16 cabin suites, 1 3-bedroom cabin* ⚹ *In-room: no a/c, kitchen (some),*

19

refrigerator, Internet. In-hotel: restaurant, bar, pool, gym, spa, some pets allowed ⊟ *AE, D, MC, V.*

$$–$$$$ ⊡ **Juniper Springs Lodge.** Tops for slope-side comfort, these condominium-style units have full kitchens and ski-in ski-out access to the mountain. Extras include gas fireplaces, balconies, and stereos with CD players; the heated outdoor pool—surrounded by a heated deck—is open year-round. If you like to be near nightlife, you'll do better at the Village, but if you don't mind having to drive to go out for the evening, this is a great spot. In summer fewer people stay here, although package deals and lower prices provide incentive. Skiers: The lifts on this side of the mountain close in mid-April; for springtime ski-in ski-out access, stay at the Mammoth Mountain Inn. **Pros:** bargain during summer; direct access to the slopes; good views. **Cons:** no nightlife within walking distance; no a/c; some complaints about service. ⊠ *4000 Meridian Blvd.* ⌂ *Box 2129, 93546* ☎ *760/924–1102 or 800/626–6684* ⊕ *www.mammothmountain.com* ⌖ *10 studios, 99 1-bedrooms, 92 2-bedrooms, 3 3-bedrooms* ♿ *In-room: no a/c, kitchen, refrigerator, Internet. In-hotel: restaurant, room service, bar, golf course, pool, bicycles, laundry facilities* ⊟ *AE, MC, V.*

$$–$$$$ ⊡ **Mammoth Mountain Inn.** If you want to be within walking distance of the Mammoth Mountain Main Lodge, this is the place. In summer the proximity to the gondola means you can hike and mountain bike to your heart's delight. The accommodations, which vary in size, include standard hotel rooms and condo units. The inn, ski lodge, and other summit facilities are likely to be razed and rebuilt within a decade, bringing more of a 21st-century ski resort feel to what's been a quaint 1950s-born resort. Meanwhile, the inn has done a respectable job with continual refurbishing. **Pros:** great location; big rooms; a traditional place to stay. **Cons:** can be crowded in ski season; won't be around for many more years. ⊠ *Minaret Rd., 4 mi west of Mammoth Lakes* ⌂ *Box 353, 93546* ☎ *760/934–2581 or 800/626–6684* ⊕ *www. mammothmountain.com* ⌖ *124 rooms, 91 condos* ♿ *In-room: no a/c, kitchen (some), refrigerator (some), Internet. In-hotel: 2 restaurants, bar, pool, laundry facilities, Wi-Fi hotspot* ⊟ *AE, MC, V.*

$–$$$
Fodor's Choice
★
⊡ **Tamarack Lodge Resort & Lakefront Restaurant.** Tucked away on the edge of the John Muir Wilderness Area, where cross-country ski trails loop through the woods, this original 1924 lodge looks like something out of a snow globe, and the lake it borders is serenely beautiful. Rooms in the charming main lodge have spartan furnishings, and in old-fashioned style, some share a bathroom. For more privacy, opt for one of the cabins, which range from rustic to downright cushy; many have fireplaces, kitchens, or wood-burning stoves. In warm months, fishing, canoeing, hiking, and mountain biking are right outside. The small and romantic Lakefront Restaurant ($$$-$$$$) serves outstanding contemporary French-inspired dinners, with an emphasis on game, in a candlelit dining room. Reservations are essential. **Pros:** rustic but not run-down; tons of nearby outdoor activities. **Cons:** thin walls; some main lodge rooms have shared bathrooms. ⊠ *Lake Mary Rd., off Hwy. 203* ⌂ *Box 69, 93546* ☎ *760/934–2442 or 800/626–6684* ⊕ *www.tamaracklodge.*

com 🌀 *11 rooms, 35 cabins* ☺ *In-room: no a/c, kitchen (some), no TV. In-hotel: restaurant, bar, Wi-Fi hotspot* ≡ *AE, MC, V.*

$$$$ 📺 **Village at Mammoth.** At the epicenter of Mammoth's burgeoning dining and nightlife scene, this cluster of four-story timber-and-stone condo buildings nods to Alpine style, with exposed timbers and peaked roofs. Units have gas fireplaces, kitchens or kitchenettes, daily maid service, high-speed Internet access, DVD players, slate-tile bathroom floors, and comfortable furnishings. The decor is a bit sterile, but there are high-end details like granite counters. And you won't have to drive anywhere: the buildings are connected by a ground-floor pedestrian mall, with shops, restaurants, bars, and—best of all—a gondola (November through mid-April only) that whisks you right from the Village to the mountain. **Pros:** central location; clean; big rooms; lots of good restaurants nearby. **Cons:** pricey; can be noisy outside. ⊠ *100 Canyon Blvd.* ☏ *Box 3459, 93546* 🖷 *760/934–1982 or 800/626–6684* ⊕ *www.mammothmountain. com* 🌀 *277 units* ☺ *In-room: no a/c, kitchen (some), Internet. In-hotel: pool, gym, laundry facilities, parking (free)* ≡ *AE, MC, V.*

SPORTS AND THE OUTDOORS

For information on winter conditions around Mammoth, call the **Snow Report** (🕿 *760/934–7669 or 888/766–9778*). The **U.S. Forest Service ranger station** (🕿 *760/924–5500*) can provide general information year-round.

BICYCLING

Mammoth Mountain Bike Park (⊠ *Mammoth Mountain Ski Area* 🕿 *760/ 934–3706* ⊕ *www.mammothmountain.com*) opens when the snow melts, usually by July, with 70-plus mi of single track trails—from mellow to super-challenging. Chairlifts and shuttles provide trail access, and rentals are available. Various shops around town also rent bikes and provide trail maps, if you don't want to ascend the mountain.

FISHING

Crowley Lake is the top trout-fishing spot in the area; Convict Lake, June Lake, and the lakes of the Mammoth Basin are other prime spots. One of the best trout rivers is the San Joaquin, near Devils Postpile. Hot Creek, a designated Wild Trout Stream, is renowned for fly-fishing (catch-and-release only). The fishing season runs from the last Saturday in April until the end of October. To maximize your time on the water, get tips from local anglers, or better yet, book a guided fishing trip with **Sierra Drifters Guide Service** (🕿 *760/935–4250* ⊕ *www.sierradrifters.com*).

Kittredge Sports (⊠ *3218 Main St., at Forest Trail* 🕿 *760/934–7566* ⊕ *www.kittredgesports.com*) rents rods and reels and also conducts guided trips.

HIKING

Hiking in Mammoth is stellar, especially along the trails that wind through the pristine alpine scenery around the Lakes Basin. Carry lots of water; and remember, you're above 8,000-foot elevation, and the air is thin. Stop at the **U.S. Forest Service ranger station** (⊠ *Hwy. 203* 🕿 *760/924–5500* ⊕ *www.fs.fed.us/r5/inyo*), on your right just before

19

the town of Mammoth Lakes, for a Mammoth area trail map and permits for backpacking in wilderness areas.

HORSEBACK RIDING

Stables around Mammoth are typically open from June through September. **Mammoth Lakes Pack Outfit** (✉ *Lake Mary Rd., between Twin Lakes and Lake Mary* ☎ *760/934–2434 or 888/475–8747* ⊕ *www. mammothpack.com*) runs day and overnight horseback trips, or will shuttle you to the high country. **McGee Creek Pack Station** (☎ *760/935– 4324 or 800/854–7407* ⊕ *www.mcgeecreekpackstation.com*) customizes pack trips or will shuttle you to camp alone. Operated by the folks at McGee Creek, **Sierra Meadows Ranch** (✉ *Sherwin Creek Rd., off Old Mammoth Rd.* ☎ *760/934–6161*) conducts horseback and wagon rides that range from one-hour to all-day excursions.

SKIING

June Mountain Ski Area. In their rush to Mammoth Mountain, most people overlook June Mountain, a compact, low-key resort 20 mi north of Mammoth. Snowboarders especially dig it. Two freestyle terrain areas are for both skiers and boarders, including a huge 16-foot-wall super pipe. Best of all, there's rarely a line for the lifts—if you want to avoid the crowds but must ski on a weekend, this is the place. And in a storm, June is better protected from wind and blowing snow than Mammoth Mountain. (If it starts to storm, you can use your Mammoth ticket at June.) Expect all the usual services, including a rental-and-repair shop, ski school, and sports shop, but the food quality is better at Mammoth. Lift tickets run $64, with discounts for multiple days. ✉ *3819 Hwy. 158, off June Lake Loop, June Lake* ☎ *760/648–7733 or 888/586–3686* ⊕ *www.junemountain.com* ↻ *35 trails on 500 acres, rated 35% beginner, 45% intermediate, 20% advanced. Longest run 2½ mi, base 7,510 feet, summit 10,174 feet. Lifts: 7.*

Fodor's Choice   If you ski only one mountain in California, make it **Mammoth Mountain**
★   **Ski Area.** One of the West's largest and best ski areas, Mammoth has more than 3,500 acres of skiable terrain and a 3,100-foot vertical drop. The views from the 11,053-foot summit are some of the most stunning in the Sierra. Below, you'll find a 6½-mi-wide swath of groomed boulevards and canyons, as well as pockets of tree-skiing and a dozen vast bowls. Snowboarders are everywhere on the slopes; there are three outstanding freestyle terrain parks of varying technical difficulty, with jumps, rails, tabletops, and giant super pipes (this is the location of several international snowboarding competitions). Mammoth's season begins in November and often lingers into May. Lift tickets cost $65. Lessons and equipment are available, and there's a children's ski and snowboard school. Mammoth runs free shuttle-bus routes around town and to the ski area, and the Village Gondola runs from the Village complex to Canyon Lodge. However, only overnight guests are allowed to park at the Village for more than a few hours. Warning: The main lodge is dark and dated, unsuited in most every way for the crush of ski season. Within a decade, it's likely to be replaced. ✉ *Minaret Rd., west of Mammoth Lakes* ☎ *760/934–2571 or 800/626–6684, 760/934– 0687 shuttle* ↻ *150 trails on 3,500 acres, rated 30% beginner, 40%*

intermediate, 30% advanced. Longest run 3 mi, base 7,953 feet, summit 11,053 feet. Lifts: 27, including 9 high-speed and 2 gondolas.

Trails at **Tamarack Cross Country Ski Center** (✉ *Lake Mary Rd., off Hwy. 203* ☎ *760/934–5293 or 760/934–2442* ⊕ *www.tamaracklodge.com*), adjacent to Tamarack Lodge, meander around several lakes. Rentals are available.

Mammoth Sporting Goods (✉ *1 Sierra Center Mall, Old Mammoth Rd.* ☎ *760/934–3239* ⊕ *www.mammothsportinggoods.com*) rents good skis for intermediates, and sells equipment, clothing, and accessories. Advanced skiers should rent from **Kittredge Sports** (✉ *3218 Main St.* ☎ *760/934–7566* ⊕ *www.kittredgesports.com*).

★ When the U.S. Ski Team visits Mammoth and needs their boots adjusted, they head to **Footloose** (✉ *3043 Main St.* ☎ *760/934–2400* ⊕ *www.footloosesports.com*), the best place in town—and possibly all California—for ski-boot rentals and sales, as well as custom insoles (ask for Kevin or Corty).

EAST OF YOSEMITE NATIONAL PARK

LEE VINING

20 mi east of Tuolumne Meadows via Hwy. 120 to U.S. 395; 30 mi north of Mammoth Lakes on U.S. 395.

Tiny Lee Vining is known primarily as the eastern gateway to Yosemite National Park (summer only; ⇨ *Chapter 20*) and the location of vast and desolate Mono Lake. Pick up supplies at the general store year-round, or stop here for lunch or dinner before or after a drive through the high country. In winter the town is all but deserted, except for the ice climbers who come to scale frozen waterfalls. You can meet these hearty souls at Nicely's restaurant, where the climbers congregate for breakfast around 8 on winter mornings.

ESSENTIALS

Visitor Information Lee Vining Chamber of Commerce (✉ *Box 130, Lee Vining 93541* ☎ *760/647–6629* ⊕ *www.leevining.com*). **Mono Lake** (✉ *Box 49, Lee Vining 93541* ☎ *760/647–3044* ⊕ *www.monolake.org*).

To try your hand at ice climbing, contact **Sierra Mountain Guides** (☎ *760/ 648–1122 or 877/423–2546* ⊕ *www.themountainguide.com*).

EXPLORING

★ Eerie tufa towers—calcium carbonate formations that often resemble castle turrets—rise from impressive **Mono Lake**. Since the 1940s, the city of Los Angeles has diverted water from streams that feed the lake, lowering its water level and exposing the tufa. Court victories by environmentalists in the 1990s forced a reduction of the diversions, and the lake has since risen about 9 feet. From April through August, millions of migratory birds nest in and around Mono Lake. The best place to view the tufa is at the south end of the lake along the mile-long **South Tufa Trail.** To reach it, drive 5 mi south from Lee Vining on U.S. 395, then 5 mi east on Highway 120. There's a $3 fee. You can swim (or

19

float) in the salty water at Navy Beach near the South Tufa Trail or take a kayak or canoe trip for close-up views of the tufa (check with rangers for boating restrictions during bird-nesting season). You can rent kayaks in Mammoth Lakes. The sensational **Scenic Area Visitor Center** (⊠ *U.S. 395* ☎ *760/647–3044*) is open daily from June through September (Sunday–Thursday 8–5, Friday and Saturday 8–7), and the rest of the year Thursday–Monday 9–4. Its hilltop, sweeping views of Mono Lake, along with its interactive exhibits inside, make this one of California's best visitor centers. Rangers and naturalists lead walking tours of the tufa daily in summer and on weekends (sometimes on cross-country skis) in winter. In town, the **Mono Lake Committee Information Center & Bookstore** (⊠ *U.S. 395 and 3rd St.* ☎ *760/647–6595* ⊕ *www. monolake.org*) has more information about this beautiful area.

WHERE TO EAT AND STAY

$-$$ ✕ **Tioga Gas Mart & Whoa Nelli Deli.** Near the eastern entrance to Yosem-
DELI ite, Whoa Nelli serves some of Mono County's best food, including
★ lobster taquitos, pizzas, and enormous slices of multilayered cakes. But what makes it special is that it's in a gas station—possibly the only one in America where you can order cocktails (a pitcher of mango margaritas, anyone?)—and outside there's a full-size trapeze where you can take lessons (by reservation). This wacky spot is well off the noisy road, and has plenty of shaded outdoor tables with views of Mono Lake; bands play here on summer evenings, and locals love it, too. ⊠ *Hwy. 120 and U.S. 395* ☎ *760/647–1088* ☐ *AE, MC, V* ⊗ *Closed mid-Nov.–mid-Apr.*

¢-$$ 🏨 **Lake View Lodge.** Lovely landscaping, which includes several inviting and shaded places to sit, is what sets this clean motel apart from its handful of competitors in town. It's also up and off the highway by a few hundred feet, which means it's peaceful as well as pretty. Open morning and early afternoon, a stand-alone coffee shop adds to the appeal. The cottages lack the main building's lake views; some have kitchens and can sleep up to six. **Pros:** attractive; clean; friendly staff. **Cons:** could use updating. ⊠ *51285 U.S. 395* ☎ *760/647–6543 or 800/990–6614* ⊕ *www.lakeviewlodgeyosemite.com* ⇆ *76 rooms, 12 cottages* ⚷ *In-room: no a/c, kitchen (some), refrigerator (some). In-hotel: Wi-Fi hotspot* ☐ *AE, D, MC, V.*

BODIE STATE HISTORIC PARK

23 mi northeast of Lee Vining via U.S. 395 to Hwy. 270 (last 3 mi are unpaved).

ⓒ Old shacks and shops, abandoned mine shafts, a Methodist church, the
Fodor'sChoice mining village of Rattlesnake Gulch, and the remains of a small China-
★ town are among the sights at fascinating **Bodie Ghost Town.** The town, at an elevation of 8,200 feet, boomed from about 1878 to 1881, as gold prospectors, having worked the best of the western Sierra mines, headed to the high desert on the eastern slopes. Bodie was a mean place—the booze flowed freely, shootings were commonplace, and licentiousness reigned. Evidence of the town's wild past survives today at an excellent museum, and you can tour an old stamp mill and a ridge that

19

contains many mine sites. Bodie, unlike Calico in Southern California near Barstow, is a genuine ghost town, its status proudly stated as "arrested decay." No food, drink, or lodging is available in Bodie. Though the park stays open in winter, snow may close Highway 270. Still, it's a fantastic time to visit: rent cross-country skis in Mammoth Lakes, drive north, ski in, and have the park to yourself. ⊠ *Museum: Main and Green Sts.* ☎ *760/647–6445* ⊕ *www.bodie.net* ✑ *Park $3, museum free* ☉ *Park: late May–early Sept., daily 8–7; early Sept.–late May, daily 8–4. Museum: late May–early Sept., daily 9–6; early Sept.–late May, hrs vary.*

SOUTH OF SEQUOIA AND KINGS CANYON: THREE RIVERS

200 mi north of Los Angeles via I–5 to Hwy. 99 to Hwy. 198; 8 mi south of Ash Mountain/Foothills entrance to Sequoia National Park on Hwy. 198.

In the foothills of the Sierra along the Kaweah River, this sparsely populated, serpentine hamlet serves as the main gateway town to Sequoia and Kings Canyon national parks (⇨ *Chapter 21, Sequoia and Kings Canyon National Parks*). Its livelihood depends largely on tourism from the parks, courtesy of two markets, a few service stations, banks, a post office, and several lodgings, which are good spots to find a room when park accommodations are full.

WHERE TO EAT AND STAY

¢ ✕ **We Three Bakery.** This friendly, popular-with-the-locals spot packs
ECLECTIC lunches for trips into the nearby national parks; they're also open for breakfast. ⊠ *43688 Sierra Dr.* ⊕ *www.wethreerestaurant.com* ☎ *559/561–4761* ⊟ *MC, V.*

¢–$$ ⬚ **Buckeye Tree Lodge.** Every room at this two-story motel has a patio facing a sun-dappled lawn, right on the banks of the Kaweah River. Accommodations are simple and well kept, and the lodge is only a quarter mile from the park gate. Book well in advance for the summer. The jointly owned Sequoia Village Inn, across the highway, is another good option (☎ *559/561–3652*); accommodation options there are cottages, cabins, and chalets. **Pros:** scenic setting; clean. **Cons:** could use an update. ⊠ *46000 Sierra Dr., Hwy. 198* ☎ *559/561–5900* ⊕ *www. buckeyetree.com* ↻ *11 rooms, 1 cottage* ⚒ *In-room: a/c. In-hotel: pool, Wi-Fi hotspot, some pets allowed* ⊟ *AE, D, DC, MC, V* ⧈ *CP.*

RAFTING

Kaweah White Water Adventures (☎ *559/561–1000 or 800/229–8658* ⊕ *www.kaweah-whitewater.com*) guides two-hour and full-day rafting trips in spring and early summer, with some Class III rapids; longer trips may include some Class IV.

Yosemite
National Park

WORD OF MOUTH

"I tried cross-country skiing for the first time in Yosemite. An avid downhill skier, I quickly learned that cross-country is more physically demanding, slower going, but scenically spectacular. I chose to use the time to find the perfect shot of Half Dome."

—photo by Sarah Corley, Fodors.com member

WELCOME TO YOSEMITE NATIONAL PARK

TOP REASONS TO GO

★ **Feel the earth move:** An easy stroll brings you to the base of Yosemite Falls, America's highest, where thundering springtime waters shake the ground.

★ **Tunnel to heaven:** Winding down into Yosemite Valley, Wawona Road passes through a mountainside and emerges before one of the park's most heart-stopping vistas.

★ **Touch the sky:** Watch clouds scudding across the bright blue dome that arches above the High Sierra's Tuolumne Meadows, a wide-open alpine valley ringed by 10,000-foot granite peaks.

★ **Walk away from it all:** Early or late in the day, leave the crowds behind and take a forest hike on a few of Yosemite's 800 mi of trails.

★ **Powder your nose:** Winter's hush floats into Yosemite on snowflakes. Wade into a fluffy drift, lift your face to the sky, and listen to the trees.

1 Yosemite Valley. At an elevation of 4,000 feet, in roughly the center of the park, beats Yosemite's heart. This is where you'll find the park's most famous sights and biggest crowds.

2 Wawona and Mariposa Grove. The park's south-eastern tip holds Wawona, with its grand old hotel and pioneer history center, and the Mariposa Grove of Big Trees, filled with giant sequoias. These are closest to the South Entrance, 35 mi (a one-hour drive) south of Yosemite Village.

3 Tuolumne Meadows. The highlight of east-central Yosemite is this wildflower-strewn valley with hiking trails, nestled among sharp, rocky peaks. It's a two-hour drive northeast of Yosemite Valley along Tioga Road (closed mid-October–late May).

4 Hetch Hetchy. The most remote, least-visited part of Yosemite accessible by auto-mobile, this glacial valley is dominated by a reservoir and veined with wilderness trails. It's near the park's western boundary, about a half-hour drive north of Big Oak Flat Entrance.

GETTING ORIENTED

Yosemite is so large that you can think of it as five parks. Yosemite Valley, famous for waterfalls and cliffs, and Wawona, where the giant sequoias stand, are open all year. Hetch Hetchy, home of less-used backcountry trails, closes after the first big snow and reopens in May or June. The subalpine high country, Tuolumne Meadows, is open for summer hiking and camping; in winter it's accessible only via cross-country skis or snowshoes. Badger Pass Ski Area is open in winter only. Most visitors spend their time along the park's south-western border, between Wawona and Big Oak Flat Entrance; a bit farther east in Yosemite Valley and Badger Pass Ski Area; and along the east–west corridor of Tioga Road, which spans the park north of Yosemite Valley and bisects Tuolumne Meadows.

20

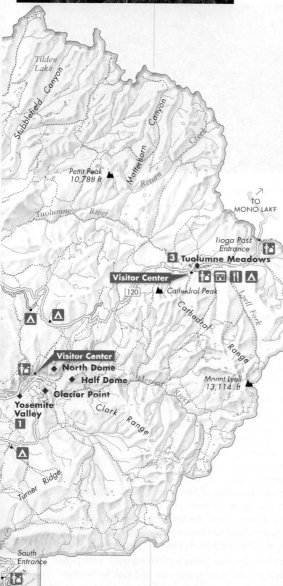

YOSEMITE NATIONAL PARK PLANNER

When to Go

During extremely busy periods—like the 4th of July—you may experience delays at the entrance gates. ■TIP➜ For less crowds, visit midweek. Or come mid-April through Memorial Day or mid-September through October, when the park is only a bit busy and the days are usually sunny and clear.

Summer rainfall is rare. In winter, heavy snows occasionally cause road closures, and tire chains or four-wheel drive may be required on the roads that remain open. The road to Glacier Point beyond the turnoff for Badger Pass is closed after the first major snowfall; Tioga Road is closed from late October through May or mid-June. Mariposa Grove Road is typically closed for a shorter period in winter.

The temperature chart below is for Yosemite Valley. In the high country, it's cooler.

AVG HIGH/LOW TEMPS

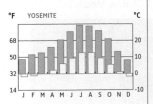

Flora and Fauna

Dense stands of incense cedar and Douglas fir—as well as ponderosa, Jeffrey, lodgepole, and sugar pines—cover much of the park, but the stellar standout, quite literally, is the *Sequoia sempervirens*, the giant sequoia. Sequoias grow only along the west slope of the Sierra Nevada between 4,500 and 7,000 feet in elevation. Starting from a seed the size of a rolled-oat flake, each of these ancient monuments assumes remarkable proportions in adulthood; you can see them in the Mariposa Grove of Big Trees. In late May the Valley's dogwood trees bloom with white, star-like flowers. Wildflowers, such as black-eyed Susan, bull thistle, cow parsnip, lupine, and meadow goldenrod, peak in June in the Valley and in July at higher elevations.

The most visible animals in the park—aside from the omnipresent western gray squirrel—are the mule deer. Though sightings of bighorn sheep are infrequent in the park itself, you can sometimes see them on the eastern side of the Sierra Crest, just off Route 120 in Lee Vining Canyon. You may also see the American black bear, which often has a brown, cinnamon, or blond coat. The Sierra Nevada is home to thousands of bears, and you should take all necessary precautions to keep yourself—and the bears—safe. For one, do not feed the bears. Bears that acquire a taste for human food can become very aggressive and destructive and often must be destroyed by rangers.

Watch for the blue Steller's jay along trails, near public buildings, and in campgrounds, and look for Golden eagles soaring over Tioga Road.

Getting Here and Around

Roughly 200 mi from San Francisco, 300 mi from Los Angeles, and 500 mi from Las Vegas, Yosemite takes a while to reach—and its sites and attractions merit much more time than what rangers say is the average visit: four hours. Most people arrive via car or tour bus, but public transportation (courtesy of Amtrak and the regional YARTS bus system) also can get you here.

Of the park's four entrances, Arch Rock is the closest to Yosemite Valley. The road that goes through it, Route 140 from Merced and Mariposa, is a scenic western approach along the Merced River. Route 41, through Wawona, is the way to come from Los Angeles. Route 120, through Crane Flat, is the most direct route from San Francisco. The only way in from the east is Tioga Road, which may be the best route in terms of scenery—though due to snowfall it's open for a frustratingly short amount of time each year (typically early June through mid-October).

Once you're in the park you can take advantage of the free shuttle buses, which make 21 stops, and run every 10 minutes or so from 9 AM to 6 PM year-round; a separate (and also free) summer-only shuttle runs out to El Capitan. Also during the summer, from Yosemite Valley you can pay to take the morning "hikers' bus" to Tuolumne or the bus up to Glacier Point. Bus service from Wawona is for people staying there and want to spend the day in Yosemite Valley. Free and frequent shuttles transport people between the Wawona Hotel and Mariposa Grove. During the snow season, buses run regularly between Yosemite Valley and Badger Pass Ski Area. For more information, visit ⊕ *www.nps. gov/yose/planyourvisit/bus.htm* or call ☎ *209/372–1240*.

There are few gas stations within Yosemite (Crane Flat, Tuolumne Meadows, and Wawona; none in the Valley), so fuel up before you reach the park. From late fall until early spring, the weather is unpredictable, and driving can be treacherous. You should carry chains. For road condition updates, call ☎ *800/427–7623* or *209/372–0200* from within California or go to ⊕ *www.dot.ca.gov*.

WHAT IT COSTS

	¢	$	$$	$$$	$$$$
Restaurants	under $8	$8–$12	$13–$20	$21–$30	over $30
Hotels	under $50	$50–$100	$101–$150	$151–$200	over $200

Restaurant prices are per person for a main course at dinner. Hotel prices are per night for two people in a standard double room in high season, excluding taxes and service charges.

Go

■ *Th* v
to Y
is a
par
terbugs looking
perfect images.

■ John Muir penned his observations of the park he long advocated for in *The Yosemite.*

■ *Yosemite and the High Sierra,* edited by Andrea G. Stillman and John Szarkowski, features beautiful reproductions of landmark photographs by Ansel Adams, accompanied by excerpts from the photographer's journals written when Adams traveled in Yosemite National Park in the early 20th century.

■ An insightful collection of essays accompany the museum-quality artworks in *Yosemite: Art of an American Icon,* by Amy Scott.

■ Perfect for beginning wildlife watchers, *Sierra Nevada Wildflowers,* by Karen Wiese, identifies more than 230 kinds of flora growing in the Sierra Nevada region.

20

By Sura Wood and Reed Parsell

By merely standing in Yosemite Valley and turning in a circle, you can see more natural wonders in a minute than you could in a full day pretty much anywhere else. Half Dome, Yosemite Falls, El Capitan, Bridalveil Fall, the meadows, Sentinel Dome, the Merced River, white-flowering dogwood trees, maybe even bears ripping into the bark of fallen trees or sticking their snouts into beehives — it's all in the Valley.

In the mid-1800s, when tourists were arriving to the area, the Valley's special geologic qualities, and the giant sequoias of Mariposa Grove 30 mi to the south, so impressed a group of influential Californians that they persuaded President Abraham Lincoln to grant those two areas to the state for protection. On Oct. 1, 1890—thanks largely to lobbying efforts by naturalist John Muir and Robert Underwood Johnson, the editor of *Century Magazine*—Congress set aside 1,500 square mi for Yosemite National Park.

PARK ESSENTIALS

ADMISSION FEES AND PERMITS
The admission fee, valid for seven days, is $20 per vehicle or $10 per individual.

If you plan to camp in the backcountry, you must have a wilderness permit. Availability of permits, which are free, depends upon trailhead quotas. It's best to make a reservation, especially if you will be visiting May through September. You can reserve two days to 24 weeks in advance by phone, mail, or fax (⌂ *P.O. Box 545, Yosemite, CA 95389* ☎ *209/372–0740* 🖷 *209/372–0739*); a $5 per person processing fee is charged if and when your reservations are confirmed. Requests must include your name, address, daytime phone, the number of people in your party, trip date, alternative dates, starting and ending trailheads, and a brief itinerary. Without a reservation, you may still get a free permit on a first-come, first-served basis at wilderness permit offices at Big Oak Flat, Hetch Hetchy, Tuolumne, Wawona, the Wilderness Center (in

Yosemite Village), and Yosemite Valley in summer; fall through spring, visit the Valley Visitor Center.

ADMISSION HOURS
The park is open 24/7 year-round. All entrances are open at all hours, except for Hetch Hetchy Entrance, which is open roughly dawn to dusk. Yosemite is in the Pacific time zone.

EMERGENCIES
In an emergency, call 911. You can also call the Yosemite Medical Clinic in Yosemite Village at 209/372–4637. The clinic provides 24-hour emergency care.

PARK CONTACT INFORMATION
Yosemite National Park ⓘ *Information Office, P.O. Box 577, Yosemite National Park, CA 95389* 🖶 *209/372–0200* ⊕ *www.nps.gov/yose.*

EXPLORING YOSEMITE NATIONAL PARK

HISTORIC SITES

★ **Ahwahnee Hotel.** Gilbert Stanley Underwood, the architect for Grand Canyon Lodge on the North Rim in Arizona, also designed the Ahwahnee. Opened in 1927, it is generally considered to be his best work. The Great Lounge, 77 feet long with magnificent 24-foot-high ceilings and all manner of Indian artwork on display, is the most special interior space in Yosemite. You can stay here (for $459 a night), or simply explore the first-floor shops and perhaps have breakfast or lunch in the lovely Dining Room. ⊠ *Ahwahnee Rd., about ¾ mi east of Yosemite Valley Visitor Center, Yosemite Village* 🖶 *209/372–1489.*

Ahwahneechee Village. This solemn smattering of re-created structures, accessed by a short loop trail, is an imagination of what Indian life might have resembled here in the 1870s. One interpretive sign points out that Miwok referred to the 19th century newcomers as "Yohemite" or "Yohometuk," which have been translated as "some of them are killers." ⊠ *Northside Dr., Yosemite Village* 🖶 *Free* ⊙ *Daily sunrise–sunset.*

Pioneer Yosemite History Center. Some of Yosemite's first structures—those not occupied by American Indians, that is—were relocated from various parts of the park and placed here in the 1950s and 1960s. You can spend a pleasurable and informative half-hour walking about them and reading the signs, perhaps springing for a self-guided-tour pamphlet (50¢) to further enhance the history lesson. Wednesdays through Sundays in the summer, costumed docents conduct free blacksmithing and "wet-plate" photography demonstrations, and for a small fee you can take a stagecoach ride. ⊠ *Rte. 41, Wawona* 🖶 *209/375–9531 or 209/379–2646* 🖶 *Free* ⊙ *Building interiors are open mid-June–Labor Day, Daily 9–5.*

★ **Wawona Hotel.** One can imagine an older Mark Twain relaxing in a rocking chair on one of the broad verandas of Yosemite's first lodge, a whitewashed series of two-story buildings from the Victorian era. Across the road is a somewhat odd sight: Yosemite's only golf course, one of the few links in the world that does not employ fertilizers or

20

other chemicals. The Wawona is an excellent place to stay or to stop for lunch, but be aware that the hotel is closed in January. ⊠ *Rte. 41, Wawona* ☎ *209/375–1425*

SCENIC STOPS

★ **El Capitan.** Rising 3,593 feet—more than 350 stories—above the Valley, El Capitan is the largest exposed-granite monolith in the world. Since 1958, people have been climbing its entire face, including the famous "nose." You can spot adventurers with your binoculars by scanning the smooth and nearly vertical cliff for specks of color. ⊠ *Off Northside Dr., about 4 mi west of the Valley Visitor Center.*

Fodor's Choice **Glacier Point.** If you lack the time, desire, or stamina to hike more than
★ 3,200 feet up to Glacier Point from the Yosemite Valley floor, you can drive here—or take a bus from the Valley—for a bird's-eye view. You are likely to encounter a lot of day-trippers on the short, paved trail that leads from the parking lot to the main overlook. Take a moment to veer off a few yards to the Geology Hut, which succinctly explains and illustrates how the Valley looked like 10 million, 3 million, and 20,000 years ago. For details about the summer-only buses, call ☎ *209/372–1240.* ⊠ *Glacier Point Rd., 16 mi northeast of Rte. 41.*

★ **Half Dome.** Visitors' eyes are continually drawn to this remarkable granite formation that tops out at more than 4,700 feet above the Valley floor. Despite its name, the dome is actually about three-quarters "intact." You can hike to the top of Half Dome on an 8.5-mi (one-way) trail whose last 400 feet must be ascended while holding onto a steel cable. To see Half Dome reflected in the Merced River, view it from Sentinel Bridge just before sundown. But stay for sunset, when the setting sun casts a brilliant orange light onto Half Dome, a stunning sight.

Hetch Hetchy Reservoir. When Congress green-lighted the O'Shaughnessy Dam in 1913, pragmatism triumphed over aestheticism. Some 2.4 million residents of the San Francisco Bay Area continue to get their water from this 117-billion-gallon reservoir, although spirited efforts are being made to restore the Hetch Hetchy Valley to its former, pristine glory. Eight miles long, the reservoir is Yosemite's largest body of water, and one that can be seen up close from several trails. ⊠ *Hetch Hetchy Rd., about 15 mi north of the Big Oak Flat entrance station.*

★ **Mariposa Grove of Big Trees.** Of Yosemite National Parks' three sequoia groves—the others being Merced and Tuolumne, both near Crane Flat well to the north—Mariposa is by far the largest and easiest to walk around. Grizzly Giant, whose base measures 96 feet around, has been estimated to be the world's 25th largest tree by volume. Perhaps more astoundingly, it's about 2,700 years old. On up the hill, you'll find many more sequoias, a small museum, and fewer people. Summer weekends are especially crowded here. Consider taking the free shuttle from Wawona. ⊠ *Rte. 41, 2 mi north of the South Entrance station.*

★ **Tuolumne Meadows.** The largest subalpine meadow in the Sierra (at 8,600 feet) is a popular way station for backpack trips along the Pacific Crest and John Muir trails. The setting is not as dramatic as Yosemite Valley, 56 mi away, but the almost perfectly flat basin, about 2½ mi long, is intriguing, and in July it's resplendent with wildflowers. The most

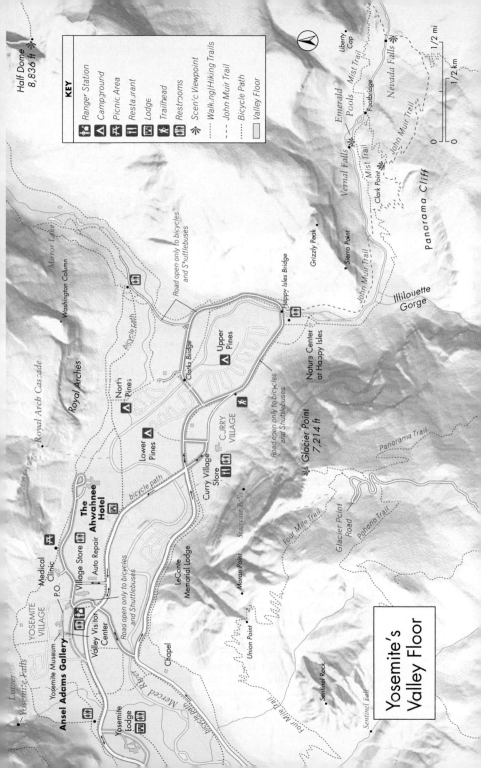

Yosemite's Valley Floor

KEY

- Ranger Station
- Campground
- Picnic Area
- Restaurant
- Lodge
- Trailhead
- Restrooms
- Scenic Viewpoint
- ⋯⋯ Walking/Hiking Trails
- ‒‒‒ John Muir Trail
- ⋯⋯ Bicycle Path
- Valley Floor

Half Dome
8,836 ft

Liberty Cap

Mist Trail

Nevada Falls

John Muir Trail

1/2 mi

1/2 km

Emerald Pools

Vernal Falls

Footbridge

Mist Trail

Clark Point

John Muir Trail

Panorama Cliff

Grizzly Peak

Sierra Point

Happy Isles Bridge

Illilouette Gorge

Mirror Lake

Washington Column

Royal Arch Cascade

Royal Arches

bicycle path

North Pines

Clarks Bridge

Upper Pines

Nature Center at Happy Isles

Road open only to bicycles and Shuttlebuses

Panorama Trail

Road open only to bicycles and Shuttlebuses

Glacier Point
7,214 ft

CURRY VILLAGE

Lower Pines

Curry Village Store

Sugarloaf Isle

Panorama Trail

Moran Point

Glacier Point Road

Pohono Trail

bicycle path

The Ahwahnee Hotel

Village Store

Auto Repair

Medical Clinic

P.O.

Ansel Adams Gallery

LeConte Memorial Lodge

Four Mile Trail

Union Point

YOSEMITE VILLAGE

Yosemite Museum

Valley Visitor Center

Road open only to bicycles and Shuttlebuses

Chapel

Sentinel Rock

Merced River

bicycle path

Lower Yosemite Falls

Yosemite Lodge

Four Mile Trail

Sentinel Fall

"This is us taking a break before conquering the top of Lembert Dome, while enjoying the beautiful view over Yosemite's high country." —photo by Rebalyn, Fodors.com member

popular day hike is up Lembert Dome, atop which you'll have breath-taking views of the basin below. Keep in mind that Tioga Road rarely opens sooner than June and usually closes by mid-October. ⊠ *Tioga Rd. (Rte. 120), about 8 mi west of the Tioga Pass entrance station.*

WATERFALLS

Yosemite's waterfalls are at their most spectacular in May and June. When the snow starts to melt (usually peaking in May), almost every rocky lip or narrow gorge becomes a spillway for streaming snowmelt churning down to meet the Merced River. By summer's end, some falls, including the mighty Yosemite Falls, dry up. They begin flowing again in late fall, and in winter they may be hung dramatically with ice. Even in drier months, the waterfalls can be breathtaking. If you choose to hike any of the trails to or up the falls, be sure to wear shoes with good, no-slip soles; the rocks can be extremely slick. Stay on trails at all times.

■ **TIP→** Visit the park during a full moon, and you can stroll in the evening without a flashlight and still make out the ribbons of falling water, as well as silhouettes of the giant granite monoliths.

Bridalveil Fall. The filmy waterfall of 620 feet is often diverted as much as 20 feet one way or the other by the breeze. It is the first marvelous view of Yosemite Valley you will see if you come in via Route 41. ⊠ *Yosemite Valley, access from parking area off Wawona Rd.*

Nevada Fall. Climb Mist Trail from Happy Isles for an up-close view of this 594-foot cascading beauty, the first major fall as the Merced River plunges out of the high country toward the eastern end of Yosemite Valley. If you don't want to hike, you can see it—distantly—from Glacier

Point. ⊠ *Yosemite Valley, access via Mist Trail from Nature Center at Happy Isles.*

Ribbon Fall. At 1,612 feet, this is the highest single fall in North America. It's also the first valley waterfall to dry up in summer; the rainwater and melted snow that create the slender fall evaporate quickly at this height. Look just west of El Capitan from the Valley floor for the best view of the fall from the base of Bridalveil Fall. ⊠ *Yosemite Valley, west of El Capitan Meadow.*

Vernal Fall. Fern-covered black rocks frame this 317-foot fall, and rainbows play in the spray at its base. You can get a distance view from Glacier Point, or hike to see it close up. ⊠ *Yosemite Valley, access via Mist Trail from Nature Center at Happy Isles.*

Fodor'sChoice
★
Yosemite Falls. Actually three falls, they together constitute the highest waterfall in North America and the fifth-highest in the world. The water from the top descends a total of 2,425 feet, and when the falls run hard, you can hear them thunder all across the Valley. When they dry up—usually in late summer—the Valley seems naked without the wavering tower of spray. ■TIP→ If you hike the mile-long loop trail (partially paved) to the base of the Lower Falls during the peak water flow in May, expect to get soaked. You can get a view of of the falls from the lawn of Yosemite Chapel, off Southside Drive. ⊠ *Yosemite Valley, access from Yosemite Lodge or trail parking area.*

VISITOR CENTERS

Le Conte Memorial Lodge. This small but striking National Historic Landmark, with its granite walls and steeply pitched shingle roof, is Yosemite's first permanent public information center. Step inside to see the cathedral-like interior, which contains a library and environmental exhibits. To find out about evening programs, check the kiosk out front, look in the park's newspaper, or visit ⊕ *www.sierraclub.org.* ⊠ *Southside Dr., about ½ mi west of Curry Village* ☉ *Memorial Day–Labor Day, Wed.–Sun. 10–4.*

Valley Visitor Center. At this center—which was overhauled in 2007—you can learn how Yosemite Valley was formed and about its vegetation, animals, and human inhabitants. Don't leave without watching the superb *Spirit of Yosemite,* a 23-minute introductory film that runs every half-hour in the theater behind the visitor center. ⊠ *Yosemite Village* ☎ *209/372-0299* ☉ *Late May–early Sept., daily 9–6; early Sept.–late May, daily 9–5.*

20

SPORTS AND THE OUTDOORS

BICYCLING

There may be no more enjoyable way to see Yosemite Valley than to ride a bike beneath its lofty granite monoliths. The eastern valley has 12 mi of paved, flat bicycle paths across meadows and through woods, with bike racks at convenient stopping points. For a greater challenge, you can ride on 196 mi of paved park roads—but bicycles are not allowed on hiking trails or in the backcountry. Kids under 18 must wear a helmet.

You can get **Yosemite bike rentals** (✉ *Yosemite Lodge or Curry Village* ☎ *209/372–1208* ⊕ *www.yosemitepark.com* ✂ *$9.50/hour, $25.50/ day* ☉ *Apr.–Oct.*) from either Yosemite Lodge or Curry Village bike stands. Bikes with child trailers, baby-jogger strollers, and wheelchairs are available.

BIRD-WATCHING

Nearly 250 bird species have been spotted in the park, including the sage sparrow, pygmy owl, blue grouse, and mountain bluebird. Park rangers lead free bird-watching walks in Yosemite Valley one day each week in summer; check at a visitor center or information station for times and locations. Binoculars are sometimes available for loan.

The Yosemite Association sponsors one- to four-day **birding seminars** (☎ *209/379–2321* ⊕ *www.yosemite.org* ✂ *$82–$254* ☉ *Apr.–Aug.*) for beginner and intermediate birders.

HIKING

The staff at the **Wilderness Center** (☎ *209/372–0740*), in Yosemite Village, provides free wilderness permits, which are required for overnight camping (advance reservations are available for $5 and are highly recommended for popular trailheads from May through September and on weekends). The staff here also provide maps and advice to hikers heading into the backcountry. From April through November, **Yosemite Mountaineering School and Guide Service** (✉ *Yosemite Mountain Shop, Curry Village* ☎ *209/372–8344*) leads two-hour to full-day treks.

EASY

★ **Yosemite Falls Trail.** This is the highest waterfall in North America. The upper fall (1,430 feet), the middle cascades (675 feet), and the lower fall (320 feet) combine for a total of 2,425 feet and, when viewed from the valley, appear as a single waterfall. The ¼-mi trail leads from the parking lot to the base of the falls. Upper Yosemite Fall Trail, a strenuous 3½-mi climb rising 2,700 feet, takes you above the top of the falls. ✉ *Trailhead off Camp 4, north of Northside Dr.*

MODERATE

★ **Mist Trail.** More visitors take this trail (or portions of it) than any other in the park other than Lower Yosemite Falls. The trek up to and back from Vernal Fall is 3 mi. Add another 4 mi total by continuing up to 594-foot Nevada Fall; the trail becomes quite steep and slippery in its final stages. The elevation gain to Vernal Fall is 1,000 feet, and to Nevada Fall an additional 1,000 feet. Merced River tumbles down both falls on its way to a tranquil flow through the Valley. ✉ *Trailhead at Happy Isles.*

★ **Panorama Trail.** Few hikes come with the visual punch that this 8½-mi trail provides. The star attraction is Half Dome, visible from many intriguing angles, but you also see three waterfalls up close and walk through a manzanita grove. Before you begin, look down on Yosemite Valley from Glacier Point, a special experience in itself. ✉ *Trailhead at Glacier Point.*

DIFFICULT

Fodor's Choice
★

John Muir Trail to Half Dome. Ardent and courageous trekkers can continue on from the top of Nevada Fall, off Mist Trail, to the top of Half Dome. Some hikers attempt this entire 10- to 12-hour, 16¾-mi round-trip trek from Happy Isles in one day; if you're planning to do this, remember that the 4,800-foot elevation gain and the 8,842-foot altitude will cause shortness of breath. Another option is to hike to a campground in Little Yosemite Valley near the top of Nevada Fall the first day, then climb to the top of Half Dome and hike out the next day; it's highly recommended that you get your wilderness permit reservations at least a month in advance. Be sure to wear hiking boots and bring gloves. The last pitch up the back of Half Dome is very steep—the only way to climb this sheer rock face is to pull yourself up using the steel cable handrails, which are in place only from late spring to early fall. Those who brave the ascent will be rewarded with an unbeatable view of Yosemite Valley below and the high country beyond. ⊠ *Trailhead at Happy Isles.*

HORSEBACK RIDING

Reservations for guided trail rides must be made in advance at the hotel tour desks or by phone. For overnight saddle trips, which use mules, go online to *www.yosemitepark.com* and fill out a lottery application for the following year. Scenic trail rides range from two hours to a full day; six-day High Sierra saddle trips are also available.

Tuolumne Meadows Stables (⊠ *Off Tioga Rd., 2 mi east of Tuolumne Meadows Visitor Center* ☎ *209/372–8427* ⊕ *www.yosemitepark.com*) runs two-, four-, and eight-hour trips—which cost $53, $69, and $96, respectively—and High Sierra four- to six-day camping treks on mules, beginning at $625. Reservations are essential. **Wawona Stables** (⊠ *Rte. 41, Wawona* ☎ *209/375–6502*) has two- and five-hour rides, starting at $53. Reservations are essential. You can tour the valley and the start of the high country on two-hour, four-hour, and all-day rides at **Yosemite Valley Stables** (⊠ *At entrance to North Pines Campground, 100 yards northeast of Curry Village* ☎ *209/372–8348* ⊕ *www.yosemitepark. com*). Reservations are required for the $53, $69, and $96 trips.

RAFTING

Rafting is permitted only on designated areas of the Middle and South Forks of the Merced River. Check with the Valley Visitor Center for closures and other restrictions.

The per-person rental fee at **Curry Village raft stand** (⊠ *South side of Southside Dr., Curry Village* ☎ *209/372–8319* ⊕ *www.yosemitepark. com* ☒ *$20.50* ☉ *Late May–July*) covers the four- to six-person raft, two paddles, and life jackets, plus a shuttle to the launch point on Sentinel Beach.

ROCK CLIMBING

Fodor's Choice
★

The one-day basic lesson at **Yosemite Mountaineering School and Guide Service** (⊠ *Yosemite Mountain Shop, Curry Village* ☎ *209/372–8344* ⊕ *www.yosemitepark.com* ☒ *$80–$190* ☉ *Apr.–Nov.*) includes some bouldering and rappelling, and three or four 60-foot climbs. Climbers must be at least 10 (kids under 12 must be accompanied by a parent or guardian) and in reasonably good physical condition. Intermediate and advanced classes include instruction in belays, self-re snow climbing, and free climbing.

ICE-SKATING

Curry Village ice-skating rink. Winter visitors have skat door rink for decades, and there's no mystery why: it's a kick ᴛᴏ ɢ across the ice while soaking up views of Half Dome and Glacier Point. ⊠ *South side of Southside Dr., Curry Village* ☎ *209/372–8319* ☑ *$8 per 2 hrs, $3 skate rental* ☉ *Mid-Nov.–mid-Mar. afternoons and evenings daily, morning sessions weekends; 12–2:30 PM on weekends as well (hrs vary).*

SKIING AND SNOWSHOEING

Badger Pass Ski Area. California's first ski resort has five lifts and 10 downhill runs, as well as 90 mi of groomed cross-country trails. Free shuttle buses from Yosemite Valley operate during ski season (December through early April, weather permitting). Lift tickets are $38, downhill equipment rents for $24, and snowboard rental with boots is $35. The gentle slopes of Badger Pass make **Yosemite Ski School** (☎ *209/372– 8430*) an ideal spot for children and beginners to learn downhill skiing or snowboarding for as little as $28 for a group lesson. The highlight of Yosemite's cross-country skiing center is a 21-mi loop from Badger Pass to Glacier Point. You can rent cross-country skis for $21.50 per day at the **Cross-Country Ski School** (☎ *209/372–8444*), which also rents snowshoes ($19.50 per day), telemarking equipment ($29), and skate-skis ($24). **Yosemite Mountaineering School** (⊠ *Badger Pass Ski Area* ☎ *209/372–8344* ⊕ *www.yosemitemountaineering.com*) conducts snowshoeing, cross-country skiing, telemarking, and skate-skiing classes starting at $30. ⊠ *Badger Pass Rd., off Glacier Point Rd., 18 mi from Yosemite Valley* ☎ *209/372–8430.*

EDUCATIONAL PROGRAMS

CLASSES AND SEMINARS

Art Classes. Professional artists conduct workshops in watercolor, etching, drawing, and other mediums. Bring your own materials or purchase the basics at the Art Activity Center, next to the Village Store. Call to verify scheduling. ⊠ *Art Activity Center, Yosemite Village* ☎ *209/372– 1442* ⊕ *www.yosemitepark.com* ☑ *Free* ☉ *Early May.–early Oct., Wed.–Sat., 10 AM–2 PM.*

Yosemite Outdoor Adventures. Naturalists, scientists, and park rangers lead multi-hour to multiday educational outings on topics from woodpeckers to fire management to pastel painting. Most sessions take place spring through fall, but a few focus on winter phenomena. ⊠ *Various locations* ☎ *209/379–2321* ⊕ *www.yosemite.org* ☑ *$82–$465.*

RANGER PROGRAMS

Junior Ranger Program. Children ages 3 to 13 can participate in the informal, self-guided Little Cub and Junior Ranger programs. A park activity handbook ($8) is available at the Valley Visitor Center or the Nature Center at Happy Isles; once your child has completed the book, a ranger

20

will present him or her with a certificate and a badge. ⊠ *Valley Visitor Center or the Nature Center at Happy Isles* ☎ *209/372–0299.*

Ranger-Led Programs. Rangers lead walks and hikes and give informative and entertaining talks on a range of topics at different locations several times a day from spring through fall. The schedule is reduced in winter, but most days you can usually find a ranger program somewhere in the park. In the evenings at Yosemite Lodge and Curry Village, lectures by rangers, slide shows, and documentary films present unique perspectives on Yosemite. On summer weekends, Camp Curry and Tuolumne Meadows Campground host sing-along campfire programs. There's usually at least one ranger-led activity each night in the Valley; schedules and locations are posted on bulletin boards throughout the park and published in the *Yosemite Guide* you receive when you enter the park.

TOURS

★ **Ansel Adams Photo Walks.** Photography enthusiasts shouldn't miss these two-hour guided camera walks that are offered three mornings each week—Tuesday, Thursday, and Saturday—by professional photographers. Some walks are hosted by the Ansel Adams Gallery, others by Delaware North; meeting points vary. All are free, but participation is limited to 15 people. Reservations are essential. To reserve a spot, call up to 10 days in advance or visit the gallery. ☎ *209/372–4413 or 800/568–7398* ⊕ *www.anseladams.com* ✉ *Free.*

DNC Parks and Resorts. The main concessionaire at Yosemite National Park, this organization operates several guided tours and programs throughout the park, including the **Big Trees Tram Tour** of the Mariposa Grove of Big Trees, the **Glacier Point Tour,** the **Grand Tour** (both Mariposa Grove and Glacier Point), the **Moonlight Tour** of Yosemite Valley, the **Tuolumne Meadows Tour,** and the **Valley Floor Tour.** ☎ *209/372–1240* ⊕ *www. yosemitepark.com* ✉ *Free.*

WHERE TO EAT

RESTAURANTS

$$$–$$$$ ✕ **Ahwahnee Hotel Dining Room.** Rave reviews about the dining room's
CONTINENTAL appearance are fully justified—it features floor-to-ceiling windows, a
Fodor's Choice 34-foot-high ceiling with interlaced sugar-pine beams, and massive
★ chandeliers. Although many continue to applaud the food, others have reported that they sense a recent dip in the quality both in the service and what is being served. Diners must spend a lot of money here, so perhaps that inflates the expectations and amplifies the disappointments. In any event, the Sunday brunch ($45) is consistently praised. Reservations are always advised, and for dinner, the attire is "resort casual." ⊠ *Ahwahnee Hotel, Ahwahnee Rd., about ¾ mi east of Yosemite Valley Visitor Center, Yosemite Village* ☎ *209/372–1489* ⚐ *Reservations essential* ▭ *AE, DC, MC, V.*

$$–$$$ ✕ **Mountain Room.** Though good, the food becomes secondary when you
AMERICAN see Yosemite Falls through this dining room's wall of windows—almost
★ every table has a view. The chef makes a point of using locally sourced, organic ingredients, so you can be assured of fresh greens and veggies here. The Mountain Room Lounge, a few steps away in the Yosemite

Lodge complex, has a broad bar with about 10 beers on tap. ⊠ *Yosemite Lodge, Northside Dr. about ¾ mi west of the visitor center, Yosemite Village* ☎ *209/372–1281* 🖃 *AE, D, DC, MC, V* ⊗ *No lunch.*

$$–$$$ ✕ **Tuolumne Meadows Lodge.** At the back of a small building that con-
AMERICAN   tains the lodge's front desk and small gift shop, this restaurant serves hearty American fare at breakfast and dinner. Let the front desk know in advance if you have any dietary restrictions, and the cooks will not let you down. ⊠ *Tioga Rd. (Rte. 120)* ☎ *209/372–8413* ⚐ *Reservations essential* 🖃 *AE, D, DC, MC, V* ⊗ *Closed late Sept.–Memorial Day. No lunch.*

$$–$$$$ ✕ **Wawona Hotel Dining Room.** Watch deer graze on the meadow while
AMERICAN   you dine in the romantic, candlelit dining room of the whitewashed
★   Wawona Hotel, which dates from the late 1800s. The American-style cuisine favors fresh California ingredients and flavors; trout is a menu staple. There's also a Sunday brunch Easter through Thanksgiving, and a barbeque on the lawn Saturday evenings in summer. A jacket is required at dinner. ⊠ *Wawona Hotel, Rte. 41, Wawona* ☎ *209/375–1425* ⚐ *Reservations essential* 🖃 *AE, D, DC, MC, V* ⊗ *Closed Jan.–mid-March.*

PICNIC AREAS

Considering how large the park is and how many visitors come here—some 3.5 million people every year, most of them just for the day—it is somewhat surprising that Yosemite has so few formal picnic areas, though in many places you can find a smooth rock to sit on and enjoy breathtaking views along with your lunch. The convenience stores all sell picnic supplies, and prepackaged sandwiches and salads are widely available. Those options can come in especially handy during the middle of day, when you might not want to spend precious daylight hours in such a spectacular setting sitting in a restaurant for a formal meal. None of these spots have drinking water available; most have some type of toilet. Good spots to hit include Cathedral Beach, Church Bowl, Swinging Bridge, and Yellow Pine.

WHERE TO STAY

■ TIP→ Reserve your room or cabin in Yosemite as far in advance as possible. You can make a reservation up to a year before your arrival (within minutes after the reservation office makes a date available, the Ahwahnee, Yosemite Lodge, and Wawona Hotel often sell out their weekends, holiday periods, and all days between May and September).

$$$$ 🏨 **The Ahwahnee.** A National Historic Landmark, the hotel is con-
Fodor's Choice   structed primarily of concrete and sugar-pine logs. Guest rooms have
★   American Indian design motifs; public spaces are decorated with art deco detailing, oriental rugs, and elaborate iron- and woodwork. Some luxury hotel amenities, including turndown service and guest bathrobes, are standard here. The Dining Room is by far the most impressive restaurant in the park and one of the most beautiful rooms in California. If you stay in a cottage room, be aware that each cottage has multiple guest rooms, though all have an en-suite bath. Even if you cannot afford to stay here, take the time to stroll about the main floor. Reservations are made through Delaware North Companies Parks and Resorts

(☎ *801/559–5000*). **Pros:** best lodge in Yosemite (if not all of California); concierge. **Cons:** expensive; some reports that service has slipped in recent years. ✉ *1 Ahwahnee Rd., about ¾ mi east of Yosemite Valley Visitor Center, Yosemite Village* 🏠 *1 Ahwahnee Rd., Yosemite National Park 95389* ☎ *559/252–4848 or 801/559–5000* ⊕ *www.yosemitepark. com* ⇔ *99 lodge rooms, 4 suites, 24 cottage rooms* ⚒ *In-room: a/c, refrigerator, Wi-Fi. In-hotel: restaurant, room service, bar, tennis court, pool, Wi-Fi hotspot* ☰ *AE, D, DC, MC, V.*

$–$$ ⊡ **Curry Village.** Opened in 1899 as a place where travelers could enjoy the beauty of Yosemite for a modest price, Curry Village has plain accommodations: standard motel rooms, cabins, and tent cabins, which have rough wood frames, canvas walls, and roofs. The tent cabins are a step up from camping, with linens and blankets provided (maid service upon request); some even have heat. The guest lounge and reservations buildings underwent a multimillion-dollar renovation the winter of 2008–2009. Happy Isles and the popular Mist Trails are a few minutes' walk away. Reservations are made through Delaware North Companies Parks and Resorts. **Pros:** comparatively economical; family-friendly atmosphere. **Cons:** can be crowded; sometimes a bit noisy. ✉ *South side of Southside Dr., Yosemite Valley* ☎ *801/559–5000* ⊕ *www.yosemitepark.com* ⇔ *18 rooms, 527 cabins* ⚒ *In-room: no a/c, no phone, no TV. In-hotel: 3 restaurants, bar, pool, bicycles* ☰ *AE, D, DC, MC, V.*

$$–$$$ ⊡ **Wawona Hotel.** This 1879 National Historic Landmark sits at Yosemite's southern end, a 15-minute drive (or free shuttle bus ride) from the Mariposa Grove of Big Trees. It's an old-fashioned New England–style estate, with whitewashed buildings, wraparound verandas, and pleasant, no-frills rooms decorated with period pieces. About half the rooms share bathrooms; those that do come equipped with robes. The romantic, candlelit dining room ($$–$$$$) lies across the lobby from the parlor, which has a fireplace, board games, and a piano, where a pianist plays ragtime most evenings. Reservations are made through Delaware North Companies Parks and Resorts. **Pros:** lovely; peaceful atmosphere; close to Mariposa Grove. **Cons:** few modern in-room amenities; half of the rooms have no baths. ✉ *Hwy. 41, Wawona* ☎ *801/559–5000* ⊕ *www.yosemitepark.com* ⇔ *104 rooms, 50 with bath* ⚒ *In-room: no a/c, no phone, no TV. In-hotel: restaurant, bar, golf course, tennis court, pool* ☰ *AE, D, DC, MC, V* ☺ *Closed Jan. and Feb.*

$–$$ ⊡ **White Wolf Lodge.** Set in a subalpine meadow, White Wolf offers rustic accommodations in tent cabins. This is an excellent base camp for hiking the backcountry. Breakfast and dinner are served home-style in the snug main building. Keep in mind that you will be seated in one of four time slots, so you might eat earlier or later than you would prefer if you do not reserve well in advance. Reservations are made through Delaware North Companies Parks and Resorts. **Pros:** quiet; convenient for hikers; good restaurant. **Cons:** far from the Valley; not much to do here other than hiking. ✉ *Off Tioga Rd. (Rte. 120), 25 mi west of Tuolumne Meadows and 15 mi east of Crane Flat* ☎ *801/559–5000* ⇔ *24 tent cabins, 4 cabins* ⚒ *In-room: no a/c, no phone, no TV. In-hotel: restaurant* ☰ *AE, D, DC, MC, V* ☺ *Closed mid-Sept.–early June.*

20

$$$ 🛏 **Yosemite Lodge at the Falls.** This lodge near Yosemite Falls, which dates from 1915, looks like a 1960s motel-resort complex, with numerous brown, two-story buildings tucked beneath the trees, surrounded by large parking lots. Rooms have two double beds; larger rooms also have dressing areas and patios or balconies. A few have views of the falls. Of the lodge's eateries, the Mountain Room Restaurant is the most formal. The cafeteria-style Food Court serves three meals a day. Many park tours depart from the main building. Reservations are made through Delaware North Companies Parks and Resorts. **Pros:** centrally located; dependably clean rooms; lots of tours leave from out front. **Cons:** can feel impersonal; appearance is little dated. ✉ *Northside Dr. about ¾ mi west of the visitor center, Yosemite Village* 🕾 *559/252–4848* ⊕ *www. yosemitepark.com* 🔊 *245 rooms* ♿ *In-room: no a/c. In-hotel: restaurant, bar, pool, bicycles, Wi-Fi hotspot* 🖃 *AE, D, DC, MC, V.*

CAMPING

The 464 campsites within Yosemite Valley are the park's most tightly spaced and, along with the 304-site campground at Tuolumne Meadows, the most difficult to secure on anything approaching short notice.

The park's backcountry and the surrounding wilderness have some unforgettable campsites that can be reached only via long and often difficult hikes or horseback rides. Delaware North operates five High Sierra Camps with comfortable, furnished tent cabins in the remote reaches of Yosemite; rates include breakfast and dinner service. The park concessionaire books the extremely popular backcountry camps by lottery; applications are due by late November for the following summer season. Phone 🕾 *801/559–4909* for more information, or check for current availability by navigating from ⊕ *www.yosemitepark.com* to the High Sierra Camps pages.

To camp in a High Sierra campground you must obtain a wilderness permit. Make reservations up to 24 weeks in advance first by visiting the park's Web site (⊕ *www.nps.gov/yose/planyourvisit/backpacking. htm*) and checking availability. For a $5 nonrefundable fee, you can make reservations by phone (🕾 *209/372–0740*) or by mail (✑ *P.O. Box 545, Yosemite, CA 95389*); make checks payable to "Yosemite Association."

Reservations are required at most of Yosemite's campgrounds, especially in summer. You can reserve a site up to five months in advance; bookings made more than 21 days in advance require prepayment. Unless otherwise noted, book your site through the central **National Park Service Reservations Office** (✑ *P.O. Box 1600, Cumberland, MD 21502* 🕾 *800/436–7275* ⊕ *www.recreation.gov* 🖃 *D, MC, V* ☉ *Daily 7–7.*

Delaware North Companies Parks and Resorts (✑ *6771 N. Palm Ave., Fresno, CA 93704* 🕾 *801/559–5000* ⊕ *www.yosemitepark.com*), which handles most in-park reservations, takes reservations beginning one year plus one day in advance of your proposed stay. Or, you can roll the dice by showing up at the front desk and asking if there have been any cancellations.

Sequoia and Kings Canyon National Parks

WORD OF MOUTH

"We headed out to Crystal Cave, which is off the General's Highway, and up a narrow road. Gorgeous drive. The entrance to the cave is a ½-mile walk down a steep trail from the parking area. The trail passes a really nice waterfall and has some good views along the way. The cave itself is spectacular."

—J_Correa

WELCOME TO SEQUOIA AND KINGS CANYON NATIONAL PARKS

TOP REASONS TO GO

★ **Gentle giants:** You'll feel small—in a good way—walking among some of the world's largest living things in Sequoia's Giant Forest and Kings Canyon's Grant Grove.

★ **Because it's there:** You can't even glimpse it from the main part of Sequoia, but the sight of majestic Mount Whitney is worth the trek to the eastern face of the High Sierra.

★ **Underground exploration:** Far older even than the giant sequoias, the gleaming limestone formations in Crystal Cave will draw you along dark, marble passages.

★ **A grander-than–Grand Canyon:** Drive the twisting Kings Canyon Scenic Byway down into the jagged, granite Kings River Canyon, deeper in parts than the Grand Canyon.

★ **Regal solitude:** To spend a day or two hiking in a subalpine world of your own, pick one of the 11 trailheads at Mineral King.

1 Giant Forest–Lodgepole Village. The most heavily visited area of Sequoia lies at the base of the "thumb" portion of Kings Canyon National Park and contains major sights such as Giant Forest, General Sherman Tree, Crystal Cave, and Moro Rock.

2 Grant Grove Village–Redwood Canyon. The "thumb" of Kings Canyon National Park is its busiest section, where Grant Grove, General Grant Tree, Panoramic Point, and Big Stump are the main attractions.

3 Cedar Grove. Most visitors to the huge, high-country portion of Kings Canyon National Park don't go farther than Roads End, a few miles east of Cedar Grove on the canyon floor. Here, the river runs through Zumwalt Meadow, surrounded by magnificent granite formations.

4 Mineral King. In the southeast section of Sequoia, the highest road-accessible part of the park is a good place to hike, camp, and soak up the unspoiled grandeur of the Sierra Nevada.

5 Mount Whitney. The highest peak in the Lower 48 stands on the eastern edge of Sequoia; to get there from Giant Forest you must either backpack eight days through the mountains or drive nearly 400 mi around the park to its other side.

General Grant Tree 180
Visitor Center 180 2
Pinehurst
Montecito-Sequoia Lodge
245
Badger

0   5 mi
0   5 km

Three Rivers

General Highway

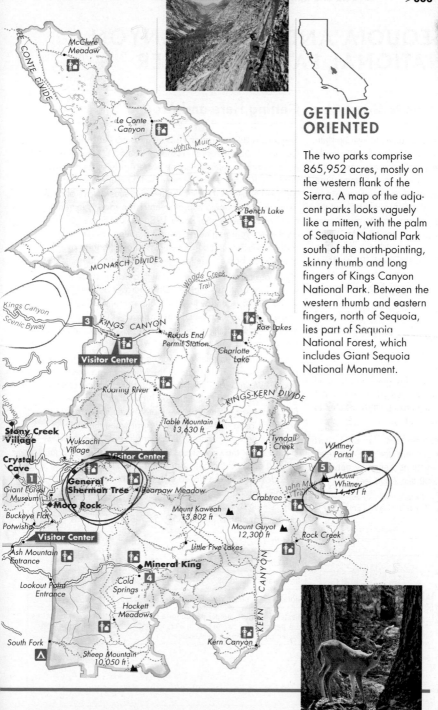

GETTING ORIENTED

The two parks comprise 865,952 acres, mostly on the western flank of the Sierra. A map of the adjacent parks looks vaguely like a mitten, with the palm of Sequoia National Park south of the north-pointing, skinny thumb and long fingers of Kings Canyon National Park. Between the western thumb and eastern fingers, north of Sequoia, lies part of Sequoia National Forest, which includes Giant Sequoia National Monument.

McClure Meadow

LE CONTE DIVIDE

Le Conte Canyon

John Muir Trail

Bench Lake

MONARCH DIVIDE

Woods Creek Trail

Kings Canyon Scenic Byway

3

KINGS CANYON

Roads End Permit Station

Rae Lakes

Charlotte Lake

Visitor Center

Roaring River

KINGS-KERN DIVIDE

Highway

Table Mountain 13,630 ft

Stony Creek Village

Wuksachi Village

Tyndall Creek

Whitney Portal

Visitor Center

5

Crystal Cave

1

General Sherman Tree

Mount Whitney 14,491 ft

Giant Forest Museum

Bearpaw Meadow

John Muir Trail

Moro Rock

Crabtree

Buckeye Flat

Mount Kaweah 13,802 ft

Potwisha

Mount Guyot 12,300 ft

Rock Creek

Visitor Center

Little Five Lakes

Ash Mountain Entrance

KERN CANYON

Mineral King

Lookout Point Entrance

4

Cold Springs

Hockett Meadows

South Fork

Kern Canyon

Sheep Mountain 10,050 ft

SEQUOIA AND KINGS CANYON NATIONAL PARKS PLANNER

When to Go

The best times to visit are late spring and early fall, when temperatures are moderate and crowds thin. Summertime can draw hoards of tourists to see the giant sequoias, and the few, narrow roads mean congestion at peak holiday times. If you must visit in summer, go during the week. By contrast, in wintertime you may feel as though you have the parks all to yourself. But because of heavy snows, sections of the main park roads can be closed without warning, and low-hanging clouds can move in and obscure mountains and valleys for days. Check road and weather conditions before venturing out mid-November to late April.

Temperatures in the chart below are for the mid-level elevations, generally between 4,000 and 7,000 feet.

Getting Here and Around

Sequoia is 36 mi east of Visalia on Route 198; Kings Canyon is 53 mi east of Fresno on Route 180. There is no automobile entrance on the eastern side of the Sierra. Routes 180 and 198 are connected by Generals Highway, a paved two-lane road that sometimes sees delays at peak times due to ongoing improvements. The road is extremely narrow and steep from Route 198 to Giant Forest, so keep an eye on your engine temperature gauge, as the incline and congestion can cause vehicles to overheat; to avoid overheated brakes, use low gears on downgrades.

If you are traveling in an RV or with a trailer, study the restrictions on these vehicles. Do not travel beyond Potwisha Campground with an RV longer than 22 feet on Route 198; take straighter, easier Route 180 instead. Maximum vehicle length on Generals Highway is 40 feet, or 50 feet combined length for vehicles with trailers.

Generals Highway between Lodgepole and Grant Grove is sometimes closed by snow. The Mineral King Road from Route 198 into southern Sequoia National Park is closed 2 mi below Atwell Mill either on November 1 or after the first heavy snow. The Buckeye Flat–Middle Fork Trailhead Road is closed mid-October–mid-April when the Buckeye Flat Campground closes. The lower Crystal Cave Road is closed when the cave closes in November. Its upper 2 mi, as well as the Panoramic Point and Moro Rock–Crescent Meadow roads, are closed with the first heavy snow. Because of the danger of rockfall, the portion of Kings Canyon Scenic Byway east of Grant Grove closes in winter. For current conditions, call ☎ 559/565-3341 Ext. 4.

AVG. HIGH/LOW TEMPS (°F)

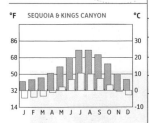

°F   SEQUOIA & KINGS CANYON   °C

WHAT IT COSTS

	¢	$	$$	$$$	$$$$
Restaurants	under $8	$8–$12	$13–$20	$21–$30	over $30
Hotels	under $70	$70–$120	$121–$175	$176–$250	over $250

Restaurant prices are per person for a main course at dinner. Hotel prices are per night for two people in a standard double room in high season, excluding taxes and service charges.

Updated by
Sura Wood
and Reed
Parsell

Although *Sequoiadendron giganteum* is the formal name for the redwoods that grow here, everyone outside the classroom calls them sequoias, big trees, or Sierra redwoods. Their monstrously thick trunks and branches, remarkably shallow root systems, and neck-craning heights are almost impossible to believe, as is the fact they can live for more than 2,500 years. Many of these towering marvels are in the Giant Forest stretch of Generals Highway, which connects Sequoia and Kings Canyon national parks.

Next to or a few miles off the 43-mi road Generals Highway are most of Sequoia National Park's main attractions and Grant Grove Village, the orientation hub for Kings Canyon National Park. The two parks share a boundary that runs west–east, from the foothills of the Central Valley to the Sierra Nevada's dramatic eastern ridges. Kings Canyon has two portions: the smaller is shaped like a bent finger and encompasses Grant Grove Village and Redwood Mountain Grove (the two parks' largest concentration of sequoias), and the larger is home to stunning Kings River Canyon, whose vast, unspoiled peaks and valleys are a backpacker's dream. Sequoia is in one piece and includes Mount Whitney, the highest point in the Lower 48 states (although it is impossible to see from the western part of the park and is a chore to ascend from either side).

PARK ESSENTIALS

ADMISSION FEES AND PERMITS
The admission fee is $20 per vehicle and $10 for those who enter by bus, on foot, bicycle, motorcycle, or horse; it is valid for seven days in both parks. U.S. residents over the age of 62 pay $10 for a lifetime pass, and permanently disabled U.S. residents are admitted free.

If you plan to camp in the backcountry, you need a permit, which costs $15 for hikers or $30 for stock users (e.g., horseback riders). One permit covers the group. Availability of permits depends upon trailhead quotas. Advance reservations are accepted by mail, fax, or e-mail for a $15 processing fee, beginning March 1, and must be made at least three weeks in advance (🖰 *HCR 89, P.O. Box 60, Three Rivers, CA 93271* ☎ *559/575–3766* 🖶 *559/565–4239*). Without a reservation, you may still get a permit on a first-come, first-served basis starting at 1 PM the day before you plan to hike. For more information on backcountry camping or travel with pack animals (horses, mules, burros, or llamas), contact the Wilderness Permit Office (☎ *530/565–3761*).

ADMISSION HOURS
The parks are open 24/7 year-round. They are in the Pacific time zone

EMERGENCIES
Call 911 from any telephone within the park in an emergency. Rangers at the Cedar Grove, Foothills, Grant Grove, and Lodgepole visitor centers and the Mineral King ranger station are trained in first aid. National Park rangers have legal jurisdiction within park boundaries: contact a ranger station or visitor center for police matters. For nonemergencies, call the parks' main number, 559/565–3341.

PARK CONTACT INFORMATION
Delaware North Park Services (🖰 *P.O. Box 89, Sequoia National Park, CA 93262* ☎ *559/565–4070 or 888/252–5757* ⊕ *www.visitsequoia.com*). This concessionaire operates the lodgings and visitor services in Sequoia, and some in Kings Canyon. **Kings Canyon Park Services** 🖰 *P.O. Box 909, Kings Canyon National Park, CA 93633* ☎ *559/335–5500 or 866/522–6966* ⊕ *www.sequoia-kingscanyon.com*. Some park services, including lodging, are operated by this company. **Sequoia and Kings Canyon National Parks** ✉ *47050 Generals Hwy. (Rte. 198), Three Rivers, CA 93271–9651* ☎ *559/565–3341* ⊕ *www.nps.gov/seki*. **Sequoia Natural History Association** 🖰 *HCR 89 P.O. Box 10, Three Rivers, CA 93271* ☎ *559/565–3759* ⊕ *www.sequoiahistory.org*. The SNHA operates Crystal Cave and the Pear Lake Ski Hut, and provides educational materials and programs. **U.S. Forest Service, Sequoia National Forest** (✉ *900 W. Grand Ave., Porterville, CA 93527* ☎ *559/338–2251* ⊕ *www.fs.fed.us/r5/sequoia*).

SEQUOIA NATIONAL PARK

EXPLORING

SCENIC STOPS
Crescent Meadow. John Muir called this the "gem of the Sierra." Take an hour or two to walk around, and see if you agree. Wildflowers bloom here throughout the summer. ✉ *End of Moro Rock–Crescent Meadow Rd., 2.6 mi east off Generals Hwy.*

★ **Crystal Cave.** One of more than 200 caves in Sequoia and Kings Canyon national parks, Crystal Cave is unusual in that it's composed largely of marble, the result of limestone being hardened under heat and pressure. It contains several impressive formations that will be easier to see once

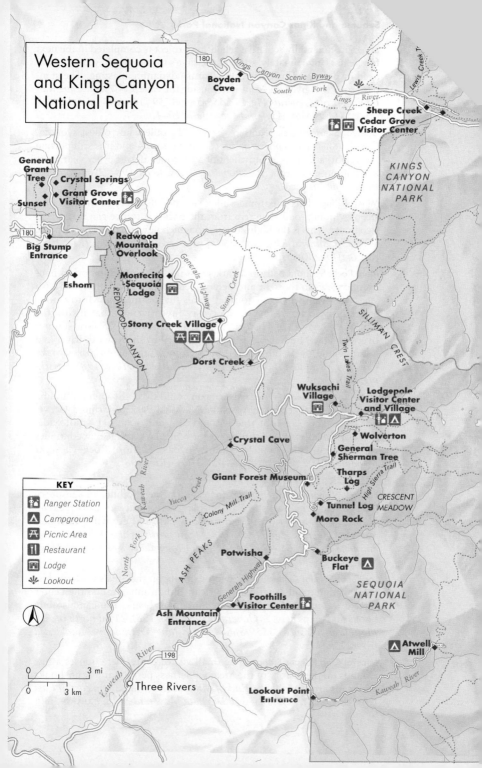

n environmentally sensitive relighting project is completed in the next ≥w years. Unfortunately, some of the cave's formations have been damged or destroyed by early 20th-century dynamite blasting. The standard tour will give you 45 minutes inside the cave. ⊠ *Crystal Cave Rd., ¡ mi west off Generals Hwy.* 🕾 *559/565–3759* ⊕ *www.sequoiahistory. org* 🖃 *$11* ⊙ *Mid-May–mid-Oct., daily 10–4.*

★ **General Sherman Tree.** Neither the world's tallest nor oldest sequoia, General Sherman is nevertheless tops in volume—and it is still putting on weight, adding the equivalent of a 60-foot-tall tree every year to its 2.7 million-pound mass. ⊠ *Generals Hwy. (Rte. 198), 2 mi south of Lodgepole Visitor Center.*

Mineral King. This subalpine valley sits at 7,800 feet at the end of a steep, winding road. The trip from the park's entrance can take up to two hours. This is the highest point to which you can drive in the park. ⊠ *End of Mineral King Rd., 25 mi east of Generals Hwy. (Rte. 198), east of Three Rivers.*

★ **Moro Rock.** Sequoia National Park's best non-tree attraction offers panoramic views to those fit and determined enough to mount its 350-ish steps. In a case where the journey rivals the destination, Moro's stone stairway is so impressive in its twisty inventiveness that it's on the National Register of Historic Places. The rock's 6,725-foot summit overlooks the Middle Fork Canyon, sculpted by the Kaweah River and approaching the depth of Arizona's Grand Canyon. ⊠ *Moro Rock– Crescent Meadow Rd., 2 mi east off Generals Hwy. (Rte. 198) to parking area.*

Tunnel Log. It's been 40 years since you could drive through a standing sequoia—and that was in Yosemite National Park's Mariposa Grove, not here. This 275-foot tree fell in 1937, and soon a 17-foot-wide, 8-foot-high hole was cut through it for vehicular passage that continues today. Large vehicles take the nearby bypass. ⊠ *Moro Rock–Crescent Meadow Rd., 2 mi east of Generals Hwy. (Rte. 198).*

VISITOR CENTERS

Foothills Visitor Center. Exhibits focusing on the foothills and resource issues facing the parks are on display here. You can also pick up books, maps, and a list of ranger-led walks, and get wilderness permits. ⊠ *Generals Hwy. (Rte. 198), 1 mi north of the Ash Mountain entrance* 🕾 *559/565–4212* ⊙ *Oct.–mid-May, daily 8–4:30; mid-May– Sept., daily 8–5.*

Lodgepole Visitor Center. Along with exhibits on the area's geologic history, wildlife, and longtime American Indian inhabitants, the center screens an outstanding 22-minute film about bears. You can also buy books and maps here. ⊠ *Generals Hwy. (Rte. 198), 21 mi north of Ash Mountain entrance* 🕾 *559/565–4436* ⊙ *June–Oct., daily 7–6; Closed from Nov.–May.*

Mineral King Ranger Station. The small visitor center here houses a few exhibits on the history of the area; wilderness permits and some books and maps are available. ⊠ *End of Mineral King Rd., 25 mi east of East Fork entrance* 🕾 *559/565–3768* ⊙ *Late May–mid-Sept., daily 8–4:30.*

CLOSE UP

Flora and Fauna

21

The parks can be divided into three distinct zones. In the west (1,500–4,500 feet) are the rolling, lower elevation foothills, covered with shrubby chaparral vegetation or golden grasslands dotted with oaks. Chamise, red-barked manzanita, and the occasional yucca plant grow here. Fields of white popcorn flower cover the hillsides in spring, and the yellow fiddleneck flourishes. In summer, intense heat and absence of rain cause the hills to turn golden brown. Wildlife includes the California ground squirrel, noisy blue-and-gray scrub jay, black bears, coyotes, skunks, and gray fox.

At middle elevation (5,000–9,000 feet), where the giant sequoia belt resides, rock formations mix with meadows and huge stands of evergreens—red and white fir, incense cedar, and

ponderosa pines, to name a few. Wildflowers like yellow blazing star and red Indian paintbrush, bloom in spring and summer. Mule deer, golden-mantled ground squirrels, Steller's jays, mule deer, and black bears (most active in fall) inhabit the area, as does the chickaree.

The high alpine section of the parks is extremely rugged, with a string of rocky peaks reaching above 13,000 feet to Mt. Whitney's 14,494 feet. Fierce weather and scarcity of soil make vegetation and wildlife sparse. Foxtail and whitebark pines have gnarled and twisted trunks, the result of high wind, heavy snowfall, and freezing temperatures. In summer you can see yellow-bellied marmots, pikas, weasels, mountain chickadees, and Clark's nutcrackers.

SPORTS AND THE OUTDOORS

The best way to see Sequoia is to take a hike. Unless you do so, you'll miss out on the up-close grandeur of mist wafting between deeply scored, red-orange tree trunks bigger than you've ever seen. If it's winter, put on some snowshoes or cross-country skis and plunge into the outscale woodland swaddled in snow. There are not too many other outdoor options: no off-road driving is allowed in the parks, and no special provisions have been made for bicycles. Boating, rafting, and snowmobiling are also prohibited.

BIRD-WATCHING

More than 200 species of birds inhabit Sequoia and Kings Canyon national parks. Not seen in most parts of the United States, the white-headed woodpecker and the pileated woodpecker are common in most mid-elevation areas here. There are also many hawks and owls, including the renowned spotted owl. Species are diverse in both parks due to the changes in elevation, and range from warblers, kingbirds, thrushes, and sparrows in the foothills to goshawk, blue grouse, red-breasted nuthatch, and brown creeper at the highest elevations. Ranger-led bird-watching tours are held on a sporadic basis. Call the park's main information number to find out more about these tours.

Contact the **Sequoia Natural History Association** (⌂ *HCR 89, P.O. Box 10, Three Rivers, CA 93271* ☎ *559/565–3759* ⊕ *www.sequoiahistory. org*) for information on bird-watching in the southern Sierra.

CROSS-COUNTRY SKIING

Pear Lake Ski Hut. Primitive lodging is available at this backcountry hut, reached by a steep and extremely difficult 7-mi trail from Wolverton. Only expert skiers should attempt this trek. Space is limited; make reservations well in advance. ⊠ *Trailhead at end of Wolverton Rd., 1½ mi northeast off Generals Hwy. (Rte. 198)* ☎ *559/565–3759* 🗲 *$38* ⊙ *Mid-Dec.–mid-Apr.*

Wuksachi Lodge. Rent skis here. Depending on snowfall amounts, instruction may also be available. Reservations are recommended. Marked trails cut through Giant Forest, just 5 mi south of the lodge. ⊠ *Off Generals Hwy. (Rte. 198), 2 mi north of Lodgepole* ☎ *559/565–4070* 🗲 *$15–$20 ski rental* ⊙ *Nov.–May (unless no snow), daily 9–4.*

HIKING

The best way to see the park is to hike it. The grandeur and majesty of the Sierra is best seen up close. Carry a hiking map—available at any visitor center—and plenty of water. Check with rangers for current trail conditions, and be aware of rapidly changing weather. As a rule of thumb, plan on trekking 1 MPH.

EASY

★ **Congress Trail.** This easy 2-mi trail is a paved loop that begins near General Sherman Tree and winds through the heart of the sequoia forest. You'll get close-up views of more big trees here than on any other Sequoia hike. Watch for the clusters known as the House and Senate. ⊠ *Trail begins off Generals Hwy. (Rte. 198), 2 mi north of Giant Forest.*

★ **Crescent Meadow Trails.** John Muir reportedly called Crescent Meadow the "gem of the Sierra." Brilliant wildflowers bloom here by midsummer, and a 1.8-mi trail loops around the meadow. A 1.6-mi trail begins at Crescent Meadow and leads to Tharp's Log, a cabin built from a fire-hollowed sequoia. ⊠ *Trail begins end of Moro Rock–Crescent Meadow Rd., 2.6 mi east off Generals Hwy. (Rte. 198).*

MODERATE

Tokopah Falls Trail. This moderate trail follows the Marble Fork of the Kaweah River for 1.75 mi one way and dead-ends below the impressive granite cliffs and cascading waterfall of Tokopah Canyon. It takes 2½ to 4 hours to make the 3.5-mi round-trip journey. The trail passes through a mixed-conifer forest. ⊠ *Trail begins off Generals Hwy. (Rte. 198), ¼ mi north of Lodgepole Campground.*

DIFFICULT

Mineral King Trails. Many trails to the high country begin at Mineral King. The two most popular day hikes are Eagle Lake and Timber Gap, both of which are somewhat strenuous. At 7,800 feet, this is the highest point to which one can drive in either of the parks. Get a map and provisions, and check with rangers about conditions. ⊠ *Trailhead at end of Mineral King Rd., 25 mi east of Generals Hwy. (Rte. 198).*

HORSEBACK RIDING

Trips take you through redwood forests, flowering meadows, across the Sierra, or even up to Mt. Whitney. Costs per person range from $25 for a one-hour guided ride to around $200 per day for fully guided trips for which the packers do all the cooking and camp chores.

Grant Grove Stables is the stable to choose if you want a short ride. ⊠ *Rte. 180, ½ Mi north of Grant Grove Visitor Center, near Grant Grove Village, Gran Grove* ☎ *559/337–2314 mid-June–Sept., 559/337–2314 Oct.–mid-June*

Horse Corral Pack Station. Hourly, half-day, full-day, or overnight trips through Sequoia are available for beginning and advanced riders. ⊠ *Off Big Meadows Rd., 12 mi east of Generals Hwy. (Rte. 198) between Sequoia and Kings Canyon national parks* ☎ *559/565–3404 in summer, 559/564–6429 in winter* ⊕ *www.horsecorralpackers.com* 🖅 *$35–$145 day trips* ☉ *May–Sept.*

Mineral King Pack Station. Day and overnight tours in the high-mountain area around Mineral King are available here. ⊠ *End of Mineral King Rd., 25 mi east of East Fork entrance* ☎ *559/561–3039 in summer, 520/855–5885 in winter* ⊕ *mineralking.tripod.com* 🖅 *$25–$75 day trips* ☉ *July–late Sept. or –early Oct.*

SLEDDING AND SNOWSHOEING

The Wolverton area, on Route 198 near Giant Forest, is a popular sledding spot, where sleds, inner tubes, and platters are allowed. You can buy sleds and saucers, starting at $8, at the **Wuksachi Lodge** (☎ *559/565–4070*), 2 mi north of Lodgepole. You can also rent snowshoes for $15–$20. Naturalists lead snowshoe walks around Giant Forest and Wuksachi Lodge, conditions permitting, on Saturdays and holidays. Snowshoes are provided for a $1 donation. Make reservations and check schedules at **Giant Forest Museum** (☎ *559/565–4480*) or **Wuksachi Lodge.**

EDUCATIONAL OFFERINGS

CLASSES AND SEMINARS

Evening Programs. In summer, the park shows documentary films and slide shows, and has evening lectures. Locations and times vary; pick up a schedule at any visitor center or check bulletin boards near ranger stations. ☎ *559/565–3341.*

★ **Seminars.** Expert naturalists lead seminars on a range of topics, including birds, wildflowers, geology, botany, photography, park history, backpacking, and pathfinding. Some courses offer transferable credits. Reserve in advance. For information and prices, pick up a course catalogue at any visitor center or contact the **Sequoia Natural History Association** (☎ *559/565–3759* ⊕ *www.sequoiahistory.org*).

Sequoia Sightseeing Tours. The only licensed tour operator in either park offers daily interpretive sightseeing tours in a 10-passenger van with a friendly, knowledgeable guide. Reservations are essential. They also offer private tours of Kings Canyon. ☎ *559/561–4189* ⊕ *www. sequoiatours.com.*

21

RANGER PROGRAMS

Free Nature Programs. Almost any summer day, half-hour to 1½-hour ranger talks and walks explore subjects such as the life of the sequoia, the geology of the park, and the habits of bears. Giant Forest, Lodgepole Visitor Center, Wuksachi Village, and Dorst Creek Campground are frequent starting points. Check bulletin boards throughout the park for the week's offerings.

🕗 **Junior Ranger Program.** This self-guided program is offered year-round for children over five. Pick up a Junior Ranger booklet at any of the visitor centers. When your child finishes an activity, a ranger signs the booklet. Kids earn a patch upon completion, which is given at an awards ceremony. It isn't necessary to complete all activities to be awarded a patch. ☎ 559/565–3341.

KINGS CANYON NATIONAL PARK

SCENIC DRIVES

★ **Kings Canyon Scenic Byway.** About 10 mi east of Grant Grove Village is Jackson View, where you'll first see Kings River Canyon. Near Yucca Point, it's thousands of feet deeper than the much more famous Grand Canyon. Continuing through Sequoia National Forest past Boyden Cavern, you'll enter the larger portion of Kings Canyon National Park and, eventually, Cedar Grove Village. Past there, the U-shaped canyon becomes broader. Be sure to allow an hour to walk through Zumwalt Meadow. Also, be sure to park and take the less-than-five-minute walks to the base of Grizzly Falls and Roaring River Falls. The drive dead-ends at a big parking lot, the launch point for many backpackers. Driving the byway takes about one hour each way (without stops).

EXPLORING

Kings Canyon National Park consists of two sections that adjoin the northern boundary of Sequoia National Park. The western portion, covered with sequoia and pine forest, contains the park's most visited sights, such as Grant Grove. The vast eastern portion is remote high country, slashed across half its southern breadth by the deep, rugged Kings River Canyon. Separating the two is Sequoia National Forest, which encompasses Giant Sequoia National Monument. The Kings Canyon Scenic Byway (Route 180) links the major sights within and between the park's two sections.

HISTORIC SITES

★ **Fallen Monarch.** This Sequoia's hollow base was used in the second half of the 19th century as a home for settlers, a saloon, and even to stable U.S. Cavalry horses. As you walk through it (assuming entry is permitted, which has not always been the case in recent years), check out how little the wood has decayed, and imagine yourself tucked safely inside, sheltered from a storm or protected from the searing heat. ✉ *Trailhead 1 mi north of Grant Grove Visitor Center.*

Kings Canyon's Cedar Grove Area

Lewis Creek

Lewis Creek Trail

Hotel Creek Trail

Hotel Creek

Granite Creek

Copper Creek Trail

North Dome
8,717 ft

Cedar Grove
Viewpoint

Roads End

Grand Sentinel Viewpoint

Cedar Grove Village and Lodge

Zumwalt Meadow

Zumwalt
Meadow
Trail

Sheep Creek

Sentinel

Motor Nature Trail

Canyon View

Moraine

South Fork Kings River

Grand Sentinel
8,508 ft

Don Cecil Trail

Canyon
Viewpoint

0   1 mi

0   1 km

SCENIC STOPS

Canyon View. There are many places along the scenic byway to pull over for sightseeing, but this special spot showcases evidence of the canyon's glacial history. Here, maybe more than anywhere else, you'll understand why John Muir compared Kings Canyon vistas with those in Yosemite. ✉ *Kings Canyon Scenic Byway (Rte. 180), 1 mi east of the Cedar Grove turnoff.*

★ **Redwood Mountain Grove.** If you are serious about sequoias, you should consider visiting this, the world's largest big-tree grove. Within its 2,078 acres are 2,172 sequoias whose diameters exceed 10 feet. Your options range from the distant (pulling off the Generals Highway onto an overlook) to the intimate (taking a 6- to 10-mi hike down into its richest regions, which include two of the world's 25 heaviest trees). ✉ *Drive 5 mi south of Grant Grove on Generals Hwy. (Rte. 198), then turn right at Quail Flat; follow it 1½ mi to the Redwood Canyon trailhead.*

VISITOR CENTERS

Cedar Grove Visitor Center. Off the main road and behind the Sentinel Campground, this small ranger station has books and maps, plus information about hikes and other things to do in the area. ✉ *Kings Canyon Scenic Byway, 30 mi east of park entrance* ☎ *559/565–3793* ⊙ *mid-May–late September, daily 9–5.*

Grant Grove Visitor Center. Acquaint yourself with the varied charms of this two-section national park by watching a 15-minute film and perusing the center's exhibits on the canyon, sequoias, and human history. Books, maps, and free wilderness permits are available, as are updates on the parks' weather and air-quality conditions. ⊠ *Generals Hwy. (Rte. 198), 3 mi northeast of Rte. 180, Big Stump entrance* ☎ *559/565–4307* ☉ *Summer, daily 8–6; mid-May–late Sept., daily 9–4:30; winter, daily 9:30–4:30.*

SPORTS AND THE OUTDOORS

CROSS-COUNTRY SKIING

Roads to Grant Grove are easily accessible during heavy snowfall, making the trails here a good choice over Sequoia's Giant Forest when harsh weather hits.

HIKING

You can enjoy many of Kings Canyon's sights from your car, but the giant gorge of the Kings River Canyon and the sweeping vistas of some of the highest mountains in the United States are best seen on foot. Carry a hiking map—available at any visitor center—and plenty of water. Check with rangers for current trail conditions, and be aware of rapidly changing weather.

If you're planning to hike the backcountry, you can pick up a permit and information on the backcountry at **Road's End Permit Station** (⊠ *5 mi east of Cedar Grove Visitor Center, at the end of Kings Canyon Scenic Byway* ☎ *No phone* ☉ *Late May–late Sept., daily 7–3:30*). You can also rent or buy bear canisters, a must for campers. When the station is closed, you can still complete a self-service permit form.

EASY

Fodor'sChoice **Zumwalt Meadow Trail.** Rangers say this is the best (and most popular)
★ day hike in the Cedar Grove area. Just 1.5 mi long, it offers three visual treats: the South Fork of the Kings River, the lush meadow, and the high granite walls above, including those of Grand Sentinel and North Dome. ⊠ *Trailhead 4½ mi east of Cedar Grove Village turnoff from Kings Canyon Scenic Byway.*

MODERATE

★ **Big Baldy.** This hike climbs 600 feet and 2 mi up to the 8,209-feet summit of Big Baldy. Your reward is the view of Redwood Canyon. The round-trip hike is 4 mi. ⊠ *Trailhead 8 mi south of Grant Grove on Generals Hwy. (Rte. 198).*

★ **Redwood Canyon Trail.** Avoid the hubbub of Giant Forest and its General Sherman Tree by hiking down to Redwood Canyon, the world's largest grove of sequoias. Opt for the trail toward Hart Tree, and you'll soon lose track of how many humongous trees you pass along the 6-mi loop. Count on spending four to six peaceful hours here—although some backpackers linger overnight (wilderness permit required). ⊠ *Trail begins off Quail Flat ✛ Drive 5 mi south of Grant Grove on Generals Hwy. (Rte. 198), then turn right at Quail Flat; follow it 1½ mi to the Redwood Canyon trailhead.*

DIFFICULT

★ **Hotel Creek Trail.** For gorgeous canyon views, take this trail from the canyon floor at Cedar Grove up a series of switchbacks until it splits. Follow the route left through chaparral to the forested ridge and rocky outcrop known as Cedar Grove Overlook, where you can see the Kings River Canyon stretching below. This strenuous 5-mi round-trip hike gains 1,200 feet and takes three to four hours to complete. For a longer hike, return via Lewis Creek Trail for an 8-mi loop. ✉ *Trailhead at Cedar Grove pack station, 1 mi east of Cedar Grove Village.*

HORSEBACK RIDING

One-day destinations by horseback out of Cedar Grove include Mist Falls and Upper Bubb's Creek. In the backcountry, many equestrians head for Volcanic Lakes or Granite Basin, ascending trails that reach elevations of 10,000 feet. Costs per person range from $25 for a one-hour guided ride to around $200 per day for fully guided trips for which the packers do all the cooking and camp chores.

> **MOUNT WHITNEY**
>
> At 14,494 feet, Mt. Whitney is the highest point in the contiguous United States and the crown jewel of Sequoia National Park's wild eastern side. Despite the mountain's scale, you can't see it from the more traveled west side of the park, because it is hidden behind the Great Western Divide. The only way to access Mt. Whitney from the main part of the park is to circumnavigate the Sierra Nevada via a 10-hour, nearly 400-mi drive outside the park. No road ascends the peak; the best vantage point from which to catch a glimpse of the mountain is at the end of Whitney Portal Road. (Whitney Portal Road is closed in winter.)

Take a day or overnight trip along the Kings River Canyon with **Cedar Grove Pack Station** (✉ *Kings Canyon Scenic Byway, 1 mi east of Cedar Grove Village* ☎ *559/565–3464 in summer, 559/337–2314 off-season* ✉ *Call for prices* ☉ *May–Oct.*). Popular routes include the Rae Lakes Loop and Monarch Divide. A one- or two-hour trip through Grant Grove leaving from **Grant Grove Stables** (✉ *Rte. 180, ½ mi north of Grant Grove Visitor Center* ☎ *559/335–9292 mid-June–Sept., 559/337–2314 Oct.–mid-June* ✉ *$35–$50* ☉ *June–Labor Day, daily 8–6*) is a good way to get a taste of horseback riding in Kings Canyon.

SLEDDING AND SNOWSHOEING

In winter, Kings Canyon has a few great places to play in the snow. Sleds, inner tubes, and platters are allowed at both the Azalea Campground area on Grant Tree Road, ¼ mi north of Grant Grove Visitor Center, and at the Big Stump picnic area, 2 mi north of the lower Route 180 entrance to the park.

Snowshoeing is good around Grant Grove, where you can take naturalist-guided snowshoe walks on Saturdays and holidays mid-December through mid-March as conditions permit.

Hiking in the Sierra mountains is a thrilling experience, putting you amid some of the world's highest trees.

WHERE TO EAT

¢–$
AMERICAN

✕ **Cedar Grove Restaurant.** For a small operation, the menu here is surprisingly extensive, with dinner entrées such as pasta, pork chops, and steak. For breakfast, try the biscuits and gravy, French toast, pancakes, or cold cereal. Burgers (including vegetarian patties) and hot dogs dominate the lunch choices. Outside, a patio dining area overlooks the Kings River. ⊠ *Cedar Grove Village* ☎ *559/565–0100* ▭ *AE, D, MC, V* ⊘ *Closed Oct.–May.*

$$–$$$
AMERICAN

✕ **Grant Grove Restaurant.** In a no-frills, open room, order basic American fare such as pancakes for breakfast or hot sandwiches and chicken for later meals. Vegetarians and vegans will have to content themselves with a simple salad. Take-out service is available. ⊠ *Grant Grove Village* ☎ *559/335–5500* ▭ *AE, D, MC, V.*

¢
CAFÉ

✕ **Lodgepole Market and Snack Bar.** The choices here run the gamut from simple to very simple, with the three counters only a few strides apart in a central eating complex. For hot food, venture into the snack bar. The deli sells prepackaged sandwiches along with ice cream scooped from tubs. You'll find other prepackaged foods in the market. ⊠ *Next to Lodgepole Visitor Center* ☎ *559/565–3301* ▭ *AE, D, DC, MC, V* ⊘ *Closed early Sept.–mid-Apr.*

$$
BARBECUE

✕ **Wolverton Barbecue.** Weather permitting, diners congregate on a wooden porch that looks directly out onto a small but strikingly verdant meadow. In addition to the predictable meats such as ribs and chicken, the all-you-can-eat buffet has sides that include baked beans, corn on the cob, and potato salad. Following the meal, listen to a ranger talk and clear your throat for a campfire sing-along. Purchase tickets at dgepole Market, Wuksachi Lodge, or Wolverton Recreation Area's ...ice. ⊠ *Wolverton Rd., 1½ mi northeast off Generals Hwy. (Rte. 198)* ...559/565–4070 or 559/565–3301 ⊟ *AE, D, DC, MC, V* ☉ *Open year ...und seven days a week.*

AMERICAN ★ **Wuksachi Village Dining Room.** Huge windows run the length of the ...igh-ceilinged dining room, and a large fireplace on the far wall warms both the body and the soul. The diverse dinner menu—by far the best in the two parks—includes filet mignon, rainbow trout, and vegetarian pasta dishes, in addition to the ever-present burgers. The children's menu is economically priced. Breakfast and lunch also are served. ⊠ *Wuksachi Village* ☎ *559/565–4070* ⌒ *Reservations essential* ⊟ *AE, D, DC, MC, V.*

WHERE TO STAY

HOTELS

$$ ⊡ **John Muir Lodge.** This modern, timber-sided lodge is nestled in a wooded area in the hills above Grant Grove Village and offers year-round accommodations. The rooms and suites all have queen-size beds and private baths, and there is a comfortable common room where you can play cards and board games, or peruse a loaner book. Look above the stone fireplace at a giant painting of Muir himself, shown relaxing on a rock by a meadow. **Pros:** common room stays warm; it's far enough from the main road to be quiet. **Cons:** check-in is down in the village. ⊠ *Kings Canyon Scenic Byway, ¼ mi north of Grant Grove Village* ⌁ *Sequoia Kings Canyon Park Services Co., PO box 907, Suite 101, Kings Canyon National Park CA 93633* ☎ *559/335–5500 or 866/522–6966* ⊕ *www.sequoia-kingscanyon.com* ⋖ *36 rooms* ⌂ *In-room: no a/c, no TV. In hotel: Wi-Fi hotspot* ⊟ *AE, D, MC, V.*

$$–$$$ ⊡ **Wuksachi Lodge.** The striking cedar-and-stone main building here is
Fodor's Choice a fine example of how a man-made structure can blend effectively with
★ lovely mountain scenery. Guest rooms, which have modern amenities, are in three buildings up the hill from the main lodge. You can usually see deer roaming around the spacious and hilly grounds, which are 7,200 feet above sea level. **Pros:** best place to stay in the parks; lots of wildlife. **Cons:** rooms can be small; main lodge is a few minutes' walk from guest rooms. ⊠ *Wuksachi Village* ☎ *559/565–4070 front desk, 559/253–2199, 888/252–5757 reservations* ⊕ *www.visitsequoia.com* ⋖ *102 rooms* ⌂ *In-room: no a/c, refrigerator, Internet, Wi-Fi. In-hotel: restaurant, bar* ⊟ *AE, D, DC, MC, V.*

CAMPING

Campgrounds in Sequoia and Kings Canyon are located in wonderful settings, with lots of shade and nearby hiking trails. But beware that party-loving "locals" from Fresno and other Central Valley cities swarm up here on Friday and Saturday nights. Only the Dorst Creek and Lodgepole campgrounds accept reservations (up to five months in advance), and none has RV hookups. Campgrounds around Lodgepole and Grant Grove get quite busy in summer with vacationing families. Permits are required for backcountry camping.

Sacramento and the Gold Country

WORD OF MOUTH

"Highway 49 travels through the California Gold Country steeped with history and small towns. . . . Much, much more interesting than taking Highway 99."

—BarbAnn

WELCOME TO SACRAMENTO AND THE GOLD COUNTRY

TOP REASONS TO GO

★ **Golden opportunities:** Marshall Gold Discovery State Park and Hangtown's Gold Bug & Mine conjure up California's mid-19th century boom.

★ **Capital connections:** The old saying "Sacramento is a nice place to live, but you wouldn't want to visit here" seems rather snarky now, with the city's downtown and midtown resurgence.

★ **That festive feeling:** Sacramento is home to the California state fair in July and many ethnic food festivals. Nevada City and environs are known for summer mountain music festivals and Victorian and Cornish winter holiday celebrations.

★ **The next Napa:** With bucolic scenery and friendly tasting rooms, the Shenandoah Valley is like Napa, without the traffic.

★ **Back to nature:** Moaning Cavern's main chamber is big enough to hold the Statue of Liberty, and Calaveras Big Trees State Park is filled with giant sequoias.

1 Sacramento and Vicinity. The gateway to the Gold Country, the seat of state government, and an agricultural hub, Sacramento plays many important contemporary roles. About 2 million people live in the metropolitan area, and the continuing influx of newcomers seeking opportunity, sunshine, and lower housing costs than in coastal California made it one of the nation's fastest-growing regions in the first half of this decade.

2 The Gold Country—South. South of its junction with U.S. 50, Highway 49 traces in asphalt the famed Mother Lode. The sleepy former gold-rush towns strung along the road have for the most part been restored and made presentable to visitors with an interest in one of the most frenzied episodes of American history.

3 The Gold Country—North. Highway 49 north of Placerville links the towns of Coloma, Auburn, Grass Valley, and Nevada City. Most are gentrified versions of once-rowdy mining camps, vestiges of which remain in roadside museums, old mining structures, and restored homes now serving as inns.

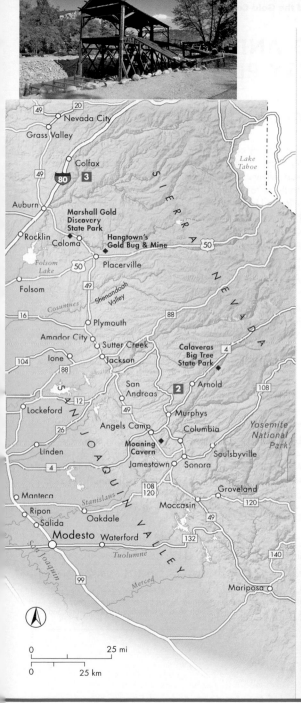

22

GETTING ORIENTED

The Gold Country is a largely laid-back and lower-tech destination for those seeking to escape glitzy Southern California and the Bay Area. Sacramento, Davis, and Woodland are in an enormous valley bordered to the east by the Sierra Nevada mountain range. Foothill communities Nevada City, Placerville, and Sutter Creek were products of the gold rush.

SACRAMENTO AND THE GOLD COUNTRY PLANNER

Exploring the Gold Country

Visiting Old Sacramento's museums is a good way to immerse yourself in history, but the Gold Country's heart lies along Highway 49, which winds the 325-mi north–south length of the historic mining area. The highway, often a twisting, hilly, two-lane road, begs for a convertible with the top down.

Timing

The Gold Country is most pleasant in spring, when the wildflowers are in bloom, and in fall. Summers are hot: temperatures of 100°F are fairly common. Sacramento winters tend to be cool with occasionally foggy and/or rainy days; many Sacramentans drive to the foothills to get some sunshine. Throughout the year Gold Country towns stage community and ethnic celebrations. In December many towns are decked out for Christmas.

Tours

Gold Prospecting Adventures, LLC (☎ 209/984–4653 or 800/596–0009 ⊕ www. goldprospecting.com), based in Jamestown, arranges gold-panning trips.

Getting Here and Around

Traveling by car is the only way to explore the Gold Country. From Sacramento, three highways fan out toward the east, all intersecting with Highway 49: I–80 heads 34 mi northeast to Auburn; U.S. 50 goes east 40 mi to Placerville; and Highway 16 angles southeast 45 mi to Plymouth. Highway 49 is an excellent two-lane road that winds and climbs through the foothills and valleys, linking the principal Gold Country towns.

About the Restaurants

American, Italian, and Mexican are common Gold Country fare, but chefs also prepare ambitious Continental, French, and California cuisine. Grass Valley's meat- and vegetable-stuffed *pasties*, introduced by 19th-century gold miners from Cornwall, are one of the region's more unusual treats.

About the Hotels

Full-service hotels, budget motels, and small inns can all be found in Sacramento. Larger towns along Highway 49—among them Placerville, Nevada City, Auburn, and Mariposa—have chain motels and inns. Many Gold Country bed-and-breakfasts occupy former mansions, miners' cabins, and other historic buildings.

WHAT IT COSTS

	¢	$	$$	$$$	$$$$
Restaurants	under $10	$10–$15	$16–$22	$23–$30	over $30
Hotels	under $90	$90–$120	$121–$175	$176–$250	over $250

Restaurant prices are for a main course at dinner, excluding sales tax of 7%–8% (depending on location). Hotel prices are for two people in a standard double room in high season, excluding service charges and 7%–8% tax.

22

Updated by
Reed Parsell

A new era dawned for California when James Marshall turned up a gold nugget in the tailrace of a sawmill he was constructing along the American River. Before January 24, 1848, Mexico and the United States were still wrestling for ownership of what would become the Golden State. With Marshall's discovery the United States tightened its grip on the region, and prospectors from all over the world came to seek their fortunes in the Mother Lode.

As gold fever seized the nation, California's population of 15,000 swelled to 265,000 within three years. The mostly young, mostly male adventurers who arrived in search of gold—the '49ers—became part of a culture that discarded many of the conventions of the eastern states. It was also a violent time. Yankee prospectors chased Mexican miners off their claims, and California's leaders initiated a plan to exterminate the local Native American population. Bounties were paid and private militias were hired to wipe out the Native Americans or sell them into slavery. California was now to be dominated by the Anglo.

The gold rush boom lasted scarcely 20 years, but it changed California forever. It produced 546 mining towns, of which fewer than 250 remain. The hills of the Gold Country were alive, not only with prospecting and mining but also with business, the arts, gambling, and a fair share of crime. Opera houses went up alongside brothels, and the California State Capitol, in Sacramento, was built with the gold dug out of the hills.

Today the Gold Country is one of California's less expensive destinations, a region of the Sierra Nevada foothills that is filled with natural and cultural pleasures. Visitors come to Nevada City, Auburn, Coloma, Sutter Creek, and Columbia not only to relive the past but also to explore art galleries, to shop for antiques, and to stay at inns full of character. Spring brings wildflowers, and in fall the hills are colored by bright red berries and changing leaves. Because it offers a mix of indoor and outdoor activities, the Gold Country is a good place to take the kids.

PLANNING

GETTING HERE AND AROUND

BY AIR

Sacramento International Airport is served by Alaska, American, Continental, Delta, Frontier, Hawaiian, Horizon Air, JetBlue, Mexicana, Southwest, United, and US Airways. A private taxi from the airport to downtown Sacramento is about $35. The cost of the Super Shuttle from the airport to downtown Sacramento is $25. Call in advance to arrange transportation from your hotel to the airport.

Contacts Sacramento International Airport (✉ *6900 Airport Blvd., 12 mi northwest of downtown off I-5, Sacramento* ☎ *916/874-0700* ⊕ *www. sacairports.org*). **Super Shuttle** (☎ *800/258-3826*).

BY BOAT

Sacramento's riverfront location enables you to sightsee while getting around by boat. Channel Star Excursions operates the *Spirit of Sacramento*, a riverboat that takes passengers on happy-hour, dinner, lunch, and champagne-brunch cruises in addition to one-hour narrated tours.

Contacts Channel Star Excursions (✉ *110 L St.* ☎ *916/552-2933 or 800/433-0263*).

BY BUS

Getting to and from SIA can be accomplished via taxi, the Super Shuttle (F By Air), or by Yolo County Public Bus 42, which operates a circular service around SIA, downtown Sacramento, West Sacramento, Davis, and Woodland. Other Gold Country destinations are best reached by private car.

Greyhound serves Sacramento, Davis, Auburn, and Placerville. It's a two-hour trip from San Francisco's Transbay Terminal, at 1st and Mission streets, to the Sacramento station, at 7th and L streets.

Sacramento Regional Transit buses and light-rail vehicles transport passengers in Sacramento. Most buses run from 6 AM to 10 PM, most trains from 5 AM to midnight. A DASH (Downtown Area Shuttle) bus and the No. 30 city bus link Old Sacramento, midtown, and Sutter's Fort.

Contacts Greyhound (☎ *800/231-2222* ⊕ *www.greyhound.com*). **Sacramento Regional Transit** (☎ *916/321-2877* ⊕ *www.sacrt.com*). **Yolo County Bus** (☎ *530/666-2837* ⊕ *www.yolobus.com*).

BY TRAIN

Several trains operated by Amtrak stop in Sacramento and Davis. Trains making the 2½-hour trip from Jack London Square, in Oakland, stop in Emeryville (across the bay from San Francisco), Richmond, Martinez, and Davis before reaching Sacramento; some stop in Berkeley and Suisun-Fairfield as well; a few venture as far south as San Jose and as far north as Auburn.

Contact Amtrak (☎ *800/872-7245* ⊕ *www.amtrakcalifornia.com*).

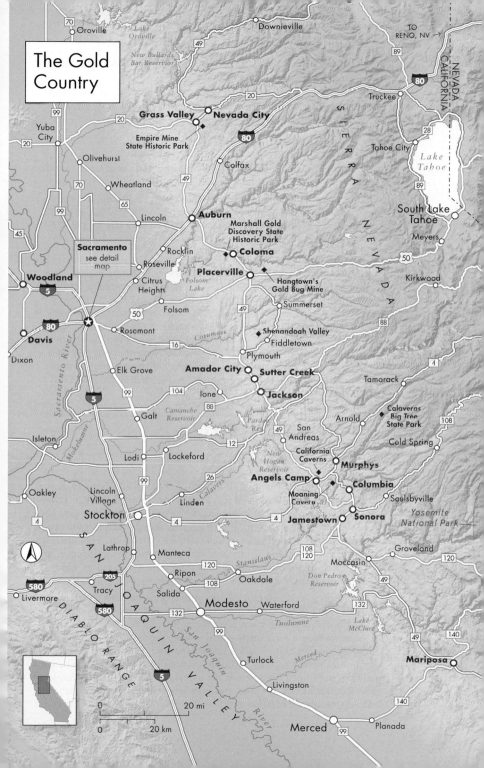

The Gold Country

HEALTH AND SAFETY

In an emergency dial 911. Each of the following medical facilities has an emergency room open 24 hours a day.

Hospitals Mercy Hospital of Sacramento (✉ *4001 J St., Sacramento* ☎ *916/453–4424*). **Sutter General Hospital** (✉ *2801 L St., Sacramento* ☎ *916/733–8900*). **Sutter Memorial Hospital** (✉ *52nd and F Sts., Sacramento* ☎ *916/733–1000*).

LODGING

A number of organizations can supply information about Gold Country B&Bs and other accommodations.

Contacts Amador County Innkeepers Association (☎ *209/267–1710 or 800/726–4667*). **Gold Country Inns of Tuolumne County** (☎ *209/533–1845*). **Historic Bed & Breakfast Inns of Grass Valley & Nevada City** (☎ *530/477–6634 or 800/250–5808*).

VISITOR INFORMATION

Contacts Amador County Chamber of Commerce & Visitors Bureau (✉ *571 S. Hwy. 49, Jackson* ☎ *209/223–0350* ⊕ *www.amadorcountychamber. com*). **El Dorado County Chamber of Commerce** (✉ *542 Main St., Placerville* ☎ *530/621–5885 or 800/457–6279* ⊕ *www.eldoradocounty.org*). **Grass Valley/Nevada County Chamber of Commerce** (✉ *248 Mill St., Grass Valley* ☎ *530/273–4667 or 800/655–4667* ⊕ *www.grassvalleychamber.com*). **Mariposa County Visitors Bureau** (✉ *5158 Hwy. 140, Mariposa* ☎ *209/966–7081 or 866/425–3366* ⊕ *www.homeofyosemite.com*). **Tuolumne County Visitors Bureau** (✉ *542 W. Stockton Rd., Sonora* ☎ *209/533–4420 or 800/446–1333* ⊕ *www.thegreatunfenced.com*).

SACRAMENTO AND VICINITY

SACRAMENTO

Driving 87 mi northeast of San Francisco (I–80 to Highway 99 or I–5) brings you to the Golden State's seat of government and to echoes of the gold-rush days. Wooden sidewalks and horse-drawn carriages on cobblestone streets lend a 19th-century feel to Old Sacramento, a 28-acre district along the Sacramento River waterfront. The museums at the north end hold artifacts of state and national significance, and historic buildings house shops and restaurants. River cruises and train rides are fun family diversions for an hour or two.

The midtown area, just east of downtown between 15th Street and the Capital City Freeway, contains many of the city's best restaurants and trendy boutiques. Midtown is a vibrant mix of genteel Victorian edifices, ultramodern lofts, and—slowed when the recession hit—a rapidly growing number of innovative restaurants and cozy wine bars. It really springs to life the second Saturday evening of every month, when art galleries hold open houses and the sidewalks are packed. A couple of intersections are lively most evenings when the weather's good; they include the corner of 20th and L streets in what's known as Lavender

22

Heights, the center of the city's gay and lesbian community. Overall, midtown is a safe and interesting place in which to take a walk, and is the city's most interesting neighborhood.

Call the **Old Sacramento Events Hotline** (☏ *916/558–3912*) for information about living-history re-creations and merchant hours.

ESSENTIALS

Visitor Information Sacramento Convention and Visitors Bureau (✉ *1608 I St., Suite 600, Sacramento* ☏ *916/808–7777* ⊕ *www.sacramentocvb.org*).

EXPLORING

⑥ California Museum for History, Women, and the Arts. California's recent first lady, Maria Shriver, took an active role in having this museum stress women's issues. Though many exhibits use modern technology, there are also scores of archival drawers that you can pull out to see the real artifacts of history and culture—from the California State Constitution to surfing magazines. Board a 1949 cross-country bus to view a video on immigration, visit a Chinese herb shop maintained by a holographic proprietor, or find familiar names inducted into the annually expanded California Hall of Fame. There's also a café that's open weekdays until 2:30 PM. ✉ *1020 O St.* ☏ *916/653–7524* ⊕ *www.californiamuseum.org* 🎟 *$8.50* ⊙ *Mon.–Sat. 10–5, Sun. noon–5.*

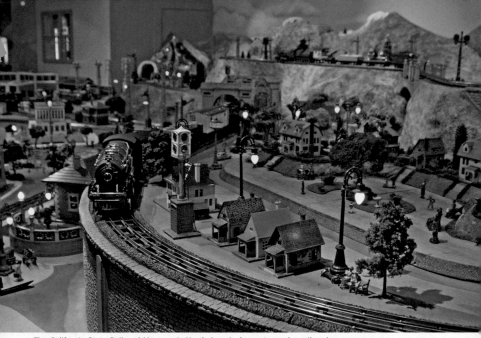

The California State Railroad Museum is North America's most popular railroad museum.

9 California State Indian Museum. Among the interesting displays at this well-organized museum a few strides from Sutter's Fort is one devoted to Ishi, the last Yahi Indian to emerge from the mountains, in 1911. Ishi provided scientists with insight into the traditions and culture of this group of Native Americans. Arts-and-crafts exhibits, a demonstration village, and an evocative 10-minute video bring to life the multi-faceted past and present of California's native peoples. ✉ *2618 K St.* ☎ *916/324-0971* ⊕ *www.parks.ca.gov* ✉ *$3* ⊘ *Daily 10–5.*

1 California State Railroad Museum. Near what was once the terminus of the transcontinental and Sacramento Valley railroads (the actual terminus **Fodor's Choice** was at Front and K streets), this 100,000-square-foot museum—the ★ best of its kind in the region, if not the country—has 21 locomotives and railroad cars on display along with dozens of other exhibits. You can walk through a post-office car and peer into cubbyholes and canvas mailbags, enter a sleeping car that simulates the swaying on the roadbed and the flashing lights of a passing town at night, or glimpse the inside of the first-class dining car. One thousand vintage toy trains constitute a much-heralded permanent exhibit, and the recently introduced "Lost Spike" is compelling. ✉ *125 I St.* ☎ *916/445-6645* ⊕ *www.csrmf.org* ✉ *$9* ⊘ *Daily 10–5.*

7 Capitol. The lacy plasterwork of the Capitol's 120-foot-high rotunda has ★ the complexity and colors of a Fabergé egg. Underneath the gilded dome are marble floors, glittering chandeliers, monumental staircases, repro-ductions of 19th-century state offices, and legislative chambers deco-rated in the style of the 1890s (the Capitol was built in 1869). Guides conduct tours of the building and the 40-acre Capitol Park, which contains a rose garden, an impressive display of camellias (Sacramento's city flower), and the California Vietnam Veterans Memorial. ⊠ *Capitol Mall and 10th St.* ☎ *916/324–0333* ⊕ *www.statecapitolmuseum.com* ⊠ *Free* ⊙ *Daily 9–5; tours hourly 10–4.*

22

❷ **Central Pacific Passenger Depot.** At this reconstructed 1876 station there's ♺ rolling stock to admire, a typical waiting room, and a small restaurant. A steam-powered train ($8) departs hourly on weekends April through September, and for special occasions October through December from the freight depot, south of the passenger depot, making a 40-minute out-and-back trip along the Sacramento riverfront. ⊠ *930 Front St.* ☎ *916/445–6645* ⊠ *$4, free with same-day ticket from California State Railroad Museum* ⊙ *Daily 10–4.*

❹ **Crocker Art Museum.** The oldest art museum in the American West has a collection of art from Europe, Asia, and California, including *Sunday Morning in the Mines* (1872), a large canvas by Charles Christian Nahl depicting aspects of the original mining industry, and the magnificent *Great Canyon of the Sierra, Yosemite* (1871), by Thomas Hill. Plans are underway to open a modern addition that will triple the facility's size. ⊠ *216 O St.* ☎ *916/264–5423* ⊕ *www.crockerartmuseum.org* ⊠ *$6, free Sun. 10–1* ⊙ *Tues.–Sun. 10–5, 1st and 3rd Thurs. 10–9.*

❽ **Governor's Mansion.** This 15-room house was built in 1877 and used ★ by the state's chief executives from the early 1900s until 1967, when Ronald Reagan vacated it in favor of a newly built home in the more upscale suburbs. Many of the Italianate mansion's interior decorations were ordered from the Huntington, Hopkins & Co. hardware store, one of whose partners, Albert Gallatin, was the original occupant. Each of the seven marble fireplaces has a petticoat mirror that ladies strolled past to see if their slips were showing. ⊠ *1526 H St.* ☎ *916/323–3047* ⊠ *$5* ⊙ *Daily 10–5; tours hourly, last tour at 4.*

QUICK BITES

The River City Brewing Co. (⊠ **Downtown Plaza** ☎ **916/447–2739**) is the best of several breweries that have cropped up in the capital city. The brewery is at the west end of the K Street Mall, between the Capitol and Old Sacramento.

❸ **Old Sacramento Visitor Information Center.** Find brochures about nearby attractions, check local restaurant menus, and get advice from the helpful staff here. ⊠ *1004 2nd St., at K St.* ☎ *916/442–7644* ⊕ *www. oldsacramento.com* ⊙ *Daily 10–5.*

❿ **Sutter's Fort.** German-born Swiss immigrant John Augustus Sutter ♺ founded Sacramento's earliest Euro–American settlement in 1839. ★ Audio speakers give information at each stop along a self-guided tour that includes a blacksmith's shop, bakery, prison, living quarters, and livestock areas. Costumed docents sometimes reenact fort life, demonstrating crafts, food preparation, and firearms maintenance. ⊠ *2701 L St.* ☎ *916/445–4422* ⊕ *www.parks.ca.gov* ⊠ *$5* ⊙ *Tues.–Sun. 10–5.*

❺ **Towe Auto Museum.** With more than 150 vintage automobiles on display, ♺ and exhibits ranging from the Hall of Technology to Dreams of Speed and Dreams of Cool, this museum explores automotive history and car culture. A 1920s roadside café and garage exhibit re-creates the early days of motoring. Friendly docents are ready to explain everything. The gift shop sells vintage-car magazines, model kits, and other car-related items. The museum is near downtown and Old Sacramento, with ample free parking. ⊠ *2200 Front St., 1 block off Broadway* ☎ *916/442–6802* ⊕ *www.toweautomuseum.org* ⊴ *$8* ☉ *Daily 10–6, Thurs. 10–9.*

WHERE TO EAT

$$–$$$ ✕ **Biba**. Owner Biba Caggiano is a nationally recognized authority on
ITALIAN Italian cuisine. The Capitol crowd flocks here for homemade ravioli,
Fodor'sChoice osso buco, grilled pork loin, and veal and rabbit specials. A pianist adds
★ to the upscale ambience nightly. ⊠ *2801 Capitol Ave.* ☎ *916/455–2422* ⊕ *www.biba-restaurant.com* ⊴ *Reservations essential* ⊟ *AE, DC, MC, V* ☉ *Closed Sun. No lunch Sat.*

¢–$ ✕ **Ernesto's Mexican Food**. Customers wait up to an hour for a table
MEXICAN on Friday and Saturday evenings at this popular midtown restaurant. Fresh ingredients are stressed in the wide selection of entrées, and the margaritas are especially refreshing. **Zocalo** (⊠ *1801 Capitol Ave.* ☎ *916/441–0303*), launched in 2004 by Ernesto's ownership, has a striking indoor-outdoor atmosphere and is a popular launching spot for nights out on the town. Its menu differs slightly from Ernesto's. ⊠ *16th and S Sts.* ☎ *916/441–5850* ⊕ *www.ernestosmexicanfood.com* ⊟ *AE, D, DC, MC, V.*

$$–$$$$ ✕ **The Firehouse**. Consistently ranked by local publications as one of the
CONTINENTAL city's top 10 restaurants, this formal and historic restaurant has a full
Fodor'sChoice bar, courtyard seating (its signature attraction), and creative American
★ cooking, such as char-grilled spring rack of lamb served with roasted French fingerling potatoes and baby artichoke and fava bean succotash. Visitors who can afford to treat themselves to a fine and leisurely meal can do no better in Old Sacramento, although competition is posed by the early 2010 debut of Ten 22, launched a block away by The Firehouse's owners. ⊠ *1112 2nd St.* ☎ *916/442–4772* ⊕ *www.firehouseoldsac.com* ⊟ *AE, MC, V* ☉ *No lunch Sat.*

$–$$$ ✕ **The Park Downtown**. Atmosphere is what it's all about at this complex
ECLECTIC of cutting-edge eateries across from Capitol Park. Ma Jong's Asian Diner has inexpensive fare, some suitable for vegetarians; the indoor-outdoor Park Lounge is a supermodern bar and dance club; and the Park To Go puts a classy spin on breakfasts and lunches for people to take away. ⊠ *1116 15th St.* ☎ *916/492–1960* ⊕ *www.theparkdowntown.com* ⊟ *AE, DC, MC, V.*

WHERE TO STAY

$$–$$$$ ⌂ **Amber House Bed & Breakfast Inn**. This B&B about a mile from the
★ Capitol encompasses two homes. The original house is a Craftsman-style home with five bedrooms, and the second is an 1897 Dutch colonial–revival home. Baths are tiled in Italian marble; some rooms have skylights, fireplaces, patios, and two-person spa tubs, or a combination of some of those features. Amber House's location has become increasingly desirable as its midtown neighborhood has blossomed with distinctive new shops and restaurants, many within 15-minutes' walking distance. **Pros:** midtown location; attentive service. **Cons:** no nearby freeway access. ⊠ *1315 22nd St.* ☎ *916/444–8085 or 800/755–6526*

⊕ *www.amberhouse.com* 🚫 *10 rooms* ♿ *In-room: a/c, Internet, Wi-Fi.*
⊟ *AE, D, DC, MC, V* ⏁ *BP.*

$$–$$$$ 🔲 **Citizen Hotel.** Billed as Sacramento's first luxury boutique hotel, the Citizen opened in 2008 downtown in the 1926 Cal Western Life building. Overnight it became a power hub for politicians, business leaders, and deep-pocketed tourists. Its Grange restaurant is attracting non-hotel guests, too, and winning praise from food critics. **Pros:** all the modern amenities with older-world charms; within easy walking distance of the Capitol and other downtown attractions. **Cons:** pricey; smallish bathrooms. ✉ *926 J St.* ☎ *916/447–2700* ⊕ *www.jdvhotels.com* 🚫 *175 rooms, 23 suites* ♿ *In-room: a/c. In-hotel: restaurant, room service, bar, gym, Wi-Fi hotspot* ⊟ *AE, D, DC, MC, V* ⏁ *BP.*

$$–$$$$ 🔲 **Hyatt Regency Sacramento.** With a marble-and-glass lobby and luxu-
★ rious rooms, this hotel across from the Capitol and adjacent to the convention center is arguably Sacramento's finest. The multitiered, glass-dominated hotel has a striking Mediterranean design. The best rooms have Capitol Park views. The service and attention to detail are outstanding. **Pros:** "important" people stay here (such as former Governor Schwarzenegger); beautiful Capitol Park is across the street. **Cons:** downtown streets can be dodgy at night; somewhat impersonal. ✉ *1209 L St.* ☎ *916/443–1234 or 800/633–7313* ⊕ *www.hyatt.com* 🚫 *500 rooms, 24 suites* ♿ *In-room: a/c. In-hotel: 2 restaurants, bar, pool, gym, laundry service, parking (paid)* ⊟ *AE, D, DC, MC, V.*

WOODLAND

20 mi northwest of Sacramento on I–5.

Woodland's downtown lies frozen in a quaint and genteel past. In its heyday it was one of the wealthiest cities in California, established in 1861 by gold seekers and entrepreneurs. Once the boom was over, attention turned to the rich surrounding land, and the area became an agricultural gold mine. The legacy of the old land barons lives on in the Victorian homes that line Woodland's wide streets. Many of the houses have been restored and are surrounded by lavish gardens.

ESSENTIALS

Visitor Information Woodland Chamber of Commerce (✉ *307 1st St., Woodland* ☎ *530/662–7327 or 888/843–2636* ⊕ *www.woodlandchamber.org*).

EXPLORING

More than 300 touring companies, including John Philip Sousa's marching band, and Frank Kirk, the Acrobatic Tramp, appeared at the **Woodland Opera House**, built in 1885 (and rebuilt after it burned in 1892). Now restored, the building is the site of concerts and, September through July, a season of musical theater. Free, guided tours reveal old-fashioned stage technology. ✉ *Main and 2nd Sts.* ☎ *530/666–9617* ⊕ *www.wohtheatre.org* ⊙ *Weekdays 10–5, weekends noon–5, tours Tues. noon–4.*

This 10-room classical-revival home of settler William Byas Gibson was purchased by volunteers and restored as the **Yolo County Historical Museum**. You can see collections of furnishings and artifacts from the

1850s to 1930s. Old trees and an impressive lawn cover the 2½-acre site off Highway 113. ✉ *512 Gibson Rd.* ☎ *530/666–1045* ⊕ *www.yolo. net/ychm/index.html* ▣ *Free* ☉ *Mon. and Tues. 10–4, Sat. noon–4.*

☙ Old trucks and farm machinery seem to rumble to life within the shed-like **Heidrick Ag History Center,** where you can see the world's largest collection of antique agricultural equipment. Also here are multimedia exhibits and a gift shop. ✉ *1962 Hays La.* ☎ *530/666–9700* ⊕ *www. aghistory.org* ▣ *$7* ☉ *Weekdays 10–5, Sat. 10–6, Sun. 10–4.*

DAVIS

10 mi west of Sacramento on I–80.

Though it began as—and still is—a rich agricultural area, Davis doesn't feel like a cow town. It's home to the University of California at Davis, whose students hang at the cafés and bookstores in the central business district, making the city feel a little more cosmopolitan. Downtown is compact and walkable; bicyclists are everywhere (and are treated with respect by drivers) throughout town. The city has long enjoyed a progressive, liberal reputation (it's been called "the People's Republic of Davis"), but a rash of 1990s-built yuppie-stocked subdivisions reflect how Davis is becoming more of a mainstream commuter community, whether residents admit it or not.

ESSENTIALS
Visitor Information Davis Chamber of Commerce (✉ *130 G St., Davis* ☎ *530/756–5160* ⊕ *www.davischamber.com*).

EXPLORING
The center of action in town is the **Davis Campus of the University of California,** which often ranks among the top 25 research universities in the United States. You can take tours of the campus, which depart from Buehler Alumni and Visitors Center. The **Mondavi Center for the Performing Arts,** a strikingly modern glass structure off I–80, offers a busy and varied schedule of performances by top-tier musical, dance and other artists. ✉ *1 Shields Ave.* ☎ *530/752–8111* ⊕ *www.ucdavis. edu* ☉ *Tours weekends at 11:30, weekdays by appointment.*

THE GOLD COUNTRY—SOUTH

PLACERVILLE

10 mi south of Coloma on Hwy. 49; 44 mi east of Sacramento on U.S. 50.

It's hard to imagine now, but in 1849 about 4,000 miners staked out every gully and hillside in Placerville, turning the town into a rip-roaring camp of log cabins, tents, and clapboard houses. The area was then known as Hangtown, a graphic allusion to the nature of frontier justice. It took on the name Placerville in 1854 and became an important supply center for the miners. Mark Hopkins, Philip Armour, and John Studebaker were among the industrialists who got their starts here.

EXPLORING

☺ **Hangtown's Gold Bug Park & Mine,** owned by the City of Placerville, centers
★ on a fully lighted mine shaft open for self-guided touring. ■**TIP→** The
self-guided audio tour is well worth the expense ($1). A shaded stream
runs through the park, and there are picnic facilities. ⊠ *North on Bedford Ave., 1 mi off U.S. 50* ☎ *530/642–5207* ⊕ *www.goldbugpark.org*
☜ *$4* ☉ *Tours mid-Apr.–Oct., daily 10–4; Nov.–mid-Apr., weekends
noon–4. Gift shop Mar.–Nov., daily 10–4.*

WHERE TO EAT AND STAY

¢ ✕**The Cozmic Cafe.** Crowds convene here at any time of day for healthful
VEGETARIAN wraps, burritos, sandwiches, salads, and the like, plus breakfasts (served
★ anytime), smoothies, and coffee drinks; vegetarians are well served here.
The portions are big, prices are low, and the ambience is among the
most distinctive in Placerville. The eatery is in the 1859 Pearson's Soda
Works Building, and extends back into the side of a mountain, into
what used to be a mineshaft. Live music here is among the best in the
foothills, and an upstairs pub beckons with local wines and microbrews;
unwind with yoga classes there before the evening's libations. ⊠ *594
Main St.* ☎ *530/642–8481* ⊕ *www.ourcoz.com* ⊟ *MC, V.*

$–$$ ⌂ **Seasons Bed & Breakfast.** A 10-minute walk from downtown, one
of Placerville's oldest homes has been transformed into a lovely and
relaxing oasis. The main house, cottages, and gardens are filled with
paintings and sculptures. Privacy is treasured here. A suite with a sitting
room and stained-glass windows occupies the main house's top floor.
One cottage has a little white-picket fence around its own mini-garden;
another has a two-person shower. **Pros:** quiet setting; attentive hosts;
great breakfasts. **Cons:** B&B environment not for everyone. ⊠ *2934
Bedford Ave.* ☎ *530/626–4420* ⊕ *www.theseasons.net* ☜ *4 rooms, 1
suite* ⟁ *In-room: a/c.* ⊟ *MC, V* ⦵ *BP.*

SHENANDOAH VALLEY

20 mi south of Placerville on Shenandoah Rd., east of Hwy. 49.

The most concentrated Gold Country wine-touring area lies in the hills
of the Shenandoah Valley, east of Plymouth. ■**TIP→** This region is gaining steam as a less-congested alternative to overrun Napa Valley. Robust
zinfandel is the primary grape grown here, but vineyards also produce
other varietals. Most wineries are open on weekend afternoons; several
have shaded picnic areas, gift shops, and galleries or museums; all have
tasting rooms.

EXPLORING

At **Charles Spinetta Winery** (⊠ *12557 Steiner Rd., Plymouth* ☎ *209/245–
3384* ⊕ *www.charlesspinettawinery.com* ☉ *Mon., Thurs., and Fri. 8–4,
weekends 9–5*), you can see a wildlife art gallery in addition to tasting
the wine.

The gallery at the Sobon-affiliated **Shenandoah Vineyards** (⊠ *12300 Steiner
Rd., Plymouth* ☎ *209/245–4455* ⊕ *www.sobonwine.com* ☉ *Daily 10–5*)
displays contemporary art, and sells pottery, framed photographs, and
souvenirs.

Sobon Estate (✉ *14430 Shenandoah Rd., Plymouth* ☎ *209/245–6554* ⊕ *www.sobonwine.com* ⊙ *Daily, 9:30–5*) operates the Shenandoah Valley Museum, illustrating pioneer life and wine-making in the valley.

AMADOR CITY

6 mi south of Plymouth on Hwy. 49.

The history of tiny Amador City mirrors the boom-bust-boom cycle of many Gold Country towns. With an output of $42 million in gold, its Keystone Mine was one of the most productive in the Mother Lode. After all the gold was extracted, the miners cleared out, and the area suffered. Amador City now derives its wealth from tourists, who come to browse through its antiques and specialty shops, most of them on or just off Highway 49.

WHERE TO STAY

$–$$$

AMERICAN

★

⚏ **Imperial Hotel.** The whimsically decorated mock-Victorian rooms at this 1879 hotel give a modern twist to the excesses of the era. Antique furnishings include iron-and-brass beds, gingerbread flourishes, and, in one room, art-deco appointments. The two front rooms, which can be noisy, have balconies. The menu at the hotel's fine restaurant ($$–$$$$) changes quarterly and ranges from country hearty to contemporary eclectic. The Imperial recently added a hilltop cottage with three suites; prices are higher, but good views, lower noise levels, and Jacuzzis help compensate. **Pros:** comfortable; good restaurant and bar; small-town charm. **Cons:** lots of noise from bordering Highway 49. ✉ *Hwy. 49,* ☎ *209/267–9172* ⊕ *www.imperialamador.com* ⇆ *6 rooms, 3 suites* ☖ *In-room: no phone, a/c, no TV. In-hotel: restaurant, bar* ⊟ *AE, MC, V* ❢⃝❙*BP.*

SUTTER CREEK

★ *2 mi south of Amador City on Hwy. 49.*

Sutter Creek is a charming conglomeration of balconied buildings, Victorian homes, and neo–New England structures. The stores on Main Street (formerly part of busy Highway 49, which thankfully has been rerouted around town) are worth visiting for works by the many local artists and craftspeople.

EXPLORING

Seek out the **Monteverde Store Museum** (✉ *3 Randolph St.*), a typical turn-of-the-20th-century emporium with vintage goods on display (but not for sale), an elaborate antique scale, and a chair-encircled potbellied stove in the corner. The store is open Thursday–Monday provided there are volunteers available. The **Sutter Creek Visitor Center** (✉ *11A Randolph St.* ☎ *209/267–1344 or 800/400–0305* ⊕ *www.suttercreek. org*) has similar hours and a helpful Web site.

WHERE TO EAT AND STAY

$$–$$$$

AMERICAN

✕ **Caffe Via d'Oro.** Tables can be hard to secure at this upscale restaurant, where short ribs, grilled duck breast, and pan-seared rainbow trout—all accompanied by seasonal vegetables—are highly recommended by the

Continued on page 840

EUREKA! CALIFORNIA'S GOLD RUSH

When James W. Marshall burst into John Sutter's Mill on January 24, 1848, carrying flecks of gold in his hat, the millwright unleashed the glittering California gold rush with these immortal words:

 "Boys, I believe I've found a gold mine!"

Before it was over, drowsy San Francisco had become the boomtown of the Golden West, Columbia's mines alone yielded $87,000,000, and California's Mother Lode—a vein of gold-bearing quartz that stretched 150 miles across the Sierra Nevada foothills—had been nearly tapped dry. Even though the gold rush soon became the gold bust, today you can still strike it rich by visiting the historic sites where it all happened.

Journey down the Gold Country Highway—a serpentine, nearly 300-mi-long two-lane route appropriately numbered 49—to find pure vacation treasure: fascinating mother lode towns, rip-roaring mining camps, and historic strike sites. In fact, in Placerville—as the former Hangtown, this spot saw so much new money and crime that outlaws were hanged in pairs—you can still pan the streams. And after you've seen the sights, the prospects remain just as golden: the entire region is a trove of gorgeous wineries, fun eateries, and Victorian-era hotels.

by: Reed Parsell and Robert I.C. Fisher

ALL THAT GLITTERED: '49ER FEVER

From imagination springs adventure, and perhaps no event in the 19th century provoked more wild adventures than the California gold rush of 1848 to 1855.

James Marshall · 1856 U.S. quarter · John Sutter

GOLD IN THEM THAR HILLS California's golden lava was discovered purely by accident. Upon finding his cattle ranch had gone to ruin while he was away fighting in the Mexican-American War, New Jersey native James W. Marshall decided to build a sawmill, with John Sutter, outside the town of Coloma, 40 miles upstream of Sutter's Fort on the American River. To better power the mill, he had a wider siphon created to divert the river water and, one morning, spotted golden flakes in the trench. Rich fur magnate Sutter tried to keep the mother strike quiet, but his own staff soon decamped to pan the streams and the secret was out. The gold rush's impact was so profound that, practically overnight, it catapulted San Francisco into one of the nation's—and the world's—wealthiest cities.

BROTHER, CAN YOU SPARE AN INGOT? After John Marshall, 37 at the time, saw his fledgling sawmill abandoned by workers who went to pan the streams, he left Coloma for almost a decade. During the 1860s he made some money as a vintner there—a dicey profession for a reported alcoholic. Eventually Marshall's wine business dried up, and he returned to prospecting, co-owning a gold mine in Kesley (near Coloma) in the 1870s. Before long, that venture failed, too. For six years starting in 1872, the state Legislature gave him a small pen-

sion as an acknowledgment of his gold rush importance, but for the last years of his life he was practically penniless. He died on Aug. 10, 1885, at age 74.

THE GOLD CRUSH Before the gold rush ended, in 1855, it is estimated that it drew 300,000 people—Americans, Europeans, and Chinese—to the Sierra Nevada foothills to seek their fortune. Sadly, accidents, disease, and skirmishes with Indians took their toll. In addition, the gold lust of '49er fever left more than a thousand murders in its wake (not counting the infamous "suspended" sentences meted out at Hangtown).

BOOM TO BUST

Jan. 24, 1848: James W. Marshall spies specks of bright rock in the streambed at his sawmill's site; Sutter certifies they are gold.
May, 1848: California's coastal communities empty out as prospectors flock to the hills to join the "forty-eighters."
Aug. 19, 1848: The *New York Herald* is the first East Coast newspaper to report a gold rush in California.
Oct. 13, 1849: California's state constitution is approved in Monterey. The state's new motto becomes "Eureka!"
1855: The California gold rush effectively ends, as digging for the precious mineral becomes increasingly difficult, and large corporations monopolize mining operations.

DID YOU KNOW?

You can still pan the streams, but any shiny stuff will usually be worthless iron pyrite. Here a young prospector tries his hand at Marshall Gold Discovery State Park.

GOING FOR THE GOLD

Marshall Gold Discovery State Park

If you want to go prospecting for the best sightseeing treasures in Gold Country, just follow this map.

Coloma

Empire Mine State Historic Park, Grass Valley: During the century that it was operating, Empire Mine produced some 5.6 million ounces of gold. More than 350 miles of tunnels were dug, most under water. Operations ceased in 1956, but today visitors to the 800-acre park can go on 50-minute guided tours of the mines and enjoy great hiking trails and picnic spots.

Marshall Gold Discovery State Historic Park, Coloma: Here's where it all began—a can't-miss gold rush site. See the stone cairn that marks the spot of James Marshall's discovery, the huge statue of him that rests on his grave site, and visit—together with crowds of schoolchildren—the updated museum, and more.

Hangtown's Gold Bug Park & Mine, Placerville: Put on a hardhat and step into the 19th century at Gold Bug, located a few miles south of Marshall's jackpot site. Take a self-guided audio tour of a mine that opened in 1888, or a special tour of a mine opened in the 1850s, and do some "placering" (panning for gold) yourself, outside the gift shop. "Fool's gold" (used for billiard tables and chalkboards) was mostly found here before digging stopped in 1942.

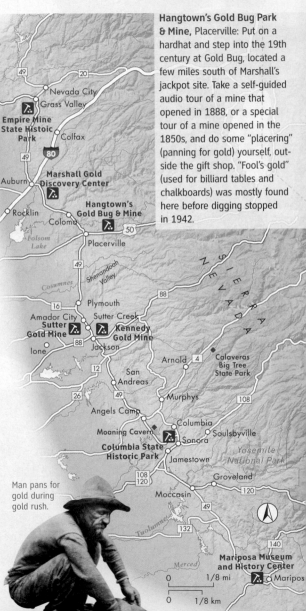

Man pans for gold during gold rush.

Sutter Gold Mine: Between Amador City and Sutter Creek off Highway 49, this is the place to see how the so-called "Forty-Niner" individual prospectors were succeeded by large, deep-pocket mining companies. One-hour tours, offered daily April through most of October, take visitors deep into a hard-rock mine, where they can see ore veins that contain gold and learn the basics of hydraulic extraction.

Kennedy Gold Mine, Jackson: At 5,912 feet below ground, this is one of the world's deepest mines. Its head frame is one of the most dominant man made sights along Highway 49's 295 miles. In operation from 1880 until World War II, the mine produced tens of millions of dollars of gold. One-hour tours, offered weekends and holidays from March through October, include a look inside the stately Mine Office.

Columbia State Historic Park. Just north of Sonora, this is the best extant example of a gold rush-era town as it appeared in the mid-19th century. During its "golden" years, Columbia yielded more than $85 million in gold. Since World War II, the town has been restored. Fandango halls, Wells Fargo stage coaches, and a costumed staff bring a working 1850's mining town to life again.

Gold dollars

Mariposa Museum and History Center, Mariposa: Find all sorts of mining equipment, including a five-stamp ore mill, at this modest museum in the gold rush region's southernmost area. Also here is the fascinating California State Mining and Mineral Museum, home to a famous 13-pound golden nugget.

A PROSPECTING PRIMER

Grab any non-Teflon-coated pan with sloping sides and head up to "them thar hills." Find a stream—preferably one containing black sand—you can stoop beside, and then:

■ Scoop out sediment to fill your pan.

■ Add water, then gently shake the pan sideways, back and forth. This allows any gold to settle at the bottom.

■ Pick out and toss away any larger rocks.

■ Keep adding water, keep shaking the pan, and slowly pour the loosened waste gravel over the rim of the pan, making sure not to upend the pan while doing so.

■ If you're left with gold, yell "Eureka!" then put it in a glass container. Your findings may not make you rich, but will entitle you to bragging rights for as long as you keep the gold handy to show friends.

■ TIP➔ If you'd rather not pan on your own, plenty of attractions and museums in the Gold Country will let you try your hand at prospecting. See listings in this chapter for more details on these historic sites.

loyal local patrons. The brick structure dates from the 1860s. ⊠ *36 Main St.* ☎ *209/267–0535* ⊕ *www. caffeviadoro.com* ☰ *AE, D, MC, V* ⊘ *Closed Mon. and Tues.*

$$ ⛱ **Eureka Street Inn.** Original redwood
★ paneling, wainscoting, beams, and cabinets as well as lead- and stained-glass windows lend the Eureka Street Inn a certain coziness. The Craftsman-style bungalow was built in 1914 as a family home. Most rooms have gas-log fireplaces, and wireless Internet is available. **Pros:** quiet location; lovely porch; engaging owners. **Cons:** only four rooms. ⊠ *55 Eureka St.,* ☎ *209/267–5500 or 800/399–2389* ⊕ *www.eurekastreetinn.com* ⤴ *4 rooms* ⚷ *In-room: a/c, no TV, Wi-Fi* ☰ *AE, D, MC, V* ⍾ *BP.*

APPLE HILL

The **Apple Hill** roadside stand sells fresh produce from more than 50 family farms in this area. During the fall harvest season (from September through December), members of the Apple Hill Growers Association open their orchards and vineyards for apple and berry picking, picnicking, and wine and cider tasting. Many sell baked items and picnic food. ⊠ *About 5 mi east of Hwy. 49; take Camino exit from U.S. 50* ☎ *530/644–7692.*

$$–$$$$ ⛱ **The Foxes Inn of Sutter Creek.** The rooms in this 1857 white-clapboard
★ house are handsome, with high ceilings, antique beds, and armoires. Five have gas fireplaces. Breakfast is cooked to order and delivered on a silver service to your room or to the gazebo in the garden. **Pros:** lovely inside and out; friendly owners. **Cons:** pricey; distracting road noise. ⊠ *77 Main St.* ☎ *209/267–5882 or 800/987–3344* ⊕ *www.foxesinn. com* ⤴ *5 rooms, 2 suites* ⚷ *In-room: a/c, DVD, Wi-Fi (some).* ☰ *AE, D, MC, V* ⍾ *BP.*

$$–$$$ ⛱ **Grey Gables Inn.** Charming yet modern, this inn brings a touch of the English countryside to the Gold Country. The rooms, named after British poets, have gas-log fireplaces. Afternoon tea and evening refreshments are served in the parlor; birds flit about the wisteria in the terraced garden. **Pros:** distinctively English feel, tasteful interiors. **Cons:** hovers over the main road, not much to do in town after dark. ⊠ *161 Hanford St.* ☎ *209/267–1039 or 800/473–9422* ⊕ *www.greygables. com* ⤴ *8 rooms* ☰ *MC, V* ⍾ *BP.*

JACKSON

8 mi south of Sutter Creek on Hwy. 49.

Jackson wasn't the Gold Country's rowdiest town, but the party lasted longer here than most anywhere else: "girls' dormitories" (brothels) and nickel slot machines flourished until the mid-1950s. Jackson also had the world's deepest and richest gold mines, the Kennedy and the Argonaut, which together produced $70 million in gold. These were deep-rock mines with tunnels extending as much as a mile underground. Most of the miners who worked the lode were of Serbian or Italian origin, and they gave the town a European character that persists to this day. Jackson has pioneer cemeteries whose headstones tell the stories of local Serbian and Italian families.

22

EXPLORING

The terraced cemetery on the grounds of the handsome **St. Sava Serbian Orthodox Church** (⊠ 724 N. Main St.) is the town's most impressive burial grounds.

The heart of Jackson's historic section is the **National Hotel** (⊠ 2 Water St. ☎ 209/233–0500), which operates an old-time saloon in the lobby. The hotel is especially active on weekends, when people come from miles around to participate in Saturday-night sing-alongs.

The **Amador County Museum**, built in the late 1850s as a private home, provides a colorful take on gold-rush life. Displays include a kitchen with a woodstove, the Amador County bicentennial quilt, and a classroom. A time line recounts the county's checkered past. The museum conducts hourly tours of large-scale working models of the nearby Kennedy Mine. ⊠ 225 Church St. ☎ 209/223–6386 ☛ Museum free; mine tours $1 ☉ Wed.–Sun. 10–4.

WHERE TO EAT

¢–$ ✕**Mel and Faye's Diner**. For more than a half-century Mel and Faye's has
AMERICAN been a local hangout, with its signature "Moo Burger" (so big it still makes cow sounds, presumably). Mel and Faye's son now runs the business and has supplemented the menu with slightly more sophisticated fare for breakfast, lunch, and dinner. ⊠ 31 Main St. ☎ 209/223–0853 ☱ MC, V ☉ Closed Tues. No dinner.

ANGELS CAMP

20 mi south of Jackson on Hwy. 49.

Angels Camp is famed chiefly for its May jumping-frog contest, based on Mark Twain's short story "The Celebrated Jumping Frog of Calaveras County." The writer reputedly heard the story of the jumping frog from Ross Coon, proprietor of Angels Hotel, which has been in operation since 1856.

EXPLORING

Angels Camp Museum houses gold-rush relics, including photos, rocks, petrified wood, old blacksmith and mining equipment, and a horse-drawn hearse. The carriage house out back holds 31 carriages and an impressive display of mineral specimens. ⊠ 753 S. Main St. ☎ 209/736–2963 ☱ $2 ☉ Jan. and Feb., weekends 10–3; Mar.–Dec., daily 10–3.

☺ **California Cavern**. A ½-mi subterranean trail winds through large chambers and past underground streams and lakes. There aren't many steps to climb, but it's a strenuous walk with some narrow passageways and steep spots. The caverns, at a constant 53°F, contain crystalline formations not found elsewhere, and the 80-minute guided tour explains local history and geology. ⊠ 9 mi east of San Andreas on Mountain Ranch Rd., then about 3 mi on Cave City Rd., follow signs ☎ 209/736–2708 ⊕ www.caverntours.com ☱ $14.25 ☉ May–Oct., daily 10–5; Nov.–Apr., weekdays 11–4, weekends 10–4.

☺ **Moaning Cavern**. A 235-step spiral staircase leads into this vast cav-
Fodor'sChoice ern. More adventurous sorts can rappel into the chamber—ropes and
★ instruction are provided. Otherwise, the only way inside is via the

45-minute tour, during which you'll see giant (and still growing) stalactites and stalagmites and an archaeological site that holds some of the oldest human remains yet found in America (an unlucky person has fallen into the cavern about once every 130 years for the last 13,000 years). ⊠ *5350 Moaning Cave Rd., off Parrots Ferry Rd., about 2 mi south of Vallecito* ☎ *209/736–2708* ⊕ *www.caverntours.com* ☑ *$14.25* ⊙ *May–Oct., daily 9–6; Nov.–Apr., weekdays 10–5, weekends 9–5.*

MURPHYS

10 mi northeast of Angels Camp on Hwy. 4.

Murphys is a well-preserved town of white-picket fences, Victorian houses, and interesting shops that exhibits an upscale vibe, with its nearby wineries and free-spending Bay Area visitors. Horatio Alger and Ulysses S. Grant came through here, staying at Murphys Historic Hotel & Lodge when they, along with many other 19th-century tourists, came to see the giant sequoia groves in nearby Calaveras Big Trees State Park.

EXPLORING

Ironstone Vineyards. ■TIP➔ Worth a visit even if you don't drink wine. Tours take you through the spectacular gardens and into underground tunnels cooled by a waterfall from a natural spring, and include a performance on a massive automated pipe organ. The winery schedules concerts during summer in its huge outdoor amphitheater, plus art shows and other events on weekends. On display is a 44-pound specimen of crystalline gold. Visit the deli for lunch. ⊠ *1894 6 Mile Rd.* ☎ *209/728–1251* ⊕ *www.ironstonevineyards.com* ⊙ *Daily 10–5; open until 6 in summer.*

WHERE TO EAT AND STAY

$$-$$$
AMERICAN

✕**Grounds.** Light entrées, grilled vegetables, chicken, seafood, and steak are the specialties at this bistro and coffee shop. Sandwiches, salads, and homemade soups are served for lunch. The crowd is friendly and the service attentive. ⊠ *402 Main St.* ☎ *209/728–8663* ▤ *MC, V.*

¢–$$

⊡**Murphys Historic Hotel & Lodge.** This 1855 stone hotel, whose register has seen the signatures of Mark Twain and the bandit Black Bart, figured in Bret Harte's short story "A Night at Wingdam." Accommodations are in the hotel and a modern motel-style addition. The older rooms are furnished with antiques, many of them large and hand carved. The hotel has a convivial old-time restaurant ($–$$$)

CALAVERAS BIG TREE STATE PARK

The **Calaveras Big Tree State Park** protects hundreds of the largest and rarest living things on the planet—magnificent giant sequoia redwood trees. Some are 3,000 years old, 90 feet around at the base, and 250 feet tall. There are campgrounds and picnic areas; swimming, wading, fishing, and sunbathing on the Stanislaus River are popular in summer. ⊠ *Off Hwy. 4, 15 mi northeast of Murphys, 4 mi northeast of Arnold* ☎ *209/795-2334* ☑ *$6 per vehicle, day use; campsites $20* ⊙ *Park daily sunrise–sunset, day use; visitor center May–Oct., daily 11–3; Nov.–Apr., weekends 11–3.*

and dark saloon, which can be noisy into the wee hours. **Pros:** loads of historical ambience; great bar; smack in the middle of downtown. **Cons:** dated; creaky. ⊠ *457 Main St.* ☎ *209/728–3444 or 800/532– 7684* ⊕ *www.murphyshotel.com* ⇆ *29 rooms, 20 with bath* ⚫ *In-room: a/c. In-hotel: restaurant, bar* ☰ *AE, D, DC, MC, V.*

COLUMBIA

14 mi south of Angels Camp via Hwy. 49 to Parrots Ferry Rd.

Columbia is the gateway for Columbia State Historic Park, which is one of the Gold Country's most visited sites.

EXPLORING

Ⓒ **Columbia State Historic Park,** known as the Gem of the Southern Mines,
Fodor's Choice comes as close to a gold-rush town in its heyday as any site in the
★ Gold Country. You can ride a stagecoach, pan for gold, and watch a blacksmith working at an anvil. Street musicians perform in summer. Restored or reconstructed buildings include a Wells Fargo Express office, a Masonic temple, stores, saloons, two hotels, a firehouse, churches, a school, and a newspaper office. At times, all are staffed to simulate a working 1850s town. The park also includes the **Historic Fallon House Theater,** where a full schedule of entertainment is presented. ⊠ *11175 Washington St.* ☎ *209/532–0150* ⊕ *www.parks.ca.gov* ▣ *Free* ⊙ *Daily 9–5.*

SONORA

4 mi south of Columbia via Parrots Ferry Rd. to Hwy. 49.

Miners from Mexico founded Sonora and made it the biggest town in the Mother Lode. Following a period of racial and ethnic strife, the Mexican settlers moved on, and Yankees built the commercial city that is visible today. Sonora's historic downtown section sits atop the Big Bonanza Mine, one of the richest in the state. Another mine, on the site of nearby Sonora High School, yielded 990 pounds of gold in a single week in 1879. Reminders of the gold rush are everywhere in Sonora, in prim Victorian houses, typical Sierra-stone storefronts, and awning-shaded sidewalks. Reality intrudes beyond the town's historic heart, with strip malls, shopping centers, and modern motels. Downtown gridlock on Highway 49 is unlikely to ease until gas prices get much, much higher.

EXPLORING

The **Tuolumne County Museum and History Center** occupies a gold rush–era building that served as a jail until 1951. Listed on the National Register of Historic Places, it houses a museum with vintage firearms and paraphernalia, a case with gold specimens, a cute exhibit on soapbox derby racing in hilly Sonora, and the historical society's and genealogical society's libraries. ⊠ *158 W. Bradford St.* ☎ *209/532–1317* ⊕ *www. tchistory.org* ▣ *Free* ⊙ *Daily 10–4.*

WHERE TO EAT AND STAY

¢ ✗ **Garcia's Taqueria.** This casual,
MEXICAN inexpensive eatery—named for and decorated in the spirit of Grateful Dead legend Jerry Garcia—serves Mexican and Southwestern fare. Vegetarians and vegans are well served here. ✉ *145 S. Washington St.* ☎ *209/588–1915* ▭ *No credit cards* ☾ *Closed Sun.*

$–$$$ ▦ **Barretta Gardens Bed and Breakfast Inn.** This inn is perfect for a romantic getaway. Its elegant Victorian rooms vary in size, but all are furnished with period pieces. The three antique filled parlors carry on the Victorian theme. The breakfast porch overlooks a fountain and mature gardens. **Pros:** lovely grounds; yummy breakfasts; romantic. **Cons:** only five rooms. ✉ *700 S. Barretta St.* ☎ *209/532–6039 or 800/206–3333* ⊕ *www.barrettagardens.com* ✍ *5 rooms* ▭ *AE, MC, V* ▯◉▯ *CP.*

A LIVING BACKDROP

If the countryside surrounding Sonora seems familiar, that's because It has been the backdrop for many movies over the years. Scenes from *High Noon*, *For Whom the Bell Tolls*, *The Virginian*, *Back to the Future III*, and *Unforgiven* were filmed here.

22

JAMESTOWN

4 mi south of Sonora on Hwy. 49.

Compact Jamestown supplies a touristy, superficial view of gold rush–era life. Shops in brightly colored buildings along Main Street sell antiques and gift items.

EXPLORING

☘ **Railtown 1897** preserves what were the headquarters and general shops of the Sierra Railway from 1897 to 1955. The railroad has appeared in more than 200 movies and television productions, including *Petticoat Junction*, *The Virginian*, *High Noon*, and *Unforgiven*. You can view the roundhouse, an air-operated 60-foot turntable, shop rooms, and old locomotives and coaches. Six-mile, 40-minute steam train rides through the countryside operate weekends in warm months and on some holiday weekends. ✉ *5th Ave. and Reservoir Rd., off Hwy. 49* ☎ *209/984–3953* ⊕ *www.railtown1897.org* ✍ *Roundhouse tour $5; train ride $8* ☾ *Apr.–Oct., daily 9:30–4:30; Nov.–Mar., daily 10–3. Train rides Apr.–Oct., weekends 11–3.*

WHERE TO STAY

$$ ▦ **National Hotel.** The National has been in business since 1859, and the furnishings—brass beds, regal comforters, and lace curtains—are authentic but not overly embellished. The saloon, which still has its original redwood bar, is a great place to linger. The popular restaurant ($–$$$) serves special sandwiches and a variety of salads and pastas for lunch. Dinners feature more upscale Continental cuisine (reservations essential). **Pros:** wonderful historic feel; great brunches—especially the crepes. **Cons:** only nine rooms. ✉ *18183 Main St.* ☎ *209/984–3446, 800/894–3446 in CA* ⊕ *www.national-hotel.com* ✍ *9 rooms* ♨ *In-room: a/c, Internet. In-hotel: restaurant, bar, Wi-Fi hotspot* ▭ *AE, D, DC, MC, V* ▯◉▯ *CP.*

MARIPOSA

50 mi south of Jamestown on Hwy. 49.

Mariposa marks the southern end of the Mother Lode. Much of the land in this area was part of a 44,000-acre land grant Colonel John C. Fremont acquired from Mexico before gold was discovered and California became a state.

EXPLORING

At the **California State Mining and Mineral Museum,** a glittering 13-pound chunk of crystallized gold makes it clear what the rush was about. Displays include a reproduction of a typical tunnel dug by hard-rock miners, a miniature stamp mill, and a panning and sluicing exhibit. ⊠ *Mariposa County Fairgrounds, Hwy. 49* ☎ *209/742–7625* ⌨ *$3* ⊙ *May–Sept., daily 10–6; Oct.–Apr., Wed.–Mon. 10–4.*

WHERE TO EAT AND STAY

$$–$$$$ ✕ **Charles Street Dinner House.** Ever since Ed Uebner moved here from
AMERICAN   Chicago to become the owner-chef in 1980, Charles Street has been firmly established as the classiest dinner joint in town—plus, it's centrally located. The extensive menu includes beef, chicken, pork, lamb, duck, and lobster; recently a few vegetarian options were added. ⊠ *Hwy. 140, at 7th St.* ☎ *209/966–2366* ⊕ *www.charlesstreetdinnerhouse.com* ⊟ *D, MC, V* ⊙ *No lunch.*

$–$$ ⊡ **Little Valley Inn.** Historical photos and old mining tools recall Mariposa's heritage at this modern B&B. A suite that sleeps five people includes a full kitchen. All rooms have private entrances, baths, and decks. The large grounds include a creek where you can pan for gold. **Pros:** quiet; comfortable; about halfway between Yosemite's western entrances. **Cons:** still about 40 minutes outside the park. ⊠ *3483 Brooks Rd., off Hwy. 49* ☎ *209/742–6204 or 800/889–5444* ⊕ *www.littlevalley. com* ⥺ *4 rooms, 1 suite, 1 cabin* ⚲ *In-room: a/c, refrigerator.* ⊟ *AE, MC, V* ⎮⦿⎮ *BP.*

THE GOLD COUNTRY—NORTH

COLOMA

8 mi northwest of Placerville on Hwy. 49.

The California gold rush started in Coloma. "My eye was caught with the glimpse of something shining in the bottom of the ditch," James Marshall recalled. Marshall himself never found any more "color," as gold came to be called.

EXPLORING

♺   Most of Coloma lies within **Marshall Gold Discovery State Historic Park.**
★   Though crowded with tourists in summer, Coloma hardly resembles the mob scene it was in 1849, when 2,000 prospectors staked out claims along the streambed. The town's population grew to 4,000, supporting seven hotels, three banks, and many stores and businesses. But when reserves of the precious metal dwindled, prospectors left as quickly as they had come. A working reproduction of an 1840s mill lies near the

spot where James Marshall first saw gold. A trail leads to a sign marking his discovery. ■**TIP➔ The museum is not as interesting as the outdoor exhibits.** ⊠ *Hwy. 49* ☎ *530/622–3470* ⊕ *www.parks.ca.gov* ⤸ *$5 per vehicle, day use* ⊙ *Park daily 8–sunset. Museum daily 10–3.*

WHERE TO STAY

$$–$$$ 🏠 **Coloma Country Inn.** Four of the rooms at this B&B on 2½ acres in the state historic park are inside an 1850s farmhouse (extensively updated in 2007). Two suites with kitchenettes are in the carriage house. Appointments include charming decor, private bathrooms, and welcoming grounds. At breakfast, the owners can direct you to tour operators leading rafting trips on the American River. **Pros:** couldn't be more convenient to the park, quiet and leisurely ambience. **Cons:** expensive, some complaints of deteriorating decor. ⊠ *345 High St.* ☎ *530/622–6919* ⊕ *www.colomacountryinn.com* ⤸ *4 rooms, 2 suites* ⚹ *In-room: a/c, kitchen, Wi-Fi* ☰ *MC, V* ⊙| *BP.*

AUBURN

18 mi northwest of Coloma on Hwy. 49; 34 mi northeast of Sacramento on I–80.

Auburn is the Gold Country town most accessible to travelers on I–80. An important transportation center during the gold rush, Auburn has a small Old Town district with narrow climbing streets, cobblestone lanes, wooden sidewalks, and many original buildings. ■**TIP➔ Fresh produce, flowers, baked goods, and gifts are for sale at the farmers' market, held Saturday morning year-round.**

EXPLORING

Auburn's standout structure is the **Placer County Courthouse**. The classic gold-dome building houses the Placer County Museum, which documents the area's history—Native American, railroad, agricultural, and mining—from the early 1700s to 1900. ⊠ *101 Maple St.* ☎ *530/889–6500* ⤸ *Free* ⊙ *Daily 10–4.*

The **Bernhard Museum Complex**, whose centerpiece is the former Traveler's Rest Hotel, was built in 1851. A residence and adjacent winery buildings reflect family life in the late Victorian era. The carriage house contains period conveyances. ⊠ *291 Auburn–Folsom Rd.* ☎ *530/889–6500* ⤸ *Free* ⊙ *Tues.–Sun. 11–4.*

The **Gold Country Museum** surveys life in the mines. Exhibits include a walk-through mine tunnel, a gold-panning stream, and a reproduction saloon. ⊠ *1273 High St., off Auburn–Folsom Rd.* ☎ *530/889–6500* ⤸ *Free* ⊙ *Tues.–Sun. 11–4.*

WHERE TO EAT

$$
ECLECTIC
★
✗ **Latitudes.** Delicious multicultural cuisine is served in an 1870 Victorian. The menu (with monthly specials from diverse geographical regions) includes seafood, chicken, beef, and turkey entrées prepared with the appropriate Mexican spices, curries, cheeses, or teriyaki sauce. Vegetarians and vegans have several inventive choices, too. Sunday brunch is deservedly popular. ⊠ *130 Maple St.* ☎ *530/885–9535* ⊕ *www.latitudesrestaurant.com* ☰ *AE, D, MC, V* ⊙ *Closed Mon. and Tues.*

22

Almost 6 million ounces of gold were extracted from the Empire Mine.

GRASS VALLEY

24 mi north of Auburn on Hwy. 49.

More than half of California's total gold production was extracted from mines around Grass Valley, including the Empire Mine, which, along with the North Star Mining Museum, is among the Gold Country's most fascinating attractions. Unlike neighboring Nevada City, urban sprawl surrounds Grass Valley's historic downtown.

EXPLORING

In the center of town, on the site of the original, stands a reproduction of the **Lola Montez House** (⊠ *248 Mill St.* ☎ *530/273–4667, 800/655–4667 in CA*), home of the notorious dancer, singer, and courtesan. Montez, who arrived in Grass Valley in the early 1850s, was no great talent—her popularity among miners derived from her suggestive "spider dance"—but her loves, who reportedly included composer Franz Liszt, were legendary. According to one account, she arrived in California after having been "permanently retired from her job as Bavarian king Ludwig's mistress," literary muse, and political adviser. She apparently pushed too hard for democracy, which contributed to his overthrow and her banishment as a witch—or so the story goes. The Grass Valley/Nevada County Chamber of Commerce is headquartered here.

The landmark **Holbrooke Hotel** (⊠ *212 W. Main St.* ☎ *530/273–1353 or 800/933–7077*), built in 1851, was host to Lola Montez and Mark Twain as well as Ulysses S. Grant and a stream of other U.S. presidents. Its restaurant-saloon is one of the oldest operating west of the Mississippi.

22

☾ The hard-rock gold mine at **Empire Mine State Historic Park** was one of
★ California's richest. An estimated 5.8 million ounces were extracted
from its 367 mi of underground passages between 1850 and 1956. On
the 50-minute tours you can walk into a mine shaft, peer into the mine's
deeper recesses, and view the owner's "cottage," which has exquisite
woodwork. With its shaded picnic areas and gentle hiking trails, this is a
pleasant place for families. ⊠ *10791 E. Empire St., south of Empire St.
exit of Hwy. 49* ☎ *530/273–8522* ⊕ *www.parks.ca.gov* ⊠ *$5* ☾ *May–
Aug., daily 9–6; Sept.–Apr., daily 10–5. Tours May–Aug., daily on hr
11–4; Sept.–Apr., weekends at 1 (cottage only) and 2 (mine yard only),
weather permitting.*

☾ Housed in the former North Star powerhouse, the **North Star Mining
Museum** displays the 32-foot-high enclosed Pelton Water Wheel, said
to be the largest ever built. It was used to power mining operations
and was a forerunner of the modern turbines that generate hydroelec-
tricity. Hands-on displays are geared to children. There's a picnic area
nearby. ⊠ *Empire and McCourtney Sts., north of Empire St. exit of
Hwy. 49* ☎ *530/273–4255* ⊠ *Donation requested* ☾ *May–mid-Oct.,
daily 10–5.*

WHERE TO EAT AND STAY

¢   ✕ **Cousin Jack Pasties.** Meat- and vegetable-stuffed pasties are a taste of
BRITISH   the region's history, having come across the Atlantic with Cornish min-
★   ers and their families in the mid-19th century. The flaky crusts practically melt in your mouth. A simple food stand, which sometimes closes
early on dreary winter days, Jack's is nonetheless a local landmark and
dear to its loyal clientele. ⊠ *Auburn and Main Sts.* ☎ *530/272–9230*
⊟ *No credit cards.*

¢–$ ⊡ **Holiday Lodge.** This modest hotel is close to many of the town's main
attractions, and its staff can help arrange historical tours of Nevada
City, Grass Valley, and the small town of Washington. **Pros:** good price;
friendly staff. **Cons:** feels a bit dated. ⊠ *1221 E. Main St.* ☎ *530/273–
4406 or 800/742–7125* ⊕ *holidaylodge.biz* ⇆ *35 rooms* ⚹ *In-room:
a/c. In-hotel: pool* ⊟ *AE, MC, V* ☖*CP.*

NEVADA CITY

4 mi north of Grass Valley on Hwy. 49.

Nevada City, once known as the Queen City of the Northern Mines,
is the most appealing of the northern Mother Lode towns. The iron-
shutter brick buildings that line the narrow downtown streets contain
antiques shops, galleries, bookstores, boutiques, B&Bs, restaurants, and
a winery. Horse-drawn carriage tours add to the romance, as do gas
street lamps. At one point in the 1850s Nevada City had a population
of nearly 10,000, enough to support much cultural activity.

ESSENTIALS

Visitor Information Nevada City Chamber of Commerce (⊠ *132 Main St.,
Nevada City* ☎ *530/265–2692* ⊕ *www.nevadacitychamber.com*).

EXPLORING

With its gingerbread-trim bell tower, **Firehouse No. 1** is one of the Gold Country's most distinctive buildings. A museum, it houses gold-rush artifacts and a Chinese joss house (temple). ✉ *214 Main St.* ☎ *530/265–5468* ✉ *Donation requested* ⊘ *Apr.–Nov., daily 11–4; Dec.–Mar., Thurs.–Sun. 11:30–4.*

The redbrick **Nevada Theatre**, constructed in 1865, is California's oldest theater building. Mark Twain, Emma Nevada, and many other notable people appeared on its stage. Several local theatrical troupes perform here, and old films are screened as well. ✉ *401 Broad St.* ☎ *530/265–6161, 530/274–3456 for film showtimes* ⊕ *www.nevadatheatre.com*

The **Miners Foundry**, erected in 1856, produced machines for gold mining and logging. The Pelton Water Wheel, a source of power for the mines (the wheel also jump-started the hydroelectric power industry), was invented here. A cavernous building, the foundry is the site of plays, concerts, weddings, receptions, and other events; call for a schedule. ✉ *325 Spring St.* ☎ *530/265–5040* ⊕ *www.minersfoundry.org.*

You can watch wine being created while you sip at the **Nevada City Winery**, where the tasting room overlooks the production area. ✉ *Miners Foundry Garage, 321 Spring St.* ☎ *530/265–9463 or 800/203–9463* ⊕ *www.ncwinery.com* ✉ *Free* ⊘ *Tastings Mon.–Sat. 11–5, Sun. noon–5.*

WHERE TO EAT AND STAY

$–$$$
AMERICAN

✕ **South Pine Cafe.** Locals flock here, especially for brunch. Although lobster and beef are on the menu, the real attention-grabbers are vegetarian entrées and side dishes, such as breakfast potatoes and apple-ginger muffins. This place is starting to take off regionally; it recently opened branches in Grass Valley and Auburn. ✉ *110 S. Pine St.* ☎ *530/265–0260* ⊕ *www.southpinecafe.com* ▭ *MC, V* ⊘ *Daily 8–3.*

$$–$$$
Fodor'sChoice
★

📷 **Red Castle Historic Lodgings.** A state landmark, this 1857 Gothic-revival mansion stands on a forested hillside overlooking Nevada City, and is a special place for those who appreciate the finer points of Victorian interior design. Its brick exterior is trimmed with white-icicle woodwork. A steep private pathway leads down through the terraced gardens into town; there's also a well-lighted set of city stairs. Handsome antique furnishings and Oriental rugs decorate the rooms. ■**TIP→** Red Castle features a delightful afternoon tea, by request, and morning breakfast buffet that is unparalleled among Gold Country B&Bs. **Pros:** friendly owners; spectacular food; fascinating architecture. **Cons:** you'll get a built-in workout walking up the hill from downtown—although many would consider that a good thing. ✉ *109 Prospect St.* ☎ *530/265–5135 or 800/761–4766* ⊕ *www.redcastleinn.com* ⇆ *4 rooms, 3 suites* ☖ *In-room: a/c.* ▭ *MC, V* ⋈ *BP.*

Lake Tahoe

WITH RENO, NEVADA

WORD OF MOUTH

"Just driving around the Lake is a very nice way to spend a day. You can stop in Emerald Bay and visit Vikingsholm, can get to South Shore and check out shops, casinos, have lunch . . . but there are also a lot of places to stop and have lunch along the way."

—crefloors

WELCOME TO LAKE TAHOE

TOP REASONS TO GO

★ **The lake:** Blue, deep, and alpine pure, Lake Tahoe is far and away the main reason to visit this high Sierra paradise.

★ **Snow, snow, snow:** Daring black diamond runs or baby bunny bumps— whether you're an expert, a beginner, or somewhere in between, there are many slopes to suit your skills at the numerous Tahoe area ski parks.

★ **The great outdoors:** A ring of national forests, recreation areas, and miles of trails make Tahoe a nature lover's paradise.

★ **Dinner with a view:** You can picnic lakeside at state parks or dine in restaurants perched along the shore.

★ **A date with lady luck:** Whether you want to roll dice, play the slots, or hope the blackjack dealer goes bust before you do, you'll find round-the-clock gambling at the casinos in Reno and on the Nevada side of the lake.

1 California Side. With the exception of Stateline, Nevada—which, aside from its casino-hotel towers, seems almost indistinguishable from South Lake Tahoe, California—the California side is more developed than the Nevada side. Here you can find both commercial enterprises—restaurants, motels, lodges, resorts, residential subdivisions— and public-access facilities, such as historic sites, parks, campgrounds, marinas, and beaches.

2 Nevada Side. You don't need a highway sign to know when you've crossed from California into Nevada: the flashing lights and elaborate marquees of casinos announce legal gambling in garish hues. But you'll find more here than tables and slot machines. Reno, the Biggest Little City in the World, has a vibrant art scene and a serene downtown RiverWalk. And when you really need to get away from the chip-toting crowds, you can hike through pristine wilderness at Lake Tahoe–Nevada State Park, or hit the slopes at Incline Village.

GETTING ORIENTED

In the northern section of the Sierra Nevada mountain range, the Lake Tahoe area covers portions of five national forests, several state parks, and rugged wilderness areas with names like Desolation and Granite Chief. Lake Tahoe, the star attraction, straddles California and Nevada and is one of the world's largest, clearest, and deepest alpine lakes. The region's proximity to the Bay Area and Sacramento to the west and Reno to the east draws hordes of thrill-seekers during ski season and summer, when water sports, camping, and hiking are the dominant activities.

TO
RENO

TO
RENO

Mtn Rose
10,776 ft.

80

80

Sugar
Bowl

Donner
Lake

Truckee

Tahoe
National
Forest

431

Northstar-
at-Tahoe

267

Rose
Knob

Kings Beach
State Recreation
Area

Incline Village

2

395

Washoe
Lake

89

Truckee

Tahoe Vista

Carnelian Bay

Ridgewood

Kings
Beach

28

Carnelian
Bay

Crystal
Bay

Crystal Bay

Brockway

Sand Harbor
Beach

Lake Tahoe
Nevada
State Park

C
A
R
S
O
N

Squaw
Peak

River

Tahoe City

Thunderbird
Lodge

Snow Valley
Peak
9,214 ft.

28

50

CALIFORNIA

NEVADA

Twin
Peaks

89

1

Lake
Tahoe
el 6,229 ft.

Glenbrook

206

Tahoe Pines

Homewood

R
A
N
G
E

Rubicon
River

Tahoma

Meeks Bay

Meyers

Sugar Pine Point
State Park

Rubicon
Bay

Cave Rock

Lakeridge

Skyland

Genoa Peak
9,150 ft.

50

206

Rubicon
Peak

89

D. L. Bliss
State Park

Zephyr
Cove

Toiyabe
National
Forest

Genoa

Emerald Bay
State Park

Emerald Bay

South Lake
Tahoe

Kingsbury

Stateline

207

El Dorado
National
Forest

Tahoe Keys

Fallen Leaf
Lake

East Peak

207

Jacks Peak

Pope-Baldwin
Recreation
Area

206

50

89

Meyers

TO
PLACERVILLE

0   5 mi

0   3 km

LAKE TAHOE PLANNER

Getting Here

The closest airport to Lake Tahoe is Reno, served by nearly a dozen airlines and all the major car-rental agencies. If you're also visiting the Bay Area or California's northern towns, fly into San Francisco, Oakland, or Sacramento airport.

Truckee, the north Tahoe resorts, and Reno are all accessible via I-80. For South Lake Tahoe, take Highway 50 from I-80 (in Sacramento). Try to travel midweek: both routes are jammed on weekends in summer and winter.

Exploring the Lake

The typical way to explore the Lake Tahoe area is to drive the 72-mi road that follows the shore through wooded flatlands and past beaches, climbing to vistas on the rugged southwest side of the lake and passing through busy commercial developments and casinos on its northeastern and southeastern edges. Another option is to actually go out on the lake on a sightseeing cruise or kayaking trip.

When to Go

A sapphire blue lake shimmering deep in the center of an ice-white wonderland—that's Tahoe in winter. But those blankets of snow mean lots of storms that often close roads and force chain requirements on the interstate. In summer the roads are open, but the lake and lodgings are clogged with visitors seeking respite from valley heat. If you don't ski, the best times to visit are early fall and late spring. The crowds thin, prices dip, and you can count on Tahoe being beautiful year-round.

Most Lake Tahoe accommodations, restaurants, and even a handful of parks are open year-round, but many visitor centers, mansions, state parks, and beaches are closed from November through May. During those months, multitudes of skiers and other winter-sports enthusiasts are attracted to Tahoe's downhill resorts and cross-country centers, North America's largest concentration of skiing facilities. Ski resorts try to open by Thanksgiving, if only with machine-made snow, and can operate through May or later. During the ski season, Tahoe's population swells on the weekends. If you're able to come midweek, you'll have the resorts and neighboring towns almost to yourself.

Unless you want to ski, you'll find that Tahoe is most fun in summer, when it's cooler here than in the scorched Sierra Nevada foothills, the clean mountain air is bracingly crisp, and the surface temperature of Lake Tahoe is an invigorating 65°F to 70°F (compared with 40°F to 50°F in winter). This is also the time, however, when it may seem as if every tourist at the lake—100,000 on peak weekends—is in a car on the main road circling the 72-mi shoreline (especially on Highway 89, just south of Tahoe City; on Highway 28, east of Tahoe City; and on U.S. 50 in South Lake). The crowds increase as the day wears on, so the best strategy for avoiding the crush is to do as much as you can early in the day. The parking lots of the Lake Tahoe Visitor Center, Vikingsholm, and Emerald Bay State Park can be jammed at any time, and the lake's beaches can be packed. September and October, when the throngs have dispersed but the weather is still pleasant, are among the most satisfying—and cheapest—months to visit Lake Tahoe. Christmas week and July 4 are the busiest times, and prices go through the roof; plan accordingly.

About the Restaurants

On weekends and in high season, expect a long wait in the more popular restaurants. And expect to pay resort prices almost everywhere. Remember, restaurants see business only 6 out of 12 months. During the "shoulder seasons" (April to May and September to November), some places may close temporarily or limit their hours, so call ahead. Also, check local papers for deals and discounts during this time, especially two-for-one coupons. Many casinos use their restaurants to attract gamblers. Marquees often tout "$8.99 prime rib dinners" or "$1.99 breakfast specials." Some of these meals are downright lousy and they are usually available only in the coffee shops and buffets, but at those prices, it's hard to complain. The finer restaurants in casinos deliver pricier food, as well as reasonable service and a bit of atmosphere. Unless otherwise noted, even the most expensive area restaurants welcome customers in casual clothes.

About the Hotels

Quiet inns on the water, suburban-style strip motels, casino hotels, slope-side ski lodges, and house and condo rentals throughout the area constitute the lodging choices at Tahoe. The crowds come in summer and during ski season; reserve as far in advance as possible, especially for holiday periods, when prices skyrocket. Spring and fall give you a little more leeway and lower—sometimes significantly lower—rates. Check hotel Web sites for the best deals.

Head to South Lake Tahoe for the most activities and the widest range of lodging options.

Tahoe City, on the west shore, has a small-town atmosphere and is accessible to several nearby ski resorts.

Looking for a taste of old Tahoe? The north shore with its woodsy backdrop is your best bet, with Carnelian Bay and Tahoe Vista on the California side.

WHAT IT COSTS

	¢	$	$$	$$$	$$$$
Restaurants	under $10	$10–$15	$16–$22	$23–$30	over $30
Hotels	under $90	$90–$120	$121–$175	$176–$250	over $250
Campgrounds	under $10	$10–$17	$18–$35	$36–$50	over $50

Restaurant prices are based on the median main course price at dinner. Hotel prices are for two people in a standard double room in high season.

Skiing and Snowboarding

The mountains around Lake Tahoe are bombarded by blizzards throughout most winters and sometimes in fall and spring; 10- to 12-foot bases are common. Indeed, the Sierra often has the deepest snowpack on the continent, but because of the relatively mild temperatures over the Pacific, falling snow can be very heavy and wet—it's nicknamed Sierra Cement for a reason. The upside is that you can sometimes ski and board as late as July (snowboarding is permitted at all Tahoe ski areas). Note that the major resorts get extremely crowded on weekends. If you're going to ski on a Saturday, arrive early and quit early. Avoid moving with the masses. eat at 11 AM or 1:30 PM, not noon. Also consider visiting the ski areas with few high-speed lifts or limited lodging and real estate at their bases: Alpine Meadows, Sugar Bowl, Homewood, Mt. Rose, Sierra-at-Tahoe, Diamond Peak, and Kirkwood. And to find out the true ski conditions, talk to waiters and bartenders—most of whom are ski bums.

The Lake Tahoe area is also a great destination for Nordic skiers. "Skinny" (i.e., cross-country) skiing at the resorts can be costly, but you get the benefits of machine grooming and trail preparation. If it's bargain Nordic you're after, take advantage of thousands of acres of public forest and parkland trails.

23

Updated
by Christine
Vovakes

Stunning cobalt-blue Lake Tahoe is the largest alpine lake in North America, famous for its clarity, deep blue water, and surrounding snowcapped peaks. Straddling the state line between California and Nevada, it lies 6,225 feet above sea level in the Sierra Nevada.

The border gives this popular resort region a split personality. About half its visitors are intent on low-key sightseeing, hiking, fishing, camping, and boating. The rest head directly for the Nevada side, where bargain dining, big-name entertainment, and the lure of a jackpot draw them into the glittering casinos.

The lake and the communities around it are the region's main draw, but other nearby destinations are gaining in popularity. Truckee, with an Old West feel and hot new restaurants, lures visitors looking for a relaxed pace and easy access to Tahoe's north shore and Olympic Valley ski parks. And today Reno, once known only for its casinos, is also drawing tourists with its buzzing arts scene, revitalized downtown riverfront, and campus attractions at the University of Nevada.

Though Lake Tahoe possesses abundant natural beauty and accessible wilderness, nearby towns are highly developed, and roads around the lake are often congested with traffic. If you prefer solitude, you can escape to the many state parks, national forests, and protected tracts of wilderness that ring the 22-mi-long, 12-mi-wide lake.

PLANNING

GETTING HERE AND AROUND
BY AIR
Reno–Tahoe International Airport, in Reno, 50 mi northeast of the closest point on the lake, is served by Alaska, American, Continental, Delta, Horizon, Southwest, United, and US Airways.

Airport Contact Reno–Tahoe International Airport (⊠ *U.S. 395, Exit 65B, 2001 E. Plumb La.Reno, NV* ☎ *775/328–6400* ⊕ *www.renoairport.com*).

BY BUS

Greyhound stops in Sacramento, Truckee, and Reno, Nevada. Blue Go runs along U.S. 50 and through the neighborhoods of South Lake Tahoe daily from morning to evening (times vary, check schedules; $2 per ride, exact change only); it also operates a 24-hour door-to-door van service to most addresses in South Lake Tahoe and Stateline for $6 per person (reservations essential). Tahoe Area Regional Transit (TART) operates buses along Lake Tahoe's northern and western shores between Tahoma and Incline Village daily, plus five shuttles daily to Truckee ($1.75 per ride, exact change only). In summer TART buses have bike racks; in winter they have ski racks. Shuttle buses run among the casinos, major ski resorts, and motels of South Lake Tahoe. South Tahoe Express runs 10 daily buses between Reno–Tahoe Airport and hotels in Stateline in winter (seven the rest of the year). Reserve online or by telephone. A nonrefundable adult ticket is $26 one-way, $46.50 round-trip.

Bus Contacts Greyhound (☎ *800/231–2222* ⊕ *www.greyhound.com*). **Blue Go** (☎ *530/541–7149* ⊕ *www.bluego.org*). **Tahoe Area Regional Transit (TART)** (☎ *530/550–1212 or 800/736–6365* ⊕ *www.laketahoetransit.com*). **South Tahoe Express** (☎ *775/325–8944 or 866/898–2463* ⊕ *www.southtahoeexpress.com*).

BY CAR

Lake Tahoe is 198 mi northeast of San Francisco, a drive of less than four hours in good weather. Avoid the heavy traffic leaving the San Francisco area for Tahoe on Friday afternoon and returning on Sunday afternoon. The major route is I–80, which cuts through the Sierra Nevada about 14 mi north of the lake. From there Highway 89 and Highway 267 reach the west and north shores, respectively. U.S. 50 is the more direct route to the south shore, taking about two hours from Sacramento. From Reno you can get to the north shore by heading south on U.S. 395 for 10 mi, then west on Highway 431 for 25 mi. For the south shore, head south on U.S. 395 through Carson City, and then turn west on U.S. 50 (50 mi total).

The scenic 72-mi highway around the lake is marked Highway 89 on the southwest and west shores, Highway 28 on the north and northeast shores, and U.S. 50 on the east and southeast. Sections of Highway 89 sometimes close during snowy periods in winter, usually at Emerald Bay because of avalanche danger, which makes it impossible to complete the circular drive around the lake. Interstate 80, U.S. 50, and U.S. 395 are all-weather highways, but there may be delays as snow is cleared during major storms. (Note that I–80 is a four-lane freeway; a large part of U.S. 50 is only two lanes with no center divider.) Carry tire chains from October through May, or rent a four-wheel-drive vehicle (most rental agencies do not allow tire chains to be used on their vehicles; ask when you book).

Contacts California Highway Patrol (☎ *530/577–1001 South Lake Tahoe* ⊕ *www.chp.ca.gov*). **Cal-Trans Highway Information Line** (☎ *800/427–7623* ⊕ *www.dot.ca.gov/hq/roadinfo*). **Nevada Department of Transportation Road Information** (☎ *877/687–6237* ⊕ *www.nevadadot.com/traveler/roads*). **Nevada Highway Patrol** (☎ *775/687–5300* ⊕ *www.nhp.nv.gov*).

BY TRAIN

Amtrak's cross-country rail service makes stops in Truckee and Reno. The *California Zephyr* stops in both towns once daily eastbound (Salt Lake, Denver, and Chicago) and once daily westbound (Sacramento and Oakland). Amtrak also operates several buses daily between Reno and Sacramento to connect with the *Coast Starlight,* which runs south to Southern California and north to Oregon and Washington.

Train Contact Amtrak (☎ *775/329–8638 or 800/872–7245* ⊕ *www. amtrakcalifornia.com*).

HEALTH AND SAFETY

In an emergency dial 911.

Hospital Contacts Barton Memorial Hospital (✉ *2170 South Ave., South Lake Tahoe* ☎ *530/541–3420*). **St. Mary's Regional Medical Center** (✉ *235 W. 6th St., Reno, NV* ☎ *775/770–3000 general information, 775/770–3188 emergency room*). **Tahoe Forest Hospital** (✉ *10121 Pine Ave., Truckee* ☎ *530/587–6011*).

TOUR OPTIONS

The 350-passenger *Tahoe Queen,* a glass-bottom paddle wheeler, departs from South Lake Tahoe daily for 2½-hour sightseeing cruises year-round by reservation and 3-hour dinner–dance cruises daily from late spring to early fall (weekly the rest of the year). Fares range from $39 to $75. A few times in winter the boat becomes the only waterborne ski shuttle in the world: $127 covers hotel transfers, a bus transfer from South Lake Tahoe or Stateline to Squaw Valley, lift ticket, and boat transportation back across the lake to South Lake. There's a full bar on board, live music, and an optional dinner.

The *Sierra Cloud,* a large 50-passenger catamaran owned by the Hyatt Hotel, cruises the north shore area morning and afternoon, May through September. The fare is $50. The 570-passenger MS *Dixie II,* a stern-wheeler, sails year-round from Zephyr Cove to Emerald Bay on sightseeing, lunch, and dinner cruises. Fares range from $39 to $65.

Also in Zephyr Cove, Woodwind Cruises operates the *Woodwind II,* a 50-passenger catamaran that sails on regular and champagne cruises April through October. Fares range from $30 to $45. Woodwind Cruises also offers half-day round-the-lake cruises aboard the *Safari Rose,* an 80-foot-long wooden motor yacht; $95 includes lunch.

Lake Tahoe Balloons conducts excursions over the lake May through October; the hour-long flights cost $250 (the entire experience takes four hours total). Soar Minden offers glider rides and instruction over the lake and the Great Basin. Flights cost $155 to $295 and depart from Minden–Tahoe Airport, a municipal facility in Minden, Nevada.

Tour Contacts Lake Tahoe Balloons (☎ *530/544–1221 or 800/872–9294* ⊕ *www.laketahoeballoons.com*). **MS Dixie II** (✉ *Zephyr Cove Marina, 760 U.S. Hwy. 50, Zephyr Cove* ☎ *775/589–4906 or 888/896–3830* ⊕ *www. laketahoecruises.com*). **Sierra Cloud** (✉ *Hyatt Regency Lake Tahoe, 111 Country Club Dr., Incline Village* ☎ *775/832–1234*). **Soar Minden** (☎ *775/782–7627 or 800/345–7627* ⊕ *www.soarminden.com*). **Tahoe Queen** (✉ *Ski Run Marina, off U.S. 50, 900 Ski Run Blvd., South Lake Tahoe* ☎ *775/589–4906 or 888/896–3830* ⊕ *www.laketahoecruises.com*). **Woodwind Cruises** (✉ *Zephyr Cove Resort,*

760 U.S. Hwy. 50, Zephyr Cove ☎ *775/588–1881 or 888/867–6394* ⊕ *www.sailwoodwind.com).*

VISITOR INFORMATION
Contacts Lake Tahoe Visitors Authority (✉ *169 U.S. Hwy. 50, Stateline* ☎ *775/588–5900 or 800/288–2463* ⊕ *www.bluelaketahoe.com).* **U.S. Forest Service** (☎ *530/587–2158 backcountry recording* ⊕ *www.fs.fed.us/r5).*

CALIFORNIA SIDE

23

SOUTH LAKE TAHOE

50 mi south of Reno on U.S. 395 and U.S. 50; 198 mi northeast of San Francisco on I–80 and U.S. 50.

The city of South Lake Tahoe's raison d'être is tourism: the casinos of adjacent Stateline, Nevada; the ski slopes at Heavenly Mountain; the beaches, docks, bike trails, and campgrounds all around the south shore; and the backcountry of Eldorado National Forest and Desolation Wilderness. The town itself, however, is disappointingly unattractive, with its mix of cheap motels, strip malls, and low-rise prefab-looking buildings that line both sides of U.S. 50. Though there are lots and lots of places to stay, we haven't recommended many because they're not cream-of-the-crop choices. The small city's saving grace is its convenient location and bevy of services, as well as its gorgeous lake views.

ESSENTIALS
Visitor Information Lake Tahoe Visitors Authority (✉ *169 U.S. Hwy. 50., Stateline* ☎ *775/588–5900 or 800/288–2463* ⊕ *www.bluelaketahoe.com).*

EXPLORING
Ⓒ Whether you ski or not, you'll appreciate the impressive view of Lake Tahoe from the **Heavenly Gondola.** Its 138 eight-passenger cars travel from the middle of town 2½ mi up the mountain in 15 minutes. When the weather's fine, you can take one of three hikes around the mountain-top and then have lunch at Adventure Peak Grill. Heavenly also offers day care for children. ✉ *Downtown* ☎ *775/586–7000 or 800/432–8365* ⊕ *www.skiheavenly.com* 🎟 *$30* ⊙ *Hrs vary; summer, daily 10–5; winter, daily 9–4.*

Fodor's Choice
★

At the base of the gondola the **Heavenly Village** is the centerpiece of South Lake Tahoe's efforts to reinvent itself and provide a focal point for tourism. Essentially a pedestrian mall, it includes some good shopping, a cinema, an arcade for kids, and the Heavenly Village Outdoor Ice Rink.

WHERE TO EAT
$-$$

ECLECTIC

✗ **Blue Angel Café.** A favorite of locals, who fill the dozen or so wooden tables, the Blue Angel serves everything from basic sandwiches, meat loaf, and vegan burgers to Mediterranean platters and Moroccan spiced lamb shanks—and best of all, the prices are extremely reasonable. This cozy café has Wi-Fi and is open daily from 11 AM to 9 PM. ✉ *1132 Ski Run Blvd.* ☎ *530/544–6544* ☰ *AE, MC, V.*

$–$$
MEXICAN

✕ **The Cantina.** The Cantina serves generous portions of traditional Mexican dishes, such as burritos, enchiladas, and tamales, as well as more stylized Southwestern cooking, including smoked chicken polenta with grilled vegetables, and crab cakes in jalapeño cream sauce. The bar makes great margaritas and serves 30 different kinds of beer. ⊠ *765 Emerald Bay Rd.* ☎ *530/544–1233* ⌕ *Reservations not accepted* ▭ *AE, D, MC, V.*

$$$–$$$$
ECLECTIC
★

✕ **Evan's.** The top choice for high-end dining in South Lake, Evan's creative American cuisine includes such specialties as seared foie gras with grilled pineapple and curried ice cream, roasted rack of lamb with citrus couscous, and daily seafood specials. Although some might find the tables a tad close to each other, the 40-seat dining room in the converted Tahoe cabin is intimate. The excellent service, world-class food, and superb wine list merit a special trip. ⊠ *536 Emerald Bay Rd.* ☎ *530/542–1990* ▭ *AE, D, MC, V* ☾ *No lunch.*

$$$–$$$$
ASIAN

✕ **Kalani's.** Fresh-off-the-plane seafood gets flown directly from the Honolulu fish market to Heavenly Village's sexiest (and priciest) restaurant. The sleek, white-tablecloth dining room is decked out with carved bamboo, a burnt-orange color palette, and a modern-glass sculpture, all of which complement contemporary Pacific Rim specialties such as melt-from-the-bone baby back pork ribs with sesame-garlic soy sauce. Sushi selections with inventive rolls and sashimi combos, plus less expensive vegetarian dishes, add depth to the menu. ⊠ *1001 Heavenly Village Way, #26* ☎ *530/544–6100* ▭ *AE, D, MC, V.*

¢–$
AMERICAN

✕ **Red Hut Café.** A vintage-1959 Tahoe diner, all chrome and red plastic, the Red Hut is a tiny place with a wildly popular breakfast menu: huge omelets; banana, pecan, and coconut waffles; and other tasty vittles. A sparkling new branch opened in South Lake Tahoe in 2009, and there's a third location in Stateline. The menu and prices are the same at each location. ⊠ *2749 U.S. 50* ☎ *530/541–9024* ⌕ *Reservations not accepted* ▭ *No credit cards* ☾ *No dinner* ⊠ *3660 Lake Tahoe Blvd.* ☎ *530/544–1595* ⊠ *227 Kingsbury Grade, Stateline, NV* ☎ *775/588–7488.*

$–$$$
ITALIAN

✕ **Scusa!** The kitchen here turns out big plates of linguine with clam sauce, veal scallopine, and chicken piccata. There's nothing fancy about the menu, just straightforward Italian-American food—and lots of it. ⊠ *1142 Ski Run Blvd.* ☎ *530/542–0100* ▭ *AE, D, MC, V* ☾ *No lunch.*

WHERE TO STAY

$$$–$$$$
Fodor'sChoice
★

⊡ **Black Bear Inn Bed and Breakfast.** South Lake Tahoe's most luxurious inn feels like one of the grand old lodges of the Adirondacks. Its great room has rough-hewn beams, plank floors, cathedral ceilings, Persian rugs, and even an elk's head over the giant river-rock fireplace. Built in the 1990s with meticulous attention to detail, the five inn rooms and three cabins feature 19th-century American antiques, fine art, and fireplaces; cabins also have kitchenettes. Never intrusive, the affable innkeepers provide a sumptuous breakfast in the morning and wine and cheese in the afternoon. **Pros:** intimate; within walking distance of several good restaurants; massive stone fireplace in great room. **Cons:** not appropriate for children under 16; pricey. ⊠ *1202 Ski Run Blvd.* ☎ *530/544–4451 or 877/232–7466* ⊕ *www.tahoeblackbear.com* ⤶ *5 rooms, 3 cabins* ⌕ *In-room: a/c, kitchen (some), DVD, Wi-Fi. In-hotel:*

Continued on page 868

TAHOE A LAKE FOR ALL SEASONS

by Christine Vovakes

Best known for its excellent skiing, Lake Tahoe is a year-round resort and outdoor sports destination. All kinds of activities are available, from snowboarding some of the best runs in North America and gliding silently along the lakeshore on cross-country skis in winter, to mountain biking through lush forests and puttering around the alpine lake in a classic yacht in summer. Whatever you do—and whenever you visit—the sapphire lake is at the center of it all, pulling you out of your posh resort or rustic cabin rental like a giant blue magnet. There are many ways to enjoy and experience Lake Tahoe, but here are some of our favorites.

(top) Heavenly Mountain Resort,
(bottom) Sand Harbor Beach.

WINTER WONDERLAND

Home to a host of world-famous Sierra resorts, Tahoe is a premier ski destination. Add sledding, ice skating, cross-country skiing, and jingly sleigh rides under the stars to the mix, and you begin to get a glimpse of Tahoe's cold-weather potential.

DOWNHILL SKIING AND SNOWBOARDING

Even if you've never made it off the bunny hill before, you should definitely hit the slopes here at least once. The Lake Tahoe region has the deepest snowpack in North America, and you can ski from Thanksgiving until it melts—which is sometimes July.

One of the top-rated resorts in the country, Olympic Valley's **Squaw Valley USA** hosted the 1960 Winter Olympics that put Tahoe on the map. A great classic resort is **Sugar Bowl,** where you can revel in a bit of Disney nostalgia while you swoop down the slopes. Walt helped start the resort, which opened in 1939 and had Tahoe's first chair lift.

Even if you're not hitting the slopes at South Lake Tahoe's **Heavenly Mountain,** be sure to take a ride on their **Heavenly Gondola** so you can take in awe-inspiring views of the frozen circle of white ice that rings the brilliant lake.

(top) Skiing in Lake Tahoe,. (above left) Cross-country skiing, (above right) Snow boarding at Heavenly Mountain.

SKI RESORT	LOCATION	TRAILS	ACRES	BEGIN.	INTER.	ADV./ EXP.
CALIFORNIA						
Alpine Meadows	Tahoe City	100	2,400	25%	40%	35%
Heavenly Mountain	South Lake Tahoe	94	4,800	20%	45%	35%
Homewood Mountain	Homewood	60	1,260	15%	50%	35%
Kirkwood	Kirkwood	65	2,300	15%	50%	35%
Northstar-at-Tahoe	Truckee	92	3,000	13%	60%	27%
Sierra-at-Tahoe	South Lake Tahoe	46	2,000	25%	50%	25%
Squaw Valley USA	Olympic Valley	170	4,000	25%	45%	30%
Sugar Bowl	Truckee	95	1,500	17%	45%	38%
NEVADA						
Diamond Peak	Incline Village	30	655	18%	46%	36%
Mt. Rose Ski Tahoe	Incline Village	61	1,200	20%	30%	50%

CROSS-COUNTRY SKIING

Downhill skiing may get all the glory here, but Lake Tahoe is also a premier cross-country (or Nordic) skiing destination. "Skinny" skiers basically have two options: pony up the cash to ski the groomed trails at a resort, or hit the more rugged (but cheaper—or free) public forest and parkland trails.

Beautiful **Royal Gorge** is the country's largest cross-country ski resort. Other resorts with good skinny skiing include **Kirkwood, Squaw Valley USA, Tahoe Donner,** and **Northstar-at-Tahoe.** Private operators **Spooner Lake Cross Country** and **Hope Valley Cross Country** will also have you shushing through pristine powder in no time.

For bargain Nordic on public trails, head to **Sugar Pine Point State Park.** Other good low-cost cross-country skiing locations include **Donner Memorial State Park, Lake Tahoe—Nevada State Park,** and **Tahoe Meadows** near Incline Village.

CAUTION⚠ Cross-country skiing is relaxing and provides a great cardiovascular workout—but it's also quite strenuous. If it's your first time out or you're not in great shape, start out slow.

SLEDDING AND TUBING

Kirkwood, Squaw Valley USA, Boreal, Soda Springs, and many other Tahoe resorts have areas where you can barrel down hills in sleds and inflatable tubes. Some good non-resort sledding spots are **Tahoe National Forest** and **Tahoe Meadows,** near Incline Village.

ICE SKATING

Want to work on your triple lutz? You can skate seasonally at **Heavenly Village Outdoor Ice Rink,** or year-round at the **South Tahoe Ice Arena.** Other great gliding spots include **Squaw Valley USA's Olympic Ice Pavilion.**

WARMING UP

To defrost your ski-stiff limbs, take a dip in a resort's heated pool, de-stress in a hotel spa…or enjoy a brandy by the fire at a cozy restaurant. Our favorite places to warm up and imbibe include Graham's of Squaw Valley and Soule Domain, near Crystal Bay.

TO
← BOREAL MOUNTAIN RESORT
← TO
← SODA SPRINGS

Donner Pass

80

Tahoe
Donner

Norden
Sugar
Bowl

Donner Lake

Donner
Memorial
State Park

80

Truckee

89

267

Northstar-
at-Tahoe

*Tahoe
National
Forest*

TO
RENO

*Mtn Rose
10,776*

TO
RENO
(30 miles)

431

Mt. Rose
Ski Tahoe

*Rose
Knob*

Diamond
Peak

Incline Village

Tahoe Vista

Carnelian Bay

Kings Beach
State Recreation
Area

*Crystal
Bay*

Kings
Beach

Crystal
Bay

Squaw
Valley
U.S.A.

Granite Chief
Wilderness

*Squaw
Peak*

Alpine
Meadows

28

*Carnelian
Bay*

Sand Harbor
Beach

Thunderbird
Lodge

*Lake Tahoe-
Nevada
State Park*

CARSON
CITY

50

Tahoe City

89

*Twin
Peaks*

*Lake
Tahoe*

CALIFORNIA
NEVADA

28

*Snow Valley
Peak
9,214*

Homewood

Homewood
Mountain

Tahoma

Sugar Pine Point
State Park

Meeks
Bay

*Rubicon
Bay*

*Rubicon
Peak*

89

D. L. Bliss
State Park

Emerald Bay
State Park

Eagle
Falls

Emerald Bay

Camp
Richardson

*Fallen Leaf
Lake*

Jacks Peak

Pope-Baldwin
Recreation
Area

Glenbrook

Cave Rock

*Genoa Peak
9,150*

50

*Toiyabe
National
Forest*

Zephyr
Cove

South Lake
Tahoe

Stateline

Tahoe Keys

East Peak

Heavenly
Mountain

207

Genoa

Minden

207

206

*El Dorado
National
Forest*

Meyers

50

89

0   5 mi
0   5 km

50

Sierra-at-
Tahoe

89

88

Kirkwood
Ski Rsort

Kirkwood

*Toiyabe
National
Forest*

431

395

*Washoe
Lake*

395

38

CARSON RANGE

Carson River

206

395

CARSON VALLEY

89

Lake Tahoe
Outdoor Activities

FROSTY CATCH

Too cold to fish? Nonsense. South Lake's Tahoe Sport Fishing runs charters year-round with crews that will clean and package your catch.

IN THE WARM CALIFORNIA SUN

Summer in Tahoe means diving into pure alpine waters, hiking a mountain trail with stunning lake views, or kayaking on glorious Emerald Bay. From tennis to golf to fishing, you can fill every waking moment with outdoor activity—or just stretch out on a sunny lakeside beach with a good book and a cool drink.

HIKING

The lake is surrounded by protected parkland, offering countless opportunities to take jaunts through the woods or rambles along lakeside trails.

One of the most unique hiking experiences in Tahoe is at Heavenly Mountain Resorts, where the **Heavenly Gondola** runs up to three nice trails. When you're done enjoying sky-high views of the lake, grab lunch at the nearby Adventure Peak Grill.

Another out-of-the-ordinary option is a romantic moonlit trek. **Camp Richardson** has lots of trails and a long curve of lake to catch the moonlight.

In **Eldorado National Forest and Desolation Wilderness,** you can hike a small portion of the famous Pacific Crest Trail and branch off to discover beautiful backcountry lakes. Nearby **Eagle Falls** has stunning views of Emerald Bay.

One of Tahoe's best hikes is a 4½-mi trail at **D.L. Bliss State Park;** it has lovely views of the lake and leads to bizarre **Vikingsholm** (*see box on next page*).

Other great places to hike in Lake Tahoe include **Sugar Pines Point State Park, Olympic Valley's Granite Chief Wilderness, Squaw Valley USA's High Camp, Donner Memorial State Park,** and **Lake Tahoe—Nevada State Park.**

You can pick up hiking maps at the **U.S. Forest Service** office at the **Lake Tahoe Visitor Center.**

HIT THE BEACH

Lake Tahoe has some gorgeous lakeside sunbathing terrain; get to perennial favorite **Kings Beach State Recreation Area** early to snag a choice spot. Or, if you never want to be far from the water, reserve one of the prime beachside spots at **D.L. Bliss State Park Campground.**

(left) Fannette Island in Emerald Bay. (right) A young man leaps off a cliff into Lake Tahoe.

MOUNTAIN BIKING AND CYCLING

You don't need to be preparing for the Tour de France to join the biking fun. While there are myriad rugged mountain biking trails to choose from, the region is also blessed with many flat trails.

Truly intrepid cyclists take the lift up **Northstar-at-Tahoe** and hit the resort's 100 mi of trails. Another good option is **Sugar Pine Point State Park,** where you can hop on a 10-mi trail to Tahoe City.

Tahoe Sports in South Lake Tahoe is a good place for bike rentals and tips for planning your trip. **Cyclepath Mountain Bikes Adventures** in Tahoe City leads guided mountain biking tours, and **Flume Trail Bikes** in Incline Village rents bikes and operates a bike shuttle to popular trails.

LAKE TOURS AND KAYAKING

One of the best ways to experience the lake is by getting out on the water.

The *Tahoe Queen* is a huge glass-bottomed paddle-wheel boat that offers sightseeing cruises and dinner-dance cruises; in winter, it's the only water-borne ski shuttle in the world. The *Sierra Cloud, MS Dixie II,* and *Woodwind I and II* also ply the lake, offering a variety of enjoyable cruises. (*See Tour Options in the Planning section at the beginning of this chapter for contact info.*)

Another enjoyable option is taking a throwback wooden cruiser from Tahoe Keys Marina in South Lake Tahoe to tour **Thunderbird Lodge,** the meticulously crafted stone mansion built in 1936 by socialite George Whittell.

For a more personal experience, rent a kayak and glide across **Emerald Bay. Kayak Tahoe** in South Lake Tahoe will have you paddling in no time.

VIKINGS?

As you kayak around Tahoe, you'll see many natural wonders…and a few manmade ones as well. One of the most impressive and strangest is **Vikingsholm,** a grand 1929 estate that looks like an ancient Viking castle. You can see it from **Emerald Bay** (which, appropriately, resembles a fjord), or hike to it via a steep one-mile trail.

(left top) Biking along the shore. (left bottom) Kayaking. (right) Steamboat cruise.

Wi-Fi hotspot, no kids under 16 ▭ *D, MC, V* ¶ *BP.*

$–$$$ **Camp Richardson.** An old-fashioned family resort, Camp Richardson is built around a 1920s lodge, with a few dozen cabins and a small inn, all tucked beneath giant pine trees on 80 acres of lakefront land on the southwest shore of Lake Tahoe. The rustic log cabin–style lodge has simple, straightforward accommodations. The cabins (one-week minimum in summer) have lots of space, fireplaces, or woodstoves, and full kitchens; some units sleep eight. The Beachside Inn has more modern amenities and sits right on the lake, but its rooms feel like an ordinary motel. Best of all, the resort sits well off the road and there's tons of space; kids have a blast here. Rates drop significantly in winter, plus you can snowshoe and zip along cross-country ski trails on the property. **Pros:** wide choice of accommodations; beautiful lakeside location. **Cons:** no phones or TVs in some rooms. ✉ *1900 Jameson Beach Rd.* ☎ *530/541–1801 or 800/544–1801* 🌐 *www.camprichardson.com* *27 lodge rooms, 40 cabins, 7 inn rooms, 200 campsites; 100 RV sites* *In-room: no phone (some), no a/c, kitchen (some), no TV (some). In-hotel: restaurant, beachfront, bicycles, Wi-Fi hotspot* ▭ *AE, D, MC, V.*

WORD OF MOUTH

"Bike trails are wonderful from Camp Richardson (near South Shore). It's like hiking in the middle of the woods, but on a bicycle. You can bike from beach to beach. Take a picnic lunch."—elnap29

$$–$$$ ★ **Inn by the Lake.** Of all the mid-range lodgings in South Lake, this one is probably the best. Across the road from a beach, the "inn" is essentially a high-end motel, with spacious, spotless rooms and suites. Beds have fluffed and freshly covered duvets; you won't find musty bedspreads here. All rooms have balconies; pricier rooms have lake views (across the road), wet bars, and kitchens. In the afternoon the staff sets out cookies and cider. **Pros:** great value; stellar service; next to a bowling alley and just a short drive from Heavenly Mountain. **Cons:** sits on Lake Tahoe Boulevard, the busy main route into town. ✉ *3300 Lake Tahoe Blvd.* ☎ *530/542–0330 or 800/877–1466* 🌐 *www.innbythelake.com* *90 rooms, 10 suites* *In-room: a/c, kitchen (some), refrigerator, Wi-Fi. In-hotel: room service, pool, gym, bicycles, laundry facilities, laundry service, Wi-Fi hotspot* ▭ *AE, D, DC, MC, V*

$$$–$$$$ ★ **Marriott's Grand Residence and Timber Lodge.** You can't beat the location of these two gigantic, modern condominium complexes right at the base of Heavenly Gondola, smack in the center of town. Though both are extremely comfortable, Timber Lodge feels more like a family vacation resort; Grand Residence is geared to upper-end travelers. Units vary in size from studios to three bedrooms, and some have amenities such as stereos, fireplaces, daily maid service, and full kitchens. Ask about vacation packages. **Pros:** central location; great for families; within walking distance of excellent restaurants. **Cons:** can be jam-packed on weekends. ✉ *1001 Park Ave.* ☎ *530/542–8400 or 800/627–7468* 🌐 *www.marriott.com* *431 condos* *In-room: a/c, kitchen (some), Wi-Fi. In-hotel: pool, gym, laundry facilities, laundry service, Wi-Fi hotspot, parking (paid)* ▭ *AE, D, MC, V.*

23

$$–$$$$ 🏠 **Sorensen's Resort.** Escape civilization by staying in a log cabin at this woodsy 165-acre resort within the Eldorado National Forest, 20 minutes south of town. You can lie on a hammock beneath the aspens or sit in a rocker on your own front porch. All but three of the cabins have a kitchen and wood-burning stove or fireplace. Some cabins are close together, and the furnishings aren't fancy (think futons as sofas), but there's a wonderful summer-camp charm about the place that makes it special. There are also five modern homes that sleep six. The resort sits on the edge of the highway, which allows it to stay open in winter—a boon for skiers—but in summer, request a cabin away from the road. **Pros:** gorgeous, rustic setting. **Cons:** nearest nightlife is 20 mi away in South Lake Tahoe. ⊠ *14255 Hwy. 88, Hope Valley* ☎ *530/694–2203 or 800/423–9949* ⊕ *www.sorensensresort.com* ⤴ *2 rooms with shared bath, 35 cabins, 5 houses* ⚬ *In-room: no phone, no a/c, kitchen (some), no TV, Wi-Fi (some). In-hotel: restaurant, children's programs (ages 3–18), Wi-Fi hotspot, some pets allowed* ⊟ *AE, D, DC, MC, V.*

$$$–$$$$ 🏠 **Tahoe Seasons Resort.** It's a 150-yard walk to California Lodge of Heavenly Mountain Resort from this all-suites time-share hotel, where every room has a two-person sunken hot tub. Most units have gas fireplaces, and some can sleep up to six people. Beautifully renovated, the resort is situated in a more residential part of town. It has a seasonal restaurant and offers shuttle service to nearby casinos. **Pros:** steps away from ski resort; a less touristy location. **Cons:** no restaurants or casinos within walking distance. ⊠ *3901 Saddle Rd.* ☎ *530/541–6700 front desk, 800/540–4874 reservations* ⊕ *www.tahoeseasons.com* ⤴ *160 suites* ⚬ *In-room: a/c, kitchen, refrigerator, DVD, Internet. In-hotel: bar, tennis courts, pool* ⊟ *AE, D, MC, V.*

SPORTS AND THE OUTDOORS

FISHING   **Tahoe Sport Fishing** (⊠ *Ski Run Marina* ☎ *530/541–5448, 800/696–7797 in CA* ⊕ *www.tahoesportfishing.com*) is one of the largest and oldest fishing-charter services on the lake. Morning trips cost $95, afternoon trips $85. Year-round outings include all necessary gear and bait, and the crew cleans and packages your catch.

GOLF   The 18-hole, par-71 **Lake Tahoe Golf Course** (⊠ *U.S. 50, between Lake Tahoe Airport and Meyers* ☎ *530/577–0788* ⊕ *www.laketahoegc.com*) has a driving range. Greens fees start at $55 and go as high as $80; a cart (mandatory Friday to Sunday) costs $25. Twilight rates drop as low as $25.

HIKING   The south shore is a great jumping-off point for day treks into nearby Eldorado National Forest and Desolation Wilderness. Hike a couple of miles on the **Pacific Crest Trail** (⊠ *Echo Summit, about 12 mi southwest of South Lake Tahoe off U.S. 50 916/285–1846 or 888/728–7245* ⊕ *www.pcta.org*). The Pacific Crest Trail leads into **Desolation Wilderness** (⊠ *El Dorado National Forest Information Center* ☎ *530/644–6048* ⊕ *www.fs.fed.us/r5/eldorado*), where you can pick up trails to gorgeous back-country lakes and mountain peaks (bring a proper topographic map and compass, and carry water and food). Late May through early September, the easiest way to access Desolation Wilderness is via boat taxi ($10 one way) across Echo **Lake from Echo Chalet** (⌧ *Echo Lakes Rd. off U.S. 50 near Echo Summit* ☎ *530/659–7207* ⊕ *www.echochalet.com*).

ICE-SKATING
❄

If you're here in winter, practice your jumps and turns at the **Heavenly Village Outdoor Ice Rink**. It's between the gondola and the cinema. ☎ *530/542–4230* ⊡ *$20, includes skate rentals* ⊙ *Nov.–Mar., daily 10–8, weather permitting.*

For year-round fun, head to the city-operated **South Tahoe Ice Arena**. You can rent equipment and sign up for lessons at this NHL regulation size indoor rink. In the evening the lights are turned low and a disco ball lights up the ice. Call ahead to check on the irregular hours. ⌧ *1176 Rufus Allen Blvd.* ☎ *530/542–6262* ⊕ *www.recreationintahoe.com/ ice_arena* ⊡ *$9, plus $3 skate rental* ⊙ *Daily.*

KAYAKING

Kayak Tahoe (⌧ *Timber Cove Marina; 3411 Lake Tahoe Blvd., behind Best Western Timber Cove Lodge* ☎ *530/544–2011* ⊕ *www.kayaktahoe. com*) has long been teaching people to kayak on Lake Tahoe and the Truckee River. Lessons and excursions (to the south shore, Emerald Bay, and Sand Harbor) are offered May through September. You can also rent a kayak and paddle solo.

MOUNTAIN
BIKING

With so much national forest land surrounding Lake Tahoe, you may want to try mountain biking. You can rent both road and mountain bikes and get tips on where to ride from the friendly staff at **Tahoe Sports Ltd.** (⌧ *4000 Lake Tahoe Blvd.* ☎ *530/542–4000* ⊕ *www.tahoesportsltd.com*).

SKIING
Fodor's Choice
★

Straddling two states, vast **Heavenly Mountain Resort**—composed of nine peaks, two valleys, and four base-lodge areas, along with the largest snowmaking system in the western United States—has terrain for every skier. Beginners can choose wide, well-groomed trails, accessed from the California Lodge or the gondola from downtown South Lake Tahoe; kids have short and gentle runs in the Enchanted Forest area all to themselves. The Sky Express high-speed quad chair whisks intermediate and advanced skiers to the summit for wide cruisers or steep tree-skiing. Mott and Killebrew canyons draw experts to the Nevada side for steep chutes and thick-timber slopes. For snowboarders and tricksters, there are four different terrain parks. True thrill-seekers will hop into the harness of the mountain's newest addition, the Heavenly Flyer, a 3,100-foot zip line with a plunging vertical drop of 525 feet. (Minors need a parent's signature on consent form.) The ski school is big and offers everything from learn-to-ski packages to canyon-adventure tours. Call about ski and boarding camps. Skiing lessons are available for children ages four and up; there's day care for infants older than six weeks. ⌧ *Ski Run Blvd., off U.S. 50, South Lake Tahoe, CA* ☎ *775/586–7000 or 800/432–8365* ⊕ *www.skiheavenly.com* ⊘ *94 trails on 4,800 acres, rated 20% beginner, 45% intermediate, 35% expert. Longest run 5½ mi, base 6,540 feet, summit 10,067 feet. Lifts: 30, including 1 aerial tram, 1 gondola, 2 high-speed 6-passenger lifts, and 7 high-speed quads.*

★

Thirty-six miles south of Lake Tahoe, **Kirkwood Ski Resort** is the hardcore skiers' and boarders' favorite south-shore mountain, known for its craggy gulp-and-go chutes, sweeping cornices, steep-aspect glade skiing, and high base elevation. But there's also fantastic terrain for

23

newbies and intermediates down wide-open bowls, through wooded gullies, and along rolling tree-lined trails. Tricksters can show off in the Stomping Grounds terrain park on jumps, wall rides, rails, and a half-pipe, all visible from the base area. The mountain gets hammered with more than 500 inches of snow annually, and often has the most in all of North America. If you're into out-of-bounds skiing, check out Expedition Kirkwood, a backcountry-skills program that teaches basic safety awareness. Kirkwood is also the only Tahoe resort to offer Cat-skiing. If you're into cross-country, the resort has 80 km (50 mi) of superb groomed-track skiing, with skating lanes, instruction, and rentals. Non-skiers can snowshoe, snow-skate, and go dogsledding or snow-tubing. The children's ski school has programs for ages 4 to 12, and there's day care for children two to six years old. ⊠ *1501 Kirkwood Meadows Dr., off Hwy. 88, 14 mi west of Hwy. 89, Kirkwood* ☎ *209/258–6000 downhill, 209/258–7248 cross-country, 209/258–7293 lodging information, 877/547–5966 snow phone* ⊕ *www.kirkwood.com* ⟳ *65 trails on 2,300 acres, rated 15% beginner, 50% intermediate, 20% advanced, 15% expert. Longest run 2½ mi, base 7,800 feet, summit 9,800 feet. Lifts: 12, including 2 high-speed quads.*

Often overlooked by skiers and boarders rushing to Heavenly or Kirk-wood, **Sierra-at-Tahoe** has meticulously groomed intermediate slopes, some of the best tree-skiing in California, and gated backcountry access. Extremely popular with local snowboarders, Sierra also has six terrain parks, including a super-pipe with 17-foot walls. For nonskiers there's a snow-tubing hill. Sierra has a low-key atmosphere that's great for families. Kids and beginners take the slow routes in the Mellow Yellow Zone. ⊠ *1111 Sierra-at Tahoe Rd., 12 mi from South Lake Tahoe off U.S. 50, near Echo Summit, Twin Bridges* ☎ *530/659–7453* ⊕ *www.sierraattahoe.com* ⟳ *46 trails on 2,000 acres, rated 25% beginner, 50% intermediate, 25% advanced. Longest run 2½ mi, base 6,640 feet, summit 8,852 feet. Lifts: 12, including 3 high-speed quads.*

Operating from a yurt at Pickett's Junction, **Hope Valley Cross Country** (⊠ *Hwy. 88, at Hwy. 89, Hope Valley* ☎ *530/694–2266* ⊕ *www.hopevalleyoutdoors.com*) provides lessons and equipment rentals to prepare you for cross-country skiing and snowshoeing. The outfit has 50 mi of trails through Humboldt–Toiyabe National Forest, 10 of which are groomed.

If you don't want to pay the high cost of rental equipment at the resorts, you'll find reasonable prices and expert advice at **Tahoe Sports Ltd.** (⊠ *4000 Lake Tahoe Blvd.* ☎ *530/542–4000* ⊕ *www.tahoesportsltd.com*.

POPE-BALDWIN RECREATION AREA

5 mi west of South Lake Tahoe on Hwy. 89.

To the west of downtown South Lake Tahoe, U.S. 50 and Highway 89 come together, forming an intersection nicknamed "the Y." If you head northwest on Highway 89 and follow the lakefront, commercial development gives way to national forests and state parks. One of these is Pope-Baldwin Recreation Area.

EXPLORING

Stroll or picnic lakeside at **Tallac Historic Site**. Then explore **Pope House,** the magnificently restored 1894 mansion of George S. Pope, who made his money in shipping and lumber and played host to the business and cultural elite of 1920s America. There are two other estates here. One belonged to entrepreneur "Lucky" Baldwin; today it houses the **Baldwin Museum,** a collection of family memorabilia and Washoe Indian artifacts. The **Valhalla** (⊕ *www.valhallatahoe.com*), with a spectacular floor-to-ceiling stone fireplace, belonged to Walter Heller. Its Grand Hall and a lakeside boathouse, refurbished as a theater, host summertime concerts, plays, and cultural activities. Docents conduct tours of the Pope House in summer; call for tour times. In winter you can cross-country ski around the site. ⊠ *Hwy. 89* ☎ *530/541–5227* ⊕ *www. tahoeheritage.org* ▧ *Free; Pope House tour $5* ⊙ *Grounds daily sunrise–sunset. Pope House and Baldwin Museum late May–mid-June, weekends 11–3; mid-June–early Sept., daily 11–4.*

℃ At **Taylor Creek Visitor Center,** operated by the U.S. Forest Service, you can visit the site of a Washoe Indian settlement; walk self-guided trails through meadow, marsh, and forest; and inspect the Stream Profile Chamber, an underground display with windows right into Taylor Creek (in fall you may see spawning kokanee salmon digging their nests). In summer U.S. Forest Service naturalists organize discovery walks and evening programs (call ahead). ⊠ *Hwy. 89, 3 mi north of junction with U.S. 50* ☎ *530/543–2674 June–Oct., 530/543–2600 year-round* ⊕ *www.fs.fed.us/r5/ltbmu/recreation/summer-index.shtml* ▧ *Free* ⊙ *Memorial Day–late Sept., daily 8–5; Oct., daily 8–4.*

EMERALD BAY STATE PARK

4 mi west of Pope-Baldwin Recreation Area on Hwy. 89.

Fodor's Choice ★ Emerald Bay, a 3-mi-long and 1-mi-wide fjordlike inlet on Lake Tahoe's shore, was carved by a massive glacier millions of years ago. Famed for its jewel-like shape and colors, it surrounds Fannette, Tahoe's only island. Highway 89 curves high above the lake through Emerald Bay State Park; from the Emerald Bay lookout, the centerpiece of the park, you can survey the whole scene. This is one of the don't-miss views of Lake Tahoe. Come before the sun drops below the mountains to the west; the light is best in mid- to late mornings, when the bay's colors really pop.

EXPLORING

A steep 1-mi-long trail from the lookout leads down to **Vikingsholm,** a 38-room estate completed in 1929. The original owner, Lora Knight, had this precise copy of a 1,200-year-old Viking castle built out of materials native to the area. She furnished it with Scandinavian antiques and hired artisans to build period reproductions. The sod roof sprouts wildflowers each spring. There are picnic tables nearby and a gray-sand beach for strolling. The hike back up is hard (especially if you're not yet acclimated to the elevation), but there are benches and stone culverts to rest on. At the 150-foot peak of Fannette Island are the ruins of a stone structure known as the Tea House, built in 1928 so that

Fjordlike Emerald Bay is quite possibly the prettiest part of Lake Tahoe.

Knight's guests could have a place to enjoy afternoon refreshments after a motorboat ride. The island is off-limits from February through June to protect nesting Canada geese. The rest of the year it's open for day use. ✉ *Hwy. 89* ☎ *530/541–6498 summer, 530/525–7277 year-round* ⊕ *www.vikingsholm.com* ✉ *Day-use parking fee $7, mansion tour $5* ⊙ *Late May–Sept., daily 10–4.*

SPORTS AND THE OUTDOORS

HIKING Leave your car in the parking lot for Eagle Falls picnic area (near Vikingsholm; arrive early for a good spot), and head to **Eagle Falls**, a short but fairly steep walk-up canyon. You'll have a brilliant panorama of Emerald Bay from this spot, near the boundary of Desolation Wilderness. If you want a full-day's hike and you're in good shape, continue 5 mi, past Eagle Lake, to Upper and Middle Velma Lakes. You can pick up trail maps from the U.S. Forest Service at their Lake Tahoe Visitor Center in summer, or at park headquarters in South Lake Tahoe year-round.

D.L. BLISS STATE PARK

3 mi north of Emerald Bay State Park on Hwy. 89.

D.L. Bliss State Park takes its name from Duane LeRoy Bliss, a 19th-century lumber magnate. At one time Bliss owned nearly 75% of Tahoe's lakefront, along with local steamboats, railroads, and banks. The park shares 6 mi of shoreline with Emerald Bay State Park; combined the two parks cover 1,830 acres, 744 of which were donated to the state by the Bliss family in 1929. At the north end of Bliss is Rubicon Point, which overlooks one of the lake's deepest spots. Short trails lead to an old lighthouse and Balancing Rock, which weighs 250,000 pounds and balances on a fist of granite. A 4.25-mi trail—one of Tahoe's premier hikes—leads to Vikingsholm and provides stunning lake views. Two white-sand beaches front some of Tahoe's warmest water. ⊠ *Hwy. 89* ☎ *530/525–7277 or 800/777–0369* ⊠ *$8 per vehicle, day use* ⊙ *Late May–Sept., daily sunrise–sunset.*

CAMPING

$$ ⚠ **D.L. Bliss State Park Campground.** In one of California's most beautiful spots, quiet, wooded hills make for blissful family camping near the lake. The campground is open June to September, and reservations are accepted up to seven months in advance. It's expensive for a campground, but the location can't be beat, especially at the beach campsites. Book early. Trailers and RVs longer than 18 feet are not allowed. ⊠ *Off Hwy. 89, 17 mi south of Tahoe City on lake side* ☎ *800/777—0369 or 800/444–7275* ⊕ *www.reserveamerica.com* ⤴ *168 sites* ⚐ *Flush toilets, drinking water, showers, bear boxes, fire pits, grills, picnic tables, public telephone, swimming (beach).*

SUGAR PINE POINT STATE PARK

8 mi north of D.L. Bliss State Park on Hwy. 89.

★ The main attraction at Sugar Pine Point State Park is **Ehrman Mansion,** a 1903 stone-and-shingle summer home furnished in period style. In its day it was the height of modernity, with a refrigerator, an elevator, and an electric stove (tours leave hourly). Also in the park are a trapper's log cabin from the mid-19th century, a nature preserve with wildlife exhibits, a lighthouse, the start of the 10-mi-long biking trail to Tahoe City, and an extensive system of hiking and cross-country skiing trails. If you're feeling less ambitious, you can relax on the sun-dappled lawn behind the mansion and gaze out at the lake. ⊠ *Hwy. 89* ☎ *530/525–7982 mansion in season, 530/525–7232 year-round* ⊠ *$8 per vehicle, day use; mansion tour $5* ⊙ *Mansion Memorial Day–Labor Day, daily 11–4.*

CAMPING

$$ ⚠ **Sugar Pine Point State Park Campground/General Creek Campground.** This beautiful and homey campground south of Tahoma, off Highway 89 is jammed in summer months. During snow season cross-country skiers and snowshoe enthusiasts enjoy the park's groomed trails. There are no hookups here; the campground is open from late May to early September only. ⊠ *Hwy. 89, 1 mi south of Tahoma* ☎ *800/777–0369 or 800/444–7275* ⊕ *www.reserveamerica.com* ⤴ *175 sites* ⚐ *Flush toilets, drinking water, showers, bear boxes, fire pits, grills.*

TAHOMA

1 mi north of Sugar Pine Point State Park on Hwy. 89; 23 mi south of Truckee on Hwy. 89.

Tahoma exemplifies life on the lake in its early days, with rustic waterfront vacation cottages that are far from the blinking lights of South Shore's casinos. In 1960 Tahoma was host of the Olympic Nordic-skiing competitions. Today there's little to do here except stroll by the lake and listen to the wind in the trees, making it a favorite home base for mellow families and nature buffs.

WHERE TO STAY

$$–$$$ **Tahoma Meadows B&B Cottages.** It's hard to beat Tahoma Meadows
★ for atmosphere and woodsy charm; it's a great retreat for families and couples. Sixteen individually decorated little red cottages sit tucked beneath towering pine trees. Inside, they're cheerful, with fun details like model ships on the shelf and a stuffed bear on the bed; some have claw-foot tubs and fireplaces. Cottages without kitchens include breakfast in the cozy, gable-roof lodge. Down-to-earth and simple, this is one of Tahoe's best hideaways. **Pros:** lovely setting; good choice for families. **Cons:** far from the casinos. ⊠ *6821 W. Lake Blvd.* ☎ *530/525–1553 or 866/525–1553* ⊕ *www.tahomameadows.com* ➔ *16 cabins* ⚒ *In-room: no phone, no a/c, kitchen (some), Wi-Fi. In-hotel: Wi-Fi hotspot, some pets allowed* ⊟ *AE, D, MC, V* ⦿❙ *BP.*

SPORTS AND THE OUTDOORS

SKIING You'll feel as though you're going to ski into the lake when you schuss down the face of **Homewood Mountain Resort**—and you could if you really wanted to, because the mountain rises right off the shoreline. This is the favorite area of locals on a fresh-snow day, because you can find lots of untracked powder. It's also the most protected and least windy Tahoe ski area during a storm; when every other resort's lifts are on wind hold, you can almost always count on Homewood's to be open. There's only one high-speed chairlift, but there are rarely any lines, and the ticket prices are some of the cheapest around—kids five to 12 ski for $10 while those four and under are free. It may look small as you drive by, but most of the resort is not visible from the road. ⊠ *5145 West Lake Blvd., (Hwy. 89), 6 mi south of Tahoe City, Homewood* ☎ *530/525–2992* ⊕ *www.skihomewood.com* ⌖ *60 trails on 1,260 acres, rated 15% beginner, 50% intermediate, and 35% advanced. Longest run 2 mi, base 6,230 feet, summit 7,880 feet. Lifts: 4 chairlifts, 3 surface lifts.*

TAHOE CITY

★ *10 mi north of Sugar Pine Point State Park on Hwy. 89; 14 mi south of Truckee on Hwy. 89.*

Tahoe City is the only lakeside town with a compact downtown area good for strolling and window-shopping. Of the larger towns ringing the lake, it has the most bona-fide charm. Stores and restaurants are all within walking distance of the Outlet Gates, enormous Lake Tahoe's only outlet, where water is spilled into the Truckee River to control the surface level of the lake. You can spot giant trout in the river from Fanny Bridge, so-called for the views of the backsides of sightseers leaning over the railing.

ESSENTIALS

Visitor Information North Lake Tahoe Resort Association (⬚ *Box 1757, Tahoe City 96145* ☎ *530/583–3494 or 888/434–1262* ⊕ *www.gotahoenorth.com*).

EXPLORING

★ The **Gatekeeper's Cabin Museum** preserves a little-known part of the region's history. Between 1910 and 1968 the gatekeeper who lived on this site was responsible for monitoring the level of the lake, using a hand-turned winch system to keep the water at the correct level. That winch system is still used today. The site is also home to a fantastic Native American basket museum that displays 800 baskets from 85 tribes and is reason enough to visit. ⊠ *130 W. Lake Blvd.* ☎ *530/583–1762* ⊕ *www. northtahoemuseums.org* ⊠ *$3* ⊙ *May–mid-June and Sept., Wed.–Sun. 11–5; mid-June–Aug., daily 11–5; Oct.–Apr., weekends 11–3.*

In the middle of town, the **Watson Cabin Living Museum**, a 1909 log cabin built by Robert M. Watson and his son, is filled with some century-old furnishings and many reproductions. Docents are available to answer questions and will lead tours with advance arrangements. ⊠ *560 N. Lake Blvd.* ☎ *530/583–8717 or 530/583–1762* ⊕ *www.northtahoemuseums. org* ⊠ *$2 donation suggested* ⊙ *Late May–June, weekends noon–4; July–early Sept., Wed.–Mon. noon–4.*

WHERE TO EAT

$$$–$$$$ ✕ **Christy Hill.** Huge windows give diners here some of the best lake views

AMERICAN in Tahoe. The menu features solid Euro–Cal preparations of fresh seafood, filet mignon, or vegetarian selections. An extensive wine list and exceptionally good desserts earn accolades, as do the gracious service and casual vibe. If the weather is balmy have dinner on the deck. In any season, this is the romantic choice for lake gazing and wine sipping. Reservations are recommended. ⊠ *Lakehouse Mall, 115 Grove St.* ☎ *530/583–8551* ═ *AE, MC, V* ⊙ *Closed Mon. No lunch.*

$$–$$$ ✕ **Fiamma.** Join the hip young singles at the little wine bar, or settle into

ITALIAN one of the comfy booths at this modern mom-and-pop trattoria that specializes in roasted and grilled meats, homemade pastas, and pizzas from the wood-fired oven. Prices run a bit high, but this is generally a good bet for a casual, easy dinner. And everything from soup stock to gelato is made from scratch. For a sure bet, stick to the crispy, delicious pizzas. ⊠ *521 N. Lake Blvd.* ☎ *530/581–1416* ═ *AE, MC, V* ⊙ *No lunch.*

¢–$ ✕ **Fire Sign Café.** Watch the road carefully or you'll miss this great little

AMERICAN diner 2 mi south of Tahoe City on Highway 89. There's often a wait

★ at the west shore's best spot for breakfast and lunch, but it's worth it. The pastries are made from scratch, the salmon is smoked in-house, the salsa is hand cut, and there's real maple syrup for the many flavors of pancakes and waffles. The eggs Benedict are delicious. ⊠ *1785 W. Lake Blvd.* ☎ *530/583–0871* ⊴ *Reservations not accepted* ═ *AE, MC, V* ⊙ *No dinner.*

$$$–$$$$ ✕ **Wolfdale's.** Going strong since 1978, Wolfdale's consistent, inspired

ECLECTIC cuisine makes it one of the top restaurants on the lake. Seafood is the

★ specialty on the changing menu; the imaginative entrées merge Asian and European cooking (drawing on the chef-owner's training in Japan) and trend toward light and healthful, rather than heavy and overdone. And everything from teriyaki glaze to smoked fish is made in-house. Request a window table, and book early enough to see the lake view from the elegantly sparse dining room. ⊠ *640 N. Lake Blvd.* 🕾 *530/583–5700* ⚓ *Reservations essential* ▭ *MC, V* ⊘ *Closed Tues. No lunch.*

WHERE TO STAY

$$–$$$$ ⊡ **Cottage Inn.** Avoid the crowds by staying just south of town in one of these charming circa-1938 log cottages under the towering pines on the lake's west shore. Cute as a button, with knotty-pine paneling, rustic pine furniture, and a gas-flame stone fireplace, each unit is decorated in old-Tahoe style while embracing you with up-to-date comfort. If you're exceptionally tall, you may find some of the sloped ceilings in the upstairs rooms a bit low (ask for a downstairs room when you book). There's also a private beach and Wi-Fi in the lobby. **Pros:** romantic, woodsy setting; each room has a fireplace; full breakfast. **Cons:** no kids under 12. ⊠ *1690 W. Lake Blvd., Box 66* 🕾 *530/581–4073 or 800/581–4073* ⊕ *www.thecottageinn.com* ↰ *22 rooms* ♿ *In-room: no phone, no a/c, DVD (some). In-hotel: beachfront, Wi-Fi hotspot, no kids under 12* ▭ *MC, V* ⊺⊙⫾ *BP.*

$$–$$$ ⊡ **River Ranch Lodge.** Tucked into a bend of the Truckee River, this intimate lodge is a short distance from major ski resorts and the town center. Each of the rooms has rustic pine furnishings and comfy bedding; most overlook the river. In summer you can watch rafts skim the rapids while enjoying the daily barbecue lunch on the patio. Fuel up for a day on the slopes with a complimentary Continental breakfast. **Pros:** beautiful site on the Truckee River; great lounge with a gorgeous curved wall of windows. **Cons:** rooms fill quickly. ⊠ *Hwy. 89, at Alpine Meadows Rd., Tahoe City* 🕾 *530/583–4264 or 866/991–9912* ⊕ *www.riverranchlodge.com* ↰ *19 rooms* ♿ *In-room: no a/c, Wi-Fi. In-hotel: restaurant, bar, Wi-Fi hotspot* ▭ *AE, MC, V* ⊺⊙⫾ *CP.*

$$$–$$$$ ⊡ **Sunnyside Steakhouse and Lodge.** The views are superb at this pretty
★   little lodge right on the lake, 3 mi south of Tahoe City. All but four rooms have balconies and locally crafted furnishings; some have river-rock fireplaces and wet bars, and some have pull-out sofas. While the lodge is great for couples, families also favor it because of its proximity to kid-friendly Homewood Mountain Resort in winter, and water sports and hiking in summer. The inviting Sunnyside Steakhouse ($$$–$$$$) echoes the design of old mahogany Chris Craft speedboats. The pricey steak, seafood, and pasta menu will thin out your wallet a bit; the Mountain Grill is a less expensive option, a good choice for those with kids in tow. Be forewarned: this is *not* a quiet place on summer weekends. The bar is a blast, and gets packed with boaters and bacchanalian revelers. **Pros:** complimentary Continental breakfast and afternoon tea; most rooms have balconies overlooking the lake. **Cons:** can be pricey for families; Wi-Fi is spotty in rooms farthest from the lobby. ⊠ *1850 W. Lake Blvd., Box 5969* 🕾 *530/583–7200 or 800/822–2754* ⊕ *www.sunnysideresort.com* ↰ *18 rooms, 5 suites* ♿ *In-room: no a/c, Wi-Fi. In-hotel: restaurant, room service, bar, beachfront, Wi-Fi hotspot* ▭ *AE, D, MC, V* ⊺⊙⫾ *CP.*

SPORTS AND THE OUTDOORS

GOLF   Golfers use pull carts or caddies at the 9-hole **Tahoe City Golf Course** (⊠ *252 N. Lake Blvd.* ☎ *530/583–1516*), which opened in 1917. ■ **TIP→** All greens break toward the lake.

Though rates vary by season, the maximum greens fees are $45 for 9 holes, $75 for 18; a power cart costs $18 to $30.

MOUNTAIN   **Cyclepaths Mountain Bike Adventures** (⊠ *1785 W. Lake Blvd.* ☎ *530/581–*
BIKING   *1171* ⊕ *www.cyclepaths.com*) is a combination full-service bike shop and bike-adventure outfitter. It offers instruction in mountain biking, guided tours (from half-day to weeklong excursions), tips for self-guided bike touring, bike repairs, and books and maps on the area.

RIVER   In summer you can take a self-guided raft trip down a gentle 5-mi
RAFTING   stretch of the Truckee River through **Truckee River Rafting** (☎ *530/583–*
↺   *7238 or 888/584–7238* ⊕ *www.truckeeriverrafting.com*). They will shuttle you back to Tahoe City at the end of your two- to four-hour trip. On a warm day, this makes a great family outing.

SKIING   The locals' favorite place to ski on the north shore, **Alpine Meadows Ski**
★   **Area**, is also the unofficial telemarking hub of the Sierra. With 495 inches of snow annually, Alpine has some of Tahoe's most reliable conditions. It's usually one of the first areas to open in November and one of the last to close in May or June. Alpine isn't the place for arrogant show-offs; instead, you'll find down-to-earth alpine fetishists. The two peaks here are well suited to intermediate skiers, with a number of runs for experts only. Snowboarders and hot-dog skiers will find a terrain park with a half-pipe, super-pipe, rails, and tabletops, as well as a boarder-cross course. Alpine is a great place to learn to ski, and has a ski school that teaches and coaches those with physical and mental disabilities. There's also an area for overnight RV parking. On Saturday, because of the limited parking, there's more acreage per person than at other resorts. ⊠ *2600 Alpine Meadows Rd., off Hwy. 89, 6 mi northwest of Tahoe City and 13 mi south of I–80* ☎ *530/583–4232 or 800/441–4423, 530/581–8374 snow phone* ⊕ *www.skialpine.com* ☞ *100 trails on 2,400 acres, rated 25% beginner, 40% intermediate, 35% advanced. Longest run 2½ mi, base 6,835 feet, summit 8,637 feet. Lifts: 13, including 1 high-speed 6-passenger lift and 2 high-speed quads.*

You can rent skis, boards, and snowshoes at **Tahoe Dave's Skis and Boards** (⊠ *590 N. Lake Blvd.* ☎ *530/583–0400*), which has the area's best selection of downhill rental equipment. If you plan to ski or board the backcountry, you'll find everything from crampons to transceivers at the **BackCountry** (⊠ *690 N. Lake Blvd.* ☎ *530/581–5861 or 888/625–8444* ⊕ *www.thebackcountry.net*).

OLYMPIC VALLEY

7 mi north of Tahoe City via Hwy. 89 to Squaw Valley Rd.; 8½ mi south of Truckee via Hwy. 89 to Squaw Valley Rd.

Olympic Valley got its name in 1960, when Squaw Valley USA, the ski resort here, hosted the winter Olympics. Snow sports remain the primary activity, but once summer comes, you can hike into the adjacent

TAHOE SPORTS TIPS

If you're planning to spend any time outdoors around Lake Tahoe, whether hiking, climbing, or camping, be aware that weather conditions can change quickly in the Sierra. To avoid a life-threatening case of hypothermia, always bring a pocket-size, fold-up rain poncho (available in all sporting-goods stores) to keep you dry. Wear long pants and a hat. Carry plenty of water. Because you'll likely be walking on granite, wear sturdy, closed-toe hiking boots, with soles that grip rock. If you're going into the backcountry, bring a signaling device (such as a mirror), emergency whistle, compass, map, energy bars, and water purifier. When heading out alone, tell someone where you're going and when you're coming back.

If you plan to ski, be aware of resort elevations. In the event of a winter storm, determine the snow level before you choose the resort you'll ski. Often the level can be as high as 7,000 feet, which means rain at some resorts' base areas but snow at others. For storm information,

check the **National Weather Service's Web page** (⊕ *www.wrh.noaa. gov/rev*). If you plan to do any backcountry skiing, check with the **U.S. Forest Service** (☎ *530/587–2158 backcountry recording*) for conditions. A shop called the **Backcountry** (☎ *530/581–5861 Tahoe City, 530/582–0909 Truckee* ⊕ *www. thebackcountry.net*), with branches in Tahoe City and Truckee, operates an excellent Web site with current information about how and where to (and where not to) ski, mountain bike, and hike in the backcountry around Tahoe.

If you plan to camp in the backcountry, you'll need to purchase a wilderness permit, which you can pick up at the **U.S. Forest Service Office** (✉ *35 College Dr., South Lake Tahoe* ☎ *530/543–2600* ⊕ *www. fs.fed.us/r5/ltbmu*) or at a ranger station at the entrance to any of the national forests. For reservations at campgrounds in California state parks, contact **Reserve America** (☎ *800/444–7275* ⊕ *www. reserveamerica.com*).

23

Granite Chief Wilderness, explore wildflower-studded alpine meadows, or lie by a swimming pool in one of the Sierra's prettiest valleys.

EXPLORING

The centerpiece of Olympic Valley is the **Village at Squaw Valley** (☎ *530/ 584–1000 or 530/584–6205, 888/805–5022 condo reservations* ⊕ *www. thevillageatsquaw.com*), a pedestrian mall at the base of several four-story ersatz Bavarian stone-and-timber buildings, where you'll find restaurants, high-end condo rentals, boutiques, and cafés. The village often holds events and festivals.

You can ride the Squaw Valley cable car to **High Camp**, which at 8,200 feet commands superb views of Lake Tahoe and the surrounding mountains. In summer, go for a hike, sit by the pool at the High Camp Bath and Tennis Club, or have a cocktail and watch the sunset. In winter, you can ski, ice-skate, or snow-tube. There's also a restaurant, lounge, and small Olympic museum. ✉ *Cable Car Bldg., Squaw Valley* ☎ *530/581–7278 High Camp, 530/583–6985 cable car* ⊕ *www.squaw.*

Squaw Valley USA has runs for skiers of all ability levels—from beginner trails to cliff drops for experts.

com ▣ Cable car $24; special packages include swimming or skating ☉ Daily; call for hrs.

WHERE TO EAT

$$–$$$$
ECLECTIC

✕ **Graham's of Squaw Valley.** Sit by a floor-to-ceiling river-rock hearth under a knotty-pine peaked ceiling in the intimate dining room in the Christy Inn Lodge. The southern European–inspired menu changes often, but expect hearty entrées such as fillet of beef and paella, along with lighter-fare small plates like grilled quail or sea scallops. You can also stop in at the fireside bar for appetizers and wine from Graham's huge and highly regarded wine list. Reservations are recommended. ⊠ *1650 Squaw Valley Rd.* ☎ *530/581–0454* ▤ *AE, MC, V* ☉ *Closed Mon. No lunch.*

$$–$$$
JAPANESE

✕ **Mamasake.** The hip and happening spot for sushi at Squaw serves stylized presentations in an industrial-warehouse-like room. In the evening, sit at the bar and watch extreme ski movies, many of which were filmed right outside the window. Or drop in from 3 PM to 5 PM to enjoy the incredibly inexpensive afternoon special: a spicy-tuna or salmon hand roll and a can of Bud for five bucks. ⊠ *The Village at Squaw Valley* ☎ *530/584–0110* ▤ *AE, D, MC, V.*

$$$–$$$$
AMERICAN
Fodor's Choice
★

✕ **PlumpJack Café.** The best restaurant at Olympic Valley is also the finest in the entire Tahoe Basin, the epitome of discreet chic and a must-visit for all serious foodies. The menu changes seasonally, but look for caramelized day boat scallops, seared Scottish salmon with piquillo peppers and roasted fennel, or grass-fed beef with a red wine reduction and potato gratin. Rather than complicated, heavy sauces, the chef uses simple reductions to complement a dish. The result: clean, dynamic, bright flavors. The wine list is exceptional for its variety and surprisingly low prices. If not for the view of the craggy mountains through the windows lining the cushy, 60-seat dining room, you might swear you were in San Francisco. A less expensive but equally adventurous menu is served at the bar. ☒ *1920 Squaw Valley Rd., Olympic Valley* ☎ *530/583–1578 or 800/323–7666* ⚓ *Reservations essential* ⊟ *AE, MC, V.*

WHERE TO STAY

$$$–$$$$
Fodor's Choice
★

PlumpJack Squaw Valley Inn. If style and luxury are a must, make PlumpJack your first choice. The two-story, cedar-sided inn near the cable car has a snappy, sophisticated look and laid-back sensibility, perfect for the Bay Area cognoscenti who flock here on weekends. All rooms have sumptuous beds with down comforters, high-end bath amenities, and hooded terry robes to wear on your way to the outdoor hot tubs. The bar is a happening après-ski destination, and the namesake restaurant (⇨ *above*) superb. PlumpJack may not have the bells and whistles of big luxury hotels, but the service—personable and attentive—can't be beat. Not all rooms have tubs: if it matters, request one. A complimentary buffet breakfast for two is included. **Pros:** small; intimate; lots of attention to details. **Cons:** not the best choice for families with small children. ☒ *1920 Squaw Valley Rd., Olympic Valley* ☎ *530/583–1576 or 800/323–7666* ⊕ *www.plumpjack.com* ⤴ *54 rooms, 5 suites* ⚐ *In-room: a/c (some), refrigerator, DVD, Wi-Fi. In-hotel: restaurant, room service, bar, pool, gym, bicycles, Wi-Fi hotspot, parking (free)* ⊟ *AE, MC, V* ⊠|*BP.*

$$$–$$$$ **The Village at Squaw Valley USA.** Right at the base of the slopes at the center point of Olympic Valley, the Village's studios and one-, two-, or three-bedroom condominiums were built in 2000 and still look fresh. Each unit comes complete with gas fireplaces, daily maid service, and heated slate-tile bathroom floors. The individually owned units are uniformly decorated with granite counters, wood cabinets, and comfortable furnishings. They're especially appealing to families, since each condo can sleep at least four people. **Pros:** family-friendly; near Village restaurants and shops. **Cons:** claustrophobia-inducing crowds. ☒ *1750 Village East Rd.,* ☎ *530/584–1000 or 866/818–6963* ⊕ *www.thevillageatsquaw.com* ⤴ *190 suites* ⚐ *In-room: no a/c, kitchen, DVD, Internet. In-hotel: laundry facilities, Wi-Fi hotspot, parking (free)* ⊟ *AE, D, DC, MC, V.*

SPORTS AND THE OUTDOORS

GOLF The **Resort at Squaw Creek Golf Course** (☒ *400 Squaw Creek Rd.* ☎ *530/583–6300* ⊕ *www.squawcreek.com*), an 18-hole championship course, was designed by Robert Trent Jones Jr. Greens fees range from $60 for afternoon play to $115 for prime time, and include the use of a cart.

HIKING The Granite Chief Wilderness and the high peaks surrounding Olympic Valley are accessible by foot, but save yourself a 2,000-foot elevation gain by riding the Squaw Valley cable car to **High Camp** (☎ *530/583–6985* ⊕ *www.squaw.com*), the starting point for a variety of hikes. Pick up trail maps at the cable car building. In late summer, High Camp offers full-moon and sunset hikes.

23

ICE-SKATING   Ice-skate from November to late September at the **Olympic Ice Pavilion**
    (⊠ *1960 Squaw Valley Rd., High Camp, Squaw Valley* ☎ *530/583–6985*
or 530/581–7246 ⊕ *www.squaw.com*). A ride up the mountain and a
skating pass cost $29, including skate rental; pay $5 extra to end your
outing in the hot tub. Prices drop after 5 PM in winter.

MINIATURE   Next to the Olympic Village Lodge, on the far side of the creek, the **Squaw**
GOLF   **Valley Adventure Center** (☎ *530/583–7673* ⊕ *www.squawadventure.com*)
has an 18-hole miniature golf course, a ropes course, and sometimes a
★   bungee-trampoline, a blast for kids.

ROCK   Before you rappel down a granite monolith, hone your skills at the
CLIMBING   **Headwall Climbing Wall** (⊠ *1960 Squaw Valley Rd., near Village at Squaw*
Valley ☎ *530/583–7673* ⊕ *www.squawadventure.com*), at the base of
the cable car.

SKIING   Known for some of the toughest skiing in the Tahoe area, **Squaw Valley**
FodorśChoice   **USA** was the centerpiece of the 1960 winter Olympics. Today it's the
★   definitive North Tahoe ski resort and among the top-three megaresorts
in California (the other two are Heavenly and Mammoth). Although
Squaw has changed significantly since the Olympics, the skiing is still
world-class and extends across vast bowls stretched between six peaks.
Experts often head directly to the untamed terrain of the infamous
KT-22 face, which has bumps, cliffs, and gulp-and-go chutes, or to the
nearly vertical Palisades, where many famous Warren Miller extreme-
skiing films have been shot. Fret not, beginners and intermediates: you
have plenty of wide-open, groomed trails at High Camp (which sits at
the *top* of the mountain) and around the more challenging Snow King
Peak. Snowboarders and show-off skiers can tear up the three fantastic terrain parks, which include a giant super-pipe. Lift prices include
night skiing until 9 PM. Tickets for skiers 12 and under cost only $10.
⊠ *1960 Squaw Valley Rd., off Hwy. 89, Olympic Valley, 7 mi northwest
of Tahoe City* ☎ *530/583–6985, 800/545–4350 lodging reservations,
530/583–6955 snow phone* ⊕ *www.squaw.com* ↶ *170 trails on 4,000
acres, rated 25% beginner, 45% intermediate, 30% advanced. Longest
run 3.2 mi, base 6,200 feet, summit 9,050 feet. Lifts: 33, including a
gondola-style funitel, a cable car, 7 high-speed chairs, and 18 fixed-
grip chairs.*

If you don't want to pay resort prices, you can rent and tune downhill
skis and snowboards at **Tahoe Dave's Skis and Boards** (⊠ *3039 Hwy. 89,
at Squaw Valley Rd.* ☎ *530/583–5665* ⊕ *www.tahoedaves.com*).

Cross-country skiers will enjoy looping through the valley's giant alpine
meadow. The **Resort at Squaw Creek** (⊠ *400 Squaw Creek Rd.* ☎ *530/
583–6300* ⊕ *www.squawcreek.com*) rents cross-country equipment and
provides trail maps.

TRUCKEE

*13 mi northwest of Kings Beach on Hwy. 267; 14 mi north of Tahoe
City on Hwy. 89.*

Formerly a decrepit railroad town in the mountains, Truckee is now the
trendy first stop for many Tahoe visitors. Around 1863 the town was

23

officially established; by 1868 it had gone from a stagecoach station to a major stopover for trains bound for the Pacific via the new transcontinental railroad. Freight trains and Amtrak's California Zephyr still stop every day at the depot right in the middle of town. Across from the station, where Old West facades line the main drag, you'll find galleries, gift shops, boutiques, old-fashioned diners, and several remarkably good restaurants. Look for outlet stores, strip malls, and discount skiwear shops along Donner Pass Road, north of the freeway. Because of its location on I–80, Truckee is a favorite stopover for people traveling from the San Francisco Bay Area to the north shore of Lake Tahoe, Reno, and points east.

ESSENTIALS

Visitor Information Truckee Donner Chamber of Commerce (✉ *10065 Donner Pass Rd., Truckee, CA* ☎ *530/587–8808* ⊕ *www.truckee.com).*

EXPLORING

Stop by the downtown **information booth** (✉ *Railroad St., at Commercial Rd.*) in the Amtrak depot for a walking-tour map of historic Truckee.

Donner Memorial State Park and Emigrant Trail Museum commemorates the Donner Party, a group of 89 westward-bound pioneers who were trapped in the Sierra in the winter of 1846–47 in snow 22 feet deep. The top of the stone pedestal beneath the monument marks the snow level that year. Only 49 pioneers survived, some by resorting to cannibalism, though none consumed his own kin. (For the full story, pick up a copy of *Ordeal by Hunger,* by George R. Stewart.) The museum's hourly slide show details the Donner Party's plight. Other displays and dioramas relate the history of railroad development through the Sierra. In the park, you can picnic, hike, camp, and go boating, fishing, and waterskiing in summer; winter brings cross-country skiing and snowshoeing on groomed trails. The day-use parking fee includes admission to the museum. ✉ *12593 Donner Pass Rd., off I–80, 2 mi west of Truckee* ☎ *530/582–7892 museum, 800/444–7275 camping reservations* ⊕ *www.parks.ca.gov* ➲ *$8 parking, day use* ☉ *Museum daily 9–4.*

OFF THE
BEATEN
PATH

Tahoe National Forest. Draped along the Sierra Nevada Crest above Lake Tahoe, the national forest offers abundant outdoor recreation: picnicking and camping in summer, and in winter, snowshoeing, skiing, and sledding over some of the deepest snowpack in the West. The **Big Bend Visitor Center** occupies a state historic landmark within the forest, 10 mi west of Donner Summit. This area has been on major cross-country routes for centuries, ever since Native Americans passed through trading acorns and salt for pelts, obsidian, and other materials. Between 1844 and 1860, more than 200,000 emigrants traveled to California along the Emigrant Trail, which passed nearby; you can see rut marks left by wagon wheels scraping the famously hard granite. Later the nation's first transcontinental railroad ran through here (and still does), as do U.S. 40 (the old National Road) and its successor, I–80. Exhibits in the visitor center explore the area's transportation history. Take the Rainbow–Big Bend exit off I–80. ✉ *49685 Hampshire Rocks Rd. (old U.S. Hwy. 40), Soda Springs* ☎ *530/426–3609 or 530/265–4531* ⊕ *www.fs.fed.us/r5/tahoe/recreation* ➲ *Free* ☉ *Hrs vary; call ahead.*

WHERE TO EAT

$$-$$$$
ECLECTIC

✕ **Cottonwood.** Perched above town on the site of North America's first chairlift, the Cottonwood restaurant is a veritable institution. The bar is decked out with old wooden skis, sleds, skates, and photos of Truckee's early days. The dining area serves an ambitious menu—everything from grilled New York strip steak to Thai red curry prawns to butternut squash enchiladas, plus fresh-baked breads and desserts—but people come here mainly for the atmosphere and hilltop views. There's live music on weekends. ⊠ *Old Brockway Rd., off Hwy. 267, ¼ mi south of downtown* ☎ *530/587–5711* ⊟ *D, MC, V* ☽ *No lunch.*

$$-$$$
ASIAN
★

✕ **Dragonfly.** Flavors are bold and zingy at this old-town, Cal-Asian spot, where every dish is artfully prepared and stylishly presented—and most importantly, well executed. The bright tones of Southeast Asian cooking inspire most dishes on the changing menu, which you can savor in the bright, contemporary dining rooms—one for sushi—or an outdoor terrace overlooking Main Street and the train depot. Lunch is a bargain, and there are lots of choices for vegetarians. Look for the staircase: the restaurant is on the second floor, not street level. ⊠ *10118 Donner Pass Rd.* ☎ *530/587–0557* ☽ *AE, D, MC, V.*

$-$$$
AMERICAN

✕ **FiftyFifty Brewing Company.** In this Truckee brewpub, warm red tones and comfy booths, plus a pint of their Donner Party Porter, will take the nip out of a cold day on the slopes. The menu includes salads, pasta, burgers, and the house specialty, a pulled pork sandwich. After 5 PM, you can tuck into entrées like barbecued ribs, steak, and caramelized yellowfin tuna. There's a full bar along with the brews, and lots of après-ski action. ⊠ *11197 Brockway Rd.* ☎ *530/587–2337* ⊟ *AE, D, MC, V.*

$$$-$$$$
ECLECTIC
★

✕ **Moody's.** Head here for contemporary-Cal cuisine in a sexy dining room with pumpkin-color walls, burgundy velvet banquettes, and art-deco fixtures. The chef-owner's earthy, sure-handed cooking features organically grown ingredients: look for ahi tuna "four ways," house-made charcuterie samplings, pan-roasted wild game, fresh seafood, and organic grass-fed steak. Lunch fare is lighter. In summer dine alfresco surrounded by flowers. Wednesday through Saturday there's music in the borderline-raucous bar that gets packed with Truckee's bon vivants. ⊠ *10007 Bridge St.* ☎ *530/587–8688* ⊟ *AE, D, MC, V.*

WHERE TO STAY

$$$-$$$$

🏨 **Cedar House Sport Hotel.** Built in 2006, Cedar House ups the ante for lodging at Tahoe. Outside, the clean, spare lines of the wooden exterior evoke a modern European feel. Inside, energy-saving heating, cooling, and lighting systems, countertops made from recycled paper, and other green features emphasize the owners' commitment to sustainability. Rooms in the three two-story satellite buildings are understatedly sexy with merlot-and-camel color schemes and mod-Italian overtones (think chrome and leather). Although not all rooms have tubs, heated-tile bathroom floors, goose-down duvets, and comfy cotton robes are luxurious extras. Ask about outdoor-sports trips when you book. Some rooms are pet friendly. **Pros:** an environmentally friendly facility that's also comfortable and hip. **Cons:** some bathrooms are on the small side. ⊠ *10918 Brockway Rd.* ☎ *530/582–5655 or 866/582–5655* ⊕ *www.*

cedarhousesporthotel.com ↵ 41 rooms ☆ In-room: no a/c, safe, refrigerator, Wi-Fi. In-hotel: bar, Wi-Fi hotspot, parking (free) ⊟ *AE, D, DC, MC, V* ⫴ *CP.*

$$$–$$$$ ⛅ **Northstar-at-Tahoe Resort.** The area's most complete destination resort is perfect for families, thanks to its many sports activities—from golf and tennis to skiing and snowshoeing—and its concentration of restaurants, shops, recreation facilities, and accommodations (the Village Mall). Lodgings range from hotel rooms to condos to private houses, some with ski-in ski-out access. The list continues to grow: Northstar has been building lots of new condos and a new Ritz-Carlton (⇨ *below*) opened in December 2009. Lodging options often include free lift tickets, on-site shuttle transportation, and complimentary access to the Swim and Racquet Club's pools, outdoor hot tubs, and fitness center. TC's Pub ($$, open winter only) serves contemporary American fare. **Pros:** vast array of lodging types; on-site shuttle, several dining options in Northstar Village. **Cons:** family accommodations are very pricey. ✉ *Hwy. 267, 6 mi southeast of Truckee, Box 129* ☎ *530/562–1010 or 800/466–6784* ⊕ *www.northstarattahoe.com ↵ 250 units ☆ In-room: a/c (some), kitchen (some), DVD, Internet (some). In-hotel: golf course, tennis courts, pool, gym, bicycle rentals, children's programs (ages 2–6), laundry facilities* ⊟ *AE, D, MC, V.*

$$$$ ⛅ **Ritz-Carlton Highlands Court, Lake Tahoe.** The first luxury hotel built in the Tahoe area in decades, the Ritz-Carlton opened in December 2009. Nestled mid-mountain on the Northstar ski resort, the hotel's plush accommodations have floor-to-ceiling windows for maximum views, plus fireplaces, cozy robes, and down comforters. Want inimitable pampering? Splurge on a pricey concierge Club Level room on the top floor of the four-story hotel. No matter which room you book, you'll enjoy access to the spa, fitness center, and heated outdoor swimming pools. Guests can ski-in ski-out or take a gondola to Northstar. In addition to 24-hour room service, dining options include a casual café lounge and the signature upscale Manzanita Restaurant ($$$–$$$$); and, of course, the many restaurants and shops at Northstar Village. **Pros:** superb service; gorgeous setting. **Cons:** prices as breathtaking as the views; must go off-site for golf and tennis. ✉ *13031 Ritz-Carlton Highlands Court* ☎ *530/562–3000 or 800/241–3333* ⊕ *www.ritzcarlton.com/laketahoe ↵ 153 rooms, 17 suites ☆ In-room: a/c, Internet, Wi-Fi. In-hotel: 3 restaurants, room service, bars, pools, gym, spa, children's programs (ages 5–12), laundry services, Internet terminal, Wi-Fi hotspot, parking (paid), some pets allowed* ⊟ *AE, D, DC, MC, V.*

$$ ⛅ **River Street Inn.** On the banks of the Truckee River, this 1885 wood-and-stone inn was at times a boardinghouse and a brothel. Now completely modernized, the uncluttered, comfortable rooms are simply decorated, with attractive, country-style wooden furniture and extras like flat-screen TVs. The cushy beds have top-quality mattresses, down comforters, and high-thread-count sheets. Bathrooms have claw-foot tubs. The affable off-site proprietors are there when you need them. **Pros:** nice rooms; good value. **Cons:** parking is a half-block from inn. ✉ *10009 E. River St.* ☎ *530/550–9290* ⊕ *www.riverstreetinntruckee.com ↵ 11 rooms ☆ In-room: no phone, no a/c, Wi-Fi. In-hotel: Wi-Fi hotspot* ⊟ *MC, V* ⫴ *CP.*

SPORTS AND THE OUTDOORS

GOLF   The **Coyote Moon Golf Course** (⊠ *10685 Northwoods Blvd.* ☎ *530/587–0886* ⊕ *www.coyotemoongolf.com*) is both challenging and beautiful, with no houses to spoil the view. Fees range from $100 to $160, including cart. **Northstar** (⊠ *Hwy. 267* ☎ *530/562–3290*) has open links–style play and tight, tree-lined fairways, including water hazards. Fees range from $40 to $80, including cart. At **Old Greenwood** (⊠ *12915 Fairway Dr., off Overland Trail exit, Exit 190, from I–80; call for specific directions* ☎ *530/550–7010* ⊕ *www.oldgreenwood.com*), north Lake Tahoe's only Jack Nicklaus signature course, the water hazards are trout streams where you can actually fish. The $100–$185 fee includes a cart.

MOUNTAIN   In summer you can rent a bike and ride the lifts up the mountain at
BIKING   **Northstar-at-Tahoe** (⊠ *Hwy. 267, at Northstar Dr.* ☎ *530/562–2268* ⊕ *www.northstarattahoe.com*) for 100 mi of challenging terrain. A ride to the mountain-biking park on the lift is $49 for ages 13 and above; $29 for ages 9–12. The season extends from July through September with varying hours; call for times.

SKIING   Several smaller resorts around Truckee give you access to the Sierra's slopes for less than half the price of the big resorts. Though you'll sacrifice vertical rise, acreage, and high-speed lifts, you can ski or ride and still have money left over for room and board. These are great places for first-timers and families with kids learning to ski.

Boreal (⊠ *Boreal/Castle Peak exit off I–80* ☎ *530/426–3666* ⊕ *www.rideboreal.com*) has 480 acres and 500 vertical feet of terrain visible from the freeway; there's also lift-served snow-tubing and night skiing until 9. **Donner Ski Ranch** (⊠ *19320 Donner Pass Rd., Norden* ☎ *530/426–3635* ⊕ *www.donnerskiranch.com*) has 505 acres and 750 vertical feet and sits across from the more challenging Sugar Bowl (⇨ *below*). **Soda Springs** (⊠ *Soda Springs exit off I–80, 10244 Soda Springs Rd., Soda Springs* ☎ *530/426–3901* ⊕ *www.skisodasprings.com*) has 200 acres and 652 vertical feet and lift-served snow-tubing. **Tahoe Donner** (⊠ *11603 Snowpeak Way* ☎ *530/587–9444* ⊕ *www.tahoedonner.com*) is just north of Truckee and covers 120 acres and 560 vertical feet; the cross-country center includes 51 trails on 114 km (71 mi) of groomed tracks on 4,800 acres, with night skiing on Wednesdays January and February.

Northstar-at-Tahoe may be the best all-around family ski resort at Tahoe. With two tree-lined, northeast-facing, wind-protected bowls, it's the ideal place to ski in a storm. Hotshot experts unfairly call the mountain "Flatstar," but the meticulous grooming and long cruisers make it an intermediate skier's paradise. Boarders are especially welcome, with awesome terrain parks, including a 420-foot-long super-pipe, a half-pipe, rails and boxes, and lots of kickers. Experts can ski the steeps and bumps off Lookout Mountain, where there's rarely a line for the high-speed quad. Northstar-at-Tahoe's cross-country center has 40 km (25 mi) of groomed trails, including double-set tracks and skating lanes. The school has programs for skiers ages four and up, and day care is available for tots two and older. The mountain gets packed on busy weekends but when there's room on the slopes, Northstar is loads of fun. (⇨ See "When to Go" at the beginning of this chapter for alternatives on busy days.) ✉ 100 Northstar Dr., off Hwy. 267, 6 mi southeast of Truckee ☎ 530/562–1010 or 800/466–6784, 530/562–1330 snow phone ⊕ www.northstarattahoe.com ⚲ 92 trails on 3,000 acres, rated 13% beginner, 60% intermediate, 27% advanced. Longest run 1.4 mi, base 6,330 feet, summit 8,610 feet. Lifts: 18, including a gondola and 6 high-speed quads.

Opened in 1939 by Walt Disney, **Sugar Bowl** is the oldest—and one of the best—resorts at Tahoe. Atop Donner Summit, it receives an incredible 500 inches of snowfall annually. Four peaks are connected by 1,500 acres of skiable terrain, with everything from gentle groomed corduroy to wide-open bowls to vertical rocky chutes and outstanding tree skiing. Snowboarders can hit two terrain parks and a 20-foot-high by 450-foot-long super-pipe. Because it's more compact than some of the area's megaresorts, there's a certain gentility here that distinguishes Sugar Bowl from its competitors, making this a great place for families and a low-pressure, low-key place to learn to ski. It's not huge, but there's some very challenging terrain (experts: head to the Palisades). There's limited lodging at the base area. This is the closest resort to San Francisco (three hours via I–80). ✉ Donner Pass Rd., 3 mi east of Soda Springs/Norden exit off I–80, 10 mi west of Truckee, Norden ☎ 530/426–9000 information and lodging reservations, 530/426–1111 snow phone, 866/843–2695 lodging referral ⊕ www.sugarbowl.com ⚲ 95 trails on 1,500 acres, rated 17% beginner, 45% intermediate, 38% advanced. Longest run 3 mi, base 6,883 feet, summit 8,383 feet. Lifts: 13, including 5 high-speed quads.

★ For the ultimate in groomed conditions, head to the nation's largest cross-country ski resort, **Royal Gorge** (✉ 9411 Hillside Dr., Soda Springs/Norden exit off I–80, Soda Springs ☎ 530/426–3871 ⊕ www.royalgorge.com). It has 308 km (191 mi) of 18-foot-wide track for all abilities, 90 trails on a whopping 9,172 acres, two ski schools, and eight warming huts. Three trailside cafés, two lodges, and a hot tub and sauna round out the facilities. Since it's right on the Sierra Crest, the views are drop-dead gorgeous, and the resort feels like it goes on forever. If you love to cross-country, don't miss Royal Gorge.

You can save money by renting skis and boards at **Tahoe Dave's** (✉ 10200 Donner Pass Rd. ☎ 530/582–0900), which has the area's best selection and also repairs and tunes equipment.

CARNELIAN BAY TO KINGS BEACH

5–10 mi northeast of Tahoe City on Hwy. 28.

The small lakeside commercial districts of Carnelian Bay and Tahoe Vista service the thousand or so locals who live in the area year-round and the thousands more who have summer residences or launch their boats here. Kings Beach, the last town heading east on Highway 28 before the Nevada border, is to Crystal Bay what South Lake Tahoe is to Stateline: a bustling California town full of basic motels and rental condos, restaurants, and shops, used by the hordes of hopefuls who pass through on their way to the casinos.

○ The 28-acre **Kings Beach State Recreation Area**, one of the largest such areas on the lake, is open year-round. The 700-foot-long sandy beach gets very crowded with people swimming, sunbathing, Jet Skiing, riding in paddleboats, spiking volleyballs, and tossing Frisbees. If you're going to spend the day, come early enough to snag a table in the picnic area; there's also a good playground. ⊠ *N. Lake Blvd., Kings Beach* ☎ *530/546–7248* 🖅 *$8 parking fee* ⊙ *Daily.*

WHERE TO EAT AND STAY

$$$–$$$$ ✕ **Gar Woods Grill and Pier.** The view's the thing at this lakeside stalwart,
ECLECTIC where you can watch the sun shimmer on the water through the dining room's plate-glass windows or from the heated outdoor deck. Grilled steak and fish are menu mainstays, but be sure to try specialties like crab chili rellenos and chicken piccata. At all hours in season, the bar gets packed with boaters who pull up to the restaurant's private pier. ⊠ *5000 N. Lake Blvd., Carnelian Bay* ☎ *530/546–3366* ⊟ *D, MC, V.*

$$–$$$ ✕ **Spindleshanks.** This handsome roadhouse, decorated with floor-to-
AMERICAN ceiling knotty pine, serves mostly classic American cooking—ribs, steaks, and seafood updated with adventurous sauces—as well as house-made ravioli. On cold nights request seating near the crackling fireplace and enjoy a drink from the full bar or the extensive wine list. Reservations are recommended. ⊠ *6873 N. Lake Blvd, Tahoe Vista* ☎ *530/546–2191* ⊟ *AE, MC, V* ⊙ *No lunch.*

$–$$$ 🛏 **Ferrari's Crown Resort.** One of the few remaining family-owned and
○ -operated motels in Kings Beach, Ferrari's has straightforward motel rooms in a resort setting, great for families with kids. Comprised of two formerly separate vintage-1950s motels, sitting side-by-side on the lake, Ferrari's is impeccably kept. It's not a fancy-pants place by any stretch, just a plain-old motel, but some of the rooms have awesome views, and for value you can't beat it. Kids love the two pools; adults enjoy the hot tubs. There are also kayak rentals on-site. **Pros:** family-friendly; lakeside location. **Cons:** older facility. ⊠ *8200 N. Lake Blvd., Kings Beach* ☎ *530/546–3388 or 800/645–2260* ⊕ *www.tahoecrown. com* 🛏 *71 rooms* 🖔 *In-room: a/c (some), kitchen (some), refrigerator, Internet, Wi-Fi. In-hotel: pools, beachfront, Wi-Fi hotspot* ⊟ *AE, D, MC, V* ⊙⧮ *CP.*

$$$–$$$$ 🛏 **Shore House.** Every room has a gas fireplace, down comforter, and
★ featherbed at this lakefront B&B in Tahoe Vista. The lovingly tended, knotty-pine-paneled guest rooms beautifully and simply capture the woodsy spirit of Tahoe, but without overdoing the pinecone motif. All have private entrances and extra touches such as bathrobes, stereo CD players, down comforters, and rubber duckies in the bathtubs; many have great views of the water. There's also a private beach. Yes, it's pricey but at how many places can you sip morning coffee while gazing out at the mist rising off the lake? **Pros:** waterfront honeymoon cottage; massage appointments available. **Cons:** pricey (even off-season). ⊠ *7170 N. Lake Blvd., Tahoe Vista* ☎ *530/546–7270 or 800/207–5160* ⊕ *www.shorehouselaketahoe.com* 🛏 *8 rooms, 1 cottage* 🖔 *In-room: no phone, no a/c, refrigerator, DVD, Wi-Fi (some). In-hotel: beachfront, Wi-Fi hotspot* ⊟ *D, MC, V* ⊙⧮ *BP.*

NEVADA SIDE

CRYSTAL BAY

1 mi east of Kings Beach on Hwy. 28; 30 mi north of South Lake Tahoe via U.S. 50 to Hwy. 28.

Right at the Nevada border, Crystal Bay has a cluster of casinos that look essentially the same, but have a few minor differences. These casinos tend toward the tacky, and most of the lodging is pretty lackluster.

23

EXPLORING

The **Cal-Neva Lodge** (⊠ *2 Stateline Rd.* ☎ *800/225–6382* ⊕ *www. calnevaresort.com*) is bisected by the state line. Opened in 1927, this joint has weathered many scandals, the largest involving former owner Frank Sinatra (he lost his gaming license in the 1960s for alleged mob connections). The secret tunnel that Frank built so that he could steal away unnoticed to Marilyn Monroe's cabin is definitely worth a look; call for tour times.

The **Tahoe Biltmore** (⊠ *5 Hwy. 28, at Stateline Rd.* ☎ *800/245–8667* ⊕ *www.tahoebiltmore.com*) has live bands with dancing on weekends.

Jim Kelley's Tahoe Nugget (⊠ *20 Hwy. 28, at Stateline Rd.* ☎ *775/831– 0455*) serves nearly 100 kinds of beer.

The **Crystal Bay Club** (⊠ *14 Hwy. 28, at Stateline Rd.* ⊕ *www. crystalbaycasino.com* ☎ *775/833–6333*) has a restaurant with a towering open-truss ceiling that looks like a wooden ship's hull.

WHERE TO EAT

$$–$$$
ECLECTIC
★
✕ **Soule Domain.** Rough-hewn wood beams and a vaulted wood ceiling lend high romance to this cozy 1927 pine-log cabin, tucked beneath tall trees, next to the Tahoe Biltmore. On the eclectic menu, chef-owner Charles Soule's specialties include curried cashew chicken, lamb ravioli, fresh sea scallops poached in champagne with kiwi and mango cream sauce, and a vegan sauté with ginger and jalapeños, but you'll find the chef's current passion in the always-great roster of nightly specials. Some find it a little pricey, but if you're looking for someplace with a solid menu, where you can hold hands by candlelight, this is it. In winter request a table near the crackling fireplace. Reservations are recommended. ⊠ *9983 Cove Ave., ½ block up Stateline Rd. from Hwy. 28, Kings Beach* ☎ *530/546–7529* ☐ *AE, D, MC, V* ⊘ *No lunch.*

INCLINE VILLAGE

3 mi east of Crystal Bay on Hwy. 28.

Incline Village, Nevada's only privately owned town, dates to the early 1960s, when an Oklahoma developer bought 10,000 acres north of Lake Tahoe. His idea was to sketch out a plan for a town without a central commercial district, hoping to prevent congestion and to preserve the area's natural beauty. One-acre lakeshore lots originally fetched

$12,000 to $15,000; today you couldn't buy even the land for less than several million.

ESSENTIALS

Visitor Information Lake Tahoe Incline Village/Crystal Bay Visitors Bureau (✉ *969 Tahoe Blvd., Incline Village* ☎ *775/832–1606 or 800/468–2463* ⊕ *www. gotahoenorth.com*).

EXPLORING

Check out **Lakeshore Drive**, along which you'll see some of the most expensive real estate in Nevada. The drive is discreetly marked: to find it, start at the Hyatt Hotel and drive westward along the lake.

Fodor'sChoice
★
George Whittell, a San Francisco socialite who once owned 40,000 acres of property along the lake, built the **Thunderbird Lodge** in 1936. You can tour the mansion and the grounds by reservation only, and though it's pricey, it provides a rare glimpse back to a time when only the very wealthy had homes at Tahoe. The lodge is accessible via a bus from the Incline Village Visitors Bureau, a catamaran from the Hyatt in Incline Village, or a 1950 wooden cruiser from Tahoe Keys Marina in South Lake Tahoe (which includes lunch). ✉ *2435 Venice Dr. E* ☎ *775/832– 8750 lodge, 800/468–2463 reservations, 775/588–1881, 888/867–6394 Tahoe Keys boat, 775/832–1234, 800/553–3288 Hyatt Incline Village boat* ⊕ *www.thunderbirdlodge.org* ◎ *$39 bus tour, $110 boat tour* ◎ *May–Oct., call for tour times.*

OFF THE BEATEN PATH
Lake Tahoe–Nevada State Park. Protecting much of the lake's eastern shore from development, Lake Tahoe–Nevada State Park comprises several sections that stretch from Incline Village to Zephyr Cove. Beaches and trails provide access to a wilder side of the lake, whether you're into cross-country skiing, hiking, or just relaxing at a picnic. The east shore gets less snow and more sun than the west shore, making it a good early- or late-season outdoor destination. One of the most likable areas is **Sand Harbor Beach** (✉ *Hwy. 28, 3 mi south of Incline Village* ☎ *775/831– 0494* ⊕ *parks.nv.gov/lt.htm*). It's so popular that it's sometimes filled to capacity by 11 AM on summer weekends. Stroll the boardwalk and read the information signs for a good lesson in the local ecology. Pets are not allowed.

WHERE TO EAT AND STAY

$$$
ECLECTIC
✕ **Frederick's.** Copper-top tables lend a chic look to the small dining room at this intimate bistro. The menu consists of a mélange of European and Asian cooking, mostly prepared using organic produce and free-range meats. Try the braised short ribs, filo wrapped crab, roasted duck with caramel pecan glaze, or the deliciously fresh sushi rolls. Ask for a table by the fire. Reservations are recommended. ✉ *907 Tahoe Blvd.* ☎ *775/832–3007* ▭ *AE, MC, V* ◎ *Closed Sun. and Mon. No lunch.*

$$$
FRENCH
★
✕ **Le Bistro.** Incline Village's hidden gem, Le Bistro serves expertly pre-pared French-country cuisine in a relaxed, cozy, romantic dining room. The chef-owner makes everything himself, using organically grown ingredients, and changes the menu almost daily. Expect such dishes as pâté de campagne, baked tomato bisque en croute, escargot, and herb-crusted roast lamb loin. Try the five-course prix-fixe menu ($48), which can be paired with their award-winning wine selections. Service

Get to Sand Harbor Beach in Lake Tahoe–Nevada State Park early; the park sometimes fills to capacity before lunchtime in summer.

is gracious and attentive. Be sure to ask directions when you book since the restaurant is hard to find. ⊠ *120 Country Club Dr., #29* ☎ *775/831–0800* ⊟ *AE, D, DC, MC, V* ⊘ *Closed Sun. and Mon. No lunch.*

¢ ✕ **T's Rotisserie.** There's nothing fancy about T's (it looks like a small
SOUTHERN   snack bar), but the mesquite-grilled chicken and tri-tip steaks are
⟳   delicious and inexpensive—a rare combination in pricey Incline Village. It's mainly a take-out spot; seating is limited. ⊠ *901 Tahoe Blvd.*
☎ *775/831–2832* ⊟ *No credit cards.*

$$$–$$$$ ⌂ **Hyatt Regency Lake Tahoe.** Once a dowdy casino hotel, the Hyatt underwent a $60 million renovation between 2001 and 2003 and is now a smart-looking, upmarket, full-service destination resort. On 26 acres of prime lakefront property, the resort has a nice range of luxurious accommodations, from tower-hotel rooms to lakeside cottages. The Lone Eagle Grille ($$$–$$$$) serves steaks and seafood in one of the north shore's most handsome lake-view dining rooms. There's also a state-of-the-art spa and fitness center. Standard rates are very high, but look for midweek or off-season discounts. **Pros:** incredible views; first-class spa. **Cons:** pricey (especially for families). ⊠ *111 Country Club Dr., at Lakeshore Dr.* ☎ *775/832–1234 or 888/899–5019* ⊕ *www.laketahoe. hyatt.com* ⟿ *422 rooms, 28 suites* ⟳ *In-room: a/c, safe, kitchen (some), refrigerator, Internet, Wi-Fi. In-hotel: 4 restaurants, room service, bars, pool, spa, beachfront, bicycles, children's programs (ages 3–12), laundry service, Wi-Fi hotspot* ⊟ *AE, D, DC, MC, V.*

SPORTS AND THE OUTDOORS

GOLF **Incline Championship** (✉ *955 Fairway Blvd.* ☎ *866/925–4653* ⊕ *www. inclinegolf.com*) is an 18-hole, par-72 Robert Trent Jones Sr. course with a driving range, both completely renovated between 2002 and 2004. The $175 greens fee includes an optional cart. **Incline Mountain** (✉ *690 Wilson Way* ☎ *866/925–4653* ⊕ *www.inclinegolf.com*) is an executive (shorter) 18-hole course; par is 58. Greens fees start at $61, including optional cart.

MOUNTAIN You can rent bikes and get helpful tips from **Flume Trail Bikes** (✉ *Spooner*
BIKING *Summit, Hwy. 28, ¾ mi north of U.S. 50, Glenbrook* ☎ *775/749–5349* ⊕ *www.theflumetrail.com*), which also operates a bike shuttle to popular trailheads. Ask about the secluded backcountry rental cabins for overnight rides.

SKIING A fun family mood prevails at **Diamond Peak**, which has many special programs and affordable rates. Snowmaking covers 75% of the mountain, and runs are groomed nightly. The ride up the 1-mi Crystal chair rewards you with some of the best views of the lake from any ski area. Diamond Peak is less crowded than the larger areas and provides free shuttles to nearby lodging. It's a great place for beginners and intermediates, and it's appropriately priced for families. However, though there are some steep-aspect black-diamond runs, advanced skiers may find the acreage too limited. For snowboarders there's a half-pipe and super-pipe. ✉ *1210 Ski Way, Incline Village* ☎ *775/832–1177* ⊕ *www. diamondpeak.com* ⌖ *30 trails on 655 acres, rated 18% beginner, 46% intermediate, 36% advanced. Longest run 2½ mi, base 6,700 feet, summit 8,540 feet. Lifts: 6, including 2 high-speed quads.*

Ski some of the highest slopes at Tahoe, and take in bird's-eye views of Reno and the Carson Valley at **Mt. Rose Ski Tahoe**. Though more compact than the bigger Tahoe resorts, Mt. Rose has the area's highest base elevation and consequently the driest snow. The mountain has a wide variety of terrain. The most challenging is the Chutes, 200 acres of gulp-and-go advanced-to-expert vertical. Intermediates can choose steep groomers or mellow, wide-open boulevards. Beginners have their own corner of the mountain, with gentle, nonthreatening, wide slopes. Boarders and tricksters have three terrain parks to choose from, on opposite sides of the mountain, allowing them to follow the sun as it tracks across the resort. Because of its elevation, the mountain gets hit hard in storms; check conditions before heading up during inclement weather or on a windy day. ✉ *22222 Mt. Rose Hwy. (Hwy. 431), 11 mi north of Incline Village, Reno* ☎ *775/849–0704 or 800/754–7673* ⊕ *www.skirose.com* ⌖ *61 trails on 1,200 acres, rated 20% beginner, 30% intermediate, 40% advanced, 10% expert. Longest run 2½ mi, base 7,900 feet, summit 9,700 feet. Lifts: 8, including 2 high-speed 6-passenger lifts.*

On the way to Mt. Rose from Incline Village, **Tahoe Meadows** (✉ *Hwy. 431*) is the most popular area near the north shore for noncommercial cross-country skiing, sledding, tubing, snowshoeing, and snowmobiling.

You'll find superbly groomed tracks and fabulous views of Lake Tahoe at **Spooner Lake Cross-Country** (⊠ *Spooner Summit, Hwy. 28, ½ mi north of U.S. 50, Glenbrook* ☎ *775/749–5349* ⊕ *www.spoonerlake.com*). It has more than 50 mi of trails on more than 9,000 acres, and two rustic, secluded cabins are available for rent for overnight treks.

TAHOE TESSIE

Local lore claims this huge sea monster slithers around Lake Tahoe. Skeptics laugh, but true believers keep their eyes peeled for surprise sightings.

23

ZEPHYR COVE

22 mi south of Incline Village via Hwy. 28 to U.S. 50.

The largest settlement between Incline Village and the Stateline area is Zephyr Cove, a tiny resort. It has a beach, marina, campground, picnic area, coffee shop in a log lodge, rustic cabins, and nearby riding stables.

EXPLORING

★ Nearby **Cave Rock** (⊠ *U.S. 50, 4 mi north of Zephyr Cove* ☎ *775/831–0494*), 75 feet of solid stone at the southern end of Lake Tahoe–Nevada State Park, is the throat of an extinct volcano. Tahoe Tessie, the lake's version of the Loch Ness monster, is reputed to live in a cavern below the impressive outcropping. Cave Rock towers over a parking lot, a lakefront picnic ground, and a boat launch. The views are some of the best on the lake; this is a good spot to stop and take a picture. However, this area is a sacred burial site for the Washoe Indians, and climbing up to the cave, or through it, is prohibited.

WHERE TO EAT AND STAY

¢ ⌘ ⚠ **Zephyr Cove Resort.** Tucked beneath towering pines at the lake's
☼ edge stand 28 cozy, modern vacation cabins ($$–$$$$) with peaked knotty-pine ceilings. While not fancy, they come in a variety of sizes, some perfect for families. Across U.S. 50, a sprawling year-round campground is geared toward RVers, but with drive-in and walk-in tent sites, too. The resort has horseback riding, snowmobiling facilities, and a marina with boat and WaveRunner rentals, all of which contribute to the summer-camp atmosphere. **Pros:** family-friendly. **Cons:** lodge rooms are very basic; can be noisy. ⊠ *760 U.S. 50, 4 mi north of Stateline* ☎ *775/589–4907 or 888/896–3830* ⊕ *www.zephyrcove.com* ⇦ *57 tent and 93 RV sites, 28 cabins* ⚐ *In-room: no a/c, kitchen (some). In-hotel: restaurant, beachfront, laundry facilities some pets allowed, flush toilets, full hookups, partial hookups, dump station, drinking water, showers, fire pits, grills, picnic tables, general store, Internet terminal, Wi-Fi hotspot* ▭ *AE, D, MC, V.*

STATELINE

5 mi south of Zephyr Cove on U.S. 50.

Stateline is the archetypal Nevada border town. Its four high-rise casinos are as vertical and contained as the commercial district of South

Lake Tahoe, on the California side, is horizontal and sprawling. And Stateline is as relentlessly indoors oriented as the rest of the lake is focused on the outdoors. This strip is where you'll find the most concentrated action at Lake Tahoe: restaurants (including typical casino buffets), showrooms with famous headliners and razzle-dazzle revues, tower-hotel rooms and suites, and 24-hour casinos.

WHERE TO EAT AND STAY

$$$-$$$$

FRENCH

★

✕ **Mirabelle.** Don't be put off by this restaurant's nondescript exterior. Inside there's a lovely, airy dining room with creamy yellow walls and white tablecloths—and some of the most delectable dishes you'll find in the Tahoe area. Enticing scents drift from the kitchen where the French Alsatian–born chef-owner personally prepares everything from puff pastry to meringues to homemade bread. Specialties include sauteed veal sweetbreads and mushrooms in a cognac veal cream sauce, garlicky escargot, and rack of lamb with fresh thyme. There's always a vegetarian entrée, and on some evenings a fixed-price menu is available for $33.50 per person. ⊠ *290 Kingsbury Grade* ☎ *775/586–1007* ⊟ *AE, MC, V* ☉ *Closed Mon. No lunch.*

$$$-$$$$

⊞ **Harrah's Tahoe Hotel/Casino.** Harrah's major selling point is that every room has two full bathrooms, each with a television and telephone, a boon if you're traveling with family. The South Shore Room hosts first-rate entertainment. Among the restaurants, the top-floor Friday's Station Steak & Seafood Grill ($$$$), with good views from every table, is a standout (but an expensive one); there's also a buffet on the 18th floor. A tunnel runs under U.S. 50 to Harveys, which Harrah's now owns. Upper-floor rooms have views of the lake or mountains, but if you really want the view, stay at Harveys instead. Cheaper rates are available midweek. **Pros:** central location; great midweek values. **Cons:** can get noisy. ⊠ *15 U.S. 50 at Stateline Ave.* ☎ *775/588–6611 or 800/427–7247* ⊕ *www.harrahstahoe.com* ⇦ *470 rooms, 62 suites* ⌂ *In-room: a/c, Internet, Wi-Fi. In-hotel: 6 restaurants, room service, pool, gym, spa, laundry service* ⊟ *AE, D, DC, MC, V.*

$$-$$$$

⊞ **Harveys Resort Hotel/Casino.** Harveys began as a cabin in 1944, and now it's Tahoe's largest casino-hotel. Premium rooms have custom furnishings, oversize marble baths, minibars, and good lake views. Although it was acquired by Harrah's and has lost some of its cachet, Harveys remains a fine property. At Cabo Wabo ($–$$), an always-hopping Baja-style cantina owned by Sammy Hagar, sip agave-style tequila while munching on tapas and shouting across the table at your date. Harveys Cabaret is the hotel's showroom. **Pros:** hip entertainment; just a few blocks south of the Heavenly Gondola. **Cons:** can get loud at night. ⊠ *18 U.S. 50, at Stateline Ave.* ☎ *775/588–2411 or 800/648–3361* ⊕ *www.harrahs.com* ⇦ *705 rooms, 38 suites* ⌂ *In-room: a/c, Internet, Wi-Fi. In-hotel: 6 restaurants, room service, pool, gym, spa* ⊟ *AE, D, DC, MC, V.*

$$-$$$$

⊞ **MontBleu.** Formerly Caesar's Tahoe, MontBleu opened in summer 2006, and the tired Roman theme is gone. In its place, you'll find a less garish—though still slightly kitschy—contemporary style. All guest rooms have luxurious bedding with down comforters; most have over-size tubs, king-size beds, two telephones, and a view of Lake Tahoe and the surrounding mountains (avoid those that overlook the parking lot's glaring lights). Famous entertainers sometimes perform in the 1,600-seat MontBleu Theater (formerly Circus Maximus). **Pros:** indoor pool; first-class spa; plush bedding. **Cons:** can get noisy. ⊠ *55 U.S. 50, Box 5800* ☎ *775/588–3515 or 800/648–3353* ⊕ *www.montbleuresort.com* ⇨ *328 rooms, 109 suites* ♻ *In-room: a/c, Internet, Wi-Fi. In-hotel: 4 restaurants, room service, pool, gym, spa, Wi-Fi hotspot* ⊟ *AE, D, DC, MC, V.*

NIGHTLIFE

23

Each of the major casinos has its own showroom, including Harrah's **South Shore Room** (☎ *775/588–6611*). They feature everything from comedy to magic acts to sexy floor shows to Broadway musicals. If you want to dance to DJ grooves and live bands, check out the scene at MontBleu's **Blu** (⊠ *55 U.S. 50* ☎ *775/588–3515*). At Harrah's, you can dance at **Vex** (⊠ *U.S. 50, at state line* ☎ *775/588–6611*). **Harveys Outdoor Summer Concert Series** (☎ *800/427–7247* ⊕ *www.harrahs.com*) presents outdoor concerts on weekends in summer with headliners such as the Eagles, Toby Keith, Stevie Wonder, Beyoncé, and James Taylor.

SPORTS AND THE OUTDOORS

One of the south shore's best, **Nevada Beach** (⊠ *Elk Point Rd., 3 mi north of Stateline via U.S. 50* ☎ *530/543–2600*) has a superwide sandy beach that's great for swimming (most Tahoe beaches are rocky). There are also picnic tables, restrooms, barbecue grills, and a campground beneath towering pines. This is the best place to watch the July 4 or Labor Day fireworks. The beach is open Memorial Day weekend through October.

On the lake, **Edgewood Tahoe** (⊠ *U.S. 50 and Lake Pkwy. 100 Lake Parkway, behind Horizon Casino* ☎ *775/588–3566 or 888/881–8659* ⊕ *www.edgewood-tahoe.com*) is an 18-hole, par-72 course with a driving range. Fees range from $140–$235, depending on the month, and include a cart (though you can walk if you wish). You can have breakfast or lunch in the bar, but the best meal at Edgewood is at the lakeview restaurant inside the clubhouse ($$$–$$$$; dinner only).

RENO

32 mi east of Truckee on I-80; 38 mi northeast of Incline Village via Hwy. 431 and U.S. 395.

Established in 1859 as a trading station at a bridge over the Truckee River, Reno grew along with the silver mines of nearby Virginia City and the transcontinental railroad that chugged through town. Train officials named it in 1868, but gambling—legalized in 1931—put Reno on the map.

Today a sign over the upper end of Virginia Street proclaims Reno THE BIGGEST LITTLE CITY IN THE WORLD. This is still a gambling town, with most of the casinos crowded into five square blocks downtown. The city has lost significant business to California's Indian casinos over the past few years, which has resulted in cheaper rooms, but mediocre upkeep; there just isn't the money coming into town that there once was.

Though parts of downtown are sketchy, things are changing. Several defunct casinos are being converted into condominiums, and downtown is undergoing an urban renewal, sparked by the development of the riverfront, with new shops, boutiques, and nongaming, family-friendly activities like kayaking on the Truckee River. Excellent restaurants have shown up outside the hotels. Temperatures year-round in this high-mountain-desert climate are warmer than at Tahoe, though it rarely gets as hot here as in Sacramento and the Central Valley, making strolling around town a pleasure.

> ### RENO'S RIVERWALK
>
> Stroll along the Truckee River and check out the art galleries, cinema, specialty shops, theater, and restaurants that line this lively refurbished section of town near Reno's casino district.

ESSENTIALS

Visitor Information Reno-Sparks Convention and Visitors Authority (✉ *4001 S. Virginia St., Reno, NV* ☎ *775/827–7600 or 800/367–7366* ⊕ *www. visitrenotahoe.com*).

EXPLORING

☾ Families with kids in tow head for **Circus Circus** (✉ *500 N. Sierra St.* ☎ *775/329–0711 or 800/648–5010* ⊕ *www.circusreno.com*). A midway above the casino floor has clowns, games, fun-house mirrors, and circus acts.

★ A few miles from downtown, the **Peppermill** (✉ *2707 S. Virginia St.* ☎ *775/826–2121 or 800/648–6992* ⊕ *www.peppermillreno.com*) is known for its excellent restaurants and neon-bright gambling areas. For cocktails, the Fireside Lounge is a blast.

Eldorado (✉ *345 N. Virginia St.* ☎ *775/786–5700 or 800/648–5966* ⊕ *www.eldoradoreno.com*) is action packed, with tons of slots, popular bar-top video poker, and good coffee-shop and food-court fare.

Harrah's (✉ *219 N. Center St.* ☎ *775/786–3232 or 800/648–3773* ⊕ *www.harrahs.com*) occupies two city blocks, with a sprawling casino and an outdoor promenade.

Silver Legacy (✉ *407 N. Virginia St.* ☎ *775/329–4777 or 800/687–8733* ⊕ *www.silverlegacy.com*) has a Victorian-theme casino, a 120-foot-tall mining rig, and video poker games that draw in the gamblers.

The **Downtown RiverWalk** (✉ *S. Virginia St. and the Truckee River* ⊕ *www. renoriver.org*) has gentrified the Reno waterfront district, replacing a seedy atmosphere with street performers, art exhibits, shops, a lovely park, and good strolling. The 2,600-foot-long Truckee River whitewater kayaking course runs right through downtown and has become a major attraction for water-sports enthusiasts. On the third Saturday of each month, from 2 to 5, local merchants host a **Wine Walk**. The cost is $20; stop inside the RiverWalk's shops, galleries, and boutiques, and they'll refill your wine glass. In July look for stellar outdoor art, opera, dance, and kids' performances as part of the monthlong **Artown festival** (⊕ *www.renoisartown.com*), presented mostly in Wingfield Park, along the river.

☾ On the University of Nevada campus, the sleekly designed **Fleischmann Planetarium** has films and astronomy shows, providing a great alternative to the glittering lights of the casinos. ✉ *1650 N. Virginia St.* ☎ *775/784–4811* ⊕ *www.planetarium.unr.nevada.edu* ✑ *Exhibits free, films and star shows $6* ☉ *Sun.–Thurs. 10:30–7, Fri. and Sat. 10:30–9.*

★ The **Nevada Museum of Art** has changing exhibits in a dramatic modern building; it's a must-see for art aficionados. ✉ *160 W. Liberty St.* ☎ *775/329–3333* ⊕ *www.nevadaart.org* ✑ *$10* ☉ *Wed. and Fri.–Sun. 10–5, Thurs. 10–8.*

☾ More than 220 antique and classic automobiles, including an Elvis Presley Cadillac and a 1949 Mercury coupe driven by James Dean in the movie *Rebel Without a Cause*, are on display at the **National Automobile Museum**. ✉ *10 S. Lake St., at Mill St.* ☎ *775/333–9300* ⊕ *www.automuseum.org* ✑ *$10* ☉ *Mon.–Sat. 9:30–5:30, Sun. 10–4.*

WHERE TO EAT

¢–$ ✗ **Bangkok Cuisine.** If you want to eat well in a pretty dining room but
THAI don't want to break the bank, come to this cute little Thai restaurant where delicious soups, salads, stir-fries, and curries are prepared by a Thai national. ✉ *55 Mt. Rose St.* ☎ *775/322–0299* ☰ *AE, D, MC, V* ☉ *No lunch Sun.*

$$$–$$$$ ✗ **Beaujolais Bistro.** Consistently spot-on Beaujolais serves earthy, country-
FRENCH style French food with zero pretension. The understated chef-owner is known for classics like beef bourguignon, roast duck, escargots, and steak frites, all lovingly prepared and seasoned just right. Less expensive small plate offerings are also on the menu. The comfortable, airy dining room has exposed brick walls, a parquet floor, and an inviting, casual vibe, making it a good choice for an unfussy meal a short walk from the casinos. ✉ *130 West St.* ☎ *775/323–2227* ☰ *AE, D, MC, V* ☉ *Closed Mon. No lunch weekends.*

¢–$$ ✗ **Chocolate Bar.** If you love chocolate, don't miss this place. Part café,
CAFÉ part cocktail bar, this hip little joint a mile from downtown makes killer truffles, chocolate fondue, fabulous fruity cocktails, gourmet appetizers and small-plate selections—and, of course, stellar hot chocolate, served at a small bar or at a dozen or so tables. It's open 4:30 PM to midnight and gets crowded on weekend evenings with twenty- and thirtysomethings. ✉ *475 S. Arlington St.* ☎ *775/337–1122* ☰ *AE, MC, V* ☉ *Closed Mon.*

WHERE TO STAY

$–$$$ 🏨 **Harrah's.** Of the big-name casino hotels in downtown Reno, double-towered Harrah's does a good job, with no surprises. The large guest rooms, decorated in blues and mauves, overlook downtown and the entire mountain-ringed valley. The dark and romantic dining room at Harrah's Steak House ($$$–$$$$; reservations essential, no lunch weekends) serves excellent prime steaks and seafood that merit a special trip by meat lovers; try the Caesar salad and steak Diane, both prepared table-side by a tuxedoed waiter. **Pros:** Harrah's sets the standard for downtown Reno; great midweek rates. **Cons:** huge property. ✉ *219 N. Center St.* ☎ *775/786–3232 or 800/648–3773* ⊕ *www.harrahs. com* ⇄ *876 rooms, 52 suites* ♿ *In-room: a/c, safe, refrigerator (some),*

23

Internet (some), Wi-Fi (some). In-hotel: 8 restaurants, room service, bars, pool, gym, spa, laundry service ▤ *AE, D, DC, MC, V.*

$-$$$ ⌗ **Peppermill.** A few miles removed from downtown Reno's flashy main
★ drag, the Peppermill generates its own glitz with a neon-filled casino that's as dazzling as any. Setting a new standard for luxury in Reno, the 600 baroque suites in the Tuscan Tower that opened in 2008 have plush king-size beds, marble bathrooms, and European soaking tubs. The casino's superior dining options include Oceano ($$–$$$), an over-the-top seafood restaurant that feels like you're eating inside an aquarium, and Romanza ($$–$$$$), with fabulous place settings of Versace china and a planetarium star show. **Pros:** casino decor is worth a special trip; good (and inexpensive) coffee shop. **Cons:** some may find the amount of neon a bit over the top. ✉ *2707 S. Virginia St.* ☎ *775/826–2121 or 800/648–6992* ⊕ *www.peppermillreno.com* ➳ *915 rooms, 720 suites* ⎙ *In-room: a/c, safe (some), refrigerator (some), Wi-Fi. In-hotel: 11 restaurants, room service, bars, pool, gym, spa, Wi-Fi hotspot* ▤ *AE, D, MC, V.*

$-$$$ ⌗ **Siena Hotel Spa Casino.** When it opened with a bang in 2001, the Siena was Reno's most luxurious hotel, breaking the floral-print mold with blond-wood furnishings and top-of-the-line beds dressed with white Egyptian-cotton linens. And you won't have to navigate past miles of slots to find the front desk, because the casino is in a self-contained room. The spa merits a special trip, as does Lexie's ($$$–$$$$; dinner only Tuesday–Saturday with a champagne brunch on Sunday), which serves terrific steaks and seafood in a sleek, river-view dining room. **Pros:** beautiful rooms; smaller-scale facility; helpful staff. **Cons:** located a few blocks from the town center. ✉ *1 S. Lake St.* ☎ *775/337–6260 or 877/743–6233* ⊕ *www.sienareno.com* ➳ *185 rooms, 29 suites* ⎙ *In-room: a/c, refrigerator, Internet, Wi-Fi. In-hotel: 3 restaurants, room service, bar, pool, gym, spa, laundry service, Wi-Fi hotspot* ▤ *AE, D, MC, V.*

The Far North

WITH LAKE SHASTA, MT. SHASTA, AND LASSEN VOLCANIC NATIONAL PARK

WORD OF MOUTH

"Bumpass Hell is a very interesting hike, the thermal features are unusual and there is a boardwalk so you can get close to the steaming holes and pools. North of the park is the gorgeous Burney Falls, real easy walk, definitely worth a visit."

—Shanghainese

WELCOME TO THE FAR NORTH

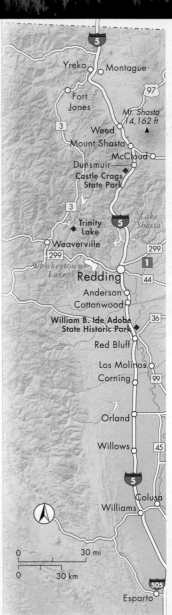

TOP REASONS TO GO

★ **Mother nature's wonders:** California's far north has more rivers, streams, lakes, forests, and mountains than you'll ever have time to explore.

★ **Rock and roll:** With two volcanoes to entice you— Lassen and Shasta—you can learn firsthand what happens when a mountain blows its top.

★ **Fantastic fishing:** Whether you like casting from a riverbank or letting your line bob beside a boat, you'll find fabulous fishing in all the northern counties.

★ **Cool hops:** On a hot day there's nothing quite as inviting as a visit to Chico's world-famous Sierra Nevada Brewery. Take the tour and then savor a chilled glass on tap at the adjacent brewpub.

★ **Shasta:** Wonderful in all its forms: lake, dam, river, mountain, forest, and town.

1 From Chico to Mt. Shasta. The far north is bisected, south to north, by I-5, which passes through several historic towns and state parks, as well as miles of mountainous terrain. Halfway to the Oregon border is Lake Shasta, a favorite recreation destination, and farther north stands the spectacular snowy peak of Mt. Shasta.

2 The Backcountry. East of I-5, the far north's main corridor, dozens of scenic two-lane roads crisscross the wilderness, leading to dramatic mountain peaks and fascinating natural wonders. Small towns settled in the second half of the 19th century seem frozen in time, except that they are well equipped with tourist amenities.

GETTING ORIENTED

24

The far north is a vast area that stretches from the upper reaches of the Sacramento Valley north to the Oregon border and east to Nevada. The region includes all or part of seven counties with sparsely populated rural farming and mountain communities, as well as thriving small cities in the valley. Much of the landscape was shaped by two volcanoes—Mt. Shasta and Mt. Lassen—that draw amateur geologists, weekend hikers, and avid mountain climbers to their rugged terrain. An intricate network of high mountain watersheds feeds lakes large and small, plus streams and rivers that course through several forests.

THE FAR NORTH PLANNER

Getting Here and Around

Both Chico and Redding have small regional airports, but for the cheapest fares fly into Sacramento airport and rent a car for your northern explorations.

Interstate 5 runs up the center of California through Red Bluff and Redding; the other main roads here are good two-lane highways that are, with few exceptions, open year-round. Check weather reports and carry detailed maps, warm clothing, and tire chains whenever you head into mountainous terrain in winter.

Contacts Caltrans Highway Information Network (☎ 800/427-7623).

When to Go

Heat scorches the valley in summer. Temperatures above 110°F are common, but the mountains provide cool respite. Fall throughout the far north is beautiful, rivaled only by the spring months when wildflowers bloom and snowmelt sends mountain creeks splashing through forests. Winter is usually temperate in the valley, but cold and snowy in high country. A few favorite tourist attractions are closed in winter.

About the Restaurants

Redding, the urban center of the far north, and college-town Chico have the greatest selection of restaurants. Cafés and simple eateries are the rule in the smaller towns, though trendy, innovative restaurants have been popping up. Dress is always informal.

About the Hotels

The far north—especially the mountainous backcountry—is gaining popularity as a tourist destination. For summer holiday weekends in towns at higher elevations that escape the valley heat, such as Mt. Shasta, Dunsmuir, and Chester, and at camping sites within state or national parks, make lodging reservations well in advance.

Rooms in Redding, Chico, and Red Bluff usually are booked solid only during popular local events. Aside from the large chain hotels and motels in Redding and Chico, most accommodations in the far north blend rusticity, simplicity, and coziness. Wilderness resorts close in fall and reopen after the snow season ends in May.

The Web site of the **California Association of Bed & Breakfast Inns** (⊕ www.cabbi.com) lists numerous bed-and-breakfasts in the far north region.

WHAT IT COSTS					
	¢	$	$$	$$$	$$$$
Retaurants	under $10	$10–$15	$16–$22	$23–$30	over $30
Hotels	under $90	$90–$120	$121–$175	$176–$250	over $250
Campgrounds	under $10	$10–$17	$18–$35	$36–$50	over $50

Restaurant prices are for a main course at dinner, excluding sales tax of 7.75%. Hotel prices are for two people in a standard double room in high season, excluding service charges and 7.25%–10% tax.

24

Updated by Christine Vovakes

The Wondrous Landscape of California's northeastern corner, relatively unmarred by development, congestion, and traffic, is the product of volcanic activity. At the southern end of the Cascade Range, Lassen Volcanic National Park is the best place to witness the far north's fascinating geology. Beyond the sulfur vents and bubbling mud pots, the park owes much of its beauty to 10,457-foot Mt. Lassen and 50 wilderness lakes.

The most enduring image of the region, though, is Mt. Shasta, whose 14,162-foot snowcapped peak beckons outdoor adventurers of all kinds. There are many versions of Shasta to enjoy—the mountain, the lake, the river, the town, the dam, and the forest—all named after the Native Americans known as the Shatasla, or Sastise, who once inhabited the region. Its soaring mountain peaks, wild rivers teeming with trout, and almost unlimited recreational possibilities make the far north the perfect destination for sports lovers. You won't find many hot nightspots or cultural enclaves, but you'll find some of the best hiking and fishing in the state.

PLANNING

GETTING HERE AND AROUND
BY AIR
Chico Municipal Airport and Redding Municipal Airport are served by United Express. Horizon Air also uses the airport in Redding.

There's no shuttle service from either airport, but taxis can be ordered. The approximate cost from the airport to downtown Redding is $28 to $30, and it's $18 from the Chico airport to downtown.

Air Contacts Chico Municipal Airport (⌧ *150 Airpark Blvd., off Cohasset Rd., Chico* ☎ *530/896–7200*). **Redding Municipal Airport** (⌧ *Airport Rd., Redding* ☎ *530/224–4320*). **Taxi Service, Chico** (☎ *530/893–4444 or 530/342–2929*). **Taxi Service, Redding** (☎ *530/246–0577 or 530/222–1234*).

BY BUS

Greyhound buses travel I–5 and interior highways, serving Burney, Chico, Red Bluff, Redding, and Susanville. Butte County Transit serves Chico, Oroville, and elsewhere. Chico Area Transit System provides bus service within Chico. The vehicles of the Redding Area Bus Authority operate daily except Sunday within Redding, Anderson, and Shasta Lake. STAGE buses serve Siskiyou County, on weekdays only, from Yreka to Dunsmuir, stopping in Mt. Shasta and other towns, and provide service in Scott Valley, Happy Camp, Hornbrook, Lake Shastina, and the Klamath River area. Lassen Rural Bus serves the Susanville, northeast Lake Almanor, and south and east Lassen County areas, running weekdays except holidays. Lassen Rural Bus connects with Plumas County Transit, which serves the Quincy area, and with Modoc County Sage Stage, which serves the Alturas area.

Bus Contacts Butte County Transit/Chico Area Transit System (☎ 530/342–0221 or 800/822–8145 ⊕ www.bcag.org/transit/index.html). **Greyhound** (☎ 800/229–9424 ⊕ www.greyhound.com). **Lassen Rural Bus** (☎ 530/252–7433). **Modoc County Sage Stage** (☎ 530/233–3883 or 233–6410). **Plumas County Transit** (☎ 530/283–2538 ⊕ www.plumastransit.com). **Redding Area Bus Authority** (☎ 530/241–2877 ⊕ www.rabaride.com). **STAGE** (☎ 530/842–8295 ⊕ www.co.siskiyou.ca.us).

BY CAR

Chico is east of I–5 on Highway 32. Lassen Volcanic National Park can be reached by Highway 36 from Red Bluff or (except in winter) Highway 44 from Redding. Highway 299 connects Redding and Alturas. Highway 139 leads from Susanville to Lava Beds National Monument. Highway 89 will take you from Mt. Shasta to Quincy. Highway 36 links Chester and Susanville.

Road Conditions Caltrans Highway Information Network (☎ 800/427–7623).

BY TRAIN

Amtrak has stations in Chico, Redding, and Dunsmuir and operates buses that connect to Greyhound service through Redding, Red Bluff, and Chico.

Train Contacts Amtrak (✉ W. 5th and Orange Sts., Chico ✉ 1620 Yuba St. (for Amtrak's Coach Starlight) or 1650 Yuba St. (Amtrak motor coach connections to Sacramento), Redding ✉ 5750 Sacramento Ave., Dunsmuir ☎ 800/872–7245 ⊕ www.amtrakcalifornia.com).

HEALTH AND SAFETY

In an emergency dial 911.

Hospitals Banner-Lassen Medical Center (✉ 1800 Spring Ridge Dr., Susanville ☎ 530/252–2000). **Enloe Medical Center** (✉ 1531 Esplanade, Chico ☎ 530/332–7300). **Mercy Medical Center** (✉ 2175 Rosaline Ave., Redding ☎ 530/225–6000).

CAMPING

■ TIP➔ Some campgrounds in California's far north get booked as much as a year in advance for July 4. Although that's not the norm, it's still a good idea to make summer reservations two to three months in advance. You can reserve a site at many of the region's campgrounds through Reserve-America and, for federal recreation reservations, Recreation.gov.

Campground Reservations ReserveAmerica (☎ 800/444–7275 ⊕ www. reserveamerica.com). **Recreation.gov** (☎ 877/444–6777 ⊕ www.recreation.gov).

VISITOR INFORMATION

Contacts Lassen County Chamber of Commerce (✉ 75 N. Weatherlow, Susanville ☎ 530/257–4323 ⊕ www.lassencountychamber.com). **Shasta Cascade Wonderland Association** (✉ 1699 Hwy. 273, Anderson ☎ 530/365–7500 or 800/474–2782 ⊕ www.shastacascade.com). **Siskiyou County Visitors Bureau** (✉ 300 Pine St., Mt. Shasta ☎ 530/926–3696 or 800/926–4865 ⊕ www. visitsiskiyou.org).

FROM CHICO TO MT. SHASTA

CHICO

180 mi from San Francisco, east on I–80, north on I–505 to I–5, and east on Hwy. 32; 86 mi north of Sacramento on Hwy. 99.

Chico (which is Spanish for "small") sits just west of Paradise in the Sacramento Valley and offers a welcome break from the monotony of Interstate 5. The Chico campus of California State University, the scores of local artisans, and the area's agriculture (primarily almond orchards) all influence the culture here. Chico's true claim to fame, however, is the popular Sierra Nevada Brewery, which keeps locals and beer drinkers across the country happy with its distinctive microbrews.

ESSENTIALS

Visitor Information Chico Chamber of Commerce (✉ 300 Salem St., Chico ☎ 530/891–5556 or 800/852–8570 ⊕ www.chicochamber.com).

EXPLORING

★ The sprawling 3,670-acre **Bidwell Park** (✉ River Rd. south of Sacramento St. ☎ 530/896–7800) is a community green space straddling Big Chico Creek, where scenes from *Gone With the Wind* and the 1938 version of *Robin Hood* (starring Errol Flynn) were filmed. The region's recreational hub, it includes a golf course, swimming areas, and paved biking, hiking, and in-line skating trails. One of the largest city-run parks in the country, Bidwell starts as a slender strip downtown and expands eastward 11 mi toward the Sierra foothills.

★ The renowned **Sierra Nevada Brewing Company**, one of the pioneers of the microbrewery movement, still has a hands-on approach to beer making. Tour the brew house and see how the beer is produced—from the sorting of hops through fermentation and bottling. You can also visit the gift shop and enjoy a hearty lunch or dinner in the brewpub (it's closed Monday), where tastings are available (for a fee). ✉ 1075 E. 20th St.

24

🖹 *530/345-2739* ⊕ *www.sierranevada.com* ✉ *Free* ⊙ *Tours Sun.–Fri. 2:30, Sat. noon–3 on the ½ hr.*

★ In **Bidwell Mansion State Historic Park** you can take a one-hour tour of most of the mansion's 26 rooms. Built between 1865 and 1868 by General John Bidwell, the founder of Chico, the home was designed by Henry W. Cleaveland, a San Francisco architect. Bidwell and his wife welcomed many distinguished guests to the distinctive pink Italianate mansion, including President Rutherford B. Hayes, naturalist John Muir, suffragist Susan B. Anthony, and General William T. Sherman. ✉ *525 The Esplanade* 🖹 *530/895–6144* ✉ *$6* ⊙ *Tues.–Wed. noon–5, weekends 11–5; last tour at 4.*

WHERE TO EAT AND STAY

$$–$$$$ ✕ **5th Street Steakhouse.** Hand-cut steak is the star in this refurbished
STEAK early 1900s building, the place to come when you're craving red meat and a huge baked potato. Exposed red brick walls warm the small dining area. A long mahogany bar catches the overflow crowds that jam the place on weekends. No reservations are accepted on Fridays and Saturdays, but it's worth the wait. ✉ *345 W. 5th St.* 🖹 *530/891–6328* ⊟ *AE, MC, V* ⊙ *No lunch.*

$$–$$$$ 🛏 **Hotel Diamond.** Crystal chandeliers and gleaming wood floors and
★ banisters elegantly welcome guests into the foyer of this restored gem in downtown Chico near the university. Some rooms are furnished with antiques that reflect the town's historic past. Johnnie's ($$–$$$$), the hotel's restaurant and bar, provides room service, and is open for lunch and dinner. **Pros:** refined; great location; excellent breakfast buffet included in room rate. **Cons:** pricey; not a good choice for families. ✉ *220 W. 4th St.* 🖹 *530/893–3100 or 866/993–3100* ⊕ *www. hoteldiamondchico.com* ⇆ *39 rooms, 4 suites* ⚫ *In-room: a/c, Internet, Wi-Fi. In-hotel: restaurant, room service, Wi-Fi hotspot* ⊟ *AE, D, MC, V* ⍐ *CP.*

$–$$ 🛏 **Johnson's Country Inn.** Nestled in an almond orchard five minutes from downtown, this Victorian-style farmhouse with a wraparound veranda is a welcome change from motel row. It's full of antique furnishings and modern conveniences. **Pros:** rural setting; beautifully maintained; serene walks. **Cons:** a car is essential. ✉ *3935 Morehead Ave.* 🖹🖹 *530/345–7829 or 866/872–7780* ⊕ *www.chico.com/johnsonsinn* ⇆ *4 rooms* ⚫ *In-room: a/c, no TV, Wi-Fi. In-hotel: Wi-Fi hotspot* ⊟ *AE, MC, V* ⍐ *BP.*

RED BLUFF

41 mi north of Chico on Hwy 99.

Historic Red Bluff is a gateway to Lassen Volcanic National Park. Established in the mid-19th century as a shipping center and named for the color of its soil, the town is filled with dozens of restored Victorians. It's a great home base for outdoor adventures in the area.

ESSENTIALS

Visitor Information Red Bluff–Tehama County Chamber of Commerce (✉ *100 Main St., Red Bluff* 🖹 *530/527-6220* ⊕ *www. redbluffchamberofcommerce.com*).

EXPLORING

★ **William B. Ide Adobe State Historic Park,** on an oak-lined bank of the Sacramento River, is named for the first and only president of the short-lived California Republic of 1846. The Bear Flag Party proclaimed California a sovereign nation, separate from Mexican rule, and the republic existed for 22 days before it was taken over by the United States. The republic's flag has survived, with only minor refinements, as California's state flag. The park's main attraction is an adobe home built in the 1850s and outfitted with period furnishings; tours are available on request. There's also a carriage shed, a blacksmith shop, and a small visitor center. ⊠ *21659 Adobe Rd.* ☎ *530/529–8599* ⊕ *www.parks.ca.gov* ☒ *$6 per vehicle* ☼ *Park and picnic facilities daily sunrise–sunset; adobe home and historic sites open Thurs.–Sun., varying hrs.*

> **RED BLUFF ROUND-UP**
>
> Check out old-time rodeo at its best during the Red Bluff Round-Up. Held the third weekend of April, this annual event attracts some of the best cowboys in the country. For more information, visit ⊕ *www.redbluffroundup.com.*

WHERE TO EAT AND STAY

$–$$$

STEAK

✕ **Green Barn Steakhouse.** You're likely to find cowboys sporting Stetsons and spurs, feasting on sizzling porterhouse, baby back ribs, and filet mignon at Red Bluff's premier steak house. For lighter fare, there's garlicky scampi or fettuccine primavera, along with fresh fish specials. As a sweet indulgence, don't miss the bread pudding with rum sauce. The lounge is usually hopping, especially when there's an event at the nearby rodeo grounds. ⊠ *5 Chestnut Ave.* ☎ *530/527–3161* ⊟ *AE, D, MC, V* ☼ *Closed Sun.*

¢–$$

▦ **The Jeter Victorian Inn.** On sunny days, breakfast is served in the garden pavilion outside this 1881 Victorian home. The four guest rooms are elegantly decorated with antiques and period furnishings; two have private baths, and the Imperial Room has a Jacuzzi. A separate cottage is also available. **Pros:** quiet residential area; within walking distance of restaurants. **Cons:** no Internet access. ⊠ *1107 Jefferson St.* ☎ *530/527–7571* ⊕ *www.jetervictorianinn.com* ⇆ *4 rooms, 3 with bath; 1 cottage* ☖ *In-room: no phone, a/c, no TV (some)* ⊟ *MC, V* ◎ *BP.*

REDDING

32 mi north of Red Bluff on I–5.

As the largest city in the far north, Redding is an ideal headquarters for exploring the surrounding countryside.

ESSENTIALS

Visitor Information Redding Convention and Visitors Bureau (⊠ *777 Auditorium Dr., Redding* ☎ *530/225–4100* ⊕ *www.visitredding.org*).

EXPLORING

☾

Fodor's Choice

★

Curving along the Sacramento River, **Turtle Bay Exploration Park** has a museum, an arboretum with walking trails, and lots of interactive exhibits for children, including a miniature dam, a gold-panning area, and a seasonal Butterfly House where monarchs emerge from their

Fisherman under Santiago Calatrava's striking Sundial Bridge in Turtle Bay Exploration Park.

cocoons. The main draw at the park, however, is the stunning **Sundial Bridge,** a modernist pedestrian footbridge designed by world-renowned Spanish architect Santiago Calatrava. The bridge's architecture consists of a translucent, illuminated span that stretches across the river, and—most strikingly—a soaring white 217-foot needle that casts a slender moving shadow, like a sundial's, over the water and surrounding trees. Watching the sun set over the river from this bridge is a magical experience. The bridge links to the Sacramento River Trail and the park's arboretum and botanical gardens. Access to the bridge and arboretum is free; a fee admits you to both the museum and the botanical gardens. ⊠ *840 Sundial Bridge Dr.* ☎ *530/243–8850 or 800/887–8532* ⊕ *www. turtlebay.org* ⊟ *$13* ⊙ *Mid-Mar.–Sept., daily 9–5; Oct.–mid-Mar., Wed.–Sat. 9–4, Sun. 10–4.*

WHERE TO EAT AND STAY

¢–$$ ✕ **Buz's Crab.** This casual restaurant in central Redding shares space with
SEAFOOD a bustling seafood market where locals snap up ocean-fresh Dungeness crab in season. The fish-and-chips is a favorite; seafood combos, including Cajun-style selections are also noteworthy. Try the wild salmon or trout charbroiled over mesquite wood. ⊠ *2159 East St.* ☎ *530/243– 2120* ⊟ *D, MC, V.*

$–$$$ ✕ **Jack's Grill.** Famous for its 16-ounce steaks, this popular bar and steak
STEAK house also serves shrimp and chicken. A town favorite, the place is usually jam-packed and noisy. ⊠ *1743 California St.* ☎ *530/241–9705* ⊟ *AE, D, MC, V* ⊙ *Closed Sun. No lunch.*

$$ ▣ **The Red Lion.** Adjacent to I–5, and close to Redding's convention
★ center and regional recreation sites, this hotel is a top choice for both

business and vacation travelers. Rooms are spacious and comfortable; a large patio surrounded by landscaped grounds is a relaxing spot to enjoy an outdoor meal or snack. Rooms have irons, ironing boards, and hair dryers, and there's a gym near the pool. The hotel's restaurant, 3-Shastas Bar and Grill ($–$$$), serves dinner only and is a popular place for locals. **Pros:** family-friendly; close to a major shopping area. **Cons:** busy area. ⊠ *1830 Hilltop Dr., Hwy. 44/299 exit off I–5* ☎ *530/221–8700 or 800/733–5466* ⊕ *www.redlion.com* ➪ *192 rooms, 2 suites* ⚓ *In-room: a/c, Wi-Fi. In-hotel: restaurant, bar, pool, gym, Wi-Fi hotspot* ⊟ *AE, D, DC, MC, V.*

SPORTS AND THE OUTDOORS

The **Fly Shop** (⊠ *4140 Churn Creek Rd.* ☎ *530/222–3555*) sells fishing licenses and has information about guides, conditions, and fishing packages.

24

WEAVERVILLE

46 mi west of Redding on Hwy. 299, called Main St. in town.

A man known only as Weaver struck gold here in 1849, and the fledgling community at the base of the Trinity Alps was named after him. With its impressive downtown historic district, today Weaverville is a popular headquarters for family vacations and biking, hiking, fishing, and gold-panning excursions.

EXPLORING

Fodor's Choice ★ Weaverville's main attraction is the **Weaverville Joss House,** a Taoist temple built in 1874 and called Won Lim Miao ("the temple of the forest beneath the clouds") by Chinese miners. The oldest continuously used Chinese temple in California, it attracts worshippers from around the world. With its golden altar, antique weaponry, and carved wooden canopies, the Joss House is a piece of California history that can best be appreciated on a guided 30-minute tour. The original temple building and many of its furnishings—some of which came from China—were lost to fire in 1873, but members of the local Chinese community soon rebuilt it. ⊠ *630 Main St.* ☎ *530/623–5284* 🎟 *Museum free; guided tour $3* ⊙ *Thurs.–Sun. 10–5; last tour at 4.*

Trinity County Courthouse (⊠ *Court and Main Sts.*), built in 1856 as a store, office building, and hotel, was converted to county use in 1865. The Apollo Saloon, in the basement, became the county jail. It's the oldest courthouse still in use in California.

★ **Trinity County Historical Park** houses the **Jake Jackson Memorial Museum,** which has a blacksmith shop, a stamp mill (where ore is crushed) from the 1890s that is still in use, and the original jail cells of the Trinity County Courthouse. ⊠ *508 Main St.* ☎ *530/623–5211* ⊙ *Late Apr.–Oct., daily 10–5; Nov. and Dec., Wed –Sat. noon–5; Jan.–late Apr., Tues. and Sat. noon–4.*

WHERE TO EAT AND STAY

$–$$$
AMERICAN
✕ **La Grange Café.** In two brick buildings dating from the 1850s (they're among the oldest edifices in town), this eatery serves buffalo and other game meats, pasta, fresh fish, and farmers' market vegetables when

they're available. There's a full premium bar, and an extensive wine list. ✉ *520 Main St.* ☎ *530/623–5325* ☰ *AE, D, MC, V* ⊘ *No lunch Sun.*

¢   🛏 **Red Hill Motel**. This 1940s-era property is popular with anglers, who appreciate the outdoor fish-cleaning area on the premises. The separate wooden lodgings, painted red and surrounded by pine trees, encircle a grassy knoll. One cozy cabin with full kitchen is good for families; two others have kitchenettes, and three have mini-refrigerators and microwaves. **Pros:** close to popular bass fishing sites; inexpensive. **Cons:** older facility; some rooms need sprucing up. ✉ *Red Hill Rd.* ☎ *530/623–4331* ☜ *4 rooms, 6 cabins, 2 duplexes* ⚴ *In-room: a/c, kitchen (some), refrigerator (some)* ☰ *AE, D, MC, V.*

SPORTS AND THE OUTDOORS

Below the Lewiston Dam, east of Weaverville on Highway 299, is the **Fly Stretch** of the Trinity River, an excellent fly-fishing area. The **Pine Cove Boat Ramp**, on Lewiston Lake, provides fishing access for those with disabilities—decks here are built over prime trout-fishing waters. Contact the **Weaverville Ranger Station** (✉ *360 Main St.* ☎ *530/623–2121*) for maps and information about hiking trails in the Trinity Alps Wilderness.

LAKE SHASTA AREA

★   *12 mi north of Redding on I–5.*

Twenty-one types of fish inhabit **Lake Shasta**, including rainbow trout and salmon. The lake region also has the largest nesting population of bald eagles in California. You can rent fishing boats, ski boats, sailboats, canoes, paddleboats, Jet Skis, and windsurfing boards at one of the many marinas and resorts along the 370-mi shoreline.

ESSENTIALS

Visitor Information Shasta Cascade Wonderland Association (✉ *1699 Hwy. 273, Anderson* ☎ *530/365–7500 or 800/474–2782* ⊕ *www.shastacascade.com*).

EXPLORING

Stalagmites, stalactites, flowstone deposits, and crystals entice people of all ages to the **Lake Shasta Caverns**. To see this impressive spectacle, you must take the two-hour tour, which includes a catamaran ride across the McCloud arm of Lake Shasta and a bus ride up Grey Rock Mountain to the cavern entrance. The caverns are 58°F year-round, making them a cool retreat on a hot summer day. The most awe-inspiring of the limestone rock formations is the glistening Cathedral Room, which appears to be gilded. During peak summer months (June through August), tours depart every half hour; in April, May, and September it's every hour. A gift shop is open from 8 to 4:30. ✉ *Shasta Caverns Rd. exit off I–5* ☎ *530/238–2341 or 800/795–2283* ⊕ *www.lakeshastacaverns.com* 💳 *$22* ⊘ *June–Aug., daily 9–4 with departures every ½ hr; Apr., May, and Sept., daily 9–3 with departures every hr; Oct.–Mar., daily 10–2 with departures every 2 hrs.*

★   **Shasta Dam** is the second-largest concrete dam in the United States (only Grand Coulee in Washington is bigger). On clear days, snowcapped Mt. Shasta glimmers on the horizon above the still waters of its namesake lake. The visitor center has computerized photographic tours of the dam construction, video presentations, fact sheets, and historical displays. Hour-long guided tours take visitors inside the dam and its powerhouse. ⊠ *16349 Shasta Dam Blvd.* ☎ *530/275–4463* ⊕ *www.usbr.gov/mp/ncao* ⊗ *Visitor center daily 8–5; call for tour times.*

WHERE TO EAT

$–$$$
SEAFOOD

✕ **Tail o' the Whale.** As its name suggests, this restaurant has a nautical theme. You can enjoy a panoramic view of Lake Shasta here while you savor house specials like prawns with fettuccine in a garlic cream sauce, or prime rib with tempura shrimp. This is a favorite spot for boaters, who anchor at a courtesy dock while they're dining. ⊠ *10300 Bridge Bay Rd., Bridge Bay exit off I–5* ☎ *530/275–3021* ⊗ *No dinner Mon. and Tues.* ⊟ *D, MC, V.*

SPORTS AND THE OUTDOORS

FISHING

The Fishin' Hole (⊠ *3844 Shasta Dam Blvd., Shasta Lake City* ☎ *530/275–4123*) is a bait-and-tackle shop a couple of miles from the lake. It sells fishing licenses and provides information about conditions.

HOUSE-
BOATING

Houseboats here come in all sizes except small. As a rule, rentals are outfitted with cooking utensils, dishes, and most of the equipment you'll need—all you supply are the food and the linens. When you rent a houseboat, you receive a short course in how to maneuver your launch before you set out. You can fish, swim, sunbathe on the flat roof, or sit on the deck and watch the world go by. The shoreline of Lake Shasta is beautifully ragged, with countless inlets; it's not hard to find privacy. Expect to spend a minimum of $350 a day for a craft that sleeps six. A three-day, two-night minimum is customary. Prices are often lower during the off-season (September through May). The **Shasta Cascade Wonderland Association** (⊠ *1699 Hwy. 273, Anderson* ☎ *530/365–7500* or *800/474–2782* ⊕ *www.shastacascade.com*) provides names of rental companies and prices for Lake Shasta houseboating. **Bridge Bay Resort** (⊠ *10300 Bridge Bay Rd., Redding* ☎ *800/752–9669*) rents houseboats, fishing boats, and patio boats.

DUNSMUIR

10 mi south of Mt. Shasta on I–5.

Castle Crags State Park surrounds the town of Dunsmuir, which was named for a 19th-century Scottish coal baron who offered to build a fountain if the town was renamed in his honor. The town's other major attraction is the Railroad Park Resort, where you can spend the night in restored railcars.

EXPLORING

★ Named for its 6,000-foot glacier-polished crags, which tower over the Sacramento River, **Castle Crags State Park** offers fishing in Castle Creek, hiking in the backcountry, and a view of Mt. Shasta. The crags draw climbers and hikers from around the world. The 4,350-acre park has 28 mi of hiking trails, including a 2.75-mi access trail to **Castle Crags Wilderness**, part of the **Shasta-Trinity National Forest.** There are excellent trails at lower altitudes, along with picnic areas, restrooms, showers, and campsites. ⊠ *6 mi south of Dunsmuir, Castella/Castle Crags exit* *off I–5; follow for ¼ mi ☎ 530/235–2684 ⛺ $8 per vehicle, day use.*

WHERE TO EAT AND STAY

FINE FISHING

The upper Sacramento River near Dunsmuir is consistently rated one of the best fishing spots in the country. Check with the chamber of commerce for local fishing guides.

$$–$$$
MEDITERRANEAN

✕**Café Maddalena**. Café Maddalena serves an adventurous Mediterranean menu with a French influence that draws in diners from nearby mountain communities, and as far away as Redding. Selections change seasonally but always feature a vegetarian offering along with fresh fish and meat entrées like seared scallops in tangerine sauce, lamb curry, and roasted quail with cardamom and pear sauce. Wines from Spain, Italy, and France complement the meals. ✉ *5801 Sacramento Ave.* ☎ *530/235–2725* ═ *AE, D, MC, V* ⊙ *Closed Mon.–Wed. and Jan. No lunch.*

$–$$
ⓒ

🚆**Railroad Park Resort**. The antique cabooses here were collected over more than three decades and have been converted into cozy motel rooms in honor of Dunsmuir's railroad legacy. The resort has a vaguely *Orient Express*–style dining room and a lounge fashioned from vintage railcars. A creek runs next to the landscaped grounds, where you'll find a huge steam engine, a restored water tower, and a spectacular view of Castle Crags. There's also an RV park and campground. **Pros:** gorgeous setting; kitschy fun. **Cons:** cabooses can feel cramped; restaurant open mid-April through September. ✉ *100 Railroad Park Rd.* ☎ *530/235–4440 or 800/974–7245* ⊕ *www.rrpark.com* ⇄ *23 cabooses, 4 cabins* ⚒ *In-room: a/c, kitchen (some), refrigerator. In-hotel: restaurant, pool, some pets allowed* ═ *MC, V.*

MT. SHASTA

34 mi north of Lake Shasta on I–5.

The crown jewel of the 2.5-million-acre Shasta-Trinity National Forest, Mt. Shasta, a 14,162-foot-high dormant volcano, is a mecca for day hikers. It's especially enticing in spring, when fragrant Shasta lilies and other flowers adorn the rocky slopes. The paved road reaches only as far as the timberline; the final 6,000 feet are a tough climb of rubble, ice, and snow (the summit is perpetually ice packed). Only a hardy few are qualified to make the trek to the top.

The town of Mt. Shasta has real character and some fine restaurants. Lovers of the outdoors and backcountry skiers abound, and they are more than willing to offer advice on the most beautiful spots in the region, which include out-of-the-way swimming holes, dozens of high mountain lakes, and a challenging 18-hole golf course with 360 degrees of spectacular views.

ESSENTIALS

Visitor Information Siskiyou County Visitors Bureau (✉ *300 Pine St., Mt. Shasta* ☎ *530/926–3696 or 800/926–4865* ⊕ *www.visitsiskiyou.org*).

24

WHERE TO EAT AND STAY

$$
ECLECTIC
✕**Lilys.** This restaurant in a white-clapboard home, framed by a picket fence and arched trellis, serves everything from steaks and pastas to Mexican and vegetarian dishes. Daily specials include prime rib and a fresh fish entrée. For innovative vegetarian fare try a roasted eggplant hoagie with three cheeses, or a *dal* burger, which is made with walnuts, fresh veggies, garbanzo beans, and rice. ⊠ *1013 S. Mt. Shasta Blvd.* ☎ *530/926–3372* ▭ *AE, D, MC, V.*

¢
CAFÉ
✕**Seven Suns Coffee and Cafe.** A favorite gathering spot for locals, this small coffee shop serves specialty wraps for breakfast and lunch, plus soup and salad selections. Pastries, made daily, include muffins and scones, and blackberry fruit bars in season. If the weather's nice, grab a seat on the patio. ⊠ *1011 S. Mt. Shasta Blvd.* ☎ *530/926–9701* ▭ *AE, MC, V.*

$$–$$$
★
⊡ **Mount Shasta Resort.** Private chalets are nestled among tall pine trees along the shore of Lake Siskiyou, all with gas-log fireplaces and full kitchens. The resort's Highland House Restaurant, above the clubhouse of a spectacular 18-hole golf course, has uninterrupted views of Mt. Shasta. Large steaks and prawn dishes are menu highlights at the restaurant. Take the Central Mount Shasta exit west from I–5, then go south on Old Stage Road. **Pros:** incredible views; romantic woodsy setting. **Cons:** kids may get bored. ⊠ *1000 Siskiyou Lake Blvd.* ☎ *530/926– 3030 or 800/958–3363* ⊕ *www.mountshastaresort.com* ⟿ *65 units* ⚑ *In-room: a/c, kitchen (some), refrigerator (some), Wi-Fi. In-hotel: restaurant, bar, golf course, spa, Wi-Fi hotspot* ▭ *AE, MC, V.*

SPORTS AND THE OUTDOORS

HIKING
The **Forest Service Ranger Station** (☎ *530/926–4511 or 530/926–9613*) keeps tabs on trail conditions and gives avalanche reports.

MOUNTAIN
CLIMBING
Fifth Season Mountaineering Shop (⊠ *300 N. Mt. Shasta Blvd.* ☎ *530/926– 3606 or 530/926–5555*) rents skiing and climbing equipment and operates a recorded 24-hour climber-skier report. **Shasta Mountain Guides** (☎ *530/926–3117* ⊕ *www.shastaguides.com*) leads hiking, climbing, and ski-touring groups to the summit of Mt. Shasta.

SKIING
☾
On the southeast flank of Mt. Shasta, **Mt. Shasta Board & Ski Park** has three triple-chair lifts and one surface lift on 425 skiable acres. It's a great place for novices because three-quarters of the trails are for beginning or intermediate skiers. The area's vertical drop is 1,390 feet, with a top elevation of 6,600 feet. The longest of the 32 trails is 1.75 mi. A package for beginners, available through the ski school, includes a lift ticket, ski rental, and a lesson. The school also runs ski and snowboard programs for children. There's night skiing for those who want to see the moon rise as they schuss. The base lodge has a simple café, a ski shop, and a ski-snowboard rental shop. The **Mt. Shasta Nordic Center,** with 25 km (15 mi) of groomed cross-country trails, is on the same road. ⊠ *Hwy. 89 exit east from I–5, south of Mt. Shasta* ☎ *530/926–8610 or 800/754–7427, 530/926–2142 Mt. Shasta Nordic Center* ⊕ *www.skipark.com; www.mtshastanordic.org* ⊙ *Winter ski season schedule: Sun.–Tues. 9–4, Wed.–Sat. 9–9.*

THE BACKCOUNTRY

MCARTHUR–BURNEY FALLS MEMORIAL STATE PARK

Hwy. 89, 52 mi southeast of Mt. Shasta and 41 mi north of Lassen Volcanic National Park.

Fodor's Choice
★
Just inside the park's southern boundary, Burney Creek wells up from the ground and divides into two falls that cascade over a 129-foot cliff into a pool below. Countless ribbonlike streams pour from hidden moss-covered crevices; resident bald eagles are frequently seen soaring overhead. You can walk a self-guided nature trail that descends to the foot of the falls, which Theodore Roosevelt—according to legend—called "the eighth wonder of the world." You can also swim at Lake Britton; lounge on the beach; rent motorboats, paddleboats, and canoes; or relax at one of the campsites or picnic areas. The camp store is open from early May to the end of October. ⊠ *24898 Hwy. 89, Burney* ☎ *530/335–2777* ☐ *$8 per vehicle, day use.*

ALTURAS

86 mi northeast of McArthur–Burney Falls Memorial State Park on Hwy. 299.

Alturas is the county seat and largest town in northeastern California's Modoc County. The Dorris family arrived in the area in 1874, built Dorris Bridge over the Pit River, and later opened a small wayside stop for travelers. Today the Alturas area is a land of few people but much rugged natural beauty. Travelers come to see eagles and other wildlife, the Modoc National Forest, and active geothermal areas.

ESSENTIALS

Visitor Information Alturas Chamber of Commerce (⊠ *522 S. Main St., Alturas* ☎ *530/233–4434* ⊕ *www.alturaschamber.org*).

EXPLORING

Modoc National Forest encompasses 1.6 million acres and protects 300 species of wildlife, including Rocky Mountain elk, wild horses, mule deer, and pronghorn antelope. In spring and fall, watch for migratory waterfowl as they make their way along the Pacific Flyway above the forest. Hiking trails lead to Petroglyph Point, one of the largest panels of rock art in the United States. ⊠ *800 W. 12th St.* ☎ *530/233–5811.*

Established to protect migratory waterfowl, the 6,280-acre **Modoc National Wildlife Refuge** gives refuge to Canada geese, sandhill cranes, mallards, teal, wigeon, pintail, white pelicans, cormorants, and snowy egrets. The refuge is open for hiking, bird-watching, and photography, but one area is set aside for hunters. Regulations vary according to season. ⊠ *1½ mi south of Alturas on Hwy. 395* ☎ *530/233–3572* ☐ *Free* ☉ *Daily dawn–dusk.*

DID YOU KNOW?

President Theodore Roosevelt supposedly called McArthur–Burney Falls "the eighth wonder of the world."

WHERE TO EAT

$$
SPANISH
✕**Brass Rail**. This authentic Basque restaurant offers hearty dinners at fixed prices that include wine, homemade bread, soup, salad, side dishes, coffee, and ice cream. Steak, lamb chops, fried chicken, shrimp, and scallops are among the best entrée selections. A full bar and lounge adjoin the dining area. ✉ *395 Lakeview Hwy.* ☎ *530/233–2906* ▬ *MC, V* ☺ *Closed Mon. No lunch Sat.*

SUSANVILLE

104 mi south of Alturas via Rte. 395; 65 mi east of Lassen Volcanic National Park via Hwy. 36.

Susanville tells the tale of its rich history through murals painted on buildings in the historic uptown area. Established as a trading post in 1854, it's the second-oldest town in the western Great Basin. You can take a self-guided tour around the original buildings and stop for a bite at one of the restaurants now housed within them; or, if you'd rather work up a sweat, you can hit the Bizz Johnson Trail and Eagle Lake recreation areas just outside of town.

ESSENTIALS

Visitor Information Lassen County Chamber of Commerce (✉ *75 N. Weatherlow, Susanville* ☎ *530/257-4323* ⊕ *www.lassencountychamber.com*).

EXPLORING

Bizz Johnson Trail follows a defunct line of the Southern Pacific Railroad for 25 mi. Known to locals as the Bizz, the trail is open for hikers, walkers, mountain bikers, horseback riders, and cross-country skiers. It skirts the Susan River through a scenic landscape of canyons, bridges, and forests abundant with wildlife. ✉ *Trailhead: 601 Richmond Rd.* ☎ *530/257-0456* ⊕ *www.blm.gov/ca/eaglelake/bizztrail.html* ▨ *Free.*

Anglers travel great distances to fish the waters of **Eagle Lake**, the second largest freshwater lake wholly in California. The Eagle Lake rainbow trout is prized for its size and fighting ability. Surrounded by high desert to the north and alpine forests to the south, the lake is also popular for picnicking, hiking, boating, waterskiing and windsurfing, and bird-watching—ospreys, pelicans, western grebes, and many other waterfowl visit the lake. On land you might see mule deer, small mammals, and even pronghorn antelope—and be sure to watch for bald eagle nesting sites. ✉ *16 mi north of Susanville on Eagle Lake Rd.* ☎ *530/257-0456 for Eagle Lake Recreation Area, 530/825-3454 for Eagle Lake Marina* ⊕ *www.blm.gov/ca/eaglelake.*

WHERE TO EAT AND STAY

¢–$
MEXICAN
✕**Mazatlan Grill**. The sauces and tortillas are prepared on-site in this friendly, family-run restaurant and lounge, which serves lunch and dinner daily. The dining room is simple and tidy, with comfortable upholstered booths. The extensive menu offers authentic, inexpensive Mexican fare ranging from fajitas and enchiladas to a vegetarian burrito. ✉ *1535 Main St.* ☎ *530/257-1800* ▬ *D, MC, V.*

¢–$
⊞ **High Country Inn**. Rooms are spacious in this two-story, colonial-style motel on the east edge of town. Complimentary Continental breakfast is

provided; more extensive dining is available next door at the Sage Hen restaurant. **Pros:** great mountain views; continental breakfast. **Cons:** must drive to town's historic center. ⊠ *3015 Riverside Dr.* ☎ *530/257–3450 or 866/454-4566* ⊕ *www.high-country-inn.com* ⇆ *66 rooms* ⚒ *In-room: a/c, refrigerator, Internet (some), Wi-Fi. In-hotel: pool, gym, Wi-Fi hotspot* ☰ *AE, D, MC, V* ⊙ *CP.*

LASSEN VOLCANIC NATIONAL PARK

45 mi east of Redding on Hwy. 44; 48 mi east of Red Bluff on Hwy. 36.

Fodor's Choice A dormant plug dome, Lassen Peak is the focus of Lassen Volcanic ★ National Park's 165.6 square mi of distinctive landscape. The peak began erupting in May 1914, sending pumice, rock, and snow thundering down the mountain and gas and hot ash billowing into the atmosphere. Lassen's most spectacular outburst occurred in 1915 when it blew a cloud of ash some 7 mi into the stratosphere. The resulting mudflow destroyed vegetation for miles in some directions; the evidence is still visible today, especially in Devastated Area. The volcano finally came to rest in 1921. Now fumaroles, mud pots, lakes, and bubbling hot springs create a fascinating but dangerous landscape that can be viewed throughout the park, especially via a hiked descent into Bumpass Hell. Because of its significance as a volcanic landscape, Lassen became a national park in 1916. Several volcanoes—the largest of which is now Lassen Peak—have been active in the area for roughly 600,000 years. The four types of volcanoes found in the world are represented in the park, including shield (Prospect Peak), plug dome (Lassen Peak), cinder cone (Cinder Cone), and composite (Brokeoff Volcano). Lassen Park Road (the continuation of Highway 89 within the park) and 150 mi of hiking trails provide access to many of these volcanic wonders. Caution is key here: signs warn visitors to stay on the trails and railed boardwalks to avoid falling into boiling water or through dangerous thin-crusted areas of the park. Although the park is closed to cars in winter, it's usually open to intrepid cross-country skiers and snowshoers. The Kohm Yah-mah-nee Visitor Center, at the southwest entrance to the park, is open year-round.

EXPLORING

Sulphur Works Thermal Area. Proof of Lassen Peak's volatility becomes evident shortly after you enter the park at the southwest entrance. Boardwalks take you over bubbling mud and boiling springs and through sulfur-emitting steam vents. ⊠ *Lassen Park Rd., 1 mi from Kohm Yah-mah-nee Visitor Center.*

Lassen Peak Hike. This trail winds 2½ mi to the mountaintop. It's a tough climb—2,000 feet uphill on a steady, steep grade—but the reward is a spectacular view. At the peak you can see into the rim and view the entire park (and much of the far north). Bring sunscreen, water, and a jacket because it's often windy and much cooler at the summit. ⊠ *Lassen Park Rd., 7 mi north of southwest entrance station.*

Lassen Scenic Byway. Beginning in Chester, this 185-mi scenic drive loops through the forests, volcanic peaks, geothermal springs, and lava fields

24

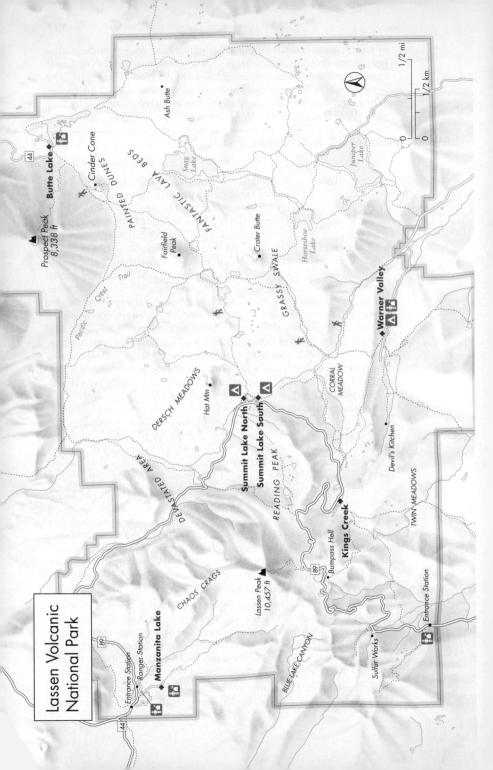

Lassen Volcanic National Park

Ash Butte

Cinder Cone

PAINTED DUNES

Snag Lake

Juniper Lake

Butte Lake

44

Prospect Peak 8,338 ft

Fairfield Peak

FANTASTIC LAVA BEDS

Crater Butte

Horseshoe Lake

GRASSY SWALE

Pacific Crest Trail

Warner Valley

DERSCH MEADOWS

Hat Mtn

CORRAL MEADOW

Summit Lake North

Summit Lake South

READING PEAK

Devil's Kitchen

DEVASTATED AREA

CHAOS CRAGS

Kings Creek

TWIN MEADOWS

Lassen Peak 10,457 ft

Bumpass Hell

89

Manzanita Lake

Ranger Station

Entrance Station

89

44

Blue Lake Canyon

Sulfur Works

Entrance Station

1/2 mi

1/2 km

0

0

of Lassen National Forest and Lassen National Park. It's an all-day excursion into dramatic wilderness; the road goes through the park and Lassen National Forest, veers southeast toward Susanville, then cuts west to make a loop around Lake Almanor before ending in Chester. The road is partially inaccessible in winter; call the Almanor Ranger District headquarters or Caltrans for current road conditions. From Chester, take Route 36 west to Route 89 north through the park (subject to closures due to snow), then Route 44 east to Route 36 west. Optionally, at Route 147, cut south to loop around Lake Almanor, and return to Route 89 north; at Route 36, turn east to return to Chester. ☎ *530/258–2141 Almanor Ranger District* ☎ *800/427–7623 Caltrans.*

Bumpass Hell Trail. Boiling springs, steam vents, and mud pots are featured on this 3½-mi round-trip hike. There's an overall descent of 700 feet from the parking lot to the base of the area. Expect to spend about three hours to do the loop. ⊠ *Lassen Park Rd., 6 mi from southwest entrance station.*

Chaos Jumbles. More than 350 years ago, an avalanche from the Chaos Crags lava domes scattered hundreds of thousands of rocks—many of them 2 to 3 feet in diameter—over a couple of square miles. ⊠ *Lassen Park Rd., 2 mi north of northwest entrance station.*

Hot Rock. This 400-ton boulder tumbled down from the summit during the volcano's active period and was still hot to the touch when locals discovered it nearly two days later. Although it's cool now, it's still an impressive sight. ⊠ *Lassen Park Rd., 7 mi south of northwest entrance station.*

WHERE TO STAY

$$$$ 🏨 **Drakesbad Guest Ranch.** At an elevation of 5,700 feet, this guest ranch is near Lassen Volcanic National Park's southern border. (It can't be reached from within the park, however; it's accessible only by a partially paved road leading out of the town of Chester.) Everything about this more-than-100-year-old property is rustic, from the comfortable furnishings, to the propane furnaces, to the kerosene lamps in lieu of electricity. Meals, casual during the day and rather elegant in the evening, are included in the room rate. The ranch begins taking reservations in mid-February for the summer season. **Pros:** a true back-to-nature experience; great for family adventures. **Cons:** difficult to get a reservation; no Internet access. ⊠ *Chester–Warner Valley Rd., north from Hwy. 36* ⊡ *Booking office: 2150 N. Main St., Suite 5, Red Bluff 96080* ☎ *530/529–1512* ⊕ *www.drakesbad.com* ⌂ *19 rooms* ⚴ *In-room: no phone, no a/c, no TV. In-hotel: restaurant, pool* ⊟ *D, MC, V* ⊘ *Closed early Oct.–early June* ⦵ *FAP.*

$$ 🏕 **Manzanita Lake Campground.** The largest of Lassen Volcanic National Park's eight campgrounds is near the northern entrance. This family-friendly site has showers, a camp store, and can accommodate vehicles up to 35 feet. Most ranger programs begin here or at nearby Loomis Museum. A trail near the campground leads east to a crater that now holds Crags Lake. Summer reservations for group campgrounds can be made up to seven months in advance. There is no running water from

the end of September until snow closes the campground. ⊠ *Off Lassen Park Rd., 2 mi east of junction of Hwys. 44 and 89* ☎ *530/595–4444* ⊕ *www.recreation.gov* ↻ *148 tent/RV sites, no hookups; 31 tent sites* ♿ *Flush toilets, dump station, drinking water, showers, fire pits, picnic tables* ▭ *D, MC, V* ☉ *Mid-May–late Oct., depending on snowfall.*

CHESTER

36 mi west of Susanville on Hwy 36.

The population of this small town on Lake Almanor swells from 2,500 to nearly 5,000 in summer as tourists come to visit. It serves as a gateway to Lassen Volcanic National Park.

ESSENTIALS

Visitor Information Chester–Lake Almanor Chamber of Commerce (⊠ *529 Main St., Chester* ☎ *530/258–2426 or 800/350–4838* ⊕ *www.lakealmanorarea. com*).

EXPLORING

Lake Almanor's 52 mi of shoreline lie in the shadow of Mt. Lassen, and are popular with campers, swimmers, water-skiers, and anglers. At an elevation of 4,500 feet, the lake warms to above 70°F for about eight weeks in summer. Information is available at the Chester–Lake Almanor Chamber of Commerce. ⊠ *529 Main St.* ☎ *530/258–2426*

WHERE TO EAT AND STAY

¢–$$ ✕ **Kopper Kettle Cafe.** Locals return again and again to this coffee shop–
AMERICAN style restaurant that serves savory home-cooked lunch and dinner, and breakfast whenever you've got a hankering for eggs with biscuits and gravy or other morning fare. A junior-senior menu, and beer and wine are available. The patio is open in summer. ⊠ *243 Main St.* ☎ *530/258–2698* ▭ *MC, V.*

¢–$ ✕ **Maria and Walker's Mexican Restaurant.** A festive atmosphere prevails
MEXICAN in this family-friendly restaurant and lounge, where traditional south-of-the-border fare is served. Lunch specials and children's plates are available. It's one of the few restaurants in the area with a full bar, a great place to enjoy a margarita at the end of a long day spent hiking. ⊠ *159 Main St.* ☎ *530/258–2262* ▭ *D, MC, V.*

$–$$ 🏨 **Best Western Rose Quartz Inn.** Down the road from Lake Almanor and close to Lassen Volcanic National Park, this small-town inn with its modern, wired rooms lets you venture into the wilderness and stay in touch with cyberspace. A large parking area accommodates motor homes and fishing boats. **Pros:** near Lake Almanor and Lassen Park; modern conveniences in a rural setting. **Cons:** on the pricey side. ⊠ *306 Main St., Chester* ☎ *530/258–2002 or 888/571–4885* ⊕ *www. bestwesterncalifornia.com* ↻ *50 rooms* ♿ *In-room: a/c, refrigerator (some), Internet. In-hotel: gym, Wi-Fi hotspot* ▭ *AE, D, MC, V* ¶○¶ *CP.*

¢–$$ 🏨 **Bidwell House.** This 1901 ranch house sits on 2 acres of cottonwood-
★ studded lawns and gardens, and has views of Lake Almanor and Mt. Lassen. Chairs and swings make the front porch inviting, and there are plenty of puzzles and games in the sunroom. Some rooms have

Lassen Volcanic National Park's King Creek Falls Hike, which takes you through forests and meadows dotted with wildflowers, is a good hike for nature photographers.

wood-burning stoves, claw-foot or Jacuzzi tubs, hardwood floors, and antiques. A separate cottage, which sleeps six, has a kitchen. The inn's three-course gourmet breakfast features blueberry-walnut pancakes. **Pros:** unique decor in each room; standout breakfast. **Cons:** not ideal for kids. ⊠ *1 Main St.* ☎ *530/258–3338* ⊕ *www.bidwellhouse.com* ⌁ *14 rooms, 2 with shared bath* ♿ *In-room: no phone, no a/c, Wi-Fi. In-hotel: Wi-Fi hotspot* ▭ *MC, V* ⦿⦿ *BP.*

QUINCY

67 mi southwest of Susanville via Hwys. 36 and 89.

A center for mining and logging in the 1850s, Quincy is nestled against the western slope of the Sierra Nevada. The county seat and largest community in Plumas County, the town is rich in historic buildings that have been the focus of preservation and restoration efforts. The four-story courthouse on Main Street, one of several stops on a self-guided tour, was built in 1921 with marble posts and staircases. The arts are thriving in Quincy, too: catch one of the plays or bluegrass performances at the Town Hall Theatre.

ESSENTIALS

Visitor Information Plumas County Visitors Bureau (⊠ *550 Crescent St., Quincy* ☎ *530/283–6345 or 800/326–2247* ⊕ *www.plumascounty.org*). **Quincy Chamber of Commerce** (⊠ *464 Main St., Quincy* ☎ *530/283–0188* ⊕ *www. quincychamber.com*).

EXPLORING

The main recreational attraction in central Plumas County, **Bucks Lake Recreation Area** is 17 mi southwest of Quincy at 5,200 feet. During warm months the lake's 17-mi shoreline, two marinas, and eight campgrounds attract anglers and water-sports enthusiasts. Trails through the tall pines beckon hikers and horseback riders. In winter much of the area remains open for snowmobiling and cross-country skiing. ⊠ *Bucks Lake Rd.* ☎ *800/326–2247* ⊕ *www.plumascounty.org.*

Plumas County is known for its wide-open spaces, and the 1.2-million-acre **Plumas National Forest**, with its high alpine lakes and crystal clear woodland streams, is a beautiful example. Hundreds of campsites are maintained in the forest, and picnic areas and hiking trails abound. You can enter the forest from numerous sites along highways 70 and 89. ⊠ *159 Lawrence St.* ☎ *530/283–2050* ☻ *U.S. Forest Service office weekdays 8–4:30.*

The cultural, home arts, and industrial history displays at the **Plumas County Museum** contain artifacts dating to the 1850s. Highlights include collections of Maidu Indian basketry, pioneer weapons, and rooms depicting life in the early days of Plumas County. There are a blacksmith shop and gold-mining cabin, equipment from the early days of logging, a restored buggy, and railroad and mining exhibits. ⊠ *500 Jackson St.* ☎ *530/283–6320* ▤ *$2* ☻ *Tues.–Sat. 9–4:30.*

WHERE TO EAT AND STAY

$–$$$

ITALIAN

✕ **Moon's.** This restored 1930 building houses a restaurant that serves such delights as honey-almond chicken, eggplant parmigiana, calamari, and Tuscan pasta. Sauces, salad dressings, pastas, breads, and desserts are all made from scratch. A verdant garden patio adds to Moon's allure. ⊠ *497 Lawrence St.* ☎ *530/283–0765* ▤ *AE, MC, V* ☻ *Closed Mon. and Tues. No lunch.*

$–$$

★

▣ **Ada's Place.** This place is actually four cottages, secluded on a quiet street one block from the county courthouse and downtown Quincy. Each is decorated with a different motif—Ruth's Garden has floral accents, while the serene Hop Sing's (which has lovely wood floors) has Oriental-art details—and each has a private yard or deck and a full kitchen. **Pros:** on-site owners' meticulous upkeep. **Cons:** a bit pricey. ⊠ *562 Jackson St.* ☎ *530/283–1954 or 877/234–2327* ⊕ *www. adasplace.com* ⇗ *4 cottages* ⌂ *In-room: a/c (some), kitchen, Wi-Fi. In-hotel: laundry facilities (some)* ▤ *MC, V.*

Travel Smart
California

WORD OF MOUTH

"Yes, the distances here in California are huge. As you'll be spending many hours in the car, make sure that you get one that's not going to be too cramped. You ought to carry bottled water with you all the time, but especially when you're driving through the desert."

—Barbara

GETTING HERE AND AROUND

Wherever you plan to go in California, getting there will likely involve driving (even if you fly). With the exception of San Diego, major airports are usually far from main attractions. (For example, four airports serve the Los Angeles area—but three of them are outside the city limits.) You'll find a similar situation in San Francisco, where it's a 30-minute-plus trip between any Bay Area airport and downtown. California's major airport hubs are LAX in Los Angeles and SFO in San Francisco, but satellite airports can be found around most major cities. When booking flights, it pays to check these locations, as you may find cheaper flights, more convenient times, and a better location in relation to your hotel. Most small cities have their own commercial airports, with connecting flights to larger cities—but service may be extremely limited, and it may be cheaper to rent a car and drive from L.A. or San Francisco.

There are two basic north–south routes in California: I–5, an interstate highway, runs inland most of the way from the Oregon border to the Mexican border; and Highway 101 hugs the coast for part of the route from Oregon to Mexico. (A slower but much more scenic option is to take California State Route 1, also referred to as Highway 1 and the Pacific Coast Highway, which winds along much of the California coast and provides an occasionally hair-raising, but breathtaking, ride.) From north to south, the state's east–west interstates are I–80, I–15, I–10, and I–8. Much of California is mountainous, and you may encounter very winding roads, frequently cliff-side, and steep mountain grades. In winter, roads crossing the Sierra east to west may close at any time due to weather, and chains may be required on these roads when they are open. Also in winter, I–5 north of Los Angeles closes during snowstorms. The flying and driving times in the following charts are best-case scenario estimates, but know that the infamous California traffic jam can occur at any time.

FROM LOS ANGELES TO:	BY AIR	BY CAR
San Diego	50 minutes	2 hours
Death Valley		5 hours
San Francisco	1 hour 25 minutes	6 hours
Monterey	1 hour 30 minutes	5 hours 30 minutes
Santa Barbara	45 minutes	1 hour 30 minutes
Big Sur		6 hours
Sacramento	1 hour 20 minutes	6 hours

FROM SAN FRANCISCO TO:	BY AIR	BY CAR
San Jose		1 hour 20 minutes
Monterey	40 minutes	2 hours 30 minutes
Los Angeles	1 hour 30 minutes	6 hours
Portland, OR	1 hour 45 minutes	10 hours
Mendocino		3 hours
Yosemite NP/ Fresno	45 minutes	4 hours
Lake Tahoe/ Reno	1 hour and 10 minutes	4 hours

▌ AIR TRAVEL

Flying time to California is less than six hours from New York and four hours from Chicago. Travel from London to Los Angeles is 12 hours or 11 hours to San Francisco and from Sydney approximately 14. Flying between San Francisco and Los Angeles takes about 90 minutes.

AIRPORTS

California's gateways are Los Angeles International Airport (LAX), San Francisco International Airport (SFO), San Diego International Airport (SAN), Sacramento International Airport (SMF), and San Jose International Airport (SJC). Oakland International Airport (OAK) is another option in the Bay Area, and other Los Angeles airports include Long Beach (LGB), Bob Hope Airport (BUR), LA/Ontario (ONT), and John Wayne Airport (SNA).

Airport Information Bob Hope Airport (☎ 818/840-8840 ⊕ www.burbankairport. com). **John Wayne Airport** (☎ 949/252-5200 ⊕ www.ocair.com). **LA/Ontario International Airport** (☎ 909/937-2700 ⊕ www. flyontario.com). **Los Angeles International Airport** (☎ 310/646-5252 ⊕ www.lawa.org/ lax). **Long Beach Airport** (☎ 562/570-2619 ⊕ www.longbeach.gov/airport). **Oakland International Airport** (☎ 510/563-3300 ⊕ www.flyoakland.com). **Sacramento International Airport** (☎ 916/929-5411 ⊕ www. sacairports.org/int). **San Diego International Airport** (☎ 619/400-2404 ⊕ www.san. org). **San Francisco International Airport** (☎ 650/761-0800 ⊕ www.flysfo.com). **San Jose International Airport** (☎ 408/277-4759 ⊕ www.sjc.org).

FLIGHTS

United, with hubs in San Francisco and Los Angeles, has the greatest number of flights into and within California. But most national and many international airlines fly here. Southwest Airlines connects smaller cities within California, often from satellite airports near major cities.

Airline Contacts Air Canada (☎ 888/247-2262 ⊕ www.aircanada.com). **Alaska Airlines/Horizon Air** (☎ 800/252-7522 ⊕ www.alaskaair.com). **American Airlines** (☎ 800/433-7300 ⊕ www.aa.com). **British Airways** (☎ 800/247-9297 ⊕ www. britishairways.com). **Cathay Pacific** (☎ 800/ 233-2742 ⊕ www.cathaypacific.com). **Continental Airlines** (☎ 800/523-3273 for U.S. and Mexico reservations, 800/231-0856 for international reservations ⊕ www.continental. com). **Delta Airlines** (☎ 800/221-1212 for U.S. reservations, 800/241-4141 for international reservations ⊕ www.delta.com). **Japan Air Lines** (☎ 800/525-3663 ⊕ www.jal.com). **JetBlue** (☎ 800/538-2583 ⊕ www.jetblue. com). **Midwest Airlines** (☎ 800/452-2022 ⊕ www.midwestairlines.com). **Northwest Airlines** (☎ 800/225-2525 ⊕ www.nwa.com). **Qantas** (☎ 800/227-4500 ⊕ www.qantas. com). **Southwest Airlines** (☎ 800/435-9792 ⊕ www.southwest.com). **Spirit Airlines** (☎ 800/772-7117 ⊕ www.spiritair.com). **United Airlines** (☎ 800/864-8331 for U.S. reservations, 800/538-2929 for international reservations ⊕ www.united.com). **US Airways** (☎ 800/428-4322 for U.S. and Canada reservations, 800/622-1015 for international reservations ⊕ www.usairways.com).

▌ BOAT TRAVEL

CRUISES

A number of major cruise lines offer trips that begin or end in California. Most voyages sail north along the Pacific Coast to Alaska or south to Mexico. California cruise ports include Los Angeles, San Diego, and San Francisco.

Cruise Lines Carnival Cruise Line (☎ 305/599-2600 or 800/227-6482 ⊕ www.carnival.com). **Celebrity Cruises** (☎ 305/539-6000 or 800/437-3111 ⊕ www. celebrity.com). **Cruise West** (☎ 888/851-8133 ⊕ www.cruisewest.com). **Crystal Cruises** (☎ 310/785-9300 or 800/446-6620 ⊕ www. crystalcruises.com). **Holland America Line** (☎ 206/281-3535 or 877/932-4259 ⊕ www. hollandamerica.com). **Norwegian Cruise Line** (☎ 305/436-4000 or 800/327-7030 ⊕ www. ncl.com). **Princess Cruises** (☎ 661/753-0000 or 800/774-6237 ⊕ www.princess.com). **Regent Seven Seas Cruises** (☎ 954/776-6123 or 800/477-7500 ⊕ www.rssc.com). **Royal Caribbean International** (☎ 305/539-6000 or 800/327-6700 ⊕ www.royalcaribbean. com). **Silversea Cruises** (☎ 954/522-4477 or 800/722-9955 ⊕ www.silversea.com).

■ BUS TRAVEL

Greyhound is the major bus carrier in California. Regional bus service is available in metropolitan areas.

Bus Information Greyhound (☎ *800/231-2222* ⊕ *www.greyhound.com*).

■ CAR TRAVEL

Three major highways—I–5, U.S. 101, and Highway 1—run north–south through California. The main east–west routes are I–15, I–10, and I–8 in Southern California and I–80 in northern California.

FROM LOS ANGELES TO	RTE.	DISTANCE
San Diego	I–5 or I–15	120 mi
Las Vegas	I–10 to I–15	290 mi
Death Valley	I–10 to I–15 to Hwy. 127 to Hwy. 190	288 mi
San Francisco	I–5 to Hwy. 156 to Hwy. 101	403 mi
Monterey	Hwy. 101 to Salinas Hwy. 68	334 mi
Santa Barbara	Hwy. 101	95 mi
Big Sur	Hwy. 101 to Hwy. 1	297 mi
Sacramento	I–5	386 mi

GASOLINE

Gasoline prices in California vary widely, depending on location, oil company, and whether you buy it at a full-serve or self-serve pump. It's less expensive to buy fuel in the southern part of the state than in the north. If you're planning to travel near Nevada, you can save a bit by purchasing gas over the border. Gas stations are plentiful throughout the state. Most stay open late (24 hours along major highways and in big cities), except in rural areas, where Sunday hours are limited and where you may drive long stretches without a chance to refuel.

ROAD CONDITIONS

Rainy weather can make driving along the coast or in the mountains treacherous. Some of the smaller routes over mountain ranges and in the deserts are prone to flash flooding. When the rains are severe, coastal Highway 1 can quickly become a slippery nightmare, buffeted by strong winds and obstructed by falling debris from the cliffs above. When the weather is particularly bad, Highway 1 may be closed due to mud and rock slides.

FROM SAN FRANCISCO TO	RTE.	DISTANCE
San Jose	Hwy. 101	50 mi
Monterey	Hwy. 101 to Hwy. 156	120 mi
Los Angeles	Hwy. 101 to Hwy. 156 to I–5	403 mi
Portland, OR	I–80 to I–505 to I–5	635 mi
Mendocino	Hwy. 1	174 mi
Yosemite NP	I–80 to I–580 to I–205 to Hwy. 120 east	184 mi
Lake Tahoe/ Reno	I–80	250 mi

Many smaller roads over the Sierra Nevada are closed in winter, and if it's snowing, tire chains may be required on routes that are open, most notably those to Yosemite and Lake Tahoe. From October through April, if it's raining along the coast, it's usually snowing at higher elevations. Consider renting a four-wheel-drive vehicle, or purchase chains before you get to the mountains. (Chains or cables generally cost $30 to $70, depending on tire size; cables are easier to apply than chains, but chains are more durable.) If you delay and purchase them in the vicinity of the chain-control area, the cost may double. Be aware that most rental-car companies prohibit chain installation on their vehicles. If you choose to risk it and do not tighten them properly, they may snap—your insurance likely will not cover any resulting damage. Uniformed chain installers on I–80 and U.S. 50 will apply them at the checkpoint for $30 or take them off for less than that. (Chain installers are independent business people, not highway employees, and set their own fees. They are not allowed to sell or rent chains.) On smaller roads, you're on your own. Always carry extra clothing, blankets, water, and food when driving to the mountains in the winter, and keep your gas tank full to prevent the fuel line from freezing.

Road Conditions Statewide Hotline (☎ 800/ GAS–ROAD [800/427–7623] ⊕ www.dot. ca.gov/hq/roadinfo).

Weather Conditions National Weather Service (☎ 707/443–6484 northernmost California, 831/656–1725 San Francisco Bay area and central California, 775/673–8100 Reno, Lake Tahoe, and northern Sierra, 805/988–6610 Los Angeles area, 858/675–8700 San Diego area ⊕ www.weather.gov).

ROADSIDE EMERGENCIES
Dial 911 to report accidents on the road and to reach the police, the California Highway Patrol (CHP), or the fire department. On some rural highways and on most interstates, look for emergency phones on the side of the road. In Los Angeles, the Metro Freeway Service Patrol provides assistance to stranded motorists under nonemergency conditions. Call #399 on your cell phone to reach them 24 hours a day.

RULES OF THE ROAD
Children under age 6 or weighing less than 60 pounds must be secured in a federally approved child passenger restraint system and ride in the back seat. Seat belts are required at all times and children must wear them regardless of where they're seated (studies show that children are safest in the rear seats). Unless otherwise indicated, right turns are allowed at red lights after you've come to a full stop. Left turns between two one-way streets are allowed at red lights after you've come to a full stop. Drivers with a blood-alcohol level higher than 0.08 who are stopped by police are subject to arrest, and police officers can detain those with a level of 0.05 if they appear impaired. California's drunk-driving laws are extremely tough—violators may have their licenses immediately suspended, pay hefty fines, and spend the night in jail. The speed limit on many interstate highways is 70 MPH; unlimited-access roads are usually 55 MPH. In cities, freeway speed limits are between 55 MPH and 65 MPH. Many city routes have commuter lanes during rush hour.

Effective July 2008, those 18 and older must use a hands-free device for their mobile phones while driving, while teenagers under 18 are not allowed to use mobile phones or wireless devices while driving. Smoking in a vehicle where a minor is present is an infraction. For more information refer to the Department of Motor Vehicles driver's handbook at ⊕ www.dmv.ca.gov/dmv.htm.

CAR RENTAL
When you reserve a car, ask about cancellation penalties, taxes, drop-off charges (if you're planning to pick up the car in one city and leave it in another), and surcharges (for being under or over a certain age, for additional drivers, or for driving across state or country borders or beyond a specific distance from your point of rental). All these things can add substantially to your costs. Request car seats and extras such as GPS when you book.

Rates are sometimes—but not always—better if you book in advance or reserve through a rental agency's Web site. There are other reasons to book ahead, though: for popular destinations, during busy times of the year, or to ensure that you get certain types of cars (vans, SUVs, exotic sports cars).

■TIP→ Make sure that a confirmed reservation guarantees you a car. Agencies sometimes overbook, particularly for busy weekends and holiday periods.

A car is essential in most parts of California. In compact San Francisco it's better to use public transportation to avoid parking headaches. In sprawling cities such as Los Angeles and San Diego, however, you'll have to take the freeways to get just about anywhere.

Rates statewide for the least expensive vehicle begin at around $73 a day and $135 a week (though they increase rapidly from here). This does not include additional fees or tax on car rentals, which is 9.75% in Los Angeles, 9.25% in San Francisco, and 8.75% in San Diego. Be sure to shop around—you can get a decent deal by carefully shopping the major car rental companies' Web sites. Also, rates are sometimes lower in San Diego; compare prices by city before you book, and ask about "drop charges" if you plan to return the car in a city other than the one where you rented the vehicle. If you pick up at an airport, there may also be a facility charge of as much as $12 per rental; ask when you book. When you're returning your rental, be aware that gas stations can be few and far between near airports.

In California, you must have a valid driver's license and be 21 to rent a car; rates may be higher if you're under 25. Some agencies will not rent to those under 25; check when you book. Non-U.S. residents must have a license with text that is in the Roman alphabet that is valid for the entire rental period. Though it need not be entirely written in English, it must have English letters that clearly identify it as a driver's license. An international license is recommended but not required.

Specialty Car Agencies In San Francisco and Los Angeles **Specialty Rentals** (☎ 800/400-8412 ⊕ www.specialtyrentals.com) ; in Los Angeles (several locations) **Beverly Hills Rent a Car** (☎ 800/479-5996 ⊕ www.bhrentacar.com) or in Los Angeles (several locations) **Midway Car Rental** (☎ 800/824-5260 ⊕ www.midwaycarrental.com).

Major Rental Agencies Alamo (☎ 800/462-5266 ⊕ www.alamo.com). **Avis** (☎ 800/331-1212 ⊕ www.avis.com). **Budget** (☎ 800/527-0700 ⊕ www.budget.com). **Hertz** (☎ 800/654-3131 ⊕ www.hertz.com). **National Car Rental** (☎ 800/227-7368 ⊕ www.nationalcar.com).

▌ TRAIN TRAVEL

One of the most beautiful train trips in the country is along the Pacific Coast from Los Angeles to Oakland via Amtrak's *Coast Starlight,* which hugs the waterfront before it turns inland at San Luis Obispo for the rest of its journey to Seattle. (Be aware that this train is frequently late arriving at and departing from Central Coast stations.) The *California Zephyr* travels from Chicago to Oakland via Denver; the *Pacific Surfliner* connects San Diego and San Luis Obispo via Los Angeles and Santa Barbara with multiple departures daily; and the *Sunset Limited* runs from Los Angeles to New Orleans via Arizona, New Mexico, and Texas.

Information Amtrak (☎ 800/872-7245 ⊕ www.amtrak.com).

ESSENTIALS

■ ACCOMMODATIONS

The lodgings we list are the cream of the crop in each price category. We always list the facilities that are available, but we don't specify whether they cost extra; when pricing accommodations, always ask what's included and what costs extra. ⇨ *For price information, see the planner in each chapter.*

Most hotels require you to give your credit-card details before they will confirm your reservation. If you don't feel comfortable e-mailing this information, ask if you can fax it (some places even prefer faxes). However you book, get confirmation in writing and have a copy of it handy when you check in.

■ **TIP→** Assume that hotels operate on the European Plan (EP, no meals) unless we specify that they use the Breakfast Plan (BP, with full breakfast), Continental Plan (CP, Continental breakfast), Full American Plan (FAP, all meals), Modified American Plan (MAP, breakfast and dinner) or are all-inclusive (AI, all meals and most activities).

BED-AND-BREAKFASTS

California has more than 1,000 bed-and-breakfasts. You'll find everything from simple homestays to lavish luxury lodgings, many in historic hotels and homes. The California Association of Bed and Breakfast Inns has about 300 member properties that you can locate and book through their Web site.

Reservation Services Bed & Breakfast.com (☎ 512/322–2710 or 800/462–2632 ⊕ *www. bedandbreakfast.com*) also sends out an online newsletter. **Bed & Breakfast Inns Online** (☎ 310/280–4363 or 800/215–7365 ⊕ *www. bbonline.com*). **BnB Finder.com** (☎ 646/205–8016 or 888/547–8226 ⊕ *www.bnbfinder. com*). **California Association of Bed and Breakfast Inns** (☎ 800/373–9251 ⊕ *www. cabbi.com*).

■ COMMUNICATIONS

INTERNET

Internet access is widely available in California's urban areas, but it's usually more difficult to get online in the state's rural areas. Most hotels offer some kind of connection—dial-up, broadband, or Wi-Fi (which is becoming much more common). Most hotels charge a daily fee (about $10) for Internet access. Cybercafés are also located throughout California.

Contacts Cybercafés (⊕ *www.cybercafes. com*).

■ EATING OUT

California has led the pack in bringing natural and organic foods to the forefront of American cooking. Though rooted in European cuisine, California cooking sometimes has strong Asian and Latin influences. Wherever you go, you're likely to find that dishes are made with fresh produce and other local ingredients.

The restaurants we list are the cream of the crop in each price category. ⇨ *For price information, see the planner in each chapter.*

CUTTING COSTS

If you're on a budget, take advantage of the "small plates" craze sweeping California by ordering several appetizer-size portions and having a glass of wine at the bar, rather than having a full meal. Also, better grocery and specialty-food stores have grab-and-go sections, with prepared foods on par with restaurant cooking, perfect for picnicking (remember, it rarely rains between May and October). At resort areas in the off-season (such as Lake Tahoe in October and May, or San Diego in January), you can often find two-for-one dinner specials at upper-end restaurants; check local papers or with visitor bureaus.

RESERVATIONS AND DRESS

Regardless of where you are, it's a good idea to make a reservation if you can. We only mention them specifically when reservations are essential (there's no other way you'll ever get a table) or when they are not accepted. For popular restaurants, book as far ahead as you can (often 30 days), and reconfirm as soon as you arrive. (Large parties should always call ahead to check the reservations policy.) We mention dress only when men are required to wear a jacket or a jacket and tie.

Online reservation services make it easy to book a table before you even leave home. OpenTable covers most states, including 20 major cities, and has limited listings in Canada, Mexico, the United Kingdom, France and elsewhere. DinnerBroker has restaurants throughout the United States as well as a few in Canada.

Contacts OpenTable (⊕ *www.opentable.com*). **DinnerBroker** (⊕ *www.dinnerbroker.com*).

WINES, BEER, AND SPIRITS

If you like wine, your trip to California won't be complete unless you sample a few of the local vintages. Throughout the state, most famously in the Napa and Sonoma valleys, you can visit wineries, many of which have tasting rooms and offer tours. Microbreweries are an emerging trend in the state's cities and in some rural areas in northern California. The legal drinking age is 21.

▮ HEALTH

Do not fly within 24 hours of scuba diving.

Smoking is illegal in all California bars and restaurants, except on outdoor patios or in smoking rooms. This law is typically not well enforced and some restaurants and bars do not comply, so take your cues from the locals. Hotels and motels are also decreasing their inventory of smoking rooms; inquire at the time you book your reservation if any are available. In addition, a tax is added to cigarettes sold

in California, and prices can be as high as $6 per pack. You might want to bring a carton from home.

▮ HOURS OF OPERATION

Banks in California are typically open weekdays from 9 to 6 and Saturday morning; most are closed on Sunday and most holidays. Smaller shops usually operate from 10 to 6, with larger stores remaining open until 8 or later. Hours vary for museums and historical sites, and many are closed one or more days a week, or for extended periods during off-season months. It's a good idea to check before you visit a tourist site.

▮ MONEY

Los Angeles, San Diego, and San Francisco tend to be expensive cities to visit, and rates at coastal and desert resorts are almost as high. A day's admission to a major theme park can run upward of $65 a head , hotel rates average $150 to $250 a night (though you can find cheaper places), and dinners at even moderately priced restaurants often cost $20 to $40 per person. Costs in the Gold Country, the Far North, and the Death Valley/ Mojave Desert region are considerably less—many fine Gold Country bed-and-breakfasts charge around $100 a night, and some motels in the Far North and the Mojave charge $70 to $90.

Prices throughout this guide are given for adults. Reduced fees are almost always available for children, students, and senior citizens.

CREDIT CARDS

Throughout this guide, the following abbreviations are used: **AE**, American Express; **D**, Discover; **DC**, Diners Club; **MC**, MasterCard; and **V**, Visa.

It's a good idea to inform your credit-card company before you travel, especially if you're going abroad and don't travel internationally very often. Otherwise, the credit-card company might put a hold on your card owing to unusual activity—not a good thing halfway through your trip. Record all your credit-card numbers—as well as the phone numbers to call if your cards are lost or stolen—in a safe place, so you're prepared should something go wrong. Both MasterCard and Visa have general numbers you can call (collect if you're abroad) if your card is lost, but you're better off calling the number of your issuing bank, since MasterCard and Visa normally just transfer you to your bank; your bank's number is usually printed on your card.

Reporting Lost Cards American Express (☎ 800/992–3404 in U.S., 336/393–1111 collect from abroad ⊕ www.americanexpress. com). **Discover** (☎ 800/347–2683 in U.S., 801/902–3100 collect from abroad ⊕ www. discovercard.com). **Diners Club** (☎ 800/234–6377 in U.S., 303/799–1504 collect from abroad ⊕ www.dinersclub.com). **MasterCard** (☎ 800/622–7747 in U.S., 636/722–7111 collect from abroad ⊕ www.mastercard.com). **Visa** (☎ 800/847–2911 in U.S., 410/581–9994 collect from abroad ⊕ www.visa.com).

▌ SAFETY

California is a safe place to visit, as long as you take the usual precautions. In large cities ask the concierge or desk clerk to point out areas on your map that you should avoid. Lock valuables in a hotel safe when you're not using them. (Some hotels have in-room safes large enough to hold a laptop computer.) Keep an eye on your handbag when you're out in public. Security is high (but mostly invisible) at theme parks and resorts.

▌ TAXES

Sales tax in California varies from about 8.25% to 9.75% and applies to all purchases except for food purchased in a grocery store; food consumed in a restaurant is taxed but take-out food purchases are not. Hotel taxes vary widely by region, from 10% to 15%.

▌ TIME

California is in the Pacific time zone. Pacific daylight time (PDT) is in effect from mid-March through early November; the rest of the year the clock is set to Pacific standard time (PST).

▌ TIPPING

Most service workers in California are fairly well paid compared to those in the rest of the country, and extravagant tipping is not the rule here. Exceptions include wealthy enclaves such as Beverly Hills, La Jolla, and San Francisco as well as the most expensive resort areas.

TIPPING GUIDELINES FOR CALIFORNIA	
Bartender	$1–$5 per round of drinks, depending on the number of drinks
Bellhop	$1–$5 per bag, depending on the level of the hotel
Hotel Concierge	$5 or more, if he/she performs a service for you
Hotel Doorman	$1–$2 if he/she helps you get a cab
Valet Parking Attendant	$1–$2 when you get your car
Hotel Maid	$1–$2 per person, per day
Waiter	15%–20% (20% is standard in upscale restaurants); nothing additional If a service charge is added to the bill
Skycap at Airport	$1–$3 per bag
Hotel Room-Service Waiter	$1–$2 per delivery, even if a service charge has been added
Taxi Driver	15%–20%, but round up the fare to the next dollar amount
Tour Guide	10% of the cost of the tour

▌ TOURS

Guided tours are a good option when you don't want to do it all yourself. You travel along with a group (sometimes large, sometimes small), stay in prebooked hotels, eat with your fellow travelers (the cost of meals sometimes included in the price of your tour, sometimes not), and follow a schedule.

But not all guided tours are an if-it's-Tuesday-this-must-be-Belgium experience. A knowledgeable guide can take you places that you might never discover on your own, and you may be pushed to see more than you would have otherwise. Tours aren't for everyone, but they can be just the thing for trips to places where making travel arrangements is difficult or time-consuming (particularly when you don't speak the language).

Whenever you book a guided tour, find out what's included and what isn't. A "land-only" tour includes all your travel (by bus, in most cases) in the destination, but not necessarily your flights to and from or even within it. Also, in most cases prices in tour brochures don't include fees and taxes. And remember that you'll be expected to tip your guide (in cash) at the end of the tour.

SPECIAL-INTEREST TOURS

BIKING

Bicycling is a popular way to see the California countryside, and commercial tours are available throughout the state. Most three- to five-day trips are all-inclusive—you'll stay in delightful country inns, dine at good regional restaurants, and follow experienced guides. The Northern California wine country, with its flat valley roads, is one of the most popular destinations. When booking, ask about level of difficulty, as nearly every trip will involve some hill work. Tours fill up early, so book well in advance.

■TIP→ Most airlines accommodate bikes as luggage, provided they're dismantled and boxed.

Contacts Napa and Sonoma Valley Bike Tours (✉ 6795 Washington St., Bldg. B, Yountville ☎ 800/707–2453 ⊕ www. napavalleybiketours.com). **Bicycle Adventures** (✉ Box 11219, Olympia, WA ☎ 800/443–6060 ⊕ www.bicycleadventures.com).

INDEX

PHOTO CREDITS

1, Yuen Kwan, Fodors.com member. 2, Som Vembar, Fodors.com member. 5, Brett Shoaf/Artistic Visuals Photography. **Chapter 1: Experience California:** 10-11, Jay Anderson, Fodors.com member. 12, Warren H. White. 13 (left), twin65a, Fodors.com member. 13 (right), univek, Fodors.com member. 14, Robert Holmes. 15 (left), vathomp, Fodors.com member. 15 (right), Charlie_Oregon, Fodors.com member. 16 (left), Jose Vigano, Fodors.com member. 16 (right), Clinton Steeds/Flickr. 17, Neil Khettry, Fodors.com member. 18, dgassa, Fodors.com member. 20, Robert Holmes. 21 (left), Valhalla I Design & Conquer, Fodors.com member. 21 (right), Lisa M. Hamilton. 22 (top and bottom left), Robert Holmes. 22 (top right), Yenwen Lu/iStockphoto. 22 (bottom right), Sheldon Kralstein/iStockphoto. 23 (top left), iStockphoto. 23 (bottom left), Corbis. 23 (right), Christophe Testi/iStockphoto. 24 (left), Aaron Kohr/iStockphoto. 24 (top right), Alan A. Tobey/iStockphoto. 24 (bottom right), Warren H. White. 25, sebastien burel/iStockphoto. 26, Robert Holmes. 27, Warren H. White. 28, Stas Volik/Shutterstock. 29 (left and right), 30, and 32, Robert Holmes. 33, Andrew Zarivny/iStockphoto. 35, Robert Holmes. 36, John Elk III/Alamy. 37 (top), Janine Bolliger/iStockphoto. 37 (bottom), Lise Gagne/iStockphoto. 38, iStockphoto. **Chapter 2: San Diego:** 39, Brett Shoaf/Artistic Visuals Photography. 40, frogger256, Fodors.com member. 41 (top), rkkwan, Fodors.com member. 41 (bottom), Steve Rabin/iStockphoto. 43 and 47, Brett Shoaf/Artistic Visuals Photography. 52, Robert Holmes. 55, Ambient Images Inc./Alamy. 56 and 58 (#16), Brett Shoaf/Artistic Visuals Photography. 58 (#7), AlanHaynes.com/Alamy. 58 (#21), Brett Shoaf/Artistic Visuals Photography. 58 (#14), Robert Holmes. 58 (#12), John Elk III/Alamy. 58 (#8), Richard Cummins/age fotostock. 58 (#19), Brett Shoaf/Artistic Visuals Photography. 60, Robert Holmes. 61 (top), Epukas/wikipedia.org. 61 (bottom), Sally Brown/age fotostock. 62, Irene Chan/Alamy. 64, Brett Shoaf/Artistic Visuals Photography. 68 and 69, SeaWorld San Diego. 75, Howard Sandler/iStockphoto. 76 and 85, George's at the Cove. 87, Starwood Hotels & Resorts. 91 (top), thalling55/Flickr. 91 (bottom), Starwood Hotels & Resorts. 94 (top), Lodge at Torrey Pines. 94 (center left and center right), La Valencia Hotel. 94 (bottom left), Grande Colonial Hotel. 94 (bottom right), Catamaran Resort Hotel and Spa. 105, Janet Fullwood. 113, Merryl Edelstein, Fodors.com member. 115, Legoland California Resort. 116, Brett Shoaf/Artistic Visuals Photography. **Chapter 3: Orange County and Catalina Island:** 119, Robert Holmes. 120, Marc Pagani Photography/Shutterstock. 121 (top), Robert Holmes. 121 (bottom), Brent Reeves/Shutterstock. 122 & 123, Robert Holmes. 129, www.ericcastro.biz/Flickr. 139, Robert Holmes. 149, Brett Shoaf/Artistic Visuals Photography. **Chapter 4: Los Angeles:** 159, Robert Holmes. 160, Kenna Love/LACVB. 161 (top), Wendy Connett/age fotostock. 161 (bottom), Scott Frances/Esto/J. Paul Getty Trust. 163, SIME/Giovanni Simeone/eStock Photo. 164 (top right), Evan Meyer/iStockphoto. 164 (center right), Kyle Maass/iStockphoto. 164 (left), iStockphoto. 164 (bottom right), Lise Gagne/iStockphoto. 165, Tom Baker/Shutterstock. 171, S. Greg Panosian/iStockphoto. 178, Universal Studios Hollywood. 179 (top), Micah May/Shutterstock. 179 (bottom), star5112/Flickr. 180, Universal Studios Hollywood. 181, Universal Studios Hollywood. 183, Alvaro Leiva/age fotostock. 190, Andy McLeod/Flickr. 195, NOIZE Photography/Flickr. 204, Jeff Morse/iStockphoto. 205 (top), Andrea Skjold/Shutterstock. 205 (bottom), wando studios inc/iStockphoto.

206, Patina Restaurant Group. 212, Four Seasons Hotels & Resorts. 215, LOOK Die Bildagentur der Fotografen GmbH / Alamy. 217 (top), Millennium Biltmore Hotel Los Angeles. 217 (center left), The Peninsula Beverly Hills. 217 (center right and bottom left), Four Seasons Hotels & Resorts. 217 (bottom right), rick/Flickr. 225, Craig Schwartz Photography. 229, steph vee/Flickr. 233, Thomas Barrat/Shutterstock. **Chapter 5: The Central Coast:** 239, TweetieV, Fodors.com member. 240, Stephen Walls/iStockphoto. 241 (top), Bart Everett/iStockphoto. 241 (bottom), Robert Holmes. 243, David M. Schrader/Shutterstock. 254, S. Greg Panosian/iStockphoto. 255, Nancy Nehring/iStockphoto. 256 (top), Richard Wong/www.rwongphoto.com/Alamy. 256 (bottom), Mats Lund/iStockphoto. 257 (top left), Witold Skrypczak/Alamy. 257 (top right), S. Greg Panosian/iStockphoto. 257 (bottom), Janet Fullwood. 258 (top left), GIPhotoStock Z/Alamy. 258 (top right), Craig Lovell/Eagle Visions Photography/Alamy. 258 (bottom) and 259 (top), S. Greg Panosian/iStockphoto. 259 (bottom), Eugene Zelenko/wikipedia.org. 262, David M. Schrader/Shutterstock. 273, Doreen Miller, Fodors.com member. 286, Robert Holmes. 300-01, Valhalla I Design & Conquer, Fodors.com member. **Chapter 6: Channel Islands National Park:** 305, Christopher Russell/iStockphoto. 306 (top), Yenwen Lu/iStockphoto. 306 (bottom), NatalieJean/Shutterstock. 307, ZanyZeus/Shutterstock. 309, ZanyZeus/Shutterstock. **Chapter 7: The Monterey Bay Area:** 313, mellifluous, Fodors.com member. 314, Janet Fullwood. 315 (top), vittorio sciosia/age fotostock. 315 (bottom), Jeff Greenberg/age fotostock. 317, Brent Reeves/Shutterstock. 318 (left), SuperStock/age fotostock. 318 (top right), CURAphotography/Shutterstock. 318 (bottom right), Michael Almond/iStockphoto. 319 (top), iStockphoto. 319 (bottom), Lise Gagne/iStockphoto. 325, Robert Holmes. 331, Holger Mette/iStockphoto. 340, laurel stewart/iStockphoto. **Chapter 8: San Francisco:** 359-63, Brett Shoaf/Artistic Visuals Photography. 364 (left), TebNad/Shutterstock. 364 (top right), Ross Stapleton-Gray/iStockphoto. 364 (bottom right), Jay Spooner/iStockphoto. 365 (top), Jay Spooner/iStockphoto. 365 (bottom), Lise Gagne/iStockphoto. 372, Robert Holmes. 375, Brett Shoaf/Artistic Visuals Photography. 376 (top), Arnold Genthe. 376 (bottom), Library of Congress Prints and Photographs Division. 377 (left), Sandor Balatoni/SFCVB. 377 (right), Detroit Publishing Company Collection, Photography Collection, Miriam and Ira D. Wallach Division of Art, Prints and Photographs, The New York Public Library, Astor, Lenox and Tilden Foundation. 378, Brett Shoaf/Artistic Visuals Photography. 379 (top), Gary Soup/Flickr. 379 (bottom), Albert Cheng/Shutterstock. 380 (top), Sheryl Schindler/SFCVB. 380 (center), Ronen/Shutterstock. 380 (bottom), Robert Holmes. 383, Walter Bibikow/age fotostock. 389, travelstock44/Alamy. 391, Brett Shoaf/Artistic Visuals Photography. 392, San Francisco Municipal Railway Historical Archives. 399, Lewis Sommer/SFCVB. 407, Robert Holmes. 415, aprillilacs, Fodors.com member. 419, Rafael Ramirez Lee/iStockphoto. 424, yummyporky/Flickr. 425 (top), Lisa M. Hamilton. 425 (bottom), Lisa M. Hamilton. 438, Queen Anne Hotel. 440 (top), George Apostolidis/Mandarin Oriental Hotel Group. 440 (center left), David Phelps/Argonaut Hotel. 440 (center right), Joie de Vivre Hospitality. 440 (bottom left), Starwood Hotels & Resorts. 440 (bottom right), Cris Ford/Union Street Inn. 441 (top), Rien van Rijthoven/InterContinental Hotels & Resorts. 441 (center left), Orchard Hotel. 441 (center right), Hotel Nikko San Francisco. 441 (bottom), The Ritz-Carlton, San Francisco. 454, Rough Guides/Alamy. 457, Robert Holmes. **Chapter 9: The Bay Area:** 459 and 460, Robert Holmes. 461, Jyeshern Cheng/iStockphoto. 463, Brett Shoaf/Artistic Visuals Photography. 467, Robert Holmes. 473, Mark Rasmussen/iStockphoto. 475, Robert Holmes. 479, S. Greg Panosian/iStockphoto. 487 and 495, Robert Holmes. **Chapter 10: The Wine Country:** 505, Robert Holmes. 506, iStockphoto. 507 and 508, Robert Holmes. 510, Warren H. White. 514, Robert Holmes. 515 (top), kevin miller/iStockphoto. 515 (bottom), Far Niente+Dolce+Nickel & Nickel. 516 (top and bottom) and 517 (top), Robert Holmes. 517 (bottom), star5112/Flickr. 518 (top left), Rubicon Estate. 518 (top right and bottom right) and 519 (top and bottom), Robert Holmes. 520 (top), Philippe Roy/Alamy. 520 (center), Agence Images/Alamy. 520 (bottom), Cephas Picture Library/Alamy. 521 (top), Napa Valley Conference Bureau. 521 (second and third from top), Wild Horse Winery (Forrest L. Doud). 521 (fourth from top), Napa Valley Conference Bureau. 521 (fifth from top), Panther Creek Cellars (Ron Kaplan). 521 (sixth from top), Clos du Val (Marvin Collins). 521 (seventh from top), Panther Creek Cellars (Ron Kaplan). 521 (bottom), Warren H. White. 522 and 525, Robert Holmes. 537, Far Niente+Dolce+Nickel & Nickel. 539, Terry Joanis/Frog's Leap. 546, Chuck Honek/Schramsberg Vineyard. 549, Castello di Amorosa. 571, Robert Holmes. **Chapter 11: The North Coast:** 579, John Redwine, Fodors.com member. 580 (all), Robert Holmes. 581 (top), Russ Bishop/age fotostock. 581 (bottom), Robert Holmes. 583, Janet Fullwood. 589, 594, and 599, Robert Holmes. **Chapter 12: Redwood National Park:** 607, iStockphoto. 608 (top), Michael Schweppe/wikipedia.org. 608 (center), Agnieszka Szymczak/iStockphoto. 608 (bottom), Natalia Bratslavsky/Shutterstock. 611, WellyWelly/Shutterstock. **Chapter 13: The Inland Empire:** 615, Mission Inn Hotel & Spa. 616, Hartford Family Wines. 617 (top), Robert Holmes. 617 (bottom), stevekc/Flickr. 619 , Edward Lin/iStockphoto. 627, Glen Ivy Hot Springs. 635, Robert Holmes. 642, Brett

Shoaf/Artistic Visuals Photography. **Chapter 14: Palm Springs:** 645, toby fraley/iStockphoto. 646, JustASC/Shutterstock. 647 (top and bottom), Robert Holmes. 649, iStockphoto. 652, William Royer/ iStockphoto. 664, David Falk/iStockphoto. 680, Brett Shoaf/Artistic Visuals Photography. **Chapter 15: Joshua Tree National Park:** 685, Eric Foltz/iStockphoto. 686 (top), Loic Bernard/iStockphoto. 686 (bottom), Eric Foltz/iStockphoto. 687 (top), Justin Mair/Shutterstock. 687 (bottom), Mariusz S. Jurgielewicz/Shutterstock. 689, Eric Foltz/iStockphoto. **Chapter 16: The Mojave Desert:** 693, Robert Holmes. 694, amygdala imagery/Shutterstock. 695, Robert Holmes. 697, San Bernardino County Regional Parks. 703, Merryl Edelstein, Fodors.com member. 708, Robert Holmes. 719, Paul Erickson/iStockphoto. **Chapter 17: Death Valley National Park:** 721, Rodney Ee, Fodors.com member. 723 (top), Igor Karon/Shutterstock. 723 (bottom), iofoto/Shutterstock. 725, Paul D. Lemke/iStockphoto. 728-29, James Feliciano/iStockphoto. 734, Rodney Ee, Fodors.com member. **Chapter 18: The Central Valley:** 737, Kim Brogan, Fodors.com member. 738, Gary Allard/iStockphoto. 739-59, Robert Holmes. **Chapter 19: The Southern Sierra:** 761, Randall Pugh, Fodors.com member. 762, Craig Cozart/iStockphoto. 763 (top), David T Gomez/iStockphoto. 763 (bottom left and bottom right), Robert Holmes. 765, christinea78, Fodors.com member. 769, moonjazz/Flickr. 776, Douglas Atmore/iStockphoto. **Chapter 20: Yosemite National Park:** 779, Sarah P. Corley, Fodors.com member. 780, Yosemite Concession Services. 781 (top), Andy Z./Shutterstock. 781 (bottom), Greg Epperson/age fotostock. 782, Thomas Barrat/Shutterstock. 783, Nicholas Roemmelt/iStockphoto. 784, Doug Lemke/Shutterstock. 788, Rebalyn, Fodors.com member. 791, Nathan Jaskowiak/Shutterstock. 795, Greg Epperson/age fotostock. 796-797, Katrina Leigh/Shutterstock. **Chapter 21: Sequoia and Kings Canyon National Parks:** 801 and 802, Robert Holmes. 803 (top), Greg Epperson/age fotostock. 803 (bottom) and 805, Robert Holmes. 811, urosr/Shutterstock. 817, Robert Holmes. **Chapter 22: Sacramento and the Gold Country:** 819 and 821 (top and bottom), Robert Holmes. 823, Andy Z./Shutterstock. 828, Marcin Wichary/Flickr. 835, Image Asset Management/age fotostock. 836 (left) and 836 (right), wikipedia.org. 836 (center), Charles Danek. 837, Ambient Images Inc./Alamy. 838 (top), Trailmix.Net/Flickr. 838 (center), oger jones/Flickr. 838 (bottom), L. C. McClure/wikipedia.org. 839 (top left), Russ Bishop/age fotostock. 839 (top center), vera bogaerts/iStockphoto. 839 (top right and bottom left), Walter Bibikow/age fotostock. 839 (bottom right), Charles Danek. 842, Janet Fullwood. 848, RickC/Flickr. **Chapter 23: Lake Tahoe:** 851, Tom Zikas/North Lake Tahoe. 852 (top), Rafael Ramirez Lee/iStockphoto. 852 (bottom) and 853, Janet Fullwood. 856, Jay Spooner/iStockphoto. 861 (top), Heavenly Mountain Resort. 861 (bottom), Jake Foster/iStockphoto. 862 (top), Lake Tahoe Visitors Authority. 862 (bottom left), iStockphoto. 862 (bottom right), Heavenly Mountain Resort. 865 and 866 (left), Andrew Zarivny/iStockphoto. 866 (right), Harry Thomas/iStockphoto. 867 (top left), Joy Strotz/Shutterstock. 867 (bottom left), iStockphoto. 867 (right), Jennifer Stone/Shutterstock. 873, Jay Spooner/iStockphoto. 880, Tom O'Neill. 891, Christopher Russell/iStockphoto. **Chapter 24: The Far North:** 899, NPS. 900 (top and bottom), Robert Holmes. 901 (top), Andy Z./Shutterstock. 901 (bottom), NPS. 903, ThreadedThoughts/Flickr. 908, Robert Holmes. 915, kathycsus/Flickr. 921, NPS.

ABOUT OUR WRITERS

Native Californian **Cheryl Crabtree**—who updated the Central Coast and Monterey Bay Area chapters and wrote On a Mission and The Ultimate Road Trip: California's Legendary Highway 1—has worked as a freelance writer since 1987. She has contributed to *Fodor's California* since 2003 and has also written for *Fodor's Complete Guide to the National Parks of the West*. Cheryl is editor of *Montecito Magazine*. She currently lives in Santa Barbara with her husband, two sons, and Jack Russell terrier.

Lisa M. Hamilton is a writer and photographer who focuses on food, farming, and travel. She lives in the Bay Area but would pretty much always rather be on a rocky beach somewhere along the North Coast. She updated our Bay Area and North Coast coverage for this edition.

A Northern California resident for 17 years, **Reed Parsell** has traveled extensively throughout the region and written hundreds of newspaper travel stories based on this experiences. A part-time copy editor and travel writer for the *Sacramento Bee*, Parsell also writes a "going green" column for *Sacramento* magazine and was the primary writer for *Fodor's InFocus Yosemite, Sequoia and Kings Canyon National Parks*. He updated our Central Valley, Southern Sierra, Sacramento and the Gold Country coverage and wrote Eureka! California's Gold Rush.

Freelance writer **Christine Vovakes**—who updated the Far North, Lake Tahoe, and Travel Smart California chapters and wrote Tahoe: A Lake for all Seasons for this edition—has also contributed to *Fodor's National Parks of the West* and *Essential USA*. Her travel articles and photographs have also appeared in many other publications, including *The Washington Post, The Christian Science Monitor, The Sacramento Bee* and the *San Francisco Chronicle*.

Sura Wood is a San Francisco-based writer who has covered the Bay Area arts and lifestyle scene in particular and the film industry in general. Her profiles, reviews, and features have appeared in *The Hollywood Reporter*, the *San Jose Mercury News, San Francisco Arts Monthly,* and many other publications. For this edition, she fact-checked our National Parks chapters, including Channel Islands, Joshua Tree, Death Valley, Yosemite, Sequoia and Kings Canyon, and Redwood National Park.

Bobbi Zane—who updated the Experience California, San Diego, Inland Empire, and Palm Springs chapters for this edition—grew up in Southern California, watching the region grow from its mostly rural roots into one of the most exciting places in the world. Her articles on Palm Springs have appeared in the *Orange County Register* and *Westways* magazine. She has contributed to *Fodor's Complete Guide to the National Parks of the West, Fodor's San Diego,* and *Escape to Nature Without Roughing It*. A lifelong Californian, Bobbi has visited every corner of the state on behalf of Fodor's.